a gift

lonely planet

Italy

Helen Gillman
Damien Simonis
Stefano Cavedoni

Italy

3rd edition

Published by

Lonely Planet Publications

Head Office: PO Box 617, Hawthorn, Vic 3122, Australia
Branches: 150 Linden St, Oakland, CA 94607, USA
10a Spring Place, London NW5 3BH, UK
71 bis rue du Cardinal Lemoine, 75005 Paris, France

Printed by

Colorcraft Ltd, Hong Kong

Photographs by

Stefano Cavedoni
G Colliva, The Image Bank
Greg Elms
Grant V Faint, The Image Bank
Rob Flynn
Photo Scala, Firenze
John Gillman
Shoot
Damien Simonis
Richard Stewart
Lauren Sunstein
Tony Wheeler
Rei Zunde

Paintings of the Galleria degli Uffizi reproduced with the permission of Italy's Ministero per i Beni Culturali e Ambientali

Front cover: One of numerous stone guardians of Roma, city of popes (Wendy Owen)

First Published

September 1993

This Edition

January 1998

Although the authors and publisher have tried to make the information as accurate as possible, they accept no responsibility for any loss, injury or inconvenience sustained by any person using this book.

National Library of Australia Cataloguing in Publication Data

Gillman, Helen
Italy
3rd ed.
Includes index
ISBN 0 86442 492 2
1. Italy - Guidebooks. I. Simonis, Damien. II. Title.

914. 504929

Helen Gillman & Stefano Cavedoni

Writing and updating Lonely Planet guides has become a family affair for Helen and Stefano, who take their four-year-old daughter, Virginia, with them on most trips. Virginia is an accomplished traveller and is the official gelato and playground tester for the Italy guide.

Helen works as a freelance journalist and editor, based in Italy. For many years she worked as a journalist in Australia (her country of birth), before moving to Italy in 1990. Helen has also written the Italy chapter in Lonely Planet's *Mediterranean Europe* and *Western Europe* shoestring guides. She has helped put together a new Lonely Planet guide to walking in Italy. When not working on guidebooks, she coordinates the publications programme of the Community Forestry Unit within the Food & Agriculture Organisation of the United Nations.

Stefano is an actor and writer. In the late 1970s, while still a university student, Stefano's career in the Italian entertainment industry was launched with a bang when his rock band, Skiantos, became a major success. After this, he wrote and performed humorous one-man shows. But, while on the stage, he was secretly thinking about travel, forests and mountains. He has worked on the Lonely Planet *Italy* guide since the 1st edition and researched and wrote many of the walks in the new Lonely Planet *Walking in Italy* guide.

Damien Simonis

Damien is a London-based journalist. With a degree in languages and several years' newspaper experience on, among others, the *The Australian* and *The Age*, he left Australia in 1989. In between stints on several London papers, including the *The Guardian*, *The Independent* and *The Daily Telegraph*, he has worked and travelled widely in Europe, the Middle East and North Africa. In addition to this guide, he has worked on travel guides to *Jordan & Syria*, *Egypt & the Sudan*, *Morocco*, *North Africa* and *Spain* as well as contributing to several shoestring guides and other publications in the UK, Australia and North America.

From the Authors

Helen Gillman & Stefano Cavedoni As with past editions of this guide, lots of friends, relatives and organisations helped out with the enormous job of updating existing information, as well as improving the guide by adding new destinations and plenty of new information. We would like to thank the following tourist organisations and staff for their valuable assistance:

ENIT (Ente Nazionale Italiana del Turismo, in particular Gigliola Lantini); Napoli EPT (a very big thank you to Aldo Cianci); Ente Sardo Industrie Turistiche (in particular Mario Pinna and Marco Grippo); APT (Azienda di Promozione Turistica) of Basilicata; Palermo APT (in particular Lia Verdina); Trapani APT (in particular Paolo Sciortino); the APTs of Catania, Siracusa, Ragusa, Cortona and Arezzo; the AAPIT di Noto (in particular Dott. Spiculia); the Pro Loco di San Gimignano; the AAST delle Isole Eolie (in particular Mimmo Ziino).

Thanks to Nicole Gillman for her help with the guide, particularly her suggestions for improvement based on her own travels in Italy. Thanks also to Sally Webb.

Damien Simonis I would like to thank, first and foremost, Daniela Antongiovanni for putting up with me – and putting me up – for a whole month in Milano. Not far behind comes Sergio Bosio, whose friendship, generosity and storage space were all invaluable. I am indebted to Luisa Cotta, as without her the travails in the refuge-hunting saga in Milano would have been disastrous rather than simply stressful. They and other friends in Milano have not only been great company, but in many cases helped out with gathering together info for this edition – often unwittingly. They include Alberto Stassi (who with Chicca Avanzini lent a much-needed hand in The Great Hundred Kilo Mailing Saga) & Anna Cerutti, John Glover, Paul & Liz Wilson, the rest of the Avanzini family, Caroline Heidler, Stephen Scott, Orietta Olivetti, Antonella Mirarchi, and Birgit & Alberto. Helen Gillman in Roma, and Vivi Giacco and Zia Cristina in Sicilia again rolled out the welcome mat which was most welcome!

Staff at several tourist offices have gone beyond the call of duty, and I would especially like to mention those at La Spezia, Spoleto, Trento, Padova, Aosta, Udine and Trieste. Also a word of thanks to John Millerchip at UNESCO in Venezia for updating information on the state of play in the lagoon city.

Maurizio the mechanic in Milano gets a vote of confidence for saving the life of my overworked little chariot, Gnomo the Renault.

Back in the UK, the LP London office, along with Michele Nayman and Steve Pearson, have all helped keep things ticking over during long absences. Thanks also to Rob van Driesum, Adrienne Costanzo and the staff in Melbourne for their flexibility and support during some trying times lately. A belated vote of thanks must also go to Geoff Leaver-Heaton in Spain, who has also been an enormous help.

Above all, my heartfelt thanks to Elisabeth Mead, who has not only been a wonderful travel companion and friend but gone to enormous lengths to help me through some unusually difficult moments, not the least of which was coping with the weirdness of one pensione dubbed by us Hotel Stupid, not to be found anywhere in this guidebook.

Finally, my share of this edition is dedicated to the memory of my mother, herself very much bitten by the wanderlust bug, and whose courage and curiosity remain a source of profound inspiration to me.

This Book

This is the 3rd edition of LP's *Italy* guide. Helen Gillman and John Gillman wrote the 1st edition and Helen and Damien Simonis updated and revamped the 2nd edition. Helen Gillman coordinated this edition, which has been updated, expanded and revised. Helen and Stefano Cavedoni wrote the Roma; Emilia-Romagna & San Marino; Campania; Puglia, Basilicata & Calabria; Sicilia; and Sardegna chapters. Damien wrote the Liguria, Piemonte & Valle d'Aosta; Lombardia & the Lakes; Trentino-Alto Adige; The Veneto; Friuli-Venezia Giulia; and Abruzzo & Molise chapters. The authors shared the introductory chapters, Toscana and Umbria & Le Marche. Ann Moffatt of the Australian National University wrote the text for the Art & Architecture chapter.

From the Publisher
This book was edited and proofed by Liz Filleul, Janet Austin and Wendy Owen, and Anne Mulvaney and Adrienne Costanzo helped with proofing. Jenny Jones coordinated the mapping, assisted by Anthony Phelan, Lyndell Taylor, Ann Jeffree and Marcel Gaston. Jenny was also responsible for layout. Simon Bracken designed the cover and Adam McCrow produced the back cover map. Thanks to Trudi Canavan and Penelope Richardson for illustrations.

Thanks
Many thanks to the following travellers who used the last edition and wrote to us with helpful hints, useful advice and interesting anecdotes:

JW Allen, J & J Anderson, Neal Ashcroft, Wanda Auerbach, Suzana Baljak, Teresa Ball, Lori Barnham, Kristie Barrow, Clare Beresford, E Berridge, Joan Bloxom, Sarah-Jane Bogue, Barbara Boone, Leontine Born, Megan Bowen-Jones, Hugh Cardiff, Eric Carlson, Peter Ceulemans, Jean Ciriani, Rachel Cohen, Natasha Colbourne, Adrienne Cole, Miguel Correia, Daniela Cremonini, Clare Currey, Tony D'Orazio, Carolyn Davies, Chris & Lucie De Vido, J Dewell, Robin Di Dominicus, Thomas Donald, L & J Dunell, Ron Edwards, Andrew Ellis, Jacob Federspiel, Inwa Fermail, Hugh Finsten, Diane Fontannaz, Anthony Forsyth, Dahlia Friedman, Ann Geroe, Jan Gillies, Alex Gilmour, Sylvie Gingras, Paul Gregory, Gary Haines, Peter Hampshire, Ingrid Haug, Addie Heuvel, Suzanne Hewitson, Stephen Iacono, George Kamory, Jon & Jan Kellogg, Andrew King, Wallson Knack, Dr D Kumar, Laya Labi, Ted & Anne Last, Douglas Lattey, Ian Lawry, Aaron Leeman-Smith, Michal Lipski, Rik Logan Tout, Micah Lowenthal, Brian Lowery, Manuel Luis, AD Macalady, Jamie MacKenzie, Sue MacKimmie, Philip Macklin, Kevin Madden, Anne Maron, Rebecca Marsden, Andrew Martinovs, MG Maubela, Gillian & Gary May, Craig McAmis, Wayne McCallum, Paul McDonnell, Judith McMillan, Stuart Messinger, Sanjeev Mohan, Kelly Noble, MJ Ogden, Martin Pagel, Lisa Pane, Corrie Pascal, F & N Pierse, Lucio Pineda, Emily Poler, Boy Pouwels, Bob Powry, Emma Prior, T & AM Purnell, Felice Rando, Bernard Ravschen, Ida Rezvani, Andreas Rogall, Helen Ruatti, David Saccon, R J Sachdev, Raymond Shamash, Nicola Shellens, Phyl Shimeld, Denis Shorr, Anna Sideris, Connie Sluski, Olivia Smales, Nick Small, Dr Sharon Smith, Christine Smith, Gary Spinks, Tom Spruetels, Steven Stahler, C Steiger, Brian Storey, Jonathon Sykes, Aurora Testai, Yvonne Trevaskis, OB Tuber, Frank Vito, Jeanette Ward, Barb Whitlock, Margaret Withers, Kris Woods, R A Zambardino, Francesco Zavarese.

Warning & Request
Things change – prices go up, schedules change, good places go bad and bad places go bankrupt – nothing stays the same. So, if you find things better or worse, recently opened or long since closed, please tell us and help make the next edition even more accurate and useful.

We value all of the feedback we receive from travellers. Julie Young coordinates a small team who read and acknowledge every letter, postcard and email, and ensure that every morsel of information finds its way to the appropriate authors, editors and publishers.

Everyone who writes to us will find their name in the next edition of the appropriate guide and will also receive a free subscription to our quarterly newsletter, *Planet Talk*. The very best contributions will be rewarded with a free Lonely Planet guide.

Excerpts from your correspondence may appear in new editions of this guide; in our newsletter, *Planet Talk*; or in updates on our Web site – so please let us know if you don't want your letter published or your name acknowledged.

Contents

SARDEGNA 763

GLOSSARY 792

INDEX 795

Boxed Asides

Map Legend

ROUTES

- Freeway, with Route Number (A5)
- Highway
- Major Road
- Minor Road
- Unsealed Minor Road
- City Highway
- City Road
- City Street
- City Lane
- Train Route, with Station
- Underground Train Route
- Metro Route, with Station (M)
- Cable Car or Chairlift
- Ferry
- Walking Track
- Path Within a Park

AREA FEATURES

- City Park, National Park
- Building
- Pedestrian Mall, Plaza
- Market
- Cemetery

BOUNDARIES

- International Boundary
- Provincial Boundary
- Disputed Boundary

HYDROGRAPHIC FEATURES

- River, Creek
- Rapids, Waterfalls
- Lake, Intermittent Lake
- Swamp

SYMBOLS

- CAPITAL — National Capital
- CAPITAL — Provincial Capital
- Capital — Regional Capital
- City — City
- Town — Town
- Village — Village
- Place to Stay
- Camping Ground
- Caravan Park
- Youth Hostel
- Hut or Chalet
- Place to Eat
- Pub or Bar
- Café
- Airport
- Ancient Wall
- Bank
- Beach
- Castle
- Cathedral, Church
- Cave, Grotto
- Cliff or Escarpment
- Embassy
- Golf Course
- Hospital
- Information
- Monument
- Mountain
- Mountain Range
- Museum
- One Way Street
- Palace
- Pass
- Petrol Station
- Police Station
- Post Office
- Ruins
- Shopping Centre
- Spring
- Telephone
- Temple
- Tomb
- Trail Head
- Transport

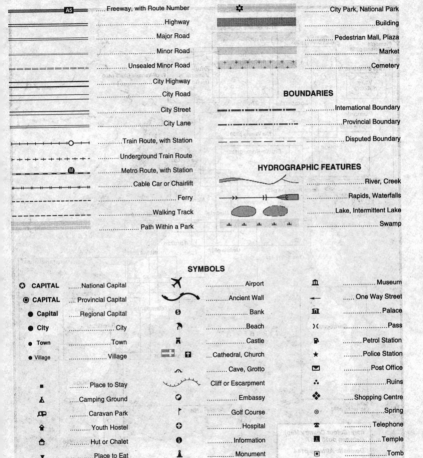

Note: not all symbols displayed above appear in this book

Map Index

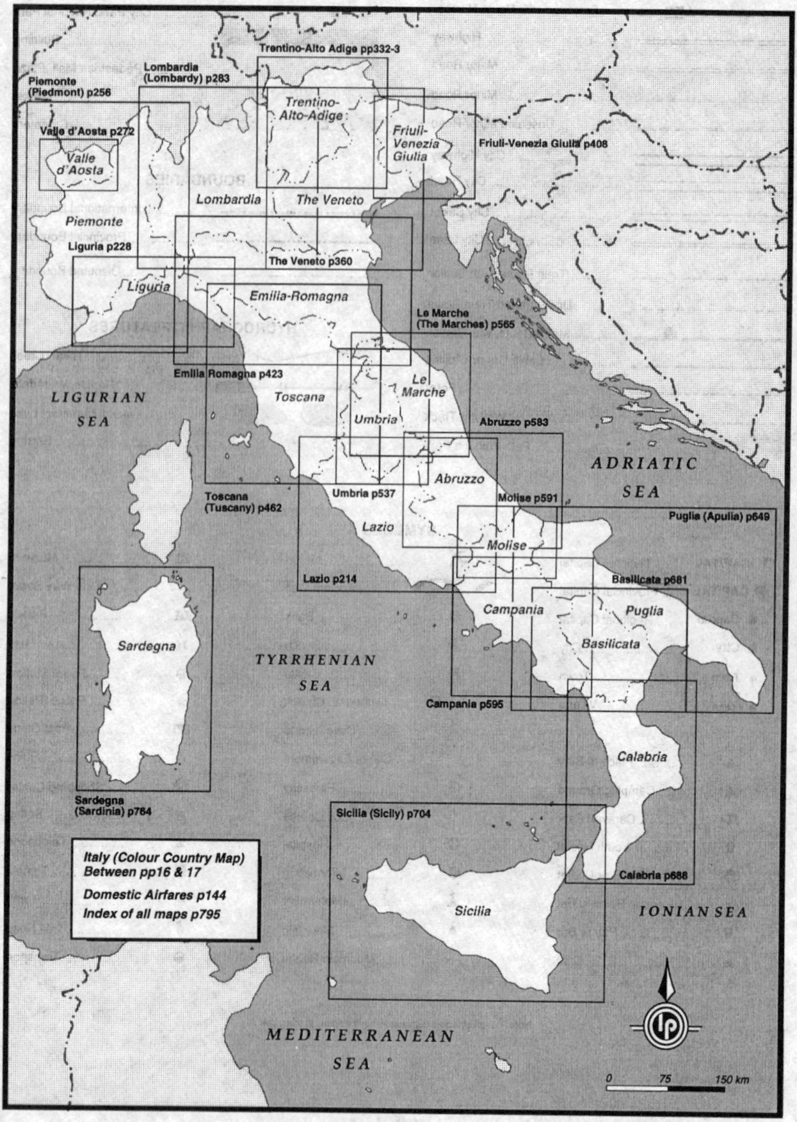

Trentino-Alto Adige pp332-3
Lombardia (Lombardy) p283
Piemonte (Piedmont) p256
Valle d'Aosta p272
Valle d'Aosta
Trentino-Alto-Adige
Friuli-Venezia Giulia
Friuli-Venezia Giulia p408
Lombardia
The Veneto
Piemonte
Liguria p228
The Veneto p360
Liguria
Emilia-Romagna
Le Marche (The Marches) p565
Emilia Romagna p423
LIGURIAN SEA
Toscana
Le Marche
Umbria
Abruzzo p583
ADRIATIC SEA
Abruzzo
Toscana (Tuscany) p462
Umbria p537
Molise p591
Puglia (Apulia) p649
Lazio
Molise
Lazio p214
Basilicata p681
Campania
Puglia
Sardegna
Basilicata
TYRRHENIAN SEA
Campania p595
Calabria
Sardegna (Sardinia) p764
Sicilia (Sicily) p704
Italy (Colour Country Map) Between pp16 & 17
Domestic Airfares p144
Index of all maps p795
Calabria p688
Sicilia
IONIAN SEA
MEDITERRANEAN SEA
0 75 150 km

Introduction

A unified nation only for the past century, Italy is a magnificently complex, if unevenly woven, tapestry.

If Roma continued to exercise extraordinary power and attract exuberant wealth as seat of the Church, its hold over the rest of the peninsula was far from complete after the collapse of the empire. City states to the north and feudal kingdoms to the south shared control and together left a legacy of unparalleled richness in diversity. To travel from Bolzano to Palermo is to cross from the rim of the Germanic universe to a realm of near North African languor.

Centuries ago, well-to-do northern Europeans were drawn to the Mediterranean light, and so the Grand Tour was born. What they found in Italy was an extraordinary cocktail: next to the awe-inspiring artistic wealth of Roma, Venezia and Firenze, they often encountered squalid decadence, poverty and spivs on the make.

The economic miracles of the past decades have transformed the country, but beneath all the style, fine food and delicious wine, there remains, happily, a certain chaotic air. Not everything is wonderful – expanding industry, poor urban planning, unchecked resort construction and what at times seems like an almost wilful indifference to the nation's art treasures have too often blighted the cities and countryside.

You could not hope to experience all the wonders of the country in even a year's non-stop travel. From the grandeur of the Dolomiti mountains to the rainbow-coloured sea of Sardegna, there is much more to the country than San Pietro and the Uffizi.

Facts about the Country

HISTORY

Italy's strategic position in the Mediterranean made it a target for colonisers and invaders, whose comings and goings over thousands of years have created a people with a diverse ethnic background. But it also gave the Romans, and later the Christian Church, an excellent base from which to expand their respective empires. Italy's history is therefore a patchwork of powerful empires and foreign domination and, from the fall of the Roman Empire until the formation of the Kingdom of Italy in 1861, the country was never a unified entity.

Prehistoric Italy

The Italian peninsula has supported human life for thousands of years. Archaeological finds show that Palaeolithic Neanderthals lived in Italy about 70,000 years ago. By around 4000 BC, Neolithic, or New Stone Age humans were no longer exclusively nomadic hunters and had started to establish settlements across the peninsula. At the start of the Bronze Age, around 1800 BC, Italy had been settled by several Italic tribes which had frequent contact with eastern and other Mediterranean cultures until they were eventually absorbed into the Roman Empire. These tribes included the Ligurians, the Venetians, the Puglians, the Sicilians, the Sardinians, the Latins, the eastern Italics and many others.

The Etruscans

Historians differ on the exact origins of the Etruscan people and when they arrived in the Italian peninsula although it is widely agreed they migrated from the Aegeo-Asian area around the end of the 12th century BC.

What is beyond doubt is that the Etruscans created a flourishing civilisation between the Arno and Tevere valleys, with other important settlements in Campania, Lazio and the Po valley. The earliest evidence of the Etruscan people in Italy was the Villanovan culture (around the 9th century BC) which centred around present-day Bologna and characterised by the practice of cremating the dead and burying the ashes in urns.

From the 7th to the 6th century BC, Etruscan culture was at its height. The nation was based on large city-states, among them Caere (Cerveteri), Tarquinii (Tarquinia), Veii (Veio), Volsinii (believed to be either Bolsena or Orvieto), Felsina (Bologna), Perusia (Perugia), Volaterrae (Volterra), Faesulae (Fiesole) and Arretium (Arezzo), collectively known as the Etruscan League. The Etruscans were predominantly navigators and traders, competing for markets in the Mediterranean against the Phoenicians and Greeks.

A good deal of what is known about the Etruscan culture has been learned from the archaeological evidence of their tombs and religious sanctuaries. Their belief in life after death necessitated the burial of the dead with everything they might need in the afterlife, such as food and drink, clothing, ornaments and weapons. Painted tombs depicting scenes of everyday life, notably those discovered at Tarquinia, near Roma, provide an important document of how the Etruscans lived.

The long period of Etruscan decline began in the 5th century BC, when they began to lose control of their trade routes to the more powerful Greeks. By the 4th century BC they had lost their northern territories to Gallic invaders and their settlements in Campania to the Samnites, confining Etruria to its original territories in central Italy. While Etruscan civilisation continued to flourish during this period, its development was by then greatly determined by its relationship with the growing power of Rome.

Rome had long been profoundly influenced by Etruscan culture and three of the seven kings who ruled Rome before the Republic were Etruscans, known as the Tarquins.

Etruscan warriors: by the 4th century BC Etruscan territories were being invaded by the Gauls

The Etruscan and Roman civilisations coexisted relatively peacefully until the defeat of Veii and its incorporation into the territory of Rome in 396 BC. During the ensuing century, Etruscan cities were either defeated or entered into peaceful alliance with an increasingly powerful Rome, although they maintained a fair degree of autonomy until 90 BC, when the Etruscans (as well as all the Italic peoples of the peninsula) were granted Roman citizenship. Thus absorbed into what was to become the Roman Empire, the separate Etruscan culture and language rapidly disappeared. Scholars of the day attached little importance to the need to preserve the Etruscan language and few translations into Latin were made. No Etruscan literature survived and the only remaining samples of the written language are related to religious and funerary customs.

Greek Colonisation

The first Greek settlements in Italy were established in the early 8th century BC – first on the island of Ischia in the Golfo di Napoli, followed by other settlements along the peninsula's southern coast and in Sicilia. What became known as Magna Graecia (Greater Greece) was, in fact, a group of independent city-states, established by colonists from the independent city-states of Greece itself. The founders of the colonies at Ischia and Cumae were from the island of Euboea; the Corinthians founded the great city of Siracusa and exiled Spartans founded the wealthy city of Taranto.

The civilisation of Magna Graecia, which flourished in territories which had previously been colonised by Pheonicians or occupied by local peoples, spanned about six centuries. The ruins of magnificent Doric temples in Italy's south (at Paestum) and in Sicilia (Agrigento, Selinunte and Segesta), and other monuments such as the Greek theatre at Siracusa, stand as testament to its splendour.

Siracusa became so powerful that Athens considered it enough of a threat to launch an attack on the city. In one of the great maritime battles in history, Siracusa managed to destroy the Athenian fleet in 413 BC. By the end of the 3rd century BC, Magna Graecia had succumbed to the might of the advancing Roman Republic, though not before playing a major role in introducing Hellenic culture to Rome.

The Roman Republic

The traditional date for the founding of Rome by Romulus is 21 April 753 BC, but the story of the first Roman Republic begins in 509 BC, after the phase of the seven kings. It is a complex, fascinating saga of a quest to create an intellectual and economic national entity from a fiercely independent, and primarily regionally focused, family and community-oriented people.

When Rome established its first Republic, it introduced a basic principle of political philosophy – that of the sovereign rights of the people. In modern Roma the initials SPQR, visible in carvings on ancient Roman monuments and stamped on municipal property to this day, stand as testimony to an ideal of continuity with the first Senate, *Senatus Populus Que Romanus*, the Senate & People of Rome.

More realistically though, during the period of the monarchy, there already existed a group of powerful families, known as the *patricii* (patricians), descendants of the *patres* (founding fathers), who wielded great influence over the rest of the population, known as the *plebeii* (plebeians). In the early years of the Republic, the patrician families managed to achieve a monopoly on public office. Hence the plebeians created their own movement, leading to what is known to scholars as the 'struggle of the orders'.

The plebeian movement was successful to the extent that the Roman statesman Cato could assume in the 2nd century BC that there were no 'formal' barriers in the way of any Roman citizen to prevent them achieving the highest office of the state. But, in reality, the control of the state always remained in the hands of the patricians and *equites* (the highest class of the non-noble rich), who constituted the vast majority of the 300 senators.

The politics of conquest favoured the patricians but also permitted the compensation of plebeians, more specifically soldiers, with parcels of land from the newly conquered territories – a system of reward which enabled the Republic to avoid internal conflict. Other peoples allied with Rome also received concrete advantages. But perhaps one of the main reasons for Rome's success was that its imperialistic exploits were based on a social system whereby every Roman citizen could participate according to his class, with the possibility of climbing the social ladder.

The Punic Wars

The use of Latin became widespread as a result of the expansion of Rome, an expansion strongly opposed by Carthage, which controlled the Mediterranean's maritime traffic in competition with Greece. Carthage engaged in three long wars with Rome, called the Punic Wars, the first of which started in 264 BC and raged for 24 years.

In 264 BC Carthage was much more powerful than Rome. Originally one of several Phoenician trading posts at the narrow point of the Mediterranean, opposite Sicilia, in what is now Tunisia, Carthage had built up a colonial empire which extended to Morocco and included western Sicilia, Corsica, Sardegna and even parts of Spain.

During the Punic Wars, the Romans were called upon for the first time to fight a war across the sea against the greatest naval power of the age. The Greek historian Polybius claimed that the Romans had no idea even of how to construct a large warship until a Carthaginian vessel was grounded and they were then able to construct a replica.

The First Punic War (264-241 BC), which Rome won, was fought over control of Sicilia. In the 20 years or so before the next war with Rome, Carthage extended its empire to Spain. In the meantime, Rome had managed to expel the Gauls from the Italian peninsula, consolidating the frontiers of Italy as we now know them.

With Spanish wealth and mercenaries, Hannibal launched his famous offensive, using elephants to cross the Alps, and sparking the Second Punic War in 218 BC. Hannibal crushed the Romans in bloody battles as he moved down the peninsula – around Lago di Trasimeno in what is now Umbria and at Cannae in what is now Puglia. He was ultimately defeated by the Roman general, Scipio, in 202 BC at Zama in North Africa, after being recalled to African soil by Carthage.

In the ensuing years, Rome added Macedonian Greece to its provinces, after decisively defeating Perseus, the son of Philip V of Macedon, in a three-year war. The Third Punic War (149-146 BC) dealt the

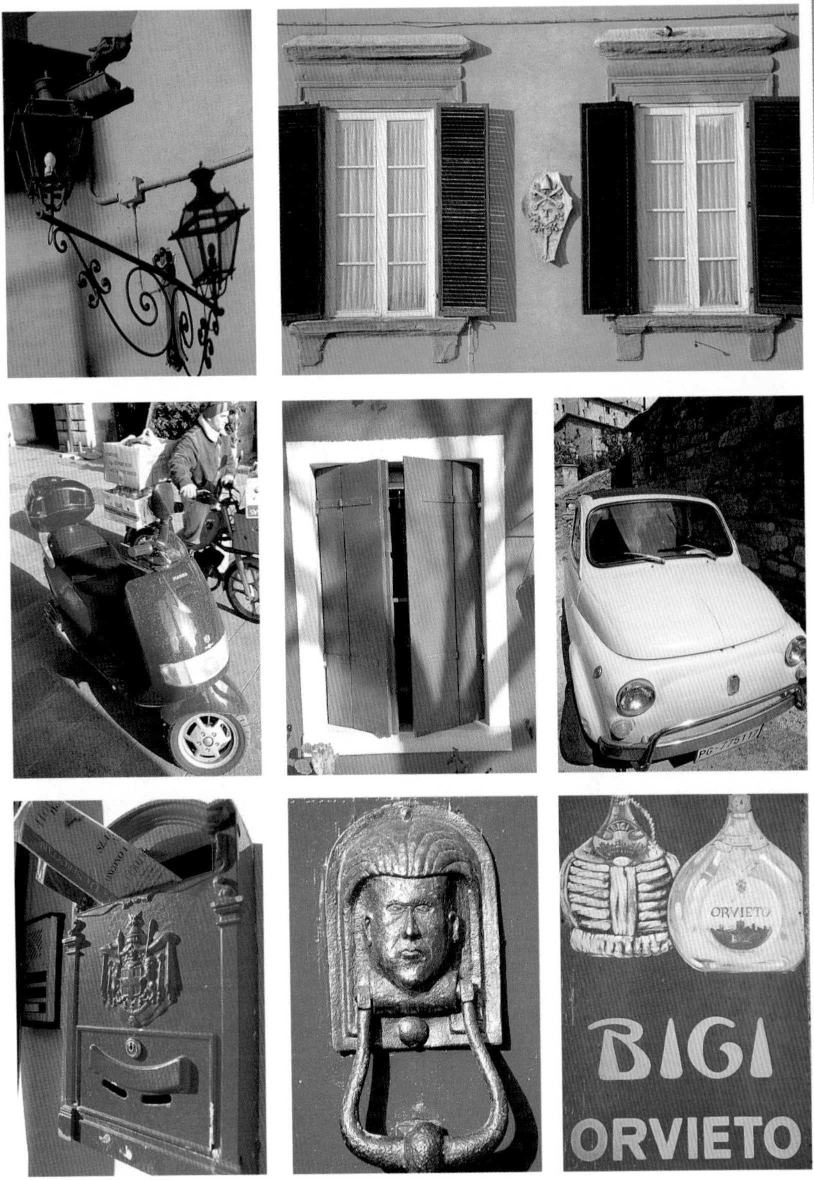

Snapshots of Italy

All photographs by Damien Simonis

GERMANY
FRANCE
SWITZERLAND
LIECHTENSTEIN
AUSTRIA
HUNGARY
SLOVENIA
CROATIA
YUGOSLAVIA
BOSNIA HERCEGOVINA
MONACO
SAN MARINO
CORSICA (FRANCE)
LIGURIAN SEA
ADRIATIC SEA
GOLFO DI VENEZIA
Golfo di Genova
VALLE D'AOSTA
PIEMONTE
LIGURIA
LOMBARDIA
TRENTINO-ALTO ADIGE
VENETO
FRIULI-VENEZIA GIULIA
EMILIA-ROMAGNA
TOSCANA
UMBRIA
LE MARCHE
LAZIO
ABRUZZO
Besancon
Basel
Zurich
Vaduz
Lucerne
Bern
Lausanne
Geneva
Innsbruck
Graz
Budapest
Klagenfurt
Nagyknizsa
Pécs
Ljubljana
Zagreb
Osijek
Trieste
Rijeka
Karlovac
Banja Luka
Zadar
Sarajevo
Spilt
Dubrovnik
Monte Bianco (4807m)
Courmayeur
Aosta
Varallo
Locarno
Bellinzona
Sondria
Livigno
Bormio
Merano
Bolzano
Brunico
Canazei
Tolmezzo
Udine
Gorizia
Pordenone
Belluno
Feltre
Trento
Riva del Garda
Lago di Maggiore
Lago di Como
Lago di Garda
Lecco
Varese
Como
Bergamo
Brescia
Milano
Biella
Ivrea
Novara
Vercelli
Modane
Susa
Torino
Briançon
Asti
Alessandria
Pavia
Voghera
Piacenza
Mantova
Verona
Vicenza
Bassano
Treviso
Venezia
Padova
Rovigo
Ferrara
Monviso (3841m)
Alba
Acqui
Fossano
Cuneo
Parma
Reggio
Modena
Bologna
Ravenna
Genova
Rapallo
Chiavari
Savona
Alassio
La Spezia
Imperia
Ventimiglia
San Remo
Nice
Cannes
Forlì
Cesena
Rimini
Pesaro
Fano
Urbino
Senigallia
Ancona
Viareggio
Lucca
Pistoia
Prato
Pisa
Firenze
Livorno
Volterra
Poggibonsi
Sansepolcro
Arezzo
Gubbio
Jesi
Fabriano
Macerata
Fermo
Cecina
Cortona
Siena
Perugia
Assisi
Lago Trasimeno
Capraia
Piombino
Elba
Foligno
Sarnano
Ascoli Piceno
Trevi
Grosseto
Lago di Bolsena
Orvieto
Spoleto
Bastia
Pianosa
Porto Santo Stefano
Orbetello
Teramo
Narni
Terni
Corno Grande (2914m)
Pescara
Montecristo
Giglio
Viterbo
Rieti
L'Aquila
Ortona
Isole Tremiti
Giannutri
Civitavecchia
Avezzano
Popoli
Sulmona
Termoli
Rodi Gargnico
Ajaccio
ROMA
Tivoli
Pescasseroli
Fiumicino
Promontorio del Gargano
Vieste
Po
Ticino
Adda
Oglio
Adige
Trebbia
Taro
Panaro
Reno
Arno
Tanaro
Tevere
Rhone
Inn
Drava
Sava
Danube
44°N
42°N

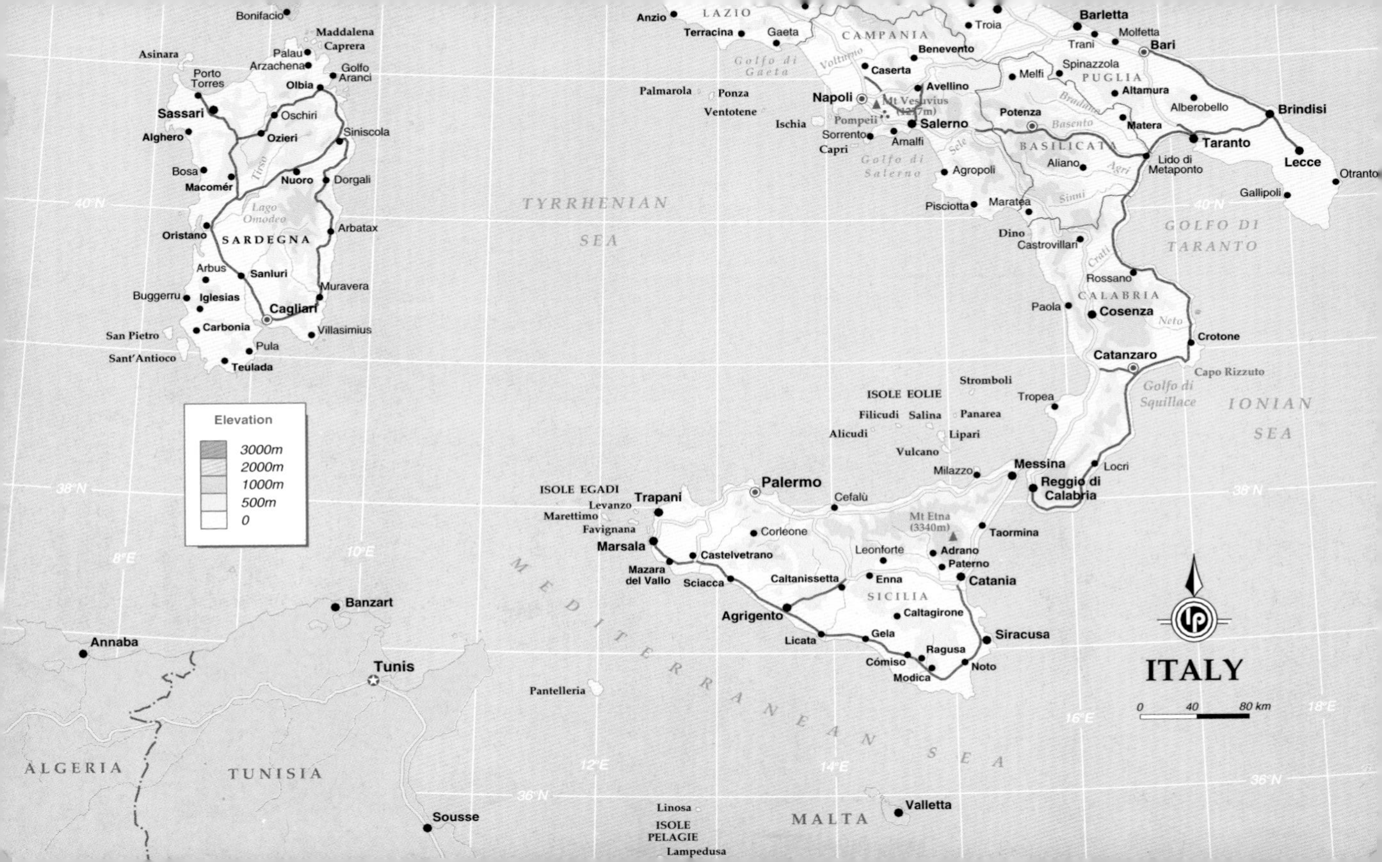
ITALY
0 40 80 km
Elevation
3000m
2000m
1000m
500m
0
TYRRHENIAN SEA
IONIAN SEA
MEDITERRANEAN SEA
GOLFO DI TARANTO
LAZIO
CAMPANIA
PUGLIA
BASILICATA
CALABRIA
SICILIA
SARDEGNA
MALTA
TUNISIA
ALGERIA
ISOLE EOLIE
ISOLE EGADI
ISOLE PELAGIE
Golfo di Gaeta
Golfo di Salerno
Golfo di Squillace
Capo Rizzuto
Mt Vesuvius
Mt Etna (3340m)
Lago Omodeo
Tirso
Volturno
Bradano
Basento
Sele
Agri
Sinni
Crati
Neto
Anzio
Terracina
Gaeta
Troia
Barletta
Molfetta
Trani
Bari
Benevento
Caserta
Melfi
Spinazzola
Altamura
Alberobello
Brindisi
Napoli
Avellino
Potenza
Matera
Pompeii
Salerno
Taranto
Lecce
Ischia
Sorrento
Amalfi
Capri
Lido di Metaponto
Aliano
Otranto
Agropoli
Gallipoli
Pisciotta
Maratea
Dino
Castrovillari
Rossano
Paola
Cosenza
Crotone
Catanzaro
Stromboli
Tropea
Filicudi
Salina
Panarea
Alicudi
Lipari
Vulcano
Milazzo
Messina
Locri
Reggio di Calabria
Palmarola
Ponza
Ventotene
Palermo
Cefalù
Trapani
Levanzo
Marettimo
Favignana
Corleone
Marsala
Castelvetrano
Leonforte
Adrano
Paterno
Taormina
Catania
Mazara del Vallo
Sciacca
Caltanissetta
Enna
Agrigento
Caltagirone
Licata
Gela
Ragusa
Siracusa
Comiso
Modica
Noto
Pantelleria
Linosa
Lampedusa
Valletta
Bonifacio
Maddalena
Caprera
Asinara
Palau
Arzachena
Golfo Aranci
Porto Torres
Olbia
Sassari
Oschiri
Alghero
Ozieri
Siniscola
Bosa
Nuoro
Dorgali
Macomér
Oristano
Arbatax
Arbus
Sanluri
Buggerru
Iglesias
Muravera
Cagliari
San Pietro
Carbonia
Villasimius
Pula
Sant'Antioco
Teulada
Banzart
Annaba
Tunis
Sousse
40°N
38°N
36°N
8°E
10°E
12°E
14°E
16°E
18°E

DAMIEN SIMONIS

DAMIEN SIMONIS

DAMIEN SIMONIS

DAMIEN SIMONIS

Carnavale
Top Left: Carnavale masks, Isola di Burano, Venezia
Top Right: Krampus, traditional spirits of the Tyrol, Udine, Friuli-Venezia Giulia
Bottom Left & Right: Participants in the Battaglia delle Arance, Carnavale in Ivrea, Piemonte

final blow to Carthage. Vengeful in victory, Rome's destruction of Carthaginian civilisation was total; little knowledge of its culture remains and no known literature survives.

With Carthage destroyed, Rome incorporated Spain into its colonies and became the dominant power in the Mediterranean.

From Republic to Empire

Until 146 BC, the history of the Roman Republic was one of external warfare but relative peace at home. The constitution, which allowed for a government of two consuls who were elected annually, and a Senate representing the ruling class, worked efficiently. Roads and aqueducts were built to link the new estates of the Roman Republic. New cities were founded across the country. The Via Appia (Appian Way) had been started as early as 312 BC, when Rome was linked to Capua, and the road was extended to Brindisi in 244 BC. The Via Flaminia was built northwards over the Apennines to Fano in 220 BC and was subsequently extended to Rimini. The Via Aurelia hugged the west coast, eventually reaching Genova, and is still in full use today, as are all the ancient consular roads.

Julius Caesar, general, statesman, historian and dictator of the Roman Empire (49-44 BC)

As well as the great wealth gained from the conquest of the Carthaginian and Hellenic worlds, Italian society found itself changed by another spoil of war, the long-term effects of which were to prove less beneficial to the Republic. To achieve the visions of its rulers and satisfy its lifestyle, Rome needed slave labour. In its last years, the Roman Republic supported around two million slaves – about 35% of the population – all of whom were completely dependent on their masters for their existence.

The influx of slave labour ensured the growth of large estates for the select few at the expense of the many small freeholdings that had characterised pre-Punic War society. The demise of smaller holdings created an agrarian disaster which brought social disruption and human misery, resulting in the Social War of 91 BC. Recognised as a last attempt by the allied peoples of the peninsula to press their claims on Rome, the revolt was resolved by force, but it resulted in Rome offering citizenship to all the peoples of its colonies.

Another, more bloody social war, was fought from 73 to 71 BC. In an attempt to secure freedom for his fellow slaves destined for the ever-popular gladiatorial games, a Tracian slave named Spartacus escaped from a school for gladiators in Capua, taking with him 200 followers. About 78 of them remained with Spartacus to form the nucleus of a force of some 70,000 runaway slaves and others. After initially repelling the Roman forces sent to suppress the uprising, Spartacus was killed and some 6000 of his followers were crucified and lined the Appian Way from Capua to Rome.

By then Rome's military greats – Gnaeus Pompeius (Pompey), Crassus (who was one of the wealthiest men in Rome), Julius Caesar, Mark Antony and Octavian – controlled the Senate and, in 60 BC, Pompey, with Caesar and Crassus, formed an unconstitutional triumvirate, effectively ending any semblance of government 'for and by the people'.

In 52 BC, Pompey finally took the title of sole consul and dictator, with the full support of Caesar, who, having secured command of the legions in Gaul, declared southern Britain part of Rome after two raids on the island Celts in 55 and 54 BC. Caesar's flagrant disregard for the authority of the Senate, which had ordered him to disband his legions and return to Rome, gained him enormous popularity, particularly among his troops.

Following his defeat of Pompey in the battle of Pharsalus, and Pompey's murder in Egypt in 48 BC, Caesar returned to Rome and was made consul and dictator. His four-year reign was marked by intense activity both in Italy and throughout the territories under Roman control. He instigated land reforms which limited individual's holdings, and framed a uniform system of local government which extended throughout Italy and the outer provinces. He also introduced the Julian calendar, which was to be used throughout Europe for many centuries.

But Caesar continued to treat the political establishment of Rome with scant respect. He increased the number of senators to 900, effectively undermining and dissipating the Senate's power and, when he was murdered on 15 March 44 BC, it was said that among his murderers were more of his friends than his enemies – including Brutus, his adopted son.

Caesar's dictatorship paved the way for further domination by Rome's military imperialists, starting with Mark Antony (consul for the year 44 BC) and followed by Caius Octavian, who had been adopted by Caesar as his son and heir. Octavian became Rome's first emperor in 27 BC, adopting the title of Augustus, the Grand One.

Augustus ruled for 45 years, a period of great advancement in engineering, architecture, administration and military arts as well as literature. He often claimed that he found Rome a city of brick and left it a city of marble. The remains of his forum are still visible opposite the Foro Romano and his mausoleum is tucked away behind the Ara Pacis in Rome.

The Augustan age enabled the blossoming of Latin literature, the foundations of which had been laid by great writers and philosophers such as Cicero (106-43 BC) and the early humorous dramatists, Plautus (c 254-184 BC) and Terence (c 195-159 BC). Virgil and the two great poets of the Augustan era, Horace (65-8 BC) and Ovid (43 BC-c 17 AD), had enormous influence on European thought and literature.

Rome's impeccable administrative system, which gave great authority to institutions, and a rigorous military discipline promoting an efficient army, favoured the development of an empire which culturally and linguistically unified many diverse peoples. By 100 AD, the city of Rome had more than 1.5 million inhabitants, and its wealth and prosperity were obvious in the rich floor mosaics, the marble temples, public baths, theatres, circuses, libraries, publishing houses, a postal service and even a telegraphic system based on light signals. Meanwhile, the empire boasted a 100,000km network of roads and a complex system of aqueducts and possessed the technology to drain large lakes and to develop sophisticated war machines.

Consolidation of Expansion

The succession of Augustus by his stepson Tiberius (14-37 AD) heralded an era which eventually was to disturb Roman imperialism, not because of any decline of military might but because of the rise of Christianity. Despite the efforts of many emperors to suppress the new religion, Christianity prospered. The Apostles and their followers travelled from Northumberland in Britain to Egypt, and from Portugal to Syria, spreading the Christian story.

Meanwhile, the Empire continued to grow and flourish, with significant cultural expansion under emperors such as Claudius, who introduced major reforms to ministerial government, created a modern system of sanitation, shops and public baths, and built aqueducts on the massive Porta Maggiore. He also created an artificial harbour at Ostia (now known as Ostia Antica) at the mouth of the Tevere, the ruins of which are visible today.

The extravagant and obviously deranged Emperor Nero (ruled 54-68 AD) is best known for the burning of Rome and his persecution of the Christians.

After a short period of instability, Emperor Vespasian, the son of a civil servant from the Italian provinces and the first of the Flavian dynasty, carried out some of the most ambitious building projects of the Empire. He started the Colosseo, which was completed by his son Titus, who succeeded him as emperor in 78 AD. He is remembered in Roman architecture by the triumphal Arco di Tito (81 AD) where the Via Sacra enters the Foro Romano.

Trajan, a Roman general, was commanding his legions in what is now Germany when he was appointed emperor by the Senate in 98 AD. He returned to Rome two years later to be crowned, but left soon after to conquer Dacia (present-day Romania), then Mesopotamia, Persia, Syria and Armenia. Under Trajan, the Roman Empire reached its point of greatest expansion: extending from present-day Kuwait to England, from the Caspian Sea to Morocco and Portugal and from North Africa to the Danube and Romania.

Trajan's architectural legacy included a new artificial harbour at Ostia to replace that built by Claudius (Trajan's harbour remains perfectly preserved in the private property of a Roman family) and the amphitheatre at Verona. The great architect Apollodorus of Damascus built a 1km-long wooden bridge over the Danube to enable Trajan to invade new territories. He also designed Trajan's forum in Rome, where the emperor placed a magnificent marble column decorated with 2000 carvings depicting his Dacian campaign. The column, which later served as Trajan's tomb, remains standing today.

His successor, Hadrian (117-138 AD), was responsible for some of Roma's most famous landmarks: he rebuilt the Pantheon after a fire, and built the vast Villa Adriana at Tivoli, near Roma, as well as Hadrian's Wall in Britain. His tomb was converted into the fortress now called Castel Sant'Angelo, in Roma.

A terrible plague swept Europe during the 2nd century and, combined with the infiltration of Eastern religions and increasing pressure from Teutonic tribes on the Rhine and Danube frontiers, Rome began to lose its grip.

With the Edict of Milano in 313 AD, Emperor Constantine gave official recognition to Christianity after having first converted to it himself. Rome was established as its headquarters. Formal recognition also sparked off a widespread building programme of cathedrals and churches throughout the land.

Division of the Empire

The Empire remained beset by civil wars as the once all-conquering Roman legions shifted their support from one would-be emperor to another. Tribes along the empire's borders took advantage of the power vacuum by grabbing ever-larger chunks of territory, and there was little Rome could do about it. The Empire was so large that it had become undefendable.

Cutting his losses and recognising the growing importance of the wealthy eastern regions of the empire, Emperor Constantine in 324 moved his capital city from Rome to Byzantium, a city on the northern shore of the Bosporus (now Turkey). He renamed it 'New Rome' but it became known as Constantinople (present-day Istanbul). Among the monuments left in Rome by Constantine are his triumphal arch between the Foro Romano and the Colosseo, and the imposing Basilica di Costantino (also known as the Basilica di Massenzio, in the forum).

The demise of the Roman Empire continued when the ruling brothers Valentian and Valens divided the empire into a western and eastern half in 364, a division that was formalised after the death of Emperor Theodosius I in 395. His son Honorius ruled the Western Roman Empire, while his other son Arcadius ruled the Eastern Roman Empire.

Separated from its Roman roots, the Eastern Roman Empire embraced Hellenistic (Greek-Egyptian) culture and developed into the mighty Byzantine

Empire, the most powerful Mediterranean state throughout the Middle Ages. It existed until the capture of Constantinople by the Turks in 1453.

The Early Middle Ages (400-600)

A population decline throughout the 2nd and 3rd centuries worsened in the 4th century through plague, famine and war.

The arrival of the Vandals in North Africa cut off Rome's corn supplies, while the western Teutonic tribe of Visigoths consolidated control of much of the northern Mediterranean coast and northern Italy. In 452, Attila the Hun, leader of a tribe from the central Asian steppes, invaded and, it is said, caused the people of Aquileia and Grado to found a city of refuge called Venezia. This city was to become a great trading and seafaring centre and the birthplace, in 1254, of one of Italy's most well known adventurers, Marco Polo.

In 476, the year traditionally recognised as the end of the Roman Empire, the last Western Roman emperor, Romulus Augustulus, was deposed by a mutinous Germanic captain of mercenaries named Odovacar (476-93).

Gothic rule in Italy reached its zenith with the Ostrogothic emperor Theodoric (493-526). The greatest of the Ostrogothic rulers, Theodoric had spent several years as a hostage in Constantinople where he acquired great respect for Roman culture. When the Eastern Roman emperor Zeno put him in charge of Italy, Theodoric, ruling from Ravenna, brought peace and prosperity to the area.

After Theodoric's death, the Eastern Roman emperor Justinian (527-565) and his wife, Theodora, reconquered Italy and laid the groundwork for the Byzantine era. Among the early examples of Byzantine art in Italy are the mosaic portraits of Justinian and Theodora in the Basilica di San Vitale at Ravenna. Though the Justinian reconquest was soon rolled back by the Lombards, Byzantine emperors and empresses managed to hold on to parts of southern Italy until the 11th century.

During the middle years of the 5th century, Pope Leo I 'the Great' (440-461), known as the founder of Catholicism, had ensured the temporal power of the papacy by persuading Attila not to attack Rome. Using a document known as the *Donation of Constantine* (which made the Western Romen Empire a gift from Constantine to the papacy forever), Leo I secured the Western Romen Empire for the fledgling Catholic Church.

In 590, Pope Gregory I, son of a rich Romen family, returned from his self-imposed exile in a monastery, having given all his wealth to the poor. He set the pattern of Church administration which was to guide Catholic services and rituals throughout history.

Gregory oversaw the Christianisation of Britain, improved conditions for slaves, provided free bread in Rome and repaired Italy's extensive network of aqueducts, as well as leaving an enormous volume of writing on which much Catholic dogma was subsequently based.

Lombard Italy & the Papal States (600-800)

Even before Gregory became pope the Lombard invasion of Italy had begun. The Lombards were a Swabian people who appear to have originally inhabited the lower basin of the Elbe but, as so often happened to conquerors of the Italian peninsula, rather than imposing their culture on the locals, they adopted the local culture. Their language did not last long after their arrival and their culture too was almost completely integrated. Their more communal concept of land and property tenure was soon overthrown by the Romans' high regard for private property, either absolute or leased, and the Lombards, who mainly settled around Milano, Pavia and Brescia, soon became city dwellers, building many churches and public baths which still grace these cities. They eventually expanded their control farther down the peninsula – taking over the important duchies of Spoleto and Benevento – although they were unable to take Roma.

A Goth (left) and a Swabian; these individuals represent just two of the different ethnic groups to invade the Italian peninsula

In an effort to unseat the Lombards, the pope invited the Franks to invade Italy, which they did in 754 and 756 under the command of their king, Pepin, disenfranchising the Lombards and establishing the Papal States, which were to survive until 1870. Using the *Donation of Constantine* as his precedent, Pepin issued the *Donation of Pepin* in 756, which gave land that was still nominally under the Byzantine Empire to Pope Stephen II and proclaimed the pope heir of the Roman emperors.

When Pepin's son and successor, Charlemagne, visited Roma in 774 he confirmed the *Donation of Pepin*. Charlemagne was crowned emperor by Pope Leo III on Christmas Day 800 in the Basilica di San Pietro, and the concept of the 'Holy Roman Empire' came into being. The bond between the papacy and the Byzantine Empire was thus forever broken and political power in what had been the Western Roman Empire shifted north of the Alps, where it would remain for more than 1000 years. But, on Charlemagne's death his successors were unable to hold together his vast Carolingian Empire. In 843, the Partition of Verdun divided the empire between his three nephews and Italy became a battleground of rival powers and states – the imperial crown was ruthlessly fought over and Roma's aristocratic families also engaged in battle for the papacy.

An Oasis of Calm

Meanwhile, the Muslim Arabs had invaded Sicilia and in 831 took Palermo as their capital, while Siracusa, an important city since the first Greek settlements, fell to them in 878. They established a splendid civilisation, restoring the fundamentals of Greek culture elaborated by Muslim scholars such as the philosopher Averroës, the physician and philosopher Avicenna, the astronomer and geographer Al Battani and the mathematician Al Kovarizmi. Cotton, sugar cane, oranges and lemons were introduced in the south, taxes there were lower, and the Sicilians lived relatively peacefully under their Arab lords for more than two centuries. Hundreds of mosques were built and the elegant, Arabian architecture survived even after Sicilia was returned to the Christian fold.

Amalfi, which had secured independence from Napoli in the 840s, soon became a major trading republic in the western Mediterranean and, with the republics of Gaeta and Napoli along with Salerno, which was still a Lombard principality, became a centre of great cosmopolitan civilisation and learning. In the 11th century, Salerno was famous for its medical school, where Greek, Hebrew, Arab and Christian teachers worked together.

While the south prospered under Arab rule, the rest of Italy was not so calm. Following the end of the Carolingian Empire in 887, warfare broke out in earnest between local Italian rulers who were divided in their support of Frankish and Germanic claimants, all absentee landlords, to the imperial title and throne. Italy became the battleground of Europe as rival factions fought for ascendancy and refugees flooded safe cities from the devastated countryside. Many of Italy's medieval hill towns developed in this period as easily defendable safe havens.

In 962, the Saxon Otto I was crowned emperor in Roma and formally founded the Holy Roman Empire. His son, Otto II, and later his grandson, Otto III, also took the title Holy Roman Emperor, cementing a tradition that was to remain the privilege of Germanic emperors until 1806.

In the early 11th century the fanatically Christian Normans began arriving, first as mercenaries in southern Italy where they fought against the Arabs, but changing allegiances as profit dictated.

The Norman & Holy Roman Eras

The campaign of Hildebrand (who was to become Pope Gregory VII in 1073) to bring the world under the rule of Christianity was, in reality, a struggle for power between Church and State. In order to be legitimate, every new emperor had to be sworn in and 'crowned' by the pope. The papacy, based in Roma, and the Holy Roman Empire, with its power base north of the Alps, were compelled to agree in order to reconstruct the political and cultural unity which had been lost with the fall of the Western Roman Empire. In reality, the two powers were in perennial conflict and the consequences of this dual leadership dominated the Middle Ages.

Both the Frankish and Germanic claimants to the crown were temporarily distracted by the summons of Christendom to recapture the Holy Land from the Muslims The First Crusade, a tragic disaster, moved primarily from the regions which are today Germany and France.

Having already established themselves firmly in Puglia and Calabria, the Normans moved into Sicilia, which they progressively managed to wrest from the Arab Muslims. But, rather than banish the Arabs, the Normans tended to assimilate Eastern traditions and systems and established what was to be a long period of religious tolerance in the south. When Roger II was crowned king of Sicilia in 1130, he established his court at Palermo, which had been the capital of the Arab emirate and, before long, church towers stood beside the domes of the mosques.

The Normans brought with them a fine appreciation of majestic spaces which are characterised by Romanesque architecture, but they liberally adapted Arab and Byzantine architectural features. The Chiesa di San Giovanni degli Eremiti at Palermo might equally pass as a mosque or a Greek or Norman basilica. King Roger's magnificent Cappella Palatina and the Cattedrale di Monreale (just outside Palermo) are excellent examples of how the Normans combined the vitality of Oriental influences with the glory of Byzantine architecture and the simple beauty of Romanesque.

Norman rule in the south gave way to Germanic claims due to the foresight of Holy Roman Emperor Frederick I (known as Barbarossa) who married off his son Henry to Constance de Hauteville, heir to the Norman throne in Sicilia. Barbarossa's grandson, Frederick II, became Holy Roman Emperor in 1220. An enlightened ruler, Frederick, who became known as Stupor Mundi (Wonder of the World), was both a warrior and a scholar. A profound admirer of Arabic culture, he allowed freedom of worship to Muslims, as well as to Jews. He studied philosophy and magic, wrote laws and earned a place in Italian history as one of the country's earliest poets. In 1224, Frederick founded the University of Napoli, with the idea of educating administrators for his kingdom. As a half-Norman southerner, Frederick rejected the tradition that Holy Roman Emperors lived north of the Alps. He moved his exotic, multicultural court (complete with Saracen guard) between Sicilia and southern Italy, where he built several castles in Puglia – notably the superb octagonal Castel del Monte.

City-States & Comuni

Between the 12th and 14th centuries, government in Italy evolved into a new kind of political institution – the city-states or city-republics, whose political organisation became known as the *comune*, or town council.

The cities of northern Italy were highly favoured commercially by their position on the 'hinge' of the Mediterranean and the European continent – they were also a long way from both the pope and the emperor. With the resulting new wealth, some cities freed themselves from feudal control. Milano, Crema, Bologna, Firenze, Pavia, Modena, Parma, Lodi and many other cities set themselves up as autonomous powers, but with the protection of either the pope or the emperor. The 'middle class' was born, composed of rich merchants and artisans who, very soon, passed from commercial rivalry to internal political struggles. These conflicts ended up favouring restricted oligarchies in which one family prevailed, charged by the city with exercising a form of government called the Signoria. The various Signorias were reinforced from within, persecuting rival families and opponents, while from without they expanded their territories at the expense of weaker neighbours.

The five great Italian regional divisions began to take shape: Il Veneto, Lombardia, Toscana, the Papal States, and the Southern Kingdom.

In the south, Charles of Anjou, who had defeated and beheaded Conradin, Frederick II's 16-year-old grandson and heir, ousted Germanic rule. French dominion under Charles brought heavy taxes, particularly on rich landowners, who did not accept such measures graciously. Although always a hated foreigner, Charles supported much-needed road repairs, reformed the coinage, imposed standard weights and measures, improved the equipment of ports and opened silver mines.

Despite his grip on papal power and his subsequent conquests of Jerusalem and Constantinople, Charles of Anjou was to become infamous throughout Italy for a popular uprising, sparked off by the assault of a Sicilian woman by a French soldier in Palermo on 30 March 1282. A crowd gathered, killing the soldier, and a widespread massacre of the French ensued as communities throughout Sicilia rose against their warlords. Known as the Sicilian Vespers, the events of this time led to the citizens of Palermo declaring an independent republic and endorsing Peter of Aragon as king, effectively separating themselves from the Neapolitan mainland and bringing themselves under Spanish rule.

The latter decades of the 13th century were marked by decreasing economic vitality as Europeans battled an invasion far more deadly than that of a mere army. The effects of plague (later to be known as the Black Death) or *la peste*, along with famine and deprivation from years of war, decimated over half the population of many major cities.

Meanwhile, in north and central Italy, the city-states were growing in importance. The Republic of Venezia increased its possessions. Trading with its powerful fleet towards the Byzantine Orient, it securely managed its own independence in the ports of Dalmatia, Greece, Cyprus and the Aegean. Marco Polo, back from the court of the Great Khan after 25 years in China, wrote the *Million* at the end of the 13th century. The commercial traffic of Genova, another 'maritime republic' and great rival of Venezia, extended as far as the Black Sea.

The legal debate of this time and the ensuing changes to Italian society, together with the dawning of a new era of powerful literary and artistic expression, were to form the basis of the humanist culture which ushered in the Renaissance.

Humanism

The artist whose works signify the breakthrough from the Byzantine or Gothic style to the Renaissance was Giotto (see the colour section on Art & Architecture). In literature, Averroës, an Arabic philosopher born in Cordova in southern Spain, resurrected Aristotle's doctrine that immortality was gained through individual efforts towards universal reason. This emphasis on the autonomy of human reason, based on the theories of the classic philosophers instead of the increasingly self-serving dogmas of the Church hierarchy, was a revolutionary philosophical position that became known as humanism.

The church had chosen to embrace only those classical philosophers whose thinking fitted its theological purposes. Humanist thinkers were, instead, making incredible discoveries of ancient Roman and Greek works, which had been transcribed by religious orders during the Middle Ages and remained hidden away – even 'lost' – in monasteries throughout Europe. These classical works were not necessarily those which were accepted by the church and they inspired great debate among intellectuals of the day.

Translated into Latin, Averroës's work became a strong influence on another interpreter of Aristotelian thought, St Thomas Aquinas, who was educated at Monte Cassino by the Benedictines and at the University of Bologna, before joining the Dominicans in 1243. Aquinas bridged the gap between the Christian belief in God and Aristotle's respect for the validity of reason with his *Summa Theologica*. This resulted in Italian Christianity never losing either its grip on the real world or its respect for good works.

The new era saw independent artisans flourish and their guilds became influential in the power structure of the cities, particularly in Firenze, which retained the trappings of the new republicanism until 1434, when the Medici family brought back a comparatively mild despotism.

The Florentine houses of Peruzzi and Bardi were the business moguls of Europe, minting some 400,000 units of their currency, the *firenze* or florin, each year. Florentine prosperity was based on the wool trade, and on finance and commerce in general. Craft and trade guilds became increasingly powerful in the affairs of the city.

The Arte della Lana (wool guild) of Firenze employed a workforce of more than 5000, but these workers were not citizens and could not take part in the elections of the Republic. In 1378, the poorest workers, the wool-carters or *ciompi*, revolted against their city fathers, taking power in the city-state for at least six weeks during which time they created new guilds to represent them.

But Europe's first working-class uprising was short-lived as a greater power struggle was taking place between the pope and the Holy Roman Emperor. This conflict formed the focal point of Italian politics in the late Middle Ages with a split into two camps – 'Guelph' (in support of the pope) and 'Ghibelline' (in support of the emperor).

Dante Alighieri, the great poet and writer whom Italians see as the father of the Italian language, even of the Italian nation, was one of the casualties of the Guelph-Ghibelline battle. A dedicated Guelph supporter, Dante was exiled from his birthplace, Firenze, in 1301 because he belonged to the wrong faction.

While the first decades of the 14th century were years of economic and cultural growth, not all cities employed the relatively liberal style of the government of Firenze. Milano, like many of the Italian *comuni*, was still strictly dominated by the *Signorie* The Della Torre family, which represented the popular party of the city-state, came into dire conflict with the Visconti family, which represented the Ghibelline nobility. Ottone Visconti had been made Archbishop of Milano in 1262, and his nephew, Matteo, was made imperial vicar by Henry VII. He subsequently destroyed the power of the Della Torre, extending Milanese control over Pavia and Cremona, and later Genova and Bologna. Giangaleazzo Visconti (1351-1402) would turn Milano from a city-state into a strong European power, and although the Visconti were unappreciated as dictators, Milano managed to resist French attempts at invasion.

The government of the Viscontis (up to 1450) and then of the Sforzas allowed Milano an economic and territorial development that extended the borders of the Signoria from Genova to Bologna and from Ticino in Switzerland to Lago di Garda. In those years of tireless labour the entire area of the Pianura Padana (the Po valley) was transformed. Massive hydraulic and irriga-

The Borgia Family

It seems surprising, if not shocking, by today's standards, that the popes of 15th-century Italy fought wars to maintain their territories, had their enemies killed, kept mistresses and even had children by them.

But, for the church to survive the effects of the Great Schism (1378-1417), when the popes resided at Avignon in France, it was considered necessary for the Pope to be noted more for his political and diplomatic skills, than for his spiritual and moral qualities. Thus he was chosen for his leadership abilities and capacity to compete with the various ferocious rulers of the peninsula at that time – in other words, the popes of the period were no saints.

The Spaniard Rodrigo Borgia was elected Pope Alexander VI in 1492, in what is said to have been the most corrupt election in papal history. He went on to establish a notoriously corrupt and immoral court and throughout his papacy he maintained a mistress, Vannozza Catanei, who bore him the infamous Borgia family. It all seemed to make little difference to the Christian pilgrims who flocked to Rome to honour Alexander in the jubilee year of 1500.

Alexander's son Cesare, who killed his own brother, terrorised Italy in a campaign to consolidate and expand the papal states. Ruthless and brilliant, he was at one point admired by Machiavelli. But his sister, Lucrezia, has gone down in history as the embodiment of Borgia cruelty, lust and avarice. It is said that Pope Alexander was obsessed with his daughter almost to the point of incest. He ensured that she lived in incredible luxury and apparently no man was worthy of her – Lucrezia had several husbands, one of whom was assassinated by Cesare. Another of her husbands was publicly declared impotent by the Pope. ■

tion projects (which included the participation of Leonardo da Vinci) converted the plain from a swampy woodland into an extremely productive agricultural collective with some of the most fertile farmland in Italy. Among other things, the cultivation of rice and mulberry was introduced. In the 15th century, parmesan cheese, a product of Parma, Reggio Emilia and Lodi, was among the most precious cheeses in Europe, and butter from the plains of Lombardia was exported as far as Roma.

The 'Babylonian Captivity'

Meanwhile, the Church was going through a profound crisis. The papacy's ongoing crusades against the Eastern infidels during the 13th century had turned into campaigns against European heretics in the 14th, campaigns which in Italy were thinly disguised grabs for wealth and prosperity by claimants from Italian ruling families and the related nobility of Europe.

Pope Boniface VIII (1294-1303) came from Italian nobility and his efforts were directed at ensuring his family's continuing wealth and power. His papal bull of 1302, *Unam Sanctum*, claimed papal supremacy in worldly and spiritual affairs – claims of temporal might which achieved its ends by eliminating heretics.

When the French pope, John XXII (1316-34) chose to base the papacy in Avignon, the Church of Rome, and indeed Roma in general, suddenly lost its *raison d'être*. Goats and cows grazed on the Campidoglio and in the Foro Romano, and residential support for the city's many churches and cathedrals disappeared. The city became a battleground for the struggles between the powerful Orsini and Colonna families. The ruling families challenged the papacy's ongoing claim to be temporal rulers of Roma and the Papal State began to fall apart.

There were seven popes in Avignon from 1305 to 1377, a period that became known as the 'Babylonian Captivity', a phrase coined by the Roman poet laureate Petrarch to castigate the evils of the French papal court.

After the failed attempt of Cola di Rienzo, a popular leader, to wrest the control of Roma from the nobility, Cardinal Egidio d'Albornoz managed to restore the Papal State with his *Egidian Constitutions*, thereby enabling Pope Gregory XI to return to Roma in 1377. When he found a ruined and almost deserted city, Gregory made La Città del Vaticano his base because it was fortified and had the formidable Castel Sant'Angelo nearby.

When Gregory died a year after returning to Roma, Roman cardinals tried to ensure their continuing power by electing as pope the unpopular Urban VI, sparking off a renegade movement of cardinals, mainly French, who, a few months later, elected a second pope, Clement VII, who set up his claim in Avignon. So began the Great Schism, and the papacy was not to be reconciled with Roma until 1417.

The Renaissance

In the 15th century, the newly influential papacy initiated the transformation of Roma. Reduced during the Middle Ages to a conglomeration of majestic ruins and wretched dwellings, the city assumed a new elegance. In 1455, Bernardo Rossellino began construction of Palazzo Venezia; Sixtus IV initiated an urban plan which was to link the areas that had been cut off from one another during the Middle Ages; Donatello, Sandro Botticelli and Fra Angelico lived and worked in Roma at this time. At the beginning of the 16th century Pope Julius II opened Via del Corso and Via Giulia and gave Bramante the task of beginning work on the second Basilica di San Pietro, which was to take more than a century to finish. In 1508, Raphael started painting the rooms in Il Vaticano which are now known as *Le Stanze di Raffaello*, while in 1512 Michelangelo began work on the vaults of the *Cappella Sistina* (Sistine Chapel).

All the great artists of the epoch were influenced by the ever more frequent discoveries of marvellous pieces of classical art, such as the *Laocoön*, found in 1506 in the area of Nero's *Domus Aurea* (the sculpture is now in the Musei del Vaticano). Roma had 100,000 inhabitants at the height of the Renaissance and had become the major centre for Italian political and cultural life. Pope Julius II was succeeded by Pope Leo X, a Medici, and the Roman Curia (or Papal Court) became the meeting place for learned men such as Baldassar Castiglione and Ludovico Ariosto.

As the Renaissance dawned, Italians found they could no longer accept the papal domination of earlier times. A remarkable treatise by the humanist Lorenzo Valla (1407-57) revealed the *Donation of Constantine* to be a forgery. Serious study of the Greek classics and the writings of others, such as Hebrew and Arabic scholars, pervaded the literary works of the later 15th century and highlighted the place of the individual in the universe.

The 15th and early 16th centuries showed unparalleled creativity and visionary accomplishments in all aspects of political, cultural and social life. In Firenze, Cosimo de' Medici, private citizen and wealthy merchant, took over the Signoria in 1434. His nephew, Lorenzo Il Magnifico (the Magnificent), is remembered in history as a great politician who counted very much on the economic and financial security of his Firenze. In his refined diplomacy he focused on building the prestige of the city by enriching it with the presence, and the works, of the greatest artists of the time. This contribution, in the wake of the innovative concepts introduced by the humanists, would combine to make Lorenzo the greatest art patron of the Renaissance.

Fluctuating between the pope and the emperor, feudal lords such as Federico da Montefeltro in Urbino, a merchant as rich as the Medici, and Francesco Sforza, military commander of Milano, turned themselves into bankers and captains of adventure. In these and other cities, revitalised by the wealth of increased commerce, the princes competed with each other for the services of artists, writers, poets and musicians.

This phenomenal creativity was disrupted in Firenze by the preaching of Savonarola, a Dominican monk who preached fire and brimstone against humanist thinking and who allied himself with the French King Charles VIII to overthrow the Medici family and declare a republic in Firenze in 1494. Although the monk eventually met a gruesome end, he wielded tremendous power in Florentine politics in the later 15th century.

The Medici, briefly reinstated, could not regain their positive influence on the Florentines who eventually rejected them, setting up a second democratic republic in 1527. In 1530 this republic was in turn overthrown when Emperor Charles V, who had sacked Roma in 1527, brought back the Medici, whose rule over Firenze for the next 210 years was, more typically, an unhappy oligarchy.

One public official of the first Florentine republic was Niccolò Machiavelli (1469-1527), whose short handbook, *The Prince*, outlined somewhat cynically the prerequisite skills for securing and retaining power. Machiavelli advocated the banishment of all foreign rule in Italy and urged the people to employ their native wit and cunning to achieve this end. He also wrote a history of Firenze, in Italian rather than Latin, although his efforts were less original than those of his contemporary and friend, Francesco Guicciardini (1483-1532).

Not all Italian states experienced the great social blossoming of the Renaissance. In the south, continuing quarrels over rulership and landholdings by the Visconti family, in league with Alfonso V of Aragon against the house of Angevin, ensured repression of the liberty and free thinking which had inspired a new sense of creativity and productivity in other parts of the country.

The Counter-Reformation

By the third decade of the 16th century, the broad-minded curiosity of the Renaissance had begun to give way to the intolerance of the Counter-Reformation. This was the response of the Church to the Reformation, a collective term for the movement led by Martin Luther that aimed to reform the Church and led to the rise of Protestantism in its many forms. The transition was epitomised by the reign of Pope Paul III (1534-49) who promoted the building of the classically elegant Palazzo Farnese in Roma but who also, in 1540, allowed the establishment of Ignatius Loyola's order of the Jesuits and the organisation in 1542 of the Holy Office. This was the final (and ruthless) court of appeal in the trials which began to gather momentum with the increased activities of the Inquisition (1232-1820), the judicial arm of the Church whose aim was to discover and suppress heresy.

Pope Paul III's fanatical opposition to Protestantism and his purging of clerical abuse, as he saw it, resulted in a widespread campaign of torture and fear. In 1559, the Church published the *Index Librorum Prohibitorum*, the Index of Prohibited Books, and the Roman Church's determination to regain papal supremacy over the Protestant churches set the stage for the persecution of intellectuals and free thinkers.

Two great Italian intellectuals who felt the brunt of the Counter-Reformation were Giordano Bruno (1548-1600) and Galileo Galilei (1564-1642). Bruno, a Dominican monk, was forced to flee Italy for Calvinist Geneva, from where he travelled extensively throughout Europe before being arrested by the Inquisition in Venezia in 1592. In 1870, the Kingdom of Italy erected a statue of Bruno in Roma's Campo de' Fiori, where he had been burnt at the stake.

An advocate of Aristotelian science, Galileo was forced by the Church to renounce his approval of the Copernican astronomical system, which held that the earth moved round the sun rather than the reverse. But where Bruno had rejected the Catholic Church, Galileo never deviated from the faith which rejected him.

However, the latter years of the 16th century were not all counterproductive. Pope Gregory XIII (1572-85) replaced the Julian calendar with the Gregorian one in 1582, fixing the start of the year on 1 January and adjusting the system of leap years to align the 365-day year with the seasons. The city of Roma was greatly embellished by the architectural and sculptural achievements of Giovanni Bernini (1598-1680).

Despite these exceptions, Italy no longer determined European cultural expression. Epidemics and wars, in particular the War of the Spanish Succession (1701-14), tossed the nation from Spanish domination in the 17th century to Austrian occupation in the 18th century, beginning with the conquest of Napoli in 1707.

The Enlightenment

The Italy of the 18th century, although mainly ruled from abroad, was set to become part of an era which broke down many of the national barriers of Europe, a development which was as much due to the intermarriage of its monarchies as to new trading laws necessitated by bad harvests in many areas of the continent. The papacy became less influential, especially following the expulsion of the Jesuits from Portugal, France and Spain.

The Enlightenment swept away the dark days of the Counter-Reformation, producing great thinkers and writers such as Cesare Beccaria (1738-94), whose masterpiece *Of Crimes & Punishments* attacked torture and capital punishment as barbarism and advocated reform of the criminal code, a proposal taken up by Grand Duke Leopold of Toscana, who abolished the death sentence.

Economic ideas advocating the liberalisation of trade laws were put forward by the influential writer Pietro Verri (1728-97) who, with his brother Alessandro, introduced reforms in schools and universities as well as in the government administration of Lombardia. Alessandro Volta (1745-1827), after whom the unit of electric potential, the volt, is named, invented the battery when he was professor of natural philosophy at the University of Bologna.

Napoleon

Italy had been the source of many enlightened political ideas, but the concept of national sovereignty had not been one of them. However, when the 27-year-old, Corsican-born French general Napoleon Bonaparte invaded Italy in 1796 and declared himself, quite unofficially, its dictator, a nationalist movement began in earnest. Inspired by the ideas of another Frenchman, Jean-Jacques Rousseau, the French leftist Jacobin movement gained significant support in Italy when, before the end of his first year of occupation, Napoleon used Italy as the base for his expedition into Egypt.

The Jacobin movement established a republic in Roma, renewing the debate about Italy as a nation and the sovereign rights of its people. This movement was dubbed the Risorgimento, or Revival, by Italian dramatist Vittorio Alfieri (1749-1803). But the mainly middle-class movement found itself unable to bring about social reforms quickly enough for the peasants, particularly the very poor of Napoli. A peasant army sacked Napoli, littering its streets with dead Jacobins.

Although having declared himself First Consul of Italy in 1799, Napoleon acceded to the calls of Italian deputies in the north to proclaim a republic and, for the first time in history, the political entity known as Italy came into being, albeit with Napoleon as its first, self-elected president.

When, in 1804, Napoleon made himself emperor of France he established the Kingdom of Italy and made himself its first sovereign , inviting Pope Pius VII to officially crown him king in Paris. Pius delayed his visit, reluctant to give his endorsement to the power brokers of the French Revolution, which had greatly curtailed the power of the Catholic Church; nor was he keen on endorsing the marriage of Napoleon to the divorcee Josephine. When the pope finally arrived several days late, Napoleon was 'not amused'. As the pope raised the emperor's crown to his head, Napoleon took it and crowned himself.

Unification

During the final years of Napoleon's domination of Italy, hopes grew that his regime would be replaced with independence and constitutional rule. It was not to be: following Napoleon's demise at Waterloo in 1815, all of the peninsula's former rulers were reinstated by the Congress of Vienna. It was a backward step that had terrible consequences for the country, but it ensured the rapid growth of secret societies which were, in the main, disaffected middle-class intellectuals.

In the south, the republican Carbonari pushed hard and often ruthlessly to ensure a valid constitution, leading a revolutionary uprising in Napoli in 1820. Another leading revolutionary figure of these secret societies was Filippo Buonarroti, who strove for independence from Austria and the establishment of a communist society devoid of private-property interests.

One of Italy's key proponents of nationhood and political freedom was a Genovan called Giuseppe Mazzini (1805-72). Having quit the Carbonari movement in 1830, Mazzini founded Young Italy, a society of young men whose aims were the liberation of Italy from foreign and domestic tyranny and its unification under a republican government. This was to be achieved through education and, where necessary, revolt by guerrilla bands.

Exiled from his homeland for his former activities with the Carbonari, Mazzini was responsible for organising a number of abortive uprisings throughout Italy during the 1830s and 1840s which left dead many of the young men who had flocked to join his Young Italy movement. Twice sentenced to death, Mazzini was to live out his days in England, from where he wrote articles and solicited as much support as he could from influential allies to raise the consciousness of Europeans about the 'Italian question'.

Count Camillo Benso di Cavour: among those who led the movement towards unification

In 1848 there were revolutions in almost every major city and town of Europe. In their newspaper, *Il Risorgimento* – one of several publications to have sprung up as the Italian nationalist movement gained ground among Italians of all classes – nationalist writer Cesare Balbo and Count Camillo Benso di Cavour of Torino pressed for a constitution. In 1848, they published their *Statuto*, advocating a two-chamber parliament with the upper chamber to be appointed by the crown and the lower chamber to be elected by educated taxpayers. In 1861, the *Statuto* was to become the constitutional basis of the Kingdom of Italy, but not before almost two more decades of warring between the European princes and their subjects had left a great many more Italians dead.

Returning to Italy in 1848 from his famous exploits in South America, where he is still remembered as a founding hero of Uruguay, Giuseppe Garibaldi (1807-82) was to become the hero Italians needed to lead them towards unification. Garibaldi's personal magnetism, the result of his respect for people, rich and poor, drew more Italians into the fight for nationhood than ever before.

Despite significant personal animosity, Garibaldi and Cavour fought side by side, each in their chosen arena, to break the stranglehold of foreign domination. The brilliant diplomacy of Cavour, coupled with the independent efforts of Garibaldi and his 'people power', finally caught the attention of European communities, particularly the British, who became staunch supporters of a free and united Italy.

When the sympathetic Piemontese monarch, King Carlo Alberto, granted a constitution based on the *Statuto* in March 1848, Cavour stood for election. In 1850 he was

Victor Emmanuel II became the first king of Italy in 1861

given three ministries – navy, commerce and finance – in the government headed by Massimo d'Azeglio. When Cavour's centre-left faction joined forces with the centre-right, headed by Urbano Rattazzi, behind d'Azeglio's back, the prime minister resigned and Cavour was asked by the king to take the top government post. As prime minister, Cavour focused on forging an alliance with the French emperor Napoleon III, in a move destined to overthrow Austrian domination of Piemonte.

Meanwhile the unification movement was literally on the move, as Garibaldi led his Expedition of One Thousand, taking Sicilia and Napoli in 1860. The Kingdom of Italy was declared on 17 March 1861 and Victor Emmanuel II, who had been king of Sardegna-Piemonte from 1849, was proclaimed king. But Italy was not completely united: Venezia remained in the hands of the Austrians and Roma was held by France.

Cavour died within six months of achieving the first parliament of the Kingdom of Italy. He had been betrayed by his French allies when Napoleon III signed the armistice of Villafranca, ending the Franco-Austrian war (fought in Italy, largely by Italians). Venezia was wrested from the Austrians in 1866 and it wasn't until the Franco-Prussian War of 1870 that Napoleon III's hold over Italy was broken. Needing all available troops, he withdrew his occupation of Roma, leaving the way clear for the Italian army to reclaim the capital.

The only resistance to the push on Roma came from the papal soldiers of Pope Pius IX who refused to recognise the Kingdom of Italy. The pope was eventually stripped of his remaining temporal powers as well as his palace, the Quirinale. The papacy regained some autonomy in the 1920s when the Fascist dictator, Benito Mussolini, restored the independent papal state, but in the interim, the papacy forbade Catholics to participate in the elections of their government.

As the 20th century dawned, the economic crisis of Europe was reflected in Italian politics by constant fluctuations as socialist democrats and right-wing imperialists gained and lost the support of the populace. When, in the general elections of 1894, Pope Pius X formally gave Catholics the right to vote (although many had already been doing just that), there was a widespread backlash against socialism. Giovanni Giolitti, one of Italy's longest serving prime ministers (heading five governments between 1892 and 1921), managed to bridge the extremes and was able to embark on parliamentary reforms which gave the vote to all literate men from the age of 21 and all illiterate men who had completed military service or were aged 30 or over. But while male suffrage had been achieved, Italian women were denied the right to vote until after WWII.

Fascism

When war broke out in Europe in July 1914, Italy chose to remain neutral rather than become caught between old enemies. But soon, senior politicians had allied themselves with the British, Russians and French, while the papacy spoke out against the 'atheist' French in favour of Catholic Austria.

In October 1914, the editor of the socialist newspaper *Avanti!* also came out strongly in favour of alignment with the Allied forces. For his views, young Benito Mussolini was forced to resign. He started his own newspaper in November, *Il Popolo d'Italia*, a propaganda publication financed by French, British and Russian interests.

In 1919 he founded the Fascist Party, with its hallmarks of the black shirt and Roman salute. These were to become the symbols of violent oppression and aggressive nationalism for the next 23 years. In 1921 the party won 35 of the 135 seats in parliament. In October 1922 the king asked Mussolini to form a government, and thus began his domination of Italy. With an expedition of 40,000 Fascist militia, he began the famous March on Roma to 'free the nation from the socialists'.

In April 1924, following a campaign marked by violence and intimidation, the Fascist Party won the national elections and Mussolini created the world's first Fascist regime. By 1925 the term 'totalitarianism' had entered the language. By the end of 1925 Mussolini had expelled opposition parties from parliament, gained control of the press and trade unions and had reduced the voting public by two-thirds. In 1929, Mussolini and Pope Pius XI signed the Lateran Pact, whereby Catholicism was declared the sole religion of Italy and the Vatican was recognised as an independent state. In return, the papacy finally acknowledged the united Kingdom of Italy.

In the 1920s, Mussolini embarked on an aggressive foreign policy, leading to skirmishes with Greece over the island of Corfu and to military expeditions against nationalist forces in the Italian colony of Libya. In 1935 Italy sought a new colonial conquest by invading Abyssinia (present-day Ethiopia) from the Italian base in Eritrea, only capturing Addis Ababa after seven months. The act was condemned by the League of Nations which imposed limited sanctions on Italy.

Fearful of international isolation, Mussolini formed the Roma-Berlin Axis with Hitler in 1936 They were soon joined by Japan and Italy entered WWII in June 1941 as an ally of Germany.

After a series of military disasters and the landing of the Allied armies in Sicilia on 10 July 1943, Mussolini was faced not only with increasing discontent among Italians and diminishing support for Fascism, but also with Hitler's refusal to assign more troops to defend southern Italy. Two weeks after the Allied landing, the King of Italy, Victor Emmanuel III, led a coup against Mussolini and had him arrested.

In the confused period that followed, now known as the '45 days', Italy erupted in a series of massive demonstrations demanding an end to the war. The king signed an armistice with the Allies that amounted to an unconditional surrender and declared war on Germany, but it was too late to prevent the effective takeover of northern Italy by Nazi troops. As the Allies moved up through the south of the Italian peninsula, the Germans began their campaign of brutal suppression in the north, prompting the formation of the Resistance.

The Germans had rescued Mussolini from his prison on the Gran Sasso in what is now Abruzzo and installed him as head of the Republic of Salò in the north. By now completely demoralised, Mussolini was nothing more than a German puppet. He was eventually captured and shot, along with his mistress, Clara Petacci, by partisans in April 1945, and hung upside down from the roof of a petrol station in Milano's Piazzale Loreto.

The Resistance

Numbering more than 100,000 by conservative estimates in early 1945, members of the Resistance managed to gain control of small areas of the north and played a significant role in liberating Firenze from the Germans in August 1944. The Nazi response to partisan attacks was savage. Whole villages were exterminated: in one of the most notorious reprisals, 1830 men, women and children were murdered by an SS battalion at Marzabotto, south of Bologna, on 1 October 1944. In Roma, in March 1944, urban partisans blew up 32 military police. In reprisal, the Germans shot 335 prisoners at the Fosse Ardeatine, just outside the city.

After Allied troops broke through German lines, northern Italy was finally liberated by the end of May 1945. The Resistance had suffered huge losses and its contribution to the Allied victory did not go unacknowledged. These people had fought not only against German and Fascist oppression, but also for an ideal of social and political change, and after the war they wanted to put change into action. The Allies, meanwhile, were wondering how to deal with what amounted to a massive, armed, left-wing movement whose leaders spoke often of 'insurrection'.

The Republic

The Resistance was disarmed, either voluntarily or by force, as Italy's political forces scrambled to regroup and the USA, through the Marshall Plan, was exerting a profound effect on the country both economically and politically. Immediately after the war there was a series of three coalition governments. The third was dominated by the newly formed Democrazia Cristiana (DC, Christian Democrats), led by Alcide de Gaspari, who remained prime minister until 1953.

In 1946, following a referendum, the constitutional monarchy was abolished and a republic established, with the DC winning the majority of votes at the first post-war elections. The Partito Comunista Italiano (PCI, Communist Party), led by Palmiro Togliatti, and the Partito Socialista Italiano (PSI, Socialist Party), led by Pietro Nenni, participated in the coalition governments until 1947, when de Gaspari formed a government which excluded the left.

Economic Recovery

By the early 1950s the country's economy had begun to show strong signs of recovery, although the more impoverished and less industrialised south lagged behind. To counter this, the government formed the Cassa per il Mezzogiorno (State Fund for the South) in 1950, which would eventually pour trillions of lire into development projects in the southern regions. When Italy became a founding member of the European Economic Community (EEC) in 1957, it signalled the beginning of the 'Economic Miracle', a period of significant economic growth which saw unemployment drop as industry expanded. A major feature of this period was the development of Italy's automobile industry and, more particularly, of Fiat in Torino, which sparked a massive migration of peasants from the south to the north in search of work.

The early 1950s also saw the formation of a new extreme right-wing party called the Movimento Sociale Italiano (MSI), which was basically neo-Fascist.

Although it was the only major party not to participate in the government of the country, the Partito Comunista nevertheless played a crucial role in Italy's social and political development well into the 1980s. The party steadily increased its share of the poll at each election and always had more 'card-carrying' members than the DC, but the spectre of European communism and the Cold War continued to undermine its chances of participating in government.

By the mid-1960s the Economic Miracle was waning and social unrest was becoming commonplace. Togliatti, the long-serving leader of the PCI, died in 1964. His policy of cooperation with the DC in the interests of national unity had played a significant role in avoiding serious social conflict. One year earlier, Aldo Moro had been appointed prime minister, a position he held until 1968. It was Moro who invited the PSI into government in 1963 and more than a decade later he was moving towards the Historic Compromise which would have allowed the communists to enter government for the first time. This prompted his kidnapping and murder by the Brigate Rosse (Red Brigades) terrorist group.

Protest & Terrorism

The late 1960s were marked by student revolt in 1967-68. Influenced by similar events in France, university students rose up in protest, ostensibly against poor conditions in the universities, but in reality in broader protest against authority and what they saw as the impotence of the left. The movement resulted in the formation of many small revolutionary groups which attempted to fill what the students saw as an ideological gap in Italy's political left wing. The uprising was closely followed in 1969 by what has become known as the Autunno Caldo (Hot Autumn), when factory workers embarked on a series of strikes and protests which continued into 1971.

But as the new decade began, a new phenomenon – terrorism – began to overshadow this turbulent era of protest and change. By 1970, a group of young left-wing militants had formed the Brigate Rosse (Le BR).

Neo-Fascist terrorists had already taken action. On 12 December 1969, a bomb exploded in a bank in Milano's Piazza Fontana, killing 16 people. Controversy and mystery shrouded this incident, but it is now certain that it was an act of right-wing extremists directed by forces within the country's secret services. The bombing formed part of what was known as the Strategy of Tension, which culminated in the 1980 bombing of the Bologna railway station by right-wing terrorists, in which 84 people died.

The Brigate Rosse were by no means the only terrorists operating in the country during the Anni di Piombo (Years of Lead) from 1973-80, but they were certainly the most prominent. While many of the BR's original members were dead or in prison by the mid-1970s, 1977 saw a major recruiting campaign give new life to the movement. The year was also marked by student protests, sparked largely by their opposition to education reforms proposed by the government. As opposed to Sessantotto (1968), this was more an anti-political than an ideological movement. Universities were occupied in Roma, Bologna and Milano and the *centro sociale* – a type of left-wing cultural centre established by 'occupying' unused buildings – had its origin in this period.

In 1978 the Brigate Rosse claimed their most important victim – Aldo Moro. During the 54 days that Moro was held captive by the BR, his colleagues laboured over whether to bargain with the terrorists to save his life, or to adopt a position of no compromise. In the end, they took the latter path and the BR killed Moro on 9 May 1978, leaving his body in the boot of a car parked in a street in the centre of Roma which was equidistant from the headquarters of the DC and the PCI.

Finally, the Carabinieri general, Carlo Alberto dalla Chiesa, was appointed to wipe out the terrorist groups. Using a new law which allowed *pentiti* (repentants) much-reduced prison sentences, he convinced key members of the groups to collaborate. In 1980, dalla Chiesa was appointed by the government to fight the Mafia in Sicilia. He and his wife were assassinated in Palermo within a few months of his taking up the job.

The 1970s in Italy also produced much positive political and social change. In 1970 the country was divided into administrative regions and regional governments were elected. In the same year divorce became legal, and efforts by conservative Catholics to have the law repealed were defeated in a referendum in 1974. In 1978 abortion was legalised, following close on the heels of anti-sexist legislation which allowed women to keep their own names after marriage.

The Historic Compromise with the communists was never to eventuate, but in 1983 the DC government was forced by its diminishing share of the electoral vote to hand over the prime ministership to a socialist. Bettino Craxi became the longest serving prime minister since De Gaspari, holding the post from 1983 to 1989. A skilled politician, Craxi continued to wield considerable power in government until he fled the country in 1993 after being implicated in the Tangentopoli national bribery scandal. Convicted in absentia on corruption charges, he remains in self-imposed exile in Tunisia.

Italy enjoyed significant economic growth

in the 1980s, during which it became one of the world's leading economic powers (see Economy later in this chapter). However, the 1990s heralded a new period of crisis for the country, both economically and politically. High unemployment and inflation rates, combined with a huge national debt and an extremely unstable lira, led the government to introduce draconian measures to revive the economy.

In this period, the PCI reached a watershed. Internal ideological disagreements led to a split in the party in the early 1990s. The old guard now goes by the title Rifondazione Comunista, under the leadership of Fausto Bertinotti. The breakaway, more moderate wing of the old party reformed itself under the title Partito Democratico della Sinistra (PDS, Democratic Party of the Left). Under the leadership of Massimo d'Alema, the party went on to become the largest in the centre-left Olive Tree coalition, which won government in 1996 (see New Beginning later in this section).

Separatist Antics

Umberto Bossi, the rambunctious leader of the Lega Nord (Northern League), is a man with a mission. He believes that Italy's rich north should no longer be forced to subsidise its poor south. Having shifted his party's platform from federalism to separatism following the 1996 elections, Bossi has done no less than call for the establishment of a separate country called Padania, which would incorporate the northern Italian regions of Veneto, Piemonte, Lombardia and Emilia-Romagna.

Bossi's antics sometimes look clownish, even surreal. In September 1996 he led a three-day march along the Po river, culminating in a rally in Venezia, at which he formally declared the independence of the 'Northern Republic of Padania'. He has since installed a government, formed a Padanian National Guard and has called on locals to refuse to pay their taxes to Roma.

While opinion polls suggest that most northerners don't want secession, support for the Northern League cannot be underestimated. The League won 10% of the national vote in the 1996 election (more than 30% in some parts of the north), making it the third-largest party in Italy. ■

Tangentopoli

The Tangentopoli scandal broke in Milano in early 1992 when a functionary of the PSI was arrested on charges of accepting bribes in exchange for public works contracts. Tangentopoli literally means 'kickback cities'; the term probably originated in journalism. Led by Milanese magistrate Antonio di Pietro, who was dubbed the 'reluctant hero', investigations eventually implicated thousands of politicians, public officials and businesspeople.

Charges ranged from bribery, making illicit political payments and receiving kickbacks, to blatant thievery. It is ironic that few ordinary Italians were surprised that many politicians, at all levels of government, were entrenched in a system whereby they demanded secret payments as a matter of course. The corruption went to the very highest levels of government and few of the country's top politicians escaped the taint of scandal.

In elections just after the scandal broke in 1992, voters expressed their discontent and the DC's share of the vote dropped by 5%. Umberto Bossi's Lega Nord (Northern League) made its first appearance as a force to be reckoned with at the national level, winning 7% of the vote on a federalist, anti-corruption platform. Following on from the elections, parliament elected the Christian Democrat, Oscar Luigi Scalfaro, a man noted for his personal integrity, as President of the Republic.

As Tangentopoli continued to unfold, the main parties – the DC and the PSI – were in tatters and the centre of the Italian political spectrum was effectively demolished. A reform of the country's electoral system of proportional representation had resulted in the introduction of a predominantly first-past-the-post voting system, like that used in the UK, in both houses of parliament.

At the 1994 national elections, voters took the opportunity to express their disgust with the old order. The elections were won by a new right-wing coalition known as the Polo della Libertà (Freedom Alliance), whose members included the newly formed Forza Italia (Go Italy) and the Neo-Fascist Alleanza Nazionale (National Alliance), as well as the federalist Northern League. Its leader, billionaire media magnate Silvio Berlusconi, who had entered politics only three months before the elections, was appointed prime minister. After a turbulent nine months in power, Berlusconi's volatile coalition government collapsed when Bossi, in an extremely controversial move, withdrew the support of his Northern League (see boxed aside).

Berlusconi himself had been notified that he was under investigation by the Milano 'Clean Hands' judges and court proceedings against him continued into 1997.

In the chaos following the fall of the Berlusconi government, Scalfaro appointed an interim government of 'technocrats' which set about confronting the country's economic problems: it introduced pension reforms as well as measures aimed at reducing the public debt.

New Beginning

The technocrats ran the country until elections were held in April 1996. By that time, the new electoral system had resulted in a fairly clear division of the parties into two main groups: centro-destra (centre-right) and centro-sinistra (centre-left). Berlusconi's party, Forza Italia, remained aligned with the National Alliance, a repackaged and sanitised MSI, led by Gianfranco Fini. Their alliance, the Polo della Libertà, has gathered other small parties of the centre right under its umbrella.

However, it was the centre-left coalition, known as the Olive Tree, which claimed victory at the 1996 elections. Led by Bolognese university professor, Romano Prodi, the coalition won 50% of the seats in the Senate and 45% in the House of Deputies. Prodi was appointed Prime Minister and immediately made two promises which have proven increasingly difficult to keep: his government would serve a full five-year term (which would be a first in Italian post-war politics) and Italy would join Europe's economic and monetary union (EMU) in the first intake in 1998. In order to achieve the latter, Prodi's government has worked hard to balance Italy's budget, drastically reducing public spending and introducing new taxes. While the results have been promising – the budget deficit and inflation were both down to levels nearing the Maastricht criteria for entry into EMU – Italy is still up against strong resistance from major EU partners, notably Germany, who continue to doubt its capacity to maintain economic stability.

The Olive Tree's biggest coalition partner is the Democratic Party of the Left, led by Massimo D'Alema, who is seen by many as waiting for the right moment to take over the prime ministership. One of the main threats to the Prodi government's stability is the fact that it relies on the far-left Rifondazione Communista (Reconstituted Communists) to maintain its majority in the House of Deputies. Efforts to reform the welfare system, privatise much of the state, and reform the electoral system, as well as Prodi's key promise to join Europe's single currency, have all met with opposition from the Rifondazione's leader, Fausto Bertinotti.

GEOGRAPHY

Italy's boot shape makes it one of the most recognisable countries in the world, with the island of Sicilia appearing somewhat like a football at the toe of the boot and Sardegna situated in the middle of the Tyrrhenian Sea to the west of the mainland.

The country is bounded by four seas, all part of the Mediterranean Sea. The Adriatic Sea separates Italy from Slovenia, Croatia and Montenegro; the Ionian Sea laps the southern coasts of Puglia, Basilicata and Calabria; and to the west of the country are the Ligurian and Tyrrhenian seas. Coastal areas vary from the cliffs of Liguria and Calabria to the generally level Adriatic coast.

More than 75% of Italy is mountainous, with the Alps stretching from the Golfo di Genova (Gulf of Genoa) to the Adriatic Sea north of Trieste and dividing the peninsula from France, Switzerland, Austria and Slovenia. The highest Alpine peak is Monte Bianco (Mont Blanc) on the border with France, standing at 4807m, while the highest mountain in the Italian Alps (le Alpi) is Monte Rosa (4634m) on the Swiss border.

The Alps are divided into three main groups – western, central and eastern – and undoubtedly are at their most spectacular in the Dolomiti (Dolomites) in the eastern Alps in Trentino-Alto Adige and the Veneto. There are more than 1000 glaciers in the Alps, remnants of the last Ice Age, which are in a constant state of retreat. The best known in the Italian Alps is the Marmolada glacier on the border of Trentino and the Veneto, a popular spot for summer skiers.

The Apennini (Appenines) form a backbone extending for 1220km from Liguria, near Genova, to the tip of Calabria and into Sicilia. The highest peak is the Corno Grande (2914m) in the Gran Sasso d'Italia group in Abruzzo. Another interesting group of mountains, the Alpi Apuane (Apuan Alps), is found in north-western Toscana and forms part of the sub-Appennini. These mountains are composed almost entirely of marble and, since Roman times, have been mined almost continuously. Michelangelo selected his blocks of perfect white marble at Carrara in the Alpi Apuane.

Lowlands, or plains, make up less than a quarter of Italy's total land area. The largest plain is the Po valley (Pianura Padana), bounded by the Alps, the Appennini and the Adriatic Sea. The plain is heavily populated and industrialised, and through it runs Italy's largest river, the Po, and its tributaries, the Reno, Adige, Piave and Tagliamento rivers. Other, smaller plains include the Tavogliere di Puglia and the Pianura Campana around Mt Vesuvius.

Italy has three active volcanoes: Stromboli (in the Isole Eolie), Vesuvius (near Napoli) and Etna (Sicilia). Stromboli and Etna are among the world's most active volcanoes, while Vesuvius has not erupted since 1944 – this is a source of concern for scientists, who estimate that it should erupt every 30 years. Etna's most recent major eruption occurred in 1992, when a trail of lava on its eastern flank threatened to engulf the town of Zafferana Etnea. The lava flow stopped before it reached the town, but not before it had destroyed orchards and a house. Related volcanic activity produces thermal and mud springs, notably at Viterbo in Lazio and in the Isole Eolie. The Campi Flegrei (Phlegraean Fields) near Napoli are an area of intense volcanic activity, including hot springs, gas emissions and steam jets.

Central and southern Italy, including Sicilia, are also subject to sometimes massive earthquakes. Messina and Reggio di Calabria were devastated in 1908 by an earthquake which had its epicentre in the sea off the coast of Sicilia. In November 1980 an earthquake south-east of Napoli destroyed several villages and killed more than 3000 people.

CLIMATE

Situated in the temperate zone and jutting deep into the Mediterranean, Italy is regarded by many tourists as a land of sunny, mild weather. The country's climate is, however, quite variable, because of the length of the peninsula and the fact that it is largely mountainous. In the Alps temperatures are lower and winters are long and severe. Generally the weather is warm from July to September, although rainfall can be high in September. While the first snowfall is usually in November, light snow sometimes falls in mid-September and the first heavy falls can occur in early October.

The Alps shield northern Lombardia and the Lakes area, including Milano, from the extremes of the northern European winter and Liguria enjoys a mild, Mediterranean climate similar to southern Italy because it has protection from both the Alps and the Appennini.

Winters are severe and summers very hot in the Po valley. Venezia can be hot and humid in summer and, although not extremely cold in winter, it can be unpleasant as the sea level rises and *acqua alta* (literally, 'high water') inundates the city.

Farther south, at Firenze, which is encircled by hills, the weather can be extreme, but as you travel farther towards the tip of the boot, temperatures and weather conditions become milder.

Roma, for instance, has an average temperature in the mid-20s (Celsius) in July/August, although the impact of the *sirocco*, a hot, humid wind blowing from Africa, can produce stiflingly hot weather in August, with temperatures in the high 30s for days on end. Winters are moderate and snow is very rare in Roma, although winter clothing (or at least a heavy overcoat) is still a requirement.

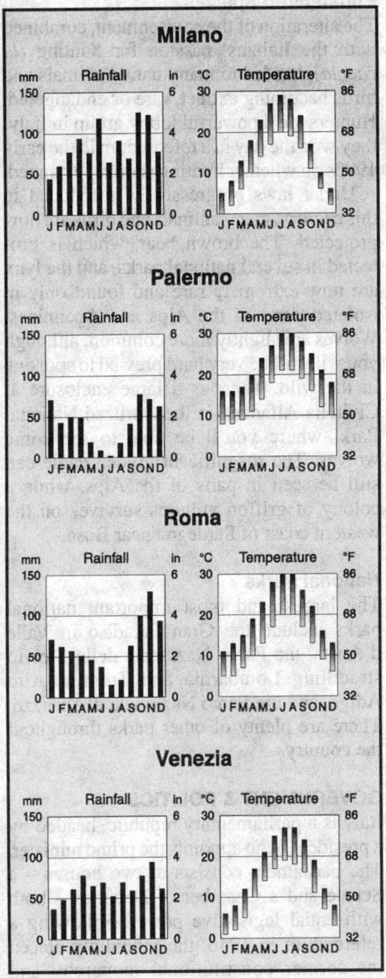

The south, Sicilia and Sardegna have a mild Mediterranean climate, with long, hot and dry summers, and moderate winters with an average temperature around 10°C. These regions are also affected by the sirocco in summer.

ECOLOGY & ENVIRONMENT

Italy is a dramatically beautiful country, but since Etruscan times humans have left their mark on the environment. Pollution problems caused by industrial and urban waste exist throughout Italy, with air pollution proving a problem in the more industrialised north of the country and in the major cities such as Roma, Milano and Napoli, where car emissions poison the atmosphere with carbon monoxide and lead. The seas, and therefore many beaches, are fouled to some extent, particularly on the Ligurian coast, in the northern Adriatic (where there is an algae problem resulting from industrial pollution) and near major cities such as Roma and Napoli. However, it is possible to find a clean beach, particularly in Sardegna. Litter-conscious visitors will be astounded by the extraordinary Italian habit of discarding and dumping rubbish when and where they like.

The Italian government's record on ecological and environmental issues is not good. The Ministry for the Environment was only created in 1986, and many environmental laws are not adequately enforced. Environmental groups say that the increase in the number of devastating floods which have hit parts of northern Italy in recent years are due not only to increased rainfall, but also to deforestation and excessive building near rivers. From 1984 to 1995, 20% of new houses were built without planning permits and environmental groups blamed this on the ministry's failure to regulate urban planning. Environmental organisations active in Italy include the Lega Ambiente (Environment League), the World Wide Fund for Nature (WWF) and the Lega Italiana Protezione Uccelli (LIPU, the Italian Bird Protection League).

FLORA & FAUNA

Flora

The long presence of humans on the Italian peninsula has had a significant impact on the environment, resulting in widespread destruction of original forests and vegetation and their replacement with crops and orchards. Aesthetically the result is not displeasing – much of the beauty of Toscana, for instance, lies in the interaction of olive groves with vineyards, fallow fields and stands of cypress and pine.

Fauna

In the Alps you might come across marmots, chamois and deer. Among the native animals in Sardegna are wild boar, the mouflon sheep, fallow deer and a variety of wild cat. Commonly available maps in national parks in the Alps and Apennines detail the local wildlife and indicate areas where they might be found.

Hunters continue to denude the countryside of birds. However, enough remain to make birdwatching an interesting pastime. A large variety of falcons and hawks are found throughout Italy, as are many varieties of small birds. The irony is that it is often easier to spot the colourful smaller birds in city parks – among the few refuges they have from the Italian hunter – than in their natural habitats in the countryside. Good spots to observe water birds include the Parco Nazionale del Circeo, just south of Roma, while you can see huge flocks of flamingoes in Sardegna, just outside Cagliari and near Oristano.

Italy is home to remarkably little dangerous fauna. It has only one poisonous snake, the viper. While the great white shark is known to exist in the waters of the Mediterranean, particularly in the southern waters, attacks are extremely rare. Italians will generally respond with a blank stare if you enquire about the presence of sharks. The seas around southern Italy and Sicilia have been used as breeding grounds since ancient times by blue-fin tuna and swordfish. The Égadi Islands, off the southern coast of Sicilia, are famous for their annual *mattanza*, the bloody netting and killing of tuna which occurs between April and July.

Endangered Species

The alteration of the environment, combined with the Italians' passion for hunting *(la caccia)*, has led to many native animals and birds becoming extinct, rare or endangered. Hunters are a powerful lobby group in Italy: they won the day in a referendum in the early 1990s on whether hunting should be banned.

Under laws progressively introduced in this century, many animals and birds are now protected. The brown bear, which is protected in several national parks, and the lynx are now extremely rare and found only in isolated parts of the Alps and Apennines. Wolves are slightly more common, although you will still be very hard pressed to spot one in the wild. There is a large enclosure at Civitella Alfadena in the Abruzzo National Park, where you'll be able to see some wolves. The magnificent golden eagle can still be seen in parts of the Alps, while a colony of griffon vultures survives on the western coast of Sardegna near Bosa.

National Parks

The largest and most important national parks include the Gran Paradiso in Valle d'Aosta, the Parco Nazionale dello Stelvio straddling Lombardia and Trentino-Alto Adige, and the Parco Nazionale d'Abruzzo. There are plenty of other parks throughout the country.

GOVERNMENT & POLITICS

Italy is a parliamentary republic, headed by a president, who appoints the prime minister. The parliament consists of two houses – a Senate and a Chamber of Deputies – both with equal legislative power. Following a referendum in 1946, the republic replaced the former constitutional monarchy and operates on the basis of a constitution which came into force on 1 January 1948.

The seat of national government is in Roma. The president resides in the Palazzo del Quirinale, the chamber of deputies sits in the Palazzo Montecitorio and the Senate in the Palazzo Madama, near Piazza Navona.

The now-defunct right-of-centre DC consistently dominated government from the formation of the republic until the party's devastating defeat in the 1994 elections. Italy's electoral system had generally forced the formation of unstable coalition governments. Since the declaration of the republic in 1946 there have been 55 governments, with an average lifespan of 11 months.

In April 1996, Italians for the first time elected a coalition government which included the Communist Party (see the History section earlier in this chapter).

Political Scandals

The heritage of consistent one-party domination was a system which Italians called *partitocrazia* (partyocracy), which operated on the basis of *lottizzazione*, by which the major parties divided control of the country's public bodies and utilities. The resulting patronage system meant that government jobs and other positions of power and influence were handed out virtually as political favours, and that no government service was excluded from potential manipulation.

The *tangenti* (kickbacks or bribes to government officials and politicians) were another unfortunate offshoot of the system. These ranged from payments by companies wanting to secure government building contracts to payments by individuals wanting to speed up bureaucracy. The Tangentopoli scandal which erupted in 1992 dramatically changed the face of Italian politics (see the History section of this chapter).

Reforms

Until reforms were introduced in 1994, members of parliament were elected by what was probably the purest system of proportional representation in the world – which was the intent of the country's intensely democratic constitution. The reforms mean that now 75% of both houses of parliament are elected on the basis of who receives the most votes in their district, basically the same system as the first-past-the-post system in the UK. The other 25% is elected by proportional representation. Italians are conscientious voters, with an average 88% turnout at the frequent elections.

In 1997, Italian politicians passed up the chance to significantly reform the country's system of government. A parliamentary commission, known as the *bicamerale*, spent six months considering reforms to Italy's 1947 constitution. But after a series of corruption scandals had all but decimated the country's ruling class, those who had been heralding a fresh start were badly disappointed. Instead of the anticipated sweeping changes to the system of government and major reforms to the judicial system, the bicamerale made a series of weak proposals which were seen by many as the result of political compromise.

The Regions

For administrative purposes Italy is divided into 20 regions which roughly correspond to the historical regions of the country. The regions are divided into provinces *(province)*, which are further divided into town councils *(comuni)*. Five regions (Sicilia, Sardegna, Trentino-Alto Adige, Friuli-Venezia Giulia and Valle d'Aosta) are autonomous or semi-autonomous, with special powers granted under the constitution. Their regional assemblies are similar to parliaments and have a wider range of economic and administrative powers than the other 15 regions.

Elections for all three tiers of local government are held simultaneously every five years.

ECONOMY

Italy's economy lay in ruins at the close of WWII, but the country wasted little time in setting about repairing the damage. By the early 1950s Italy had regained prewar levels of production. The boom of the 1950s and early 1960s, known as the Economic Miracle, relied to a great extent on the masses of workers who migrated from the poorer south of the country to the industrial north, providing an ample but low-paid workforce.

Today, services account for 48% of GDP, industry 35%, agriculture 4%, and public administration 13%. The latter figure is revealing, for a bloated and costly bureaucracy has been a considerable drain on Italy's resources since before Mussolini's time. Since 1945 this costly parasite has tended, if anything, to grow.

Most raw materials for industry and more than three-quarters of energy needs are imported. Tourism remains an important source of income. In 1996, estimated takings were about US$27.5 million – Italy ranked No 4 in the international tourist receipts stakes, with France and Spain just ahead and the US way out in front on US$64.5 million.

Following sustained growth of 3% through much of the 1980s, Italy became the fifth-largest economy in the world, made possible largely by the national gift for producing entrepreneurs. Next to the big names such as Agnelli (Fiat), De Benedetti (Olivetti) and Berlusconi (media), numerous ordinary Italians run their own business. Some 90% of Italian firms have fewer than 100 workers and many of these are family businesses.

Some would say they succeed in spite of those who govern them. Massive public debt, widespread corruption and an arcane legal and tax system have always combined to brake economic progress. Foreign firms have long found all this and the country's seemingly endless political wrangling a strong deterrent to investment in Italy.

Many of the country's top business people have been implicated in the Tangentopoli corruption scandals.

Worse, as the European Union, of which Italy was a founding member, has moved to closer integration, Italy has spun into something of a crisis over whether it will be included in the first wave of single currency countries. Since the severe economic crisis of 1992-93, successive governments have managed to impose a series of draconian measures to pull the economy into line – prompted more than anything by fear of being left out of the 'new Europe'. By early 1997, however, the European Commission was issuing encouraging statements to the effect that, if Italy could maintain a steady diet of heavy government spending cuts, slicing the massive public debt and privatisation of national enterprises, the country might just manage to join the single currency. Tentative steps down that path have been taken, with Telecom partly privatised and ENEL, the state-run energy body, long slated for privatisation.

In spite of all the efforts since WWII to promote growth in the poor south, the gap between north and south remains as great as ever. The desperate poverty of the past is a memory, and regions like Puglia and Abruzzo have seen real economic progress, but the fact remains that Italy's richest regions (Piemonte, Emilia-Romagna and Lombardia) are all northern, and its poorest (Calabria, Campania and Sicilia) are all southern.

Unemployment in the south is double the national average of about 12% (and three times the level in the north). Infrastructure remains poorer and several attempts to establish industry in the south have come to little, in spite of the trillions of lire poured into the *Mezzogiorno* (south) in the form of subsidies, tax breaks and loans.

POPULATION & PEOPLE

The population of Italy is 58.3 million, according to 1995 estimates. The birth rate was put at 10.89 per thousand in 1995, one of the lowest in Europe and below the EU average of about 12 per thousand – surprising given the Italians' preoccupation with children and family. Although demographers have been predicting a continuing fall in the numbers, a slight increase in the birth rate in the past five years combined with immigration may well keep the population steady. More children are born in the south than in the north – for instance, the birth rate in Emilia-Romagna is half that of Campania.

Heavily populated areas include those around Roma, Milano and Napoli, Liguria, Piemonte and parts of Lombardia, the Veneto and Friuli-Venezia Giulia. The most densely populated spot in Italy – in fact the most populous in the world after Hong Kong – is Portici, a suburb of Napoli, located directly under Mt Vesuvius.

There is only a small minority of non-Italian-speaking people, which includes German-speakers in Alto Adige (in the province of Bolzano) and a tiny French-speaking minority in the Valle d'Aosta. Slovene is spoken by some people around Trieste and along the border with Slovenia. In the south are pockets of Greeks and Albanians, descendants of immigrants in the 14th and 15th centuries.

Italy has traditionally been a country of emigrants, as Italians have left in search of work, travelling mainly to the USA, Argentina, Brazil, Australia and Canada. Southern Italians have also traditionally moved to the north of the country, to work in the factories of Piemonte and Lombardia.

In recent years, however, it has become a country of immigration. Long coastlines, the country's proximity to Africa and a fairly relaxed attitude to enforcement of immigration laws by Italian authorities has made Italy an easy point of entrance into Europe, particularly for Africans. It is estimated that more than 1.5 million immigrants now live in Italy. Illegal immigrants are known in Italy as *extracomunitari*. This state of affairs has come to worry not only the Italians but the rest of the European Union. In early 1997 tougher immigration rules were approved by parliament, envisaging a more determined programme of expulsion for illegal migrants.

Italians, however, are still more concerned with the traditional hostility of northern Italians towards southerners. Many northerners are resentful that the richer north in effect subsidises the poorer south, and their concerns are finding a strong voice in the success of the Northern League, which has attracted considerable electoral support with its policies opposing the use of tax revenues to pay for public projects in the south. It is now concentrating on calls for secession of the north, dubbed Padania, from the rest of the country.

EDUCATION

The Italian state-school system is free of charge and consists of several levels. Attendance is compulsory from the ages of six to 14 years, although children can attend a *scuola materna* (nursery school) from the ages of three to five years before starting the *scuola elementare* (primary school) at six. After five years they move on to the *scuola media* (secondary school) until they reach the age of 14.

The next level, the *scuola secondaria superiore* (higher secondary school), is voluntary and lasts a further five years until the student is 19 years old. It is, however, essential if young people want to study at university. At this level there are several options: four types of *liceo* (humanities-based school), four types of technical school, and teacher-training school.

The government is in the process of reforming the education system. The standards of education in the state-run system compare well with those in other countries, although the system does have its problems, compounded by relatively low standards in teacher-training and poor government management. Officially at least, only 3% of Italians over the age of 15 cannot read or write.

Private schools in Italy are run mainly by religious institutions, notably the Jesuits.

Italy has a long tradition of university education and can claim to have the world's oldest university, established at Bologna in the 11th century. Courses are usually from four to six years, although students are under no obligation to complete them in that time. Students in fact often take many more years to fulfil their quota of exams and submit their final thesis. Attendance at overcrowded lectures is optional and for scientific courses, practical experimentation is done. Students therefore tend to study at home from books. All state-school and university examinations are oral, rather than written.

Italy produces far fewer graduates per capita than most other countries in the West. Despite that, unemployment among graduates is estimated at higher than 40%.

ARTS

Literature

Roman The roots of ancient Latin literature lie in simple popular songs, religious rites and official documents. As Latin evolved and Rome came into contact with the Greek world, the emerging empire's upper classes began to acquire more sophisticated tastes. Plautus (259-184 BC) adapted classic Greek themes to create his own plays – a step forward from the translations of Greek literature that had come before.

Rome's classical period didn't occur until well into the 1st century BC. Cicero (106-43 BC) stands out in the early years of this time, as the Roman Republic collapsed into civil war and gave way to dictatorial government. Cicero's writing, infused with political *engagement*, explored new terrain in Latin prose with works such as *Brutus*. More concerned with affairs of the heart, particularly his own, Catullus (c 84-54 BC) devoted his creative power to passionate love poetry. Julius Caesar combined conquest with commentary in recording his campaigns in Gaul and the disintegration of the Republic.

The reign of Augustus marked the emergence of a new wave of intellectuals. Among the greats was Virgil, whose epic poem, *The Aeneid*, links the founding of Rome with the fall of Troy. Some years later, Ovid addressed love in his poems, *Amores*, annoyed Emperor Augustus with descriptions of lewd lifestyles in *Ars Amatoria* after the emperor's daughter had been banished for vice, and wrote about transformation myths in *Metamorphoses*. Horace toed the martial line while Livy chronicled the emergence of the new empire.

Seneca (4 BC-65 AD), a Spanish philosopher, introduced a more introspective, even existential note to Latin writing in the early years of the Christian era. Petronius (died 66 AD) conveyed the decadence of the age of Nero in his *Satyricon*, although only a fragment still exists. It is to Pliny the Younger (62-113 AD) that we owe first-hand descriptions of the disaster of Pompeii. The years following the downfall of Nero are detailed in the *Histories* of Tacitus (55-120 AD), while his *Annales* reveal the astounding court intrigues of the early emperors. Marcus Aurelius' *Meditations* were the musings of the last philosopher-king of the crumbling empire.

Middle Ages From before the final collapse of Rome until well into the Middle Ages, creative literary production declined, kept barely alive in western Europe by clerics and erudites who debated theology, wrote history, translated or interpreted classical literature and used Latin as their lingua franca.

Latin had, however, already ceased to be a living language. The genius of Dante, probably the greatest figure in Italian literature, confirmed the Italian vernacular (in its Florentine form) as a serious medium for poetic expression, culminating in his *Divina Commedia* – an allegorical masterpiece that takes his protagonist on a search for God through Hell, Purgatory and Paradise. His Latin work *De Monarchia* reflects his preference for a return of imperial power and his vision of a world where the roles of pope and emperor complemented each other.

Another master of this time was Petrarch (Francesco Petrarca, 1304-74), son of a lawyer exiled from Firenze at the same time as Dante. Petrarch was crowned poet laureate in Roma in 1341 after earning a reputation throughout Europe as a classical scholar. His epic poem, *Africa*, and the sonnets of *Il Canzoniere* are typical of his formidable lyricism, which has had a permanent influence on Italian poetry. His talent for self-examination in an individual, style was unprecedented.

Giovanni Boccaccio (1313-75) completes the triumvirate. Author of *Il Decamerone*, 100 short stories ranging from the bawdy to the earnest which chronicled the exodus of 10 young Florentines from their plague-ridden city, Boccaccio is considered the first Italian novelist.

Renaissance The 15th century produced several treatises on architecture and politics, but perhaps more important was the feverish study and translation of Greek classics and the work of more recent Hebrew and Arabic scholars. The advent of the printing press accelerated the spread of knowledge. In Italy the industry was developed above all in Venezia, where Aldo Manuzio (c 1450-1515) flooded the market with Greek classics from his famous Aldine Press and introduced italic type in 1501, along with the octavo, half the size of a standard quarto page and more suitable for printed books.

Machiavelli's *Il Principe* (The Prince), although purely political, has proved the most lasting of the Renaissance works. Surprisingly for many, Machiavelli was also an accomplished playwright, whose *Mandragola* is a masterpiece. See the History section.

Machiavelli's contemporary Ludovico Ariosto (1474-1533) is arguably the star of the Italian Renaissance. His *Orlando Furioso* is a subtle tale of chivalry, told in exquisite verse and laced with subplots. Torquato Tasso (1544-95) continued a tradition of narrative poetry with his *Gerusalemme Liberata*, for which he drew inspiration from Italy's increasingly precarious political situation towards the end of the century.

To the 19th Century At a time when French playwrights ruled the stage, the Venetian, Carlo Goldoni (1707-93), attempted to bring Italian theatre back into the limelight, combining realism and a certain literary discipline with a popular feel rooted in the *commedia dell'arte*, the tradition of improvisational theatre based on a core of set characters.

The heady winds of Romanticism that prevailed in Europe in the first half of the 19th century did not leave Italy untouched. In the small town of Recanati in Le Marche, Giacomo Leopardi began penning verses heavy with longing and melancholy, but equally erudite although he was largely self-taught. The best of them, the *Canti*, constitute a classic of Italian verse.

Poetry remained the main avenue of literary expression for much of the century, but Milano's Alessandro Manzoni (1785-1873) changed all that with his *I Promessi Sposi* (The Betrothed), a historical novel on a grand scale. Manzoni laboured hard to establish a narrative language accessible to all Italians, lending the manuscript a barely disguised nationalist flavour lost on no-one when it appeared in the 1840s. In 1881, Giovanni Verga announced the arrival of the realist novel in Italy with *I Malavoglia*.

20th Century The turbulence of political and social life in Italy throughout most of this century has produced a wealth of literature, much of it available in translation for English speakers.

Theatre In Sicilia, Luigi Pirandello (1867-1936) began his career writing novels and short stories along realist lines, but soon moved to theatre. With such classics as *Sei Personaggi in Cerca d'Autore* (Six Characters in Search of an Author) he threw into question every preconception of what theatre should be. A Nobel-prize winner in 1934, Pirandello's influence continues to assert itself in the West; from Brecht to Beckett, few modern playwrights could claim to have escaped his influence.

Modern Italian theatre is much the junior member of Italy's literary family. Its most enduring contemporary representative is Dario Fo (1926-), who from the 1950s to this day has written, directed and performed. Often a one-man show, but also in company (most often with Franca Rame), his work is laced with political and social critique. He has had a number of hits in London's West End, including *Accidental Death of an Anarchist*, *Can't Pay, Won't Pay* and *Mistero Buffo*.

Poetry Gabriele d'Annunzio (1863-1938) is in a class of his own. An ardent nationalist, his often virulent poetry was perhaps not of the highest quality, but his voice was a prestige tool for Mussolini's Fascists.

Giuseppe Ungaretti (1888-1970), whose

creative and personal baptism of fire took place on the battlefields of WWI, produced a robust, spare poetry, far from the wordy complexity of his predecessors. The sum of his work is contained in *Vita d'un Uomo* (Life of a Man).

Two other 'hermetic' poets stand out, both Nobel-prize winners. Eugenio Montale (1896-1981) is less accessible than Ungaretti, and devoted much of his time after WWII to journalism. Sicilian poet Salvatore Quasimodo (1901-68) reached a high point after WWII, when he believed poetry could and should empathise with human suffering. The myth exploded; his later work is heavy with melancholy and nostalgia.

Fiction Italy's richest contribution to modern literature has been in the novel and short story. Torino especially has produced a wealth of authors. Cesare Pavese, born in a Piemonte farmhouse in 1908, took Walt Whitman as his guiding light. Involved in the anti-Fascist circles of prewar Torino, his greatest novel, *La Luna e Il Falò* (The Moon and the Bonfire), was published in 1950, the year he took his life.

Like Pavese, the Torino doctor Carlo Levi (1902-75) experienced internal exile in southern Italy under the Fascists. The result was a moving account of a world oppressed and forgotten by Roma, *Cristo si è Fermato a Eboli* (Christ Stopped at Eboli).

Primo Levi, a Torino Jew, ended up in Auschwitz during the war. *Se Quest'è Un Uomo* (If This is a Man) is the dignified account of his survival, while *La Tregua* (The Truce) recounts his long road back home through eastern Europe. In 1996 the latter was made into a decent film (although not entirely faithful to the book) starring John Turturro and directed by Francesco Rosi. Born in 1919, Levi committed suicide in 1987.

Palermo-born Natalia Ginzburg (1916-90) spent most of her life in Torino. Much of her writing is semi-autobiographical. *Tutti I Nostri Ieri* (All Our Yesterdays), *Valentino* and *Le Voci della Sera* (Voices in the Evening) are just three novels among a palette of prose, theatre and essays. Her particular gift is in capturing the essence of gestures and moments in everyday life.

A writer of a different ilk is Italo Calvino (1923-85), who was born in Cuba. A resistance fighter and then Communist Party member until 1957, Calvino's works border on the fantastical, thinly veiling his main preoccupations with human behaviour in society. *I Nostri Antenati* (Our Ancestors), a collection of three such tales, is perhaps his greatest success.

Alberto Moravia (1907-90) describes Roma and its people in his prolific writings. Such novels as *La Romana* (A Woman of Roma) convey the detail of place and the sharp sense of social decay that make his story-telling so compelling.

Unique is *Il Gattopardo* (The Leopard), the only work of lasting importance by Sicilia's Giuseppe Tomasi di Lampedusa (1896-1957). Set at the time of Italian unification, it is a moving account of the decline of the virtually feudal order in Sicilia, embodied in the slow ruin of Prince Fabrizio Salina, later played by Burt Lancaster in Luchino Visconti's 1963 film.

Leonardo Sciascia (1921-89) has dedicated most of his career to his native Sicilia, attacking all facets of its past and present in novels and essays. His first great success was *Il Giorno della Civetta* (The Day of the Owl), a kind of whodunit illustrating the extent of the Mafia's power.

The novels of Roma's Elsa Morante (1912-85), characterised by a subtle psychological appraisal of her characters, can be seen too as a personal cry of pity for the sufferings of individuals and society. Her 1948 novel *Menzogna e Sortilegio* (Lie and Incantation) brought her to prominence. In it she recounts the slow decay of the southern Italian noble family.

Italian literature of the 1980s was dominated by Bologna intellectual Umberto Eco (1932-), who shot to popularity with his first and best known work, *Il Nome della Rosa* (The Name of the Rose), which was also made into a successful film with Sean Connery. Subsequent novels, though heavily marketed, have failed to make the same impact.

Pisan-born Antonio Tabucchi (1943-) is emerging as a writer of some stature, with more than a dozen books to his credit. Possibly one of his most endearing works is *Sostiene Pereira*, set in prewar Lisbon and made into a charming film starring Marcello Mastroianni – one of his last performances.

Marina Jarre (1925-), born in Latvia, has been turning out adult and children's literature from her home in Torino since the 1950s. Among her better known, more recent works are *Padri Lontani* (Distant Fathers, 1987) and *Tre Giorni alla Fine di Luglio* (Three Days at the End of July, 1993).

Another rising star of the Italian literary scene is Susanna Tamaro. Born in Trieste in 1957, her latest novel, *Anima Mundi*, is probably her best. Also worth keeping an eye on is Lara Cardella (1969-), who in her early 20s had an enormous success with *Volevo i Pantaloni* (I Wanted Pants), the story of an adolescent dealing with a world much dominated by males. The sequel, *Volevo i Pantaloni 2*, predictably dealing with the same character as an adult, is not as rewarding, but Cardella has other titles to her name and it's early days yet in her career.

Music

Classical Music & Opera The Italians have played a pivotal role in the history of music: they invented the system of musical notation in use today; a 16th-century Venetian printed the first musical scores with movable type; Cremona produced violins by Stradivari and others; and Italy is the birthplace of the piano.

The 16th century brought a musical revolution in the development of opera, which began as an attempt to recreate the drama of ancient Greece. The first successful composer, Claudio Monteverdi (c 1567-1643), drew from a variety of sources.

In the 17th and early 18th centuries, instrumental music became established, helped by the concertos of Arcangelo Corelli (1653-1713) and Antonio Vivaldi (1675-1741). Vivaldi, whose best known work is *The Four Seasons* created the concerto in its present form while he was teaching in Venezia. Domenico Scarlatti (1685-1757) wrote more than 500 sonatas for harpsichord and Giovanni Battista Sammartini (1700-75) experimented with the symphony.

Verdi, Puccini, Bellini, Donizetti and Rossini, composers from the 19th and early 20th centuries, are all stars of the modern operatic era. Giuseppe Verdi (1813-1901) became an icon midway through his life and his achievements include *Aïda* and one of the most popular operas of all, *La Traviata*. Rossini's *Barber of Seville* is an enduring favourite, with a lively score, and *Madame Butterfly* ensures Puccini a firm place in musical history.

The composer Gian Carlo Menotti (1911-) is also famed for creating the Spoleto Festival of Two Worlds, at Spoleto in Umbria.

Contemporary Opera The main opera season in Italy runs from December to June. The country's premier opera theatres include La Scala in Milano, San Carlo in Napoli, the Teatro dell'Opera in Roma and La Fenice in Venezia. With restoration partially complete, Sicilia's prestigious Teatro Massimo in Palermo is now finally back in action. Tenor Luciano Pavarotti (1935-) is today's luminary of Italian opera.

Canzone Napoletana If a great many rock and pop greats in the English-speaking world have their roots in the blues tradition, Italian popular music has much the same relation to the *canzone Napoletana* (Neapolitan song).

By the late 18th century, an annual pilgrimage in September to the Chiesa di Santa Maria di Piedigrotta, in Pozzuoli, had become an occasion for merriment and song. At a time when the Neapolitan dialect had the status of a language in its own right, bands played in impromptu competitions that soon began to produce what could be considered the year's top hits. In 1840 came the first real classic, *Te Voglio Bene Assaje*, a song that remains enshrined in the city's musical imagination. But surely the best known Neapolitan song remains *O Sole Mio*.

Contemporary Music Few modern Italian singers or groups have made any impact outside Italy. The best vocalist to emerge since the war is probably Mina. During the 1960s she cut dozens of records. Many of her songs were written by Giulio Rapetti, better known as Mogol, the undisputed king of Italian songwriters.

The 1960s and 1970s produced various *cantautori* (singer songwriters), vaguely reminiscent of some of the greats of the UK and USA. Lucio Dalla, Vasco Rossi and Pino Daniele have been successfully hawking their versions of protest music since the early 1970s. While not of the stature of, say, Bob Dylan, the strength of their music lies in lyrics occasionally laced with venom portraying the shortcomings of modern Italian society. Daniele, whose Neapolitan roots are clearly on display, brings an unmistakably bluesy flavour to his music.

Much softer and less inclined towards social critique, but highly popular since the end of the 1960s, is Lucio Battisti. Some of the early music will make your hair stand on end (*very* 1970s), but Battisti is highly regarded, even by younger generations.

Ivano Fossati is another well-established cantautore, but some of his most agreeable material is purely instrumental.

Zucchero (Adelmo Fornaciari) is a phenomenon on the Italian music scene. Starting out as a session musician with the likes of Joe Cocker, he has aimed at both the Italian and international market as few other Italians have, earning a lot of sour grapes along the way. He sings many of his songs in Italian *and* English, and is known in the UK and USA as Sugar and was clever enough to earn further fame by doing *Senza una Donna* with Paul Young.

Other names to look out for include Luca Carboni, Francesco de Gregori, Antonello Venditti, Fiorella Mannioa, Claudio Baglioni and the group RAF. In the early 1990s, Eros Ramazzotti emerged as one of the country's top male artists, while the somewhat saccharine Laura Pausini is probably the most commercially successful female vocalist of the moment.

For what it's worth, Italian hip-hop and house productions are much appreciated by connoisseurs, and there is a flourishing market in home-grown rap. A particularly popular exponent of the latter is Jovanotti. Other home-grown hip-hop bars include Neffa, Frankie-Hi-Nrg, Space One, Spaghetti Funk, Solo Zippo, Chief & Soci and La Famiglia. There are also some decent Indie-style bands in circulation, such as Litfiba. A lighter sound comes from Pooh, a band that appeared in the mid-90s.

Cinema

Born in Torino in 1904, the Italian film industry originally made an impression with silent spectaculars. By 1930 it was virtually bankrupt and Mussolini began moves to nationalise the industry. These culminated in 1940, when Roma's version of Hollywood, Cinecittà, was ceded to the state. Set up in 1937, this huge complex was fitted out with the latest in film equipment. Half the nation's production took place here – 85 pictures in 1940 alone.

Abandoned later in the war, Cinecittà only went timidly back into action in 1948 – its absence had not bothered the first of the neo-realist directors. In 1950 an American team arrived to make *Quo Vadis?*, and for the rest of the 1950s film-makers from Italy and abroad moved in to use the site's huge lots. By the early 1960s, however, this symbol of Italian cinema had again begun to wane as location shooting became more common.

Neo-Realism Even before the fall of Mussolini in 1943, those who were about to launch Italy's most glorious era of the silver screen were at work. Luchino Visconti (1906-76) came to cinema late, after meeting Jean Renoir, the French film-maker, in France in 1936. His first film, *Ossessione*, based on James Cain's *The Postman Always Rings Twice*, was one of the earliest examples of the new wave in cinema.

In the three years following the close of hostilities in Europe, Roberto Rossellini (1906-77) produced a trio of neo-realist masterpieces. The first, in 1945, was *Roma Città*

Stars of the Screen

One of Italy's earliest international stars was Rudolph Valentino (actually Rodolfo Pietro Filiberto Guglielmi), whose brief career in Hollywood from about 1920 until his death in 1926 spanned 10 silent movies. A migrant from Puglia in southern Italy, he was a true American success story, arriving at the age of 18 and working as a waiter and professional dance partner before being 'discovered'.

Among Italy's greatest actors since WWII is Marcello Mastroianni (died in 1996), who starred in *La Dolce Vita* and countless other films, including Robert Altman's *Prêt-à-Porter*. Of similar stature but less known outside Italy is Vittorio Gassman. Now a grand old man of Italian cinema, he most recently appeared as a New York gangland boss in the American flick *Sleepers*. Others include Anna Magnani, who won an Academy Award for *The Rose Tattoo*; Gina Lollobrigida *(Go Naked in the World* and *Come September)*; and, of course, Sophia Loren, whose innumerable films include *It Started In Naples*, *Houseboat* and *Boy on a Dolphin*.

The undisputed king of film comedy was long Totò, who, until his death in 1967 was for Italy what Chaplin became for the Anglo-Saxon world. That he never achieved similar international recognition can perhaps be attributed to the special appeal for Italian audiences of his quick Naples wit, the kind of thing that does not translate well.

Who, however, has not seen at least one 'spaghetti western' with 160kg Bud Spencer and his thin, blue-eyed counterpart, Terence Hill? The names are pseudonyms and these cowboys are all-Italian. From 1970, when *They Called Him Trinity* came out, until 1986, they kept Italy and much of the rest of the world in stitches with their version of how the West was won. They tried again in late 1994 with *Botte di Natale*, a box office flop.

The contemporary scene has thrown up few actors of international stature. But there are some names to watch. Massimo Troisi (see also the main Cinema section in this chapter) brought a striking human touch to his characters – always Neapolitan. He died young and unexpectedly during the editing of arguably his best film – *Il Postino*. One who occasionally appears out of the Italian context is Roberto Benigni, a highly popular Tuscan comedian who starred in Jim Jarmusch's *Down by Law*. ■

Aperta (Rome Open City), set in German-occupied Roma and starring Anna Magnani. For many cinophiles the film marks the true beginning of Neo-Realism, uniting a simplicity and sincerity peculiar to Italian film-making; often heart-rending without ever descending into the bathos to which so many Hollywood products fall victim.

Paisà (1946) follows the course of war from Sicilia to the Po river in a series of powerful vignettes, while *Germania Anno Zero* (Germany Year Zero, 1947) pulls no punches in looking at a country left crushed by the war it had launched.

Vittorio de Sica (1901-74) kept the neo-realist ball rolling with another classic in 1948, *Ladri di Biciclette* (Bicycle Thieves), the story of a man's frustrated fight to earn a crust and keep his family afloat. It is one of 10 films he made from 1939 to 1950.

1950s to the 1970s Federico Fellini (1920-94) took the creative baton from the masters of neo-realism and carried it into the following decades. His disquieting filmic style is more demanding of audiences, abandoning realistic shots for pointed images at once laden with humour, pathos and double-meaning – all cleverly capturing not only the Italy of the day, but the human foibles of his protagonists. Fellini's greatest international hit was *La Dolce Vita* (1968), with Anita Ekberg and Marcello Mastroianni. Others include *8½* (1963), *Satyricon* (1969), *Roma* (1972) and *Amarcord* (1973). Fellini's wife, Giulietta Masina, starred in many of his pictures.

Luchino Visconti, meanwhile, continued to make movies until his death, including the memorable adaptation of Tomasi di Lampedusa's *Il Gattopardo*.

Michelangelo Antonioni (1912-) began directing in 1950; his films explore existential themes and individual crises, reaching a climax with *Blow-up* in 1967. Pier Paolo Pasolini's (1922-75) themes are altogether different, preoccupied at first with the condition of the subproletariat in films like

Accattone (1961) and *Teorema* (1968), and later with human decay and death *(Il Decamerone*, *I Racconti di Canterbury* and *Il Fiore delle Mille e Una Notte)*.

In 1974, Lina Wertmüller (1928-) angered feminists with her work, *Swept Away* (or in Italian, *Travolti da un Insolito Destino nell'Azzurro Mare di Agosto*!). Bernardo Bertolucci (1941-) first made an international hit with *Last Tango in Paris* (1972).

1980 to the Present Bertolucci's foreign profile has continued to grow with blockbusters like *The Last Emperor* (1987), *The Sheltering Sky* (1990), *Little Buddha* (1992) and *Stealing Beauty* (1996). Another director who has done a lot of work outside Italy is Franco Zeffirelli (1923-), among whose better known films are *Othello* (1986), *Young Toscanini* (1988), *Hamlet* (1990) and *Jane Eyre* (1995). He was also behind the TV epic *Jesus of Nazareth* (1977).

Paolo (1931-) and Vittorio Taviani (1929-) got started in the 1960s and in 1976 produced *Padre Padrone*, a heart-rending account of peasant life in Sardegna and one man's escape. Their biggest hits of the 1980s were *Good Morning Babilonia* (1986), an account of the creation of WD Griffiths' *Intolerance*, and *Kaos* (1984), inspired by stories by Luigi Pirandello.

A wonderful homage to film-making is *Nuovo Cinema Paradiso* (1988), by Giuseppe Tornatore (1956-). Tornatore was back in 1995 with *L'Uomo delle Stelle* (The Starmaker), the story of a fraud touring around Sicilia and peddling hopes of a screen career in Cinecittà.

Nanni Moretti (1953-), who first came to the silver screen in the late 1970s, has proven a highly individualistic actor-director. *Caro Diario* (Dear Diary), his whimsical, self-indulgent, autobiographical three-part film won the prize for best director at Cannes in 1994. One of the most striking Italian films to have emerged in recent years is *Il Postino e Pablo Neruda* (The Postman – and Pablo Neruda), starring Massimo Troisi. Released in 1995 and directed by the UK's Michael Radford, it recounts the exile of the poet Pablo Neruda in a small southern Italian fishing village and his encounter with the local postman. Troisi died during the making of the film.

Maurizio Nichetti (1948-) has also brought some wonderful entertainment to the screen with *Volere Volare* (Wanting to Fly, 1990), in which the main protagonist, a cartoonist, finds himself turning into a cartoon character. The year before he had brought out *Ladri di Saponette*, an acid attack on publicity in which people watching the classic movie *Ladri di Biciclette* (constantly broken up by ads) end up *entering* the film they are viewing.

SOCIETY & CONDUCT

It is difficult to make blanket assertions about Italian culture, if only because Italians have only lived as one nation for little over 100 years. Prior to unification, the peninsula was long subject to a widely varied mix of masters and cultures. This lack of unity also contributed to the maintenance of local dialects and customs. Indeed it was really only the advent of national TV that began the spread of a 'standard' Italian. Previously it was not unusual to find farmers and villagers who spoke only their local dialect.

Italians at a World Cup football match may present a patriotic picture, but even today the bulk of Italians tend to identify more strongly with their region or even home town than with the nation – a phenomenon known to some as *campanilismo* (which could loosely translate as an attachment to one's local bell tower!). An Italian is first and foremost a Sicilian or Tuscan, or even a Roman, Milanese or Neapolitan, before being Italian.

Confronted with a foreigner, however, Italians will energetically reveal a national pride difficult to detect in the relationships they have with each other.

Stereotypes

Foreigners may think of Italians as passionate, animated people who gesticulate wildly when speaking, love to eat and drive like maniacs. There's a little more to it than that, however.

The Italian journalist Luigi Barzini defined his compatriots as a hard-working, resilient and resourceful people, who are optimistic and have a good sense of humour. If there is a 'national' stereotype, Barzini's description is probably closer to the truth. Italians are also passionately loyal to their friends and families – all-important qualities, noted Barzini, since 'a happy private life helps people to tolerate an appalling public life'.

Italians have a strong distrust of authority and when they are confronted with a silly rule, an unjust law or a stupid order (and they are regularly confronted with many of them), they do not complain or try to change rules, but rather try to find the quickest way around them.

Family

The family remains of central importance in the fabric of Italian society, particularly in the south. Most young Italians tend to stay at home until they marry, a situation admittedly partly exacerbated by the lack of affordable housing. Still, modern attitudes have begun to erode the traditions. Statistics show that one in three married couples have no children and one in nine children is born out of wedlock. In Milano, more than one third of families are headed by a single parent and two-thirds of these by a woman.

Dos & Don'ts

Italians tend to be very tolerant but, despite an apparent obsession with (mostly female) nakedness, especially in advertising, are not excessively free and easy.

In some parts of Italy, particularly in the

Mummy's Boys

The rough charm of the unshaven Latin lover, mounted jauntily on his Vespa, is an inescapable Italian image, one redolent of the man's man, someone seductively in charge of his own life. The truth is perhaps a little less macho.

According to figures published in 1997 by Istat (Istituto Centrale di Statistica), the country's main statistics body, most Italian men actually constitute an *esercito di mammoni* (army of mummy's boys). Forget Oedipus – these boys know where their bread is buttered. Perhaps they are not so different from men the world over, but the numbers are certainly telling.

If you can believe Istat, 70% of single Italian men remain at home with mum (and dad) even after their 35th birthday. Granted, this is partly caused by problems of unemployment, the cost of housing and so on. Of the remainder who do move out of home, some 42% do not shift more than 1km away – only 20% dare to move more than 50km beyond the maternal home. Of all these 'independent' single men, 70% manage to stop by mum's place every day of the week. The unkind might be led to believe (as indeed was the author of at least one newspaper story on the subject) that apart from filial devotion, the lads might well bring with them a bag of dirty washing and time the visit to coincide with lunch . . .

But even if the washing and lunch are taken care of by the wife – not an uncommon situation among Italian couples – those men who are married still find time to pop in to see mamma at least a few times a week. And when marriage fails, a quarter of the soon-to-be ex-husbands go home to mother, as opposed to 17% of wives. ■

south, women will be harassed if they wear skimpy or see-through clothing – one female traveller reported that she was hissed at, jeered and spat on by locals when she arrived in Assisi wearing a tight miniskirt.

Topless sunbathing, while not uncommon on some Italian beaches, is not de rigueur – women should look around before dropping their tops. Nude sunbathing is likely to be offensive anywhere but on appropriately designated beaches. Walking the streets near beaches in a bikini or skimpy costume is also not on – on the Venezia Lido you'll be fined.

In churches you are expected to dress modestly, and those that are major tourist attractions, such as St Peter's in Roma and St Francis' in Assisi, enforce strict dress codes. Churches are places of worship – if you visit one during a service, try to be as inconspicuous as possible.

The police and carabinieri (see also Dangers & Annoyances in the Facts for the Visitor chapter) have the right to arrest you for 'insulting a state official' if they believe you have been rude or offensive to them – so be diplomatic in your dealings with them!

THE MAFIA

It is an understatement to note that the Mafia knows no limits, but in Italy one wonders just who runs the country – the government or the Mafia? As an English journalist noted, 'Everyone knows that the Mafia and the establishment are intertwined, and that this marriage is one of the pillars of political life in Italy. The Mafia is not only omnipotent, it is omnipresent'. The multiple crises that have rocked Italy's political establishment, from the stream of revelations linking Mafia figures to politicians, through to Tangentopoli (see History earlier in this chapter), have only served to increase peoples' awareness of the problem.

In Italy, the term 'mafia' can be used to describe five distinct organised crime groups: the original Sicilian Mafia, also known as the Cosa Nostra; the Calabrian 'Ndrangheta; the Camorra of Napoli; and two relatively new organisations, the Sacra Corona Unita (United Holy Crown) and La Rosa (the Rose) in Puglia. These groups operate both separately and together.

Their activities range from contraband to protection rackets and on to monopolising lucrative contracts in just about any field. It was inevitable that they should also move into the hard narcotics trade, and at a 1989 meeting in Nice, the Sicilian Mafia, the 'Ndrangheta and the Camorra met representatives of the Colombian and Venezuelan drug cartels and carved up the world's heroin and cocaine markets.

By the early 1990s, the combined estimated worth of the Italian mafia groups was around L100,000 billion, or about 12% of GNP. The EU shudders at the prospect of Mafia money being laundered legitimately as European borders come down.

Cosa Nostra

The Sicilian Mafia has its roots in the oppression of the Sicilian people and can claim a history extending back to the 13th century. Its complex system of justice is based on the code of silence known as *omertà*.

Mussolini managed to virtually wipe out the Mafia, but from the devastation of WWII grew the modern version of the organisation, known as Cosa Nostra, which has spread its tentacles worldwide and is far more ruthless and powerful than its predecessor. It is involved in drug-trafficking and arms deals, as well as finance, construction and tourist development, not to forget public-sector projects and Italian politics. Few Italians doubt the claim that the Mafia's tentacles extend into almost every part of the country, and well beyond.

The early 1990s saw a virtual firestorm of Mafia violence in Sicilia, seen by many as a push by the Cosa Nostra to once and for all wipe out its opposition. Two anti-Mafia judges were assassinated in Palermo in separate bomb blasts, and the murders were interpreted as messages from the Mafia that it could kill with impunity. The assassinations, however, had the opposite effect, as the Italian government, long lethargic and even reluctant in its efforts to combat the Cosa Nostra, was finally moved to take action.

One early result of this feverish anti-Mafia activity was the arrest of Salvatore 'Toto' Riina, the Sicilian godfather. Riina, head of the powerful Corleonese clan, had been the world's most wanted man since 1969. When he was arrested, it was discovered that he had never left Sicilia and had, in fact, been living in the centre of Palermo with his family. More recently, the venerable ex-prime minister Giulio Andreotti, one of the longest serving and most dominant political figures in post-war Italy, was put on trial in Palermo for alleged links with the Mafia. Andreotti was also on trial in Perugia for alleged complicity in the 1979 murder of journalist Carmine Pecorelli. Another breakthrough came in May 1996 with the arrest of Giovanni ('The Pig') Brusca and his brother Vincenzo. Brusca was the man believed to have taken power after Riina's arrest and was implicated in the murder of anti-Mafia judge, Giovanni Falcone, as well as in the 1993 bombings in Firenze, Roma and Milano, which damaged monuments and works of art and killed several people.

The policy of clemency for *pentiti*, arrested Mafia members who grass (that's how Andreotti went down), has raised uncomfortable questions. On more than one occasion the pentiti have been found to be lying. And however much improved the judicial activity, the Mafia is still alive and well, so much so that it is claimed Riina is running it from inside his jail cell.

'Ndrangheta

Until the late 1980s, the 'Ndrangheta was a disorganised group of bandits and kidnappers; today it controls an organised crime network specialising in arms, drug-dealing and construction. In the 1970s, 16-year-old oil heir J Paul Getty III was kidnapped and held by the 'Ndrangheta, having his ear severed before his release. The organisation continues to kidnap for profit. With its base in the villages of Calabria, the 'Ndrangheta is notorious for its savage violence: in the early 1990s there was an average of one execution a day.

Camorra

This secret society grew to power in Napoli in the 19th century. It was all but completely suppressed around the turn of the century, but enjoyed a renaissance after WWII, dealing mainly in contraband cigarettes. After the 1980 earthquake, the Camorra diverted hundreds of millions of dollars of the aid money that poured in for reconstruction around Napoli and built an empire that has since diversified into drugs, construction, finance and tourist developments. It has worked closely with the Sicilian Mafia.

As the Camorra clans began to fragment in the mid-90s, their internecine squabbles over territory left a trail of death across Napoli. To make matters worse, 20 policemen from the Napoli *questura* stood accused in early 1997 of collusion with the Camorra. The mayor of Napoli at that time, Antonio Bassolino, was not surprised that the Camorra's tentacles had reached into the ranks of the police.

'It would have been strange had that not been the case – there is not one sector of society that has been spared by the system of corruption in Campania,' he said. Nor was the mayor impressed when, in mid-1997, Roma decided to send 600 troops into Napoli to protect sensitive points of the city and free up police to pursue the bandits. But for Antonio Bassolino, this was a case of too little, too late.

Sacra Corona Unita & La Rosa

Puglia had managed to escape the clutches of organised crime that had terrorised the rest of the south, but by the late 1980s the Mafia had arrived in the form of the Sacra Corona Unita in the south of the region and La Rosa in the north. As a natural gateway to Eastern Europe through its main ports of Bari and Brindisi, Puglia was a natural target following the collapse of communism. It quickly supplanted Napoli as a base for the Mafia's smuggling activities, chiefly in contraband cigarettes and an early consequence of its activities has been a massive upsurge in the number of heroin addicts in Bari, Brindisi and Taranto.

RELIGION

Some 85% of Italians professed to be Catholic in a census taken in the early 1980s. Of the remaining 15%, there were about 500,000 evangelical Protestants, about 140,000 Jehovah's Witnesses, and other, small groups, including a Jewish community in Roma and the Valdesi (Waldenses) – Swiss-Protestant Baptists living in small communities in Piemonte. There are also communities of orange-clad followers of the Bhagwan Rajneesh, known in Italy as the *arancioni*.

The big surprise on this front is the growth of the Muslim population, estimated at 700,000, and thus the second largest religious community in Italy after the Catholics. A fitting symbol for this novelty in the heart of Christendom was the inauguration in 1995 of the first mosque in Roma.

Although the fabric of Italian life is profoundly influenced by the presence of the Catholic Church, surprisingly few Italian Catholics practise their religion. Church attendance is low – an average of only 25% attend Mass regularly – and many children are never baptised. But first communion remains a popular event, the majority of Italian couples prefer to be married in a church, and religious festivals never fail to attract a large turn-out. Italians are also well acquainted with the saints and keenly follow the activities of the pope.

Stray Flock

Most Italians claim to be Catholic, but ask them about the *malocchio* (evil eye) and see what happens. Most will make a simple hand movement – index and little finger pointing down, with the middle and ring fingers folded under the thumb – which is designed to ward off evil spirits. Others, if pressed, might admit to wearing amulets. A pregnant woman might wear a chicken's neck hanging around her own neck – to ensure that her child is not born with the umbilical cord around its neck. Insurance agents can have difficulty discussing life insurance policies with clients – many of them don't want to discuss their eventual death, or the possibility of suffering serious accidents. Sociologists call this phenomenon Catholic paganism. ■

LANGUAGE

Although many Italians speak some English because they study it in school, English is more widely understood in the north, particularly in major centres such as Milano, Firenze and Venezia, than in the south. Staff at most hotels, pensioni and restaurants usually speak a little English, but you will be better received if you at least attempt to communicate in Italian.

Italian is a Romance language related to French, Spanish, Portuguese and Romanian. The Romance languages belong to the Indo-European group of languages, which include English. Indeed, as English and Italian share common roots in Latin, you will recognise many Italian words.

Modern literary Italian began to develop in the 13th and 14th centuries, predominantly through the works of Dante, Petrarch and Boccaccio, who wrote chiefly in the Florentine dialect. The language drew on its Latin heritage and many dialects to develop into the standard Italian of today. Although many dialects are spoken in everyday conversation, standard Italian is the national language of schools, media and literature, and is understood throughout the country.

There are 58 million speakers of Italian in Italy; half a million in Switzerland, where Italian is one of the official languages; and 1.5 million speakers in France, Slovenia and Croatia. As a result of migration, Italian is also spoken in the USA, Argentina, Brazil and Australia.

Visitors to Italy with more than the most fundamental grasp of the language need to be aware that many older Italians still expect to be addressed by the third person formal, ie *lei* instead of *tu*. Also, it is not considered polite to use the greeting *ciao* when addressing strangers, unless they use it first; it's better to say *buongiorno* (or *buonasera*, as the case may be) and *arrivederci* (or the more polite form, *arrivederla)*. We have used the formal address for most of the phrases. The informal address appears in brackets. Italian, like other Romance languages, has masculine and feminine forms. These two forms appear separated by a slash, the feminine form first.

See LP's *Italian Phrasebook* for a comprehensive list of words and phrases.

Pronunciation

Italian is not difficult to pronounce once you learn a few easy rules. Although some of the more clipped vowels, and stress on double letters, require careful practice for English speakers, it is easy enough to make yourself understood.

Vowels

Vowels are generally more clipped than in English:

a	as the second 'a' in 'camer**a**'
e	as in 'd**ay**' but a shorter sound
i	as in '**i**nn'
o	as in 'd**o**t'
u	as in 'c**oo**k'

Consonants

The pronunciation of many Italian consonants is similar to that of English. The following sounds depend on certain rules:

c	like 'k' before 'a', 'o' and 'u'. Like the 'ch' in 'choose' before 'e' and 'i'
ch	hard 'k' sound
g	hard, like the 'g' in 'get' before 'a', 'o'and 'u'. Like the 'j' in 'job' before 'e' and 'i'.
gh	hard, as in 'get'
gli	like the 'lli' in 'million'
gn	like the 'ny' in 'canyon'
h	always silent
r	a rolled 'rrr' sound
sc	like the 'sh' in 'sheep'before 'e'. Hard like the 'sch' sound in 'school'and 'i'. Before 'h', 'a', 'o' and 'u'.
z	like the 'ts' in 'lights'. Like the 'ds' in 'beds' when the first letter of a word.

Note that when 'ci', 'gi' and 'sci' are followed by 'a', 'o' or 'u', the 'i' is not pronounced unless the accent falls on the 'i'. Thus the name 'Giovanni' is pronounced 'joh-*vahn*-nee'.

Stress

Double consonants are pronounced as a longer, often more forceful sound than a single consonant.

Stress often falls on the second-last syllable, as in *spa-ghet-ti*. When a word has an accent, the stress is on that syllable, as in *cit-tà*, 'city'.

Language Problems

Please write it down.	*Può scriverlo, per favore?*
Can you show me (on the map)?	*Me lo puo mostrare (sulla carta/ pianta)?*
I (don't) understand.	*(Non) Capisco.*
Do you speak English?	*Parla (Parli) inglese?*
Does anyone speak English?	*C'è qualcuno che parla inglese?*
How do you say ... in Italian?	*Come si dice ... in italiano?*
What does ... mean?	*Che vuole dire ...?*

Paperwork

name	*nome*
nationality	*nazionalità*
date of birth	*data di nascita*
place of birth	*luogo di nascita*
sex (gender)	*sesso*
passport	*passaporto*
visa	*visto consolare*

Greetings & Civilities

Hello.	*Buongiorno/Ciao.*
Goodbye.	*Arrivederci/Ciao.*
Yes.	*Sì.*
No.	*No.*
Please.	*Per favore/Per piacere.*
Thank you.	*Grazie.*
That's fine/You're welcome.	*Prego.*
Excuse me.	*Mi scusi (Scusami).*

Sorry (forgive me).	*Mi scusi/Mi perdoni.*

Small Talk

What is your name?	*Come si chiama? (Come ti chiami?)*
My name is ...	*Mi chiamo ...*
Where are you from?	*Di dov'è/Di dove sei?*
I am from ...	*Sono di ...*
How old are you?	*Quanti anni ha (hai)?*
I am ... years old.	*Ho ... anni.*
Are you married?	*È sposato/a?*
I'm (not) married.	*(Non) sono sposata/o.*
I (don't) like ...	*(Non) Mi piace ...*
Just a minute.	*Un momento.*

Getting Around

I want to go to ...	*Voglio andare a ...*
What time does ... leave/arrive?	*A che ora parte/ arriva ...?*
the boat	*la barca*
the bus (city bus)	*l'autobus*
the bus (intercity)	*il pullman/il corriere*
the train	*il treno*
the aeroplane	*l'aereo*
the first	*il primo*
the last	*l'ultimo*
one-way ticket	*un biglietto di solo andata*
return ticket	*un biglietto di andata e ritorno*
1st class	*prima classe*
2nd class	*seconda classe*
platform number	*binario numero*
station	*stazione*
ticket office	*biglietteria*
timetable	*orario*
train station	*stazione*
The train has been cancelled/delayed.	*Il treno è soppresso/ in ritardo.*
I'd like to rent ...	*Vorrei noleggiare ...*
a car	*una macchina*

Useful Signs

CAMPEGGGIO	*CAMPING GROUND*
OSTELLA PER LA GIOVENTU	*YOUTH HOSTEL*
INGRESSO/ ENTRATA	*ENTRANCE*
USCITA	*EXIT*
COMPLETO	*NO VACANCIES/ FULL*
PENSIONE	*GUEST HOUSE*
ALBERGO	*HOTEL*
INFORMAZIONE	*INFORMATION*
VIETATO FUMARE	*NO SMOKING*
APERTO	*OPEN*
CHIUSO	*CLOSED*
POLIZIA/ CARABINIERI	*POLICE*
QUESTURA	*POLICE STATION*
TELEFONO	*TELEPHONE*
GABINETTO/ BAGNI	*TOILETS*

a bicycle	*una bicicletta*
a motorcycle	*una motocicletta*

Directions

Where is ...?	*Dov'è ...?*
Go straight ahead.	*Si va/(Vai) sempre diritto.*
Turn left.	*Gira a sinistra.*
Turn right.	*Gira a destra.*
at the next corner	*al prossimo angolo*
at the traffic lights	*al semaforo*
behind	*dietro*
in front of	*davanti*
far	*lontano*
near	*vicino*
opposite	*di fronte a*

Around Town

I'm looking for ...	*Cerco ...*
a bank	*un banco*
the church	*la chiesa*
the city centre	*il centro (città)*
the ... embassy	*l'ambasciata di ...*
my hotel	*il mio albergo*
the market	*il mercato*

the museum	*il museo*
the post office	*la posta*
a public toilet	*un gabinetto/ bagno pubblico*
the telephone centre	*il centro telefonico*
the tourist infomation office	*l'ufficio di turismo/ d'informazione*

want to exchange some money/ travellers' cheques.	*Voglio cambiare del denaro/degli assegni per viaggiatori.*

·each	*la spiaggia*
·ridge	*il ponte*
astle	*il castello*
athedral	*il duomo/la cattedrale*
hurch	*la chiesa*
sland	*l'isola*
nain square	*la piazza principale*
narket	*il mercato*
nosque	*la moschea*
·ld city	*il centro storico*
·alace	*il palazzo*
uins	*le rovine*
ea	*il mare*
quare	*la piazza*
ower	*la torre*

ccommodation

I'm looking for a ...	*Cerco un ...*
hotel	*albergo*
guesthouse	*pensione*
youth hostel	*ostello per la gioventù*

Vhere is a cheap hotel?	*Dov'è un albergo che costa poco?*
Vhat is the address?	*Cos'è l'indirizzo?*
Could you write the address, please?	*Può scrivere l'indirizzo, per favore?*
Do you have any rooms available?	*Ha camere libere/ C'è una camera libera?*

I would like ...	*Vorrei ...*
a bed	*un letto*
a single room	*una camera singola*
a double room	*una camera matrimoniale*
room with two beds	*una camera doppia*
a room with a bathroom	*una camera con bagno*
to share a dorm	*un letto in dormitorio*

How much is it per night/per person?	*Quanto costa per la notte/ ciascuno?*
Can I see it?	*Posso vederla?*
Where is the bathroom?	*Dov'è il bagno?*
I am/We are leaving today.	*Parto/Partiamo oggi.*

Food

breakfast	*prima colazione*
lunch	*pranzo/colazione*
dinner	*cena*
restaurant	*ristorante*
grocery store	*un alimentari*

What is this?	*(Che) cos'è?*
I would like the set lunch.	*Vorrei il menu turistico.*
Is service included in the bill?	*È compreso il servizio?*
I am a vegetarian.	*Sono vegetariana/o.*

Shopping

I would like to buy ...	*Vorrei comprare ...*
How much is it?	*Quanto costa?*
I don't like it.	*Non mi piace.*
Can I look at it?	*Posso dare un'occhiata?*

I'm just looking.	*Sto solo guardando.*
Do you accept credit cards/ travellers' cheques?	*Accetta carte di credito/assegni per viaggiatori?*
It's cheap.	*Non è cara/o.*
It's too expensive.	*È troppo cara/o.*

more	*più*
less	*meno*
smaller	*più piccola/o*
bigger	*più grande*

Time & Dates

What time is it?	*Che ora è?/Che ore sono?*
It is 8 o'clock ...	*Sono le otto...*
in the morning	*di mattina*
in the afternoon	*di pomeriggio*
in the evening	*di sera*
today	*oggi*
tomorrow	*domani*
yesterday	*ieri*
Monday	*lunedì*
Tuesday	*martedì*
Wednesday	*mercoledì*
Thursday	*giovedì*
Friday	*venerdì*
Saturday	*sabato*
Sunday	*domenica*
January	*gennaio*
February	*febbraio*
March	*marzo*
April	*aprile*
May	*maggio*
June	*giugno*
July	*luglio*
August	*agosto*
September	*settembre*
October	*ottobre*
November	*novembre*
December	*dicembre*

Numbers

0	zero
1	uno
2	due
3	tre
4	quattro
5	cinque
6	sei
7	sette
8	otto
9	nove
10	dieci
11	undici
12	dodici
13	tredici
14	quattordici
15	quindici
16	sedici
17	diciassette
18	diciotto
19	diciannove
20	venti
21	vent'uno
22	ventidue
30	trenta
40	quaranta
50	cinquanta
60	sessanta
70	settanta
80	ottanta
90	novanta
100	cento
1000	mille
2000	due mila
one million	un milione

Health

I am ill.	*Mi sento male.*
It hurts here.	*Mi fa male qui.*
I'm ...	*Sono ...*
diabetic	*diabetica/o*
epileptic	*epilettica/o*
asthmatic	*asmatica/o*
I'm allergic ...	*Sono allergica/o ...*
to antibiotics	*agli antibiotici*
to penicillin	*alla penicillina*
antiseptic	*antisettico*
aspirin	*aspirina*
condoms	*preservativi*
contraceptive	*anticoncezionale*
diarrhoea	*diarrea*
medicine	*medicina*
sunblock cream	*crema/latte solare (per protezione)*
tampons	*tamponi*

Emergencies

Help!	*Aiuto!*
Call a doctor!	*Chiami/Chiama un dottore/un medico!*
Call the police!	*Chiami/Chiama la polizia!*
Go away!	*Vai via! (informal)*

Italian
Art & Architecture

The Galleria degli Uffizi in Firenze, the Renaissance offices of the Medici, houses an overwhelming number of great paintings and epitomises the wealth of Italian art. But it is atypical as, in Italy, most art is still *in situ* – buildings, fountains and gardens, sculpture, paintings and mosaics in churches, city mansions (*palazzi*) and country villas. What sets the art of Italy apart is the lasting influence of its ancient Greek and Roman culture. This humanistic tradition has been so strong that the more anti-classical elements in later styles, like the flatness and distorted proportions of Romanesque sculpture and the pointed arches of Gothic art, have been less common in Italy than north of the Alps. The Renaissance and Baroque period, especially, involved a revival of the artistic styles of the classical world. In the 18th century, artists and scholars flocked to Roma and Napoli to study models for their neoclassical style of art and to visit the places described in classical literature.

Title Page: Detail of the gilded stucco decoration of the vaulted ceiling of the Capella Paolina, 1617, Palazzo Quirinale, Roma. An angel of the apocalypse carrying a chalice, monstrance and a book with seven seals. The cappella is in the wing of the Palazzo Quirinale designed by Carlo Maderno for Pope Paul V at the beginning of the 17th century. (photograph by G Colliva, The Image Bank)

GRANT V FAINT, THE IMAGE BANK

Right: The head of Constantine, from a colossal statue (colossus) which originally stood at his basilica in the Foro Romano; marble, 10m high; 4th century AD; now in the Musei del Palazzo dei Conservatori, Campidoglio, Roma.

TIMELINE

1500-1000 BC	1000-800 BC	700s BC	600s BC
Bronze Age • Cultures of the Siculi, Sicani and Elymi in Sicilia • Minoan and Mycenaean cultures in southern Greece and Crete	• Early Etruscan (Villanovan) culture around Bologna • Nuraghic culture in Sardegna	• First Greek colonies in southern Italy and Sicilia • Geometric style in Greek art • 753: Foundation of Rome • Etruscan settlements at Tarquinia and Cerveteri • Oscan settlement at Pompeii	• Further Greek colonies including Gela in Sicilia and Posidonia (Paestum) in southern Italy • 616-510: Etruscan kings in Rome

The 1st millennium BC

A typical hilltop town in central Italy is likely to have a history dating back to the Etruscans. Only in the 1st century BC did the Romans finally administer all of Italy and, by then, the other Italic peoples like the Etruscans, Samnites, Daunians and Lucanians were losing, or had already lost, their identity and any distinctive art forms.

While there are archaeological remains in Italy dating back to the fourth millennium in Italy, the earliest, well preserved Italian art is from the first millennium BC, from three cultures. These are Etruscan, in what is now roughly-speaking Toscana (Tuscany); Latin, including Roman, in Lazio; and the culture of the area called Magna Grecia, in southern Italy and Sicilia, where city-states were founded in the 8th and 7th centuries BC by Greek colonists who settled alongside the Italic peoples.

The Etruscans

Most evidence of Etruscan art has come from their tombs, richly furnished with carved stone sarcophagi, frescoes, fabulous gold jewellery, ceramics and bronzes. It appears to have been a personal or religious art rather than a public art. The earliest form, made circa 1000-650 BC, is also known as Villanovan. Characteristic pottery is metallic-looking, dull, black bucchero ware or sometimes red ware, produced from the 7th century, usually with relief decoration. Otherwise, Etruscan pottery closely follows the styles of Greek pottery. The decoration was painted in a clay slip fired black.

The 7th century BC saw geometric and oriental motifs with lions and sphinxes, but by the end of the century there was a growing interest in the human figure. In the 5th century, figures in clay colour were painted on a black background. Terracotta and stone sculpture and bronze figurines often followed Greek styles, from the rather stiff figures of the Archaic period (6th century) to the almost idealised naturalism of the Classical (5th and 4th centuries). Finally, a more naturalistic and even expressive realism surfaced in the Hellenistic period (from 323 BC to 31 BC). The representation of nudity was generally avoided, but naturalism occurs in portraiture and in figures like the terracotta winged horses at Tarquinia.

The Etruscans were famous for metalwork. Fine examples are the early 6th-century she-wolf in Roma's Musei Capitolini and the 4th-century two-headed chimera from Arezzo in Firenze's Museo Archeologico. Few such large bronze sculptures survive, but there are many figurines, some naturalistic, others strangely attenuated, and many bronze mirrors with incised figure decoration on the back. Also indicative of personal art is the technically superb gold jewellery employing filigree work and granulation.

Etruscan winged horses – architectural decoration from the Ara della Regina temple in Tarquinia; terracotta, 115cm high, 3rd century BC; Museo Nazionale Tarquinese, Tarquinia (photograph by Lauren Sunstein)

600s BC *cont*
- Earliest painted tombs at Tarquinia
- Orientalising style in Greek and Etruscan art, eg lion motifs

500s BC
- c. 550: Earliest Greek Doric temple at Paestum
- 510-27: Roman Republic established with Senate and two consuls
- Archaic period in Greek and Etruscan art; focus on the human figure

400s BC
- Doric temples at Paestum and in Sicilia
- Greeks fight Carthaginian encroachment into Sicilia
- 480-323: Classical period of Greek art
- 447-32: Parthenon, on Acropolis in Athens

The cemeteries of Tarquinia and Cerveteri (ancient Caere) are large archaeological sites containing tombs hewn out of the local volcanic tufa; at Tarquinia they are painted, often depicting banquets and dancing. The Museo Nazionale di Villa Giulia in Roma, the Museo Etrusco Gregoriano in il Vaticano and the Museo Archeologico in Firenze have the richest collections of Etruscan art, including sarcophagi with mythological scenes in relief and the carved, figures of the deceased couple on the lids.

The Latins

The gold jewellery and incised cylindrical bronze urns found at Palestrina, south-west of Roma, are now attributed to the local Latins rather than Etruscan settlers in the area, and excavations at Lavinio on the coast of Lazio, just north of Anzio, have produced large terracotta statues.

Like the Greeks, the early Romans built temples of stone. There are examples in Roma by the Tevere and, though not so well preserved, in Largo Argentina. They differ from Greek temples in having a high podium with steps and columns only at the front, forming a deep porch. Instead of the Doric columns with cushion-like capitals and no bases, the Romans favoured Ionic columns with volute capitals and Corinthian columns with acanthus leaf capitals, both types with bases. All three types were usually fluted. The Etruscans used the Tuscan column which was unfluted and had a rounder version of a Doric capital plus a base. There is a strong Hellenistic influence in the symmetry of the great hillside sanctuary of circa 80 BC at Palestrina (ancient Praeneste) near Roma, but its concrete, rather than dry stone construction is an Italian innovation. Egyptian influence is apparent in the Nilotic mosaic found nearby and now included in the site museum.

Greek Temple E, doric style, Selinunte, Sicilia; limestone; 490-480 BC; re-erected

DAMIEN SIMONIS

The Greeks

Greek temples in southern Italy and Sicilia, at Paestum, Metaponto, Agrigento, Siracusa (the present duomo), Selinunte and Segesta, are Doric, from the 6th and 5th centuries, with steps and colonnades on all four sides. The three at Paestum, south of Napoli, inspired 18th-century European architects before the classical temples of Athens became well known. Near Selinunte are ancient quarries with some monolithic columns cut, but not removed, from the surrounding rockface. The temple at Segesta remained unfinished, its columns unfluted. The bosses for lifting the stones with ropes were left on and the internal walls and columns were never constructed. Also at Segesta there is a Greek theatre, typically built into the hillside.The red-figure potttery of the 4th century, found in tombs, was locally made. At Canossa, ceramics were decorated with bright pigments, sometimes gilded. Gold was again used for jewellery, as in Greece. The largest collections of Italian Greek art are in Taranto, Palermo and il Vaticano. The finds are mainly of the 5th to 2nd centuries BC after which Roman influences predominate.

300s BC
- 390: Gauls sack Rome and leave Italy
- Etruscan-style temple of Jupiter, Juno and Minerva on Capitolino, Roma
- Servian walls to protect Roma
- Peace between Romans and Etruscans
- 323 -31: Hellenistic period of Greek art (from death of Alexander the Great to defeat of Cleopatra, Ptolemaic Greek ruler of Egypt)

200s BC
- Roman defeat of Samnites and Vulci
- 246-201: Wars between Romans and Carthaginians fought mainly in Sicilia
- Sicilia, Sardegna and Spain under Roman rule

100s BC
- North Africa and Greece under Roman rule

1st cent BC
- 64: Syria under Roman rule
- 44: Assassination of Julius Caesar

The Roman Empire: 27 BC – circa 600 AD

From the 1st century BC Italians, using vulcanic pozzolana, made a quick-curing, strong concrete for vaults and domes. It was used especially in Roma to roof vast areas like the Pantheon (118-128 AD) which consists of a hemispherical dome 43.2m in diameter set on a drum of the same height and lit from above by an oculus 9m in diameter. Pumice was used in the concrete at the top to reduce the weight. Brick-faced concrete was also used for multistorey apartment blocks and basilicas (public halls) like that of Maxentius/Constantine in the Foro Romano. Huge vaults covered the hot baths and other rooms in complexes like the Terme di Caracalla and di Diocleziano opposite the Stazione Termini. Dry stone masonry was used for temples, as at Brescia (73 AD); for aqueducts, and for the vaulted substructures to support the seating of theatres and amphitheatres. Examples are the Teatro di Marcello and the Colosseo (80 AD) in Roma and the amphitheatres at Verona, Lucca and Capua.

Equestrian statues and portraits, carved reliefs and monumental arches were erected in many towns, commemorating individuals and historical events. These include the Ara Pacis (Altar of Peace) of Augustus (13 BC-9 BC) and the columns of Trajan and Marcus Aurelius in Roma and the arches at Aosta, Ancona, Rimini, Benevento and Roma. The Arco di Costantino (c. 315 AD) incorporates sculpture from earlier Roman imperial monuments.

The largest collections of Roman sculpture are in the Musei del Vaticano and the Musei Capitolini in Roma. Many of the statues are Roman marble copies or variants of Greek religious statuary, made famous by ancient writings on art and then fancied by the Romans for secular use in piazzas, public bath buildings, gardens and private mansions. Romans even had statues made of themselves in the guise of Greek gods or heroes, like the statue of a matron posing as Venus with Cupid, dated to the 2nd century AD, and the idealised figure of Hadrian's lover Antinoüs, both in il Vaticano.

ROB FLYNN

LAUREN SUNSTEIN

Right: The River Nile – detail; Roman floor mosaic from the Forum of Praeneste (Palestrina), c. 80 BC; Museo Archeologico Nazionale Prenestino, Palestrina, Lazio

Left: The Villa dei Misteri, Pompeii; 60-50 BC, fresco

1st century BC *cont*
- 31: Octavianus (Augustus) defeats Antony and Cleopatra; Egypt under Roman rule
- 27 BC-AD 14: Augustus, 1st Roman emperor

1st cent AD
- 64: Fire in Rome under Emperor Nero
- 79: Eruption of Vesuvio and destruction of Pompeii and Herculaneum
- 80: Colosseo, amphitheatre, Roma

100s
- Pantheon, temple of all the gods, Roma
- Villa Adriana at Tivoli, the Castel Sant'Angelo in Roma
- Column and Forum of Emperor Trajan, Roma
- Column and statue of emperor Marcus Aurelius, Roma

200s
- Terme di Caracalla, Roma
- Aurelian walls to protect Rome

All the major Greek artistic styles were available to the Romans: the austere Archaic figures which experimented with the human form, the more naturalistic, idealised classical ones popular again in the age of Augustus and, finally, the over-sweet representations of children or brutally realistic scenes of agony or old age produced in the Hellenistic period. Today, there is more interest in the Romans's own sculpture commemorating their history and citizens or made for specific architectural settings while, still drawing on Greek precedents. The context for such use of statuary can still be appreciated in the remains of the Villa Adriana (2nd century) at Tivoli.

Major public buildings, villas and apartment blocks were decorated with frescoes and mosaics such as survive still at Pompeii and Herculaneum (modern Ercolano) and at Roma's ancient port of Ostia. Some are still in situ; many, cut from their context, are in the Museo Archeologico in Napoli, along with other objects preserved by the eruption of Vesuvio in 79 AD: garden statues, furniture, glassware, and bronze and silver vessels.

Roman wall-paintings, including those of the catacombs in Roma, were in true fresco technique with water-based pigments applied to plaster while still wet. The frescoes represent four styles: the first imitates stone-work; the second creates illusions of architectural settings (eg the Villa dei Misteri, Pompeii, and the Villa at Oplontis) and dates to the last century BC; the third has a pattern of delicate architectural tracery combined with imitations of

Below Left: Antinoüs, Hadrian's lover, in the guise of Bacchus, from a villa near Palestrina; marble, c. 130 AD; Museo Pio-Clementino, il Vaticano; the drapery, originally of bronze, was restored by Thorvaldsen in marble

Below Right: Venus Felix and Cupid – dedicated by Sallustia and Helpidus, mid-2nd century AD; marble, 214m high; Belvedere courtyard, Musei del Vaticano

LAUREN SUNSTEIN

LAUREN SUNSTEIN

300s
Late Antique art: c. 300-600

- Basilica of Maxentius/Constantine in Foro Romano
- 306-337: Constantine 1st Christian emperor; Arco di Costantino built
- First Christian basilicas in Rome: San Giovanni in Laterano, Santa Croce, and San Pietro
- 330: Byzantium renamed Constantinople; becomes residence of the Eastern Roman emperors until 1453
- 374-97: St Ambrose bishop of Milano

400s

- Vandals enter Roman Empire through Gaul and Spain and settle in Northern Africa
- 452: Attila and his Huns sack northern Italian cities
- 455: Vandals sack part of Roma
- 476: Last Roman emperor deposed
- 493-540 : Ostrogoths rule Italy

panel paintings; and the fourth, from the mid-1st century, combines features of the second and third styles and is the most common. This style survives because much of Pompeii and Herculaneum (like the Casa dei Vettii, Pompeii) was redecorated following the earthquake in 62 AD which preceded the eruption of 79. Later frescoes, to be found at Ostia and in the catacombs, tend towards simpler decoration and are often on a white ground.

Coloured marble veneers and mosaics were also used: first, black and white mosaic tesserae (cubes) on floors. Later, they were coloured, as in the villa at Piazza Armerina south of Enna in Sicilia and in the early churches of Aquileia and Grado near Trieste. By the 4th century, glass tesserae were used to splendid effect in the apses of the early Christian churches of Roma, (Santa Costanza, Santa Pudenziana, SS Cosma e Damiano and Santa Maria Maggiore) and in Ravenna (San Vitale, Sant'Apollinare Nuovo, and Sant'Apollinare in Classe). The old Basilica di San Pietro in Roma, rebuilt in the Renaissance, would have been similar to the vast basilicas of Santa Maria Maggiore and San Giovanni in Laterano, which featured a long nave with clerestory windows culminating in a wide apse, four, rather than two, side aisles and ceilings lower than that of the nave.

There are late, carved ivories in the bishop's throne in Ravenna (Museo Arcivescovile), 5th-century carved wooden doors on Santa Sabina, Roma, and painted illustrations in manuscripts like those in the Biblioteca Vaticana, displayed in the Salone Sistino (Sistine Hall) of the Musei del Vaticano. These are precursors of art forms which were to predominate in the medieval period.

Early Medieval: circa 600-1050 AD

The Middle Ages, from the point of view of Renaissance scholars, meant the entire period which followed the classical, late antique and early Christian past and was dominated by the Church and monasteries. Now, the Middle Ages is generally divided into an early period, then Romanesque and Gothic styles, which both first evolved north of the Alps. The transitions are not clear cut, especially in Italy where the influence of the classical past militated against extreme innovation and led almost naturally to the Renaissance.

In the early medieval centuries, wealth was often invested by individuals and the Church in land or luxury objects. Examples include the gold altar-front in Sant'Ambrogio, Milano (c. 850, which shows scenes from the lives of Christ and St Ambrose), and the large series of carved ivory panels, now in the duomo of Salerno. Illuminated manuscripts copied in Italy transmitted classical humanist styles across Europe to regions otherwise strongly influenced by the more linear, less naturalistic artistic traditions of the Anglo-Saxons, Franks and Germans. The duomo of Milano contains a gold book-cover, set with cloisonné enamels, given by Archbishop Aribert (1018-45).

Angel in vault and two martyrs in lunette; Chapel of San Zenone, Chiesa di Santa Prassede, Roma; mosaic, c. 820

LAUREN SUNSTEIN

500s
- 540: Byzantines recover Italy from Ostrogoths; rule Ravenna until 751
- Ravenna churches decorated with mosaics
- 568: Lombard invasion; established states centred on Pavia, Spoleto and Benevento; Italy fragmented until 19th century unification
- Byzantine rule through local governors in Sicilia until 9th century
- Byzantine rule in south eastern Italy, Bari to Otranto, until 11th century
- 590-604: Gregory I the Great pope, reorganises the Church

600s
Early Medieval art c. 600-1050
- Growing power of Papal State in central Italy

Following the Lombard and Frankish invasions of the 6th century, there was little building on the same scale until the Romanesque period. However, gems include the small church at Castelseprio, north-east of Milano, painted in an almost impressionistic style, and the frescoed and elaborately stuccoed Tempietto di Santa Maria in Valle at Cividale del Friuli, east of Udine. Both were decorated in about the 8th century.

The Greeks in the south built some small, cross-shaped and domed churches in the Byzantine style with fresco decoration on a blue ground. Three survive from the 10th to 11th centuries: the Cattolica at Stilo, San Marco, Rossano and San Pietro, Otranto. In Roma, the tradition of mosaic decoration of churches continued into the 9th century in Santa Prassede, Santa Maria in Domenica and Santa Cecilia in Trastevere.

Below Left: The Archangel Michael – detail; mosaic, 1143; Chiesa di Santa Maria dell'Ammiraglio, La Martorana, built by George of Antioch, Palermo, Sicilia

Below Right: St Peter consecrates St Hermagoras bishop, c. 1200; fresco, crypt of the Basilica di San Pietro, Aquilea

Romanesque: circa 1050-1200

The term Romanesque dates from the 19th century only and initially referred to the revival of buildings whose size and structure resembled those of the Roman Empire. It applies to the 11th-century Norman period of architecture in England, southern Italy and Sicilia. The stone vaulted naves supported by massive piers, typical of Romanesque churches north of the Alps, made little impact in Italy, where the basilican style of

REI ZUNDE

DAMIEN SIMONIS

700s
- 751: Ravenna falls to the Lombards and then is under the Papacy
- 774: Lombard capital of Pavia taken by the Frank Charlemagne

800s
- 800: Charlemagne crowned Holy Roman Emperor in Roma; capital at Aachen
- Arabs take Sicilia from Byzantines and ravage coast of Italy up to Roma

900s
- 962: Otto I of Saxony crowned Holy Roman Emperor
- Byzantine-style churches at Stilo, Ortranto, & Rossano, southern Italy

1000s
Romanesque art c. 1050-1200s
- 1054: Schism between Western and Byzantine churches
- 1063-93: San Marco, Venezia

late antiquity survived, with columns, sometimes from ancient buildings, in the nave. Large basilicas were built in Puglia at Bari, Molfetta, Trani, Barletta, Bitonto, and Canosa, often with typically Romanesque blind arcading on the exterior walls and whimsical sculptural ornament. The basilica of Sant'Angelo in Formis, near Capua, rebuilt in the 11th century under the patronage of the Benedictine monastery of Montecassino, shows Byzantine influence with frescoes of agitated figures on a blue ground. By the 13th century, the Norman rulers in the south had succumbed to the German Hohenstaufen dynasty, epitomised in Puglia by the great octagonal keep of Frederick II, Castel del Monte.

In multicultural Sicilia, where the Normans had overcome the Muslims, at Cefalú, Monreale and Palermo there are basilicas and domed churches with vast areas of wall mosaic in the Byzantine style, with Christ, the Virgin and archangels in dominant positions and rows of biblical scenes. There are also magnificent mosaics in Roma in the apses of San Clemente and Santa Maria in Trastevere, and throughout San Marco in Venezia. That five-domed basilica was built under Byzantine influence in the second half of the 11th century; the Gothic elements on the façade are later additions. Cast bronze doors, with religious scenes, on the Chiesa di San Zeno Maggiore in Verona, and in the south at Trani and Ravello, imitated those at Amalfi, Montecassino and San Paolo fuori le Mura in Roma, imported from Constantinople.

Below Left: The Torre di Pisa (Leaning Tower), 1063-1350; marble

Below Right: Façade of Chiesa di San Michele in Foro, Lucca, Toscana; 11th-12th century

DAMIEN SIMONIS

DAMIEN SIMONIS

1000s *cont*
- 1063-1350: Pisa baptistry, duomo and campanile
- 1071: Normans capture Bari; end of Byzantine rule in south-eastern Italy
- 1073: Sant' Angelo in Formis, near Capua
- 1091: Norman settlers control southern Italy and Sicilia
- 1097: First Crusade; capture of Jerusalem from Turks

1100s
- Churches with Byzantine-style mosaics in Sicilia
- Norman churches of Puglia, southern Italy
- 1176: Lombard cities gain independence from German emperor
- 1196-1215: Siena Duomo

1200s (Duecento)
- Late Romanesque and early Gothic art
- German Hohenstaufen, then French Angevin rule in Sicilia
- 1204: Fourth Crusade

There are many modest 11th-13th century Romanesque basilican churches throughout Italy, with rounded arch forms echoing those of classical and late antiquity, and traces of fresco. In San Pietro at Civate, south of Lago di Como and in the crypts of the cathedrals at Aquileia (c. 1200) in the Veneto and Anagni (c. 1255), south-east of Roma frescoes are extensive. The figures have the linear modelling of the period but, again due to the influence of antiquity and Byzantium, are less abstract and contorted than some murals north of the Alps. Some of the Romanesque churches have free-standing campanili. The most stunning complex must be the liberally carved marble cathedral, baptistry and bell-tower at Pisa. The Chiesa di San Michele in Foro at Lucca has galleries on the façade, as at Pisa, but also an inlay of fantastic animals and grotesque carvings above the capitals. Overlooking Firenze, San Miniato al Monte (1062) has colourful marble veneers forming bold geometric patterns on the façade and inside. Geometrically patterned pavements of inlaid Cosmati work were made by cutting up ancient coloured marble veneers and porphyry columns. Carved animal and human figures and mosaic tesserae, some gilded, often decorate fonts, pulpits and columns of cloisters; examples are at Monreale in Sicilia, Santa Sofia in Benevento and San Paolo fuori le Mura in Roma.

Large-scale stone sculpture appeared in the early 12th century for the first time since antiquity, but was less naturalistic, characterised by flatness and stylised folds. Examples include the marble ambo of Sant'Ambrogio in Milano, reliefs by the sculptor Wiligelmo in the façade of Modena cathedral, and the figures framing the doors of cathedrals in Cremona, Ferrara and Verona and the Chiesa di San Zeno Maggiore, Verona.

Gothic: circa 1200-1400

Gothic (meaning barbarian or Germanic) was a derogatory term applied in the Renaissance to late medieval architecture, which the Renaissance replaced with a style more deliberately based on classical models. Gothic architecture and sculpture developed first in France from the mid-12th century and is characterised by pointed arches and vaults, often accentuated by ribbing. Walls with large, stained-glass windows were supported from the outside by flying buttresses and the downward thrust of pinnacles.

Statue of San Michele added in 14th century, Foro Lucca, Toscana; Romanesque church of the 11th-12th century

DAMIEN SIMONIS

Because of the influence of antiquity, the pointed arches of Gothic architecture never flourished in Italy to the same extent as they did north of the Alps. Sant'Antonio in Padova, begun in 1231, is roofed with domes, influenced by the earlier San Marco in nearby Venezia. Until recently, the upper and lower churches of San Francesco at Assisi (1228-53) had great expanses of wall with frescoes by leading painters including, probably, Cimabue (Cenni di Pepi, d. 1302) and, in the first part of the 14th century, Simone Martini, Pietro Lorenzetti and Giotto di Bondone and his pupils (see the section on Assisi in Umbria & Le Marche for details). In Padova, Giotto's frescoes in the Scrovegni or 'Arena' Chapel (1305), built on the site of the old Roman amphitheatre, continue to present narrative scenes in rows on a blue ground and a Last Judgment fills the west wall. But volume has started to triumph over flatness in figures and there is a more realistic representation of three-dimensional depth in the architectural settings.

In Roma there is only one Gothic church, Santa Maria sopra Minerva, but in the north, the finest Gothic includes the duomo (1196-1215) of Siena; (its altarpiece, made in 1311 by Duccio di Buoninsegna, consisting of many

1200s *cont*

- 1204-126:1 Crusaders hold Constantinople
- 1210: St Francis of Assisi founds the Franciscan Order
- 1220: St Dominic founds the Dominican order at Bologna
- 1222: Foundation of the University of Padova
- 1225-1274: St Thomas Aquinas, Dominican theologian
- 1228-53: Upper and lower churches of San Francesco, Assisi
- 1270-97: Nicola Pisano and son Giovanni sculpt Pisa baptistry
- 1271: Marco Polo's journey to China
- 1290: Duomo of Orvieto is begun; continued by Lorenzo Maitano
- 1294: Duomo of Firenze is begun by Arnolfo di Cambio
- 1298-1310: Palazzo della Signoria (Palazzo Vecchio), Firenze

icon-like scenes, is now in the Museo dell'Opera del Duomo), and the duomo of Milano, begun in the 14th century but completed in the 19th. The Dominican and Franciscan orders often built vast, Gothic churches on the outskirts of the medieval city, like Santa Maria Novella and Santa Croce in Firenze. The building of the duomo of Orvieto, and the production of its stained glass, is well documented and the plans for the Gothic façade (circa 1310) by the architect Lorenzo Maitano have survived. They indicate the reliefs on the piers between the doors and the rose window and pinnacles.

Sculpture now also showed a greater interest in classical naturalism and depth, as in the marble reliefs in the 13th-century pulpits by Nicola Pisano (d. 1278) in the Pisa Baptistry and Siena Duomo and those by his son Giovanni (d. 1314) in the duomo of Pisa and Sant'Andrea in Pistoia. Giovanni also carved sculpture for the exterior of the Pisa Baptistry and Siena Duomo. The grace and vertical linearity of Gothic architecture was also reflected in tombs, tabernacles over altars and reliquaries for the remains of saints.

With the growth of trade and city government, town halls were built, like the Palazzo del Popolo in Todi (1213-1267) and Palazzo del Capitano in Orvieto (c. 1250), both still in the Romanesque style, and the Palazzo Pubblico in Siena, begun in 1298. In the latter there are frescoes by Simone Martini of the Maestà (Virgin in majesty; 1315) and of the *condottiere* Guidoriccio da Fogliano riding between the two towns he liberated, painted

Below Left: Pinnacles on the Duomo, Milano

Below Right: 13th century Gothic additions to the 11th century facade of the Basilica di San Marco, Venezia, and replacement mosaics of the 19th century

DAMIEN SIMONIS

DAMIEN SIMONIS

1300s (Trecento)
Gothic art

- Writers:
  Dante Alighieri (1265-1321), Petrarch (1304-74), Boccaccio (1313-75)
- Spanish Aragonese rule in Sicilia
- 1297-1310: Palazzo Pubblico, Siena
- 1312-1447: Visconti family rule in Milano
- 1305: Giotto's Scrovegni frescoes, Padova
- 1308-11: Duccio's Maestà altarpiece for duomo, Siena
- 1309-78: Babylonian captivity: popes based at Avignon in France
- 1338-9: Ambrogio Lorenzetti's frescoes in Palazzo Pubblico, Siena
- 1340s: Palazzo Ducale (Doges' Palace) begun, Venezia
- 1347: Bubonic plague, the Black Death, strikes Europe
- 1378-1417: Schism in Western Church (rival popes)
- 1386: Duomo of Milano begun

Giotto, Ognissanti Madonna; c. 1310; tempera on panel; Galleria degli Uffizi, Firenze (Photo Scala, Firenze)

Sandro Botticelli, Allegory of Spring (Primavera), 1478; tempera and oil on panel; Galleria degli Uffizi, Firenze (Photo Scala, Firenze)

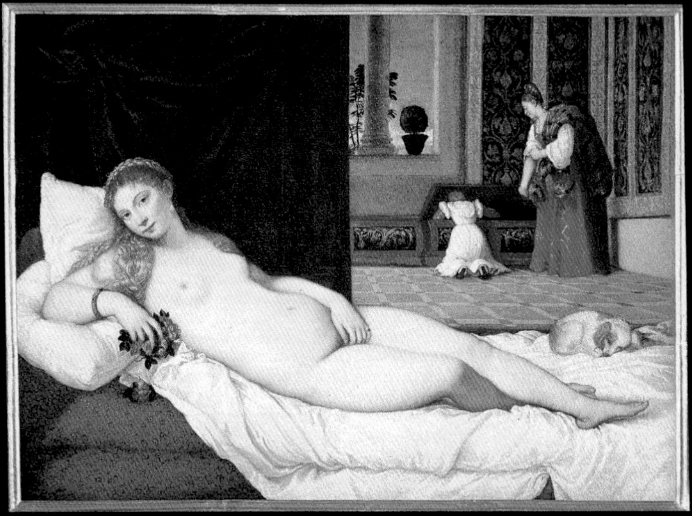

Titian (Tiziano Vecelli), Venus of Urbino (La Venere di Urbino), 1538; oil on

in 1328. There are also frescoes of good and bad government by Ambrogio Lorenzetti (1339). Firenze has the fortress-like Bargello (1255), which now houses Florentine sculpture, and the Palazzo della Signoria, also known as the Palazzo Vecchio (1298-1310). Also on the Piazza della Signoria is the Loggia della Signoria (also known as the Loggia dei Lanzi) of 1376-82, used now for sculpture. The nearby Orsanmichele (1337) is a colonnaded market building with a chapel by Andrea Orcagna (1349-59). In Venezia, the Doges' palace, the Palazzo Ducale, which houses a superb collection of arms and armour, is of the 14th and early 15th century. The Gothic style in Italy lingered longest in Venezia and the Porta della Carta, facing the Piazzetta San Marco, with its statue of Venezia as Justice and the four virtues is dated 1438-43. The elegant Gothic Ca' d'Oro on the Canal Grande was built between 1420-34. The Palazzo Davanzati in Firenze is a good example of late medieval townhouse Nearby San Gimignano has houses with towers.

Icon paintings were traditionally painted on wooden panels with tempera (pigments in an egg binder); backgrounds were often of gold leaf. From the late 12th century large wooden crucifixes for churches were painted and big panels showing the Virgin and Child appeared at the turn of the 13th century. The *Rucellai Madonna*, an early work by Duccio (c.1285), is a gentler-looking version of a Byzantine type and can be compared with the *Ognissanti Madonna* by Giotto (c. 1310). Both are in the Galleria degli Uffizi. Giotto makes the figures of the angels overlap to indicate recession and the drapery has volume; nevertheless, the steps of the throne are still in inverted perspective (becoming wider as they recede) and a frontal view of the throne is achieved only by showing the arms awkwardly splayed.

Altarpieces in the 14th century became less like Byzantine icons, less formulaic, and with larger individual panels and greater unification of the picture space. This can be seen in the elegant *Annunciation* (1333) in the Uffizi, painted by Simone Martini, who later worked at the papal court in Avignon. Ambrogio Lorenzetti's *Presentation in the Temple* (1342), also in the Uffizi, shows a lively interest in perspective, but there is no consistent vanishing point, a concept only mastered in the next century.

Renaissance: circa 1400-1600

Secular art achieved more prominence as aristocratic families and churchmen indulged in a grander life style. Portraiture flourished, with sculpted busts and figures on innumerable tombs. Early Renaissance portrait paintings (of which there are examples in the Palazzo Pitti, Firenze) were often in profile, influenced by Roman coins. Thus, in 1465, Piero della Francesca painted both Battista Sforza, of the powerful Milanese family, and Duke Federigo da Montefeltro of Urbino (now in the Uffizi). The wood-panelled studiolo in the palace of this scholarly soldier-duke is an illusionistic treat with inlay used to depict cupboards, books and musical instruments (1479).

Domes, vaults and arches provide the key to Renaissance architecture. The arcade of Filippo Brunelleschi's Ospedale degli Innocenti (Foundling Hospital; 1419-44), in Firenze, has a pleasing geometry and blue and white terracottas of babes in swaddling clothes by Andrea della Robbia (1487) decorate the roundels. Brunelleschi's bold experiment in 1436 in spanning the duomo of Firenze with a double-skinned, segmented dome (45.5m x 91m high) was followed by other domes: the Tempietto of Donato Bramante (c. 1504-10) beside the Chiesa di San Pietro in Montorio on the Gianicolo

1400s (Quattrocento)
Renaissance art

- Sforzas rule in Milano, Medici in Firenze, Gonzagas in Mantova, Estensi in Ferrara, Malatestas in Rimini, Federigo da Montefeltro in Urbino; Spanish (Aragonese) control in southern Italy
- 1425-52: Ghiberti's bronze Porta del Paradiso, east door of the Baptistry, Firenze
- 1427: Masaccio's frescoes in Cappella Brancacci, Santa Croce, Firenze
- 1430-64: Alberti's treatises on painting, architecture and sculpture
- 1434: Jan van Eyck's *Arnolfini Marriage*, Flemish, using oil-based paint
- 1436: Brunelleschi's dome for the duomo of Firenze
- 1438-39 : Council of Ferrara-Firenze; Byzantines seek help against Turks
- 1438-47: Fra Angelico's frescoes in the Convent of San Marco, Firenze

in Roma, and the large, centrally planned church of Santa Maria della Consolazione near Todi. The latter was begun in 1508 when Bramante was designing the Basilica di San Pietro. Originally conceived as centrally planned and domed, the basilica was finally built in the form of a long Latin cross with a large dome designed by Michelangelo Buonarroti (1475-1564) with 42m-wide double skin and completed by Giacomo della Porta in 1590.

In the second half of the 16th century the Jesuit order, founded by the Spaniard St Ignatius Loyola in 1534, built as its main church in Roma the Gesú (1568-75), whose mannerist façade, designed by della Porta, has more pronounced architectural elements than earlier Renaissance churches. These create a greater contrast between surfaces and a play of light and shade and if the building is scarcely striking now it is because it has been so frequently copied, as was the interior designed by Giacomo Barozzi da Vignola, with its wide nave and side chapels instead of aisles.

REI ZUNDE

Duomo, Firenze, Santa Maria del Fiore; detail of lantern of dome (exterior); Filippo Brunelleschi and others, 1467.
(Brunelleschi died in 1446 and several others worked on the lantern, adapting his design.)

A palazzo in the city was a very visible sign of a family's success. Some of the grandest Renaissance palazzi are in Firenze (Rucellai and Strozzi) and Roma (Venezia, Cancelleria, Farnese and Spada). Well-proportioned, and often embellished with classical columns, some retain their furnishings or have become art museums. Country villas were usually less pretentious. However, whereas in the 15th century Leonbattista Alberti had applied classical forms to church façades, as at Mantova (Sant'Andrea and San Sebastiano) and Rimini (Tempio Malatestiano), Andrea Palladio in the mid-16th century, applied ancient Roman temple design to the façades of his churches in Venezia and also his villas in Vicenza and the Veneto. His Villa Barbaro at Maser, east of Bassano del Grappa, has playful illusionistic frescoes by Paolo Veronese (1560s) and the Villa Rotonda, outside Vicenza, was a cardinal's party-house imitating the Pantheon in Roma.

Brunelleschi's experiments with optics and perspective were discussed by his fellow architect Alberti in *On Painting* (1435). Also in this period, Masaccio produced a tour de force when he used a central vanishing point in his fresco of *The Holy Trinity* (1427) in Santa Maria Novella, Firenze. To achieve depth he also painted figures in the foreground more sharply and used strong light from one direction to create greater contrasts of light and shadow (chiaroscuro), as evident in his frescoes, including the *Tribute Money*, in the Brancacci Chapel in Santa Maria del Carmine, Firenze (1427).

Fra Angelico (Guido di Pietro; 1387-1455) painted frescoes in the cells of his Dominican convent of San Marco in Firenze, as well as a large Annunciation (1440s). Walls started to be used for a single scene rather than being divided horizontally and vertically as Giotto had done in the Arena Chapel. Benozzo Gozzoli decorated a small chapel in the Palazzo Medici-Riccardi in Firenze with a fresco of tapestry-like richness continuing right around the walls (1459) and showing the three Magi travelling through luxuriant countryside. Such interest in landscape had not occurred in Italian painting since antiquity. In Mantova, in the Gonzagas' ducal palace, Andrea

1400s *cont*

- 1445-50: Donatello's Gattamelata equestrian statue, Padova
- 1450: Alberti designed Tempio Malatestiano, Rimini
- 1450: Gutenberg's invention of the printing press
- 1453: Fall of Constantinople to the Ottoman Turks
- 1459: Gozzoli's fresco, Palazzo Medici-Riccardi, Firenze
- 1454-66: Piero della Francesca's frescoes, San Francesco, Arezzo
- 1465-74 : Mantegna's frescoes in Camera degli Sposi, Palazzo Ducale, Mantova
- 1478: Botticelli's painting *Primavera*, Galleria degli Uffizi, Firenze
- 1480s: Lower frescoes of Cappella dii Sistina (Botticelli, Perugino, Ghirlandaio)
- 1490: Aldo Manuzio establishes printing press in Venezia
- 1492: Columbus' discovery of America

Mantegna (1431-1506) painted the illusion of a dome with oculus in the vault of the *Camera degli Sposi*. On the walls he depicted members of the family with their courtiers, servants and hounds (1465-74).

Oil painting, first used by Jan van Eyck and other Flemish painters in the first half of the 15th century, was only slowly adopted in Italy, initially combined with tempera. However, it was in northern Italy that canvas was first used for major paintings, a memorable example being Mantegna's foreshortened *Dead Christ* (1466) in the Brera Gallery in Milano. There are two large paintings of classical mythology by Sandro Botticelli (1445-1510) commissioned for a Medici prince and now in the Uffizi: the *Birth of Venus* of circa 1482 was painted on canvas, while *Primavera* (Spring) of 1478 is painted on a panel of poplar, using both tempera and oil. Renaissance scholars interpreted the figures in this work as allegories for the moral qualities required of a humanist prince.

In Roma, when Baldassare Peruzzi built and helped decorate what is now the Villa Farnesina across the Tevere (1508-11), he incorporated in the frescoes a horoscope of the patron, the banker Agostino Chigi, and grotesques like those found at that time in the excavations of Nero's Golden House on Monte Celio. Raffaello Sanzio (Raphael; 1483-1520) captured the new humanist spirit in his frescoes in the apartment of Pope Julius II in il Vaticano. In *The School of Athens* (depicting philosophers and mathematicians), he repeated the curvature of the vaulted room in his painted architectural setting (1512). Raphael's religious art also reflected the new humanism. His tender *Madonna with the Goldfinch* in the Uffizi (1507) has a landscape background and sympathetically captures the difference in age of the children, the young John the Baptist and the still younger Christ.

In the refectory adjoining the church of Ognissanti in Firenze is a fresco of the *Last Supper* by Domenico del Ghirlandaio (1480) which creates the illusion of the Apostles sitting in the convent's refectory with a garden beyond.The *Last Supper* by Leonardo da Vinci (1452-1519) in the refectory of Santa Maria delle Grazie in Milano, painted at the end of the century (1495-98), has the participants so engrossed it draws the viewer right into the drama. About the same time, Luca Signorelli (c. 1441-1523) decorated a chapel in the duomo of Orvieto with the *Resurrection of the Dead.* Its images of naked figures rising from their graves, stretching their muscular limbs, reflects the intellectual climate of the Renaissance. In the Piccolomini

LAUREN SUNSTEIN

Constellation of Perseus, beheading the gorgon Medusa, and Fame with her trumpet; Loggia della Galatea, Villa Farnesina, Roma; ceiling fresco by Baldassare Peruzzi, who built the villa for the banker Agostino Chigi in 1508-11

1400s *cont*

- 1495-98: Leonardo da Vinci's *Last Supper*, Cenacolo Viinciano, Santa Maria delle Grazie, Milano

1500s
High Renaissance and Mannerist art

- Popes Julius II (1503-13), and the Medici Leo X (1513-21) & Clement VII, patrons of the arts
- 1501-04: Michelangelo's statue of *David*, Firenze
- 1506: Bramante appointed architect for rebuilding of San Pietro, Roma
- 1508-12: Michelangelo's Cappella Sistina ceiling, il Vaticano
- 1510-14: Frescoes in the Stanze Raffaello, il Vaticano
- 1516-18: Titian's *Assumption of the Virgin*, Santa Maria Gloriosa dei Frari, Venezia
- 1517: Luther in Wittenberg signals German Reformation
- 1527: Sacking of Roma by troops of Emperor Charles V

LAUREN SUNSTEIN

Grotesques, c. 1511; Villa Farnesina, Roma, detail of a fresco (the frescoes were by the leading painters in Roma, Sebastiano del Piombo, Sodoma, Raphael and Giulio Romano as well as Peruzzi)

Library, off the side aisle of the Duomo in Siena, Bernardino di Betto, known as Pinturicchio, depicted in vertical, page-like panels (1509) highlights in the career of Aeneas Silvio Piccolomini, who later became Pope Pius II (1458-64), and gave his home town of Pienza a square harmoniously flanked by a cathedral and palaces designed in the 1460s by Bernardo Rossellino.

In 1550, Giorgio Vasari (1511-1574), who painted frescoes in the Palazzo Vecchio in Firenze, wrote *The Lives of the Most Excellent Painters, Sculptors and Architects*, which is still influential. Vasari stressed the fundamental importance to painting of drawing and line at a time when, in Venezia, more emphasis was being placed on colour, notably by Tiziano Vecelli (Titian; 1493-1576), Tintoretto (Jacopo Robusti, 1518-94), and Veronese (Paolo Caliari, 1528-88). Titian painted the huge panel of the *Assumption of the Virgin* (1516-18) above the altar of the Franciscan church of Santa Maria Gloriosa dei Frari, in which the composition is built up with colours as much as by form. The artist was sought after as a painter of portraits and produced sensuous paintings like the *Venus of Urbino.* The softness and light hues of the reclining nude and the bedding are contrasted with deep plum-coloured fabrics and a strong, vertical line provocatively divides the picture into two fields of colour (1538; Uffizi). Near the Frari in Venezia is the Scuola di San Rocco which houses Tintoretto's large-scale cycle of biblical scenes, including the 12m-wide *Crucifixion*, in which a pool of light in the centre is ringed by a crowd of figures. Veronese's most striking canvas is probably the 13m *Feast in the House of Levi* (1573), in the Galleria d'Accademia, Venezia, which depicts the Last Supper, with Christ seated at a banquet with a crowd in contemporary Venetian dress in a lavish palazzo.

The most striking examples of the mannerist style of the 16th century are the dramatically foreshortened statuesque figures of Michelangelo's Cappella Sistina ceiling (1508-12). Shadows are achieved not by deeper hues but by a change of colour, sometimes to a sharp green. Michelangelo returned to Roma a few years after it had been sacked in 1527 by mercenaries of Emperor Charles V, and continued work in the chapel, painting *The*

- 1534: St Ignatius Loyola founds Society of Jesus (Jesuits)
- 1535-50: Palazzo Farnese, Roma (Antonio da Sangallo the Younger and Michelangelo)
- 1536-41: Michelangelo's *Last J udgment*, Cappella Sistina, Roma
- 1550: Vasari's treatise *The Lives of the Most Excellent Painters, Sculptors & Architects*
- 1550: Palladio's Villa Rotonda, Vicenza
- 1565-87: Tintoretto's cycle of paintings in the Scuola di San Rocco, Venezia

1600s
Baroque art

- 1624: Bernini's statue of *Apollo & Daphne*, Villa Borghese, Roma
- 1655: Bernini's *Fontana dei Quattro Fiumi*, Piazza Navona, Roma
- 1656-67: Bernini's colonnade in front of San Pietro, Roma

REI ZUNDE

Michelangelo's David, detail of hand; marble, 1504; the Galleria dell'Accademia, Firenze (copy in Piazza della Signoria)

Last Judgment with even more contorted figures, seemingly suspended across the east wall (1536-41). Other 16th-century artists who used rich colours and a stylish, sometimes contrived manner, especially in relation to perspective, were Correggio (1489-1534), Giulio Romano (1492-1546) who decorated the Gonzaga's Palazzo del Tè in Mantova in 1530, Pontormo (1494-1557), Bronzino (1503-72), Parmigianino (1503-40), Giambologna, (1529-1608) and, later in the century, Annibale Carracci (1560-1609), who decorated the Palazzo Farnese in Roma (1597), and Caravaggio (1573-1610).

The cast bronze doors of Firenze's Baptistry show the progression from the Gothic style of sculpture of Andrea Pisano (south side, 1336) to the Renaissance masterpieces of Lorenzo Ghiberti (1378-1455) on the north and, on the east side, the innovative and almost painterly gilded Porta del Paradiso. Many of the bronze statues by Ghiberti's prolific contemporary Donatello (Donato Bardi, 1386-1466) are in the Museo del Bargello in Firenze and his large equestrian statue of Gattamelata (1453), the first since antiquity, is outside the Basilica di Sant'Antonio in Padova. The Colleoni statue by Andrea del Verrocchio (1481) is outside the burial church of the doges, SS Giovanni e Paolo, in Venezia. Sculptors worked often in Carrara marble. The most famous example is Michelangelo's over-lifesize statue of *David* (1504) in Firenze, which exhibits the slight distortions (large head and hands) and exaggerated musculature typical of the late, mannerist phase of the Renaissance. Distinctive terracotta sculpture was produced by three generations of the della Robbia family (15th to mid-16th century) using blue and white enamel glazes, sometimes with the addition of yellow and green. Lavishly coloured scenes also decorate the white, tin-glazed ceramics (maiolica) of Faenza (museum), Gubbio, Castel Durante and Deruta.

Baroque: 17th century

The two great names connected with Roma, city of baroque churches and fountains are the architect Francesco Borromini (1599-1667) and architect and sculptor Gianlorenzo Bernini (1598-1680). Borromini created an oval-shaped interior in the church of San Carlo alle Quattro Fontane (1634) and set a spiral campanile on his church of Sant' Ivo della Sapienza. Outside Borromini's church of Sant'Agnese in Agone, in the Piazza Navona, Bernini set an ancient Egyptian obelisk above a fountain flanked by four river gods. Near the Pantheon he set a small obelisk on the back of an elephant; and for the parapets of the Tevere bridge to the Castel Sant'Angelo (the mausoleum of the emperor Hadrian) he designed 10 angels, carving two himself. His most dramatic sculptures, like the twisting figures of Apollo pursuing Daphne, now in the gallery of the Villa Borghese, are intended to be viewed from all sides. In the church of Santa Maria della Vittoria, Bernini's *Ecstasy of St Theresa* is given an added theatrical touch with figures of the Cornaro family, who look down from flanking balconies.

Carlo Maderno designed the massive facade of the Basilica di San Pietro (1612), Bernini its curving colonnade (1656-1667), the baldacchino over the altar, the setting for the throne and tombs for Urban VIII and Alexander VII.

In the south, architecture and sculpture converge at Lecce, in Puglia. Because the buildings are of a soft sandstone which hardens on exposure to the air, ornately carved doorways and balconies were readily incorporated in many churches and houses, like the Chiesa di Santa Croce (1549-1679).

Paintings in the 17th century, like those by the precocious Caravaggio

1700s
Rococo & Neoclassical art

- Bourbon rule of southern Italy and Sicilia
- 1723-68: Canaletto's views of Venezia
- 1740s: Tiepolo's frescoes in Palazzo Labia, Venezia
- 1748: First excavations at Pompeii
- 1778: La Scala opera house, Milano
- 1796-1814: Napoleon and French rule in Italy

1800s
19th-century art

- 1805: Canova's marble statue of Paulina Borghese, Villa Borghese
- 1870: Italian Unification under King Victor Emanuel II of Piemonte after defeat of Austrians in north & Bourbons in south and French withdrawal from Roma
- 1865-78: Galleria Vittorio Emanuele II, Milano
- 1871: Roma declared capital of Italy
- 1885-1911: Monument to Victor Emanuel II and Italian unity, Roma

STEFANO CAVEDONI

DAMIEN SIMONIS

Above Left: Angel on the Ponte Sant'Angelo, Roma, marble,1688; designs by Bernini

Above Right: Basilica of Santa Croce, Lecce; 1549-1679; detail of entablature

(1573-1610) and José Ribera who spent most of his life in Napoli (1591-1652), tended to be sombre, with flashes of luminosity, like those of the Dutch artist Rembrandt (1606-69). Other painters used a bright palette: the émigré Claude from Lorraine (1600-82), in his serene Italian landscapes, and Pietro da Cortona (1596-1669), in his allegorical ceiling in the Palazzo Barberini, Roma. The rococo (1728) piazza of Sant'Ignazio, with its curved façades, gives the Chiesa di Sant'Ignazio, the second Jesuit church of Roma, a theatrical setting to complement its trompe l'œil ceiling by Andrea Pozzo (1691-94).

Baroque furniture featured ebony veneers, spiral legs and stretchers. Exuberantly carved softwoods were gilded. Tables with mosaics of lapis lazuli and other coloured stones, were made in il Vaticano for European courts. Firenze, Venezia, Milano and Genova were renowned for lace-making; Venetian glass was blown and twisted into complex forms.

18th to 20th centuries

In the 18th century, the Kingdom of Naples was ruled by the Spanish dynasty, the Bourbons, who built the Palazzo Reale di Capodimonte which now houses the art collection of the Farnese family of Roma. At Caserta, north of Napoli, vast royal palace and grounds were designed by Luigi Vanvitelli.

1900s
Modern and Post-Modern art

- 1909: Futurist Manifesto and artists under Boccioni form Futurist movement
- 1914-18: WWI; Italy gains the Trentino and Trieste from Austria
- 1922: Formation of a Fascist government under Mussolini
- 1929 Città del Vaticano becomes an independent state
- 1933 Hitler comes to power in Germany
- 1938 Building begins on EUR, Roma
- 1939-45 WW II: Italy aligns with Germany and enters war in 1940
- 1946 Italy votes to become a republic
- 1957 Italy a member of the European Economic Community
- 1958-63 Papacy of John XXIII

Excavations began at Pompeii and Herculaneum and, as interest in classical antiquities and mythology revived, Italy became the focus of the Grand Tour. Young French artists awarded the Prix de Rome studied at the French Academy in Roma. The opera theatre La Scala opened in Milano in 1778. Napoli's San Carlo had opened in 1738, but was rebuilt after fire in 1816.

The Spanish Steps (1726) created a focal point for visitors, artists and writers and the appeal of Roma was enhanced abroad by Giovanni Battista Piranesi's etchings of the city and its ancient Roman ruins (1745). Venezia was similarly served by the paintings of Canaletto (Giovanni Antonio Canal; 1697-1768). The asymmetrical, ornamental Rococo style of the mid-18th century is well illustrated by the 1745 frescoes of Giambattista Tiepolo in the Palazzo Labia, Venezia. The neoclassical style which followed is represented by the sculptures of Antonio Canova (1757-1822) and Bertel Thorvaldsen (1768-1844)who worked in Roma with commission from all over Europe. Most famous example of their work is Canova's figure of Napoleon's sister, Paolina Borghese, as Venus, in the Villa Borghese.

The beginning of modern architecture is epitomised in the 19th-century iron and glass-roofed shopping galleries. The most famous is the Galleria Vittorio Emanuele in Milano (1865-78), but there are others in Napoli, Genova and Torino. The response to the great white marble 'wedding-cake' monument to Victor Emanuel II in Roma (1885-1911), built to celebrate Italian unity, is not always enthusiastic. With huge colonnade and quadrigas alluding to ancient precedents, it anticipates grandiose schemes of the Fascist era like the Foro Italico sports centre at the foot of Monte Mario (1928-31) and EUR (Esposizione Universale di Roma). This district, on the outskirts of Roma, (1938) has a classicizing, axial monumentality, massive statues and underutilised museums.

Italian painting and sculpture since Italian unification in 1870 is most readily found in the Galleria Nazionale d'Arte Moderna in Roma, but also in Milano and Torino. There are works by the Italian Futurists, inspired by urbanism, industry and the idea of progress, such as Umberto Boccioni (1882-1916) and Giacomo Balla (1871-1958) who aligned themselves with the Futurist Manifesto (1909) of the writer Emilio Marinetti, and Carlo Carrà (1881-1996), who had much in common with Cubists like Pablo Picasso. Giorgio Morandi (1890-1964) consistently depicted bottles and jars as forms rather than objects, while the Surrealist Giorgio de Chirico (1888-1978) painted visionary empty streetscapes with elements disconcertingly juxtaposed, often incorporating allusions to classical antiquity.

Present generation Italian artists, Sandro Chia (b. 1946) and Francesco Clemente (b. 1952) have worked in Italy and abroad, the latter combining fantasy with trompe l'œil naturalism. Works of art since WWII should also include the tomb of Pope John XXIII (d. 1963), by Emilio Greco, in the Basilica di San Pietro; the buildings in which Pier Luigi Nervi introduced concrete reinforced with mesh, like the Pirelli skyscraper in Milano (1958) and the Palazzetto dello Sport and Stadio Flaminio, built for the 1960 Roma Olympics; post-modernist works like Aldo Rossi's cemetery in Modena (1971); the viaducts soaring over Genova and mountain ravines; and the achievements of leading Italian fashion houses, car manufacturers and designers of everyday domestic items, leather goods and furnishings, should also be noted.

Ann Moffatt, Australian National University, Canberra

Further reading:

Nancy H Ramage & Andrew Ramage, *Roman Art, Romulus to Constantine, 2nd ed*, Laurence King, 1995
Richard Krautheimer, *Roma, Profile of a City, 312-1308*, Princeton UP, 1980
John White, *Art and Architecture in Italy: 1250-1400*, Penguin, 1976
Frederick Hartt, *A History of Italian Renaissance Art*, Thames & Hudson, 1979
Bruce Cole, *Italian Art 1250-1550. The relation of Renaissance art to life and society*, New York, Harper & Row, 1987
Rudolf Wittkower, *Art and Architecture in Italy 1600-1750* Penguin, 3rd ed. 1973

Facts for the Visitor

PLANNING

When to Go

The best time to visit Italy is in the low season, from April to June and in September/October, when the weather is usually good, prices are lower and there are fewer tourists. The weather is warm enough for beach-goers from June to September. Late July and August is the time to avoid Italy, when the weather boils, prices are inflated and the country swarms with holiday-makers. Most of the country goes on vacation in August, abandoning the cities (and leaving many shops, hotels and restaurants closed) and packing out the coast and mountains. Finding a place to stay by the sea or in the hills without booking months in advance can be especially difficult at this time.

July and September are the best months for hiking in the Alps and Appennini (like everything else, walking trails and *rifugi* (refuges) are crowded in August). During these months the weather is generally good, although you should always allow for cold snaps. Rifugi usually open from late June to the end of September for hikers and at Easter (March/April) for skiers.

A mild climate usually makes winter a reasonable time to visit Italy's southern regions and Sardegna, but in recent years areas like Puglia, Calabria and Sicilia have all been hit hard by freezing conditions, heavy rain and snow.

What Kind of Trip?

Virtually anything is possible in Italy, and how you approach it will depend on your budget, time, how well you know the country and whether or not you have specific interests. The top tourist cities (such as Roma, Venezia and Firenze) are popular destinations for short excursions from Europe – many firms offer travel and accommodation packages for this kind of weekend break.

The budget traveller could spend months slowly touring around the whole country, using local transport and sticking to youth hostels and basic *pensioni*. Those with less time might prefer instead to concentrate on a single region (Toscana or the island of Sicilia, for instance) or make up an itinerary taking in some of the great cities. Having your our own vehicle is a great advantage, allowing you to explore the backblocks – and Italy is great motorcycling country.

Skiers often spend a week or two on the slopes in the mountains of northern Italy and pretty much ignore the rest of the country.

There is no shortage of organised tour possibilities. They reduce hassle but can be restricting and pricey – see Organised Tours in the Getting There & Away chapter. Some tours are theme-based, such as art tours or cookery courses in rural Italy. Another approach is to undertake language and culture courses in cities like Perugia and Firenze and fit in travel around study.

Maps

Small-Scale Maps Michelin has a series of good fold-out country maps. No 988 covers the whole country on a scale of 1:1,000,000. You could also consider the series of area maps at 1:400,000 – Nos 428 to 431 cover the mainland, 432 Sicilia and 433 Sardegna. These cost L10,000 each in Italy. The Touring Club Italiano (TCI) also publishes a decent map covering Italy, Switzerland and Slovenia at 1:800,000.

Road Atlases If you are driving around Italy, the AA's *Big Road Atlas – Italy*, available in the UK for UK£9.99, is scaled at 1:250,000 and includes 39 town maps. In Italy, de Agostini's *Atlante Stradale d'Italia* (1:600,000) contains city plans and sells for L24,500. For L43,000 the same publisher offers the more comprehensive *Atlante Turistico Stradale d'Italia* (1:250,000). The Touring Club Italiano publishes an *Atlante Stradale d'Italia* (1:200,000), divided into three parts – Nord, Centro and Sud. Each costs L34,000.

City Maps City maps in this book, combined with tourist office maps, are generally adequate. More detailed maps are available at good bookshops (like Feltrinelli) or newspaper stands. Excellent city plans and maps are published by the Istituto Geografico de Agostini, the Touring Club Italiano and Michelin. Other decent city map publishers include FMB (with the yellow covers) and Milano's Vincitorio Editore. The Touring Club Italiano publishes *200 Piante di Città* for L20,000, a handy booklet of street plans covering pretty much any city that might otherwise be a source of confusion.

Hiking Maps Maps of walking trails in the Alps and Appennini are available in major bookshops – but the best by far are the Touring Club Italiano bookshops (especially the head office in Milano). Otherwise you can usually locate maps of specific zones once you are in the area. The best hiking maps are the 1:25,000 scale series published by Tabacco, which mainly cover the north. Kompass also publishes 1:25,000 scale maps of various parts of Italy, as well as a 1:50,000 series and several in other scales (including one at 1:7500 of Capri!). Edizioni Multigraphic Firenze produces a series of walking maps concentrating mainly on the Appennini. All cost around L8000 to L10,000 each. The series of *Guide dei Monti d'Italia*, grey hardbacks published by the TCI and Club Alpino Italiano, are exhaustive walking guides containing maps.

What to Bring

Pack as little as possible. A backpack is an advantage since petty thieves prey on luggage-laden tourists with no free hands. Backpacks whose straps and openings can be zipped inside a flap are less awkard and more secure than the standard ones.

Suitcases with portable trolleys may be fine in airports but otherwise you won't get far on foot with them. If you must carry a suitcase/bag, make sure it is lightweight and not too big. Pack a bag and test it out before leaving – could you carry it for a few km? Remember that most everyday necessities can be found easily in Italy – there is no need to stock up in advance and drag it all around with you.

A small pack (with a lock) for day trips and sightseeing is preferable to a handbag or shoulder bag, especially in the southern cities where motorcycle bandits are particularly active.

Clothes Except in the mountains, Italy is uniformly hot in summer but variable in winter. In most areas, during July and August a light jacket will do for cool evenings. In winter you will need a heavy coat, hat, gloves and scarf for the north, while in Sicilia a lined raincoat would do. Roma has a mild climate, so you will need heavy woollens only in January/February.

Italians dress up just to do the daily food shopping, so if you plan to hang around in cafés and bars or enjoy some of the nightlife you'll feel more comfortable with a set of casually dressy clobber – jeans and T-shirts will give you the decided air of a bum by local standards.

You'll need a pair of hardy, comfortable walking shoes with rubber soles – trainers are fine except for going out, so something a little more presentable, though casual, might cover all bases.

People planning to hike in the Alps should bring the necessary clothing and equipment, in particular a pair of hiking boots (lightweight and waterproof). Even in high summer you will need warm clothing on long hikes or if you plan to go to high altitudes on cable cars – even if it's sweltering in the valley the temperature can drop to below zero at 3000m. Inexperienced hikers should check with a local mountaineering group for a list of essentials before leaving home. Otherwise, the list provided in the Dolomites section of the Trentino-Alto Adige chapter should be adequate.

Unless you plan to spend large sums in dry-cleaners and laundries, pack a portable clothesline. Many pensioni and hotels ask guests not to wash clothes in the room, but such rules are rarely enforced. Consider packing a light travel iron or crease-proof clothes.

Useful Items Apart from any special personal needs, consider the following:

- an under-the-clothes money belt or shoulder wallet, useful for protecting your money and documents in cities
- a towel and soap, often lacking in cheap accommodation
- a small Italian dictionary and/or phrasebook
- a Swiss army knife
- minimal unbreakable cooking, eating and drinking gear if you plan to prepare your own food and drinks
- a medical kit (see Health)
- a padlock or two to secure your luggage to racks and to lock hostel lockers
- a sleeping sheet to save on sheet rental costs if you're using youth hostels (a sleeping bag is unnecessary unless you're camping)
- an adapter plug for electrical appliances
- a torch (flashlight)
- an alarm clock
- sunglasses

Basic drugs are widely available and indeed many items requiring prescriptions in countries like the USA can be obtained easily over the counter in Italy. If you require specific medication, it's easier to bring it with you. Condoms can cost L30,000, or more, for 12 but as little as L12,000 in supermarkets.

SUGGESTED ITINERARIES

However you decide to approach the country, and whatever itinerary you map out, remember that the determined monument zealot could spend days and in some cases weeks in any one Italian city. No human being can 'do' all of Italy, probably not even in a lifetime dedicated to the project! So do some research before you go and assemble a package of cities, monuments and countryside you particularly wish to see and build in time for detours, long lunches and the unexpected!

Short Trips

A week is not a long time in Italy but speedy travellers have been known to arrive in Roma and undertake a whistle-stop tour of the tried and true. After a couple of days in Roma you could make for Firenze by train, spend two nights there (allowing time for a quick excursion to Siena or Pisa) and then push on to Venezia where another two days would allow you to sample the place. The ultra-keen might stop for a day en route in Bologna. Such a trip could be a one-way proposition or end with a return trip by rail to the point of departure (eg Roma).

With two weeks the options widen a little. The same route could be used as a basis, with further side trips thrown in to suit. Between Roma and Firenze, Perugia suggests itself as a stop, while Firenze itself can be used as a base for a whole range of exploratory touring – why not try the medieval village of San Gimignano? It is one among many in the Tuscan and Umbrian countryside which is worth poking about in.

Digging Deeper

Those who know Italy or simply want to 'specialise' a little could devote three to four weeks to one or two regions. Sicilia, for example, offers plenty. Arriving by charter flight in Palermo you could undertake a circuit taking in (heading east) Cefalù, the Isole Eolie (where you could easily chew up a week alone), Taormina, Mt Etna, Syracuse, Ragusa, Agrigento, Trapani (for the Isole Egadi), Erice and the Riserva Naturale dello Zingaro. Speedy travellers can accomplish this in less time but that still leaves the villages and hill country of the interior – a world little observed by foreigners. Another area to consider for a concentrated visit is Campania. Basing yourself in Italy's fascinating southern metropolis, Napoli (itself worthy of several days' investigation), you could easily spend a week or two taking in the wonders of: Vesuvio (Mt Vesuvius); the ancient cities of Pompeii, Herculaneum and, further south, Paestum; the captivating islands of Capri, Ischia and Procida; the seaside resort of Sorrento and the dazzling Amalfi coast; and the regal town of Caserta.

A 'Grand Tour'

Of course those with a full month or more have unlimited options. Backpackers often wander into the north of Italy from France and make their way south to Brindisi to catch a boat on to the next obvious destination – the Greek isles. You might begin with some exploration of the Ligurian coast, including the chic Portofino and charming Cinque Terre then head eastward for Bologna and on to Venezia. Or you could simply maintain a straightforward south-easterly course. This would allow you to take in Pisa, Firenze, Siena, Perugia, perhaps some excursions in the Tuscan and Umbrian countryside, Roma and Napoli before cutting east across to Brindisi and the ferries for Greece. This alone could make a full schedule for a month, but those intent on 'seeing everything' could squeeze in more spots en route.

THE BEST & THE WORST

Coming up with a Top 10 hit list for Italy is a little like trying to find the 10 shiniest gold ingots in Fort Knox. Bearing that in mind, you could try the following:

1. Firenze
2. Isole Eolie
3. Amalfi coast
4. Siena
5. Italian food
6. Le Cinque Terre
7. Ancient ruins of Roma, Pompeii & Paestum
8. Venezia
9. Parco Naturale di Fanes-Sennes-Braies (in the Dolomiti)
10. Carnevale in Ivrea (Piemonte)

The authors felt they could live without a second dose of the following:

1. Potenza
2. Reggio di Calabria
3. Italian bureaucracy
4. Italian drivers
5. Autostrada tolls
6. Roman men
7. Driving through fog in the Po valley
8. Catania
9. Italian beaches in August (so packed you cannot breathe!)
10. Italian queues

TOURIST OFFICES

Local Tourist Offices

The quality of tourist offices in Italy varies dramatically. One office might have enthusiastic staff but no useful printed information, while indifferent and even hostile staff in another might keep a gold mine of brochures hidden under the counter.

Three tiers of office exist: regional, provincial and local. The names of tourist boards vary throughout the country, but they all offer basically the same services.

Regional offices are generally concerned with promotion, planning, budgeting and other projects far removed from the daily concerns of the humble tourist. Provincial offices are known either as the Ente Provinciale per il Turismo (EPT) or, more commonly, as the Azienda di Promozione Turistica (APT) and usually have information on both the province and the town. Local offices generally only have info about the town you're in and go by various names. Increasingly common is IAT (Informazioni e Assistenza ai Turisti), but you may also come across AAST (Azienda Autonoma di Soggiorno e Turismo) offices. These are the places to go if you want specific information about bus routes, museum opening times etc.

In many small towns and villages the local tourist office is called a Pro Loco, often similar to the IAT or AAST offices but on occasion little more than a meeting place for the local elderly men.

Most offices of the EPT, APT and AAST will respond to written and telephone requests for information about hotels, apartments for rent etc.

Tourist offices are generally open Monday to Friday from 8.30 am to 12.30 or 1 pm, and from 3 to around 7 pm. Hours are usually extended in summer when some offices also open on Saturday afternoons or on Sunday.

Information booths at most major train stations and some smaller stations tend to keep similar hours but in some cases only operate in summer. They can usually provide a map *(pianta della città)*, list of hotels *(elenco degli alberghi)* and information on the major sights *(informazioni sulle attrazioni turistiche)*. Many will help you find a hotel.

English, and sometimes French or German, is spoken at offices in larger towns and major tourist areas. German is of course spoken in Alto Adige. Printed information is generally provided in a variety of languages.

If you are landing in Roma you can obtain limited information about the major destinations throughout the country from the EPT office, Via Parigi 11, 00185 Roma, and at the headquarters of Italy's national tourist office, ENIT (Ente Nazionale Italiano per il Turismo), Via Marghera 2, 00185 Roma. Both are near Roma's central train station, Stazione Termini.

The addresses and telephone numbers of local, provincial and some useful regional tourist offices are listed under towns and cities throughout this book.

Tourist Offices Abroad

Information on Italy is available from the Italian State Tourist Office in the following countries:

Australia
: Alitalia, Orient Overseas Building, Suite 202, 32 Bridge St, Sydney (☎ 02-9247 1308)

Canada
: 1, Place Ville Marie, Suite 1914, Montreal, Québec H3B 3M9 (☎ 514-866 7667)

UK
: 1 Princes St, London W1R 8AY (☎ 0171-408 1254; 0891-600280)

USA
: 630 Fifth Avenue, Suite 1565, New York, NY 10111 (☎ 212-245 4822)
: 124000 Wilshire Blvd, Suite 550, Los Angeles CA 90025 (☎ 310-82 02977)
: 401 North Michigan Ave, Suite 3030, Chicago, IL 60611 (☎ 312-644 0990)

Sestante-CIT (Compagnia Italiana di Turismo), Italy's national travel agency, also has offices throughout the world (known as CIT or Citalia outside Italy). It can provide extensive information on travelling in Italy and will organise tours, as well as book individual hotels. CIT can also make train bookings, including sector bookings (such as Roma-Napoli), and sells Eurail passes and discount passes for train travel in Italy. Sestante-CIT offices include:

Australia
: 263 Clarence St, Sydney 2000 (☎ 02-9267 1255)
: Level 4, 227 Collins St, Melbourne 3000 (☎ 03-9650 5510)

Canada
: 1450 City Councillors St, Suite 750, Montreal, Quebec H3A 2E6 (☎ 514-845 4310)
: 111 Avenue Rd, Suite 808, Toronto M5R 3I8 (☎ 416-927 7712)

France
: 5 Boulevard des Capucines, Paris 75002 (☎ 01-44 51 39 00)

Germany
: Komödienstrasse 49, Köln D-50667 (☎ 0221-207090)

UK
: Marco Polo House, 3-5 Lansdowne Rd, Croydon, Surrey CR9 1LL (☎ 0181-686 0326)

USA
: 342 Madison Ave, Suite 207, New York, NY 10173 (☎ 212-697 2497)
: 6033 West Century Blvd, Suite 980, Los Angeles, CA 90045 (☎ 310-338 8615)

Italian cultural institutes in major cities throughout the world have extensive information on study opportunities in Italy.

VISAS & DOCUMENTS

Passport

Citizens of the 15 European Union member states can travel to Italy with their national identity cards alone. People from countries that do not issue ID cards, such as the UK, must have a valid passport. All non-EU nationals must have a full valid passport.

If you've had the passport for a while, check that the expiry date is at least some months off, otherwise you may not be granted a visa (if you need one). If you travel a lot, keep an eye on the number of pages you have left in the passport. US consulates will generally insert extra pages into your passport if you need them, but others tend to require you to apply for a new passport. If your passport is nearly full when you are preparing to leave home, do yourself a favour and get a new one before you leave.

Visas

EU citizens require only a passport or national identity card to stay in Italy for as long as they like. Citizens of many other countries, including the US, Canada, Australia, New Zealand, Japan and South Africa, do not need a visa if entering as tourists for up to three months. Since passports are often not stamped on entry, that three-month rule can generally be interpreted flexibly, since no-one can prove how long you have been in the country. The only time you are likely to have your passport stamped is when you arrive by air – although even at Roma's airport there's a good chancethey won't stamp it. If your passport has been stamped and you wish to stay longer, you can play safe by leaving the country and re-entering – in that case you will have to make sure a new entry stamp goes into the passport, as it's likely you won't be stamped out either.

If you are entering Italy for any reason other than tourism (for instance, study) or if you plan to remain in the country for an extended period, you should insist on having the entry stamp. Without it you could encounter problems when trying to obtain a *permesso di soggiorno* – in effect, permission to remain in the country for a nominated period – which is essential for everything from enrolling at a language school to applying for residency in Italy.

Italy is not yet a full member of the Schengen Area – a group of seven EU countries including France which have reciprocal free movement without (theoretically) passport controls.

EU Citizens EU citizens supposedly do not require any permits to live, work or start a business in Italy. They are, however, advised to register with a *questura* (police station) if they take up residence – in accordance with an anti-mafia law which aims at keeping a watch on everyone's whereabouts in the country. Failure to do so carries no consequences, although some landlords may be unwilling to rent out a flat to you if you cannot produce proof of registration. Those considering long-term residence will eventually want to consider getting a permesso di soggiorno, a necessary first step to acquiring a *carta d'identità,* or residence card. See also the Permesso di Soggiorno section later. While you're at it, you'll need a *codice fiscale* (tax file number) if you wish to be paid for most work in Italy.

Study Visas Non-EU citizens who want to study at a university or language school in Italy must have a study visa. These visas can be obtained from your nearest Italian embassy or consulate. It should be noted that you will normally require confirmation of your enrolment, payment of fees and proof of adequate funds to support yourself before a visa is issued. The visa will then cover only the period of the enrolment. This type of visa is renewable within Italy but, again, only with confirmation of ongoing enrolment and proof that you are able to support yourself – bank statements are preferred.

Work Permits

Non-EU citizens wishing to work in Italy will need to obtain a work permit *(permesso di lavoro)*. If you intend to work for an Italian company and will be paid in lire, the company must organise the permesso and forward it to the Italian consulate in your country – only then will you be issued an appropriate visa.

If non-EU citizens intend to work for a non-Italian company or will be paid in foreign currency, or wish to go freelance, they must organise the visa and permesso in their country of residence through an Italian consulate. This process can take many months – so look into it early.

It is in any case advisable to seek detailed information from an Italian embassy or consulate on the exact requirements before attempting to organise a legitimate job in Italy. Many foreigners, however, don't bother with such formalities, preferring to work 'black' in areas such as teaching English, bar work and seasonal jobs. See the section on Work later in this chapter.

Permesso di Soggiorno

Visitors are technically obliged to report to a *questura* if they plan to stay at the same address for more than one week, to receive a *permesso di soggiorno* (residence permit). Tourists who are staying in hotels are not required to do this, because hotel-owners are required to register all guests with the police.

A permesso di soggiorno only becomes a necessity (for non-EU citizens at any rate) if you plan to study, work (legally) or live in Italy. Obtaining one is never a pleasant experience. It involves enduring long queues, rude police officers and the frustration of arriving at the counter (after a two-hour wait) to find that you don't have all the necessary documents.

The exact requirements, such as documents and official stamps *(marche da bollo)*, vary from city to city. In general, you will need a valid passport, containing a visa stamp indicating your date of entry into Italy; a special visa issued in your own country if you are planning to study; four passport-style photographs; and proof of your ability to support yourself financially.

It is best to go to the questura to obtain precise information on what is required. Sometimes there is a list posted, otherwise you will need to join a queue at the information counter.

The main Roma questura, in Via Genova, is notorious for delays and best avoided if possible. This problem has been solved by decentralisation: in Roma it is now possible to apply at the questura closest to where you are staying.

Photocopies

Make photocopies of all important documents, especially your passport. This will help speed replacement if they are lost or stolen. Other documents to photocopy might include your airline ticket and credit cards. Also record the serial numbers of your travellers' cheques (cross them off as you cash them in). All this material should be kept separate from the documents concerned, along with a small amount of emergency cash. Leave extra copies with someone reliable at home. If your passport is stolen or lost, notify the police and obtain a statement, and then contact your embassy or consulate as soon as possible.

Travel Insurance

Don't, as they say, leave home without it. It will cover you for medical expenses, luggage theft or loss, and for cancellation of and delays in your travel arrangements. Cover depends on your insurance and type of ticket, so ask both your insurer and ticket-issuing agency to explain where you stand. Ticket loss is also covered by travel insurance, but keep a separate record of your ticket details (see the previous Photocopies information). Buy travel insurance as early as possible. If you buy it the week before you fly or hop on the bus, you may find, for example, that you are not covered for delays to your trip caused by strikes or other industrial action.

Travel insurance papers, and the international medical aid numbers that generally accompany them, are valuable documents, so treat them like air tickets and passports. Keep the details (photocopies or hand-written) in a separate part of your luggage.

Paying for your ticket with a credit card often provides limited travel accident insurance, and you may be able to reclaim the payment if the operator doesn't deliver. Ask your credit card company what it will cover.

Hostel Card

A valid HI hostelling card is required in all associated youth hostels (Associazione Italiana Alberghi per la Gioventù) in Italy. You can get this in your home country or at youth hostels in Italy. In the latter case you apply for the card and must collect six stamps in the card at L5000 each. You pay for a stamp on each of the first six nights you spend in a hostel. With six stamps you are considered a full international member.

Student, Teacher & Youth Cards

An ISIC (International Student Identity Card) or similar card will get you discounted entry prices into some museums and other sights and is an asset for other purposes. It

Italian Consulates & Embassies

The following is a selection of Italian diplomatic missions abroad. Bear in mind that Italy maintains consulates in additional cities in many of the countries listed below:

Australia
Level 45, The Gateway, 1 Macquarie Place, Sydney (☎ 02-9247 8442)
509 St Kilda Rd, Melbourne (☎ 03-9867 57 44)
Austria
Ungargasse 43, Vienna (☎ 01-713 5671)
Belgium
Rue de Livourne 38, Brussels (☎ 02-537 1934)
Canada
136 Beverley St, Toronto (☎ 416-977 1566)
3489 Drummond St, Montreal (☎ 514-849 8351)
Croatia
Meduliceva Ulica 22, Zagreb (☎ 051-27 51 85)
Denmark
Engskiftevo 4, Copenhagen (☎ 18 34 44)
France
17 rue du Conseiller Collignon, Paris (☎ 01-44 30 47 00)
Germany
Karl Finkelnburgstrasse 49-51, Bonn (☎ 0228-82 00)
Greece
Odos Sekeri 2, Athens (☎ 01-361 1722)
Japan
Mte 2-chome 5/4, Tokyo (☎ 03-34 53 52 91)
Netherlands
Herengracht 609, Amsterdam (☎ 020-524 0043)
New Zealand
34 Grant Rd, Thorndon, Wellington (☎ 04-73 53 39)
Norway
Inkognitosten 7, Oslo (☎ 55 22 33)
Slovenia
Snezniska Ulica 8, Ljubljana (☎ 061-21 48 14)
South Africa
796 George Ave, Pretoria (☎ 012-43 55 41)
Spain
Calle Lagasca 98, Madrid (☎ 91-577 6529)
Sweden
Oakhill Djurgarden, Stockholm (☎ 08-24 58 05)
Switzerland
Elfenstrasse 14, Bern (☎ 031-352 41 51)
Tunisia
3 Rue de Russie, Tunis (☎ 01-34 18 11)
UK
14 Three Kings Yard, London (☎ 0171-312 2209)
USA
12400 Wilshire Blvd, West Los Angeles (☎ 213-820 06 22)
690 Park Ave, New York (☎ 212-737 9100) 2590 Webster St, San Francisco (☎ 415-931 4924)

Foreign Consulates & Embassies In Italy

Foreign embassies are all based in Roma, although many countries maintain consulates in other big cities. The following are all in Roma (telephone area code 06):

Australia
Via Alessandria 215 (☎ 85 27 21)
Austria
Via Pergolesi 3 (☎ 855 82 41)
Consulate: Viale Liegi 32 (☎ 855 29 66)
Belgium
Via dei Monti Parioli 49 (☎ 360 95 11)
Canada
Via G B de Rossi 27 (☎ 44 5 9 81)
Consulate: Via Zara 30 (☎ 455 24 21)
Croatia
Via SS Cosma e Damiano 26 (☎ 33 25 02 42)
Denmark
Via dei Monti Parioli 50 (☎ 320 04 41)
Finland
Via Lisbona 3 (☎ 841 98 14)
France
Piazza Farnese (☎ 68 60 11)
Visas: Via Giulia 251 (☎ 68 80 64 37)
Germany
Via Po 25c (☎ 88 47 41)
Greece
Via Mercadante 36 (☎ 855 31 00)
Ireland
Piazza Campitelli 3 (☎ 697 91 21)
Israel
Via Michele Mercati 14 (☎ 36 19 81)
Japan
Via Q Sella 50 (☎ 48 90 39 05)
Netherlands
Via Michele Mercati 8 (☎ 322 11 41)
New Zealand
Via Zara 28 (☎ 440 29 28)
Norway
Via Terme Deciane 7 (☎ 575 58 33)
Slovenia
Via L Pisano 10 (☎ 808 10 75)
South Africa
Via Tanaro 14 (☎ 841 97 94)
Spain
Largo Fontanella Borghese 19 (☎ 687 81 72)
Consulate: Via Campo Marzio 34 (☎ 687 14 01)
Sweden
Piazza Rio de Janeiro 3 (☎ 44 19 41)
Switzerland
Via Barnarba Oriani 61 (☎808 36 41)
Consulate: Largo Elvezia 15 (☎ 808 83 71)
Tunisia
Via Asmara 5-7 (☎860 30 60)
Consulate: Via Egadi 13 (☎ 87 18 80 06)
UK
Via XX Settembre 80a (☎ 482 54 41)
USA
Via Vittorio Veneto 119a-121 (☎ 4 67 41)

For other foreign embassies in Roma and consulates in other cities, look under 'Ambasciate' or 'Consolati' in the telephone book or, in Roma, check the English *Yellow Pages*. Tourist offices will also generally have a list.

can help for cheap flights out of Italy and can also come in handy for such things as cinema and theatre and other travel discounts.

Some travel agents may issue cards with certain discounted air tickets without even asking to see proof of student status. More legitimately, the cards are available from many student and budget travel offices, including the following:

Australia
Student Services Australia, 1st Floor, 20 Faraday St, Carlton (☎ 03-9348 1777)

Canada
Travel Cuts, 187 College St, Toronto (☎ 416-977 3703)
Voyages Campus, Université McGill, 3480 Rue McTavish, Montreal (☎ 514-398 0647)

UK
Cards are best obtained from STA and Campus Travel offices – see under Air in the Getting There & Away chapter

USA
CIEE, 205 East 42nd St, New York (☎ 212-661 1414)
1093 Broxton Ave, Los Angeles (☎ 213-208 3551)
312 Sutter St, San Francisco (☎ 415-421 3473)

Similar cards are available to teachers (ITIC). They are good for various discounts and carry a travel insurance component.

You can get information on travel problems, medical or legal emergencies and the like on an international free ISIC/ITIC help line. For the UK dial ☎ 0181-666 9205. Cardholders can reverse the charges.

If you're aged under 26 but not a student you can apply for a FIYTO (Federation of International Youth Travel Organisations) card or Euro 26 card (in the UK known as the Under 26 Card), which gives much the same discounts as ISIC.

The head office of FIYTO is in Denmark, at Islands Brygge 81, DK-2300 Copenhagen S, where you can write to request a brochure. Otherwise, the organisations listed above for the USA and Canada will issue the cards.

Both types of card are issued by student unions, hostelling organisations and some youth travel agencies (like Campus Travel in the UK). They don't always automatically entitle you to discounts, but you won't find out until you flash the card.

In Italy, any office of the Centro Turistico Studentesco e Giovanile (CTS) will issue ISIC, ITIC and Euro 26 cards if you join the CTS itself for L43,000. See also the Useful Organisations section.

CUSTOMS

You can import, without paying duty, two cameras and 10 rolls of film; a movie or TV camera with 10 cartridges of film; a portable tape recorder and 'a reasonable amount' of tapes; a CD player; a pair of binoculars; sports equipment, including skis; one bicycle or motorcycle (not exceeding 50 cc); one portable radio and one portable TV set (both may be subject to the payment of a licence fee) and personal jewellery.

Limits on duty free imports include: up to 200 cigarettes; 50 cigars; two litres of wine and a litre of liquor. There is no limit on the amount of lire you can import.

MONEY

The best thing to do is to take a combination of travellers' cheques and credit cards.

Costs

Italy isn't cheap. Accommodation charges and high entrance fees for many museums and monuments keep daily expenditure high. A *very* prudent backpacker might scrape by on around L60,000 a day, but only by staying in youth hostels, eating one simple meal a day (at the youth hostel), making sandwiches for lunch, travelling slowly to keep transport costs down and minimising the number of museums and galleries visited.

One rung up, you can get by on L100,000 per day if you stay in the cheaper pensioni or small hotels, and keep sit-down meals and museums to one a day. Lone travellers may find even this budget hard to maintain, since single rooms tend to be pricey.

If money is no object, you'll find your niche in Italy. There's no shortage of luxury hotels, expensive restaurants and shops. Realistically, a traveller wanting to stay in comfortable lower to mid-range hotels, eat two square meals a day, not feel restricted to one museum a day and be able to enjoy the odd drink and other minor indulgences should reckon on a minimum daily average of L200,000 to L250,000 a day – possibly more if you are driving.

A basic breakdown of costs per person during an average day for the bottom to lower middle-range traveller could be: accommodation L20,000 (youth hostel) to L50,000 (single in pensione or per person in comfortable double); breakfast L3000 (coffee and croissant); lunch (sandwich and mineral water) L5000; bottle of mineral water L1500; public transport (bus or underground railway in a major town) up to L5000; entrance fee for one museum up to L12,000; cost of long-distance train or bus travel (spread over three days) L15,000 to L20,000; and sit-down dinner L14,000 to L30,000.

Accommodation Budget travellers can save by staying in youth hostels (open to people of all ages) or camping grounds. If you are travelling in a group and staying in pensioni or hotels, always ask for triples or quads. The cost per person drops the more people you have in a room. Avoid, where possible, pensioni and hotels that charge for a compulsory breakfast. A cappuccino and brioche at a bar cost less and are probably better.

If you plan to ski, it may be cheaper to organise accommodation as part of a White Week (Settimana Bianca) skiing package. These deals offer accommodation, meals and a ski pass.

Food In Italian bars, prices can double (sometimes even triple) if you sit down and are served at the table. Stand at the bar to drink your coffee or eat a sandwich – or buy a sandwich or slice of pizza and head for the nearest piazza.

Read the fine print on menus (usually posted outside eating establishments) to check the cover charge *(coperto)* and service fee *(servizio)*. These can make a big difference to the bill and it is best to avoid restaurants that charge both. Shop in supermarkets and *alimentari* (grocery shops) for picnic lunches and the odd meal in your room.

Travelling If travelling by train and you have time to spare, take a *regionale* or *diretto*: they are slower but cheaper than the Intercity trains, for which you have to pay a supplement (*un supplemento*). See the Getting Around chapter for information about these different types of trains and about various discounts on train travel.

When catching ferries (such as to Sardegna, Corsica or Greece), travelling deck class *(passaggio ponte)* in summer (when available) is cheapest.

In the cities, where you need to use a lot of public transport, buy a daily tourist ticket (up to L5000).

Other Cost-Savers Aerograms (on sale only at the post office for L850) are the cheapest way to send international mail.

At museums, never hesitate to ask if there are discounts for students, young people, children, families or the elderly. When sightseeing, buy a *biglietto cumulativo* where possible: a combined ticket that allows entrance to a number of associated sights for less than the cost of separate admission fees.

Avoid buying food and drinks at service stations on the autostrade, where they can be up to 30% dearer. Petrol tends to be slightly more expensive on the autostrade.

Carrying Money

Petty theft is a problem throughout Italy and tends to get worse the farther south you travel. Keep only a limited amount of your money as cash and the bulk in more easily replaceable forms such as travellers' cheques or plastic. If your accommodation has a safe, use it. If you must leave money and documents in your room, divide the former into several stashes and hide them in different places. Lockable luggage is a good deterrent.

On the streets, keep as little on you as necessary. The safest thing is a shoulder wallet or under-the-clothes money belt or pouch. External money belts tend to attract attention to your belongings rather than deflect it. If you eschew the use of any such device, keep money in your *front pockets* and watch out for people who seem to brush close to you – there is an infinite number of tricks employed by teams of delinquents, whereby one distracts your attention and the other deftly empties your pockets.

Cash

There is little advantage in bringing foreign cash into Italy. True, exchange commissions are often lower than for travellers' cheques, but the danger of losing the lot far outweighs such petty gains.

It is worth bringing some lire with you into the country (especially if you're arriving by air) to avoid the hassles of changing money on arrival.

Travellers' Cheques

These are a safe way to carry money and are easily cashed at banks and exchange offices throughout Italy. Always keep the bank receipt listing the cheque numbers separate from the cheques and keep a list of the numbers of those you have already cashed – this will reduce problems in the event of loss or theft. Check the conditions applying to such circumstances before buying the cheques.

If you buy your travellers' cheques in lire (which you should only do if your trip is to be restricted to Italy alone), there should be no commission charge when cashing them. Most hard currencies are widely accepted, although you may have occasional trouble with the New Zealand dollar. Buying cheques in a third currency (such as US dollars if you are not coming from the USA), means you pay commission when you buy the cheques and again when cashing them in Italy.

Get most of the cheques in largish denominations to save on per-cheque exchange charges.

Travellers using the better known cheques, such as Visa, American Express and Thomas Cook, will have little trouble in Italy. American Express, in particular, has offices in all the major Italian cities and agents in many smaller cities. If you lose your Amex cheques, you can call a 24-hour toll free number (☎ 167-87 20 00) anywhere in Italy.

Take along your passport when you go to cash travellers' cheques.

Credit/Debit Cards & ATMs

Carrying plastic (whether a credit or debit card) is the simplest way to organise your holiday funds. You don't have large amounts of cash or cheques to lose, you can get money after hours and on weekends and the exchange rate is better than that offered for travellers' cheques or cash exchanges. By arranging for payments to be made into your card account while you are travelling, you can avoid paying interest.

Major credit cards, such as Visa, MasterCard, Eurocard, Cirrus and Euro Cheques cards, are accepted throughout Italy.

They can be used for many purchases (including in many supermarkets) and in hotels and restaurants (although pensioni and smaller trattorie and pizzerie tend to accept cash only). Credit cards can also be used in ATMs *(bancomat)* displaying the appropriate sign or (if you have no PIN number) to obtain cash advances over the counter in many banks – Visa and MasterCard are among the most widely recognised for such transactions. Check charges with your bank but, as a rule, there is no charge for purchases on major cards and a 1.5% charge on cash advances and ATM transactions in foreign currencies.

It is not uncommon for ATMs in Italy to reject foreign cards. Don't despair or start wasting money on international calls to your bank. Try a few more ATMs displaying your credit card's logo at major banks before assuming the problem lies with your card rather than with the local system.

If your credit card is lost, stolen or swallowed by an ATM, you can telephone toll-free to have an immediate stop put on its use. For MasterCard the number in Italy is

☎ 1678-6 80 86, or make a reverse-charges call to St Louis in the USA on ☎ 314-275 66 90; for Visa, phone ☎ 1678-2 10 01 in Italy. Otherwise, call ☎ 1678-2 20 56 to have any card blocked.

American Express is also widely accepted (although not as common as Visa or MasterCard). Amex's full-service offices (such as in Roma and Milano) will issue new cards, usually within 24 hours and sometimes immediately, if yours has been lost or stolen. Some American Express offices have ATMs that you can use to obtain cash advances if you have made the necessary arrangements in your own country.

The toll-free emergency number to report a lost or stolen American Express card varies according to where the card was issued. Check with American Express in your country or contact American Express in Roma on ☎ 06-7 22 82, which itself has a 24-hour cardholders' service.

International Transfers

One reliable way to send money to Italy is by 'urgent telex' through the foreign office of a large Italian bank, or through major banks in your own country, to a nominated bank in Italy. It is important to have an exact record of all details associated with the money transfer, particularly the exact address of the Italian bank to where the money has been sent. The money will always be held at the head office of the bank in the town to which it has been sent. Urgent-telex transfers should take only a few days, while other means, such as telegraphic transfer, or draft, can take weeks.

It is also possible to transfer money through American Express and Thomas Cook. You will be required to produce identification, usually a passport, in order to collect the money. It is also a good idea to take along the details of the transaction. It is inadvisable to send cheques by mail to Italy, because of the unreliability of the country's postal service.

A more recent and speedy option is to send money through Western Union (toll free ☎ 1670-13839). This service functions in Italy through the Mail Boxes Etc chain of stores which you will find in the bigger cities. The sender and receiver have to turn up at a Western Union outlet with passport or other form of ID and the fees charged for the virtually immediate transfer depend on the amount sent.

Currency

Italy's currency is the lira (plural: lire). The smallest note is L1000. Other denominations in notes are L2000, L5000, L10,000, L50,000 and L100,000. Coin denominations are L50, L100 (two types of silver coin), L200 and L500. You might occasionally find yourself in possession of *gettoni* (telephone tokens). They are legal tender and have the same value as a L200 coin but are being withdrawn from circulation.

Remember that, like other Continental Europeans, Italians indicate decimals with commas and thousands with points.

Currency Exchange

Australia	A$1	=	L1294.81
Canada	C$1	=	L1279.79
France	1FF	=	L289.790
Germany	DM1	=	L974.950
Japan	¥100	=	L14.6593
New Zealand	NZ$1	=	L1127.00
United Kingdom	UK£1	=	L2804.00
USA	US$1	=	L1772.00

Changing Money

If you need to change cash or travellers' cheques, be prepared to queue (this is when you'll wish you had a credit card to stick in the nearest friendly ATM!).

You can change money in banks, at the post office or in special change offices. Banks are generally the most reliable and tend to offer the best rates. However, you should look around and ask about commissions. These can fluctuate considerably and a lot depends on whether you are changing cash or cheques. While the post office charges a flat rate of L1000 per cash transaction, banks charge L2500 or even more. Travellers' cheques attract higher fees. Some banks charge L1000 *per cheque* with a

L3000 minimum, while the post office charges a maximum L5000 per transaction. Other banks will have different arrangements again, and in all cases you should compare the exchange rates too. Exhange booths often advertise 'no commission', but the rate of exchange can often be inferior to that in the banks.

Balanced against the desire to save on such fees by making occasional large transactions should be a healthy fear of pickpockets – you don't want to be robbed the day you have exchanged a huge hunk of money to last you weeks!

Tipping & Bargaining

You are not expected to tip on top of restaurant service charges, but it is common to leave a small amount. If there is no service charge, the customer might consider leaving a 10% tip, but this is by no means obligatory. In bars, Italians often leave any small change as a tip, often only L100 or L200. Tipping taxi drivers is not common practice, but you should tip the porter at higher class hotels.

Bargaining is common throughout Italy in flea markets, but not in shops. At the Porta Portese market in Roma, for instance, don't hesitate to offer half the asking price for any given item. Don't be deterred by stallholders who dismiss you with a wave of the arm: the person at the next stall will be just as likely to accept your offer after a brief (and obligatory) haggle. While bargaining in shops is not acceptable, you might find that the proprietor is disposed to give a discount if you are spending a reasonable amount of money. It is quite acceptable to ask if there is a special price for a room in a pensione if you plan to stay for more than a few days.

Taxes & Refunds

Value-added tax, known as IVA (Imposta di Valore Aggiunto) is slapped on to just about everything in Italy and hovers around 19%. Tourists who are residents of countries outside the EU may claim a refund on this tax if the item was purchased for personal use and cost more than a certain amount (L360,000 in 1997). The goods must be carried with you and you must keep the fiscal receipt.

The refund only applies to items purchased at retail outlets affiliated to the system – these shops display a 'Tax-free for tourists' sign. Otherwise, ask the shopkeeper. You must fill out a form at the point of purchase and have the form stamped and checked by Italian customs when you leave the country. You then return it by mail within 60 days to the vendor, who will make the refund, either by cheque or to your credit card. At major airports and some border crossings you can get an immediate cash refund at specially marked booths.

Receipts

Laws aimed at tightening controls on the payment of taxes in Italy mean that the onus is on the buyer to ask for and retain receipts for all goods and services. This applies to everything from a litre of milk to a haircut. Although it rarely happens, you could be asked by an officer of the Fiscal Police (Guardia di Finanza) to produce the receipt immediately after you leave a shop. If you don't have it, you may be obliged to pay a fine of up to L300,000.

POST & COMMUNICATIONS

Italy's postal service is notoriously slow, unreliable and expensive. Don't expect to receive every letter sent to you, or that every letter you send will reach its destination.

Stamps & Post Offices

Stamps *(francobolli)* are available at post offices and authorised tobacconists (look for the official *tabacchi* sign: a big 'T', often white on black). Since letters often need to be weighed, what you get at the tobacconist's for international air mail will occasionally be an approximation of the proper rate. Main post offices in the bigger cities are generally open from around 8 am to at least 5 pm. Many open on Saturday mornings too. Tobacconists keep regular shopping hours.

Postal Rates

The cost of sending a letter air mail *(via*

aerea) depends on its weight and where it is being sent. Letters up to 20g cost L1350 to Australia and New Zealand, L1250 to the USA and L750 to EU countries (L850 to the rest of Europe). Postcards cost the same. Aerograms are a cheap alternative, costing only L850 to send anywhere. They can be purchased at post offices only.

Sending letters express *(espresso)* costs a standard extra L3000, but may help speed a letter on its way.

If you want to post more important items by registered mail *(raccomandato)* or by insured mail *(assicurato)*, remember that they will take as long as normal mail. Raccomandato costs L3400 on top of the normal cost of the letter. The cost of assicurato depends on the weight of the object and is not available to the USA.

Sending Mail

An air-mail letter can take up to two weeks to reach the UK or the USA, while a letter to Australia will take between two and three weeks. Postcards will take even longer because they are low-priority mail. One of the authors of this book sent a postcard from Australia for Christmas – it got tangled up in the Italian postal system and did not arrive until September of the *following* year.

The service within Italy is no better: local letters take at least three days and up to a week to arrive in another city. A 1988 survey on postal efficiency in Europe found that next-day delivery did not exist in Italy. Sending a letter express (see Postal Rates above) can help.

In Roma you can avoid this frustration by using the Vatican post office in St Peter's Square. It has an excellent record for prompt delivery but doesn't accept poste restante mail.

Express Mail Urgent mail can be sent by Express Mail Service (EMS), also known as CAI Post. A parcel weighing 1kg will cost L34,000 in Europe, L54,000 to the USA and Canada, and L80,000 to Australia and New Zealand. EMS is not necessarily as fast as private services. It will take four to eight days for a parcel to reach Australia and two to four days to reach the USA. Ask at post offices for addresses of EMS outlets.

Couriers International couriers such as DHL, Federal Express and UPS operate in Italy. Look in the telephone book for addresses. Note that if you are having articles sent to you by courier in Italy, you may well be obliged to pay IVA of up to 19% to retrieve the goods.

Receiving Mail

Poste restante is known as *fermo posta* in Italy. Letters marked thus will be held at the counter of the same name in the main post office in the relevant town. Poste restante mail should be addressed as follows:

John SMITH,
Fermo Posta,
37100 Verona
Italy

Postcodes are provided throughout this guide. You will need to pick up your letters in person and present your passport as ID.

American Express card or travellers' cheque holders can use the free client mail-holding service at American Express offices in Italy. You can obtain a list of these from American Express offices inside or outside Italy. Take your passport when you go to pick up mail.

Telephone

The orange public pay phones liberally scattered about Italy come in at least four types. Increasingly, the most common accept only telephone cards *(carte/schede telefoniche)*, although you will still find plenty that accept cards and coins (L100, L200 and L500). Rare now are the ones that accept only *gettoni*, tokens worth L200. Some card phones now also accept special Telecom credit cards and even commercial credit cards. Among the latest generation of pay phones are those that also send faxes. If you call from a bar or shop, you may still encounter old-style metered phones, which count *scatti*, the units used to measure the length of a call.

Phones can be found in the streets, train stations and some big stores as well as in Telecom offices. Some of the latter are staffed, and a few have telephone directories for other parts of the country. Where these offices are staffed it is possible to make international calls and pay at the desk afterwards. Addresses of telephone offices are listed throughout the book.

You can buy phonecards at post offices, tobacconists, newspaper stands and from vending machines in Telecom offices. To avoid the frustration of trying to find fast-disappearing coin telephones, always keep a phonecard on hand. They come with a value of L5000, L10,000 and L15,000.

Costs Rates, particularly for long-distance calls, are among the highest in Europe. There are four different rates for local and national phone calls and two to three rates for international calls. The cheapest time for domestic calls is from 10 pm to 8 am. It is a little more complicated for international calls but, basically, the cheapest off-peak time is 11 pm to 8 am and most or all of Sunday, depending on the country called.

A local call *(comunicazione urbana)* from a public phone will cost L200 for three to six minutes, depending on the time of day you call (8.30 am to 1 pm, Monday to Friday, is peak call time).

Rates for long distance calls within Italy *(comunicazione interurbana)* depend on the time of day and the distance involved. At the worst, one minute will cost about L580 in peak periods.

If you need to call overseas, beware of the cost – even a call of less than five minutes to Australia after 11 pm will cost around L15,000 from a private phone (more from a public phone). Calls to most of the rest of Europe cost about L800 per minute, and closer to L1200 from a public phone.

Travellers from countries that offer direct dialling services paid for at home country rates (such as AT&T in the USA and Telstra in Australia) should think seriously about taking advantage of them.

Domestic Calls Telephone codes all begin with 0 and consist of up to four digits. Codes are provided throughout the guide. The code is followed by a number of anything from four to eight digits. Drop the 0 when calling in the same town or area. The above does not include mobile phone numbers and free phone numbers *(numeri verdi*, which usually begin with 167 or 1678). For directory enquiries, dial 12.

Area codes are listed under cities and towns in this book. Important telephone area codes include: Roma 06, Milano 02, Firenze 055, Napoli 081, Cagliari 070, Venezia 041 and Palermo 091.

Domestic Telephone Numbers

The telephone system in Italy seems to be in a constant state of overhaul, which means that telephone numbers change with alarming regularity. Often there will be a message giving you the new number, but only in Italian. Domestic operators also generally speak only Italian. If a telephone number is going to change, the new number will often be listed in brackets after the existing number in the telephone book. It will be preceded by the word *prenderà*.

International Calls Direct international calls can easily be made from public telephones by using a phonecard. Dial 00 to get out of Italy, then the relevant country and city codes, followed by the telephone number. Useful country codes are: Australia 61, Canada and USA 1, New Zealand 64, and the UK 44. Codes for other countries in Europe include: France 33, Germany 49, Greece 30, Ireland 353, and Spain 34. Other codes are listed in Italian telephone books.

To make a reverse charges (collect) international call from a public telephone, dial ☎ 170. For European countries dial ☎ 15. All operators speak English.

Easier, and often cheaper, is using the Country Direct service in your country. You dial the number and request a reverse charges call through the operator in your country. Numbers for this service include:

Australia (Telstra)	☎ 172 10 61
Australia (Optus)	☎ 172 11 61
Canada	☎ 172 10 01
France	☎ 172 00 33
New Zealand	☎ 172 10 64
UK (British Telecom)	☎ 172 00 44
UK (British Telecom Chargecard Operator)	☎ 172 01 44
USA (AT&T)	☎ 172 1011
USA (MCI)	☎ 172 10 22
USA (Sprint)	☎ 172 18 77
USA (IDB)	☎ 172 17 77

For international directory enquiries call ☎ 176.

International Phonecards Several private companies now distribute international telephonecards, mostly linked to US phone companies such as Sprint and MCI. You call the number provided, which connects you with a US-based operator, through whom you can then place your international call at rates generally lower (by as much as 40% compared with standard peak hour rates) than the standard Italian rates. A recorded message will tell you before your call goes through how much time you have left on the card for that call. The cards come in a variety of unit 'sizes', and are sold in some bars and tobacconists in the bigger cities – look out for signs advertising them.

Calling Italy from Abroad The country code for Italy is 39. Always drop the initial 0 from area codes.

Telegram
These dinosaurs can be sent from post offices or dictated by phone (☎ 186) and are an expensive, but sure, way of having important messages delivered by the same or next day.

Fax
There is no shortage of fax offices in Italy but the country's high telephone charges make faxes an expensive mode of communication. To send a fax within Italy you can expect to pay L3000 for the first page and L2000 for each page thereafter, plus L50 a second for the actual call. International faxes can cost L6000 for the first page and L4000 per page thereafter, and L100 a second for the call. You can imagine what this can mean with a slow fax machine at peak rates! Faxes can also be sent from some Telecom public phones.

Email
Italy has been a little slower than some parts of Western Europe to march down the Infobahn, nevertheless, email has definitely arrived. If you are travelling with your laptop in Italy and want access to the Internet you will need to have a server that operates in Italy too. CompuServe has nodes in Roma and Milano as well as slow-access numbers in other towns. You will need to stay in hotels with a modern phone in the room and even then you will need to get advice before leaving home on measures to protect your modem – many hotel PABX phone systems can fry both modem and computer.

Italy also has a growing number of Internet cafés. These allow you to log in to the Net for an average L10,000-15,000 an hour and in many cases permit you to send email (receiving is harder, unless you have your own email account to log on to). This type of café can be found in several of the bigger cities.

BOOKS
Most books are published in different editions by different publishers in different countries. As a result, a book might be a hardcover rarity in one country while it is readily available in paperback in another. Fortunately, bookshops and libraries search by title or author, so your local bookshop or library is best placed to advise you on the availability of the following recommendations.

Lonely Planet
Mediterranean Europe on a shoestring and *Western Europe on a shoestring* include chapters on Italy and are recommended for

hose planning further travel in Europe. Also published by Lonely Planet, the *Italian phrasebook* lists all the words and phrases you're likely to need when travelling in Italy. A new guide to walking in Italy will be published in 1998.

Guidebooks

The paperback Companion Guides are excellent and include *Rome* by Georgina Masson, *Venice* by Hugh Honour, *Umbria* by Maurice Rowdon, *Tuscany* by Archibald Lyall and *Southern Italy* by Peter Gunn. The Blue Guide series gives very good detailed information about the art and monuments of Italy. If you can read in Italian you can't go past the excellent red guides of the Touring Club Italiano.

For information on hiking and climbing, try the guides published by Cicerone Press, Cumbria. Titles include *Walking in the Dolomites* and *Walking in the Central Italian Alps*, both by Gillian Price; *Classic Climbs in the Dolomites*, by Lele Dinoia and Valerio Casari (translated by Al Churcher); and *Selected Climbs in Northern Italy*, by Al Churcher.

Travel

There are endless books written by travellers to Italy. For a potted idea of how the great writers saw the country, it's worth reading *Venice: the Most Triumphant City* compiled by George Bull (hardback) and *When in Rome: the Humorists' Guide to Italy*.

Three Grand Tour classics are Johann Wolfgang von Goethe's *Italian Journey*, Charles Dickens' *Pictures from Italy*, and Henry James' *Italian Hours*. DH Lawrence wrote three short travel books while living in Italy, now combined in one volume entitled *DH Lawrence and Italy*.

Others include: *Venice* by James Morris; *The Stones of Florence* and *Venice Observed* by Mary McCarthy; *On Persephone's Island* by Mary Taylor Simeti; *Siren Land* and *Old Calabria* by Norman Douglas; *North of Naples, South of Rome* by Paolo Tullio; *The Golden Honeycomb* by Vincent Cronin (travels through Sicilia); and, *A Traveller in Southern Italy* by HV Morton. Although written in the 1960s the latter remains a valuable guide to the south and its people. Morton also wrote *A Traveller in Italy* and *A Traveller in Rome*.

History & Politics

For in-depth research there is Edward Gibbon's masterpiece, *History of the Decline and Fall of the Roman Empire* (available in six hardback volumes, or an abridged, single-volume paperback). Other, simpler history books include: *The Oxford History of the Roman World* edited by John Boardman, Jasper Griffin & Oswyn Murray; *Daily Life in Ancient Rome* by Jerome Carcopino; Robert Graves' classics *I, Claudius* and *Claudius the God*; *Italy: A Short History* by Harry Hearder; *Concise History of Italy* by Vincent Cronin; *History of the Italian People* by Giuliano Procacci; *The Oxford Dictionary of Popes* compiled by JND Kelly; *Rome: Biography of a City* by Christopher Hibbert, and by the same author, *Venice: the Biography of a City* and *The Rise and Fall of the House of the Medici*. *A History of Contemporary Italy: Society and Politics 1943-1988* by Paul Ginsburg, is an absorbing and very well written book which will help Italophiles place the country's modern society in perspective.

Art

The Penguin Book of the Renaissance by JH Plumb, *Painters of the Renaissance* by Bernard Berenson, and Giorgio Vasari's *Lives of the Artists* should be more than enough on the Renaissance. Other worthwhile books include *A Handbook of Roman Art*, edited by Martin Henig; *Roman Architecture* by Frank Sear; and *Art and Architecture in Italy 1600-1750* by Rudolf Wittkower (hardback).

There is also a series of guides to Italian art and architecture, published under the general title World of Art. These include: *Palladio and Palladianism* by Robert Tavernor; *Michelangelo* by Linda Murray; *Italian Renaissance Sculpture* by Roberta JM Oleson; *Roman Art and Architecture* by

Mortimer Wheeler. See also the Art & Architecture chapter for other guides.

General

The Mafia *The Honoured Society* by Norman Lewis is an excellent introduction to the subject. *Excellent Cadavers: The Mafia and the Death of the First Italian Republic* by Alexander Stille is a shocking and absorbing account of the Mafia in Sicilia, focusing on the years leading up to the assassinations of anti-Mafia judges Giovanni Falcone and Paolo Borsellino in 1992 and the subsequent fall of Italy's 'First Republic'.

People For background on the Italian people and their culture there is the classic by Luigi Barzini, *The Italians*. *Italian Labyrinth* by John Haycraft looks at Italy in the 1980s. *Getting it Right in Italy: A Manual for the 1990s* by William Ward aims, with considerable success, to provide accessible, useful information about Italy, while also providing a reasonable social profile of the people. *An Italian Education* by Tim Parks is an often hilarious account of the life of an expatriate in Verona.

Food *The Food of Italy* by Waverley Root is an acknowledged classic.

ONLINE SERVICES

There is a page on Italy on Lonely Planet's website (www.lonelyplanet.com). Another good place to start is *Excite Reviews* (www.excite.com). Call it up and key in Italy and it will give you a long selection of sites related to Italy, as well as brief reviews and ratings. Chiantinet (www.chiantinet.it) is an excellent site with lots of information about the Chianti area and links to other sites. Alfanet (www.alfanet.it) has a Welcome Italy page, with a link to information about Roma. Roma's municipal government, the *comune*, has a web page which doubles as a source of information for residents and tourists. Its address is www.comune.roma.it. Planet Italy(www.planetitaly.com) has some interesting information.

FILMS

If you want to get in the mood before heading off to Italy, here are a few suggestions: *Roman Holiday* (Gregory Peck and Audrey Hepburn scootering around Roma); *Three Coins in a Fountain* (three American women get their men at the Fontana di Trevi); *It Happened in Naples* (Sophia Loren); *Come September* (Rock, Gina, Sandra and Bobby romp around the Amalfi Coast); *The Agony & the Ecstasy* (Charleton Heston as Michelango); *A Room with a View* (not a view in the world can beat the one from Fiesole over Firenze); *Stealing Beauty* (dumb film, but a great Tuscan travelogue); and *The Pink Panther* (set in Cortina and Roma).

NEWSPAPERS & MAGAZINES

The major English-language newspapers available in Italy are the *Herald Tribune* (L2800), an international newspaper available from Monday to Saturday, and *The European* (L3500), available on Friday. *The Guardian* (L2800 on airmail paper), *The Times* (L4500) and the *Daily Telegraph* (L3300), as well as the various tabloids, are sent from London; outside major cities, such as Roma and Milano, they are generally a few days old. *Time*, *Newsweek* (both L5400) and the *The Economist* (L8000) are available weekly.

RADIO & TV

Vatican Radio (526 AM, 93.3 FM and 105 FM) broadcasts the news in English at 7 am,8.30 am, 6.15 pm and 9.50 pm. Pick up a pamphlet at the Vatican information office. RAI (846 AM) broadcasts news in English from 1 to 5 am at three minutes past the hour. You can pick up the BBC World Service on medium wave at 648 kHz, short wave at 6195 kHz, 9410 kHz, 12095 kHz, 15575 kHz, and on long wave at 198 kHz, depending on where you are and the time of day. Voice of America (VOA) can usually be found on short wave at 15205 kHz.

At the time of writing, CNN was broadcast on Telemontecarlo (TMC) nightly from around 3 am. On Channel 41, known as

Autovox, the American PBS McNeill Lehrer News Hour was broadcast nightly at around 8 pm. Sky Channel and CNN by satellite are also available in many better hotels.

There is also a French-language TV channel, Antenne 2, which can be received on Channel 10 if you are watching TV in some places along the Tyhrennian coast.

VIDEO SYSTEMS

Italy uses the PAL video system (the same as in Australia and throughout Europe, except in France). This system is not compatible with NTSC (used in the United States, Japan and Latin America) or Secam (used in France and other French-speaking countries). However, modern video players are often multi-system and can read all three.

PHOTOGRAPHY & VIDEO

A roll of 36 exposure 100 ASA Kodak film costs around L8000. It costs around L18,000 to have 36 exposures developed and L12,000 for 24 exposures. A roll of 36 slides costs L10,000 and L7000 for development.

There are numerous outlets which sell and process films but beware of poor quality processing. A roll of film is called a *pellicola* but you will be understood if you ask for 'film'. Many places claim to process films in one hour but you will rarely get your photos back that quickly – count on late the next day if the outlet has its own processing equipment, or three to four days if it hasn't. Tapes for video cameras are often available at the same outlets or can be found at stores selling electrical goods.

TIME

Italy operates on a 24-hour clock which will take some getting used to for travellers used to a 12-hour clock. Daylight-saving time starts on the last Sunday in March, when clocks are put forward one hour. Clocks are put back an hour on the last Sunday in September. Ensure that when telephoning home you also make allowances for daylight-saving in your own country.

European countries such as France, Germany, Austria and Spain are on the same time as Italy. Greece, Egypt and Israel are one hour ahead. When it's noon in Roma, it's 11 pm in Auckland, 11 am in London, 6 am in New York, 7 pm in Perth, 3 am in San Francisco, 9 pm in Sydney, and 6 am in Toronto.

ELECTRICITY

The electric current in Italy is 220V, 50Hz, but make a point of checking with your hotel management because in some areas – for instance, in some older hotels in Roma, they may still use 125V.

Power points have two or three holes and do not have their own switches, while plugs have two or three round pins. Some power points have larger holes than others. Italian homes are usually full of plug adapters to cope with this anomaly.

Make sure you bring plug adapters for your appliances. It is a good idea to buy these *before* leaving home as they are virtually impossible to get in Italy. If you do forget, there is always the option of taking your appliance to an electrical store and having them replace the foreign plug with an Italian one. Travellers from the USA need a voltage converter (although many of the more expensive hotels have provision for 110 V appliances such as shavers).

WEIGHTS & MEASURES

Italy uses the metric system. Basic terms for weight include *un etto* (100g) and *un chilo* (1kg). Travellers from the USA will have to cope with the change from pounds to kg, miles to km and gallons to litres. A standard conversion table can be found at the back of this book.

Note that Italians indicate decimals with commas and thousands with points.

LAUNDRY

Coin laundrettes, where you can do your own washing, are catching on in Italy and you'll find them in most of the main cities. A load will cost around L8000. Dry-cleaning *(lavasecco)* charges range from around L6000 for a shirt to L12,000 for a jacket. Be careful, though – the quality can be unreliable.

TOILETS

Public toilets are not exactly widespread in Italy. Most people use the toilets in bars and cafés – although you might need to buy a coffee first!

HEALTH

The quality of medical treatment in public hospitals varies throughout Italy. Basically, the farther north, the better the care.

Private hospitals and clinics throughout the country generally provide excellent services but are expensive for those without medical insurance. That said, certain treatments in public hospitals may also have to be paid for and in such cases can be equally costly.

Your embassy or consulate in Italy can provide a list of recommended doctors in major cities; however, if you have a specific health complaint, it would be wise to obtain the necessary information and referrals for treatment before leaving home.

The public health system is administered by local centres generally known as Unità Sanitaria Locale (USL), or also USSL (Unità Socio Sanitaria Locale), usually listed under 'U' in the telephone book (sometimes under 'A' for Azienda USL). Under these headings you'll find long lists of offices – look for Poliambulatorio (polyclinic) and the telephone number for Accetazione Sanitaria. You need to call this number to make an appointment – there is no point in just rolling up. Opening hours vary widely, with the minimum generally being about 8 am to 12.30 pm Monday to Friday. Some open for a couple of hours in the afternoon and on Saturday mornings too.

For emergency treatment, go straight to the Casualty *(pronto soccorso)* section of a public hospital, where you'll also receive emergency dental treatment. In major cities you are likely to find doctors who speak English, or a volunteer translator service. Often, first aid is also available at train stations, airports and ports.

Medical Cover

Citizens of EU countries are covered fo emergency medical treatment in Italy on pre sentation of an E111 form. It is necessary t obtain information about this from you national health service before leaving home Treatment in private hospitals is not covered Australia also has a reciprocal arrangemen with Italy so that emergency treatment i covered – Medicare in Australia publishes a brochure with the details. The USA, Canad and New Zealand do not have reciproca arrangements and citizens of these countrie will be required to pay for any treatment ir Italy themselves. Advise medical staff of any reciprocal arrangements *before* they begir treating you.

Predeparture Preparations

Health Insurance A travel insurance policy to cover theft, loss and medical problems is wise. There are a wide variety of policies and your travel agent will have recommendations. The international student travel policies handled by STA Travel or student travel organisations are usually good value Some policies offer lower and higher medical expenses options but the higher one is chiefly for countries like the USA, where medical costs are extremely high.

Check the small print. Some policies specifically exclude 'dangerous activities' which can include scuba diving, motorcycling, skiing and even trekking. If such activities are on your agenda you don't want that sort of policy. A locally acquired motorcycle licence may not be valid under your policy.

You may prefer a policy that pays doctors or hospitals direct rather than you having to pay on the spot and claim later. If you have to claim later make sure you keep all documentation. Some policies ask you to call back (reverse charges) to a centre in your home country where an immediate assessment of your problem is made.

Check if the policy covers ambulances or an emergency flight home. If you have to stretch out you will need two seats and somebody has to pay for them!

Medical Kit A small, straightforward medical kit is a wise thing to carry. A possible kit list includes:

- Aspirin or paracetamol (acetaminophen in the US) – for pain or fever.
- Antihistamine (such as Benadryl) –
- useful as a decongestant for colds, allergies, to ease the itch from insect bites or stings or to help prevent motion sickness.
- Antiseptic such as povidone-iodine (eg Betadine)
- Calamine lotion or Stingose spray –
- to ease irritation from bites or stings.
  Bandages and Band-aids for minor injuries.
  Scissors, tweezers and a digital thermometer.
- Insect repellent, sunscreen, and chap stick.
- Loperamide (eg Imodium) or Lomotil –
- for diarrhoea.
- prochlorperazine (eg Stemetil) or metaclopramide (eg Maxalon) – for nausea and vomiting.
- Antidiarrhoea medication should not be given to children under the age of 12.

General Preparations

Make sure you are healthy before you leave home. If you are embarking on a long trip, make sure your teeth are OK: dentists are particularly expensive in Italy.

If you wear glasses, take a spare pair and your prescription. If you lose your glasses, you will be able to have them replaced within a few days by an optician *(ottico)*.

If you require a particular medication, take an adequate supply as well as the prescription, with the generic rather than the brand name, as it will make getting replacements easier.

No vaccinations are required for entry into Italy unless you have been travelling through a part of the world where yellow fever or cholera may be prevalent.

Basic Rules

Care in what you eat and drink is the most important health rule; stomach upsets are the most likely travel health problem, but in Italy the majority of these upsets will be relatively minor and probably due to overindulgence in the local food.

However, it pays to be careful with certain foods in Italy. In recent years there have been incidences throughout the country of salmonella poisoning related to infected eggs. Therefore, raw eggs and foods containing them should be avoided.

Water Tap water is drinkable throughout Italy although Italians themselves have taken to drinking the bottled stuff. The sign *acqua non potable* tells you that water is not drinkable (eg in trains and at some camping grounds). Drinking water from drink fountains is safe unless there is a sign telling you otherwise.

Nutrition Make sure your diet is well balanced. You will have little trouble finding good-quality fruit and vegetables in Italy.

Everyday Health A normal body temperature is 98.6°F or 37°C; more than 2°C (4°F) higher is a 'high' fever. A normal adult pulse rate is 60 to 80 beats per minute (children 80 to 100, babies 100 to 140). You should know how to take a temperature and a pulse rate. As a general rule the pulse increases about 20 beats per minute for each °C (2°F) rise in fever.

Many health problems can be avoided by taking care of yourself. Avoid climatic extremes: keep out of the sun when it's hot, dress warmly when it's cold. You can avoid insect bites by covering bare skin when insects are around, by screening windows or beds or by using insect repellents. Seek local advice: if you're told the water is unsafe due to jellyfish (a common occurrence in some parts of the country) don't go in.

Environmental Hazards

Sunburn In the south of Italy during summer or at high altitude in the Alps you can get sunburnt surprisingly quickly, even through cloud. Use a sunscreen, a hat and some barrier cream for your nose and lips. Calamine lotion is good for mild sunburn. Protect your eyes with good quality sunglasses.

Prickly Heat Prickly heat is an itchy rash caused by excessive perspiration trapped under the skin. It usually strikes people who have just arrived in a hot climate and whose pores have not yet opened sufficiently to cope with greater sweating. Keeping cool by bathing often, using a mild talcum powder or even resorting to air-conditioning may help until you acclimatise.

Heat Exhaustion Dehydration or salt deficiency can cause heat exhaustion. Take time to acclimatise to high temperatures and make sure you get sufficient liquids. Salt deficiency is characterised by fatigue, lethargy, headaches, giddiness and muscle cramps and in this case salt tablets may help.

Heatstroke This serious and sometimes fatal condition can occur if the body's heat-regulating mechanism breaks down and the body temperature rises to dangerous levels. Long, continuous periods of exposure to high temperatures can leave you vulnerable to heatstroke. You should avoid excessive alcohol or strenuous activity when you first arrive.

The symptoms are feeling unwell, not sweating much or at all and a high body temperature (39°C to 41°C or 102°F to 106°F). Where sweating has ceased, the skin becomes flushed and red. Severe, throbbing headaches and lack of coordination will also occur and the sufferer may become confused or aggressive. Eventually the victim will become delirious or convulse. Hospitalisation is essential but meanwhile, get patients out of the sun, remove their clothing, cover them with a wet sheet or towel and then fan them continuously.

Fungal Infections Hot-weather fungal infections are most likely to occur on the scalp, between the toes or fingers, in the groin and on the body (ringworm). You get ringworm (which is a fungal infection, not a worm) from infected animals or by walking on damp areas, like shower floors.

To prevent fungal infections, wear loose, comfortable clothes, avoid artificial fibres, wash frequently and dry carefully. If you do get an infection, apply an antifungal powder.

Cold Too much cold is just as dangerous as too much heat, particularly if it leads to hypothermia. Cold combined with wind and moisture is particularly risky. If you are trekking at high altitudes or in a cold, wet environment, be prepared.

Hypothermia occurs when the body loses heat faster than it can produce it and the core temperature of the body falls. It is surprisingly easy to progress from very cold to dangerously cold through a combination of wind, wet clothing, fatigue and hunger, even if the air temperature is above freezing.

Symptoms of hypothermia are exhaustion, numb skin (particularly toes and fingers), shivering, slurred speech, irrational or violent behaviour, lethargy, stumbling, dizzy spells, muscle cramps and violent bursts of energy. Irrationality may take the form of sufferers claiming they are warm and trying to take off their clothes.

To treat hypothermia, first get the patient out of the wind and/or rain, remove their clothing if it's wet and replace it with dry, warm clothes. Give them hot liquids – not alcohol – and some high-kilojoule, easily digestible food. This should be enough for the early stages of hypothermia but if it has gone further it may be necessary to place victims in warm sleeping bags and get in with them.

Altitude Sickness Altitude or mountain sickness (AMS) occurs at high altitudes where the lack of oxygen affects most people to some extent. There is no hard and fast rule as to how high is too high: AMS has been fatal at altitudes of 3000m, although 3500 to 4500m is the usual range. Very few treks or ski runs in the Alps reach heights of 3000m or more – Mont Blanc (Monte Bianco) on the border with France is one exception – so it's unlikely to be a major concern.

Headaches, nausea, dizziness, a dry cough, insomnia, breathlessness and loss of appetite are all signs to heed. Mild altitude problems will generally abate after a day or so, but if the symptoms persist or become worse the only treatment is to descend – even 500 metres can help.

Motion Sickness Eating lightly before and during a trip will reduce the chances of motion sickness. If you are prone to motion sickness try to find a place that minimises disturbance – near the wing on aircraft, close to midships on boats, near the centre on buses. Fresh air usually helps, reading or cigarette smoke doesn't. Commercial anti-motion-sickness preparations, which can cause drowsiness, have to be taken before the trip commences; when you're feeling sick it's too late. Ginger (available in capsule form) and peppermint (including mint-flavoured sweets) are natural preventatives.

Infectious Diseases

Diarrhoea Despite all your precautions, you may still have a bout of mild travellers' diarrhoea. Dehydration is the main danger with any diarrhoea, particularly for children, so fluid replenishment is the number one treatment. Weak black tea with a little sugar, soda water or soft drinks allowed to go flat and diluted 50% with water are all good. With severe diarrhoea a rehydrating solution is necessary to replace minerals and salts and you should see a doctor. Stick to a bland diet as you recover.

Hepatitis Hepatitis is a general term for inflammation of the liver. The symptoms are fever, chills, headache, fatigue, feelings of weakness and aches and pains, followed by loss of appetite, nausea, vomiting, abdominal pain, dark urine, light-coloured faeces, jaundiced (yellow) skin and the whites of the eyes may turn yellow. Hepatitis A is transmitted by contaminated food and drinking water. You should seek medical advice but there is not much you can do apart from resting, drinking lots of fluids, eating lightly and avoiding fatty foods. People who have had hepatitis should avoid alcohol for some time after the illness as the liver needs time to recover.

Hepatitis B is spread through contact with infected blood, blood products or body fluids, for example through sexual contact, unsterilised needles and blood transfusions, or contact with blood via small breaks in the skin. Other risk situations include getting a tattoo, or body piercing. Hepatitis B may lead to long term problems.

There is no treatment for hepatitis but vaccination against the disease is readily available in most countries.

Rabies Rabies is still found in Italy, but only in isolated areas of the Alps. It is caused by a bite or scratch by an infected animal. Dogs are noted carriers. Any bite, scratch or even lick from a mammal in an area where rabies does exist should be cleaned immediately and thoroughly. Scrub with soap and running water and then clean with an alcohol solution. Medical help should be sought immediately.

Sexually Transmitted Diseases Gonorrhoea, herpes and syphilis are among these diseases; sores, blisters or rashes around the genitals, discharges or pain when urinating are common symptoms. In some STDs, such as wart virus or chlamydia, symptoms may be less marked or not observed at all especially in women. Syphilis symptoms eventually disappear completely but the disease continues and can cause severe problems in later years. While abstinence from sexual contact is the only 100% effective prevention, using condoms is also effective. The treatment for gonorrhoea and syphilis is with antibiotics. The different sexually transmitted diseases each require specific antibiotics. There is no cure for herpes or AIDS.

HIV/AIDS HIV, the Human Immunodeficiency Virus, develops into AIDS, Acquired Immune Deficiency Syndrome, which is a fatal disease. Any exposure to blood, blood products or body fluids may put the individual at risk. The disease is often transmitted through sexual contact or dirty needles – vaccinations, acupuncture, tattooing and body piercing can be potentially as dangerous as intravenous drug use.

Needles used in Italian hospitals are reliable.

If you require treatment or tests for a suspected STD or for HIV/AIDS, head for the nearest USL or public hospital. Each USL area has its own Family Planning Centre (Consultorio Familiare) where you can go for contraceptives, pregnancy tests and information about abortion; these are listed under each USL office in the telephone book, otherwise ask at the USL office. See the Emergency section in the Rome chapter for further information.

The fear of HIV infection should never preclude treatment for serious medical conditions.

Insect-Borne Diseases

Leishmaniasis This is a group of parasitic diseases transmitted by sandfly bites, found in coastal parts of Italy. Cutaneous leishmaniasis affects the skin tissue, causing ulceration and disfigurement and visceral leishmaniasis affects the internal organs. The disease rarely causes serious illness but, if it is suspected, seek medical advice.

Avoiding sandfly bites is the best precaution against this disease.

Lyme Disease Lyme disease is an infection transmitted by ticks that can be acquired throughout Europe, including the forested areas of Italy. The illness usually begins with a spreading rash at the site of the tick bite and is accompanied by fever, headache, extreme fatigue, aching joints and muscles and mild neck stiffness. If untreated, these symptoms usually resolve over several weeks but over subsequent weeks or months disorders of the nervous system, heart and joints may develop. The response to treatment is best early in the illness. Medical help should be sought.

Cuts, Bites & Stings

Cuts & Scratches Skin punctures can easily become infected in hot climates and may be difficult to heal. Treat any cut with an antiseptic such as povidone-iodine. Where possible avoid bandages and Band-aids, which can keep wounds wet.

Bites & Stings Bee and wasp stings are usually painful rather than dangerous. Calamine lotion will give relief, or use ice packs to reduce the pain and swelling.

Snakes Italy's only dangerous snake, the viper, is found throughout the country (except in Sardegna). To minimise your chances of being bitten, always wear boots, socks and long trousers when walking through undergrowth where snakes may be present. Don't put your hands into holes and crevices and be careful when collecting firewood.

Viper bites do not cause instantaneous death and an antivenene is widely available in pharmacies. Keep the victim calm and still, wrap the bitten limb tightly, as you would for a sprained ankle, and attach a splint to immobilise it. Then seek medical help, if possible with the dead snake for identification. Don't attempt to catch the snake if there is even a remote possibility of being bitten again. Tourniquets and sucking out the poison are now comprehensively discredited.

Jellyfish Italian beaches are occasionally inundated with jellyfish. Their stings are painful but not dangerous. Dousing in vinegar will de-activate any stingers that have not 'fired'. Calamine lotion, antihistamines and analgesics may reduce the reaction and relieve the pain.

Lice All lice cause itching and discomfort. They make themselves at home in your hair, clothing or in pubic hair. You catch lice through direct contact with infected people or by sharing combs, clothing and the like. Powder or shampoo treatment will kill the lice and infected clothing should then be washed in very hot water.

Leeches & Ticks Leeches may be present in damp forest conditions; they attach themselves to your skin to suck your blood. Trekkers often get them on their legs or in their boots. Salt or a lighted cigarette end will make them fall off. Do not pull them off as the bite is then more likely to become infected. An insect repellent may keep them away. Vaseline, alcohol or oil will persuade a tick to let go.

Always check your body if you have been walking through a tick-infested area. In recent years there have been several reported deaths in Sardegna related to tick bites and health authorities have yet to pinpoint to cause.

Women's Health

Gynaecological Problems Sexually transmitted diseases are a major cause of vaginal problems. Symptoms include a smelly discharge, painful intercourse and sometimes a burning sensation when urinating. Male sexual partners must also be treated. Medical attention should be sought and remember in addition to these diseases HIV or hepatitis B may also be acquired during exposure. Besides abstinence, the best thing is to practise safe sex using condoms.

Antibiotic use, synthetic underwear, sweating and contraceptive pills can lead to fungal vaginal infections when travelling in hot climates. Maintaining good personal hygiene and wearing loose-fitting clothes and cotton underwear will help to prevent these infections.

Fungal infections, characterised by a rash, itch and discharge, can be treated with a vinegar or lemon-juice douche, or with yoghurt. Nystatin, miconazole or clotrimazole pessaries or vaginal cream are the usual treatment.

Pregnancy Most miscarriages occur during the first three months of pregnancy, so this is the most risky time to travel as far as your own health is concerned. Miscarriage is not uncommon and can occasionally lead to severe bleeding. The last three months of pregnancy should also be spent within reasonable distance of good medical care. A baby born as early as 24 weeks stands a chance of survival, but only in a good, modern hospital. Pregnant women should avoid all unnecessary medication. Additional care should be taken to prevent illness and particular attention should be paid to diet and nutrition. Alcohol and nicotine, for example, should be avoided.

Women travellers often find that their periods become irregular or even cease while they're on the road. Remember that a missed period in these circumstances doesn't necessarily indicate pregnancy. There is a Consultorio Familiare attached to each USL (listed in the telephone book), where you can seek advice and have a test to determine whether you are pregnant or not.

If you use contraceptive pills, don't forget to take time zones into account and beware that the pills may not be absorbed if you suffer intestinal problems. Ask your physician about these matters. If you think you've run into problems in Italy, contact the nearest Consultorio Familiare.

WOMEN TRAVELLERS

Italy is not a dangerous country for women, but women travelling alone will often find themselves plagued by unwanted attention from men. This attention usually involves catcalls, hisses and whistles and, as such, is more annoying than anything else. Lone women will also find it difficult to remain alone – you will have Italian men harassing you as you walk along the street, drink a coffee in a bar or try to read a book in a park. Usually the best response is to ignore them, but if that doesn't work, politely tell them that you are waiting for your husband *(marito)* or boyfriend *(fidanzato)* and, if necessary, walk away.

Avoid becoming aggressive as this almost always results in an unpleasant confrontation. If all else fails, approach the nearest member of the police or carabinieri.

Basically, most of the attention falls into the nuisance/harassment category. However, women on their own should use their common sense. Avoid walking alone in deserted and dark streets and look for hotels which are centrally located and within easy walking distance of places where you can eat at night (unsafe areas for women are noted throughout this book). Women should also avoid hitchhiking alone.

Women will find that the farther south

they travel, the more likely they are to be harassed. It is advisable to dress more conservatively in the south, particularly if you are travelling to small towns and villages. In cities where there is a high petty-crime rate, such as Roma, Napoli, Palermo, Siracusa and Bari, women on their own are regarded as prime targets for bag-snatchers and should be very careful about walking in deserted streets.

Roma is one of the worst cities when it comes to overattentive males. Watch out for men with wandering hands on crowded buses. Either keep your back to the wall or make a loud fuss if someone starts fondling your backside.

Recommended reading is the *Handbook for Women Travellers* by M & G Moss and the *Women Travel* Rough Guide.

GAY & LESBIAN TRAVELLERS

Homosexuality is legal in Italy and well tolerated in major cities, particularly in the north. However, overt displays of affection by homosexual couples could attract a negative response in smaller towns. Friendships between Italian men tend to involve physical contact that most Anglo-Saxons would find excessive, so the sight of two men (or two women) walking down a street arm in arm is not unusual.

Cities such as Roma, Firenze and Milano have several gay discos, which may be listed in newspaper listings sections but can be more reliably tracked down through local gay organisations or the national monthly gay magazine *Babilonia* which, along with the annual *Guida Gay Italia*, is available at most newsstands. The national organisation for gay men is AGAL (☎ 051-644 70 54; fax 644 67 22), which is affiliated with the Communist Party's youth section, at Piazza di Porta Saragozza 2, 40123, Bologna. The corresponding organisation for lesbians is based in Roma: CLI Co-ordinamento Lesbiche Italiano (☎ 06-686 42 01), Via San Francesco di Sales 1/A. The bimonthly newsletter for lesbians, *Bolletino delle Connessioni Lesbiche Italiane*, is available here.

Babilonia is published monthly, and *Guida Gay Italia* is published annually. Both provide extensive information and are available at newspaper stands. More information about gay and lesbian discos can be found in the Entertainment section of the major city sections.

DISABLED TRAVELLERS

The Italian State Tourist Office in your country may be able to provide advice on Italian associations for the disabled and what help is available in the country. It may also carry a small brochure, *Services for Disabled People*, published by the Italian railways, which details facilities at stations and on trains. The Italian travel agency, CIT, can advise on hotels with special facilities, such as ramps etc. It can also request that wheelchair ramps be provided on arrival of your train if you book travel throughCIT.

In Italy itself you may also be able to get help. The Associazione Italiana Disabili (☎ 02-55 01 75 64), Via S Darnaba 29, Milano, can offer advice on holidaying for the handicapped.

The UK-based Royal Association for Disability & Rehabilitation (RADAR) publishes a useful guide called *Holidays & Travel Abroad: A Guide for Disabled People*, which provides a good overview of facilities available to disabled travellers throughout Europe. Contact RADAR (☎ 0171-250 3222) 250 City Rd, London EC1V 8AS.

SENIOR TRAVELLERS

Senior citizens are entitled to discounts on public transport and on admission fees at some museums in Italy. It is always important to ask. The minimum qualifying age is generally 60 years. You should also seek information in your own country on travel packages and discounts for senior travellers, through senior citizens' organisations and travel agents. Consider booking accommodation in advance to avoid inconvenience.

TRAVEL WITH CHILDREN

Successful travel with children can require a special effort. Don't try to overdo things by packing too much into the time available, and make sure activities include the kids as well. Remember that visits to museums and galleries can be tiring, even for adults. Children might also be more interested in some of the major archaeological sites, such as Pompeii, or the Colosseo and the Forum in Roma, and Greek temples in the south and Sicilia. If travelling in northern Italy, you might want to make a stopover at *Gardaland*, the amusement park near Lago di Garda in Lombardia. Allow time for the kids to play, either in a park or in the hotel room; taking a toddler to a playground for an hour or so in the morning can make an amazing difference to their tolerance for sightseeing in the afternoon. When travelling long distances by car or train etc, take plenty of books and other activities, such as colouring pencils and paper. Include older children in the planning of the trip – if they have helped to work out where they will be going, they will be much more interested when they get there.

Discounts are available for children (usually under 12 years of age) on public transport and for admission to museums, galleries etc.

There are special sections on activities for families in the chapters on Roma, Firenze and Venezia, as well as in several other cities and towns. These include activities which might interest the kids and usually point out where you can find a playground for young children. Always make a point of asking at tourist offices if they know of any special family or children's activities and for suggestions on hotels which cater for kids. Families should book accommodation in advance, where possible, to avoid inconvenience.

Chemists *(farmacie)* sell baby formula in powder or liquid form as well as sterilising solutions, such as Milton. Disposable nappies are widely available at supermarkets, chemists (where they are more expensive) and sometimes in larger *cartolerie* (stores selling papergoods). A pack of around 30 disposable nappies (diapers) costs around L18,000. Fresh cow's milk is sold in cartons in bars (which have a 'Latteria' sign) and in supermarkets. If it is essential that you have milk you should carry an emergency carton of UHT milk, since bars usually close at 8 pm. In many out-of-the-way areas in southern Italy the locals use only UHT milk.

Many car-rental firms rent out children's safety seats; however it is strongly advised that you book them in advance.

For more information, see Lonely Planet's *Travel with Children* by Maureen Wheeler.

DANGERS & ANNOYANCES

Theft

This is the main problem for travellers in Italy. Pickpockets and bag-snatchers operate in most major cities and are particularly active in Napoli and Roma. The best way to avoid being robbed is to wear a money belt under your clothing. You should keep all important items, such as money, passport, other papers and tickets, in your money belt at all times. If you are carrying a bag or camera, ensure that you wear the strap across your body and have the bag on the side away from the road to deter snatch thieves who often operate from motorcycles and scooters. Since the aim of young motorcycle bandits is often fun rather than gain you are just as likely to find yourself relieved of your sunglasses – or worse, of an earring. Motorcycle bandits are very active in Napoli, Roma, Siracusa and Palermo.

You should also watch out for groups of dishevelled-looking women and children. They generally work in groups of four or five and carry paper or cardboard which they use to distract your attention while they swarm around and riffle through your pockets and bag. Never underestimate their skill – they are lightning fast and very adept. Their favourite haunts are in and near major train stations, at tourist sights (such as the Colosseum) and in shopping areas. If you notice that you have been targeted by a group, either take evasive action, such as crossing the street, or shout *va via!* (go away!) in a loud, angry voice.

Pickpockets often hang out on crowded buses (the No 64 in Roma, which runs from

Stazione Termini to the Vatican, is notorious) and in crowded areas such as markets. There is only one way to deter pickpockets: simply *do not* carry any money or valuables in your pockets, and be very careful about your bags.

Be careful even in hotels and don't leave valuables lying around your room. You should also be cautious of sudden friendships, particularly if it turns out that your new-found *amico* or *amica* wants to sell you something. Parked cars are also prime targets for thieves, particularly those with foreign number plates or rental company stickers. Try removing the stickers, or cover them and leave a local newspaper on the seat to make it look like a local car.

Never leave valuables in your car – in fact, try not to leave anything in the car if you can help it and certainly not overnight. It is a good idea to pay extra to leave your car in supervised car parks, although there is no guarantee it will be completely safe. Throughout Italy, particularly in the south, service stations along the autostradas are favourite haunts of thieves who can clean out your car in the time it takes to have a cup of coffee. If possible, park the car where you can keep an eye on it. In recent years there have been isolated incidences of armed robberies on the autostrada south of Napoli, where travellers have been forced off the road, or tricked into pulling over, and have then been robbed at gunpoint.

When driving in cities you also need to beware of snatch thieves when you pull up at traffic lights. Keep the doors locked and, if you have the windows open, ensure that there is nothing valuable on the dashboard. Car theft is a major problem in the regions of Campania and Puglia, particularly in the cities of Napoli, Bari, Foggia and Brindisi. Beware also of unofficial parking attendants who say you can leave your car double-parked as long as you leave them your keys: you might return to find that both the attendant and your car have disappeared.

Horror tales abound about women being dragged to the ground by thieves trying to snatch their bags, of people losing wallets, watches and cameras on crowded buses or in a flurry of newspaper-waving children. These things really do happen! Certainly even the most cautious travellers are still prey to expert thieves, but there is no need to be paranoid. By taking a few basic precautions, you can greatly lessen the risk of being robbed.

Unfortunately, some Italians practise a more insidious form of theft: short-changing. Numerous travellers have reported losing money in this way. If you are new to the Italian currency, take the time to acquaint yourself with the denominations. When paying for goods, or tickets, or a meal, or whatever, keep an eye on the bills you hand over and then count your change carefully. One popular means of short-changing goes something like this: you hand over L50,000 for a newspaper which costs L2800; you are handed change for L10,000 and, while the person who sold you the paper hesitates, you hurry off without counting it. If you'd stayed for another five seconds, the rest of the change probably would have been handed over without your needing to say anything.

In case of theft or loss, always report the incident at the questura within 24 hours and ask for a statement, otherwise your travel insurance company won't pay out.

In case of emergency, you can contact the police throughout Italy on ☎ 113.

Traffic & Pedestrians

Italian traffic can at best be described as chaotic, at worst downright dangerous, for the unprepared tourist. Drivers are not keen to stop for pedestrians, even at pedestrian crossings, and are more likely to swerve. Italians simply step off the footpath and walk through the (swerving) traffic with determination – it is a practice which seems to work, so if you feel uncertain about crossing a busy road, wait for the next Italian. In many cities, roads which appear to be for one-way traffic have special lanes for buses travelling in the opposite direction – always look both ways before stepping onto the road.

Pollution

Italy has a poor record when it comes to

environmental concerns. Few Italians would think twice about dropping litter in the streets, illegally dumping household refuse in the country or driving a car or motorcycle with a faulty or nonexistent muffler.

Tourists will be affected in a variety of ways by the surprising disregard Italians have for their country, which is of considerable natural and artistic beauty. Noise and air pollution are problems in the major cities, caused mainly by heavy traffic. A headache after a day of sightseeing in Roma is likely to be caused by breathing carbon monoxide and lead, rather than simple tiredness. While cities such as Roma, Firenze and Milano have banned normal traffic from their historic centres, there are still more than enough cars, buses and motorcycles in and around the inner city areas to pollute the air.

Particularly in summer, there are periodic pollution alerts. The elderly, children and people with respiratory problems are warned to stay indoors. If you fit into one of these categories, keep yourself informed through the tourist office or your hotel proprietor.

When booking a hotel room it is a good idea to ask if it is quiet – although this might mean you will have to decide between a view and sleep.

One of the most annoying things about Roma is that the footpaths are littered with dog's poo – so be careful where you plant your feet.

Italy's beaches are generally heavily polluted by industrial waste, sewage and oil spills from the Mediterranean's considerable sea traffic. There are clean beaches in Sardegna, Sicilia, the less populated areas of the south and around Elba.

Italian-Style Service

It requires a lot of patience to deal with the Italian concept of service. What for Italians is simply a way of life can be horrifying for the foreigner – like the bank clerk who wanders off to have a cigarette just as it is your turn (after a one-hour wait) to be served, or the postal worker who has far more important work to do at a desk than to sell stamps to customers. Anyone in a uniform or behind a counter (including police officers, waiters and shop assistants) is likely to regard you with imperious contempt. Long queues are the norm in banks, post offices and any government offices.

It pays to remain calm and patient. Aggressive, demanding and angry customers stand virtually no chance of getting what they want.

LEGAL MATTERS

For many Italians, finding ways to get around the law (any law) is a way of life. They are likely to react with surprise, if not annoyance, if you point out that they might be breaking a law. Few people pay attention to speed limits, few motorcyclists and many drivers don't stop at red lights – and certainly not at pedestrian crossings. No-one bats an eyelid about littering or dogs pooping in the middle of the footpath – even though many municipal governments have introduced laws against these things. But these are minor transgressions when measured up against the country's organised crime, the extraordinary levels of tax evasion and corruption in government and business.

The average tourist will probably have a brush with the law only after being robbed by a bagsnatcher or pickpocket.

Drugs

Italy has introduced new drug laws which are lenient on drug users and heavy on pushers. If you're caught with drugs which the police determine are for your own personal use, you'll be let off with a warning – and, of course, the drugs will be confiscated. If, instead, it is determined that you intend to sell the drugs in your possession, you could find yourself in prison. It's up to the discretion of the police to determine whether or not you're a pusher, since the law is not specific about quantities. The sensible option is to avoid illicit drugs altogether.

Drink Driving

The legal limit for blood alcohol level is 0.08% and breath tests are now in use. See

Road Rules in the Getting Around chapter for more information.

Police

If you run into trouble in Italy, you're likely to end up dealing with either *la polizia* (police) or the *carabinieri* (military police). The police are a civil force and take their orders from the Ministry of the Interior, while the carabinieri fall under the Ministry of Defence. There is a considerable duplication of their roles, despite a 1981 reform of the police forces which intended to merge the two. Both forces are responsible for public order and security which means that you can call either in the event of a robbery, violent attack etc.

The carabinieri wear a dark-blue uniform with a red stripe and drive dark-blue cars with a red stripe. They are well trained and tend to be helpful. You are most likely to be pulled over by the carabinieri rather than the police when you are speeding etc. Their police station is called a *caserma*.

The police wear powder-blue pants with a fuchsia stripe and a navy-blue jacket and drive light blue cars with a white stripe, with 'polizia' written on the side. Tourists who want to report thefts, and people wanting to get a residence permit, will have to deal with them. Their headquarters are called the questura, and addresses and telephone numbers are given in the Emergency sections throughout this book.

Other varieties of police in Italy include the *vigili urbani*, basically traffic police, who you will have to deal with if you get a parking ticket, or your car is towed away; and the *guardia di finanza*, who are responsible for fighting tax evasion and drug smuggling. It is a long shot, but you could be stopped by one of them if you leave a shop without a receipt for your purchase.

> **Warning**
> While Italy's policemen and women are generally helpful, they don't consider themselves public servants. If you become too demanding, rude or difficult they'll treat you at the very least with imperious contempt. At worst, they have the right to arrest you if they feel you have insulted them.

Your Rights

Italy still has some anti-terrorism laws on its books which could make life very difficult if you happen to be detained by the police. You can be held for 48 hours without a magistrate being informed and you can be interrogated without the presence of a lawyer. It is difficult to obtain bail and you can be held legally for up to three years without being brought to trial. These same laws require that all foreigners must report to the police within eight days of arriving in the country, even if you are here only for a holiday (see Visas & Documents).

BUSINESS HOURS

Business hours vary from city to city, but generally shops are open Monday to Friday from around 9 am to 1 pm and 3.30 to 7.30 pm (or 4 to 8 pm). In some cities, grocery shops might not reopen until 5 pm and, during the warmer months, they could stay open until 9 pm. They close on Thursday or Monday afternoons (depending on which town you're in) and often on Saturday afternoons. Shops, department stores and supermarkets also close for a half day during the week – it varies from city to city, but is usually either Monday morning or Thursday afternoon. Department stores, such as Coin and Rinascente, and most supermarkets now have continuous opening hours, from 9 am to 7.30 pm Monday to Saturday. Some even open from 9 am to 1 pm on Sunday.

Banks tend to open Monday to Friday from 8.30 am to 1.30 pm and 3.30 to 4.30 pm, although hours can vary. They are closed at weekends, but it is always possible to find an exchange office open in the larger cities and in major tourist areas.

Major post offices open Monday to Saturday from 8.30 am to 6 or 7 pm Monday to Saturday. Smaller post offices generally open Monday to Friday from 8.30 am to 2 pm and on Saturday from 8.30 am to midday.

Pharmacies are usually open from 9 am to 12.30 pm and 3.30 to 7.30 pm. They are always closed on Sunday and usually on Saturday afternoon. When closed, pharmacies are required to display a list of pharmacies in the area which are open.

Bars (in the Italian sense, ie coffee-and-sandwich places) and cafés generally open from 7.30 am to 8 pm, although some stay open after 8 pm and turn into pub-style drinking and meeting places. Discos and clubs might open around 10 pm, but often there'll be no-one there until around midnight. Restaurants open from midday to 3 pm and 7.30 to 11 pm (later in summer and in the south). Restaurants and bars are required to close for one day each week, which varies between establishments.

Museum and gallery opening hours vary, although there is a trend towards continuous opening hours from 9.30 am to 7 pm. Many close on Monday.

PUBLIC HOLIDAYS

Most Italians take their annual holidays in August, deserting the cities for the cooler seaside or mountains. This means that many businesses and shops close for at least a part of the month, particularly during the week around Ferragosto (Feast of the Assumption) on 15 August. Larger cities, notably Milano and Roma, are left to the tourists, who may be frustrated that many restaurants and clothing and grocery shops are closed until early September.

National public holidays include the following: Epiphany (6 January); Easter Monday (March/April); Liberation Day (25 April); Labour Day (1 May); Feast of the Assumption (15 August); All Saints' Day (1 November); Feast of the Immaculate Conception (8 December); Christmas Day (25 December); and the Feast of Santo Stefano (26 December).

Individual towns also have public holidays to celebrate the feasts of their patron saints. See the following section and Festivals on the next page for details.

SPECIAL EVENTS

Italy's calendar bursts with cultural events ranging from colourful traditional celebrations, with a religious and/or historical flavour, through to festivals of the performing arts, including opera, music and theatre.

Many towns celebrate the feasts of their patron saints in eye-catching fashion. They include: the Feast of St Mark on 25 April in Venezia; the Feast of St John the Baptist on 24 June in Firenze, Genova and Torino; the

Jousting tournaments occur during many festivals

Festivals

These are some of Italy's main festivals.

February/March/April

Carnevale

During the period before Ash Wednesday many towns stage carnivals and enjoy their last opportunity to indulge before Lent. The carnival held in Venezia during the 10 days before Ash Wednesday is the most famous, but more traditional and popular carnival celebrations are held at Viareggio on the north coast of Toscana and at Ivrea, near Torino.

Sartiglia

This is the highlight of carnival celebrations at Oristano, in Sardegna, on the Sunday and Tuesday before Lent. It involves a medieval tournament of horsemen in masquerade.

Festival of the Almond Blossoms

This traditional festival features a historical pageant and fireworks held at Agrigento, Sicily, in early March.

Le Feste di Pasqua

Holy Week in Italy is marked by solemn processions and passion plays. On Holy Thursday at Taranto, in Puglia, there is the Procession of the Addolorata and on Good Friday the Procession of the Mysteries, when statues representing the Passion of Christ are carried around the town. One of Italy's oldest and most evocative Good Friday processions is held at Chieti in Abruzzo in Sicilia. The week is marked by numerous events, including a Procession of the Mysteries at Trapani and the celebration of Easter according to Byzantine rites at Piana degli Albanesi, near Palermo. Women in colourful 15th-century costume give out Easter eggs to the public.

Scoppio del Carro

Held in Florence in the Piazza del Duomo at noon on Easter Sunday, this event features the explosion of a cart full of fireworks – a tradition dating back to the Crusades and seen as a good omen for the city if it works.

May

Feast of San Nicola

On 2 and 3 May, the people of Bari, in Puglia, participate in a procession in traditional costume to re-enact the delivery of the bones of their patron saint to Dominican friars. The next day a statue of the saint is taken to sea.

Festival of Snakes

Held at Cocullo in Abruzzo on May 5, this famous and still very traditional festival honours the town's patron saint, San Domenico. His statue is draped with live snakes and carried in procession.

Feast of San Gennaro

Three times a year (the first Sunday in May, 19 September and 16 December) the faithful gather in Napoli's Duomo to wait for the blood of Saint Januarius to liquefy – if the miracle occurs it is considered a good omen for the city.

Corsa dei Ceri

This exciting, traditional candle race is held at Gubbio in Umbria on 15 May. Groups of men carrying huge wooden shrines race uphill to the town's basilica, dedicated to the patron saint, Ubaldo.

Cavalcata Sarda

Hundreds of Sardi wearing colourful traditional costume gather at Sassari on the second-last Sunday in May for this Sardinian cavalcadeto mark a victory over the Saracens in the year 1000.

Palio della Balestra

The Palio of the Crossbow, held in Gubbio on the last Sunday in May, is a crossbow contest between the men of Gubbio and Sansepolcro, who dress in medieval costume and use antique weapons. There is a rematch at Sansepolcro on the first Sunday in September.

Maggio Musicale Fiorentino

This music festival is held in Firenze in May and June.

June

Regatta of the Four Ancient Maritime Republics

This event sees a procession of boats and a race between the four historical maritime rivals – Pisa, Venezia, Amalfi and Genova. The event rotates between the four towns.

Feast of Sant'Antonio

Fans of St Anthony, patron saint of Padova and of lost things, might want to attend the procession of the saint's relics held annually on 13 June.

Infiorata

To celebrate Corpus Domini on 21 June, some towns decorate a selected street with colourful designs made with flower petals. Towns include Genzano, near Roma, and Spello in Umbria.

Gioco del Ponte
Two groups in medieval costume contend for the Ponte di Mezzo, a bridge over the Arno river, in Pisa.

Festival dei Due Mondi
The Festival of Two Worlds, an international arts event held in June and July at Spoleto, a beautiful hill town in Umbria, was created by Gian Carlo Menotti and features music, theatre, dance and art exhibitions.

July

Il Palio
The pride and joy of Siena, this famous traditional event is held twice a year – on 2 July and 16 August – in the town's beautiful Piazza del Campo. It involves a dangerous bareback horse race around the piazza, preceded by a parade of supporters in traditional costume.

Ardia
More dangerous than the Palio, this impressive and chaotic horse race at Sedilo in Sardegna on 6 and 7 June celebrates the victory of the Roman Emperor Constantine over Maxentius in 312 AD (the battle was actually at the Ponte Milvio in Roma). A large number of horsemen race around town while onlookers shoot guns into the ground or air.

Festa del Redentore
Fireworks and a procession over the bridge to the Church of the Redeemer on Giudecca Island in Venezia mark the feast of the Redemeer on the third weekend in July.

Umbria Jazz
Held at Perugia in Umbria in July, this week-long festival features performers from around the world.

International Ballet Festival
This festival, held at Nervi, near Genova, features international performers.

August

Quintana
This historical pageant features a parade of hundreds of people in 15th-century costume, followed by a spectacular jousting tournament. It is held at Ascoli Piceno in Le Marche on the first Sunday in August.

I Candelieri
The festival of candelabra is held on 14 August at Sassari in Sardegna and features town representatives in medieval costume carrying huge wooden columns through the town. It celebrates the Feast of the Assumption to honour a vow made in 1652 to end a plague.

Il Palio
This repeat of Siena's famous horse race is held on 16 August.

Festa del Redentore
Held at Nuoro in Sardegna, this folk festival and parade is attended by thousands of people from all over the island, who dress in traditional regional costume.

International Film Festival
Held at the Lido, Venezia, the festival attracts the international film scene.

September

Living Chess Game
The townspeople of Marostica in the Veneto dress as chess figures and participate in a match on a chessboard marked out in the town square. Games are held in even years on the first weekend in September.

Palio della Balestra
A rematch of the crossbow competition between Gubbio and Sansepolcro is held at Sansepolcro.

Regata Storica
This historic gondola race along Venezia's Canal Grande is preceded by a parade of boats decorated in 15th-century style. It is held on the first Sunday in September.

Giostra della Quintana
This medieval pageant involves a parade and jousting event with horsemen in traditional costume. It is held on the second Sunday in September.

Feast of San Gennaro
On 19 September the faithful of Napoli gather for the second time to await the miraculous liquefaction of Saint Januarius' blood. They gather again on 16 December.

October

Feast of San Francesco d'Assisi
Special religous ceremonies are held in the churches of San Francesco and Santa Maria degli Angeli in Assisi on 3 and 4 October.

November

Feast of the Madonna della Salute
Held in Venezia on 21 November, this procession over a bridge of boats across the Canale Grande to the Chiesa di Santa Maria della Salute to give thanks for the city's deliverance from plague in 1630.

Feast of Santa Cecilia
A series of concerts and exhibitions takes place in Siena to honour the patron saint of musicians.

December

Feast of San Nicola
Various religious ceremonies as well as traditional folk celebrations take place at Bari on 6 December.

Christmas
During the weeks preceding Christmas there are numerous processions, religious events etc. Many churches set up elaborate cribs or nativity scenes known as *presepi*.

Feast of Saints Peter & Paul in Roma on 29 June; the Feast of San Gennaro (Janarius) in Napoli on 19 September; and the Feast of St Ambrose in Milano on 7 December. Religious festivals are particularly numerous in Sicilia and Sardegna, notably Le Feste di Pasqua (Easter Week) in Sicilia.

Among the important opera seasons are those at Verona's Arena and at La Scala in Milano. Major music festivals include Umbria Jazz in Perugia and Maggio Musicale Fiorentino in Firenze, while the Festival of Two Worlds (Festival dei Due Mondi) in Spoleto is worth visiting. As well as Carnevale, Venezia offers an international film festival and the Biennale visual arts festival, the latter held every odd year.

If you wish to time your visit with a particular festival, contact the Italian State Tourist office in your country or write to ENIT in Roma (see the Tourist Offices Abroad section) for dates. ENIT publishes an annual booklet, *An Italian Year*, which lists most festivals, music, opera and ballet seasons, as well as art and film festivals.

ACTIVITIES

If the museums, galleries and sights are not enough for you there are numerous options for getting off the beaten tourist track. From mountaineering to courses in the history of art, Italy offers a wide range of outdoor and cerebral pursuits.

Hiking & Mountaineering

The Alps, in particular the spectacular Dolomiti, offer well-marked trails and strategically placed rifugi for long-distance hikers. With careful planning it is possible to walk for as many days as you want, without carrying large quantities of supplies, by staying and buying your food at the rifugi. However, hikers still need to be well prepared in the Alps – even at the height of summer the weather can change suddenly. Hikers planning to tackle longer and more difficult trails, particularly at high altitudes, should ensure that they leave basic details of their route with someone. They should also be well informed on weather predictions and prepared for cold weather, rain and snow (the first snow can fall in September). See the section on Trekking in the Dolomiti in the Trentino-Alto Adige chapter for more information.

Guided treks are a good idea for inexperienced walkers.

The Appennini also have good walking trails and interesting areas include the Parco Nazionale d'Abruzzo and La Sila (Sila massif) in Calabria. The Alpi Apuane in Toscana also have well-marked and challenging trails. In Sardegna, the rugged landscape offers some spectacular hikes in the eastern ranges, such as Gennargentu, and the gorges near Dorgali. See the relevant sections to obtain further information.

Skiing

There are numerous excellent ski resorts in the Italian Alps and, again, the Dolomiti provide the most dramatic scenery. Options include downhill *(lo sci)* and cross-country *(sci di fondo)* skiing, as well as ski mountaineering *(sci alpinismo)* – only for the adventurous and advanced, where skiers head well away from the organised runs and combine their mountaineering and skiing skills.

Skiing is quite expensive because of the costs of ski lifts and accommodation but a Settimana Bianca package can reduce the expense. It is not expensive, on the other hand, to hire ski equipment – and this factor should be weighed up against the inconvenience of bringing your own gear. Cross-country skiing costs less because you don't pay for the lifts.

The season in Italy generally extends from December to late March, although at higher altitudes and in particularly good years it can be longer. There is year-round skiing in areas such as the Marmolada glacier in Trentino-Alto Adige and on Monte Bianco (Mont Blanc) and the Matterhorn (Monte Cervino) in the Valle d'Aosta.

The five major (read: most fashionable and expensive) ski resorts in Italy are Cortina d'Ampezzo in the Veneto; Madonna di Campiglio, San Martino di Castrozza and

Canazei all in Trentino; and Courmayeur in the Valle d'Aosta. There are many other, less expensive resorts which also offer excellent facilities (see the Alpine sections of the northern Italy chapters for more information).

Water Sports

Windsurfing and sailing are extremely popular in Italy, and at most beach resorts it is possible to rent boats and equipment. There are also various diving schools, but the scenery above water is much more interesting. See the Things to See & Do and Activities sections throughout this book for boat and windsurfing equipment hire at water resorts.

Cycling

This is a good option for people who can't afford a car but want to see some of the more out-of-the-way places. The only problem is that more than 75% of Italy is mountainous or hilly, so you will need some stamina and a good bike. A mountain bike would be a good idea, enabling you to tackle some of the Alpine trails as well. Cycling and mountain biking are becoming increasingly popular in Italy and you'll find that most tourist offices will be able to offer information on bike hire, mountain bike trails and guided mountain bike rides. People planning to cycle around Italy could easily bring their own bikes, or might consider buying one once they arrive in Italy (see the Bicycle section of the Getting Around chapter for details). Bikes can be transported on aeroplanes for a surprisingly low fee and, within Italy, they can be transported free on ferries to Sicilia and Sardegna, and relatively cheaply on trains. The hills of Toscana are very popular for cycling, particularly around Firenze and Siena, from where you could explore the hills around Fiesole, San Gimignano and Chianti, just to name a few possibilities. A bike would be particularly useful for exploring Sardegna. In Umbria, areas such as the Valnerina and the Piano Grande at Monte Vettore have beautiful trails and quiet country roads to explore. Serious cyclists will know where to go for the most challenging routes – the torturous, winding road up to the Passo Stelvio is one of the most famous. Mountain bikers have endless possibilities and are well catered for by tourist offices throughout the country, with information and maps of trails.

COURSES

Travelling to Italy to study the language is becoming increasingly popular. Courses are offered by private schools and universities throughout Italy and are a great way to learn Italian while enjoying the opportunity to live in an Italian city or town.

Among the cheapest options is the Università per Stranieri in Perugia, where the cost per month is L260,000 (compared to an average of L600,000 at a private school in Firenze). Individual schools and universities are listed under the relevant towns throughout this book. Accommodation can usually be arranged through the school.

Many schools also offer courses in painting, art history, sculpture, architecture and cooking; however, all these courses can be expensive at an average of L600,000 a month.

It is also possible to undertake serious academic study at an Italian university, although obviously only if you have a very good command of the language.

Italian cultural institutes will provide information about study in Italy, as well as enrolment forms. Otherwise, check with travel agencies in your country for organised study tours to Italy. In England, an organisation called Italian Study Tours (☎ 0171-482 3767), 35 Murray Mews, London NW1 9RH, organises small groups to study the language in a Tuscan farmhouse for one week.

The more adventurous traveller might want to take a course in rock climbing, ski mountaineering, or hang-gliding, just to name a few of the possibilities. Mountain guide groups offering courses are listed in the Alpine sections of the northern Italy chapters, or you can always get information from local tourist offices in the relevant areas.

WORK

It is illegal for non-EU citizens to work in Italy without a work permit, but trying to obtain one can be time consuming. EU citizens are allowed to work in Italy, but they still need to obtain a permesso di soggiorno from the main questura in the town where they have found work. See the Visas & Documents section for more information about these permits. New immigration laws require foreign workers to be 'legalised' through their employers, which can apply even to cleaners and babysitters. The employers then pay pension and health insurance contributions. This doesn't mean that 'black' work can't still be found.

Working Holiday

The best options, once you're in the country, are trying to find work in a bar, nightclub or restaurant during the tourist season. Babysitting is a good possibility. In the major cities you may be able to pick up a summer job accompanying a family on their annual beach holiday – you could look in magazines such as *Wanted in Rome*, or even place an advertisement. Another option is au pair work, organised before you come to Italy. A useful guide is *The Au Pair and Nanny's Guide to Working Abroad* by S Griffith & S Legg (Vacation Work, paperback). By the same publisher is *Work Your Way Around the World* by Susan Griffith.

Teaching English

The easiest source of work for foreigners is teaching English, but even with full qualifications an American, Australian, Canadian or New Zealander might find it difficult to secure a permanent position. Most of the larger, more reputable schools will hire only people with work permits, but their attitude can become more flexible if demand for teachers is high and they come across someone with good qualifications. The more professional schools will require a TEFL (Teaching English as a Foreign Language) certificate. It is advisable to apply for work early in the year, in order to be considered for positions available in October (language school years correspond roughly to the Italian school year: late September to the end of June).

There are numerous schools throughout the country which hire people without work permits or qualifications, but the pay is usually low (around L15,000 an hour). It is more lucrative to advertise your services and pick up private students (although rates vary wildly, ranging from as low as L15,000 to up to L50,000 an hour). In a large city like Roma the average rate is around L30,000, while in smaller provincial towns, where the market is more limited, even qualified private teachers will have to charge as low as L15,000 to L20,000 in order to attract students. Although you can get away with absolutely no qualifications or experience, it might be a good idea to bring along a few English grammar books (including exercises) to help you at least appear professional.

Most people get started by placing advertisements in shop windows and on university notice boards, or in a local publication, such as *Wanted in Rome* or *Porta Portese* in Roma or *Secondamano* in Milano. All are available at newspaper stands.

Street Performers

Busking is common in Italy although, theoretically, buskers require a municipal permit. Italians tend not to stop and gather around street performers, but they are usually quite generous.

Other Work

There are plenty of markets around the country where you can set up a stall and sell your wares, although you may need to pay a fee. Selling goods on the street is also illegal unless you have a municipal permit and it is quite common to see municipal police moving people along. Another option is to head for beach resorts in summer, particularly if you have handcrafts or jewellery you want to sell.

ACCOMMODATION

Prices for accommodation quoted in this book are intended as a guide only. There is generally a fair degree of fluctuation in hotel prices throughout Italy, depending on the season and whether establishments raise prices when they have the opportunity. It is not unusual for prices to remain fixed for years on end, and in some cases they even go down: but it is more common that they rise by around 5% or 10% annually. Always check room charges before putting your bags down.

Reservations

It's a good idea to book a room if you're planning to travel during peak tourist periods such as summer. Hotels usually require confirmation by fax or letter, as well as a deposit. Fax numbers for larger hotels in major cities are listed in this book. Tourist offices will generally send out on request information about hotels, camping, apartments etc, if you need more options than we provide. Another option is to use one of the local hotel booking services – you'll find some listed under Roma and Firenze.

Camping

Most camping facilities in Italy are major complexes with swimming pools, tennis courts, restaurants and supermarkets. Like hotels, they are graded according to a star system. Prices at even the most basic camping grounds can be surprisingly expensive once you add up the various charges for each person, a site for your tent or caravan and a car, but they generally still work out cheaper than a double room in a one-star hotel. Average prices are L8000 to L12,000 per adult, L6000 to L8000 for children aged under 12 years, and from L10,000 for a site. You'll also often have to pay to park your car and there is sometimes a charge for use of the showers, usually around L1000.

Locations are usually good, ranging from beach or lakeside, to valleys in the Alps. In major cities, camping grounds are often a long way from the historic centres, and the inconvenience, plus the additional cost of needing to use public transport, should be weighed up against the price of a hotel room.

Independent camping is generally not permitted in Italy and you might find yourself disturbed during the night by the carabinieri. But, out of the main summer tourist season, independent campers who choose spots not visible from the road, don't light fires, and who try to be inconspicuous, shouldn't have too much trouble. Always get permission from the landowner if you want to camp on private property. Camper vans are very popular in Italy (see the Getting Around chapter for details on renting them).

Full lists of camping grounds in and near cities and towns are usually available from local tourist offices. In Sicilia and Sardegna the regional tourist boards publish annual booklets listing all facilities throughout the islands. The Touring Club Italiano publishes an annual book listing all camping grounds in Italy, *Campeggi e Villagi Turistici in Italia* (L22,000), and the Istituto Geografico de Agostini publishes the annual *Guida di Campeggi in Europa* (L20,000), both available in major bookshops in Italy.

Hostels

Hostels in Italy are called *ostelli per la gioventù* and many are run by the Associazione Italiana Alberghi per la Gioventù (AIG), which is affiliated to Hostelling International (HI). An HI card is not always required, but it is recommended that you have one. Membership cards can be purchased at major hostels, from CTS (student and youth travel centre) offices, from AIG offices throughout Italy, and of course from a HI-affiliated office in your home country. Pick up a booklet on Italian hostels, with details of prices, locations etc, from the AIG national head office (☎ 06-487 11 52), Via Cavour 44, Roma.

Many Italian hostels are beautifully located, some in castles and villas. Many have bars and with few exceptions they have restaurants, kitchens (for self-catering) or both. Nightly rates vary from L13,000 to L24,000 and the cost per night often includes breakfast. If not, breakfast will cost around

L2000. In some hostels there is an extra charge for use of heating and hot water, usually around L1000. A meal will cost from L12,000.

Accommodation is in segregated dormitories, although some hostels offer family rooms (at a higher price per person).

Hostels are generally closed from 9 am to 3.30 pm, although there are many exceptions. Check-in is from 6 to 10.30 pm, although some hostels will allow you a morning check-in, before they close for the day (it is best to check beforehand). Curfew is 10.30 or 11 pm in winter and 11.30 pm or midnight in summer. It is usually necessary to pay before 9 am on the day of your departure, otherwise you could be charged for another night.

Pensioni & Hotels

It is very important to remember that prices quoted in this book are intended as a guide only. Hotels and pensioni are allowed to increase charges twice a year, although many don't. Travellers should always check on prices beforedeciding to stay. Make a complaint to the local tourist office if you believe you're being overcharged. Many proprietors employ various methods of bill-padding, such as charging for showers, or making breakfast compulsory.

There is often no difference between a *pensione* and an *albergo*; in fact, some hotels use both titles. However, a pensione will generally be of one to three-star quality, while an albergo can be awarded up to five stars. *Locande* (similar to pensioni) and *alloggi*, also known as *affittacamere*, are generally cheaper, but not always. Locande and affittacamere are not included in the star classification system, although in some areas (such as the Isole Eolie and in the Alps) the standard of affittacamere is very high.

While the quality of accommodation can vary a great deal, one-star hotels/pensioni tend to be very basic and usually do not have a private bathroom attached to rooms. Standards at two-star places are often only slightly better, but rooms will generally have private bathroom. Once you arrive at three

stars you can assume that standards will be reasonable, although quality still varies dramatically. Four and five-star hotels are usually part of a group of hotels and offer facilities such as room service, laundry and dry-cleaning. For the average traveller it is really an unnecessary expense to go above three-star hotels.

Overall, prices are highest in Roma, Firenze, Milano and Venezia, and at other major tourist destinations. They also tend to be higher in northern Italy than in the south, and prices can skyrocket in the high season at beach resorts and during the ski season in the Alps.

A single room *(camera singola)* is uniformly expensive in Italy, costing from around L40,000. A double room with twin beds *(camera doppia)*, and a double with a double bed *camera matrimoniale* cost from around L60,000. It is much cheaper to share with two or more people. In most parts of Italy, proprietors will charge no more than 15% of the cost of a double room for each additional person.

Tourist offices have booklets listing all pensioni and hotels, including prices (although they might not always be up to date). Ask for lists of locande and affittacamere.

Agriturismo

This is a holiday on a working farm and is becoming increasingly popular in Italy. Traditionally the idea was that families rented out rooms in their farmhouses, and it is still possible to find this type of accommodation. However, more commonly it is a restaurant in a restored farm complex, with rooms available for rent. All *agriturismo* establishments are operating farms and you will usually be able to sample the local produce.

Agriturismo is well organised in Trentino-Alto Adige, Toscana and Umbria and increasingly so in parts of Sicilia and Sardegna, and local tourist offices will usually have information. For detailed information on all facilities in Italy, contact Agriturist (☎ 06-6 85 21), Corso Vittorio Emanuele 89, 00186 Roma. It publishes a book with all agriturismo listings throughout the country (L35,000), available at the office and in selected bookshops.

Rifugi

If you are planning to hike in the Alps, Appennini or other mountains in Italy, obtain information on the network of *rifugi* (refuges). There are various kinds of rifugi, which are detailed in the relevant Alpine sections of the northern Italy chapters. The average price per person for an overnight stay plus breakfast is from around L18,000 to around L40,000. Accommodation is generally in dormitories and meals are available. The locations of rifugi are marked on good hiking maps and it should be noted that most are open only from July to September. Some are close to chair lifts and cable-car stations, which means they are usually expensive and crowded with tourists. Others are at high altitude, involving hours of hard walking or climbing from the nearest village or another rifugio. These tend to be cheaper and, in general, are used by serious trekkers and mountaineers. It is important to book a bed in advance, otherwise you could find yourself walking for an unplanned extra few hours to the next rifugio. Additional information, including telephone numbers, can be obtained from local tourist offices.

Religious Institutions

Known as *casa religione di ospitalità*, these institutions offer accommodation in major cities and often in monasteries in the country. The standard is usually good, but prices are no longer low. You can expect to pay about the same as for a one-star hotel, if not more. Information can be obtained through local tourist offices, or through the archdiocese of the relevant city. Associazione Cattolica al Servizio della Giovane (or Protezione della Giovane) can organise accommodation for women in hostels. The organisation has offices in most major towns, and often at major train stations, although these can be open at irregular hours.

Student Accommodation

People planning to study in Italy can usually organise accommodation through the school or university they will be attending. Options include a room with an Italian family, or a share arrangement with other students in an independent apartment. Some Italian universities operate a *casa dello studente*, which houses Italian students throughout the school year and lets out rooms to others during the summer break (July to the end of September). It can be very difficult to organise a room in one of these institutions. The best idea is to attempt to book a room through your own university, or contact the relevant Italian university directly.

Landmark Trust

If you fancy staying in the building where the poet Keats died, one of Palladio's villas, or the poet Browning's house, contact the Landmark Trust in the UK. Established as a charity in 1965, the trust restores and conserves a host of architectural marvels in the UK, as well as three in Italy: the third-floor apartment where Keats died in Piazza di Spagna, Roma; the Casa Guidi in Firenze where Browning lived; and the Villa Saraceno, near Vicenza, an early Palladio commission. For any further information, contact The Landmark Trust (☎ 0628-825 925), Shottesbrooke Maidenhead, Berkshire SL6 3SW, UK. For information on Palladio's villa you should contact Lorella Graham at the Villa Saraceno (☎ 0444-89 13 17), Finale di Agugliaro, Vicenza.

Rental Accommodation

Finding rental accommodation in the major cities can be difficult and time-consuming, but not impossible. There are rental agencies which will assist, for a fee, (some agencies are listed in the major city sections). Prices are higher for short-term rental. A small apartment anywhere near the centre of Roma will cost around L1,800,000 a month and it is usually necessary to pay a bond (generally at least one month in advance). Apartments and houses *(villas)* for rent are listed in local publications such as the weekly *Porta Portese* in Roma. You will find that many owners want to rent to foreigners because it is short term, or because they intend to charge a high rent. Another option is to answer an advertisement in any of the local publications to share an apartment.

In major resort areas, such as the Isole Eolie and other parts of Sicilia, the coastal areas of Sardegna and in the Alps, the tourist offices have lists of local apartments and villas for rent. Most offices will be more than cooperative if you telephone beforehand for information on how to book an apartment.

People wanting to rent a villa in the countryside can seek information from specialist travel agencies in their own country, or contact an organisation in Italy directly. One of the major companies in Italy is Cuendet, which has villas in Toscana, Umbria, the Veneto, Roma, Le Marche, the Amalfi Coast, Puglia, Sicilia and Sardegna. This reliable company publishes a booklet listing all the villas in its files, many with photos. Prices for a villa for four to six people range from around US$400 a week in winter up to US$1200 a week in August.

For details, write to Cuendet & Cie spa, Strada di Strove 17, 53035 Monteriggioni, Siena (☎ 0577-57 63 10, fax 0577-30 11 49, email cuede@tin.it), and ask them to send you a copy of their catalogue (US$15).

In the UK, you can order Cuendet's catalogues and make reservations by calling ☎ 0800-891 573 toll free. In the USA, Cuendet bookings are handled by Rentals in Italy (☎ 805-987 5278, fax 805-482 7976), 1742 Calle Corva, Camarillo, California 93010.

CIT offices throughout the world also have lists of villas and apartments available for rent in Italy. In Australia, try an organisation called Cottages & Castles (☎ 03-862 1142), 11 Laver St, Kew 3101, Victoria.

Don't expect to land in Italy and find an apartment or villa immediately – unless you are staying for an indefinite period, you might find that your holiday is taken up with flat-hunting.

FOOD

Eating is one of life's great pleasures for Italians. Be adventurous and don't ever be intimidated by eccentric waiters or indecipherable menus and you will find yourself agreeing with the locals, who believe that nowhere in the world is the food as good as in Italy and, more specifically, in their own town.

Regional Cuisines

What the world regards as Italian cooking is really a collection of regional cuisines *(cucine)*. While the eating habits of Italians are now fairly homogeneous, cooking styles continue to vary notably from region to region and significantly between the north

and south. In the north the food is rich and often creamy, while in Sicilia, for example, it is spicier.

The regional specialities of Emilia-Romagna, including *tagliatelle al ragù* (and its adaptation, *spaghetti bolognese), lasagne* and *tortellini* are among the best known Italian dishes, and the best *prosciutto* (cured ham) comes from Parma, which is also the home of *parmigiano reggiano* (parmesan cheese).

Liguria is the home of *pesto*, a delicious uncooked pasta sauce of fresh basil, garlic, oil, pine nuts and cheese, ground together with a mortar and pestle. Also try the *farinata*, a tart made with chick-pea flour, and the *focaccia*, a flat bread.

In Piemonte the cuisine is influenced to some extent by nearby France. It is often delicate and always flavoursome. *Tartufo bianco* (white truffle) is used in a wide variety of dishes. Traditional dishes make good use of game birds and animals, including chamois, pheasant and quail, as well as more unusual meats, such as horse, donkey and frog (there is even such a dish as frog risotto).

In Trentino-Alto Adige the cuisine has a heavy Austrian influence, and alongside minestrone and spaghetti, you will find *canerdeli* (a soup with noodles in it), goulash soup and Wiener schnitzel. Local specialities include smoked meats, eaten with heavy, black rye bread.

In the Veneto, try the boiled meats and the bitter red lettuce *(radicchio trevisano)*, eaten baked, or in risotto or with pasta. Risotto comes in many varieties in the Veneto: with mushrooms, zucchini, sausage, quail, trout and other seafood, chicken, spring vegetables and, not to be missed, *risotto nero*, coloured and flavoured with the ink of squid.

In Toscana and Umbria the locals use a lot of olive oil and herbs, and regional specialities are noted for their simplicity, fine flavour and the use of fresh produce.

In Toscana, try *bistecca fiorentina*, a huge T-bone steak usually three to four cm thick. It is quite acceptable, and in fact advisable, to order one steak for two people. Among the staples of Tuscan cuisine are small white *cannellini* beans, although all types of beans are widely used. There is also a wide range of soups, from the simple *acquacotta*, which translates as 'cooked water', to the rich *minestrone alla fiorentina*, flavoured with pork and chicken giblets. Don't miss the incredibly rich *panforte*, Siena's famous Christmas fruitcake.

In Umbria both the tartufo (truffle) and the *porcini* mushrooms (like the French *cèpes)* are abundant and both turn up in pasta, rice and a large number of other dishes. While many Umbrian dishes are based upon vegetables, the locals eat more meat than any other Italians, and a local speciality is *porchetta*, a whole roast piglet stuffed with rosemary. Umbrian cakes and pastries are worth a try, as are the chocolates produced by the Perugina factory at Perugia, notably the famous *baci* (chocolate-coated hazelnuts).

In and around Roma, traditional pasta includes spaghetti *carbonara* (with egg yolk, cheese and bacon) and *alla matriciana* (with a sauce of tomato, bacon and a touch of chilli). Offal is also popular in Roma – if you can stomach it, try the pasta *pajata*, made with the entrails of very young veal, considered a delicacy since they contain the mother's congealed milk.

As you go farther south, the food becomes hotter and spicier and the *dolci* (cakes and pastries) sweeter and richer. Don't miss the experience of eating a pizza in Napoli (where it was created), or the *melanzane parmigiana* (eggplant layered with a tomato sauce and mozzarella and baked), another classic Neapolitan dish. A favourite *dolce* in Napoli is *sfogliatelle*, layers of fine pastry with a ricotta filling.

The food of Puglia is simple and hearty, featuring a lot of vegetables. Try the *orecchiette* (pasta in the shape of 'little ears' with a sauce of sautéed green vegetables). Another popular local dish is made from puréed broad beans topped with chicory. The Pugliesi also eat a lot of seafood.

In Sicilia, try the *pesce spada* (swordfish, usually sliced into thick steaks and cooked

Pasta al Dente

Cooking good pasta according to the Italian way is no mean feat. First, the pasta has to be of the highest quality, second it has to be cooked for precisely the correct length of time, so that it is *al dente*, which means that it is firm. Italians almost always add salt to the boiling water before adding the pasta and they never throw in *(buttare)* the pasta until everyone who is going to eat is present. Don't complain if your pasta takes a while to arrive when you are in a restaurant – you'll need to wait the 10 to 12 minutes it takes to cook.

Farfalle

Fusilli

Gnocchi

Italian pasta is infinitely varied. It comes in a dazzling variety of shapes and sizes, ranging from spaghetti and linguine to tube pasta such as *penne* and rigatoni, shell-shaped *(conchiglie)*, bow-shaped *(farfalle*, which means butterflies), corkscrew-shaped *(fusilli)* and many others.

Packet, or dried pasta, is made with high-quality durum wheat and water. On the other hand, fresh egg pasta *(pasta all'uovo*, or *fatto a mano*) is made with eggs and flour and is used to make stuffed pasta such as tortellini and ravioli, or cut into strips called tagliatelle (thinner strips are also called *taglionini* or *tagliarini*).

Egg pasta is usually served with a richer, creamier sauces than those which usually accompany dried pasta and are most likely to be tomato based.

Sampling the great variety of pasta sauces you'll find in Italy can make eating a lot of fun during your trip, particularly if you are adventurous enough to try traditional local recipes in the various regions or towns you visit.

Pasta sauce ingredients traditionally vary quite dramatically between the north and south of the country. In the north, they are richer, often creamy and often use red meat (such as the delicious *ragù* of Bologna, known outside Italy as *bolognese)*, while, as you head farther south, they tend to use more vegetables and, on the coast, lots of seafood.

Ravioli

Rigatoni

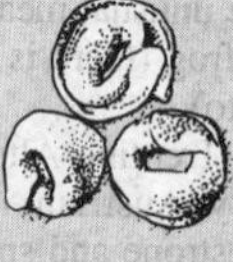

Tortellini

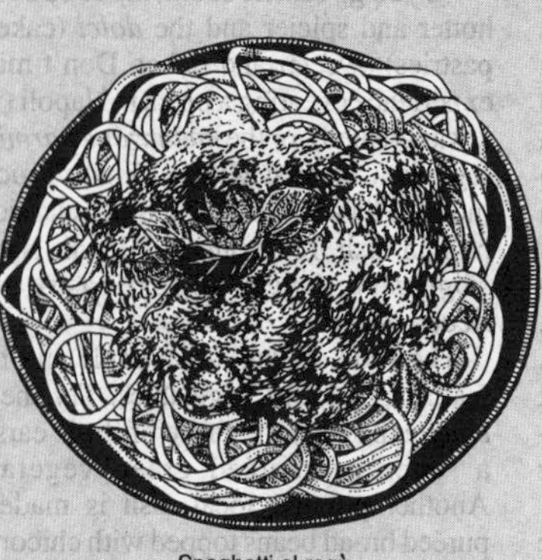

Spaghetti al ragù

In Puglia, for instance, a typical pasta dish is *orecchiette con cime di rapa*, ear-shaped pasta served with turnip tops which have been sautéed in oil with chilli and garlic. In Sicily, eggplant is a popular addition to tomato-based pasta sauces. See the section on Food for some other traditional pasta dishes.

Freshly grated cheese is the magic ingredient for most pasta. Parmesan *(parmigiano)* is the most widely used, particularly in the north. Look for the name 'Parmigiano Reggiano' on the rind to ensure you're getting the genuine parmesan because there is also the similar, but lower-quality *grana padano*. In Sardegna and around Roma there is a tendency to use the sharp *pecorino*, an aged sheep's cheese, while *ricotta salata* (salted ricotta), is widely used in the south and in Sicilia. ■

on an open grill). *Pasta con le sarde* (pasta with sardines) is popular in Palermo. Eggplant is popular in Sicilia, turning up in pasta or as *melanzane alla siciliana*, filled with olives, anchovies, capers and tomato.

The Sicilians are masters when it comes to their dolci. Don't leave the island without trying *cassata*, a rich sponge cake filled with a cream of ricotta cheese, liqueur and candied fruits. Another speciality is *cannoli*, tubes of sweet pastry filled with a rich cream, often made from a mixture of cream cheese, honey and almond paste with bits of candied fruit. Also try the assortment of *paste di mandorle* (almond pastries) and the *zabaione*, native to Marsala.

Another speciality is *marzapane* (marzipan), which Sicilian pastry chefs whip into every imaginable shape. Sicilian gelato is absolutely heavenly.

Sardegna's best known dish is *porcheddu*, baby pig roasted on a spit. Try also the *carte musica*, a thin, crisp bread eaten warm and sprinkled with salt and oil. *Pecorino sardo* is a sharp, aged sheep's cheese which the Sardi sprinkle on their pasta instead of parmigiano.

Where to Eat

Eateries are divided into several categories. A *tavola calda* (literally 'hot table') usually offers cheap, pre-prepared meat, pasta and vegetable dishes in a self-service style. A *rosticceria* usually offers cooked meats, but often has a larger selection of takeaway food. A *pizzeria* will of course serve pizza, but usually also a full menu. An *osteria* is likely to be either a wine bar offering a small selection of dishes, or a small *trattoria*. A trattoria is basically a cheaper version of a *ristorante* (restaurant), which in turn generally has a wider selection of dishes and a higher standard of service. The problem is that many of the establishments that are in fact restaurants call themselves trattorie and vice versa for reasons best known to themselves. It is best to check the menu, usually posted by the door, for prices.

Don't judge the quality of a ristorante or trattoria by its appearance. You are likely to eat your most memorable meal at a place with plastic tablecloths in a tiny back street, a dingy piazza or on a back road in the country.

And don't panic if you find yourself in a trattoria which has no printed menu: they are often the ones which offer the best and most authentic food and have menus which change daily to accommodate the availability of fresh produce. Just hope that the waiter will patiently explain the dishes and cost.

Most eating establishments have a cover charge, usually around L2000 to L3000, and a service charge of 10% to 15%. Restaurants usually open for lunch from 12.30 to 3 pm, but many are not keen to take orders after 2 pm. In the evening, opening hours vary from north to south. They eat dinner earlier in the north, usually from 7.30 pm, but in Sicilia you will be hard-pressed to find a restaurant open before 8.30 pm.

Numerous restaurants offer tourist menus, with an average price of L20,000 to L30,000 (usually not including drinks). Generally the food is of a reasonable standard, but choices will be limited and you can usually get away with paying less if you want only pasta, salad and wine.

After lunch and dinner, head for the nearest *gelateria* (ice-cream parlour) to round off the meal with some excellent *gelati*, followed by a *digestivo* (digestive liqueur) at a bar.

For a light lunch, or a snack, most bars serve *panini* (rolls), and there are numerous outlets where you can buy pizza by the slice *(a taglio)*. Another option is to go to one of the many alimentari and ask them to make a panino with the filling of your choice. At a *pasticceria* you can buy pastries, cakes and biscuits.

Fast food is becoming increasingly popular in Italy. There are McDonald's outlets throughout the country as well as numerous other chain restaurants and US-style hamburger joints.

Eating Customs

Italians rarely eat a sit-down breakfast *(colazione)*. They tend to drink a cappuccino, usually *tiepido* (warm), and eat a croissant (*cornetto*) or other type of pastry while standing at a bar.

Lunch *(pranzo)* is traditionally the main meal of the day and many shops and businesses close for three to four hours every afternoon to accommodate the meal and siesta which is supposed to follow.

A full meal will consist of *antipasto*, which can vary from *bruschetta*, a type of garlic bread with various toppings, to fried vegetables, or *prosciutto e melone* (cured ham wrapped around melon). Next comes the *primo piatto*, a pasta or risotto, followed by the *secondo piatto* of meat or fish. Italians often then eat an *insalata* (salad) or *contorno* (vegetable side-dish), and round off the meal with fruit (occasionally with a sweet) and *caffè*, often at a bar on the way back to work.

The evening meal *(cena)* was traditionally a simpler affair, but habits are changing because of the inconvenience of travelling home for lunch every day.

Vegetarian Food

Vegetarians will have no problems eating in Italy. While there are very few restaurants devoted to them, vegetables are a staple of the Italian diet. Most eating establishments serve a good selection of *antipasti* and *contorni* (vegetables prepared in a variety of ways), and the farther south you go, the more excellent vegetable dishes you will find. Vegetarian restaurants and grocery shops are listed throughout this book.

Stand or Sit?

Remember that as soon as you sit down in Italy, prices go up considerably, since you have to pay for the service. A cappuccino at the bar will cost around L1200 to L1500, but if you sit down you will pay anything from L2500 to L8000 and more than L12,000 in Piazza San Marco in Venezia. Italians rarely sit down in bars and, consequently, many bars do not even have seating. In some bars, where it is obvious that no-one is serving the tables, you can sometimes sit down without paying extra. ■

Self-Catering

If you have access to cooking facilities, it is best to buy fruit and vegetables at open markets, and salami, cheese and wine at alimentari or *salumerie*, which are a cross between grocery stores and delicatessens. Fresh bread is available at a *forno* or *panetteria* (bakeries which sell bread, pastries and sometimes groceries) and usually at alimentari. There are also supermarkets in most towns and they are listed throughout this book.

Food Glossary

This glossary is intended as a brief guide to some of the basics and by no means covers all of the dishes you are likely to encounter in Italy. Names and ingredients of dishes often vary from region to region, and even pizza toppings can change. Most travellers to Italy will already be well acquainted with the various Italian pastas, which include spaghetti, fettucine, penne, rigatoni, gnocchi, lasagne, tortellini and ravioli. The names are the same in Italy and no further definitions are given here.

Useful Words

bill/cheque	*il conto*
boiled	*bollito*
cooked	*cotto*
cooked over hot coals	*alla brace*
firm (as all good pasta should be)	*al dente*

fried	*fritto*
grilled	*alla griglia*
knife/fork/spoon/teaspoon	*coltello/forchetta/cucchiaio/cucchiaino*
menu	*menù*
plate	*piatto*
raw	*crudo*
restaurant	*ristorante*
roasted	*arrosto*
smoked	*affumicato*
waiter/waitress	*cameriere/a*
well done (cooked)	*ben cotto*

Staples

bread	*pane*
butter	*burro*
cheese	*formaggio*
chilli	*peperoncino*
cooked cornmeal	*polenta*
cream	*panna*
egg/eggs	*uovo/uova*
honey	*miele*
jam	*marmellata*
lemon	*limone*
oil	*olio*
olives	*olive*
pepper	*pepe*
rice	*riso*
rice cooked with wine and stock	*risotto*
salt	*sale*
sugar	*zucchero*
vinegar	*aceto*
wholemeal bread	*pane integrale*

Meat & Fish

anchovies	*acciughe*
beef	*manzo*
chicken	*pollo*
clams	*vongole*
cod	*merluzzo*
crab	*granchio*
cutlet or thin cut of meat, usually crumbed and fried	*cotoletta*
dentex (type of fish)	*dentice*
lamb	*agnello* or *abacchio*
liver	*fegato*
lobster	*aragosta*
mackerel	*sgombro*
mussels	*cozze*
octopus	*polpo*
oysters	*ostriche*
prawns	*gamberi*
rabbit	*coniglio*
sardines	*sarde*
sausage	*salsiccia*
sole	*sogliola*
squid	*calamari*
steak	*bistecca*
swordfish	*pesce spada*
tripe	*trippa*
tuna	*tonno*
turkey	*tacchino*
veal	*vitello*

Vegetables

artichokes	*carciofi*
asparagus	*asparagi*
cabbage	*verza, cavolo*
carrots	*carote*
chicory	*cicoria*
eggplant	*melanzane*
onion	*cipolla*
peas	*piselli*
peppers	*peperoni*
potatoes	*patate*
spinach	*spinaci*
string beans	*fagiolini*

Fruit

apples	*mele*
bananas	*banane*
cherries	*ciliegie*
grapes	*uva*
oranges	*arance*
peaches	*pesche*
pears	*pere*
strawberries	*fragole*

Soups & Antipasti

brodo	broth
carpaccio	very fine slices of raw meat
insalata caprese	sliced tomatoes with mozzarella and basil
insalata di mare	seafood, generally crustaceans
minestrina in brodo	pasta in broth

minestrone	vegetable soup
olive ascolane	stuffed, deep-fried olives
prosciutto e melone	cured ham with melon
ripieni	stuffed, oven-baked vegetables
stracciatella	egg in broth

Pasta Sauces

al ragù	meat sauce (bolognese)
arrabbiata	tomato and chilli
carbonara	egg, bacon and black pepper
alla matriciana	tomato and bacon
napoletana	tomato and basil
panna	cream, prosciutto and sometimes peas
pesto	basil, garlic and oil, often with pine nuts
vongole	clams, garlic and oil, sometimes with tomato

Pizzas

All pizzas listed have a tomato and sometimes mozzarella base.

capricciosa	olives, prosciutto, mushrooms, artichokes
frutti di mare	seafood
funghi	mushrooms
margherita	oregano
napoletana	anchovies
pugliese	tomato, mozzarella and onions
quattro formaggi	with four types of cheese
quattro stagioni	the same as a capricciosa, but sometimes with egg
verdura	mixed vegetables (usually zucchini, eggplant and sometimes carrot and spinach)

DRINKS

Nonalcoholic Drinks

Coffee The first-time visitor to Italy is likely to be confused by the many ways in which the locals consume their caffeine. The boxed aside on Caffè Society is a basic guide, although there can be variations from north to south.

Tea Italians don't drink a lot of tea *(tè)* and generally only in the late afternoon, when they might take a cup with a few *pasticcini* (small cakes). You can order tea in bars, although it will usually arrive in the form of a cup of warm water with an accompanying tea bag. If this doesn't suit your taste, ask for the water *molto caldo* or *bollente* (boiling). Good-quality packaged teas, such as Twinings tea bags and leaves, as well as packaged herbal teas, such as camomile, are often sold in alimentari and some bars. You can find a wide range of herbal teas in a herbalist's shop *(erboristeria)*, which sometimes also stocks health foods.

Granita *Granita* is a drink made of crushed ice with fresh lemon or other fruit juices, or with coffee topped with fresh whipped cream.

Water While tap water is reliable throughout the country, most Italians prefer to drink bottled mineral water *(acqua minerale)*. It will be either sparkling *(frizzante)* or still *(naturale)* and you will be asked in restaurants and bars which you would prefer. If you want a glass of tap water, ask for *acqua dal rubinetto*, although simply asking for *acqua naturale* will also suffice.

Alcoholic Drinks

Wine & Spirits Wine *(vino)* is an essential accompaniment to any meal, and *digestivi* are a popular way to end one. Italians are very proud of their wines and find it hard to believe that anyone else in the world could produce wines as good as theirs. Many Italians drink alcohol only with meals and the

Caffè Society

An *espresso* is a small amount of very strong black coffee. You can ask for a *doppio espresso*, which means double the amount, or a *caffè lungo* (although this can sometimes mean a slightly diluted espresso). If you want a long black coffee (as in a weaker, watered-down version), ask for a *caffè Americano*. If you are in an isolated village in Sardegna where they have no name for diluted coffee, try asking for an *espresso con molta acqua calda* (coffee with a lot of hot water). A *corretto* is an espresso with a dash of grappa or some other spirit and a *macchiato* is espresso with a small amount of milk – on the other hand, *latte macchiato* is milk with a spot of coffee. *Caffè freddo* is a long glass of cold black coffee.

Then, of course, there is the *cappuccino*, coffee with hot, frothy milk – if you want it without the froth, ask for a *caffè latte* or a cappuccino *senza schiuma*. Italians tend to drink cappuccino only with breakfast and during the morning. They never drink it after meals or in the evening and, if you order one after dinner, don't be surprised if the waiter asks you two or three times, just to make sure that he or she heard correctly. You will also find it difficult to convince bartenders to make your cappuccino hot, rather than lukewarm. Ask for it *molto caldo* and wait for the same 'tut-tut' response that you attracted when you ordered a cappuccino after dinner. ■

foreign custom of going out for a drink is still considered unusual although, in some parts of Italy, it is common to see men starting their day with a grappa for breakfast and continuing to consume strong drinks throughout the day.

Wine is reasonably priced and you will rarely pay more than L15,000 for a good bottle of wine, although prices range up to more than L30,000 for really good quality. There are three main classifications of wine – *DOCG; (denominazione d'origine controllata e garantita)*, *DOC; (denominazione di origine controllata)* and *vino da tavola* (table wine) – which will be marked on the label. A DOC wine is produced subject to certain specifications, although the label does not certify quality. DOCG is subject to the same requirements as normal DOC but it is also tested by government inspectors. While there are table wines better left alone, there are also many which are of excellent quality, notably the Sicilian Corvo red and white.

Although some excellent wines are produced in Italy, most trattorie stock only a limited selection of bottled wines and generally only cheaper varieties. Most people tend to order the house wine *(vino della casa)* or the local wine *(vino locale)* when they go out to dinner.

The styles of wine vary throughout the country, so make a point of sampling the local produce in your travels. Try the many varieties of the famous Chianti wines produced in Toscana, as well as the white Vernaccia of San Gimignano and the excellent Brunello di Montalcino and Vin Nobile of Montepulciano; the Soave in Verona and Valpolicella around Venezia. Piemonte and Trentino-Alto Adige both produce excellent wines, notably the Barolo in Piemonte. The wines of Orvieto in Umbria are good. In Roma try the local Frascati and other wines of the Castelli Romani. Sicilia is the home of Marsala.

Before dinner, Italians might drink a Campari and soda, or a fruit cocktail, usually pre-prepared and often without alcohol *(analcolico)*. After dinner try a shot of grappa, a very strong, clear brew made from grapes, or an *amaro*, a dark liqueur prepared from herbs. If you prefer a sweeter liqueur, try an almond-flavoured *amaretto* or the sweet aniseed *sambuca*. On the Amalfi coast and the islands of the Golfo di Napoli the fragrant local lemons are used to produce *limoncello*.

Beer The main local labels are Peroni, Dreher and Moretti, all very drinkable and cheaper than the imported varieties. If you want a local beer, ask for a *birra nazionale*, which will be either in a bottle or on tap. Italy also imports beers from throughout Europe and the rest of the world. All the main German beers are, for instance, available in bottles or cans; English beers and Guinness are often found on tap *(alla spina)* in *birrerie* (bars specialising in beer), and Australians might be pleased to know that you can even find a Foster's and a Castlemaine XXXX. There has lately been a proliferation of pubs which specialise in beers from all around the world.

ENTERTAINMENT

Cinemas

There is no shortage of cinemas in Italy, but quite a dearth of original language ones. Even in a city like Milano only three cinemas show subtitled original language movies, and then only once a week. The dubbing industry has a justifiably proud reputation in Italy, but that doesn't help foreigners who don't want to hear John Cleese spout Italian. The only other option in larger cities is the foreign cultural centres, which often put on film cycles. It costs around L12,000 to see a movie.

Discos

Discos are expensive – entrance charges range from around L30,000 to up to L100,000 for hotspots in places such as Rimini during summer. This usually covers the cost of the first drink, although after that you will pay up to L6000 just for a glass of wine. They are usually enormous, with big dance floors and the music is the usual Top 40 fare. There are gay and lesbian discos and nightclubs in most cities.

Nightclubs

These places are usually smaller, smokier, more crowded, and with less dancing space than discos. They are also more likely to play alternative music and attract an older, 'hipper' crowd. The entrance fee varies from free to around L20,000.

Opera

There are opera seasons in the major cities, including Roma, Milano (although La Scala will be closed for renovations for a few years) and Bologna. In summer, there are special seasons at the Arena in Verona and in Piazza Siena in Roma. An opera is also usually performed as part of the Festival of Two Worlds at Spoleto in June and July. A ticket to the opera costs from L50,000 to more than L100,000 for the best seats.

Theatre

If you can understand Italian, you'll have plenty of options in all of the major cities. Performances in languages other than Italian are hard to come by, although in Roma the Agora has an international season. Tourist offices should be able to help out with information. In summer, there are performances of Greek theatre in Sicilia at Siracusa (biannually), Taormina, Segesta and Palazzolo Acreide. A ticket costs from L30,000 upwards.

Classical Music

The main concert seasons are usually during the winter months, although there are always plenty of classical music concerts included in major summer entertainment festivals, such as Roma's Estate Romana.

Rock

The world's major performers are constantly passing through Italy. Keep an eye on local newspapers if it is important that you don't miss any of them. Major venues and how to book tickets are listed under the major cities throughout the book.

Jazz

Italians love jazz and some of the numerous jazz venues in major cities are listed throughout the book. The country's premium jazz festival is Umbria Jazz, held in Perugia in July and Orvieto in December/January.

Pubs & Bars

The Italian version of an Irish pub has taken off in a big way. Basically places where you can get Guinness on tap or select from a big range of international beers, they are becoming more numerous by the month in major cities such as Roma, Firenze and Milano. Some pubs, in particular those where you are likely to meet up with other young foreigners, are listed under the major cities in this book.

SPECTATOR SPORT

Football

Il calcio excites Italian souls more than politics, religion, good food and dressing up all put together. Football (soccer) is one of the great forces in Italian life, so if you can get to one of the big games you'll be in for a treat. Spirits run wild and at times overflow, as when Fiorentina fans stoned the Juventus players' bus as it arrived in Firenze for a match in February 1997. Generally, Italian crowds have not yet plumbed the depths reached by the worst of the UK's football hooligans, but violence is definitely a problem.

Eighteen teams tough out the Italian football honours in Serie A (the top division). Serie B teams consist of a further 20 teams, while another 90 teams dispute the medals at Serie C level, itself split up into several more manageable sub-competitions.

Predictably enough, Serie A is dominated by an elite group of teams *(squadre)* that generally take honours. Among the championship teams, well known to football fans beyond Italy too, are Juventus (based in Torino), Inter Milano and AC Milan, Sampdoria (based in Genova) and Napoli.

Of course, not everyone can be champ all the time. At the close of the 1996-97 season it could be said that Napoli and AC Milan in particular had not made their fans terribly happy. The former has not quite been the same since the days when Argentina's Diego Maradona injected an extra spark into an already gifted team's game. Berlusconi was at a loss to explain the miserable performance of AC Milan, which finished well down the table.

Juventus and Sampdoria, both traditionally strong, were the teams to watch in 1996-97. Although the former maintained its lead in the table for much of the season, it has the unfortunate tendency of winning in low-scoring games and, on occasion, coming away with a draw because of some late-game slackness after dominating pretty much the entire match. That alone kept fans *(tifosi)* guessing about who would come out on top of the table until much later in the season than might otherwise have been the case.

Whatever the form or place on the ladder of the various teams, some local derbies make for particularly hot clashes – for instance when AC Milan and rivals Inter come face to face, or when Roma takes on Lazio. Both are traditionally sell-out excuses for a little sporting lunacy – with tifosi even more vociferous than usual. Tickets for games start at around L20,000 and can rise to L100,000. They are best purchased through specific ticketing agencies, some of which are listed in this guide; if not listed, the local tourist office can tell you where to find them.

Italy is one of the world's leading football nations and has won the World Cup three times.

Motor Racing

The Italian Formula One Grand Prix races are held at the Monza autodrome, just north of Milano, each September. The San Marino Grand Prix (to all intents and purposes, if not technically, an Italian race) is held at the five-km Imola circuit in May. Ayrton Senna lost his life during this race in 1994.

Italy is one of the homes of prestige motor racing. Monza has been a venue since 1922, and Italy has provided some of the world's greatest driving machines. Ferrari, more than any other manufacturer, continues to dominate the Grand Prix in the popular imagination, even if it has not been in the winner's circle so often in recent years. Alfa Romeo has also been up there and, for a while back in the 50s, Maserati was on top, until the company ran into difficulties in 1958. Maserati has continued to contribute motors, as have Lamborghini and Lancia. Bugatti also surfaced briefly in the 50s, but never took line honours. Ferrari's main competitors continue to be the Williams, Benetton and McLaren outfits. Few of the top name drivers nowadays are Italians, and patriotism plays little role in deciding who drives for which team – Ferrari's 1997 drivers were Germany's Michael Schumacher and the UK's Eddie Irvine.

Every few years the administrators of the circuit have to do battle with Monza town authorities to renew the rent agreement. They did so in 1997, guaranteeing the Monza track as the exclusive site for Formula One racing into the next millennium.

Next to the present track is the crumbling reminder of more dangerous days: a circuit with slopes at such a steep gradient and scene of enough accidents to convince all concerned it should be closed – it was last used in 1969. This crumbling dinosaur has long been slated for demolition but as yet remains an intact, if overgrown, curio for bicycleiders doing more relaxed circuits of the adjacent Parco di Monza.

The classic Italian race was the long distance Mille Miglia, run annually (interrupted by WW II) from 1927 to 1957. Nowadays it's still held as a nostalgic competition in which vintage racing cars career 1000 miles around Italy from Brescia to Roma and back again.

Tickets for the Monza Grand Prix go on sale months in advance and cost up to L400,000 for a good seat in the grandstand; a spot on the grass costs L75,000. For information on where to obtain tickets, call the autodrome direct in Monza on ☎ 039-2 48 21, or a FIA Formula One Grand Prix racing organisation in your country.

Cycling

Second only to the Tour de France, the Giro d'Italia is *the* event on the summer cycling calendar. Little wonder, since Italy has a long record of producing world-class riders.

The race was first held in 1909 and has been staged every year since, interrupted predictably enough by the two world wars. Initially a mostly Italian affair, it is perhaps not surprising that the 1909 winner, Luigi Ganna, was followed by a long succession of Italian victors. Only in 1950 did a non-Italian finally break the home side's long winning streak, when the Swiss Hugo Koblet took the finishing line honours. In total, the Giro has been won by non-Italians 24 times, and by Italian riders 55 times. The latest Italian winner was Ivan Gotti in 1997.

This event is one of the few things in life that are free: if you want to watch, find out when the race is passing a location convenient to you and wait for the cyclists – it's as simple as that.

Skiing

Most people would probably rather do it than watch it, but skiing is something of a prestige spectator sport in Italy. Maybe that has something to do with the fact that Italy has some stars who are particularly good at it. The brash Alberto Tomba (*Tomba la bomba!* – 'the bomb is falling!') has for the past decade been one of the world's most popular skiers, despite (or because of) off-piste antics. Tomba has won Olympic gold medals as well as the World Cup. Another world beater from Italy is Deborah Compagnoni who, at the 1997 world championships in Sestriere, won two gold medals, taking her career total to five. The latest star to emerge from Italy's ranks in those championships was Isolde Kostner – another gold winner. Meanwhile, Albertissimo was already considering moving into the more comfortable world of film and sports commentary ... and training new stars. Several Italian ski fields host annual World Cup competitions. It doesn't cost anything to watch – just a fortune to find accommodation!

THINGS TO BUY

Shopping in Italy is probably not what you are used to back home. The vast proportion of shops are small businesses, and large department stores and supermarkets tend to be very thin on the ground. If you need necessities such as underwear, pantyhose, pyjamas, T-shirts, toiletries, etc, head for one of the large retail stores, such as Standa, Upim, Oviesse or Rinascente. Otherwise, you can pick up underwear, pantyhose and pyjamas in a haberdashery *(merceria)*, toiletries and condoms in a pharmacy *(farmacia)* or sometimes in an alimentari, and items such as T-shirts in a normal clothing store. Supermarkets also stock toiletries and condoms. Hardware items can be purchased at a *ferramenta*, and air-mail paper, note pads, pens, greeting cards etc at a paper-goods shop *(cartoleria)*.

Clothing

Italy is synonymous with elegant, fashionable and high-quality clothing. The problem is that most of the better quality clothes are very expensive. However, if you can manage to be in the country during the summer sales in July and August and the winter sales in December and January, you can pick up incredible bargains. By mid-sale, prices are often slashed by up to 60% and 70%. Generally speaking, Roma, Firenze and Milano have the greatest variety of clothing, shoes and accessories. Main shopping areas are detailed under the relevant cities throughout this book. Fashions tend to be conservative and middle-of-the-range, and cheaper clothing can be downright boring for English, US and Australian travellers accustomed to a wide variety of styles and tastes.

The same applies to shoes. Expect to pay dearly (although still considerably less than at home) for the best quality at shops such as Beltrami and Pollini. Again, prices drop dramatically during the sales, but expect to have some difficulty finding shoes to fit if you take a larger size.

Italy is particularly noted for the quality of its leather goods, so plan to stock up on bags, wallets, purses, belts and gloves. At markets such as Porta Portese in Roma you can find some incredible second-hand bargains. The San Lorenzo leather market in Firenze has a vast array of leather goods, including jackets, bags, wallets and belts, although the variety can be limited, and you should check carefully for quality before buying.

Glassware & Ceramics

Some might call the famous and expensive Venetian glass grotesque – and it is certainly an acquired taste. Shops all over Venezia are full of it and if you listen to the claims of the shop assistants, most of it (except for the glass in *their* shop) is not the real thing. If you want to buy Venetian glass, shop around and compare prices and quality. The merchandise at the larger factories is generally not cheaper, but you can be sure it is authentic. And remember you will probably have to pay customs duty on your purchase when you arrive home. For more information see the Things to Buy information in the Venezi section of the Veneto chapter.

Ceramics and pottery are less costly an more rustic. There is a great diversity o traditional styles throughout Italy, associate with villages or areas, where designs hav been handed down over the centuries. Majo centres include: Deruta, near Perugia i Umbria; Faenza, in Emilia-Romagna; Viet sul Mare, near Salerno at the start of th Amalfi coast; and Grottaglie, near Taranto i Puglia. Sicilian pottery is particularly inter esting. Caltagirone and Santo Stefano d Camastra are two important ceramic produc ing towns.

Souvenirs & Handcrafts

The beautiful Florentine paper goods, wit their delicate flower design, and Venetiar paper goods, with a marbled design, are reasonably priced and make wonderful gifts Specialist shops are dotted around both Firenze and Venezia, although it is possible to buy these paper goods in cartolerie throughout the country.

Popular jewellery tends to be chunky and cheap-looking, but if they can afford it, Italians love to wear gold. The best known haunt for tourists wanting to buy gold in Italy is the Ponte Vecchio in Firenze, lined with tiny shops full of both modern and antique jewellery. Jewellery and ornaments carved from coral can be found at Torre del Greco just out of Napoli, and on the west coast of Sardegna, although overharvesting and pollution threaten this once thriving industry.

Local handcrafts include lace and embroidery, notably on the Isola Maggiore in Lago di Trasimeno, Umbria, and the woodcarvings of the Val Gardena in Trentino-Alto Adige.

Getting There & Away

If you live outside Europe, flying is the easiest way to get to Italy. Competition between the airlines means you should be able to pick up a reasonably priced fare, even if you are coming from as far away as Australia. If you live in Europe, chances are you'll be going to Italy overland, but don't ignore the flight option, as you can often find enticing deals from major European hubs.

AIR

Always reconfirm your onward or return bookings by the specified time – at least 72 hours before departure on international flights. Otherwise you risk turning up at the airport only to find you've missed your flight because it was rescheduled, or that you've been classified as a 'no show'.

Airports & Airlines

Italy's main international gateway is Roma's Leonardo da Vinci (Fiumicino) airport, but regular international flights also serve Milano's Malpensa and Linate airports. Plenty of flights from other European cities are available direct to most regional capitals.

The country's national airline is Alitalia, but many international airlines (including most European ones) also serve Italy.

Buying Tickets

The plane ticket will probably be the single most expensive item in your budget, and buying it can be intimidating. Start early: some of the cheapest tickets have to be bought months in advance, and some popular flights sell out quickly. Talk to recent travellers and look at ads in newspapers, magazines (including the Italian press in your home country), on TV teletext services and, where possible, the Internet. Always watch for special offers. Then telephone travel agents for bargains. Check out the fare, the route, the duration of the journey and any restrictions on the ticket.

Official cheap tickets include advance-purchase tickets, budget fares, Apex and super-Apex and so on. Unofficial discount tickets are released by the airlines through selected travel agents and it is worth shopping around to find them. Sometimes the discount special deals have bonuses attached, such as a free flight within Europe, free accommodation for the first few nights, or a free stopover. Discounted tickets are available only from travel agents. Airlines can provide information on routes and timetables, and their low-season, student and senior citizens' fares can be competitive.

Return tickets usually work out much cheaper than two one-way tickets (Italy is not the place to buy your ticket home because cheap tickets, particularly one-way, can be difficult to find). If Italy is only one stop on your grand world tour, consider buying a Round-the-World (RTW) ticket. (see the Air Travel Glossary for details.) Prices start at about UK£900, A$1800 or US$1300, depending on the season. RTWs can get a bit complicated, so ensure that your travel agent has made your bookings correctly and filled you in on all of the ticket's restrictions and conditions.

If you are travelling to Italy from the USA or South-East Asia, or you have decided to fly home from London in the hope of finding a cheaper fare there, you will probably find that the cheapest flights are being advertised by obscure agencies whose names haven't yet reached the telephone directory. Many such firms are honest and solvent, but a few rogues will take your money and disappear, only to reopen elsewhere a month or two later under a new name. If you feel suspicious about a firm, don't give them all the money at once – leave a deposit of 20% or so and pay the balance when you get the ticket. If they insist on cash in advance, go somewhere else. Once you have the ticket, ring the airline to confirm that you are actually booked on the flight.

Many travellers prefer to pay more than

Air Travel Glossary

Apex Tickets Apex stands for Advance Purchase Excursion fare. These tickets are usually between 30 and 40% cheaper than the full economy fare, but there are restrictions. You must purchase the ticket at least 21 days in advance and must be away for a minimum period and return within a maximum period. Stopovers are not allowed and, if you have to change your dates of travel or destination, there will be extra charges to pay. These tickets are not fully refundable – if you have to cancel your trip, the refund is often considerably less than what you paid for the ticket. Make sure you take out travel insurance to cover yourself in case you have to cancel your trip unexpectedly – for example, due to illness.

Baggage Allowance This will be written on your ticket; you are usually allowed one 20kg item, plus one item of hand luggage. Some airlines which fly transpacific and transatlantic routes allow for two pieces of luggage (there are limits on their dimensions and weight).

Bucket Shops At certain times of the year and/or on certain routes, many airlines fly with empty seats. This isn't profitable and it's more cost-effective for them to fly full, even if that means having to sell a certain number of drastically discounted tickets. They do this by off-loading them onto bucket shops (UK) or consolidators (USA), travel agents which specialise in discounted fares. The agents, in turn, sell them to the public at reduced prices. These tickets are often the cheapest you'll find, but you can't purchase them directly from the airlines. Availability varies widely, so you'll not only have to be flexible in your travel plans, you'll also have to be quick off the mark as soon as an advertisement appears in the press.

Bucket-shop agents advertise in newspapers and magazines and there's a lot of competition so it's a good idea to telephone first.

Bumped Just because you have a confirmed seat doesn't mean you're going to get on the plane – see Overbooking.

Cancellation Penalties If you have to cancel or change an Apex or other discount ticket, there may be heavy penalties; insurance can sometimes be taken out against these penalties. Some airlines impose penalties on regular tickets as well, particularly against 'no show' passengers.

Check In Airlines ask you to check in a certain time ahead of the flight departure (usually two hours on international flights). If you fail to check in on time and the flight is overbooked, the airline can cancel your booking and give your seat to somebody else.

Confirmation Having a ticket written out with the flight and date on it doesn't mean you have a seat until the agent has confirmed with the airline that your status is 'OK'. Prior to this confirmation, your status is 'on request'.

Courier Fares Businesses often need to send their urgent documents or freight securely and quickly. They do it through courier companies. These companies hire people to accompany the package through customs and, in return, offer a discount ticket which is sometimes a phenomenal bargain. In effect, what the courier companies do is ship their freight as your luggage on the regular commercial flights. This is a legitimate operation – all freight is completely legal. There are two shortcomings, however: the short turnaround time of the ticket, usually not longer than a month; and the limitation on your luggage allowance.

Discounted Tickets There are two types of discounted fares – officially discounted (such as Apex – see Promotional Fares) and unofficially discounted (see Bucket Shops). The latter can save you more than money – you may be able to pay Apex prices without the associated Apex advance booking and other requirements. The lowest prices often impose drawbacks, such as flying with unpopular airlines, inconvenient schedules, or unpleasant routes and connections.

Economy Class Tickets Economy-class tickets are usually not the cheapest way to go, though they do give you maximum flexibility and they are valid for 12 months. If you don't use them, most are fully refundable, as are unused sectors of a multiple ticket.

Full Fares Airlines traditionally offer first class (coded F), business class (coded J) and economy class (coded Y) tickets. These days there are so many promotional and discounted fares available that few passengers pay full fare.

Lost Tickets If you lose your airline ticket, an airline will usually treat it like a travellers' cheque and, after inquiries, issue you with a replacement. Legally, however, an airline is entitled to treat it like cash, so if you lose a ticket, it could be forever. Take good care of your tickets.

MCO An MCO (Miscellaneous Charges Order) is a voucher for a value of a given amount, which resembles an airline ticket, and can be used to pay for a specific flight with any IATA (International Air Transport Association) airline. MCOs, which are more flexible than a regular ticket, may satisfy the irritating onward ticket requirement, but some countries are now reluctant to accept them. MCOs are fully refundable if unused.

No Shows No shows are passengers who fail to show up for their flight. Full-fare no shows are sometimes entitled to travel on a later flight.

Open Jaw Tickets These are return tickets which allow you to fly to one place but return from another and to travel between the two 'jaws' by any means of transport, at your own expense. If available, this can save you backtracking to your arrival point.

Overbooking Airlines hate to fly with empty seats and, since every flight has some passengers who fail to show up, they often book more passengers than they have seats available. Usually the excess passengers balance those who fail to show up, but occasionally somebody gets bumped. If this happens, guess who it is most likely to be? The passengers who check in late.

Promotional Fares These are officially discounted fares, such as Apex fares, which are available from travel agents or direct from the airline.

Reconfirmation You must contact the airline at least 72 hours prior to departure to 'reconfirm' that you intend to be on the flight. If you don't do this, the airline can delete your name from the passenger list and you could lose your seat.

Restrictions Discounted tickets often have various restrictions on them, such as necessity of advance purchase, limitations on the minimum and maximum period you must be away, restrictions on breaking the journey or changing the booking or route etc.

Round-the-World Tickets These tickets have become very popular in the last few years; basically, there are two types – airline tickets and agent tickets. An airline RTW ticket is issued by two or more airlines that have joined together to market a ticket which takes you around the world on their combined routes. It permits you to fly pretty well anywhere you choose, using their combined routes, as long as you don't backtrack, ie keep moving in approximately the same direction east or west. Other restrictions are that you (usually) must book the first sector in advance and cancellation penalties then apply. There may be restrictions on how many stopovers you are permitted. The RTW tickets are usually valid for 90 days to up to a year.

The other type of RTW ticket, the agent ticket, is a combination of cheap fares strung together by an enterprising travel agent. These may be cheaper than airline RTW tickets, but the choice of routes will be limited.

Stand-by This is a discounted ticket where you only fly if there is a seat free at the last moment. Stand-by fares are usually only available directly at the airport but sometimes they may also be handled by an airline's city office. To give yourself the best possible chance of getting on the flight you want, get there early and have your name placed on the waiting list. It's first come, first served.

Student Discounts Some airlines offer student-card holders 15% to 25% discounts on their tickets. The same often applies to anyone under the age of 26. These discounts are generally only available on ordinary, economy-class fares.

Tickets Out An entry requirement for many countries is that you have an onward or return ticket, in other words, a ticket out of the country. If you're not sure what you intend to do next, the easiest solution is to buy the cheapest onward ticket to a neighbouring country or a ticket from a reliable airline which can later be refunded if you do not use it.

Transferred Tickets Airline tickets cannot be transferred from one person to another. Travellers sometimes try to sell the return half of their ticket, but officials can ask you to prove that you are the person named on the ticket. This may not be checked on domestic flights, but on international flights, tickets are usually compared with passports.

Travel Periods Some officially discounted fares, Apex fares in particular, vary with the time of year. There is often a low (off-peak) season and a high (peak) season. Sometimes there's an intermediate or shoulder season as well. At peak times, when everyone wants to fly, both officially and unofficially discounted fares will be higher, or there may simply be no discounted tickets available. Usually the fare depends on your outward flight – if you depart in the high season and return in the low season, you pay the high-season fare.

the rock-bottom fare in order to fly with a major airline, or to avoid 'milk-run' flights with several stopovers before they land in Roma. However, few travellers want to pay full airline fares, and there are numerous better-known travel agents offering bargain fares. Firms such as STA Travel, which has offices worldwide, Council Travel in the USA, Travel CUTS in Canada, and Flight Centres International in Australia, are not going to disappear overnight, leaving you clutching a receipt for a nonexistent ticket.

Use the fares quoted in this book as a guide only. They are approximate and based on the rates advertised by travel agents at the time of writing and are likely to have changed by the time you read this.

Travellers with Special Needs

If you have a broken leg, are a vegetarian or require a special diet (such as kosher food), or you are travelling in a wheelchair, taking a baby or your dog, terrified of flying or have some other special need, let the airline know as soon as possible so that they can make arrangements accordingly. You should remind them when you reconfirm your booking (at least 72 hours before departure) and again when you check in at the airport. It may also be worth ringing round the airlines before you make your booking to find out how they can handle your particular needs. Some airlines publish brochures on the subject. Ask your travel agent for details.

Guide dogs for the blind will often have to travel in a specially pressurised baggage compartment, away from their owner. They will be subject to the same quarantine laws (six months in isolation etc) as any other animal when entering or returning to countries currently free of rabies, such as Britain or Australia.

Deaf travellers can ask for airport and in-flight announcements to be written down for them.

Children aged under two travel for 10% of the standard fare (or free on some airlines), as long as they don't occupy a seat. They don't get a baggage allowance either. 'Skycots', baby food and nappies (diapers) should be provided by the airline if requested in advance. Children aged between two and 12 can usually occupy a seat for half to two-thirds of the full fare and do get a baggage allowance. Pushchairs (strollers) can often be carried as hand luggage.

The USA

The North Atlantic is the world's busiest long-haul air corridor and the flight options are bewildering. Several airlines fly direct to Italy, landing at either Roma or Milano. These include Alitalia, TWA and Delta. However, if your trip will not be confined to Italy, consult your travel agent on whether cheaper flights are available to other European cities.

The *New York Times*, the *LA Times*, the *Chicago Tribune* and the *San Francisco Examiner* produce weekly travel sections in which you'll find any number of travel agents' ads. Council Travel and STA Travel have offices in major cities nationwide. The magazine *Travel Unlimited* (PO Box 1058, Allston, MA 02134) publishes details of cheap air fares.

Standard fares on commercial airlines are expensive and probably best avoided. However, travelling on a normal scheduled flight can be more secure and reliable, particularly for older travellers and families, who might prefer to avoid the potential inconveniences of the budget alternatives.

Discount and rock-bottom options from the USA include charter flights, stand-by and courier flights. Stand-by fares are often sold at 60% of the normal price for one-way tickets. Airhitch (☎ (212) 864-2000; email airhitch@netcom.com), 2641 Broadway, New York, NY 10025, specialises in this sort of thing. You will need to give a general idea of where and when you need to go, and a few days before your departure you will be presented with a choice of two or three flights. They have several other offices in the USA, including Los Angeles (☎ (310) 726-5000), as well as others in London, Paris, Amsterdam, Prague, Madrid and Bonn. You can contact their Roma representative on ☎ 06-77 20 86 55.

Courier flights are where you accompany freight or a parcel to its destination. A New York-Roma return on a courier flight can cost about US$300 to US$400 in the low season (more expensive from the US west coast). Generally courier flights require that you return within a specified period (sometimes within one or two weeks, but often up to one month). You will need to travel light, as luggage is usually restricted to what you can carry on to the plane (the parcel or freight you carry comes out of your luggage allowance), and you may have to be a US resident and apply for an interview before they will take you on. Most flights depart from New York.

A good source of information on courier flights is Now Voyager (☎ (212) 431-1616), Suite 307, 74 Varrick St, New York, NY 10013. This company specialises in courier flights, but you must pay an annual membership fee (around US$50), which entitles you to take as many courier flights as you like. Phone after 6 pm to listen to a recorded message detailing all available flights and prices. The Denver-based Air Courier Association (☎ (303) 278-8810) also does this kind of thing. You join the association which is used by international air freight companies to provide the escorts.

Prices drop as the departure date approaches. It is also possible to organise the flights directly through the courier companies. Look in your Yellow Pages under Courier Services.

Charter flights tend to be significantly cheaper than scheduled flights. Reliable travel agents specialising in charter flights, as well as budget travel for students, include STA and Council Travel, both of which have offices in major cities. Reputable agencies specialising in cheap fares include:

STA
48 East 11th St, New York, NY 10003
(☎ (212) 477-7166)
914 Westwood Blvd, Los Angeles, CA 90024
(☎ (213) 824-1574)
166 Geary St, Suite 702, San Francisco, CA
94108 (☎ (415) 391-8407)

Council Travel
148 West 4th St, New York, NY 10011
(☎ (212) 254-2525)
205 East 42nd St, New York, NY 10017
(☎ (212) 661-1450)
1093 Broxton Ave, Los Angeles, CA 90024
(☎ (213) 208-3551)
Suite 407, 312 Sutter St, San Francisco, CA
94108 (☎ (415) 423473)

For the truly hi-tech traveller, another potential source of info and flights are the travel forums open to users of the Internet and assorted computer information and communication services. They are a step further down the travellers' superhighway from TV Teletext services – another source of flights and fares.

Low season return airfares from Roma to New York were around L660,000 at the time of writing, and L890,000 to Los Angeles. Low season open return tickets from New York to Roma or Milano go for as little as US$500.

If you can't find a particularly cheap flight, it is always worth considering getting a cheap Transatlantic hop to London and prowling around the bucketshops there. See The UK & Ireland later in this section and make some calculations.

Canada

Both Alitalia and Air Canada have direct flights to Roma and Milano from Toronto and Montreal. Travel CUTS, which specialises in discount fares for students, has offices in all major cities. Otherwise scan the budget travel agents' ads in the *Toronto Globe & Mail*, the *Toronto Star* and the *Vancouver Province*. See the previous section for information on courier flights. For courier flights originating in Canada, contact FB on Board Courier Services (☎ 514-633 0740 in Toronto or Montreal, or ☎ 604-338 1366 in Vancouver). Airhitch (see the USA section) has stand-by fares to/from Toronto, Montreal and Vancouver. Low season return fares from Roma to Toronto start from around L700,000.

The UK & Ireland

London is one of the best centres in the world for discounted air tickets. The price of RTW tickets, especially, is about the best available anywhere and tickets can be had for under UK£1000.

For the latest fares, check out the travel page ads of the Sunday newspapers, *Time Out*, *TNT*, and *Exchange & Mart*. All are available from most London newsstands. Another good source of information on cheap fares is the magazine *Business Traveller*. Those with access to Teletext on television will find a host of travel agents advertising. As in North America, the Internet is another possible source of information.

Most British travel agents are registered with ABTA (Association of British Travel Agents). If you have paid for your flight with an ABTA-registered agent who then goes bust, ABTA will guarantee a refund or an alternative. Unregistered bucket shops are riskier but sometimes cheaper.

The Globetrotters Club (BCM Roving, London WC1N 3XX) publishes a newsletter called *Globe* which covers obscure destinations and can help you to find travelling companions.

One of the more reliable, but not necessarily cheapest, agencies is STA (☎ 0171-361 6161 for European flights). It has several offices in London, as well as branches on many university campuses and in cities such as Bristol, Cambridge, Leeds, Manchester (☎ 0161-834 0668) and Oxford. The main London branches are:

86 Old Brompton Rd, London SW7 3LH
117 Euston Rd, London NW1 2SX
38 Store St, London WC1E 7BZ
Priory House, 6 Wrights Lane, London W8 6TA
11 Goodge St, London, W1

A similar place is Trailfinders (☎ 0171-937 5400 for European flights). Its short haul booking centre is at 215 Kensington High St. Other offices are at 42-50 Earls Court Rd, London W8 6FT and 194 Kensington High St, London W8 7RG (☎ 0171-938 3232). The latter offers an inoculation service and a research library for customers. It also has agencies in Bristol, Birmingham, Glasgow and Manchester.

Campus Travel is in much the same league and has the following branches in London:

52 Grosvenor Gardens, London SW1W 0AG (European flights on ☎ 0171-730 3402)
University College of London, 25 Gordon St, London WC1H 0AH (☎ 0171-383 5377)
YHA Adventure Shop, 174 Kensington High St, London W8 7RG (☎ 0171-938 2188)
YHA Adventure Shop, 14 Southampton St, London (☎ 0171-836 3343)
South Bank University, Keyworth St, London SE1 (☎ 0171-401 8666)

The two flag airlines linking the UK and Italy are British Airways (☎ 0171-434 4700; 24 hour line (local rate) ☎ 0345-222111), 156 Regent St, London W1R, and Alitalia (☎ 0171-602 7111), 27 Piccadilly, London W1V 9PF. They operate regular flights (usually several a day) to Roma, Milano, Venezia, Firenze, Torino, Napoli and Pisa, as well other cities, including Palermo, during the summer. Normal fares on a scheduled flight to Roma are UK£249 one way and UK£498 return on either airline. However, Apex and other special fares are a better option and can cost considerably less. Alitalia's cheapest high season return fare to Roma, for instance, is UK£259 plus departure tax. The fare differences between destinations tend not to be great, but the main cities are cheapest.

One option is to take a direct charter flight from London to Roma or Milano. Italy Sky Shuttle (☎ 0181-748 1333), 227 Shepherd's Bush Rd, London W6 7AS, specialises in charter flights to 22 destinations in Italy from London, Birmingham, Manchester, Glasgow and Edinburgh. An open return in August (high season) from London to Milano is UK£224, while a similar ticket to Roma costs UK£236. It can also organise a one week fly/drive deal which, in high season, costs UK£196 for a small car (Ford Fiesta or similar) and the above quoted airfares.

Italy Sky Shuttle also has offices in Italy,

from where you can buy tickets for charter flights to Britain. If you're booking a charter flight, remember to check what time of the day or night you'll be flying; many charter flights arrive very late at night. If you're flying in to Roma by charter, you will probably land at Ciampino airport, from where there is no public transport into the city centre after about 11 pm.

Another specialist in flights and holidays to Italy is Skybus Italia (☎ 0171-373 6055), 24A Earl's Court Gardens, London SW5 0TA. It has high season return flights to Roma starting from UK£184 plus UK£21 in departure tax.

Still cheaper fares can be found, and it is well worth shopping around. Major airlines sometimes discount flights to fill seats. At the time of writing, for instance, STA had a return fare with BA to Roma, with a two-month limit, for UK£144 plus UK£11.30 in departure tax.

Occasionally, special deals worth investigating do arise. For instance, until April 1997 Alitalia was offering people under 26 (and students under 31 with valid ISIC) a Europa Pass from London and Dublin. The pass was valid for up to six months and allowed unlimited one-way flights to all the airline's European and Mediterranean destinations for UK£59 per flight, with a minimum of four flights. The first flight had to be *to* Italy and the last flight back to the UK or Ireland *from* Italy. Internal flights in Italy could be had for UK£39 a pop.

You needn't necessarily fly from London, as many good deals are as easily available from other major centres in the UK.

Flying as a courier (see also The USA section), might be a possibility – you'll have to go through the Yellow Pages to find companies that do this.

If you're coming from Ireland, it might be worth comparing what is available direct and from London – getting across to London first may save you a few quid.

Continental Europe

Air travel between Italy and other places in Continental Europe is worth considering if you are pushed for time. Short hops can be expensive, but good deals are available from some major hubs.

Several airlines, including Alitalia, Qantas and Air France, offer cut-rate fares on legs of international flights between European cities. These are usually cheap, but often involve flying at night or early in the morning. Days on which you can fly are restricted.

France Voyages et Découvertes (☎ 01-42 61 00 01), 21 rue Cambon, is a good place to start hunting down the best airfares in Paris. There are plenty of regular flights between Paris and Roma or Milano. From Roma the CTS agency has return fares for students starting from L270,000.

Germany In Munich, a great source of travel information and equipment is the Därr Travel Shop (☎ 089-28 20 32) at Theresienstrasse 66. In Berlin, Kilroy Travel-ARTU Reisen (☎ 030-310 00 40), at Hardenbergstrasse 9, near Berlin Zoo (with five branches around the city) is a good travel agent. In Frankfurt a/M, you might try SRID Reisen (☎ 069-70 30 35), Bergerstr. 118. Return flights between Roma and Berlin can cost from about L400,000.

Greece Shop around the travel agents in the backstreets of Athens between Syntagma Square and Omonia Square.

Netherlands Amsterdam is a popular departure point. Some of the best fares are offered by the student travel agency NBBS Reiswinkels (☎ 020-620 5071). Its fares are comparable to those of London bucket shops, and return flights between Amsterdam and Roma start at about UK£170 for students. NBBS Reiswinkels has branches in Brussels, Belgium, as well.

Spain In Madrid one of the most reliable budget travel agents is Viajes Zeppelin (☎ 547 79 03; fax 542 65 46) Plaza de Santo Domingo 2. Return flights to Roma in low season start at about 30,000 ptas.

Africa

Italy being an unlikely place to look for cheap tickets, it makes an even less likely source of budget air tickets to Africa. Tunisia is the most popular North African destination for Italians, so you might dig up something for Tunis; typically, return tickets from Roma to Tunis cost upwards of L300,000.

Australia

STA Travel and Flight Centres International are major dealers in cheap airfares, although heavily discounted fares can often be found at your local travel agent. Scan the ads in the Saturday travel sections of the Melbourne *Age* and the *Sydney Morning Herald*.

Qantas and Alitalia are joined by a host of other European and Asian airlines flying between Australia and Italy. Many of the European airlines throw in a return flight to another European city so, for instance, BA will fly you return to London with a London-Roma-London flight included in the price.

Discounted return fares on mainstream airlines through reputable agents can be surprisingly cheap. Low season fares average around A$1800 return but can go as low as A$1400 with airlines like Garuda. High season fares range from A$1700 with Garuda to A$2600 with Qantas.

Qantas and Alitalia fly from Melbourne and Sydney to Roma three times a week. Flights from Perth are generally a few hundred dollars cheaper.

The following are some addresses for agencies offering good-value fares:

STA Travel
  224 Faraday Street, Carlton, Vic 3053 (☎ 03-9347 6911)
  1st Floor, 732 Harris Street, Ultimo, NSW 2007 (☎ 02-212 1255)
  Hackett Hall, University of Western Australia, Crawley, WA 6009 (☎ 09-380 3779; freephone ☎ 1800-637 444)

Flight Centres International
  Bourke Street Flight Centre, 19 Bourke Street, Melbourne, Vic 3000 (☎ 03-9650 2899)
  Martin Place Flight Centre, Shop 5, State Bank Centre, 52 Martin Place, Sydney, NSW 2000 (☎ 02-9235 0166)
  City Flight Centre, 25 Cinema City Arcade Perth, WA 6000 (☎ 09-325 9222)

CIT
  263 Clarence St, Sydney, NSW 2000 (☎ 02-9267 1255)
  227 Collins St, Melbourne, Vic 3000 (☎ 03-9650 5510)
  Level 9 QV1 Building, 250 St Georges Terrace, Perth, WA 6000 (☎ 09-322 1096)

New Zealand

STA Travel and Flight Centres International are popular travel agents in New Zealand. The cheapest fares to Europe are routed through the USA and a RTW ticket may be cheaper than a return. Otherwise, you can fly from Auckland to pick up a connecting flight in Melbourne or Sydney. Air New Zealand can fly you to Bangkok to connect with a Thai Airways flight to Roma, to Singapore to connect with a Singapore Airlines flight, or to Hong Kong to connect with a Cathay Pacific flight. Garuda flies from Auckland to Roma via Jakarta.

Useful addresses include:

Flight Centres International
  Auckland Flight Centre, Shop 3A, National Bank Towers, 205-225 Queen St, Auckland (☎ 09-309 6171)

STA Travel & International Travellers Centre
  10 High St, Auckland (☎ 09-309 0458)

Campus Travel
  Gate 1, Knighton Rd, Waikato University, Hamilton (☎ 07-838 4242)

Asia

Bangkok is probably the best Asian capital to trawl for bucket shops with cheap flights to Roma.

LAND

Not quite all roads lead to Roma, but there are plenty of options for entering Italy by train, bus or private vehicle.

Bus

If you are travelling by bus, train or car to Spain it will be necessary to check whether you require visas to the countries you intend to pass through. Eurolines, in conjunction with local bus companies across Europe, is the main international carrier.

You can find Eurolines offices in Italy at:

Roma
- Lazzi Express, Via Tagliamento 27/r (☎ 06-884 08 40)
- Agenzia Elios, Circonvallazione Nomentana 574, Lato Stazione Tiburtina (☎ 06-44 23 39 28)

Milano
- Autostradaleviaggi, Piazza Castello 1 (☎ 02-72 00 13 04)

Firenze
- Autostazione, Piazza Stazione 1, on the corner of Piazza Adua (☎ 055-21 51 55)

Torino
- Autostazione Comunale, Corso Inghilterra (☎ 011-433 25 25)

Venezia
- Agenzia Brusutti, Piazzale Roma 497/e (☎ 041-522 97 73)

The UK From the UK bus is probably the cheapest, if least comfortable, option. Eurolines (☎ 0171-730 8235), 52 Grosvenor Gardens, Victoria, London SW1, runs buses twice a week (Wednesday and Saturday) at 9.30 am for Milano (23½ hours), Roma (33 hours) and other destinations. Up to four services run in summer. Other destinations include Torino, Genova, Firenze, Rimini and Ancona. The lowest youth/under-26 fares from London to Roma are UK£81 one way and UK£127 return. The full adult fares are UK£91/137. To Milano the respective fares are UK£71/107 and UK£78/120. The single biggest disadvantage of the bus is that you can't get off along the way. Fares rise in the peak summer season.

The same company offers the option of a Eurolines Pass. A pass valid for 30/60 days costs UK£229/279 (UK£199/249 for under-26s and senior citizens) and allows unlimited travel between 18 European cities, including Roma, Milano and Firenze.

Austria Eurolines' main office in Vienna is at Autobusbahnhof Wien-Mitte, Schalter 2 (Window 2), Hauptstrasse 1b (☎ 01-712 04 53). SITA (see Germany later) has a weekly service from Vienna to Padova with connections for Venezia. SITA tickets can be bought in Vienna at Fangokur Reisen, Wipplingerstrasse 12 (☎ 533-1360).

France Eurolines has offices in several French cities. In Paris they are at 28 Ave du Général de Gaulle (☎ 01-49 72 51 51). The adult low season one-way/return fares to Paris from Milano are L122,000/195,000; from Roma L169,000/270,000. Local services cross the frontier at some points.

Germany Eurolines and associated companies have stations at major cities across Germany, including Hamburg, Frankfurt and Munich. For the latter, head for Deutsche Touring GmbH, Amulfstrasse 3 (Stamberger Bahnhof) (☎ 089-545 87 00). Otherwise, SITA has buses between Frankfurt /main and Padova, with connections possible for destinations further into Italy. In Frankfurt, SITA is at Am Römerhof 17 (☎ 069-790 3240).

Netherlands Eurolines is at Rokin 10 in Amsterdam (☎ 020-627 51 51). The adult one-way/return fare from Milano to Amsterdam is L150,000/240,000.

Slovenia Regular cross-border services connect Gorizia with Nova Gorica, from where there are services all over Slovenia.

Spain Eurolines and associated companies have representatives across the country, including the Estación Sur de Autobuses (91-528 11 05), Calle de las Canarias 17, in Madrid and the Estación Autobuses de Sants (☎ 93-490 40 00), Calle del Viriato s/n, Barcelona. There are at least two weekly services between Roma and Madrid, with stops en route. Fares vary, but from Milano to Madrid can cost adults L213,000/386,000 one way and return.

Train

Train travel is a convenient and simple means of travelling from most parts of Europe to Italy. It is certainly a popular way of getting around for backpackers and other young travellers, and even the more well-heeled travellers will find European trains a comfortable and reliable way to reach their destination.

If you plan to travel extensively by train in Europe it might be worth getting hold of the *Thomas Cook European Timetable*, which gives a complete listing of train schedules and indicates where supplements apply or where reservations are necessary. It is updated monthly and is available from Thomas Cook offices and agents worldwide.

EuroCity (EC) trains run from major destinations throughout Europe – including Paris, Geneva, Zürich, Frankfurt, Vienna and Barcelona – direct to major Italian cities. On overnight hauls you can book a *cuccetta* (known outside Italy as a *couchette* or sleeping berth) for around UK£15 for most international trains. In 1st class there are four bunks per cabin and in 2nd class there are six bunks. Sleepers are more expensive, but also much more comfortable.

It is always advisable to book a seat on EuroCity trains, or for any long-distance train travel to/from Italy. Trains are often extremely overcrowded, particularly in summer, and you could find yourself standing in the passageway for the whole trip!

When crossing international borders on overnight trips, train conductors will usually collect your passport before you go to sleep and hand it back the following morning.

Discount Tickets Those under 26 can get Wasteels or BIJ (Billet International de Jeunesse) tickets. They amount to the same thing and, from London at any rate, represent a surprisingly small saving on normal tickets. In Italy, BIJ tickets can be purchased at Transalpino offices at most major train stations and most travel agents. Always check them out, because in Continental Europe they can be a good deal.

Wasteels also offers those under 26 a series of set-route passes valid for unlimited stops over two months. One of these Mini-Tour tickets includes Italy. Leaving from London, for instance, the ticket would take you through Belgium, Switzerland, Italy and back to London through France. It costs UK£190.

Check out any rail discounts for children and seniors over 60. In the UK, seniors can get a special international rail travel card (valid only for trips that cross at least one border). Seniors pay UK£5 for the card, but they must already have a British Rail card (UK£16). The pass entitles you to roughly 30% off standard fares. The card is known in Italy as Carta Rail Europ Senior.

People aged over 26 might ask about Rail Inclusive Tour (RIT) tickets. These are for either 1st or 2nd class and carry a discount of 20%. They must be purchased in conjunction with other tourist services, such as a reservation for a minimum of three nights accommodation at the city of arrival. CTS and Sestante CIT can also provide information about these tickets.

For information about train discounts within Italy, see the Getting Around chapter.

Eurail Pass This pass is for non-European residents, which means you are not entitled to one if your passport shows you have been in Europe continuously for six months or more (in which case consider the better value InterRail card instead). For some reason people over 26 pay for a 1st-class pass and those under 26 for a 2nd-class pass. Plan to spend a lot of time on trains – even Eurail says you need to do at least 2400 km within two weeks before you start to get value for money. The cards are good for travel in 17 European countries, but forget it if you intend to travel mainly in Italy.

The standard passes are expensive. You can get one valid for 15 or 21 days, or for one, two or three months. The 15-day pass costs UK£329, or UK£411 for over-26s. The one-month pass costs UK£479 or UK£659 for over-26s and the three-month pass for over-26s (not available to those under 26) costs UK£1155! Treat it like gold, as it is virtually impossible to obtain replacement cards or refunds in the event of loss or theft.

Eurail also offers Flexipasses, with which the traveller is entitled to 10 or 15 days' rail travel over a two-month period. These cost respectively UK£343/461 for those under 26 in 2nd class and UK£483/636 for over-26s in 1st class. Eurail Saverpass is for two or more people travelling together and is available for 15 or 21 days or one month (minimum of three people from April 1 to September 30). The price per person is UK£355, UK£454 and UK£560 respectively. There are other passes for combined rail travel and car rental too.

In spite of their cost, the passes do not include all high speed train supplements but are good for travel on most ferries, such as those between Italy and Greece.

People generally purchase Eurail passes in their country of origin, but in London you *may* be able to get them at the rail centre. If not, the French Railways (0171-493 9731) office does sell them. You'll find its office at 179 Piccadilly W1V 0BA.

InterRail Pass If you are resident in any European country in the InterRail network, think about an InterRail pass. The InterRail map of Europe is divided into zones, one of which is composed of Italy, Greece, Slovenia and Turkey. The ticket is designed for people under 26 (there is a ticket for older people, but Italy does not recognise it). Fifteen days' unlimited 2nd-class travel in one zone costs UK£185. Better value is the one-month ticket for two zones for UK£220 (which from the UK would get you across France too). If you think you can stand careering around virtually all of Europe, you could go for the one-month all-in UK£275 ticket. Bear in mind that you must pay part of the fare on certain high speed trains such as the Pendolino.

Cardholders get discounts on travel in the country of residence where they purchase the ticket, as well as on a variety of other services such as ferry travel.

In the UK you can buy InterRail cards at the International Rail Centre (☎ 0171-834 2345) at Victoria Station, or several other mainline stations.

Europass This is a comparatively new rail pass for non-Europeans, which provides between five and 15 days' unlimited travel within a two-month period. Youth (aged under 26) and adult passes are available and can be purchased at the same outlets as for Eurail passes. You choose from a list of combinations of adjacent countries. The combinations range from three to five countries. A youth pass for one of the five-country combinations for 15 days costs UK£375. Adults can save a little on the standard pass prices by purchasing a pass for two people.

Euro-Domino You can also get Euro-Domino (known as Freedom in the UK) passes for any one of 25 European countries, valid for three, five or 10 days' travel over a month. For Italy, a 1st class, 10-day pass costs UK£329. Second class is UK£239 and a youth version (under 26) costs UK£179. This is a more attractive option than Eurail if you intend to spend a decent amount of time exploring Italy rather than rocketing all over the Continent. But again, you would need to be on trains a good amount of the time to get full value out of the pass. On balance, you are better off with an InterRail card if you can get one.

Italian Rail Passes A couple of Italian rail passes can be purchased in the UK. The Italy Railcard allows eight, 15, 21 or 30 days' unlimited travel on the country's network. Most high speed supplements (except the Pendolino and ETR trains) are covered. Fares in 2nd class range from UK£110 for eight days to UK£190 for 30 days. Alternatively, you could buy a Kilometric Card. With this pass you can travel up to 3000 km or make up to 20 trips, whichever comes first. The pass can be shared by up to five people and is valid for two months from the first trip. It includes *no* supplements for high speed trains and costs UK£88 in 2nd class.

Car Transport Some of the main international services include transport for private cars – an option worth examining to save wear and tear on your vehicle before it arrives in Italy.

The UK Travelling from the UK, you have a choice of train tickets covering the channel crossing by ferry, the faster Seacat, or the Eurostar train through the Channel Tunnel, which speeds up the initial part of the journey. Several routes are also available, via Paris and southern France or swinging from Belgium down through Germany and Switzerland.

The cheapest standard fares to Roma on offer at the time of writing were UK£93/157 one-way/return for students and those under 26, while the full adult fares were UK£108/176. To Milano the respective fares were UK£79/130 and UK£90/140.

Austria Regular trains on two lines connect Italy with main cities in Austria.

France & Spain Standard one-way, 2nd-class fares from Roma include L167,400 to Paris and L169,500 through France to Barcelona. The luxury high speed Artesia service using the French TGV and Italian ETR-460 trains connects Paris with Milano and Torino – at a price.

Slovenia Two lines connect Italy with Slovenia.

Switzerland The fast Pendolino ETR470 Cisalpino trains run at speeds of up to 200 kmh from Milano to major Swiss destinations, including Basel, Geneva, Lausanne and Berne. One-way fares in 2nd class range up to L114,500 to Basel.

Car & Motorcycle

Coming from the UK, you can take your car across to France by ferry or the Channel Tunnel car train, Le Shuttle. The latter runs around the clock, with up to four crossings (35 minutes) an hour in high season. You pay for the vehicle only and fares vary according to time of day and season. The cheapest normal fare is UK£109 return for a car and UK£45 for a motorcycle (ranging up to UK£159 and UK£55 respectively for Club class). You can book in advance (☎ 0990-353535), but the service is designed to let you just roll up and get on the next train.

The main points of entry to Italy are the Mont Blanc tunnel from France at Chamonix, which connects with the A5 for Torino and Milano; the Grand St Bernard tunnel from Switzerland, which also connects with the A5; and the Brenner Pass from Austria, which connects with the A22 to Bologna. Mountain passes in the Alps are often closed in winter and sometimes in autumn and spring, making the tunnels a less scenic, but more reliable way to arrive in Italy. In any event, make sure you have snow chains in winter. Along the coast from France, you can take the outrageously expensive A12 or the scenic but often clogged Via Aurelia (SS1).

Paperwork & Preparations Proof of ownership of a private vehicle should always be carried (Vehicle Registration Document for UK-registered cars) when driving through Europe. As of July 1996, all EU member states' driving licences are fully recognised throughout the Union, regardless of your length of stay. The old-style UK green licence is officially only accepted with a translation issued by the Italian consulate, although you are unlikely to have any problems without it. Otherwise you can get an International Driving Permit, also advisable for non-EU licences (see Documents in the Facts for the Visitor chapter).

Third party motor insurance is a minimum requirement in Italy and throughout Europe, and it is compulsory to have a Green Card, an internationally recognised proof of insurance, which can be obtained from your insurer. Also ask your insurer for a European Accident Statement form, which can simplify matters in the event of an accident. Never sign statements you can't read or understand – insist on a translation and sign that only if it's acceptable.

A European breakdown assistance policy is a good investment, such as the AA Five Star Service or the RAC Eurocover Motoring Assistance. In Italy, assistance can be obtained through the Automobile Club

Italiano. See Car, Organisations section in Getting Around chapter for details.

Every vehicle travelling across an international border should display a nationality plate of its country of registration. A warning triangle (to be used in the event of a breakdown) is compulsory throughout Europe. Recommended accessories are a first-aid kit, a spare bulb kit and a fire extinguisher.

In the UK, you can obtain further information can be obtained from the RAC (☎ 0181-686 0088 or 0345-331133) or the AA (☎ 01256-20123).

Rental There is a mind-boggling variety of special deals and terms and conditions attached to car rental. However, there are a few pointers to help you through. Multinational agencies – Hertz, Avis, Budget and Europe's largest rental agency, Europcar – will provide a reliable service and good standard of vehicle.

However, if you walk into an office and ask for a car on the spot, you will always pay high rates, even allowing for special weekend deals. National and local firms can sometimes undercut the multinationals but be sure to examine the rental agreement carefully (although this might be difficult if it is in Italian).

Planning ahead and prebooking a rental car through a multinational agency before leaving home will enable you to find the best deals. Prebooked and prepaid rates are always cheaper, and there are fly/drive combinations and other programmes that are worth looking into. You will simply pick up the vehicle on your arrival in Italy (or other European city) and then return it to a nominated point at the end of the rental period. Ask your travel agent for information, or contact one of the major rental agencies. Holiday Autos has good rates for Europe, for which you need to prebook; its main office is in the UK (☎ 0990 300400).

Another possibility if you don't know when you will want to rent is to call back home (more or less affordable to the UK and the US) and reserve through an agent there. This way you get the benefits of booking from home. One US reader suggested taking out American Automobile Association membership before leaving home – companies such as Hertz often have discounts for AAA members booking a car through a US office.

No matter where you rent, make sure you understand what is included in the price (unlimited kilometres, tax, insurance, collision damage waiver etc) and what your liabilities are. The minimum rental age in Italy is 21 years. A credit card is usually required.

Motorcycle and moped rental is common in Italy and there are specialist rental agencies in most cities (see Car & Motorcycle, Rental in the Getting Around chapter).

Purchase It is illegal for nonresidents to purchase vehicles in Italy. The UK is probably the best place to buy, as second-hand prices are good. Whether buying privately or from a dealer, if you are English speaking, the absence of language difficulties will help you to establish exactly what you are getting for your money. Bear in mind that you will be getting a left-hand drive car (ie steering wheel on the right) if you buy in the UK. If you want a right-hand drive car and can afford to buy new, prices are relatively low in Belgium, the Netherlands and Luxembourg. Paperwork can be tricky wherever you buy, and many countries, including Italy, have compulsory roadworthiness checks on older vehicles, which can add considerably to initial purchase costs.

Camper Van A popular way to tour Europe is for three or four people to band together and buy a camper van. This mode of holidaying is extremely popular in Italy. London is the usual embarkation point. Look at the ads in London's free magazine *TNT* if you want to form a group or buy a van. Private vendors gather on a daily basis at the Van market in Market Rd, London N7 (near Caledonian Rd tube station). Some second-hand dealers offer a 'buy-back' scheme for when you return from Europe but, if you have the time, buying and reselling privately is more advantageous. Obviously, a great advantage of travelling in a camper van is the flexibility, but a disadvantage is that they can be difficult to manoeuvre around towns.

If you want to rent, organise it before reaching Italy, as it is next to impossible to hire vans there. At the time of writing, Avis offered a deal on camper van rental from around US$106 a day for a four-berth van, but does not rent camper vans in Italy itself. Details are available through Sestante CIT offices abroad.

Motorcycling Europe is made for motorcycle touring and Italy is no exception. Motorcyclists literally swarm into the country in summer to tour the winding, scenic roads, particularly in mountainous areas. Wearing crash helmets is compulsory in Italy, as it is throughout Europe. It is worth noting that motorcyclists rarely have to book ahead for ferries. You will be able to enter restricted traffic areas in Italian cities without any problems and Italian traffic police generally turn a blind eye to motorcycles parked on footpaths.

Anyone considering joining a motorcycle tour from the UK might want to join the International Motorcyclists Tour Club (UK£19 per annum plus UK£3 joining fee). The club counts 400 members, and in addition to holidays on the Continent, it also has social weekends! The present secretary, James Clegg, can be contacted on ☎ 01484-66 48 68.

SEA

Ferries connect Italy to Greece, Turkey, Tunisia and Malta. There are also services to Corsica, Toulon and Marseille (France), and Durrës and Vlora (Albania). Ticket prices vary according to the time of year and are at their most expensive during summer. Prices for cars, camper vans and motorcycles vary according to the size of the vehicle and bicycles can sometimes be taken free of charge. Eurail and InterRail pass holders pay only a supplement on the Italy-Greece route, but must travel with approved companies. Ticket prices are competitive on the heavily serviced Brindisi-Greece route and travellers wanting to pick up the best deals can shop around in Brindisi.

For detailed information, see the Getting There & Away sections for: Brindisi, Bari and Ancona (ferries to/from Greece, Albania, Croatia and Turkey); Otranto (to/from Albania); Napoli (to/from Tunisia and Corsica); Trapani (to/from Tunisia via Pantelleria); Syracusa (to/from Malta); Porto Torres (to/from Marseille and Toulon), Livorno, La Spezia and Santa Teresa di Gallura (to/from Corsica); Genova (to/from Corsica, Tunisia & Malta); and Trieste (to/from Albania, Croatia and Greece).

DEPARTURE TAXES

The departure tax payable when you leave Italy by air is factored into your airline ticket.

ORGANISED TOURS

There are many options for organised travel to Italy. The Italian Tourist Office can sometimes provide a list of tour operators noting what each specialises in. Offices of CIT (see the Tourist Offices section in the Facts for the Visitor chapter) abroad can also help. What follows is a guide only to the kinds of options available and should not be read as an endorsement of any of the mentioned companies. It is always worth shopping around for value, but such tours rarely come cheap. Tours can save you hassles, but they do rob you of independence.

Under-35s

Top Deck Travel (☎ 0171-370 4555), 131-135 Earls Court Rd, London SW5 9RH, and Contiki Travel Ltd (☎ 0171-637 0802), c/o Royal National Hotel, Bedford Way, London WC1H 0DG, do a range of coach tours for young people across Europe – they are generally aimed at the high-speed, party-minded crowd.

In the USA, New Frontiers (☎ 800-366-63 87), 12 East 33rd St, New York, offers rail travel packages and other tours in Italy.

Tours for Seniors

For people aged over 60, Saga Holidays offers holidays ranging from cheap coach tours to luxury cruises. You will find offices in Britain (☎ 0800-300 500), Saga Building, Middelburg Square, Folkestone, Kent CT20 1AZ; the USA (☎ 0617-451 6808), 120 Boyleston St, Boston, MA 02116; and Australia (☎ 02-957 4222), Level 4, 20 Alfred St, Milsons Point, Sydney 2061.

Walking Tours

Several companies offer organised walking tours in selected areas of the continent. Explore Worldwide (☎ 01252-31 94 48), 1 Frederick St Aldershot, Hants GU11 1LQ, is one. Other names to look for in the UK include Exodus (0181-673 0859) and Ramblers (0171-733 1133).

Short Breaks

Kirker Travel Ltd (☎ 0171-231 3333), 3 New Concordia Wharf, Mill St, London SE1 2BB, offers pricey short breaks from London in exclusive hotels in the main cities of Italy. Such a trip starts at about UK£340 per person for three nights in twin accommodation with airfare, transfers and breakfast included. Depending on the hotel you choose, the price can rise considerably.

A less opulent version can be organised through Italia Tours Ltd (☎ 0171-371 1114), 205 Holland Park Ave, London W11 4XBT.

Other Tours

There are two other organisations in the Air Travel Group (see Air above): Magic of Italy, which organises anything from resort holidays and short city breaks to opera tours and coach trips, and Italian Escapades, which specialises more in package deals.

There are plenty of more focused possibilities. Tasting Italy (☎ 0181-964 5839), 97 Bravington Rd, London W9 3AA, offers one-week trips led by cooking instructors. You cook and eat your way to a better understanding of a chosen region.

> **Warning**
>
> The information in this chapter is particularly vulnerable to change: prices for international travel are volatile, routes are introduced and cancelled, schedules change, special deals come and go, and rules and visa requirements are amended. Airlines and governments seem to take a perverse pleasure in making price structures and regulations as complicated as possible. You should check directly with the airline or a travel agent to make sure you understand how a fare (and ticket you may buy) works. In addition, the travel industry is highly competitive and there are many lurks and perks.
>
> The upshot of this is that you should get opinions, quotes and advice from as many airlines and travel agents as possible before parting with your hard-earned cash. The details given in this chapter should be regarded as pointers and are not a substitute for your own careful, up-to-date research.

Getting Around

AIR

Domestic Air Services

Travelling by plane is expensive within Italy and it makes much better sense to use the efficient and considerably cheaper train and bus services. The domestic lines are Alitalia and Meridiana.

The main airports are in Roma, Pisa, Milano, Napoli, Catania and Cagliari, but there are other, smaller airports throughout Italy. Domestic flights can be booked through agencies such as Sestante CIT, CTS and normal travel agencies.

Alitalia offers a range of discounts for young people, families, the elderly and weekend travellers, as well as occasional special promotional fares. It should be noted that airline fares fluctuate and that special deals sometimes only apply when tickets are bought in Italy, or for return fares only. The Airfares Chart will give you an idea of return fares at the time of writing. Barring special deals, a one-way fare is generally half the cost of the return fare.

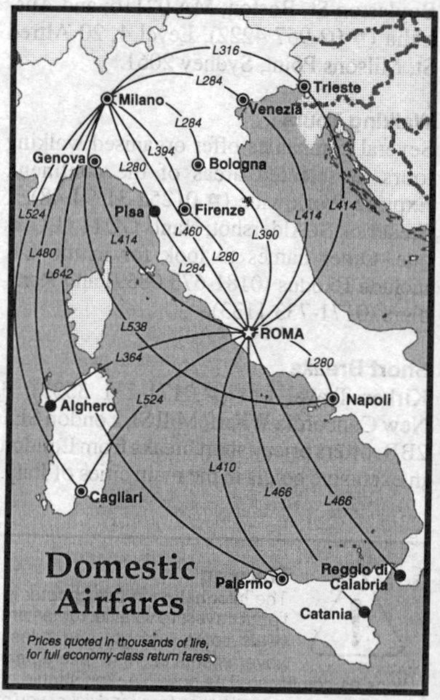

Domestic Airfares

Prices quoted in thousands of lire, for full economy-class return fares

BUS

Bus travel within Italy is provided by numerous companies and services vary from local routes linking small villages to fast and reliable major intercity connections. By utilising the local services, it is possible to arrive in just about any location throughout the country. Buses can be a cheaper and faster way to get around if your destination is not on major train lines.

It is usually possible to get bus timetables for the provinces and intercity services from local tourist offices. In larger cities most of the main intercity bus companies have ticket offices or operate through agencies and buses leave from either a bus station *(autostazione)* or from a particular piazza or street. Details are provided in the individual towns and city sections. In some smaller towns and villages tickets are sold in bars – just ask for *biglietti per il pullman* – or on the bus. Note that buses almost always leave on time.

Major companies which run long-haul services include Marozzi (Roma to Brindisi); SAIS and Segesta (Roma to Sicilia); Lazzi and SITA (from Lazio, Tuscany and other regions to the Alps – Lazzi also runs international services). See the Getting There & Away sections of Roma and Firenze as well as the Getting There & Away chapter for more information.

Reservations & Costs

It is usually not necessary to make reservations on buses, although it is advisable in high season for overnight or long-haul trips. Phone numbers and addresses of major bus companies are listed throughout this book.

xamples of ticket prices include: Roma-alermo L50,000; Roma-Siena L22,000.

RAIN

ravelling by train in Italy is simple, cheap nd generally efficient. The Ferrovie dello tato (FS) is the partially privatised state ain system and there are several private ain services throughout the country. There re several types of trains. Some stop at all tations, such as a *regionale* or *inter-egionale*; other, faster trains, such as the ntercity (IC), or EuroCity (EC), stop only at najor cities and you must pay a supplement ɔ the normal fare. Then there's the very fast rain, the ETR450, known as the *Pendolino*, new express service between Napoli, Roma, Firenze, Bologna and Milano.

Travellers should note that a new ticket alidation system has been introduced by the 'S whereby tickets must be punched by nachines installed at the entrance to all train latforms. The machines are yellow and easy ɔ find. The rule does not apply to tickets urchased outside Italy.

There are also several private train lines in taly, which are noted throughout this book. 'here are left-luggage facilities at all train tations. They are often open 24 hours a day ut, if not, they usually close only for a ouple of hours after midnight. They open even days a week and charge from L1500 or each piece of luggage.

rain Passes

t is not worth buying a Eurail or Inter-Rail ass if you are going to travel only in Italy, ince train fares are reasonably cheap. The 'S offers its own discount passes for travel vithin the country. These include the Carta 'erde for young people aged 12 to 26 years. t costs L40,000, is valid for one year and ntitles you to a 20% discount on all train ravel, but you'll need to do a fair bit of ravelling to get your money's worth. Chil-lren aged between four and 12 years are utomatically entitled to a 50% discount, and nder four years they can travel for free. The Carta d'Argento entitles people aged 60 ears and over to a 20% discount on 1st and 2nd class travel for one year. It also costs L40,000. You can buy a kilometric ticket *(biglietto chilometrico)*, which is valid for two months and allows you to cover 3000km, with a maximum of 20 trips. It costs L206,000 (2nd class) and you must pay the supplement if you catch an Intercity train. Its main attraction is that it can be used by up to five people, either singly or together. The Italy Railcard and the Kilometric Card can be bought in the UK; see Train/Italian Rail Passes in Getting There & Away chapter.

Classes

There are 1st and 2nd classes on all Italian trains, with a 1st class ticket costing a bit less than double the price of 2nd class. On the Pendolino, 2nd class is much like 1st class on other trains.

Reservations

It is recommended that you book train tickets for long trips, particularly if you're travelling on weekends or during holiday periods, otherwise you could find yourself standing in the corridor for the entire journey. Reservations are obligatory for the Pendolino. You can get timetable information and make train bookings at most travel agents, including CTS and Sestante CIT, or you can simply buy your ticket on arrival at the station. There are special booking offices for the Pendolino at the relevant train stations. If you are doing a reasonable amount of travelling, it is worth buying a train timetable. There are several available, including the official FS timetables, which are available at newspaper stands in or near train stations for around L5000.

Costs

To travel on the Intercity and EuroCity trains, you are required to pay a *supplemento*, an additional charge determined by the distance you are travelling. For instance, on the Intercity train between Roma and Firenze you will pay an extra L15,000. On the Pendolino, it is obligatory to make a booking, since they don't carry standing room passengers. The cost of the ticket includes the supplement and booking fee. The one-way fare from Roma to Firenze on the Pendolino is L46,000 in 2nd class and L73,000 in 1st class. The difference in price between the Pendolino (1½ hours) and the cheaper Intercity (around two hours) is only L9000. For the extra money you get a faster, much more comfortable service, with an airline-type snack thrown in. The Pendolino always takes priority over other trains, so there's no risk of long delays in the middle-of-nowhere.

Always check whether the train you are about to catch is an Intercity, and pay the supplement before you get on, otherwise you will pay extra on the train. On overnight trips within Italy it can be worth paying extra for a *cuccetta* (L23,000). It is possible to take your bicycle in the baggage compartment on some trains (L10,000).

Some price examples for one-way train fares (including supplements) are: Roma-Firenze L62,000 (1st class) and L37,000 (2nd class); Venezia-Milano L55,000 (1st class), L35,000 (2nd class); Firenze-Venezia L50,000 (1st class), L42,000 (2nd class).

CAR & MOTORCYCLE

Driving Licence & Vehicle Papers

If you want to rent a car or motorcycle, you will generally need to produce your driving licence. Certainly you will need to produce it if you aare pulled over by the police or *carabinieri*, who, if it's a non-EU licence, may well want to see an International Driving Permit. This is available from automobile clubs throughout the world, usually valid for 12 months and must be kept with your proper licence.

If driving your own vehicle in Italy you need an International Insurance Certificate, also known as a Green Card (Carta Verde). Your third party insurance company will issue this. For further details, see the Car & Motorcycle section in the Getting There & Away chapter.

Roads

Roads are generally good throughout the country and there is an excellent network of autostradas. The main north-south link is th Autostrada del Sole, which extends fro Milano to Reggio di Calabria (called the A from Milano to Napoli and the A3 fro Napoli to Reggio di Calabria). Drive usually travel at very high speed in the lef hand fast lane on the autostradas, so use th lane only to pass other cars. You will pay toll to use Italy's network of autostradas. F example, it will cost you approximatel L30,000 from Roma to Bologna, dependin on the size of your car. Travellers with tim to spare could consider using the system state roads *(strade statali)*, which are ofte multi-lane, dual carriageways and toll-fre They are represented on maps as 'SS'. Th provincial roads *(strade provinciali)* a sometimes little more than country lanes, b provide access to some of the more beautif scenery and the many towns and village They are represented as 'SP' on maps.

Road Rules

In Italy, as throughout Continental Europ people drive on the right side of the road an overtake on the left. Unless otherwise ind cated, you must give way to cars comin from the right. It is compulsory to wear se belts if fitted to the car (front seat belts on a cars, rear seat belts on cars produced after 2 April 1990). If caught without seat belts, yo will be required to pay a L58,000 fine on th spot, although this doesn't seem to dete Italians, many of whom use them only on th autostradas.

Random breath tests now take place i Italy. If you're involved in an accident whil under the influence of alcohol, the penaltie can be severe. The limit on blood-alcoho content is 0.08%. Speed limits, unless other wise indicated by local signs, are: o autostradas 130km/h for cars of 1100cc c more, 110km/h for smaller cars and fo motorcycles under 350cc; on all main, non urban highways 110km/h; on secondary non-urban highways 90km/h; and in built-u areas 50km/h. Speeding fines follow EU standards and are L59,000 for up to 10km/ over the limit, L235,000 for up to 40km/h ıd L587,000 for more than 40 km/h. riving through a red light costs L117,000.

You don't need a licence to ride a moped ıder 50cc, but you should be aged 14 years over, and a helmet is compulsory up to age ; you can't carry passengers or ride on ıtostradas. The speed limit for a moped is) km/h. To ride a motorcycle or scooter up 125cc, you must be at least 16 years old ıd have a licence (a car licence will do). elmets are compulsory for everyone riding motorcycle bigger than 50cc. For motor- 'cles over 125cc you need a motorcycle :ence. There is no lights-on requirement for otorcycles during the day.

ental

ar It is cheaper to arrange car rental before aving your own country, for instance rough some sort of fly/drive deal. Most ajor firms, including Hertz, Avis and udget, will arrange this, and you simply ck up the vehicle at a nominated point hen you arrive in Italy. Foreign offices of ;stante CIT can also help to organise car or ımpervan rental before you leave home ee the section on Rental in the Getting here & Away chapter).

You will need to be aged 21 years or over 3 years or over for some companies) to rent car in Italy and you will find the deal far ısier to organise if you have a credit card. lost firms will accept your standard licence, ›metimes with an Italian translation (which ın usually be provided by the agencies emselves) or International Driving Permit.

At the time of writing, Avis offered a ›ecial weekend rate for unlimited lometres which compared well with rates fered by other firms: L238,000 for a Fiat no or Renault Clio, or L328,000 for a Fiat rava, from Friday 9 am to Monday 9 am. laggiore Budget offered a weekend deal of 177,000 for a Renault Clio, with a limit of 50km. The same car for five days, with ılimited mileage, costs L540,000, plus 108,000 for each additional day.

ampervan It is difficult, if not just about ›wnright impossible, to rent a campervan once you are in Italy. See Car & Motorcycle in the Getting There & Away chapter for information about renting campervans before you arrive.

Motorcycle You'll have no trouble renting a small motorcycle such as a scooter (Vespa) or moped. There are numerous rental agencies in cities, where you'll also usually be able to rent larger motorcycles for touring, and at tourist destinations such as seaside resorts. The average cost for a 50cc scooter (for one person) is around L60,000 per day and L300,000 per week. For a 125cc (two people) you will pay from around L80,000 per day and L400,000 per week. For a moped (virtually a motorised bicycle) you'll pay around L45,000 per day and L220,000 per week. Most agencies will not rent motorcycles to people under the age of 18 years. Note that many places require a sizeable deposit and that you could be responsible for reimbursing part of the cost of the bike if it is stolen. Always check the fine print in the contract. See the Road Rules section for more details about age, licence and helmet requirements. Rental agencies are listed

under the major cities in this book. Most tourist offices can provide information about renting a car or motorcycle, otherwise look in the local *Yellow Pages* (*Pagine Gialle*).

Purchase

Car It 's very dificult for foreigners to buy a car in Italy, as the law requires that you must be a resident to own and register one. You can get around this is by having a friend who is a resident of Italy buy one for you.

It is possible to buy a cheap, small 10-year-old car for as little as L1,500,000, ranging up to around L7,000,000 for a reasonable five-year-old Fiat Uno, and up to L10,000,000 for a two-year-old Fiat Uno. The best way to find a car to buy is to look in the classified section of local newspapers. If you buy a car in another country and need any assistance or advice in Italy, contact the ACI (Automobile Club of Italy, see the Organisations section below).

Motorcycle The same laws apply to owning and registering a motorcycle. The cost of a second-hand Vespa ranges from L500,000 to L1,500,000, and a moped will cost from L300,000 to L1,000,000. Prices for more powerful bikes start at L1,500,000.

City Driving

Driving in Italian towns and cities is quite an experience and may well present the unprepared with headaches. The Italian attitude to driving bears little comparison to the English concept of traffic in ordered lanes (a normal two-lane road is likely to carry three or four lanes of traffic), and the farther south you travel, the less drivers seem to pay attention to road rules. Instead, the main factor in determining right of way is whichever driver is more forceful, or *prepotente*.

If you must drive in an Italian city, particularly in Roma or Napoli, remain calm, keep your eyes on the car in front of you and you should be OK. Most roads are well signposted and once you arrive in a city or village, follow the *centro* (city centre) signs. Be extremely careful where you park your car. In major cities it will almost certainly be towed away and you will pay a heavy fine if you leave it in an area marked with a sign reading *Zona Rimozione* (Removal Zone) and featuring a tow truck. A stopover in a medieval hill town will generally mean leaving the car in a car park some distance from the town centre.

Parking

It is a good idea to leave your car in a supervised car park if you have luggage, but even then it is a risk to leave your belongings in an unattended car. Car parks are indicated in major city sections in this book; they are denoted throughout Italy by a sign bearing a white 'P' on a blue background.

Petrol

The cost of petrol in Italy is very high, at around L1900 per litre (slightly less for unleaded petrol). Petrol is called *benzina*, unleaded petrol is *benzina senza piombo* and diesel is *gasolio*. If you are driving a car which uses LPG (liquid petroleum gas), you will need to buy a special guide to service stations which have *gasauto* or GPL. By law these must be located in nonresidential areas and are usually in the country or on city outskirts, although you'll find plenty on the autostradas. GPL costs around L900 per litre.

Organisations

The Automobile Club Italiano (ACI) no longer offers free roadside assistance to tourists. Residents of the UK and Germany should be able to organise assistance abroad through their home-country organisations, which entitles them to use ACI's emergency assistance number ☎ 116 for a small fee. Without it, you'll pay a minimum fee of L150,000 if you call ☎ 116. ACI has offices at Via Marsala 8, Roma (☎ 06-4 99 81); and Corso Venezia 43, Milano (☎ 02-7 74 51).

BICYCLE

Rental

Bikes are available for rent in most Italian towns and many places have both city and mountain bikes. Rental costs for a city bike range from L15,000 a day to around

L100,000 per week. A good mountain bike will cost more. See Getting Around in each city section for more information.

Purchase

If you shop around, bargain prices range from L190,000 for a woman's bike without gears to L400,000 for a mountain bike with 16 gears, but you will need to pay a lot more for a very good bike. A good place to shop for bargains is Tacconi Sport, which has large outlets near Perugia, Arezzo, Trento and in the Republic of San Marino. It buys in bulk and has some great bargains.

Planning

If you plan to bring your own bike, check with your airline for any additional costs. The bike will need to be disassembled and packed for the journey.

A primary consideration on a cycling tour is to travel light, but you should take a few tools and spare parts, including a puncture repair kit and a spare inner tube. Panniers are essential to balance your possessions on either side of the bike frame. A bike helmet is a very good idea, as is a very solid bike lock and chain, although even that might not prevent your bike from being stolen if you leave it unattended. Theft of mountain bikes is a major problem in the big cities.

There are organisations that can help you plan your bike tour, or through which you can organise guided tours. In England, you should contact the Cyclists' Touring Club (☎ 01483-417 217), Cotterell House, 69 Meadrow, Godalming, Surrey GU7 3HS. It can supply information to members on cycling conditions, itineraries and cheap insurance. Membership costs £25 per year or £12.50 for students and people aged under 18. There are also organisations in Italy which can offer guided bike tours, including I Bike Italy (see the Firenze section of the Toscana chapter).

Travelling with a Bicycle

Bikes can be taken very cheaply on trains (L10,000), although only some trains will actually carry them. Fast trains (IC, EC etc) will generally not accommodate bikes and they must be sent as registered luggage. This can take a few days and will probably mean that your bike won't be on the same train that you travel on. It might be an idea to send your bike in advance, if possible. Check with the FS or a travel agent for more information.

The European Bike Express is a coach service where cyclists can travel with their machines. It runs in summer from north-east England to Italy or Spain, with pick-up/drop-off points en route.

The return fare is £149 (£139 for CTC members); phone ☎ 01642-251 440 in the UK for details. See the Activities section in the Facts for the Visitor chapter for suggestions on places to cycle.

HITCHING

Hitching is never safe in any country, and we don't recommend it. Travellers who decide to hitchhike should understand they are taking a small, but potentially serious, risk. People who do choose to hitchhike will be safer if they travel in pairs and let someone know where they are planning to go. It is illegal to hitchhike on Italy's autostradas, but quite acceptable to stand near the entrance to the toll booths. It is not a major pastime in Italy, but Italians are friendly people and you will generally find a lift. A man and a woman travelling together is probably the best combination. Women travelling alone should be extremely cautious about hitching anywhere in Italy.

Never hitchhike where drivers can't stop in good time or without causing an obstruction. You could also approach drivers at petrol stations and truck stops. Look presentable, carry as little luggage as possible and hold a sign in Italian, indicating your destination. It is sometimes possible to arrange lifts in advance – ask around at youth hostels. The International Lift Centre in Firenze (☎ 055-28 06 26) as well as Enjoy Roma (see Tourist Offices under Information in the Roma chapter) may be able to help. Dedicated hitchhikers might also like to get hold of Simon Calder's *Europe – a Manual for Hitchhikers*.

WALKING

Check with tourist offices in each city for information about local groups which organise walking tours. In the UK, Ramblers Holidays (☎ 01707-331133) organises walking holidays. Numerous mountain guide groups throughout the Alps offer guided hikes, ranging from nature walks to demanding week-long treks which may or may not require some mountaineering skills. Information about mountain guides can always be obtained from tourist offices throughout the Alps: many guides are also listed in the Alpine sections of the northern Italy chapters.

BOAT

Large ferries *(navi)* service the islands of Sicilia and Sardegna, and smaller ferries *(traghetti)* and hydrofoils *(aliscafi)* service areas such as the Isole Eolie, Elba, the Tremiti Islands, Capri and Ischia. The main embarkation points for Sardegna are Genova, Livorno, Civitavecchia and Napoli; for Sicilia the main points are Napoli and Villa San Giovanni in Calabria. The main points of arrival in Sicilia are Palermo and Messina; in Sardegna they are Cagliari, Arbatax, Olbia and Porto Torres.

Tirrenia Navigazione is the major company servicing the Mediterranean and it has offices throughout Italy. The FS also operates ferries to Sicilia and Sardegna. Travellers can choose between cabin accommodation (men and women are usually segregated in 2nd class, although families will be kept together) or a *poltrona*, an airline-type armchair. Deck class is available only in summer and only on some ferries, so ask when making your booking.

Detailed information is provided in the Getting There & Away sections of the Sicilia and Sardegna chapters, as well as in the Getting There & Away sections of other relevant destinations. Many services are overnight and all ferries carry vehicles (generally it is possible to take a bicycle free of charge). Restaurant, bar and recreation facilities, including cinemas, are available on the larger, long-haul ferries.

LOCAL TRANSPORT

All major cities have good transport systems – bus and underground train systems are usually integrated, although in Venezia your only options are by boat or on foot.

Bus

In the cities, bus services are usually frequent and reliable. You must always buy bus tickets before you board the bus and validate them once aboard. It is common practice among Italians and many tourists to ride buses for free by not validating their tickets – just watch how many people rush to punch their tickets when an inspector boards the bus. However, if you get caught with an unvalidated ticket, you will be fined up to L50,000 on the spot. Efficient provincial and regional bus services also operate between towns and villages. Tourist offices will provide information on urban public transport systems, including bus routes and maps of the subway systems.

Subway

There are subways in Milano (MM), Roma and Napoli (Metropolitana). You must buy tickets and validate them before getting on the train.

Bus & Subway Tickets

Tickets are sold at most tobacconists, at many newspaper stands and at ticket booths or dispensing machines at bus stations (for instance, outside Stazione Termini in Roma where many of the city buses stop) and in the subways. The tickets are valid for both buses and the subways in Roma, Milano and Napoli. Tickets are different from city to city and generally cost from L1500 to L2000 for one hour to 75 minutes. Most cities offer 24-hour tourist tickets which can mean big savings.

Taxi

Taxis in Italy are expensive (even the shortest taxi ride in Roma costs around L10,000) and it is generally possible to catch a bus instead. If you need a taxi, you can usually find them on taxi ranks at train and bus stations or you can telephone (radio-taxi phone numbers are listed throughout this book in the Getting Around sections of the major cities). However, if you book a taxi by phone, you will be charged for the trip the driver makes to reach you. Taxis will rarely stop when hailed on the street and generally will not respond to telephone bookings if you are calling from a public phone.

Rates vary from city to city. A good indication of the average is Roma, where the flagfall is L6400 (for the first 3km), then L1200 per km. There is a L3000 supplement from 10 pm to 7 am and L1000 from 7 am to 10 pm on Sunday and public holidays. The limit on the number of people is four or five depending on the size of the taxi.

Be aware of the Roma airport supplement – L15,000 on travel to and from the airport, because it is outside the city limits.

Watch out also for taxi drivers who take advantage of new arrivals and stretch out the length of the trip, and consequently the size of the fare.

ORGANISED TOURS

People wanting to travel to Italy on a fully organised tour have a wide range of options, and it is best to discuss these with your travel agent. Foreign offices of CIT (see the Tourist Offices section in the Facts for the Visitor chapter) can provide information and organise package tours. Student or youth travel agencies will be able to recommend companies which specialise in tours for young people. An outfit called Tracks offers budget coach/camping tours for under US$40 per day, plus food fund. It has a London office (☎ 0171-937 3028) and is represented in Australia and New Zealand by Adventure World: in North America, call ☎ 800-233 6046. In London, Contiki (☎ 0181-290 6422) and Top Deck (☎ 0171-370 4555) offer hotel-based coach tours for the 18-to-35-years age group. Both have offices in North America, Australia and South Africa.

For people who are aged over 50, Saga Holidays offers holidays ranging from cheap coach tours to luxury cruises. You will find offices in Britain (☎ 0800-300 500), Saga Building, Middelburg Square, Folkestone, Kent CT20 1AZ. Saga also operates in the USA as Saga International Holidays (☎ 617-262 2262), 222 Berkeley St, Boston, MA 02116, and in Australia as Saga Holidays Australasia (☎ 02-9957 5660), Level One, 110 Pacific Highway, North Sydney, NSW 2060.

Being in a tour group removes most of the hassles associated with travelling – such as where to sleep and eat and how to get around. However, it also takes away your independence and opportunities to make interesting detours or to take your time savouring the sights, so make sure you weigh up the pros and cons carefully before deciding on a guided tour.

Once in Italy, it is often less expensive and usually more enjoyable to see the sights independently, but if you are in a hurry or prefer guided tours, go to the CIT office (in all major cities). Apart from package tours of Italy, they organise city tours for an average price of L40,000. Local tourist offices can generally assist with information on other local agencies which offer tours.

Roma

'I now realise all the dreams of my youth,' wrote Goethe on his arrival in Roma (Rome) in the winter of 1786. Perhaps Roma today is more chaotic, but certainly no less romantic or fascinating. In this city a phenomenal concentration of history, legend and monuments coexists with an equally phenomenal concentration of people busily going about everyday life. It is easy to pick the tourists, because they are the only ones to turn their heads as the bus passes the Colosseo.

Modern-day Roma is a busy city of about four million residents and, as the capital of Italy, it is the centre of national government. Tourists usually spend their time in the historic centre, thereby avoiding the sprawling and architecturally anonymous suburbs.

While the look of central Roma is most obviously defined by the Baroque style of the many fountains, churches and palaces, there are also ancient monuments, beautiful churches and buildings of the medieval, Gothic and Renaissance periods, as well as the architectural embellishments of the post-Risorgimento and Fascist eras.

Realistically, a week is probably a reasonable amount of time to explore the city. Whatever time you devote to Roma, put on your walking shoes, buy a good map and plan your time carefully, and the city will seem less overwhelming than it first appears. It is best to avoid Roma during August, when the weather is suffocatingly hot and humid, making sightseeing an unpleasant pastime. Most Romans head for the beaches or mountains at this time to take their summer holidays, leaving half the city closed down.

HIGHLIGHTS

- Visiting San Pietro & Il Vaticano, especially on Sunday mornings and at Easter
- Reconstructing ancient history amid the ruins of the Foro Romano & the Palatino
- Giving the thumbs up sign at the Colosseo
- Eating a gelato as you gaze at the beautiful fountains, along with artists, pigeons, Romans and tourists of the world in beautiful Piazza Navona
- Watching little boys fish for coins in the Fontana di Trevi as their older brothers fish for foreign women
- Wandering through the ruins of the ancient Roman port city of Ostia Antica
- Cooling off in Roma's heat at the lush summer playground of Tivoli

History

In Roma, there is visible evidence of the two great empires of the western world: the Roman Empire and the Christian Church. From the Foro Romano and the Colosseo to the Basilica di San Pietro and Il Vaticano and in almost every piazza, lies history on so many levels that the saying 'Rome, a lifetime is not enough' must certainly be true.

It is generally agreed that Roma had its origins in a group of Etruscan, Latin and Sabine settlements on the Palatino,

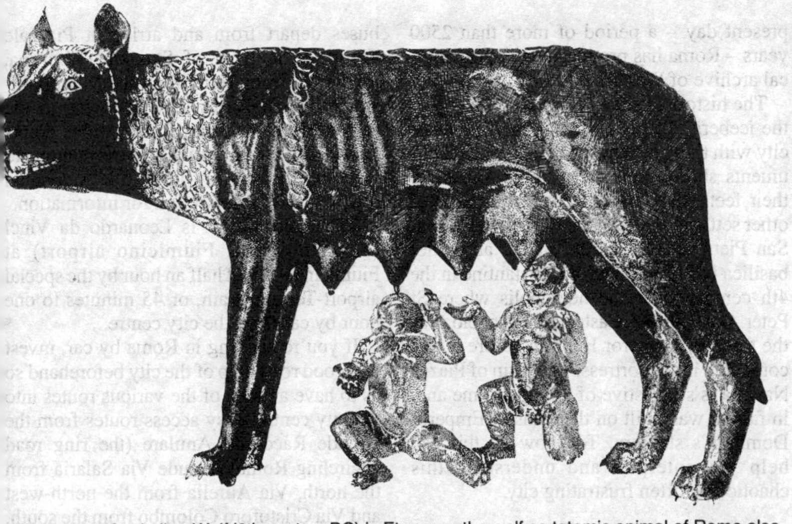

The bronze *Capitoline Wolf* (6th century BC) is Etruscan; the wolf as totemic animal of Rome also has links to Etruscan mythology. Romulus and Remus were added during the Renaissance.

Esquilino and Quirinale hills. These and surrounding hills constitute the now-famous seven hills of Rome. Ancient Romans put the date of their city's foundation as 21 April 753 BC and, indeed, archaeological discoveries have confirmed the existence of a settlement on the Palatino in that period. It is, however, the legend of Romulus and Remus which prevails. The twin sons of Rhea Silvia and the war god Mars, according to legend they were raised by a she-wolf after being abandoned on the banks of the Tevere (Tiber) river. The myth says Romulus killed his brother during a battle over who should govern, and then established the city of Rome on the Palatino.

Later, Romulus, who had established himself as the first king of Rome, disappeared one day, enveloped in a cloud that was believed to have carried him back to the domain of the gods.

From the legend grew an empire which eventually controlled almost the entire world known to Europeans at the time, an achievement described by a historian of the day as 'without parallel in human history'. The 18th-century historian, Edward Gibbon, wrote that Roma comprised the most beautiful part of the earth and its most civilised people. He further wrote that the most prosperous and happy period of human existence took place between the death of Emperor Domitian in 96 AD and the ascent of Emperor Commodus in 180 AD. Perhaps Gibbon neglected to consider the lives of the thousands of slaves who served the Roman aristocracy.

Roma has always inspired wonder and awe in its visitors. Its ruined, but still imposing, monuments represent a point of reference for a city which, through the imperial, medieval, Renaissance and Baroque periods, has undergone many transformations. As such, the cultured and well-to-do Europeans who, from the mid-17th century onwards, rediscovered Roma, found in the Eternal City a continuity from the pagan to the Christian worlds. In fact, from the time of the Roman Empire, through the development of Christianity to the present day – a period of more than 2500 years – Roma has produced an archaeological archive of Western culture.

The historical sites of Roma are the tip of the iceberg. Tourists wandering around the city with their eyes raised to admire its monuments should know that about 4m under their feet exists another city, with traces of other settlements deeper still. The Basilica di San Pietro stands on the site of an earlier basilica built by Emperor Constantine in the 4th century over the necropolis where St Peter was buried. Castel Sant'Angelo was the tomb of Emperor Hadrian before it was converted into a fortress. The form of Piazza Navona is suggestive of a hippodrome and, in fact, it was built on the ruins of Emperor Domitian's stadium. To know all this can help you interpret and understand this chaotic and often frustrating city.

Orientation

Roma is a vast city, but the historic centre is quite small. Most of the major sights are within a reasonable distance of the central railway station, Stazione Termini. It is, for instance, possible to walk from the Colosseo, through the Foro Romano and the Palatino, up to Piazza di Spagna and across to Il Vaticano in one day, although such a crowded itinerary is hardly recommended even for the most dedicated tourist. One of the great pleasures of being in Roma is wandering through the many beautiful *piazzas*, stopping now and again for a caffè and *pasta* (cake). All the major monuments are west of the train station, but make sure you use a map. While it can be enjoyable to get off the beaten track in Roma, it can also be very frustrating and time-consuming.

In planning your itinerary, check which museums and monuments are open only in the morning. Several itineraries are proposed later in this chapter.

Most new arrivals in Roma will end up at Stazione Termini, the terminus for all international and national trains. The station is commonly referred to as Termini. The main city bus station is in Piazza dei Cinquecento, directly in front of the station. Many Intercity buses depart from and arrive at Piazzale Tiburtina, in front of Stazione Tiburtina accessible from Termini on the Metropolitana Linea B. Buses serving towns in the region of Lazio depart from various points throughout the city, usually corresponding to stops on the subway lines. See individual towns in the Lazio section for information.

The main airport is Leonardo da Vinci (also known as Fiumicino airport) at Fiumicino – about half an hour by the special airport-Termini train, or 45 minutes to one hour by car from the city centre.

If you're arriving in Roma by car, invest in a good road map of the city beforehand so as to have an idea of the various routes into the city centre: easy access routes from the Grande Raccordo Anulare (the ring road encircling Roma) include Via Salaria from the north, Via Aurelia from the north-west and Via Cristoforo Colombo from the south. Normal traffic is not permitted into the city centre, but tourists are allowed to drive to their hotels (you will need a booking and your hotel will give you a special pass.) Without a pass your car could be towed away. There is unsupervised parking available along the Lungotevere (beside the Tevere river) and on the periphery of the historic centre at L2000 per hour. The main car park is at the Villa Borghese. (See the Getting Around section in this chapter.)

The majority of cheap hotels and *pensioni* are concentrated around Stazione Termini, but if you are prepared to go the extra distance, it is only slightly more expensive and definitely more enjoyable to stay closer to the city centre. The area around the train station, particularly to the west, is seedy and can be dangerous at night, but the sheer number of hotels makes it the most popular area for budget travellers and tour groups.

Maps Invest L6000 in the street map and bus guide simply entitled *Roma*, which is published by Editrice Lozzi in Roma; it is available at any newspaper stand in Termini. It lists all streets, with map references, as well as all bus routes. There is also an excellent free map, called *Roma Città*, which details the city's public transport routes. Pick it up at the tourist office. People with their own cars could buy a book of road maps for Italy.

Information

Tourist Offices There is an information office (EPT, ☎ 487 12 70) opposite platform No 4 at Stazione Termini which is open daily from 8.15 am to 7.15 pm. The main EPT office (☎ 06-48 89 92 53) is at Via Parigi 11 and is open Monday to Saturday from 8.15 am to 7.15 pm. Walk north-west from Stazione Termini through Piazza dei Cinquecento and Piazza della Repubblica; Via Parigi runs to the right from the top of the piazza, about a five minute walk from the station. The office has information on accommodation, museums, festivals and concert seasons, as well as details on local and intercity transport. Brochures and, sometimes, maps and hotel lists for other Italian cities are available at this office. There's also a branch office in the arrivals hall at Fiumicino airport.

A good alternative is Enjoy Rome (☎ 445 18 43; fax 445 07 34), Via Varese 39 (a few minutes walk north-east of the train station), a privately run tourist office brimming with information about the city and its surrounds. It offers a free-of-charge hotel reservation service and can also organise alternative accommodation, such as rental apartments. There's always someone who speaks English and staff are always very keen to help. The office is open Monday to Friday from 8.30 am to 1 pm and 3.30 to 6 pm and on Saturday from 8.30 am to 1 pm. Enjoy Rome publishes a very useful *Roma* city guide, with lots of practical information.

Tourist information booths can also be found at Largo Corrado Ricci, opposite the entrance to the Foro Romano; Largo Goldoni, on Via del Corso at the end of Via Condotti; and next to the Palazzo del Esposizione in Via Nazionale.

Foreign Embassies For addresses and telephone numbers, see Foreign Embassies in the Facts for the Visitor chapter. All embassies and consulates are listed in the Roma telephone book under 'Ambasciate'. The Australian, New Zealand and Canadian embassies can be reached from Stazione Termini on bus No 36, which travels along Via Nomentana. This bus also passes the British Embassy. Both the US and British embassies are easily accessible on foot from the station. The French Embassy and consulate are in Roma's historic centre and also easily reached on foot.

Money Banks are open Monday to Friday from 8.30 am to 1.30 pm and usually from 2.45 to 3.45 pm. You will find a bank and several exchange offices at Stazione Termini. There is also an exchange office (Banco di Santo Spirito) at Fiumicino airport, to the right as you exit from the customs area. Numerous other exchange offices are scattered throughout the city, including American Express in Piazza di Spagna and Thomas Cook in Piazza Barberini and Piazza della Repubblica.

Most people use *bancomats* (ATMs) these days to get cash advances on their credit cards and you should have no problems in Roma. It is straightforward, and most bancomats give you the option of conducting the transaction in English, French or German. Visa card holders should have no problems at most banks, but you could have problems with MasterCard. Go directly to a branch of the Banca Commerciale Italiana or the Deutsche Bank, Largo Tritone 161, to avoid wasting time. The head office of the Banca Commerciale, at Via del Corso 226, at Piazza Venezia, is also a good place to receive money transfers; the closest branch to Stazione Termini is at Largo Santa Susanna 124, through Piazza della Repubblica, just before Via Barberini. Western Union is expanding its money transfer facilities worldwide and there is an office downstairs at Stazione Termini, at the Fertravel Travel Agency (☎ 48 36 95).

Post See the Facts for the Visitor chapter for more detailed information about postal services in Italy.

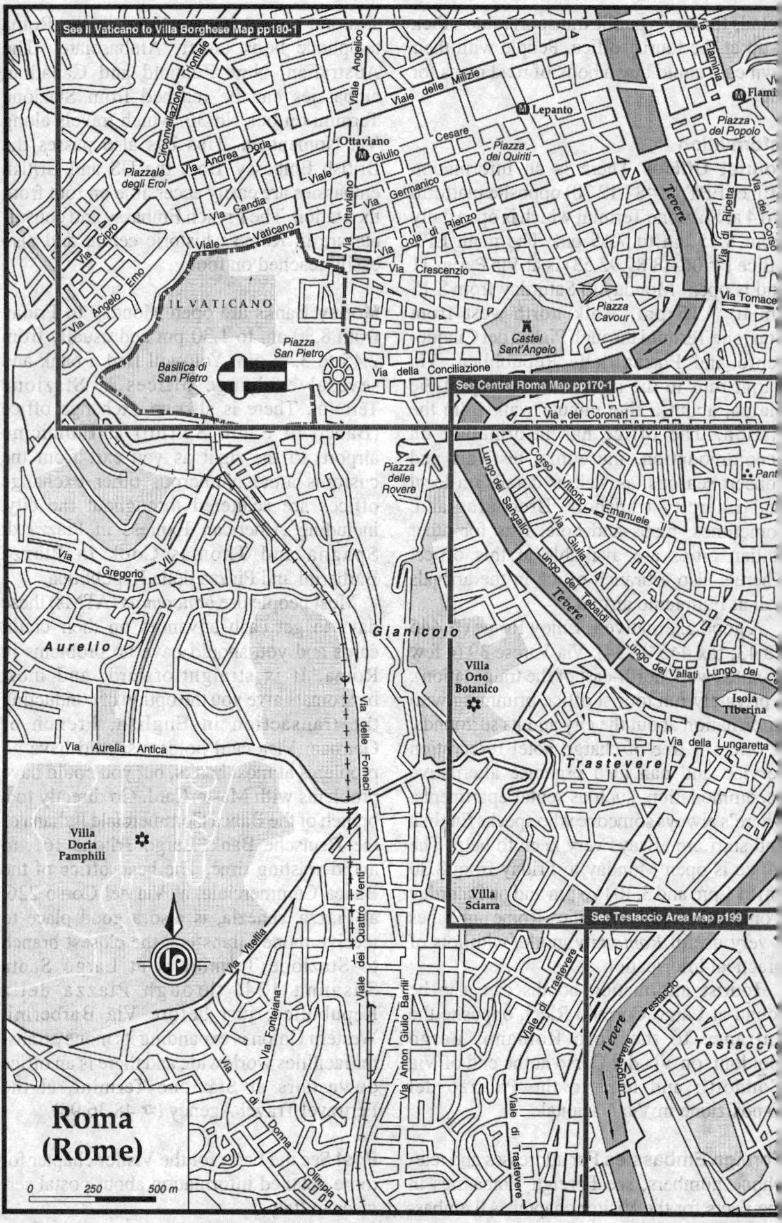
See Il Vaticano to Villa Borghese Map pp180-1
See Central Roma Map pp170-1
See Testaccio Area Map p199
Circonvallazione Trionfale
Viale Angelico
Viale delle Milizie
Lepanto
Via Flaminia
Flaminio
Piazza del Popolo
Ottaviano
Giulio
Cesare
Piazza dei Quiriti
Via Andrea Doria
Piazzale degli Eroi
Viale
Via Germanico
Tevere
Via di Ripetta
Via del Corso
Via Candia
Via Ottaviano
Via Cola di Rienzo
Viale Vaticano
Via Cipro
Via Crescenzio
Via Angelo Emo
IL VATICANO
Piazza Cavour
Via Tomacelli
Castel Sant'Angelo
Piazza San Pietro
Basilica di San Pietro
Via della Conciliazione
Via dei Coronari
Pantheon
Piazza delle Rovere
Lungo dei Sangallo
Corso Vittorio Emanuele
Via Giulia
Lungo dei Tebaldi
Tevere
Via Gregorio VII
Gianicolo
Aurelio
Lungo dei Vallati
Lungo dei Cenci
Villa Orto Botanico
Isola Tiberina
Via delle Fornaci
Via Aurelia Antica
Via della Lungaretta
Trastevere
Villa Doria Pamphili
Villa Sciarra
Via Vitellia
Viale dei Quattro Venti
Viale di Trastevere
Via Testaccio
Tevere
Lungotevere
Testaccio
Via Fonteiana
Via Anton Giulio Barrili
Via di Donna Olimpia
Roma (Rome)
0 250 500 m

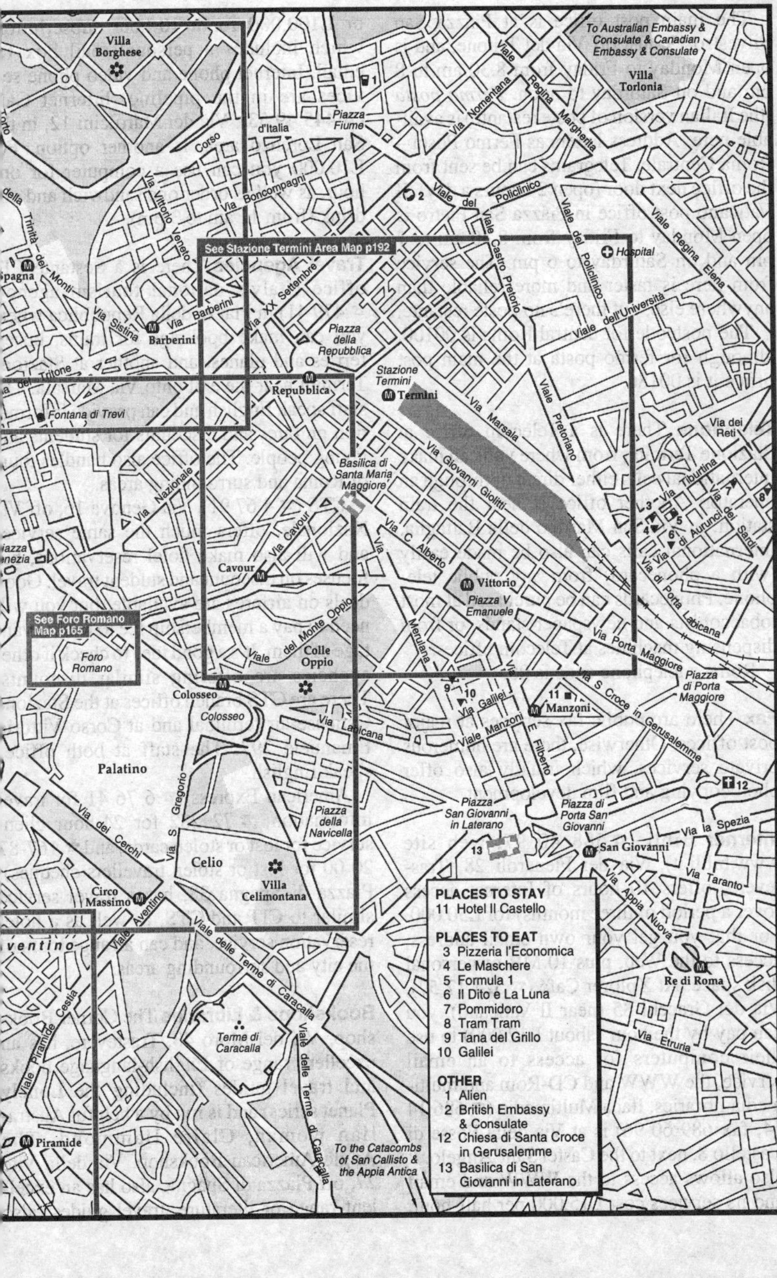
To Australian Embassy & Consulate & Canadian Embassy & Consulate
Villa Torlonia
Villa Borghese
Piazza Fiume
d'Italia
Corso
Via Nomentana
Viale Regina Margherita
Via Boncompagni
Via Vittorio Veneto
Viale del Policlinico
Viale Castro Pretorio
Viale Regina Elena
della Trinità dei Monti
Spagna
Via Sistina
Via Barberini
Barberini
Via XX Settembre
See Stazione Termini Area Map p192
Hospital
Viale dell'Università
Piazza della Repubblica
Stazione Termini
Termini
Repubblica
del Tritone
Fontana di Trevi
Via Marsala
Viale Pretoriano
Via dei Reti
Via Nazionale
Basilica di Santa Maria Maggiore
Via Giovanni Giolitti
Via Tiburtina
Via dei Sardi
Via degli Aurunci
Via di Porta Labicana
Via Cavour
Via C Alberto
Cavour
Vittorio
Piazza V Emanuele
iazza enezia
See Foro Romano Map p165
Foro Romano
Viale del Monte Oppio
Colle Oppio
Via Merulana
Via Porta Maggiore
Piazza di Porta Maggiore
Colosseo
Via Labicana
Via Galilei
Manzoni
Viale Manzoni
Via S Croce in Gerusalemme
Via E Filiberto
Palatino
Via S Gregorio
Via dei Cerchi
Piazza della Navicella
Piazza San Giovanni in Laterano
Piazza di Porta San Giovanni
San Giovanni
Via la Spezia
Via Taranto
Celio
Villa Celimontana
Circo Massimo
Viale Aventino
Via Appia Nuova
ventino
Viale delle Terme di Caracalla
Re di Roma
Terme di Caracalla
Via Etruria
Viale Piramide Cestia
Piramide
To the Catacombs of San Callisto & the Appia Antica
PLACES TO STAY
11 Hotel Il Castello
PLACES TO EAT
3 Pizzeria l'Economica
4 Le Maschere
5 Formula 1
6 Il Dito e La Luna
7 Pommidoro
8 Tram Tram
9 Tana del Grillo
10 Galilei
OTHER
1 Alien
2 British Embassy & Consulate
12 Chiesa di Santa Croce in Gerusalemme
13 Basilica di San Giovanni in Laterano

The main post office is at Piazza San Silvestro 19, just off Via del Tritone, and is open Monday to Friday from 8.30 am to 8 pm and on Saturday to noon. *Fermo posta* (the Italian version of poste restante) is available here. Address letters as Fermo Posta – Roma Centrale. Telegrams can be sent from the office next door (open 24 hours a day). Il Vaticano post office in Piazza San Pietro is open Monday to Friday from 8.30 am to 7 pm and on Saturday to 6 pm. The service from here is faster and more reliable than anywhere else, but there's no poste restante.

The postcode for central Roma is 00100, although for fermo posta at the main post office it is 00186.

Telephone There is a Telecom office at Stazione Termini, from where you can make international calls either direct or through an operator. Another office is near the train station, in Via San Martino della Battaglia. International calls can also be made easily (with a phonecard) from any public telephone. Phonecards can be purchased at most tobacconists and newspaper stands, or from dispensing machines at Telecom offices.

Roma's telephone code is 06.

Fax There are public fax services at major post offices. Otherwise, there are numerous private services, which usually also offer photocopying and film development.

Internet Bibli (☎ 588 40 97; web site www.bibli.it), Via dei Fienaroli 28, Trastevere, offers 10 hours of Internet access (over a period of three months) for L50,000. For that you get your own email address, access to the Web, plus 10 MB of personal disk space. At Xplorer Café (☎ 324 17 57), Via dei Gracchi 85 (near Il Vaticano), you can pay by the hour (about L12,000) to use their computers for access to an email service, the WWW and CD-Rom and multimedia libraries. Itaca Multimedia (☎ 686 14 64; fax 689 60 96) is at Via della Fosse di Castello 8, next to the Castel Sant'Angelo. It also allows access to the WWW and email and its services cost L15,000 per half-hour, or L100,000 for a 10-hour subscriptio which includes a personal mail box f email. Internet phone and video phone se vices are in the pipeline. Internet Ca (☎ 445 49 53), Via dei Marrucini 12, in t San Lorenzo area, is another option. F L10,000 you can use a computer for o hour, as well as order one sandwich and o drink (from 11 am to 3 pm).

Travel Agencies There is a Sestante CI office (Italy's national tourism agenc ☎ 479 41) in Piazza della Repubblica whe you can make bookings for trains, buse ferries and planes, and another at Stazior Termini near the exit onto Via Marsala. Th staff speak English and can provide informa tion on fares and discounts for students an young people. The office also handles tou of Roma and surrounding areas.

CTS (☎ 4 67 91), Via Genova 16, off Vi Nazionale, offers much the same service and will also make hotel reservations, bu focuses on discount and student travel. Goo deals on airfares are available, but you wi need to pay a membership fee to take advan tage of them. It's a good idea to check if othe agencies are offering similar discounts There are CTS branch offices at the Stazion Ostiense air terminal and at Corso Vittori Emanuele 297. The staff at both office speak English.

American Express (☎ 6 76 41 for trave information; ☎ 72 282 for 24-hour clien service for lost or stolen cards; and ☎ 167-87 20 00 for lost or stolen travellers cheques) Piazza di Spagna 38, has a travel service similar to CIT and CTS, as well as a hote reservation service, and can arrange tours o the city and surrounding areas.

Bookshops & Libraries The Corner Bookshop, Via del Moro 48, Trastevere, has an excellent range of English-language books and travel guides (including the Lonely Planet series) and is run by a helpful Australian woman, Claire Hammond. The Anglo-American Bookshop, Via della Vite 27, off Piazza di Spagna, also has an excellent range of literature, travel guides (also cluding Lonely Planet) and reference ooks and is also the Thomas Cook agent for aly. The Lion Bookshop is now closed. eltrinelli International, Via VE Orlando 84, ust off Piazza della Repubblica, has an xtensive range of books for adults and chil-ren in English, Spanish, French, German nd Portuguese, plus lots of guidebooks for oma and Italy, as well as for the rest of the orld (Lonely Planet guides included). See lso Feltrinelli in Largo Argentina. The conomy Book & Video Center, Via Torino 36, also has a good selection of books, as ell as second-hand paperbacks.

The British Council (☎ 47 81 41), Via elle Quattro Fontane 20, allows free public se of its large reference library. It has closed own its lending service and, in 1997, was n the process of setting up a multimedia nformation service. This will offer such ser-ices as use of CD-Roms, Internet access and erhaps email facilities.

aundry There are coin laundrettes, Onda lu, at Via Principe Amedeo 70b, near the rain station; Via Milazzo 8a/b; Via amarmora 10; and Via delle Cave 28/32.

ledical Services Emergency medical treat-nent is available in the casualty sections of ublic hospitals, including: Policlinico Jmberto I (☎ 4 99 71), Viale del Policlinico 55, near Stazione Termini; and Policlinico Gemelli (☎ 33 01 51), Largo A Gemelli 8 some distance from the centre). For skin roblems go to Ospedale San Gallicano ☎ 588 23 90), Via San Gallicano, in Trastevere. The hospital also has a venereal liseases clinic. For HIV/AIDS treatment, ontact Ospedale Spallanzani (☎ 58 23 76 9), Via Portuense 332. For information bout abortion, go to the free clinic at Ospedale San Camillo (☎ 5 87 01), Cir-convallazione Gianacolense. There is a gynaecological clinic, known by its acronym AIED (☎ 884 0661), at Via Salaria 58, where oreign women can seek medical assistance. English-speaking doctors work there twice a veek: phone for appointments.

The American Hospital (☎ 2 25 51), Via E Longoni 69, is private and you should use its services only if you have health insurance and have consulted your insurance company. Roma's paediatric hospital is Bambino Gesù (☎ 68 59 23 51) on the Gianicolo (Janiculum hill) at Piazza Sant'Onofrio.

In general, the casualty sections of Roma's hospitals give free treatment to emergency patients. However, if you are admitted, or are referred to a specialist, you may be charged a fee. See the Health section in Facts for the Visitor for further details.

Your embassy will be able to recommend where to go for medical treatment and should be able to refer you to doctors who speak your language. For an ambulance, call ☎ 51 00, or ☎ 118.

There is a pharmacy (☎ 488 00 19) which is open 24 hours a day, just outside Stazione Termini, at Piazza dei Cinquecento 51. Inside the station a pharmacy opens daily from 7.30 am to 10 pm (closed in August). For recorded information (only in Italian) on other 24-hour pharmacies in Roma, call ☎ 19 21. Otherwise, closed pharmacies are required by law to post a list in their windows of others open nearby.

Emergency The questura (police station, ☎ 46 86) is at Via San Vitale 15. The Ufficio Stranieri (Foreigners' Bureau ☎ 46 86 29 87) is around the corner at Via Genova 2. It is open 24 hours a day and thefts can be reported here. You need to go here if you want to apply for a permesso di soggiorno. For immediate police attendance, call ☎ 112 or 113.

Dangers & Annoyances Thieves are very active around Stazione Termini, at major sights such as the Colosseo and Foro Romano, and in the city's more expensive shopping streets, such as around Piazza di Spagna. Be careful in crowded shops and watch out for motorcycle-riding bag and camera snatchers. Pickpockets like to work on crowded buses (the No 64 from Stazione Termini to San Pietro is notorious and the No 27 from Stazione Termini to the Colosseo is not much better). For more comprehensive information on how to avoid being robbed see the Dangers & Annoyances section in the Facts for the Visitor chapter.

Although Roma's traffic is nowhere near as chaotic as in Napoli, many drivers, particularly motorcyclists, do not stop at red lights. Don't expect them to stop at pedestrian crossings either. The accepted mode of crossing a road is to step into the traffic and walk at a steady pace. If in doubt, follow a Roman.

The heavy traffic also means heavy pollution which, in summer, under certain conditions, can rise to such high levels that elderly people, children and people with respiratory complaints are warned to stay indoors. Check with your hotel for daily information.

Other Information If you need a wash when you arrive in Roma, there are public baths downstairs at Stazione Termini (follow the 'diurno' signs) open from 6.40 am to 8 pm. Showers cost L12,000.

Also inside Termini is a new 24-hour multi-purpose store, in the style of an American drugstore. Here you can get just about anything you need any time of the day, seven days a week.

Suggested Itineraries

Try not to overdo it if you have only a short time in Roma, and remember there is much more to the city than Roman ruins – it's worth making the time to have at least one long lunch at a little trattoria or pizzeria in one of the many piazzas.

One Day
: San Pietro and Musei del Vaticano in the morning; Piazza del Campidoglio, Foro Romano, Palatino, Via dei Fori Imperiali and the Colosseo in the afternoon (the Foro Romano closes at 2 pm in winter and 5 pm in summer).

Two Days
: As above for the first day; then on the second day, a visit to one of the catacombs (such as San Callisto) on the Via Appia Antica (Appian Way) in the morning and, in the afternoon, a wander around the historic centre of Roma to see the Scalinata della Trinità dei Monti (Spanish Steps), Fontana di Trevi, the Pantheon and Piazza Navona, where you can stop for a well-earn coffee before planning the evening's activities

Three Days
: As above for the first two days; then on the thi day, visit some of Roma's more interestir churches (see the tour outlined in the boxed asic on Mosaics) but adding Santa Maria Maggio and San Giovanni in Laterano.

One Week
: All of the above, plus visits to some of the fo lowing: the Musei Capitolini, the Galleria Borgh ese (and a walk through the Villa Borghese), th Museo Nazionale di Villa Giulia and the Term di Caracalla (Caracalla Baths), as well as a da trip out of Roma, to one or more of the followin – Tivoli (Villa Adriana and Villa d'Este), Osti Antica (ancient Roman port town) or Tarquini (painted Etruscan tombs). Or, if you want break, take time out to wander around th Aventino (Aventine Hill) or Celio (Celian Hill where you can picnic in a park.

Piazza del Campidoglio

Designed by Michelangelo in 1538 an located on the Campidoglio (Capitoline hill) this piazza is bordered by three palaces: th Palazzo dei Conservatori on the south side the Palazzo dei Senatori at the rear, and th Palazzo Nuovo. The palace façades wer also designed by Michelangelo. It was o this hill, which was the seat of the ancien Roman government and is now the seat o the city's municipal government, that Brutu spoke of the death of Julius Caesar and wher Nelson hoisted the British flag in 179 before he prevented Napoleon from enterin the city. For the greatest visual impact approach the piazza from Piazza d'Aracoel

Recognising the Four Evangelists

The four evangelists, Matthew, Mark, Luke and John, who wrote the gospels which record events in the life of Christ, are very often represented in early Christian art with symbols. Matthew is depicted as an eagle, Mark as a lion, Luke as a bull and John as a man. Look for the symbols of the evangelists in mosaics and in bas-relief decorations and on capitals in Romanesque churches. ■

and ascend the *cordonata*, a stepped ramp also designed by Michelangelo.

The bronze equestrian statue of Emperor Marcus Aurelius in the centre of the piazza is a copy of the original, which has been restored and is now displayed inside the Palazzo del Museo Capitolino.

Musei Capitolini (Capitoline Museums) is the title used to describe the two museums in the Palazzo del Museo Capitolino and the Palazzo dei Conservatori opposite. The most famous piece is the *Capitoline Wolf*, an Etruscan bronze statue from the 6th century BC. Romulus and Remus were added in 1509. It stands in the Sala della Lupa on the 1st floor of the Palazzo dei Conservatori. Also of interest in this wing are the *Spinario*, a statue of a boy taking a thorn from his foot, dating from the 1st century BC, and a bronze bust of Julius Caesar's assassin, Brutus. Both are in Room 3 on the 1st floor.

The inner court of the ground floor contains the fascinating remains of a colossal statue of Emperor Constantine – the head, a hand and a foot – which were removed from the Basilica di Costantino in the Foro Romano. You can look at these without having to pay for admission into the museum.

Major works in the **Museo Nuovo** in the Palazzo del Museo Capitolino, include the impressive *Dying Gaul* in Room 1 on the 1st floor, and the *Capitoline Venus*, a Roman copy of a 3rd-century BC Greek original, in Room 7. Well worth a look is the collection of busts of Roman emperors and other famous people of the day.

The museums are open Tuesday to Saturday from 9 am to 7 pm and Sunday from 9 am to 1 pm. Admission is L10,000.

If you walk to the right of Palazzo del Senato on Via del Campidoglio you'll see one of the best views in Roma – a panorama of the Foro Romano. To the left of the palace is Via di San Pietro in Carcere, and the ancient Roman **Carcere Mamertino** (Mammertine Prison), where prisoners were put through a hole in the floor to starve to death. St Peter was believed to have been imprisoned here and to have created a miraculous stream of water to baptise his jailers. It is now the site of Chiesa di San Pietro in Carcere.

The **Chiesa di Santa Maria in Aracoeli** is between the Piazza del Campidoglio and Monumento Vittorio Emanuele II at the highest point of the hill. It is accessible either by a long flight of steps from the Piazza d'Aracoeli, or from behind the Palazzo del Museo Capitolino.

Built on the site where legend says the Tiburtine Sybil told Augustus of the coming birth of Christ, it features frescoes by Pinturicchio in the first chapel of the south aisle. The church is noted for a statue of the baby Jesus said to have been carved from the wood of an olive tree from the garden of Gethsemane. The statue was stolen in 1994 and a replica is on display.

Piazza Venezia

The piazza is overshadowed by one of Italy's more unusual monuments, dedicated to Victor Emmanuel II. Often referred to by Italians as the *macchina da scrivere* (typewriter) – because it resembles one – the monument was built to commemorate Italian unification. It incorporates the **Altare della Patria** (Altar of the Fatherland) and the tomb of the unknown soldier. Considered out of harmony with its surroundings, the monument has prompted many calls for its demolition. On the west side of the piazza is the Renaissance **Palazzo Venezia**, which was partially built with materials quarried from the Colosseo. Mussolini used it as his official residence and made some of his famous speeches from the balcony. Major exhibitions are held here. The **Museo di Palazzo Venezia**, entrance at Via del Plebiscito 118, has an interesting collection of paintings, jewellery, precious ceramics and sculptures in wood, bronze and marble. The museum is open Tuesday to Saturday from 9 am to 1.30 pm and Sunday to 12.30 pm.

Actually part of the Palazzo Venezia, but facing onto Piazza San Marco, the **Basilica di San Marco** was founded in the 4th century in honour of St Mark the Evangelist. After undergoing several major transformations over the centuries, the church has a Renaissance façade, a Romanesque bell tower and a largely Baroque interior. The main attraction is the 9th-century mosaic in the apse, which depicts Christ with saints and Pope Gregory IV.

The **Palazzo Doria Pamphili** is just north of Piazza Venezia on the corner of Via del Corso and Via del Plebiscito. Inside you will also find the **Galleria Doria Pamphili**, which contains the private collections of the Doria and Pamphili families, including paintings by Titian, Tintoretto and Caravaggio, as well as a collection of sculptures. The Gallery is open daily, except Thursday from 10 am to 5 pm. Admission is from Piazza del Collegio Romano 1 and costs L10,000 for the gallery and L5000 to visit the private apartments.

Linking Piazza Venezia with the Colosseo is the Via dei Fori Imperiali, an unfortunate project of Mussolini's which saw many 16th-century buildings destroyed and part of the Velia hill levelled. The road, which runs over part of the Foro di Traiano, was opened in 1933 after only superficial excavations and studies had been undertaken. It has been proposed that the road should be closed between Via Cavour and Piazza Venezia. At present, traffic is limited and the entire

Mosaics in Roma

Few tourists know that 'hidden' in Roma's medieval churches are some of the most beautiful Byzantine-style mosaics in Italy. Most of these mosaics decorate the apses of the city's important churches, such as Santa Maria Maggiore, Santa Maria in Trastevere and San Clemente. The oldest mosaics date from the 4th century (Mausoleo di Santa Costanza and Chiesa di Santa Pudenziana), the period in which the Roman art of mosaic-making was evolving into the early Christian and Byzantine styles. Those depicting Santa Costanza retain some characteristics of Roman mosaics: a white background, geometric composition and ornamental motifs.

During the reign of Emperor Constantine, who had legalised the Christian religion, many churches were being built and ornamental mosaic became the main form of decoration. Often used to cover vast areas of wall inside these new churches, they were a form of architectural tapestry which, with their uneven tesserae of coloured glass and gold, brilliantly reflected light to create strong effects and sharp contrasts of colour.

Roma's early-Christian mosaics also illustrate the progression from the naturalism of Roman art to the symbolism of Christian art, reflected, for example, in the various ways in which Jesus Christ was represented. A very early Christian mosaic, in a mausoleum under the Basilica di San Pietro, shows Christ in the form of Apollo. In Chiesa di Santa Pudenziana (390 AD) he is represented enthroned between the apostles, but his magisterial air is reminiscent of Jupiter and the apostles are dressed as Roman senators. By the 9th century, as in Chiesa di Santa Prassede, he has become the 'Lamb' and the faithful his 'flock'.

The mosaics of Roma's medieval churches are a fascinating and often overlooked treasure for the tourist who might not have time to visit Ravenna or Monreale. The following is a suggested itinerary of some of the lesser known churches. The mosaics in major churches are described later in this chapter.

The **Mausoleo di Santa Costanza** was built in the mid-4th century by Costantia, daughter of Constantine, as a mausoleum for herself and her sister Helen. This round church is in the same grounds as **Basilica di Sant'Agnese Fuori le Mura**, on Via Nomentana, a few km north of the centre (catch bus No 60 from Piazza Venezia). As well as the fascinating paleochristian mosaics on the barrel-vaulting of the ambulatory, the 7th-century mosaic of St Agnes and popes Symmachus and Honorius I in the apse of the basilica are also worth taking a look at.

Tradition says that **Chiesa di Santa Pudenziana**, one of the oldest churches in Roma, was founded on the site of a house where St Peter was given hospitality. The structure actually incorporated the internal thermal hall of the house. The mosaic in the apse dates from 390 AD and is the earliest of its kind in Roma but, unfortunately, was partially destroyed by a 16th-century restoration. The church is in Via Urbana.

Basilica di SS Cosma e Damiano, on Via dei Fori Imperiali, harbours magnificent 6th-century

stretch from the Colosseo to Piazza Venezia becomes a pedestrian zone on most Sundays.

Foro di Traiano

Designed by Apollodorus of Damascus for Emperor Trajan and constructed at the beginning of the 2nd century AD, the Foro di Traiano (Trajan's Forum) was the last of the forums. It was a vast complex, measuring 300 by 185m, extending from what is now Piazza Venezia, and comprised a basilica for the judiciary, two libraries – one Greek and one Latin – a temple, a triumphal arch in honour of the emperor, and the **Colonna di Traiano** (Trajan's Column). Restored in the late 1980s, the column was erected to mark the victories of Trajan over the Dacians, who lived in what is now Romania. It was built to house the ashes of the emperor, which were contained in a golden urn placed on a marble slab at the base of the column. The urn, along with the ashes, disappeared during one of the barbarian sacks of Roma.

The column is decorated with a spiral series of reliefs depicting the battles between the Roman and Dacian armies, which are regarded as among the finest examples of ancient Roman sculpture. A golden statue of Trajan once topped the column, but it was lost during the Middle Ages and replaced with a statue of St Peter. Apart from the

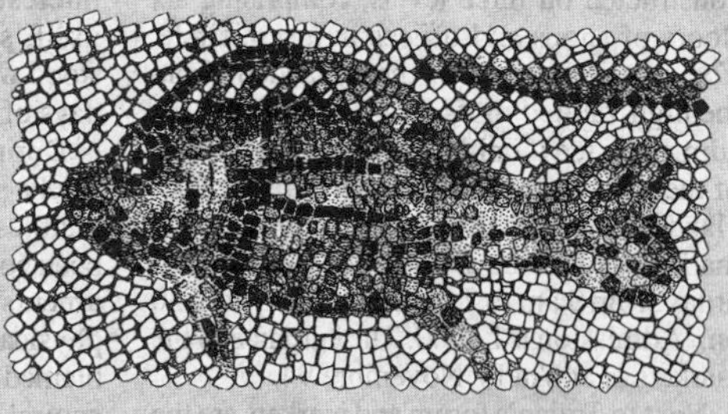

mosaics on the triumphal arch (Christ as the Lamb enthroned, surrounded by candlesticks and angels, as well as the symbols of the Evangelists) and in the apse of the saints Cosma and Damian being presented to Christ by saints Peter and Paul and, underneath, Christ as the Lamb, with the 12 apostles also represented as lambs. Bethlehem and Jerusalem are represented on either side.

The 9th-century **Chiesa di Santa Prassede**, in Via Santa Prassede, was founded in honour of St Praxedes, sister of St Pudentiana, by Pope Paschal I, who transferred the bones of 2000 martyrs there from the catacombs.The rich mosaics of the apse date from the 9th century and feature Christ in the centre of the semi-dome, surrounded by saints Peter, Pudentiana and Zeno (to the right) and saints Paul, Praxedes and Paschal (to the left). Underneath is Christ the Lamb and his flock. The **Cappella di San Zenone** (Chapel of St Zeno), inside the church, is the most important Byzantine monument in Roma, built by Paschal I as a mausoleum for his mother. Known as the Garden of Paradise, the chapel has a vaulted interior completely covered in mosaics, including the *Madonna with Saints*, *Christ with Saints* and, in the vault, *Christ with Angels*. The pavement of the chapel is one of the earliest examples of opus sectile (polychrome marble), and in a small niche on the right are fragments of a column brought from Jerusalem in 1223 and said to be the column at which Christ was scourged.

Across the Tevere, in Piazza dei Mercanti, is the **Basilica di Santa Cecilia in Trastevere,** built in the 9th century by Paschal I over the house of St Cecilia, where she was martyred in 230. The impressive mosaic in the apse was executed in 870 and features Christ giving a blessing. To his right are saints Peter, Valerian (husband of St Cecilia) and Cecilia. To his left are Saints Paul, Agatha and Paschal. The holy cities are depicted underneath. The baldacchino over the main altar was carved by Arnolfo di Cambio, and the statue of St Cecilia in front of the altar is by Stefano Maderno. This finely carved statue depicts with considerable compassion the body of the saint as she was found when her tomb was opened in 1599. Of great interest are the excavations of Roman houses, one of which was perhaps the house of St Cecilia, underneath the church. These ruins of ancient houses are accessible from the room at the end of the left aisle, as you enter the church. There is a 13th-century fresco of the *Last Judgment* by Pietro Cavallin in the convent, only on view on Tuesday and Thursday from 10 to 11.15 am and on Sunday from midday to 12.30 pm. ■

The Roman Basilica

This type of building was introduced into the Foro Romano in the 2nd century BC. A large covered space devoted to public meetings and legal and administrative activities, a basilica usually had an apse, a long hall and two aisles. The design was adapted for the first Christian basilicas. ■

column, all that remains of the grand imperial forum are some of the pillars which once formed part of the Basilica Ulpia, the largest basilica built in Ancient Rome.

By comparison, the **Mercati di Traiano** (Trajan's Markets) are well preserved. Also designed by Apollodorus, the markets were constructed on three levels, comprising six floors of shops and offices in a semicircle. You can get an idea of their grandeur from the high vaulted roofs. It's worth paying the admission fee if only to reach the high levels of the market, from where there are spectacular views across to the Foro Romano. The markets and forum are open Tuesday to Saturday from 9 am to 7 pm and Sunday to 1.30 pm. Admission is L4000. The entrance to the markets is at Via IV Novembre 94.

Next to Trajan's forum and markets are the **forums of Augustus** and **Nerva**, although very little remains of either complex. The 30m-high wall behind the Foro d'Augusto was built to protect the area from the fires which frequently swept through the area known as the Suburra (suburb).

There is a delightful walkway beneath the loggia of the Casa dei Cavalieri di Rodi (ancient seat of the Knights of St John of Jerusalem), which is between the forums of Trajan and Augustus and accessible from either Via dei Fori Imperiali or Piazza del Grillo. In summer the three forums are illuminated at night.

Across the Via dei Fori Imperiali is the Foro di Cesare, which was built by Julius Caesar at the foot of the Campidoglio. Again, very little remains to give an idea of the original structure.

Foro Romano & Palatino

The commercial, political and religious centre of Ancient Rome, the Foro Romano (Roman Forum) stands in a valley between the Capitoline and Palatine hills. Originally marshland, the area was drained during the early Republican era and became a centre for political rallies, public ceremonies and Senate meetings. The forum was constructed over 900 years, with later emperors erecting buildings next to those from the Republican era. Its importance declined along with the Roman Empire after the 4th century AD, and the temples, monuments and buildings constructed by successive emperors, consuls and senators fell into ruin, eventually leading to the site being used as pasture land. In the Middle Ages the area was known as the Campo Vaccino (literally, cow field), an interesting example of history repeating itself, since the valley in which the forum stood was used as pasture land in the earliest days of the city's development.

During medieval times the area was extensively plundered for its stone and precious marbles. Many temples and buildings had been converted to other uses and other monuments lay half revealed. Ironically, the physical destruction of Ancient Rome can be blamed not on the invading barbarians or natural disasters such as earthquake, but on the Romans themselves. Over the centuries, in the name of progress, the Romans dismantled the ancient city brick by brick and marble block by marble block in order to build their own palaces, churches and monuments.

During the Renaissance, with the renewed appreciation of all things classical, the forum provided inspiration for artists and architects. The area was systematically excavated in the 18th and 19th centuries, and excavations are continuing. You can watch archaeological teams at work in several locations.

You can enter the forum from Via dei Fori Imperiali. Opening hours vary according to the season; in summer it's open Monday to Saturday from 9 am to 6 pm, and to 3 pm in winter, and year-round on Sunday to 1 pm.

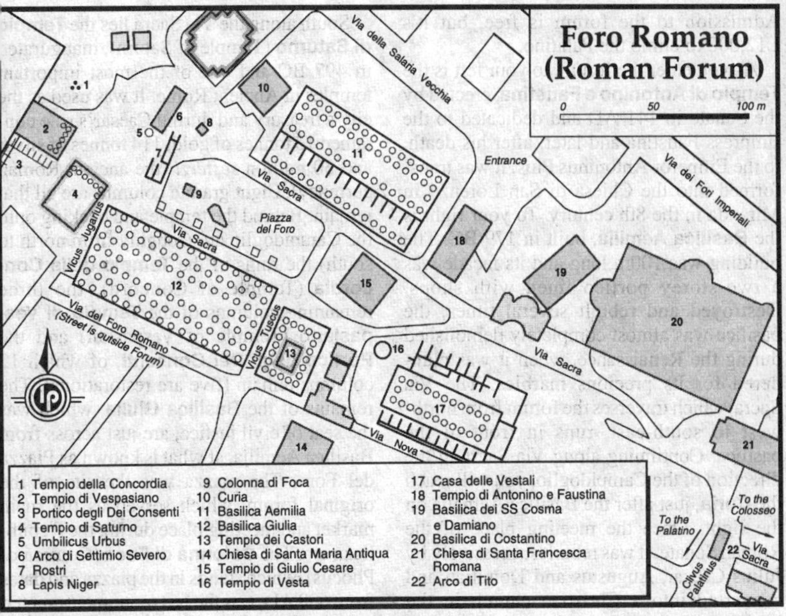
Foro Romano
(Roman Forum)
0
50
100 m
Via della Salaria Vecchia
Entrance
Via dei Fori Imperiali
Via Sacra
Piazza
del Foro
Vicus Jugarius
Vicus Tuscus
Via del Foro Romano
(Street is outside Forum)
Via Nova
To the
Colosseo
To the
Palatino
Clivus
Palatinus
1 Tempio della Concordia
2 Tempio di Vespasiano
3 Portico degli Dei Consenti
4 Tempio di Saturno
5 Umbilicus Urbus
6 Arco di Settimio Severo
7 Rostri
8 Lapis Niger
9 Colonna di Foca
10 Curia
11 Basilica Aemilia
12 Basilica Giulia
13 Tempio dei Castori
14 Chiesa di Santa Maria Antiqua
15 Tempio di Giulio Cesare
16 Tempio di Vesta
17 Casa delle Vestali
18 Tempio di Antonino e Faustina
19 Basilica dei SS Cosma
e Damiano
20 Basilica di Costantino
21 Chiesa di Santa Francesca
Romana
22 Arco di Tito

The Foro Romano as it would have looked in ancient times.

Admission to the forum is free, but it's L12,000 to climb the Palatino.

As you enter the forum, to your left is the **Tempio di Antonino e Faustina**, erected by the Senate in 141 AD and dedicated to the Empress Faustina and later, after his death, to the Emperor Antoninus Pius. It was transformed into the Chiesa di San Lorenzo in Miranda in the 8th century. To your right is the **Basilica Aemilia**, built in 179 BC. The building was 100m long and its façade was a two-storey portico lined with shops. Destroyed and rebuilt several times, the basilica was almost completely demolished during the Renaissance, when it was plundered for its precious marbles. The Via Sacra, which traverses the forum from north-west to south-east, runs in front of the basilica. Continuing along Via Sacra in the direction of the Campidoglio, you will reach the **Curia**, just after the Basilica Aemelia on the right. Once the meeting place of the Roman Senate, it was rebuilt successively by Julius Caesar, Augustus and Domitian and converted into a Christian church in the Middle Ages. The church was dismantled and the Curia restored in the 1930s. The bronze doors are copies – the Roman originals were moved by Borromini to San Giovanni in Laterano.

In front of the Curia is the famous **Lapis Niger**, a large piece of black marble which covered a sacred area legend says was the tomb of Romulus. Down a short flight of stairs (rarely open to the public), under the Lapis Niger, is the oldest known Latin inscription, dating from the 6th century BC.

The **Arco di Settimio Severo** (Arch of Septimus Severus) was erected in 203 AD in honour of this emperor and his sons and is considered one of Italy's major triumphal arches. A project to renovate the arch left it exactly half cleaned in 1988 when the money ran out. Work is now underway to clean the other half. To the south is the Rostrum, used in ancient times by public speakers and once decorated with the rams of captured ships. A circular base stone, the *umbilicus urbis*, beside the arch marks the symbolic centre of Ancient Rome.

South along the Via Sacra lies the **Tempio di Saturno** (Temple of Saturn), inaugurated in 497 BC and one of the most important temples in Ancient Rome. It was used as the city's treasury and during Caesar's rule contained 13 tonnes of gold, 114 tonnes of silver and 30 million *sesterzi* (the ancient Roman currency). Eight granite columns are all that remain. Behind the temple and backing onto the Campidoglio are (roughly from north to south) the ruins of the **Tempio della Concordia** (Temple of Concord), the three remaining columns of the **Tempio di Vespasiano** (Temple of Vespasian) and the **Portico degli Dei Consenti**, of which 12 columns remain (five are restorations). The remains of the **Basilica Giulia**, which was the seat of civil justice, are just across from Basilica Aemilia, at what is known as Piazza del Foro. The piazza was the site of the original forum, which served as the main market and meeting place during the Republican era. The **Colonna di Foca** (Column of Phocus), which stands in the piazza and dates from 608 AD, was the last monument erected in the forum. It honoured the Eastern Emperor Phocus who donated the Pantheon to the church. At the south-eastern end of the piazza is the **Tempio di Giulio Cesare** (Temple of Julius Caesar), which was erected by Augustus in 29 BC on the site where Caesar's body was burned and Mark Antony read his famous speech. Back towards the Palatino is the **Tempio dei Castori** (Temple of Castor & Pollux), built in 489 BC to mark the defeat of the Etruscan Tarquins and in honour of the Heavenly Twins, or Dioscuri, who miraculously appeared to the Roman troops during an important battle. The temple was restored during the 1980s.

In the area south-east of the temple is the **Chiesa di Santa Maria Antiqua**, the oldest Christian church in the forum. Inside the church are some early Christian frescoes. This area, including the church, has been closed to the public since 1992. Back on the Via Sacra is the **Casa delle Vestali** (House of the Vestals), home of the virgins who tended the sacred flame in the adjoining

Tempio di Vesta. The six virgin priestesses, aged between six and 10 years were selected from patrician families. They had to serve in the temple for 30 years and during this time they were bound by a vow of chastity. If the flame in the temple went out it was seen as a bad omen and the responsible priestess would be flogged. If a priestess lost her virginity she was buried alive, since her blood could not be spilled, and the offending man was flogged to death.

The next major monument is the vast **Basilica di Costantino**, also known as the Basilica di Massenzio. The Emperor Maxentius initiated work on the basilica and it was finished in 315 AD by Constantine. Its impressive design provided inspiration for Renaissance architects, possibly including Michelangelo. The **Arco di Tito** (Arch of Titus), at the Colosseo end of the forum, was built in 81 AD in honour of the victories of the emperors Titus and Vespasian against Jerusalem. This arch, along with that of Constantine, was once incorporated into the medieval Frangipani fortress.

From here, follow the Clivio Palatino to the right to reach the Palatino, the mythical founding place of Roma. Wealthy Romans built their homes here during the Republican era and it later became the realm of the emperors. Like those of the forum, the temples and palaces of the Palatino fell into ruin and in the Middle Ages a few churches and castles were built over the remains. During the Renaissance, members of wealthy families established their gardens on the hill, notably Cardinal Alessandro Farnese, who had his **Orti Farnesiani**, Europe's first botanical gardens, laid out over the ruins of the Domus Tiberiana. Excavations are being carried out at the site. South-west of the gardens is the **Tempio della Magna Mater**, also known as the Tempio di Cibele (Temple of Cybele], built in 204 BC to house a black stone connected with the Asiatic goddess of fertility, Cybele. East of here is the **Casa di Livia**, thought to have been the house of the wife of Emperor Augustus, and decorated with frescoes. In front of the Casa di Livia is the **Casa d'Augusto**, the actual residence of Augustus – the two constructions were most likely part of the same complex. The Casa d'Augusto is still being excavated and is closed to the public but can sometimes be visited by appointment; ask at the entrance to the Palatino. Several rooms have frescoes which are very well-preserved and of significant interest. Farther east are the remains of the **Domus Flavia**, the residence of Domitian, and the vast **Domus Augustana**, which was the private residence of the emperors. Continuing east you will find the **Stadio**, probably used by the emperors for private games and events, and next to it are the ruins of the **Terme di Settimio Severo**.

Opening hours are the same as for the forum.

Chiesa di SS Cosma e Damiano & Chiesa di Santa Francesca Romana

East towards the Colosseo along Via dei Fori Imperiali, past the Foro Romano entrance, is the 6th-century Basilica di SS Cosma e Damiano. The church once incorporated a large hall which formed part of Vespasian's Forum of Peace. In the apse are 6th-century mosaics, among the most beautiful in Roma, which were restored in 1989. In a room off the 17th-century cloisters is a vast Neapolitan nativity scene *(presepio)*, dating from the 18th century. Past the Basilica di Costantino there is a small stairway leading to Chiesa di Santa Francesca Romana. Built in the 9th century over an earlier oratory, the church incorporates part of theTempio di Venere e Roma (Temple of Venus and Rome). It has a lovely Romanesque bell tower. There is a 12th-century mosaic in the apse of the Madonna and child and saints, as well as a 7th-century painting of the Madonna and child above the high altar. During restoration works in 1949, another painting of the Madonna and child was discovered beneath the 7th-century work. Dating from the early 5th century and probably taken from the Chiesa di Santa Maria Antiqua in the Foro Romano, this precious painting is now in the sacristy.

Colosseo

Construction of the Colosseo (Colosseum) was started by Emperor Vespasian in 72 AD in the grounds of Nero's private Domus Aurea. Originally known as the Flavian Amphitheatre, after the family name of Vespasian, it was inaugurated by his son Titus in 80 AD. The massive structure could seat more than 80,000, and the bloody gladiator combat and wild beast shows held there, when thousands of wild animals were slashed to death, give some insight into Roman people of the day. The games held to mark the inauguration of the Colosseo lasted for 100 days and nights, during which some 5000 animals were slaughtered. The Emperor Trajan once held games which lasted for 117 days, during which some 9000 gladiators fought to the death.

In the Middle Ages the Colosseo became a fortress, occupied by two of the city's warrior families: the Frangipani and the Annibaldi. Its reputation as a symbol of Roma, the eternal city, also dates to the Middle Ages when Christian pilgrims are said to have predicted that when the Colosseo fell, Roma would also fall. Damaged several times by earthquake, it was later used as a quarry for travertine and marble for the Palazzo Venezia and other buildings. Pollution and the vibrations caused by traffic and the Metro have also taken their toll. Restoration works have periodically been carried out, the latest starting in 1992. Partly financed by the Banco di Roma, the project is expected to take 10 years and every effort will be made to keep the Colosseo open to the public during this time.

Opening hours in winter are Monday to Friday from 9 am to 3 pm, in summer to 7 pm, and on Sunday to 1 pm. At the time of writing, a general admission charge of L10,000 was introduced by the Colosseo; visitors are given a card with a magnetic strip to gain entry.

Arco di Costantino

On the west side of the Colosseo is the triumphal arch built to honour Constantine following his victory over Maxentius at the

Gladiators

These men, who fought to the death in bloody battles at the Colosseo, were usually prisoners of war or young slaves who had been offered the chance to become gladiators because of their physical strength or prowess in battle. While the risks were great, so were the potential rewards. Successful gladiators were considered heroes; they were trained in military-style gladiator schools and their standard of living was usually much higher than that of the average slave. Battles between gladiators, and between gladiators and wild animals, were often great spectacles enhanced by elaborate scenery. The animals were brought into the arena from cages in the rooms below by a system of rope-pulled elevators: as many as 100 animals could appear at once. If it happened that a gladiator managed to disarm his opponent, he would turn to the public (or to the emperor if he was present) for the verdict on the fate of his foe. The famous thumbs-down meant death. Thumbs-up meant appreciation of the valour of the vanquished, who would thus be spared. ■

battle of the Milvian Bridge (near the present-day Zona Olimpica, north-west of the Villa Borghese) in 312 AD. Its decorative reliefs were taken from earlier structures. Incorporated into the Frangipani fortress, the arch was 'liberated' in 1804. Major restoration was completed in 1987.

Walk back towards Via dei Fori Imperiali and turn left into the Via Sacra, towards the Arco di Tito and one of the Foro Romano exits. Just before the gate, head uphill to the left for another panoramic view of the forum.

Esquilino

The Esquilino (Esquiline hill) covers the area stretching from the Colosseo across Via Cavour, which links Via dei Fori Imperiali with Stazione Termini. Not the best known of Roma's seven hills, it incorporates the Parco del Colle Oppio, now a haunt of homeless people and drug users, but once the site of part of Nero's fabled **Domus Aurea** (Golden House). Nero had the palace built after the fire of 64 AD. It was a vast complex of buildings covering an area of some 50 hectares, stretching from the Colle Oppio to the Celio and the Palatino. The gardens, which contained a lake and game animals, occupied the valley where the Colosseo now stands.

After Nero's death in 68 AD, his successors were quick to destroy the complex, which had occupied a major part of Ancient Rome's centre. Vespasian drained the lake to build the Colosseo, Domitian demolished the buildings on the Palatino and Trajan built his baths over the buildings on the Colle Oppio. During the Renaissance, artists descended into the ruins of the wing of the Domus Aurea on the Colle Oppio to study its architectural features and the rich paintings which adorned its walls. Unfortunately, the ruins have been closed indefinitely for conservation reasons.

From the Colle Oppio, follow the Via Terme di Tito and turn left into Via del Monte to reach the **Basilica di San Pietro in Vincoli**, built in the 5th century by the Empress Eudoxia, wife of Valentinian III, to house the chains of St Peter. Legend has it that when a second part of the chains was returned to Roma from Constantinople, the two pieces miraculously joined together. While the presence of the chains makes the church an important place of pilgrimage, the church offers another great treasure – Michelangelo's unfinished tomb of Pope Julius II, with his powerful *Moses* and unfinished statues of *Leah* and *Rachel* on either side. Michelangelo was frustrated for many years by his inability to find time to complete work on the tomb. In the end, Pope Julius was buried in the Basilica di San Pietro without the great tomb he had envisioned and the unfinished sculptures which were to have adorned it are in the Louvre and the Galleria dell'Accademia in Firenze. A flight of steps through a low arch leads down from the church to Via Cavour.

Basilica di Santa Maria Maggiore

One of Roma's four patriarchal basilicas (the others are San Pietro, San Giovanni in Laterano and San Paolo Fuori Le Mura), Santa Maria Maggiore was built on a summit of the Esquilino in the 5th century, during Pope Sixtus III's era. Its main façade was added in the 18th century, preserving the 13th-century mosaics of the earlier façade. The interior is Baroque and the bell tower Romanesque. The basilican form of the vast interior, a nave and two aisles, remains intact and the most notable feature is the cycle of mosaics dating from the 5th century which decorate the triumphal arch and nave. They depict biblical scenes, in particular events in the lives of Abraham, Jacob and Isaac (to the left), and Moses and Joshua (to the right). Note also the Cosmatesque pavement, dating from the 12th century. The sumptuously decorated Cappella Sistina, last on the right, was built in the 16th century and contains the tombs of popes Sixtus V and Pius V. Opposite is the Cappella Borghese, (or Cappella Paolina) also full of elaborate decoration, erected in the 17th century by Pope Paul V. The *Madonna and Child* above the altar is believed to date from the 12th to the 13th century.

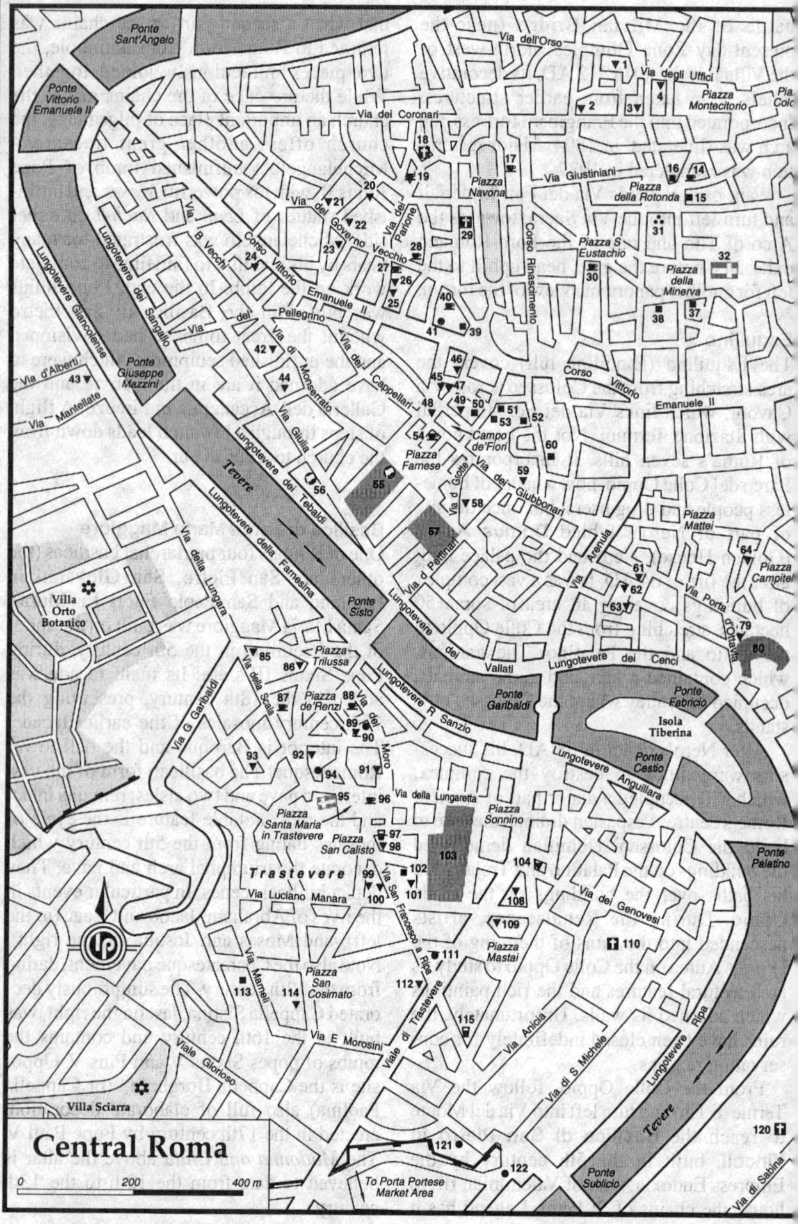
Ponte Sant'Angelo
Ponte Vittorio Emanuele II
Via dell'Orso
Via degli Uffici
Piazza Montecitorio
Via dei Coronari
Piazza Navona
Via Giustiniani
Piazza della Rotonda
Corso Rinascimento
Piazza S Eustachio
Piazza della Minerva
Via del Governo Vecchio
Via dei Parione
Via B Vecchi
Corso Vittorio Emanuele II
Lungotevere dei Sangallo
Lungotevere Gianicolense
Via del Pellegrino
Via di Monserrato
Via dei Cappellari
Ponte Giuseppe Mazzini
Via d'Alberti
Via Mantellate
Via Giulia
Campo de'Fiori
Piazza Farnese
Via d Grotte
Via dei Giubbonari
Via d Pettinari
Via Arenula
Piazza Mattei
Piazza Campitelli
Via Porta d'Ottavia
Tevere
Lungotevere dei Tebaldi
Lungotevere della Farnesina
Via della Lungara
Ponte Sisto
Lungotevere dei Vallati
Lungotevere dei Cenci
Ponte Garibaldi
Ponte Fabricio
Isola Tiberina
Ponte Cestio
Villa Orto Botanico
Piazza Trilussa
Via della Scala
Piazza de'Renzi
Via del Moro
Lungotevere R Sanzio
Lungotevere Anguillara
Via G Garibaldi
Via della Lungaretta
Piazza Sonnino
Piazza Santa Maria in Trastevere
Piazza San Calisto
Trastevere
Via Luciano Manara
Via San Francesco a Ripa
Via dei Genovesi
Ponte Palatino
Piazza Mastai
Via Mameli
Piazza San Cosimato
Viale di Trastevere
Via E Morosini
Via Anicia
Via di S Michele
Lungotevere Ripa
Viale Glorioso
Villa Sciarra
Ponte Sublicio
Via di Sabina
To Porta Portese Market Area
Central Roma
0 200 400 m
1 2 3 4 14 15 16 17 18 19 20 21 22 23 24 25 26 27 28 29 30 31 32 37 38 39 40 41 42 43 44 45 46 47 48 49 50 51 52 53 54 55 56 57 58 59 60 61 62 63 64 79 80 85 86 87 88 89 90 91 92 93 94 95 96 97 98 99 100 101 102 103 104 108 109 110 111 112 113 114 115 120 121 122

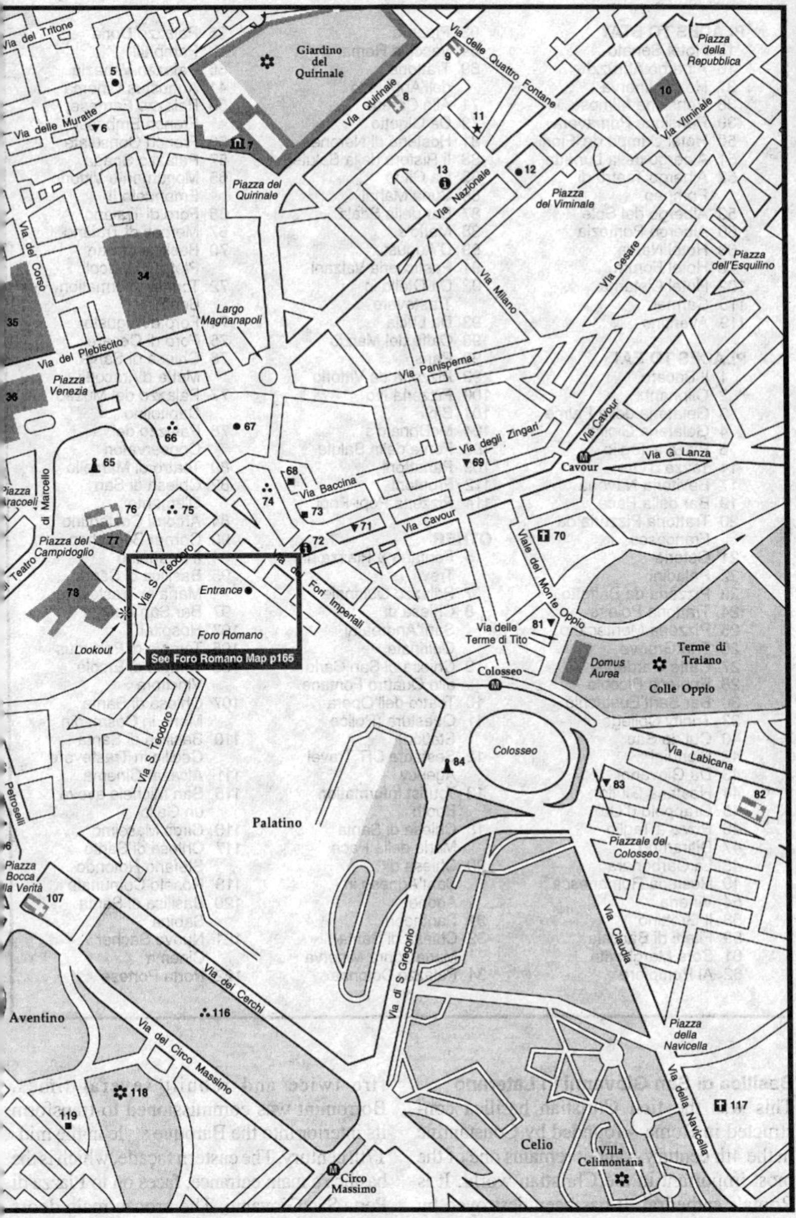
Via del Tritone
Giardino del Quirinale
Via delle Quattro Fontane
Piazza della Repubblica
Via Quirinale
Via delle Muratte
Via Viminale
Via Nazionale
Piazza del Quirinale
Piazza del Viminale
Via del Corso
Via Cesare
Piazza dell'Esquilino
Via Milano
Largo Magnanapoli
Via del Plebiscito
Piazza Venezia
Via Panisperna
Via degli Zingari
Via Cavour
Via G Lanza
Cavour
Via Baccina
Piazza Aracoeli
Via del Teatro di Marcello
Piazza del Campidoglio
Via S Teodoro
Entrance
Foro Romano
Lookout
See Foro Romano Map p165
Via dei Fori Imperiali
Viale del Monte Oppio
Via delle Terme di Tito
Colosseo
Domus Aurea
Terme di Traiano
Colle Oppio
Via Labicana
Palatino
Piazzale del Colosseo
Petroselli
Piazza Bocca della Verità
Via Claudia
Via dei Cerchi
Via di S Gregorio
Aventino
Via del Circo Massimo
Piazza della Navicella
Via della Navicella
Celio
Villa Celimontana
Circo Massimo
5
6
7
8
9
10
11
12
13
34
35
36
65
66
67
68
69
70
71
72
73
74
75
76
77
78
81
82
83
84
107
116
117
118
119

PLACES TO STAY
15 Hotel Senato
16 Albergo Abruzzi
37 Hotel Minerva
38 Pensione Mimosa
39 Pensione Primavera
50 Hotel Campo de' Fiori
51 Albergo della Lunetta
52 Albergo Teatro di Pompeo
53 Albergo del Sole
60 Albergo Pomezia
68 Hotel Nerva
73 Hotel Forum
102 Hotel Cisterna
113 Carmel
119 Aventino

PLACES TO EAT
1 Il Bacaro
2 Oliphant
3 Gelateria della Palme
4 Gelateria Giolitti
6 Pizza a Taglio
14 Tazza d'Oro
17 Bevitoria Navona
19 Bar della Pace
20 Trattoria Pizzeria da Francesco
21 Osteria
22 Paladini
23 Pizzeria da Baffetto
24 Trattoria Polese
25 Pizzeria Montecarlo
26 The Groove
27 Caffè Gardenia
28 Enoteca Piccolo
30 Bar Sant'Eustachio
33 Trinity College
40 Cul de Sac
42 Pierluigi
43 Da Giovanni
44 Hostaria Giulio
45 Grappolo d'Oro
46 Pizza a Taglio
47 Ditirambo
48 La Carbonara
49 Hosteria Romanesca
54 Vineria
58 Il Grottino
59 Filetti di Baccalà
61 Sora Margherita
62 Al Pompiere
63 Piperno
64 Vecchia Roma
69 Trattoria dell'Angeletto
71 Alle Carette
79 Da Gigetto
81 Hosteria di Nerone
83 Il Ristoro della Salute
85 Da Gildo
86 Suria Mahal
87 Bar della Scala
88 Mario's
89 D'Augusto
91 Pasticceria Valzani
92 Da Otello in Trastevere
93 Da Lucia
96 Caffé del Marzio
98 Paris
99 Pizzeria da Vittorio
100 Pizzeria Ivo
101 Bibli
104 McDonald's
108 Fonte della Salute
109 Panattoni
112 Frontoni
114 Pizzeria Popi-Popi

OTHER
5 Fontana & Piazza di Trevi
7 Palazzo Quirinale
8 Chiesa di Sant'Andrea al Quirinale
9 Chiesa di San Carlo alle Quattro Fontane
10 Teatro dell'Opera
11 Questura (Police Station)
12 Sestante CIT Travel Agency
13 Tourist Information Booth
18 Chiesa di Santa Maria della Pace
29 Chiesa di Sant'Agnese in Agone
31 Pantheon
32 Chiesa di Santa Maria sopra Minerva
34 Palazzo Colonna
35 Palazzo Doria Pamphili
36 Palazzo Venezia
41 Augustus Cinema
55 Palazzo Farnese; French Embassy
56 French Consulate
57 Palazzo Spada
65 Monumento Vittorio Emanuele II
66 Foro di Traiano
67 Mercati di Traiano
70 Basilica di San Pietro in Vincoli
72 Tourist Information Booth
74 Foro d'Augusto
75 Foro di Cesare
76 Chiesa di Santa Maria d'Aracoeli
77 Palazzo del Museo Capitolino
78 Palazzo dei Conservatori
80 Teatro di Marcello
82 Chiesa di San Clemente
84 Arco di Costantino
90 Corner Bookshop
94 Il Pasquino
95 Basilica di Santa Maria in Trastevere
97 Bar San Calisto
103 Hospital
105 Tempio di Portunus
106 Tempio di Ercole Vincitore
107 Chiesa di Santa Maria in Cosmedin
110 Basilica di Santa Cecilia in Trastevere
111 Alcazar Cinema
115 San Michele aveva un Gallo
116 Circo Massimo
117 Chiesa di Santo Stefano Rotondo
118 Roseto Comunale
120 Basilica di Santa Sabina
121 Nuovo Sacher Cinema
122 Porta Portese

Basilica di San Giovanni in Laterano

This was the first Christian basilica constructed in Roma – founded by Constantine in the 4th century – and it remains one of the most important in the Christian world. It is Roma's cathedral. It has been destroyed by fire twice and rebuilt several times. Borromini was commissioned to transform its interior into the Baroque style in the mid-17th century. The eastern façade, which is the basilica's main entrance, faces on to Piazza di Porta San Giovanni. The bronze main doors were moved here by Borromini from the Curia in the Foro Romano. The northern façade, which faces on to Piazza San Giovanni in Laterano, was damaged by a bomb attack in 1993 and was still under restoration in 1997. The beautiful 13th-century **cloister** was decorated by the Cosmati family. The **baptistry** was also built by Constantine. The heads of Saints Peter and Paul are contained in a tabernacle over the papal altar. The **Palazzo Laterano**, which adjoins the basilica, was the papal residence until the pope moved to Avignon in the 14th century. It was largely destroyed by fire in 1308 and most of what remained was demolished in the 16th century. The building on the eastern side of Piazza di Porta San Giovanni contains the **Scala Santa** and the **Sancta Sanctorum**. The Scala Santa (Holy Stairs) is said to be from the palace of Pontius Pilate in Jerusalem and people are allowed to climb it only on their knees. The Sancta Sanctorum was the popes' private chapel and contains 13th-century frescoes and mosaics. It can only be visited with a guide (L5000).

Celio

The Celio (Celian hill) is accessible either from Via di San Gregorio or, from the other side, from Via della Navicella. The **Villa Celimontana** is a large public park on top of the hill, perfect for a quiet picnic. There is also a children's playground. The 4th-century **Chiesa di SS Giovanni e Paolo**, in the piazza of the same name on Via di San Paolo della Croce, is dedicated to two Romans, Saints John and Paul, who had served in the court of Emperor Constantine II and were beheaded by his anti-Christian successor, Emperor Julian, for refusing to serve as officers in his court. The church was built over their houses. Walk downhill along the Clivio di Scauro, an atmospheric road dating from the 1st century BC. The 8th-century **Chiesa di San Gregorio Magno** was built in honour of Pope Gregory the Great on the site where he dispatched St Augustine to convert the people of Britain to Christianity. The church was remodelled in the Baroque style in the 17th century.

The fascinating **Chiesa di Santo Stefano Rotondo** is on Via di S Stefano Rotondo, just across Via della Navicella from the Villa Celimontana. Inside are two rings of antique granite and marble columns. The circular wall is lined with frescoes depicting the various ways in which saints were martyred. The vivid scenes are quite grotesque and you might not make it through all 34 of them. Watch out for a little priest pointing to your shoes – he is worried you will dirty the polished wooden floor.

At the base of the Celio, near the Colosseo, is the **Basilica di San Clemente** in Via San Giovanni in Laterano. Dedicated to one of the earliest popes, the church defines how history in Roma exists on many levels. The 12th-century church at street level was built over a 4th-century church which was, in turn, built over a 1st-century Roman house containing a late 2nd-century temple to the pagan god Mithras (imported to Roma by soldiers returning from the East). Further, it is believed that foundations from the Republican Rome era lie beneath the house. It is possible to visit the first three levels. In the medieval church, note the marble choir screen, originally in the older church below, and the early Renaissance frescoes by Masolino in the Capella di Santa Caterina, depicting the life of St Catherine of Alexandria. The stunning mosaics in the apse date from the 12th century. On the triumphal arch are Christ and the symbols of the four Evangelists. In the apse itself is depicted the Triumph of the Cross, with 12 doves symbolising the apostles. Figures around the cross include the Madonna and St John, as well as St John the Baptist and other saints encircled by a vine growing from the foot of the cross.

While little remains of the church below (which was destroyed by Norman invaders in the 11th century), some Romanesque frescoes remain. Descend farther and you arrive at the Roman house and temple of Mithras.

Terme di Caracalla & Circo Massimo

The baths are a huge complex on Via delle

Terme di Caracalla, south of the Celio, accessible by bus Nos 160 and 628 from Piazza Venezia. Covering 10 hectares, Caracalla's Baths could hold 1600 people and had shops, gardens, libraries and entertainment. Begun by Antonius Caracalla and inaugurated in 217 AD, the baths were used until the 6th century AD. From the 1930s until 1993 they were an atmospheric venue for opera performances in summer. These have now been banned to prevent further damage to the ruins. The baths are open Tuesday to Saturday from 9 am to 5.30 pm in summer, and from 9 am to 3 pm in winter, and to 1 pm on Sunday and Monday. Admission is L8000.

At the foot of the Palatino is the **Circo Massimo** (Circus Maximus). There is not much to see here: only a few ruins remain of what was once a chariot racetrack big enough to hold more than 200,000 people.

Aventino

South of the Circo Massimo is the Aventino (Aventine hill), best reached from Via di Circo Massimo by either Via di Valle Murcia or Clivo dei Pubblici to Via di Santa Sabina. (It is also easily accessible by bus No 27 from Stazione Termini and the Colosseo, or on the Metro Linea B, disembarking at the Circo Massimo train station). Along the way, you will pass the **Roseto Comunale**, a beautiful public rose garden, best seen obviously when the roses are in bloom from spring into summer, and the pretty, walled **Parco Savello**, planted with orange trees. There is a stunning view of Roma from the park. Next to the park is the 5th-century **Basilica di Santa Sabina**. Of particular note is the carved wooden door to the far left as you stand under the 15th-century portico facing the church. Also dating from the 5th century, the door features panels depicting biblical scenes and the crucifixion scene is one of the oldest in existence. Farther south along Via Santa Sabina is the Piazza Cavalieri di Malta and the **Priorato di Malta**. Look through the keyhole in the central door of the entrance for a surprising view of the property's private garden.

Towards the Jewish Ghetto

The recently refurbished **Chiesa di Santa Maria in Cosmedin**, in Piazza Bocca della Verità, is regarded as one of the finest medieval churches in Roma. It has a 12th-century, seven-storey bell tower and its interior, including the beautiful floor, was heavily decorated with inlaid marble. There are 12th-century frescoes in the aisles. Under the portico is the famous **Bocca della Verità** (Mouth of Truth), a large disk in the shape of a mask which probably once served as the cover of an ancient drain. Legend says that if you put your right hand into the mouth while telling a lie, it will snap shut. Opposite the church are two tiny Roman temples: the round Tempio di Ercole Vincitore and the Tempio di Portunus. Both were consecrated as churches in the Middle Ages.

Off the piazza, towards the Palatino, is the Arco di Giano (Arch of Janus), a four-sided Roman arch which once covered a crossroads, and the medieval **Chiesa di San Giorgio in Velabro**. The church's portico has been rebuilt following a 1993 bomb attack by the Mafia.

From Piazza Bocca della Verità, follow Via Petroselli to reach the **Teatro di Marcello**, built around 13 BC to plans by Julius Caesar and dedicated by Emperor Augustus. It was converted into a fortress and residence during the Middle Ages, and a palace built on the site in the 16th century preserved the original form of the theatre. In recent years open air concerts have been held there nightly in summer.

From the theatre, head north along Via Montanara to Piazza Campitelli and then take Via dei Funari to Piazza Mattei. In the piazza is the **Fontana delle Tartarughe** (Fountain of the Tortoises), a fountain designed by Giacomo della Porta and sculpted in bronze by Taddeo Landini in the 16th century. The tortoises were added in the 17th century and are thought to be by Gian Lorenzo Bernini.

The area just south of here, around Via del Portico d'Ottavia, is known as the Jewish Ghetto. In the 16th century Pope Paul IV ordered the confinement of Jewish people in this area, marking the beginning of a period of intolerance which continued well into the 19th century. Follow Via del Portico d'Ottavia to the river and the 19th-century **synagogue**. Along the way note the medieval houses. There is a 15th-century house at No 1 which incorporates pieces of ancient Roman sculpture in its façade.

From the ghetto area, you can reach the **Isola Tiberina** across the **Ponte Fabricio**, which was built in 62 BC and is Roma's oldest standing bridge. The island has been associated with healing since the 3rd century BC when the Romans adopted Aesculapius, the Greek god of healing, as their own and erected a temple to him on the island. Today it is the site of the Ospedale Fatebenefratelli. The Chiesa di San Bartolomeo was built in the 10th century on the ruins of the Roman temple. It has a Romanesque bell tower and a marble well-head, believed to have been built over the same spring which provided healing waters for the temple. The **Ponte Cestio**, built in 46 BC, connects the island to Trastevere. It was rebuilt in the late 19th century. The remains of a bridge to the south of the island are part of the **Ponte Rotto** (Broken Bridge), which was Ancient Rome's first stone bridge.

Trastevere

The settlement at Trastevere was, in early times, separate from Roma. Although it was soon swallowed by the growing city, this sense of separation continued during medieval times when the area, on the other side of the river, developed its own identity. It is said that even today many of the old people of Trastevere rarely cross the river to the city. In recent years it has become a fashionable place to live and is always very busy on weekends and during summer, when tourists and Romans alike flock here to eat in the many trattorie or to drink at the numerous bars.

The **Basilica di Santa Maria in Trastevere**, in the lovely piazza of the same name, is believed to be the oldest place of worship dedicated to the Virgin in Roma. Although the first basilica was built on this site in the 4th century AD, the present structure was built in the 12th century and features a Romanesque bell tower and façade, with a mosaic of the Virgin from the 12th century. The impressive interior features 21 ancient Roman columns. Of particular interest are the 17th-century wooden ceiling and the vibrant 12th-century mosaics in the apse and on the triumphal arch. Note the richly patterned dress of the Madonna in the apse. There is a badly deteriorated painting of the Madonna and angels dating from the Byzantine era, displayed in a room to the left of the altar.

Also well worth visiting is the **Basilica di Santa Cecilia in Trastevere** (see the boxed aside on Mosaics in this chapter).

Via Giulia

This street, running parallel to the Tevere river, was designed by Donato Bramante, who was commissioned by Pope Julius II to create a new approach to San Pietro. It is lined with Renaissance palaces, antique shops and art galleries.

Palazzo Spada

South of the Campo de' Fiori on Piazza Capodiferro, this 16th-century palace has an elaborately decorated façade. It was restored by Francesco Borromini a century later, after Cardinal Bernardino Spada had acquired the palace. Note the optical illusion created by Borromini's trompe l'œil colonnade, which he built to give an idea of greater space in linking two courtyards within the palace. The **Galleria Spada** contains the private collection of the Spada family, which was acquired by the state in 1926 and features works by Titian, Andrea del Sarto, Guido Reni and Caravaggio. It is open Tuesday to Saturday from 9 am to 7 pm and Sunday to 1.30 pm. Admission is L8000.

Campo de' Fiori

This is a lively piazza where a flower and vegetable market is held every morning except Sunday. Now lined with bars and trattorie, the piazza was in fact a place of execution during the Inquisition. The monk

Giordano Bruno was burned at the stake for heresy in the piazza in 1600 and his statue now stands at its centre.

Nearby is the **Palazzo Farnese**, in the piazza of the same name. A magnificent Renaissance building, it was started in 1514 by Antonio da Sangallo with work carried on by Michelangelo and completed by Giacomo della Porta. Built for Cardinal Alessandro Farnese (later Pope Paul III), the palace is now the French Embassy. The piazza has two fountains, which were enormous granite baths taken from the Terme di Caracalla.

Piazza Navona

Lined with Baroque palaces this vast and beautiful piazza was laid out on the ruins of Domitian's stadium and holds three fountains, including Bernini's masterpiece, the **Fontana dei Fiumi** (Fountain of the Rivers), in the centre, depicting the Nile, Ganges, Danube and the Rio Plata. The piazza is a popular gathering place for Romans and tourists alike. Take time to relax on one of the stone benches and watch the artists who gather in the piazza to do their work, have your *tarocchi* (tarot cards) read, or pay top prices to enjoy a drink at one of the outdoor cafés, such as Tre Scalini. Facing the piazza is the Chiesa di Sant'Agnese in Agone, its façade designed by Bernini's bitter rival, Borromini. It is traditionally held that the statues of Bernini's Fontana dei Fiumi are shielding their eyes in disgust from Borromini's church, but the truth is that Bernini completed the fountain two years before his contemporary started work on the façade.

The Pantheon

This is the best preserved building of Ancient Rome. The original temple was built by Marcus Agrippa, son-in-law of Augustus, in 27 BC and dedicated to the planetary gods. Although the temple was rebuilt by Emperor Hadrian around 120 AD, Agrippa's name remained inscribed over the entrance, leading historians to believe it was the original building until excavations in the 1800s revealed traces of the earlier temple.

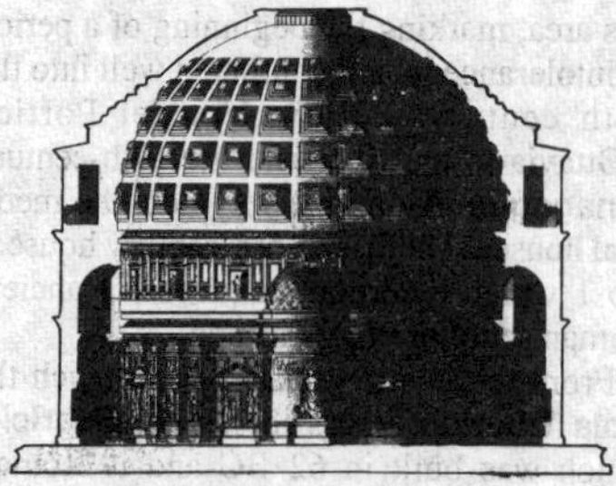

Cross-section of the Pantheon

After being abandoned under the first Christian emperors, the temple was given to the church by the Eastern emperor, Phocus, in 608 AD and dedicated to the Madonna and all martyrs. (A column was erected in honour of Phocus in the Foro Romano to mark the occasion.) Over the centuries the temple was consistently plundered and damaged. The gilded bronze roof tiles were removed by an emperor of the Eastern empire and, in the 17th century, the Barberini pope, Urban VIII, had the bronze ceiling of the portico melted down to make the *baldacchino* (canopy) over the main altar of San Pietro and 80 cannons for Castel Sant'Angelo.

The height and diameter of the building's interior both measure 43.3m and the extraordinary dome is considered the most important achievement of ancient Roman architecture.

The Italian kings, Victor Emmanuel II and Umberto I, and the artist Raphael are buried here. The Pantheon is in the Piazza della Rotonda and is open Monday to Saturday from 9 am to 6.30 pm and Sunday and holidays to 1 pm. Admission is free.

Chiesa di Santa Maria Sopra Minerva

In Piazza della Minerva, just east of the Pantheon, this 13th-century Dominican church was built on the site of an ancient temple of Minerva. It was heavily restored in the Gothic style in the 19th century. It con-ains a number of important art treasures, ncluding Michelangelo's statue the *Risen Christ*, to the left of the high altar, as well as vibrant frescoes by Filippo Lippi in the Cappella Caraffa (the last chapel in the south transept) depicting events in the life of St Thomas Aquinas, and a beautiful *Annunciation*. The body of St Catherine of Siena, minus her head (which is in the Chiesa di San Domenico in Siena) lies under the high altar. In the piazza in front of the church is a delightful Bernini statue of an elephant supporting an Egyptian obelisk.

Piazza Colonna

Just off Via del Corso, near its intersection with Via del Tritone, Piazza Colonna features the imposing **Colonna di Marco Aurelio** (Column of Marcus Aurelius), erected around 190 AD and decorated with bas-relief sculptures depicting military victories by the emperor.

Fontana di Trevi

This high-Baroque fountain is one of Roma's most famous monuments. Completely dominating a tiny piazza, it was designed by Nicola Salvi in 1732. Its water is supplied by one of Roma's earliest aqueducts. Work to clean the fountain and its water supply was completed in 1991, but the effects of pollution have already dulled the brilliant white of the clean marble. The famous custom is to throw a coin into the fountain (over your shoulder while facing away) to ensure you return to Roma. If you throw a second coin you can make a wish. The terraces around the fountain are always packed with tourists throwing coins.

Piazza di Spagna & Scalinata della Trinità dei Monti

The piazza, church and famous Scalinata della Trinità dei Monti (Spanish Steps) have long provided a gathering place for foreigners. Built with a legacy from the French in 1725, but named after the Spanish Embassy to the Holy See, the steps lead to the French church, Trinità dei Monti.

In the 18th century the most beautiful women and men of Italy gathered here, waiting to be chosen as an artist's model. In May each year the steps are decorated with pink azaleas. To the right as you face the steps is the house where Keats died in 1821, now the **Keats-Shelley Memorial House**. It is open Monday to Friday from 9 am to 1 pm and 2.30 to 5.30 pm. Admission is L5000. In the piazza is the boat-shaped fountain called the **Barcaccia**, believed to be by Pietro Bernini, father of the famous Gian Lorenzo. One of Roma's most elegant shopping streets, **Via Condotti**, runs off the piazza towards Via del Corso. The famous **Caffè Greco** is at No 86, where artists, musicians and the literati used to meet, including Goethe, Keats, Byron and Wagner.

Piazza del Popolo

This vast piazza was laid out in the early 16th century at the point of convergence of the three roads – Via di Ripetta, Via del Corso and Via del Babuino – which form a trident at what was the main entrance to the city from the north. The two Baroque churches that divide the three roads are Santa Maria dei Miracoli (bordering Via di Ripetta) and Santa Maria in Montesanto. The piazza was redesigned in the neoclassical style by Giuseppe Valadier in the early 19th century. In the piazza's centre is an obelisk brought by Augustus from Heliopolis, in ancient Greece, and moved to the piazza from the Circo Massimo in the mid-16th century. To the east is a ramp leading up to the **Pincio hill**, which affords a stunning view of the city.

The **Chiesa di Santa Maria del Popolo**, next to the Porta del Popolo at the northern end of the piazza, was originally a chapel built in 1099 on the site where Nero was buried. It was enlarged in the 13th century and rebuilt during the early Renaissance. In the 17th century the interior was renovated by Bernini. The Cappella Chigi (the second chapel in the north aisle after you enter the church) was designed by Raphael for the famous banker Agostino Chigi. Raphael died, thus leaving the chapel unfinished. It was completed more than 100 years later by Bernini. The apse was designed by Donato Bramante and contains the tombs of Cardinal Ascanio Sforza and Cardinal Girolamo Basso della Rovere, both signed by the Florentine sculptor Andrea Sansovino. The frescoes in the vault are by Bernardino Pinturicchio. In the first chapel to the left of the high altar are two paintings by Caravaggio, the *Conversion of St Paul* and the *Crucifixion of St Peter*.

Villa Borghese

This beautiful park, just north-east of the Piazza del Popolo, was once the estate of Cardinal Scipione Borghese. The main entrance is from Piazzale Flaminio, although it is also accessible through the park at the top of the Pincio hill. Take a picnic to the park if the tourist trip starts to wear you down and certainly take the kids there for a break. The cardinal's 17th-century villa houses the **Museo e Galleria Borghese**, which reopened in mid-1997 following a decade-long restoration project. A sculpture section on the ground floor features numerous important classical works and several sculptures by Bernini and Canova. In Room 1 is Canova's famous statue of Pauline Borghese (wife of Camillo Borghese and sister of Napoleon Bonaparte] depicted as Venus Victrix. The picture gallery on the 1st floor has finally been relocated from the Istituto di San Michele a Ripa in Trastevere, where it had been temporarily housed for several years. The gallery is open Tuesday to Saturday from 9 am to 7 pm and Sunday to 1 pm. Admission is L10,000.

Also in the park are **Zoological Gardens**, north-west along Viale dell'Uccelliera from the museum. The animals are poorly housed and there are discussions underway on the possible closure of the zoo.

Just outside the park, on Viale delle Belle Arti, is the **Galleria Nazionale d'Arte Moderna**, which houses an impressive collection of Italian art from the 19th century to the present day. It is open Tuesday to Saturday from 9 am to 7 pm and Sunday to 1 pm. Admission is L8000.

Museo Nazionale Etrusco di Villa Giulia

Situated in the 16th-century villa of Pope Julius III at the top end of the Villa Borghese in the Piazzale di Villa Giulia, this museum houses the national collection of Etruscan treasures, many found in tombs at sites throughout Lazio. If you plan to visit Etruscan sites near Roma, a visit to the museum before setting out will give you a good understanding of Etruscan culture. Of particular note is the statue of Apollo found at Veio, and the *Sarcophagus of the Married Couple*, containing a husband and wife, from a tomb at Cerveteri. The museum is open Tuesday to Saturday from 9 am to 7 pm and Sunday to 1.30 pm. Admission is L8000.

Around Via Vittorio Veneto

This street was Roma's hot spot in the 1960s where film stars could be seen at the expensive sidewalk cafés. It's still the city's most fashionable street, although the atmosphere of Fellini's Roma is long dead. The **Chiesa di Santa Maria della Concezione** is an austere 17th-century church, but the Capuchin cemetery beneath (access is on the right of the church steps) features a bizarre display of the bones of some 4000 monks, used to decorate the walls of a series of chapels from 1528 to 1870.

In the centre of **Piazza Barberini**, at the southern end of Via Veneto, is the spectacular **Fontana del Tritone** (Fountain of the Triton), created by Bernini in 1643 for Pope Urban VIII, patriarch of the Barberini family. It features a Triton blowing a stream of water from a conch shell. He is seated in a large scallop shell which is supported by four dolphins. In the north-east corner of the piazza is another fountain, the **Fontana delle Ap** (Fountain of the Bees), created by the same artist for the Barberini family, whose crest which features three bees, can be seen on many buildings throughout Roma.

The 17th-century **Palazzo Barberini**, in Via delle Quattro Fontane, is well worth a visit, although it is partly closed for restoration. Carlo Maderno was commissioned by Pope Urban VIII to build the palace and both Bernini and Borromini worked on its conruction for the Barberini family. The palace ouses the **Galleria Nazionale d'Arte ntica**. The collection includes paintings by aphael, Caravaggio, Filippo Lippi and lolbein. A highlight is the ceiling of the nain salon of the palace (part of the gallery), ntitled the *Triumph of Divine Providence*, ainted by Pietro da Cortona. The palace and allery are open Tuesday to Saturday from 9 m to 2 pm, and Sunday to 1 pm. Admission s from Via delle Quattro Fontane 13 and osts L8000.

alazzo del Quirinale to Piazza della epubblica

he Palazzo del Quirinale, in the piazza of he same name, is the official residence of the resident of the republic. Built and added to rom 1574 to the early 18th century, the alace was the summer residence of the opes until 1870, when it became the royal alace of the kings of Italy. The palace is pen to the public on the second and fourth unday of the month, from 8.30 am to 1.30 m. Arrive early, since it is usually not posible to join the queue after about 11.30 am. Admission is free.

Along Via del Quirinale are two excellent xamples of Baroque architecture: the hurches of **Sant'Andrea al Quirinale**, esigned by Bernini, and **San Carlo alle Quattro Fontane**, designed by Borromini. The Chiesa di Sant'Andrea is considered one f Bernini's masterpieces. He designed it vith an elliptical floor plan, and with a series f chapels opening on to the central area. The nterior is decorated with polychrome narble, stucco and gilding. Note the cherubs vhich decorate the lantern of the dome. The Chiesa di San Carlo was the first church lesigned by Borromini in Roma and was ompleted in 1641. The small cloister was lso designed by Borromini. The church tands at the intersection known as **Quattro Fontane**, after the late 16th-century founains at its four corners.

From this intersection walk south-east long Via delle Quattro Fontane and turn left nto Via Nazionale to reach Piazza della Repubblica. Formerly known as Piazza Esedra, it follows the line of the exedra of the adjacent Terme di Diocleziano. The fountain in its centre, the Fontana delle Naiadi, was erected at the turn of the century.

Terme di Diocleziano

Started by Emperor Diocletian, these baths were completed in the early 4th century. The complex of baths, libraries, concert halls and gardens was the largest in Ancient Rome, covering about 13 hectares and with a capacity of 3000 people. The baths' *calidarium* (hot room) extended into what is now Piazza della Repubblica. After the aqueduct which fed the baths was destroyed by invaders in about 536 AD, the complex fell into disrepair. However, large sections of the baths were incorporated into the Chiesa di Santa Maria degli Angeli, which faces Piazza della Repubblica, and the Museo Nazionale Romano, facing Piazza dei Cinquecento. The baths are open Tuesday to Saturday from 9 am to 2 pm and Sunday to 1 pm. Entry is L12,000.

The **Basilica di Santa Maria degli Angeli** was designed by Michelangelo and incorporates what was the great central hall and *tepidarium* ('lukewarm room') of the original baths. During the following centuries his work was drastically changed and little evidence of his design, apart from the great vaulted ceiling, remains. An interesting feature of the church is a double meridian in the transept, one tracing the polar star and the other telling the precise time of the sun's zenith, visible at midday (solar time). The church is open from 7.30 am to 12.30 pm and 4 to 6.30 pm. Through the sacristy is an entrance to a stairway leading to the upper terraces of the ruins. A plaque near the stairway records the traditional belief that the baths were built by thousands of Christian slaves.

The **Museo Nazionale Romano**, which opened in 1889 and incorporated several halls of the ancient baths, houses a valuable collection of ancient art, including Greek and Roman sculpture. It also contains the *Ludovisi Throne*, a 5th-century BC Greek sculpture, and frescoes taken from the Villa

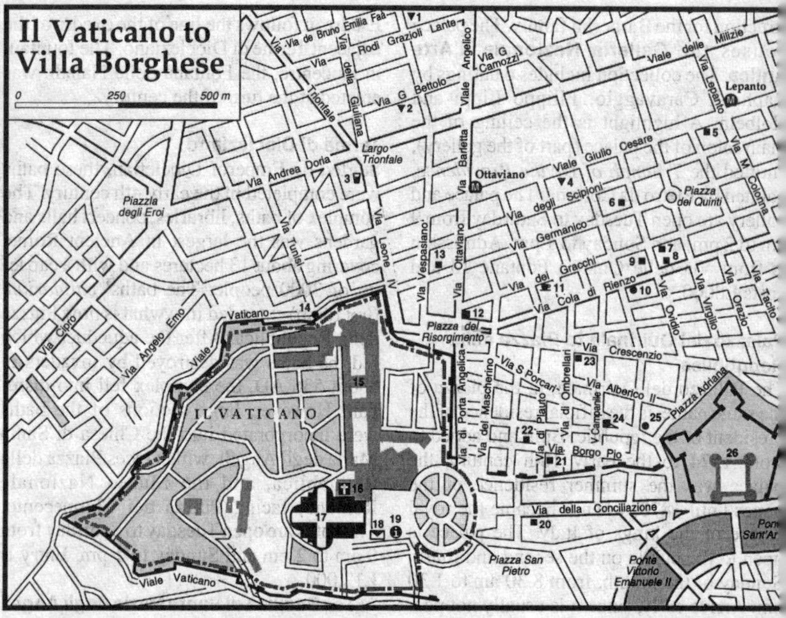

di Livia at Prima Porta (just north of Roma). Much of the museum has been closed for many years and only a fraction of its collection has been on public view. Fortunately, this situation is changing: the museum has taken over the former Collegio Massimo, diagonally across Piazza dei Cinquecento, and the collection has been divided between the two sites. At the time of writing, many rooms were closed. The museum is open Tuesday to Saturday from 9 am to 2 pm and Sunday to 1 pm. Entry is L12,000 and covers entrance to both buildings.

Il Vaticano

After unification, the Papal States of central Italy became part of the new Kingdom of Italy, causing a considerable rift between the church and state. In 1929, Mussolini, under the Lateran Treaty, gave the pope full sovereignty over what is now the Città del Vaticano (Vatican City).

The city has its own postal service, currency, newspaper, radio station, train station and army of Swiss Guards, responsible for security. The corps was established in 1506 and its uniform was probably designed by Michelangelo.

Information & Services The tourist office (☎ 69 88 44 66), in Piazza San Pietro to the left of the basilica, is open daily from 8.30 am to 7 pm and has general information about San Pietro and il Vaticano. Guided tours of il Vaticano can be organised at the tourist office.

Il Vaticano post office, said to provide a much faster and more reliable service than the normal Italian postal system, is a few doors from the tourist office (there is another outlet on the other side of the piazza). Letters can be posted in Vaticano post boxes only if they carry Vaticano stamps.

Papal Audiences The pope usually gives a public audience every Wednesday at 11 am

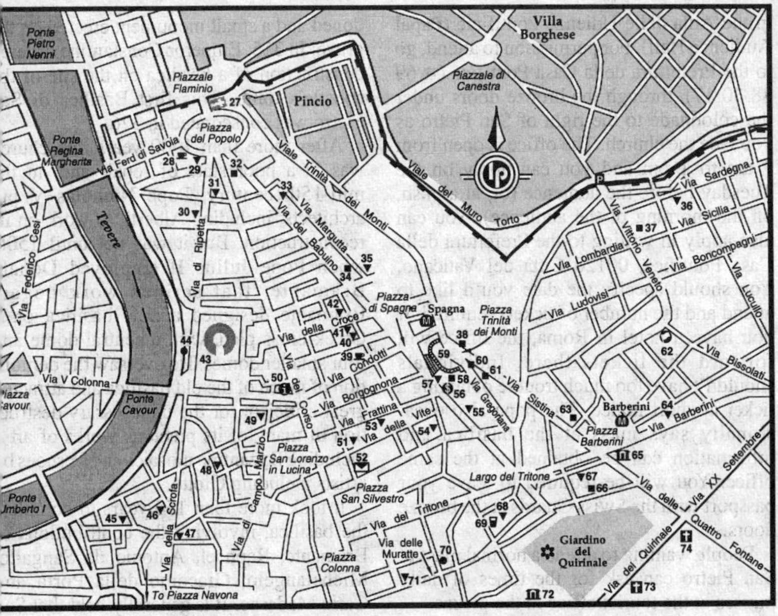

PLACES TO STAY

- 5 Pensione Valparaiso
- 6 Hotel Giuggioli, Pensione Lady & Pensione Nautilus
- 7 Hotel Ticino
- 8 Hotels Joli & Florida
- 9 Pensione San Michele
- 12 Pensione Ottaviano
- 13 Hotel Amalia
- 20 Hotel Columbus
- 21 Hotel Bramante
- 22 Hotel Sant'Anna
- 23 Hotel Prati
- 24 Hotel Adriatic
- 32 Pensione Fiorella
- 34 Hotel Forte
- 37 Hotel Pensione Merano
- 38 Hassler Villa Medici & Trinità dei Monti Church
- 58 Hotel Scalinata di Spagna
- 60 Hotel Gregoriana
- 61 Hotel Pensione Suisse
- 63 Hotel Sistina
- 66 Hotel Julia

PLACES TO EAT

- 1 Pizzeria Giacomelli
- 2 Osteria dell'Angelo
- 4 Il Tempio della Pizza
- 28 Caffè Rosati
- 29 Dal Bolognese
- 30 Caffè Sogo
- 31 Paneformaggio
- 33 Margutta Vegetariano
- 35 Osteria Margutta
- 36 Andrea
- 39 Caffè Greco
- 40 Al 34
- 41 Fior Fiore
- 42 Otello alla Concordia
- 45 Il Convivio
- 46 La Campana
- 47 M&M Volpetti
- 48 El Toulà
- 49 Pizzeria Il Leoncino
- 51 Centro Macrobiotico Italiano
- 53 Mario
- 54 Sogo Asahi
- 55 McDonald's
- 57 Babington's Tea Rooms
- 64 Tullio
- 67 Colline Emiliane
- 68 Golden Crown
- 71 Al Moro

OTHER

- 3 Alexanderplatz
- 10 Castroni
- 11 Xplorer Café
- 14 Entrance to the Musei Vaticano
- 15 Musei del Vaticano
- 16 Cappella Sistina
- 17 Basilica di San Pietro
- 18 Vatican Post Office
- 19 Vatican Tourist Office
- 25 Itaca Multimedia
- 26 Castel Sant'Angelo
- 27 Chiesa di Santa Maria del Popolo
- 43 Mausoleo d'Augusto
- 44 Ara Pacis
- 50 Tourist Information Booth
- 52 Main Post Office
- 56 American Express Office
- 59 Scalinata della Trinità dei Monti (Spanish Steps)
- 62 US Embassy & Consulate
- 65 Palazzo Barberini
- 69 Metropolis
- 70 Fontana di Trevi
- 72 Palazzo del Quirinale
- 73 Chiesa di Sant'Andrea al Quirinale
- 74 Chiesa di San Carlo alle Quattro Fontane

in the Aula delle Udienze Pontificie (Papal Audience Hall). For permission to attend, go to the Prefettura della Casa Pontifica (☎ 69 88 30 17), through the bronze doors under the colonnade to the right of San Pietro as you face the church. The office is open from 9 am to 1 pm and you can apply on the Tuesday before the audience (or, at a push, on the morning of the audience). You can also apply in writing to the Prefettura della Casa Pontifica, 00120 Città del Vaticano. You should specify the date you'd like to attend and the number of tickets required. If you have a hotel in Roma, the office will forward the tickets there. Individuals shouldn't have too much trouble obtaining a ticket at short notice. The pope also occasionally says mass at the basilica and information can be obtained at the same office. You will be required to leave your passport with the Swiss Guards at the bronze doors.

People wanting to attend a normal mass at San Pietro can ask for the times of daily masses at the tourist office in the piazza.

Piazza San Pietro Bernini's piazza is considered a masterpiece. Laid out in the 17th century as a place for the Christians of the world to gather, the immense piazza is bounded by two semicircular colonnades, each of which is made up of four rows of Doric columns. In the centre of the piazza is an obelisk brought to Roma by Caligula from Heliopolis in ancient Egypt. When you stand on the dark paving stones between the obelisk and either of the fountains, the colonnade on that side appears to have only one row of columns.

Basilica di San Pietro In the same area where the church (St Peter's Basilica) now stands, there was once the Circo Vaticano, built by Nero. It was probably in this stadium that St Peter and other Christians were martyred between 64 and 67 AD. The body of the saint was buried in an anonymous grave next to the wall of the circus, and his fellow Christians built a humble 'red wall' to mark the site. In 160 AD the stadium was abandoned and a small monument erected on th grave. In 315, Emperor Constantine ordere construction of a basilica on the site of th apostle's tomb. This first Basilica di Sa Pietro was consecrated in 326.

After more than 1000 years, the churc was in a poor state of repair and, in th mid-15th century, Pope Nicholas V p architects, including Alberti, to work on i reconstruction. But it was not until 150 when Pope Julius II employed Donat Bramante, that serious work begar Bramante designed a new basilica on Greek cross plan, with a central dome an four smaller domes. He oversaw the demol tion of much of the old basilica and attracte great criticism for the unnecessary destru tion of many of its precious works of art including Byzantine mosaics and frescoes b artists including Giotto.

It took more than 150 years to complet the basilica, involving the contributions c Bramante, Raphael, Antonio da Sangallc Michelangelo, Giacomo della Porta an Carlo Maderno. It is generally held that Sa Pietro owes most to Michelangelo, who too over the project in 1547 at the age of 72 an was responsible for the design of the dome He died before the church was completed.

The façade and portico were designed b Carlo Maderno, who took over the projec after Michelangelo's death. He was als instructed to lengthen the nave towards th piazza, effectively altering Bramante's orig inal Greek cross plan to a Latin cross Restoration work on the façade began i 1997 and is expected to take at least tw years. Work will consist mainly of cleanin the travertine marble and repairing damag caused by age and pollution.

The cavernous interior, decorated b Bernini and Giacomo della Porta, can hol up to 60,000 people. It contains treasure including Michelangelo's superb *Pietà*, a the beginning of the right aisle, sculpte when he was only 25 years old and the only work to carry his signature (on the sash across the breast of the Madonna). It is now protected by bulletproof glass after having been attacked in 1972 by a hammer-wielding

Michaelangelo sculpted the Pietà when he was 25

andal. The red porphyry disk just inside the ıain door marks the spot where Charle-ıagne and later emperors were crowned by ıe pope.

Bernini's Baroque *baldacchino* (canopy) ands 29m high in the centre of the church ıd is an extraordinary work of art. The ronze used to make it was taken from the antheon. The high altar, which only the ope can use, stands over the site of St eter's grave.

Michelangelo's **dome**, a majestic archi-ctural masterpiece, soars 119m above the igh altar. Its balconies are decorated with liefs depicting the so-called Reliquie Mag-iori (major relics) – the lance of St onginus, which he used to pierce Christ's de; the cloth of St Veronica, which bears a ıiraculous image of Christ; and a piece of ıe True Cross, collected by St Helena, the ıother of Emperor Constantine. Entry to the ome is to the right as you climb the stairs to ıe atrium of the basilica. Access to the roof f the church is by elevator (admission .6000) or stairs (admission L5000). From there, ascend the stairs to the base of the dome for a view down into the basilica. From here, a narrow staircase leads eventually to the top of the dome and San Pietro's lantern, from where you have an unequalled view of Roma. It is well worth the effort, but bear in mind it is a long and tiring climb. You can climb the dome from 8 am to one hour before the basilica closes.

To the right as you face the high altar is a famous bronze statue of St Peter, believed to be a 13th-century work by Arnolfo di Cambio. The statue's right foot has been worn down by the kisses and touch of pil-grims.

The entrance to the **Sacre Grotte Vatic-ane** (Sacred Grottoes) the resting place of numerous popes, is next to the pier of St Longinus (one of four piers supporting the arches at the base of Michelangelo's cupola) to the right as you approach the papal altar. The tombs of many early popes were moved here from the old Basilica di San Pietro, and later popes, including John XXIII, Paul VI and John Paul I, are buried here. The grottoes are open daily from 8 am to 6 pm (April to September) and 8 am to 5 pm (September to March).

The excavations beneath San Pietro, which began in 1940, have uncovered part of the original church, an early Christian cem-etery and pagan tombs. Archaeologists believe they have also found the tomb of St Peter; the site of the empty tomb is marked by a shrine and a wall plastered with red. Nearby is another wall, scrawled with the graffiti of pilgrims, under which were found the bones of an elderly, strongly built man. Pope Paul VI declared these to be the bones of St Peter.

The excavations can be visited only by appointment, which can be made either in writing or in person at the Ufficio Scavi (☎ 69 88 53 18), in Piazza Braschi. Address your letter to Ufficio Scavi, 00120, Città del Vaticano, Roma, and stipulate the date you'd like to visit. The office will then get back in contact with you to confirm the time and date. You need to book at least one week ahead. The office is open from Monday to

Saturday from 8 am to 5 pm. Small groups are taken most days between 9 am and midday and 2 and 5 pm. It costs L10,000 to visit the excavations with a guide.

Dress regulations are stringently enforced at San Pietro. It is forbidden to enter the church in shorts (men included), or wearing a short skirt, or with bare shoulders.

Musei del Vaticano From San Pietro, follow the wall of il Vaticano north to the museums' entrance. They are open Monday to Saturday from 8.45 am to 1 pm. In summer, and at Easter, they stay open Monday to Friday to 4 pm and Saturday to 1 pm. Admission is L15,000. The museums are closed on Sunday and holidays, but open on the last Sunday of every month from 9 am to 2 pm (free admission, but queues are always very long). A regular bus service runs from outside the Arco delle Campane (to the left of the basilica just near the tourist office) to the museum about every half-hour from 8.45 am to 12.45 pm. A ticket costs L2000 and it is certainly the easiest way to make the journey. The bus passes through an area of il Vaticano and its gardens.

The museums contain an incredible collection of art and treasures accumulated by the popes, and you will need several hours to see the most important areas and museums. One visit is probably not enough to appreciate the full value of the collections and it's worth trying to make at least two visits if you have the time. There are four 'one-way' itineraries which il Vaticano has mapped out with the aim of simplifying visits and containing the huge number of visitors. It is basically compulsory that you follow the itineraries, but you can make some deviations if you want.

Another point to note is that the Cappella Sistina comes towards the end of a full visit. If you want to spend most of your time in the chapel, or you want to get there early to avoid the crowds, it is possible to walk straight there and then walk back to the Quattro Cancelli to pick up one of the itineraries. Most tour groups (and there are many!) head straight to the chapel and it almost always very crowded. It is als important to note that, while the museun don't officially close until 1 pm, the guar at the Cappella Sistina often refuse to l people in well before then. Of great assistan and well worth the L10,000 investment, is th *Guide to the Vatican Museums and City*, o sale at the Musei. See the Cappella Sistir section.

The **Museo Gregoriano Egizio** (Egyp tian museum) contains many pieces take from Egypt in Roman times. The collectic is small, but there are interesting pieces.

Il Vaticano's enormous collection o ancient sculpture is contained in a series o galleries. The long corridor which forms th **Museo Chiaramonti** contains hundreds o marble busts, while the **Braccio Nuov** (New Wing) contains important work including a famous statue of Augustus, an a statue depicting the Nile as a reclining go with 16 babies playing on him, which a supposed to represent the number of cubi the Nile rose when in flood.

The **Museo Pio-Clementino** is in the Be vedere Pavilion and accessible through th Egyptian Museum. In the Cortile Ottagon (Octagonal Courtyard), which forms part o the gallery, is part of il Vaticano sculptu collection: the *Apollo Belvedere*, a 2nd century Roman copy in marble of 4th-century BC Greek bronze, considere one of the great masterpieces of classica sculpture and, notably, the *Laocoön*, depic ing a Trojan priest of Apollo and his two son in mortal struggle with two sea serpent When discovered in 1506 on the Esquilin (Michelangelo was said to be present), th sculpture was recognised from description by the Roman writer Pliny the Elder an purchased by Pope Julius II.

In the Sala delle Muse (Room of th Muses) is the *Belvedere Torso*, a Gree sculpture of the 1st century BC, which wa found in the Campo de' Fiori during the tim of Pope Julius II and was much admired b Michelangelo and other Renaissance artist In the Sala a Croce Greca (Greek Cros Room) are the porphyry sarcophagi o ɔnstantine's daughter, Constantia, and his other, St Helena.

Up the next flight of the Simonetti stair-se is the **Museo Gregoriano Etrusco** truscan Museum) which contains arte-cts from Etruscan tombs of southern ruria. Of particular interest are those ɔm the Regolini-Galassi tomb, discov-ed in 1836 south of Cerveteri. Those ıried in the tomb included a princess, and nong the finds on display are gold jewell-y, and a funeral carriage with a bronze d and funeral couch. There is also a llection of Greek vases and Roman anti-ıities in the museum.

Through the **Galleria degli Arazzi** (Tap-try Gallery) and the **Galleria delle Carte eografiche** (Map Gallery) are the magnifi-nt **Stanze di Raffaello**, the private artments of Pope Julius II. Raphael ainted the Stanza della Segnatura and the anza d'Eliodoro, while the Stanza ll'Incendio was painted by his students to s designs and the ceiling was painted by his master, Perugino. In the Stanza della Segnatura is one of Raphael's masterpieces, *The School of Athens*, featuring philosophers and scholars gathered around Plato and Aristotle. The lone figure on the steps is Diogenes and is believed to be a portrait of Michelangelo, who was painting the Cappella Sistina at the time. Opposite is *Disputation on the Sacrament*, also by Raphael. In the Stanza d'Eliodoro is another Raphael masterpiece, *Expulsion of Heliodorus from the Temple*, on the main wall (to the right as you enter from the sala dei Chiaroscuri), which depicts Julius' military victory over foreign powers. To the left is *Mass of Bolsena*, showing Julius II paying homage to the relic of a 13th-century miracle at Orvieto. Next is *Leo X Repulsing Attila*, by Raphael and his school, and on the fourth wall is *Liberation of St Peter*, which depicts St Peter being freed from prison, but is actually an allusion to Pope Leo's imprisonment after the battle of Ravenna (also the real subject of the Attila fresco).

Rapahel's fresco *The School of Athens* (1510-11), Stanza della Segnatura, il Vaticano, Roma

From Raphael's rooms, go down the stairs to the **Appartamento Borgia**, but only to see the ceiling in the first room, decorated with frescoes by Bernardino Pinturicchio. It really isn't worth visiting the collection of modern religious art.

Cappella Sistina The private papal chapel, completed in 1484 for Pope Sixtus IV, the Cappella Sistina (Sistine Chapel) is used for some papal functions and for the conclave which elects the popes. But the chapel is best known for one of the most famous works of art in the world: Michelangelo's wonderful frescoes of the *Creation* on the barrel-vaulted ceiling, and the *Last Judgment* on the end wall. Both have been restored (the ceiling was unveiled after a 10-year restoration project in 1990 and work on the *Last Judgment* was completed in 1994) and the rich, vibrant colours used by Michelangelo have been brought back to the surface.

Michelangelo was commissioned by Pope Julius II to paint the ceiling and although very reluctant to take on the job (he never considered himself a painter), he started work on it in 1508. The complex and grand composition which Michelangelo devised to cover the 800sq m of ceiling took him four years to complete. He worked on scaffolding which the restorers believe was inserted into holes under the windows. The restorers also learned much about the way in which the artist worked and how his painting skill developed as he progressed through the great project.

Vasari records Michelangelo's suffering and frustration, as well as his problems with an impatient Pope Julius and the fact that he did the work almost entirely alone, after dismissing in disgust the Florentine masters he had gathered to help him.

Twenty-four years later Michelangelo was commissioned by Pope Clement VII to paint the *Last Judgment* (the pope died shortly afterwards and the work was executed under Pope Paul III). Two frescoes by Perugino were destroyed to make way for the new painting, which caused great controversy in its day. Criticism of its dramatic, swirli mass of predominantly naked bodies w summarily dismissed by Michelangelo, wh depicted one of his greatest critics, Paul II master of ceremonies, as Minos with ass ears. As with the *Creation*, the *Last Judg ment* was blackened by candle smoke a incense, but it was also damaged by po restorations and by the addition of clothes cover some of the nude figures. One Michelangelo's students, Daniele da Vo terra, was commissioned by Pius IV to do t cover-up job.

The walls of the chapel were painted b famous Renaissance artists including Bot celli, Domenico Ghirlandaio, Pinturicch and Luca Signorelli. Even if you find it ha to drag your attention away from Mic elangelo's frescoes, take time to apprecia these paintings, which were executed in t late 15th century and depict events in the li of Moses (to the right with your back to t *Last Judgment)* and Christ (to the left). No particularly Botticelli's *Burning Bush* on t right wall, as well as his *Cleansing of t Leper*, Domenico Ghirlandaio's *Calling Peter and Andrew* and Perugino's *Chri Giving the Keys to St Peter*.

Castel Sant'Angelo

Originally the mausoleum of Emper Hadrian, this building was converted into fortress for the popes in the 6th century AD It was named Castel Sant'Angelo by Pop Gregory the Great in 590 AD, after he saw vision of an angel above the structure heral ing the end of a plague in Roma. The fortre was linked to the Vatican palaces in 1277 b a wall and passageway, used often by t popes to escape to the fortress in times threat. During the 16th-century sacking Roma by Emperor Charles V, hundreds people lived in the fortress for months.

Castel Sant'Angelo is open daily from am to 7 pm (closed the second and four Tuesday of the month). Admission is L800

Hadrian built the **Ponte Sant'Ange** across the Tevere river in 136 AD to provi an approach to his mausoleum. It collaps

1450 and was subsequently rebuilt, incorporating parts of the ancient bridge. In the 7th century, Bernini and his pupils sculpted e figures of angels which now line the edestrian-only bridge.

ra Pacis

ross the Ponte Sant'Angelo from the castle nd turn left along the Lungotevere to reach e Ara Pacis (Altar of Augustan Peace), culpted and erected during the four years fter Augustus' victories in Spain and Gaul. 'he marble altar is enclosed by a marble creen decorated with reliefs – historical cenes on the sides and mythological scenes n the ends, all protected in a glass building.)f particular interest are the stories related o the discovery and eventual reconstruction f the Ara Pacis.

Sculpted marble panels were first nearthed in the 16th century and sections vere acquired by the Medici, il Vaticano and ven the Louvre. More panels were nearthed in the early 19th century during xcavations under a palace at the corner of /ia del Corso and Via di Lucina. The Italian overnment began acquiring the various anels from all over the world and continued xcavations until the surrounding palaces vere in danger of collapse. It was not until Aussolini ordered the excavation to be esumed that the remainder of the monument vas unearthed and the Ara Pacis reconstructed at its present site.

The monument is open Tuesday to Saturday from 9 am to 7 pm and Sunday from 9 am to 1.30 pm. Admission is L4000.

Beyond the monument is the **Mausoleo d'Augusto** (Mausoleum of Augustus), built by the emperor for himself and his family. It vas originally faced with marble and was converted into a fortress during the Middle Ages. It then served various purposes until estored to its original state in 1936.

Other Basilicas & Churches

The **Chiesa di San Paolo Fuori le Mura** is n Via Ostiense, some distance from the city centre (take Metro Linea B to San Paolo). The original church was built in the 4th century AD by Emperor Constantine over the burial place of St Paul and, until the construction of the present-day Basilica di San Pietro, was the largest church in the world. The church was destroyed by fire in 1823 and the present structure was erected in its place. The beautiful cloisters of the adjacent Benedictine abbey, decorated with 13th-century mosaics, survived the fire.

The **Chiesa di Santa Croce in Gerusalemme**, in the piazza of the same name (take Metro Linea A to San Giovanni) dates from the 4th century but was completely remodelled in Baroque style in the 18th century. A modern chapel inside the church contains what are said to be fragments of the cross on which Christ was crucified. The fragments were found by St Helena in the Holy Land.

The **Chiesa di San Lorenzo Fuori le Mura** is dedicated to the martyred St Lawrence. The original structure was built by Constantine, but the church was rebuilt on many occasions. Of note are the 13th-century pulpits and bishop's throne. The remains of Saints Lawrence and Stephen are in the church crypt.

The opening hours of Roma's churches vary, but they are generally open from 7 or 8 am to midday, and 4 to 7 pm.

Gianicolo & Villa Doria Pamphili

Go to the top of the Gianicolo hill, between the Basilica di San Pietro and Trastevere, for a panoramic view of Roma. This is a good place to take the kids if they need a break. At the top of the hill, just off Piazza Garibaldi there is a permanent merry-go-round and pony rides, and on Sunday a puppet show is often held In the piazza there is a small bar. Catch bus No 41 from Via della Conciliazione in front of San Pietro to reach Piazza Garibaldi, or walk up the steps from Via Mameli in Trastevere. Bus No 41 (from the end of Corso Vittorio Emanuele where it meets the Lungotevere) will also take you within easy walking distance of the nearby **Villa Doria Pamphili**, the largest park in Roma and a lovely quiet spot for a walk and a picnic. Ask for directions to the lake inside the park, which is home to a large population of ducks, a few herons and some strange little rodents known as *nutrie*. A short distance from the southern end of the lake is a children's playground. Built in the 17th century for the Pamphili family, the villa is now used for official government functions.

Via Appia Antica

Known to ancient Romans as the *regina viarum* (queen of roads), the Via Appia Antica (Appian Way) extends from the Porta San Sebastiano, near the Terme di Caracalla, to Brindisi on the coast of Puglia. It was started around 312 BC by the censor Appius Claudius Caecus, but did not connect with Brindisi until around 190 BC. The first section of the road, which extended 90km to Terracina, was considered revolutionary in its day because it was almost perfectly straight – perhaps the world's first autostrada.

Every Sunday, a long section of the Via Appia Antica becomes a no-car zone. You can walk or ride a bike from the Porta di San Sebastiano for several km.

Monuments along the road near Roma include the catacombs and Roman tombs. The **Chiesa di Domine Quo Vadis** is built at the point where St Peter is said to have met Jesus Christ as he was leaving Roma. Peter consequently returned to Roma, where he was martyred.

Circo di Massenzio This circus, built around 309 AD by Emperor Maxentius, is better preserved than the Circo Massimo. In front of the circus is the **Tomba di Romolo** (Tomb of Romulus), built by the same emperor for his son, and next to both are the ruins of the imperial residence. The circus is open Tuesday to Saturday from 9 am to 1.30 pm and Sunday until 12.30 pm.

Tombe di Cecilia Metella Farther along Via Appia is this famous tomb of a Roman noblewoman. The tomb was incorporated into the castle of the Caetani family in the early 14th century. It is open Tuesday to Saturday from 9 am to 6 pm in summer (to 4 pm in winter and to 1 pm on Sunday and Monday. Admi sion is free.

Not far past the tomb is a section of tl actual ancient road, excavated in the mi 19th century. It is very picturesque, lin with fragments of ancient tombs. Althou it is in an area where the rich have built th villas, the road is in a bad state – littered wi rubbish and the ruins vandalised. It is advi able not to wander there alone after dark.

To get to Via Appia Antica, catch bus N 218 from Piazza San Giovanni in Lateran

Catacombe

There are several catacombs along and ne Via Appia – km of tunnels carved out of tl soft tufa rock, which were the meeting a burial places of early Christians in Ron from the 1st century to the early 5th centur People were buried, wrapped in simple whi sheets, and usually placed in rectangul niches carved into the tunnel walls, whi were closed with marble or terracotta slab

To get to the area of the catacombs cat bus No 218 from Piazza San Giovanni Laterano (at the Basilica di San Giovanni Laterano) or Metro Linea A from Stazio Termini to the Colli Albani train station a then bus No 660 to the Via Appia Antica.

Catacombe di San Callisto These cat combs at Via Appia Antica 110 are the large and most famous and contain the tomb of th martyred St Cecilia (although her body w moved to the Basilica di Santa Cecilia Trastevere). There is also a crypt containin the tombs of seven popes martyred in the 3 century. In the 20km of tunnels explored date, archaeologists have found the sepu chres of some 500,000 people.

The catacombs are open daily excep Wednesday, from 8.30 am to midday an 2.30 to 5.30 pm. Admission is with a guid only and costs L8000. The catacombs a closed in February.

Basilica & Catacombe di San Sebastian The basilica was built in the 4th century ov the catacombs, which were used as a sa haven for the remains of saints Peter and Pa uring the reign of the Emperor Vespasian, ho repressed and persecuted the Christians. t Sebastian was buried here in the late 3rd entury. Admission to the catacombs is with guide only. They contain early Christian vall paintings and symbolic decorations. he church and catacombs, at Via Appia ntica 136, just past the main entrance to the 'atacombs of San Callisto, are open Friday Wednesday from 8.30 am to midday and .30 to 5.30 pm. Admission is L8000. The atacombs are closed in November.

'atacombe di San Domitilla Among the argest and oldest catacombs in Roma, they vere established on the private burial ground f Flavia Domitilla, niece of the Emperor Domitian and a member of the wealthy 'lavian family. They contain Christian wall aintings and the underground Chiesa di SS Nereus e Achilleus. The catacombs are situated in Via delle Sette Chiese 283 (take bus No 218) and are open Friday to Wednesday rom 8.30 am to midday and 2.30 to 5.30 pm. Admission is L8000. These catacombs close n January.

Mausoleo delle Fosse Ardeatine

If you walk back to Via Ardeatine and turn right to reach the **Mausoleo delle Fosse Ardeatine**, you will come to the site of one of the worst Nazi atrocities in Italy during WWII. After a brigade of Roman urban partisans blew up 32 German military police in Via Rasella, the Germans took 335 prisoners, who had no connection with the incident, to the Ardeatine Caves and shot them. The Germans used mines to explode sections of the caves and thus bury the bodies. After the war, the bodies were exhumed, identified and reburied in a mass grave at the site, now marked by a huge concrete slab and sculptures. The massacre continues to anger and distress Italians: at the time of writing, two of the alleged perpetrators were on trial in Roma.

EUR

This acronym, which stands for Esposizione Universale di Roma, has become the name of a peripheral suburb of Roma, interesting for its many examples of Fascist architecture, including the **Palazzo della Civiltà del Lavoro** (Palace of the Workers), a square building with arched windows known as the Square Colosseum. Mussolini ordered the construction of the satellite city for an international exhibition to have been held in 1942. Work was suspended with the outbreak of war and the exhibition was never held; however, many buildings were completed during the 1950s.

The **Museo della Civiltà Romana**, Piazza G Agnelli, reconstructs the development of Roma with the use of models. It's open Tuesday to Saturday from 9 am to 7 pm and Sunday to 1.30 pm. Admission is L5000. Also of interest is the **Museo Nazionale Preistorico Etnografico Luigi Pigorini**, Piazza Marconi 14. Its Museo Preistorico covers the development of civilisation in the region, while its ethnographical collection includes exhibits from around the world. The museum is open Tuesday to Friday from 9 am to 1.30 pm, Saturday to 7 pm, and Sunday to 12.30 pm. Admission is L8000.

EUR is accessible on the Metro Linea B.

Family Activities

Sightseeing in Roma will wear out adults – so imagine how the kids feel! If the weather isn't too hot, children of all ages should appreciate a wander through the Foro Romano and up to the Palatino. Also take them to visit the port city, Ostia Antica. Another interesting, if not tiring, experience is the climb to the top of the dome of Basilica di San Pietro for a spectacular view of the city. There is a Luna Park at EUR, as well as a couple of museums which older children might find interesting (see previous section). Another museum which might amuse the kids is the **Museo delle Paste Alimentari** (Pasta Museum), Piazza Scanderbeg, (just near Palazzo del Quirinale), which traces the history of pasta.

During the Christmas period Piazza Navona is transformed into a festive market place, with stalls selling puppets, figures for nativity scenes and Christmas stockings.

Most churches set up nativity scenes – many of them elaborate arrangements which will fascinate kids and adults alike. The most elaborate is an 18th-century Neapolitan presepio at the Basilica di SS Cosma e Damiano.

If you can spare the money, take the family on a tour of Roma by horse and cart. You'll pay through the nose at around L180, 000 for what the driver determines is the 'full tour' of the city. Make sure you agree on a price and itinerary before you get in the cart – even though prices are supposedly regulated, horror stories abound about trusting tourists who forgot to ask the price!

Fortunately the city has plenty of parks. Take a break for a picnic lunch and an afternoon in the Villa Borghese. Near the Porta Pinciana there are bicycles for rent, as well as pony rides, mini-train rides and a merry-go-round. In the Villa Celimontana, on the western slopes of the Celio (entrance from Piazza della Navicella), is a lovely public park and a children's playground. See the earlier section on the Gianicolo & the Villa Doria Pamphili for more ideas on activities for small children.

Language Courses

The Dante Alighieri school (☎ 687 37 22), Piazza Firenze 27, 00186, is Roma's best known Italian language school. It offers intensive one-month courses (eight hours a week) for L260,000, or two-month courses (four hours a week) for the same price. Write or phone for a programme and enrolment forms. The Centro Linguistico Dante Alighieri (☎ 44 23 14 00; fax 44 23 10 07), Piazza Bologna 1, offers courses in Italian language and culture. One-month intensive courses cost L950,000 (80 hours) or L650,000 (60 hours). A one-month course of 20 hours costs L250,000. The school will send out brochures and enrolment forms on request.

Organised Tours

Bus Several agencies in Roma offer guided bus tours of the city in languages including English, French, Spanish, Japanese and German. Appian Line (☎ 48 78 66 01), Piazza Esquilino 6, has a good range of tou[rs] of the city, as well as Tivoli, the Caste[lli] Romani and excursion tours to other ma[in] tourist destinations in Italy. Vastours (☎ 48 43 09), Via Piemonte 34, and Carrani (☎ 48 05 10), Via V E Orlando 95, offer simil[ar] tours. Prices range upwards from L30,0[00] for a two-hour tour. American Express (☎ 76 41), Piazza di Spagna 38, also operat[es] tours of the city, in English only. Anoth[er] option is the ATAC Bus No 110, whic[h] leaves from Piazza dei Cinquecento, in fro[nt] of Termini daily at 3.30 pm (2.30 pm i[n] winter). A three-hour tour costs L15,000.

Walking Walk through the Centuries (☎ 32 17 33), Via Silla 10, offers several guide[d] three hour walking tours, which cos[t] L30,000, or L25,000 if you're under 2[6]. Information is also available at Enjoy Rom[a] (see Tourist Offices). Secret Walks (☎ 39 7[?] 87 28), Via dei Quattro Cantoni 6, will hel[p] you discover some of Roma's hidden trea[-]sures.

Special Events

Although Romans desert their city i[n] summer, particularly in August, when th[e] weather is relentlessly hot and humid, cul[-]tural and musical events liven up the plac[e] and many performances and festivals ar[e] held in the open. The Comune di Rom[a] coordinates a diverse series of concerts, per[-]formances and events throughout summe[r] under the general title of Estate Roman[a] (Roman Summer). The series usually fea[-]tures major international performers an[d] kicks off in early June with a gargantua[n] Festa della Musica (Music Festival). Infor[-]mation is published in Roma's dail[y] newspapers. Otherwise tourist offices hav[e] details.

One of the more interesting and pleasan[t] summer events is the jazz festival in the Vill[a] Celimontana, a lovely park on top of th[e] Celio (entrance is from Piazza dell[a] Navicella). Organised by Alexanderplatz the festival doesn't feature big names bu[t] there are open-air tables and cold-beer stalls

The Festa de Noantri, in honour of Ou[r]

ady of Mt Carmel, is held in Trastevere in ıe last two weeks of July and, if you stick ɔ Viale di Trastevere, is not much more than line of street stalls. Head for the back treets, however, and you will find street heatre and live music. Locals eat their meals n the street.

The Festa di San Giovanni is held on 23 nd 24 June in the San Giovanni area and eatures much dancing and eating in the treets. Part of the ritual is to eat stewed nails and suckling pig.

The focus is also religious during Holy Week and events include the famous procesion of the cross between the Colosseo and he Palatino on Good Friday, and the pope's lessing of the city and the world in Piazza San Pietro on Easter Sunday.

The Spanish Steps become a sea of lowers during the Spring Festival in April.

Keep an eye out for Italian Cultural Heriage Week, which in recent years has been ıeld in mid-April. Museums, galleries, ırchaeological zones and monuments overseen by the Ministero dei Beni Culturali can be visited free of charge throughout the week and numerous monuments normally closed to the public open their doors.

Places to Stay

Roma has a vast number of pensioni and hotels, but it is always best to book. While summer is the peak period, tourists and pilgrims flock to Roma year-round. If you haven't already booked, go to the tourist office at Stazione Termini or Fiumicino airport, the main EPT office or Enjoy Rome (see Tourist Offices). A hotel booking service is available free of charge for new arrivals in Roma. Called HR Hotel Reservations, the service is offered by a consortium of Roma hotel owners and has booths at Fiumicino airport in the International Arrivals Hall, at Stazione Termini opposite Platform 10, and on the Autostrada del Sole at the Tevere Ovest service station. The service operates daily from 7 am to 10 pm; phone ☎ 699 10 00. It will also make bookings at hotels in other major Italian cities.

Avoid the people at the train station who claim to be tourism officials and offer to find you a room.

The Associazione Cattolica Internazionale al Servizio della Giovane (also known as Protezione della Giovane), downstairs at Stazione Termini, is usually open from 9 am to 1 pm and 2 to 8 pm, and offers young women accommodation. If the office is closed, try contacting the head office (☎ 488 00 56) at Via Urbana 158, which runs parallel to Via Cavour, off Piazza Esquilino.

Most of the budget pensioni and larger hotels which cater for tour groups are located near Stazione Termini. The area south-west (to the left as you leave the station) can be noisy and unpleasant. It teems with pickpockets and snatch thieves and women may find it unsafe at night. To the north-east you can find accommodation in quieter and somewhat safer streets in a more pleasant residential area. However, the historic centre of Roma is far more appealing and the area around il Vaticano is much less chaotic; both of these areas are only a short bus or Metro ride away.

You will often find three or four budget pensioni in the same building, although many are small establishments of 12 rooms or less which fill up quickly in summer. The sheer number of budget hotels in the area should, however, ensure that you find a room.

Most hotels will accept bookings in advance, although some demand a deposit for the first night. Many Roman pensioni proprietors are willing to bargain the price of a room. Generally, prices go down if you stay for more than three days. Prices quoted here are for the high season (June to September).

Places to Stay – bottom end

Unless otherwise stated, the prices quoted for hotels in this section are for rooms without a shower or bath. Many pensioni charge an extra L1000 to L2000 for use of the communal bathroom.

Camping All of Roma's camping grounds are a fair distance from the centre. *Seven Hills* (☎ 30 31 08 26), Via Cassia 1216,

charges L9500 per person, per day. It costs L8000 per tent and L10,000 per person, and an extra L5000 if you have a car. It is open from 15 March to 30 October. It's a bit of a hike from Termini: catch the Metro Linea A to Ottaviano, walk to Piazza del Risorgimento and take bus No 907 (ask the driver where to get off). From Via Cassia it is a 1km walk to the camping ground. A good option is *Village Camping Flaminio* (☎ 333 26 04), Via Flaminia 821, which is about 15 minutes from the city centre by public transport. It costs L13,000 per person and L12,400 for a site. Tents, caravans and bungalows are available for rent. From Stazione Termini catch bus No 910 to Piazza Mancini, then bus No 200 to the camping ground. At night, catch bus No 24N from Piazzale Flaminio (just north of Piazza del Popolo).

Hostel The HI *Ostello Foro Italico* (☎ 323 62 67) is at Viale delle Olimpiadi 61. Take Metro Linea A to Ottaviano, then bus No 32 to Foro Italico. It has a bar, restaurant and garden and is open all year. It is closed from 9.30 am to midday. Breakfast and showers are included in the price, which is L23,000 per night. A meal costs L14,000.

PLACES TO STAY
1 Hotel Montecarlo
3 Hotel Castelfidardo
4 Hotel Floridia
5 Albergo Mari 2
6 Papa Germano
7 Pensione Katty
8 Hotel Harmony
10 Pensione Lachea, Hotel Pensione Dolomiti & Tre Stelle
11 Albergo Sandra
12 Hotel Positano
13 Pensione Restivo
15 Pensione Ester
16 Hotel Pensione Gabriella & Hotel Ventura
17 Hotel Venezia
18 Hotel Piemonte
19 Pensione Giamaica
23 Fawlty Towers
24 Hotel Rimini
35 Hotel Pensione Oceania
36 Hotel Pensione Seiler
39 Hotel Elide
44 Hotel Galatea
47 Pensione Everest
48 Hotel Giada
51 Hotel Dina
53 Albergo Onella & Home Sweet Home
54 Hotel Acropoli
56 Hotel Palladium
57 Hotel Kennedy
58 Hotel Igea
60 Hotel Sandy
65 Hotel d'Este

PLACES TO EAT
20 Da Gemma alla Lupa
21 Trattoria da Bruno
26 La Piazza
34 Dagnino
45 Il Golosone
52 Hosteria Angelo

OTHER
2 Trimani
9 Telecom Office
14 Hospital (Policlinico Umberto I)
22 Enjoy Rome Tourist Office
25 Telecom Office
27 CIT Travel Agency
28 EPT Tourist Branch Office
29 Urban Bus Station
30 Museo Nazionale Romano & Terme di Diocleziano
31 Chiesa di Santa Maria degli Angeli
32 EPT Tourist Office
33 Feltrinelli
37 CIT Travel Agency
38 Eurojet Travel Agency
40 British Council Library
41 Teatro dell'Opera
42 Questura (Police Station)
43 CTS Travel Agency
46 Chiesa di Santa Pudenziana
49 24-Hour Pharmacy
50 Italian Youth Hostels Association
55 Laundromat
59 Basilica di Santa Maria Maggiore
61 Fiddler's Elbow
62 Chiesa di Santa Prassede
63 Marconi
64 Druid's Den
66 Circolo degli Artisti

The Associazione Italiana Alberghi per la Gioventù (Italian Youth Hostels Association; ☎ 487 11 52), Via Cavour 44, has information about all youth hostels in Italy, and will assist with bookings to stay at universities during summer. You can also join HI here.

Religious Institutions There are a number of religious institutions in Roma, including near Stazione Termini and il Vaticano. However, they have strict curfews. If you want to stay in one, you can apply to the nearest Catholic archdiocese in your home town. Otherwise, try the *Domus Aurelia delle Suore Orsoline* (☎ 39 37 64 80), Via Aurelia 218 (about 1km from San Pietro, which has singles/doubles with a bathroom for L60,000/90,000. From Stazione Termini catch bus No 64 to Largo Argentina, then No 46 to Via Aurelia. The *Padri Trinitari* (☎ 638 38 88), Piazza Santa Maria alle Fornaci, very close to the Basilica di San Pietro, has singles/doubles for L70,000/120,000 and triples for L145,000, including breakfast.

Villa Bassi (☎ 581 53 29) is at the top of the Gianicolo hill in the Monte Verde area at Via Giacinto Carini 24, very close to both Trastevere and Il Vaticano. Take bus No 75 from Stazione Termini. Clean, simple singles/doubles are L55,000/80,000, L100,000 for a triple and L120,000 a quad.

Pensioni & Hotels Roma has a wide range of pensioni and hotels in this price range.

North-East of Termini To reach the pensioni in this area, head to the right as you leave the train platforms, onto Via Marsala, which runs alongside the station. At Via Marghera 17 is the *Hotel Rimini* (☎ 446 19 91) with singles/doubles with a bathroom for L80,000/120,000 with breakfast. Off Via Vicenza, at Via Magenta 13, *Pensione Giamaica* (☎ 49 01 21) has OK singles/doubles for L50,000/75,000. *Fawlty Towers* (☎ 445 03 74), Via Magenta 39, offers hostel-style accommodation. A bed is L25,000, or L27,000 with a shower, single rooms are L50,000 and doubles are from L70,000. Run by the people at Enjoy Rome (see under Tourist Offices), it offers lots of information about Roma. Added bonuses are the sunny terrace and satellite TV.

Nearby in Via Palestro are several reasonably priced pensioni. *Pensione Restivo* (☎ 446 21 72), Via Palestro 55, has large singles/doubles for L50,000/80,000. There is a midnight curfew. *Pensione Katty* (☎ 444 12 16), Via Palestro 35, has basic rooms for L50,000/70,000. *Pensione Ester* (☎ 495 71 23), Viale Castro Pretorio 25, has large, comfortable doubles for L70,000 and triples for L90,000.

The recently restored *Hotel Pensione Gabriella* (☎ 445 02 52), Via Palestro 88, has doubles with bathroom for L130,000. In the same building is *Hotel Ventura* (☎ 445 19 51; fax 446 00 34), with recently renovated singles/doubles for up to L80,000/100,000.

At Via San Martino della Battaglia 11, there are three good pensioni. *Pensione Lachea* (☎ 495 72 56) has large, clean doubles/triples for L60,000/80,000. *Hotel Pensione Dolomiti* (☎ 49 10 58) has a helpful management and singles/doubles for L45,000/60,000 including breakfast; a triple is L80,000. Downstairs is *Tre Stelle* (☎ 446 30 95) with singles/doubles for L80,000/110,000 and triples for L140,000.

Albergo Sandra (☎ 445 26 12), Via Villafranca 10 (which runs between Via Vicenza and Via San Martino della Battaglia) is clean with dark, but pleasant rooms. Singles/doubles cost L60,000/80,000, including the cost of a shower. Prices go down according to the length of your stay.

Albergo Mari 2 (☎ 474 03 71; fax 482 83 13), Via Calatafimi 38, has singles/doubles for L50,000/100,000 or up to L70,000/140,000 with a bathroom. *Papa Germano* (☎ 48 69 19), Via Calatafimi 14a, is one of the more popular budget places in the area and has singles/doubles for L50,000/75,000 and doubles with a bathroom for L90,000. Nearby, at Via Montebello 45, is *Hotel Floridia* (☎ 481 70 64) with singles/doubles for L65,000/90,000. Pensione Ascot (☎ 474 16 75), Via Montebello 22, has singles/double with a bathroom for L75,000/100,000. Don' worry about the porn cinema opposite; th hotel itself is fine.

Hotel Castelfidardo (☎ 446 46 38), Vi Castelfidardo 31, off Piazza dell'Indipen denza, is one of Roma's better one-sta pensioni. It has singles/doubles for L60,000 75,000, and triples for L95,000. A double/triple with a private bathroom cost L90,000/125,000. Across Via XX Settem bre, at Via Collina 48 (a 10-minute wal from the train station), is *Pensione Erco* (☎ 474 54 54) with singles/doubles wit bathroom for L80,000/120,000 and triple for L160,000. In the same building is *Pen sione Tizi* (☎ 474 32 66) with singles doubles for L50,000/70,000. Triples ar L120,000 with a shower.

South-West of Termini This area is decidedly seedier, but prices remain the same. A you exit the train station, follow Via Giobert to Via G Amendola, which becomes Vi Filippo Turati. This street and the parallel Vi Principe Amedeo harbour a concentration o budget pensioni and you shouldn't have any trouble finding a room. The area improves a you head away from the train station and towards the Colosseo and Foro Romano.

A good choice in the area is *Hotel Kenned* (☎ 446 53 73), Via F Turati 62, which has very comfortable singles/doubles fo L80,000/110,000. At Via Cavour 47, the main street running south-west from the piazza in front of Termini, is the *Pension Everest* (☎ 488 16 29), also clean and simple with rooms for L50,000/90,000. *Hote Sandy* (☎ 488 45 85), Via Cavour 136, has dormitory beds for L28,000 a night. *Hotel I Castello* (☎ 77 20 40 36), Via Vittorio Amedeo II 9, is close to the Manzoni Metro stop, south of Termini. It has beds in dorm rooms for L28,000.

Off Via Nazionale is the *Hotel Elid* (☎ 488 39 77), Via Firenze 50, which has well-maintained rooms. A single costs L60,000. A double/triple with bathroom costs L110,000/160,000. Ask for room No 18, which has an elaborate, gilded ceiling

'otel Galatea (☎ 474 30 70), Via Genova 4, is through the grand entrance of an old alace. Its well-furnished singles/doubles :e good value at L70,000/89,000. A triple osts around L165,000. With bathroom, ooms are L80,000/118,000/210,000 respec-vely.

'ity Centre Really economical hotels in .oma's historical centre basically don't xist. But, in the areas around Piazza di pagna, Piazza Navona, the Pantheon and 'ampo de' Fiori, you do have the conve-ience and pleasure of staying right in the entre of historic Roma. The easiest way to et to Piazza di Spagna is on the Metro Linea . to Spagna. To get to Piazza Navona and ie Pantheon area, take bus No 64 from iazza dei Cinquecento, in front of Stazione ermini, to Largo di Torre Argentina.

One of the most centrally located 'lower'-riced hotels is the *Pensione Primavera* ☎ 68 80 31 09), Piazza San Pantaleo 3, on 'orso Vittorio Emanuele II, just south of iazza Navona. A magnificent entrance leads) a pleasant, recently renovated establish-ient where a double costs L130,000 and iples are L60,000 per person, including reakfast. *Albergo Abruzzi* (☎ 679 20 21), iazza della Rotonda 69, overlooks the Pan-ieon. You couldn't find a better location, but ie rooms can be very noisy until late at night 'hen the piazza is finally deserted. ingles/doubles are L87,000/120,000 and se of the communal shower is free. Book-igs are essential throughout the year.

Pensione Mimosa (☎ 68 80 17 53) at Via anta Chiara 61, off Piazza della Minerva, as singles/doubles for L70,000/105,000 nd triples are L145,000. Prices include reakfast.

Albergo della Lunetta (☎ 686 10 80), 'iazza del Paradiso 68, on the north side of 'ampo de' Fiori, has doubles for L100,000 r L140,000 with a shower. Bookings are ssential. *Albergo Pomezia* (☎ 686 13 71), 'ia dei Chiavari 12, which runs off Via dei Giubbonari from Campo de' Fiori, is reason-bly priced given its location, with doubles/ riples for L100,000/150,000, breakfast included. Use of the communal shower is free.

Near Piazza di Spagna is *Pensione Fiorella* (☎ 361 05 97), Via del Babuino 196, with very clean singles/doubles for L59,000/ 95,000, including breakfast.

Near Il Vaticano & Trastevere Although there aren't many bargains in this area, it is comparatively quiet and still close to the main sights. Bookings are an absolute neces-sity because rooms are often filled with people attending conferences etc at il Vaticano. The simplest way to reach the area is on the Metro Linea A to Ottaviano. Turn left into Via Ottaviano, and Via Germanico is a short walk away. Otherwise, take bus No 64 from Stazione Termini to the Basilica di San Pietro and walk away from the basilica, north along Via di Porta Angelica, which becomes Via Ottaviano after the Piazza del Risorgimento. This is a five-minute walk.

The best bargain in the area is *Pensione Ottaviano* (☎ 39 73 72 53), Via Ottaviano 6, near Piazza del Risorgimento. It has dormi-tory beds for L28,000 per person and doubles for L80,000. The owner speaks English. *Hotel Giuggioli* (☎ 324 21 13), Via Germanico 198, is very small, but a delight. A double costs L110,000, or L130,000 with bathroom. Rooms are well furnished. There are other pensioni in the same building. *Pen-sione Lady* (☎ 324 21 12), on the 4th floor, has large, clean singles/doubles for L90,000/110,000. *Pensione Nautilus* (☎ 324 21 18), on the 2nd floor, has doubles for L80,000 and triples for L120,000. Doubles with bathroom are an extra L20,000.

Pensione San Michele (☎ 324 33 33), Via Attilio Regolo 19, off Via Cola di Rienzo, has average singles/doubles for L50,000/ 80,000. At Via Giulio Cesare 47, near the Lepanto Metro stop, is *Pensione Valparaiso* (☎ 321 31 84) with clean, simple singles/ doubles for the same prices as the San Michele.

In Trastevere is the *Carmel* (☎ 580 99 21), Via Mameli 11, with singles/doubles for L80,000/100,000 with bathroom.

Places to Stay – middle
All rooms in this section have private bathroom unless otherwise stated.

Near Stazione Termini To the south-west of the train station, at Via Principe Amedeo 97, is the *Hotel Igea* (☎ 446 69 11). It has singles/doubles for L120,000/160,000 and triples for L190,000. *Hotel Acropoli* (☎ 488 56 85) in the same street at No 67 has singles/doubles for L70,000/150,000. *Hotel Dina* (☎ 474 06 94; fax 445 37 77), Via Principe Amedeo 62, is clean with a friendly management. Singles/doubles are L70,000/110,000. At No 47 is the *Hotel Sweet Home* (☎ 488 09 54), with singles/doubles for L120,000/150,000, including breakfast. In the same building is recently renovated *Albergo Onella* (☎ 488 52 57). Its singles/doubles cost up to L140,000/ 240,000, breakfast included.

Hotel Palladium (☎ 446 69 17; fax 446 69 37), Via Gioberti 36, has large double rooms for L280,000; singles are L230,000 and triples L350,000. The *Hotel d'Este* (☎ 446 56 07; fax 446 56 01), Via Carlo Alberto 4b, is a stone's throw from Santa Maria Maggiore and is one of the better medium-range hotels in the area. It has beautifully furnished, comfortable singles/doubles for up to L160,000/200,000.

North-west of the train station, in Via Firenze, off Via Nazionale, there are a couple of good-value hotels. *Hotel Pensione Seiler* (☎ 488 02 04; fax 488 06 88) at No 48 has clean but basic rooms; all have a TV and the price includes breakfast. Singles/doubles are L110,000/170,000. Triples/quads are also available. *Hotel Pensione Oceania* (☎ 482 46 96; fax 488 55 86) at No 38, is an ideal family hotel – although it is on the expensive side. Simply furnished singles/doubles are L170,000/230,000, and triples/quads are L295,000/345,000. A room for five is L390,000. During winter the hotel offers a 20% discount and a 10% discount can be negotiated at other times.

North-east of the train station is *Hotel Harmony* (☎ 48 67 38), Via Palestro 13, which has singles/doubles for L100,000/160,000. *Hotel Positano* (☎ 49 03 60; fax 4 01 78) at Via Palestro 49, has clean, pleasar doubles/triples for up to L160,000/220,00(

City Centre *Albergo del Sole* (☎ 687 94 46) Via del Biscione 76, off Campo de' Fiori, ha big rooms and a roof terrace. Singles doubles cost L115,000/160,000 or L90,00(130,000 without bathroom. *Hotel Campo de Fiori* (☎ 68 80 68 65), Via del Biscione 6 i – as its name suggests – just off the Camp de' Fiori. It has interestingly furnished room on its six floors (but there is no lift), as we as a roof garden with a great view. Double are L190,000/240,000 or L120,000/180,00 without a bathroom.

Near Piazza di Spagna is *Hotel Pension Suisse* (☎ 678 36 49), Via Gregoriana 56. I has good-quality singles/doubles fo L120,000/180,000 and triples L240,00(Closer to Piazza del Popolo is *Hotel Margutta* (☎ 322 36 74), Via Laurina 34, off Vi del Corso. It has spotless rooms, and prices which are negotiable, include breakfas There are no singles and a double costs up t L147,000, a triple L195,000 and a qua L230,000. *Hotel Forte* (☎ 320 76 25), Vi Margutta 61 (parallel to Via del Babuino), i comfortable and quiet. Singles cost L100,00 and doubles are L150,000.

Hotel Pensione Merano (☎ 482 17 96) i a lovely old place, well located at Vi Vittorio Veneto 155. It has singles/double for L105,000/150,000 and triples fo L190,000, including breakfast. *Hotel Juli* (☎ 488 16 37), Via Rasella 29, off Via dell Quattro Fontane near Piazza Barberini, is no-frills place but quiet and clean. Singles doubles are L130,000/220,000. The pric includes breakfast and all rooms have television.

Near Il Vaticano & Trastevere Virtuall next to the wall of Il Vaticano off Via de Corridori is *Hotel Bramante* (☎ 68 80 6 26), Vicolo delle Palline 24. It has rooms o reasonable quality. Singles/doubles ar L120,000/160,000. Without bathroom, the cost L88,000/120,000. *Hotel Prati* (☎ 68 53 57), Via Crescenzio 89, has singles doubles for L95,000/150,000 and triples for L195,000. Singles/doubles without bathroom are L75,000/95,000. *Hotel Adriatic* (☎ 686 96 68), Via Vitelleschi 25 (the continuation of Via Porcari, off Piazza del Risorgimento), has modern rooms and is good value with singles/doubles at L105,000/145,000; rooms without bathroom are L85,000/110,000. A triple costs L195,000, or L148,000 without bathroom.

At Via Cola di Rienzo 243 there are two good-quality hotels, both excellent value for their location and prices. *Hotel Joli* (☎ 324 18 54) is on the 6th floor. It has large rooms and is ideal for families. Singles/doubles are L80,000/120,000 and triples L160,000. *Hotel Florida* (☎ 324 18 72) is on the 2nd floor and has singles/doubles for L65,000/135,000 and triples for L157,000. Discounts are available out of the high season.

Hotel Ticino (☎ 324 32 51), Via dei Gracchi 161, has comfortable rooms and some are big enough for families. There are showers but no toilets in the rooms, and prices include breakfast. Singles/doubles are L75,000/130,000 and triples are L175,000 without bathroom.

Hotel Amalia (☎ 39 72 82 07), Via Germanico 66, near the corner of Via Ottaviano, has a beautiful courtyard entrance and clean, sunny rooms. Singles/doubles are L80,000/100,000 with use of the communal shower; triples are L135,000. Singles/ doubles with bathroom are L130,000/ 200,000, and triples are L270,000.

In Trastevere there is the *Hotel Cisterna* (☎ 581 72 12), Via della Cisterna 7-9, off Via San Francesco a Ripa. It has average, comfortable rooms. Singles/doubles L120,000/160,000 and triples are L215,000.

Places to Stay – top end

There is no shortage of expensive hotels in Roma, but many, particularly those near Stazione Termini, are geared towards large tour groups and, while certainly offering all conveniences, tend to be a bit anonymous. The following three and four-star hotels have been selected on the basis of their individual charm, as well as value for money and location. All rooms are with bathroom, telephone and TV. Breakfast is usually included in the price, but it is wise to check.

Aventino If you prefer quieter surroundings and don't mind being a bit out of the centre of town, try the *Aventino* (☎ 574 35 47), Via San Domenico 10. It has pleasant singles/ doubles for up to L170,000/240,000.

Near Stazione Termini *Hotel Venezia* (☎ 445 71 01; fax 495 76 87), Via Varese 18, on the corner of Via Marghera, is beautifully furnished in antique style. Singles/doubles cost L174,000/242,000 and triples L320,000. Prices drop in the low season. At *Hotel Montecarlo* (☎ 446 00 00; fax 446 00 34), Via Palestro 17a, singles/doubles cost L170,000/250,000, triples L347,000. It also offers generous discounts on rooms in the low season. *Hotel Piemonte* (☎ 445 22 40; fax 445 16 49), Via Vicenza 34, has very pleasant singles/doubles for up to L150,000/210,000. On the other side of the train station is *Hotel Giada* (☎ 488 58 63), Via Principe Amedeo 9. It is a very pleasant establishment with singles/doubles for L190,000/230,000. Discounts are offered in the off season and during August.

At the end of Via Cavour, in the area close to the Foro Romano, are two very good hotels. Both are in Via Tor de' Conti, which runs behind the Via dei Fori Imperiali and their location is hard to beat. *Hotel Nerva* (☎ 678 18 35), at No 3, has singles/doubles for up to L220,000/300,000. *Hotel Forum* (☎ 679 24 46), at No 25, is a four-star hotel, with singles/doubles from L280,000/400,000. It also has a rooftop terrace with stunning views.

City Centre Near Piazza di Spagna are several of Roma's better hotels. The *Gregoriana* (☎ 679 42 69), Via Gregoriana 18, has long been an institution for the fashionable set. Its rooms are not numbered, but instead adorned with letters by the 1930s French fashion illustrator Erté. Singles/doubles cost up to L210,000/360,000 and triples cost L380,000. Magnificently located at the top of the Spanish Steps, at Piazza Trinità dei Monti 17, is *Hotel Scalinata di Spagna*, which has a roof terrace overlooking the city. It is usually booked up for months in advance, so it's worth contacting them early. It has singles/doubles for up to L230/380,000. Opposite is the high-class *Hassler Villa Medici* (☎ 678 26 51), one of Roma's top hotels. Doubles cost up to L650,000 per night. Around the corner at Via Sistina 136 is the small *Hotel Sistina* (☎ 474 41 76) with singles/doubles for L240,000/340,000.

Another of Roma's top hotels is *Minerva* (☎ 69 94 18 88; fax 679 41 65), Piazza della Minerva 69. It is run by Holiday Inn, and for around L600,000 a double, you get absolute luxury and comfort. It has a rooftop terrace with a splendid view of the Pantheon. *Hotel Senato* (☎ 678 43 43), Piazza della Rotonda 73, overlooks the Pantheon. Its comfortable rooms are L195,000/295,000. The rooms are also reasonably quiet, considering the hotel's position. The *Albergo Teatro di Pompeo* (☎ 687 28 12), Largo del Pallaro 8, near Campo de'Fiori, has plenty of old world charm – in fact parts of the hotel go back as far as the Roman Republic. It has very comfortable doubles from L270,000.

Near Il Vaticano *Hotel Columbus* (☎ 686 52 45), Via della Conciliazione 33, is in a restored 15th-century palace in front of Basilica di San Pietro. It has singles/doubles for L230,000/320,000 and triples for L400,000. The elegant *Hotel Sant'Anna* (☎ 68 80 16 02), Borgo Pio 133, is also near il Vaticano. It has doubles for L260,000 and triples for L290,000.

Rental Accommodation

Apartments near the centre of Roma are expensive and you can expect to pay a minimum of L1,500,000 a month. A good way to find a shared apartment is to buy *Wanted in Rome* or *Porta Portese* at newspaper stands. A room in a shared apartment will cost at least L600,000 a month, plus bills. There are also agencies, known as *agenzie immobiliari*, specialising in short-term rentals in Roma, which charge a fee for their services. They are listed in *Wanted in Rome*.

Places to Eat

Roma offers a pretty good range of eating places: there are some excellent establishments offering typical Roman fare to suit a range of budgets, as well as some good, but usually fairly expensive, restaurants offering international cuisines such as Indian, Chinese, Vietnamese and Japanese. The best areas to look for good trattorie are Trastevere and between Piazza Navona and the Tevere. During summer these areas are lively and atmospheric and most establishments have outside tables. Meal times are generally from 12.30 to 3 pm and from 8 to 11 pm, although in summer many restaurants stay open later. If you want to be sure of finding a table (especially if you want one outside), either drop into the restaurant during the day and make a booking or arrive before 8.30 pm.

Antipasto dishes in Roma are particularly good and many restaurants allow you to make your own mixed selection. Typical pasta includes: bucatini all'Amatriciana, with a usually very salty sauce of tomato and pancetta (cured bacon), topped with pecorino Romano (matured sheep's cheese); penne all'arrabbiata, which has a hot sauce of tomatoes and chilli; spaghetti carbonara, with pancetta, eggs and cheese. Saltimbocca alla Romana (slices of veal and ham) and abbacchio (roast lamb seasoned with rosemary) are classic meat dishes, which are followed by a wide variety of vegetables. During winter, try the carciofi alla Romana (artichokes stuffed with mint or parsley and garlic), or carciofi alla giudia, which are deep-fried. Offal is also very popular in Roma, and a local speciality is the pajata (pasta with a sauce of chopped veal intestines).

Always remember to check the menu posted outside the establishment for prices, cover and service charges. Expect to pay under L25,000 per person at a simple trattoria, up to L50,000 at an average restaurant and around L100,000 or more at Roma's top eating places. These prices are for a full meal ncluding entrée, main, dessert and wine. ìating only a pasta and salad and drinking ne house wine at a trattoria can keep the bill lown. If you order meat or, particularly, fish 'ou will push up the bill substantially.

Good options for cheap, quick meals are t the hundreds of bars around the city, where andwiches cost L2500 to L5000 taken at the bar (al banco), or at takeaway pizzerie, where slice of freshly cooked pizza, sold by veight, can cost as little as L1500. Bakeries re numerous in the Campo de' Fiori area and re another good choice for a cheap snack. Try a piece of pizza bianca, a flat bread resembling focaccia, which costs from around L1500 a slice. See the Sandwiches & Snacks section for details.

For groceries and supplies of cheese, prosciutto, salami and wine, shop at alimentari. For fresh fruit and vegetables there are numerous outdoor markets, notably the lively daily market in Campo de' Fiori, although it is expensive. Cheaper food markets are held in Piazza Vittorio Emanuele near Stazione Termini, in Piazza Testaccio on the other side of the Aventino from the

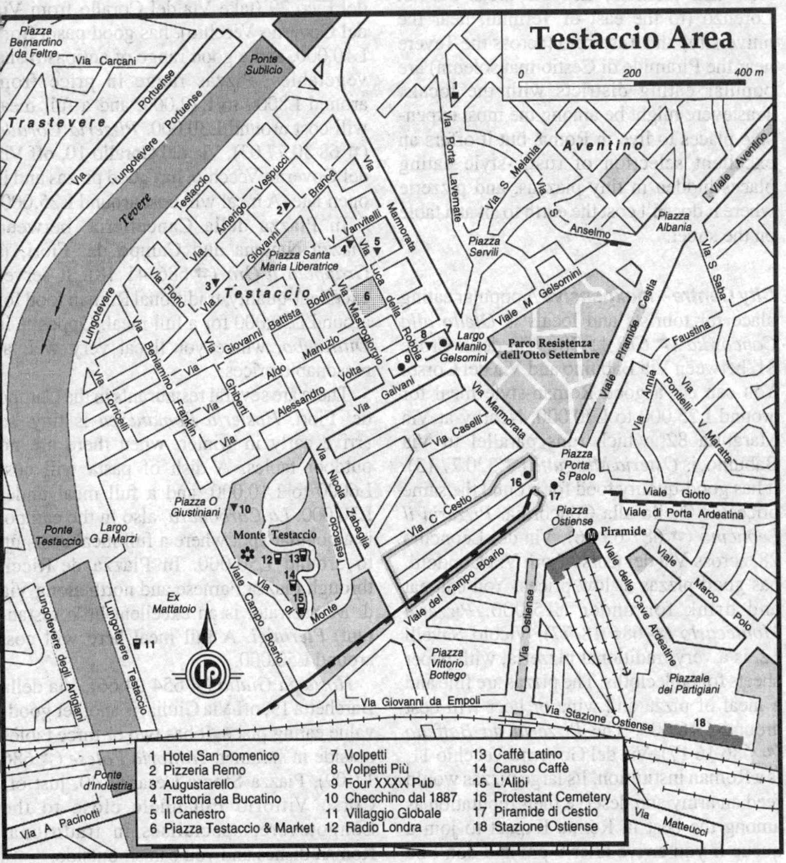

Circo Massimo, and in Via Andrea Doria, near Largo Trionfale, north of il Vaticano. The huge wholesale food markets in Via Ostiense, some distance from the city centre, are open Monday to Saturday from 10 am to around 1 pm.

Restaurants, Trattorie & Pizzerie Generally the restaurants near Stazione Termini are to be avoided if you want to pay reasonable prices for good-quality food. The side streets around Piazza Navona and Campo de' Fiori harbour many good-quality, low-priced trattorie and pizzerie, and the areas of San Lorenzo (to the east of Termini, near the university) and Testaccio (across the Tevere near the Piramide di Cestio mausoleum) are popular eating districts with the locals. Trastevere might be among the most expensive places to live in Roma, but it offers an excellent selection of rustic-style eating places hidden in tiny piazzas, and pizzerie where it doesn't cost the earth to sit at a table on the street.

City Centre – inexpensive A popular eating place for tourists and locals is *Otello alla Concordia* (☎ 679 11 78), Via della Croce 81, between Via Babuino and Via del Corso. You can eat a good Roman-style meal for around L25,000 to L30,000. Nearby at Via Margutta 82, which runs parallel to Via Babuino, is *Osteria Margutta* (☎ 320 77 13). It has good-quality food for around the same prices as Otello alla Concordia. *Pizzeria il Leoncino* (☎ 687 63 06), Via del Leoncino 28, across Via del Corso from Via Condotti, has good pizzas at low prices. You can eat and drink for under L15,000. *Pizzeria Montecarlo* (☎ 686 18 77), Vicolo Savelli 12, is a very traditional pizzeria, with paper sheets for tablecloths. The pizzas are fine and a meal of pizza and wine or beer will cost around L16,000. The *Pizzeria da Baffetto* (☎ 686 16 17), Via del Governo Vecchio 11, is a Roman institution. Its large pizzas would feed an army and deserve their reputation as among the best in Roma. Expect to join a queue if you arrive after 9 pm and don't be surprised if you end up sharing a table. Pizzas cost around L8000 to L12,000, a litre of wine costs L8000 and the cover charge is only L1500. Farther along the street at No 1? is a tiny, nameless *osteria* (no telephone), run by Antonio Bassetti, where you can eat an excellent meal for around L20,000. The consistently good food and low prices make it one of the best-value eating places in Roma. There is no written menu, but don't be nervous: even when very busy, the owner waiter will try to explain (in Italian) the dishes.

Trattoria Pizzeria da Francesco, Piazza del Fico 29 (take Via del Corallo from Via del Governo Vecchio), has good pasta from L10,000, and a good range of antipasto and vegetables. Pizzas range in price from around L8000 to L12,000, and a full meal will cost around L30,000. *Pizzeria Corallo* (☎ 68 30 77 03), Via del Corallo 10, off Via del Governo Vecchio, has good pizzas and is open late. A meal will cost around L25,000.

In Piazza della Cancelleria, between Piazza Navona and Campo de' Fiori, is *Grappolo d'Oro* (☎ 686 41 18). It serves excellent-quality, traditional Roman food for around L30,000 for a full meal. Opposite is *Ditirambo*, where you'll eat very well at reasonable prices.

There are several restaurants in the Campo de' Fiori. *Hosteria Romanesca* is tiny, so arrive early in winter, when there are no outdoor tables. A dish of pasta will cost L6000 to L10,000, and a full meal under L30,000. *La Carbonara*, also in the campo, is a popular spot where a full meal costs up to around L50,000. In Piazza de'Ricci, through Piazza Farnese and north along Via di Monserrato, is an excellent little restaurant, *Pierluigi*. A full meal here will cost around L50,000.

Hostaria Giulio (☎ 654 04 66), Via della Barchetta 19, off Via Giulia, is another good-value eating place. It has two or three tables outside in summer. *Trattoria Polese* (☎ 686 17 09), Piazza Sforza Cesarini 40, just off Corso Vittorio Emanuele close to the Lungotevere, specialises in traditional Roman dishes and you can sit outside.

Along Via Giubbonari, off Campo de' Fiori, is *Filletti di Baccalà* (☎ 686 40 18) in Largo dei Librari, off Via dei Cappellari, which serves only deep-fried cod fillets and wine. You can satisfy moderate hunger and thirst for under L10,000. *Il Grottino*, Via delle Grotte 27, off Via dei Giubbonari near Campo de' Fiori, serves reasonable pizzas for around L6000 to L9000, a litre of wine costs L5000 and the coperto is L1500. A full meal will cost under L25,000.

On the other side of Via Arenula, in the Jewish quarter, is *Sora Margherita* (☎ 686 40 02), Piazza delle Cinque Scole 30, which serves traditional Roman and Jewish food in simple surroundings. A meal will cost under L25,000. Also in the Jewish quarter is *Al Pompiere* (☎ 686 83 77), at Via Santa Maria de' Calderari 38. Its food is great – try the carciofi alla giudia (deep-fried artichokes) – and prices are reasonable. A full meal should cost around L30,000. *Da Gigetto* (☎ 686 11 06), Via del Portico d'Ottavia 21a, is a local institution.

City Centre – mid-range The very popular *Mario* (☎ 678 38 18), Via della Vite 55, off Piazza di Spagna, offers Tuscan food for around L65,000 a full meal. Another good restaurant in the area is *Al 34* (☎ 679 50 91), Via Mario de' Fiori 34, which has a menu combining Roman cooking with regional dishes from throughout Italy. A full meal will cost around L55,000. The widely known *Dal Bolognese* (☎ 361 14 26), Piazza del Popolo 1, is in a prime position to attract tourists, but maintains high culinary standards and reasonable prices. You must book if you want a table outside in summer. A full meal will cost up to L70,000.

Near the Fontana di Trevi is *Al Moro* (☎ 678 34 95), Vicolo delle Bollette 13, which runs between Via dei Crociferi and Via delle Muratte. A good-quality, traditional Roman meal will come to less than L60,000. *Tullio* (☎ 475 85 64), Via San Nicola da Tolentino 26, which runs off Piazza Barberini, serves Roman and Tuscan dishes. It is of a high standard and a full meal will cost between L60,000 and L70,000. Also near Piazza Barberini is *Colline Emiliane* (☎ 481 75 38), Via degli Avignonesi 22, a spartan-looking trattoria which serves superb Emilia-Romagnan food. A full meal will cost around L55,000.

At Via degli Spagnoli 27, a few streets north of the Pantheon, is *Il Bacaro* (☎ 686 41 10), a tiny trattoria whose menu reflects what is available fresh on any given day. A meal will cost around L50,000. *La Campana* (☎ 686 78 20), Vicolo della Campana 18, at the top end of Via della Scrofa, is believed to be Roma's oldest restaurant and is certainly a favourite. A full meal will cost around L60,000. *Il Cardinale – GB* (☎ 686 93 36), Via delle Carceri 6, which runs off Via Giulia, is another well-known restaurant with superb food. A full meal should come to less than L80,000.

Vecchia Roma (☎ 686 46 04), Piazza Campitelli 18, has a well-deserved reputation for good food. Its outside tables are extremely popular in summer. A full meal will cost from L70,000. *Piperno* (☎ 654 27 72), Via Monte de' Cenci 9, which has a menu combining Roman and Jewish cooking and is considered one of Roma's better mid-range restaurants. A full meal will cost from L85,000.

City Centre – expensive *Andrea* (☎ 482 18 91), Via Sardegna 24-28, close to Via Vittorio Veneto, is one of Roma's most popular top restaurants. A full meal will be in the range of L100,000. *Il Convivio* (☎ 686 94 32), Via dell'Orso 44, a little north of Piazza Navona, is an elegant restaurant with a creative menu. A full meal will cost around L100,000. *El Toulà* (☎ 687 34 98), Via della Lupa 29, is one of Roma's most prestigious restaurants, which is reflected in the prices – more than L130,000 for a full meal.

West of the Tevere – inexpensive The main concentration of good-value restaurants is in Trastevere and the Testaccio district. Most establishments around San Pietro and il Vaticano are geared towards tourists and can be very expensive. *Osteria dell'Angelo* (☎ 38 92 18), Via G Bettolo 24, is in the Trionfale area – walk along Via Leone IV from il Vaticano. A hearty Roman meal can be had for around L30,000. *Pizzeria Giacomelli* (☎ 38 35 11), Via di Bruno Emilia Faà 25, is off Via della Giuliana past Largo Trionfale. The pizzas are good, big and cheap. *Il Tempio della Pizza* (☎ 321 69 63), Viale Giulio Cesare 91, is open late and has reasonably-priced, good-quality food.

In Trastevere's maze of tiny streets there are any number of pizzerie and cheap trattorie. The area is beautiful at night and most establishments have outside tables. It is also very popular, so arrive before 9 pm unless you want to queue for a table.

Mario's (☎ 580 38 09), Via del Moro 53, is a local favourite for its cheap pasta (around L8000 to L10,000) but you can find better quality elsewhere. *D'Augusto* (☎ 580 37 98), nearby in Piazza dei Renzi 15, is another great spot for a cheap meal. Try the homemade fettucine. If you arrive early there is also a good selection of vegetables. A meal with wine will cost L15,000 to L20,000. *Da Otello in Trastevere*, Via della Pelliccia 47-53, has excellent antipasto. A hearty meal should cost between L25,000 and L30,000.

Da Giovanni (☎ 686 15 14), Via della Lungara 41, is a good 10-minute walk from the centre of Trastevere. It is a popular eating place and you will probably have to wait for a table. The food is basic but the prices are good. *Da Gildo* (☎ 580 07 33), Via della Scala 31, is a pizzeria/trattoria with a range of pizzas and good-quality food. A full meal will cost around L25,000. Nearby, at Vicolo del Mattinato 2, is *Da Lucia* (☎ 580 36 01), which offers an excellent range of antipasto and pasta. In summer it has outside tables. A full meal will cost around L40,000. *Pizzeria Ivo* (☎ 581 70 82), Via San Francesco a Ripa 158, has outdoor tables, but the pizza could be bigger for the price (from L7500 to L10,000). The bruschetta is an excellent start to the meal. The house wine comes in bottles and is not a bargain at L8000. *Pizzeria Popi-Popi*, Via delle Fratte di Trastevere, just off Piazza San Cosimato, is very popular among young people, who flock to its outside table in summer. The pizzas are average but chea *Pizzeria da Vittorio*, Via San Cosimato 14 is tiny and you will have to wait if you arriv after 9 pm. A delicious bruschetta and pizz with wine will cost around L18,000. At Vial di Trastevere 53 is *Panattoni* (☎ 580 09 19 open late and always crowded, it is one c the more popular pizzerie in Trastevere. Yo can eat there for around L15,000.

You won't find a noisier, more popula pizzeria in Roma than *Pizzeria Remo* (☎ 57 62 70), Piazza Santa Maria Liberatrice 44, i Testaccio. A meal will cost around L16,000 *Augustarello* (☎ 574 65 85), Via G Branc 98, off the piazza, specialises in offal dishes A full meal should cost around L20,000 *Trattoria da Bucatino*, Via Luca dell Robbia 84, is a popular Testaccio eatin place, with pasta from L7000 to L10,000 an pizzas for around the same prices. It als serves Roman fare. A full meal will cos around L30,000.

West of the Tevere – mid-range to expensive *Paris* (☎ 581 53 78), Piazza San Calist 7, has developed a reputation for excellen cuisine. A meal will cost up to L70,000.

In Testaccio is *Checchino dal 188* (☎ 574 63 18), Via di Monte Testaccio 30 which serves superb Roman food – which means, of course, lots of offal. It was selectec in 1994 as one of the best restaurants in Italy by the international newspaper, the *Herald Tribune*. A full meal will cost around L75,000.

San Lorenzo to the Foro Romano – inexpensive As Roma's university district, eating places in San Lorenzo are influenced by the student population. One of the more popular places, *Pizzeria l'Economica*, Via Tiburtina 44, serves local fare and good pizzas at prices students can afford. *Formula 1* (☎ 445 38 66), Via degli Equi 13, is another good-value pizzeria, as is *Le Maschere* (☎ 445 38 05), Via degli Umbri 8; both are popular with students. One of the area's more famous trattorie is *Pommidoro* (☎ 445 26 92), Piazza dei Sanniti 44; an excellent meal will cost around L40,000. *Tram Tram*, Via dei Reti 44, has excellent food at moderate prices.

If you have no option but to eat near Stazione Termini, try to avoid the tourist traps offering overpriced full menus. There are many tavole calde in the area, particularly to the west of the train station, which offer panini and pre-prepared dishes for reasonable prices. There is a self-service in the station complex, *La Piazza*, where you can eat good food at reasonable prices. There are a few good-value restaurants in the area. *Da Gemma alla Lupa* (☎ 49 12 30), Via Marghera 39, is a simple trattoria with prices to match: a full meal will cost around L27,000. *Trattoria da Bruno*, Via Varese 29, has good food at reasonable prices. *Hosteria Angelo*, Via Principe Amedeo 104, is a traditional trattoria with very reasonable prices. *Galilei* (☎ 731 56 42), Via Galilei 12, between the train station and Basilica di San Giovanni in Laterano, is a good, cheap pizzeria. Towards the Colosseo, at Via delle Terme di Tito 96, is *Hostaria di Nerone* (☎ 474 52 07). Popular with tourists, it has good food and a full meal will cost under L25,000. Another decent pizzeria is *Alle Carrette* (☎ 679 27 70), Vicolo delle Carrette 14, off Via Cavour near the Foro Romano; a pizza and wine will come to around L15,000. *Trattoria dell'Angeletto* is an excellent restaurant in the piazza of the same name, just off Via Cavour. It has outside tables and, while the service can get a bit slow when they're busy, the food is good.

San Lorenzo to the Foro Romano – mid-range *Tana del Grillo* (☎ 731 64 41), Via Alfieri 4-8, off Via Merulana, a few streets north of Piazza San Giovanni in Laterano, offers Ferrara cuisine, as well as the usual Roman fare. A full meal will cost from L35,000 to L40,000. *Il Dito e La Luna* (☎ 494 07 26), Via dei Sabelli 47-51, in the San Lorenzo district, serves hearty, good-quality meals for around L45,000.

Foreign Restaurants These are not exactly abundant, but there are some very good restaurants in Roma which serve international cuisine. Chinese food is very popular, but the food is often heavily salted and can leave a lot to be desired.

Golden Crown (☎ 678 98 31), Via in Arcione 85, between Via del Tritone and the Palazzo del Quirinale, is a good choice; a solid meal will cost up to L40,000. For an excellent Japanese meal, head for *Sogo Asahi* (☎ 678 60 93), Via di Propaganda 22, near Piazza di Spagna. It is expensive, however, at around L70,000 a head. There's a sushi bar, for which you have to book. *Suria Mahal* (☎ 589 45 54), Piazza Trilussa, in Trastevere, is an Indian restaurant where a delicious meal will cost around L45,000.

Tex Mex food can be found at *Oliphant*, on the corner of Via della Scrofa and Via delle Coppelle. If all you really want is a Big Mac, you'll find McDonald's outlets in Piazza della Repubblica (with outside tables), Piazza di Spagna and Viale di Trastevere (between Piazza Sonnino and Piazza Mastai). At *Marconi*, Via Santa Prassede 1, just in front of Santa Maria Maggiore, you can munch on fish & chips, baked beans and other assorted stodgy English dishes.

Vegetarian Restaurants All trattorie serve a good selection of vegetable dishes, but there are other options for vegetarians in Roma. *Centro Macrobiotico*, Via della Vite 4, requires a L8000 membership fee and dishes start at L10,000. At *Margutta Vegetariano* (☎ 678 60 33), Via Margutta 19, which runs parallel to Via del Babuino, décor and prices are upmarket and a meal will cost no less than L40,000. *Il Canestro*, Via Luca della Robbia 47, Testaccio, is another good option. A full meal will cost around L35,000.

Cafés Remember that prices skyrocket in cafés as soon as you sit down, particularly in major tourist haunts such as near Piazza di Spagna or the Pantheon, where a cappuccino at a table can cost as much as L10,000. The same cappuccino taken at the bar will cost around L1600. The narrow streets and tiny piazzas in the area between Piazza Navona and the Tevere offer a number of popular cafés and bars.

Those seeking the best coffee in Roma should go to the *Tazza d'Oro*, just off Piazza della Rotonda in Via degli Orfani, and *Bar Sant'Eustachio*, Piazza Sant'Eustachio, near the Pantheon. Fashionable (and expensive) places to drink coffee or tea are the *Caffè Greco*, Via dei Condotti 86, near Piazza di Spagna, *Babington's Tea Rooms*, Piazza di Spagna 23 and *Caffè Rosati* in Piazza del Popolo.

At *Caffè del Marzio*, Piazza Santa Maria in Trastevere, you will pay L5000 for a cappuccino if you sit down outside, but it's worth it as this is one of Roma's most beautiful and atmospheric piazzas.

Sandwiches & Snacks *Paladini*, Via del Governo Vecchio 29, might look like a rundown alimentarie but it makes mouthwatering pizza bianca on the premises, filled with whatever you want, for around L5000. Try the prosciutto and fig – an unusual combination but delicious. In Via di Ripetta (which runs off Piazza del Popolo, parallel to Via del Corso) there are several bars and takeaways with good fare. *Caffè Sogo*, Via di Ripetta 242, has Japanese snacks, as well as coffee etc. Next door is a tiny Japanese grocery.

Paneformaggio, Via di Ripetta 7, and *M & M Volpetti*, Via della Scrofa 31, near Piazza Navona, are upmarket sandwich bars/rosticcerie where you can buy gourmet lunch snacks for above-average prices. Closer to Termini is *Il Golosone*, Via Venezia, off Via Nazionale, a sandwich bar and tavola calda where you can sit down without paying extra. Another option is *Dagnino*, Galleria Esedra, off Via VE Orlando.

Among the more famous sandwich outlets in Roma is *Frontoni* in Viale di Trastevere, on the corner of Via San Francesco a Ripa, opposite Piazza Mastai. It makes its panini with both pizza bianca and bread and you can choose from an enormous range of fillings. Sandwiches are sold by weight and a generously filled one will cost around L6000. It also has excellent pizza by the slice. It is worth making a special trip to Testaccio, to eat lunch at *Volpetti Più*, Via A Volta 8. It is a tavola calda, so you don't pay extra to sit down. The pizza by the slice is extraordinarily good and there are plenty of pasta, vegetable and meat dishes.

Takeaway pizza by the slice is very popular in Roma and there are numerous outlets all over the city. Usually you can judge the quality of the pizza simply by taking a look. Some good places are *Pizza Rustica* in Campo de' Fiori, *Pizza a Taglio*, Via Baullari, between Campo de'Fiori and Via V Emanuele II, and *Pizza a Taglio* in Via delle Muratte, just off Piazza di Trevi. Near Piazza di Spagna, at Via della Croce 18, is *Fior Fiore*.

Gelati *Gelateria Giolitti*, Via degli Uffici del Vicario 40, has long been a Roman institution. It was once the meeting place of the local art crowd and writers. Today it remains famous for its fantastic gelati. *Gelateria della Palma*, around the corner at Via della Maddalena 20, has a huge selection of flavours and some say the gelati is better than at Giolitti; a cone with three flavours costs around L2500. Both establishments also have cakes and pastries. *La Fonte della Salute*, Via Cardinal Marmaggi 2-6 in Trastevere, has arguably the best gelati in Roma. An atmospheric spot for a good gelati is *Il Ristoro della Salute* in the Piazza del Colosseo. Buy a cone or a frullato (fruit drink) and wander across the road to the Colosseo.

Bread & Pastries *Bernasconi*, Largo di Torre Argentina 1, is a reasonably good pasticceria. *Bella Napoli*, a bar/pasticceria that specialises in Neapolitan pastries, is at Via Vittorio Emanuele 246. *Valzani*, Via del Moro 37 in Trastevere, is one of Roma's best pasticcerie, as is *Antonini*, Via Sabotino 21-29, near Piazza Mazzini in Prati. *La Dolceroma*, Via del Portico d'Ottavia 20 (between the Teatro di Marcello and Via Arenula), specialises in Austrian cakes and pastries. In the same street at No 2 is the kosher bakery *Il Forno del Ghetto*, a very ɪpular outlet for cakes and pastries. You ill need to look for the street number as ere is no sign. Near Stazione Termini is *ınella l'Arte del Pane*, Largo Leopardi 2-) (on Via Merulana), with a big variety of ıstries and breads.

rocery Shops Hundreds of small outlets the centre of Roma sell cheese, salami, ead and groceries. There is also a growing ımber of supermarkets in Roma's suburbs. ne of the easiest to get to from the centre is ıe *Standa* in Viale Trastevere. The follow-ıg are some of Roma's better known astronomic establishments.

Billo Bottarga, Via di Sant'Ambrogio 20, ear Piazza Mattei, specialises in kosher ood and is famous for its bottarga (roe of ına or mullet). *Castroni*, Via Cola di Rienzo 96, in Prati near il Vaticano, has a wide election of gourmet foods, packaged and esh, including international foods (desper-te Aussies will find Vegemite here). It also as an outlet at Via delle Quattro Fontane 38, ff Via Nazionale. *Gino Placidi*, Via della Maddalena 48, near the Pantheon, is one of entral Roma's best alimentari. *Ruggeri*, Campo de' Fiori 1, has a good range of heese and meats, and *Strega Cavour*, Via Marianna Dionigi 19, near Piazza Cavour in l Vaticano area, combines a bar and well-tocked alimentare. *Volpetti*, Via Marmorata 47, in Testaccio, has high-quality cheese and neats.

Health Foods Buying muesli, soy milk and he like can be expensive in Italy. The fol-owing outlets have a good range of roducts, including organic fruit and vegeta-bles at relatively reasonable prices.

L'Albero del Pane, Via Santa Maria del Pianto 19, in the Jewish quarter, has a wide range of health foods, both packaged and fresh. It has an outlet for organic fruit and vegetables at Via dei Baullari 112, just off Campo de' Fiori. *Emporium Naturae*, Viale Angelico 2 (take Metro Linea A to Ottaviano), is a well-stocked health-food supermarket. *Il Canestro*, Via Luca della Robbia 47, in Testaccio near the market, also has a large selection of health food, as well as fresh fruit and vegetables and takeaway food.

Entertainment

Roma's primary entertainment guide is *Trovaroma*, a weekly supplement in the Thursday edition of the newspaper *La Repubblica*. Considered the bible for what is happening in the city, it provides a com-prehensive listing, but in Italian only. The newspaper also publishes a daily listing of cinema, theatre and concerts. *Roma C'è* is a good guide to weekly events. It is published in English and is available at newsstands. *Metropolitan* and *Wanted in Rome* are fort-nightly magazines in English which review what is happening within Roma's English-speaking community and have entertainment listings, as well as details on bars, pubs etc. Both are available at various outlets, includ-ing the Economy Book & Video Center. See the Information section for Roma for addresses. They are also available at various newspaper stands in the city centre, includ-ing at Largo Argentina and Piazza Santa Maria in Trastevere.

Cinemas Films are screened daily in English at *Il Pasquino* (☎ 580 36 22), Vicolo del Piede 19, in Trastevere, just off Piazza Santa Maria in Trastevere. On Monday nights you can see films in their original language at *Alcazar* (☎ 588 00 99), Via Merry del Val, off Viale Trastevere. The *Nuovo Sacher* (☎ 581 81 16) at Largo Ascianghi, between the Porta Portese area and Trastevere, shows films in their original language on Monday and Tuesday. The *Augustus*, Corso Vittorio Emanuele 203, has a regular programme of films in English, usually screened on Tuesday evenings. Drop in at the cinema and ask for details.

A popular form of entertainment in the hot Roman summer is outdoor cinema. In July at the Castel Sant'Angelo, on the Tevere, two huge screens are erected to show films in Italian. Screens are also set up at other loca-tions, including on the Celio, but films are usually shown only in Italian. Check *Trovaroma* for details.

Discos Roman discos are expensive. Expect to pay up to L40,000 to get in, which may or may not include one drink. Hot spots include *Alien*, Via Velletri 13; *Piper '90*, Via Tagliamento 9; and *Gilda*, Via Mario de'Fiori 97.

Nightclubs *Discobar*, Via degli Avignonesi (near Piazza Barberini); *The Groove*, Vicolo Savelli 10 (near Piazza Navona); and *Circolo degli Artisti*, Via Lamarmora 28 (near Piazza Vittorio Emanuele II) are all in the centre and very popular among young foreigners and Italians. Testaccio is alive with nightclubs, most on Via di Monte Testaccio. One of the more interesting and popular places is *Radio Londra*, and others include *Akab*, *Caruso Caffè* and Caffè Latino. In the same area is *Villaggio Globale*, Lungotevere Testaccio (accessible from Largo G B Marzi at the Ponte Testaccio), an alternative hangout for people who really know the meaning of 'angst'. This is one of several *centri sociali* in Roma, a type of squatters' club frequented by ageing hippies, new-age types and people who are still into punk and 'grunge' etc. Common throughout Italy, these places are often associated with extreme left-wing political activity, although in Roma they are principally places of entertainment.

Opera The opera season at the *Teatro dell'Opera*, Piazza Beniamino Gigli, starts in November. In summer, opera is performed outdoors in Piazza Siena, in the Villa Borghese park.

Theatre English language theatre is performed periodically at the International Theatre – Teatro Agora (☎ 687 41 67), Via della Penitenza 33, in Trastevere. Other theatres occasionally perform plays in English. Check *Wanted in Rome*, *Trovaroma* etc for details.

Classical Music Concerts are held at the *Auditorio di Santa Cecilia*, Via della Conciliazione 4, during the winter months and in the gardens at *Villa Giulia* in summer. The are also seasons at the *Accademia Filarmonica*, Via Flaminia 18, and the *Teat Olimpico*, Piazza G da Fabriano 17. Fro June to September, there are concerts in th ruins of the *Teatro di Marcello*, Via di Teat Marcello 44, near Piazza Venezia, eve evening at 9 pm. For information call ☎ 4 48 00. In December and January free co certs of sacred music are held in some Roma's churches. The programme is gene ally excellent and not to be missed. Check Roma C'è for details.

Rock Rock concerts are held throughout th year and are advertised on posters plastere around the city. Concerts by major perform ers are usually held at the *Palazzo dello Spo* or *Stadio Flaminia*, both a good distan from the city centre. For information an bookings, contact the ORBIS agency (☎ 48 74 03) in Piazza Esquilino near Stazior Termini.

Jazz For jazz and blues, try *Alexanderplat* Via Ostia 9 (open nightly) or, in summer, th *Villa Celimontana* park; *Folkstudio*, Vi Frangipane 42; *Big Mama*, Via Sa Francesco a Ripa 18, in Trastevere; or th *Four XXXX Club*, Via Galvani 29, Testacci

Pubs & Bars Pubs are the new big thing i Roma. They offer a big selection of beers an many have Guinness on tap. A favourit haunt of young foreigners, they're als popular with the locals. In the centre, try *Th Drunken Ship*, Campo de' Fiori 20 or *Trinit College*, Via del Collegio Romano 6. Nea Termini, there's *Cirrosy's*, Via Lamarmor 29; *Marconi*, Via Santa Prassede 9 (here yo can get fish & chips, baked beans etc); th *Druid's Den*, Via San Martino ai Monti 28 or the *Fiddler's Elbow*, Via dell'Olmata 43.

There are also plenty of places to enjoy glass of wine. The *Vineria* in Campo de Fiori, also known as *Giorgio's*, has a wide selection of wine and beers and was once the gathering place of the Roman literati. Today it is less glamorous but is still a good place to drink (although cheap only if you stand a ıe bar). *Caffè Gardenia*, Via del Governo 'ecchio 98, has snacks for around L6000, nd live jazz. *Enoteca Piccolo*, at No 75 in ıe same street, is a pleasant wine bar with nacks available. Off Via del Governo 'ecchio, in Via della Pace, is the *Bar della 'ace*, a popular place for the young 'in' rowd, but you pay high prices to drink there. *'ul de Sac*, Piazza Pasquino 73, just off 'iazza Navona at the start of Via del Governo 'ecchio, is a popular wine bar which also erves excellent food.

The *Bevitoria Navona*, Piazza Navona 72, harges reasonable prices (around L2500 for glass of average wine and up to L10,000 or better quality wine – although expect to ay higher prices to sit outside). *Trimani*, Via 'ernaia 37, near Stazione Termini, is another ood wine bar and serves good-quality food.

In Trastevere there is the *Bar San Calisto* n the piazza of the same name, with tables utside. This bar is seedy, but cheap, and you an sit down without paying extra. A much nore comfortable place to drink is the *San Michele aveva un Gallo* in Via San Francesco a Ripa, across Viale Trastevere near the corner of Piazza San Francesco d'Assisi. You can also eat light meals here.

Gay & Lesbian Venues Roma's top gay disco is *L'Alibi*, Via di Monte Testaccio 44. Women are allowed in only if accompanied by a man. Another choice for gays is the bar/disco *L'Angelo Azzurro*, Via Cardinal Merry del Val 13, in Trastevere (Friday evenings are for women only).

Spectator Sport

Football matches are played at the Stadio Olimpico at Foro Italico, north of the city centre. You'll find information in one of the local daily newspapers, such as *La Repubblica* or *Il Messaggero*.

Things to Buy

Don't feel bad if you find that Roma's shop windows are competing with its monuments for your attention. Just make sure you allocate plenty of time (as well as funds) for shopping. Roma's main shopping districts include: the Piazza di Spagna area for the main clothing, shoes and leathergoods designers (Via Condotti, Via Frattina, Via delle Vite, Via Borgognona, Via del Corso etc); Via Nazionale and surrounds for a good mix of affordable clothing; the Via Veneto area for the top names; Via dei Coronari for antiques; Via del Governo Vecchio for second-hand and alternative clothing. If you can time your visit to coincide with the sales, you'll pick up some marvellous bargains. The winter sales run from early January to around mid-February and the summer sales from August through September. Shops usually open from around 9.30 am to 1 pm and then 3.30 pm to around 8 pm. There is a trend towards continuous opening hours from 9.30 am to 7.30 pm, but usually only the larger shops or department stores have these hours.

Clothing, Shoes & Leathergoods The big designer names for clothing include: Armani, Via Condotti 77; MaxMara, Via Condotti 17, Via Frattina 28 and Via Nazionale 28; Fendi, Via Borgognona 36; Mila Schön, Via Condotti 64; Cenci, Via Campo Marzio 1-7.

For shoes and leathergoods, there's: Gucci, Via Condotti 8; Ferragamo, Via Condotti 73; Pollini, Via Frattina 22; Bruno Magli, Via Veneto 70; Beltrami, Via Condotti 18; Fratelli Rossetti, Via Borgonogna 5; Raphael Salato, Via Veneto 149, and Mandarina Duck, Via di Propaganda 1, just off Piazza di Spagna. More affordable shops include: Benetton, Sisley and Stefanel, which are on just about every street corner, and Max & Co, Via Condotti 46. For cut price designer wear, head for Discount Systems, Via del Viminale 35.

Antiques, Design & Furniture Wander along Via dei Coronari and Via dei Banchi Nuovi if you're interested in antiques. Antique prints can be found at Alinari, Via Aliberti 16, and Nardecchia, Piazza Navona 25. Designer furniture can be found on Via del Babuino. If you're looking for Italian design homewares, try Limentani, Via Portico d'Ottavia 47.

Kids For children's clothes, shop at La Cicogna, Via Frattina 139 or PrèNatal, Via Nazionale 45. For toys, head for Città del Sole, Via della Scrofa 65, or Piazza della Chiesa Nuova 18.

Markets Everyone flocks to Porta Portese market every Sunday morning. A mish mash of new and old, the market has all manner of incredible deals – but you have to drive a hard bargain. The market extends for a few km along the side streets parallel to Viale Trastevere. Be extremely careful of pick-pockets and bag snatchers. The excellent market in Via Sannio, near Porta San Giovanni, sells new and second-hand clothes. It is open Monday to Saturday until around 1 pm. For prints, antiques and books, head for the market at Piazza Fontanella Borghese, held every morning except Sunday.

Getting There & Away

Air The main airport is Leonardo da Vinci (☎ 6 01 21), also known as Fiumicino, after the town nearby. The other airport is Ciampino, where many national and some international, including charter, flights arrive. See the Getting Around section in this chapter for details on getting to/from the airports, and the Getting There & Away chapter for information on flights to/from Roma.

All the airlines have counters in the departure hall at Fiumicino, but their main offices are located in the area around Via Veneto and Via Barberini, north of Stazione Termini. They include:

Alitalia
  Via Bissolati 20 (☎ 65 62 82 22)
Air France
  Via Sardegna 40 (☎ 48 79 11)
Air New Zealand
  Via Bissolati 54 (☎ 488 07 61)
British Airways
  Via Bissolati 54 (☎ 52 49 15 12)
Cathay Pacific
  Via Barberini 3 (☎ 487 01 50)
Qantas
  Via Bissolati 35 (☎ 48 64 51)
Singapore Airlines
  Via Barberini 11 (☎ 481 89 43)
TWA
  Via Barberini 67 (☎ 4 72 11)
United Airlines
  Via Bissolati 54 (☎ 48 90 41 40)

Bus The main station for Intercity buses is in Piazzale Tiburtina, in front of Stazione Tiburtina. Catch the Metropolitana Linea B from Termini to Tiburtina. Buses run by various companies go to cities throughout Italy. COTRAL buses, which service the Lazio region, depart from numerous points throughout the city, depending on their destinations. The company is linked with Roma's public transport system, which means that the same ticket is valid for city and regional buses, trams, the Metro, and train lines. For more detailed information about which companies go to which destinations, go to Stazione Tiburtina, or the Eurojet agency in Piazza della Repubblica 54 (where you can buy tickets for some bus lines). Enjoy Rome or the EPT office can also help (see Tourist Offices in this chapter).

Some useful bus lines include:

COTRAL
  Via Ostiense 131 (☎ 591 55 51)
  Services throughout Lazio. Buses for Palestrina and Tivoli depart from Rebibbia Metro station on Linea B; buses for Bolsena, Saturnia, Toscana and Viterbo depart from Saxa Rubra, on the Ferrovia Roma Nord train line; buses for the Castelli Romani depart from Anagnina, the last stop on the Metro Linea A; buses for the beaches south of Roma depart from the EUR-Fermi station on the Metro Linea B; for Bracciano, Cerveteri and Tarqunia take a bus from the Lepanto stop on Metro Linea A. Also see under individual destinations in the Around Roma section
ARPA, SIRA, Di Fonzo, Di Febo & Capuani
  Services to Abruzzo, including L'Aquila, Pescasseroli and Pescara
  Information at Piazzale Tiburtina
Bonelli
  Services to Emilia-Romagna, including Ravenna and Rimini
  Information at Piazzale Tiburtina

zzi
Services to other European cities and the Alps
Via Tagliamento 27r (☎ 884 08 40)

rosi
Services to Calabria
Information at Eurojet (☎ 474 28 01)

arozzi
Services to Bari and Brindisi, (via towns including Alberobello and Matera) Sorrento, the Amalfi coast and Pompeii
Information at Eurojet (☎ 474 28 01)

AIS & Segesta
Services to Sicilia
Information at Piazza della Repubblica or Piazzale Tiburtina (☎ 481 96 76)

na
Services to Siena
Information at Eurojet (☎ 474 28 01)

JLGA
Services to Perugia and Assisi, as well as to Fiumicino airport
Information at Eurojet (☎ 474 28 01 or ☎ 075-500 96 41)

ain Almost all trains arrive at and depart om Stazione Termini. There are regular nnections to all the major cities in Italy and urope. Examples of one-way costs for tercity trains (rapido supplement included) om Roma are as follows: Firenze L36,000; Iilano L67,000); Venezia L61,000; and apoli L27,000. For train information, ring 1478-880 88 from 9 am to 5 pm (in Italian nly) or go to the information office at the ain station (English is spoken). Timetables an be bought at most newspaper stands in nd around Termini and are particularly seful if you are travelling mostly by train. ervices at Stazione Termini include ggage storage beside tracks 1 and 22 L1500 per item per day), telephones and oney exchange facilities. See the Roma nformation section for further details. ickets for city buses and the Metro can be urchased at tobacconists inside the train ation. There are eight other train stations cattered throughout Roma. Some northound trains depart from or stop at Stazione Ostiense and Stazione Trastevere. Remember to validate your train ticket in the yellow achines on the station platforms. If you on't, you may be forced to pay a fine on the ain.

Car & Motorcycle The main road connecting Roma to the north and south of Italy is the Autostrada del Sole, which extends from Milano to Reggio di Calabria. On the outskirts of the city it connects with the Grande Raccordo Anulare, the ring road encircling Roma. From here, there are several exits into the city.

If you are approaching from the north, take the Via Salaria, Via Nomentana or Via Flaminia exits. From the south, Via Appia Nuova, Via Cristoforo Colombo and Via del Mare (which connects Roma to the Lido di Ostia) all provide reasonably direct routes into the city. The Grande Raccordo Anulare and all arterial roads in Roma are clogged with traffic on weekday evenings from about 5 to 7.30 pm, and on Sunday evenings, particularly in summer, all approaches to Roma are subject to traffic jams as Romans return home after weekends away.

The A12 connects the city to Civitavecchia and then along the coast to Genova (it also connects the city to Fiumicino airport). Signs from the centre of Roma to the autostrada can be vague and confusing, so invest in a good road map. It is best to stick to the arterial roads to reach the Grande Raccordo Anulare and then exit at the appropriate point.

The main roads out of Roma basically follow the same routes as the ancient Roman consular roads. The seven most important are:

Via Aurelia (SS1), which starts at il Vaticano and leaves the city to the north-east, following the Tyrrhenian coast to Pisa, Genova and France;
Via Cassia (SS2), which starts at the Ponte Milvio and heads north-west to Viterbo, Siena and Firenze;
Via Flaminia (SS3), which also starts at the Ponte Milvio, and goes north-west to Terni, Foligno and over the Appennini into Le Marche, ending on the Adriatic coast at Fano;
Via Salaria (SS4), which heads north from near Porta Pia in central Roma to Rieti and into Le Marche, and ends at Porto d'Ascoli on the Adriatic coast;
Via Tiburtina (SS5), which links Roma with Tivoli and Pescara, on the coast of Abruzzo;
Via Casilina (SS6), which heads south-east to Anagni and into Campania, terminating at Capua near Napoli;

Via Appia Nuova (SS7), the most famous of the consular roads, which heads south along the coast of Lazio into Campania, and then goes inland across the Appennini into Basilicata, through Potenza and Matera to Taranto in Puglia and on to Brindisi.

Hitching It is illegal to hitchhike on the autostrada, so it is necessary to wait on main roads near autostrada entrances. To head north on the A1, take bus No 319 from Stazione Termini, get off at Piazza Vescovio and then take bus No 135 to Via Salaria. To go south to Napoli on the A2, take the Metropolitana to Anagnina and wait in Via Tuscolana. There is an International Lift Centre in Firenze (☎ 055-28 06 26) which matches people up. Hitching is not recommended, particularly for women, either alone or in groups.

Getting Around

To/From the Airports From Fiumicino airport, access to the city is via the airport-Stazione Termini direct train (follow the signs to the train station from the airport arrivals hall), which costs L13,000. The train arrives at and leaves from track No 22 at Termini. Tickets can be bought from vending machines at Fiumicino and Termini, or from the Alitalia office at track 22, or at the airport. The first direct train leaves the airport for Termini at 7.38 am, then runs hourly (half-hourly at certain times of the day) from 8.08 am until 10.08 pm. From Termini to the airport, trains start at 6.52 am and run hourly and half-hourly until 9.22 pm. Another train stops at Trastevere, Ostiense and Tiburtina stations (L7000). From Fiumicino, trains run from 6.28 am to 12.13 am and from Ostiense from 5.22 am until 11.22 am. The train does not stop at Termini. From midnight to 5 am a bus runs from Stazione Tiburtina (accessible by bus No 42N from Piazza dei Cinquecento in front of Termini) to the airport. The airport is connected to the city by an autostrada. Follow the signs for Roma out of the complex and exit from the autostrada at EUR. From there, you'll need to ask directions to reach Via Cristoforo Colomb which will take you directly into the centr

If you arrive at Ciampino airport, blu COTRAL buses (running between 5.45 a and 10.30 pm) will take you to the Anagni Metropolitana stop, from where you ca catch the subway to Stazione Termini. If yo arrive late or very early, you have litt option other than to catch a taxi.

Ciampino airport is connected to Roma b the Via Appia Nuova.

Bus The city bus company is ATAC an most of the main buses terminate in Piazz dei Cinquecento at Stazione Termini. At th information booth in the centre of the piazz you can obtain a map which outlines the bu routes. The Lozzi map of Roma provides good enough guide to these bus routes. Se also the Roma Information section in th chapter.

Another central point for the main bu routes is Largo di Torre Argentina, nea Piazza Navona. Buses generally run fro about 6 am to midnight, with limited service throughout the night on some routes Regular travellers to Roma should note tha some bus routes have been changed in th past few years.

Travel on Roma's buses, subway and sub urban railways is now part of the sam system and the same tickets are valid for a three modes of transport. This means indi vidual tickets are now considerably mor expensive, but if you manage to get th intended mileage out of them, the savings a high. Singles tickets cost L1500 for 7 minutes.

Tickets must be purchased *before* you ge on the bus or train and then validated in th machine as you enter. The fine for travellin

> **Warning**
> Pickpockets are active on crowded buses, particularly those popular with tourists. The No 64, for example, is notorious and the No 27 is also a popular route for thieves.

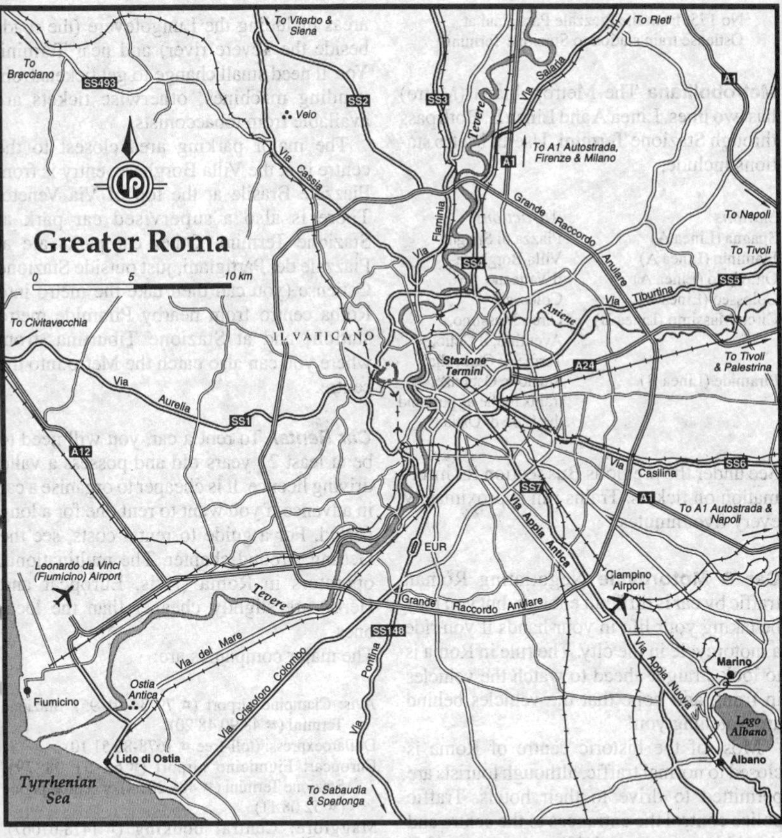

without a validated ticket is L50,000 and inspectors are growing tired of the same old explanations from tourists that they 'didn't know'. Tickets can be obtained in Piazza dei Cinquecento, at tobacconists, at newspaper stands and from vending machines at main bus stops. Daily tickets cost L6000, weekly tickets L24,000 and monthly tickets L50,000. These tickets are valid for city and regional buses, trams, the metro and train lines.

Useful buses include:

No 64, from Stazione Termini to the Basilica di San Pietro
No 27, from Stazione Termini to the Colosseo, Circo Massimo and the Aventino
No 44, from Piazza Venezia to Trastevere
No 218, from Piazza San Giovanni in Laterano to the Via Appia Antica
No 3 or 910, from Stazione Termini to the Villa Borghese
No 36, from Stazione Termini along Via Nomentana (for foreign embassies)

On weekdays there are special buses which run from the main car parks into the city centre. They include:

No 116, from the Villa Borghese to Piazza della Repubblica

No 175, from the Piazzale Partigiani at Ostiense train station to Stazione Termini

Metropolitana The Metropolitana (Metro) has two lines, Linea A and Linea B. Both pass through Stazione Termini. Useful Metro stations include:

Stations	*Attractions*
Spagna (Linea A)	Piazza di Spagna
Flaminio (Linea A)	Villa Borghese
Ottaviano (Linea A)	il Vaticano
Colosseo (Linea B)	Colosseo
Circo Massimo (Linea B)	Circo Massimo, Aventino, il Celio, Terme di Caracalla
Piramide (Linea B)	Stazione Ostiense, trains to the airport and the Lido di Ostia

See under the previous Bus section for information on tickets. Trains run approximately every five minutes.

Car & Motorcycle Negotiating Roman traffic by car is difficult enough, but you may be taking your life in your hands if you ride a motorcycle in the city. The rule in Roma is to look straight ahead to watch the vehicles in front, and hope that the vehicles behind are watching you!

Most of the historic centre of Roma is closed to normal traffic, although tourists are permitted to drive to their hotels. Traffic police control the entrances to the centre and should let you through if you have a car full of luggage and mention the name of your hotel. The hotel management should provide a pass which allows you to park in the centre. Traffic police are getting very tough on illegally parked cars. At best you'll get a heavy fine (around L200,000), at worst a wheel brace or your car towed away. In the event that your car goes missing after it was parked illegally, always check first with the traffic police (☎ 6 76 91). You will have to pay about L180,000 to get it back, plus a hefty fine.

A new parking system has been introduced around the periphery of Roma's city centre. Spaces are denoted by a blue line in areas including the Lungotevere (the road beside the Tevere river) and near Termini. You'll need small change to get tickets from vending machines, otherwise tickets are available from tobacconists.

The major parking area closest to the centre is at the Villa Borghese; entry is from Piazzale Brasile at the top of Via Veneto. There is also a supervised car park at Stazione Termini. Other car parks are at Piazzale dei Partigiani, just outside Stazione Ostiense (you can then take the metro into Roma centro from nearby Piramide metro station] and at Stazione Tiburtina, from where you can also catch the Metro into the centre.

Car Rental To rent a car, you will need to be at least 21 years old and possess a valid driving licence. It is cheaper to organise a car in advance if you want to rent one for a long period. For a guide to rental costs, see the Getting Around chapter. The multinational operators in Roma (Avis, Europcar and Hertz) are slightly cheaper than the local ones.

The major companies are:

Avis: Ciampino airport (☎ 79 34 01 95), Stazione Termini (☎ 48 90 48 20)
Dollaroexpress: (toll-free ☎ 1678-86 51 10)
Europcar: Fiumicino airport (☎ 65 01 08 79), Stazione Termini (☎ 488 28 54) or central phone (☎ 52 08 11)
Maggiore: Central booking (☎ 1478-67067), Fiumicino airport (☎ 65 01 06 78), Stazione Termini (☎ 488 00 49)

Motorcycle & Bicycle Rental Motorcycles (as well as scooters or mopeds) and bicycles can be rented at Happy Rent (☎ 481 81 85), Piazza Esquilino 8. It rents motorcycles up to 850cc, as well as cars and minivans (baby seats are available for both cars and bicycles). Another option is I Bike Roma (☎ 322 52 40), Via Veneto 156. A 50 cc motorcycle costs around L60,000 per day or L300,000 per week; a bicycle costs L15,000 per day. Bicycles are also usually available for rent in Piazza Sonnino, in Trastevere, in Piazza del Popolo and at the Villa Borghese. For more information on rental costs, see the Getting Around chapter.

Taxi Taxis are on radio call 24 hours a day in Roma. Cooperativa Radio Taxi Romana (☎ 3570) and La Capitale (☎ 4994) are two of the many operators. Major taxi ranks are at the airports and Stazione Termini and also at Largo Argentina in the historical centre. There are surcharges for luggage, night service, public holidays and travel to and from Fiumicino airport. The taxi flagfall is L6400 (for the first 3km), then L1200 per km. There is a L3000 supplement from 10 pm to 7 am and L1000 from 7 am to 10 pm on Sunday and public holidays. There is a L15,000 supplement on travel to and from Fiumicino airport because it is outside the city limits. This means the fare will cost around L70,000. If you telephone for a taxi, the driver will turn on the meter immediately and you will pay the cost of travel from wherever the driver was when the call was received.

Lazio

Roma demands so much of your time and concentration that most tourists forget the city is part of the Lazio region. Declared a region in 1934, the Lazio area (known as Latium in English) has, since ancient Roman times, been an extension of Roma. Through the ages, the rich built their villas in the Lazio countryside and many towns developed as the fiefs of noble Roman families, such as the Orsini, Barberini and Farnese. Even today, Romans build their weekend and holiday homes in the picturesque areas of the region (the pope, for instance, has his summer residence at Castelgandolfo, south of Roma) and Romans continue to migrate from their chaotic and polluted city to live in the Lazio countryside. This means the region is relatively well-served by public transport, and tourists can take advantage of this to visit places of interest.

While the region does not abound in major tourist destinations, it does offer some worthwhile day trips from the city. A tour of Etruria, the ancient land of the Etruscans, which extended into northern Lazio, is highly recommended. Visits to the tombs and museums at Cerveteri and Tarquinia provide a fascinating insight into Etruscan civilisation. The ruins of Villa Adriana (Hadrian's villa), near Tivoli, and of the ancient Roman port at Ostia Antica, are both easily accessible from Roma, as is the medieval town of Viterbo, north of the capital. In summer, tired and overheated tourists can head for the lakes north of Roma, including Bracciano, Bolsena and Vico, which are somewhat preferable to the polluted beaches near the city, or head south of Roma to the relatively clean, sandy beaches of Sabaudia or Sperlonga.

There are some hill-top towns south of Roma which are worth visiting, such as Anagni (and the remarkable frescoes in its Romanesque cathedral), Alatri and those of the Castelli Romani in the hills just past Roma's outskirts. People interested in Italy's involvement in WWII might want to visit Monte Cassino, the scene of a major battle during the dying stages of the war.

If you have your own transport, try to avoid day trips out of Roma on Sunday during summer. On your return in the evening you are likely to find yourself in traffic jams extending for many km, even on the autostrada.

OSTIA ANTICA

The Romans founded this port city at the mouth of the Tevere river in the 4th century BC and it became a strategically important centre of defence and trade. It was populated by merchants, sailors and slaves, and the ruins of the city provide a fascinating contrast to the ruins at Pompeii, which was populated by wealthy Romans. After barbarian invasions and the outbreak of malaria it was abandoned, but Pope Gregory IV re-established the city in the 9th century AD.

Information about the town and ruins is available at the EPT office in Roma.

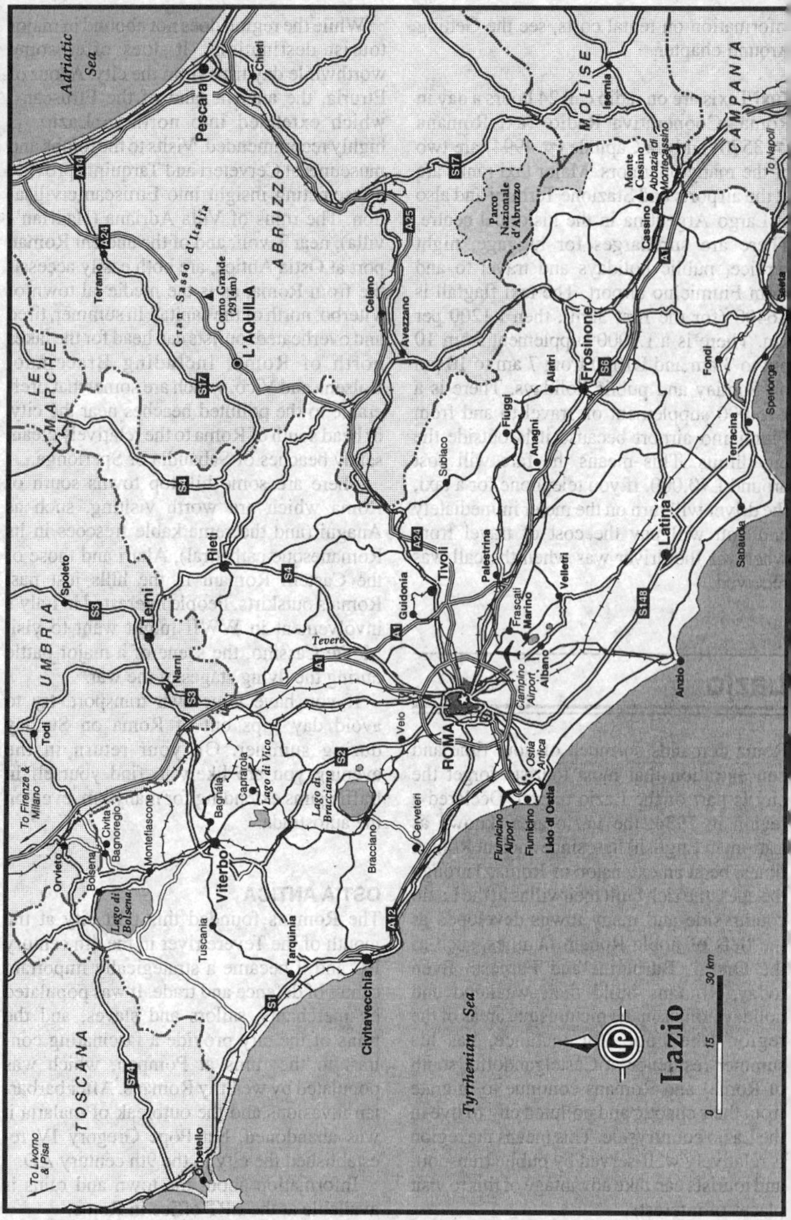
Lazio
0 15 30 km
Tyrrhenian Sea
Adriatic Sea
TOSCANA
UMBRIA
LE MARCHE
ABRUZZO
MOLISE
CAMPANIA
ROMA
To Livorno & Pisa
To Firenze & Milano
To Napoli
Orbetello
Civitavecchia
Tarquinia
Tuscania
Viterbo
Lago di Bolsena
Bolsena
Orvieto
Civita Bagnoregio
Montefiascone
Bagnaia
Caprarola
Lago di Vico
Lago di Bracciano
Bracciano
Cerveteri
Veio
Todi
Narni
Terni
Spoleto
Rieti
Tevere
Guidonia
Tivoli
Palestrina
Subiaco
Frascati
Marino
Albano
Velletri
Ciampino Airport
Fiumicino Airport
Fiumicino
Lido di Ostia
Ostia Antica
Anzio
Latina
Sabaudia
Terracina
Sperlonga
Fondi
Gaeta
Anagni
Fiuggi
Alatri
Frosinone
Cassino
Monte Cassino
Abbazia di Montecassino
Parco Nazionale d'Abruzzo
Isernia
Avezzano
Celano
L'AQUILA
Gran Sasso d'Italia
Corno Grande (2914m)
Teramo
Pescara
Chieti
A1
A12
A14
A24
A25
S1
S2
S3
S4
S6
S17
S74
S148

Things to See & Do

The ruins are quite spread out and you will need a few hours to wander through them. Admission to the city is through the **Porta Romana**, which leads you onto Ostia Antica's main thoroughfare, the **Decumanus Maximus**. The Porta Marina, at the other end of the road, once opened onto the seafront. Of particular note in the excavated city are the **Terme di Nettuno** (Neptune's Baths), to your right just after entering the city. Take a look at the black-and-white mosaic depicting Neptune and Amphitrite. Next is a **Roman theatre** built by Agrippa, which could hold 2700 people. It was restored in 1927 and is now used for staging classical performances and concerts. Behind the theatre is **Piazzale delle Corporazioni**, where Ostia's merchant guilds had their offices, each distinguished by mosaics depicting their wares.

Returning to the Decumanus Maximus, you reach the **forum**, the **Tempio di Roma e Augusto**, with its statue of Roma Vincitrice (Victorious Rome), and the **Tempio Rotondo**. Follow the Vico del Pino and Via del Tempio Rotondo to the Cardo Maximus to reach the **Domus Fortuna Annonaria**, the heavily decorated home of one of Ostia's wealthier citizens. Opposite, in the area next to the **Grandi Horrea** (warehouses), are private houses, including the well-preserved **Casa di Diana**.

Continue along the Via dei Dipinti to reach Ostia Antica's **museum**, which houses statues, mosaics and wall paintings found at the site. The ruins are open daily from 9 am to one hour before sunset year-round. Admission is L8000.

Getting There & Away

To get to Ostia Antica, take the Metro Linea B to Piramide, then the Ostia Lido train from Ostiense. Trains leave every half-hour and the trip takes about 20 minutes. Buy a ticket which covers both the Metro and the Ostia train. The ruins are also easy to reach by car from Roma. Take the Via del Mare, a fast superstrada which runs parallel to the Via Ostiense.

TIVOLI

Set on a hill by the Aniene river, Tivoli was a resort town of the ancient Romans and became popular as a summer playground for the rich during the Renaissance. While the majority of tourists are attracted by the terraced gardens and fountains of the Villa d'Este, the ruins of the spectacular Villa Adriana, built by the Roman emperor Hadrian, are far more interesting.

The AAST office (☎ 0774-31 12 49) is in Largo Garibaldi, near the COTRAL bus stop. It is open in summer from 8 am to 6 pm and in winter to 3 pm.

Things to See & Do

The **Villa Adriana** was built in the 2nd century AD as the summer residence of the Emperor Hadrian and was influenced by the classical architecture of the day. It was successively plundered by barbarians and Romans for building materials, and many of its original decorations were used to embellish the Villa d'Este. However, enough remains to give an idea of its former splendour. You will need about four hours to wander through the vast ruins, and you'll be exhausted before you've seen even half the place. Take a break for a picnic, or lunch at the bar in the visitors' centre, before resuming your tour.

Highlights include the **Villa dell'Isola** (Villa of the Island), where Hadrian is supposed to have spent his more pensive moments; the **Palazzo Imperiale** and its **Piazza d'Oro** (Golden Square); and the floor mosaics of the **Hospitalia**. Although very little remains of Hadrian's **Piccole e Grandi Terme** (Small and Large Baths), it is easy to work out their layout and imagine their former grandeur. Take a look at the model of the villa in the small visitors' centre to get an idea of the extent of the complex. The villa is open in the warmer months from 9 am to 7 pm (last admission at 6 pm) and in winter to around 4 pm. Admission is L8000.

The Renaissance **Villa d'Este** was built in the 16th century for Cardinal Ippolito d'Este, grandson of the Borgia pope, Alexander VI, on the site of a Franciscan monastery. The villa's beautiful gardens are decorated with numerous fountains, which are its main attraction. You will wander through the cardinal's villa on the way to the gardens. Rather than paying too much attention to the fairly drab rooms, take a look out of the windows for a bird's-eye view of the gardens and fountains. Opening hours are the same as for the Villa Adriana. Admission is L8000.

Getting There & Away
Tivoli is about 40km east of Roma and accessible by COTRAL bus, which leaves from Via Tiburtina. Take Metro Linea B from Stazione Termini to Rebibbia; the bus leaves from outside the station every 15 minutes. The bus also stops at the Villa Adriana, about 1km from Tivoli. Otherwise, from Tivoli's Piazza Garibaldi catch local bus No 4 to Villa Adriana. The fastest route by car is on the Roma-L'Aquila autostrada (A24).

ETRUSCAN SITES

Lazio has several important Etruscan archaeological sites, most within easy reach of Roma by car or public transport. These include Tarquinia (one of the major Etruscan League city-states), Cerveteri, Veio and Tuscania. The tombs and religious monuments discovered throughout the area yielded the treasures which can now be seen in museums including the Villa Giulia and il Vaticano. The smaller museums at Tarquinia and Cerveteri are also well worth a visit.

The sheer number of tombs in the area has long supported the illegitimate industry of the *tombaroli* (tomb robbers), who have been plundering the sites for centuries and selling their 'discoveries' on the black market. It is said that, since many tombs are still to be excavated, a good number of tombaroli remain active. Prospective buyers of illicit Etruscan artefacts should, however, beware: another notorious activity of the tombaroli is the manufacture of fake treasures.

If you have the time, a few days spent touring at least Tarquinia and Cerveteri, combined with visits to their museums and the Villa Giulia should constitute one of your most fascinating experiences in Italy. A useful guidebook to the area, *The Etruscans* is published by the Istituto Geografico de Agostini and has a map. If you really want to lose yourself in a poetic journey, take along a copy of DH Lawrence's *Etruscan Places* (published by Penguin in the compilation *DH Lawrence and Italy)*.

Tarquinia

Believed to have been founded in the 12th century BC, and home of the Tarquin kings who ruled Roma before the creation of the republic, Tarquinia was an important economic and political centre of the Etruscan League. The town has a small medieval centre, with a good Etruscan museum, but the major attractions here are the painted tombs of its burial grounds.

Orientation & Information By car or bus you will arrive at the Barriera San Giusto, just outside the main entrance to the town. See Getting There & Away in this section. The AAST office (☎ 0766-85 63 84) is on your left as you walk through the medieval ramparts, at Piazza Cavour 1. It's open Monday to Saturday from 8 am to 2 pm. It is possible to see Tarquinia on a day trip from Roma, but if you want to stay overnight in the medieval town, it is advisable to make a booking.

Tarquinia's telephone code is ☎ 0766.

Things to See The 15th-century Palazzo Vitelleschi, located in Piazza Cavour, houses the **Museo Nazionale Tarquiniese** and a significant collection of Etruscan treasures, including frescoes removed from the tombs. There is a beautiful terracotta frieze of winged horses, taken from the temple, **Ara della Regina**. Numerous sarcophagi found in the tombs are also on display. At any one time, sections of the museum are likely to be closed to the public. The museum is open Tuesday to Sunday from 9 am to 7 pm. Admission is L8000.

The famous painted tombs are at the **necropolis**, also open from 9 am to 7 pm and entrance is L8000 (ask for directions from

Etruscan sculpture from the 6th century BC

the museum, a 15 to 20-minute walk away). Almost 6000 tombs have been excavated, of which about 60 are painted, and only a handful are open to the public. Excavation of the tombs started in the 15th century and still continues today. Unfortunately, exposure to air and human interference has led to serious deterioration in many tombs and they are now enclosed and maintained at constant temperatures. The painted tombs can be seen only through glass partitions.

DH Lawrence, who studied the tombs before measures were taken to protect them, wrote extensive descriptions of the frescoes he saw, and it is well worth reading his *Etruscan Places* before seeing the tombs of Tarquinia. Entering the famous Tomb of the Leopards, Lawrence noted how, despite the extensive destruction of the tombs through vandalism and neglect, the colours of the wall paintings were still fresh and alive.

If you have a car, ask for directions to the remains of the Etruscan acropolis, on the crest of the Civita hill nearby. There is little evidence of the ancient city, apart from a few limestone blocks which once formed part of the city walls, since the Etruscans generally used wood to build their temples and houses. However, a large temple, the **Ara della Regina**, was discovered on the hill and has been excavated this century.

If you have time, wander through the pleasant medieval town of Tarquinia. There are several churches worth a look, including the late 13th-century Chiesa di San Francesco, in Via Porta Tarquinia, and the beautiful Romanesque Chiesa di Santa Maria di Castello, in the citadel at the north-west edge of town.

Places to Stay & Eat There is a camping ground by the sea at Tarquinia Lido, *Tusca Tirrenia* (☎ 8 82 94), Viale Neriedi.

There are no budget options in the old town if you want to stay overnight, and it can be difficult to find a room if you don't book well in advance. The *Hotel San Marco* is the only hotel in the medieval section of town. It has newly renovated singles/doubles for L65,000/100,000. The *Hotel all'Olivo* (☎ 85 73 18), Via Togliatti 15 in the newer part of town is a 10-minute walk downhill from the medieval centre. Singles/doubles are L60,000/85,000. Closer to the centre, but more expensive, is *Hotel Tarconte* (☎ 85 65 85), Via Tuscia 23, with doubles costing more than L100,000, including breakfast. At Tarquinia Lido is *Hotel Miramare* (☎ 8 80 20), Viale dei Tirreni 36, with singles/doubles for L55,000/75,000.

There are few places to eat in Tarquinia, but for a good, cheap meal, go to *Trattoria Arcadia*, Via Mazzini 6. *Cucina Casareccia* is opposite at No 5.

Getting There & Away Buses leave approximately every hour for Tarquinia from Via Lepanto in Roma, near the Metro Linea A Lepanto stop, arriving at Tarquinia at the Barriera San Giusto, a few steps away from the tourist office. You can also catch a train from Roma, but Tarquinia's train station is at Tarquinia Lido, approximately 3km from the centre. You will then need to catch one of the regular local buses to the Barriera San Giusto. Buses leave from the Barriera for Tuscania, near Tarquinia, every few hours. If you are travelling by car, take the autostrada for Civitavecchia and then the Via Aurelia

(SS1). Tarquinia is about 90km north-west of Roma.

Cerveteri

Ancient Caere was founded by the Etruscans in the 8th century BC and enjoyed a period of great prosperity as a commercial centre from the 7th to 5th century BC. The main attractions here are the tombs known as *tumoli*, great mounds of earth with carved stone bases. Treasures taken from the tombs can be seen in the Musei del Vaticano, the Museo di Villa Giulia and the Louvre. The Pro Loco tourist office is at Via delle Mura Castellane.

The main necropolis area, **Banditaccia**, is open daily, except Monday, from 9 am to one hour before sunset. Admission is L8000. It's accessible by local bus in summer only from the main piazza in Cerveteri, otherwise it is a pleasant 3km walk west from the town. You can wander freely once inside the area, although it is best to follow the recommended routes to see the best preserved tombs. One of the more interesting is the Tomba dei Rilievi, which is decorated with painted reliefs of household items. The tomb has been closed to avoid further damage to its paintings but can be viewed through a glass window. Follow the signs o the Tomba dei Capitali and the Tomba dei Vasi Greci. Signs detailing the history of the main tombs are in Italian only.

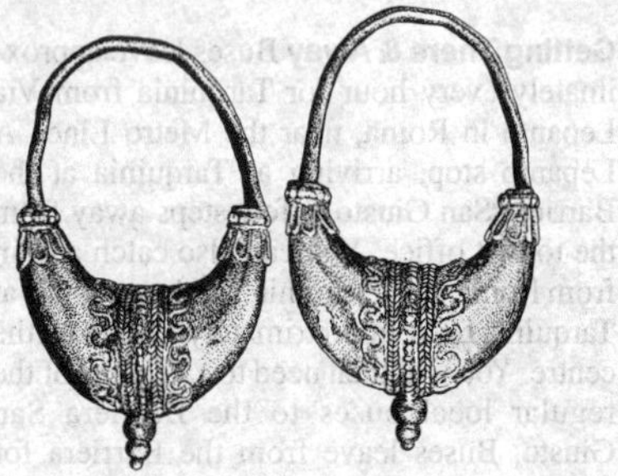

Etruscan ear-rings from the Cerveteri tombs

There is also a small **museum** in Cerveteri which contains an interesting display of pottery and sarcophagi. It is in the Palazzo Ruspoli and is open daily, except Monday from 9 am to 2 pm. Admission is free.

Cerveteri is only about 40 minutes north-west of Roma and accessible by COTRAL bus from Via Lepanto, outside the Lepanto stop on Metro Linea A. Otherwise, catch the Roma-Pisa train, which stops at Cerveteri. By car take either Via Aurelia or the Civitavecchia autostrada (A24).

Veio

Your visit to Etruria should include Veio which is just north of Roma. This was the largest of the Etruscan League cities. Its proximity to Roma meant there was a traditional rivalry between the two cities and after a siege lasting 10 years, it finally fell under Roma's dominion in 396 BC and was destroyed. It became a municipium under Augustus, but eventually declined in importance and was abandoned.

Little evidence remains of the city. The only things to see are the remains of a swimming pool and the lower section of a temple. However, important finds were made during excavations of the site in the 18th century, including the famous statue of Apollo, now in the Museo di Villa Giulia in Roma.

By car, leave Roma on the Via Cassia and exit at Isola Farnese. Signs will point you towards Veio. Otherwise, take bus No 201 (for Olgiata) from Piazza Mancini, near the Ponte Milvio, to Isola Farnese and ask the bus driver to let you off at the road to Veio (although there is probably not enough to see at Veio to warrant the trouble of taking public transport).

CIVITAVECCHIA

There is little to recommend this busy port and industrial centre to tourists, other than the ferries which leave daily for Sardegna. Established by Emperor Trajan in 106 AD as the port town of Centumcellae, it was later conquered by the Saracens, but regained importance as a papal stronghold in the 16th century. The medieval town was almost

›mpletely destroyed by bombing during /WII. In 1995, the town hit the headlines hen a 43cm-high statue of the Madonna, ›cated in the private garden of a local ımily, started crying tears of blood. Origi-ılly brought from Medgugori (part of the ›rmer Yugoslavia) the statue is now in the ›cal Chiesa di Sant'Agostino. Tests ›vealed the tears were in fact human blood ıd the statue continues to attract crowds of ilgrims – although il Vaticano is yet to rule n the authenticity of the 'miracle'.

›rientation & Information

he port, and therefore the departure point ›r ferries, is a quick walk from the train :ation. As you leave the station, turn right ıto Viale Garibaldi and follow it along the ›afront. The APT office (☎ 0766-2 53 48) , at Viale Garibaldi 42 and is open Monday › Friday from 8 am to 1 pm and 4 to 7 pm nd Saturday from 9 am to 1 pm. From June › September there is also an information ›ooth at the port, open seven days a week.

The town's telephone code is ☎ 0766.

laces to Stay & Eat

here should be no need to spend the night ı Civitavecchia. It is easily accessible from .oma and, to save time and money, it is ›etter to catch a night ferry to Sardegna. If ›ou get stuck, try *Hotel Traghetto* (☎ 2 59 0), Via Braccianese, just near the port. ingles/doubles are L77,000/99,000, break-ıst included.

For a meal, head for one of the pizzerias long the waterfront, or try *Trattoria da 'itale* at Viale Garibaldi 26. It is not overly xpensive to eat on the ferry (full restaurant ıeals, as well as snacks, are available), but is a good idea to bring supplies on board if ›ou want to save money. There is a grocery ıop near the station at Civitavecchia and a ıarket every morning from Monday to Sat-ırday in Via Doria.

›etting There & Away

ivitavecchia is on the main train line ›etween Roma (1½ hours) and Genova ²½ hours). By car it is easily reached from Roma on the A12. If arriving from Sardegna with your car, simply follow the A12 signs from the Civitavecchia port to reach the auto-strada for Roma.

Ferries to/from Sardegna Tirrenia operates ferries to Olbia (seven hours), Arbatax (nine hours) and Cagliari (12 hours). Departure times and prices change annually and it is best to check with a travel agent, or with Tirrenia directly, for up-to-date information. At the time of writing, a one-way fare to Olbia was L42,000 for a seat (poltrona), L58,000 for a bed in a 2nd-class cabin, L78,000 for a bed in a 1st-class cabin and L120,000 for a small car. The company also operates fast boats (in summer only) which take only 3½ hours from Civitavecchia to Olbia. Tickets are considerably more expen-sive: L102,000 per person and L140,000 for a small car. Tickets can be purchased at travel agents, including CIT, or at the Tirrenia office in Roma (☎ 06-474 20 41), Via Bissolati 41, and at the stazione marittima in Civitavecchia.

The Ferrovie dello Stato (FS) also runs several ferries a day to Sardegna, docking at Golfo Aranci (about 20km north of Olbia and accessible by bus or train). Tickets can be purchased at travel agents, at Stazione Termini in Roma, or the stazione marittima in Civitavecchia.

VITERBO

Founded by the Etruscans and eventually taken over by Roma, Viterbo developed into an important medieval centre and in the 13th century became the residence of the popes.

Papal elections were held in the town's Gothic Palazzo Papale and stories abound about the antics of impatient townspeople anxious for a decision. In 1271, when the college of cardinals had failed to elect a new pope after three years of deliberation, the Viterbesi first locked them in a turreted hall of the palazzo, removed its roof and put the cardinals on a starvation diet. Only then did the cardinals manage to elect Gregory X.

Although badly damaged by bombing

during WWII, Viterbo remains Lazio's best preserved medieval town and is a pleasant base for exploring northern Lazio. For travellers with less time, Viterbo is an easy day trip from Roma.

Apart from its historical appeal, Viterbo is famous for its therapeutic hot springs. The best known is the sulphurous Bulicame pool, mentioned by Dante in his *Divine Comedy*.

Orientation & Information

As with most historic centres in Italy, the town of Viterbo is neatly divided between newer and older sections. Hotels are in the newer part of town, and you must cross the Piazza del Plebiscito, with its 15th and 16th-century palaces, before reaching medieval Viterbo and the real reason for your visit. There are train stations north and south-east of the town centre; both are just outside the town walls. The station for intercity buses is located somewhat inconveniently at Riello, a few km out of town.

The EPT office (☎ 0761-30 47 95) is at Piazza San Carluccio in the medieval quarter and is open Monday to Saturday from 9 am to 1 pm and 1.30 to 3.30 pm. Hours are extended in summer.

The main post office is in Via F Ascenzi, just off Piazza del Plebiscito. The Telecom office is at Via Cavour 28, off the other side of the piazza.

Viterbo's postcode is 01100 and its telephone code is 0761.

Things to See & Do

Piazza del Plebiscito The piazza is enclosed by 15th and 16th-century palaces, the most imposing of which is the **Palazzo dei Priori**, with an elegant 17th-century fountain in its courtyard. Many rooms are decorated with frescoes, notably the Sala Reggia, which is decorated with a late-Renaissance fresco depicting the myths and history of Viterbo.

Cattedrale di San Lorenzo & the Palazzo Papale The 12th-century cathedral in Piazza San Lorenzo was rebuilt in the 14th century to a Gothic design, although the interior has just been restored to its original Romanesqu[e] simplicity. Also in the piazza is the Palazz[o] Papale, built in the 13th century with the ai[m] of enticing the popes away from Roma. I[ts] beautiful and graceful loggia is in the earl[y] Gothic style. The part facing the valley col[-] lapsed in the 14th century and you can se[e] the bases of some of the columns. The ha[ll] in which papal conclaves were held is at th[e] top of the steps. If it is not open, ask at th[e] curia.

Piazza Santa Maria Nuova From th[e] Palazzo Papale, head back to the Piazza del[la] Morte and take Via Cardinale la Fontaine t[o] this piazza. The Romanesque church of th[e] same name was restored to its original for[m] after sustaining bomb damage in WWII. Th[e] cloisters, which are believed to date from a[n] earlier period, are worth a visit.

The Medieval Quarter Via San Pellegrin[o] takes you through the medieval quarter int[o] **Piazza San Pellegrino**. The extremely well[-] preserved buildings which enclose this tin[y] piazza are considered the finest group o[f] medieval buildings in Italy.

Other Sights Built in the early 13th century, [t]he **Fontana Grande**, in Piazza Fontan[a] Grande, is the oldest and largest of Viterbo'[s] Gothic fountains.

Back at the entrance to the town is th[e] **Chiesa di San Francesco**, in the piazza o[f] the same name, a Gothic building which wa[s] restored after suffering serious bom[b] damage during WWII. The church contain[s] the tombs of two popes: Clement IV (wh[o] died in 1268) and Adrian V (who died i[n] 1276). Both tombs are lavishly decorated[,] notably that of Adrian, which feature[s] Cosmati work, a mosaic technique used i[n] the 12th and 13th centuries.

The **Museo Civico** has reopened after [a] 10-year restoration project. It is housed in th[e] convent of the Chiesa di Santa Maria dell[a] Verità, just outside the Porta della Verità o[n] the north-east side of town. Among th[e] works in the museum are the lovely *Pietà* b[y] Sebastiano del Piombo along with a Roma[n]

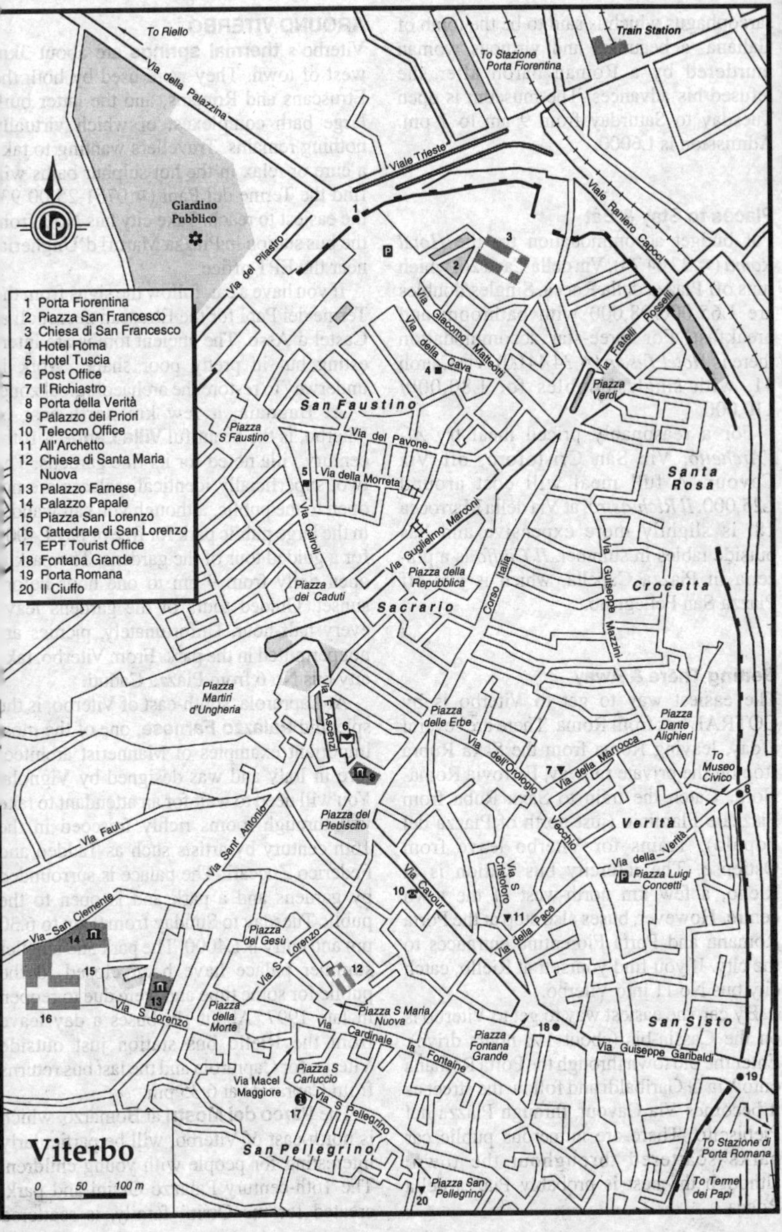
Viterbo
1 Porta Fiorentina
2 Piazza San Francesco
3 Chiesa di San Francesco
4 Hotel Roma
5 Hotel Tuscia
6 Post Office
7 Il Richiastro
8 Porta della Verità
9 Palazzo dei Priori
10 Telecom Office
11 All'Archetto
12 Chiesa di Santa Maria Nuova
13 Palazzo Farnese
14 Palazzo Papale
15 Piazza San Lorenzo
16 Cattedrale di San Lorenzo
17 EPT Tourist Office
18 Fontana Grande
19 Porta Romana
20 Il Ciuffo
To Riello
Via della Palazzina
To Stazione Porta Fiorentina
Train Station
Viale Trieste
Giardino Pubblico
Via del Pilastro
Viale Raniero Capoci
Via Fratelli Rosselli
Via Giacomo Matteotti
Via della Cava
Piazza Verdi
San Faustino
Piazza S Faustino
Via del Pavone
Via della Morreta
Via Cairoli
Via Guglielmo Marconi
Santa Rosa
Piazza della Repubblica
Corso Italia
Via Guiseppe Mazzini
Crocetta
Piazza dei Caduti
Sacrario
Piazza Martiri d'Ungheria
Via Ascenzi
Piazza delle Erbe
Via dell'Orologio
Via della Marrocca
Piazza Dante Alighieri
To Museo Civico
Piazza del Plebiscito
Via Faul
Via Sant' Antonio
Vecchio
Verità
Via della Verità
Piazza Luigi Concetti
Via S Cristoforo
Via Cavour
Via della Pace
Via San Clemente
Piazza del Gesù
Via S Lorenzo
Piazza della Morte
Piazza S Maria Nuova
Via Cardinale la Fontaine
Piazza Fontana Grande
San Sisto
Via Guiseppe Garibaldi
Piazza S Carluccio
Via Macel Maggiore
Via S Pellegrino
San Pellegrino
Piazza San Pellegrino
To Stazione di Porta Romana
To Terme dei Papi
0 50 100 m

sarcophagus which is said to be the tomb of Galiana, a beautiful and virtuous woman murdered by a Roman baron after she refused his advances. The museum is open Tuesday to Saturday from 9 am to 7 pm. Admission is L6000.

Places to Stay & Eat

For budget accommodation try the *Hotel Roma* (☎ 22 64 74), Via della Cava 26, which runs off Piazza della Rocca. Singles/doubles are L65,000/98,000 with bathroom and breakfast. For three-star accommodation there is *Hotel Tuscia* (☎ 34 44 00), Via Cairoli 41, with singles/doubles for L80,000/110,000.

For a reasonably priced meal try *All'Archetto*, Via San Cristoforo, off Via Cavour. A full meal will cost around L25,000. *Il Richiastro*, at Via della Marrocca 18, is slightly more expensive and has outside tables in summer. *Il Ciuffo* is a pizzeria in Piazza Capella, which is just off Piazza San Pellegrino.

Getting There & Away

The easiest way to get to Viterbo is by COTRAL bus from Roma. There are several a day, leaving Roma from the Saxa Rubra stop on the private railway, Ferrovia Roma-Nord. Catch the train to Saxa Ruba from Piazzale Flaminio (just north of Piazza del Popolo). Trains for Viterbo leave from Ostiense. The intercity bus station is at Riello, a few km north-west of the town centre. However, buses also stop at the Porta Romana and Porta Fiorentina entrances to the city. If you find yourself at Riello, catch city bus No 11 into Viterbo.

By car, the easiest way to get to Viterbo is on the Cassia-bis (about 1½ hours drive). Enter the old town through the Porta Romana onto Via G Garibaldi and follow the street as it becomes Via Cavour, through Piazza del Plebiscito. There are numerous public car parks scattered throughout the town, although the best is probably Piazza della Rocca.

AROUND VITERBO

Viterbo's **thermal springs** are about 3km west of town. They were used by both the Etruscans and Romans, and the latter built large bath complexes, of which virtually nothing remains. Travellers wanting to take a cure or relax in the hot sulphur baths will find the Terme dei Papi (☎ 0761-25 00 93) the easiest to reach. Take city bus No 2 from the bus station in Piazza Martiri d'Ungheria near the EPT office.

If you have a car, follow the signs from the Terme dei Papi for the Etruscan necropoli at Castel d'Asso. The ancient tombs are interesting but in pretty poor shape. Work is underway to restore the archaeological zone.

At Bagnaia, a few km north-east of Viterbo, is the beautiful **Villa Lante**, a 16th century villa noted for its fine gardens. The two, superficially identical, palaces are not open to the public, although you can wander in the large public park for free or pay L4000 for a guided tour of the gardens. The park is open daily from 9 am to one hour before sunset. Guided tours of the gardens leave every half-hour. Unfortunately, picnics are not permitted in the park. From Viterbo, take city bus No 6 from Piazza Caduti.

At Caprarola, south-east of Viterbo, is the splendid **Palazzo Farnese**, one of the most important examples of Mannerist architecture in Italy and was designed by Vignola. You will need to wait for an attendant to take you through rooms richly frescoed in the 16th century by artists such as Taddeo and Federico Zuccari. The palace is surrounded by gardens and a park and is open to the public Tuesday to Sunday from 9 am to 6.30 pm and entry is L4000. The park and smaller summer palace have been closed to the public for some time and were due to reopen in late 1997. About six buses a day leave from the Riello bus station just outside Viterbo for Caprarola and the last bus returns from Caprarola at 6.35 pm.

The **Parco dei Mostri** at Bomarzo, which is north-east of Viterbo, will be particularly interesting for people with young children. The 16th-century Palazzo Orsini and park, created for the Orsini family, is scattered with gigantic and grotesque sculptures including an ogre, a giant and a dragon. Also of interest are the octagonal *tempietto* (little temple) and the crooked house, built without use of right angles. The park is open from dawn to sunset and admission is L12,000. To get there from Viterbo, catch the COTRAL bus from the stop near Viale Trento to Bomarzo, then follow the signs to Palazzo Orsini.

Another interesting detour from Viterbo is the tiny, hill-top medieval town of **Civita di Bagnoregio**, near its newer Renaissance counterpart, Bagnoregio, (north of Viterbo). In a picturesque area of tufa ravines, Civita is known as the 'dying town' because continuous erosion of its hill has caused the collapse of many buildings. Abandoned by its original residents, who moved to Bagnoregio, most of the buildings in the town were purchased by foreigners and artisans and, in recent years, Civita has been restored and developed into a minor tourist attraction.

Regular COTRAL buses connect Bagnoregio with Viterbo. From the bus stop, ask for directions to Civita, which has been recently connected to Bagnoregio's outskirts by a pedestrian bridge.

THE LAKES

There are three large lakes north of Roma, all of which are extremely popular recreational spots in summer for hot Romans. The shores of the lakes never seem to get as crowded as Lazio's beaches and their hilly, leafy environment makes them more attractive swimming destinations.

Bracciano

Close to Roma, this lake is easily accessible by train or bus. Visit the **Castello Orsini-Odelscalchi** in the medieval town, or head for the lake for a swim. For picnic supplies there is an alimentare in Piazza Roma, or you can dine at the excellent little trattoria *del Castello* (☎ 99 80 43 39), in the piazza by the castle.

COTRAL buses, which depart roughly every half-hour from outside the Lepanto Metro stop, arrive in Piazza Roma in the centre of the town of Bracciano. You can also catch a train from the San Pietro station, next to Il Vaticano, off Via Aurelia.

Lago di Vico

This lake, close to Viterbo, is a nature reserve with various recreational facilities, including canoeing. There is a camping ground, *Natura* (☎ 0761-61 23 47), at the lakeside about 3km from the town of Caprarola. It is open from June to December and bookings are essential in summer. The town is accessible by train from Roma's Trastevere station. Catch the Viterbo train and change at Capranica-Sutri. Otherwise catch a COTRAL bus from Viterbo to Caprarola.

Bolsena

Too far from Roma to warrant a day trip, Bolsena is, however, close to Viterbo. The town was the scene of a miracle in 1263, when a doubting priest was convinced of transubstantiation when blood dripped from the host he was holding during a mass. Pope Urban IV founded the festival of Corpus Domini to commemorate the event. There's a tourist office (☎ 0761-79 99 23), Piazza Matteotti 9. The town also has a web site: www.pelagus.it/bolsena/bolsena.html (in English and Italian). Bolsena is a very popular destination in summer.

There are numerous hotels and camping grounds by the lake, including *Villaggio Camping Lido* (☎ 79 92 58) and *Hotel Eden* (☎ 79 90 15).

Bolsena has an interesting medieval section, with a 12th-century castle which now houses a museum. Of particular interest are the 11th-century **Chiesa di Santa Cristina** and the **catacombs** beneath it. Just before the entrance to the catacombs is the **altare del miracolo**, where the miracle of Bolsena occurred. The catacombs are of particular interest because they contain tombs which are still sealed.

If you're touring the area by car, it is worth heading on to **Montefiascone**, noted for its white wine, Est, Est, Est. Visit the **duomo** and the nearby Romanesque church of

Sant'Andrea. On the road to Orvieto is the Romanesque church of **San Flaviano**.

From Viterbo, catch one of the regular COTRAL buses to Bolsena.

SOUTH OF ROMA

The Castelli Romani

Just past the periphery of the city are the Colli Albani (Alban Hills) and the 13 towns of the Castelli Romani. A summer resort area for wealthy Romans since the days of the Empire, its towns were mainly founded by popes and patrician families. Castel Gandolfo and Frascati are perhaps the best known; the former is the summer residence of the pope and the latter is famous for its crisp white wine. The other towns are Monte Porzio Catone, Montecompatri, Rocca Priora, Colonna, Rocca di Papa, Grottaferrata, Marino, Albano Laziale, Ariccia, Genzano and Nemi.

The area has numerous villas, including the 16th-century **Villa Aldobrandini** at Frascati, which was designed by Giacomo della Porta and built by Carlo Maderno, and has a beautiful garden. The ancient site of **Tusculum**, near Frascati, is preceded by a stretch of ancient Roman road. There is little to see here but you can take in the excellent view. At Grottaferrata is a 15th-century **Abbazia** and museum.

Nemi is worth a visit to see the pretty **Lago di Nemi**, in a volcanic crater. In ancient times there was an important sanctuary beside the lake, where the goddess Diana was worshipped. Today, very little remains of this massive temple complex, but it is possible to see the niche walls of what was once an arcade portico. New excavations at the site have recently started. The incongruous-looking building at the edge of the lake, near the ruins of the temple, has an interesting story attached to it. It was built by Mussolini to house two ancient Roman boats (one 73m long, the other 71m), which were recovered from the bottom of the lake when it was partly drained in 1927-32. The official story is that retreating German troops burned the ships on June 1, 1944. Locals tell a different story, but you'll have to go there to find out!

There is a delightful trattoria in the town of Nemi, the *Trattoria la Sirena del Lago* (☎ 06-936 80 20), located literally on the edge of a cliff and overlooking the lake. Signs will direct you there from the centre of town. A simple, but excellent meal will cost less than L30,000.

It is really best to tour this area by car: you could see most of the more interesting sights on an easy day trip from Roma. However most of the towns of the Castelli Romani, including Nemi, are accessible by COTRAL bus from the Anagnina station on Metro Linea A. Trains also leave from the Lazio platform at Stazione Termini for Frascati, Castelgandolfo and Albano Laziale, from where you could catch a bus to Nemi.

Palestrina

A town has existed on this site since as early as the 7th century BC, making it one of the oldest in the region. Known in ancient times as Praeneste, it is certainly worth visiting especially to see the massive **Santuario della Fortuna Primigenia**. Built by the ancient Romans on a series of terraces which cascade down the hill, the sanctuary was topped by a temple on the summit. The **Palazzo Colonna Barberini** now stands at this point and houses the **Museo Archeologico Nazionale Prenestino**. Extensive work is being carried out on the museum, and it will eventually house an important collection of Roman artefacts. Of particular interest is the spectacular **Barberini mosaic**, dating from the second century BC. It depicts the Nile in flood and it is fascinating to study the numerous individual scenes. Also, the view from the sanctuary is really excellent and this on its own should warrant a visit to this town.

Palestrina is accessible from Roma by COTRAL bus from the Rebibbia station on Metro Linea B.

Anagni & Alatri

These medieval towns are in an area about 40 minutes south of Roma, known as the Ciociaria. **Anagni**, birthplace of a number of medieval popes, is of particular interest for

GREG ELMS

TONY WHEELER

ROB FLYNN

Roma
Top Left: Fontana dei Fiumi, Piazza Navona
Top Right: Spanish Steps
Bottom: View of Piazza San Pietro from the Basilica di San Pietro

DAMIEN SIMONIS

Manorola Village, Cinque Terre, Liguria

its lovely Lombard-Romanesque cathedral, built in the 11th century. Its pavement was laid by Cosmati marble workers of the Middle Ages. In the crypt is an extraordinary series of vibrant frescoes, painted by three Benedictine monks in diverse periods during the 13th century. Depicting a wide range of subjects, the frescoes are considered a major example of medieval painting at the crucial stage of its transition from the Byzantine tradition to the developments which culminated in the achievements of Giotto. The frescoes were recently unveiled after a four-year restoration project and certainly warrant a day trip from Roma. The crypt's pavement was also laid by the Cosmati. Visits to the crypt can be made with a guide only, but you should not need to wait any longer than 10 minutes.

Alatri has a couple of interesting churches, including the 13th-century Chiesa di Santa Maria Maggiore in its main piazza. Its ancient **acropolis** is surrounded by massive 6th-century BC walls, built by the town's original inhabitants, the Ernici.

Anagni is easily accessible from Roma's Stazione Termini on the Cassino-Caserta-Napoli train line. For Alatri, catch the train to Frosinone and then a bus to Alatri.

Along the Coast

Beaches close to Roma include Fregene, the Lido di Ostia and the long stretch of sand dune-lined beach between Ostia and Anzio. However, they really are not terribly inviting and the water tends to be heavily polluted. You'll need to go further south to Sabaudia and Sperlonga to find cleaner, more attractive spots for a swim. Sabaudia has the added attraction of sand dunes and the **Parco Nazionale del Circeo**, a wetlands nature reserve along the coast. It is accessible by COTRAL bus from outside the EUR-Fermi stop on Roma's Metropolitana Linea B.

Sperlonga This small, increasingly touristy, medieval hilltop town has a pretty beach. The main attraction in the area is the **Grotta di Tiberio**, a cave with a circular pool used by the Roman emperor. The remains of his villa are in front of the cave. Statues found in the cave are housed in the nearby museum

The Battle of Monte Cassino

'If you let me use the whole of our bomber force against Cassino we will whip it out like a dead tooth.' The US Major General was speaking of a key WWII German stronghold between Napoli and Roma. This 'stronghold' was the ancient **Abbazia di Montecassino**, a Benedictine monastery founded by St Benedict in 529. Destroyed and rebuilt three times – in 581, 883 and 1349 – each time on a grander scale, the abbey posed a formidable physical and psychological obstacle for the allied forces. For six long months in late 1943 and early 1944 the Germans used this position to prevent the Allies' Fifth Army from reaching Roma, with huge loss of life on both sides. Crowning the 518m-high Monte Cassino, the abbey, built of stone, with walls 3m thick and about 50m high, still housed members of the Benedictine order, as well as many refugees and a priceless collection of illustrated manuscripts and Latin literature. The Germans eventually ensured that most of these treasures were moved to safety at il Vaticano. As the deadly stand-off continued into 1944, the plan to destroy the abbey was developed. Although there was strong opposition to the plan, on grounds that the abbey was a precious part of Italy's cultural and religious heritage, the decision was made to bomb Monte Cassino in February 1944. About 300 monks and refugees died in the first attack, having been unable to evacuate the monastery despite Allied warnings. The bombing, however, failed to destroy the massive structure and, just over one month later another 1000 tons of explosive were dropped on the abbey and the Cassino area. The abbey was destroyed, but the Germans held their position and what had been described as the 'greatest concentration of air power in the world' had failed. It was not until 18 May, two months later, that Polish troops took the monastery and raised their flag there. Many of the 4000 Polish soldiers who died in the battle to take Monte Cassino are buried in a cemetery nearby. The monastery was rebuilt in medieval style and parts of it are open to the public.

Cassino is accessible from Roma on the Cassino-Caserta-Napoli train line. ■

and include a large group in the style of the *Lacoön* (in the Musei del Vaticano).

If you want to stay, try the *Albergo Major* (☎ 0771-54 92 44), Via Romita. It charges L90,000 a double with bathroom, breakfast included, and is open year-round. In high season, half board costs L110,000 per person.

To get there from Roma, catch the local train to Napoli (not the Intercity) and get off at Fondi. There are buses approximately every hour to Sperlonga from the station. Otherwise, it's about L25,000 by taxi.

The Pontine Islands

International tourists are yet to discover this group of small islands between Roma and Napoli. Only two of the islands – Ponza and Ventotene – are inhabited, and both are popular summer holiday spots for Italians. Ponza is the larger of the two and has a number of hotels and plenty of good restaurants. There are OK beaches at Ponza town and at the other main settlement on the island, Le Forna. The island is ecologically in pretty poor shape. Almost every inch of the hilly island was terraced and used for farming, and now there's a lot of erosion. Birdhunting is virtually an obsession for the locals; migrating birds pass over on their journeys between Europe and Africa. Ventotene has a very small permanent population and limited accommodation facilities. Basically, neither of the islands has the fascination or wild beauty of the Isole Eolie or Egadi islands (off Sicilia), but they're pleasant and handy to Roma.

There's a tourist office in Ponza's main town (☎ 0771-800 31). Hotels on Ponza include *Hotel Mari* (☎ 0771-8 01 01), Corso Pisacane, in Ponza town, which has singles/doubles for up to L100,000/180,000 with bathroom, breakfast included. However, numerous locals rent out rooms for much less and you'll find them touting at the port. An excellent place to eat is the *Ristorante da Ciro* (☎ 0771-80 83 88), Via Calacaparra, a km or so past the town of Le Forna. A meal of fresh seafood will cost less than L40,000.

There's a regular local bus service on Ponza. Otherwise, you can rent a small motorcycle at the port, either at one of the numerous outlets, or from one of the touts who will meet you at the ferry. The islands are accessible by car ferry or hydrofoil from Anzio, Terracina or Formia (timetable information is available from most travel agents).

Liguria, Piemonte & Valle d'Aosta

The north-western corner of Italy has long been a political, economic and intellectual engine room for the country. It was here that the movement for Italian unity took wing; Piemonte was the cradle of Italy's industrial success and birthplace of its labour movements, while the Piemonte capital, Torino, was for much of this century a hotbed of intellectual activity. A little farther south, Genova was long a major city port, open to the rest of the world for centuries and today regaining importance.

Torino and Genova resonate with past glories, but they are only one side of the coin. From the ski pistes and walking trails of the Valle d'Aosta and northern Piemonte to the Ligurian coast and magic of the Cinque Terre (Five Lands), this corner of the country is a microcosm of the best Italy has to offer in natural beauty.

HIGHLIGHTS

- Walking between the picturesque coastal villages of the Cinque Terre, with dinner in Vernazza
- The portside aquarium in Genova
- *Trenette al pesto* and a seafood main in a Genovese trattoria
- Hiking all or part of the Grande Traversata delle Alpi
- Orange hurling at Carnevale in Ivrea
- *Caffè* life in Torino
- Skiing in Courmayeur or just getting the cable car to Monte Bianco

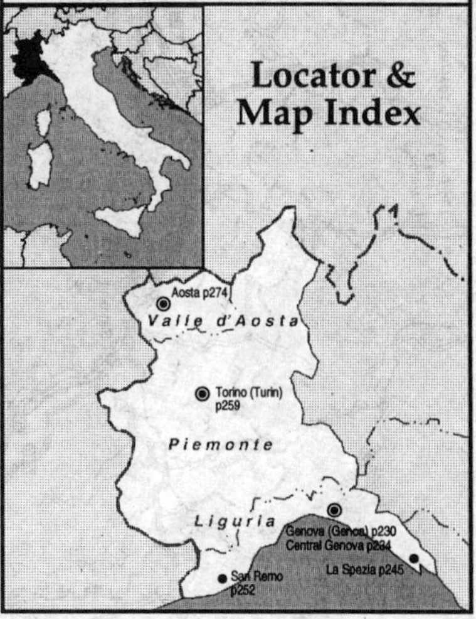

Liguria

The Ligurian coast was inhabited by Neanderthals about one million years ago, and many remains have been unearthed in the area. The locals say they were lured by the beaches, which still exert a hold over the hundreds of thousands of tourists who flock to this narrow coastal region each year. There is more to Liguria, however, than its beaches. Stretching from the French border in the west to La Spezia in the east, the coast is dotted with resorts and medieval towns; the mountainous hinterland hides hilltop villages, the occasional piste and plenty of scope for walkers and climbers. Genova, regional capital and one-time sea power, is an important port and a much overlooked attraction in its own right.

Liguria has been ruled by the Greeks, Saracens, Romans, Venetians, Lombards and the French, and strong early trade influences from as far afield as Sicilia, Northern Africa and Spain are evident.

Cuisine is marked by the products of the Mediterranean climate – fresh herbs, extra virgin olive oil and seafood. Among its culinary creations are *pesto, focaccia* and *farinata*, a chickpea flour bread. A visit to the Cinque Terre is not complete without trying its delicious but rare dessert wine,

LIGURIA

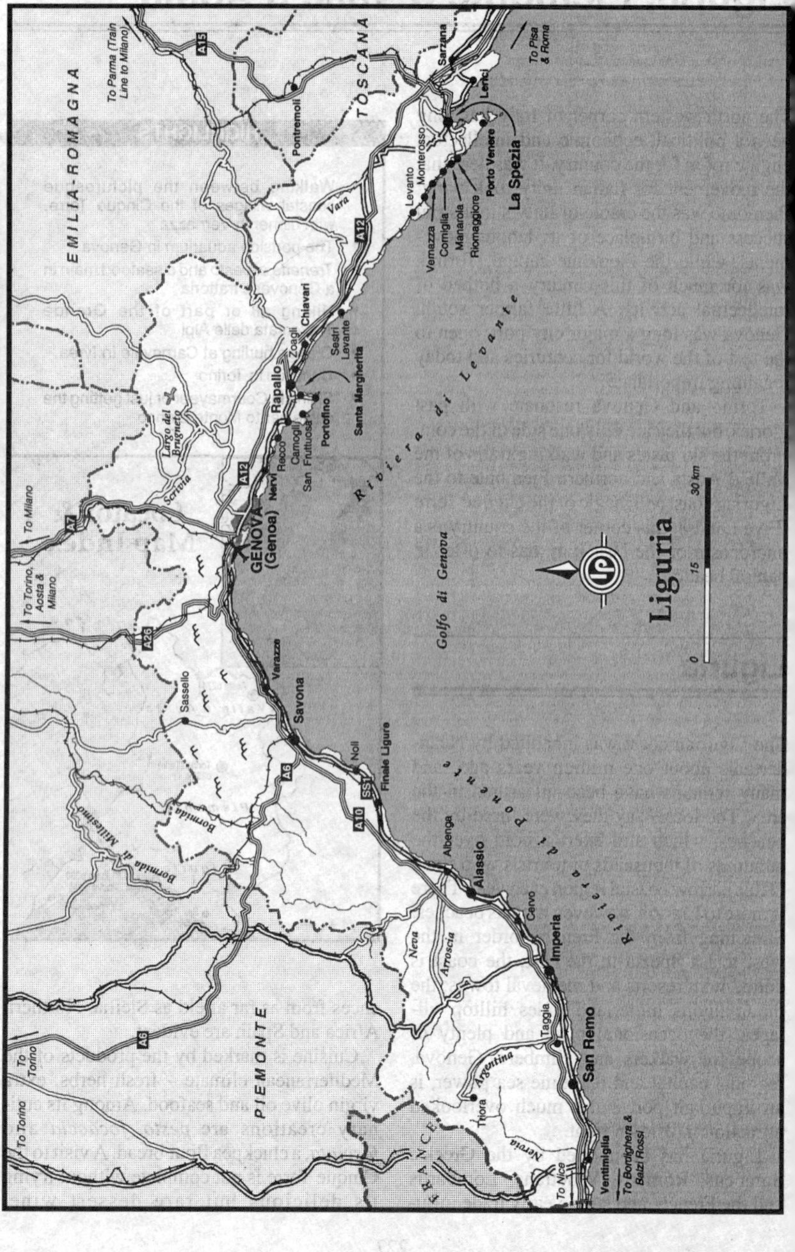

Liguria
0
15
30 km
EMILIA-ROMAGNA
TOSCANA
PIEMONTE
FRANCE
To Parma (Train Line to Milano)
To Pisa & Roma
To Milano
To Torino, Aosta & Milano
To Torino
To Torino
To Nice
To Bordighera & Balzi Rossi
A15
A12
A7
A26
A6
A10
SS1
Pontremoli
Sarzana
Lerici
Monterosso
Levanto
Vernazza
Corniglia
Manarola
Riomaggiore
Porto Venere
La Spezia
Vara
Chiavari
Zoagli
Sestri Levante
Rapallo
Santa Margherita
Portofino
Camogli
San Fruttuosa
Recco
Nervi
Largo del Brugneto
Scrivia
GENOVA (Genoa)
Riviera di Levante
Golfo di Genova
Varazze
Sassello
Savona
Noli
Finale Ligure
Bormida
Bormida di Millesimo
Albenga
Alassio
Riviera di Ponente
Cervo
Imperia
Neva
Arroscia
Taggia
San Remo
Argentina
Triora
Nervia
Ventimiglia

ciacchetrà. The Riviera di Ponente is also ell known for its wine.

A train line follows the coast from the rench frontier to La Spezia and beyond, onnecting all points along the way. By road ou have the choice of good (and expensive) utostradas; the A10 west of Genova, the 12 east or the Via Aurelia (SS1), an often ongested but more picturesque state ighway.

ENOVA

ravellers who write off Genova (Genoa) as imply a dirty port town and bypass it for the oastal resorts do the city and themselves a isservice. Once a mighty maritime republic nd the birthplace of Christopher Columbus, ie city known as *La Superba* (the proud, aughty), has admittedly lost some of its loss over the centuries, but none of its fasination. Genova might have had a still reater story behind it had the town founders een fit to lend an ear to Columbus' exploraion ideas; but instead Spain became a enaissance superpower on the back of ealth discovered in the Americas. This idn't stop Genova from celebrating the 00th anniversary of the discovery of merica with an Expo in 1992. The Expo ave the city something of a facelift and conomic heart-starter, although it ended up eing a bit of a disaster when a serious flood evastated parts of the city.

The labyrinth of narrow alleys at the heart f the old city near the port is a scrappy zone f some ill-repute, but it is undeniably intersting – full of visiting sailors, prostitutes, elinquents and longtime residents. Turn a orner and you stumble across medieval hurches or well-to-do Renaissance resiences converted into museums. During the ay, the seamier side of Genovese life mixes t with the fashionable set. At night, however, entral Genova empties and becomes a ecidedly uninviting neighbourhood.

listory

enova was founded in the 4th century BC, nd possibly derives its name from the Latin *ianua* (door). A key Roman port, it later became a mercantile power, although often subject to the domination of others. Genova was occupied by the French in 774, the Saracens in the 10th century and even by the Milanese in 1353. A famous victory over Venezia in 1298 led to a period of rapid growth, but quarrels between the noble families of the city – the Grimaldis, the Dorias and the Spinolas – caused much internal disruption.

Genova reached its peak in the 16th century under the rule of imperial admiral Andrea Doria, and managed to benefit from Spain's American fortunes by financing Spanish exploration. Coinciding happily with the Renaissance, Genova's golden age lasted into the following century and produced innumerable magnificent palaces and great works of art. The feverish activity attracted masters of the calibre of Rubens, Caravaggio and Van Dyck. Galeazzo Alessi (1512-72), who designed many of the city's splendid buildings, is ranked with Andrea Palladio. The age of exploration left the writing on the wall, however, and as the importance of the Mediterranean declined, so too did Genova's fortunes.

A leading participant in the Risorgimento – the process of Italian unification and independence in the 19th century – Genova was also the first northern city to rise against the Germans and the Italian Fascists towards the close of WWII, liberating itself before the arrival of Allied troops.

After the war, the city expanded rapidly along the coast and swallowed numerous villages along the way. But after the boom years of the 1960s it began to decline as big industry folded and port activity dropped. The waterfront and city centre were allowed to decay.

The city may now have turned a corner. Vast amounts of money were poured into improvements for the Columbus Festival in 1992, and the largely privatised and restructured port operations are registering big increases in container business – a sign that Genova may yet recover some of its glory as a trading port.

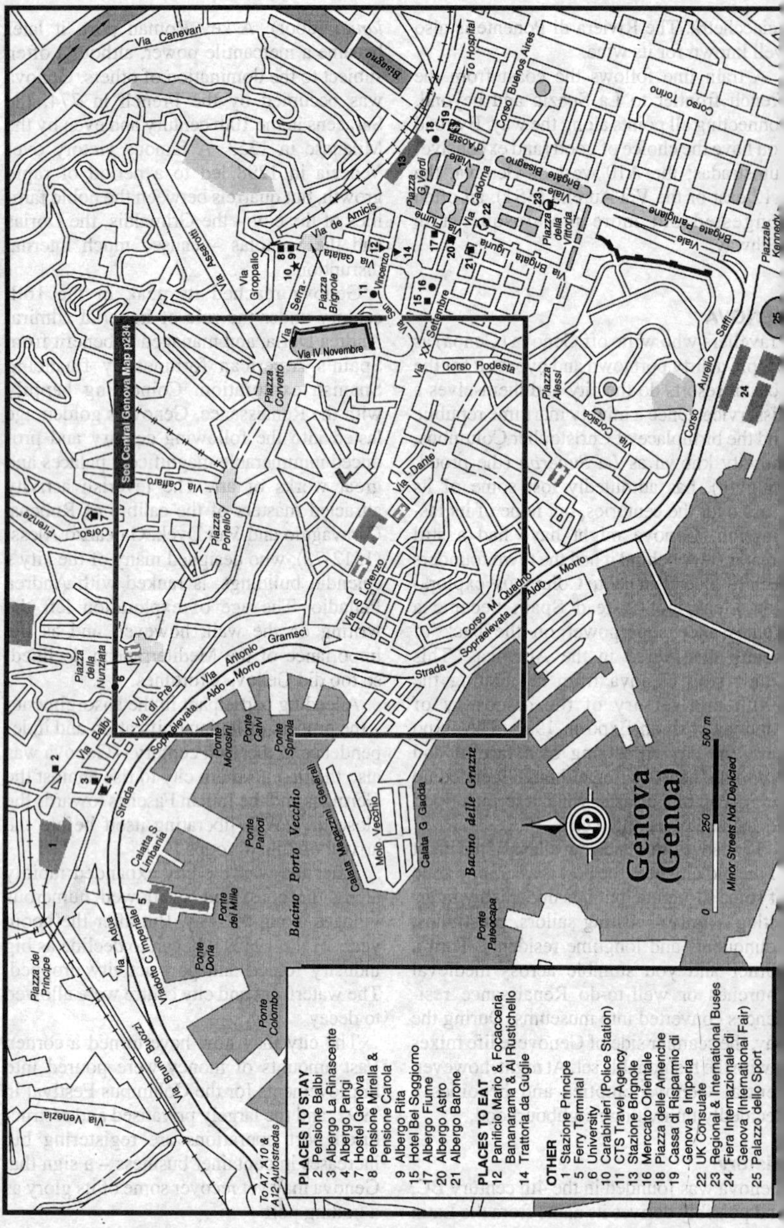
Genova
(Genoa)
Minor Streets Not Depicted
0
250
500 m
See Central Genova Map p234
To A7, A10 & A12 Autostradas
To Hospital
Bacino Porto Vecchio
Bacino delle Grazie
Via Canevari
Bisagno
Via Assarotti
Via Groppallo
Via de Amicis
Via Serra
Piazza Brignole
Via Galata
Via San Vincenzo
Piazza G Verdi
Viale G Fiume
Corso Buenos Aires
Viale d'Aosta
Corso Torino
Via Cadorna
Brigate Bisagno
Viale Brigata Liguria
Piazza della Vittoria
Brigate Partigiane
Piazzale Kennedy
Via XX Settembre
Corso Podestà
Piazza Alessi
Corso Aurelio Saffi
Via Corsica
Via Dante
Piazza Corvetto
Via IV Novembre
Via Caffaro
Piazza Portello
Corso Firenze
Via S Lorenzo
Corso M Quadrio
Aldo Morro
Strada Sopraelevata
Via Antonio Gramsci
Via di Pré
Piazza della Nunziata
Via Balbi
Piazza del Principe
Via Adua
Viadotto C Imperiale
Calatta S Limbania
Ponte Morosini
Ponte Calvi
Ponte Spinola
Ponte Parodi
Ponte dei Mille
Ponte Doria
Ponte Colombo
Calata Magazzini Generali
Molo Vecchio
Calata G Gadda
Ponte Paleocapa
Via Bruno Buozzi
Via Venezia
PLACES TO STAY
2 Pensione Balbi
3 Albergo La Rinascente
4 Albergo Parigi
7 Hostel Genova
8 Pensione Mirella & Pensione Carola
9 Albergo Rita
15 Hotel Bel Soggiorno
17 Albergo Fiume
20 Albergo Astro
21 Albergo Barone
PLACES TO EAT
12 Panificio Mario & Focacceria, Bananarama & Al Rustichello
14 Trattoria da Guglie
OTHER
1 Stazione Principe
5 Ferry Terminal
6 University
10 Carabinieri (Police Station)
11 CTS Travel Agency
13 Stazione Brignole
16 Merccato Orientale
18 Piazza delle Americhe
19 Cassa di Risparmio di Genova e Imperia
22 UK Consulate
23 Regional & International Buses
24 Fiera Internazionale di Genova (International Fair)
25 Palazzo dello Sport

Orientation

Genova stretches along the Ligurian coast for some 30km and is served by 15 train stations. It can seem overwhelming on arrival, but the city centre is quite compact, tucked in between the two main train stations, Principe and Brignole. The main boulevard, Via XX Settembre, starts a short walk south of Stazione Brignole and spills into the city's focal point, Piazza de Ferrari. This stretch offers the better cheap accommodation. The APT office is on Via Roma, north of Piazza de Ferrari.

West towards the port and stretching around the waterfront towards Stazione Principe are the oldest Genovese quarters, within a maze of narrow lanes, or *caruggi*. Most of the city's monuments are here, but Genova is no museum – a classic and somewhat weather-beaten port, the streets hum with activity, not all of it salubrious. The Stazione Principe area, close to the port, is dodgy ground for newcomers – local buses run between it and Stazione Brignole.

It is easier to walk around the old city as most traffic is banned from the centre. Car parks are well signposted.

Information

Tourist Offices The main IAT information office (☎ 2 48 71) is in the Palazzina Santa Maria near Il Bigo on the waterfront and is open daily from 9 am to 6.30 pm. There are branch offices at the airport and Stazione Principe, open Monday to Saturday from 8 am to 8 pm, and smaller offices in Nervi and Arenzano, which have irregular opening hours. Pick up its walking tours booklet, *Genova, The Old City*.

Foreign Consulates The British Consulate (☎ 56 48 33) is at Piazza Vittoria 15 and the French Consulate (☎ 20 08 79) at Via Garibaldi 20.

Money Most banks will give cash advances and change travellers' cheques, and there are plenty of ATMs. The Banca Carige, on Piazza delle Americhe near Stazione Brignole, can change money and has user-friendly ATMs. Plenty of banks with change and ATM facilities are scattered about the city.

Post & Communications The main post office is in Via Dante, just off Piazza de Ferrari. It is open Monday to Saturday from 8.15 am to 7.40 pm. Genova's postcode is 16100.

The most convenient Telecom office, at the main post office, is open from 6 am to 10 pm. There's another at Stazione Brignole, open daily from 8 am to 9.30 pm. Genova's telephone code is ☎ 010.

Travel Agencies CTS (☎ 56 43 66) is at Via San Vincenzo 119. CIT (☎ 29 19 53) has an office at Via XXV Aprile 16.

Bookshops Bozzi, Via Cairoli 2, has a good selection of English and French-language books. Feltrinelli's store at Via Bensa 32r also has a reasonable range.

Gay & Lesbian Information Arci Gay (☎ 277 07 39) is at Via San Luca 11/4.

Laundry There's an Onda Blu laundry at Via Gramsci 181r.

Emergency & Medical Services The questura (☎ 5 36 61) is on Via Diaz, or for immediate police attendance, call ☎ 113. For an ambulance, call ☎ 570 59 51. The Ospedale San Martino (☎ 3 53 51) is at Via Benedetto XV. The Guardia Medica Regione Liguria (☎ 35 40 22) operates an after-hours, home-visit medical service from 8 pm to 8 am. The Ghersi pharmacy (☎ 54 16 61), Corte Lambruschini 16/18/r, right by the huge Naca Carige building off Piazza delle Americhe, is open night and day.

Piazza de Ferrari

Flanked by the **Teatro Carlo Felice**, the imposing **Borsa** (former stock exchange) and **Palazzo Ducale**, Piazza de Ferrari is the focal point of Genova and an obvious starting point for exploration of the city. The palace, once the seat of the city's rulers, has been opened up for cultural exhibitions and houses a couple of good restaurants.

Cattedrale di San Lorenzo
A stone's throw west of the Palazzo Ducale, whose main entrance faces Piazza Matteotti, is the city's cathedral. Its distinctively Genovese black and white striped Gothic marble façade, fronted by twisting columns and almost gaudy decoration, is something of a shock every time you turn a corner to see it. Construction and embellishment were carried out over several hundred years. Begun in the 12th century, its bell tower and cupola weren't erected until the 16th century. Inside, the **Cappella del Battista** once housed relics of St John the Baptist.

Look out for the museum, which houses the *Sacro Catino*, a cup allegedly given to Solomon by the Queen of Sheba and used by Jesus at the Last Supper. Other relics include the polished quartz platter upon which Salome is said to have received John the Baptist's head. The museum was closed for restoration at the time for writing.

Porta Soprana & Casa di Colombo
Head back south-east through Piazza Matteotti and you will find the impressive remains of Genova's city walls. Porta Soprana was originally raised in 1155, although what you see is the restored version. In Genova's heyday, the city was considered virtually impregnable on the landward side because of its walls.

In the gate's shadow, on Piazza Dante, is a much rebuilt house said to be the birthplace of Columbus, or at least the spot where his father lived. There are conflicting opinions about the authenticity of the claims, so some healthy scepticism seems in order.

Via Garibaldi & Palazzi
Skirting the northern edge of what were then the city limits, Via Garibaldi clearly marks a break between the Middle Ages and the

The Ocean Blue
From an early age, Christopher Columbus (or Cristoforo Colombo to his compatriots) showed signs of having a bad case of what we might call the 'travel bug'. Steeped in Marco Polo's writings and Pliny's *Natural History*, he conceived an ambitious project to reach the Orient by sailing west instead of east. Adventurous as Genova's rulers may have been, this was too much, so Columbus went off to Spain where he received a more sympathetic hearing. Cristóbal Colón, as the Spaniards know him, set off with the three ships *Niña*, *Pinta* and *Santa Maria* on 3 August 1492 and two months later landed in the Bahamas. In the following eight years, he discovered Cuba, Haiti, Jamaica and some of the Antilles, still convinced he was in Asia.

Sent back to Spain on charges of committing atrocities (although subsequent Spanish colonisers evidently developed a thicker skin in this regard), he made one last voyage in 1502-4, tracking the central American coast and reaching Colombia. When he died a forgotten and embittered man two years later in Valladolid, Spain, he still had no idea he had discovered a new world. Today, of course, he's everyone's hero, from Genova to the USA and from Spain to Latin America. ■

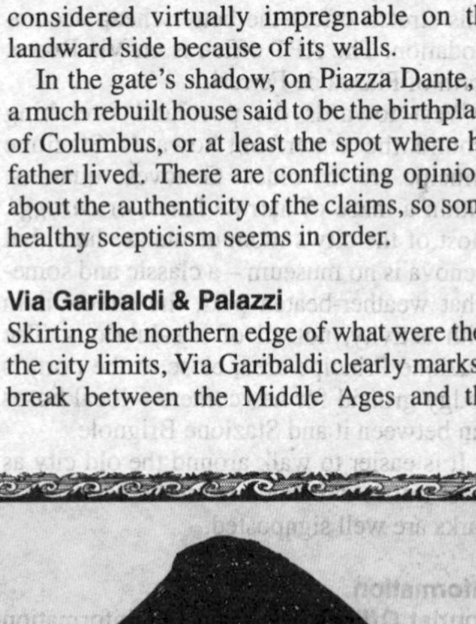

Renaissance, and between poor and rich. Lined with magnificent, if somewhat blackened and unkempt *palazzi*, it is the place to admire the pick of Genova's museums.

The **Galleria di Palazzo Rosso** is open Tuesday to Sunday from 9 am to 1 pm (Wednesday and Saturday to 7 pm). Admission costs L6000. It boasts works from the Venetian and Genovese schools and several canvasses by Van Dyck. The **Galleria di Palazzo Bianco** (same hours and admission fee as Palazzo Rosso) features works by Flemish, Spanish and Dutch masters, displaying Genova's international cultural links, but there is plenty of home-grown material too, with the likes of Caravaggio and Antonio Pisanello. Look also for Dürer's *Portrait of a Young Boy*.

Many of the buildings on Alessi's grand boulevard house banks or other public facilities. Wander in if the gates are open. At No 9, the **Palazzo Doria Tursi**, Genova's town hall since 1848, was built in 1564. It houses the relics of two famous Genovese – fragments of the skeleton of Columbus and one of Niccolò Paganini's violins, played occasionally at concerts. The **Palazzo Podestà**, Via Garibaldi 7, has magnificent frescoes in the courtyard.

The Genius of Genova

Born in 1782, Niccolò Paganini already knew just about all there was to know about the violin by his 13th year. Two years later, after learning composition in Parma, he launched his concert career, which, in the following 40 years, was to take him to every corner of Italy and to the great stages of Europe.

Paganini didn't just play a mean violin. He was a virtuoso on the guitar as well and from the violin extracted chords, harmonies, arpeggios and rhythms hitherto undreamed of. A prolific composer, he shared his genius with posterity, leaving behind six concertos, 24 quartets for violin, viola, guitar and other strings, 12 sonatas for violin and guitar and a long list of further sonatas. Liszt and Chopin applied much of what they learned from Paganini's genius to the piano.

The virtuoso spent the last days of his restless life a little farther along the coast from his native Genova, in Nice, France, where he died in 1840. He is now buried in Parma. ■

Museums

Not far from Via Garibaldi, heading into the old town, is the **Galleria Nazionale di Palazzo Spinola**, Piazza Superiore di Pellicceria 1, a 16th century mansion housing Italian and Flemish Renaissance works. It is open Tuesday to Saturday from 9 am to 7 pm, Monday to 1 pm and Sunday from 2 to 7 pm. Admission is L8000. The **Galleria di Palazzo Reale**, Via Balbi 10, also features Renaissance works. It is open Wednesday to Saturday from 9 am to 6.30 pm; the rest of the week to 1.30 pm. Admission is L8000.

The **Museo d'Arte Orientale**, set in gardens next to Piazzale Mazzini, has one of the largest collections of Oriental art in Europe. It is open Tuesday, Thursday to Saturday and every second Sunday from 9 am to 1 pm. Admission is L4000. The city also boasts a **Museo d'Arte Moderna** (closed at the time of writing) in the suburb of Nervi, and a museum of pre-Columbian art, the **Museo Americanistico F Lunardi**, in the Villa Gruber on Corso Solferino.

Churches

The **Santissima Annunziata del Vestato**, Piazza della Nunziata, is a rich example of 17th-century Genovese architecture and is still being restored after virtually being destroyed in WWII bombing raids. Look up at the trompe l'œil in the dome. The **Chiesa di San Siro**, Via San Siro, also badly damaged in WWII, dates to the 4th century, but was rebuilt in the 16th century.

The **Chiesa di San Donato**, Strada S Agostino, was built in the 11th century in

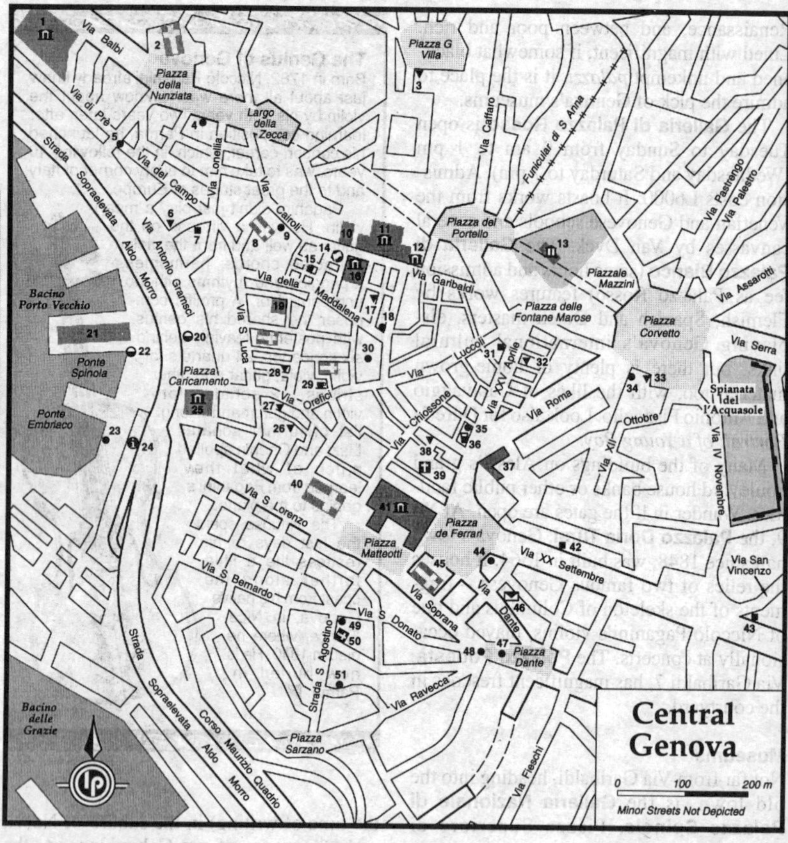

pure Romanesque style, but was enlarged in the 12th and 13th centuries. The church of the Doria family, **Chiesa di San Matteo**, in Piazza Matteotti, was founded in 1125. Doria's sword is preserved under the altar and his tomb is in the crypt. The **Chiesa del Gesù**, which is also known as Chiesa di Sant'Ambrogio, is nearby.

Old City

Medieval Genova is a maze of twisting lanes and dank blind alleys, the core of which is bound by Porta dei Vacca on the waterfront, and vias Cairoli, Garibaldi, XXV Aprile and the Porta Soprana around the inland periphery. Beyond this it straggles along the coast in both directions, especially at the northern end with the seedy Via di Prè.

The best way to explore the area is simply to wander about. Most of the prostitution and lowlife seem to be concentrated in the zone west of **Via San Luca**, itself a hip thoroughfare full of cafés and bars which ends at its southern end at Piazza Bianchi. East off the piazza is Via degli Orefici, where you'll find market stalls, especially for second-hand books (there are some gems in the line of

PLACES TO STAY	OTHER	
7 Albergo Rio	1 Palazzo Reale	25 Palazzo San Giorgio
31 Hotel Metropoli	2 Santissima Annunziata del Vestato	30 Piazza Lavagna & Flea Market
42 Bristol Palace	4 Feltrinelli Bookshop	34 APT Tourist Office
43 Albergo Soana	5 Porta dei Vacca	35 CIT Travel Agency
	8 Chiesa di San Siro	36 Britannia Pub
PLACES TO EAT	9 Bozzi Bookshop	37 Teatro Carlo Felice
3 Rosticceria	10 Palazzo Bianco	39 Chiesa di San Matteo
6 Trattoria Le Maschere	11 Palazzo Doria Tursi	40 Cattedrale di San Lorenzo
15 Trattoria Carletto	12 Palazzo del Podestà	41 Palazzo Ducale
17 Trattoria Vittorio	13 Museo d'Arte Orientale	44 Borsa
26 La Santa	14 French Consulate	45 Chiesa del Gesù
27 A Ved Romanengo (Pastry Shop)	16 Palazzo Rosso	46 Post Office
28 Trattoria da Walter	18 Coin Laundrette	47 Casa di Colombo
29 Café Royal	19 Palazzo Spinola	48 Porta Soprana
32 Trattoria da Maria	20 AMT Bus Station	49 Caffetteria Le Corbusier
33 Mancini & C Pasticceria	21 Aquarium	50 Chiesa di San Donato
38 Ristorante Bruno	22 Port Tours	51 Teatro della Tosse
	23 Il Bigo	
	24 IAT Information Office	

Fascist-era newspapers and magazines), more cafés and a couple of great restaurants and pasticcerie. As for Via di Prè, it is seedy but not really all that interesting.

As busy as it is in daylight, just about everything shuts at night, exceptions being some very good eateries and the 24-hour prostitution and drug trade.

Porto Antico

The 1992 Expo left the Genovese waterfront with some lasting attractions, and the area known as the Porto Antico continues to be developed.

Stars of the **aquarium** (among the largest in Europe and well worth a visit) include sharks, dolphins and penguins. Located on Ponte Spinola, it's open Tuesday to Friday from 9.30 am to 6.30 pm and on weekends and holidays until 8 pm. In summer it also opens on Monday. Admission is L14,000.

A hundred metres south along the pier is **Il Bigo**, a derrick built for the sole purpose of hoisting a cylindrical lift 200m into the air and allowing its occupants a bird's-eye view of the city. This costs L5000 and it operates Tuesday to Saturday from 11 am to 1 pm and 2.30 to 4 pm (Sunday and holidays until 5 pm). There's an ice-skating rink next door.

The frescoed Palazzo San Giorgio, just back from the waterfront, has undergone several changes of career over the centuries. Now home to the port authority, it was once a bank. Marco Polo was imprisoned here for a stint and spent his time working on *Il Milione*.

Spianata dell'Acquasole

This park, beside Viale IV Novembre, is a pleasant distraction from the chaos of the streets of central Genova, and the swings and rides provide welcome relief for kids bored silly by museums.

Organised Tours

It is possible to organise guided tours of the city or elsewhere in the region through travel agents such as Viatur.

In summer, the Cooperativo Battellieri del Porto di Genova runs tours of the port from near the Aquarium for L10,000 at 3.15 pm.

Places to Stay – bottom end

Camping The camping grounds on the outskirts of the city are all easily accessible by bus from Stazione Brignole. *Villa Doria* (☎ 696 96 00), Via al Campeggio Villa Doria 15, on the way to Pegli, is open all year and can be reached by bus No 1, 2 or 3 from Piazza Caricamento, on the waterfront. Farther on is the *Caravan Park la Vesima* (☎ 619 96 72), Via Rubens 50r. Catch bus

LIGURIA

No 95 from Voltri (which you can reach on bus No 1).

Hostels & Hotels The HI *Hostel Genova* (☎ 242 24 57), Via Costanzi 120, is in the Righi area, north of Genova's old centre. B&B is L22,000 and a meal costs L14,000. Catch bus No 40 to the end of the line from Stazione Brignole or No 35 from Stazione Principe, after which you have to connect with No 40. The hostel is closed from 20 December to 1 January.

The *Casa della Giovane* (☎ 20 66 32), Piazza Santa Sabina 4, is off Piazza della Nunziata, a short walk east of Stazione Principe, and usually has cheap beds for women.

Although the old city, Stazione Principe and the port areas have a fair smattering of budget places, you'll generally get better value and a greater feeling of security near Stazione Brignole and Via XX Settembre.

Near Stazione Brignole are a couple of hotels in a lovely old building at Via Groppallo 4. Turn right as you leave the train station and walk up Via de Amicis to Piazza Brignole. To your right is Via Groppallo. *Pensione Mirella* (☎ 89 37 22) has singles/doubles for L37,000/65,000. The *Pensione Carola* (☎ 839 13 40), on the 3rd floor, is better with clean, well-kept rooms for up to L45,000/75,000. Up the road at No 8, the *Albergo Rita* has been refurbished and offers a range of rooms, some with private bathroom, from L45,000/65,000 up.

Down Via Fiume in front of the train station, *Albergo Fiume* (☎ 570 54 60) has decent, clean rooms from L40,000/70,000. Single rooms with a toilet are L65,000, and it's one of the few budget hotels to accept credit cards. The showers are admirable.

Head farther down Via Fiume and turn right into Via XX Settembre and you'll come to *Albergo Astro* (☎ 58 15 33) at No 3, a simple but comfortable place on the 5th floor with rooms starting from L45,000/80,000.

Right across the road at No 2, *Albergo Barone* (☎ 58 75 78) is good value at L45,000/70,000.

Closer to Piazza de Ferrari, at No 23 Via XX Settembre, *Albergo Soana* (☎ 56 28 14) offers quite decent singles/doubles, the latter with shower, for L50,000/80,000. When they're cheeky, the doubles can go as high as L120,000. Ear plugs are useful in some rooms because of street noise.

Near Stazione Principe is *Pensione Balbi* (☎ 28 09 12), Via Balbi 21-3, with singles/doubles for L35,000/60,000. Most of the singles are permanently occupied, but there are several hotels in a similar category on the same street.

If you want to mix it with prostitutes, sailors and so forth, head for Via di Prè. *Albergo Parigi* (☎ 25 21 72), Via di Prè 72, has secure rooms for L30,000/50,000. *Albergo La Rinascente* (☎ 26 11 13), at No 59, charges the same but shouldn't.

Places to Stay – middle

If you want to spend a little more money, you cannot go past *Hotel Bel Soggiorno* (☎ 58 14 18), Via XX Settembre 19. Singles/doubles with a bathroom, TV and mini-bar start at L75,000/110,000.

Albergo Rio (☎ 29 05 51), Via Ponte Calvi 5, charges L75,000/90,000 if you stay for a couple of nights.

The *Hotel Metropoli* (☎ 28 41 41) in Piazza delle Fontane Marose has rooms from L110,000/145,000, including breakfast. The rooms are spotless and the location is hard to beat.

Places to Stay – top end

One of the grand old establishments of Genovese hospitality is the *Bristol Palace* (☎ 59 25 41; fax 56 17 56), Via XX Settembre 35. Rooms range from L140,000 to L350,000.

Places to Eat

Local Cuisine The bulk of the good eating is to be done in the old city, although there are exceptions. Don't leave town without trying a pasta with pesto genovese (a sauce of basil, garlic, parmesan cheese and pine nuts), torta pasqualina (made with spinach, ricotta cheese and eggs), pansoti (spinach ravioli with a thick, creamy hazelnut sauce), trenette (a spaghetti with pesto and potato) and, of course, focaccia. If you're cooking your own meals, stock up in the Mercato Orientale on Via XX Settembre.

Restaurants Some of the best and cheapest takeaways are at the *Rosticceria* on the corner of Spianata Castelletto and Piazza Goffredo Villa. You can take away a hot and filling serve of pasta, sold by weight, for a few thousand lire. Try the trenette al pesto.

Via San Vincenzo, near Stazione Brignole, is a short but busy food street. *Al Rustichello*, No 59r, is about the 'poshest' joint, where a main will cost L15,000 or more. For cheaper snacks try *Panificio Mario*, No 61; the down-to-earth farinata specialists *Trattoria da Guglie*, No 64; or the *focacceria* at No 61a. You could finish with a delicious ice cream from *Bananarama*, at No 65.

The waterfront area around Piazza Caricamento is lined with cheap eateries and restaurants, including a couple of Chinese places. Less informal, and wedged in at the corner of Via Sottoripa and Via Ponte Calvi, is *Trattoria Le Maschere*.

A good place is *Trattoria da Maria*, Vico Testa d'Oro 14, off Via XXV Aprile, where a meal costs L13,000, including wine. It's a basic little place and full of simple charm.

The *Gran Caffè Ducale* in the Palazzo Ducale on Piazza de Ferrari offers expensive coffee but great set menus, including several Ligurian specialities, for L25,000. It should not be confused with the more expensive joint upstairs.

Trattoria da Walter at Vico Colalanza 2r concentrates on Genovese specialities. Pasta starts at L7000. The lane is off Via San Luca.

Hidden away in the nearby Vico degli Indoratori (No 5) just south of Via degli Orefici, *La Santa* is more expensive if you eat à la carte but has a reputation for good regional cooking. It has a tourist set menu for L18,000 (not including drinks). Nearby, *Café Royal*, Via degli Orefici 70, is a bright and popular place for light food and drinks.

Seafood is inevitably a speciality in some restaurants. The *Trattoria Vittorio*, Vico del Duca 24, offers a limited but tasty range, and a full meal will cost around L30,000.

Looser purse strings will open up still more mouth-watering pleasures. The tiny *Trattoria Carletto*, Vico del Tempo Buono 5r, costs about L50,000 a head, but they know their fish – the family running this place lend it an atmosphere reminiscent of a Fellini film. *Ristorante Bruno*, Vico Casana 9, falls into a similar category, but the offerings are more limited.

If you feel like heading right out of town (you'll need to take a taxi) *Il Primopiatto*, Via del Tritone 12 R, just in from the waterfront in the Sturla area east of the International Fair, is highly recommended.

LIGURIA

Cafés & Pasticcerie Away from the waterfront, central Genova all but shuts down in the evening – 'better to go home and sleep' was the advice of one local.

Mangini & C, on Via Roma at Piazza Corvetto, is renowned as Genova's finest pasticceria. *A Ved Romanengo*, Via degli Orefici 31, has been serving scrumptious pastries since 1805. Nearby, Via San Luca and Campetto are good hunting grounds for cafés and snackbars during the day, but dead at night. The posh spot in the Borsa building opposite the post office is an experience on its own.

Entertainment

Opera The opera house, *Teatro Carlo Felice* (☎ 58 93 29), Piazza de Ferrari, opened in 1991 on the site of the original opera house (heavily bombed in WWII) and has a year-round programme.

Theatre The IAT usually has full theatre programmes and booking details for the city's main stages. The Genova Theatre Company performs throughout the year at the *Politeama Genovese* (☎ 839 35 89), Via Piaggio, and at the *Teatro della Corte* (☎ 570 24 72), Corte Lambruschini. The main season is from January to May.

The stage of *Teatro della Tosse* (☎ 247 07 93), Piazza Renato Negri 4, first saw action in 1702, when it was built as the Teatro

Sant'Agostino. Some time later, Casanova walked the boards here.

Cinema Three cinema clubs show films in their original language on selected nights. They are: *Cineclub Chaplin* (☎ 88 00 69), Piazza Cappuccini 1; *Fritz Lang* (☎ 21 97 68), Via Acquarone 64; and *Cineclub Lumière* (☎ 50 59 36), Via Vitale 1. They cost L6000 to join and it's about L6000 to see a film.

Bars & Discos If you like cocktails, you could try *Caffetteria le Corbusier* in Piazza San Donato, which is open until 1 am. Those sick of Italian lager might pop in to the *Britannia Pub* on Vico Casana; the Guinness is L3500 a pint.

A popular disco is *Mako*, Corso Italia 28r. You can find a few others, especially in summer, farther south-east along the waterfront in the Lido area.

Getting There & Away

Air The Cristoforo Colombo international airport at Sestri Ponente, 6km west of the city, has regular domestic and international connections but, for the latter, Milano and Pisa have cheaper options. For flight information, telephone ☎ 601 54 10 or your airline.

Bus Buses for international destinations leave from Piazza della Vittoria, as do limited interregional services and buses for other locations in Liguria.

Train Genova is directly connected by train to Torino, Milano, Pisa and Roma, and it makes little difference which of the two train stations (Principe or Brignole) you choose. The exception to the rule is for trips along the two Rivieras. West to San Remo and Ventimiglia, for instance, there are more departures from Stazione Principe than Brignole.

Car & Motorcycle The A12 connects Genova with Livorno in Toscana and with the A11 for Firenze. The A7 goes to Milano, the A26 to Torino and the A10 to Savona and the French border. Hitchhikers should ask at Stazione Brignole for bus routes to autostrada on/off ramps. You may have more luck on the SS1 heading in either direction along the coast, or the SS35 heading north to Alessandria (and on to Torino). Drivers who hate tolls and are in no hurry should also consider these roads.

Boat The city's busy port is an important embarkation point for ferries to Sicilia, Sardegna, Corsica and Elba. Most of the maritime activity is from June to September only.

Major companies are:

Corsica Ferries
: Piazza Dante 5a (☎ 59 33 01)
: for Corsica (cheapest one-way fare to Bastia is L42,000)

Tirrenia
: Pontile Colombo (☎ 275 80 41)
: for Sardegna (deck class to Porto Torres or Olbia L50,000 in the low season); from Sardegna you can connect to Sicilia

Grandi Navi Veloci (Grimaldi group)
: Via Fieschi 17 (☎ 58 93 31)
: for Sardegna (low-season deck class to Porto Torres L72,000) and Sicilia (low-season deck class to Palermo L120,000). Sicilia service all year around; to Sardegna in summer only

Grandi Traghetti (Grimaldi group)
: Via Fieschi 17 (☎ 58 93 31)
: for Tunisia and Malta (cheapest one-way fare to either Tunis or Malta is L154,000)

Corsica Marittima
: c/o GSA/Cemar, Via XX Settembre 2-10 (☎ 58 95 95) for Corsica (low-season deck fare L42,000 to Bastia), Sardegna (via Corsica with option of stay in Corsica before picking up a Moby Lines ferry from Bonifacio to Sardegna – Santa Teresa di Gallura); Tunisia (return fares to Tunis start at L334,000)

Moby Lines
: Imbarco Ponte Assereto (☎ 25 27 55)
: for Corsica (one-way low-season daylight deck class to Bastia L39,000) and Sardegna via Corsica (overland between Bastia and Bonifacio). The services run from March to September.

See also the Getting There & Away sections for Sicilia and Sardegna.

Ferries go to towns along the Riviera di

Levante, including Camogli, Portofino, the Cinque Terre, Santa Margherita and San Fruttuoso, from June to September. Co-operativa Battellieri del Porto di Genova (☎ 26 57 12) ferries leave from Calata Zingari, just west of the Stazione Marittima, and cost up to L35,000 return. Servizio Marittimo del Tigullio, based in Santa Margherita (☎ 0185-28 46 70), also runs occasional summer services between Genova and Portofino. Alimar (☎ 25 67 75) runs Marexpress, a summertime catamaran service to Portofino and Monte Carlo. Frequency depends largely on demand.

Getting Around

The Airport An airport bus service, the Volabus (☎ 59 94 14), leaves from Piazza Verdi, outside Stazione Brignole, and stops at Stazione Principe.

Bus AMT buses (☎ 599 74 14) operates services throughout the city. Main termini include the two train stations, Piazza della Vittoria and Piazza Caricamento. Buses No 33 and 37 link these stations. A ticket valid for 90 minutes costs L1500, or an all day ticket L5000 – they can be used on mainline trains within the city limits (as far as Voltri and Nervi) too. The same ticket can be used on the Art Bus, which runs every 20 to 25 minutes on a route designed for tourists, taking in the two train stations, Piazza de Ferrari and the waterfront.

Taxi For a taxi, call Radiotaxi on ☎ 59 66.

AROUND GENOVA

Hidden behind the industrial wasteland of Genova's west is **Pegli**, a victim of the city's growth. It lies in a sheltered harbour and offers magnificent views of the city and coastline. The Museo Navale is in the Villa Doria at Piazza Bonavino. The Museo Archeologico, Via Pallavicini, in the Villa Pallavicini, presents a comprehensive overview of Ligurian prehistory. The villa itself is set in a magnificent park modelled on the Genovese gardens of the Renaissance.

On Genova's eastern edge, **Nervi** has also been absorbed by the growing city. Renowned for its outdoor International Ballet Festival at the Teatro ai Parchi in July, and an outdoor cinema in the rose garden (Cinema nel Roseto) at the same venue in August, Nervi still manages to retain its own identity.

Recco, a little farther east, is the scene of an enormous fireworks display in the first week of September. Take a train there, as traffic is so tight you could spend a whole evening looking for a parking spot.

RIVIERA DI LEVANTE

The coast east of the portside sprawl of Genova is not as heavily developed as the western side of the capital and even rivals Campania's Amalfi coastline in beauty. A sprinkling of small resorts and villages, especially the Cinque Terre, retain a real charm despite their evident popularity, and the surrounding countryside is visually dramatic.

Camogli

Wandering through the alleyways and the long, cobbled streets of Camogli, it is hard not to be taken aback by the painstaking trompe-l'oeuil decoration – house after house sports meticulously painted columns, balustrades and even windows. Although a feature of many Ligurian towns, Camogli seems to take special pride in this genre of civic art. The esplanade, Via Garibaldi, is a colourful place for a stroll and really comes to life on the second Sunday in May, when local fishermen celebrate the Sagra del Pesce, frying hundreds of fish for all and sundry in 3m pans along the waterfront.

Camogli means 'house of wives', from the days when the women ran the town while their husbands were at sea. The town was also a strong naval base and at one stage boasted a fleet larger than Genova's.

Information To the right when you leave the train station is the APT office (☎ 0185-77 10 66) at Via XX Settembre 33. It's supposed to be open Monday to Saturday from 8.40 am to 12.10 pm and 3.40 to 6.10 pm, but don't bet on it. Camogli's telephone code is ☎ 0185.

Activities Luigi Simonetti Nautica (☎ 77 19 21), Via Garibaldi 59, hires out canoes, pedal boats, rowing and motor boats. B&B Mare Sport (☎ 77 27 51), Via Garibaldi 197A, operates a diving centre.

Places to Stay & Eat The *Albergo la Camogliese* (☎ 77 14 02), Via Garibaldi 55, has singles/doubles from L60,000/90,000. The *Augusta* (☎ 77 05 92), Via P Schiaffino 100, has singles/doubles from L80,000/100,000 in the high season, while the *Selene* (☎ 77 01 49), Via Cuneo 15, has rooms for L60,000/90,000.

Like accommodation, eating out is expensive, with most waterfront restaurants charging high prices for ordinary food. Try *Il Faulo*, Via Garibaldi 98, which specialises in Genovese fare and has a vegetarian menu. Pasta starts at around L13,000. Smaller, less expensive trattorie are tucked into the laneways away from the water, so you'll need to explore.

Getting There & Away Camogli is on the Genova-La Spezia train line, and services are regular. Tigullio buses head for Rapallo, Santa Margherita and Portofino Vetta along a pretty drive known as La Ruta. Drivers can reach Camogli from the A12 or the Via Aurelia (SS1). In summer ferries connect Camogli with other towns on the Portofino promontory and the Cinque Terre. See the following Santa Margherita section.

Santa Margherita

In a sheltered bay on the east side of the Portofino promontory on the Golfo di Tigullio, Santa Margherita is an attractive resort town and a potential base for exploring the area – although those on a tight budget are better off getting a hotel in Rapallo, 3km away. From the jumble of one-time fishing families' houses on the waterfront you can admire the million-dollar yachts at their moorings.

Once home to a considerable coral-fishing fleet that roamed as far as Africa, Santa Margherita is now better known for its orange blossoms and lace.

From the train station, head downhill to the port, then along Via Gramsci to Piazza Caprera, from where most buses depart.

Information The IAT office (☎ 0185-28 74 85), Via XXV Aprile 2b, just off Piazza Caprera, is open daily from 8.30 am to 12.30 pm and 2.30 to 5.30 pm. It's open from 9.30 am on Sunday and holidays and has extended hours in summer.

The post office is at Via Roma 36 and is open Monday to Friday from 8.10 am to 5.30 pm and Saturday morning. The postcode is 16038 and the phone code ☎ 0185.

For the police, call ☎ 113 or the Carabinieri (☎ 28 71 21) in Via Vignolo. The Ospedale Civile di Rapallo (☎ 68 31) is at Rapallo in Piazza Molfino. For an ambulance call ☎ 28 70 19; for a night doctor (Guardia Medica) call ☎ 6 03 33.

Activities Santa Margherita is a sports playground, with the list headed by sailing, water-skiing and diving. Ask at the tourist office, the big hotels or on the waterfront – and have a fat wallet handy.

Places to Stay & Eat A central and relatively cheap place to sleep is *Albergo Annabella* (☎ 28 65 31), Via Costasecca 10 (just off Piazza Mazzini), where rooms start at L45,000/65,000. Handily placed between the water and the train station is *Albergo Azalea* (☎ 28 81 60), Via Roma 60. Singles/doubles start at L50,000/70,000.

At *Trattoria San Siro*, Corso Matteotti 137 (15 minutes from the seashore), a full meal will cost around L25,000. Try the pansoti. *Trattoria da Pino*, Via Jacopo Ruffini, is quite cheap, while at *Ristorante da Alfredo*, Piazza Martiri della Libertà 38, near the water, pizzas start at L7000. It's one of several similar places on the esplanade. *Simonetti*, Via Bottaro 51, has good gelati.

Getting There & Away Santa Margherita is on the Genova-La Spezia train line. By car,

The A12 passes Rapallo before cutting inland towards Santa Margherita. Viale E Rainusso, which runs off Piazza Vittorio Veneto, joins the Via Aurelia (SS1), the secondary road to Genova, which is the best bet for hitchhikers. Buses leave Piazza Martiri della Libertà for Portofino.

In summer, the Servizio Marittimo del Tigullio (☎ 28 46 70) operates ferries from near the bus stop to Portofino (L9000 return). Other ferries service San Fruttuoso (L17,000 return) and the Cinque Terre (L30,000 return). Some services begin in spring and run into October, but dry up in winter.

You can hire bicycles and motor scooters at Agrifogli, Piazza Martiri della Libertà 40, or from a place opposite the IAT office.

Paraggi

Two km short of Portofino, there's little here but a couple of hotels and one of the area's few slivers of white, sandy beach.

Portofino

Dubbed by the Italian press the 'richest promontory in Italy', Portofino and its environs is home (or holiday home) to the mega-rich and powerful. Anyone who is anyone has a villa here, and a host of movers and shakers wheel, deal and play in Portofino. Entrepreneur and short-lived prime minister Silvio Berlusconi pays a fortune here for a villa he hardly ever visits (he prefers Sardegna, considered by many as rather brash).

For all this, a certain haughty disdain on the part of long-standing residents lends the town a healthy air of restraint, and the huddle of pastel-coloured houses around the modest portside piazza are a delight. In summer the piazza, fronted by unassuming but expensive cafés and boutiques, is awash with glitterati as film stars flock to the most 'happening' spot in all Liguria.

Information The IAT office (☎ 0185-26 90 24), Via Roma 35, just back from the port, is open daily from 9 am to midday and 3 to 6 pm. It can advise on water sports and accommodation, which is scarce and expensive.

The telephone code for Portofino is ☎ 0185.

Things to See & Do Near the **Chiesa di San Giorgio** a flight of stairs leads up to the 16th-century **castle** of the same name. Built over an existing fort by the Genovese, under some pressure from their Spanish allies, it occasionally saw action, particularly when occupied by Napoleon and taken by the English in 1814. It offers a great view, but for a still better outlook continue to the **lighthouse**, an hour's walk there and back.

Boats can be hired from Giorgio Mussini & C (☎ 26 93 27), Calata Marconi 39.

Places to Stay & Eat The 'cheapest' lodgings are at *Piccolo Hotel* (☎ 26 90 15), Via Duca degli Abruzzi 35 – singles/doubles cost L110,000/160,000 and upwards. The cover charge alone at most restaurants would equal some travellers' daily meal allowance, while a cup of coffee at a table will cost L5000 or more at the waterfront cafés. Don't despair. *Pizzeria El Portico*, Via Roma 21, has pizzas from L8000 and the *Panificio Canale*, at No 30, has decent pastries for about L3000 a slice.

Getting There & Away Portofino can be reached by bus from Santa Margherita, and in summer ferries criss-cross the gulf from most towns along the coast (see Santa Margherita above). Drivers must park at the entrance to the town (L6000 for the first hour) as cars are banned farther in.

San Fruttuoso

Accessible either by foot from Camogli or Portofino (an exhilarating cliffside walk that takes up to 2½ hours each way from either town), or by ferry (all year round from Camogli), San Fruttuoso is a fascinating village dominated by the **Abbazia di San Fruttuoso di Capodimonte**, a Benedictine abbey with medieval origins. Built as a resting place for bishop St Fructuosus, martyred in Spain in 259, the abbey was rebuilt in the mid-1200s with the assistance of the Doria family, who used it as a family crypt.

It fell into decay with the decline of the religious community, and in the 1800s was divided into small living quarters by local fishermen. The Dorias donated the abbey and hamlet to the Italian Environmental Protection Foundation in 1983 and it was renovated three years later at a cost of L3.5 billion. It's open daily from 10 am to 6 pm in summer but otherwise opening hours are irregular. It closes altogether in November and December and opens on weekends only in January and February. Admission is L5000.

Perhaps more fascinating is the bronze statue of Christ, *Il Cristo degli Abissi*, lowered 15m to the sea bed by locals in 1954 as a tribute to divers lost at sea and to bless the waters. You must dive to see it, but locals say if the waters are calm it can be viewed from a boat. A replica in a fish tank is on show in the church adjoining the abbey. A religious ceremony is held over the statue every August.

Rapallo

Rapallo is a major resort, but often overlooked for the more illustrious Santa Margherita and Portofino. A bigger place, it has an air of bustle independent of tourists that the other towns farther down the promontory lack – all the more so on Thursday, which is market day at Piazza Cile.

Rapallo has Roman origins and even boasts a bridge supposedly used by Hannibal during the Carthaginian invasion of Italy in 218 BC.

More recently, Rapallo enjoyed a brief period of international popularity in the treaty-signing business. In 1920, the Italo-Yugoslav Treaty that defined the borders of the two countries was signed here, and two years later the Russians and Germans sealed a peace deal that lasted all of 19 years.

Information The IAT office (☎ 0185-23 63 46) is through the town centre at Via Diaz 9 and is open daily from 8.30 am to 12.30 pm and 2.30 to 5.30 pm. The telephone code for Rapallo is ☎ 0185.

Things to See & Do A *funivia* (follow the signs from Corso Assereto) goes to **Montallegro**, a sanctuary built on the spot where the Virgin Mary reportedly appeared on 2 July 1557. A circuitous 10km road also leads to the site. Just off the Lungomare Vittoria Veneto lies a 16th-century **castle**.

You can join up for PADI dive courses with Marco Maglia (☎ 26 04 98) or just call for advice on dive sites. Are submarines your thing? The Tritone 2 does underwater jaunts in summer. Get in touch with Portofino Coast (☎ 23 01 85), Via Lamarmora 17/6, but don't expect budget rates.

Places to Stay & Eat For the camping grounds in the hills near Rapallo take the Savagna bus from the train station. *Miraflores* (☎ 26 30 00), Via Savagna 12, is open from April to October, and *Rapallo* (☎ 26 20 18), Via San Lazzaro 4, is open only in summer. The cheap-end pick of the many hotels in Rapallo is *Bandoni* (☎ 5 04 23), Via Marsala 24, situated right on the waterfront with singles/doubles from L35,000/65,000. *Albergo Centro* (☎ 23 10 58), Vico Piazza Venezia 1, is simple but fine, with rooms costing L35,000/60,000 with private bath.

Vesuvio, Lungomare Vittorio Veneto 29, has pizzas from L8000, while *Da Monique*, at No 5 on the same street, has a set seafood meal for L35,000. A slightly more intimate atmosphere makes the *Hostaria Vecchia Rapallo*, Via Fratelli Cairoli 24, a block farther back from the water, a pleasant alternative. A main will cost about L25,000.

Getting There & Away Regular buses connect Rapallo with Santa Margherita (every 20 minutes; L1400) and Camogli. The trip in both directions is more pleasant than by train. In summer, ferries connect Rapallo to other towns on the coast. See the Santa Margherita section earlier.

Chiavari to Levanto

The stretch of coast between the Portofino promontory and the Cinque Terre can come as a bit of a letdown, wedged as it is between two such beauty spots. It does have some of he Riviera di Levante's best beaches, but the esorts of Sestri Levante, Deiva and Levanto et predictably crowded in summer.

Cinque Terre

f you miss the five villages of the mountainide Cinque Terre – Monterosso, Vernazza, Corniglia, Manarola and Riomaggiore – you will have bypassed some of Italy's most extraordinary country. But blink as the train tips between tunnels and miss them you will.

The mountains, covered wherever possible by terraced vineyards (the locals have set up ingenious monorail mechanisms to ferry themselves up and the grapes back down), drop precipitately into the Mediterranean. They leave little room for the tiny fishing villages that clutter the coves, are tucked into ravines or perched on top of sharp ridges. Fishing and viniculture have been the two main sources of income over the centuries, but tourism now plays a pivotal role too – the position of the villages has hopefully saved them from the thoughtless resort development that blights much of the Ligurian coast. Oddly, the area is popular more with foreign than Italian tourists, for whom it is still largely 'undiscovered'.

Ask at the IAT office in La Spezia and you may well be told all accommodation has been booked out in the Cinque Terre, but plenty of people rent out rooms on a more or less official basis – if you miss the telltale signs, 'camere' and 'affittacamere', ask around in the bars. Prices are not low but neither are they extortionate. Food is not cheap either, and often mediocre. Try to lay your hands on some local vintages, such as the nationally renowned white and dessert wines, Morasca, Chiaretto del Faro and the heavenly, sweet Sciacchetrà.

You can drive to all five villages, but cars are not permitted beyond the entrance to each town. Note that some of the road between Vernazzo and Monterosso is in very poor condition – mules are much better transport. Occasional buses go close to the towns, but the local La Spezia-Genova trains are regular and by far the most convenient way to get to and around the Cinque Terre.

Better than trains, buses or cars for those with the time is a scenic path reopened in late 1994 and connecting all the villages. There are a few slightly strenuous sections, but the dramatic views of the towns and coast more than compensate for any sweating you might do.

The Cinque Terre shares the same phone code as La Spezia – ☎ 0187.

Monterosso Huge statues carved into the rocks overlook one of the few beaches in the Cinque Terre – a grey, pebbly affair. Monterosso gets its name from the unusual red colouring of the nearby cliff faces, but it is the least attractive of the villages. It's expensive too. *Albergo Punta Mesco* (☎ 81 74 95), Via Molinelli 35 (just past the rail bridge), a few minutes walk from the beach, has singles/doubles for L60,000/98,000 in the high season. The beachside hotels start at about L100,000 a single with breakfast in the high season.

Vernazza Possibly the most fetching of the villages, Vernazza makes the most of the sea, with a promenade and piazza on the water. The road winding away from the centre is choked with tiny vineyards and patches of lemon grove. Head for the **Castello Doria**, which has sweeping views from the tower of the town and surrounding coast.

Del Capitano (☎ 81 22 01), Piazza G Marconi 21 (ask at the bar), has singles/doubles in the high season for L50,000/70,000. *Da Sandro* (☎ 81 22 23), Via Roma 62, is much the same. *Pensione Sorriso* (☎ 81 22 24), Via Gavino 4, offers rooms with breakfast for L70,000/90,000. All have restaurants. For waterside views you could try the immodestly priced restaurant and bar in the Belforte, a tower which stands watch over the sea. The train station is in the middle of town.

Corniglia Balanced precariously along a ridge high above the sea, Corniglia is quite an uphill hike from the train station. Fourstorey houses, narrow lanes and stairways are woven together on the hill, and topped by

La Torre, a medieval lookout from which you can look south-east to Manarola.

On the path to Manarola, behind the train station, is the *Villaggio Marino Europa* (☎ 81 22 79), a row of self-contained bungalows sleeping up to six people. Open from June to the end of September, they can be rented for a minimum of three days and are cheaper in June and September. Local wine grower Domenico Spora (☎ 81 22 93) is just one of several people offering rooms – a quick walk around town will throw up several options. The Spora rooms start at L35,000 per person. *A Cantina de Mananan*, Via Carruggio 117, is a cosy little osteria where pasta starts at L10,000 and seafood at L13,000.

Manarola Perhaps lacking some of the atmosphere of Corniglia and Vernazza, Manarola is nonetheless a captivating village. If you're game for a good uphill hike, take the path off Via Rollandi, near Piazza Castello, through vineyards to the top of the mountain. On a clear day you can see all the villages. The affittacamere run by Gianni Capellini (☎ 73 67 65), Via Discovolo 6, near the church, has big, modern rooms with views for L60,000 a double. He also has an apartment with a kitchen and terrace overlooking the town for L60,000 a day. There are several small restaurants by the water.

Riomaggiore The Via dell'Amore (Lovers' Lane) straggles along the cliffside from Manarola to Riomaggiore – a mess of houses slithering down a ravine that forms the main street, with tiny fishing boats lining the shore and stacked in the small square. The older part of town is a few minutes walk south of the train station, through a long tunnel.

Up on the hillside is *Soggiorno Alle Cinque Terre* (☎ 92 05 87), Via de Gasperi 1. In the high season, singles/doubles go for L50,000/70,000. The owners have other rooms in the town and an office on Via Colombo (you can't miss the 'camere/Zimmer/rooms' sign). Signora Anna Michielini (☎ 92 04 11) rents rooms at Via Colombo 143, and has apartments, each with a kitchen and bathroom, for L35,000 per person. A stroll down this street will reveal several similar deals. Most restaurants are along Via Colombo, which runs from the waterfront through the centre of the village. Try *Veciu Muin*, Via Colombo 83, for a good pizza. Or try *La Lanterna*, where a meal overlooking the cove will cost about L35,000 a head.

La Spezia

La Spezia sits at the head of the gulf of the same name – also known as the Gulf of Poets in deference to Byron, Dante, DH Lawrence, Shelley, George Sand and others who were drawn here by its beauty. A decision late last century to establish Italy's largest naval base in La Spezia propelled it from minor port to busy provincial capital; the street grid and venerable public buildings are largely a product of that time. It's still a navy town, with the ubiquitous blue sailor's uniform a constant reminder.

Orientation The city is sandwiched between the naval base to the west and the commercial port to the east. The main street and scene for the ritual passeggiata is the narrow Via Prione, running from the train station to the palm-lined Viale Italia on the waterfront.

Information The IAT office (☎ 0187-77 09 00), Viale G Mazzini 45, is open Monday to Saturday from 9.30 am to 12.30 pm and 3.30 to 6.30 pm. There is another office (☎ 0187-71 89 97) at the train station. It is closed on Sunday afternoons and, oddly, Monday.

Several banks have offices in the centre and most are open from 8 am to 1 pm and 2.30 to 4 pm. Quite a few have ATMs that take Visa and MasterCard.

The post office in Piazza Giuseppe Verdi is open Monday to Saturday from 8.15 am to 7.40 pm. La Spezia's postcode is 19100. An unstaffed Telecom office at Via da Passano 50 is open daily from 7 am to 11 pm. You'll find a similar office at the train station. The telephone code for La Spezia and much of the surrounding province is ☎ 0187.

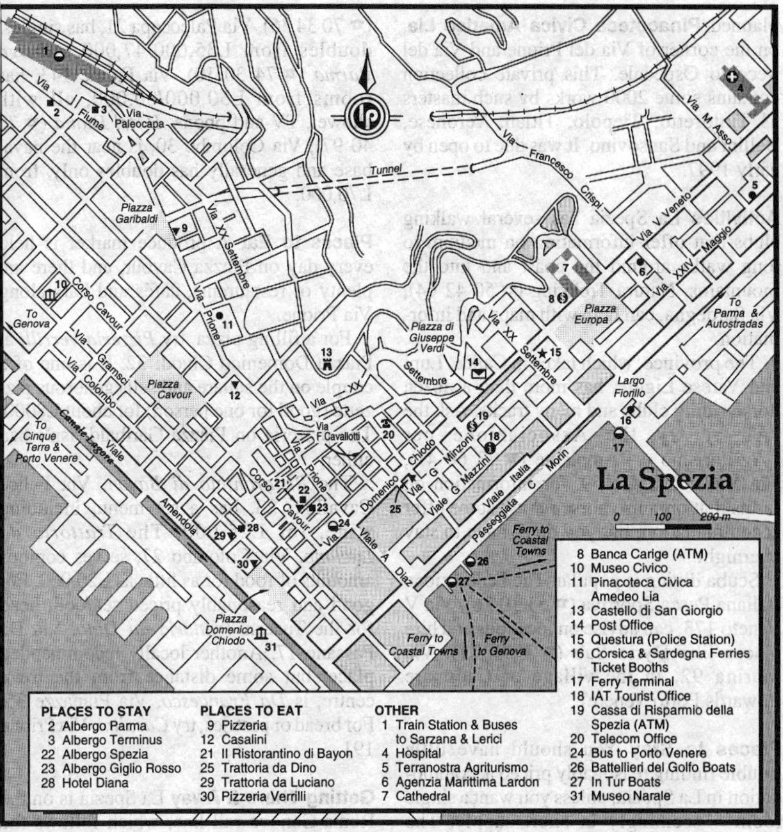

There's an Onda Blu laundry at Via dei Mille 21.

For emergency police attendance, call ☎ 113. The questura (☎ 77 24 11) is at Via XX Settembre 4. For an ambulance, call ☎ 70 21 21, or for out of hours medical help call ☎ 73 05 00.

Things to See The city's **Museo Navale**, Piazza Domenico Chiodo, is open Monday to Saturday from 2 to 6 pm; Monday, Tuesday, Wednesday and Saturday from 9 am to noon; and Sunday from 8.30 am to 1.15 pm. Admission is L2000. Founded in 1870, following the transfer of the Genovese maritime museum to La Spezia, it hosts a phalanx of *polene*, the colourful busts or statuettes that graced the prows of vessels, and loads of model ships. The adjoining naval base is open to the public one day a year, 19 March, also the festival of the town's patron saint, San Giuseppe.

The most interesting part of the **Museo Civico**, Via Curtatone 9, off Corso Cavour, is the archaeology department, containing a hotchpotch of Bronze and Iron Age objects and squat, ancient Ligurian *statue-stelae*.

If it opens, the star museum will be the

planned **Pinacoteca Civica Amedeo Lia**, on the corner of Via del Prione and Via del Vecchio Ospedale. This private collection contains some 2000 works by such masters as Tintoretto, Tiepolo, Titian, Veronese, Bellini and Sansovino. It was due to open by early 1997.

Activities La Spezia has several walking clubs that offer information on medium to long walks around the coast and into the mountains. Natura Trekking (☎ 50 42 64), Via Sardegna, can help with maps and information.

The province, which takes in Calice, Luni and Varese Ligure, has more than a dozen horse-riding clubs and many tracks. Ask the IAT or try the Associazione per l'Agriturismo e l'Ambiente (☎ 73 60 41), Via XXIV Maggio 69, for information on farms that organise horse riding; some offer accommodation, but you don't have to stay overnight.

Scuba diving is popular. The Federazione Italiana Pesca Sportiva (☎ 51 10 26), Via V Veneto 173, can advise on locations and hire places like Dyria Sub (☎ 2 91 71), Via Marina 92, in the village of Cadimare (towards Porto Venere).

Places to Stay You should have little trouble finding reasonably priced accommodation in La Spezia, unless you want a single room – seemingly in short supply. The town's proximity to the Cinque Terre, Porto Venere and Lerici makes it a perfect base, especially as the limited accommodation in the surrounding area often fills up. There is no camping ground in La Spezia, but plenty in the surrounding towns. You might also ask at the IAT office about agriturismo options.

Albergo Giglio Rosso (☎ 73 13 74), Via Carpenino 31, has perfectly adequate, if slightly dingy, singles/doubles for L32,000/42,000 – most likely you'll be told there are no singles. *Albergo Spezia* (☎ 73 51 64), Via Felice Cavallotti 31, is a block away and has singles/doubles from L38,000/49,000 – same problem here with snaring a single. Opposite the train station, *Albergo Terminus* (☎ 70 34 36), Via Paleocapa 21, has singles/doubles from L35,000/47,000. *Albergo Parma* (☎ 74 30 10), Via Fiume 143, has rooms from L50,000/80,000, all with shower, TV and phone. *Hotel Diana* (☎ 73 40 97), Via Colombo 30, is near the naval base and generally has doubles only, from L70,000.

Places to Eat A produce market is held every day on Piazza Cavour, and there are plenty of restaurants, cafés and bars along Via Prione.

For a filling pizza, try *Pizzeria Verrilli* at Piazza Domenico Chiodi 32. It is one of a couple on the square and sells generous pizzette (good for one person) for about L8000. The pizzeria on Piazza Garibaldi isn't bad either.

The *Ristorantino di Bayon*, Via Felice Cavallotti 23, has a set menu, including wine, for L25,000. The *Trattoria da Luciano*, Via Colombo 27, serves copious amounts of food for as little as L20,000. For good and reasonably priced seafood, head for the Tuscan *Trattoria da Dino*, Via Da Passano 17. Another locally recommended place, but some distance from the town centre, is *Da Francesco*, Via Pianazze 35. For bread or pastries, try *Casalini*, Via Prione 191.

Getting There & Away La Spezia is on the Roma-Genova rail line, which follows the coast, and is also connected to Milano, Torino and Pisa. The Cinque Terre and other coastal towns are easily reached by train, but other towns close to La Spezia can only be reached by ATC buses (☎ 52 25 22). These include Porto Venere (from Via Domenico Chiodi), Sarzana and Lerici (both from the train station). Buy your tickets from tobacconists.

Cyclists might like to know that most trains passing through the Apenninni to Parma have bicycle storage.

The A12 runs past La Spezia to Genova and Livorno, and the A15 to Parma also connects with the main north-south route, the A1. Hitchhikers can catch the Lerici bus and get off at Via Valdilocchi in the port area, a main access to the A12 and A15. The SS1 passes through the city and connects with the SS62 for Parma and the north.

Ferries leave La Spezia for coastal towns and Genova during the summer months, and occasionally on pleasant weekends through the rest of the year. Navigazione Golfo dei Poeti (☎ 96 76 76; office in Lerici), Gruppo Battellieri del Golfo (☎ 2 10 10) at Banchina Revel off Passeggiata C Morin, In Tur (☎ 73 29 87) at Viale Mazzini 21, and Baracco (☎ 96 69 55) at Via San Bernardino 1, all offer services.

From April to October, Corsica Ferries (☎ 77 80 97), Largo Fiorillo, runs the occasional ferry to Bastia in Corsica. Tirrenia Navigazione runs fast summer services to Sardegna. Contact Agenzia Marittima Lardon (☎ 55 11 11) at Via S Bartolomeo 93.

Porto Venere

It is worth catching the bus from La Spezia for the razor-clam soup Porto Venere has contributed to Ligurian fare. Roma founded Portus Veneris on the western shore of the Golfo di La Spezia as a base on the route from Gaul to Spain. From the brightly coloured houses along the waterfront, narrow staircases and cobbled paths lead up the hillside towards the **Chiesa di San Lorenzo**, erected in the 12th century and subsequently altered. It lies in the shadow of **Castello Doria**, built in the 16th century on the site as part of the Genovese Republic's defence system. The views from its magnificent terraced gardens are superb.

At the end of the waterfront quay is the 13th century **Chiesa di San Pietro**, built in the Genovese Gothic style with black and white bands of marble, and the **Grotta Arpaia**, once a haunt of Byron, with views towards the Cinque Terre. A plaque celebrates the poet's exploits as a swimmer – he once made a dash from Porto Venere to Lerici.

Just off the promontory lie three tiny islands, Palmaria, Tino and Tinetto. Navigazione Golfo dei Poeti runs trips around the islands for L12,000 in summer, and you can hire local boats from the waterfront (haggling advised) to take you to Palmaria and the grottoes along its western shore.

Fishing is supposedly Porto Venere's mainstay (a likely story). You can buy all the tackle and gear you want at Lucky Nautica Sport (☎ 79 21 98), Calata Doria 38. It hires out kayaks (L7000 an hour) and boats (L25,000 an hour).

Places to Stay & Eat Only 12km south of La Spezia, Porto Venere is a straightforward day trip – a good thing as neither accommodation nor food is cheap. If you do want to stay, *Albergo Il Genio* (☎ 79 06 11), in a former castle at the start of the waterfront, has singles/doubles from L95,000/110,000.

Ristorante Miramare and *Taverna di Venere* are among the half-dozen or so restaurants along Calata Doria, by the sea. The former has a good seafood set meal for L30,000 including wine; the latter a less impressive set menu for L25,000. Or try *Bar al Naviglio*, Via Olive 73, away from the quay and a relatively cheap place for lunch. *Pizzaccia*, in Via Cappellini 94, the street leading from Albergo Il Genio to San Pietro, has takeaway pizza slices from L2000.

Lerici

At the southern end of the Riviera di Levante, 10km from La Spezia, Lerici is an exclusive summer refuge for wealthy Italians, a town of villas with manicured gardens set into the surrounding hills and equally well-kept bathing boxes built into the cliffs along the beach. Make your way up to the 12th century **Castello Lerici** for outstanding views of the town and the occasional art exhibition.

If you plan to stay in the area, jump off the bus at **San Terenzo**, a pleasant village (also dominated by a Genovese castle) half an hour's walk from Lerici. In 1822, Percy Bysshe Shelley set sail from here for Livorno (Leghorn), a fateful voyage that cost him his life on the return trip when his boat sank off the coast near Viareggio.

A pleasant 4km walk or bus ride from

Lerici along the Fiascherino road takes you past some magnificent little bays towards Tellaro. The area was a haunt of DH Lawrence in the year before the outbreak of WWI. When you reach a huge illuminated sign reading 'Eco del Mare', make for the nearby *spiaggia libera*, the euphemism for a public beach – most others in the area are private.

Tellaro is a quiet fishing hamlet with pink and orange houses cluttered about narrow lanes and tiny squares. Weave your way to the Chiesa di San Giorgio, sit on the rocks and watch the world go by.

You can hire canoes and kayaks at Via Arpaia 8, quayside in Lerici, or call Gianni on ☎ 96 62 09.

Places to Stay & Eat Three camping grounds are based in the hills around Lerici. The *Gianna* (☎ 96 64 11), Via Fiascherino (just short of the village), is open from Easter to the end of September. *Maralunga* (☎ 96 65 89), at Via Carpanini 61, on the road from Lerici to Tellaro, and *Senato Park* (☎ 98 83 96), Via Senato 1, both open on 1 June and close at the end of September. The camping grounds can be reached by bus from Piazza PG Garibaldi in Lerici.

Hotels include *Albergo delle Ondine* (☎ 96 51 31), Via Fiascherino 1, in a good spot at the top of Tellaro. Singles/doubles are L40,000/70,000, or L85,000 for doubles with private bathroom. Outside Tellaro at Via Fiascherino 57 is the affittacamere *Armando Sarbia* (☎ 96 50 49), with doubles for L50,000, or L40,000 if you stay for several days. In San Terenzo, the *Pensione Pino* (☎ 97 05 95), Via Garibaldi 12, has singles/doubles from L30,000/65,000, or L60,000/80,000 with bath.

There are a few pleasant trattorias in San Terenzo. Try *La Palmira*, Via Angelo Trogu, where you can dine well for about L30,000. *Fuoco e Fiamme*, Piazza Brusacà, has pizzas from L9000.

Val di Magra

South-east of La Spezia, the Val di Magra forms the easternmost tongue of Ligurian territory before you reach Toscana. **Sarzana**, a short bus ride from La Spezia, was once an important outpost of the Genovese republic. In the cathedral you can see the world's oldest crucifix, painted on wood. In the chapel is a phial said to have contained the blood of Christ. Nearby, the fortress of Sarzanello (also known as Castruccio Castracani) offers magnificent views. A pretty detour is to the hillside hamlet of **Castelnuovo Magra**, with a medieval castle.

Diehard fans of all things Roman may be interested in **Luni**, about 6km south-east of Sarzana (1km off the SS1 towards the coast; it's not well signposted). Established as a Roman colony in 177 BC on the site of an Etruscan village, it thrived until the 13th century. Excavations have revealed the amphitheatre, forum, temple and other remnants of a classic Roman town, but the ruins are not in top condition. The site and a small museum are open daily from 9 am to 7 pm. Admission is L4000.

RIVIERA DI PONENTE

Stretching west from Genova to France, this part of the Ligurian coast is more heavily developed than the eastern side and attracts package tour groups from northern Europe and Italian summer holiday-makers en masse. However, some of the resorts are not bad at all; several of Genova's historical maritime rivals retain the architectural trappings of a more glorious past, and the mountains, hiding a warren of hilltop villages, promise cool air and pretty walking and driving circuits.

Savona

From west or east, it is the sprawl of the port's facilities that first strikes you when approaching Savona, although with a population of only 70,000, it doesn't match the chaos of its longtime rival, Genova. The two cities have been opponents since the Punic Wars, and the Genovese destroyed the town in 1528, proving their dominance. Now a provincial capital and bishopric, Savona suffered heavy bombing raids during WWII.

The small medieval centre, dominated by the Baroque **Cattedrale di Nostra Signora Assunta**, still survives.

Orientation The train station is in a newer part of town, south-east of the Letimbro river. Via Collodi, to the right of the train station as you walk out, and Via Don Minzoni, to the left, both lead across the river towards the leafy Piazza del Popolo (which serves as a drug-addicts' hang-out). From here, Via Paleocapa, Savona's elegant main boulevard, runs to the waterfront.

Information The APT office (☎ 019-82 05 22), Via Paleocapa 23, is open Monday to Saturday from 9 am to 12.30 pm and 3 to 6 pm. The telephone code for Savona is ☎ 019 and you'll find telephones on Piazza Mameli.

Places to Stay & Eat Savona has two youth hostels. The first is in the *Fortezza Priamar* (☎ 81 26 53), Corso Mazzini, on the waterfront, and charges L19,000 for B&B (open all year). Take bus No 2 from the train station. The other, *Villa de' Franceschini* (☎ 26 32 22), Via alla Strà 29, Conca Verde, charges L15,000 for B&B; telephone on arrival in Savona for its private bus. It opens from 15 March to 30 September.

Otherwise, things are grim for the small spender. *Albergo Ghione* (☎ 82 18 20), Piazza del Popolo 51/r, has a few singles/doubles going as 'cheaply' as L50,000/80,000. If you have no joy here, try *Albergo Riviera Suisse* (☎ 85 08 53), Via Paleocapa 24, where rooms out of season can start as low as L45,000/65,000.

A smattering of restaurants, trattorias and cafés can be found along Via Paleocapa and in the city centre. *Ristorante da Nicola*, Via XX Settembre 43, offers local specialities, with pasta from L8000 – it's also the town's oldest pizzeria.

Getting There & Away Apart from the trains, SAR and ACTS buses leave from Piazza del Popolo and the train station.

Apenninni Savonesi

About a 40-minute bus ride from Savona, **Sassello** is a tranquil mountain resort close to the regional boundary with Piemonte. A pleasant circuit from Savona to Genova, if you have your own transport, takes you along winding mountain roads to Sassello and past several towns, including Rossiglione, just inside Piemonte. Sassello's modest monuments include the Bastia Soprano, a Doria family castle. **Acqui Terme**, 32km farther north-east in Piemonte, is an ancient spa built around the ruins of a Roman water system. Enjoy a bath in the natural hot spring.

Noli

For 600 years an independent republic, the seaside town of Noli has little of the Riviera di Ponente's made-to-measure resort atmosphere. Dominated by the ruined walls of the medieval republic, which run up a hill behind the old town and peak in a fort designed to watch for invaders from North Africa, the town sells itself as the original home of a Ligurian culinary singularity: *trofie* (tiny pasta shreds made from potato flour and eaten with pesto sauce). The claim is disputed by Recco, a town east of Genova. Fishing remains one of Noli's mainstays, and the waterfront is often converted into an impromptu seafood market.

The APT office (☎ 019-74 89 31) is at Corso Italia 8, on the waterfront.

Again, cheap accommodation is in short supply here, although outside summer you can often bargain down. *Villa Salvarezza* (☎ 019-74 89 98), Via Vescovado 7, has simple singles/doubles from L35,000/55,000. Otherwise, about the lowest rates seem to hover around L50,000/75,000. At this level try *Albergo Rino* (☎ 74 80 59), Via Cavalieri di Malta 3.

For meals, try *Ristorante Ferrari*, Via Colombo 88. Great gelati are to be had at *Pappus*, Piazza Manin 12.

Buses run from Finale Ligure and Savona. For even better beaches, stop off in **Varigotti**, just past Noli on the way south to Finale Ligure.

LIGURIA

Finale Ligure

With a good beach and affordable accommodation, Finale Ligure is worth considering as a base for the Riviera di Ponente. If climbing rocks is your idea of fun, pack your ropes and head for the hinterland, where several areas offer good free climbing, and well-organised clubs produce maps of the best climbs.

Finale Ligure is divided into three areas. Finalborgo, away from the coast on the Pora river, is the original centre of the region. A clutter of twisting alleys behind medieval walls, it is the most interesting part of the Finale triad. Also atmospheric is the waterfront Finale Marina area, where most accommodation and restaurants can be found. Finale Pia, towards Genova, runs along the Sciusa river and is rather suburban. The train station is at Piazza Vittorio Veneto, at the western end of Finale Marina. Walk straight down Via Saccone for the sea.

Information The APT office (☎ 019-69 25 81), opposite the beach at Via San Pietro 14, is open Monday to Saturday from 8.30 am to 1 pm and 3.30 to 6.30 pm. The telephone code for Finale Ligure is ☎ 019.

Activities Rock-climbing in the area immediately inland is popular. Rockstore in Via Nicotera, Finalborgo, hires out climbing gear and gives free advice. Another good place to seek information and meet other climbers is the nearby Caffè Centrale.

Places to Stay & Eat There are two camping grounds open all year: *La Foresta* (☎ 69 81 03) and *San Martino* (☎ 69 82 50), both in the same area about 7km north-east of town. ACTS buses run past from the centre. There's a *youth hostel* (☎ 69 05 15) at Via Caviglia 46. It costs L18,000 a night, including breakfast.

The APT can sometimes advise on private rooms or mini-apartments in private houses.

The town boasts 130 hotels, quite a few offering rooms at about L35,000/50,000. *Marita* (☎ 69 29 04), Via Saccone 17, is close to the train station and starts at L35,000/65,000 for singles/doubles.

Pizzeria Le Petit, Via San Pietro 3, ha specials galore and pizzas starting at L6000 *Trattoria la Tavernetta*, Via Colombo 37 does great trofie al pesto.

Getting There & Away SAR buses along th coast leave from opposite the train station.

Getting Around Regular local buses link Finale Marina to Finalborgo. You can hire bicycles for L4000 an hour or L16,000 a day at Oddone (☎ 69 42 15), Via Colombo 22. I also has mountain bikes.

Albenga

Albenga's medieval centre sets it apart from many of the resorts farther west. Settled as far back as the 5th century BC, Albenga grew from its Roman roots to become an independent maritime republic in the Middle Ages despite being destroyed several times by barbarian invaders. In the 13th century it threw in its lot with Genova.

The Pro Loco tourist office (☎ 0182-55 9C 58) is in Via Ricci, and is open Monday to Saturday from 9 am to noon and 3 to 6.30 pm. The telephone code is ☎ 0182.

Things to See Albenga's **Museo Diocesano**, featuring a painting by Caravaggio, is near the 5th century **baptistry** and Romanesque **cathedral**. The baptistry is somewhat unusual, if only because the 10 sided exterior breaks with the usual octagonal shape that characterises its counterparts throughout northern Italy. The **Museo Navale Romano**, Piazza San Michele, has a collection of 1st-century amphoras, or wine urns, recovered in 1950 from the wreck of a Roman cargo vessel 4km offshore. It is one of the world's oldest discovered shipwrecks.

Places to Stay & Eat There are some 20 camping grounds in the area around Albenga. The *Florida* (☎ 5 06 37) and *Delfino* (☎ 5 19 98), both on Via Aurelia (SS1), are reasonably close to the train station.

Albergo Italia (☎ 5 04 05), Viale Martiri della Libertà 8, is in a handy location. Rooms with breakfast cost L45,000/70,000. *Da Romano* (☎ 5 04 08), Piazza Corridoni 2, has doubles only for L55,000, or L65,000 with a bathroom – they are OK but not special.

Trattoria la Bifora, Via delle Medaglie d'Oro 20, is in the historic heart of town and has pizzas starting at L6000. *Ristorante La Rocca*, Via Roma 72, does great things with swordfish and other seafood. If you don't want fish, try any of their pasta, with sauce 'alla Rocca'.

Getting There & Away Albenga is served by trains and SAR buses (main stop on Piazza del Popolo) along the coast.

Alassio

As well as 3km of white beaches, Alassio boasts its own version of Baci, a delicious chocolate concoction that falls somewhere between a truffle and a biscuit. Not as well known as Perugia's version, Alassio's contribution is still money well spent – head for *Caffè Talmone*, Via Mazzini 107. One of the more pleasant beach resorts on this mountainous stretch of the Ligurian coast, there is no shortage of hotels should you decide to stay.

The IAT office (☎ 0182-64 03 46) is at Via Gibb 26, and a prominently placed billboard outside the train station lists accommodation and other information. The SAR Autolinee bus information office (☎ 64 05 96) at Piazza della Libertà can organise excursions around the Isola Gallinara nature reserve (you can't step onto the island), as well as day trips inland to Monte Carlo and other destinations. The telephone code is ☎ 0182.

Cervo

Past Capo Cervo on the way south-west to Imperia, this small fishing village, dominated by the ring of walls and towers around the medieval centre, makes for a pretty stop.

Imperia

Dominated by lines of hothouses on the surrounding hillside, Imperia is the main city of the westernmost province of Liguria, commonly known as the Riviera dei Fiori because of the area's flower-growing industry – said to be among the most extensive in Europe. Imperia was founded in 1923 by Mussolini when he bridged the Impero river and unified the towns of Porto Maurizio (to the west) and Oneglia (to the east), although they retain the air of separate towns.

Trains stop at Oneglia and Porto Maurizio stations, but the latter is the handiest. From the train station, head up the hill to Viale Matteotti, or through an underpass to the waterfront, which eventually leads to Corso Garibaldi. Buses connect both train stations, and bus No 3 runs through Porto Maurizio.

Information The APT office (☎ 0183-29 49 47) is at Viale G Matteotti 54a. A post and Telecom office is at Via San Maurizio 13 and 15. Imperia's telephone code is ☎ 0183.

Things to See Porto Maurizio, the older of the two towns, is dominated by the **Cattedrale di San Maurizio**, a large neoclassical cathedral in Piazza del Duomo at the highest point on the hill. Across the square, the small **Museo Navale Internazionale del Ponente Liguria** is open only for a couple of hours on Wednesday and Saturday evenings.

Places to Stay & Eat The camping grounds, *Eucalyptus* (☎ 6 15 34) and *La Pineta* (☎ 6 14 98), are just off the coast road (SS1) and can be reached by buses No 2 or 3 from both train stations. There are several others in the area.

The *Pensione Paola*, Via Rambaldo 30 (☎ 6 29 96), has simple singles/doubles from L22,000/44,000, while the nearby *Pensione Ambra* (☎ 6 37 15), at No 9, charges L35,000/56,000. They will probably insist on half or even full board.

Pizzamania, Via XX Settembre 39, has pizza by the slice and is good for lunch. There are several restaurants and cafés along the esplanade, Via Scarincio. The poshest is the *Lanterna Blù* at No 32, with set menus starting at L45,000.

Getting There & Away Apart from the trains, buses for the coast stop virtually in front of the tourist office. Tickets are sold in the café next door.

San Remo

San Remo gained prominence as a resort for Europe's social elite, especially British and Russian, in the mid-to-late 1800s when the likes of Empress Maria Alexandrovna (mother of Nicholas II, the last tsar) held court here. Today, while a few hotels thrive as luxury resorts, many from that period are long past their prime and are cut off from the beach by the railway line.

Orientation The old centre, La Pigna, is just north of Corso Matteotti, San Remo's main strip, where the wealthy take their evening stroll. Farther east, past Piazza Colombo and Corso Giuseppe Garibaldi, is the seedier area. Corso Matteotti meets San Remo's other famous strip, Corso Imperatrice, at Piazzale Battisti near the train station.

Information The APT office (☎ 0184-57 15 71) is at Largo Nuvoloni 1, just near the corner of Corso Imperatrice. It's open Monday to Saturday from 8 am to 7 pm and Sunday from 9 am to 1 pm. There are plenty of banks around, especially along Via Roma.

The main post office is at Via Roma 156 and is open Monday to Saturday from 8.15 am to 7.40 pm. The postcode for central San Remo is 18038. Public telephones are located at the train station, and if you want the latest telephone books for most of the country go to the tourist office. San Remo's telephone code is ☎ 0184.

In an emergency, ring the police on ☎ 113. The questura (☎ 50 77 77) is at Via del Castillo 5. For medical assistance, head for the Ospedale Generale (☎ 53 61), Via Giovanni Borea 56.

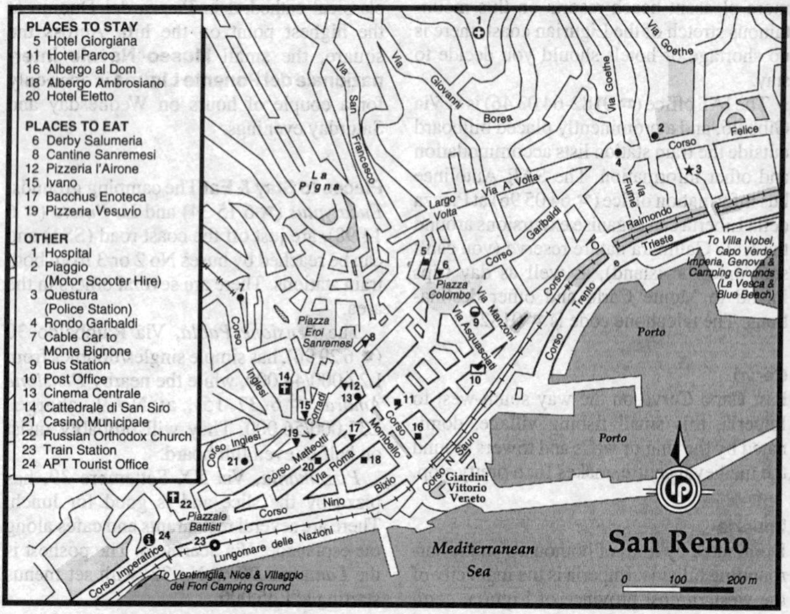

hings to See The **Russian Orthodox hurch** in Piazza Nuvoloni was built for the ussian community who followed Tsarina lexandrovna to San Remo. The church, ith its onion-shaped domes, was designed 1906 by Josef Choussef, who 20 years ater planned Lenin's mausoleum in loscow. It is open daily from 7 am to 12.30 m and 3.30 to 7 pm.

Italy's principal **flower market** is held in orso Garibaldi from June to October, daily rom 6 to 8 am. Go along and watch the renetic bidding.

Monte Bignone is a short drive from the entre, or a cable-car ride (if it's working) rom Corso degli Inglesi, and offers views ver San Remo and as far as Cannes.

The **Villa Nobel**, where the Swedish nventor of dynamite and originator of the Nobel prizes, Alfred Nobel, lived and died, s at Corso Cavalotti 112, but is closed for estoration.

ctivities Water-sport enthusiasts can hire vindsurfing gear at Morgana (☎ 50 36 47), Corso Salvo d'Acquisto.

pecial Events In February, budding and stablished talents congregate for the Festival della Canzone Italiana. It is *the* music event, and although much of the music is depressingly middle-of-the-road, more than a few local success stories have emerged from the festival.

Places to Stay There are many hotels in San Remo, and with luck you may strike a reasonable deal. The tourist office has a full list, but don't take too much notice of the prices. Summer is difficult, and some places shut for holidays in September.

There are three camping grounds worth considering: *Blue Beach* (☎ 51 32 00), Via al Mare 183, 5km east of town near the small town of Bussana; *La Vesca* (☎ 51 37 75), Corso Mazzini 80, a little closer to town; and *Villaggio dei Fiori* (☎ 66 06 35), 2km west at Via Tiro a Volo 3. All can be reached by bus from the train station.

The *Albergo al Dom* (☎ 50 14 60), Corso Mombello 13, is a homely place with singles/doubles in the low season starting at L35,000/65,000. The doubles have shower and toilet. Not far off, the *Albergo Ambrosiano* (☎ 57 71 89), Via Roma 36, has OK doubles ranging from L50,000 to L80,000. *Hotel Parco* (☎ 50 96 40), Via Roma 93, has decent if unspectacular rooms for L35,000/50,000.

Closer to Piazza Colombo, the *Hotel Giorgiana* (☎ 50 69 30), in a big block at Via San Francesco 37, has rooms for about L35,000/60,000.

For something a little more upmarket, *Hotel Eletto* (☎ 50 04 08; fax 50 68 58), Corso Matteotti 44, has a whole range of rooms, the best of which come in at L90,000/120,000.

Places to Eat Try the local cuisine at *Cantine Sanremesi*, Via Palazzo 7. It is an old tavern and about the only place with its kind of time-worn character in San Remo. Many cheaper trattorie are around Piazza Colombo and Piazza Eroi Sanremesi. The *Pizzeria l'Airone*, at Piazza Eroi Sanremesi 12, feels tucked away and offers a reasonable set menu for L20,000.

Another place with a cosy atmosphere, *Ivano*, just down from the Cattedrale di San Siro at Via Corradi 39, offers good-value meals. Another pleasant, if pricier, location is the *Pizzeria Vesuvio* at No 5. For modestly priced food and a few glasses of wine, you could try the *Bacchus Enoteca* at Via Roma 65. To make your own food, head for the *Derby Salumeria* on Piazza Colombo.

Entertainment With more than 20 clubs, San Remo jumps at night. First and foremost is the grand *Casinò Municipale*, Corso degli Inglesi 18, with its 'American Games', cabaret shows, roof garden and nightclub – bring your chequebook! The *Odeon Music Hall*, Corso Matteotti 178, is where all the groovy young things go to dance. The tourist office has a list of nightclubs and might be able to advise you on the most happening locations. More sedate are the cafés and bars lining Corso Matteotti.

Getting There & Away San Remo is on the Genova-Ventimiglia train line and is easily accessible by regular trains from either city. Riviera Trasporti buses (☎ 59 27 06) leave from the train station and the main bus station near Piazza Colombo for the French border, Imperia and inland. Other companies operate from the same bus station to destinations such as Torino and Milano. By car, you can reach San Remo quickly on the A10 or more scenically – and less expensively – by following the SS1 along the coast.

Getting Around The Piaggio agent, Bianchi Emilio (☎ 54 13 17), Corso Felice Cavalotti 39, hires out scooters and motorcycles. In summer, head down to Giardini Vittorio Veneto, by the old port, to hire bicycles.

Valle Argentina

The so-called 'silver valley' stretches away from **Taggia**, a charming little place a few km inland from the San Remo-Imperia road, into thickly wooded mountains that seem light years from the coastal resorts. Buses from San Remo go as far as **Triora**, 33km from San Remo and 776m above sea level. This haunting medieval village, the scene of celebrated witch trials and executions in the 16th century, dominates the surrounding valleys, and the trip alone is worth it. Those with their own transport can explore plenty of other villages, each seemingly more impossibly perched on hill crests than the one before.

Ventimiglia

Coming in from the splendidly rich end of the French Riviera, arrival in Ventimiglia can be a bit of a letdown. The town is jaded, the grey, pebbly beach is nothing special and the limpid blue water of Nice is far away. But this is also its charm – none of the ritzy or package-tour crowd hang about here. Typical of this frontier area, French almost seems to have equal status with Italian.

The train station is at the head of Via della Stazione, which continues to the waterfront as Corso della Repubblica. Corso Genova, which runs past the Roman ruins, is the main eastern exit from the city, while its continuation to the west, Via Cavour, runs through the centre and heads to France.

Information The APT office (☎ 35 11 83), Via Cavour 61, opens Monday to Saturday from 8 am to 7 pm. There are several banks (some with ATMs) and also an exchange booth at the train station. The telephone code is ☎ 0184.

Things to See Ventimiglia's **Roman ruins**, including an amphitheatre, date from the 2nd and 3rd centuries, when it was known as Albintimulium. The ruins straddle Corso Genova, a couple of km east of the train station, but are only for diehards. The train lines and traffic kill any atmosphere.

Squatting on a hill on the west bank of the Roia river is the medieval town. A 12th century **cathedral** on Via del Capo rises above the surrounding lanes and neglected houses. There are some breathtaking views of the coast from Corso Giuseppe Verdi.

Places to Stay The camping ground, *Roma* (☎ 23 90 07), Via Peglia 9, is near the town centre. *Albergo Cavour* (☎ 35 13 66), Via Cavour 3, has singles/doubles for L40,000/60,000 (add L10,000 for a room with bathroom). *Albergo XX Settembre* (☎ 35 12 22), Via Roma 16, can come in quite cheap if you're lucky – at L25,000/ 45,000. It has a popular restaurant downstairs. Near the waterfront on Corso della Repubblica 12 is *Hotel Villa Franca* (☎ 35 18 71), which offers reasonable rooms for L45,000/75,000 – but the price is considerably more if you take breakfast.

The *Hotel Posta* (☎ 35 12 18), Via Sottoconvento 15, is a step up in quality at L60,000/100,000.

Places to Eat A series of pizza restaurants lines the beach on Passeggiata G Oberdan. A nicely placed one is *Il Terrazzino*, which offers pretty views across to the old town and an unspectacular, if comparatively cheap, set menu for L18,900. *Pizza 'al Giro'*, Via Cavour 56, sells pizza by the slice and ocaccia for L1500. Several other down-to-arth places are located around Via Roma nd Piazza della Libertà or along Via Cavour. For a cosier atmosphere, try the *Pergola* (set menu for L19,000) at Via Roma 6a. Ice ream places abound – one with a huge hoice of flavours is *Haiti*, Via Roma 28c.

Getting There & Away By bus, Riviera Trasporti (☎ 35 12 51), next to the tourist office, connects the city with towns along the oast and into France – frequency drops out of the high season. Trains connect the city with Genova, Nice, Cannes and Marseilles. The A10 (toll) and Via Aurelia (SS1) link the own with Genova and the French border, while the SS20 heads north for France.

Getting Around Eurocicli (☎ 35 18 79), Via Cavour 70b, hires out bicycles and tandems.

Bordighera
A few km east of Ventimiglia on the San Remo bus, is built-up Bordighera. Apart from being a one-time favourite haunt of ich, British seaside lovers – the collection of charming and costly hotels attests to this - Bordighera's fame rests on a centuries-old monopoly of the Holy Week palm business. Il Vaticano selects its branches exclusively from the palms along the promenade, Lungomare Argentina.

Balzi Rossi
Right by the Ponte San Lodovico crossing into France, 8km west of Ventimiglia, is the Balzi Rossi ('red rocks') Stone Age site. To enter (with a guide only) the grottoes where Cro-Magnon people once lived, you must buy a ticket for the small **Museo Preistorico**, which features the Triple Burial (a grave of three Cro-Magnon), pots of weapons, and animal remains from the period. It is open daily from 9 am to 7 pm and admission is L4000. The Riviera Trasporti bus to France that leaves Via Cavour three times a day (except Sunday) drops you right there.

Villa Hanbury
Overlooking the coast by the village of Mortola are the Giardini Botanici Hanbury. Established last century by Sir Thomas Hanbury, an English noble, the tumbledown gardens surround his Moorish-style mausoleum. It's open from 9 am to 6 pm in summer but hours reduce in the off season. Admission is L8500. You can get the No 1A bus from Via Cavour in Ventimiglia. The bus goes on to the Ponte San Luigi frontier post, from where you could walk down to the Balzi Rossi.

Piemonte

Its position against the French and Swiss Alps has helped forge in Piemonte (Piedmont) an identity quite separate from the rest of Italy. The region's neat and tidy northernmost reaches could easily be Swiss, while Torino's grand squares, arcades and sophisticated café life owe more to French influence than anything 'typically Italian'.

The House of Savoy, which ruled Piemonte during the early 11th century, created one of Europe's grand cities in Torino. Victor Emmanuel II and the Piemontese statesman Count Camillo Cavour were instrumental in achieving Italian unification, and succeeded in making Torino the capital of Italy, albeit briefly, from 1861.

Much of Italy's industrial boom this century has its roots in the region, particularly in and around Torino, where Fiat started making cars. Today, Piemonte is second only to Lombardia in industrial production and is one of the country's wealthiest regions.

Piemonte cuisine is heavily influenced by French cooking and uses marinated meats and vegetables. *Bagna caoda* (meat dipped in oil, anchovies and garlic) is popular during winter, and the white truffles of Piemonte are considered the best in Italy. The region accounts for two-thirds of Italy's rice production, so it comes as no surprise that risotto is popular in Piemonte. The crisp climate is

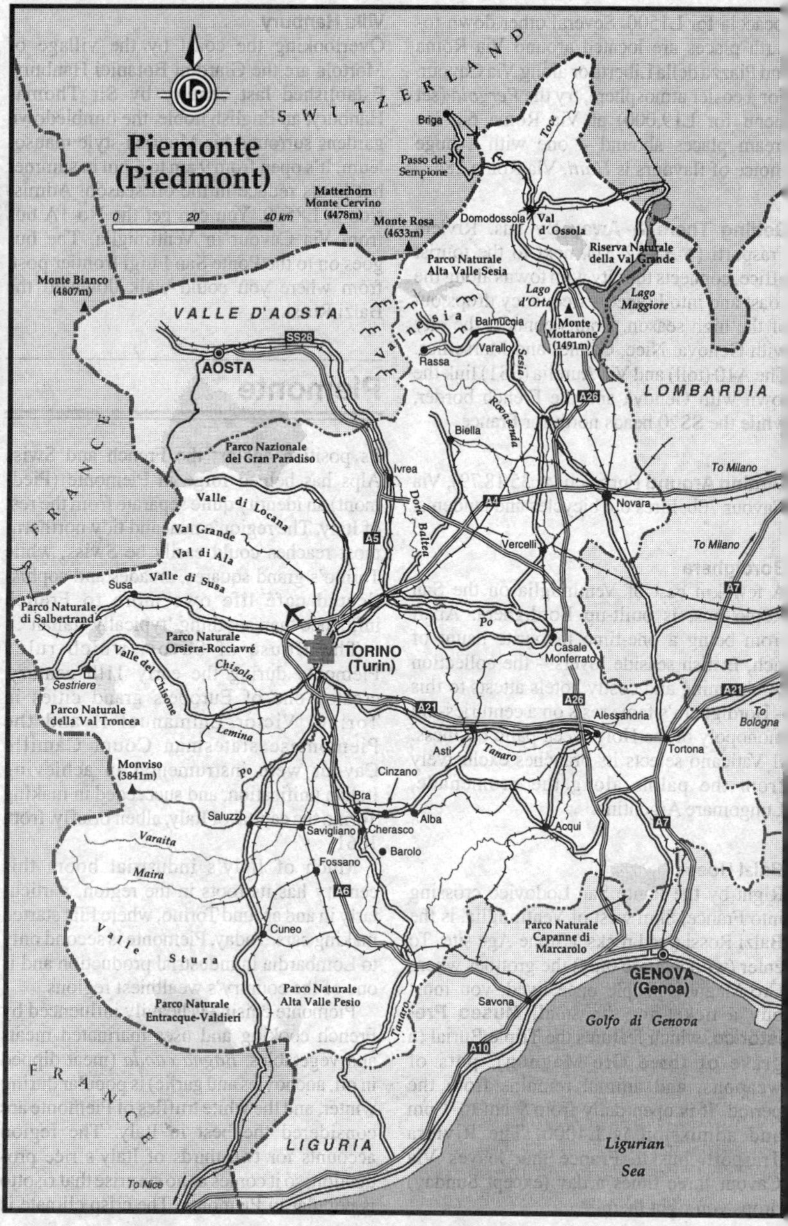
Piemonte
(Piedmont)
0 20 40 km
SWITZERLAND
Briga
Passo del Sempione
Toce
Matterhorn
Monte Cervino
(4478m)
Monte Rosa
(4633m)
Domodossola
Val d' Ossola
Riserva Naturale della Val Grande
Parco Naturale Alta Valle Sesia
Lago d'Orta
Lago Maggiore
Monte Mottarone
(1491m)
Monte Bianco
(4807m)
VALLE D'AOSTA
Valnesia
Balmuccia
Varallo
Rassa
Sesia
SS26
AOSTA
LOMBARDIA
A26
Rovasenda
Biella
FRANCE
Parco Nazionale del Gran Paradiso
Ivrea
To Milano
Valle di Locana
A4
Novara
Dora Baltea
A5
Val Grande
Val di Ala
Vercelli
To Milano
Valle di Susa
A7
Susa
Parco Naturale di Salbertrand
Po
Parco Naturale Orsiera-Rocciavré
Casale Monferrato
Valle del Chisone
Chisola
TORINO
(Turin)
Sestriere
A26
A21
A21
To Bologna
Parco Naturale della Val Troncea
A21
Alessandria
Lemina
Asti
Tanaro
Tortona
Monviso
(3841m)
Po
Cinzano
Bra
Alba
Saluzzo
Savigliano
Cherasco
Acqui
Varaita
Barolo
Fossano
A7
Maira
A6
Valle Stura
Cuneo
Parco Naturale Capanne di Marcarolo
GENOVA
(Genoa)
Parco Naturale Alta Valle Pesio
Parco Naturale Entracque-Valdieri
Savona
Tanaro
Golfo di Genova
A10
FRANCE
LIGURIA
Ligurian Sea
To Nice

DAMIEN SIMONIS

DAMIEN SIMONIS

JOHN GILLMAN

LAUREN SUNSTEIN

Top: Pastel-coloured houses of Portofino, Liguria
Middle: La Salita al Castello, Saluzzo (south of Torino), Piemonte
Bottom: Fishing nets in Camogli, Liguria
Right: Vernazzo, Cinque Terre, Liguria

DAMIEN SIMONIS

DAMIEN SIMONIS

DAMIEN SIMONIS

Milano
Top Left: Cupola, Certosa di Pavia (Gothic monastery south of Milano)
Top Right: The 19th-century Palazzo della Veneranda Fabbrica, Piazza del Duomo
Bottom: Detail of the duomo

no hindrance to wine-making, and you can find some good reds, notably those from the vineyards of Barolo and Barbera, and sparkling wines from Asti.

Centrally located, Torino is an ideal base for exploring the region. The area's main attraction is the Grande Traversata delle Alpi (GTA), a walk of more than 200km through the Alps from the Ligurian border to Lago Maggiore in the north-east of the region.

Activities

Walking Allow yourself a couple of weeks to complete the Grande Traversata delle Alpi, or a couple of days for smaller sections. The walk starts in the area of Viozene, in the south of Piemonte, and follows a network of Alpine *rifugi* north through the province of Cuneo, the Valle di Susa and the Parco Nazionale del Gran Paradiso and across the north of the region, before ending on the banks of Lago Maggiore at Cannobio.

The best months for walking are late June into September, although by the end of summer (officially 21 September) the weather can be unpredictable.

A fold-out map entitled *Percorsi e Posti Tappa GTA* (Routes & Places to Stop), which lists names and locations of rifugi and emergency information, is available from the APT or the CAI in Torino. The information is in Italian only, but addresses and details are easily deciphered. All rifugi are open from July to September, and some remain open through winter for cross-country skiers – many are located in or near villages.

The paths described are clearly marked and generally within the grasp of moderately fit people, and in various places link with optional walks inside French territory.

In addition, readers of Italian can purchase a wide range of detailed guides to specific areas published by the CAI.

Emergency There is a 24-hour mountain rescue service. If you're in difficulty and you can get to a phone, call ☎ 118. In dire situations where a helicopter is sent in, signal for help by raising both arms above your head (one up and one down by your side means you don't need help).

Horse Riding The Alpitrek map, *A Cavallo Tra Val & Valsangone*, provides similar information for horse-riding tracks through the Piemontese Alps. It is available from the Valle di Susa APT office in Oulx. A second map, *In Piemonte a Cavallo*, with routes starting at Albissola on the Ligurian coast, is available from the APT in Torino or the Associazione Nazionale Turismo Equestre Piemonte (☎ 011-54 74 55) in Torino, Via Bertola 39.

Quite a number of places organise horse-riding treks or less exacting rides through some of the region's valleys and national parks. A popular approach is to book places in an agriturismo or rifugio where horse riding is an option. Alpe Plane (☎ 0330-68 52 78), in Sauze di Cesana, down the southern slopes from Sestriere in the Valle del Chisone, is one such place. However, it is best to check the alternatives with individual tourist offices first.

Adventure Sports Activities as diverse as white-water rafting, bungee jumping and mountain-bike treks are organised by various groups throughout Piemonte, principally in the summer months. For paragliding, for instance, contact Marco Borio (☎ 0338-631 68 70), a representative of Volo Libero Valle Elvo, Regione Campra, 7, 13050 Graglia (near Biella in northern Piemonte).

These groups have a habit of coming and going, so get details of companies doing this kind of thing from tourist offices.

Skiing Skiing is possible in the north and west of Piemonte – consult skiing entries in this chapter for more details. The tourist offices in these areas have copious amounts of information on pistes, rifugi and ski hire.

TORINO

A gracious city of wide boulevards, elegant arcades and grand public buildings, Torino (Turin) is built beside a pretty stretch of the Po river. Although much of the industrial and

PIEMONTE

PIEMONTE

suburban sprawl, especially west and south of the city centre, is predictably awful, the city is blessed with a green belt in the hills east of the river, with views to the snow-covered Alps west and north.

The Savoy capital from 1574, and for a brief period after unification the seat of Italy's parliament, Torino is also the birthplace of Italian industry. Giants like Fiat (Fabbrica Italiana di Automobili Torino) and Olivetti lured hundreds of thousands of impoverished southern Italians to Torino and housed them in vast company-built and owned suburbs, such as Mirafiori to the south. Fiat's owner, Gianni Agnelli, is one of the country's most powerful men, but Torino itself is a left-wing bastion. Industrial unrest on Fiat's factory floors spawned the Italian Communist Party under the leadership of Antonio Gramsci and, in the 1970s, the left-wing terrorist group, the *Brigate Rosse* (Red Brigades).

History

It is unclear whether the ancient city of Taurisia began as a Celtic or Ligurian settlement. Like the rest of northern Italy, it eventually came under the sway of Roma, which was succeeded by the Goths, Lombards and Franks.

When Torino became capital of the House of Savoy, it pretty much shared the dynasty's fortunes thereafter. The Savoys annexed Sardegna in 1720, but Napoleon virtually put an end to their power and occupied Torino in 1798. Torino suffered Austrian and Russian occupation before Victor Emmanuel I restored the House of Savoy and re-entered Torino in 1814. Nevertheless, Austria remained the true power throughout northern Italy until unification, when Torino became capital, an honour it passed on to Firenze three years later.

Torino adapted quickly to its loss of political significance, becoming a centre for industrial production during WWI and later a hive of trade-union activity. Today, it is Italy's second largest industrial city after Milano.

Orientation

The north-facing Stazione Porta Nuova is the point of arrival for most travellers. Trams and buses out the front of the station connect with most parts of the historic centre, which is quite spread out. From the station, walk straight ahead over the main east-west route, Corso Vittoria Emanuele II, through the grand Piazza Carlo Felice and north along Via Roma until you come to the broad, café-lined Piazza San Carlo. Piazza Castello and the Duomo (which contains the Shroud of Turin) are farther north along Via Roma. The Mole Antonelliana dominates the horizon to the east, leading to Via Po (the student area), Piazza Vittorio Veneto and the mighty Po river.

Information

Tourist Office The APT office (☎ 53 51 81) is at Via Roma 226, under the colonnade at the south-west corner of Piazza San Carlo. It opens daily from 9 am to 7.30 pm, while the smaller IAT office at Stazione Porta Nuova closes half an hour earlier (and does not open at all on Sunday). Informa Giovani (☎ 011-442 49 76), Via Assarotti 2, publishes a magazine for young people, *Città di Torino Informa Giovani*, and has a range of information from travel to services for the disabled.

Foreign Consulates The UK has a representative (☎ 650 92 02) at Via Saluzzo 60. The French consulate (☎ 83 52 52) is located at Via Bogino 8.

Money There is a bank with an ATM and an exchange booth at Stazione Porta Nuova. Banks are located along Via Roma and in Piazza San Carlo. Quite a few ATMs around the city accept Visa, MasterCard and Eurocard.

Post & Communications The main post office is at Via Alfieri 10 and is open Monday to Friday from 8.15 am to 5.30 pm, and Saturday from 8.15 am to 1 pm. There's a branch at Stazione Porta Nuova. The postcode for central Torino is 10100.

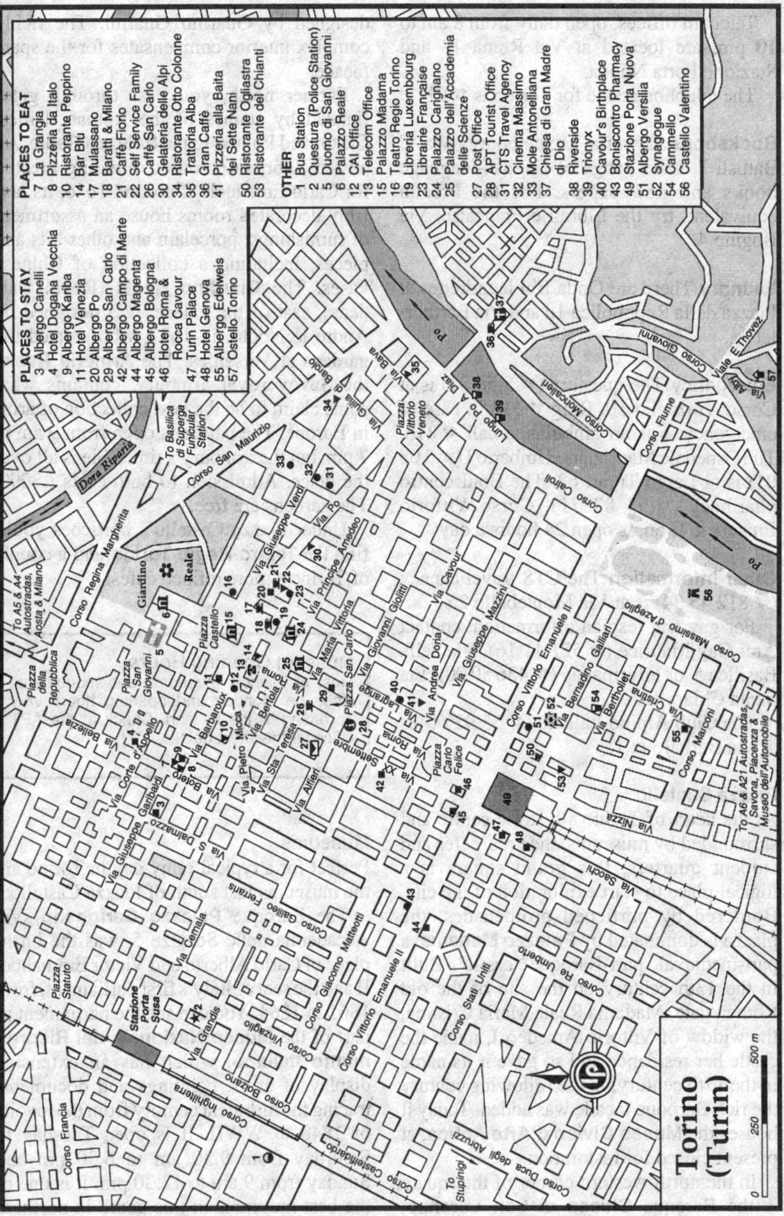
Torino
(Turin)
0 250 500 m
PLACES TO STAY
3 Albergo Canelli
4 Hotel Dogana Vecchia
9 Albergo Kariba
11 Hotel Venezia
20 Albergo Po
29 Albergo San Carlo
42 Albergo Campo di Marte
44 Albergo Magenta
45 Albergo Bologna
46 Hotel Roma & Rocca Cavour
47 Turin Palace
48 Hotel Genova
55 Albergo Edelweis
57 Ostello Torino
PLACES TO EAT
7 La Grangia
8 Pizzeria da Italo
10 Ristorante Peppino
14 Bar Blu
17 Mulassano
18 Baratti & Milano
21 Caffè Fiorio
22 Self Service Family
26 Caffè San Carlo
30 Gelateria delle Alpi
34 Ristorante Otto Colonne
35 Trattoria Alba
36 Gran Caffè
41 Pizzeria alla Baita dei Sette Nani
50 Ristorante Ogliastra
53 Ristorante del Chianti
OTHER
1 Bus Station
2 Questura (Police Station)
5 Duomo di San Giovanni
6 Palazzo Reale
12 CAI Office
13 Telecom Office
15 Palazzo Madama
16 Teatro Regio Torino
19 Libreria Luxembourg
23 Librairie Française
24 Palazzo Carignano
25 Palazzo dell'Accademia delle Scienze
27 Post Office
28 APT Tourist Office
31 CTS Travel Agency
32 Cinema Massimo
33 Mole Antonelliana
37 Chiesa di Gran Madre di Dio
38 Riverside
39 Trionyx
40 Cavour's Birthplace
43 Boniscontro Pharmacy
49 Stazione Porta Nuova
51 Albergo Versilia
52 Synagogue
54 Cammello
56 Castello Valentino
To A5 & A4 Autostradas, Aosta & Milano
To Basilica di Superga Funicular Station
To A6 & A21 Autostradas, Savona, Piacenza & Museo dell'Automobile
To Stupinigi
Giardino Reale
Dora Riparia
Po
Stazione Porta Susa
Piazza Statuto
Piazza della Repubblica
Piazza San Giovanni
Piazza Castello
Piazza San Carlo
Piazza Carlo Felice
Piazza Vittorio Veneto
Corso Regina Margherita
Corso San Maurizio
Corso Vittorio Emanuele II
Corso Massimo d'Azeglio
Corso Moncalieri
Corso Francia
Via Po
Via Roma
Via Garibaldi
Via Nizza
Via Sacchi

Telecom offices, open daily from 8 am to 10 pm, are located at Via Roma 18 and Stazione Porta Nuova.

The telephone code for Torino is ☎ 011.

Bookshops Libreria Luxembourg, Via C Battisti 7, has a range of English-language books and newspapers. For the French equivalent, try the Librairie Française, Via Bogino 4.

Laundry There are Onda Blu laundrettes at Piazza della Repubblica 1d and Via Berthollet 2g.

Emergency The questura (☎ 5 58 81) is at Corso Vinzaglio 10. Ring ☎ 113 in case of emergency. For an ambulance call ☎ 118. The Ospedale Mauriziano Umberto I (☎ 5 08 01) is at Largo Turati 62. The Boniscontro pharmacy (☎ 53 82 71), Corso Vittorio Emanuele II 66, is open 24 hours a day.

Other Information The CTS travel agency (☎ 812 45 34) is at Via Montebello 2.

For gay and lesbian information, contact Arci Gay Maurice (☎ 521 11 16), Via della Basilica 5, or Informagay (☎ 436 50 00), Via Santa Chiara 1.

The Club Alpino Italiano (☎ 53 92 60) is at Via Barbaroux 1.

Piazza Castello

At the heart of Torino's historic centre and surrounded by museums, theatres, cafés and student quarters, this grand square is a logical place to start exploration of the city. Bordered by porticoed promenades, the piazza is dominated by **Palazzo Madama**, a part-medieval, part-Baroque 'castle'. Built in the 13th century on the site of the old Roman gate, Madama Reale Maria Cristina, the widow of Vittorio Amedeo I, made the castle her residence and so gave it its name in the 17th century; in the following century the rich Baroque façade was added. Today it houses the **Museo Civico d'Arte Antica**, at present closed for restoration.

In the north-western corner of the square is the Baroque **Chiesa di San Lorenzo**, designed by Guarino Guarini. The richly complex interior compensates for the spare façade.

Farther north, you pass through gates flanked by statues of the Roman deities Castor and Pollux, to the **Palazzo Reale**. An austere, apricot-coloured building erected for Carlo Emanuele II around 1646, its lavishly decorated rooms house an assortment of furnishings, porcelain and other bits and pieces, including a collection of Chinese vases. The **Giardino Reale** (Royal Gardens), east of the palace, was designed by Andre le Noôtre in 1697, who created the gardens at Versailles. The **Armeria Reale**, the Savoy royal armoury, contains what some claim to be the best collection of arms in Europe. The palace is open from 9 am to 7 pm, but the armoury's timetable is all over the place. Admission to both costs L8000. The gardens are free.

Under Piazza Castello's porticoes you'll find the **Teatro Regio Torino** and a couple of Torino's more refined cafés.

> **Museum Opening Hours**
> Most of Torino's museums and monuments close on Monday and opening hours vary according to the season. Check at the APT office for the latest details.

Museums

Perfect for a typical rainy day in Torino are the museums just south of Piazza Castello.

The Baroque **Palazzo Carignano**, Via Accademia delle Scienze 5, was the birthplace of Carlo Alberto and Victor Emmanuel II and the seat of Italy's first parliament, from 1861 to 1864. You can see the parliament as part of the **Museo Nazionale del Risorgimento Italiano**, which has an extensive display of arms, paintings and documents tracing the turbulent century from the revolts of 1848 to WWII. It is open Tuesday to Saturday from 9.30 am to 6.30 pm and Sunday from 9 am to 12.30 pm. It is one of the best museums in this genre in northern

Italy but will be of limited interest to those who don't read Italian. Admission is L8000. On the subject of the Risorgimento, one of its prime architects, Camillo Benso di Cavour, was born and died at Via Lagrange 25.

On the street of the same name and housing the **Museo Egizio** is the **Palazzo dell'Accademia delle Scienze.** The museum was established in the late 18th century and is considered one of the best museums of ancient Egyptian art after those in London and Cairo. It is open Tuesday to Saturday from 9 am to 2 pm (although on Tuesday and Thursday it stays open to 7 pm) and admission is L12,000. In the same building is the **Galleria Sabauda**, housing the Savoy collection, including works by Italian, French and Flemish masters. It's open Tuesday to Saturday from 9 am to 2 pm and admission is L6000.

Farther afield is the **Galleria Civica d'Arte Moderna e Contemporanea**, Via Magenta 31, dedicated to 19th and 20th-century artists including Renoir, Courbet, Klee and Chagall. Opening times vary. Admission is L8000.

For modern art of a more metallic sheen, head for the **Museo dell'Automobile**, Corso Unità d'Italia 40 (south along Via Nizza). Among its 400 masterpieces is one of the first Fiats and the Isotta Franchini driven by Gloria Swanson in the film *Sunset Boulevard*. It's open Tuesday to Sunday from 10 am to 6.30 pm. Admission is L10,000. Bus No 34 goes there from beside Stazione Porta Nuova.

Back in central Torino, the **Museo della Marionetta**, Via Santa Teresa 5, contains puppets and costumes tracing the history of marionette theatre from the 17th century. If it's open (which seems to be a matter of chance), you may be lucky enough to see a performance as well.

Duomo di San Giovanni

Torino's cathedral, west of the Palazzo Reale off Via XX Settembre, houses the **Shroud of Turin** in which Christ's body was supposedly wrapped after his crucifixion. Carbon dating in 1988 dated it to the 13th or 14th century, but current scientific research indicates that a fire in 1532 (in which the shroud caught alight) may have had an impact on the carbon dating, making it unreliable evidence. Despite the numerous tests that have been undertaken since the 19th century, no-one has been able to explain the images of the back and front of a man imprinted in the cloth. Certainly, the thousands who flock to see it don't seem to mind the continuing debate over its authenticity.

The shroud is usually in the **Cappella della Santa Sindone** (Chapel of the Holy Shroud), but has been temporarily stored in the arcivescovado in the wake of a fire that damaged the chapel. The shroud is expected to be back in place some time in 1998. The chapel itself is topped by Guarino Guarini's honeycomb-like black marble dome, and a copy of the shroud adorns the walls of a nearby chapel. Luigi Gagna's copy of Da Vinci's *Last Supper*, above the doors, is considered the best ever produced.

Piazzas

The great squares and elegant boulevards lend Torino its air of reserved majesty. Via Roma, Torino's main shopping thoroughfare since 1615, heads south from Piazza Castello to the grandiose **Stazione Porta Nuova**, built by Mazzucchetti in 1865. If you have a few minutes around the station, head east a few blocks to admire the Oriental strangeness of the 19th-century **synagogue** on Piazzetta Primo Levi.

Walking south you first emerge in **Piazza San Carlo**, known as Torino's drawing room and home to several renowned cafés. Surrounded by the characteristic porticoes (central Torino boasts some 18km of them), its southern end is capped by two Baroque churches, Chiesa di San Carlo and Chiesa di Santa Cristina. Farther down Via Roma you reach **Piazza Carlo Felice**, at once piazza and garden. The latter, like Via Nizza which continues south off the piazza past the train station, has seen better days. Now the main axis of Torino's seedier side of life, Via Nizza and the surrounding area is worth exploring but dodgy territory at night.

Via Po & Around

The hip young scene, revolving around Torino's university, can be freely indulged in the cafés and trattorie along and around Via Po, which connects Piazza Castello and the river via Piazza Vittorio Veneto.

The single most remarkable sight in the area is the **Mole Antonelliana**, a couple of blocks north of Via Po on Via Montebello. Intended as a synagogue when it was started in 1863, this extraordinary structure comes as something of a shock when you first see it from the surrounding narrow streets. Capped by an aluminium spire, it is a display of engineering as an art form (in a similar vein perhaps to the Eiffel Tower) – and quite a spectral sight when lit up at night. At the time of writing the lift to the top was closed, as work was being completed on a new museum to be dedicated to the history of cinema.

Walking south along the Po river, you will come to the **Castello del Valentino**, a mock medieval castle built in the 17th century. The carefully designed, French-style park around it was first opened in 1856 and is one of the most celebrated in Italy – particularly by in-line skaters, cyclists and smooching young romancers. In 1884 a minor Disney-style medieval castle and *borgo* (village) were built for the Esposizione Generale Italiana. The castle and borgo were reopened after restoration in 1996. You can wander the borgo at will, while entry to the castle (Tuesday to Sunday from 9 am to 7 pm) costs L5000.

East from Piazza Vittorio Veneto, across the Po, is the **Gran Madre di Dio** church, built between 1818 and 1831 to commemorate the return of Victor Emmanuel I from exile. Set into the hills, its dome is an unmistakable landmark, but the church is usually closed to the public.

Basilica di Superga

In 1706, Vittorio Amedeo I promised to build a basilica to honour the Virgin Mary if Torino was saved from besieging French and Spanish armies. The city was saved and architect Filippo Juvarra built the church on a hill across the Po river to the north-east of central Torino. It became the resting place of the Savoys, whose lavish tombs make for interesting viewing.

The spot is now better known as a football shrine. The tomb of the Torino football team, all killed when their plane crashed into the basilica in 1949, is at the rear. The basilica is reached by the No 15 tram. Take it to the end of the line and connecting funicular.

If you have a vehicle, the drive up through the thickly wooded Pino Torinese helps give the lie to the belief that Torino is little more than a polluted, industrial town.

La Palazzina di Caccia di Stupinigi

A visit to the Savoys' sprawling hunting lodge, tucked away in manicured grounds beyond the Fiat plants and Mirafiori suburb, is a must. It is slowly being restored with Fiat money and many parts of the building are in original condition. Check with the APT because opening times vary. Take bus No 41 from Corso Vittorio Emanuele II, which runs along the north side of Stazione Porta Nuova. It is open daily from 10 am to 7 pm (an hour longer on weekends) and admission costs L10,000.

Castello di Rivoli

The mainly 17th century preferred residence of the Savoy family lies just outside central Torino in Rivoli. It now houses a contemporary art gallery and hosts various temporary exhibits. It is open Tuesday to Friday from 10 am to 5 pm, and to 7 pm on weekends; entry costs L10,000. Take bus No 36 along Corso Francia from near Porta Susa train station.

Markets

Every morning until about midday, Piazza della Repubblica, north of the city centre, fills to the cries and smells of the main food and clothes market. On Saturday Piazza d'Albera, on the north-eastern corner of

Piazza della Repubblica, becomes an antique collector's heaven.

Places to Stay – bottom end

Finding a room can be difficult in Torino, and finding a cheap one even harder. Call the APT office in advance for a suggestion, although the staff won't make a reservation. The IAT at Stazione Porta Nuova will provide a map and directions to your hotel.

Camping & Hostel The *Campeggio Villa Rey* (☎ 819 01 17), Strada Superiore Val San Martino 27, is away from the centre. Check with the APT for directions and opening times.

The youth hostel, *Ostello Torino* (☎ 660 29 39), Via Alby 1, is in the hills east of the Po river and can be reached by bus No 52 from Stazione Porta Nuova. Ask the driver for the right stop. B&B is L18,000 and a meal L14,000.

Hotels Near Stazione Porta Nuova, *Albergo Magenta* (☎ 54 26 49), Corso Vittorio Emanuele II 67, has rooms starting at L50,000/65,000. *Albergo Versilia* (☎ 65 76 78), Via Sant'Anselmo 4, is not bad at L45,000/65,000. *Albergo Edelweis* (☎ 669 01 17), Via Madama Cristina 34, will put you up for L45,000/ 55,000 a single/double.

Albergo Canelli (☎ 54 60 78), Via San Dalmazzo 7, off Via Garibaldi, has bare but serviceable rooms starting as low as L25,000/35,000. In the same pleasant area, *Albergo Kariba* (☎ 54 22 81), Via San Francesco d'Assisi 4, charges L40,000/ 60,000/90,000 for singles/doubles/triples in slightly more comfortable digs. *Albergo Po* (☎ 812 50 71), Via Po 4, is scruffy but in a great location. Rooms can start as low as L22,000/27,000.

Albergo San Carlo (☎ 562 78 46), at No 197 on the piazza of the same name, has singles/doubles from L60,000/80,000 and L110,000 for a triple – the location is hard to beat. *Albergo Bologna* (☎ 562 01 91), Corso Vittorio Emanuele II 60, just across from Stazione Porta Nuova, is in a similar class but is often full. Singles without private bath are L50,000, but the rooms with private bath are well overpriced at L90,000/120,000.

A good but not terribly cheap choice is *Albergo Campo di Marte* (☎ 54 53 61), Via XX Settembre 7, which also has singles/ doubles from L70,000/90,000.

Places to Stay – middle to top end

With a little extra to spend, the *Hotel Dogana Vecchia* (☎ 436 67 52; fax 436 71 94), Via Corte d'Appello 4, has well-kept rooms for L100,000/120,000 with breakfast. Mozart and Verdi were among its more distinguished guests. If you get lucky, it may have a few cheaper rooms without private bath.

The three-star *Albergo Roma & Rocca Cavour* (☎ 561 27 72), Piazza Carlo Felice 60, charges about L140,000 for a single and L170,000 for a double – all in sumptuous style. Weekend rates drop and, again, it has a couple of not so hot rooms going more cheaply. *Hotel Genova* (☎ 562 94 00), Via Sacchi 14, is not much classier but charges L170,000/220,000.

Hotel Venezia (☎ 562 30 12), Via XX Settembre 70, has rooms from L143,000/ 190,000, but prices can come down in winter.

The city's most luxurious hotel is *Torino Palace* (☎ 562 55 11; fax 561 21 87), Via Sacchi 8, with singles/doubles starting at L280,000/330,000.

Places to Eat

Torino's cuisine is heavily influenced by the French, and the massive migration to the city of southern Italians brought traditions of cooking unmatched anywhere else in the north. Try risotto alla piemontese (with butter and cheese) or zuppa canavesana (turnip soup) and finish with a Savoy favourite, panna cotta (baked cream). The wines are largely from the Asti region or the Barolo vineyards.

Via Nizza near Stazione Porta Nuova is loaded with cheap eateries and takeaway joints. The area around Via Po is great for cheaper restaurants full of students.

Restaurants One of the better self-service restaurants is *La Grangia*, Via Garibaldi 21, where you can eat a full meal for L12,000. Another is *Family*, Via Bogino 2, off Via Po, open for lunch only. There are a few others in a more takeaway line on Via Po itself.

Close to Stazione Porta Nuova, *Ristorante del Chianti*, Via Saluzzo 13 (parallel to Via Nizza), has a set menu for L12,000. Not far away, you can experiment with Sardinian cuisine at the *Ristorante Ogliastra* at Via B Galliari – a full meal should cost less than L30,000 per person with wine.

Ristorante Peppino, Via Mercanti 7, is a popular and cheerful place with an extensive menu. A full meal will set you back around L25,000.

A cheap place to eat is *Ristorante Otto Colonne*, Via Guilia di Barolo 5, near Via Po, with pasta from L8000 and meat dishes from L10,000. *Trattoria Alba*, Via Bava 2, off Piazza Vittorio Veneto, is a busy, modestly priced restaurant offering solid serves of tasty food – a good meal with wine costs about L25,000.

Pizzeria alla Baita dei Sette Nani, Via A Doria 5, is said to be the best in Torino, with pizzas from L6500. Crowds queue for hours to get in. *Pizzeria da Italo*, Via Botero 7, has scrummy pizzas, done in the Turinese style, and great salads.

Cafés & Bars Perhaps partly due to Torino's legacy of French and Austrian involvement, and maybe also as a result of the indifferent weather, the city has a flourishing and chic café life. Piazzas Castello and San Carlo are loaded with establishments patronised by the well-to-do (where a coffee can easily cost you L4000 or more) and there is a great choice along Via Po. Torino's long list of literary luminaries and political potentates have certainly not wanted for places to chat the day away.

Caffè Fiorio, Via Po 8, was a favourite haunt of Camillo Cavour; it's been operating since 1780. *Mulassano*, Piazza Castello, established in 1900, is a true belle époque relic and is popular with the theatre mob from the nearby Teatro Regio Torino. A couple of steps away is the slightly older and more elegant *Baratti & Milano*.

Caffè San Carlo, on Piazza San Carlo once played host to a riotous gaggle of pre-unification patriots and other dangerous persons. Today it is more bankers' territory. *Gran Caffè*, just across the Po river at Piazza Gran Madre di Dio, makes for a tranquil change of atmosphere.

Gelaterie There are plenty of gelaterie to choose from. The *Gelateria delle Alpi*, Via Po 18, and *Gelateria Fiorio*, Via Po 8, are among the best. *Bar Blu* on the corner of Piazza Castello and Via Roma is also good.

Entertainment

On Friday, the newspaper *La Stampa* has an entertainment insert, *Torino Sette*, which lists what's on around town. The city organises Punta Verdi – a series of summer concerts and films in various parks and theatres from June until August, and plenty of free music events in September – the APT has all the programmes. Free midday concerts are usually staged from February to April.

Theatre The cheapest tickets for the opera season at *Teatro Regio Torino*, Piazza Castello, go on sale for a minimum of L20,000 an hour before the performances begin, but you'll generally need to queue well before. When they sell out, it is often possible to see the performance for free live on TV in the Teatro Piccolo Regio next door.

There are theatres throughout the city. Check *Torino Sette* and the APT office for programmes.

Cinema *Cinema Massimo*, on Via Massimo near the Mole Antonelliana, offers an eclectic mix of films, mainly in English, or with subtitles.

Nightclubs The nightclubs are among the country's best. Many require membership but you can often join temporarily. The scene changes quickly – pick up the free booklet *News Spettacolo* at the APT office to get an idea of what's happening. Ai Murazzi, the arcaded riverside area along the Po between

Ponte Vittorio Emanuele I and Ponte Umberto I, is a popular place for late-night entertainment. *Riverside*, Via Murazzi Po 35, puts on an alternative mix of jazz, blues and Latin music. Noisier stuff booms at *Trionyx*, Lungo Po Murazzi 53. Via Principe Tommaso has a few happening spots. *Cammello*, at No 11, is a beacon, pumping out music and alcohol from 5 pm to 5 am. There are also several places strung out along the length of the seemingly never-ending Corso Francia. Two noticeable trends have emerged in Torino – an affection for Irish-style pubs and Latin American night spots – check *News Spettacolo* to get an idea of options.

Getting There & Away

Air Torino is served by Caselle international airport (☎ 567 63 61 for flight information), north-west of the city, which has connections to European and national destinations.

Bus International and inter-regional buses terminate at the main bus station at Corso Inghilterra 1. Other stations serving Piemonte can be found at Corso Marconi and near Piazza Repubblica.

Train The main train station (☎ 561 33 33) is Stazione Porta Nuova, Piazza Carlo Felice. Regular trains connect Torino with Milano, Aosta, Venezia, Genova and Roma.

Car & Motorcycle Torino is a major autostrada junction. The A4 connects with Milano, the A5 with Aosta, the A6 with Savona and the Ligurian Coast and the A21 with Piacenza. If you're heading for Genova, take the A21 and then the A7 rather than the expensive and sometimes dangerous A6. For hitchhikers, the SS29 heads for Asti, the SS24 for Susa and the SS11 east for Milano.

Getting Around

The Airport The SADEM bus company (☎ 311 16 16) runs a service to the airport every half-hour from the bus station.

Bus & Tram The city boasts a dense network of buses and trams run by Trasporti Torinesi (free call ☎ 167-019152), which has an information booth at Stazione Porta Nuova. Day tickets (L4200) are available and good value if you use the local transport a lot.

The company also runs Navigazione sul Po (☎ 576 42 22), which operates boat rides on the river from June to September.

Car Rental Major rental agencies include Avis (☎ 50 11 07), Corso Turati 15, and Europcar (☎ 650 36 03), Via Madama Cristina 72.

Taxi Call ☎ 57 37 or 57 30 if you need a cab.

PIEMONTE

VALLE DI SUSA

West of Torino and easily accessible by car, bus and train, the Valle di Susa takes in the old town of Susa and several ski resorts, including the glamorous but overdeveloped Sestriere. It is also known as Val. There are some beautiful spots and a few pleasant mountain villages, but they can be thronged in ski season and on weekends. The roads often get clogged with miles of traffic jams on Friday and Sunday as Torino's weekend escapees pile in and out of the city. Walking possibilities are good, but better in the north and around the Parco Nazionale del Gran Paradiso.

The area's telephone code is ☎ 0122.

Sacra di San Michele

Perched atop Monte Pirchiriano at the mouth of the Valle di Susa, high above the road from Torino, this brooding Gothic-Romanesque abbey dates back to the 11th century. The closest town is Avigliana, a short train ride from Torino, which is connected to the abbey by bus (there are about three a day). A better route is to continue by train to Sant'Ambrogio, at the foot of the hill, and tackle the 90-minute walk up. Check opening times with the APT in Torino before setting out.

Susa

On the busiest route between Torino and France, Susa started life as a Celtic town (a Druid well remains as testimony) before falling under the sway of Roma. The modest Roman ruins make it a pleasant stop on the way to the western ski resorts.

In addition to remains of a Roman **aqueduct**, an **amphitheatre** still in use and the **Arco d'Augusto**, the early 11th-century **Duomo di San Giusto** is a rare medieval survivor in Piemonte, and is finally having some long overdue restoration.

Albergo Stazione (☎ 62 22 26), Corso Stati Uniti 2, is as close as Susa comes to cheap, with singles/doubles for L45,000/ 65,000.

Sapar buses connect Susa with Torino, Oulx and other valley destinations.

Exilles

Worth a brief look is the forbidding **fort** overlooking the quiet village of Exilles, 14km west of Susa. Of obscure medieval origins, its military role only ended in 1943. It's generally open from 2 to 7 pm, but you should check with an APT office in the area before making a special trip. Sapar buses stop here.

Oulx

Nothing much in itself, Oulx is a good place to get information on skiing, hiking and other activities throughout the Valle di Susa. The APT office (☎ 83 15 96), Piazza Garambois 5, is the main tourist office for the valley and can help with lodgings, Settimana Bianca packages and walking details. Regular trains run from Torino, and Sapar buses connect with destinations along the Susa and Chisone valleys.

Cesana Torinese

Eleven km from the resort of Sestriere, Cesana makes a much cosier base than its better known neighbour, and offers several cheaper accommodation possibilities. The IAT office (☎ 8 92 02) is at Piazza V Amedeo 3. Three or four daily buses make the run up to Susa and back.

Sestriere

Conceived by Mussolini and built by the Agnelli clan (of Fiat fame), Sestriere is a cultural desert that has grown to become one of Europe's most fashionable ski resorts. The mountains here are pleasant indeed, and there are several villages on either side of Sestriere that could make more appealing bases, unless of course you feel a need to be seen here in your après-ski garb.

The IAT office (☎ 75 54 44) is at Piazza Agnelli 11, and has information on skiing and accommodation. Summer activities include hiking, free climbing and mountain bike riding. Out of season, only a couple of three-star hotels remain open.

Buses connect the resort with Oulx, Susa and Torino.

SOUTHERN PIEMONTE

The roads south of Torino to Liguria mark the divide between the low hills and dull plains of most of eastern Piemonte from the slopes that rise in the west to the southern French Alps. It is an area little frequented by foreign tourists, where numerous valleys slice paths west towards France (only a few offer access across the border). Not as high as the mountains of the north, the area still provides good hiking opportunities, and skiing in winter.

Cuneo

Cuneo is a mildly interesting provincial capital and transport junction between Torino and Liguria. The old town lies in the northern wedge of the city, presenting a faded if pleasant picture, although there is not too much to delay the sightseer. Cuneo is useful as a base for exploring the southern valleys of Piemonte, especially for those without their own transport. If you have wheels, a better alternative is Saluzzo, 33km north.

The bus station is handily located at the northern tip of the old town, which peters out at the vast central square, Piazza di Duccio Galimberti. The train station lies to the south-west on Piazzale Libertà.

Information The APT office (☎ 6 66 15), Corso Nizza 17, has extensive information about the province. The town's telephone ode is ☎ 0171, and there are Telecom ffices on Via Massimo d'Azegli and Via Carlo Emanuele III.

Places to Stay & Eat *Albergo Ciriegia* (☎ 69 27 03), Corso Nizza 11, has decent singles/doubles from L40,000/70,000. *Albergo Cavallo Nero* (☎ 69 20 17), Via Seminario 8, charges L50,000/70,000, or L20,000 more with a bathroom.

This hotel also has a restaurant, or you could try a pizza at the cosy *Ristorante Capri* on the other side of Piazza Seminario. *Ristorante Tre Citroni*, Via Bonelli 2, is more formal, with set menus for you to splurge on at around L60,000. Piazza di Duccio Galimberti and Corso Nizza are the best places to look for cafés.

Getting There & Away Cuneo's big plus is transport. There are regular trains to Saluzzo, Torino, San Remo, Ventimiglia, and Nice in France. There is a second train station for the Cuneo-Gesso line, serving small towns in the valley. Various bus companies run services to Saluzzo, Torino, Imperia, Savona and along the Valle Stura. By car, take the A6 from Torino towards Savona and exit at Fossano, or the SS20.

Around Cuneo

Among the valleys that radiate westwards from Cuneo, the **Valle Stura** (the longest) leads to the Colle della Maddalena crossing into France. The surrounding mountains offer skiing when snowfalls are good, and several rifugi for trekkers. The same can be said of the bare rock mountain slopes that feature along the **Valle Gesso**.

Another attractive option is the **Valle Maira**, which starts to the north-west of Cuneo. **Dronero**, a pretty medieval village with houses topped by precarious-looking grey slate roofs, marks the start of the climb upwards and west.

Saluzzo

About 60km south of Torino, Saluzzo warrants a one-day trip and is a good base for closer exploration of the valleys and castles of southern Piemonte. Once a feisty medieval stronghold, the town maintained its independence until the Savoys won it in a 1601 treaty with France. One of Saluzzo's better known sons was General Carlo dalla Chiesa, whose implacable pursuit of the Mafia lead to his assassination in 1982.

Information The APT office (☎ 4 67 10), Via Griselda 6, has a range of information about the surrounding valleys.

The telephone code is ☎ 0175.

Things to See Cobbled lanes twist upwards to La Castiglia, the sombre castle (for a time used as a prison this century) of the Marchesi, Saluzzo's medieval rulers. La Salita al Castello is lined with houses from the period. Commanding views over the old town's burnt-red tiled rooftops is the **Torre Civica**, a restored 15th-century tower that was part of the old *municipio* (town administration). For L2500 you can climb to the top. Pass the contemporary church and convent of San Giovanni on the same square and you reach the **Museo Civico di Casa Cavassa** (L5000), a fine example of a 16th-century noble's residence. The museum and Torre Civica are open Wednesday to Sunday and a combined admission ticket costs L6000.

Places to Stay & Eat There is no really cheap accommodation in Saluzzo. *Albergo Persico* (☎ 4 12 13), Vicolo Mercati 10, has rooms for L60,000/85,000. Failing that, the *Perpoin* (☎ 4 23 83), Via Spielberg 19, is good but still pricier at L90,000/130,000.

The latter has its own restaurant, and there are plenty of little pizzerias scattered over the lower part of town. If you want to splash out, try *La Taverna di Porti Scür* (meaning 'dark porticoes'), Via Alessandro Volta 14, a dim, low-ceilinged restaurant with medieval ambience. For a drink in style, head for the *Bistrot La Drancia*, in the shadow of La Castiglia's walls.

Getting There & Away There are regular bus

Mushroom Magic

When autumn comes to Piemonte, it's time to *andare a funghi* – go mushroom-picking. Mushrooms, especially the popular *porcini* (boletus) and the much harder to come by *tartufo* (truffle), also known as *tuber magnatum*, are considered something of a delicacy. So prized are mushrooms that the town of Alba celebrates the Fiera del Tartufo for a couple of weeks each mid-October. This is a delightful occasion for the palate, when Alba's best wines and rival vintages from Asti and the Langhe are brought out to accompany mouthwatering mushroom and truffle recipes that date back to the 17th century. The markets overflow with great slabs of porcini – some as big as 2kg have been found by avid pickers and that's a lot of mushroom. Porcini and other specimens sprout in the dark oak and chestnut forest floors on sunny days immediately following a good burst of rain. Truffles, on the other hand, incubate for several months, and those who know where to look often take specially trained truffle-sniffing dogs. If you head off mushroom-picking yourself, let someone in the know examine them before you gobble them up – many species are dangerous. ■

PIEMONTE

and train connections from Torino and Cuneo. Buses also run up the Po Valley.

Around Saluzzo

A few minutes drive south of Saluzzo is one of the more easily accessible castles in the region, that of **Manta** – inquire at the APT office for up-to-date information.

The Po river doglegs north a few km west of Saluzzo, and the valley westward to its source, below **Monviso** (3841m), is an enticing excursion. Should you want to hike around the mountain, there are rifugi, and a few hotels in the nearby town of **Crissolo**. Take your passport in case you want to cross into France.

Alba

Solid red-brick towers rise above the heart of Alba, a wine town that has kept enough of its medieval past to make it a worthwhile stop.

First settled in Neolithic times, Alba's modern claims to fame include cooking with truffles, and a Palio on donkey-back – inaugurated in 1932 as a snub to nearby Asti, eternal rival in all things including wine production. Towards the end of WWII, the town's citizens proclaimed Alba an independent republic for 23 days after partisans liberated it from the Germans.

Orientation & Information The tumbledown Piazza del Risorgimento, dominated by the 15th-century Cattedrale di San Lorenzo, leads into Via Vittorio Emanuele II, Alba's main street and a busy pedestrian zone. It in turn is capped by the ample Piazza Savona, whose porticoed footpaths are lined with chic cafés.

The APT office (☎ 0173-3 58 33), Piazza Medford, can help with suggestions on wineries to seek out in the region. They might be able to advise which of the many privately owned castles and medieval manors in the surrounding Langhe and Roero regions can be visited.

Places to Stay & Eat About the cheapest place in town is *Albergo Piemonte* (☎ 0173-44 13 54), Piazza Rossetti 6, which has

Cin Cin

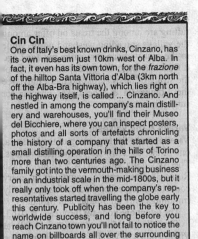

One of Italy's best known drinks, Cinzano, has its own museum just 10km west of Alba. In fact, it even has its own town, for the *frazione* of the hilltop Santa Vittoria d'Alba (3km north off the Alba-Bra highway), which lies right on the highway itself, is called ... Cinzano. And nestled in among the company's main distillery and warehouses, you'll find their Museo del Bicchiere, where you can inspect posters, photos and all sorts of artefacts chronicling the history of a company that started as a small distilling operation in the hills of Torino more than two centuries ago. The Cinzano family got into the vermouth-making business on an industrial scale in the mid-1800s, but it really only took off when the company's representatives started travelling the globe early this century. Publicity has been the key to worldwide success, and long before you reach Cinzano town you'll not fail to notice the name on billboards all over the surrounding countryside. ■

singles/doubles starting at L40,000/65,000. The *Leon d'Oro* (☎ 0173-44 19 01), Piazza Marconi 2, is similar. There are several cafés and trattorias on Piazza Savona and along Via Vittorio Emanuele II.

Getting There & Away Alba can be reached by bus from Torino, Cuneo and Asti (30km to the north-east).

Cherasco

The quiet medieval town of Cherasco, some 23km west of Alba on the confluence of the rivers Stura di Demonte and Tanaro, boasts a commanding position in the wine-growing hill region of Le Langhe. The local castle was built in 1348 by Luchino Visconti, and in September the place comes to life for the traditional celebratory bonfire *(falò)* at harvest time. More important however is the snail – a central part of Langhe cuisine. Some people come here just to savour this delicacy, and a good place to do so is the tiny and welcoming *Osteria della Rosa Rossa* (☎ 0172-48 81 33). A meal will cost you from about L30,000, and you may well need to book ahead. Cherasco is on the Alba-Bra (a few km north) bus line.

EASTERN PIEMONTE

Asti

Settled long before it was made a Roman colony in 89 BC, the town has had a more turbulent history than its subdued aspect might suggest. An independent city state in the 13th and 14th centuries, it subsequently was passed around between Spain, Austria, Napoleon's France and finally the Savoys, prior to unification.

The largely flat lands around Asti produce grapes that make some of Italy's top sparkling wines.

Information The APT office (☎ 53 03 57), Piazza Alfieri 34, in the centre of town, has information about the town and can assist with itineraries for the wine areas.

The telephone code is ☎ 0141 and there's a Telecom office on the same square.

Things to See & Do The **cathedral**, Piazza Cattedrale, is a large, 14th-century, Gothic construction. The city's other noteworthy church is the **Chiesa di San Secondo**, Asti's patron saint. During the late 13th century, the region became one of Italy's wealthiest, and some 100 towers of the period stand as reminders of its glorious past.

Special Events On the third Sunday of every September, 21 jockeys spur their horses around a chaotic course in the regional wine centre of Asti; the prize a banner known as the Palio. The medieval horse race, revived in 1967 and dating back to the 13th century, comes at the end of a week-long wine festival.

Places to Stay & Eat September is a difficult time to find a place to stay. The nearest camping ground is *Campeggio Umberto Cagni* (☎ 27 12 38), Via Valmanera 78, off Corso Volta. *Albergo Antico Paradiso* (☎ 21 43 85), Corso Torino 329, has singles/doubles with shower from L40,000/75,000, and the *Cavour* (☎ 53 02 22), Piazza Marconi

12, has a few singles/doubles for L50,000/70,000, or L60,000/93,000 with a bathroom.

Asti is something of a culinary centre and has restaurants to suit most budgets; try on and around Piazza Alfieri or pick up a list from the APT office.

Getting There & Away Trains run to Torino and Genova, and the region's bus station is just near the train station. By car, you can take the A21 Torino-Piacenza autostrada. It is also an easy drive from Genova on good roads, starting with the SS35.

NORTHERN PIEMONTE

Head north-east from Torino towards Milano, and you'll pass through wide plains that largely typify eastern Piemonte – some of it so flat and wet it's good for growing rice, as is evident on the approaches to Vercelli. Take a left here and aim north; the landscape quickly changes as the lower slopes preceding the Swiss Alps come into view. Skiing (even in summer!), hiking and white-water rafting are among the treats on offer among the valleys spreading west and north, while to the east you can you strike out for Lago d'Orta and Lago Maggiore, the first two of the string of lakes across northern Italy. See the Lombardia & The Lakes chapter for further information.

Varallo & the Valsesia

Varallo marks the beginning of the Valsesia, one of the less crowded Piemontese valleys. The APT della Valsesia (☎ 5 12 80), Corso Roma 38, has plenty of pamphlets on every conceivable aspect of the area. It's open daily (mornings only on Sunday and Monday).

The telephone code for the area is ☎ 0163.

The *Albergo Monte Rosa* (☎ 5 11 00), at Via Regaldi 4 in Varallo, is a delightful place and all the rooms face tree-covered hills. Immaculate singles/doubles cost L45,000/80,000.

Varallo makes sense as a starting point if only by virtue of being a railhead and bus

Battle of the Oranges

The mildly charming plains town of Ivrea, 35km north-east of Torino explodes out of its year-round torpor to celebrate the Battaglie delle Arance (Battle of the Oranges) in February – the highpoint of its Carnevale celebrations.

The story goes that, back in medieval times, a miller chose another miller's pretty young daughter for his wife. So far so good. But the nasty tyrant, like many other feudal rulers, reserved for himself the right to the first round with any woman in town to be married. A feisty individual, the miller's daughter was so upset by this that she sparked a revolt by the impoverished townspeople. On foot and armed only with stones, they launched themselves against the tyrant's troops, pelting them as they rode around the town in horse-drawn carts. This desperate rising went into the town's folk history and centuries later provided an excuse for rival gangs from different parts of town to stage an annual riot around Carnevale.

When Napoleon occupied this part of Italy at the beginning of the 19th century, his administrators decided to order everyone to wear red revolutionary bonnets. Just what immediate effect this had on the Carnevale celebrations is hard to say, but the red bonnet became mandatory millinery for anyone on foot at the time of Carnevale. Napoleon's men also put a stop to the fatal nature of the brawling, ordering that from then on the re-enactment of the famous uprising was to be carried out with oranges.

And so today, for three days running in early February, teams of 'revolutionaries' wait at four different piazzas for roaming carts laden with helmeted 'soldiers' – and they pound each other with tonnes of oranges specially imported from Sicilia for the occasion. In the midst of the mayhem, a colourful costume procession featuring the miller's daughter *(la mugnaia)*, medieval characters and Napoleonic troops slips and slides its way along a slimy carpet of squashed orange (well mingled with horse manure). Beware – *anyone* on the ground caught not wearing some kind of red headgear is considered fair game for a massive orange assault by the 'rebel' squads.

Ivrea is an easy day trip from Torino, accessible by regular trains and occasional buses. The centre of town, where all the fun takes place, is a few minutes' walk from the train station. ■

line junction. A narrow winding road also links the valley directly with the pretty **Lago d'Orta**. Again, see the Lombardia & the Lakes chapter for details.

The Valsesia to Monte Rosa From Varallo, at 450m, you can follow the valley up towards Monte Rosa and the Swiss frontier, where some peaks exceed 4000m. **Alagna** is the last town along the valley, and you can get detailed local skiing information there at Monterosa Ski. Some 20 *rifugi* dot the area, the Capanna Osservatorio Regina Mergherita at Punta Gnifetti being the highest at 4559m. A cable car at Alagna climbs to Punta Indren (3260m), from where it is possible (in summer at least) to hike to various of the several peaks. Get expert local advice on what can be safely undertaken before setting out, as some of the trails require expert Alpine skills and gear.

Some 25 Alpine guides are on the books at Alagna – inquire at the IAT tourist office (☎ 92 29 88), Piazza Grober.

Domodossola

The last main stop before Switzerland, Domodossola might once have been an attractive pre-Alpine town, but the suburban spread and hotels have ruined the effect. Those intending to explore the surrounding valleys should make haste to do so and leave this place behind them.

Information The APT delle Ossola office (☎ 0324-48 13 08), Corso P Ferraris 49, has detailed information about walking and skiing. It's open Monday to Friday from 9 am to noon and 2 to 5 pm. Most resorts are well organised and offer Settimana Bianca packages. The Comunità Montana Valle Ossola (☎ 4 63 91) is also a useful place to get information. The telephone code for the area is ☎ 0324.

Places to Stay & Eat *Albergo Domus* (☎ 24 23 25), Via Cuccioni 12, is the town's cheapest hotel, and very central, with singles/doubles from L30,000/50,000. *Albergo La Pendola* (☎ 24 37 04) is further away from the centre and train station. It has singles from L35,000 or doubles with a bathroom for L75,000. Both have restaurants. Otherwise, the *Trattoria Romana*, Via Binda 16, is not unreasonable and specialises in French and Roman cuisine.

Getting There & Away Trains regularly run to Milano, and Novara for Torino. You can also board international trains to Switzerland (including the charming run to Locarno – a trip well worth doing), France, Germany and even the Czech Republic from here.

The bus station is in front of the train station. Milano is 125km south-east, and Torino 168km south-west of Domodossola.

Valle d'Aosta

Covering a mere 3262sq km and with a population of only 117,000, the Valle d'Aosta is the smallest of the Italian regions, but also one of the wealthiest. The Valdestans, as they are called, still speak the Franco-Provençal patois, and French is afforded equal rights with Italian. To the east of the region, villagers cling to the German dialect, Tich. The valley has always been an important passageway through the Alps and is lined with castles. The opening of the Monte Bianco (Mont Blanc) tunnel in 1965, which connects Courmayeur in the west to the French resort of Chamonix, turned what had been a quiet valley into a major road-freight thoroughfare and one of Europe's premier skiing areas. Unfortunately, over-development and pollution soon followed, although you can certainly still 'get away from it all' in the valleys running off Valle d'Aosta.

Valle d'Aosta enjoys self-governing status, stemming from its binational origins, which means 90% of local taxes are spent in the province.

The region shares, with France, Europe's highest mountain, Monte Bianco (Mont Blanc, 4807m) and, with Switzerland, the

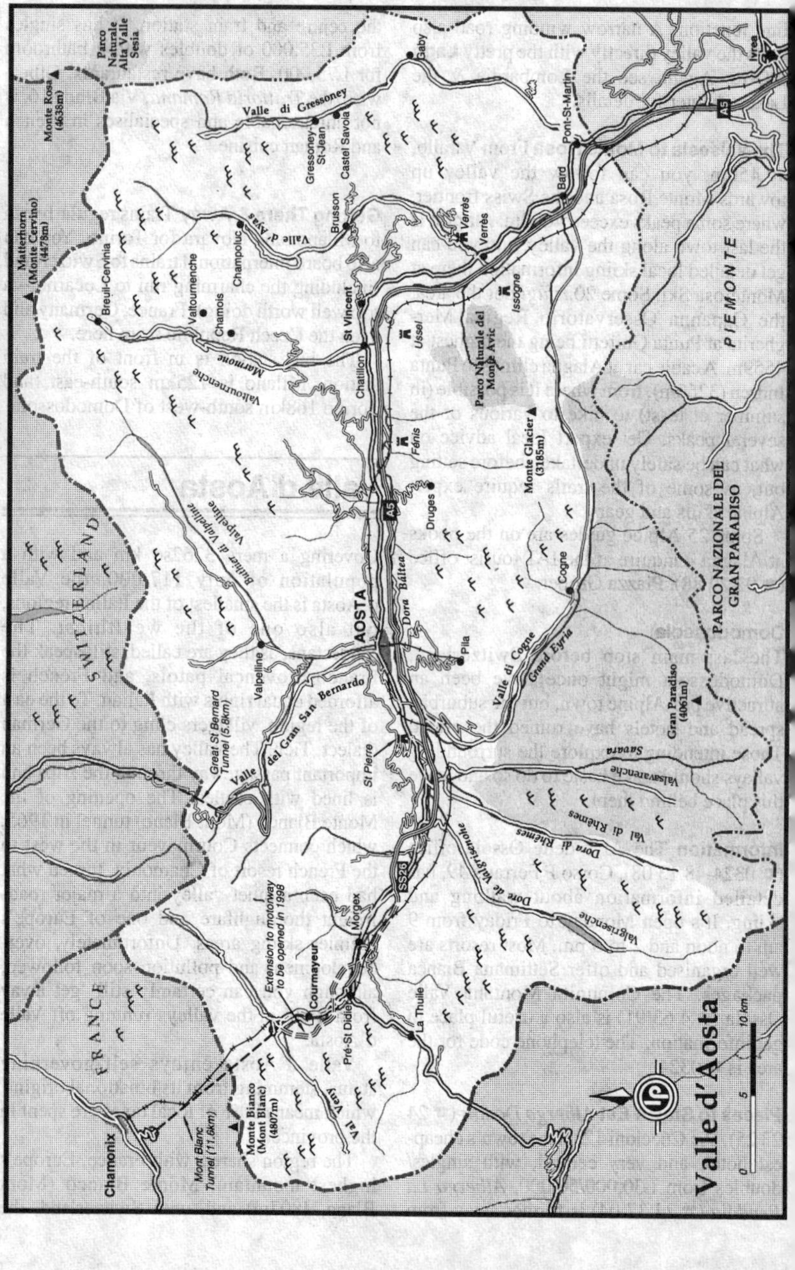
Valle d'Aosta
0
5
10 km
Chamonix
Mont Blanc Tunnel (11.6km)
Monte Bianco (Mont Blanc) (4807m)
FRANCE
SWITZERLAND
Courmayeur
Pré-St Didier
La Thuile
Val Veny
Morgex
Extension to motorway to be opened in 1998
SS26
Great St Bernard Tunnel (5.8km)
Valle del Gran San Bernardo
St Pierre
Valpelline
Buthier di Valpelline
AOSTA
A5
Pila
Dora Báltea
Valle di Cogne
Grand Eyvia
Cogne
Gran Paradiso (4061m)
PARCO NAZIONALE DEL GRAN PARADISO
Savara
Valsavarenche
Val di Rhêmes
Dora di Rhêmes
Dora de Valgrisenche
Valgrisenche
Druges
Fénis
Monte Glacier (3185m)
Parco Naturale del Monte Avic
Chatillon
St Vincent
Ussel
Issogne
Verrès
Bard
Pont-St-Martin
Ivrea
PIEMONTE
Gaby
Valle di Gressoney
Gressoney-St-Jean
Castel Savoia
Brusson
Valle d'Ayas
Champoluc
Marmore
Valtournenche
Chamois
Breuil-Cervinia
Matterhorn (Monte Cervino) (4478m)
Monte Rosa (4638m)
Parco Naturale Alta Valle Sesia

Matterhorn (Monte Cervino, 4478m). It also takes in Monte Rosa (4638m) and the Gran Paradiso (4061m), which it shares with Piemonte. Its resort towns – Courmayeur, Breuil-Cervinia, La Thuile, Gressoney St Jean and Cogne – and valleys offer a feast of year-round activities. Some towns, such Breuil-Cervinia, are anonymous, custom-built resort towns but others, such as Cogne, retain their mountain village character.

There is plenty of good hiking in areas such as the Parco Nazionale del Gran Paradiso. More adventurous (and expert) mountaineers might want to tackle Monte Bianco. It is possible to reach 3462m by cable car, from where trekkers can set off across the ice to the peak (4807m), although this is for expert climbers only – tourists should stay very close to the rifugio.

Plenty of good information is available at the tourist offices in the region about walking trails and mountain rifugi and huts. Many trails will take you to high altitudes, so it is necessary to be well prepared with the correct clothing and footwear, good maps and other essentials. For advice on what to take on long treks see the section on Trekking in the Dolomiti in the Trentino-Alto Adige chapter. As in Piemonte, ☎ 118 is the number to call in case of emergency in the mountains.

Human settlement in the Valle d'Aosta dates to 3000 BC and Neolithic and early Bronze Age remains have been discovered. Early Roman sites dot the valley, and Aosta is known as the Roma of the Alps.

The cuisine of the Valle d'Aosta makes liberal use of the local cheese, Fontina, a curious cross between Gouda and Brie. Traditional dishes include *valpellineuntze*, a thick soup of cabbage, bread, beef broth and Fontina, and *carbonada con polenta*, traditionally made with the meat of the chamoix, although beef is now generally used. *Mocetta* (dried beef) is popular. The valley also boasts numerous small, government-subsidised cooperative vineyards, most producing whites, reds and *rosatos* (rosé). These wines are generally dry and fruity.

AOSTA

Aosta is the capital and only major city of the region, and has a population of about 37,000. It lies at the centre of the valley, with the Dora Baltea river on its southern boundary and the Buthier river on its eastern side, and is the transport hub for the region. It has limited attractions, but is a jumping-off point to the region's 11 valleys and their resorts.

Orientation

From Piazza Manzetti, outside the train station, Via G Carducci, to the west, and Via Giorgio Carrel, to the east, follow the Roman wall around the city. Viale della Stazione and Via Olletti lead from the train station into the town centre. The former goes to Piazza Narbonne, which houses the main post office and bus station, and the latter to Piazza Chanoux, the main square.

The city is laid out on a grid following the Roman pattern and most of the historic centre is closed to traffic. Via de Tillier, west of Piazza Chanoux, is Aosta's main boulevard and has a good selection of restaurants, bars, cafés and fashion shops.

Information

Tourist Office The APT office (☎ 23 66 27) is at Piazza Chanoux 8 and is open daily from 8 am to 1 pm and 3 to 8 pm. It is open on Sunday year-round from 8 am to 1 pm and also during the winter and summer high seasons from 3 to 8 pm. It has information on skiing conditions and cheap package deals and can assist with accommodation. The Valle d'Aosta APT has an office in Roma, at Via Sistina 3 (☎ 06-474 41 04).

Money Exchange booths are located in Piazza Chanoux and there are banks along Viale della Stazione.

Post & Communications The main post office is on Piazza Narbonne and is open Monday to Friday from 8.15 am to 7.30 pm and Saturday to 1 pm. The postcode for central Aosta is 11100.

There is a Telecom office at Viale della

VALLE D'AOSTA

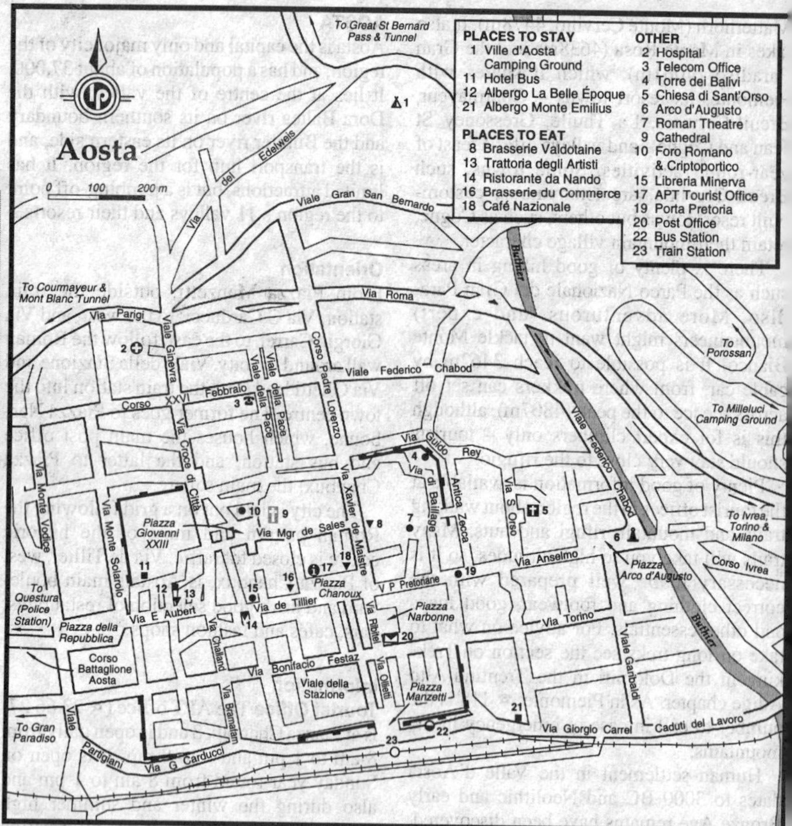

Pace 9 which is open Monday to Friday from 8.15 am to 12.15 pm and 2 to 5 pm.

Aosta's telephone code is ☎ 0165.

Bookshop Libreria Minerva, Via de Tillier 34, has Istituto Geografico Centrale hiking maps covering pretty much all the Valle d'Aosta region. They are on a 1:25,000 scale and sell for L12,000 apiece.

Laundry You'll find a laundry at Via Chambery 60.

Emergency Call ☎ 113 for immediate police attendance or contact the questura (☎ 26 21 69), Via Battaglione Aosta 169. For medical attention, call ☎ 30 41, or the Ospedale Regionale (☎ 4 14 00), Viale Ginevra. For an ambulance, call ☎ 30 42 11.

Things to See

The main attractions are the Roman ruins. The **Arco d'Augusto** is placed in a straight axis between the Porta Pretoria (the main gate to the Roman city) and the Buthier river bridge at the end of Via Anselmo. The arch ears a crucifix, added during medieval imes. Walk the 300m westwards from the ridge to the gate and head north along Via i Baillage to the **Roman theatre**. Part of its 2m-high façade remains intact and performances are often held in the well-preserved ower section. All that remains of the **Foro Romano**, another couple of blocks westvards beneath the Piazza Giovanni XXIII, is colonnaded walkway known as the **Criptoportico**. The **Torre dei Balivi**, at the orner of the Roman wall, was used until ecently as a prison.

The **cathedral**, also in Piazza Giovanni XXIII, has a neoclassical façade which belies the impressive Gothic interior. The carved wooden choir stalls are particularly beautiful. Two floor mosaics in the church, dating from the 12th to 14th centuries, are also worth studying. The cathedral has a museum with religious treasures from hroughout the region.

The **Chiesa di Sant'Orso** located in Via Sant' Orso dates from the 10th century but vas altered on several occasions, notably n the 15th century, when Giorgi di Challant of the ruling family ordered the original frescoes covered and a new roof nstalled. Remnants of the frescoes can be viewed by climbing up into the cavity between the original and 15th-century ceilings. Ask the church attendant for a our. The interior and the magnificently carved choir are Gothic and recent excavaions have unearthed the remains of an earlier church, possibly from the 8th century. The Romanesque cloister with ornately carved capitals representing bibical scenes is to the right of the church.

Activities

Rock-climbing can be conducted on the rocks known as Adrénaline, Polyester and Lipstick. For information, call Cooperativa Interguide (☎ 4 09 39), Via Monte Emilius 13. Centro Volo Valle d'Aosta (☎ 26 24 42) can set you up for hang-gliding or paragliding.

The tourist office can advise on walking trails or put you in contact with an Alpine guide if you prefer not to go it alone.

Special Events

Each October thousands of Valdestans come together to watch cow fights. Known traditionally as the Bataille de Reines (Battle of the Queens), the event is organised along the lines of a beauty contest. Knockouts start in March, when locals from across the region prime their best bovines for battle, and end with the finals on the third Sunday in October, when the queen of the cows is crowned. This might seem a bit strange, but it is a tradition from the days when cows returning from mountain fields would tussle with each other. The losing cow is not injured and the match ends when one pulls away. The queen sells for millions of lire.

The Foire de Sant' Orso, the annual wood fair held on 30 to 31 January in honour of the town's patron saint, brings together craftspeople from all over the valley who display their carvings and then present an item to the saint at Chiesa di Sant'Orso. It is held near the Porta Pretoria.

Places to Stay

Accommodation in Aosta is generally expensive and difficult to find, particularly during the high seasons around Christmas and Easter. Cheaper and more pleasant lodgings can be found in the hinterland, which is usually accessible by bus. Check with the APT. There are no hostels in the region.

The *Ville d'Aosta* camping ground (☎ 36 13 60), Viale Gran San Bernardo 76, is just north of the town centre and opens from June to September. *Milleluci* (☎ 23 52 78), about 1km east of Aosta, is open all year and can be reached by bus No 11.

In Aosta, try the hotel *Albergo La Belle Époque* (☎ 26 22 76), Via d'Avise 18 (off Via E Aubert), which has singles/doubles starting at L30,000/50,000, and up to L25,000 more with private bathroom in the high season. *Albergo Mochettaz* (☎ 4 37 06), about 1km east of the town centre at Corso Ivrea 107, has singles/doubles for L37,000/57,000. *Albergo Monte Emilius* (☎ 3 56 92),

Via Giorgio Carrel 11, has rooms from L50,000/ 80,000. *Hotel Bus* (☎ 4 36 45), Via Malherbes 18, on the south side of Piazza Giovanni XXIII, is for the fuller wallet with good rooms costing as much as L88,000/ 127,000.

If you have a car, try *Hotel Hirondelle* (☎ 5 11 10), which is 8km into the hills from Aosta at Arpuilles and has great views of the city and mountains. Singles/doubles range up to L45,000/75,000.

Almost all hotels in Aosta offer Settimana Bianca packages.

Places to Eat

The penny-conscious will find several self-service restaurants around that won't hurt too much.

Otherwise, *Ristorante da Nando*, Via de Tillier 41, is reasonably priced, as is *Brasserie du Commerce*, Via de Tillier 10. Tucked away at Via Maillet 3, the *Trattoria degli Artisti* is recommended – L35,000 should see your way through a satisfying meal. At the top end is *Brasserie Valdotaine*, Via Xavier de Maistre 8.

Café Nazionale, Piazza Chanoux, is one of the classier places to enjoy your morning macchiato.

Things to Buy

Tradition has it that Sant'Orso gave carved, wooden shoes known as *sabo* to the city's poor. Valdestans continue to carve shoes, tiny houses and ceremonial pots which are still widely used. Shops throughout the city, particularly along Via Porte Pretoriane, sell these goods.

Getting There & Away

Air Aosta has a small airport which services commuter flights. The airports at Torino and Geneva are both about an hour away by car.

Bus Buses to Milano, Roma, Firenze, Torino and Geneva leave from the bus station (☎ 26 20 27) virtually opposite the train station. Other services cover most of the region – buses to Courmayeur are particularly frequent.

Train The town is serviced by trains from most parts of Italy, via Torino and Milano. Most travellers to and from Milano must change trains at Chivasso. A limited train service connects Aosta with Pré-St Didier about 5km short of Courmayeur.

Car & Motorcycle The A5 from Torino and Milano terminates east of the city and continues along its northern edge as Via Roma and then Via Parigi, which connects with the Monte Bianco (Mont Blanc) tunnel. Viale Gran San Bernardo, also to the north, connects Aosta with the Great St Bernard Tunnel and Switzerland. The A5 will eventually connect with the Monte Bianco tunnel. Aosta has several large car parks, including one opposite the train station.

Hitching Hitchhikers should have no trouble on Viale Gran San Bernardo, Via Roma or Via Parigi.

Getting Around

The town is quite small and all sites are easily reached on foot.

Navetta (shuttle) buses run through town from the train station. Taxis can be reached on ☎ 3 18 31.

AROUND AOSTA

If you need a break from the slopes, the Aosta valley is peppered with castles, many of them Romanesque and Gothic, just waiting to be explored. Each castle is within view of the next, and messages used to be flagged along the valley. Heading east from Aosta is the magnificently restored **Castello di Fénis**, formerly of the Challant family and featuring rich frescoes, as well as period graffiti. It was never really used as a defensive post, but rather served as a plush residence. Past St Vincent, the sober **Castello di Verrès** is more the real thing, doing sentinel duty atop its rocky perch. About 1km south of the Dora river, below the town of Verrès, you'd hardly know the restored 15th-century **Castello d'Issogne** was a castle – it looks for all the world like a stately home. Farther down the valley still, owards Pont St Martin, the fortress of **Bard** vas a no-nonsense military outpost given hort shrift by Napoleon on his first cam-aign into Italy. Once at Pont St Martin, you ould strike north for Gressoney St Jean. Just ear the town is the fairy-tale **Castel Savoia**, egun in 1900 for the Italian royals.

Heading west towards Monte Bianco from Aosta, the **Castello di Saint Pierre**, which ouses a natural history museum, is the main tem of interest on the castle route.

Entry to all but Bard is L4000 each, and n each case people are sent through at half-hourly intervals. A ceiling of 20 to 50 visitors n any half-hour period is imposed, so you nay have to wait if there's a crowd. Bard is free, and many other castles reduced to ruins invite impromptu scrambles for the true buff. The Aosta APT has full timetable information.

Probably the only reason to visit **St Vincent**, Valle d'Aosta's second biggest city, is for its casino and as a stopping-off point for the Valle d'Ayas and Valtournenche, which leads to the Matterhorn.

PILA

This is the closest resort to Aosta (about 18km south) and prices are quite reasonable. There is a village at Pila, but most services, such as the tourist office, police and medical services, are handled from Aosta. The telephone code is ☎ 0165.

Activities

Skiing Pila is among the largest ski areas in the valley, with more than 80km of runs, including about 10km for cross-country skiing. It is serviced by 15 lifts, including four cable ways, one of which connects the village with Aosta. It offers challenging and difficult black runs and has a competition slalom course, but also caters for beginners with many easy runs. The highest slope reaches 2700m, in the shadow of Gran Paradiso.

Walking This is not one of the best areas for walking if you like high Alpine country, but the lower slopes leading down into the Dora Baltea valley provide picturesque and easy walks. Of the two rifugi in the Charvensod area a few km south of Aosta, one opens all year. Some lifts operate in summer for walkers or day-trippers.

Places to Stay

Aosta is a cheaper bet than Pila. The *Soleil et Neige* camping ground (☎ 5 99 48), open all year, is about 7km from the resort on the way to Aosta. *Hotel La Nouva* (☎ 52 10 05) has singles/doubles for L55,000/80,000 in the high season. *Albergo Chacaril*, (☎ 52 12 15) has rooms for L60,000/110,000 (considerably less in off season). The best Settimana Bianca deals are in Aosta.

Getting There & Away

Two roads, one from Aosta and the other from Gressan, a town about 6km west of Aosta, lead to Pila. A cable car connects Aosta with the village. SVAP buses Nos 4 and 5 go from Aosta to Charvensod and Gressan respectively, but there is no bus service to Pila.

COURMAYEUR & MONTE BIANCO

With much of the original village intact and set against the backdrop of Monte Bianco (Mont Blanc), Courmayeur is one of the more picturesque of the skiing resorts in Valle d'Aosta. It is also one of the most expensive. Out of season, wealthy Milanese and Turinese women leave their fur coats in a local furrier's vault – minks and ermines are too valuable to be worn in the streets of their home cities. The resort has more than 140km of downhill and cross-country skiing runs and a feast of summer activities, including skiing, horse riding, hang-gliding, canoeing and 280km of mountain walking trails. A cable-car service leaves from La Palud, near Courmayeur, for Punta Helbronner (3462m) on Monte Bianco – an extraordinary 20-minute ride. It is also possible to organise guided treks up the mountain. See the Activities section for details.

Information

Tourist Office The APT office (☎ 84 20 60), Piazzale Monte Bianco 13, opens daily from 9 am to 7 pm in summer. In winter it opens Monday to Friday from 9 am to 12.30 pm and 3 to 6.30 pm; weekends from 9 am to 7.30 pm. The Associazione Operatori Turistici del Monte Bianco (☎ 0165-84 23 70), Piazzale Monte Bianco 3, can assist with accommodation.

The telephone code is ☎ 0165.

Emergency For police assistance, phone ☎ 113. For medical attention and ambulance, phone ☎ 80 96 80 or go to the Pronto Soccorso at the Ospedale Regionale d'Aosta (☎ 30 42 56).

Activities

Skiing Monte Bianco has skiing year-round. The Ski Club Courmayeur Monte Bianco (☎ 84 24 41) is at Piazzale Monte Bianco, and there is a skiing school (☎ 84 24 77) at Strada Regionale 51. The best bet if you are just skiing is to book a Settimana Bianca package through an agent such as CIT. Most ski runs, chairlifts and ski lifts can be reached via the Courmayeur, Dolonne and Val Veny cable cars. For details, check with the APT or the cable-way station in Val Veny (☎ 84 35 66), or Cableways Monte Bianco in La Palud (☎ 8 99 25).

Walking & Climbing The APT has a basic map of walking trails in the Valdigne and on Monte Bianco. You would however be better off with the IGC 1:25,000 map No 107. If you walk the higher trails on Monte Bianco, or want to walk on the glaciers, go properly equipped and consider hiring a guide. Many people who take the Punta Helbronner cable way are completely unprepared for what awaits them at almost 3500m. Even if it's sweltering in the valley, it could be -10°C at Punta Helbronner. Moral of the story: take heavy winter clothes. Head up early in the morning, because by early afternoon heavy weather usually descends on the summit area.

You can continue from Punta Helbronner down to Chamonix in France (bring your passport and check if you need a visa to enter France). The return fare from La Palud to Punta Helbronner varies according to the season, starting at L39,000 and reaching L44,000. You can do a round trip either way between La Palud and Chamonix – the return leg is by bus. Mont Blanc Tour Operator, Piazzale Monte Bianco 3, in Courmayeur, sells tickets.

The Società Guide di Courmayeur (mountain guide association; ☎ 84 20 64), Piazza Henry 2, organises activities including rock-climbing courses and a seven-day guided trek up Monte Bianco.

Many rifugi and huts are located along walking trails in the mountains around Courmayeur. They are marked on all walking maps. Those offering hotel-style service and accommodation are usually only open in summer. Unattended huts, or *bivacchi*, are open year-round. The APT publishes a guide to the different huts.

Mountain Biking To rent a bike, go to Noleggio Ulisse (☎ 84 22 55), in front of the Courmayeur chairlift, or Club des Sports (☎ 8 95 70), in Planpincieux.

Other Activities The Scuola di Canoa e Rafting Courmayeur (☎ 80 00 88) can advise on canoeing. If you want to go ballooning, contact the Club Aérostatique Mont Blanc (☎ 76 55 25).

Places to Stay & Eat

During peak seasons, accommodation in Courmayeur is very expensive if you aren't on a package deal, but the towns along the valleys, of La Palud, Dolonne, Entrèves, La Saxe, Plan Ponquet, Val Ferret, Pré-St Didier and Morgex, offer reasonably priced rooms. Contact the APT office or the local hotel association, the Associazione Operatori Turistici del Monte Bianco for assistance.

Campers can head for *CAI Mont Blanc* (☎ 8 92 15) in Val Veny (open August and September only), and *Val Veny-Cuignon* (☎ 86 90 73; open July to September), both within easy reach of Courmayeur where

Albergo Serena (☎ 84 22 63), Via Villair 3, has rooms from L45,000/70,000 in the high season (doubles with private bathroom L85,000). In La Palud, *Albergo La Quercia* (☎ 8 99 31) charges from L50,000 to L70,000 for doubles. There are good food shops along Via Roma, in the old part of town. Most restaurants are also along Via Roma. *Café des Guides*, Viale Monte Bianco 2, is a popular spot for a snack.

Getting There & Away

Three trains a day from Aosta terminate at Pré-St Didier, with bus connections to the main bus station at Piazzale Monte Bianco, outside the tourist office. Courmayeur is serviced by long haul buses from Milano, Torino and Geneva. Local buses connect the resort with Aosta and surrounding towns and villages. By car, take the SS26 from Aosta. The trip from Chamonix through the Monte Bianco tunnel for a small car costs L43,000 (or L54,000 return).

VALTOURNENCHE

Stretching from the Valle d'Aosta to the Matterhorn, the Valtournenche takes in several smaller and reasonably priced skiing areas – Antey-St André, Chamois, La Magdeleine and Torgnon – and culminates in the resorts of Valtournenche and Breuil-Cervinia. The latter is the second-largest resort in Valle d'Aosta and is modern, purpose-built, expensive and pretty ugly, although it offers some of the best skiing in Europe.

Information

Tourist Office The Matterhorn Central Valley APT office (☎ 0166-54 82 66) is in Antey-Saint-André and the Breuil-Cervinia office (☎ 0166-94 91 36) is at Via Carrel 29. In the town of Valtournenche, the APT office (☎ 0166-9 20 29) is at Via Roma 45.

The telephone code for the valley is ☎ 0166.

Mountain & Alpine Guides For guides, contact the Società Guide del Cervino (☎ 94 81 69), Via Carrel.

Activities

Skiing There are several resorts in the valley, all well equipped with downhill and cross-country runs. From Breuil-Cervinia, eight cable ways and 18 lifts take skiers into breathtaking terrain. Summer skiing is also possible as several cable ways and lifts continue to operate, taking skiers on to the Plateau Rosa. This resort introduced Valle d'Aosta to night skiing, in the Campetto area. For details, contact the tourist office or Sciovia (ski lift) Crétaz (☎ 94 86 76). In Breuil-Cervinia, you can arrange lessons with the Cielo Alto ski school (☎ 94 84 51).

Walking Basic walking maps are available at the tourist office, but if you want to tackle the Matterhorn you need to be properly dressed and equipped. Get a 1:25,000 walking map, such as the IGC map No 108.

Places to Stay

Campers in Valtournenche should make for *Glair-Lago di Maen* ground (☎ 9 20 77). In Breuil-Cervinia, *Albergo Leonardo Carrel* (☎ 94 90 77) has rooms for L50,000/67,000, while *Hotel Sporting* (☎ 94 91 12) has nothing for under L100,000/120,000. If you're heading there to ski, it is best to arrange a Settimana Bianca package.

Getting There & Away

Buses operate from Aosta to the resorts and most ski areas in the valley. Savda (☎ 0165-36 12 44) operates services from Courmayeur, Aosta and Châtillon to Breuil-Cervinia, and on to other resort villages. Dinotours (☎ 015-2 22 15) also operates bus services in the valley.

GRAN PARADISO NATIONAL PARK

The Parco Nazionale del Gran Paradiso was Italy's first national park, established in 1922 after Victor Emmanuel II gave his hunting reserve to the state. It incorporates the valleys around the Gran Paradiso (4061m), three of which are in the Valle d'Aosta: the Valsavarenche, Val di Rhêmes and the beautiful Valle di Cogne (check out IGC map No 102). On the Piemonte side of the mountain

VALLE D'AOSTA

the park incorporates the valleys of Soana and Orco. In 1945, the ibex had been almost hunted to extinction and there were only 419 left in the park. Today due to conscious policy there are almost 4000.

Excellent cross-country trails line the Valle di Cogne, but the park is really devoted to summer activities. There are numerous well-marked trails and rifugi. The main point of departure for the Gran Paradiso mountain is Pont in the Valsavarenche.

If you are interested in a guided, four day trek in the park, contact the Società Guide del Gran Paradiso-Valsavarenche (☎ 9 51 03) or the tourist office. The tourist office in Cogne publishes a brief walking guide.

Valle di Cogne is the most picturesque, unspoiled valley with a good range of accommodation in the village.

The telephone code for the whole area is ☎ 0165.

Information

Tourist Offices The Gran Paradiso Mountain Community Tourist Office (☎ 9 50 55) is at Loc Champagne 18, Villeneuve. Cogne's APT (☎ 7 40 40) is at Piazza Chanoux 36. Both have plenty of information about summer and winter activities. If you want a mountain guide, try the APT or the Società Guide di Cogne (☎ 7 43 61), Via Cavagnet 10. Les Amis du Paradis (the Friends of Paradise Association, ☎ 7 48 35), in Cogne, has reams of information about the area.

Emergency For police, call ☎ 113, or in Cogne call ☎ 7 40 24, and in Saint-Pierre call ☎ 90 30 16. First-aid is available in Saint-Pierre (☎ 90 38 11) and Cogne (☎ 74 91 07).

Places to Stay

If you're camping, *Al Sole* (☎ 7 42 37) in the Lillaz area, Valle di Cogne, is open all year. In Valsavarenche, *Camping Pont Breuil* (☎ 9 54 58), at Pont, is open June to September.

Hotels in Cogne include the *Albergo Stambecco* (☎ 7 40 68), Via Clementina 21, which charges as little as L25,000/40,000 and as much as L40,000/80,000, depending on the rooms and season. *Hotel du Solei*l (☎ 7 40 33), Viale Cavagnet 24, has singles/doubles for anything up to L50,000/96,000. *Hotel au Vieux Grenier* (☎ 7 40 02), Via Limnea Borealis 32, charges a minimum of around L50,000/90,000.

Getting There & Away

Several bus companies operate reliable services between valley towns and Cogne, and on to Aosta and beyond. Cogne can also be reached by cable car from Pila.

AROUND MONTE ROSA

The Valle di Gressoney, the first of the Valle d'Aosta's eastern valleys, and the parallel Valle d'Ayas, are dominated by the massive Monte Rosa (4633m). Both valleys are picturesque and also very popular in both summer and winter.

In Valle di Gressoney, stay in Gressoney St-Jean, a pretty mountain village by a lake which has retained its traditional atmosphere. Gressoney-La-Trinité is higher up the valley and therefore closer to the main walking trails and ski runs, but is these days basically taken over by anonymous tourist facilities.

In Valle d'Ayas, the main resort is Champoluc at the head of the valley, but Brusson is also a good option, particularly if you're interested in easy half or one-day walks. Serious walkers may want to invest in the IGC map No 101.

Information

Tourist Offices APT offices are in Champoluc (☎ 30 71 13), Brusson (☎ 30 02 40), La Trinité (☎ 36 61 43) and St Jean (☎ 35 51 85). For information about mountain guides, contact the tourist offices, or the Società Guide di Champoluc-Ayas (☎ 30 89 60).

Telephone The telephone code in the higher valley (including Champoluc, Brusson, La Trinité, St Jean and Verrès) is ☎ 0125. Lower down it becomes ☎ 0166. All numbers listed in this section require the upper valley code.

mergency For police call ☎ 113. In Brusson, ☎ 30 01 32, in St Jean ☎ 35 51 92, nd in Verrès ☎ 92 93 24. For an ambulance nywhere in the valley, call ☎ 80 70 67.

Places to Stay

For camping, *Sole e Neve* (☎ 30 66 10) in Morenex, Valle d'Ayas, is open all year as is *a Pineta* (☎ 35 53 70) at Gressoney-St-Jean n the Valle di Gressoney. Hotels in the Valle l'Ayas include *Albergo Cré-Forné* (☎ 30 71 7) in Crest, with singles/doubles from .35,000/45,000, and *Hotel Beau Site* (☎ 30 1 44), Via Trois Villages 2, in Brusson. The atter charges L35,000/55,000.

In Gressoney-St-Jean, the *Hotel Grünes Vasser* (☎ 35 54 03), Strada Regionale 41, No 14, has singles/doubles for L45,000/70,000. *Hotel Lyskamm* (☎ 35 54 36), Strada Statale 505, No 1, has more upmarket rooms for L65,000/100,000. At Gressoney-La-Trinité, try the *Gasthaus Lysjoch* (☎ 36 61 50), Loc. Föhre 4, where rooms start at L70,000/120,000.

Getting There & Away

The train to Aosta stops in St Vincent and Verrès, from where you can catch a bus to either valley. SAVDA operates bus No 33 along the Valle di Gressoney and bus No 35 from Verrès to Champoluc. Bus No 40 connects Aosta with Champoluc, via Col de Joux. Leave the A5, SS26 or Aosta-Torino/Milano train at Pont-St-Martin and swing north for the Valle di Gressoney.

Lombardia & the Lakes

From the Alps to the lush plains of the Po river, Lombardia's (Lombardy's) often fractious political history is in part reflected in its geographical diversity. Beyond the financial metropolis of Milano, the region is peppered with affluent towns that conserve a distinct character inherited from the city-states period. Mantova, Cremona, Bergamo, Brescia and Pavia have wealth and style, but the northern clime and a degree of orderly self-satisfaction make them a little staid in comparison with cities farther south. The hard-working people of Milano have created Italy's economic and fashion capital; a businesslike place that more closely resembles the great cities of northern Europe.

Italy's richest and most developed region offers its populace numerous escape routes. The most popular is the stretch of enchanting lakes from Lago d'Orta to Lago di Garda.

Lombardia formed part of the Roman province of Gallia Cisalpina (Cisalpine Gaul) before it fell to barbarian tribes and later to the Germanic Lombards (Langobards). Interference by the Franks under Barbarossa in the 12th century ended when the cities united under the Lega Lombarda (Lombard League). After the Lega collapsed, Lombardia was divided among very powerful families – the Viscontis, Sforzas, Gonzagas and Scaligers and later invaded by Venetians, Habsburg Austria and Napoleon.

Lombard cuisine relies heavily on rice and polenta and features butter, cream and cheese from the Alpine pastures. Gorgonzola originated just outside Milano. Pasta is fresh and usually stuffed with squash, meat, cheese or spinach. As a dessert it can contain raisins or candied fruit. Meats are predominantly pork and veal – *cotoletta alla milanese* (fillet of veal fried in breadcrumbs) is famous.

Lombardia's sparkling wines are among Italy's best – the Franciacorta red is mellow, the white fruity and dry. The region around Lago di Garda also produces good wines.

HIGHLIGHTS

- The Duomo in Milano, Italy's most extravagant Gothic church. Climb up to the roof for views to the mountains
- A night at the opera, La Scala
- Jazz and drinks in Milano's Navigli district
- A visit to the magnificent Certosa di Pavia monastery south of Milano
- Boat rides on Lago di Como with a stop in Bellagio for lunch
- Wandering the Città Alta of Bergamo and hearing the strange *bergamasco* dialect

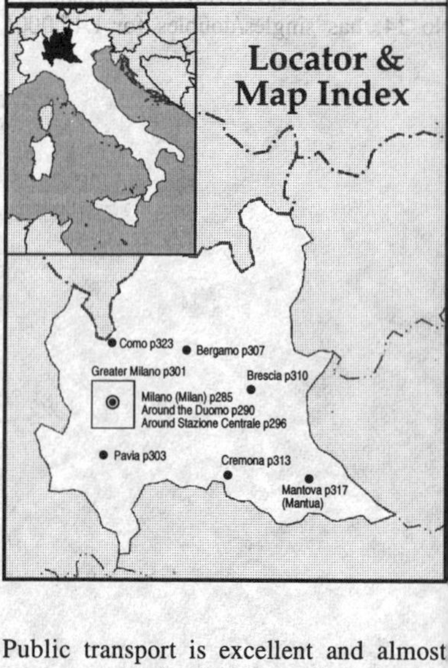

Public transport is excellent and almost every town can be reached easily by road or rail.

Milano

Obsessed with work and money, the Milanese run their busy metropolis with comparative efficiency and aplomb. Indeed, Milano

Milan) is synonymous with style – the country's economic engine room, it is also the world's design capital and rivals Paris as a leading fashion centre.

As Notre Dame cathedral is for Paris, so Milano's duomo is this city's most striking symbol. But however much Milano feels it should be the country's leading city (and not a few Milanese have a healthy disregard for Roma), it is smaller than the ancient imperial capital whose population rapidly overtook Milano's after WWII. But Milano is home to Italy's stock market, most of the country's major corporations and the nation's largest concentration of industry. The city and surrounding zone generate almost a quarter of Italy's tax revenue.

Milano's business and political leaders have long railed against corrupt and inefficient government in Roma and the subsidies directed to the south. This sense of protest spawned a separatist party in the late 1980s, the Northern League, which, under the whimsical direction of Umberto Bossi, has had its political ups and downs. Milano's city council is one of several in the League's hands, but the Disney-style proclamation of an independent northern

republic of Padania in late 1996 was something of a flop.

Meanwhile, years after Tangentopoli (see History in the Facts about the Country chapter), Milano's judges continue to form the core of those pursuing political, business and fashion industry figures over bribery cases, often involving tax inspectors of the Guardia di Finanza. The slick entrepreneur, short-lived prime minister and present opposition leader Silvio Berlusconi has himself had these judges on his tail since 1994, but charges have yet to be laid.

Milano is distinctly sophisticated. Shopping, whether of the window variety or, for those who can afford it, the real thing, is of almost religious significance. Theatre and cinema flourish, the city is top on most international music tour programmes, and the club scene is busy.

Food is another of Milano's joys. Immigrants from the rest of Italy and abroad have introduced a surprisingly eclectic cuisine – it's not quite London or New York, but in precious few other Italian cities can you find Korean and African food, or Malaysian specialities side by side with Sicilian, Tuscan and Lombard dishes.

The Milanese are proud of their city, but it can seem daunting and uninviting to outsiders. Make yourself at home by spending a few days wandering the shopping arcades and back streets, the exclusive boutique area of Monte Napoleone and the chic Brera district, or groovy Navigli to the south. And stay away in August, when the city shuts down as the population seeks to escape the stifling summer humidity.

History

Milano is said to have been founded by Celtic tribes who settled along the Po river in the 7th-century BC. In 222 BC, Roma's legions marched into the territory, defeated the Gallic Insubres and occupied the town, which they knew as Mediolanum ('middle of the plain'). Mediolanum's key position on the trade routes between Roma and north-western Europe ensured its continued prosperity and it was here in 313 AD that Constantine I made his momentous edict granting Christian freedom of worship.

The city survived centuries of chaos, afte waves of barbarian invasions, to form *comune* in the 11th century. The city-state governed by a council involving all classes entered a period of rapid growth, but soo found itself squabbling with neighbourin towns. The Holy Roman emperor, Frederic Barbarossa, decided to exploit the local con flicts and besieged Milano in 1162. The cit and its allies formed the Lega Lombarda an exacted revenge in 1176.

From the mid-13th century, the city wa ruled by a succession of important familie – the Torrianis, the Viscontis and finally th Sforzas. Under the latter two it enjoyed con siderable wealth and power. It came unde Spanish rule in 1535, and passed to Austri under the Treaty of Utrecht of 1713, signe at the end of the War of the Spanish Succes sion. Legacies of the reign of Maria Theres of Austria are still evident, particularly th dull-yellow (her favourite colour) façades o La Scala and the royal palace.

Napoleon made Milano the capital of hi Cisalpine Republic in 1797 and, five year later, of his Italian Republic, crownin himself King of Italy and Milano there i 1805. Austria again occupied the town i 1814, but this time the occupation was short lived. Troops of Victor Emmanuel II an Napoleon III crushed the Austrian forces at th Battle of Magenta in 1859 and Milano wa incorporated into the nascent Kingdom of Italy

Heavily bombed in WWII, the city wa rebuilt and quickly grew to acquire it modern industrial prominence.

Orientation

Milano is a sprawling metropolis, but mos attractions are concentrated in the centre between the duomo and the Castello Sforzesco. The duomo is an unmistakable focal point for your explorations, whether or foot or by public transport. The city is serviced by an efficient underground railway the Metropolitana Milanese. It is easy to ge lost, so a map is essential.

Milano
(Milan)
0 250 500 m
See Around Stazione Centrale Map p296
See Around the Duomo Map p290
Piazzale Lagosta
Stazione Porta Garibaldi
Garibaldi FS
Via Melchiorre Gioia
Piazza Duca d'Aosta
Gioia
Stazione Centrale
Piazza Caiazzo
Caiazzo
Loreto
Stazione Centrale
Via Pisani
Via Dom Scarlatti
Via Dom Vitruvio
Lima
Piazza Lima
Via B Marcello
Via Tadino
Corso Buenos Aires
Via Pasubio
Via Crispi
Largo la Foppa
Moscova
Via Moscova
Repubblica
Piazza della Repubblica
Viale Tunisia
Viale Vittorio Veneto
Piazza VIII Novembre
Piazzale Oberdan
To Hard Disk Café
Piazza Sempione
Turati
Via Turati
Via Filippo
Via Manin
Giardini Pubblici
Porta Venezia
Parco Sempione
Via Legnano
Corso Garibaldi
Via Fatebenefratelli
Piazza Cavour
Lanza
Via Pontaccio
Palestro
Via Borgospesso
Castello Sforzesco
Via Mercato
Viale Brera
Via della Spiga
Via S Damiano
Corso Venezia
Viale Maino
Cadorna
Cairoli
Via A Manzoni
Monte Napoleone
Monte Napoleone
Stazione Nord
Piazzale Cadorna
Via Dante
Via Broletto
Piazza della Scala
San Babila
Piazza San Babila
Piazzale del Tricolore
Corso Magenta
V Meravigli
Piazza Cordusio
Duomo
C V Emanuele II
To Cenacolo Vinciano & Chiesa Santa Maria delle Grazie
Piazza del Duomo
V Orefici
Largo Augusto
Sant' Agostino
Piazza Diaz
Corso Porta Vittoria
Via Torino
Piazza Missori
Missori
Via San Barnaba
V Correnti
Largo Carrobbio
Via Francesco Sforza
Piazza Resistenza Partigiana
Porta Ticinese
Via M d Armi
Via S Sofia
Corso di Porta Romana
Crocetta
Viale Caldara
Navigli
Corso Italia
Piazza Card Ferrari
Viale G d'Annunzio
Corso Columbo
Viale Gorizia
Via Quadronno
Corso Porta Vigentina
Porta Romana
Piazzale XXIV Maggio
Viale Galeazzo
Viale B d'Este
Via Vigevano
Alzaia Naviglio Grande
Naviglio Grande
Ripa Ticinese
Corso S Gottardo
Via Trelie
Lodi
Str Alz Naviglio Pavese
Via Cardinale A Sforza
Via G Meda
Via Giambologna
Via Liguria
Via Tibaldi
1 Alitalia
2 The Dickens Inn
3 Antica Trattoria della Pesa
4 Teatro Smeraldo & Shocking
5 Cinema Anteo
6 La Bataclan
7 Mail Boxes
8 French Consulate
9 Conservatorio Giuseppe Verdi
10 Chiesa di Sant'Eustorgio
11 CTS Travel Agency
12 Ipotesi Disco
13 Osteria del Pallone
14 Medoro
15 Rococò Caffè
16 Gelateria Rinomata
17 Il Barcone
18 Cristal
19 Il Golossone
20 Löwen Nacht & Maya
21 Le Scimmie
22 Arcigay
23 Propaganda

Apart from the centre, the main areas of interest for tourists are the Brera, immediately north of the duomo, which takes in many galleries and fashionable shopping streets, and Navigli to the south.

From Stazione Centrale (there is a Metropolitana station here), built in 1931 and a classic of the Fascist era, you emerge on Piazza Duca d'Aosta – the scruffy green patch in front of the station. (This is a junkies' hang-out and it's inadvisable to hang about here.) A good orientation point is the Pirelli building, a slender skyscraper to your right as you leave the train station. The area behind the station is occupied mainly by offices, and many of the better hotels are clustered here as well. To the south-east of Stazione Centrale, Via Dom Vitruvio leads to the main area for budget hotels. It meets Piazza Lima at the intersection of Corso Buenos Aires and becomes Via Plinio.

To get from Piazza Duca d'Aosta to the centre, walk south-west along Via Pisani, through the enormous park-lined Piazza della Repubblica, and along Via F Turati to Piazza Cavour. From here, take Via A Manzoni, which runs off the south-west side of the piazza. This takes you through the exclusive Monte Napoleone fashion district and on to Piazza della Scala, with its opera house. From there the glass-domed Galleria Vittorio Emanuele II leads to Piazza del Duomo. The APT office is at the south-east corner of this piazza.

To reach the city centre from the main budget hotel area east of Stazione Centrale, head south along the broad Corso Buenos Aires and its extension, Corso Venezia, and then veer right into Corso Vittorio Emanuele II from Piazza San Babila.

Via Orefici leads off the south-west corner of Piazza del Duomo, later becoming Via Dante as it approaches Castello Sforzesco, while Via Torino branches off southwards from the same corner towards Navigli.

LOMBARDIA

Information

Tourist Office The main branch of the APT (☎ 72 52 41 30) is at Via Marconi 1, in Piazza del Duomo, where you can pick up the useful *Milan is Milano* and *Milano Mese* brochure[s]. It has a copy of the *Pagine Gialle – Turism[o]*, a bilingual Yellow Pages you can loo[k] through at leisure. The office is ope[n] Monday to Saturday from 8 am to 8 pm an[d] on Sunday and holidays from 9 am to 12.3[0] pm and 1.30 to 5 pm. There is a branch offic[e] (☎ 669 05 32) at Stazione Centrale, als[o] open seven days a week.

The Comune di Milano (Milano Cit[y] Council) operates an information offic[e] (☎ 869 07 34) in Galleria Vittorio Emanue[le] II, just off Piazza del Duomo. It's especiall[y] good for finding out about cultural even[ts] and other activities in and around the city.

If you're lucky, one of the above office[s] may just have copies of a good free visitor[s'] guide (with lots of listings and a mini-map) called *Milano – Dove, Come, Quando*.

Foreign Consulates Many countries hav[e] consulates in Milano, including the following:

Australia
: Via Borgogna 2 (☎ 77 70 42 17; outside offic[e] hours emergency 0368-321 56 48)

Canada
: Via Vittorio Pisani 19 (☎ 6 75 81). Open Monda[y] to Friday from 9 am to 12.30 pm and 1.30 to [5] pm.

France
: Via Mangili 1 (☎ 655 91 41)

UK
: Via San Paolo 7 (☎ 72 30 01). Open Monday t[o] Friday from 9.15 am to 12.15 pm and 2.30 to 4.3[0] pm.

USA
: Via P Amadeo 2-10 (☎ 29 03 51). Open Monda[y] to Friday from 9 am to midday and 2 to 4 pm.

Money Banks in Milano are open Monda[y] to Friday from 8.30 am to 1.30 pm and fo[r] one hour in the afternoon, often from 2.45 t[o] 3.45 pm. The Banca Nazionale delle Comunicazioni, Stazione Centrale, is open Monday to Saturday from 8.35 am to 2.05 pm – it has a 24-hour cash-changing machine. The Exact exchange booth at the station is open seven days a week from 7 am to 10.30 pm. Watch the commission.

The Banca Commerciale Italiana has a 4-hour booth with a cash-changing achine inside on the corner of Via Manzoni nd Piazza della Scala – you need a cash (or redit) card to get in, but the ATMs probably von't accept it for withdrawals. There are veekend exchange offices at both airports. he Sestante CIT office in Galleria Vittorio manuele II changes money. American xpress (☎ 72 00 36 94), Viale Brera 3, is pen Monday to Friday from 9 am to 5 pm.

For Western Union money transfers, there re 16 Mail Boxes Etc stores scattered about he city. A central one (☎ 29 00 22 45) is at ia Moscova 13.

Post & Communications The main post ffice is on Piazza Cordusio, although the ffice (and parcel post) at Via Cordusio 4 is pen longer hours: Monday to Friday from .15 am to 7.40 pm and Saturday to 5.40 pm. ax and telegraph services are open 24 hours day. There are branches at Stazione Centrale and both airports. The postcode for entral Milano is 20100.

The main Telecom office is in Galleria Vittorio Emanuele II and is open daily from am to 9.30 pm. Another office at Stazione Centrale, open the same hours, has telephone irectories for Italy, the UK, Germany, rance and other European countries.

Telecom's drawn-out number-changing rogramme in Milano (generally from seven o eight-digit numbers) may yet cause confusion – if in doubt, directory inquiries is on ☎ 12 (but they speak Italian only). The telephone code for Milano is ☎ 02.

Email The Hard Disk Café, Corso Sempione 44 (www.hdc.it), is an Internet café where you can send email and surf the Net.

To receive email you'd have to log in to your own email address – or you can become a member of the Internet Club, in which case the Hard Disk will provide you with an address. Net time costs L10,000 an hour until 9 pm.

Travel Agencies For student and budget travel, CTS has offices at Via S Antonio 2 (☎ 58 30 41 21), Corso di Porta Ticinese 100 (☎ 837 26 74) and Via di V Peroni 21 (☎ 70 63 20 59). Sestante CIT (☎ 86 37 01) is in the Galleria Vittorio Emanuele II.

Bookshops The American Bookstore (☎ 72 02 00 30), Via Camperio 16, has a good selection of English books. Alternatively try the English Bookshop (☎ 469 44 68), Via Ariosto. For French go to the Ile de France Libreria Francese (☎ 76 00 17 67), Via San Pietro all'Orto 10. You could also try Feltrinelli, Via Manzoni 12, which has books in a variety of languages.

For an extensive range of guidebooks, including Lonely Planet, and the best map selection (including complete sets of the Kompass and Tabacco 1:25,000 walking series), head for the Touring Club Italiano bookshop (☎ 8 52 61) at Corso Italia 10.

Publications Those planning to hang around in Milano for a long time may want to pick up the monthly *The Informer*, available at the American Bookstore. It is particularly good for advice on bureaucracy, and you can access back issues on its website.

Another very useful monthly free publication you should pick up is *Hello Milano*. It is packed with listings, maps and practical info.

If you're planning to live here, *Milanopass* has 300-plus pages of listings info. You'll find it in most bookshops for L19,000.

Gay & Lesbian Information For information on gay activities, call Arci Gay/Centro d'Iniziativa Gay (☎ 58 10 03 99), Via Torricelli 19. The staff can advise on other associations in Milano and throughout Italy. Babilonia (☎ 569 64 68) publishes several magazines for gays, including the monthly *Babilonia*, available at most newspaper stands.

Laundry There are a few laundrettes *(lavanderie)* around the Stazione Centrale area, including Onda Blu at Via Scarlatti 19 and Acqua e Sapone on Via Tadino – see the Around Stazione Centrale map.

There are other Onda Blu laundrettes at Via Piero della Francesca 68; Corso Plebisciti 7; Via Adige 3; Via Paisiello 4; and Via Savona Fronte Civico 1.

Consumer Aid The Comitato Difesa Consumatori (☎ 696 15 50), Via Valassina 22, operates Pronto Soccorso Vacanze, a legal service for tourists who have serious disputes with hotels, camping grounds, travel agencies and the like. The service is available from 1 July to 30 September.

Emergency & Medical Services For a police emergency, call ☎ 113. The questura (☎ 6 22 61) is at Via Fatebenefratelli 11. Some staff speak English. For an ambulance, call ☎ 118, and for first aid, call the Italian Red Cross on ☎ 38 83.

The Ospedale Maggiore Policlinico (☎ 5 50 31) is at Via Francesco Sforza 35, close to the city centre. All-night pharmacies include one at Stazione Centrale (☎ 669 09 35) and Ticinese (☎ 89 40 34 33), Corso S Gottardo 1.

Dangers & Annoyances Milano's main shopping areas are popular haunts for pickpockets and thieves – including the kids-with-cardboard crowd, who operate in the same way as their *confrères* in Roma and other cities. The same streets are also patrolled by police, so don't hesitate to make a racket if you are hassled.

Other Information For lost property *(oggetti smarriti)*, contact the Milano City Council (☎ 546 52 99), at Via Friuli 39. Otherwise try Linate airport (☎ 756 04 86), Malpensa airport (☎ 40 09 90 09) or the Ufficio Oggetti Rinvenuti at Stazione Centrale (☎ 63 71 26 67).

The Duomo

Milano's navel, Piazza del Duomo, has the atmosphere of London's Piccadilly Circus but the latter's statue of Eros doesn't quite compare with Milano's most visible monument, the duomo . The world's fourth largest church, it was commissioned by Gian Galeazzo Visconti in 1386.

The first glimpse of this late-Gothic wonder is certainly memorable, with its marble façade shaped into pinnacles, statues and pillars, the whole held together by a web of flying buttresses. The Milanese pay a special tax to fund the ongoing works. Some 135 spires and 3200 statues have somehow been crammed onto the roof and into the façade and masons add a new piece every few years.

The central spire is capped by a gilded copper statue of the Madonna, 108m above the ground. The forest of spires, statuary and pinnacles generally distracts observers from an interesting omission – Milano's duomo is one of very few churches of any importance without a bell tower. The huge brass doors at the front bear the marks of bombs that fell near the church during WWII.

Inside are 15th-century stained-glass windows on the right and newer copies on the left. You will notice a definite contrast between the two. A nail stored high above the altar is said to have come from Christ's Cross and is displayed once a year, in September. Originally lowered using a device made by da Vinci called the *nigola*, it is now retrieved with more modern means. The nigola is stored near the roof on the right-hand side as you enter the church. Note the trompe l'œil ceiling. The 158-step climb to the roof of the duomo (L6000) is worth the effort – for some locals it serves as a sunbathing terrace. There's also a lift for L8000. The entrance is outside the church on the north flank.

Around the Duomo

At the **Museo del Duomo**, Piazza del Duomo 14, you can study more closely the church's six centuries of history, in addition to a rich collection of sculptures, some made for the duomo, from the 14th to the 19th centuries. It is open daily, except Monday, from 9.30 am to 12.30 pm and 3 to 6 pm. Admission is L8000.

The **Civico Museo d'Arte Contemporanea**, in the restored Palazzo Reale, south of the duomo, is dedicated to works by Italian futurists and lesser known modern Italian artists. It's open Tuesday to Sunday from 9.30 am to 5.30 pm.

Virtually destroyed in bombing raids during WWII and rebuilt afterwards, the cruciform **Galleria Vittorio Emanuele II** leads north off Piazza del Duomo. The galleria, designed by Giuseppe Mengoni, was one of the first buildings in Europe to employ mainly iron and glass as structural elements. The four mosaics around the central octagon represent Europe, Asia, Africa and North America. The galleria became known as 'il salotto di Milano' (Milano's drawing room) thanks to elegant cafés like Savini (something of a contrast to the less exclusive hamburger joint opposite).

South-west of Piazza del Duomo, the **Pinacoteca Ambrosiana**, Piazza Pio XI 2 (MM1: Cordusio), is one of the city's finest galleries and contains Italy's first real still life, Caravaggio's *Fruit Basket*, as well as works by Giovanni Tiepolo, Titian and Raphael. The library contains many protected da Vinci manuscripts. The gallery was due to reopen in late 1997. Behind lies the **Chiesa di San Sepolcro**, begun in 1030 and featuring a Romanesque crypt. It was dedicated to the Holy Sepulchre during the second crusade.

South of the duomo, and best viewed from its roof, is one of Milano's more memorable skyscrapers, the **Torre Velasca**, a 20 storey building topped by a six storey protruding block. A classic late-1950s design by Studio BBPR, this building should be seen. Apparently the duomo offered some inspiration.

La Scala & Around

Walk north through the Galleria Vittorio Emanuele II from Piazza del Duomo to Piazza della Scala, dominated by a monument dedicated to da Vinci, and **Teatro alla Scala**. La Scala, as it is most commonly known, opened on 3 August 1778 and was the venue for innumerable operatic first nights throughout the 19th and early 20th centuries. Heavily damaged in WWII, it was reopened in 1946 under the baton of Arturo Toscanini, who came from New York after a 15 year absence from Italy. It is now closed for refurbishment and due to reopen in mid-1999. The adjoining **Museo Teatrale alla Scala** boasts such curiosities as Verdi's death mask (complete with the maestro's facial hairs). When open, you can wander into the opera house from the museum, which is open Monday to Saturday from 9 am to midday and 2 to 6 pm and Sunday from 9.30 am to 12.30 pm and 2.30 to 6 pm from March to October only. Admission is L5000.

The **Palazzo Marino**, between Piazza della Scala and Piazza San Fedele, was begun in 1558 by Galeazzo Alessi and is a masterpiece of 16th-century residential architecture. For those who intend to explore Milano at greater length, it is worth bearing in mind that there are more than 60 grand *palazzi* scattered about the city centre – a far cry from the several hundred that were still standing at the end of the 19th century, but impressive enough.

North-east along Via Manzoni is the **Museo Poldi-Pezzoli**, a rich collection bequeathed to the city in 1881 by nobleman Giacomo Poldi-Pezzoli. Works by Raphael and Bellini figure among the paintings on display and there are collections of jewellery, sundials, tapestries and some bronzework. It is open daily, except Monday, from 9.30 am to 12.30 pm and 2.30 to 6 pm (a little longer on Saturday; closed also Sunday afternoon from April to September). Admission is L10,000.

Castello Sforzesco

At the north end of Via Dante looms the imposing Castello Sforzesco (MM1: Cadorna or Cairoli, or MM2: Cadorna). Originally a Visconti fortress, it was entirely remodelled by Francesco Sforza in the 15th century, and da Vinci had a hand in designing the defences. Its modern museums hold excellent sculpture collections, including Michelangelo's *Pietà Rondanini*. Other collections include an applied arts display and a decent picture gallery that includes works by Bellini, Giovanni Tiepolo, Andrea Mantegna, Correggio, Titian and a Van Dyck. You can also visit a museum devoted to ancient Egyptian artefacts. The castle museums are open Tuesday to Sunday from 9.30 am to 5.30 pm. Admission is free. Behind the castle, the **Parco Sempione** is a

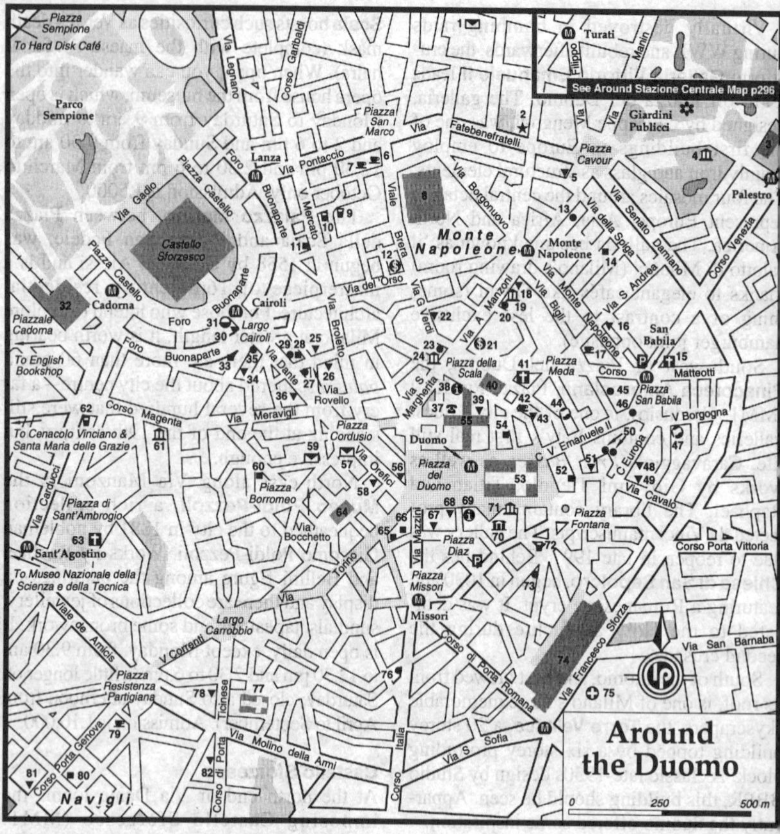

47 hectare park featuring a sadly neglected arena inaugurated by Napoleon. A fun park and (more discretely) drug dealers compete here for strollers' attention.

Palazzo di Brera

The sprawling 17th-century Palazzo di Brera, in the street of the same name east of the Castello Sforzesco, houses the **Pinacoteca di Brera** (MM2: Lanza). Its extensive treasure of paintings has continued to grow since the gallery was inaugurated at the beginning of the 19th century, and represents Milano's single most impressive collection. Andrea Mantegna's masterpiece, *The Dead Christ*, is just one of the better known works on display. Also represented are Raphael, Bellini (look for his *Madonna and Child*), Giovanni Tiepolo, Rembrandt, Goya, Caravaggio, Van Dyck, El Greco and many more. There are also regular temporary exhibitions. It is open Tuesday to Saturday from 9 am to 5.30 pm and Sunday to 12.30 pm. Admission is L8000.

Cenacolo Vinciano

Leonardo da Vinci's masterful mural depicting the Last Supper is in the Cenacolo

PLACES TO STAY

- 11 Albergo Comercio
- 14 Hotel Manzoni
- 28 Hotel London
- 33 Hotel Cairoli
- 52 Hotel Nuovo
- 54 Grand Hotel Duomo
- 60 Albergo Vecchia Milano
- 65 Hotel Speronari
- 66 Albergo Rio
- 80 Albergo Cantore

PLACES TO EAT

- 5 Brek
- 6 Caffè Il Beverin
- 7 Orient Express
- 16 Cova
- 17 Sunflower Bar & Milan Point
- 18 Don Lisander
- 22 Suntory
- 25 Vecchia Napoli
- 26 San Tomaso
- 30 Viel (Gelati Place)
- 34 Antica Osteria Milanese
- 36 Ciao
- 39 Caffè Savini
- 42 Luini
- 43 Ristorante di Gennaro
- 48 Ciao
- 49 Trattoria da Bruno
- 51 Panino Gusto
- 56 Amico
- 58 Peck Delicatessen
- 67 Pizzeria Dogana
- 68 Ciao
- 78 Black Friars
- 79 Caffè Cucchi
- 81 Milanodoc
- 82 Osteria dell'Operetta

OTHER

- 1 Mail Boxes
- 2 Questura (Police Station)
- 3 Museo Civico di Storia Naturale
- 4 Civica Galleria d'Arte Moderna
- 8 Palazzo di Brera
- 9 Club 2
- 10 Biblos
- 12 American Express
- 13 British Council
- 15 Chiesa di San Babila Museo di Milano
- 19 Museo Poldi-Pezzoli
- 20 Feltrinelli Bookshop
- 21 Banca Commerciale Italiana 24-Hour Booth
- 23 Teatro alla Scala
- 24 Museo Teatrale
- 27 Chiariva
- 29 Instituto Cervantes (Spanish Cultural Centre)
- 31 Main Bus Station & Malpensa Shuttle Bus
- 32 Stazione Nord
- 35 American Bookstore
- 37 Telecom Office
- 38 Comune di Milano
- 40 Palazzo Marino
- 41 Chiesa di San Fedele
- 44 UK Consulate
- 45 Ill de France Bookshop
- 46 Milanoticket
- 47 Australian Consulate
- 50 Cinemas
- 53 Duomo
- 55 Galleria V Emanuele II
- 57 Main Post Office
- 59 Post Office
- 61 Civico Museo Archeologico
- 62 Bar Magenta
- 63 Basilica di Sant'Ambrogio
- 64 Pinacoteca Ambrosiana
- 69 APT Tourist Office
- 70 Palazzo Reale
- 71 Museo del Duomo
- 72 Bar dell'Università
- 73 CTS Travel Agency
- 74 Università Statale
- 75 Hospital
- 76 Touring Club Italiano Bookshop
- 77 Chiesa di San Lorenzo Maggiore & Piazza Vetra

Vinciano (Vinciano Refectory), next to the **Chiesa di Santa Maria delle Grazie** (MM1: Conciliazione, or MM2: Cadorna). Painted between 1495 and 1498 in the refectory (the word *cenacolo* means refectory, the place where Christ and the 12 Apostles celebrated the Last Supper, and any mural depicting this scene!) of the Santa Maria delle Grazie convent, da Vinci's famous work is believed to capture the moment when Jesus uttered, 'One of you will betray me'. Recently, it has been argued that da Vinci believed Jesus had a twin. The basis for this contention can be seen in the painting, which depicts two virtually identical Christs.

Restoration of the *Last Supper* began in 1977 and is proceeding slowly, but centuries of damage from floods, bombing and decay have left their mark. It was the method employed by restorers last century that caused most damage – their alcohol and cotton wool removed a layer from the painting. Much of the building was destroyed during WWII, and it was a miracle that the wall with the mural was left standing at all. It is open Tuesday to Sunday from 8 am to 2 pm and at L12,000 the admission price is distressingly steep, especially considering that between you and the mural stands a complex piece of scaffolding upon which restorers go about their business.

South of Castello Sforzesco

The **Civico Museo Archeologico**, Corso Magenta 15 (MM2: Cadorna), features substantial Roman, Greek, Etruscan, Gandhara (ancient north-west Indian) and medieval sections and is housed in the Monastero Maggiore, which is attached to the Chiesa di San Maurizio. It contains frescoes by B Luini and is open daily, except Monday, from 9.30 am to 5.30 pm. Admission is free.

A Saint of the World

When the future St Ambrose was appointed Bishop of Milano in 374, to great public acclaim, his credentials were hardly in order – he hadn't even been baptised. Small matter; this former governor of Liguria had impressed everyone with his skills in umpiring between Catholics and Arians, and so he received all the sacraments and the mitre in an unusually accelerated procedure.

At that time, Milano was the effective capital of the western half of the crumbling Roman Empire, and Ambrose became a leading figure in imperial politics. He and the Western emperor, Gratian, embarked on a crusade to eradicate paganism and the Arian heresy.

His influence became such that he was later able to challenge the authority of Theodosius – the Eastern emperor and guarantor of the Western empire after Gratian's assassination – with impunity. In one incident, the emperor had ordered Christians responsible for burning down a synagogue to rebuild it. Ambrose demanded the order be revoked and, threatening to thump the pulpit and stir popular feeling on the issue, convinced the emperor to see things his way.

Ambrose, the public functionary who had never been a priest, turned out to be a powerful and charismatic bishop. He incarnated the triumph of spiritual over secular power, presaging the Church's future political role in European affairs and inspiring the composition of the *Te Deum*. He died in 397. ■

LOMBARDIA

A short stroll south, the Romanesque **Basilica di Sant'Ambrogio** – dedicated to Milano's patron saint, St Ambrose – dominates the piazza of the same name. Founded in the 4th century by Ambrose, Bishop of Milano, the church has been repaired, rebuilt and restored several times since and is a bit of a hodgepodge of styles. The shorter of the two bell towers dates to the 9th century, as does the remarkable ciborium under the dome inside. It is believed that at least parts of the columns inside date to St Ambrose's time. The saint is buried in the crypt. The attached museum houses relics dating to the earliest days of the basilica's existence, and opens daily from 10 am to noon and 3 to 5 pm (mornings only on Tuesday; afternoons only on Saturday and public holidays). Entry to the museum is L3000.

The **Museo Nazionale della Scienza e della Tecnica**, Via San Vittore 21 (MM2: Sant'Ambrogio), is one of the world's largest technology museums and features a room dedicated to da Vinci's scientific work. The museum is open daily, except non-holiday Mondays, from 9.30 am to 5.00 pm (Saturday and public holidays to 6.30 pm). Admission is L10,000.

Around Piazza Cavour

The **Civica Galleria d'Arte Moderna**, Via Palestro 16 (MM1: Palestro), in the 18th-century Villa Reale, which Napoleon temporarily called home, has a wide range of 19th century works including many from th Milanese neoclassical period. It open Tuesday to Sunday from 9.30 am to 5.30 pm (entry free). In the grounds you can see mor recent work in the **Padiglione d'Arte Contemporanea**. The nearby **Chiesa di San Babila** is said to have been built on the sit of a paleo-Christian church dating to 46 AD

Around Navigli

The **Chiesa di San Lorenzo Maggiore** Piazza Vetra, an early Christian church buil between 355 and 372 on the site of a Roman building, features several 3rd-century columns. The **Chiesa di Sant'Eustorgio** Piazza Sant'Eustorgio, was built in the 9th century and altered in the 11th century, an features a 15th century Cappella Portinar (Chapel of St Peter Martyr). Donato Bramante designed the baptistry.

Language Courses

The Linguadue School of Italian (☎ 29 51 9 72), Corso Buenos Aires 43, offers individual or group courses in Italian. It is one o several language schools in Milano.

Work

If you are so taken with Milano that you' like to live there, one possible source of work s teaching English. There are many schools, ›ut competition is stiff and the pay unspectacular. The British Council (☎ 77 22 21), Via Manzoni 38, is not in the habit of employing people who simply walk in, but hey might be able to point you in other directions.

For other nationalities, the first stop should be the relevant cultural centre: the German Goethe Institut, Via San Paolo 10 (☎ 76 00 58 71); the Centre Culturel Français, Corso Magenta 63 (☎ 48 59 19 11); and the Instituto Cervantes for Spain (☎ 72 02 34 50), Via Dante 12.

Organised Tours

Guided tours to the city can be organised through the Centro di Guide Turistiche (☎ 869 20 69), Piazza Marconi 1.

The Autostradale bus company has a three-hour bus tour of the city from the tourist office. Departures are at 9.30 am daily except Monday and tickets cost a rather extravagant L50,000. Better value is perhaps the Ciao Milano tourist tram, a vintage piece from the 20s that runs four times a day past the main points of interest. It costs L30,000 and you can get on and off as you please.

CIT organises day trips to lakes Maggiore and Como by bus and ferry.

Special Events

If you needed any convincing of the special place that St Ambrogio occupies in the city's iconography, a quick look around will reveal the omnipresence of the adjective *ambrosiano*, from banks to shops and advertising. See the boxed aside in this section. St Ambrose's Day, 7 December, is Milano's biggest feast day. Until late 1993, religious celebrations and a traditional street fair were held around the Basilica di Sant'Ambrogio, but it appears that from now on they will take place at the Fiera di Milano (MM1: Fiera), Milano's trade, conference and exhibition centre. La Scala also marks the occasion by opening its opera season on this day.

The first 10 days of June are devoted to the Festa del Naviglio, a smorgasbord of parades, music and other performances.

Milano plays year-round host to fairs of all sorts – autumn seems the heaviest time for the fashion variety.

Places to Stay

Milano's hotels are among the most expensive and heavily booked in Italy. The area around Stazione Centrale abounds with cheapish one and two-star joints, but quality varies and you'll be lucky to find singles/doubles for less than L50,000/70,000. The popularity of the city as a trade-fair and exhibition venue means hotel owners charge what they like – and get away with it. When fairs are on it can be difficult to find a room anywhere.

The main tourist office will make recommendations but not bookings – the Stazione Centrale office is more helpful in this respect, and will call around if things are tight. Chiariva (☎ 8 50 41), Via Dante 8, will book hotels of three star rating and up.

The APT has lists of private rooms, student accommodation, religious institutions and boarding houses. Most are rented by the month. It also offers a deal called Weekend Milano – discounted weekend packages in some of the better hotels.

Places to Stay – bottom end

Camping The *Campeggio Città di Milano* (☎ 48 20 01 34) is a fair distance from the centre at Via G Airaghi 61. Go to the MM1 De Angeli train station, west of the city centre, and take bus No 72 (phone ahead first). By car, exit the Tangenziale Ovest at San Siro-Via Novara. Otherwise, the nearest *camping ground* is in Monza (☎ 039-38 77 71), open April to September.

Hostels & Religious Institutions The HI youth hostel, *Ostello Pietro Rotta* (☎ & fax 39 26 70 95), is at Viale Salmoiraghi 1. B&B is L23,000. Take the MM1 in the direction of Molino Dorino and get off at QT8 (the name of the station and surrounding area) or take bus No 90 or 91. An HI card is compulsory, but you can buy a card and stamps there (effectively amounts to L30,000 for full membership).

The *Protezione della Giovane* (☎ 29 00 01 64), Corso Garibaldi 123, east of Parco Sempione, is for women aged between 16 and 25. Beds cost from L35,000.

Hotels – Stazione Centrale & Corso Buenos Aires Most of the cheaper hotels near the station will not take bookings. One of the nicest places is the *Hotel Due Giardini* (☎ 29 52 10 93), Via Settala 46. The rooms are simple and not rock bottom in price (starting at L60,000/80,000), but those at the back are separated from the outside world by a cheerful garden – you'd never know you were in a big city.

In Via Dom Vitruvio, to the left of Piazza Duca d'Aosta as you leave the train station, there are two cheaper options. The *Albergo Salerno* (☎ 204 68 70), at No 18, has singles/doubles for L45,000/70,000. The *Albergo Italia* (☎ 669 38 26), at No 44, costs L45,000/65,000 – but the rooms are pretty spartan.

LOMBARDIA

Around the corner from the Salerno, in something of a red light area, is the *Hotel Paradiso* (☎ 204 94 48), Via Benedetto Marcello 85. It has singles/doubles for L60,000/80,000. Doubles with bathroom are L100,000.

The *Hotel Valley* (☎ 669 27 77), Via Soperga 19, is not in a great location, but the rooms are reasonable and the staff friendly. Singles/doubles with bathroom, TV and phone cost L70,000/100,000. There are singles without bathroom for L60,000.

East of Corso Buenos Aires at Via Gaspare Spontini 6 is *Hotel Del Sole* (☎ 29 51 29 71), with singles/doubles for L45,000/60,000 and triples for L80,000.

A 10-minute walk south-east of the train station, *Hotel Nettuno* (☎ 29 40 44 81), Via Tadino 27, has singles/doubles for L44,000/64,000 and others with bathroom for L53,000/84,000.

Down near Piazza della Repubblica, *Hotel Casa Mia* (☎ 657 52 49), Viale Vittorio Veneto 30, has something of a family atmosphere. Singles/doubles cost L70,000/100,000. The *Verona* (☎ 66 98 30 91), at Via Carlo Tenca 12 (also close to Piazza della Repubblica), is L70,000/90,000 – thi includes TV and breakfast, and you ca bargain down on longer stays in singl rooms. Up the road towards Stazione Cen trale, *Hotel Boston* (☎ 669 26 35), Via L Petit 7, has similar rooms for L80,000/130,00 – if you bargain.

Two other possibilities are located in th one building at Viale Tunisia 6. *Hotel Sa Tomaso* (☎ 29 51 47 47), on the 3rd floor, ha overpriced singles/doubles for L65,000 90,000. On the 6th floor, *Hotel Kennedy* (☎ 2 40 09 34) has better rooms for L60,000/80,00 (or L110,000 with bathroom).

Closer to the city centre, in an interestin location near lots of restaurants and we away from the seedy atmosphere of the trai station, is *Hotel Tris* (☎ 29 40 06 74), Vi Sirtori 26, which has singles/doubles fron L50,000/80,000 and triples from L120,000

There is a crowd of low and middle-leve places along Via Napo Torriani as well.

Hotels – city centre The *Albergo Com mercio* (☎ 86 46 38 80), Via Mercato 1, ha singles/doubles for L50,000/60,000 wit shower, but it's often full. From Piazz Cordusio, walk up Via Broletto, whic becomes Via Mercato. The entrance to th hotel is around the corner in Via delle Erbe Within spitting distance of Piazza de Duomo is *Hotel Speronari* (☎ 86 46 11 25) Via Speronari 4, with comfortable singles doubles from L60,000/80,000. *Hotel Nuov* (☎ 86 46 05 42), Piazza Beccaria 6, is als in a great location, to the south just off Cors Vittorio Emanuele II, and rooms withou own bath cost L50,000/70,000.

Hotels – Navigli The *Albergo Cantor* (☎ 835 75 65), Corso Genova 25, is close t Milano's Bohemian zone. Fairly simpl singles/doubles are L40,000/65,000.

Places to Stay – middle to top end

Stazione Centrale & Corso Buenos Aire
The *Hotel Fenice* (☎ 29 52 55 41; fax 29 5 39 42), Corso Buenos Aires 2, in the uppe three star category, has singles/doubles fron L170,000/230,000. The city's most elegan

hotel is with little doubt the *Albergo Excelsior Gallia* (☎ 6 78 51), Piazza Duca d'Aosta 9. Rooms here start at L335,000/390,000, or quite a bit more for luxury rooms.

City Centre The *Albergo Vecchia Milano* (☎ 87 50 42), Via Borromei 4, near Piazza Borromeo, is a good but slightly expensive two star deal, offering singles/doubles with bathroom and breakfast for L105,000/165,000. *Hotel London* (☎ 72 02 01 66; fax 805 70 37), Via Rovello 3 (off Via Dante), looks swanky but charges reasonable rates. Singles/doubles are L90,000/130,000, or L110,000/160,000 with bathroom. *Albergo Rio* (☎ 87 41 14), Via Mazzini 8, in a great location just off Piazza del Duomo, has singles/doubles with breakfast for L110,000/180,000.

In a nice location near Castello Sforzesco is *Hotel Cairoli* (☎ 80 13 71), Via Porlezza 4 (just off Via Camperio). Rooms cost L135,000/205,000 with breakfast.

If you want to mix it with the big spenders, *Hotel Manzoni* (☎ 76 00 57 00; fax 78 42 12), Via Santo Spirito 20, is close to Armani & Co. A room here is L162,000/202,000.

The *Grand Hotel Duomo* (☎ 88 33; fax 86 46 20 27), on the north side of the cathedral, is one of the city's better hotels and a room will set you back L385,000/525,000 with breakfast.

Places to Eat

Italians say Lombard cuisine is designed for people who don't have time to waste because they are always in a hurry to work. Fast-food outlets and sandwich bars are popular and cluttered around Stazione Centrale and the duomo.

The city has a strong provincial cuisine. Polenta (a cornmeal porridge similar to American grits) is served with almost everything, and risotto dominates the first course of the city's menus. Try cotoletta alla milanese or ossobuco (veal shank). Polenta also figures on the sweets menu, but torta di tagliatelle, a cake made with egg pasta and almonds, might be more inviting.

Via Speronari is one of the better areas to shop for bread, salami, cheese and wine. There is also a fresh produce market on weekends at Via Benedetto Marcello. The Super Sconto supermarket on Via Panfilo Castaldi, just off Corso Buenos Aires, is not a bad place for picking up supplies.

Bar snacks are an institution in Milano and most lay out their fare daily from 5 pm.

Restaurants – Stazione Centrale For snacks try *Spontini Bar* on Via Spontini (technically Corso Buenos Aires 60), or head next door to *Spontini Pizzeria*. *Ciao*, Corso Buenos Aires 7, is part of a chain (there are others in Corso Europa and at Via Dante 5), but the food is good quality and relatively cheap, with pasta from L5000 and salads for around L4000. *Brek* and *Amico* are similar chains and make quick, cheap, but superior alternatives to hamburger-style fast food. Several have been marked on the maps. *Ristorante Primavera d'Oriente*, Via Palestrina 13, offers a standard Chinese meal from L13,500. This is one of many Chinese establishments dotted about the city.

Trattoria da Polpetta (☎ 29 40 05 50), near the Via Vittorio Veneto end of Via Tadino and on the corner of Via Panfilo Castaldi, is a small eatery where a full meal with wine will cost about L40,000. Virtually across the road is about the only chance you'll get in Italy to eat Korean – the *Ristorante Seoul* (☎ 29 40 60 62), Via Tadino 1, serves a full meal for around L35,000. Around the corner at Via Panfilo Castaldi 42, you can have a taste of Africa at the *Ristorante Ebony*. A little walking in the back streets around here will turn up quite a few other little restaurants.

Particularly recommended for its Tuscan dishes is *Il Faro* (☎ 284 68 38), a bit of a walk north-east of Stazione Centrale at Piazzale San Materno 8 (MM1: Piazzale Loreto). One Metro stop farther east is *Ristorante Cuccuma*, on the corner of Via Pacini and Via Fossati (MM2: Piola). This eccentrically lit Neapolitan place offers excellent seafood and pizzas, often accompanied by someone singing soppy Italian hits. *Ristorante da Oscar*, Via Palazzi 4, is the place to head to for seafood – L15,000

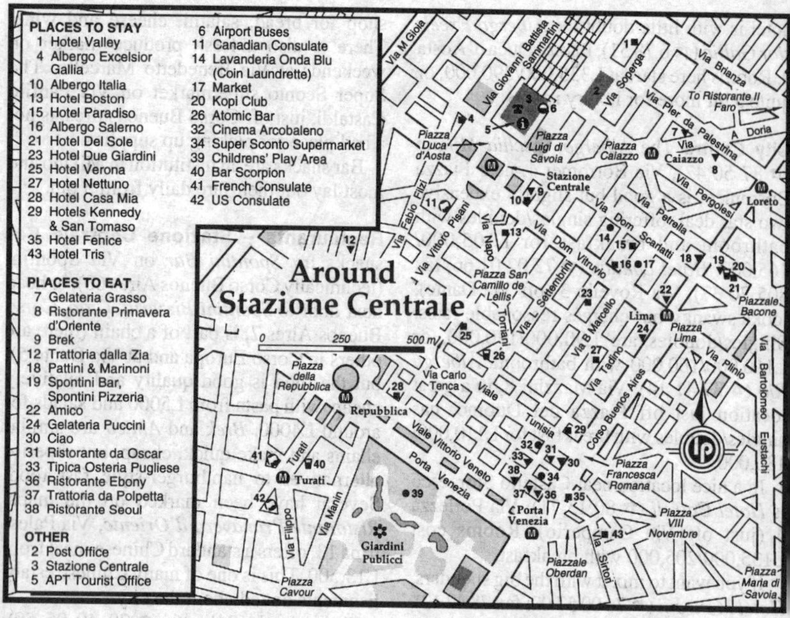

will get a gargantuan helping of pasta with watery delights mixed in – it's unlikely you'll need a second course. For southern Italian feasting wrap your mouth around the goodies in the *Tipica Osteria Pugliese*, Via Tadino 5. The self-serve antipasti are enough to make you drop the main courses. Ask for a plate of bruschette too and for dessert their divine torta al limone (lemon pie).

Trattoria dalla Zia, Via Gustavo Fara 5, is a good little Tuscan restaurant not far from Stazione Centrale. Heading farther west towards Stazione Porta Garibaldi and Corso Como is the area haunted at night by a certain Milanese high society crew, all seemingly in search of the most expensive drink. You can find a couple of good places here.

For about L50,000, you too can munch where Ho Chi Minh once sampled the best of Lombard food, at the *Antica Trattoria della Pesa* (☎ 655 57 41), Via Pasubio 10. You might want to have a drink afterwards at *The Dickens Inn*, the 'pub' next door.

There are several self-service places along Via Pisani, including the often packed *Bar Scorpion* at No 28.

Restaurants – city centre The first Milanese pizza was cooked at *Ristorante di Gennaro*, Via S Radegonda 14, east of Piazza alla Scala.

The *Trattoria da Bruno*, Via Cavallotti 15, off Corso Europa, is popular and has a set-price lunch for L17,000. *Pizzeria Dogana*, on the corner of Via Capellari and Via Dogana, near the duomo, has pasta and pizza for around L10,000.

Bar dell'Univesità, Via Larga 8 (just south of the duomo), has great-value pizza slices (al trancio). *San Tomaso*, Via San Tomaso 5 (near Via Rovello), features live jazz and specialises in salads for up to L12,000. Close by is *Vecchia Napoli*, Via San Tomaso on the corner of Via Rovello, with pizzas from L10,000.

A good place to make for after the movies is *Panino Giusto* (aka *House of Sandwich*), on Piazza Beccaria.

A highly recommended place is the charming *Antica Osteria Milanese*, Via Camperio 12, where mains start at L18,000.

One of the city's posher restaurants is *Don Lisander* (☎ 76 02 01 30), Via Manzoni 12A, which serves Milanese risotto and a host of Tuscan dishes. It is relatively expensive, with main dishes starting at L32,000.

If Japanese is your thing, head to *Suntory* (☎ 869 30 22), Via Verdi 6. It's not cheap though. A better and less expensive alternative is *Ristorante Wu* (☎ 46 89 99), Via Ranzoni 6 (MM1: Amendola Fiera or tram No 24). It also does good Szechuan food.

Restaurants – Navigli There is any number of eateries in and around the Navigli area, and the accompanying cafés and bars make it surely the most pleasing part of Milano to pass an evening. One outstanding spot, where a full meal with wine will come to as much as L50,000, is the *Osteria del L'Operetta*, Corso di Porta Ticinese 70. A more modest alternative is the *Osteria del Pallone*, on the corner of Via Vigevano and the Alzaia Naviglio Grande.

Cafés, Bars & Snack Joints In the Stazione Centrale area is *Pattini & Marinoni*, Corso Buenos Aires 53, which sells bread, as well as pizza by the slice for about L3000. The street is loaded with small cafés and places to grab a quick panino.

Close to the city centre is one of Milano's oldest fast-food outlets – *Luini*, Via S Radegonda 16, off Piazza del Duomo. It sells panzerotti (pizza dough stuffed with tomatoes, garlic and mozzarella) for L3000.

Cova, Via Monte Napoleone 8, in the Monte Napoleone shopping district, is an elegant but expensive tearoom where you can mix it with wealthy Milanese. Close by is another haunt of the fashion-conscious, the slightly less expensive *Sunflower Bar* at Via Pietro all'Orto 8.

Just south of Piazza San Marco, *Caffè Il Beverin* is a pleasant place for a drink, with tables spilling onto the cobbled Viale Brera. It also has food. Around the corner at Via Fiori Chiari 8, *Orient Express* is a rather chic spot for a post antique-browsing drink or, on Sunday, brunch (if you can get in).

South of the duomo, in and around Navigli, is a happening part of town, and there are plenty of cafés and bars to check out. *Cucchi*, at the northern end of Corso Genova, is a fine place for piazza-watching. Head farther south still and you turn up *Rococó*, a cool bistro on the corner of Via Casale and the Alzaia Naviglio Grande. Around the corner at No 48 on the latter street is *Medoro*, a similar bohemian locale where you can get great crêpes.

Gourmet Takeaway For gourmet takeaway, head for *Peck*. Its rosticceria is at Via Cesare Cantù 11 (just west of Piazza del Duomo), where you can pick up fine cooked meats and vegetables. Its three storey food store is at Via Spadari 9. Established in 1883, it is one of Europe's elite gourmet outlets – if anything, more tempting than London's Harrods or Fortnum & Mason – and a mecca famous since 1920 for its home-made ravioli. Wandering around in here (strongly advised) will open your eyes to undreamed of culinary delights, ranging from cheeses (up to 3500 variations on Parmigiano alone) to freshly prepared meals ready to take home, and fine wines (three quarters of them Italian) that can cost anything from US$10 to US$1000!

Gelaterie There are any number of places to pick up gelati. A popular one in the trendy Navigli area is *Gelateria Rinomata*, on Viale Gorizia (on the south side of Ripa di Porta Ticinese) by the Darsena. Nearby, on Piazza Antonio Cantore, *Milanodoc* is also good – try its soya-based gelati.

Near Stazione Centrale, at Viale Andrea Doria, on the corner of Via Palestrina, is *Gelateria Grasso*, a fine tribute to 1970s architecture and an even better one to good gelati. If you'd like a crêpe as well, head for the *Gelateria Puccini*, Corso Buenos Aires 33.

A classic place is *Viel*, near the Castello Sforzesco and a favourite late-night haunt for young Milanese.

LOMBARDIA

Entertainment

Milano has Italy's best clubs, a handful of cinemas screening English-language films, and a fabulous year-round cultural calendar, topped by La Scala's opera season. The main season for theatre and concerts opens in October. The summer months are usually crammed with musical and theatrical events.

Jazz festivals are held at various times of the year – check with the APT for the latest details.

The tourist office has entertainment listings, as do most daily newspapers. Pick up *Milano Mese*, a monthly entertainment guide from the tourist office. For some clue to what's happening in the club scene, *Corriere della Sera* has a good liftout, *ViviMilano*, on Wednesday. *La Repubblica* is better for day-to-day information on events and also has a good liftout on Friday. Both papers are fine for cinema listings.

Live in Italia is a free monthly you can sometimes dig up in the tourist office. It lists upcoming gigs, although these are mostly international acts. *Hello Milano* (see Information earlier) is also good if you can get it.

The free *No Sleep* monthly mag is a night owl's guide to Milano's club scene. It is free and can be picked up in some bars, including the Hard Disk Café (see Email under Information earlier).

A good place to get tickets (and an idea of what's on) is the Milano ticket booth on Via Vittorio Emanuele II.

Cinema English-language films are shown once a week at the following cinemas: *Anteo* (☎ 659 77 32), Via Milazzo 9 (MM2: Moscova); *Arcobaleno* (☎ 29 40 60 54), Viale Tunisia 11 (MM1: Porta Venezia); and *Mexico* (☎ 48 95 18 02), Via Savona 57 (MM2: Porta Genova). A couple of other cinemas occasionally put on original language *(lingua originale)* films.

Nightclubs *Ipotesi* is a popular disco on Piazzale XXIV Maggio, at the northern end of Navigli. At Bastioni di Porta Nuova 12, *Shocking* is practically always open, attracting different crowds with thematic changes in music each evening. Admission costs up to L30,000. A more economical option is *La Bataclan*, a short walk away at Piazzale Biancamano 2. *Factory*, Via Ricciarelli 11, has just about everything, including a speakers' corner and hair stylist. It roams from hip-hop and reggae to more classic rock and Goth nights. *Milano In*, Via dei Missaglia 46/3, is a fairly posh place that often hosts cabaret-style acts, open until 2.30 am. Admission is around L20,000.

Opera La Scala's main opera season opens on 7 December, but there is theatre, ballet and concerts all year save the last week or two of July and all of August. The box office (☎ 72 00 37 44) is in the portico in Via Filodrammatici, on the left-hand side of the building, and is open daily from midday to 7 pm and until 15 minutes after curtains on performance nights. Book well in advance, as most performances sell out months before. Your only hope may be the 200 standing-room tickets that go on sale at the entrance to the opera house museum 45 minutes before the scheduled starting time. These can cost as little as L5000. The best seats in the house on premier night can be as much as L1,500,000! CIT offices abroad will book tickets. Note that pre-booked tickets carry a 20% surcharge.

Note At the time of publication La Scala was shut for refurbishment, and performances will be held in alternative theatres until well into 1999.

Theatre At least another 50 theatres are active in Milano – check the newspapers and ask at the tourist office.

Classical Music The *Chiesa di San Maurizio* in the Monastero Maggiore hosts concerts, usually involving small classical ensembles, throughout the year.

The *Conservatorio Giuseppe Verdi* (☎ 76 00 17 55), Via Conservatorio 12, is the venue for many classical music concerts.

Rock Concerts Live music can sometimes be seen at discos like *Propaganda*, Via

Castelbarco 11, and *Rolling Stone*, Corso XXII Marzo 32. Another venue to watch is the *Teatro Smeraldo*, Piazza XXV Aprile 10. Bigger concerts tend to be held at the *Palatrobis* (☎ 72 00 33 70), Viale Elia 33, near the San Siro stadium, or the Forum di Assago, farther out of town.

Bars & Pubs There are two areas in particular to search for a drink, some music and the madding crowd. Otherwise, good bars are sprinkled at distant intervals across the city.

Brera The Brera (predictably located around Viale Brera) comes alive at night as crowds swirl through the narrow lanes and into watering holes where a beer will cost anything from L8000 to L20,000, depending on the bar and whether or not they have music (usually of the smoke-filled piano bar variety). Among the more popular of these places are *Biblos*, Via Madonnina 17, and *Club 2*, Via Formentini 2. As you might have guessed, this is the expensive part of town.

Navigli & Porta Ticinese Alternatively you can head south for Navigli via (roughly) Corso di Porta Ticinese.

One pleasant bar you could start with is *Black Friars* (for Guinness), Corso di Porta Ticinese 16. Or peek into *Luca's Bar*, tucked in by the arch where Corso di Porta Ticinese and Via Molino delle Armi intersect.

The focal point for the truly busy nightlife is Via A Sforza, which runs along the Naviglio Pavese (canal). Starting south and moving up, you'll find *Le Scimmie*, No 49, a well-established jazz bar. At No 41, *Maya* comes equipped with a Mexican restaurant and Latin music bar. A German flavour is injected into *Löwen Nacht* next door. *Il Golossone*, No 29, is a more sedate and stylish place for a drink, while at *Cristal* you can sip an apéritif on a boat. Where the often filthy dribble of water ends is an even bigger floating bar/café, *Il Barcone*.

Elsewhere Another traditional meeting place for Milanese night owls is the *Bar Magenta*, Via Carducci 13, a short walk south of Castello Sforzesco. A good new place is *Kopi Club*, Via Spontini 6, not far from Stazione Centrale. Also within walking distance of the station is *Atomic Bar*, Via Casati 24, a cool place with a vaguely grungy New York feel and mean drinks for L10,000.

Spectator Sport

Football Milano's two teams, Inter Milano and AC Milan, play on alternate Sundays during the football season, at San Siro stadium, also known as Meazza because it is in Piazza Meazza. Tram No 24 and buses Nos 95, 49 and 72 go direct. Or take the metro and get off at MM1: Lotto, from where a free shuttle bus runs to the stadium. Tickets are available at the stadium or, for AC Milan matches, from Milan Point (☎ 79 64 81), Via San Pietro all'Orto 8, or branches of the Cariplo bank. For Inter matches, tickets are sold at Banca Popolare di Milano branches (or call ☎ 7 70 01). The cost ranges from L25,000 to L65,000.

Motor Racing The Italian Grand Prix is held at the Monza autodrome each September. The track is several km out of town and can be reached along Viale Monza from Piazzale Loreto.

Things to Buy

Every item of clothing you ever wanted to buy, but could never afford, is in Milano. The main streets for clothing, footwear and accessories are behind the duomo around Corso Vittorio Emanuele II, and between Piazza della Scala and Piazza San Babila.

For upmarket and exclusive fashions, head for Via della Spiga, the boutique mecca Via Monte Napoleone or Via Borgospesso which runs between the two – all in an area known as the Quadrilatero d'Oro (Golden Quad), or Monte Napo to the in-crowd. Gianfranco Ferré is at Via della Spiga 11 and Krizia at No 23. Around the corner in Via Sant'Andrea you will find Armani, Trussardi and Kenzo. Versace, Valentino, Ungaro, Ferretti, Louis Vuitton and Cartier are cluttered along Via Monte Napoleone.

The areas around Via Torino, Corso XXII

Design

Milano is the world's design capital, although you have to search it out as shops and galleries are spread throughout the city, and most products are made for export. Although the city began to make a name for itself in the design of modern furniture before WWII, it wasn't until after the war, when the city took off as an industrial powerhouse, that the design business came into its own.

The magazine *Interni* occasionally publishes a foldout guide called *Interni Annual*, which lists the names and addresses of most design shops and galleries, as well as a list of upcoming design fairs and exhibitions (of which there are many). The magazine, along with many others (such as *Abitare*, *Domus* and *Casa Bella*) that have grown on the back of the industry, are on sale at newspaper stands.

Serious shoppers or design buffs and students wanting to find out where the best showrooms are could look at *A Key to Milan*, a city guidebook published by Hoepli (available in most bookshops for L27,000). It has a good introductory section on the subject, with a selected list of top showrooms. ■

LOMBARDIA

Marzo and Corso Buenos Aires are less expensive. Markets are held around the canals, notably on Viale Papiniano on Tuesday and Saturday mornings. There is a flea market in Viale Gabriele d'Annunzio on Saturday and a decent antique market in Brera at Via Fiori Chiari every third Saturday of the month. Milano's version of Portobello Rd, a huge market where you can buy just about anything, is held on the last Sunday of each month on the Alzaia Naviglio Grande and Ripa di Porta Ticinese (tram No 19).

Getting There & Away

Air International flights use Malpensa airport, about 50km north-west of the city. Domestic and European flights use Linate airport, about 7km east. The city is served by an increasing number of flights from the USA and many cities in Europe. For flight information on both airports call ☎ 785 22 00.

Major airlines include Alitalia (☎ 2 68 51/2/3), Corso Como 15, and British Airways (☎ 80 98 92), Corso Italia 8.

Bus Bus stations are scattered across the city, so unless you know exactly what you want and where you're going, you're better off with the train. Bear this in mind when deciding how to get to Milano as well. Eurolines, Autostradale and several other national and regional companies operate from Piazza Castello, in front of Castello Sforzesco (MM2: Cairoli), to many national and international destinations.

Train You can catch a train from Stazione Centrale (☎ 1478-8 80 88) to all major cities in Italy and throughout Europe. The bulk of the trains from here carry some kind of supplement (plus a fine if you did not pay the supplement before embarkation). There are regular trains for Venezia, Firenze, Bologna, Genova, Torino and Roma.

FNM trains from Stazione Nord (☎ 48 06 67 71) in Piazzale Cadorna connect Milano with Como, Erba and Varese. Stazione Porta Garibaldi (☎ 655 20 78) has mostly regional trains which service destinations such as Lecco, Como, Varese, Bergamo, Cremona, Mantova, the Valtellina and the north-west. It is always worth comparing departure possibilities from Centrale and Porta Garibaldi. All these train stations are on the MM2 line.

Car & Motorcycle Milano is the major junction of Italy's motorways, including the Autostrada del Sole (A1) to Reggio di Calabria in southern Italy; the A4, also known as the Milano-Torino (west to Torino) and the Serenissima (east to Verona and Venezia); the A7 south to Genova; and the A8 and A9 north to the lakes and Swiss border. The city is also a hub for smaller national roads, including the SS7 (Via Emilia), which runs south through Emilia-Romagna, and the SS11, which runs east-west from Torino to Brescia.

All these roads meet with the Milano ring road, known as the Tangenziale Est and the Tangenziale Ovest. From here, follow the signs into the city centre. It should be noted that the A4 in particular is an extremely busy road, where numerous accidents can hold up traffic for hours. From October to April all

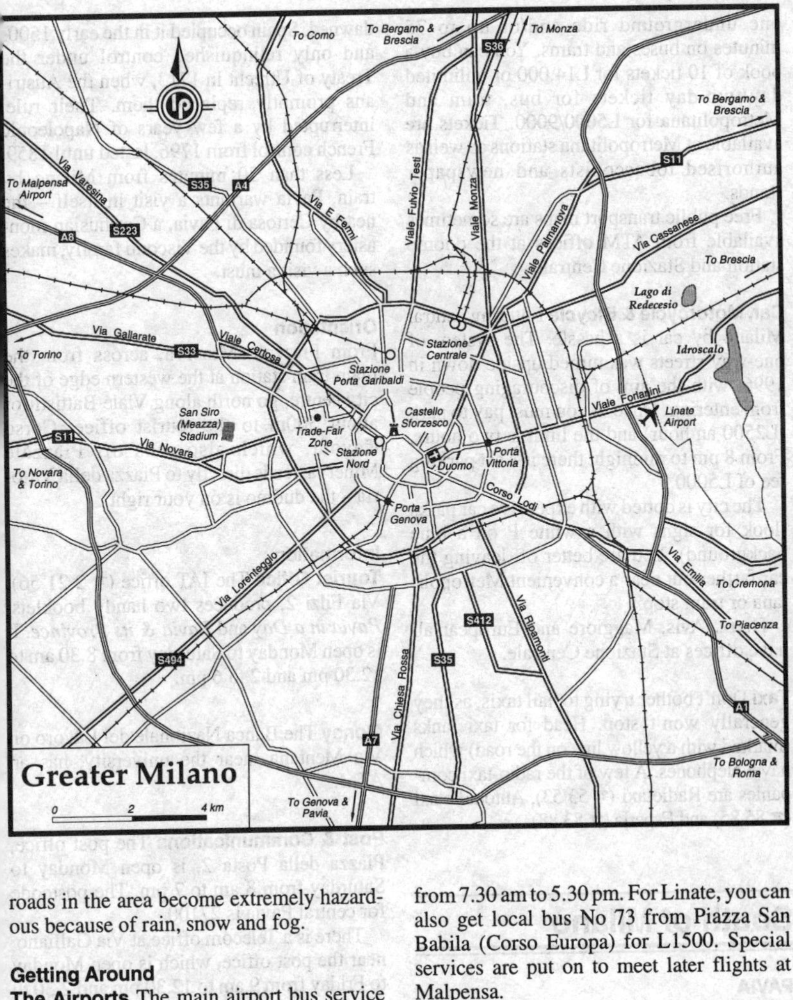

roads in the area become extremely hazardous because of rain, snow and fog.

Getting Around

The Airports The main airport bus service leaves from Piazza Luigi di Savoia, on the east side of Stazione Centrale. STAM buses (☎ 66 98 45 09) run to Linate airport every 20 to 30 minutes from 5 am to 9 pm (L4500, 20 minutes), and to Malpensa airport (Malpensa Shuttle; ☎ 40 09 92 60) every 30 to 60 minutes (L12,000, 75 minutes) from 5.15 am to 8.30 pm. A separate service operates between Piazza Castello and Malpensa from 7.30 am to 5.30 pm. For Linate, you can also get local bus No 73 from Piazza San Babila (Corso Europa) for L1500. Special services are put on to meet later flights at Malpensa.

Metropolitana, Tram & Bus Milano's public transport system (ATM ☎ 669 70 32) is efficient. Its Metropolitana consists of three underground lines (red MM1, green MM2 and yellow MM3). It is the most convenient way to get around, but you may find ATM buses and trams useful too. A Metropolitana ticket costs L1500 – good for one underground ride and/or up to 75 minutes on buses and trams. You can buy a book of 10 tickets for L14,000 or unlimited day/two-day tickets for bus, tram and Metropolitana for L5000/9000. Tickets are available at Metropolitana stations as well as authorised tobacconists and newspaper stands.

Free public transport maps are sometimes available from ATM offices at the duomo station and Stazione Centrale.

Car, Motorcycle & Bicycle Entering central Milano by car is a hassle. The system of one-way streets was turned upside down in 1996, with the aim of discouraging people from entering. Once in you must pay to park (L2500 an hour) and the limit is two hours. From 8 pm to midnight there is a set parking fee of L5000.

The city is dotted with expensive car parks (look for signs with a white P on a blue background). You are better off leaving the car farther out near a convenient Metropolitana or tram stop.

Hertz, Avis, Maggiore and Europcar all have offices at Stazione Centrale.

Taxi Don't bother trying to hail taxis, as they generally won't stop. Head for taxi ranks (marked with a yellow line on the road) which have telephones. A few of the radio-taxi companies are Radiotaxi (☎ 53 53), Autoradiotaxi (☎ 85 85) and Esperia (☎ 83 88).

LOMBARDIA

South of Milano

PAVIA

Virtually a satellite of Milano, Pavia is nonetheless a thriving industrial and agricultural centre on the banks of the Ticino river, perhaps best known for its prestigious university. Originally the Roman Ticinum, Pavia later rivalled Milano as the capital of the Lombard kings until the 11th century. Like many cities of the north, Pavia became a pawn of power politics as the Renaissance dawned. Spain occupied it in the early 1500s and only relinquished control under the Treaty of Utrecht in 1713, when the Austrians promptly replaced them. Their rule, interrupted by a few years of Napoleonic French control from 1796, lasted until 1859.

Less than 30 minutes from Milano by train, Pavia warrants a visit in itself – the nearby Certosa di Pavia, a Carthusian monastery founded by the Visconti family, makes such a visit a must.

Orientation

From Piazzale Minerva, across from the main train station at the western edge of the city centre, go north along Viale Battisti for about 500m to the tourist office. Corso Cavour, which also runs off Piazzale Minerva, leads directly to Piazza della Vittoria – the duomo is on your right.

Information

Tourist Office The IAT office (☎ 2 21 56), Via Filzi 2, produces two handy booklets, *Pavia in a Day* and *Pavia & its Province*. It is open Monday to Saturday from 8.30 am to 12.30 pm and 2 to 6 pm.

Money The Banca Nazionale del Lavoro on Via Mentana, near the university, has an ATM.

Post & Communications The post office, Piazza della Posta 2, is open Monday to Saturday from 8 am to 7 pm. The postcode for central Pavia is 27100.

There is a Telecom office at Via Galliano, near the post office, which is open Monday to Friday from 9 am to 12.30 pm and 2.30 to 6 pm.

The telephone code for Pavia is ☎ 0382.

Emergency For a police emergency, call ☎ 113. The questura (☎ 51 21) is at Piazza Italia 5. For medical assistance, go to the Ospedale San Matteo (☎ 50 11), Piazza Golgi 2; for emergencies, ring ☎ 47 23 51, and at night call ☎ 52 76 00.

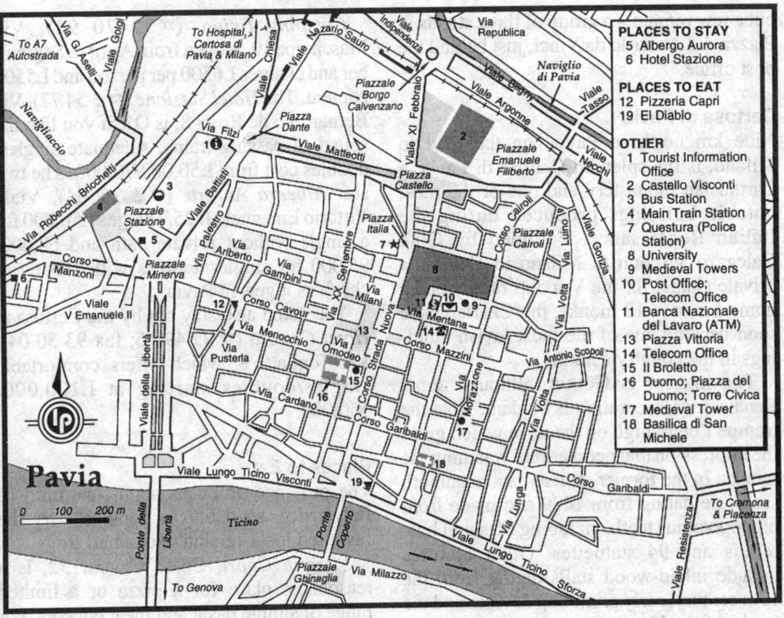

Castello Visconti

Watching over the northern end of the medieval city, this forbidding castle (only two of its original four massive towers remain) was only ever used as a residence. It was built in 1360 for Galeazzo II Visconti and now houses the Museo Civico, Museo del Risorgimento and a small gallery of modern art. The castle and museums are open Tuesday to Saturday from 9 am to 1 pm and Sunday from 9.30 am to 12.30 pm. Admission is L5000.

University

On Corso Strada Nuova is the University of Pavia, which started life as a school in the 9th century and was elevated to university status in 1361. Among its notable graduates were Christopher Columbus (whose ashes are purportedly kept in a safe in the director's office) and the self-taught physicist Alessandro Volta, who discovered the electric volt.

Churches

The **duomo**, started in 1488, boasts the third largest dome in Italy, but it was only completed last century. Both da Vinci and Donato Bramante contributed to the church's design. Parts of the duomo look the worse for wear – in 1989 its bell tower simply fell over, killing four people.

The Romanesque **Basilica di San Michele**, built on the site of a 7th-century church in 1090, was long a preferred location for European coronations. Barbarossa was crowned Holy Roman emperor here in 1155. Although deteriorated, the façade is a masterwork of Romanesque. The statues and restrained floral sculpting on the arches over the main entrance are as pleasing to the eye today as they must have been almost a millennium ago.

Medieval Towers

Pavia once boasted some 100 medieval watch towers. Most have been demolished, but a few remain – a group of three stands in Piazza di Leonardo da Vinci, just behind the post office.

Certosa di Pavia

Nine km north of Pavia, on the road to Milano, is the splendid Certosa di Pavia, a Carthusian monastery and one of the most notable buildings produced during the Italian Renaissance. Founded by Gian Galeazzo Visconti of Milano in 1396 as a private chapel for the Visconti family and a home for only 12 monks, the Charterhouse soon became one of the most lavish buildings in the country's north.

The interior is Gothic, although some Renaissance decoration is evident. Note the trompe l'oeuil high on the nave which gives the impression that people were watching the monks. In the former sacristy is a mammoth sculpture dating from 1409 and made from hippopotamus teeth, including 66 small bas-reliefs and 94 statuettes. Other features include inlaid-wood stalls dating from the 15th century, early plumbing devices and the tombs of the Viscontis.

The small cloisters to the right offer good photo angles of the church, particularly from behind the Baroque fountain. Behind the 122 arches of the larger cloisters are 24 cells, each a self-contained living area for one monk. Several are open to the public.

The Certosa is open Tuesday to Sunday from 9.30 to 11.30 am and 2.30 to 4.30 pm (or as late as 6 pm from May to September). Admission is free although you are encouraged to leave a donation.

To get there by car from Milano, take the SS35 to Pavia and turn off at Torre del Mangano. The Certosa is well signposted. SGEA buses leave from Piazza Castello in Milano and from Via Trieste in Pavia, near the train station. The Certosa, a 10-minute walk from the bus stop, is also on the Milano-Pavia train line.

Places to Stay

Choice of accommodation is decidedly limited, making a day trip from Milano the most straightforward option.

Camping Ticino (☎ 52 70 94), Via Mascherpa 10, is open from April to September and charges L6500 per person and L5500 per tent. The *Hotel Stazione* (☎ 3 54 77), Via Bernardino de Rossi 8, is OK if you like the sound of passing trains. Adequate singles/doubles cost from L50,000/70,000. The two star *Albergo Aurora* (☎ 2 36 64), Viale Vittorio Emanuele II 25, charges L50,000 for a single without private bath and 68,000/95,000 for singles/doubles with. That's as cheap as it gets in Pavia.

You could also stay out by the Certosa at *Hotel Certosa* (☎ 93 49 45; fax 93 30 04), Via Togliatti 8, which offers comfortable singles/doubles starting at L100,000/150,000.

Places to Eat

The province produces about one-third of Italy's rice, so risotto is popular – try the favoured local version with small frogs.

Pizzeria Capri, Corso Cavour 32, is a reasonable place for a pizza or a limited range of simple pasta and meat courses. For something different, try the local version of Tex-Mex at *El Diablo*, Piazzale Ponte Ticinese 6. It has good salads for L10,000. The presence of the university gives Pavia a bit of jump, with a few good bars around the campus.

Getting There & Away

The city's bus station is on Via Trieste, right by the train station. SGEA buses run hourly to Milano and also to Certosa di Pavia. Pavia can also be reached direct from Genova, Piacenza, Cremona and Ventimiglia. By car, take the A7 autostrada from Milano and exit at the Bereguardo or Gropello C turn-off. The SS35 from Milano is a better bet for hitchhikers.

Getting Around

The town is small, but SGEA buses Nos 3 and 6 run from the train station through the main square, Piazza della Vittoria. Most cars are banned from the centre and there are car parks near the station.

East of Milano

BERGAMO

Virtually two cities, Bergamo's walled hilltop *città alta* (upper town) is surrounded by the *città bassa* (lower town), a sprawling modern addition to this magnificent former outpost of the Venetian empire. Although Milano's skyscrapers to the south-west are visible on a clear day, Bergamo's dialect and traditions echo more faithfully those of Venezia, which controlled the city for 350 years until Napoleon arrived at the gates. Despite its wealth of medieval, Baroque and Renaissance architecture, the city is not a big tourist destination.

Orientation

Viale Papa Giovanni XXIII, which becomes Viale Roma and then Viale Vittorio Emanuele II uphill towards the old town, forms the principal axis of the city. It is capped at the southern end by the train and bus stations, and the main tourist, post and telephone offices and several banks are all located on or near this central boulevard. These services are duplicated in the upper town. Viale Vittorio Emanuele II swings east around the old town walls to enter the upper town at Porta di Sant'Agostino. You can also take a funicular up for the last leg.

Piazza Vecchia is the focal point of the upper town, and the main street is Via B Colleoni.

Information

Tourist Offices In the lower town, the APT is at Piazzale Marconi 7 (☎ 24 22 26), in the west wing of the train station building, while in the upper town it is at Vicolo Aquila Nera 2 (☎ 23 27 30). Both are open Monday to Friday from 9 am to 12.30 pm and 2.30 to 5.30 pm. The lower town office has a hotel list posted on the door.

Money You'll find several banks in the lower end of town and a couple on Via B Colleoni near the tourist office in the città alta.

Post & Communications The main post office in the lower town is at Via Masone 2A, beyond Piazza della Libertà. It is open Monday to Friday from 8.15 am to 8 pm and Saturday from 8.30 am to 12.30 pm. A branch office on Via San Lorenzo in the upper town is open from 8 am to 1.30 pm (5.30 pm in summer). The postcode is 24100.

The Telecom office is in Largo Porta Nuova, near Piazza Vittorio Veneto, and is open from 9 am to 12.30 pm and 2.30 to 6 pm. In the upper town, the Telecom office is just next to the Agnello d'Oro hotel on Piazzetta San Pancrazio.

The telephone area code is ☎ 035.

Emergency For police emergency, call ☎ 113. The questura is on Via A Noli. The Ospedale Maggiore (☎ 26 91 11) is at the western edge of town, along Via Garibaldi and its continuation, Via Mazzini. For an ambulance, call ☎ 40 20 00.

Things to See

If you have limited time, head straight to the città alta. Bus No 1 from the train station goes to the funicular.

Piazza Vecchia The heart of medieval Bergamo is hard to miss. Whichever way you enter the walled hilltop town, you'll soon find yourself in this gracious square. The white porticoed building on Via Colleoni, which forms the north side of the piazza, is the 17th-century **Palazzo Nuovo**, now a library and the square's least interesting feature. Turn instead to the south and you will face the imposing arches and columns of the **Palazzo della Ragione**, first built in the 12th century, but largely reconstructed four centuries later. The lion of St Mark is a reminder of Venezia's long reign. Note the sun clock in the pavement beneath the arches. The building occasionally hosts exhibitions, and on summer Sunday afternoons traditional puppeteers take over below. Their art dates to the 16th century and contributed much to the Venetian commedia dell'arte. Next to the palazzo, the **Torre Civica** still tolls the 10 pm curfew. For L2000 you can

LOMBARDIA

climb to the top for wonderful views of the city. From March to September it is open daily, otherwise only on weekends and holidays.

Tucked in behind these secular buildings is the core of Bergamo's spiritual life, the Piazza del Duomo. Oddly enough, the modest Baroque **duomo**, which is dedicated to St Alexander, very much plays second fiddle to the neighbouring **Chiesa di Santa Maria Maggiore**, an imposing Romanesque church begun in 1137 and whose weather-worn exterior hides a lavish Baroque interior. Gaettano Donizetti, a 19th-century composer and native son of Bergamo, lies buried here. The extravagant add-on is the gaudy Renaissance **Cappella Colleoni**, built by the condottiere of the same name as a funeral chapel – he in fact was not buried here. All churches are open from 9 am to midday and from 2 to 6 pm. Admission is free.

The octagonal **baptistry** was built inside Santa Maria Maggiore in 1340, but transferred outside late last century.

Lookouts A stroll downhill along Via Colleoni and then Via Gombito, the latter marked by a 12th-century **tower** of the same name, takes you along medieval 'main street' towards the funicular, and left to **La Rocca**, a fortress which houses the small **Museo Civico del Risorgimento e della Resistenza**. The views from the adjoining park are worth the effort. For more spectacular views, take the funicular to Monte San Vigilio from Porta di Sant'Alessandro, at the opposite end of the upper town.

Accademia Carrara Some time should be made for the art gallery of the Accademia Carrara, most pleasantly reached on foot from the upper town through the Porta di Sant'Agostino and down the cobbled Via D Noca. Founded in 1780, it contains an impressive range of Italian masters, particularly of the Venetian school. An early *St Sebastian* by Raphael is worth looking out for, and there are works by Botticelli, Lorenzo Lotto, Andrea Mantegna, Giovanni Tiepolo, Titian and Canaletto. It is open daily, except Tuesday, from 9.30 am to 12.30 pm and 2.30 to 5.30 pm. Admission is L5000.

Città Bassa If heading back to the station for a train to Milano, you could do worse than hover about the series of squares that make up the centre of the lower town. Piazza Matteotti was redesigned in 1924 by a Fascist favourite, Marcello Piacentini.

The **Teatro Donizetti**, close to Piazza Cavour, was built in the shape of a horseshoe in the 18th century and dedicated to the composer in 1897, the centenary of his birth.

Activities

The CAI, Via Ghislanzoni 15, has details about winter sports, hiking and gentle walks in the Bergamo Alps, which rise to 1000m close to the town.

The tourist office also produces several maps of hiking trails in the Bergamo province, many of them numbered and quoted with approximate walking times. The Libreria Lorenzelli, Viale Papa Giovanni XXIII 72, has a range of hiking and cycling guidebooks in Italian devoted to the area.

Places to Stay

Bergamo is an easy day trip from Milano but if you want to stay, arrive early or telephone ahead – what hotels there are can fill distressingly quickly.

A few cheaper hotels – often full with migrant workers from the south – are scattered about the lower town, but if you have a little extra, a few excellent options can be found up the hill. The APT has a list of camping grounds and *rifugi* in the nearby Bergamo Alps, and agriturismo farms and houses throughout the province.

The *Ostello Città di Bergamo* (☎ 36 17 24), Via Galileo Ferraris 1, is several km from the lower town. Take bus No 14 from the train station. B&B is L22,000, or you can opt for L25,000 a head in a double or L30,000 a single.

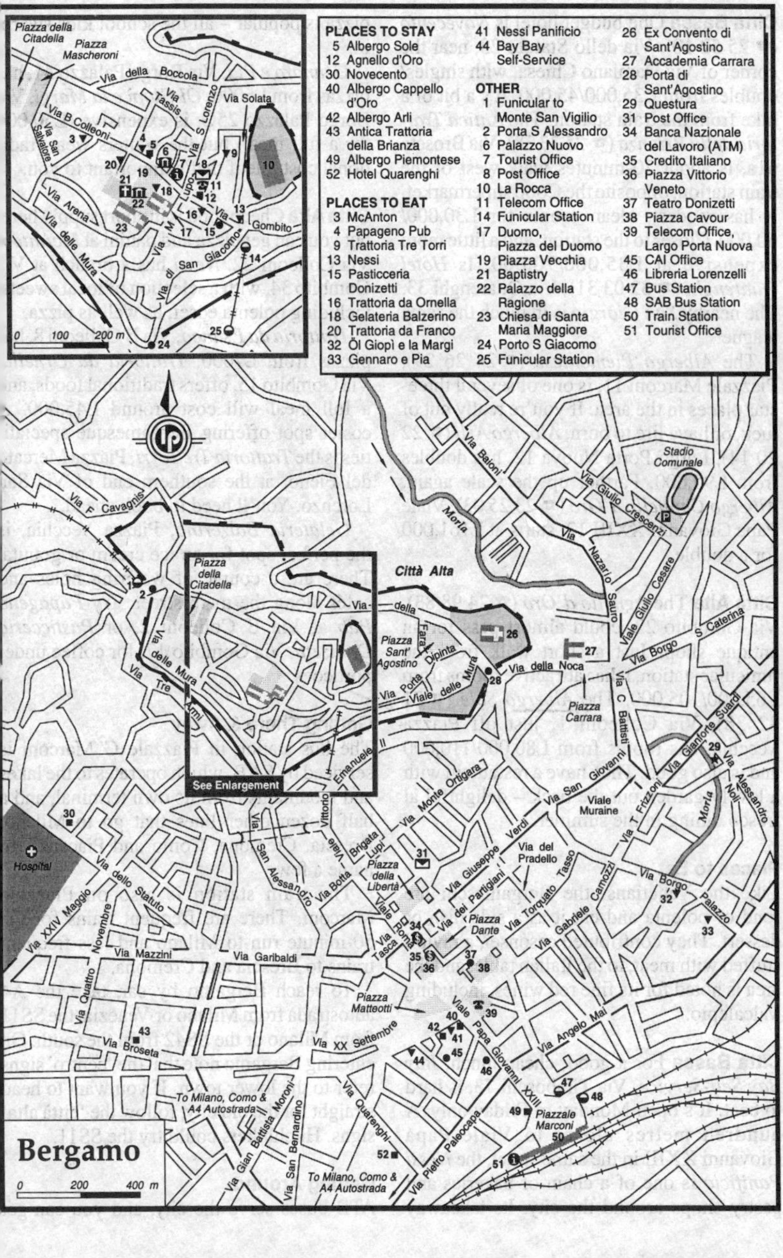
Bergamo
0 200 400 m
PLACES TO STAY
5 Albergo Sole
12 Agnello d'Oro
30 Novecento
40 Albergo Cappello d'Oro
42 Albergo Arli
43 Antica Trattoria della Brianza
49 Albergo Piemontese
52 Hotel Quarenghi
PLACES TO EAT
3 McAnton
4 Papageno Pub
9 Trattoria Tre Torri
13 Nessi
15 Pasticceria Donizetti
16 Trattoria da Ornella
18 Gelateria Balzerino
20 Trattoria da Franco
32 Öl Giopì e la Margi
33 Gennaro e Pia
41 Nessi Panificio
44 Bay Bay Self-Service
OTHER
1 Funicular to Monte San Vigilio
2 Porta S Alessandro
6 Palazzo Nuovo
7 Tourist Office
8 Post Office
10 La Rocca
11 Telecom Office
14 Funicular Station
17 Duomo, Piazza del Duomo
19 Piazza Vecchia
21 Baptistry
22 Palazzo della Ragione
23 Chiesa di Santa Maria Maggiore
24 Porto S Giacomo
25 Funicular Station
26 Ex Convento di Sant'Agostino
27 Accademia Carrara
28 Porta di Sant'Agostino
29 Questura
31 Post Office
34 Banca Nazionale del Lavoro (ATM)
35 Credito Italiano
36 Piazza Vittorio Veneto
37 Teatro Donizetti
38 Piazza Cavour
39 Telecom Office, Largo Porta Nuova
45 CAI Office
46 Libreria Lorenzelli
47 Bus Station
48 SAB Bus Station
50 Train Station
51 Tourist Office
Piazza della Citadella
Piazza Mascheroni
Via della Boccola
Via Solata
Via B Colleoni
Via Arena
Via delle Mura
Via di San Giacomo
Via Gombito
0 100 200 m
See Enlargement
Città Alta
Piazza Sant'Agostino
Stadio Comunale
Via Baioni
Via Giulio Crescenzi
Via Nazario Sauro
Viale Giulio Cesare
Via Borgo S Caterina
Via della Noca
Piazza Carrara
Via C Battisti
Via Gianforte Suardi
Via Alessandro Noli
Morla
Via F Cavagnis
Via Tre Armi
Viale Vittorio Emanuele II
Via Monte Ortigara
Via San Giovanni
Viale Muraine
Via T Frizzoni
Via del Pradello
Via Giuseppe Verdi
Via Torquato Tasso
Via Gabriele Camozzi
Via Borgo Palazzo
Hospital
Via XXIV Maggio
Via dello Statuto
Via San Alessandro
Via Botta
Viale Brigata Lupi
Piazza della Libertà
Viale Roma
Via Tasca
Via dei Partigiani
Piazza Dante
Via Mazzini
Via Garibaldi
Via Quattro Novembre
Piazza Matteotti
Via Broseta
Via XX Settembre
Viale Papa Giovanni XXIII
Via Angelo Mai
Piazzale Marconi
Via Quarenghi
Via Pietro Paleocapa
To Milano, Como & A4 Autostrada
Via Gian Battista Moroni
Via San Bernardino
To Milano, Como & A4 Autostrada

LOMBARDIA

Città Bassa One budget hotel is *Novecento* (☎ 25 52 10), Via dello Statuto 23, near the corner of Via Damiano Chiesa, with singles/doubles from L35,000/45,000. It's a bit of a hike from the train station. The *Antica Trattoria della Brianza* (☎ 25 33 38), Via Broseta 61a, is about 20-minutes walk west of the train station, opposite the Coop supermarket. It has modest, clean rooms for L30,000/60,000. Closer to the station, and a little more expensive at L35,000/70,000, is *Hotel Quarenghi* (☎ 32 03 31), Via Quarenghi 33. The nearby *San Giorgio* is in much the same league.

The *Albergo Piemontese* (☎ 24 26 29), Piazzale Marconi 11, is one of several three-star places in the area. If you're really out of luck, or have lire to burn, *Albergo Arli* (☎ 22 20 14), Largo Porta Nuova 12, has doubles from L95,000. Farther up the scale again, *Albergo Cappello d'Oro* (☎ 23 25 03), Viale Papa Giovanni XXIII 12, starts at L161,000 for a double.

Città Alta The *Agnello d'Oro* (☎ 24 98 83), Via Gombito 22, could almost pass for an antique shop. Just a short walk from the funicular station, it has attractive rooms from L65,000/105,000. The *Albergo Sole* (☎ 21 82 38), Via Colleoni 1, just off Piazza Vecchia, has rooms from L80,000/110,000 and is also good. They have a restaurant with a lovely garden out the back – delightful al fresco dining in the summer.

Places to Eat

Like the Venetians, the Bergamaschi are fond of polenta and eat it as a side dish or dessert. They contributed casonsei, a ravioli stuffed with meat, to the Italian table, and the area is noted for its fine red wines, including Valcalepio.

Città Bassa For a good, cheap lunch, *Bay Bay Self-Service*, Via Tiraboschi 73, is hard to beat. It's open Monday to Friday only. A hundred metres closer to Viale Papa Giovanni XXIII in the same street, the *Nessi Panificio* is one of a chain of bakeries and pastry shops around the city. Its takeaway pizza is popular – all the school kids swarm in.

Gennaro e Pia, Via Borgo Palazzo 41, has pizzas from L6000. *Öl Giopì e la Margì*, Via Borgo Palazzo 25G, is expensive (L50,000 for a full meal) but the waiters wear traditional costume if that's important to you.

Città Alta Cheap food is in short supply here but you can get pizza and panini at *McAnton*, Via Colleoni 22. *Nessi* has a branch at Via Gombito 34, with a selection of local sweets including polenta eösei, as well as pizza.

Trattoria da Franco, Via B Colleoni 8, has pizzas from L7000. *Trattoria da Ornella*, Via Gombito 15, offers traditional foods, and a full meal will cost around L45,000. A cosier spot offering Bergamesque specialities is the *Trattoria Tre Torri*, Piazza Mercato del Fieno, at the southern end of Via San Lorenzo. You'll need to book ahead.

Gelateria Balzerino, Piazza Vecchia, is the perfect spot for an ice cream or granita. There are a couple of watering holes and cafés along the main street. Try *Papageno Pub* at Via B Colleoni 2, or *Pasticceria Donizetti*, Via Gombito 17, for coffee under porticoes.

Getting There & Away

The bus station in Piazzale G Marconi is serviced by SAB, which operates to the lakes and mountains from its own terminal, and a half dozen other lines that go to Milano, Brescia, Cremona, Como and Piacenza, to name a few.

The train station is also on Piazzale Marconi. There are frequent trains for the 50-minute run to Milano and less frequent trains to Brescia and Cremona.

To reach Bergamo by car, take the A4 autostrada from Milano or Venezia, the SS11 from Milano or the SS42 from the south. On entering Bergamo note that the 'centro' signs refer to the lower town. If you want to head straight for the old city, follow the 'città alta' signs. Hitchhikers could try the SS11.

Getting Around

ATB buses serve the city, and you can get

ree route maps from the office on Largo 'orta Nuova. Bus No 1 connects the train tation with the funicular to the città alta. Bus No 3 runs from Porta Sant'Alessandro in the città alta to Via Pietro Paleocapa in the lower own. You can buy tickets valid for an hour's ravel on buses and funiculars for L1400 or an all-day ticket for L4400. There are nachines at the train and funicular stations.

AROUND BERGAMO

There are several small ski resorts in the Bergamo Alps, notably around the **Val Brembana**, reached from Bergamo along Via Nazario Sauro, and **Val Seriana**, reached by way of Via Santa Caterina from the lower town. Each valley boasts seven or eight Alpine rifugi for summer and winter activities (details from the Bergamo APT), many walking tracks and reasonably priced accommodation.

VALTELLINA

Covering the band of Alps across Lombardia's north, the Valtellina is one of Italy's least attractive Alpine regions, although it does have some acceptable skiing and is well set up for walking.

The APT Valtellina has offices in Bormio (☎ 0342-90 33 00), Via Stelvio 10; in Sondrio (☎ 0342-51 25 00), Via C Battisti 12; in Aprica (☎ 0342-74 61 13), Corso Roma 150; in Madesimo (☎ 0343-5 30 15), Via Carducci 27; and in Livigno (☎ 0342-99 63 79), Via Dala Gesa 65. Pick up a copy of *Trekking in Valtellina*, which details walks and provides rifugio information for the area.

Trains leave Milano for Sondrio, a regional transport hub, and buses connect with the resorts and towns.

BRESCIA

With a population of 190,000, Brescia is a somewhat scruffy provincial capital, arms production centre and transport hub. Although rough around the edges, its student life gives the place a bit of life noticeably lacking in some other Lombard towns, and there are a few sights worth stopping for.

When Roma took control of the Gallic town in 225 BC, Brescia (the name derives from a word meaning hill) already had hundreds of years of now obscure history behind it. Charlemagne and his successors ruled Brescia in the 9th century, and the following 1000 years brought a succession of outside rulers. As revolution swept Europe in 1848-49, Brescia was dubbed 'The Lioness' for its 10 day anti-Austrian uprising – an unsuccessful prelude to its participation in the movement towards Italian unification a decade later.

Orientation

From the train and bus stations on the south-western edge, the city centre is a 10-minute walk along Viale della Stazione and Corso dei Martiri della Libertà towards Piazza della Vittoria.

Information

Tourist Office The APT (☎ 4 34 18) is at Corso Zanardelli 34. It is open Monday to Friday from 9 am to 12.30 pm and 3 to 6 pm and Saturday from 9 am to 12.30 pm. Another tourist information office has opened on Piazza della Loggia. It opens Monday to Saturday from 9.30 am to 6.30 pm.

Money There are plenty of banks in Brescia. The Banca San Paolo di Brescia on Corso Zanardelli and the Banca Credito Agrario Bresciano on Piazza Paolo VI both have reliable ATMs.

Post & Communications The main post office is in Piazza della Vittoria and is open Monday to Friday from 8.15 am to 5.30 pm and Saturday from 8.15 am to 1 pm. The postcode for central Brescia is 25100.

The Telecom office is at Via Moretto 46 and is open Monday to Friday from 9 am to 12.30 pm and 2.30 to 6 pm. The telephone code for Brescia is ☎ 030.

Laundry There's an Onda Blu laundry at Via Solferino 8f.

Emergency & Medical Services The questura (☎ 3 74 41) is on Via Botticelli. For

PLACES TO STAY	23 Spizzico	16 Duomo Nuovo
4 Albergo Vellia	27 Don Rodriguez	17 Piazza Paolo VI
10 Hotel Nuovo Orologio		18 Duomo Vecchio
20 Hotel Vittoria	**OTHER**	19 Banca Credito Agrario Bresciano
26 Albergo Regina e Due Leoni	1 Colle Cidneo & Castle	21 Piazza della Vittoria
28 Albergo Rigamonti e Mansione	2 Torre della Pallata	22 Piazza del Mercato
31 Albergo Solferino	8 Capitoleum; Museo Civico Età Romano	24 Tourist Office
	9 Monastero di Santa Giulia; Basilica di San Salvatore	25 Banca San Paolo di Brescia (ATM)
PLACES TO EAT		29 Telecom Office
3 Yo	11 Piazza della Loggia	30 Pinacoteca Civica Tosio–Martinengo
5 Manhattan	12 Post Office	32 Bus Station
6 Caffetteria la Torre	13 Tourist Office	33 Train Station
7 Al Frate	15 Il Broletto	
14 Hosteria La Vineria		

mergencies call ☎ 113. The Ospedale Civile (☎ 3 99 51) is in Piazzale Ospedale at the northern edge of the city. You can get an ambulance on ☎ 200 25 22. There's an all-night pharmacy at Via Einaudi 9.

Colle Cidneo & Castle

Brescia's historic centre is dominated by the Colle Cidneo, surmounted by a rambling castle that has been the core of the city defences for centuries. Torre Mirabella, the main round tower, was built by the Viscontis in the 13th century; the rest is a hotchpotch of add-ons and alterations completed by Brescia's long series of outside overlords. The castle houses two museums. The **Museo delle Armi** and the **Civico Museo del Risorgimento** are open daily, except Monday, from 10 am to 12.30 pm and 3 to 5 pm (hours vary slightly in summer and on weekends). Admission to each is L5000. The former is said to contain one of Italy's most extensive weapons collections. The latter deals with Italian unification history. You can wander the grounds and much of the castle walls (a smoochers' hang-out) from 8 am to 8 pm.

Cathedrals & Piazzas

The most compelling of Brescia's religious monuments is the **Duomo Vecchio**, or Rotonda, an 11th-century Romanesque basilica built over a 6th-century circular structure on Piazza Paolo VI. The form of the church is uncommon and there are hints, like the mosaics, of an even earlier Roman presence on the site. Next door, the Renaissance **Duomo Nuovo** dwarfs its elderly neighbour, but is of less interest. Also on the square is **Il Broletto**, a medieval town hall with an 11th-century tower.

North-west of Piazza Paolo VI is Piazza della Loggia, dominated by the squat 16th-century **loggia**, in which Palladio had a hand. The **Torre dell'Orologio**, with its exquisite astrological timepiece, is modelled on the one in Venezia's Piazza San Marco.

Finally, the Fascist era **Piazza della Vittoria** is well worth a look. Laid out in 1932 by Piacentini, the square and its buildings (like the post office) are a perfect example of the period's monumentalism.

Roman Ruins & Museums

Evidence of the Roman presence in Brescia is still visible today. Along Via dei Musei, at the foot of the castle, are the now partly restored and rather impressive remains of the **Capitolium**, a Roman temple built in 73 AD that houses the modest **Museo Civico Età Romana**. Hours and admission are the same as for the Museo delle Armi.

In some respects more intriguing is the jumbled **Monastero di Santa Giulia & Basilica di San Salvatore**. Roman mosaics have been unearthed here as well. The star piece of the collection is the 8th-century Croce di Desiderio, a Lombard cross encrusted with hundreds of jewels. Hours and admission are as above.

On Piazza Moretto, the **Pinacoteca Civica Tosio-Martinengo** features works by artists of the Brescian school as well as Raphael. Again, hours and admission are the same as for the other museums.

Special Events

The International Piano Festival, held from early April until June, is staged in conjunction with nearby Bergamo, while the Estate Aperta festival of music and other activities occupies the summer months. The city's opera season is in October and November.

Places to Stay

There should be no problems finding accommodation, particularly in summer.

Albergo Solferino (☎ 4 63 00), Via Solferino 1, is near the station and has basic singles/doubles from about L30,000/50,000. Closer to the centre of town is the similar *Albergo Vellia* (☎ 375 64 72), Via Calzavellia 35.

Among the better budget choices is *Hotel Nuovo Orologio* (☎ 377 28 78), Via Cesare Beccaria 17, just off Piazza Paolo VI. Some singles are pokey though, and they start at L45,000. Doubles start at L65,000. The hotel has a bar and TV room.

Albergo Regina e Due Leoni (☎ 375 78 81),

LOMBARDIA

near the tourist office in Corso Zanardelli, charges L40,000/70,000.

Another reasonable choice in the same range is *Albergo Rigamonti e Mansione* (☎ 4 81 52), Contrada Mansione 6. They have a range of rooms, with singles starting at L32,000 and doubles going as a high as L65,000 with private bathroom.

Places to Eat

For fresh produce, locals head for Piazza del Mercato. Risotto and beef dishes are common in Brescia and the region offers many good wines, including those from Botticino, Lugana and Riviera del Garda.

There is a collection of cheap snack places at the bus station, or you can try *Spizzico*, on the corner of Via IV Novembre and Via X Giornate, for huge fast-food-style pizza slices at about L4500. *Don Rodriguez*, Via Cavallotti 6, has moderately priced pizzas.

A few steps away at Via X Giornate 4, *Hosteria La Viniera* not only offers moderately priced meals (try the polenta e funghi) but doubles as a wine boutique, or enoteca.

The happening area is along Corso Mameli and Via dei Musei. There are plenty of restaurants, cafés and bars, lent a bit of buzz by the student population.

If you're prepared to part with L40,000-plus, *Al Frate*, Via dei Musei 25, serves up well-presented regional dishes – it's often full.

Caffetteria la Torre and the *Manhattan* bar are busy student haunts. For yoghurt gelato, go straight to *Yo*, Corso Mameli 63.

Getting There & Away

The main bus station is near the train station, but most runs serve Brescia province and lakes Garda and Iseo. Only a few buses run to Milano and Bergamo.

If you're coming by train from Roma, change at Verona. From Milano, frequent trains take 50 minutes. There are quite a few to Cremona, Venezia, Verona and Bergamo.

By car, the A4 and SS11 go west to Milano and east to Lago di Garda and Verona, while the A21 and SS45 head south to Cremona.

CREMONA

Home of the Stradivarius violin, Cremona today jealously maintains its centuries-old status as premier exponent of the delicate art of making the perfect string instrument. All the great violin-making dynasties started here – Amati, Guarneri and Stradivari – and there are plenty of opportunities for getting better acquainted with the subject. Not that Cremona is Italy's only centre for violin makers – rivals in nearby cities like Bologna will assure you the only thing better about the Cremonese product is the publicity. For centuries an independent city-state, Cremona also boasts a compact but impressive city centre, meriting a stopover if not necessarily an overnight stay. It is an easy day trip from Milano, Mantova, Brescia and Piacenza.

Orientation

The town is small and easy to navigate. From the train station, walk straight south along Via Palestro to the central area around Piazza Cavour, Piazza della Pace and Piazza del Comune. Bus No 1 goes to Piazza Cavour from the train station, but you'll probably travel just as fast on foot.

Information

Tourist Office The APT office (☎ 2 32 33) is at Piazza del Comune 5, opposite the duomo, and is open Monday to Saturday from 9.30 am to 12.30 pm and 3 to 6 pm; Sunday and holidays from 9.45 am to 12.15 pm. Ask if the discount entry scheme to all Cremona's museums is still in effect.

Money The Banca Popolare di Cremona on Piazza del Comune has a money-changing machine, while the Banca Nazionale del Lavoro's ATM off Piazza Roma is reliable.

Post & Communications The post office is at Via Verdi 1, and it is open Monday to Friday from 8 am to 7 pm and Saturday to 1 pm. The postcode for central Cremona is 26100.

The Telecom office, Via Cadolini 3, is open Monday to Friday from 9 am to 12.30

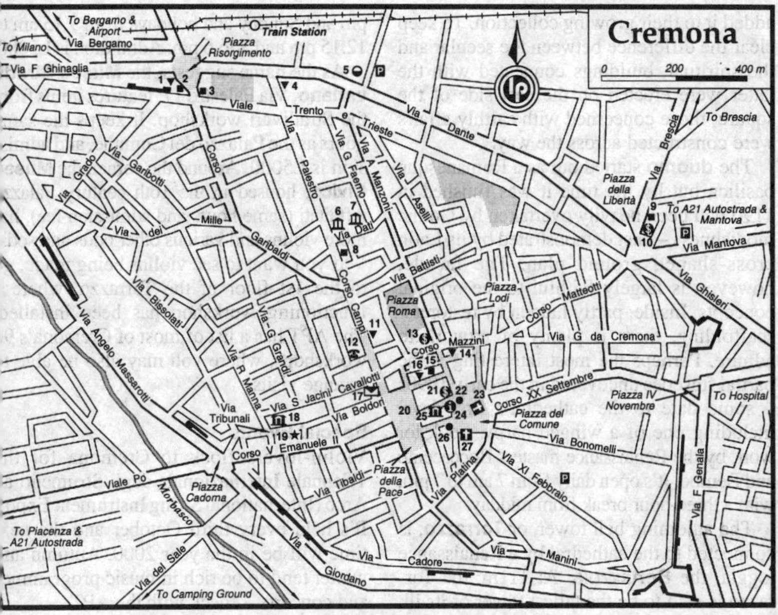

PLACES TO STAY
- 2 Albergo Bologna
- 3 Albergo Ideale
- 8 Albergo Touring
- 9 Albergo Brescia
- 15 Hotel Astoria

PLACES TO EAT
- 1 La Bersagliera
- 4 Taboga Fast Food
- 11 Ristorante Marechiaro
- 14 Ristorante Centrale
- 16 Ristorante Fou-Lú

OTHER
- 5 Bus Station
- 6 Museo Stradivariano
- 7 Museo Civico
- 10 Credito Romagnolo (ATM)
- 12 Telecom Office
- 13 Banca Nazionale del Lavoro
- 17 Post Office
- 18 Palazzo di Giustizia
- 19 Questura (Police Station)
- 20 Piazza Cavour
- 21 Banca Popolare di Cremona
- 22 Torrazzo
- 23 Duomo
- 24 APT Tourist Office
- 25 Palazzo Comunale
- 26 Loggia dei Militi
- 27 Baptistry

m and 2.30 to 6 pm. The telephone code for Cremona is ☎ 0372.

Emergency & Medical Services For police emergency, call ☎ 113. The questura (☎ 48 81) is at Via Tribunali 6. For an ambulance call ☎ 118. The public hospital (☎ 40 51 11) is on Largo Priori.

Piazza del Comune

Even if violins do not ring your bell, the rust-red heart of Cremona, **Piazza del Comune**, makes at least a brief stop in this quiet town worthwhile. Quiet is the word – most museums are closed on Monday and city ordinances limiting traffic in the centre have so emptied the zone that shopkeepers groaning over the stay-away effect have told the authorities '*basta!*' (enough!).

Medieval Cremona, like most Lombard towns, was an independent *comune* until the 14th century, when the Viscontis of Milano added it to their growing collection. To keep clear the difference between the secular and the spiritual, buildings connected with the latter were erected on the east side of the square; those concerned with earthly affairs were constructed across the way.

The **duomo** started out as a Romanesque basilica but by the time it was finished in 1190 had been heavily overtaken by Gothic modishness – best demonstrated by its Latin cross-shaped ground plan. The façade, however, is largely faithful to the original concepts. Inside, partly hidden by restorers' scaffolding, there is plenty of artwork to admire. Perhaps the most interesting is the partial frescoes uncovered in the early 1990s – some date to the cathedral's first days, including one of a winged harpy. Look for work by the Renaissance masters Boccaccino and Bembo. It's open daily from 7 am to 7 pm, with a three-hour break from midday.

The adjoining bell tower, or **Torrazzo**, is connected to the cathedral by a Renaissance loggia, the **Bertazzola**. At 111m, the Torrazzo is said to be the tallest tower of its ilk in Italy. It is open from 10.30 am to 7 pm. Admission is L5000. To the south is the 12th-century **baptistry** which, like many Italian medieval baptistries, has an octagonal base. Alluding to renewal and hence baptism and resurrection, the figure eight appears in much religious decoration – its use in this kind of architecture is no coincidence.

Across the square are the **Palazzo Comunale** and, just to its south, the smaller porticoed **Loggia dei Militi**, both dating from the 13th century. The former was and remains the town hall, while the latter housed the town's militia.

LOMBARDIA

Violin Museums & Workshop

While you're at the Palazzo Comunale, take a look at the violin collection, featuring two Amatis, two Guarneris and a 1715 Stradivarius. A local maestro occasionally plays the instruments to keep them in working order. To find out if and when he might do so, call the town hall switchboard (☎ 40 71) for an appointment. The collection can be viewed Monday to Saturday from 8.30 am to 5.45 pm and Sunday and holidays from 9.15 am t
12.15 pm and 3 to 6 pm. Admission is L500

As the name suggests, the **Museo Stradi variano**, Via Palestro 17, features items fro the Stradivari workshop. It keeps the sam hours as the Palazzo del Comune, and admis sion is L5000. Around the corner, the **Muse Civico**, housed in the 16th century Palazz Affaitati (same hours and admission fee), ha more violins and various other odds and sods

If you want to see violins being made, g to the 1st floor of the Torrazzo, where functioning workshop has been installed The APT has a list of most of Cremona's 9 workshops, where you may also be able t arrange visits.

Special Events

Violin-lovers flock to Cremona for th Triennale Internazionale degli Strumenti a Arco (International String Instrument Expo) It's held every third October and the nex time will be in the year 2000. Autumn an winter tend to be rich in music programme and concerts – check with the APT.

Places to Stay

The *Camping Parco al Po* (☎ 2 71 37), Vi Lungo Po Europa, has sites from L7000 pe person, plus L5000 per tent. Head south west from Piazza Cavour.

Albergo Bologna (☎ 2 42 58), at Piazz Risorgimento 7 near the train and bus sta tions, has small singles for L30,000. Not fa off in Viale Trento e Trieste, *Albergo Ideal* (also known as *Rada*, ☎ 3 86 68) has singles doubles for L35,000/50,000 and a poke room for L30,000. Closer to the centre *Albergo Touring* (☎ 3 69 76), Via Palestro 3 has singles/doubles for L35,000/ 60,000. I you're driving in, *Albergo Brescia* (☎ 43 4 15), Via Brescia 7, is handy. Decent singles doubles cost L35,000/50,000. Located in small lane near Piazza Cavour, *Hotel Astori* (☎ 46 16 16), Via Bordigallo 19, has com fortable singles/doubles with three-star mo cons for L75,000/100,000.

Places to Eat

Cremona's gifts to Italian cuisine includ

ollito (boiled meats) – there are several arieties and cotechino with polenta is the peciality. Mostarda, often served with your ollito, consists of fruit in sweet mustardy oo. Sounds unpalatable, but it's really not ad at all.

For quick snacks, head for *Taboga Fast ood*, Via Palestro 51, near the train station. The *Ristorante Marechiaro*, Corso Campi 9, serves standard Italian fare, including izzas for about L9000. *La Bersagliera*, iazza Risorgimento 12, is similar.

With a little more money, you could try the ine *Ristorante Centrale*, Via Pertusio 4, off Corso Mazzini. It's a popular and charming pot where you can try cotechino, admire uman-size jars of mostarda and drool over uge drums of fresh local cheese. You can at well for about L35,000. If you need a hange, go to *Ristorante Fou-Lú*, the Chinese establishment on Via Bordigallo, ust north of Piazza Cavour.

Getting There & Away

The bus station is off Via Dante, east of the train station. Various companies run to Milano, Brescia and Bergamo, and occasionally long-distance buses heading for Genova, Trieste and Venezia call in here.

By train (☎ 2 22 37), the city can be reached from Milano via Treviglio, from Mantova, Pavia and Brescia, or from the south by changing at Piacenza.

If you're driving, the most direct road from Milano is the SS415 (Paullo exit); the A21 takes you to Brescia, where it joins with the A4.

MANTOVA

On the shores of lakes Superiore, Mezzo and Inferiore (a glorified widening of the Mincio river), Mantova (Mantua) is a serene and beautiful city. However, industrial sprawl from its booming petrochemical industry has scarred the surrounding countryside and left the lakes heavily polluted. The city can be visited as a day trip from as far afield as Milano but, to do it justice, spend the night.

History

Mantova was settled by the Etruscans in the 10th-century BC and later prospered under Roman rule. It passed to the House of Gonzaga in 1328, flourishing under one of the foremost Renaissance dynasties and attracting the likes of Petrarch, Antonio Pisanello, Andrea Mantegna, Giulio Romano and Rubens. The golden days of 'La Gloriosa' came to a mean end when Austria took control in 1708. Vienna's troops stayed in control (aside from the predictable Napoleonic interlude at the end of the 18th century) until 1866.

Orientation

The old part of the city is on a small peninsula at the southern edge of the three lakes, while the newer districts spread around their shores. From the train station in Piazza Don Leoni, head a short distance to the right for Largo di Porta Pradella. From there, take a sharp turn left up Corso Vittorio Emanuele II for a 10-minute walk to the city centre. The heart of the centre is a string of five piazzas, capped at the northern end by the sprawling complex of the Palazzo Ducale.

Information

Tourist Office The helpful APT office (☎ 32 82 53), Piazza Mantegna 6, produces a range of information about trips throughout the province. It is open Monday to Saturday from 8.30

The Chaste & Royal Poet

Dryden called Virgil 'the chastest and royalest of poets'. Born 70 years before Christ on his parents' farm just outside Mantova, Virgil is that city's most illustrious son and one of Roma's greatest poets. Of the three works he left behind, *The Aeneid* is the most exalted. An epic in the great tradition of the ancient Sumerian myth, Gilgamesh, and Homer's *Iliad* and *Odyssey*, the tale is a fantastic account of the foundation of Roma, loaded with symbolism and told with unsurpassed virtuosity. The inspiration of countless poets since, Virgil comes to life as Dante's 'sweet master' in the Florentine's *Divine Comedy*, 14 centuries after Virgil's death. ■

am to 12.30 pm and 3 to 6 pm; Sunday from 9.30 am to 12.30 pm.

Money Banks are located throughout the city centre and open from 8.20 am to 1.20 pm and 3.20 to 4.20 pm. Some have extended hours on Thursday.

Post & Communications The main post office is on Piazza Martiri di Belfiore, along Via Roma south of Piazza Marconi. It is open Monday to Friday from 8.30 am to 7 pm and Saturday from 8.20 am to 1.20 pm. The postcode for central Mantova is 46100.

There is a Telecom office on Via XX Settembre which is open Monday to Friday from 9 am to 12.30 pm and 2.30 to 6 pm. The telephone code for Mantova is ☎ 0376.

Emergency & Medical Services For police emergency, call ☎ 113. The questura (☎ 20 51) is at Piazza Sordello 46. For an ambulance call ☎ 118 or ☎ 22 02 20. The public hospital (☎ 20 11) is on Via Albertoni, at the southern end of the old town.

Palazzo Ducale

Also known as the Reggia dei Gonzaga, after the longtime rulers of Mantova, the Palazzo Ducale occupies a great chunk of the north-eastern corner of the city. Its walls hide three piazzas, a park, a basilica and a total of 450 rooms – an imposing demonstration of the pride and wealth of the Gonzagas, although from Piazza Sordello you would never guess the extent of what lies behind. The centrepiece is the **Castello di San Giorgio**, which contains a museum. The Gonzagas were avid art collectors, as the visitor soon realises. The highpoint is Andrea Mantegna's Camera degli Sposi, a series of fine frescoes in one of the castle's towers. This part of the complex is open daily from 9 am to 2 pm and also Tuesday to Saturday from 2.30 to 6 pm (7 pm in summer). Admission is L12,000. You are free to wander the rest of the area at will. Occasionally other exhibitions are held in the cellars of the outer walls, so it is worth wandering outside the city gates and along the palace's lakeside fortifications.

Churches

The Baroque cupola of the **Basilica di Sant'Andrea**, on Piazza Mantegna, looms majestically over the city in much the same way that St Paul's dominates east London. Designed by Leon Battisti Alberti in 1472, Mantova's principal place of worship houses a much disputed relic: containers said to hold earth soaked by the blood of Christ's spear wound. The very Roman soldier responsible for the wound is said to have scooped up the earth and buried it in Mantova after leaving Israel. The containers are paraded around the town in a grand procession on Good Friday. There is no dispute about the tomb of the painter Andrea Mantegna, also to be found inside the basilica.

East of the basilica, across the 15th-century colonnaded Piazza delle Erbe, is the 11th-century Romanesque **Rotonda di San Lorenzo**, sunk below the level of the piazza and believed to be on the site of a Roman temple dedicated to Venus.

The **duomo**, on Piazza Sordello, pales somewhat before the magnificence of the basilica. Its origins lie in the 10th century but there is little to see of them. The façade was erected in the mid-18th century, while the decoration inside was done by Giulio Romano after a fire in 1545.

Piazzas

Past the 13th-century Palazzo della Ragione on Piazza delle Erbe is the **Palazzo Broletto**, which dominates the neighbouring Piazza del Broletto. In a niche on the façade is a figure said to represent Virgil.

Enter Piazza Sordello from the south and on your left you have the grand house of the Gonzagas' predecessors, the Bonacolsi clan. Hapless prisoners used to be dangled in a cage from the tower – aptly known as the **Torre della Gabbia** (Cage Tower). Behind the duomo lies the **Casa di Rigoletto**, which Verdi used as a set model for most of his operas.

Palazzo del Te

Mantova's other Gonzaga palace, at the southern edge of the centre along Via Roma and Via Acerbi, is a grand villa built by

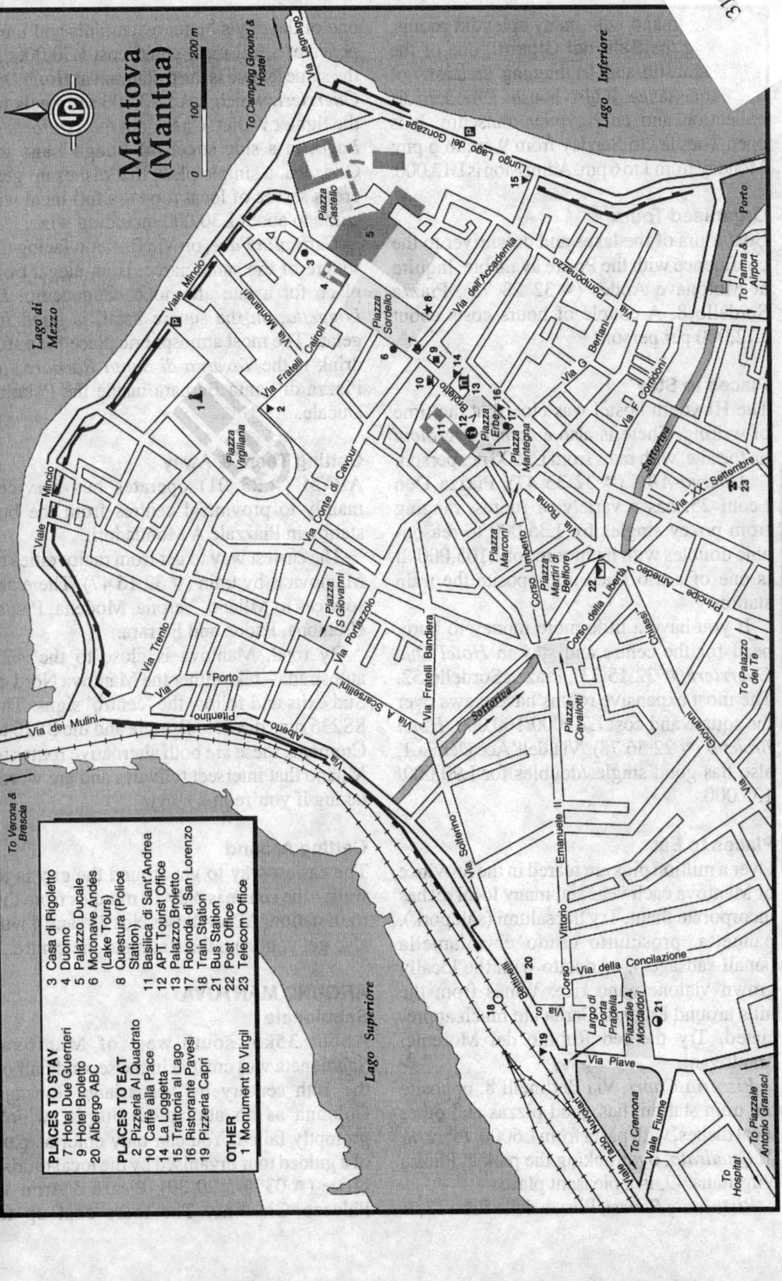
Mantova
(Mantua)
0
100
200 m
PLACES TO STAY
7 Hotel Due Guerrieri
9 Hotel Broletto
20 Albergo ABC
PLACES TO EAT
2 Pizzeria Al Quadrato
10 Caffè alla Pace
14 La Loggetta
15 Trattoria al Lago
16 Ristorante Pavesi
19 Pizzeria Capri
OTHER
1 Monument to Virgil
3 Casa di Rigoletto
4 Duomo
5 Palazzo Ducale
6 Motonave Andes (Lake Tours)
8 Questura (Police Station)
11 Basilica di Sant'Andrea
12 APT Tourist Office
13 Palazzo Broletto
17 Rotonda di San Lorenzo
18 Train Station
21 Bus Station
22 Post Office
23 Telecom Office
Lago di Mezzo
Lago Superiore
Lago Inferiore
To Verona & Brescia
To Camping Ground & Hostel
To Parma & Airport
To Palazzo del Te
To Cremona
To Hospital
To Piazzale Antonio Gramsci
Piazza Castello
Piazza Sordello
Piazza Virgiliana
Piazza Erbe
Piazza Mantegna
Piazza Marconi
Piazza Martiri di Belfiore
Piazza Cavallotti
Piazza S Giovanni
Largo di Porta Pradella
Piazzale A Mondadori
Porto
Via Legnago
Lungo Lago dei Gonzaga
Viale Mincio
Via Montanari
Via Fratelli Cairoli
Via Conte di Cavour
Via dell'Accademia
Via Pomponazzo
Via G Bertani
Via F Corridoni
Via XX Settembre
Sottoriva
Via Roma
Corso Umberto
Corso della Libertà
Via Chiassi
Principe Amedeo
Via Giovanni
Via Trento
Via Portazzolo
Via Fratelli Bandiera
Via A Scarsellini
Via dei Mulini
Via Pitentino
Via Alberto
Via Solferino
Corso Vittorio Emanuele II
Via della Concilazione
Via Bettinelli
Via Piave
Viale Fiume
Viale Tazio Nuvolari

LOMBARDIA

Giulio Romano with many splendid rooms, including the **Sala dei Giganti**, one of the most fantastic and frightening creations of the Renaissance. It also houses a modern art collection and an Egyptian museum. It is open Tuesday to Sunday from 9 am to 6 pm; Monday from 1 to 6 pm. Admission is L12,000.

Organised Tours

Boat tours of the lakes and downriver to the confluence with the Po are available. Inquire at Motonave Andes (☎ 32 28 75), Piazza Sordello 8. A couple of hours costs about L12,000 per person.

Places to Stay

The HI youth hostel was closed at the time of writing. There is also a *camping ground* on the site, with rates from L5000 per person.

Albergo ABC (☎ 32 33 47), Piazza Don Leoni 25, has a variety of rooms, ranging from pokey singles for L35,000 to reasonable doubles with bathroom for L105,000. It is one of a trio lined up opposite the train station.

If you have a little more money to burn, head for the centre and stay in *Hotel Due Guerrieri* (☎ 32 15 33), Piazza Sordello 52. The most expensive rooms have views over the square and cost L70,000/100,000. *Hotel Broletto* (☎ 22 36 78), Via dell'Accademia 1, also has good singles/doubles for L90,000/135,000.

Places to Eat

Over a million pigs are reared in the province of Mantova each year and many local dishes incorporate them. Try the salumi (salt pork), pancetta, prosciutto crudo or salamella (small sausages), or risotto with the locally grown vialone nano rice. Wines from the hills around Lago di Garda are much appreciated. Try the red Rubino dei Morenici Mantovani.

Pizzeria Capri, Via Bettinelli 8, opposite the train station, has good pizzas and other local dishes, with pasta from L6000. *Pizzeria Al Quadrato*, overlooking the park at Piazza Virgiliana 49, is a pleasant place.

Ristorante Pavesi, Piazza delle Erbe 13, is one of the city's better restaurants and inexpensive; a full meal could cost L30,000. I the same league is the restaurant at *Hotel Du Guerrieri*, which has L22,000 set meals fc the tighter wallet. Check out the *Trattoria d Lago*, in a side street off Lungo Lago de Gonzaga, a simple place that dishes up generous serves of local food – a full meal wi come to about L30,000 including wine.

Caffè alla Pace, on Via Broletto facing th square of the same name, is an elegant ol place for a late afternoon cappuccino. *L Loggetta*, on the square itself, is good fo gelati. The most atmospheric place for a sti drink is the *Taverna di Santa Barbara*, o Piazza di Santa Barbara inside the Palazz Ducale.

Getting There & Away

APAM (☎ 23 01) operates bus service mainly to provincial centres from the bu station in Piazzale A Mondadori.

The easiest way to get from major cities t Mantova is by train (☎ 32 16 47). There ar services to Milano, Verona, Modena, Pavia Cremona, Padua and Ferrara.

By road, Mantova is close to the A2 autostrada – take either the Mantova Nord o Sud exits and follow the 'centro' signs. Th SS236 runs direct to Brescia and the SS10 t Cremona; these are both alternative routes t Milano that intersect tollways and are wort taking if you're in a hurry.

Getting Around

The easiest way to get around the city is t walk – the centre is only 10 minutes from the train station. APAM buses Nos 2M and 4 wil also get you from the station to the centre.

AROUND MANTOVA

Sabbioneta

About 35km south-west of Mantova, Sabbioneta was created in the second half of the 16th century by Vespasiano Gonzaga Colonna as an attempted Utopia, which promptly failed. You can only enter as part of a guided tour organised by the local tourist office (☎ 0375-5 20 39), Piazza d'Armi 1, Palazzo Giardino. The tours cost up to

L10,000, depending on how many of Sabbioneta's five 16th-century monuments you care to visit. Admission to the 19th-century synagogue (L3000) and Museo d'Arte Sacra (L3000) are extra. Several buses run there from Mantova.

San Benedetto Po

The Benedictine abbey in this small Po valley town, 21km south-east of Mantova, was founded in 1007. Little remains of the original buildings, although the Chiesa di Santa Maria still sports a 12th-century mosaic. The star attraction is the Correggio fresco discovered in the refectory in 1984. There are buses from Mantova.

The Lakes

Where the Lombard plains rise into the Alps, northern Italy is pocked by a series of lakes, among the most beautiful of Italy's natural attractions. Unfortunately, the secret has been out for at least a century – the prices and summer crowds can detract from the pleasure. The lakes are not only the playground of the Milanoese rich; tourists from all over northern Europe converge on their favourites. Lakes Garda, Como and Maggiore are especially busy, although even the minor lakes are hardly immune.

Most are within easy reach of Milano and provincial centres such as Bergamo and Brescia. There are plenty of camping grounds, some hostels and hotels in all budget categories, as well as many rifugi in the mountains.

LAGO MAGGIORE

The largest, and generally regarded as the most captivating of the lakes, Maggiore (also known as Lago Verbano) is indeed stunning in parts, although its shores are flatter and less spectacular than those of some of its pre-Alpine confrères. Fed principally by the Ticino and Tresa rivers, Lago Maggiore is about 65km long. The area becomes stiflingly overcrowded in the high season, a good time to stay well away.

The lake's northern reaches are in Swiss territory, as are some of the better walking areas, so consult the Ente Turistico di Locarno e Valli (☎ 091-751 03 33), Largo Zorzi, 6601 Locarno, Switzerland.

Stresa

Extremely popular with British and German tourists, mostly of the package tour variety, this resort town on the lake's western shore is like one great English tearoom – prim and not unattractive, but somehow insipid. Although commonly touted as a base for the Isole Borromee and the lake in general, the islands can be reached from other points around the lake.

Information The APT del Lago Maggiore (☎ 3 01 50) is at Via Principe Tomaso 70/72, and in summer is open seven days a week (mornings only on weekends; closed Sunday in winter). Other tourist offices are at Arona, Baveno and Verbania.

The telephone code for the area is ☎ 0323.

Things to See & Do Apart from the Isole Borromee, you could take a cable car west to the summit of Monte Mottarone, the highest peak in the vicinity (1491m). Modest skiing possibilities are an added attraction to the views, and the nearby **Parco del Mottarone** offers some pleasant walking. The cable car runs daily from about 9 am to 5 pm, or you can drive up through the park (L6000 per car for the round trip). The **Villa Pallavicino**, a huge garden with a zoo where the animals roam relatively freely, offers superb views of the lake and the surrounding mountains. Admission is L10,500.

Places to Stay & Eat The nearest camping ground is the *Sette Camini Residence* (☎ 2 01 83), Via Pianezza 7, a few km from Stresa at Gignese. There are some 40 camping grounds up and down the western shore of the lake – check with the APT in Stresa. Hotels are plentiful, but must be booked well in advance for summer or long weekends.

THE LAKES

Orsola Meublé (☎ 3 10 87), Via Duchessa di Genova 45, has singles/doubles costing from L40,000/ 60,000. *Albergo Vidoli* (☎ 3 11 76), Via G Leopardi 19, has singles/doubles from L30,000/L45,000, or L55,000 for a double with bathroom. There are 23 hotels in the three to five star range. The *Speranza au Lac* (☎ 3 11 78), Piazza Imbarcadero, has rooms from L166,000/ 232,000. Alternatively, pick up an agriturismo guide in the Stresa APT.

Eating can be an expensive exercise in Stresa, but one moderate option is *Chez Osvaldo*, Via Anna Bolongaro 59. Pasta costs around L9000 and mains up to L16,000 – try the scaloppine panna e mele, veal done in an apple and cream sauce. They also have rooms for rent. A Spanish cook at the *Ristorante del Pescatore*, Vicolo del Poncivo 3, will whip up a paella for two for L53,000.

Getting There & Away Stresa lies on the Domodossola-Milano train line. Buses leave from the waterfront for destinations around the lake and elsewhere, including Milano, Novara and Lago d'Orta. By car, the A8 autostrada connects Milano with Varese, south-east of Lago Maggiore. Exit at Legnano for the SS33 road, which passes the lake's west shore and continues to the Simplon pass. The A26 from Milano has an exit for Lago Maggiore, via Arona.

Navigazione Lago Maggiore (☎ 0322-4 66 51) operates ferries and hydrofoils around the lake, connecting Stresa with Arona, Angera, Baveno, Cannobio, Pallanza, the islands and Locarno (Switzerland). A variety of day tickets (starting at L9000 and rising depending on destinations) are available for unlimited trips, but most unhurried visitors find normal single-trip tickets better value. Services are reduced in autumn and winter.

Isole Borromee

These islands (Borromean Islands) can be reached from various points around the lake, but Stresa and Baveno are the best step-off points. The four islands, Bella, Pescatori (or Superiore), Madre and San Giovanni, form the lake's most beautiful corner.

Isola Bella has long played host to famous holiday-makers – Wagner, Stendhal, Byron and Goethe among them. The **Palazzo Borromeo** is the main draw card. Built in the 17th century for the Borromeo family, the sumptuous palace contains works by Giovanni Tiepolo and Van Dyck, Flemish tapestries and sculptures by Canova. The gardens are magnificent and contain plants from around the world – although you must pay L13,000 to see it all. **Isola Madre** provides fertile ground for Italy's tallest palm trees, an 18th-century palace and even more lavish gardens than Isola Bella. Admission is L13,000.

Isola dei Pescatori retains some of its original fishing-village atmosphere. The *Albergo Belvedere* (☎ 3 00 47) on this island opens mid-March to mid-October and charges L80,000 for a double with breakfast.

Western Shore to Switzerland

Stresa is not the only town on Lago Maggiore, and it is worth considering the alternatives. The choice depends a little on your tastes, and you will never really escape the feeling of being in a somewhat artificial environment. **Verbania**, the biggest town on the lake, offers plenty of accommodation in most classes, but it's the least inviting place to hang about. **Cannero Riviera**, farther north, is a small lakeside village and a good spot for a tranquil break. Just off the coast lie some tiny islets that, before being taken over by the Borromeo family in the 15th century, had served as a den for thieves who operated in the area in the 12th century. More interesting is **Cannobio**, 5km short of the Swiss border – the town's spotless cobblestone streets and the waves of Swiss day-trippers could leave you wondering if you've already crossed the frontier! Swiss francs are acceptable here.

Camp sites dot the coast and Cannero and Cannobio have about 20 hotels between them – check the APT in Stresa or branches in Arona, Baveno or Verbania for a list. A car ferry links Intra (Verbania) to Laveno on the east coast, and all the western shore towns are connected by ferry and bus.

LAGO D'ORTA

Only 15km long and about 2.5km wide, Lago d'Orta is one of the smaller of the Italian lakes. It is actually in the Piemonte region and is separated from its more celebrated eastern neighbour, Lago Maggiore, by Monte Mottarone. Its still waters are surrounded by lush woodlands and are not yet swarming with visitors like the big lakes, but it can still become congested on weekends and in summer.

Orta San Giulio

This is undoubtedly the prettiest of the lake's towns and suffers less than places like Stresa from the blandness born of over-tourism. It is difficult to beat sipping a coffee over the morning paper in one of the cafés on the lakeside square. It is the obvious choice as a base, not only for Lago d'Orta but arguably for Maggiore as well (if you have a vehicle at any rate) – which you can reach via Monte Mottarone and its **national park**.

Information The APT del Lago d'Orta (☎ 91 19 37), Via Olina 9-11, can advise on hiking in the area. The telephone code is ☎ 0322.

Things to See & Do Regular launches make the short trip (L3500 a head return) to the **Isola San Giulio**, named after a Greek evangelist who earned his saintly status by ridding the island of an assortment of snakes and monsters late in the 4th century. A 12th-century basilica dominates the island. The **Sacro Monte**, behind Orta San Giulio, is dotted with a series of small chapels erected to St Francis of Assisi over a 200 year period from 1591 – it makes for a pleasant stroll above the town.

The small village of **Armeno**, at the foot of Monte Mottarone, is worth visiting, not least for its umbrella museum.

Places to Stay & Eat The hitch in Orta San Giulio can be finding a place to stay, especially in the high season and on weekends. *Camping Cusio* (☎ 9 02 90), Via G Bosco, is near the lake shore, and there are others in the area – ask the APT.

Taverna All'Antico Agnello (☎ 9 02 59) is an old establishment full of character, with fine singles/doubles from L40,000/70,000 and triples from L80,000. Try for room No 8, the only one with a lake view. It also has a moderately expensive restaurant that is so good even hotel guests need to book in advance.

Pizzeria Campana, Via Giacomo Giovanetti 41, has about the cheapest food in town – which is not that cheap. The pizzas are great, but the pasta average.

In Armeno, the *Madonna di Luciago* (☎ 90 01 92) has singles/doubles from L40,000/70,000. You may find cheaper rooms by asking the locals.

If all else fails, the APT has a list of places around the lake.

Getting There & Away Orta San Giulio is just off the Novara-Domodossola train line, and can also be reached by bus from Stresa. From the south, take the SS32 from Novara, in Piemonte, or the road to Borgomanero, also from Novara, which is not as interesting but much quicker.

LAGO DI COMO

Marie Henri Beyle first set foot on the shores of Lago di Como as a 17 year old conscript under Napoleon. Years later, as Stendhal, he wrote in *La Chartreuse de Parme* that the blue-green waters of the lake and the grandeur of the Alps made it the most beautiful place in the world. Pliny the Elder and Pliny the Younger were born here, but are not known to have gushed about the area to the same degree as Stendhal. In any case, many people would no doubt consider Como's other famous son as having done quite a deal more for the world. Alessandro Volta, born in 1745, came up with, well, the battery.

The whole centre becomes one great antiques market on the last Saturday of every month – a nice excuse for a day trip by train from Milano.

Known also as Lago Lario, this immense body of water is enchantingly beautiful, as are its tiny waterside villages, some accessible only by boat. Today, the waters are murky and swimming, although permitted in parts, is inadvisable.

Como

Como gets a lot of bad press, but has the advantage over many other lakeside towns of being a real city (population about 90,000) with its own life. The people you mingle with in the streets just might be Italians – even locals – and not the usual crowd of package tourists crated in from northern Europe. The town offers a few attractions in its own right, and is a good base from which to make excursions around the lake.

Orientation From the main train station at Piazzale San Gottardo, walk east to Piazza Cacciatori delle Alpi, and continue along Via Garibaldi to Piazza Volta. The main square, Piazza Cavour, which overlooks the lake, is about 50m farther east along Via Fontana. Tourist boats depart from in front of the piazza, and regular ferries from along the shore. East of Piazza Cavour along Lungo Lario Trieste is the bus station and Stazione Ferrovia Nord Milano (FNM), a smaller train station running shuttles to Milano. The funicular for the mountain settlement of Brunate is farther along.

Information The APT office (☎ 26 97 12) is at Piazza Cavour 16 and is open Monday to Saturday from 9 am to 12.30 pm and 2.30 to 6 pm. There is a smaller office in the central train station.

The Credito Italiano just off Piazza Cavour is good for exchange.

The post office is at Via Gallio 6 and is open Monday to Friday from 8.15 am to 5.30 pm and Saturday from 8.15 am to 1 pm. The postcode for central Como is 22100.

The Telecom office is on a small square off Via Albertolli, south of Piazza Cavour. It is open weekdays 9 am to 12.30 pm and 2.30 to 6 pm. Como's telephone code is ☎ 031.

For police emergency, call ☎ 113. The questura (☎ 31 71) is at Viale Roosevelt 7. The Ospedale Sant'Anna (☎ 58 51 11) is at Via Napoleona 60. In an emergency call ☎ 118.

Duomo From Piazza Cavour, walk along the arcaded Via Plinio to Piazza del Duomo and the marble-faced cathedral, built and repeatedly altered from the 14th to the 18th centuries. The duomo combines elements of Romanesque, Gothic, Renaissance and Baroque design and is crowned with a high octagonal dome. Next to it is the polychromatic **town hall**, altered in 1435 to make way for the cathedral.

Churches & Museums The **Basilica di San Fedele**, named after the saint who brought Christianity to the Como region, first went up in the 6th century. It has since undergone various changes, including those in the bell tower and façade this century – although the original lines of the basilica have been largely respected. It's on Via Vittorio Emanuele II, as are the Palazzo Giovio and Palazzo Olginati – the former housing the **Museo Archeologico**, with important prehistoric and Roman remains, and the latter the **Museo Storico** (aka Museo Garibaldi), with mementos from Garibaldi's period – he actually stayed in this building for a time. Both are open daily from 9.30 am to 12.30 pm and 2 to 5 pm, except Monday and Sunday afternoons. The **Pinacoteca Civica**, a small art gallery, is at Via Diaz 86.

Brunate East of Piazza Cavour along the waterfront is the funicular railway station for Brunate. Tickets are L3900 one way or L7000 return. Check the timetable for the last car before you leave. Brunate, at 720m, overlooks Como and the lake and offers a pleasant walk and excellent views from the small town of San Maurizio.

Hiking Around Como The tourist office has produced a hiking map of the area with a 50km walk from Cernobbio, near Como, to Sorico, near the lake's northern edge. It can be broken into four stages. The map shows the location of rifugi and some camping grounds. Maps for other walks are available, but mostly in Italian. Try also the CAI (☎ 26 41 77), Via Volta 56.

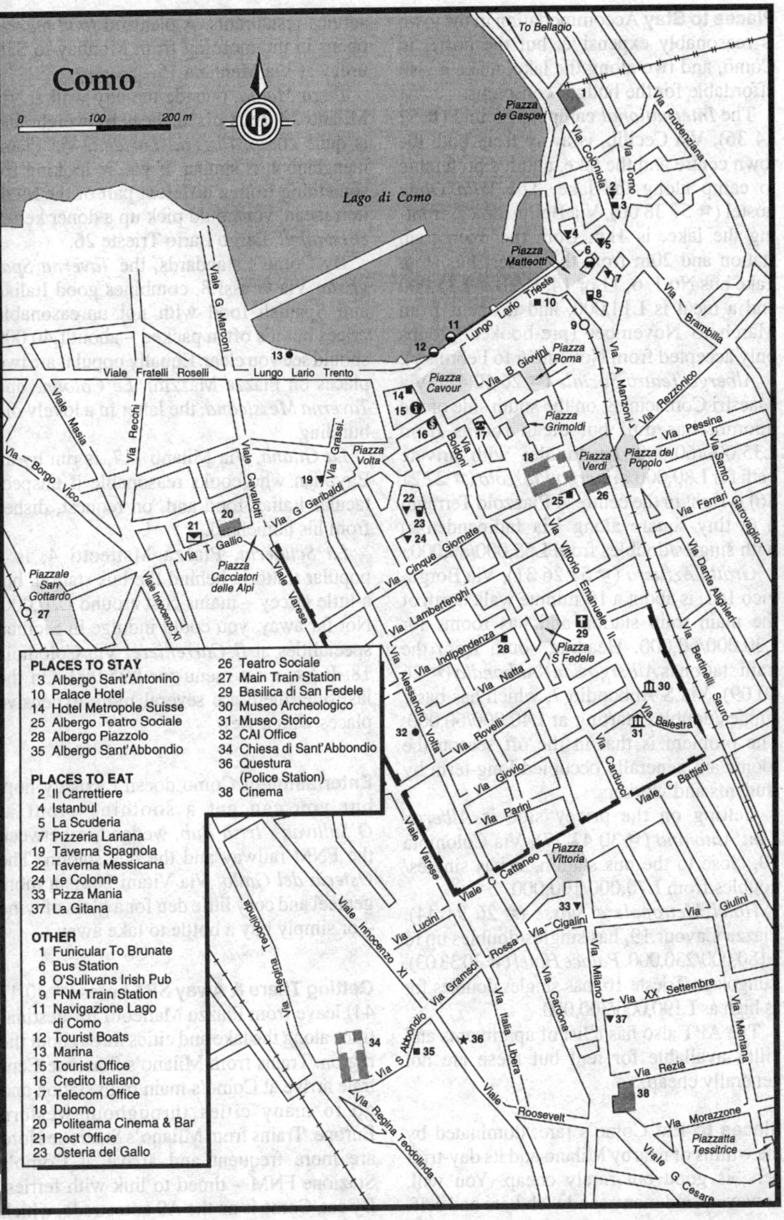
Como
0
100
200 m
Lago di Como
To Bellagio
Piazza de Gasperi
Piazza Matteotti
Piazza Roma
Piazza Cavour
Piazza Grimoldi
Piazza Volta
Piazza Verdi
Piazza del Popolo
Piazza Cacciatori delle Alpi
Piazzale San Gottardo
Piazza S Fedele
Piazza Vittoria
Piazzatta Tessitrice
Via Prudenziana
Via Coloniola
Via Torno
Via Brambilla
Lungo Lario Trieste
Lungo Lario Trento
Viale G Marconi
Viale Fratelli Roselli
Via A Manzoni
Via Rezzonico
Via Pessina
Via B Giovini
Via Boldoni
Via Grassi
Via Recchi
Viale Masia
Via Borgo Vico
Viale Cavallotti
Via G Garibaldi
Via T Gallio
Viale Innocenzo XI
Viale Varese
Via Cinque Giornate
Via Lambertenghi
Via Indipendenza
Via Alessandro Volta
Via Natta
Via Rovelli
Via Giovio
Via Parini
Via Vittorio Emanuele II
Via Carducci
Viale C Battisti
Via Balestra
Via Bertinelli
Via Sauro
Via Dante Alighieri
Via Garovaglio
Via Santo
Via Ferrari
Viale C Cattaneo
Via Lucini
Via Rossa
Via Cigalini
Via Giulini
Via Gramsci
Via Milano
Via Cardona
Via Italia Libera
Via XX Settembre
Via Mentana
Via Rezia
Via S Abbondio
Via Regina
Via Regina Teodolinda
Viale Roosevelt
Via Morazzone
Viale G Cesare
PLACES TO STAY
3 Albergo Sant'Antonino
10 Palace Hotel
14 Hotel Metropole Suisse
25 Albergo Teatro Sociale
28 Albergo Piazzolo
35 Albergo Sant'Abbondio
PLACES TO EAT
2 Il Carrettiere
4 Istanbul
5 La Scuderia
7 Pizzeria Lariana
19 Taverna Spagnola
22 Taverna Messicana
24 Le Colonne
33 Pizza Mania
37 La Gitana
OTHER
1 Funicular To Brunate
6 Bus Station
8 O'Sullivans Irish Pub
9 FNM Train Station
11 Navigazione Lago di Como
12 Tourist Boats
13 Marina
15 Tourist Office
16 Credito Italiano
17 Telecom Office
18 Duomo
20 Politeama Cinema & Bar
21 Post Office
23 Osteria del Gallo
26 Teatro Sociale
27 Main Train Station
29 Basilica di San Fedele
30 Museo Archeologico
31 Museo Storico
32 CAI Office
34 Chiesa di Sant'Abbondio
36 Questura (Police Station)
38 Cinema

THE LAKES

Places to Stay Accommodation in the town is reasonably expensive, but the hostel in Como, and two along the lake, make a visit affordable for the budget-conscious.

The *International* camping ground (☎ 52 14 36), Via Cecilio, is away from both the town centre and the lake, and it's preferable to camp along the lake. The *Villa Olmo* hostel (☎ 57 38 00), Via Bellinzona 2, fronting the lake, is 1km from the main train station and 20m from the closest bus stop. Take bus No 1, 6, 11 or 14. B&B is L15,000 and a meal is L14,000, and it opens from March to November (pre-booked groups only accepted from November to February).

Albergo Teatro Sociale (☎ 26 40 42), Via Maestri Comacini 8, on the south side of the duomo, has dull but clean rooms from L35,000/60,000, or doubles with private bath for L80,000. *Albergo Piazzolo* (☎ 27 21 86) is right in the centre at Piazzolo Terragni 6 (a tiny square along Via Indipendenza) with singles/doubles from L55,000/80,000.

Grotta Azzurra (☎ 57 26 31), Via Borgovico 161, is about a 10-minute walk north of the main train station and has rooms for L30,000/60,000. Heading south from the train station is *Albergo Sant'Abbondio* (☎ 26 40 09), Via S Abbondio 7, which has basic singles/doubles starting at L40,000/60,000. The problem is that in the off season the rooms are generally occupied long-term by students and workers.

Getting on the pricey side is *Albergo Sant'Antonino* (☎ 30 42 77), Via Coloniola 10, close to the bus station. It has singles/doubles from L70,000/100,000.

Hotel Metropole e Suisse (☎ 26 94 44), Piazza Cavour 19, has singles/doubles up to L180,000/230,000. *Palace Hotel* (☎ 30 33 03), Lungolago Trieste 16, has singles/doubles for as high as L190,000/300,000.

The APT also has a list of apartments and villas available for rent but these are not generally cheap.

Places to Eat Como's fare, dominated by the whims of nearby Milano and its day-trippers, is good but rarely cheap. You will, however, find many sandwich bars and self-service restaurants. A plentiful *food market* opens in the morning from Monday to Saturday at Via Mentana 15.

Pizza Mania, outside the city wall at Via Milano 20, sells pizza slices by weight and is quite cheap. *Pizzeria Lariana*, Via Fiammenghino 4, is similar. If you're looking for something from a different part of the Mediterranean, you could pick up a doner kebab at *Istanbul*, Largo Lario Trieste 26.

By Como's standards, the *Taverna Spagnola*, Via Grassi 8, combines good Italian and Spanish food with not unreasonable prices but it's often packed – about L40,000 should see you clear. Equally popular are two places on Piazza Mazzini, *Le Colonne* and *Taverna Messicana*, the latter in a lovely old building.

La Gitana, Via Milano 117, is run by an Egyptian who cooks reasonable if unspectacular Italian food and, on request, dishes from his homeland.

La Scuderia, Piazza Matteotti 4, is a popular trattoria behind the bus station, but a little pricey – mains cost around L20,000. Not far away, you could indulge in Sicilian specialities at *Il Carrettiere*, Via Coloniola 18. It has a set menu for L25,000. On the lakeside, there are several more expensive places with a view.

Entertainment Como doesn't exactly hop, but you can get a soothing stout at *O'Sullivan's Irish Pub*, wedged in between the FNM railway and the bus station. The *Osteria del Gallo*, Via Vitani 20, is a more genteel and cosy little den for a glass of wine – or simply buy a bottle to take away.

Getting There & Away SPT buses (☎ 30 47 44) leave from Piazza Matteotti for destinations along the lake and cities throughout the region. Trains from Milano's Stazione Centrale arrive at Como's main train station and go to many cities throughout western Europe. Trains from Milano's Stazione Nord are more frequent and arrive at Como's Stazione FNM – timed to link with ferries. By car, Como is on the A9 autostrada, which connects with Milano's ring road, as does the SS35, the best bet for hitchhikers.

Ferries and hydrofoils criss-cross the lake. Navigazione Lago di Como (☎ 57 92 11), Piazza Cavour, operates boats all year. A day ticket allowing unlimited trips is L26,000. A day cruise around the lake with lunch on the boat is L47,000.

Around Como

Looking like an inverted 'Y', Lago di Como is 51km long and lies at the foot of the Rhetian Alps. Its myriad towns can easily be explored by boat, or bus from Como, and are worth at least a two day visit. Highlights include the **Villa d'Este** at Cernobbio, a monumental 16th-century villa that is now a hotel; the **Isola Comacina**, the lake's sole island, where Lombard kings took refuge from invaders; and the **Villa Carlotta** near Tremezzo, with its magnificent gardens. The towns farther north are lesser tourist attractions.

There are two youth hostels on Lago di Como, numerous camping grounds and many reasonably priced hotels. The *Ostello La Primula* (☎ 0344-3 23 56), Via IV Novembre 86, at Menaggio, about halfway up the lake on the western side, is close to the bus stop on the route from Como. It charges L15,000 a night. Farther north is the *Ostello Domaso* (☎ 0344-9 60 94), Via Case Sparse 12, at Domaso, which is the same price and on the same bus route. Both are open from March to October. Check with the APT in Como for lists of the 50 or so camping grounds, hotels and agriturismo facilities along the lake.

Bellagio Considered the 'pearl' of the lake, Bellagio is indeed a pretty little town sitting more or less on the point where the western and eastern arms of the lake split and head south. The 30km drive from Como is itself rewarding, but the trip down the east side towards Lecco is less so. The only drawback is the inevitable feeling you're sharing the pleasure with just a few too many other outsiders – would the real residents of Bellagio please stand up?

Albergo Roma (☎ 95 04 24) is neatly situated in the town and has singles/doubles starting at L40,000/65,000 – it's about as cheap as Bellagio gets, and opens from March to November only.

The lake's only car ferries connect the east and west shores in this area, stopping at Bellagio.

LAGO DI GARDA

The largest and most popular of the Italian lakes, Garda lies between the Alps and the Po valley, so enjoys a temperate climate. At its northern reaches, Garda is hemmed in by craggy mountains and resembles a fjord. As it broadens towards the south, the lake takes on the appearance of an inland sea.

There are many large villages around the lake, but most are heavily developed and unpleasant. The picturesque but Disneyland-like resort of Sirmione is worth visiting, as is Gardone Riviera on the lake's western edge. At the northern end, Riva del Garda is a good base for walking in the nearby Alps. If you are staying, a good brochure for information is *Garda Doc*.

Getting There & Away

Buses leave Verona, Brescia, Mantova and Milano for the main towns on the lake. Desenzano del Garda is on the main Milano-Venezia train line. By car, the A4 autostrada and the SS11, which connect Milano with Venezia, pass the southern edge of the lake, and the A22 runs parallel with the lake's eastern shore, connecting Verona with Trento. Riva can be reached by exiting the A22 at Rovereto Sud.

Getting Around

Navigazione sul Lago di Garda (☎ 030-914 13 21), Piazza Matteotti 2, in Desenzano, operates ferries between most towns on the lake. It has offices or booths in all towns it serves and operates all year. Ask at tourist offices for timetables. Fares range from L2000 to L20,200, depending on the length of the trip and whether you get the *battello* (ferry) or *aliscafo* (hydrofoil).

Sirmione

Catullus, the Roman poet, celebrated Sirmione – a narrow peninsula jutting out from the southern shore of the lake – in his writings, and his name is still invoked in connection with the place. It is a popular bathing spot and is often jammed tight with tourists. In spite of this, Sirmione retains a comparatively relaxed atmosphere. The area of interest (watch for the castle) is an islet attached by a bridge to the rest of the peninsula.

Information The main tourist office (☎ 91 62 45), Viale Marconi 2, has information on hotels and activities such as walking, skiing, windsurfing and horse riding. There is a Telecom office on Piazza Carducci. The telephone code is ☎ 030.

Things to See & Do The Roman villa and baths known as the **Grotte di Catullo** probably had nothing to do with the Roman poet, although Catullus and his family did have a villa in the area. The extensive ruins occupy a prime position on the northern, quieter end of the Sirmione island. The site is open Tuesday to Sunday from 9 am to 6.45 pm (4.30 pm in winter). Admission is L8000.

The **Castello Scaligero**, also known as the Rocca Scaligera, was built by Verona's ruling family, the Scaligeri, as a stronghold on the lake in 1250. There's not a lot inside, but the views from the tower are good. It's open daily from 9 am to 6.30 pm in summer; 9 am to 1 pm from Tuesday to Sunday in winter. Admission is L8000.

You can go for a watery spin around the island. Plenty of boats leave from near the castle – at about L20,000 per person. All sorts of vessels will also make any manner of trip around the lake – at a price.

It is possible to swim at the small beaches on the town's eastern side and an array of water activities can be arranged in the town. Windsurfers could try calling Claudio Lana on ☎ 0338-624 36 50. He is an instructor and can provide details of windsurf schools and hire. Or call Martini (☎ 91 62 08). The Yachting Club Sirmione (☎ 990 40 78) can assist with boating. Several places hire out pedalos and kayaks.

Places to Stay & Eat It is hard to believe there are close to 100 hotels crammed in here. Book ahead or stay away in summer and at long weekends. There are four camping grounds near the town and the APT can advise on others around the lake. *Campeggio Sirmione* (☎ 91 90 45), on the foreshore at Via Sirmioncino 9, is one of the largest.

Hotels include the *Albergo Progresso* (☎ 91 61 08), Via Vittorio Emanuele 18, which is as cheap as you'll find in the heart of old Sirmione. You'll pay L40,000/65,000 for singles/doubles. The *Albergo degli Oleandri* (☎ 990 57 80), on Via Dante 31, near the castle, is in a shady, pleasant location and has rooms for L65,000/85,000 including breakfast. The *Albergo Sirmione* (☎ 91 63 31; fax 91 65 58), Piazza Castello 19, has rooms for up to L160,000/260,000. Bear in mind that these and most other hotels shut from the end of October to March.

The *Osteria al Pescatore*, Via Piana 18, is one of the better, reasonably priced restaurants and there is loads of takeaway food to be found, especially around Piazza Carducci. This is also where the bulk of the cafés and gelati joints are.

Around Sirmione

Sirmione is about 5km east of Desenzano del Garda, the lake's largest town and a main transport hub (but not really worth a visit). Farther north from Desenzano del Garda is Salò, which gave its name to Mussolini's puppet republic in 1943, after the dictator was rescued from the south by the Nazis. The CAI has an office in Salò, at Via San Bernardino 26, with information on walks and Alpine rifugi in the surrounding mountains.

Heading east, kids will be excited to hear of **Gardaland** (☎ 045-644 97 77), Italy's equivalent of Disneyland. Adults and children over 10 years pay L28,000 to enter in the high season and get sick on the various rides. Only toddlers get in for free. The nearest train station is at Peschiera del Garda.

The remaining 2km are covered in a free bus. If that's not enough, you could try the **Parco Natura Viva**, a zoo and educational park a little farther north between Bussolengo and Pastrengo, but this time there's no free bus. Driving is really the only answer.

Gardone Riviera

On the western edge of the lake at the head of a small inlet, Gardone Riviera is a popular resort. It retains a hint of its past as the lake's most elegant holiday spot but has succumbed to development and the problems of being a group tourist destination.

The APT office (☎ 2 03 47) is at Corso Repubblica 35. The town's telephone code is ☎ 0365.

Things to See A visit to the town is a must to see **Il Vittoriale**, the exotic villa of Italy's controversial 20th-century poet and screeching nationalist, Gabriele d'Annunzio. He moved in here in 1922 because, he claimed, he wanted to escape the world, which made him ill. Protagonist of clamorous but ineffectual wartime stunts in WWI – he flew a lone raid to drop leaflets over Vienna – he died in 1938 and is buried near the villa among his wartime companions.

One of d'Annunzio's most triumphant and more bizarre feats was to capture, with a band of his soldiers, a battleship from the fledgling Yugoslavia shortly after WWI, when Italy's territorial claims had been partly frustrated in postwar peace talks. The ship's bow protrudes from the villa's gardens and adds to the kitsch flavour of the residence. **D'Annunzio's villa** is at the north-eastern edge of town and is open daily from 8 am to 8.30 pm in summer (April to September) and from 9 am to 12.30 pm and 2 to 6 pm in winter. Admission is L16,000 to both the grounds and house. The town also features **botanical gardens**, on the road to d'Annunzio's villa.

Some pleasant and easy walks can be undertaken from here heading inland to the rifugi at **Monte Spino** or **Monte Pizzicolo**. Ask at the APT for more details.

Places to Stay & Eat The *Albergo Nord* (☎ 2 07 07), Via Zanardelli 18, has singles/doubles from L35,000/60,000 and is in a good location. *Villa Fiordaliso* (☎ 2 01 58), Via Zanardelli 132, was a favourite of Mussolini's mistress, Clara Petacci. It is also one of the lake's most beautiful hotels and best restaurants. Rooms cost from L250,000 and food is expensive. For more modest food, try *Pizzeria Sans Souci*, near the tourist office, which has pizzas from L8000.

Gargnano & Villa

Gargnano is really just another lake resort town. Mussolini was based here for the short life of his Repubblica Sociale Italiana (or Repubblica di Salò). He was guarded by German SS units and the republic was a fiction, as northern Italy was occupied territory after Italy signed an armistice with the Allies in September 1943. The republic lasted until 25 April 1945, when the last German troops were finally cleared from Italy. Mussolini and Petacci were lynched three days later near Lago di Como.

Just a couple of km south of Gargnano is Villa. It's an unremarkable place, but it may interest some to know that DH Lawrence spent a good deal of time here writing *Twilight in Italy*, commonly classed as travel writing but just as much a circuit through David Herbert's pelvic theories.

Riva del Garda

The most popular of the resort towns around Lago di Garda, Riva is at its northern edge. It has a pleasant old centre of cobbled laneways and squares and a nice position on the lake. Links with the Germanic world are evident not only in the bus and car loads of Germans and Austrians, but also in its history. Riva was part of Habsburg Austria until it was incorporated into Italy after WWI, and was annexed briefly by Nazi Germany in the closing years of WWII. While the likes of DH Lawrence were hanging about on the western shore, central European luminaries such as Nietzsche, Kafka and Thomas Mann were wont to put their feet up in Riva.

Information The APT office (☎ 55 44 44) is in the Giardino di Porta Orientale, opposite the 'castle'. It can advise on accommodation and sporting activities. The telephone code is ☎ 0464.

Things to See Three km north of town is the **Cascata Varone**, a 100m waterfall fed by the Lago di Tenno. Admission to the waterfall area is L5000. Opening hours vary – check with the APT.

Activities Riva is one of Italy's most popular spots for windsurfing and has four schools that hire out equipment. Bouwmeester Windsurfing Centre (☎ 55 17 30), care of the Hotel Pier, or Nautic Club Riva (☎ 55 24 53), Viale Rovereto 132 also run sailing classes.

The APT has a list of people who can help with information on free-climbing in the area. For mountain bike hire, try Centro Cicli Pederzolli (☎ 55 18 30), Viale Canella, or Girelli (☎ 55 66 02), Viale Damiano Chiesa 15/17. You're looking at L25,000 for a day.

Speedy Gonzales (☎ 55 20 89) runs boat excursions on the lake at L15,000 per person per hour. Boats leave from near the APT. Moby Dick runs competition excursions for the same price from the same spot.

The town is a great starting point for walks around Monte Rocchetta, which dominates the northern end of Lago di Garda.

Places to Stay & Eat Several camping grounds dot the waterfront, including *Campeggio Bavaria* (☎ 55 25 24), Viale Rovereto 100. There is an HI youth hostel, the *Benacus* (☎ 55 49 11), at Piazza Cavour 10, in the centre of town. It costs L16,000 for B&B and is open 1 March to 31 October.

Hotels are plentiful, but during summer it is advisable to book. *La Montanara* (☎ 55 48 57), Via Montanara 18, is one of the cheapest places and located in a narrow laneway in the centre. Singles/doubles are L26,000/52,000 and doubles with bathroom L56,000. The hotel also offers half and full board and has a pleasant trattoria. The nearby *Albergo Vittoria* (☎ 55 43 98), Via Dante 39, has rooms with bath costing L42,000/73,000, although a few cheaper ones are available if you push. *Hotel Portici* (☎ 55 54 00), Piazza III Novembre 19, offers rooms for L76,000/120,000 in the high season, although you may be obliged to take full board in the high season. *Hotel Sole* (☎ 55 26 86; fax 55 28 11), at No 35 overlooking the lake, was Nietzsche's favourite and has rooms ranging from L170,000 to L240,000.

The town has many takeaway places and good delicatessens for picnic supplies. *Leon d'Oro*, Via Fiume 26, has various Trentino dishes (including strangolapreti – 'strangle the priest') and prices are average. At *Country Stube*, Piazza III Novembre 11, you can eat hamburgers washed down with a wide range of bottled beers. For an exceptional wood oven pizza, head straight for *Bella Napoli*, Via dei Fabbri 34. There are plenty of lakeside cafés and pastry shops.

Getting There & Away The bus station is in Viale Trento, in the newer part of town, a 10-minute walk from the lake. Regular APT buses connect Riva with Verona, leaving Verona from the Porta Nuova bus station. Atesina buses connect Riva with Trento. Other buses serve stops around the lake.

LAGO D'ISEO & VALLE CAMONICA

Probably the least known of the large Italian lakes, Iseo is possibly the least attractive. Although shut in by mountains, it is scarred in the north-east (around Lovere and Castro) by industry and a string of tunnels.

At the southern end of the Valle Camonica, the lake is fed by the Oglio river and marks the boundary between the provinces of Bergamo and Brescia – getting information about one side from the other tourist office is not easy! Farther south stretches the Franciacorta, a patch of rolling countryside that produces a good wine. The mountainous hinterland offers decent walking possibilities. Check with the APT in the lake towns, or at Bergamo or Brescia.

Getting There & Around

Buses connect the lake with Brescia and Bergamo. There are also trains from Brescia to Iseo and several other towns on the lake. Navigazione sul Lago d'Iseo (☎ 035-97 14 83), based in Costa Volpino, operates ferries between (south to north) Sarnico, Iseo, Monte Isola, Lovere and Pisogne. The timetable is substantially reduced in winter and fares range from L2000 to L9300 per trip. Buses also connect towns around the lake.

Iseo

A pleasant, if somewhat dull, spot fronting the southern end of the lake, Iseo boasts the first monument erected to Garibaldi. The APT del Lago d'Iseo (☎ 98 02 09) is at Lungolago Marconi 2. The telephone code for the east (Brescia) side of the lake, starting with Iseo, is ☎ 030, and ☎ 035 on the other side (there are a couple of exceptions).

The area is well supplied with accommodation, particularly camping grounds. Iseo has 18 sites, including the *Belvedere* (☎ 98 90 48), Via Risorgimento. About the cheapest hotel in the centre of town is *Albergo Milano* (☎ 98 04 49), Lungolago Marconi 4, with singles/doubles at L70,000/90,000.

Monte Isola

The best thing to do here is get a boat to Europe's biggest lake island, Monte Isola. Few vehicles are allowed on the streets, so the fishing village is quite peaceful. It has six hotels and a camping ground, *Campeggio Monte Isola* (☎ 982 52 21), Via Goce.

Eastern Shore

If Iseo seems a little empty and you want to stay on the mainland, there are a few smaller towns farther north. **Sulzano** is small and quiet, and on the ferry run to Monte Isola. Farther up the road is **Marone**, from where a side road winds up into the mountains to **Zone**. Walking is the attraction and there are a few rifugi about – inquire at the APT.

Western Shore

The northern end of the lake you can forget, although some of the drives through the blasted rock face at the water's edge is enjoyable. **Riva di Solto** is a fairly unspoiled village on the western shore, although **Sarnico**, towards the southern end of the lake, is better, with hotels and restaurants.

Valle Camonica

The Valle Camonica weaves its way from the north of Lago d'Iseo to the vast **Parco dell'Adamello** and farther north, to the **Parco Nazionale dello Stelvio**. The area borders on Trentino-Alto Adige and takes in the better parts of the Lombard Alps. The two national parks offer many walks of varying difficulty and are dotted with Alpine rifugi. See the Trentino-Alto Adige chapter.

About halfway between Darfo Boario Terme and Edolo, lovers of rock-carving will have a field day. The **Parco Nazionale delle Incisioni Rupestri** at Capo di Monte is a 30 hectare open-air museum containing a representative spread of engravings going as far back as the Bronze Age. The valley is littered with such carvings. The park is open daily, except Monday, from 9 am to sunset; admission costs L6000.

The area from Edolo north offers some reasonable **skiing** in winter, particularly near Ponte di Legno, at the northern end of the valley, and the nearby Passo del Tonale.

The area is part of the province of Brescia, and Brescia's APT is a good place to obtain walking, camping and rifugi information. In the valley there are tourist offices at Darfo Boario Terme (☎ 0364-53 16 09), Edolo (☎ 0364-7 10 65) and Ponte di Legno (☎ 0364-9 11 22).

THE LAKES

Trentino-Alto Adige

This autonomous Alpine region, incorporating much of the spectacular limestone Dolomiti mountain range, is best thought of as two distinct areas. Its provinces, Trentino and Alto Adige, are culturally, linguistically and historically separate.

Alto Adige, or Südtirol (South Tyrol), in the north was part of the Tyrol area of Austria until ceded to Italy in 1918. The people, mostlyof Germanic descent, predictably favour the German language (68%) over Italian (28%), although Ladin (4%), an ancient Latin-based language is also spoken in some zones, mainly the Val Badia (Gadertal) and the Val Gardena (Grödnertal). See also the boxed aside in the Val Badia section.

Trentino, to the south of Alto Adige, was a reluctant part of the Austrian and Austro-Hungarian empires for about a century until returned to Italy after WWI. The population here is strongly Italian, although German is widely spoken (more to accommodate the realities of modern tourism than a sign of nostalgia for the days of Austrian rule!).

The marriage of Trentino to Alto Adige, Italian to Tyrolean, has at times created friction, and extreme right-wing political parties have always done well here. Alleanza Nazionale, the dignified descendant of the fascist MSI party, has strong support in the area, but in Alto Adige the Südtiroler Volkspartei (SVP) is the top party by far. One of its primary aims is the preservation and development of German and Ladin ethnic groups, but more extreme elements want to secede from Italy. Bombings of railways, power stations and military installations that shook the region in the 1950s, 60s and 80s were attributed to radical secessionists.

Only in 1992 was a long haggled-over deal covering the area's statutes and privileges formally agreed to by Italy and Austria, with the UN's blessing. By the mid-90s, however, the SVP was pushing to have Alto Adige made a separate region, in complete contravention of the 1992 package and much

HIGHLIGHTS

- Trekking in the Parco Naturale Fanes-Senes-Braies
- Skiing in the Brenta group, the Val di Fassa or just about anywhere in the Dolomiti!
- Strudel & German coffee in one of Bolzano's Tyrolean cafés
- Mixing with the beautiful (rich) people in Cortina d'Ampezzo
- Mountain-biking in the Alpi di Siusi

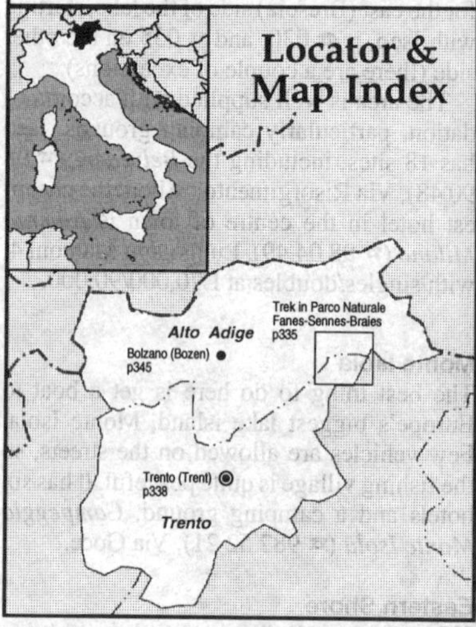

to the alarm of the people of Trentino, who fear being swallowed up by other regions (such as the Veneto) and losing the benefits gained through Trentino-Alto Adige's joint status as an autonomous region.

Politics aside, tourism throughout Trentino-Alto Adige is highly organised and travellers will have little difficulty finding good accommodation and extensive information on their choice of activity, including walking, trekking and skiing.

The types of accommodation here range

from hotels and pensioni (which tend to insist on half or full board), through *garnis* (basically B&Bs) to *rifugi* (mountain huts), which can be anything from expensive hotel/restaurants at the top of chairlift routes to simple *bivacchi* (spartan mountain huts). Prices vary greatly according to the season and most Alpine rifugi open only from late June to late September. If you plan on walking in the mountains during August, book a bed at the rifugi before you set out.

Information

The two provincial tourist offices are the APT del Trentino at Trento and the APT for Südtirol at Bolzano. Both are extremely helpful and have loads of information about the region. See town sections for details. The APT del Trentino has other offices in Roma (☎ 06-36 09 58 42), care of Touring Club Italiano, Via del Babuino 20, and in Milano (☎ 02-86 46 12 51), Piazza Diaz 5. There is also a 24-hour toll-free information service you can call from anywhere in Italy on ☎ 167-01 05 45.

Inquiries to the Internet can be posted to apt@lii.unitn.it, or check out Trentino's website: www.patio.cs.unitn.it/apt.

Getting There & Away

If you want to fly direct into the area, the two nearest airports are Verona and Innsbruck (Austria). The latter is actually closer to the pick of the mountains. If no financially acceptable options present themselves to these two airports, you might check out flights to Munich (Germany), so long as you don't mind then doing the train trip south to Bolzano (or taking an express bus to Merano).

Public transport in Trentino-Alto Adige is excellent. The two main companies are SAD in Alto Adige and Atesina in Trentino. The main towns and many ski resorts can be reached direct from major Italian cities – including Roma, Firenze, Bologna, Milano and Genova. Long-haul bus companies operating such routes include Lazzi, SITA and STAT. Information about the services is available from tourist offices and bus stations throughout Trentino-Alto Adige, or from the following offices: Lazzi Express (☎ 06-884 08 40), Via Tagliamento 27B, Roma; SITA (☎ 055-21 47 21), Autostazione, Via Santa Caterina da Siena 17, Firenze – go to Piazza Adua 1, Firenze, for information about the Lazzi/SITA joint service, called ALPI Bus (☎ 055-21 51 55); and STAT (☎ 010-58 71 81), Piazza della Vittoria 30, Genova.

TREKKING IN THE DOLOMITI

The Dolomiti, stretching across Trentino-Alto Adige into the Veneto, provide the most spectacular opportunities for walkers in the Italian Alps – from half-day strolls to

An Alpine Coral Reef

The Dolomiti account for a vast portion of the eastern Alps and are divided between Trentino, Alto Adige and the Veneto. (These regions/provinces are now all part of Italy, but during WWI were split by the border, and hence the front line of combat, between Italy and Austria-Hungary.) These spectacular, spiky peaks take their name from the French geologist De Dolomieu, who was the first to identify their composition of sedimentary limestone formed from calcium carbonate and magnesium. The Dolomiti are actually ancient coral reefs, a fact that makes them seem all the more extraordinary. During the Triassic period, the entire area was covered with tropical forest and a shallow, warm sea. After millions of years, the sea receded at the same time as the Alps were being formed, raising what had once been the seabed to heights of 2000m and 3000m. During the Ice Age, the coral reefs and rocks were eroded by glaciers which, together with normal atmospheric erosion, shaped the fantastic formations we see today in the Dolomiti. Among the pinnacles, towers and dramatic sheer drops of these mountains it is not unusual to find marine fossils. Coral reefs are always fascinating, but particularly so when reincarnated as Alpine peaks. ■

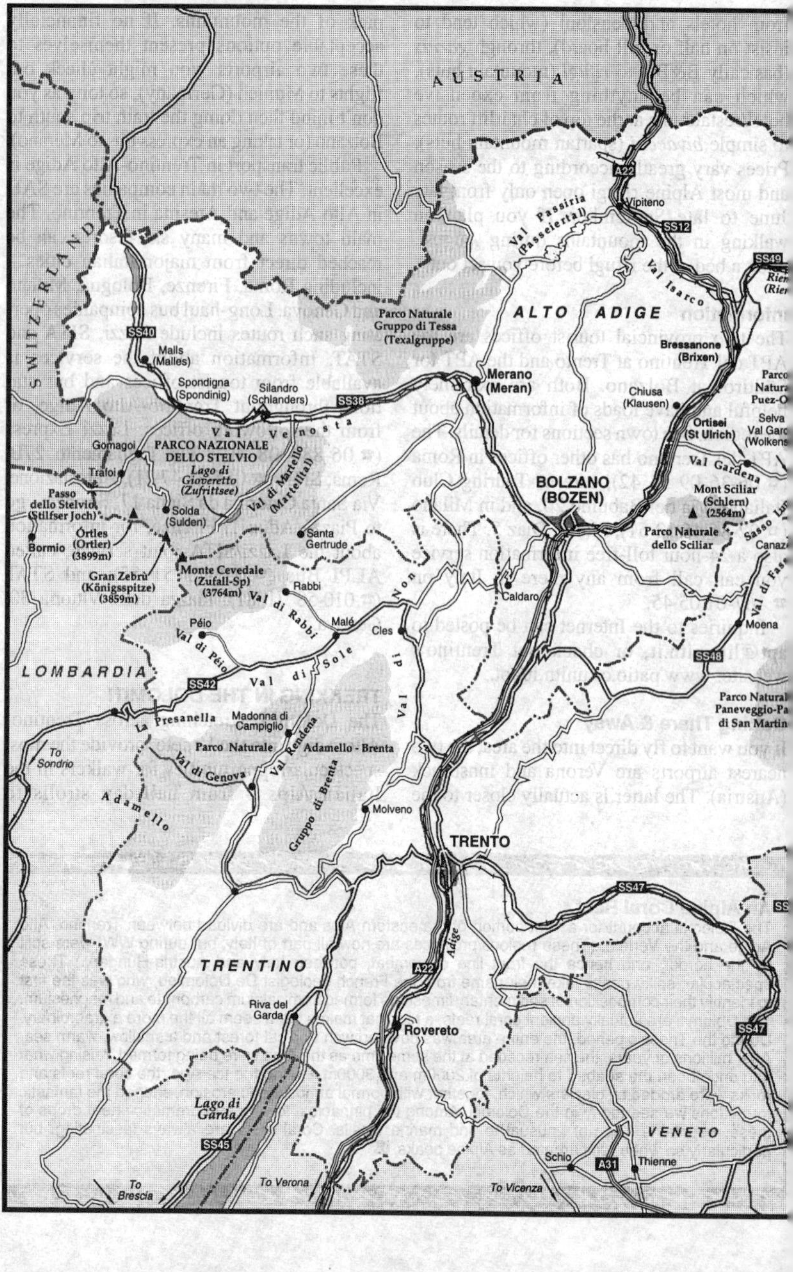
AUSTRIA
SWITZERLAND
ALTO ADIGE
LOMBARDIA
TRENTINO
VENETO
A22
SS12
SS49
SS40
SS38
SS42
SS48
SS47
SS45
A31
Vipiteno
Val Passiria (Passeiertal)
Val Isarco
Parco Naturale Gruppo di Tessa (Texalgruppe)
Malls (Malles)
Spondigna (Spondinig)
Silandro (Schlanders)
Merano (Meran)
Bressanone (Brixen)
Chiusa (Klausen)
Ortisei (St Ulrich)
Selva Val Gardena (Wolkenstein)
Val Gardena
Val Venosta
Gomagoi
PARCO NAZIONALE DELLO STELVIO
Lago di Gioveretto (Zufrittsee)
Val di Martello (Martelltal)
Trafoi
Passo dello Stelvio (Stilfser Joch)
Solda (Sulden)
Bormio
Ortles (Ortler) (3899m)
Gran Zebrù (Königsspitze) (3859m)
Monte Cevedale (Zufall-Sp) (3764m)
Santa Gertrude
Rabbi
Val di Rabbi
BOLZANO (BOZEN)
Mont Sciliar (Schlern) (2564m)
Parco Naturale dello Sciliar
Caldaro
Val di Non
Cles
Malé
Péio
Val di Péio
Val di Sole
Moena
Parco Naturale Paneveggio-Pale di San Martino
La Presanella
Madonna di Campiglio
Parco Naturale Adamello - Brenta
Val Rendena
Val di Genova
To Sondrio
Adamello
Gruppo di Brenta
Molveno
TRENTO
Adige
Riva del Garda
Rovereto
Lago di Garda
To Brescia
To Verona
To Vicenza
Schio
Thienne

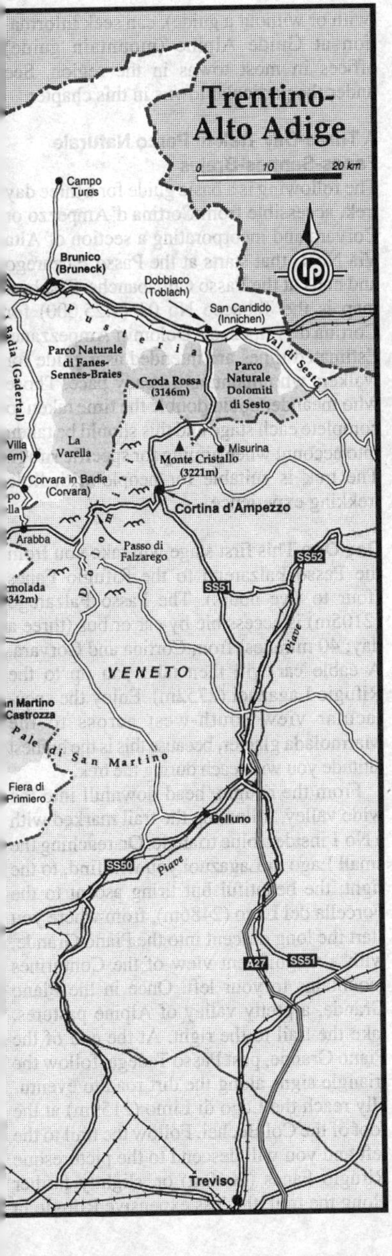

walks/treks that can include more demanding routes requiring mountaineering skills.

Trails are generally well marked with numbers on red-and-white painted bands (on trees and rocks along the trails), or inside different coloured triangles for the Alte Vie (High Routes). Numerous rifugi offer overnight lodgings and refreshments. Tourist offices usually have maps with roughly marked trails, but walkers planning anything more than the most basic itinerary should use detailed maps. Tourist office staff can advise on the trails' degree of difficulty.

Preparations

If you plan a serious trek, invest in a good map. The best are the Tabacco 1:25,000 maps, which provide extensive detail on trails, altitudes and gradients, as well as marking all rifugi and bivacchi. They are widely available throughout the Dolomiti. An alternative is the Kompass series.

The walking season is from end of June to the end of September and, depending on weather conditions, sometimes into October – although rifugi close around 20 September.

Always check weather predictions before setting out and ensure you are prepared for high-altitude conditions. In the Alps the weather can suddenly change from hot and sunny to cold and wet even in mid-August. Changes usually occur in the afternoon, so it is best to set out earlyy. Even on the shortest, most popular trails at the height of summer, make sure you have good walking shoes, a warm jacket and plenty of water.

The following is a list of items to carry on high-altitude treks of more than one day:

- comfortable, waterproof walking/trekking boots (already worn in)
- light, comfortable backpack
- anorak (or pile/wind jacket)
- change of T-shirt, underwear and socks (wool and cotton)
- shorts and long pants
- gloves, wool or pile hat, or headband, and scarf
- water bottle with at least 1L per person
- hooded raincoat or poncho
- torch (flashlight) and batteries, a pocket knife, a lightweight thermal blanket (for emergencies), tissues, sunglasses and, if necessary, a sheet or

sleeping bag. You could also bring along a pair of slippers or thongs to wear at rifugi. Carry some lightweight, energy-producing food.

Trekking Areas

The best areas to walk in the Dolomiti include:

- the Brenta group (Dolomiti di Brenta) accessible from either Molveno to the east or Madonna di Campiglio to the west
- the Val di Genova and the Adamello group also accessible from Madonna di Campiglio (the Brenta and Adamello groups form the Parco Naturale Adamello-Brenta)
- the Sella group accessible from either the Val Gardena to the west or the Val Badia to the east
- the Alpe di Siusi, the Sciliar and the Catinaccio group accessible from Siusi and Castelrotto
- the Pale di San Martino accessible from San Martino di Castrozza
- the area around Cortina which straddles Trentino and the Veneto and features the magnificent Parco Naturale di Fanes-Sennes-Braies, and, to the south, Monte Pelmo and Monte Civetta
- the Sesto Dolomiti north of Cortina towards Austria

There are four Alte Vie in the Dolomiti – treks that can take up to two weeks to complete. The routes link up pre-existing trails and, in some places, have created new trails to make difficult sections easier to traverse.

Each route links a chain of rifugi and you can opt to walk only certain sections:

- Alta Via No 1 crosses the Dolomiti from north to south, from the Lago di Braies to Belluno
- Alta Via No 2 extends from Bressanone to Feltre and is known as the High Route of Legends, because it passes through Odle, the mythical kingdom of ancient Ladino fairy tales
- Alta Via No 3 links Villabassa and Longarone
- Alta Via No 4 goes from San Candido to Pieve di Cadore

The Alte Vie are marked by numbers inside triangles – blue for No 1, red for No 2 and orange/brown for No 3 (No 4 is marked by the normal numbers on red-and-white bands). Booklets mapping out the routes in detail are available at the APT di Belluno, in the Veneto, or the APT in Trento.

People wanting to undertake guided treks, or to tackle the more difficult trails that combine mountaineering skills with walking (with or without a guide), can seek information at Guide Alpine (mountain guide) offices in most towns in the region. See under the particular towns in this chapter.

A Three-Day Trek in Parco Naturale Fanes-Sennes-Braies

The following is a basic guide for a three day trek, accessible from Cortina d'Ampezzo or Corvara and incorporating a section of Alta Via No 1, that starts at the Passo Falzarego and ends at the Passo Cimabanche. The best map is the Tabacco No 03 (1:25,000) for Cortina d'Ampezzo e Dolomiti Ampezzane. Estimated times are intended as a guide for walkers who maintain a steady pace. Those who meander could double the time taken to complete each stage and this should be taken into account when aiming for specific rifugi. The trek is suitable for people with little trekking experience.

Day One This first stage will take you from the Passo Falzarego to the Rifugio Fanes (four to five hours). The Passo Falzarego (2105m) is accessible by car or bus (three a day; 40 minutes) from Cortina and Corvara. A cable car will then take you up to the Rifugio Lagazuoi (2752m). Enjoy the spectacular view south-west across to the Marmolada glacier, because this is the highest altitude you will reach during the trek.

From the rifugio, head downhill into the wide valley, following the trail marked with a No 1 inside a blue triangle. On reaching the small Lago di Lagazuoi you will find, to the right, the beautiful but tiring ascent to the Forcella del Lago (2486m), from where you start the long descent into the Piano Grande, with a magnificent view of the Conturines mountains to your left. Once in the Piano Grande, a pretty valley of Alpine pastures, take the trail to the right. At the end of the Piano Grande, past Passo Tadega, follow the triangle signs along the dirt road to eventually reach the Lago di Limo (2159m) at the foot of the Col Bechei. Follow the trail to the left and you will descend to the picturesque Rifugio Fanes (2060m) or, slightly farther along the trail, the less expensive Rifugio la

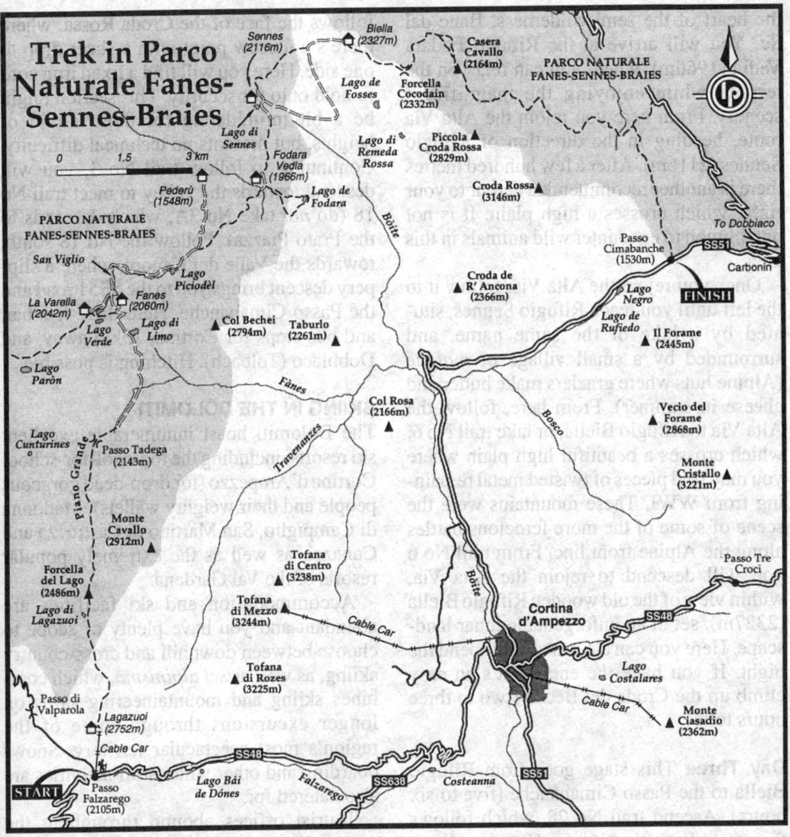

Varella (2042m). You can eat a meal and spend the night at either one. If you still have the energy, explore the beautiful Fanes high plain, taking trail No 12 to Lago Paron through enchanting scenery of limestone-white and a thousand shades of green, dotted with the colours of Alpine flowers.

Day Two This stage will take you from Rifugio Fanes to Rifugio Biella (five to six hours). Again following the blue triangular Alta Via signs, head down into the small valley of the San Vigilio river until you reach Lago Piciodèl on your right. Shortly after the lake, again on your right, is a trail that can be taken in preference to the Alta Via route, which, at this point, becomes a long descent to the Rifugio Pederù (1548m), from where you would have to ascend to 2000m following a road heavily used by 4WD vehicles ferrying tourist groups to the rifugio. For those who want to finish their trek now, a road descends from the rifugio into the Val Badia. The detour, on the other hand, is an atmospheric route which, although tiring at times, is not difficult. The unnumbered trail leads off to the right just after a river of gravel and follows the lake before ascending into the heart of the semi-wilderness, Banc dal Se. You will arrive at the Rifugio Fodara Vedla (1966m), where you can relax on the terrace while enjoying the magnificent scenery. From here you rejoin the Alta Via route, heading in the direction of Rifugio Sennes (2116m). After a few hundred metres there is another recommended detour to your right, which crosses a high plain. It is not uncommon to encounter wild animals in this area.

Once you rejoin the Alta Via, follow it to the left until you reach Rifugio Sennes, situated by a lake of the same name, and surrounded by a small village of *malghe* (Alpine huts where graziers make butter and cheese in summer). From here, follow the Alta Via to Rifugio Biella, or take trail No 6, which crosses a beautiful high plain where you may find pieces of twisted metal remaining from WWI. These mountains were the scene of some of the more ferocious battles along the Alpine front line. From trail No 6 you will descend to rejoin the Alta Via, within view of the old wooden Rifugio Biella (2327m), set in an unforgettable lunar landscape. Here you can eat a meal and spend the night. If you have the energy, it's an easy climb up the Croda del Becco (two to three hours total).

Day Three This stage goes from Rifugio Biella to the Passo Cimabanche (five to six hours). Ascend trail No 28, which follows the crest above the rifugio. Here you leave the Alta Via, which descends to the Lago di Braies, a short distance north. The route instead heads south-east towards the majestic Croda Rossa, a beautiful mountain inhabited by golden eagles. Trail No 28 follows the crest until it reaches the Forcella Cocodain, a mountain pass at 2332m. From here you descend to the left, in a northerly direction on the slope of the Prato Piazza. After a short distance you pick up trail No 3 and continue the descent until you reach an intersection with trail No 4. Continuing to follow No 3 to the right, you will reach the Casera Cavallo at 2164m. From here the trail starts to ascend, always towards the right. It follows the face of the Croda Rossa, where there's a narrow point with a sheer drop to one side. Here you will find a fixed iron cord to hold onto for security. This section might be a bit intimidating for those afraid of heights, but presents no technical difficulty. Continuing to follow trail No 3, you will descend towards the valley to meet trail No 18 (do *not* take No 3A, which descends to the Prato Piazza). Follow the No 18 south, towards the Valle dei Canopi, where a slippery descent brings you to the SS51 road and the Passo Cimabanche. Here there is a bar, and bus stops for Cortina, 15km away, and Dobbiaco (Tolbach). Hitching is possible.

SKIING IN THE DOLOMITI

The Dolomiti boast innumerable excellent ski resorts, including the too-cool-for-school Cortina d'Ampezzo (for drop-dead gorgeous people and their weighty wallets), Madonna di Campiglio, San Martino di Castrozza and Canazei, as well as the extremely popular resorts of the Val Gardena.

Accommodation and ski facilities are abundant and you have plenty of scope to choose between downhill and cross-country skiing, as well as *sci alpinismo*, which combines skiing and mountaineering skills on longer excursions through some of the region's most spectacular territory. Snowboarding and other white-stuff activities are also catered for.

Tourist offices abound throughout the region, but the best for general information, including on ski pass prices and Settimana Bianca (white week) deals are the APT del Trentino in Trento and the APT for Alto Adige/Südtirol Dolomiti in Bolzano. See the Trento and Bolzano sections.

The high season is generally from Christmas to early January and then from early February to April, when prices go up considerably – Settimana Bianca packages are a big money-saver. See the Skiing section in the Facts for the Visitor chapter.

If you want to go it alone, but plan to do a lot of skiing, invest in a ski pass. Most resort areas offer their own passes for unlimited use of lifts at several resorts for a nominated period (average price in the 1996/97 high season for a six day pass in the most popular resorts was around L250,000). However, the best value is the Superski Dolomiti pass which allows access to 464 lifts and more than 1180km of ski runs. In the 1996/97 high season a Superski pass for seven days cost L296,000 (or L258,000 from 1 January to 1 February and again from 16 March). Ring Dolomiti Superski (☎ 0471-79 53 98), Via Meisules-Str 183, Selva (Alto Adige), for information or pick up brochures at tourist offices throughout the region.

For the latest information on snow in the area, you can call ☎ 0461-91 66 66. In case of emergency in the mountains, call either ☎ 118 or ☎ 0461-23 31 66 for Soccorso Alpino.

The average cost of ski and boot hire is from L18,000 to L25,000 a day for downhill skis and up to L18,000 for cross-country skis and boots. In an expensive resort like Cortina, however, prices jump to as high as L35,000 a day to rent downhill skis and boots.

Ski schools operate at all resorts. A six-day course can cost up to L180,000, while private lessons will cost at least L40,000 an hour.

OTHER ACTIVITIES

Come summer, you can ditch walking for such pastimes as mountain biking, hang-gliding and rock-climbing. Tourist offices can help you find trails, bike rental outlets and hang-gliding schools.

Gruppi Guide Alpine (Mountain Guides Groups) can be found in most towns and villages – many are listed in this chapter. If no group is listed for a particular area, the local tourist office will assist.

These groups organise guided treks (ranging from family nature walks to challenging treks of up to seven days at high altitudes), rock-climbing courses or can even send the kids away for a few days of adventure. Many groups also offer guided mountain-bike and horse-riding tours.

Families are well catered for throughout the region, but particularly in Alto Adige. Many tourist offices organise special activities for kids in the summer and winter high seasons and some guides groups offer special courses and treks for youngsters. Most of the resort towns in Alto Adige have sports centres and playgrounds and many hotels are equipped for children (with cots, high chairs, special menus, playrooms etc).

Some information is given in this chapter, including some suggested family walks, but contact tourist offices for more details.

Trentino

TRENTO

This calm, well-organised provincial capital is a good place to start any exploration of the province. Its tourist offices have extensive information on the town and Trentino, and it is convenient for public transport throughout the province.

Known as Tridentum under the Romans, Trento (Trent) later passed from the Goths to the Lombards and was eventually annexed to the Holy Roman Empire, when it was known as Trento or Trient. For eight centuries from 1027 it was an episcopal principality, during a period marked by political and territorial conflict with the rulers of Tyrol. The Council of Trent (1545-63) considered the restructuring of the Catholic Church here and launched the Counter-Reformation.

Orientation

The train station and adjacent bus station are close to Trento's compact historical centre, as well as to most accommodation. Turn right as you leave the train or bus station and follow Via Andrea Pozzo, which becomes Via Cavour, to the central Piazza del Duomo.

Information

Tourist Offices Cross the park in front of the train station and turn right to reach the APT office (☎ 98 38 80) at Via Alfieri 4. It's open Monday to Friday from 9 am to midday and 3 to 6 pm and on Saturday to midday. From mid-June to mid-September, it opens Sunday from 10 am to midday. The office has loads of information in English about the town, including maps.

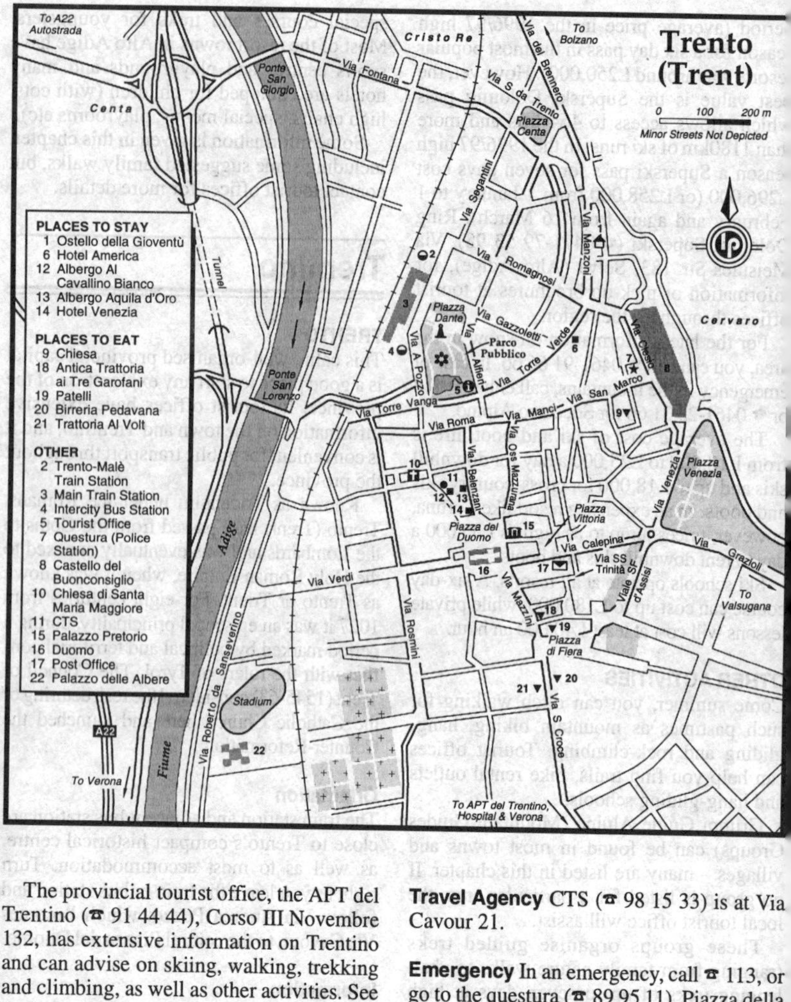

The provincial tourist office, the APT del Trentino (☎ 91 44 44), Corso III Novembre 132, has extensive information on Trentino and can advise on skiing, walking, trekking and climbing, as well as other activities. See the introduction to this chapter for its Roma and Milano offices.

Post & Communications Trento's main post office is in Via Calepina, at Piazza Vittoria, east of Piazza del Duomo. The postcode for central Trento is 38100.

Trento's telephone code is ☎ 0461.

Travel Agency CTS (☎ 98 15 33) is at Via Cavour 21.

Emergency In an emergency, call ☎ 113, or go to the questura (☎ 89 95 11), Piazza della Mostra, off Via San Marco near the Castello del Buonconsiglio.

Ospedale Santa Chiara (☎ 90 31 11) is in Largo Medaglie d'Oro, south-east of the centre, off Corso III Novembre. In a medical emergency, call ☎ 118.

Things to See & Do
The Piazza del Duomo, flanked by the

Romanesque **duomo** and the 13th-century **Palazzo Pretorio** and tower, is the natural place to start a tour of Trento. The Council of Trent was held in the duomo (as well as in the Chiesa di Santa Maria Maggiore). In the cathedral's transept are fragments of medieval frescoes, and two colonnaded staircases flank the nave. The foundations of an early Christian church were discovered in the late 1970s beneath the cathedral. The area is open Monday to Saturday from 10 am to midday and 2.30 to 6 pm. Admission is L2000, or you can pay L5000 for a combined ticket that includes the **Museo Diocesano** in the Palazzo Pretorio. This houses paintings depicting the Council of Trent, as well as a collection of Flemish tapestries. Opening hours are the same as for the duomo.

On the other side of the piazza are two Renaissance houses, known as the **Case Rella**, their façades decorated with frescoes. In the centre of the piazza is the 18th-century **Fontana di Nettuno**.

From the piazza, head north along Via Belenzani or Via Oss Mazzurana and turn right into Via Manci to reach the **Castello del Buonconsiglio**. The castle, home of the bishop-princes who once ruled Trento, incorporates the 13th-century Castello Vecchio and the Renaissance Magno Palazzo. Inside the castle is the **Museo Provinciale d'Arte**. The castle and museum are open Tuesday to Sunday from 9 am to midday and 2 to 5 pm. Admission is L7000.

Ask the APT about the castles in the valleys around Trento.

Places to Stay

The *Ostello della Gioventù* (☎ 23 45 67), Via Manzoni 17, is near the Castello del Buonconsiglio and charges L20,000 a night with breakfast.

Hotel Venezia (☎ 23 41 14), Piazza del Duomo 45, has singles/doubles with bathroom for L57,000/82,000. *Albergo Al Cavallino Bianco* (☎ 23 15 42), Via Cavour 29, has rooms for L42,000/68,000 without private bath and L63,000/92,000 with. *Albergo Aquila d'Oro* (☎ 98 62 82), Via Belenzani 76, has good rooms with bathroom for L120,000/170,000. *Hotel America* (☎ 98 30 10), Via Torre Verde 50, is an excellent option if you don't mind the expense. It has comfortable singles/doubles for L130,000/160,000.

The APT office has information on agriturismo accommodation in the area.

Places to Eat

You will have no problem finding a decent place to eat: the town teems with pizzerias, trattorias and restaurants. *Antica Trattoria ai Tre Garofani*, Via Mazzini 15, is a simple place which also serves pizzas. A good set menu costs L25,000.

Patelli, Via Dietro le Mura 5, off Via Mazzini, serves fine and unusual Italian dishes, and a full meal will cost around L35,000. For that German beer hall feeling, complete with stags' heads mounted on the wall and hearty food, you can't go past the *Birreria Pedavana*, Via Santa Croce 15. Across the road at No 16, *Trattoria Al Volt* has a delicious strudel della nonna for dessert.

Chiesa, Parco San Marco, on Via San Marco, is one of Trento's better restaurants and an excellent meal will come to around L80,000.

Getting There & Away

Bus From the bus station in Via Andrea Pozzo, intercity buses leave for destinations including Madonna di Campiglio, San Martino di Castrozza, Molveno, Canazei and Riva di Garda. Timetables are posted at the bus station. You can also pick up a full guide to Trentino's public transport from the APT del Trentino.

Train Regular trains connect Trento with Verona, Venezia, Bologna and Bolzano. The Trento-Malé train line (station next to the main station) connects the city along scenic routes with Cles in the Val di Non, and with Andalo and Molveno.

Car & Motorcycle Trento is easily accessible from Verona in the south and Bolzano in the north on the A22.

DOLOMITI DI BRENTA

This majestic group of jagged peaks is isolated from the main body of the Dolomiti and provides good walking opportunities. It is probably best suited to experienced trekkers wanting to test their mountaineering skills. North-west of Trento, and part of the Parco Naturale Adamello-Brenta, the group is easily accessible from either Molveno or Madonna di Campiglio. People should plan their routes, since many trails at higher altitudes incorporate *vie ferrate* (climbing trails with permanent steel cords) for which you will need harnesses and ropes. The group's most famous trail is the Via Bocchetta di Tuckett, opened up by 19th-century climber Francis Fox Tuckett, which runs from Molveno to Cima Brenta and includes sections of vie ferrate.

There are excellent skiing facilities at Madonna di Campiglio, and near Molveno is the well-equipped ski resort, Andalo.

Molveno

This village is in a very picturesque position by the Lago di Molveno, overshadowed by the towering Brenta group. It became famous in the 19th-century as a base for English and German mountaineers who came to open up trails into the group.

Information The APT office (☎ 58 69 24) is at Piazza Marconi 7 and is open Monday to Saturday from 9 am to 12.30 pm and 3.30 to 7 pm and Sunday from 9 am to midday. The staff can help you find accommodation (although in August you should book in advance) and can advise on walking trails. Also in the piazza is the office of the Gruppo Guide Alpine (☎ 58 60 86).

There is a tourist medical service *(ambulatorio medico)* provided by the *comune* (☎ 59 60 45) during the day in the Palazzo Comunale. If a medical emergency occurs at night, phone the Guardia Medica on ☎ 58 56 37.

The telephone code for the village is ☎ 0461.

Activities From the top of the village, a *cabinovia* (two seater cable car) will take you up to the Rifugio Pradel (1400m), from where you take trail No 340 to the Rifugio Croz dell'Altissimo (1430m), a pleasant and easy one-hour walk. Take trail No 340 to the Rifugio Selvata (1630m), then trail No 319 to the rifugi Tosa and Tommaso Pedrotti (2491m and about four hours walk).

From here most of the trails are difficult and you will need to be prepared for vie ferrate or for traversing glaciers. It is best to seek detailed information locally and take a carefully planned route using a good map.

For a less demanding walk, there is a path around the lake which starts at the camping ground. Making the entire circle of the lake will take about three and a half hours, but half the route is on the road, so it might be best to double back when the trail ends.

The Gruppo Guide Alpine organises guided treks, some incorporating vie ferrate as well as rock-climbing courses and, in winter, ski-mountaineering. Of interest to families might be the five-day mountaineering courses for kids aged from eight to 15 years. The course is offered weekly from June to October.

Places to Stay & Eat The tourist office will provide a list of the mountain rifugi and their telephone numbers to help you plan your trek. If you want to stay in Molveno, there is *Camping Spiaggia Lago di Molveno* (☎ 58 69 78), which charges up to L9500 per person and L13,000 for a space.

Prices do not vary greatly among the various hotels in town and many require that you take full board. Average prices for full board are from L60,000 per person in May and June, and around L100,000 per person in the high season (July/August). Try the *Zurigo* (☎ 58 69 47), Via Rio Massò 2, or *Europa* (☎ 58 89 37), Via Nazionale 11. The *Hotel Ariston* (☎ 58 69 07) is right in the centre of town on Piazza San Carlo. The *Grand Hotel Molveno* (☎ 58 69 34) is in a lovely position out of town by the lake. Full board is around L140,000 in the high season.

ietting There & Away Molveno is accesible by FTM or Atesina bus from Trento. ıtesina buses also connect Molveno with ⁄ilano in July and August, leaving from ʼiazza Castello in Milano on Saturday nd/or Sunday.

ladonna di Campiglio

)ne of the top ski resorts in the Alps, ⁄ladonna di Campiglio (often simply called ⁄ladonna) sprawls along the Valle Rendena, n the other side of the Brenta group. Ski lifts re plentiful, as are opportunities for crossountry and Alpine skiing.

nformation The APT office (☎ 44 20 00) is n the centre of the village, off Piazza Brenta ılta. It has loads of information about skiing nd walking in the area and can advise on ccommodation. It will mail out hotel lists nd other information on request. The office f the Gruppo Guide Alpine (☎ 44 26 34) is cross the street (open only after 4 pm) and brochures on its summer excursions are vailable at the tourist office.

A tourist medical service (☎ 44 07 55 or)368-96 30 07) operates during the winter and summer high seasons. This tends to change each season, so check with the tourist office.

The telephone code for the village is ☎ 0465.

Activities A network of chairlifts and cable cars will take you from the village to the numerous ski runs or, in summer, to the walking trails. A few km out of the village at Campo Carlo Magno is a cable car (in two stages) up to the Passo Grosté, from where trekkers can set off into the Brenta group. (The return trip on the cable car will cost L38,000.) The Via delle Bocchette (trail No 305) leaves from the Rifugio Grosté at the cable car station. This is the via ferrata for which the Brenta group is famous and only experienced mountaineers with the correct equipment should attempt it. Otherwise, take trail No 316 to Rifugio del Tuckett and Rifugio Sella. From there, take trail No 328 and then No 318 (sentiero Bogani) to the Rifugio dei Brentei Maria e Alberto (four to five hours from Grosté). All trails heading higher into the group from here cross glaciers and special equipment is needed.

Near Madonna is the Val Genova, often described as one of the most beautiful valleys in the Alps. A series of spectacular waterfalls along the way confirms its reputation as great walking country, and it's just as tempting for a picnic. Four rifugi strung out along the valley floor also make staying an option. In August the valley is closed to normal traffic and half-hourly buses ferry walkers and tourists to the Rifugio Adamello at the end of the road, from where you can take trail No 241 to the end of the valley (2000m) beneath a huge, receding glacier. The trail then climbs steeply to the Rifugio Caduti dell'Adamello (3020m) at the edge of the glacier.

Places to Stay & Eat Virtually none of Madonna's accommodation will suit the pockets of budget travellers. Most places require that you pay for half or full board and in the high season may be reluctant to accept bookings for less than seven days. *Garni Bucaneve* (☎ 44 12 71) is south of the village, near Piazza Palù, and has singles/doubles for L100,000/180,000. The *Bellavista* (☎ 44 10 34), a pleasant establishment uphill from the tourist office, near the Funivia Pradalago, charges up to L200,000 per person per day for full board. *La Fontanella* (☎ 44 33 99) is a few km out of town towards the Val Genova and has a magnificent view of the Brenta group. Prices range up to about L140,000 per person per day for full board.

In the Val Genova, the *Rifugio Fontanabona* (☎ 50 11 75) and the *Rifugio Stella Alpina* (☎ 50 12 16) are both in lovely settings. B&B costs around L50,000 and full board around L80,000 per person. Both have excellent restaurants and are open from 20 June to 20 September.

In Madonna, try *Ristorante/Pizzeria Le Roi*, Via Cima Tosa, near Piazza Brenta Alta, where a full meal will cost around L35,000. Around the corner is *Bar Dolomiti*, where hot sandwiches for L4500 should be sufficient for lunch. In the summer and winter high seasons you could try one of the malghe, such as *Malga Ritorto* (☎ 44 24 70), accessible by car in summer and by 'snow cat' service in winter.

Getting There & Away Madonna di Campiglio is accessible from Trento's bus station by regular Atesina bus. Autostradale and SIA have weekend services from Milano, while Lazzi and SITA between them run services from cities including Roma, Firenze and Bologna.

VAL DI NON

The Val di Non is a picturesque valley of apple orchards and castles accessible from Trento by Trento-Malé train or bus. The main town is Cles, dominated by the Castel Cles. The Pro Loco tourist office is in Corso Dante, just off the main road through town. If you want to stay here on your way north, try the *Antica Trattoria* (☎ 0463-42 16 31), Via Roma, which has singles/doubles for up to L60,000/84,000 with bathroom in the high season. The *Cristallo* (☎ 0463-42 13 55), Corso Dante, has rooms for L70,000/100,000 with bathroom.

SAN MARTINO DI CASTROZZA

Huddled at the foot of the imposing Pale di San Martino – mountains so stark and grey-white that they virtually glow in the dark – San Martino is another of Trentino's top ski resorts. The mountains are part of the Parco Naturale Paneveggio-Pale di San Martino, noted for its Alpine vegetation and wildlife, including the roe deer, chamois, marmot, wildfowl and birds of prey such as the golden eagle. It is a magnificent area for skiing or walking, and both San Martino di Castrozza and nearby Fiera di Primiero are well equipped for tourists.

Information

The APT office (☎ 76 88 67), Via Passo Rolle 167, has plenty of info and can advise on walking trails. You can telephone or write to request information about hotels or apartments. The office is open in the high season (summer and winter) from Monday to Saturday from 9 am to 12.30 pm and 3 to 7 pm and Sunday from 9.30 am to 12.30 pm. The Guide Alpine staff a desk in the same building daily from 5 to 7 pm.

San Martino's telephone code is ☎ 0439.

The nearest hospital is at Feltre, although a tourist medical service is available during summer and winter at San Martino (☎ 76 87 39) and Primiero. Full details are available at the tourist office.

Activities

The area has excellent ski runs and is part of the extensive Superski Dolomiti; during winter a special ski bus connects the valley with the various runs. The Pale di San Martino has well-marked trails and a reasonable map is available at the tourist office. A chairlift and cable car will take you to the Rifugio Rosetta (2600m), from where you can choose between several relatively easy walks or treks requiring mountaineering skills.

The more ambitious can check out activities with the Guide Alpine. It organises mountaineering ascents (Pala di San Martino, Cima della Madonno and Sass Maor), a 120km-long, high-altitude skiing excursion, as well as walks along vie ferrate and rock-climbing courses.

Places to Stay & Eat

Prices vary according to the season and many places will require that you pay for half or full board. They may also be reluctant to accept bookings for less than seven days. The tourist office will advise on apartments to rent and has a full list of rifugi in the area.

The *Suisse* (☎ 6 80 87), Via Dolomiti 1, has singles/doubles with shower for L40,000/80,000. *Biancaneve* (☎ 6 81 35) is nearby at No 14 and charges about L50,000 per person for B&B. The newly renovated *Hotel Plank* (☎ 76 89 76), Via Laghetto, charges L165,000 per person for full board. Good Settimana Bianca deals are available.

For meals, try *Da Anita*, a cosy place in the centre of San Martino at Via Dolomiti. Slightly out of town, along Via Fontanelle, are *Ristorante Le Fontanelle* and *Caffè Col*.

Local food is served at the various malghe around San Martino, which have developed into proper restaurants. Try the traditional-style *Malga Venegiota* (☎ 0462-57 60 44), accessible by a short trail from the Malga Juribello near Passo Rolle.

Getting There & Away
Atesina serves San Martino from Trento and Canazei (via Predazzo). Long-haul services connect it with Firenze, Roma (Lazzi and SITA) and Bologna (Dolomiti Express), to name a few.

CANAZEI

This popular ski resort in the Val di Fassa is surrounded by the striking peaks of the Gruppo di Sella to the north, the Catinaccio (Rosengarten) to the west and the Marmolada to the south-east. Canazei, a modern town, and a series of others down the valley to Vigo di Fassa, are geared to summer and winter tourism, although some locals still make a traditional living from dairy farming.

Skiing possibilities include a range of downhill and cross-country runs, as well as some challenging Alpine tours and the Sella Ronda network. The Marmolada glacier provides summer skiing. Walkers can approach the Catinaccio group from Vigo di Fassa, 11km south of Canazei. The best approach to the Sella group is from the Passo Pordoi, where a cable car will take you up to almost 3000m.

Information The Canazei AAST office (☎ 60 11 13), Via Roma 34, has information on skiing, walking and accommodation.

The telephone code for Canazei is ☎ 0462.

Places to Stay & Eat There are hundreds of hotels, garnis and rooms for rent in the Val di Fassa, and plenty enough in Canazei itself. It is advisable to book in August and during the peak ski season. The tourist office can provide details on rooms and apartments for rent.

The *Camping Marmolada* (☎ 60 16 60) is in the town centre and open in summer and winter.

Finding cheap places to stay is not always easy – and many places prefer you to stay for seven days. There is a cluster of cheaper possibilities on Via Dolomiti in Canazei. *Garni Christian* (☎ 60 13 88), at No 150, charges L50,000 a night per person for half board. *Hotel Giardino delle Rose* (☎ 60 22 21), at No 174, charges the same, as does *Garni Centrale* (☎ 60 23 40) at No 176. *Garni Ciamorc* (☎ 60 24 26), Via Pareda 41, is another decent option in the same price bracket.

There is a supermarket at Via Dolomiti 120, and numerous bars and *paninoteche*. The *Osteria La Montanara*, Via Dolomiti 147, serves good meals for around L30,000. Opposite, at No 168, is the *Pizzeria/Ristorante Italia*, where pizzas cost from L8000.

Getting There & Away Canazei can be reached by Atesina bus from Trento and by Servizi Autobus Dolomiti (SAD) bus from Bolzano and the Val Gardena. Buses do not cross the high mountain passes (such as Sella) in winter.

GRUPPO DI SELLA

The Sella group, in the western Dolomiti, straddles the border between Trentino and Alto Adige, close to Cortina d'Ampezzo in the Veneto and the spectacular Parco Naturale di Fanes-Sennes-Braies. To the west is the spiky Sasso Lungo, which extends to the Alpe di Siusi in Alto Adige. To the east is the Val Badia and its main town, Corvara, while to the south lies the Val di Fassa.

The zone is well equipped for skiers, and, by following a network of runs known as the Sella Ronda, you can make a day-long skiing tour of the valleys surrounding the Sella group. Full details are available at tourist offices.

The walking trails of the Sella and Sasso Lungo can be reached from Canazei or the Val Gardena resorts by bus to Passo Sella or Passo Pordoi. At Passo Sella (2240m), from which you enjoy a magnificent view across the Alps, a cable car runs to the Rifugio T Demetz (2996m) on the Sasso Lungo. From here you can pick up trail No 525, which traverses the mountain's jagged peaks to the Alpe di Siusi. From Passo Pordoi (2242m), take the cable car up to Sasso Pordoi (2952m). Here you can get onto the Alta Via No 2, which crosses the group, heads down to the Passo Gardena and then continues into the breathtaking Parco Naturale Puez-Odle.

Alternatively you can take trail No 638 to the Rifugio Piz Fass on Piz Boé (3152m). Continuing along No 638 you will reach a combined chairlift and cable car service down to Corvara in the Val Badia. The cable car and chairlift are open from 8.30 am to 5.30 pm, with a break for lunch (from about 12.15 to 2 pm), and are closed all day Monday. Use a good map (such as Tabacco, 1:25,000 scale) and plan carefully.

The Sella also offers challenging walks, some incorporating vie ferrate, for people with mountaineering experience. For further information on the Sella, the Val Gardena and the Val Badia see the following section on Alto Adige.

Alto Adige

This orderly Alpine fairyland owes more to its largely Austrian heritage than to its recent Italian history. Alto Adige (Südtirol) is a year-round attraction for skiers, climbers, trekkers, walkers or just plain ordinary folk looking to appreciate its natural splendour.

BOLZANO

The provincial capital, Bolzano (Bozen) is unmistakably Austrian. Forget your *cappuccino* and *brioche* and tuck into some *Sachertorte* with *deutscher Kaffee*. You'll hear Italian and German spoken (both languages are compulsory subjects in school), but aside from concessions to the former in street, hotel and restaurant signs, there are precious few reminders of Italian rule here. The town's small historic centre, with its engaging Tyrolean architecture and arcade streets, harbours numerous outdoor café and restaurants, making it a very pleasan place to spend a few days.

Settled in the Middle Ages, Bolzano wa an important market town that became pawn in the power battles between th bishops of Trento and the counts of Tyrol During the first decades of the 19th centur it passed, with the rest of the Tyrol, fron Bavaria, to Austria, to Napoleon's kingdon of Italy and, finally, again to Austria. Alon with the Südtirol, Bolzano passed to Italy after WWI and was declared the capital o the province in 1927.

Orientation

The old-town centre is Piazza Walthe (Waltherplatz), a few minutes walk along Viale Stazione from the train station on Via Garibaldi. The intercity bus station is on Vi Perathoner, between the train station and the piazza.

Information

Tourist Offices The AST office (☎ 0471-97 56 56) is at Piazza Walther 8 and is open Monday to Friday from 8.30 am to 6 pm (9 am to 12.30 pm and 2.30 to 6 pm in winter) and Saturday from 9 am to 12.30 pm.

The provincial tourist office for Alto Adige (☎ 0471-99 38 08) is at Piazza Parrocchia (Pfarrplatz) 11 and is open Monday to Friday from 9 am to midday and 3 to 5.30 pm (5 pm in winter). Here you can pick up information about accommodation, activities and transport, as well as walking and trekking possibilities. The office's Alpine information desk can help further with planning treks and climbs.

Money Money can be changed at all banks in Bolzano. On weekends, from 7 am to 8 pm, an exchange office opens at the train station.

Post & Communications The post office, Via della Posta, opens Monday to Friday

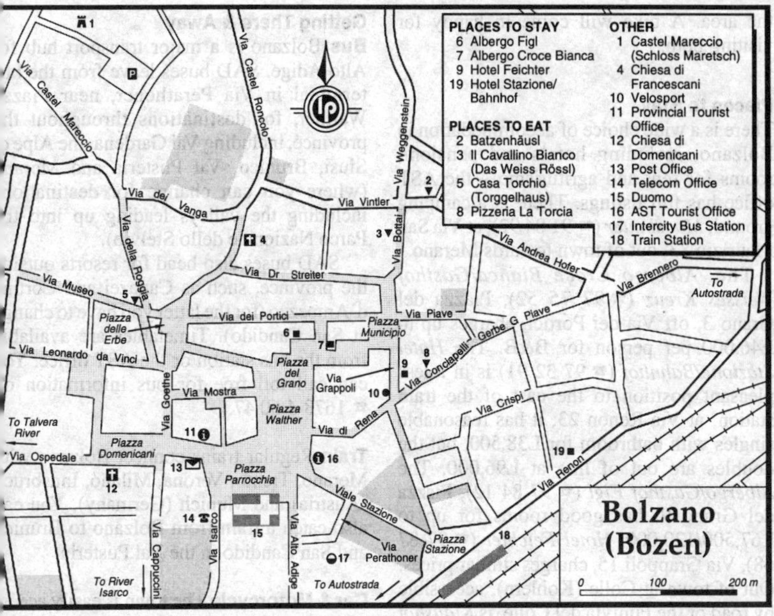

om 8.15 am to 7.15 pm; Saturday from 9 m to 1 pm. The Telecom office, Piazza arrocchia 15, is open daily from 7 am to 10 m. The postcode for central Bolzano is 9100 and the telephone code is ☎ 0471.

mergency For immediate police attenance, call ☎ 113. The questura (☎ 94 76 11) at Via Marconi 33. The Ospedale egionale San Maurizio (☎ 90 81 11) is in ia Lorenze Böhler, some distance from the own centre off the road to Merano, and ccessible on city bus No 8 from the train ation.

hings to See & Do

Vhile away a few hours at one of the many utdoor cafés in Piazza Walther or along the ide streets that lead to Piazza delle Erbe Obstplatz). Otherwise, rent a bike from 'elosport, Via Grappoli (Weintraubengasse) 6, near Piazza Walther.

The AST office offers a Visitor's Pass to tourists who spend at least three nights in town. It includes free admission to some sights and a guided tour of the town.

Start with the Gothic **duomo** in Piazza Parrocchia and the nearby **Chiesa di Domenicani** with its cloisters and chapel featuring 14th-century frescoes of the Giotto school. Take a walk along the arcaded **Via dei Portici** (Laubengasse), through the charming Piazza delle Erbe (the German Obstplatz explains what this square is – the daily fresh produce market), to reach the 14th-century **Chiesa di Francescani** in Via dei Francescani. It features beautiful cloisters and a magnificent Gothic altarpiece in the Cappella della Beata Vergine (Virgin's Chapel), carved by Hans Klocker in 1500. There are several castles in the town: the 13th-century **Castel Mareccio** (Schloss Maretsch) is along Via della Roggia from Piazza delle Erbe. **Castel Roncolo** (Schloss Runkelstein), out of town on the road to Sarentino (Sarnthein), is the best of a trio in the area. A bike will come in handy for visiting both.

Places to Stay

There is a wide choice of accommodation in Bolzano, including hotels and pensioni, rooms for rent and agriturismo – the AST office has full listings. There is a camping ground, *Moosbauer* (☎ 91 84 92), at Via San Maurizio 83, out of town towards Merano.

The *Albergo Croce Bianca/Gasthof Weisses Kreuz* (☎ 97 75 52), Piazza del Grano 3, off Via dei Portici, charges up to L46,000 per person for B&B. The *Hotel Stazione/Bahnhof* (☎ 97 32 91) is in a less pleasant position to the east of the train station, at Via Renon 23; it has reasonable singles with bathroom for L38,500, but the doubles are out of line at L96,000. The *Albergo/Gasthof Figl* (☎ 97 84 12), Piazza del Grano 9, has good rooms for up to L67,500/120,000. *Hotel Feichter* (☎ 97 87 68), Via Grappoli 15, charges similar prices. Out of town at Colle (Kohlern), accessible by road or the Funivia del Colle, is *Klaushof* (☎ 97 12 94), which offers B&B for a more affordable L40,000 per person.

Places to Eat

You can pick up supplies of fruit and vegetables, bread and cheese etc from the open-air market held every morning from Monday to Saturday at Piazza delle Erbe. In the same area are numerous bakeries, pastry shops and cafés, as well as a small supermarket. While you can eat pizza and pasta if you wish, Bolzano's best restaurants specialise in Tyrolean food. The *Cavallino Bianco (Das Weiss Rössl)*, Via Bottai, is extremely popular and reasonably priced at around L30,000 for a full meal. *Pizzeria La Torcia*, Via dei Conciapelli 25, is cheap and has pasta too. *Casa Torchio (Torrgelhaus)*, just off Piazza dell Erbe at Via Museo 2, is a wonderful place with antique glass windows and excellent local specialities at reasonable prices. *Batzenhäusl*, Via Andrea Hofer 30, is one of the city's better restaurants. A full meal will cost up to L50,000.

Getting There & Away

Bus Bolzano is a major transport hub fo Alto Adige. SAD buses leave from the bu terminal in Via Perathoner, near Piazz Walther, for destinations throughout th province, including Val Gardena, the Alpe d Siusi, Brunico, Val Pusteria and Meran (where you can change for destination including the valleys leading up into th Parco Nazionale dello Stelvio).

SAD buses also head for resorts outsid the province, such as Canazei and Cortin d'Ampezzo (for the latter you have to chang at San Candido). Timetables are availabl from the bus station or the AST office. Yo can call toll free for bus information o ☎ 1678-4 60 47.

Train Regular trains connect Bolzano wit Merano, Trento, Verona, Milano, Innsbruc (Austria) and Munich (Germany). You ca also catch a train from Bolzano to Brunic and San Candido in the Val Pusteria.

Car & Motorcycle The town is easily acces sible from the north and south on the A22 The road to Merano is one long traffic jar in busy periods. There's no way to avoid i so try driving at lunch or dinnertime to a least miss the rush hours.

MERANO

Merano (Meran) is a rather sedate littl place, its typically Tyrolean centre clean an well tended. The Terme di Merano, complex of therapeutic baths and treatments is the main attraction and most tourists ten to be of older age groups. Merano is close t the Parco Naturale Gruppo di Tess (Texalgruppe), the Parco Nazionale dell Stelvio and the spectacular Ortles mountai range, so you might use the town as a stop over on your way to higher altitudes.

The train and intercity bus stations are i Piazza Stazione (Bahnhofsplatz), a 10 minute walk from the centre of town. As yo leave the train station, turn right into Vi Europa (Europaallee) and at Piazza Mazzin (Mazziniplatz) take Corso della Libert (Freiheitsstrasse) to the town centre.

formation

he Azienda di Cura e Soggiorno (☎ 23 52 3), Corso della Libertà 35, has information bout the city.

The main post office and Telecom office e at Via Roma (Romastrasse) 2, on the her side of the river from the historic entre. The town's telephone code is ☎ 0473.

For police emergency, call ☎ 113. The spedale Provinciale (☎ 4 61 11) is at Via oethe 50, along Via O Huber (Huberstrasse) om Corso della Libertà.

hings to See & Do

he historic centre of the town is around the caded Via dei Portici (Laubengasse) and e Piazza del Duomo – take any of the reets off Corso della Libertà near the tourist ffice (leading away from the river). The **erapeutic baths** *(Kurbad* or *terme)* offer full range of treatments, including radon aths (cost L38,000), hydromassages .50,000) and physiotherapy. The complex open all year from Monday to Saturday.

If you're interested in women's clothing ast and present, drop in to the **Museo della onna (Frauenmuseum)** at Via dei Portici 3.

Beer-lovers might be interested in a visit the **Forst Brewery**, at Forst just out of lerano.

laces to Stay

ccommodation is abundant in Merano – k at the tourist office for full hotel and artment lists, including those equipped for ildren (with services such as baby cots, abysitting and playrooms). Most establish-ents in the centre are expensive, although e *Pension Tyrol* (☎ 44 97 19), off Corso ella Libertà at Via XXX Aprile (30 prilstrasse) 8, has reasonable rooms start-g at about L45,000/60,000 for doubles ingles are hard to get). The price includes eakfast.

Villa Pax (☎ 23 62 90), Via Leichter 3, arges up to L33,000 per person. To reach from Corso della Libertà, cross the river at azza D Rena and follow Via Cavour to Via ante, turn right and then left into Via Leichter. *Pensione Tyrol* (☎ 44 97 19), Via XXX Aprile 8, has rooms for up to L47,000 per person. *Villa Fanny* (☎ 23 35 20), Via Giardini 2, charges L60,000 per person for B&B. The *Graf von Meran/Conte di Merano* (☎ 23 21 81), Via delle Corse 78, is just near the Via dei Portici. Its lovely rooms, breakfast included, can cost up to L110,000 per person.

Places to Eat

The *Ristorante Forsterbräu*, Corso della Libertà 90, has an internal garden/courtyard and serves typical Tyrolean food at reasonable prices. A full meal could cost under L40,000. *Picnic Grill*, Via delle Corse 26, is even more economical, with pizzas and pre-prepared food. Two restaurants in Via dei Portici serve excellent Tyrolean fare at higher prices: *Algunder Weinstube* at No 232 and *Terlaner Weinstube* at No 231. A full meal at either will cost at least L30,000. Another good one with a cavernous feel about it is *Haisrainer* at No 100 – a main costs L20,000.

Getting There & Away

Merano is easily accessible by bus or train from Bolzano (about 40 minutes). SAD buses also connect the town with Katharinaberg and other villages that give access to the Tessa group, as well as to Silandro (Schlanders) and the valleys leading up into the Ortles range and the Parco Nazionale dello Stelvio. See the section on the Parco Nazionale dello Stelvio for bus information. A direct bus connects Merano and Munich (Germany) every Saturday from late March to early November for DM45.

PARCO NAZIONALE DELLO STELVIO

If you can tear yourself away from the Dolomiti, this major national park offers fantastic walking possibilities: at low altitudes in the pretty valleys, Val d'Ultimo (Ultental), Val Martello (Martelltal) and Val di Solda (Suldental); and at high altitudes on spectacular peaks such as the Gran Zebru (Königspitze) (3859m), Cevedale (3769m) and the breathtaking Ortles (Ortler)

(3905m), all part of the Ortles range. There is a network of well-marked trails, including routes over some of the range's glaciers. The park incorporates one of Europe's largest glaciers, the Ghiacciaio dei Forni.

The glaciers permit year-round skiing and there are well-serviced runs at Solda and the Passo Stelvio. The Passo Stelvio is the second-highest pass in the Alps and is approached from Trafoi on one of Europe's most spectacular roads, a series of tight switchbacks with at times nerve-wrackingly steep gradients. The road is famous among cyclists, who flock to the park every summer to tackle the ascent.

The village of **Trafoi** marks the start of about 15km of switchbacks up to the pass. If you want to stay here, there is a *camping ground* (☎ 0473-61 15 33) and several hotels, including the *Hochleiten* (☎ 0473-61 17 91) which charges L38,000 for B&B, and the *Madatsch* (☎ 0473-61 17 67), with half board for up to L100,000.

SAD buses (line 102) operate to Stelvio village. From Merano change at Spondigna (Spondinig). Buses to the pass operate in summer only.

The park straddles Alto Adige and Trentino and can be approached from Merano (from where you have easy access to the Val d'Ultimo, Val Martello, Val di Solda and the Passo Stelvio), or from the Val di Sole in Trentino, which gives easy access to the Valle di Péio and the Val di Rabbi and high trails up to the Forni glacier.

Val di Solda

The village of Solda (Sulden), at the head of the Val di Solda (Suldental), is a small ski resort and a base for walkers and climbers in summer. Challenging trails lead you to high altitudes, including the No 28, which crosses the Cima Madriccio (Madritschspitze) (3263m) into the Val Martello. The tourist office at Solda (☎ 0473-61 30 15) has information on accommodation and activities.

At Solda try *Pension Nives* (☎ 0473-61 32 20), which offers B&B for up to L35,000 per person, or half board for up to L60,000. At the top end, *Parc Hotel* (☎ 0473-61 31 33) has lovely rooms and good food for up t L132,000 per person for half board. Th village virtually closes down from Octob to Christmas.

Solda is accessible by SAD bus on week days during summer only. From Merano yo need to change at Spondigna (Spondinig).

Val Martello

This picturesque valley is a good choice fo relatively low altitude walks, with spectacu lar views of some of the park's high peak The real beauty of the valley is that th environment is unspoiled by ski lifts an downhill ski runs. It is a popular base fo tackling the glaciers: guided treks can b organised through the valley's Pro Loco offic (☎ 0473-74 45 98). In winter there is exceller

Red deer can be found in the Parco Naturale dello Stelvio and, except when mating, live in sexually segregated herds

ross-country skiing, and climbers can crawl p the valley's frozen waterfalls from anuary to March. In spring the valley ttracts ski mountaineers, since there is no anger of avalanches.

People with children might like to take ail No 20 up into the Val di Peder. It is an asy walk, with some lovely picnic spots long the way and the chance to see animals ncluding chamois and deer.

The *Schoenblick* (☎ 0473-73 04 76) is igh in the valley and offers B&B from 37,000 per person. For further accommoation, inquire at the Pro Loco.

The road into the valley is open throughut the year, and SAD bus 107 runs to lartello village from Silandro. In summer ne bus proceeds to the Rifugio Genziana Enzianhütte).

alle di Péio

rom Péio (also spelt Péjo) Terme (1393m), ctually inside Trentino province, chairlifts perate to the Rifugio Doss dei Cembri 2400m), from where you can pick up trail lo 105 to the Rifugio Mantova al Vioz 3535m) at the edge of the Forni glacier. If ou want to climb Monte Vioz (3645m) or ontinue onto the glacier, you will need the ppropriate equipment.

The tourist office at Malé (☎ 0463-90 12 0), Piazza Regina Elena, has extensive nformation on these valleys, including ccommodation, transport and sporting ctivities, and will advise on walking trails nd ski facilities.

Ferrovia Trento-Malé buses connect Péio 'erme with Madonna di Campiglio and with Malé in the Val di Sole. Malé is on the 'rento-Malé train line.

AL GARDENA

'his enchanting Alpine valley (Grödental) s hemmed in by the towering peaks of the 'arco Naturale Puez-Odle, the imposing ella group and Sasso Lungo and the gentle lopes and pastures of the Alpe di Siusi, the argest high plain in the Alps. It is one of the nore popular skiing areas in the Alps ecause of its relatively reasonable prices and excellent facilities. Be warned though that the valley and its ski runs are packed in ski season. In the warmer months, walkers have easy access to trails at high and low altitudes. See Activities in this section for details.

The valley's main towns, Ortisei (St Ulrich), Santa Cristina (St Christina) and Selva (Wolkenstein), all offer lots of accommodation. Along with the Alpe di Siusi, the Val Gardena provides excellent facilities for families. The well-organised tourist offices run activities for children in summer and winter, and you'll find sports centres and well-equipped playgrounds.

Along with Val Badia (Gadertal), the Val Gardena is an enclave that has managed to preserve the ancient Ladin language and culture, and a rich tradition in colourful legends. See the boxed aside in the Val Badia section later in this chapter. The ancient tradition of woodcarving is also maintained and the valley's artisans are famed for their statues, figurines, altars and toys. Beware of mass-produced imitations.

Information

There are tourist offices in each of the towns: Ortisei (☎ 79 63 28), Santa Cristina (☎ 79 30 46) and Selva (☎ 79 51 22). All have extensive information on accommodation, ski facilities and walking trails. A guidebook in English is available for each town, along with information on guided treks and rock-climbing schools.

The telephone code for the valley is ☎ 0471.

Activities

In addition to its own fine downhill ski runs, the valley also forms part of the Sella Ronda, a network of runs connecting the Val Gardena, Val Badi and Val di Fassa. Areas like the Vallunga, near Selva, offer good cross-country skiing. Alpine skiers should consult the tourist office for detailed information. Stunning trails are on offer around Forcella Pordoi and Val Lasties in the Sella group, and on the Sasso Lungo.

This is walkers' paradise, with endless

possibilities from the challenging Alte Vie of the Sella group and the magnificent Parco Natural Puez-Odle (Naturpark Puez-Geisler), to picturesque family strolls in spots like the Vallunga. Just behind Selva, the valley is home to some over-friendly horses who like to harass picnicking tourists. The walk to the end of the valley and back will take three to four hours. It is possible to continue from the end of the valley, along trail No 14, to pick up the Alta Via No 2. From here you can continue up into the Odle group, or double back into the Puez group and on to the Sella.

A Full-Day Trek in the Puez-Odle This is a full day walk (about eight hours) at high altitude through the Alpe di Cisles, an extraordinarily beautiful landscape dominated by the Odle and Puez groups. As with all walks, make sure you carry a good map: the Tabacco 1:25,000 No 05 is recommended. Also ensure that you carry the correct items of clothing and plenty of water (see under Trekking in the Dolomiti) and notify your hotel of your planned route.

From Ortisei (about 1250m) in the Val Gardena, take the funivia to Seceda (2456m). This is the highest point you will reach during the walk and there is a memorable view – one of the most spectacular in the Dolomiti. Behind you is the Odle group, a series of spiky pinnacles. Take trail No 2a, which follows the slope and passes through what most people would consider a typical Alpine environment – lush green, sloping pastures dotted with wooden malghe, which herders use as summer shelters. This type of environment is in fact unusual at such high altitude. Following trail No 2a through the scenic Alpe di Cisles, you will come to an area known as Prera Longia. Huge boulders with surreal forms dot the landscape – who knows how long ago they fell from the mountains. It's highly likely that you'll see marmots, roe deer and certainly lots of birds here. Follow trail No 2a until you arrive in a valley: at this point you need to descend into the valley (continuing along trail No 2a and making sure you don't follow the signs for Rifugio Firenze) then go up the other side following the sign for Forces de Sieles. It's a 200m descent and then a very tiring 400m uphill. At this point the trail becomes No 2 (there are several trails which branch off to the right – don't follow them), which will bring you to the Forces de Sieles (2505m).

Continue on trail No 2: following it to the left you'll reach a short section of vie ferrate. Don't panic, you don't need any equipment, just hold onto the cord if you need help to cross this steep section. After a short distance, the trail joins the Alta Via No 2 (signed with the number 2 inside a triangle). Following the trail to the right, you'll pass a crest and then descend to a small high plain, almost like a rocky balcony above the Vallunga – you are directly beneath the Puez group at this point, the highest peak of which is the Cima Puez at 2913m. Continue along the trail, heading towards Rifugio Puez (Puezhütte) but, before you get there, you'll find trail No 4, which descends into a broad valley and eventually reaches the Vallunga and trail No 4-14. This is virtually a small road; follow it to the right and meander down the pretty Vallunga, with its Alpine vegetation. If you walk quietly, you should come across quite a few animals. The contrast between the majesty of the high mountains and the gentle environment of the valley creates a memorable effect and provides a fitting end to the walk. Once you arrive at the end of the valley, it will take another 15 minutes or so to reach the town of Selva, from where you catch a bus back to Ortisei.

Places to Stay

The valley has hundreds of hotels and pensioni, but it is still advisable to book in advance, particularly during August and at Christmas and Easter. Many places will require half or full board, but there are also plenty of B&Bs and affittacamere, as well as apartments for rent. The tourist offices have full lists, including photos and prices, so write or phone to request a booklet in advance. If you arrive in Ortisei without a booking and the tourist office is closed, an ectronic table outside the office has the test info on hotel vacancies.

rtisei There are plenty of budget places, ich as *Gran Cësa* (☎ 79 74 22), Via itadella-Strasse 67, which offers B&B for p to L40,000 per person.

Panoramik (☎ 79 64 95), Via Vidalong-trasse 9, has B&B for around L60,000 per erson in peak season, while *Alpenhotel ainell* (☎ 79 61 45), Via Vidalong-Strasse 9, offers half board for L100,000 to 135,000 per person in high season.

anta Cristina Try *Affittacamere Mauron* ☎ 79 37 04), Via Plesdinaz-Strasse 77, hich charges up to L33,000 for B&B. *Garni Tyrol* (☎ 79 20 58), Via Plesdinaz-trasse 113, charges around L40,000 per erson for B&B all year round. *Haus Walter* ☎ 79 33 37), Via Val-Strasse 6, is simple and harges up to L52,000 for B&B. *Pensione Bellavista* (☎ 79 20 39) is set back from the own at Via Plesdinaz-Strasse 65 and offers alf board for up to L78,000 per person, as vell as B&B. In the centre of town is *Hotel Post* (☎ 79 20 78), Via Dursan-Strasse 17, which offers half board for up to L170,000 er person.

Selva About the cheapest place is *Plochof* ☎ 79 55 88), on the edge of town at Via Daunëi-Strasse 71. It charges up to L32,000 er person. *Garni Katiuscia* (☎ 79 55 08) is ear the Vallunga, a fair walk from town but n a lovely position, at Via Larciunëi-Strasse 38. B&B is up to L50,000 a person. *Garni Zirmei* (☎ 79 52 12), Via Col da Lech-Strasse 60, charges up to L57,000 for B&B.

Getting There & Away

The Val Gardena is accessible from Bolzano by SAD bus, as well as from Canazei (only in summer). Regular buses connect the towns along the valley and you can reach the Alpe di Siusi either by bus or cable car. Full timetables are available at the tourist offices or from the SAD office in Antoniusplatz, Ortisei.

Information about long-distance bus services (Lazzi, SITA and STAT) to major cities throughout Italy can be obtained at Tourdolomit Viaggi in Ortisei (☎ 79 61 35).

ALPE DI SIUSI & PARCO NATURALE DELLO SCILIAR

There's something magical about the view across the Alpe di Siusi (Seiser Alm) to the Sciliar (Schlern): the green undulating pastures end dramatically at the foot of these towering peaks. It is a particularly spectacular scene in an area that certainly doesn't lack scenery. The Alpe di Siusi (1700m to 2200m), the largest plateau in Europe, forms part of what is known as the Altipiano dello Sciliar, which also incorporates the villages of Castelrotto (Kastelruth) and Siusi (Seis), lower down at about 1000m.

There is something for walkers of all ages and expertise in this area. The gentle slopes of the Alpe di Siusi are perfect for families with young kids, and you won't need much more than average stamina to make it to the Rifugio Bolzano al Monte Pez (Schlernhaus) (2457m), just under Monte Pez, the Sciliar's summit. If you're after more challenging walks, the jagged peaks of the Catinaccio group and the Sasso Lungo (Langkofel) are nearby. These mountains are famous among climbers worldwide.

Information

Tourist Offices The area is popular in both summer and winter and its tourist offices are highly organised. All local offices will send out information, hotel lists and prices etc. There are three offices of the Associazione Turistica Sciliar: Castelrotto (☎ 0471-70 63 33), Piazza Kraus 1; Siusi (☎ 0471-70 70 24), Via Sciliar 8; and at Compatsch in the Alpe di Siusi (☎ 0471-72 79 04). Pick up the brochure which lists local services.

Emergency In a medical emergency phone ☎ 118 or ☎ 0471-70 65 55. The Guardia Medica Turistica (☎ 0471-70 54 44) is based at Telfen, between Castelrotto and Siusi.

Activities

There's no shortage of organised activities or information about how to organise your own. In winter the area offers excellent skiing: downhill, cross-country and ski-mountaineering. It forms part of the Superski Dolomiti network. As in the Val Gardena, the area gets pretty crowded during peak periods. Ask at the tourist office about walking trails open during the snow season.

In summer, the trails of the Alpe di Siusi are crowded with walkers, but as soon as you get to higher altitudes they start to thin out. Using a good map and following the tourist office recommendations, you could spend days taking leisurely walks in the Alpe di Siusi, stopping for picnics or planning your walks to ensure that you reach a malgha for a lunch break. The tourist offices organise low-priced guided walks of varying length and difficulty. There are also plenty of good trails for mountain bikers. Apart from the trek outlined in this section, there are plenty of challenging trails, including several vie ferrate. The Catinaccio group can also be approached from the Val di Fassa.

Activity Courses The Scuola Alpina Dolomiten (☎ 0471-70 53 43), Via Vogelweider (Vogelweidergasse) 6, Castelrotto, has a summer programme which includes a seven-day guided trek across the Dolomiti from the Alpe di Siusi to the Tre Cime di Lavaredo. Also offered is a week of free-climbing (for experts), a rock-climbing course for beginners, a mountain-bike 'safari' from Bolzano to Sesto, and an expedition on horseback. In winter, a beginners' ski-mountaineering course is on offer, as well as a 'Skisafari' for experts, both on and off runs, through the Alpe di Siusi, Val Gardena, Val Badia to Cortina, the Marmolada, the Val di Fassa and finishing at the Alpe di Siusi.

A Three-Day Trek in the Sciliar & Catinaccio

This is a basic guide for a three day trek through the Alpe di Siusi, up to the Sciliar and across to the Catinaccio d'Antermoia (Kessel-Kgl) and the famous Torri del Vajolet (Vajoletturme) and Cima Catinaccio (Rosengarten).

The walk starts and ends at Compatsch (Compaccio) (1820m), easily accessible by car or bus from the town of Siusi. It is an
interesting walk, in particular for the co
trasts between the gentle green slopes of th
Alpe di Siusi and the Gothic pinnacles an
rocky towers of the Catinaccio group, whic
give the impression of a fairy-tale castle.

As with all of the treks/walks detailed i
this book, make sure you are correct
dressed and equipped. The information he
should be used as a guide only and yo
should use Tabacco 1:25,000 map No 05. (
this is not available, a different map, als
produced by Tabacco, may be available
the provincial tourist office in Bolzano.) Th
second day of the walk is demanding an
may present some difficulties for walke
with no experience. However, if you are fi
healthy and cautious you should have n
trouble. Book in advance to sleep at the sma
Rifugio Passo Santner.

Day One This first stage will take you fro
Compatsch to the Rifugio Bolzano (2450m
(three to four hours). From the big car par
at Compatsch, take the trail marked No 1
and follow it until you reach the deviation t
the left for Malga Saltner (Saltnerhütte) (tra
No 5). You will be walking through th
western part of the Alpe di Siusi, a vast an
beautiful area of undulating green pastures
packed full of tourists in summer. Stop at th
Saltnerhütte (1832m) for a drink before tack
ling the ascent to the Sciliar. Follow trail N
5, which becomes trail No 1, known as th
Sentiero dei Turisti, which snakes its way u
to the Sciliar high plain. The ascent is tiring
but by no means difficult, although yo
should watch out for falling rocks dislodge
by chamois. There is a great view across th
Alpe di Siusi to the Sasso Lungo, the Sell
group and Le Odle (3025m at the highes
peak). Once you arrive at Rifugio Bolzan
(2450m), if you have the energy, climb th
nearby Monte Pez (2563m). From its summi
you have a 360° view: to the north you ca
see the Alps stretching into Austria; to th
north-east you see Le Odle, Puez (2913m
and Sassongher (2665m); to the east is th
Sella group (3152m), Sasso Lungo (3181m
and Sasso Piatto (2964m); south-east yo

can see the Catinaccio group, where you'll be heading on day two.

Day Two This tract will take you from Rifugio Bolzano to Rifugio Passo Santner (Santnerpasshütte) under the summit of the Rosengarten (a tough five to six hours). Head back along trail No 1 for a short distance, then turn right onto trail No 3-4, which crosses the Sciliar high plain in the direction of the Catinaccio group, completely dominating the landscape. You will pass the Cima di Terrarossa and the spectacular, jagged peaks of the Denti di Terrarossa. Keep to trail No 3-4 (don't take No 3, which heads to the right at a certain point) to reach the Rifugio Alpe di Tires (2440m), then go south on trail No 3a-554, ascend to the Passo Alpe di Tires and continue for the Passo Molignon (2596m).

From here you start the difficult and very steep descent on a *ghiaione* (river of gravel) into the lunar landscape of a valley. Before reaching the valley floor the trail forks. Keep to the left and stay on trail No 554, which will take you up to Rifugio Passo Principe (2599m), under the Catinaccio d'Antermoia (3200m). You can take a break at this tiny refuge. From here, descend into the valley along the comfortable trail No 584. You'll arrive at the rifugi Vajolet and Preuss (2243m), from where you take trail No 542s up to the Rifugio Re Alberto (2621m). This tract is better described as a climb and inexperienced mountaineers will find it quite challenging. There are plans to install an iron cord for safety reasons, which would significantly reduce the excitement of the ascent.

Once at the top you will be in a wide valley with the Torri del Vajolet, famous among climbers, to your right and the peak of the Rosengarten to your left. Follow trail No 542s up to Rifugio Passo Santner, perched on a precipice under the Rosengarten, with an almost sheer drop down into the Val di Tires. It is one of the most spectacularly located rifugi in the Alps, and has just two rooms, each with four beds. Climbers flock here in summer. The trail 542s becomes a via ferrata where it descends from the rifugio. If you intend to tackle either the ferrata or a climb, make sure you are properly equipped.

Day Three The section from Rifugio Passo Santner back to Compatsch will take six to seven hours. Return down to Rifugio Vajolet along trail No 542s and return to Passo Principe. Instead of continuing for Passo Molignon, remain on trail No 584 to reach Passo d'Antermoia (2770m) and then descend to Lago d'Antermoia (2490m) and shortly afterwards the refuge of the same name. Here the trail becomes No 580, which heads east to the Passo Dona (2516m) and then descends towards the Alpe di Siusi. After a relatively short distance the No 580 veers to the right (east), but you will instead continue straight ahead and, at the next fork, take trail No 555, which will take you in a westerly direction along the northern slopes of the Molignon group. At the base of the Molignon, the trail joins a dirt road (trail No 532) near the group of herders' shelters known as Malga Dòcoldaura (2046m). Follow No 532 to the Casa del TCI Sciliar, then go straight ahead along trail No 7, which will take you all the way down to Compatsch. (At Rifugio Molignon, the trail becomes a small road and some distance ahead it becomes trail No 7-12.)

Places to Stay

There are plenty of hotels and pensioni, but bookings are recommended during the summer and winter high seasons. If you're travelling with kids, ask the tourist office for information on hotels equipped for, or offering special deals for, children. There's a choice between places in the villages, or up on the Alpe di Siusi. If you choose to stay in the Alpe di Siusi, there is a regular bus service. In summer normal traffic is banned from the plateau. See Getting Around in this section.

Try *Albergo Zallinger* (☎ 72 79 47), Saltria 74, at the foot of the Sassopiatto (Plattkofel). Half board per person per day costs up to L68,000. In Castelrotto, *Garni Villa Rosa* (☎ 70 63 27), St Annaweg 3, offers B&B in double rooms for L33,000 to

L50,000 per person, depending on the season. It's about 10 minutes' walk to the centre. The traditional-style *Gasthof zum Wolf* (☎ 70 63 32) is right in the centre of Castelrotto at Oswald von Wolkensteinstrasse 5, and offers comfortable B&B from L55,000 to L90,000 per person in a double, depending on the season – they may insist on half board (an extra L15,000 per person). In most hotels you pay L8000 extra for single occupancy.

Getting There & Away

The Altipiano dello Sciliar is accessible by SAD bus from Bolzano, the Val Gardena and Bressanone. By car, exit the Brennero autostrada (A22) at Bolzano Nord or Chiusa.

Getting Around

From May to October the roads of the Alpe di Siusi are closed to normal traffic. Tourists with a booking at a hotel in the zone, who are staying for five days or more, can obtain a special permit from the tourist office at Compatsch to drive from 6 pm to 9 am. It is best to organise your pass before arriving in the area; ask your hotel owner for assistance. A regular bus service operates from Castelrotto and Siusi to Compatsch and from there on to the Alpe di Siusi. Tourists staying in hotels in the area will be given a special *Favorit* card which entitles them to free bus travel.

VAL BADIA

Along with the Val Gardena, Val Badia (Gadertal) is one of the last strongholds of the ancient Ladin culture and language. Most local kids (as well as adults) are aware of the Ladin legends, richly peopled by giants, kings, witches, fairies and dragons. Many are centred on the nearby Fanes high plain, which forms part of the magnificent Parco Naturale Fanes-Sennes-Braies. This is one of the most evocative places in the Dolomiti and can be reached easily from the Alta Val Badia, either on foot or by funivia from Passo Falzarego. The towns in the valley include Colfosco (Colfosch), La Villa (La Ila), San Cassiano (San Ciascian) and Corvara.

Corvara

This ski resort is an excellent base for walkers wanting to tackle the peaks enclosing the Alta Badia. Corvara was the central town of the Ladin tribes and today is a pleasant little town, with a well-organised tourist office and plenty of accommodation.

The AAST tourist office (☎ 83 61 76) is in the town's main street and open Monday

ALTO ADIGE

The Ladin Tradition

The Ladin language and culture trace their ancestry to around 15 BC, when the people of the Central Alps were forcibly united into the Roman province of Rhaetia. The Romans, of course, introduced Latin to the province, but the original inhabitants of the area, with their diverse linguistic and cultural backgrounds, modified the language to such an extent that, by around 450 AD, it had evolved into an independent Romance language, known as raeto-romanic. At one point the entire Tyrol was Ladin, but today the language and culture are confined mainly to the Val Gardena and the Val Badia, where about 90% of the locals declared in the 1981 census that they belonged to the Ladin language group. Along with German and Italian, Ladin is taught in schools and the survival of the Ladin cultural and linguistic identity is protected by law.

The Ladin culture is rich in vibrant poetry and legends, set amid the jagged peaks of the Dolomiti and peopled by fairies, gnomes, elves, giants, princesses and heroes. Passed on by word-of-mouth for centuries and often heavily influenced by Germanic myths, many of these legends were in danger of being lost. In the first decade of this century, journalist Carlo Felice Wolff, who had lived most of his life at Bolzano, undertook a major project: he spent 10 years gathering and researching the local legends, listening as the old folk, farmers and shepherds recounted the legends and fairy tales. The originality of the legends he eventually published is that, instead of simply writing down what he was told, Wolff reconstructed the tales from the many different versions and recollections he gathered. ■

o Saturday from 8 am to midday and 3 to 7 pm and Sunday from 10 am to midday. It has extensive information on ski facilities, walking trails, accommodation and transport.

For medical assistance, go to the Croce Bianca (☎ 83 64 44), set back from Corvara's main street just near the tourist office. In an emergency, the nearest public hospital is in Brunico (☎ 0474-58 11 11).

Corvara's telephone code is ☎ 0471.

Activities Corvara is on the Sella Ronda ski trail and is part of the Superski Dolomiti network. From the town, you can reach the Passo Falzarego by SAD bus and then take the cable car up into the Fanes-Sennes-Braies park. See the section on Trekking in the Dolomiti. Otherwise, you can pick up trail No 12 from near La Villa, or trail No 11, which joins Alta Via No 1, at the Capanna Alpina, a few km off the main road between Passo Valparola and San Cassiano. Either trail will take you up to the Alpe di Fanes and the two rifugi, Lavarella and Fanes.

A combination of cabinovia and chairlift will take you from Corvara up into the Sella group at Vallon (2550m) and you'll get a a spectacular view across to the Marmolada glacier. From Vallon you can traverse the Sella or follow the trail that winds around the valley at the top of the chairlift (about one hour). A good area for family walks is around Prelongiá (Prelungé) (2138m). Catch the funivia from La Villa and then take trail No 4 and trail No 23 to reach Prelongiá. Trail No 23 will take you down to Corvara. Horse riding, mountain biking and hang-gliding are also popular activities in the valley.

Places to Stay & Eat The tourist office can assist,otherwise try the *Garni Laura* (☎ 83 63 40), back from the main road near the tourist office, which has B&B for up to L40,000 per person. *Ciasa Blancia* (☎ 83 62 96), Via Sassongher 52, offers half board for up to L100,000 per person per day. *La Tambra* (☎ 83 62 81), Via Sassongher 2, is a pleasant, 'children-friendly' hotel. It offers full board for up to L155,000 per person per day. Full meals at *Ristòrante/Pizzeria La Tambra* cost under L35,000.

Getting There & Away SAD buses connect Corvara with Bolzano, Merano, Brunico, the Val Gardena, the Passo Sella and Passo Pordoi, Canazei and the Passo Falzarego (note that buses do not cross the high passes in winter).

CORTINA D'AMPEZZO

Across the Fanes-Conturines mountains from the Val Badia is the jewel of the Dolomiti, Cortina d'Ampezzo. Italy's most famous, fashionable and expensive ski resort, Cortina is actually situated in the Veneto, but has been included here because of its central location in the Dolomiti. It is one of the best equipped, and certainly the most picturesque, resorts in the Dolomiti. If you are on a tight budget, the prices for accommodation and food will be prohibitive, even in the low season. However, camping grounds and Alpine rifugi (open only during summer) provide more reasonably priced alternatives.

Situated in the Ampezzo bowl, Cortina is surrounded by some of the most stunning mountains in the Dolomiti, including Monte Cristallo, the Marmarole group, Monte Sorapiss and the Tofanes. To the south are Monte Pelmo and Monte Civetta. Facilities for both downhill and cross-country skiing are first class and the small town's population swells dramatically during the ski season, as the rich and famous pour in. The town is also busy during the summer months, since the area offers great possibilities for trekking and climbing, with well-marked trails and numerous rifugi.

Information

The main APT office (☎ 32 31) is at Piazzetta San Francesco 8, in the town centre. It has information on accommodation, ski facilities and hiking trails. It can also provide a full listing of apartments and rooms for rent. There is a small information office at Piazza Roma 1.

Cortina's Gruppo Guide Alpine (☎ 47 40 or 86 85 05), based at Piazzetta San Francesco 5 in summer, is open from 8 am to midday and 4 to 8 pm. Apart from the usual rock-climbing courses and guided treks for adults, the guides also offer a range of courses and hikes for children.

Cortina's telephone code is ☎ 0436.

Activities

Apart from the three day trek through Fanes-Sennes-Braies detailed in the Trekking in the Dolomiti section, the Dolomiti around Cortina offer a network of spectacular trails. A series of three cable cars (L84,000 return) will take you from Cortina up to the Tofana di Mezzo (3243m) in summer only, from where all the trails are difficult and incorporate vie ferrate, for which you will need to be properly equipped. Note that the cable cars were out of action in the summer of 1997 but should be running again in 1998. You can link up with the Alta Via No 1 either at the Passo Falzarego, or at the evocative Passo Giau, with the spiky Croda da Lago to the east and the Cinque Torri to the north-west. To get to the Passo Giau, catch a bus from Cortina to Pocol and then hitch a ride.

Another possibility is to take the local bus from Cortina east to Passo Tre Croci (1805m) and take trail No 215 (which is a section of Alta Via No 3) up to the Rifugio A Vandelli (1928m) in the heart of the Sorapiss group. From here the Alta Via No 3 continues up to 2316m and then to the left, as trail No 242. This section incorporates a section of vie ferrate, as does trail No 215, which heads off to the right.

Not far from Cortina, and accessible by Dolomiti Bus in summer, are the Tre Cime di Lavaredo, one of the most famous climbing locations in the world and also a panoramic place to walk. The fact that you can arrive by bus literally at the foot of the Tre Cime means the area is crawling with tourists in the high season.

A Family Walk from Rifugio Ra Stua to Forcella Lerosa This is a good walk for families because the climb is not too steep, is fairly short – around four hours up and back, including a picnic stop – and there are lots of animals and birds along the way. The area is easily accessible from either the Val Pusteria or Cortina, by car or public transport – from Cortina or Dobbiaco take the SS51.

Arriving from Cortina, take the small road to the left at the first switchback – if you are approaching from Dobbiaco it is the first switchback after Passo Cimabanche. During summer, from mid-June to mid-September, the road up to Ra Stua is closed to normal traffic. You can walk the 2km to 3km from the car park (1420m) to Ra Stua (1670m), or use the reasonably priced minibus service which operates in summer from Albergo Fiàmes, a few km north of Cortina, to the Rifugio Ra Stua.

Use the Tabacco 1:25,000 map for Cortina d'Ampezzo e Dolomiti Ampezzane.

If you decide to walk, take the track that heads uphill from the eastern side of the switchback and follows the slope of the Croda de R'Ancona. The track doesn't have a number but is marked on the map.

Rifugio Ra Stua is at the beginning of the Val Salata, a lovely Alpine environment and perfect for a family walk. Before heading off for a walk in the valley, make sure you let the people running the rifugio know where you are going and check on the departure time of the last minibus.

More serious trekkers can walk to the end of the Val Salata, ascend to the Lago di Sennes (2116m) and pick up the walk through the Parco Naturale Fanes-Sennes-Braies which is detailed earlier in this chapter. However, for our walk, head along the Val Salata for about 150m and take the dirt road to your right, which ascends for about 250m, then turn right to take track No 8. Another 250m ahead the track forks – follow the track to the right: it is longer, but much easier and more scenic. There is a series of switchbacks winding uphill past ancient fir trees and at certain points there are panoramic views across the Fanes high plain. Always keep to the left. You will reach a small valley where, if you approach quietly, you might see the resident marmots, chamois and squirrels. Follow trail No 8 around the valley. In front of you now is the majestic Croda Rossa (3146m), one of the most beautiful peaks in the Dolomiti. The trail will bring you to a wide valley, near the pass, Forcella Lerosa (2020m). There's a little wooden house and a water fountain.

One option is to turn right, still following No 8, to reach the pass. Take the dirt road to the right (still No 8). After a picturesque walk of roughly 4km you will reach the SS51, closer to Dobbiaco and just before Passo Cimabanche.

Alternatively you can turn left at the wooden house and follow the trail back down to Ra Stua. This route is much shorter but less attractive than the ascent – so, there is always the option to return the way you came.

Back at the Rifugio Ra Stua, try the fantastic hot chocolate topped with fresh cream.

Places to Stay

The *International Camping Olympia* (☎ 50 57) is a few km north of Cortina at Fiames and is open all year. There are no budget hotels in Cortina. *Pension Fiames* (☎ 23 66), Via Fiames 13, is about as cheap and basic as it gets, with rooms ranging up to L110,000 for a double in the high season. *Pension Montana* (☎ 33 66), Corso Italia 94, goes up to L150,000 with breakfast. *Albergo Cavallino* (☎ 26 14), Corso Italia 142, is in the heart of the town and charges up to L90,000 per person, with breakfast.

Places to Eat

There are numerous good eating places in and around Cortina, though many are very expensive. The Standa supermarket in Via Franchetti is a good place to shop if you have access to a kitchen. For a good pizza, head for *Il Ponte*, Via Franchetti 8. The *Ristorante Croda Café*, Corso Italia 186, has reasonably priced meals. *El Zoco*, Via Cademai 18, specialises in grills – don't expect much change from L40,000.

Getting There & Away

Cortina's bus station is in Via Marconi. SAD buses connect Cortina with Dobbiaco, where you can change for Brunico and Bolzano. Dolomiti Bus travels to Belluno, Pocol and Passo Falzarego. There are also bus services to Venezia and Padua (ATVO), Bologna and Milano (Zani), and Firenze and Roma (a combination of Lazzi and SITA). Local services connect the town with the camping ground at Fiames, and Pocol (from where you can hitch to Passo Giau).

As mentioned in the walk to Ra Stua, a minibus service connects Fiames to the Malga Ra Stua daily from 8 am to 6 pm from mid-July to mid-September. A special service for mountain bikers and their bikes also operates from Fiames to various locations. Phone ☎ 86 70 88 for information.

VAL PUSTERIA & DOLOMITI DI SESTO

On the northern edge of the Dolomiti, this valley (Pustertal) is bordered by the magnificent Parco Naturale Fanes-Sennes-Braies and, farther north, by the Parco Naturale delle Dolomiti di Sesto, which includes some of the area's most famous peaks – among them the Tre Cime di Lavaredo. The valley is easily reached from the Val Badia (Gadertal) and Cortina d'Ampezzo along the spectacular Valle di Landro (Höhlensteintal). Its main town is Brunico (Bruneck), a pleasant market town with excellent transport connections that makes a good base for excursions into Fanes-Sennes-Braies. More picturesque options are San Candido (Innichen) and Sesto (Sexten) at the base of the Dolomiti di Sesto.

Information

The tourist office in Brunico (☎ 55 57 22) is at the bus station in Via Europa. In San Candido, the tourist office (☎ 91 31 49) is in Piazza del Magistrato, and in Sesto the office (☎ 71 03 10) is in the main street, Via Dolomiti. All have plenty of information about ski facilities and walking possibilities and will send out brochures on accommodation etc.

There is an excellent public hospital at Brunico (☎ 58 11 11).

The telephone code for the valley is ☎ 0474.

Activities

Easy to get to from the Val Pusteria is the beautiful Lago di Braies, a perfect spot for a picnic, followed by a leisurely walk around the lake. More serious walkers might like to tackle part of the Alta Via No 1, which starts here. The Fanes-Sennes-Braies park is more easily approached from the Val Badia or from Passo Falzarego.

At the other end of the valley, towards Austria, are the Dolomiti di Sesto, where there are some spectacular trails. Good areas for family walks are the Valle Campo di Dentro (Innerfeldtal), near San Candido, and the Val Fiscalina (Fischleintal), near Sesto. Both valleys are very popular spots for cross-country skiing in winter.

From Val Fiscalina, it is a long, but easy walk along trail No 102 to Rifugio Locatelli (Drei Zinnen-Hütte), from where you will be able to get a great view of the Tre Cime di Lavaredo (Drei Zinnen). You can continue to the Tre Cime along trail No 101 and then down to Rifugio Auronzo (2320m). From there you can catch a Dolomiti Bus down to the Valle di Landro. This is one of the highest rifugi in the Dolomiti that can be reached by road.

All of the trails around the Tre Cime are easy enough for first-time walkers and for families. In fact, in July and August the trails here are more like autostradas; they are literally packed with tourists, since it is possible to get there by car or bus.

If you do want to walk here, don't be fooled by the crowded trails into thinking that you don't need suitable clothing, water etc. Remember you are walking at high altitude and the weather conditions can change dramatically at any time, so always carry a warm jacket and water and wear proper walking shoes.

Another option for serious walkers is to take trail No 103 from the Val Fiscalina up to Rifugio Comici (Zsigmondy-Hütte) and then trail No 101 to Rifugio Pian di Cengia (Büllele-Joch-Hütte) and then to Rifugio Locatelli.

Places to Stay

In Brunico, the *Krone-Corona* (☎ 8 52 67), Via Ragen di Sopra (Oberragen) 8, is in the old town centre. It charges L52,000 per person for B&B in the high season. In San Candido, *Residence Obermüller-Fauster Melchior* (☎ 91 34 12), Via Castello (Burgweg) 8, is in a picturesque position at the back of the town. It has rooms and apartments at reasonable prices, up to L35,000 per person per day. *Villa Waldheim* (☎ 91 31 87), Via Pascolo (Am Erschbann) 1, offers half board for up to L96,000 per person per day.

Getting There & Away

By SAD bus you can reach Brunico and San Candido from Bolzano and Merano, the Val Badia and San Vigilio di Marebbe, the Val Gardena (on the Innsbruck bus) and Cortina. Catch a bus from Brunico or San Candido to Dobbiaco, from where you can catch a bus to the Lago di Braies. To get to the Rifugio Auronzo at the Tre Cime di Lavaredo, catch the Cortina bus from San Candido or Dobbiaco then, from Cortina, catch the bus for Misurina and the Tre Cime.

By train, you can reach the Val Pusteria from Bolzano, via Fortezza (where a change is necessary). By road, the valley is easily accessible from the Val Badia, from Cortina via the Valle di Landro, and from the A22.

The Veneto

Most travellers to the Veneto are so dazzled by Venezia that they neglect the rest of the region. The region certainly deserves lots of time, but yyou should try to set aside extra days to see Giotto's extraordinary frescoes at Padova and to take in an opera at Verona's Roman Arena.

Vicenza, which was the home town of the architect Palladio, is also well worth a stop-over, perhaps on your way to the northern reaches of the Veneto for a visit to Cortina, one of the world's most famous ski resorts, and for some trekking in the eastern Dolomiti.

The region's cuisine is founded on rice and corn. Polenta is fried, served with hearty game stews and included in other main-course dishes across the region. Risotto is cooked with almost everything the country-side and lagoon have to offer, from baby peas to shellfish and game, although a local favourite is risotto flavoured with the ink of *seppia* (cuttlefish).

One of the Veneto's best known contributions to the Italian table is *tiramisù*, a rich dessert of mascarpone cheese, Marsala, sponge and chocolate. The wine list provides some of Italy's most popular wines, including Soave, a fine white that is well known in the USA, the UK and Australia. The light, sparkling Prosecco and Bardolino red wines are also known widely. Of course, the Bellini, a cocktail of Prosecco and fresh peach juice, has come a long way since Giuseppe Cipriani first mixed one at Harry's Bar in Venezia in the 1950s.

Getting around is easy. The A4, which runs between Torino and Venezia, bisects the region and there is an efficient bus and train network which means that few parts are out of reach.

For information on the Veneto region you can call from anywhere in Italy free on ☎ 167-01 41 96. You can also call up http://www.portve.interbusiness.it/wetvenice/wetvenice.html on the Internet.

HIGHLIGHTS

- A gondola ride along the canals – if you can afford it!
- Visiting the Venetian islands of Murano (for the glass) and Burano (for the colours)
- A seafood meal in a Venetian *osteria*, preceded by a Bellini cocktail at aperitif hour
- The unrivalled mosaics in the Basilica di San Marco
- A glass (or two) of *fragolino*, the Veneto's sweet, 'bootleg' strawberry wine
- A little tour of Palladio's neoclassical villas
- Catching an opera at Verona's Arena

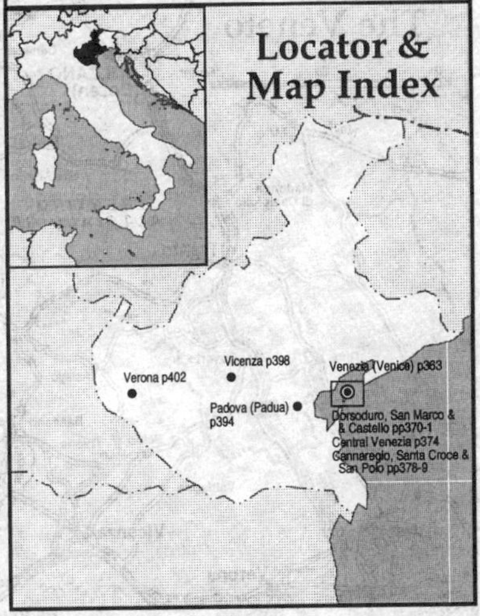

Venezia

Perhaps no other city in the world has inspired the superlatives that have been heaped upon Venezia (Venice) by great writers and travellers through the centuries.

Forget that Venezia is no longer a great

maritime republic and that its buildings are in serious decay and constantly threatened by rising tides. Today, Byron might be reluctant to take his daily swim along the Canal Grande: it is too dirty. But the thoughts of Henry James are as true today as they were a century ago: 'Dear old Venice has lost her complexion, her figure, her reputation, her self-respect; and yet, with it all, has so puzzlingly not lost a shred of her distinction.' 'La Serenissima', the Most Serene Republic, remains a singular phenomenon.

The secret to really seeing and discovering the romance and beauty of Venezia is to *walk*. Parts of Cannaregio, Dorsoduro and Castello are empty of tourists even in the high season. You could become lost for hours in the narrow, winding streets between the Ponte dell'Accademia and the train station, where the signs that point towards San Marco and the Ponte di Rialto never seem to make any sense at all – but what a way to pass the time!

The city's busiest months are between June and September, during Carnevale, which takes place in February, and at Easter, but it is always a good idea to make a hotel booking.

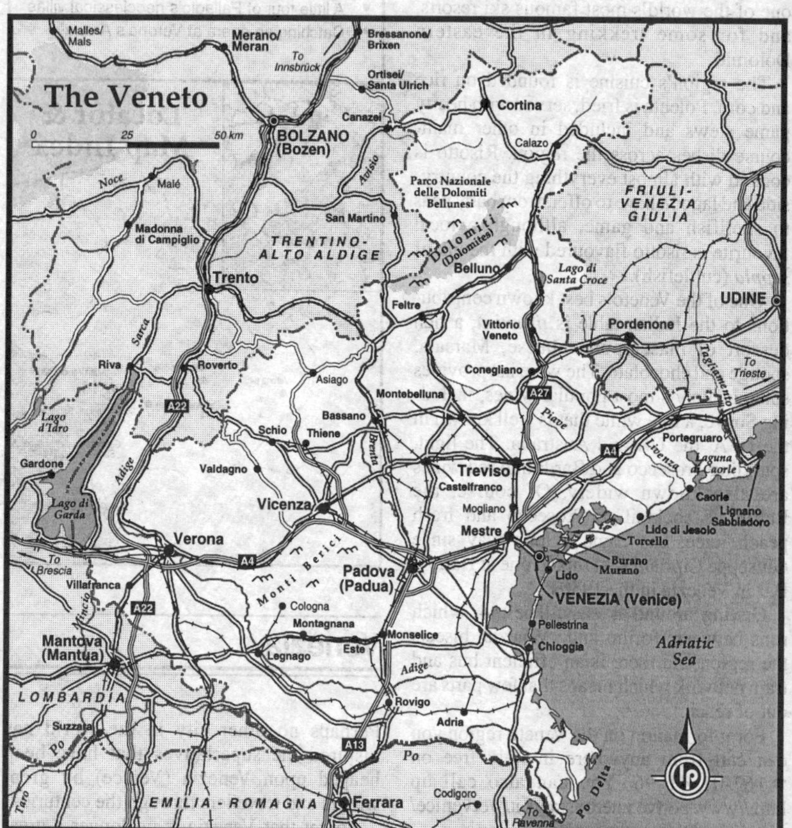

Acque Alte

Venezia can be flooded by high tides during winter. Known as *acque alte*, these occur mainly from November to April and flood low-lying areas of the city such as Piazza San Marco. The serious floods are announced several hours before they reach their high point by 16 sirens throughout the city and islands. In some areas you can see the water rising up over the canal border although most of the water actually bubbles up through drains. The best thing to do is buy a pair of gumboots *(stivali di gomma)*, and continue sightseeing. Raised walkways are set up in Piazza San Marco and other major tourist areas of the city (you can pick up a brochure with a map of the *passerelle* at the tourist office), but the floods usually last only a few hours. If the flood level exceeds 1.20m, then you can be in trouble, as even the walkways are no use at that level.

Venezia's flooding problems are compounded by the fact that the city is actually sinking: it sank by 26cm in the first 80 years of this century. Another major concern is that the waters of the canals are incredibly polluted. Until 20 years ago, the Adriatic Sea's natural tidal currents flushed the lagoons and kept the canals relatively clean. But the dredging of a 14m-deep canal in the 1960s, to allow tankers access to the giant refinery at Marghera, changed the currents. Work is now underway to clean the sludge from the city canals. As though all this were not enough, the salt water – even when clean – is corroding the city's foundations. Alarm bells are ringing – if efforts are not made to counteract the corrosion, the city fathers have warned that canalside buildings could start to collapse.

A project to install three massive floodgates at the main entrances to the lagoon was approved by the Italian government in the 1980s, but so far nothing has been done. The gates would be designed to protect the city from disaster-level floods (around 1.9m: the average incidence of acque alte is around 50cm). As late as October 1994, the Association of Private Committees for the Safeguarding of Venezia reminded the Italian government of its unfulfilled commitment to this project and in late 1996 the rightwing parties of Silvio Berlusconi's Polo della Libertá demanded action to implement the project.

In Venezia itself, opinion on the plan is divided and the local council has stalled on the project. Some environmentalists have attacked the project, but in the 10 years since it was proposed no-one has produced a comprehensive environmental impact study. See the Saving Venezia section for more information. ■

History

The barbarian invasions of the 5th and 6th centuries saw the people from the Roman towns of the Veneto and along the Adriatic coast flee to the marshy islands of the Venetian lagoon.

In the 6th century, the islands began to form a type of federation, with each community electing representatives to a central authority, though its leaders were subject to the Byzantine rulers in Ravenna. Byzantium's hold over Italy grew weaker early in the 8th century and in 726 AD the people of Venezia elected their first doge, a type of magistrate, whose successors would lead the city for more than 1000 years. In 828, Venetian merchants stole the remains of St Mark from Alexandria and brought them triumphantly to the lagoon city. Work began immediately on construction of the Basilica di San Marco to house the apostle's remains.

By late in the 10th century, Venezia had become an important trading city and a great power in the Mediterranean, prospering out of the chaos caused by the First Crusade, launched in 1095. During the 12th century, the city continued to profit from the crusades and at the beginning of the 13th century, under Doge Enrico Dandolo, Venezia led the Fourth Crusade to Constantinople. Venezia not only kept most of the treasures plundered from Constantinople, it also kept most of the territories won during the crusade, consolidating a maritime might that made it the envy of other powers. In 1271, Venetian merchant and explorer Marco Polo set out on his overland trip to China, returning by sea over 20 years later.

During much of the 13th and 14th centuries, the Venetians struggled with Genova for maritime supremacy, a tussle that culminated in Genova's defeat in 1380 during an epic siege at Chioggia. Their maritime power consolidated, the Venetians turned their attentions to dominating the mainland, capturing most of the Veneto and portions of what is now Lombardia and Emilia-Romagna. But the increasing power of the Turks forced the Venetians to deploy forces to protect their interests elsewhere. The fall of Constantinople in 1453 and Morea in 1499 gave the Turks control of access to the Adriatic Sea. The rounding of Africa's Cape of Good Hope in 1498 by the Portuguese explorer Vasco da Gama opened an alternative trade route to the Mediterranean. These events could not fail to adversely affect Venezia, robbing its ports of much of their importance.

But Venezia remained a formidable power. At home, the doges, the Signory and the much-feared judicial Council of Ten, which was responsible for internal security, ruled with an iron fist. The Signory, also known as the Senate, was the main governing council from which the members of all other governing committees were appointed. The doge was the only politician who could sit on all committees. Following a decree of 1297, only citizens whose ancestors had served on the Maggior Consiglio (Great Council) between 1172 and 1297 could serve on any of these committees, an act which virtually ensured that Venezia's aristocracy had a firm hold on power. (For further information on the Great Council see the Palazzo Ducale section in this chapter.)

All Venetians were encouraged to spy for the security of the state, on other Venetians and in every city, port and country where the Venetian Republic had an interest. Acts considered to be against the state were punished swiftly and brutally: no public trial and execution, a body would just turn up on the street as an example to other potentially wayward citizens.

Venezia was remarkably cosmopolitan, its commerce attracting people of all nationalities, races and creeds. Although Venezia limited the commercial and social activities of its Jewish community, which it concentrated in one of Europe's earliest ghettoes, it did nothing to stifle the Jewish religion. Similarly, the Armenians were permitted religious freedom for centuries and given protection during the Inquisition.

The city's wealth was made all the more conspicuous by the luxury goods traded and produced there. Venezia had a monopoly in Europe on the making of what is now known as Murano glass; its merchants had also reintroduced the art of making mosaics, and Venetian artisans made fine silks and lace.

But even as her people wallowed in their well being, Venezia was on the wane. Both the Turks and Roma made gains at the republic's expense during the 16th and 17th centuries, and in 1669 Venezia lost Crete to the Turks after a 25-year battle: its last stronghold in the Mediterranean was gone. Finally, in 1797 the Great Council abolished the constitution and opened the gates to Napoleon, who in turn handed Venezia to the Austrians. Napoleon returned in 1805, incor-

Saving Venezia

Floods, neglect, pollution and many other factors have contributed to the degeneration of Venezia's monuments and artworks. Since 1969, however, a group of private international organisations, in conjunction with UNESCO which adminsters their programme, has been working to repair the damage. The Joint UNESCO-Private Committees Programme for the Safeguarding of Venezia has raised millions of dollars for restoration work in the city: from 1969 to 1992 nearly 80 monuments and more than 800 works of art were restored. During the four years to 1995 alone, the programme funded more than 70 restoration projects, including work on seven of Venezia's churches. Major restoration projects completed include the Chiesa di Madonna dell'Orto, the façade of the Chiesa di San Zulian and the polyptych by Giovanni Bellini in the Basilica di SS Giovanni e Paolo. The funding is provided by 24 private committees representing 12 countries. Apart from restoration works, the programme also funds specialist courses for trainee restorers in Venezia. ■

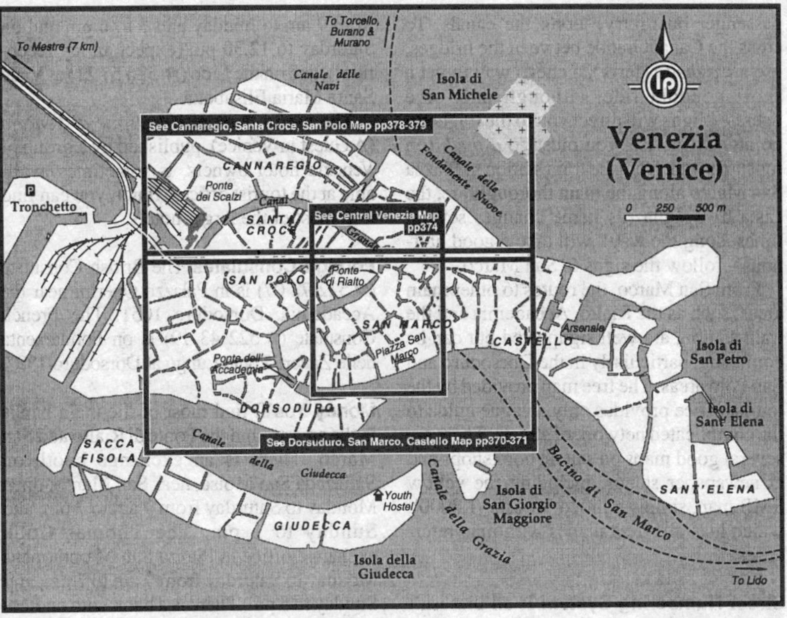

porating the city into his Kingdom of Italy, but it reverted to Austria after his fall. The movement for Italian unification spread quickly through the Veneto and, after several rebellions, the city was united with the Kingdom of Italy in 1866. The city was bombed during WWI but suffered only minor damage during WWII, when most attacks were aimed at the neighbouring industrial regions of Mestre and Marghera.

The city's prestige as a tourist destination grew during the 19th century, just as it was surpassed as a trade port by Trieste. Today, Venezia's permanent population of 75,000 (less than half that of the 1950s) is swollen by up to 25 million visitors every year, the majority of whom are day-trippers. The total population of the Comune di Venezia, including those living on the mainland in Mestre, is around 330,000.

Orientation

Venezia is built on 117 small islands and has some 150 canals and 409 bridges. Only three bridges cross the Canal Grande (Grand Canal): the Rialto, the Accademia and the Scalzi. The city is divided into six quarters *(sestieri)*: Cannaregio, Castello, San Marco, Dorsoduro, San Polo and Santa Croce. A street is called a *calle* (sometimes shortened to *ca')*, *ruga* or *salizzada*; little side streets can be called *caletta* or *ramo*; a street beside a canal is called a *fondamenta*; a canal is a *rio*; and a street which follows the course of a filled-in rio is a *rio terrà*. A quay is a *riva* and where a street passes under a building (something like an extended archway) it is called a *sottoportego*. The only square in Venezia called a piazza is San Marco – all the others are called a *campo*. On maps you will find the following abbreviations: Cpo for Campo, Sal for Salizzada, cl or C for Calle and Fond for Fondamenta.

No cars are permitted on the islands, although ferries transport them to the Lido, and all public transport is by *vaporetto* (small passenger boat/ferry) along the canals. To cross the Canal Grande between the bridges, use a *traghetto* (ferry), a cheap way to get a short gondola ride, although only five operate. Signs will direct you to the traghetto points. Otherwise, you must go *a piedi* (on foot). To walk from the train station to Piazza San Marco along the main thoroughfare, the Lista di Spagna (its name changes several times along the way), will take a good half-hour – follow the signs to San Marco.

From San Marco, the routes to other main areas, such as the Rialto, Accademia and the train station, are well signposted but can be confusing, particularly in the Dorsoduro and San Polo areas. The free map provided by the tourist office provides only a vague guide to the complicated network of streets. There are several good maps on sale in bookshops and at newspaper stands, including the yellow FMB map, simply entitled *Venezia* (L8000), which lists all street names with map references.

Street Numbering System If all that isn't confusing enough, Venezia also has its own style of street numbering. Instead of a system based on individual streets, there is instead a long series of numbers for each *sestiere*. For instance, a hotel might give its address as San Marco 4687, which doesn't help you much. This is really the postal address, so ask the hotel owner for the actual name of the street. As much as possible, we give actual street names plus the sestiere numbers throughout the book.

Information

Tourist Offices Venezia's main APT office (☎ 529 87 27) is in the Palazzetto Selva in the ex-Giardini Reali. From Piazza San Marco, walk to the waterfront and turn right. The office is about 100 metres ahead. The young staff will assist with information on hotels, transport and things to see and do in the city. The office is open Monday to Saturday from 9.30 am to 12.30 pm and 2 to 5 pm (9.40 am to 3.20 pm in winter). There is a smaller office at the train station (☎ 71 90 78), which is open from Monday to Friday from 9 am to midday and 3 to 6 pm and on Saturday to 12.30 pm (expect an icy reception!), and on the Lido (☎ 526 57 21) at Viale Santa Maria Elisabetta.

The useful booklet *Un Ospite di Venezia* (A Guest in Venice), published by a group of Venezia hotel owners, is sometimes available at the tourist offices. If not, you can find it in most of the larger hotels.

Foreign Consulates The British Consulate (☎ 522 72 07) is in Palazzo Querini near the Accademia, Dorsoduro 1051. The French Consulate (☎ 522 43 19) is on Fondamenta delle Zattere Ponte Lungo at Dorsoduro 1397.

Money You'll find most of the main banks in the area around the Ponte di Rialto and San Marco. There is an exchange booth on Salizzada San Moisè, near San Marco, open Monday to Saturday from 9 am to 7 pm, and Sunday to 1 pm. The Thomas Cook exchange office in Piazza San Marco opens Monday to Saturday from 9 am to 7 pm, and Sunday to 5 pm. There is a bank with endless queues at the train station, and an Exact Change booth in the platform area offers good rates and opens daily from 8 am to 10 pm. You'll find another Exact Change booth On Campo San Bartolomeo near the Ponte di Rialto.

The American Express office (☎ 520 08 44) is at Salizzada San Moisè (exit from the western end of Piazza San Marco on to Calle Seconda dell'Ascensione). For American Express card holders there's also an express cash machine. The office is open Monday to Friday from 9 am to 5.30 pm, and Saturday to 12.30 pm. Thomas Cook has two offices, one at Piazza San Marco (☎ 522 47 51) and the other at Riva del Ferro 5126 (☎ 528 72 58), near Ponte di Rialto.

Post & Communications The main post office is at Salizzada del Fontego dei Tedeschi, just near the Ponte di Rialto. It opens Monday to Saturday from 8.15 am to 7 pm. Stamps are available at windows No 11 and 12 in the central courtyard. There is a branch post office at the western end of San

Marco. The address for poste restante mail is 30100 Venezia.

There is a staffed Telecom office next to the post office, open Monday to Friday from 8.30 am to 12.30 pm and 4 to 7 pm. There is also a bank of telephones nearby on Calle del Galiazzo. Other unstaffed offices can be found on Strada Nova on the corner of Corte dei Pali, and just off Campo San Luca.

If you need to send or receive email, try Media Service (☎ 71 78 85), Calle del Megio 1764, in Sestiere San Polo.

The telephone code for Venezia is ☎ 041.

Travel Agencies For budget student travel, contact CTS (☎ 520 56 60), Ca' Foscari 3252, Dorsoduro. Transalpino is near the train station, and CIT (☎ 534 13 88) is at Via Giardino 5 in the Arsenale area.

Bookshops A good selection of English-language guides and books on Venezia is available at Studium, Calle de la Canonica 337a, off Piazza San Marco. San Giorgio, Calle Larga XXII Marzo 2087 (west of San Marco), has a reasonable range of literature in English.

Gay & Lesbian Information Arci Gay NOVE (☎ 72 18 42), Santa Croce 1507, can provide info on meeting-places and entertainment.

Youth Information The InformaGiovani office (☎ 041-534 62 68) at Mestre, Viale Garibaldi 155, can provide information

Venezia in a Nutshell

Uneven alleys turn porticoed corners and end in tiny bridges arched over muddied canals. Others lead nowhere. Still others take you along wider waterways and, often enough, you'll emerge from a lane to behold yet another wonder of Venezia before you – one of its more than 200 churches, or some grand palatial residence. Cheerful *osterie* are tucked away in the most unlikely spots, colourful markets abound and the bustling main streets throng with crowds of locals and visitors window-shopping, parading or simply racing to get from point A to B. Venezia is unique for many reasons but where else in the world can you immerse yourself in such activity without having your ears assaulted by the roar of cars? Instead, here you are carried along by the tramp of feet, the music of human discourse echoing through the narrow streets and canals, the lap of the water and the hum of the vaporetti. You could spend months here and never tire of learning your way through the labyrinth. Give yourself as much time as you can.

The main tourist areas are Piazza San Marco, the Rialto and the streets of souvenir shops which connect the two, as well as the main thoroughfare connecting the train station and San Marco. It is easy to escape the crowds. Head for the tranquil streets and squares of Dorsoduro and San Polo – while the hordes are cramming into the Basilica di San Marco, you will be virtually alone admiring Tintoretto's paintings in the Scuola San Rocco or Titian's masterpieces in the adjacent Frari. If you go to the sestiere of Castello, farther away from San Marco, you'll discover relatively little-visited monuments such as the massive Gothic Chiesa dei SS Giovanni e Paolo. Cannaregio, if you keep away from the main thoroughfare, is really worth exploring.

Before you do anything else, catch the No 1 vaporetto along the Canal Grande, Venezia's main 'street' (see the Canal Grande section for a description of the outstanding grand buildings, or *palazzi*, along the waterway). ■

ranging from assistance for the disabled to courses offered in the city. They have a branch office in the Assessorato alla Gioventù.

Medical Services The Ospedale Civile (☎ 529 45 17) is at Campo SS Giovanni e Paolo. For an ambulance, call ☎ 523 00 00. Current information on all-night pharmacies is listed in *Un Ospite di Venezia*.

Emergency For police emergencies, call ☎ 113. The questura (☎ 523 60 00) is in Mestre. There is a special Carabinieri number for foreigners in trouble – call ☎ 520 47 77.

Lost Property For property lost on trains call ☎ 78 52 38; for property left on vaporetti call ☎ 272 21 79. Otherwise call the municipal government *(comune)* on ☎ 270 82 25.

Rolling Venice Concession Pass If you are aged between 14 and 29, take your passport and a colour photograph to the Assessorato alla Gioventù (☎ 274 76 37), Corte Contarina 1529 (just west of Piazza San Marco), and pick up the Rolling Venice card. It offers significant discounts on food, accommodation, entertainment, public transport, museums and galleries, and costs L5000. The office opens on Monday, Thursday and Friday from 10 am to 1 pm and on Tuesday and Thursday from 3 to 6 pm. You can also pick up the pass at: Associazione Italiana Alberghi per la Gioventù (☎ 520 44 14), Calle del Castelforte 3103, San Polo; Oltrex Viaggi (☎ 524 28 40), Piazzale Roma 466; and Agenzia Arte e Storia (☎ 524 02 32), Campo della Lana 659, Santa Croce. It is also available at the tourist offices listed earlier from July to September.

Museum Opening Hours Check with the APT for the latest variations on opening days and hours, as exceptions tend to be greater than any perceptible rule.

Special Tickets The comune offers a special ticket for L17,000 that covers entry to the Palazzo Ducale (Doge's Palace), Museo Correr, the Museo Vetrario on Murano, Consorzio Merletti di Burano (lace museum) and the rather minor Museo Mocenigo, dedicated to textiles. The ticket is valid for several months and can be purchased from any of these museums, but is only worth it if you are sure to visit the Palazzo Ducale, Museo Correr and at least one other museum.

Canal Grande

Described by French writer Philippe de Commines in the 15th century as 'the finest street in the world, with the finest houses', the Canal Grande is a little dilapidated these days but still rivals the world's great boulevards. It weaves for 3.5km through the city like a huge, upside-down 'S', with a depth of about 6m and a width ranging from 40m to 100m. Taking a vaporetto is the only way to see the incredible parade of buildings, including more than 100 palazzi, which date from the 12th to the 18th centuries. Board vaporetto No 1 in Piazzale Roma and try to grab a seat on the deck at the back.

Not far past the train station and Canale di Cannaregio (the city's second-largest canal) and just after the Riva di Biasio stop (to the right) is one of the most celebrated Veneto-Byzantine buildings, the **Fondaco dei Turchi**. Once a Turkish warehouse and now the Museo Civico di Storia Naturale (Natural History Museum), it was badly restored in the 19th century. It is recognisable by the three-storey towers on either side of its colonnade.

Continue past the Rio Terrà della Maddalena to the **Palazzo Vendramin Calergi** on the left. Richard Wagner died here in 1883 and it is now a fine Renaissance winter home for the casino. Farther on and to the right, just after the San Stae stop, is the **Ca' Pesaro**, Baldassare Longhena's Baroque masterpiece built between 1679 and 1710. Longhena died worrying about the cost and it was only completed after his death. It houses the Galleria d'Arte Moderna and Museo Orientale.

Shortly after, to the left, is the **Ca' d'Oro** (Golden House), acclaimed as the most

VENETO

beautiful Gothic building in Venezia (see the Cannaregio section below). To the right as the boat turns for the Ponte di Rialto (Rialto Bridge) is the **Pescheria** (fish market) on the Campo della Pescaria, built in 1907. Opposite the fish market is the **Palazzo Michiel dalle Colonne**, with its distinctive colonnade.

On the right, just after the fish market, are the **Fabbriche Nuove di Rialto**, built in 1554 by Jacopo Sansovino as public offices for trade and commerce. Next door is the city's produce market and then the **Fabbriche Vecchie di Rialto**, built in 1522 as a courthouse. Just before the Ponte di Rialto, on the left bank, the **Fondaco dei Tedeschi** was once the most important trading house on the canal and now serves as the main post office. It was rebuilt after a fire in 1505 and frescoes by Titian and Giorgione once adorned its façade.

The stone **Ponte di Rialto** was built in the late 16th century by Antonio da Ponte, who won the commission in a public competition over architects including Palladio. The Renaissance **Palazzo Grimani**, on the left after the bridge and just before the Rio di San Luca, was designed by Sanmicheli. Farther along the same bank, the **Palazzo Corner-Spinelli** was designed in the same period by Mauro Cordussi. On the right, as the canal swings sharply to the left, is the late-Gothic **Ca' Foscari**, commissioned by Doge Francesco Foscari. One of the finest mansions in the city, it is followed on the left by the 18th-century **Palazzo Grassi**. Now owned by Fiat, it is used as a cultural and exhibition centre. Opposite, the massive **Ca' Rezzonico**, designed by Baldassare Longhena, houses the city's collection of 18th-century art.

You are now approaching the last of the canal's three bridges, the wooden **Ponte dell'Accademia**, built in 1930 to replace a metal 19th-century structure. Past it and on the right is the unfinished **Palazzo Venier dei Leoni**, where American heiress Peggy Guggenheim lived until her death in 1979. It is home to her collection of modern art. Two buildings along is the delightful **Palazzo Dario**, built in 1487 and recognisable by the multi-coloured marble façade and its many chimneys.

On the left bank, at the Santa Maria del Giglio stop, is **Palazzo Corner**, an imposing, ivy-covered residence also known as the Ca' Grande and designed in the mid-16th century by Jacopo Sansovino. On the right, before the canal broadens into the expanse facing San Marco, is the magnificent **Basilica di Santa Maria della Salute** by Baldassare Longhena.

San Marco

Piazza San Marco Napoleon thought of Piazza San Marco as the finest drawing room in Europe. Enclosed by the basilica and the arcaded Procuratie Vecchie and Nuove, the square plays host to competing flocks of pigeons and tourists. Stand and wait for the bronze *Mori* to strike the bell of the 15th-century Torre dell'Orologio, which rises above the entrance to the Mercerie, the main thoroughfare from San Marco to the Rialto. Or sit and savour a coffee at Florian or Quadri, 18th-century cafés across from each other on the piazza – expect to pay at least L10,000 for a cappuccino (more if there is music).

Basilica di San Marco The basilica embodies a magnificent blend of architectural and decorative styles, dominated by the Byzantine and ranging through Romanesque to Renaissance.

Venetian merchants stole the body of St Mark the Evangelist from Alexandria, Egypt, in 828 AD and brought it to Venezia for Doge Giustiniano Participazio, who bequeathed a huge sum of money to build a basilica fitting for such an estimable theft. The honourable merchants were doing nothing more than fulfilling a pious portent – for legend had it that an angel once appeared to St Mark and told him he would be laid to rest in Venezia.

The original church was destroyed by fire in 932 and rebuilt, but in 1063 Doge Domenico Contarini decided it was poor in comparison to the splendid Romanesque

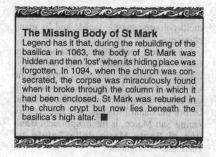

The Missing Body of St Mark

Legend has it that, during the rebuilding of the basilica in 1063, the body of St Mark was hidden and then 'lost' when its hiding place was forgotten. In 1094, when the church was consecrated, the corpse was miraculously found when it broke through the column in which it had been enclosed. St Mark was reburied in the church crypt but now lies beneath the basilica's high altar. ■

churches being raised in mainland cities and had it demolished.

The new basilica, built on the plan of a Greek cross, with five bulbous domes, was modelled on Constantinople's (destroyed) Church of the Twelve Apostles and consecrated in 1094. It was actually built as the doges' private chapel and remained so until it became Venezia's cathedral in 1807.

For more than 500 years, the doges enlarged and embellished the church, adorning it with an incredible array of treasures plundered from the East, in particular Constantinople during the crusades.

The arches above the doorways in the **façade** boast fine mosaics. The one on the left end of the façade, depicting the arrival of St Mark's body in Venezia, was completed in 1270. The three arches of the main doorway are decorated with Romanesque carvings, dating from around 1240.

On the balcony, or *loggia*, above the main door are copies of four gilded bronze horses: the originals, on display inside, were stolen when Constantinople was sacked in 1204, during the Fourth Crusade. Napoleon removed them to Paris in 1797, but they were returned after the fall of the French Empire.

Through the doors is the **narthex**, or vestibule, its domes and arches decorated with mosaics, mainly dating from the 13th century. The oldest mosaics in the basilica, dating from around 1063, are in the niches of the bay in front of the main door from the narthex into the church proper. They feature the Madonna with the Apostles.

The **interior** of the basilica is dazzling: if you can take your eyes off the glitter of the mosaics, take time to admire the 12th-century marble pavement, an infinite variety of geometrical whimsy (it has subsided in places, making the floor uneven).

The lower level of the walls is lined with precious eastern marbles, and above this decoration the extraordinary feast of gilded **mosaics** begins. Work started on the mosaics in the 11th century and continued until well into the 13th century. Later mosaics were added in the 14th and 15th centuries in the baptistry and side chapels and, as late as the 18th century mosaics were being added or restored.

The mosaics include the 12th-century Ascension in the central dome; those on the arch between the central and west domes, dating from the same period and including Christ's Passion, the Kiss of Judas and the Crucifixion; the early 12th-century mosaics of the Pentecost in the west dome; the lunette over the west door depicting Christ between the Virgin and St Mark (13th century); the 13th-century Agony in the Garden on the wall of the right aisle; the 13th-century work in the central dome depicting the miraculous rediscovery of the body of St Mark; the early 12th-century mosaics in the dome of the left transept portraying the life of St John the Evangelist; those in the east dome depicting the Religion of Christ as foretold by the Prophets (12th century); and those between the windows of the apse depicting the four patron saints of Venezia, which are among the earliest mosaics in the basilica.

To the right of the high altar is the entrance to the sanctuary. St Mark's body is contained in a sarcophagus beneath the altar. Behind the altar is one of the basilica's greatest treasures, the exquisite **Pala d'Oro**, a gold, enamel and jewel-encrusted altarpiece made in Constantinople for Doge Pietro Orseolo I in 976. It was enriched and reworked in Constantinople in 1105, enlarged by Venetian goldsmiths in 1209 and again reset in the 14th century. Among the almost 2000 precious stones which adorn it are emeralds, rubies, amethysts, sapphires and pearls.

The **Tesoro** (Treasury), accessible from he right transept, contains most of the booty rom the 1204 raid on Constantinople, ncluding a thorn said to be from the crown vorn by Christ. Admission to the Pala d'Oro s L3000 and L4000 to the Tesoro.

Through a door at the far right end of the arthex is a stairway leading up to the **Galle-ia**, which contains the original gilded ronze horses and the **Loggia dei Cavalli** L3000). The Galleria affords wonderful iews of the church's interior, while the loggia offers equally splendid vistas of the square.

Although the church is open for longer ours, tourists are restricted to visiting Monday to Saturday between 9 am to 5 pm the paying attractions open 45 minutes ater) and Sunday and holidays from 2 to 5 om. The best (but most crowded) times to go re when the mosaics are illuminated: Monday to Friday from 11 am to noon, and am to 5 pm on weekends.

The basilica's 99m-tall **bell tower** is in Piazza San Marco. It was built in the 10th entury but suddenly collapsed on 14 July 1902 and was later rebuilt brick by brick. You can pay L6000 to get to the top. It opens laily from 9.30 am to 5.30 pm.

Procuratie The former residence and offices of the Procurators of St Mark, who were esponsible for the upkeep of the basilica, the **Procuratie Vecchie** were designed by Mauro Codussi and occupy the entire north side of the Piazza San Marco.

On the south side of the piazza are the **Procuratie Nuove**, planned by Jacopo Sansovino and completed by Vincenzo Scamozzi and Baldassare Longhena. Napoleon converted this building into his royal palace and demolished the church of San Geminiano at the western end of the piazza to build the wing commonly known as the Ala Napoleonica, which housed his ballroom.

The Ala Napoleonica is now home to the **Museo Correr** (combined entrance ticket with Palazzo Ducale), dedicated to the art and history of Venezia. The museum also takes in the modest **Museo del Risorgimento**, on the 2nd floor, tracing the fall of the Venetian Republic and Italian unification.

Piazzetta di San Marco Stretching from Piazza San Marco to the waterfront, the piazzetta features two columns bearing statues of the Lion of St Mark and St Theodore, the city's two emblems. Originally a marketplace, the area was also a preferred location for public executions and political meetings.

Palazzo Ducale Not only the doges' official residence, as the name suggests, the Palazzo Ducale was also the seat of the republic's government and housed government officials and the prisons. Established in the 9th century, the building began to assume its present form 500 years later, with the decision to build the massive **Sala del Maggior Consiglio** to house the members of the Great Council, who ranged in number from 1200 to 1700. It was inaugurated in 1419.

The palace's two magnificent Gothic façades in white Istrian stone and pink Verona marble face the water and Piazzetta di San Marco. Much of the building was damaged by fire in 1577, but it was successfully restored by Antonio da Ponte (who designed the Ponte di Rialto).

The main entrance, the 15th-century **Porta della Carta** (Paper Door), to which government decrees were fixed, was carved by Giovanni and Bartolomeo Bon. From the courtyard, the **Scala dei Giganti** (Giants' Staircase) by Antonio Rizzo takes its name from the huge statues of Mars and Neptune, by Sansovino, which flank the landing.

Past Sansovino's **Scala d'Oro** (Golden Staircase) are rooms dedicated to the various doges, including the **Sala delle Quattro Porte** on the 3rd floor, where ambassadors would be kindly requested to patiently await their ducal audience. The room's ceiling was designed by Palladio and the frescoes are by Tintoretto. Off this room is the **Anticollegio**, which features four Tintorettos and the *Rape of Europa* by Veronese. Through here, the ceiling of the splendid **Sala del Collegio** features a series of artworks by Veronese.

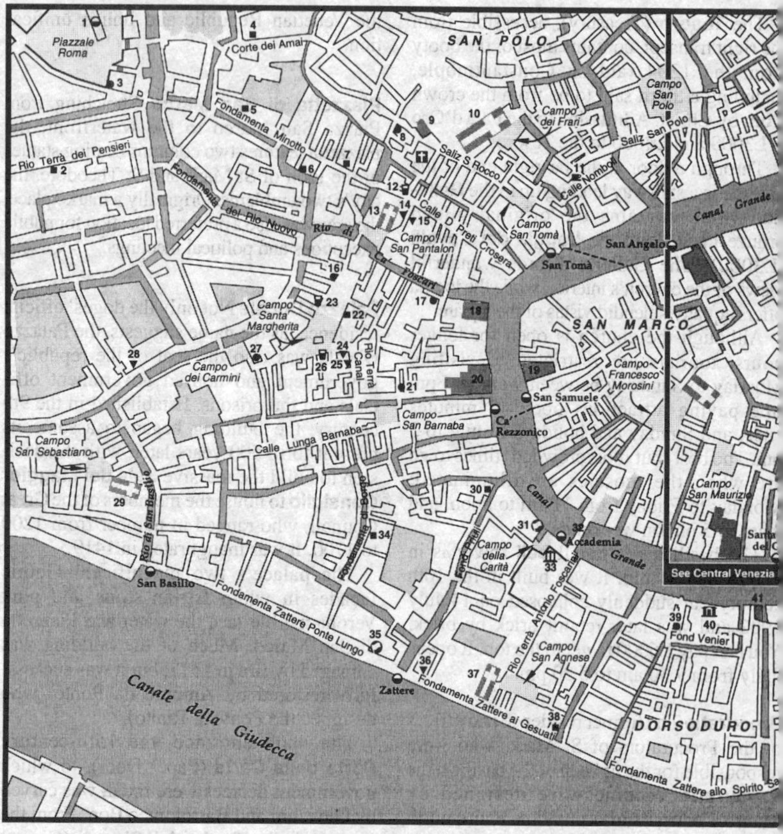

PLACES TO STAY
2 Domus G B Giustinian
4 Hotel al Gallo
5 Locanda Salieri & Brodo di Giuggiole
6 Hotel dalla Mora
7 Albergo Casa Peron
22 Albergo Antico Capon
30 Albergo Accademia Villa Maravege
34 Antica Locanda Montin
38 Pensione Seguso
44 Foresteria Valdese
49 Locanda Il Piave da Mario
51 Albergo Corona
52 Hotel Bridge
54 La Residenza
57 Londra Palace
58 Albergo Paganelli
59 Hotel Doni
61 Danieli

PLACES TO EAT
11 Bar ai Nomboli
14 Crepizza
15 Da Silvio
24 Gelateria il Doge
25 L'Incontro
28 Da Codroma
36 Gelati Nico
45 Osteria al Mascaron
46 Pizzeria da Egidio
53 Trattoria alla Rivetta
60 Al Vecchio Penasa

OTHER
1 Intercity Bus Station
3 Oltrex Viaggi (Rolling Venice)
8 Associazione Italiana Alberghi per la Gioventù
9 Scuola Grande di San Rocco
10 Chiesa di Santa Maria Gloriosa dei Frari

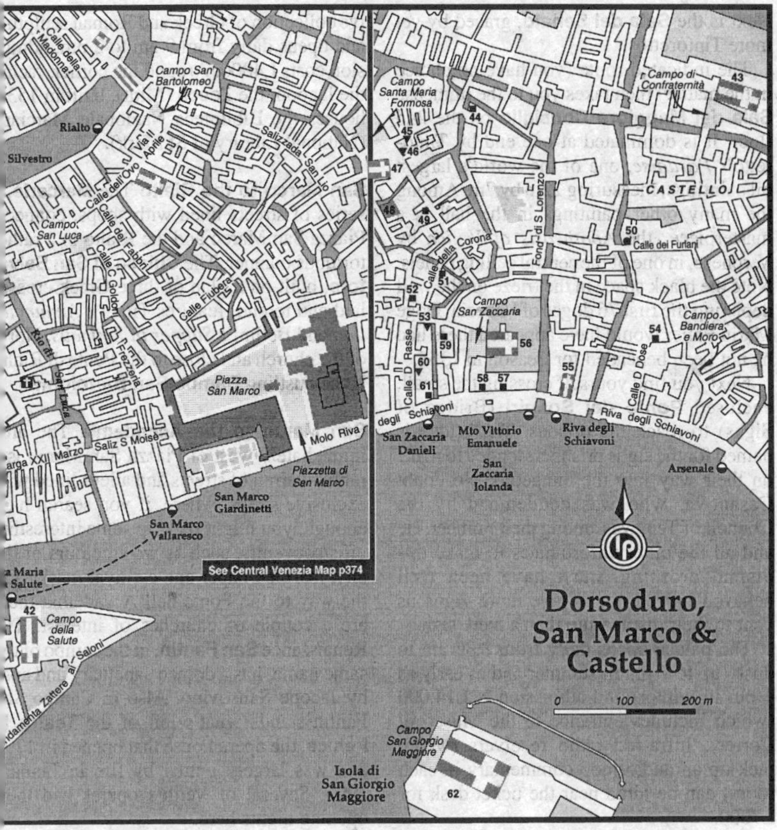

12	Caffè Blue Music	31	British Consulate	43	Chiesa di San Francesco della Vigna
13	Chiesa di San Pantalon	32	Ponte dell'Accademia (Accademia Bridge)	47	Chiesa di Santa Maria Formosa
16	Supermarket	33	Galleria dell'Accademia	48	Palazzo Querini-Stampalia
17	CTS	35	French Consulate	50	Scuola di San Giorgio degli Schiavoni
18	Ca' Foscari	37	Chiesa dei Gesuati	55	Chiesa di Santa Maria della Pietà
19	Palazzo Grassi	39	Il Pavone	56	Chiesa di San Zaccaria
20	Ca' Rezzonico	40	Palazzo Venier dei Leoni & Peggy Guggenheim Collection	62	Chiesa di San Giorgio Maggiore
21	Ca' Macana	41	Palazzo Dario		
23	Il Caffè	42	Basilica di Santa Maria della Salute		
26	Green Pub				
27	Scuola Grande dei Carmini				
29	Chiesa di San Sebastiano				

Next is the **Sala del Senato**, graced by yet more Tintorettos.

The indicated route (you have no choice in the matter) then takes you to the immense **Sala del Maggiore Consiglio** on the 2nd floor. It is dominated at one end by Tintoretto's *Paradise*, one of the world's largest oil paintings, measuring 22m by 7m. Among the many other paintings in the hall is a masterpiece, the *Apotheosis of Venice* by Veronese, in one of the central ceiling panels. Note the black space in the frieze on the wall depicting the first 76 doges of Venezia. Doge Marin Falier would have appeared there had he not been beheaded for treason in 1355.

Next you find yourself crossing the small, enclosed **Ponte dei Sospiri** (Bridge of Sighs) to reach the prisons. The bridge is named for the sighs prisoners tended to make on their way into the dungeons. No doubt Casanova, who was condemned by the Council of Ten, was among their number. He and all the other unfortunates to make this dismal crossing, must have been well behaved indeed not to give more vigorous vent to their displeasure than a mere sigh.

The palace opens daily from 8.30 am to dusk (up to 7 pm in summer and as early as 4 pm in winter) and admission is L14,000 (which includes entrance to the Museo di Correr). Infra-red radio receivers (which pick up an audio-loop commentary in each room) can be hired near the ticket desk for L7000.

Guided tours, known as *itinerari segreti* (secret itineraries) of lesser known areas of the palace, including the original prisons, can be joined. As a rule the tours are conducted in Italian.

Libreria Sansoviniana Described by Palladio as the most sumptuous palace ever built, this building was designed by Jacopo Sansovino in the 16th century. It takes up the entire west side of the Piazzetta di San Marco and houses the **Libreria Marciana** (aka the Libreria Vecchia, or Old Library) and the **Museo Archeologico**. The library can only be visited with special permission (call ☎ 520 87 88). The museum has an impressive collection of Greek and Roman sculptu and opens daily from 9 am to 2 pm; admi sion costs L4000. Around the corner, facir the lagoon, the **Zecca** (Mint), built in 153 houses the Biblioteca Nazionale Marciar (National Library of St Mark).

San Marco to the Rialto The **Mercerie,** series of streets lined with shops, connec Piazza San Marco and the Rialto in a rath tortuous manner. The **Chiesa di San Salv tore**, built on a plan of three Greek cross laid end to end, features Titian's *Annunci tion* and Bellini's *Supper in Emmaus*. Nor of the church and close to the Ponte di Rial is the bustling **Campo San Bartolomeo**.

San Marco to the Accademia The are immediately west of Piazza San Marco is rabbit warren of streets and alleys lined wi exclusive shops, where, if you search har enough, you might pick up some interestin gifts/souvenirs, such as watercolours of th city, marbled paper and carnival masks. O the way to the Ponte dell'Accademia the are a couple of churches of interest. Th Renaissance **San Fantin**, in the campo of th same name, has a domed sanctuary and aps by Jacopo Sansovino. Also in Campo Sa Fantin stands what's left of the **Teatro Fenice**, the opera house that opened in 179 and was largely gutted by fire in Januar 1996. Several of Verdi's operas had the opening nights here.

Return to Calle Larga XXII Marzo an turn right for the **Chiesa di Santa Maria de Giglio**, also known as Santa Mari Zobenigo. Its Baroque façade features map of European cities as they were in 167 Proceed to Campo Francesco Morosini (c Campo Santo Stefano) and the Gothi **Chiesa di Santo Stefano**. Of particular not are three paintings by Tintoretto in the sac risty: the *Last Supper*, the *Washing of th Feet* and the *Agony in the Garden*.

Dorsoduro

Galleria dell'Accademia This is a must fo anyone with even a passing interest in ar The former church and convent of Sant

[M]aria della Carità, with additions by Palla[di]o, hosts a collection that follows the [pr]ogression of Venetian art from the 14th to [th]e 18th centuries.

Room 1 contains works by the early 14th-[ce]ntury painter Paolo Veneziano, including [th]e *Coronation of the Virgin*. The main [fe]ature of Room 2, which covers the late 15th [a]nd early 16th centuries, is Carpaccio's altar[p]iece *The 10,000 Martyrs of Mt Ararat*. It [a]lso contains works by Giovanni Bellini. [R]ooms 4 and 5 feature Andrea Mantegna's *[S]t George*, several paintings of the Madonna [a]nd Child by Giovanni Bellini and [G]iorgione's fabulous *La Tempesta*. Rooms 6 [to] 10 contain works of the High Renaissance, [in]cluding Tintoretto and Titian, but one of [th]e highlights is Paolo Veronese's *Christ in [th]e House of Levi* in Room 10. Originally [c]alled *The Last Supper*, the painting's name [w]as changed because the leaders of the [I]nquisition objected to its depiction of char[a]cters such as drunkards and dwarfs. The [r]oom also contains one of Titian's last works, *Pietà*. In Room 13 are a number of works [b]y the 18th-century painter Giambattista [T]iepolo. Giovanni Bellini and Carpaccio [a]ppear again in subsequent rooms and the [c]ollection ends in Room 24 with Titian's [b]eautiful *Presentation of the Virgin*.

The gallery is open Friday to Sunday only [f]rom 10.30 am to 1.30 pm. Entry costs [L]12,000.

[P]eggy Guggenheim Collection Peggy [G]uggenheim called the unfinished Palazzo [V]enier dei Leoni home for 30 years until she [d]ied in 1979. She left behind a collection of [w]orks by her favourite modern artists, repre[s]enting most of the major movements of the [2]0th century. Picasso, de Chirico, Kan[d]insky, Ernst, Chagall, Klee, Mirò, Dalì, [P]ollock, Rothko and Bacon are all repre[s]ented. The collection is open daily, except [T]uesday, from 11 am to 6 pm, and entry costs [L]10,000. Take a wander around the sculpture [g]arden, where Miss Guggenheim and many [o]f her pet dogs are buried.

[S]anta Maria della Salute Dominating the entrance to the Canal Grande, this beautiful church was built in the 17th century in honour of the Virgin Mary, who was believed to have delivered the city from an outbreak of plague that had killed more than a third of the population. Inside Baldassare Longhena's octagonal church, Titian and Tintoretto left their mark in the Great Sacristy. Every year, on 21 November, a procession takes place from Piazza San Marco to the church to give thanks for the city's good health.

The Zattere The Fondamenta delle Zattere runs along the Canale della Giudecca from Punta della Salute to the Stazione Marittima. It is a popular passeggiata location. The main sight is the 18th-century Santa Maria del Rosario, or **Chiesa dei Gesuati**, designed by Giorgio Massari. Tiepolo's ceiling frescoes tell the story of St Dominic. At the end of the Zattere, over Rio di San Basilio, the **Chiesa di San Sebastiano** was the local church of Paolo Veronese, who provided most of the paintings and lies buried in the church.

Ca' Rezzonico This 17th-18th-century mansion, its façade on the Canal Grande, houses the **Museo del Settecento Veneziano**. Designed by Baldassare Longhena and completed by Massari, it was home to several notables over the years, including the poet Robert Browning, who died there. The museum houses a collection of 18th-century art and furniture and is also worth visiting for the views over the Canal Grande and the fine ceiling frescoes by Tiepolo – notably the *Allegory of Merit* in the Throne Room. The museum opens daily, except Friday, from 9 am to 4 pm. Admission costs up to L12,000, depending on what temporary exhibitions are on.

Scuola Grande dei Carmini Tiepolo also had a hand in this 16th-century building, near the church of the same name, just west of Campo Santa Margherita. In the Salone, nine ceiling paintings depict the virtues surrounding the *Virgin in Glory*. It opens Monday to

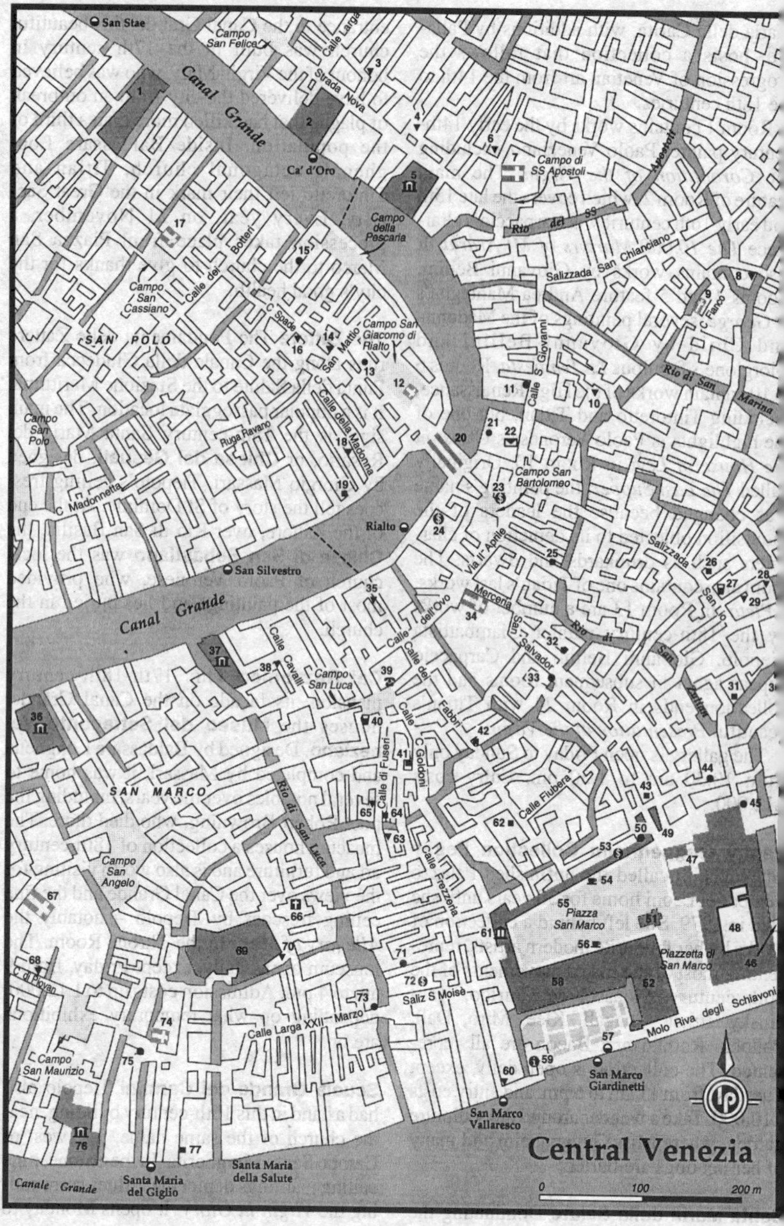
Central Venezia
San Stae
Campo San Felice
Calle Larga
Strada Nova
Canal Grande
Ca' d'Oro
Campo di SS Apostoli
Apostoli
Rio dei SS
Campo della Pescaria
Calle dei Botteri
Salizzada San Chianciano
C Fiarco
Campo San Cassiano
C Spade
Campo San Giacomo di Rialto
C San Mattio
SAN POLO
Rio di San Marina
Calle S Giovanni
Calle della Madonna
Ruga Ravano
Campo San Polo
Campo San Bartolomeo
C Madonnetta
Rialto
Via II' Aprile
Salizzada
San Lio
San Silvestro
Merceria
Calle dell'Ovo
Rio di San Zulian
San Salvador
Calle Cavalli
Campo San Luca
Calle dei Fabbri
Calle di Fuseri
C Goldoni
SAN MARCO
Rio di San Luca
Calle Fiubera
Piazza San Marco
Campo San Angelo
Calle Frezzeria
Piazzetta di San Marco
C di Piovan
Saliz S Moisè
Calle Larga XXII Marzo
Molo Riva degli Schiavoni
Campo San Maurizio
San Marco Giardinetti
San Marco Vallaresco
Santa Maria del Giglio
Santa Maria della Salute
Canale Grande
0
100
200 m

PLACES TO STAY

- 19 Locanda Sturion
- 25 Locanda San Salvador
- 26 Hotel da Bruno
- 30 Locanda Silva
- 31 Hotel Riva
- 32 Pensione Al Gazzettino
- 41 Serenissima
- 42 Al Gambero
- 43 Hotel ai do Mori
- 62 Hotel Noemi
- 64 Locanda Casa Petrarca
- 77 Gritti Palace

PLACES TO EAT

- 3 Osteria dalla Vedova
- 4 Trattoria Enoteca alla Bomba
- 6 Pizzeria Casa Mia
- 8 Osteria da Alberto
- 10 Osteria al Milion
- 14 Cantina do Mori
- 16 Cantina do Spade
- 18 Trattoria alla Madonna
- 28 Cip Ciap
- 29 Osteria alle Testiere
- 35 Antica Carbonera
- 38 Enoteca Il Volto
- 54 Caffè Quadri
- 56 Caffè Florian
- 60 Harry's Bar
- 63 Ristorante da Ivo
- 65 Zorzi
- 68 Pasticceria Marchini
- 70 Vino Vino

OTHER

- 1 Ca' Pesaro
- 2 Ca' d'Oro
- 5 Palazzo Michiel dalle Colonne
- 7 Chiesa dei SS Apostoli
- 9 Chiesa di Santa Maria dei Miracoli
- 11 Grizzo
- 12 Chiesa di San Giacomo di Rialto
- 13 Food Market
- 15 Fish Market
- 17 Chiesa di San Cassiano
- 20 Ponte di Rialto (Rialto Bridge)
- 21 Fondaco dei Tedeschi
- 22 Main Post Office & Telecom Office
- 23 Exact Change
- 24 Thomas Cook
- 27 Nave di Oro Vinaria
- 33 Agenzia Kele & Teo
- 34 Chiesa di San Salvatore
- 36 Palazzo Corner-Spinelli
- 37 Palazzo Grimani
- 39 Telecom Phone Office
- 40 Black Jack Bar
- 44 Veneziartigiana
- 45 Studium (Bookshop)
- 46 Bridge of Sighs (Ponte dei Sospiri)
- 47 Basilica di San Marco
- 48 Palazzo Ducale
- 49 Torre dell'Orologio
- 50 Intras travel agent
- 51 Bell Tower
- 52 Libreria Sansoviniana
- 53 Thomas Cook Exchange Office
- 55 Procuratie Vecchie
- 57 Boat to Airport
- 58 Procuratie Nuove
- 59 Tourist Office
- 61 Museo Correr
- 66 Chiesa di San Fantin
- 67 Chiesa di Santo Stefano
- 69 Teatro la Fenice
- 71 Assessorato alla Gioventù
- 72 American Express
- 73 San Giorgio (Bookshop)
- 74 Chiesa di Santa Maria del Giglio
- 75 Legatoria Piazzesi
- 76 Palazzo Corner (Ca' Grande)

;aturday from 9 am to noon and 3 to 6 pm. \dmission is L5000.

A short walk north of Campo Santa /largherita along Calle della Chiesa and over he bridge will bring you into Campo San 'antalon. In the campo is the **Chiesa di San 'antalon**, with its stark, unfinished façade. .ook inside at the ceiling painting by Gian \ntonio Fumiani depicting events in the life of San Pantaleone. The artist died in a fall rom the scaffolding as he was finishing the painting and is buried in the church.

San Polo

Santa Maria Gloriosa dei Frari One of the highlights of a visit to Venezia, this massive Gothic church is rich in art treasures. It was built for the Franciscans in the 14th and 15th centuries and decorated by an illustrious array of artists. Titian, who is buried in the church, painted the dramatic *Assumption* over the high altar. Another of his masterpieces, the *Madonna di Ca' Pesaro*, hangs above the Pesaro altar (last on the left before the choir). Also of note are the beautiful triptych by Bellini in the apse of the sacristy; the statue of John the Baptist by Donatello in the first chapel to the right of the sanctuary; and a painting of St Mark and other saints by Vivarini, in the second-last chapel to the left of the sanctuary. The church opens Monday to Saturday from 9 am to noon and 2.30 to 6 pm, and on Sunday from 3 to 6 pm. Admission is L2000 (free on Sunday and holidays).

Scuola Grande di San Rocco Built for the Confraternity of St Roch in the 16th century and decorated with more than 50 paintings by Tintoretto, this is one of Venezia's great surprises. Tintoretto won a competition to decorate the school and spent 23 years on the extraordinary series of paintings. The ground floor hall, where you enter, was the last to be painted and features a series on the life of the Virgin Mary, starting on the left wall with the *Annunciation* and ending with the *Assumption* opposite. Up the grand staircase, designed by Scarpagnino, is the main hall. Tintoretto painted Old Testament episodes in the ceiling panels and a remarkable series of New Testament scenes around the walls. Pick up one of the hand-held mirrors so you can study the ceiling paintings without getting a sore neck. The small **Sala dell'Albergo**, off the main hall, contains the cycle's most striking paintings, including the *Glorification of St Roch* in the centre of the ceiling. The *Crucifixion* occupying an entire wall of the room is a masterpiece.

In summer the school is open Monday to Friday from 9 am to 5 pm (in winter from 10 am to 4 pm). Entry costs L8000.

Towards the Rialto Heading for Ponte di Rialto from the Frari, you soon arrive in the vast **Campo San Polo**, the city's largest square after Piazza San Marco. Locals bring their children here to play, so if you are travelling with small kids they might appreciate some social contact, while you take a cappuccino break. The area around the **Ponte di Rialto**, bursting with the life of the daily produce market, was one of the earliest settled locations in Venezia. Rialto, or *rivo alto*, means high bank and the spot was considered one of the safest in the lagoon. There has been a market here for almost 1000 years – the **Fabbriche Vecchie** along the Ruga degli Orefici and the **Fabbriche Nuove**, running along the Canal Grande, were built by Scarpagnino after a fire destroyed the old markets in 1514. Although there has been a bridge at the Rialto since the foundation of the city, the present stone one by Antonio da Ponte was completed in 1592.

Virtually in the middle of the market, off the Ruga degli Orefici, is the **Chiesa di San Giacomo di Rialto**. According to local legend it was founded on 25 March 421, the same day as the city.

Towards the Train Station Tintoretto fa
will want to visit the **Chiesa di Sa
Cassiano** in the campo of the same nam
north-west of the Rialto. The sanctuary
decorated with three of Tintoretto's pain
ings, the *Crucifixion*, the *Resurrection* ar
the *Descent into Limbo*. The Renaissan
Ca' Pesaro, its façade facing the Can
Grande, houses the **Museo d'Arte Moderr**
on the ground floor. Started in 1897, t
collection includes works purchased fro
the Venezia Biennale art festival, held eve
even-numbered year, and is one of the large
collections of modern art in Italy. The galle
was closed at the time of writing. The **Muse
Orientale**, in the same building on the to
floor, features a collection of Asian ar
Eastern oddments.

Continuing north-west past the Chiesa
San Stae is the **Fondaco dei Turchi**, a 12t
century building used as a warehouse b
Turkish merchants and now housing t
Museo Civico di Storia Naturale. If
reopens, take the kids there to see t
impressive 12m-long crocodile. Headin
south, the 13th-century **Chiesa di Sa
Giacomo dell'Orio**, near the square of t
same name, is worth a visit. Of particul
interest is the Old Sacristy, whose walls an
ceilings are decorated with a cycle of pain
ings depicting the *Mystery of the Euchari*
by Palma Giovane.

Cannaregio

The long pedestrian thoroughfare connec
ing the train station and Piazza San Marc
crawls with tourists heading from one to th
other – few venture off it into the peacef
back lanes.

The Carmelite **Chiesa dei Scalzi** (lite
ally 'barefoot') is next to the train statio
and recognisable by the scaffolding coverin
its façade. There are damaged frescoes b
Tiepolo in the vaults of two of the sid
chapels. Along the Lista di Spagna, the othe
wise uninspiring 18th-century **Chiesa
San Geremia** contains the body of St Luc
who was martyred in Siracusa in 304 AI
Her body was stolen by Venetian merchan
from Constantinople in 1204 and moved t

an Geremia after the Palladian church of ınta Lucia was demolished in the 19th ntury to make way for the train station.

hetto Nuovo Most easily accessible from e Fondamenta Pescaria, next to the Canale Cannaregio, through the Sottoportico del hetto, this was the world's original ghetto. he area was once a foundry and it is tempt-g to think that the Venetian word for undry *('getto')* gave rise to what would ecome an unpleasant addition to Europe's ıltural vocabulary. The city's Jews were dered to move to the small island, which ecame known as the Ghetto Nuovo, in 516. They were locked in at night by Chris-an soldiers and forced to follow a set of ıles limiting their social and economic ctivities, but they retained full freedom of ligious expression. Extreme overcrowding ombined with building height restrictions ıeans that some apartment blocks have as any as seven storeys, but with very low eilings. In 1797 Jews were allowed to leave e ghetto to live wherever they chose. The **useo Ebraico** (Jewish Museum) in ampo Ghetto Nuovo opens daily from 10 m to 4 pm, and entry costs L4000. Guided ours of the ghetto and three of its syn-gogues leave from the museum hourly etween 10.30 am and 3.30 pm daily, except aturday, and cost L10,000. Of the 500 or so ews still living in Venezia, only about 30 main in the ghetto.

Cross the iron bridge from the Campo di hetto Nuovo to reach the Fondamenta degli rmesini and turn right. This is a truly peace-ul part of Venezia, almost completely empty f tourists. There are some interesting bars nd a couple of good restaurants along the ondamenta.

adonna dell'Orto This 14th-century hurch was Tintoretto's parish church and ontains many of his works, notably the *Last udgment* and the *Making of the Golden Calf* the choir and the *Vision of the Cross to St eter* and the *Beheading of St Paul*, which lank an *Annunciation* by Palma Giovane in he apse. On the wall at the end of the right aisle is Tintoretto's *Presentation of the Virgin in the Temple*. The artist is buried in the church.

Gesuiti This Jesuit church (its proper name is Santa Maria Assunta) dates from the early 18th century. Its Baroque interior features walls with inlaid marble in imitation of curtains. Titian's *Martydom of St Lawrence* is on the first altar on the left, balanced by Tintoretto's *Assumption* in the north transept.

Santa Maria dei Miracoli This particularly beautiful Renaissance church, designed by Pietro Lombardo, boasts magnificent sculptures. Pietro and Tullio Lombardo executed the carvings on the choir.

SS Apostoli This church, at the eastern end of the Strada Nova, is worth visiting for the 15th-century Cappella Corner by Mauro Codussi, which features a painting of St Lucy by Tiepolo (removed for restoration in 1994).

Ca' d'Oro This magnificent Gothic structure, built in the 15th century, was named Ca' d'Oro (Golden House) for the gilding that originally decorated the sculptural details of the façade. Visible from the Canal Grande, the façade has been covered and under restoration for some years. It houses the **Galleria Franchetti's** impressive collection of bronzes, tapestries and paintings, and opens daily from 9 am to 2 pm. Entry costs L4000.

Castello

Santa Maria Formosa This church is in the middle of one of Venezia's most appealing squares, Campo Santa Maria Formosa, a few minutes north-east of Piazza San Marco. Rebuilt in 1492 by Mauro Cordussi on the site of a 7th-century church, it contains an altarpiece by Palma Giovane depicting St Barbara.

Palazzo Querini-Stampalia This 16th-century palace was donated to the city in 1868 by Count Gerolamo Querini. On its 2nd floor, the **Museo della Fondazione Querini-Stampalia** has a collection of paintings and Venetian furniture. It opens Tuesday

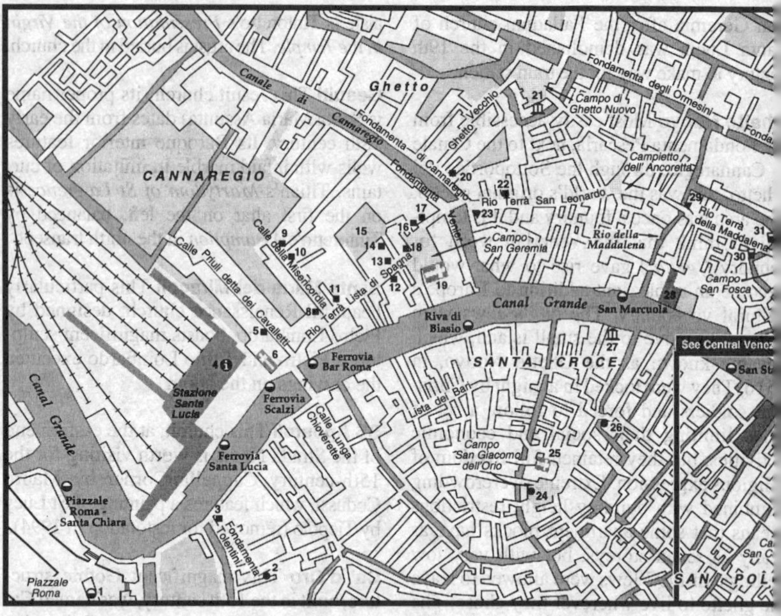

PLACES TO STAY

3 Hotel Canal
5 Hotel Abbazzia
8 Hotel Atlantide
9 Hotel Villa Rosa
10 Hotel Santa Lucia
11 Locanda Antica Casa Carettoni
12 Albergo Adua
13 Hotel Minerva & Nettuno
14 Hotel Rossi
16 Hotel al Gobbo
17 Hotel San Geremia
18 Alloggi Calderan
20 Alloggi Biasin
22 Arcadia

PLACES TO EAT

23 Trattoria alla Palazzina
29 Ristorante al Ponte
32 Paradiso Perduto
34 Ristorante Arabo

OTHER

1 Intercity Bus Station
2 Agenzia Arte e Storia (Rolling Venice)
4 Tourist Office
6 Chiesa dei Scalzi
7 Ponte dei Scalzi (Scalzi Bridge)
15 Park & Playground
19 Chiesa di San Geremia
21 Ghetto Nuovo & Jewish Museum
24 Arci Gay
25 Chiesa di San Giacomo dell'Orio
26 Media Service
27 Fondaco dei Turchi & Museo Civico di Storia Naturale
28 Palazzo Vendramin Calergi
30 Caffè Poggi
31 Wine Bar
33 Chiesa della Madonna dell'Orto
35 Standa Supermarket
36 Gesuiti
37 Hospital
38 Chiesa dei SS Giovanni e Paolo

to Sunday from 10 am to 1 pm and 3 to 6 pm. Admission is L10,000.

SS Giovanni e Paolo This huge Gothic church, founded by the Dominicans, rivals the Franciscans' Frari in size and grandeur. Work started on the church in 1333, but i was not consecrated until 1430. Its vast inte rior is divided simply into a nave and tw aisles, separated by graceful, soaring arches The beautiful stained-glass window in th south transept (the largest in Venezia) wa

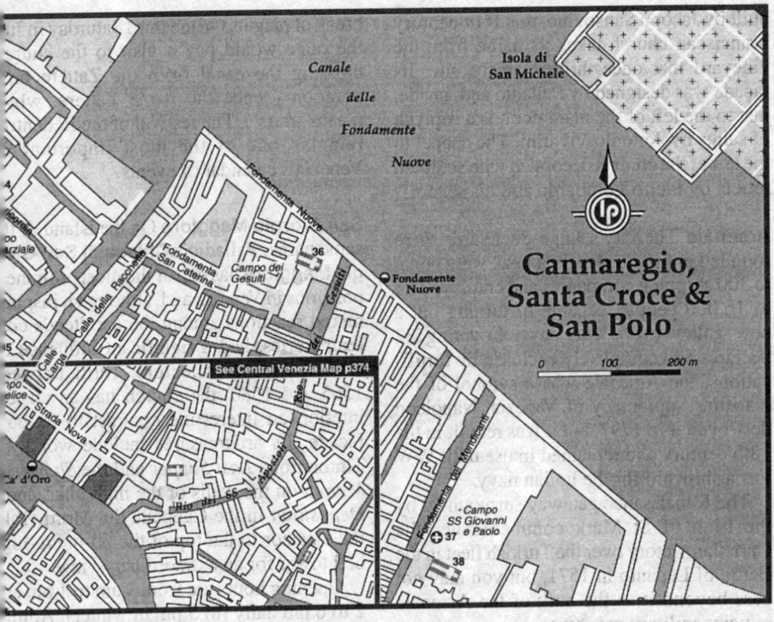

ıade in Murano to designs by Bartolomeo ivarini and Girolomo Mocetto in the 15th ɛntury.

Around the walls, many of the tombs of 5 doges were sculpted by prominent Gothic ıd Renaissance artists. Look out for iovanni Bellini's polyptych of St Vincent ɛrrer over the second altar of the right aisle; ill in its original frame, it also features an *ssumption* and *Pietà*. There are several aintings by Paolo Veronese in the Cappella el Rosario at the end of the north transept, ıcluding ceiling panels and an *Adoration of ıe Shepherds* on the west walls.

an Zaccaria The mix of Gothic and enaissance architectural styles make this 5th-century church interesting. Most of the othic façade is by Antonio Gambello, hile the upper part, in Renaissance style, is y Codussi. On the second altar of the north isle is Giovanni Bellini's *Madonna with aints and an Angel Musician*.

Riva degli Schiavoni This walkway extends along the waterfront from the Palazzo Ducale to the Arsenale at the far south-eastern end of Castello. The exclusive hotels that line it have long been favourites for Venezia's more affluent visitors. About halfway along is Chiesa di Santa Maria della Pietà, known as **La Pietà**, where concerts are held regularly. Vivaldi was concert-master here in the early 18th century. Look for the ceiling fresco by Tiepolo.

Scuola di San Giorgio degli Schiavoni The school was established by Venezia's Slavic community in the 15th century and this building was erected in the 16th century. The walls of the ground floor hall are decorated with a series of superb paintings by Vittore Carpaccio, depicting events in the lives of the three patron saints of Dalmatia: George, Tryphone and Jerome.

San Francesco della Vigna Designed and

built by Jacopo Sansovino, this 16th-century Franciscan church takes its name from the vineyard that once thrived on the site. Its façade was designed by Palladio and, inside, just to the left of the main door, is a triptych of saints by Antonio Vivarini. The chapel to the left of the choir is decorated with sculpted reliefs by Pietro Lombardo and his school.

Arsenale The city's huge dockyards were founded in 1104 and at their peak were home to 300 shipping companies and employed up to 16,000 people, capable of turning out a new galley every 100 days. Covering 32 hectares and completely enclosed by fortifications, the Arsenale was a symbol of the maritime supremacy of Venezia. Napoleon destroyed it in 1797, but it was rebuilt in the 18th century and remained in use until WW I as a shipyard for the Italian navy.

The Renaissance gateway surmounted by the Lion of St Mark commemorates the Christian victory over the Turkish fleet in the Battle of Lepanto in 1571, but you may not pass beyond it as the bulk of the Arsenale remains military property.

The **Museo Storico Navale**, back towards the San Marco Canal on the far side of the Rio dell'Arsenale, covers the republic's maritime history with a huge exhibition of paraphernalia, model boats, costumes and weapons, and is well worth visiting. Among the exhibits are Peggy Guggenheim's gondola, one of the oldest remaining in the city. The museum is open Monday to Saturday from 9 am to 1 pm, and entry is L2000.

At the eastern edge of Venezia, the islands of **San Pietro** and **Sant'Elena** are worth walking through to see how the locals live.

Islands of the Lagoon

Giudecca Originally known as *spinalunga* (long spine) because of its shape, Giudecca's present name probably derives from the Jewish community that lived here in the 13th century. Rich Venetians later built their villas on the island. Its main attraction is the **Redentore** church, built by Palladio in 1577 after the city was saved from a savage outbreak of plague. On the third Saturday in Ju the doge would pay a visit to the churc crossing the canal from the Zattere on pontoon (hence the name Zattere, whic means 'rafts'). The festival of the Redento remains one of the most important c Venezia's calendar of events.

San Giorgio Maggiore On the island of th same name, Palladio's **Chiesa di San Giogio Maggiore** has one of the most promine positions in Venezia and, although it inspire mixed reactions among the architect's cotemporaries, had a significant influence c Renaissance architecture. Built betwee 1565 and 1580, the church has an auste interior, an interesting contrast to its bo façade. Its art treasures include works b Tintoretto: a *Last Supper* and the *Shower* *Manna* on the walls of the high altar, and *Deposition* in the Cappella dei Morti. Tak the elevator to the top of the 60-metre-hig bell tower for an extraordinary view.

Opening hours are from 9 am to 1 pm an 2 to 6 pm daily (to 5 pm in winter). Admission is free, although you are encouraged t make an offering.

San Michele The city's cemetery was estab lished on Isola di San Michele unde Napoleon and is maintained by the Francis cans. The **Chiesa di San Michele in Isola** begun by Codussi in 1469, was among th city's first Renaissance buildings.

Murano The people of Venezia have bee making crystal and glass (the differenc between the two lies in the amount of lea employed) since as early as the 10th centur when the secrets of the art were brought bac from the East by merchants. The industr was moved to the island of Murano in th 13th century. Venezia had a virtual monopo ly on the production of what is now know as Murano glass and the methods of the cra were such a well-guarded secret that it wa considered treason for a glass worker t leave the city. The incredibly elaborat pieces produced by the artisans can rang rom the beautiful to the grotesque – but, as he Italians would say, *i gusti son gusti* (each o his own). Watching the glassworkers in ction is certainly interesting.

The **Museo Vetrario** contains some exqui-ite pieces and is open every day except Vednesday from 10 am to 4 pm. Entry is L8000.

The nearby **Chiesa dei SS Maria e Donato** is a fascinating example of Vene-ian-Byzantine architecture. Founded in the th century and rebuilt 500 years later, the hurch was originally dedicated to the Virgin Mary; it was rededicated to St Donato after is bones were brought there from Cephalonia, along with those of a dragon he upposedly had killed (four of the 'dragon' ones are hung behind the altar). The hurch's magnificent mosaic pavement was aid in the 12th century, and the impressive nosaic of the Virgin Mary in the apse dates rom the same period.

The island can be reached on vaporetto No 12, 13 or 52 from Fondamente Nuove (No 52 also leaves from San Zaccaria and Piazzale Roma).

Burano Famous for its lace industry, Burano s a pretty fishing village, its streets and canals lined with bright, pastel-coloured houses. The **Consorzio Merletti di Burano** s a museum of lace-making and is open Tuesday to Saturday from 9 am to 6 pm, and on Sunday from 10 am to 4 pm (in winter daily but Monday from 10 am to 4 pm). Entry costs L5000. If you plan to buy lace on the sland, choose with care and discretion, as these days much of the cheaper lace is mported from China.

Take vaporetto No 12 from Fondamente Nuove or No 14 from San Zaccaria.

Torcello This delightful little island, with its overgrown main square and sparse, scruffy-looking buildings and monuments, was at its peak from the mid-7th century to the 13th century, when it was the seat of the Bishop of Altinum and home to some 20,000 people. Rivalry with Venezia and a succession of malaria epidemics systematically reduced the island's splendour and its population. Today, fewer than 80 people call the island home.

The island's Veneto-Byzantine cathedral, **Santa Maria Assunta**, shouldn't be missed. Founded in the 7th century, it was Venezia's first cathedral. It was rebuilt early in the 11th century and contains magnificent Byzantine mosaics.

On the west wall of the cathedral is a vast mosaic depicting the Last Judgment, but the cathedral's great treasure is the mosaic of the Madonna in the semi-dome of the apse. Starkly set on a pure gold background, the figure is one of the most stunning works of Byzantine art you will see in Italy. The cathedral opens daily from 10 am to 12.30 pm and 2 to 6.30 pm. Admission is L1500.

The adjacent tiny **Chiesa di Santa Fosca** was founded in the 11th century to house the body of Santa Fosca. Across the square, in the Palazzo del Consiglio, is the **Museo di Torcello**, which tells the history of the island. It opens Tuesday to Sunday from 10 am to 12.30 pm and 2 to 6.30 pm. Entry costs L3000.

Take vaporetto No 12 from Fondamente Nuove or No 14 from San Zaccaria.

The Lido The main draw here is the beach, but the water is heavily polluted and the public areas of the waterfront are unkempt and dirty. Alternatively, you can pay a small fortune (between L20,000 and L80,000) to rent a chair and umbrella in the more easily accessible and cleaner areas of the beach. The Lido forms a land barrier between the lagoon and the Adriatic Sea. For centuries, the doges trekked out here to fulfil Venezia's Marriage to the Sea ceremony by dropping a ring into the shallows, celebrating Venezia's close relationship to the sea. The Lido became a fashionable seaside resort around the turn of this century and its more glorious days are depicted in Thomas Mann's novel *Death in Venice*. The rows of modern apartments and hotels ensure the beaches are crowded, particularly with holidaying Italians and Germans, but the Lido is far from fashionable these days.

The Lido's snappy **Palazzo del Cinema** hosts Venezia's international film festival each September and the **casinò** packs them in during the summer months. Apart from that, there is little to draw you here, unless you are passing through on your way to Chioggia. The Lido can be reached by vaporetto No 1, 6, 11, 52 or 82 and vehicle ferry No 17 from Tronchetto.

Chioggia The second most important city in the lagoon after Venezia, Chioggia lies at the southern end of the lagoon. Invaded and destroyed by the Venetian Republic's maritime rival, Genova, in the late 14th century, the medieval core of modern Chioggia is a crumbly but not uninteresting counterpoint to its more illustrious patron to the north. In no way cute like Murano or Burano, Chioggia is a firmly practical town, its big sea fishing fleet everywhere in evidence. If your time is limited in Venezia, you can live without Chioggia – the trip can take about two hours each way. City bus No 1, 2, 6 or 7 connects Chioggia with the Sottomarina, saving you the 15-minute walk.

A highlight of the trip is the bus ride from the Lido, which takes you along the giant sea wall. Bus No 11 leaves from Gran Viale Santa Maria Elisabetta, outside the tourist office on the Lido; it boards the car ferry at Alberoni and then connects with a steamer at Pellestrina which will take you to Chioggia. Or you can take a bus from Piazzale Roma. The APT (☎ 40 10 68) is on the waterfront at the Sottomarina.

Courses

The Società Dante Alighieri (☎ 528 91 27), Ponte del Purgatorio, Arsenale, offers intensive and longer Italian-language courses from September to June. Monthly courses start at L330,000.

The Cini Foundation (☎ 528 99 00) runs seminars on subjects relating to the city, in particular music and art. Otherwise, try InformaGiovani (see Information earlier) for information on other courses available in Venezia.

Family Activities

The kids will certainly enjoy a trip down the Canal Grande on vaporetto No 1. If you can afford a gondola, at least treat them to a sho trip across the canal on a traghetto. They wi probably also enjoy a trip to the island particularly to see the glass-making demon strations on Murano. Older kids might enjo watching the big ships pass along the Canal della Giudecca, so take them to Gelati Nic on the Fondamenta Zattere, where you ca relax for half an hour or so.

Children of all ages will enjoy watchin the Mori strike the hour on the Law Courts clock tower in Piazza San Marco. In summe you could spend a few hours on the beach a the Lido, stopping for gelati on the way home

There are public gardens at the eastern en of Castello, at the Giardini vaporetto stop There is also a small playground tucked i behind the Lista di Spagna just befor Campo San Geremia.

Organised Tours

A local group organises guided visits to S Mark's Basilica daily from Monday to Sat urday at 11 am. Call ☎ 520 48 88 fo information. Consult *Un Ospite di Venezi* for details of visits to other churches and site in the city. The APT has an updated list o authorised guides, who will take you on a walking tour of the city. The going rate i L164,000 for a three-hour tour for up to 2 people.

Travel agents all over central Venezia car put you onto one of several city tours ranging from guided walks for L23,000 to gondola rides with serenade for L50,000 a person.

Special Events

The major event of the year is Carnevale when Venetians don spectacular masks and costumes for a 10-day street party in the run-up to Ash Wednesday.

The APT publishes a list of annual events including the many religious festivals staged by almost every church in the city. One is held in early July at the Chiesa del Redentore (see the Giudecca Island section), and another at the Basilica di Santa Maria della alute each November (see the Dorsoduro ection).

The city next hosts the Historical Regatta f the Four Ancient Maritime Republics in une 1998. The former maritime republics of enova, Pisa, Venezia and Amalfi take turns host this colourful event. The annual egatta del Redentore, held each July on the anal Grande, is another celebration of the ty's former maritime supremacy.

The Venezia Biennale, a major exhibition f international visual arts, started in 1895 nd has been held every even-numbered year nce early this century. However, the 1992 stival was postponed until 1993 so there ould be a festival on the Biennale's 100th nniversary in 1995. It is held from June to ctober in permanent pavilions in the iardini Pubblici, as well as in other locaons throughout the city. Major art xhibitions are held at the Palazzo Grassi and ou will find smaller exhibitions in various enues around the city throughout the year.

The Venezia International Film Festival, aly's version of Cannes, is organised by the iennale and held annually in September at e Palazzo del Cinema on the Lido.

laces to Stay

will come as no great surprise to hear that enezia is an expensive place to stay, in spite f the huge choice of accommodation. Even the depths of low season, only a handful f one-star pensioni offer singles/doubles ithout private bath for around L45,000/ 8,000. Otherwise, you should be prepared pay an average of more like L60,000/ 0,000 for decent rooms without private athroom. Expect to pay in the vicinity of 150,000 for a quality lower-mid range ouble with private bath. Hotel proprietors re inclined to pad the bill by demanding xtra for a compulsory and generally unsatsfactory breakfast.

Budget travellers have the option of the outh hostel on the Giudecca and a variety f religious institutions, mostly open in ummer only.

Most of the top hotels are around San Marco and along the Canal Grande, but it is possible to find some great bargains tucked away in tiny streets and on side canals in the heart of the city. There are lots of hotels near the train station, but it is a good 30-minute walk to San Marco. The Dorsoduro area is quiet and relatively tourist-free.

It is advisable to book well in advance year-round in Venezia, particularly in September, at Carnevale and on weekends.

The Associazione Veneziana Albergatori has offices at the train station, in Piazzale Roma and at the Tronchetto car park, and will book you a room, but you must leave a small deposit. It opens from 8 am and does not accept reservations. New arrivals at the train station will be descended on by agents for many of the hotels nearby. They are generally legitimate, but check with the APT before booking.

By the time you have this guide in your hands, inflation will have sent prices up, but in Venezia more than elsewhere hotel rates also vary wildly for a range of other reasons. They depend on the season (high season means top dollar), weekend versus weekday rates (the latter are cheaper), position (rooms overlooking canals are generally dearer than others) and, finally, proprietors' whim. The prices that follow should be regarded as an orientation at best – hotel owners in some cases quote different prices for the same rooms in the space of five minutes – we've tried them out! Where possible, plan ahead and shop around. Consider using Padova (see below) as a base, or at least for a day or two while you get oriented in Venezia (it's only 37 km away), and so give yourself time to find and book a place that suits.

Places to Stay – bottom end

Camping There are numerous camping grounds, many with bungalows, at Litorale del Cavallino, the coast along the Adriatic Sea, north-east of the city. The tourist office in San Marco has a full list, but you could try the *Marina di Venezia* (☎ 530 09 55), Via Montello 6, at Punta Sabbioni, which is open from April to the end of September.

Hostels The HI *Ostello Venezia* (☎ 523 82 11) is on Giudecca, at Fondamenta delle Zitelle 86. It's open to members only, although you can buy a card there. B&B is L23,000 and full meals are available for L14,000. Take vaporetto No 82 or 52 from the train station or Piazzale Roma to Zitelle. The hostel is closed between 9.30 am and 1.30 pm. The *Istituto Canossiano* (☎ 522 21 57), nearby at Fondamenta del Piccolo 428, has beds for women only from L18,000 a night. Take vaporetto No 52 to Sant'Eufemia on Giudecca.

The *Foresteria Valdese* (☎ 528 67 97), Castello 5150, is in an old mansion near Campo Santa Maria Formosa. Head east from the square on Calle Lunga, cross the small bridge and the Foresteria is in front of you. It has a couple of dorms with beds for L25,000 per night, with breakfast included (less if you stay for a few nights). A bed in a private room is L32,000, with breakfast included. Book well ahead.

Domus G B Giustinian (☎ 71 06 17), Santa Croce 326a, is near the Rio Terrà dei Pensieri in Dorsoduro, and has beds for L19,000 a night. It opens from July to September only.

Hotels & Pensioni – Cannaregio There is plenty to choose from here, with many hotels a stone's throw from the train station.

Locanda Antica Casa Carettoni (☎ 71 62 31), Lista di Spagna 130, has singles/doubles for L45,000/68,000 and there's no extra charge for use of the communal shower.

Just off the Lista di Spagna, at Calle della Misericordia 358, *Hotel Santa Lucia* (☎ 71 51 80) is in a newish building with rooms for up to L60,000/90,000 without private bath. At No 389, *Hotel Villa Rosa* (☎ 71 65 69) has singles/doubles going for as much as L70,000/90,000 without private bath but including breakfast. *Albergo Adua* (☎ 71 61 84), Lista di Spagna 233a, about 50 metres past Casa Carettoni, is a real find. Singles/doubles are around L50,000/70,000. The *Hotel Minerva & Nettuno* (☎ 71 59 68), Lista di Spagna 230, has rooms for L59,000/85,000, or L77,000/125,000 with privat bathroom. Breakfast is included.

The *Hotel Rossi* (☎ 71 51 64) is also nea the train station, in the tiny Calle delle Pro curatie off the Lista di Spagna. It has pleasar singles/doubles starting at L60,000/90,00 including breakfast in low season.

At *Hotel al Gobbo* (☎ 71 50 01), in Camp San Geremia, the compulsory breakfas bumps up the prices. Singles without ow bath are L65,000 and doubles with bath cos L110,000.

Hotel San Geremia (☎ 71 62 45), in th same square, is a friendly establishmen Small singles/doubles are L60,000/90,00(an extra L20,000 with a bathroom. There ar bigger rooms for families and a few room with small balconies (usually heavil booked).

Also in Campo San Geremia is *Allogg Calderan* (☎ 71 53 61), with small but clea singles/doubles without private bath hover ing around L40,000/65,000 in the low seasor Triples and quads cost L90,000/ 120,000.

The *Hotel Marte* (☎ 71 63 51), Fonda menta Venier, has rooms which start fron L60,000/80,000. *Alloggi Biasin* (☎ 71 7 31), Fondamenta di Cannaregio 1252, acros the Ponte delle Guglie, is run by the sam people for the same price.

Hotels & Pensioni – San Marco Althoug the most heavily touristed part of Venezia Sestiere San Marco offers some surprisingl good quality budget pensioni.

Just off Piazza San Marco is *Hotel ai d Mori* (☎ 520 48 17), Calle Larga 658. It ha pleasant rooms, some with views of th basilica and one even has a terrace. The mos expensive double goes for L115,000, with variety of descending prices for other rooms

Al Gambero (☎ 522 43 84), Calle de Fabbri 4685, is in a great location off Piazz San Marco, and has been recommended b readers. Singles/doubles are L61,000/ 100,00 including breakfast. Book well in advance.

Hotel Noemi (☎ 523 81 44), Calle de Fabbri 909, has basic singles/doubles fo L55,000/75,000 and a triple for L93,000. T get to these hotels from Piazza San Marco

DAMIEN SIMONIS

DAMIEN SIMONIS

DAMIEN SIMONIS

DAMIEN SIMONIS

Church Detail
Top Left: Detail of the Abbazia di Pomposa, Emilia-Romagna
Top Right: Detail of the Chiesa di San Michele, Ruvo di Puglia, Puglia
Bottom Left: Detail of the duomo, Galleria di Vittorio Emanuele II, Milano, Lombardia
Bottom Right: Detail from the doors of the Basilica di San Marco, Venezia, the Veneto

SHOOT

SHOOT

Top & Bottom: The Dolomiti, Trentino-Alto Adige

take the sottoportego next to Caffè Quadri and then turn left into Calle dei Fabbri.

One of the nicest places to stay in this area is *Locanda Casa Petrarca* (☎ 520 04 30), San Marco 4386, with singles/doubles for L75,000/85,000. Extra beds in a room cost an additional 35%, and doubles with a bathroom cost L110,000. The friendly owner speaks English. To get there, find Campo San Luca, follow Calle dei Fuseri, take the second left and then turn right into Calle Schiavone. The *Locanda San Salvador* (☎ 528 91 47), San Marco 5264, charges about the same. It is just off Campo San Bartolomeo in Calle del Galiazzo.

Pensione Al Gazzettino (☎ 528 65 23), San Marco 4971, is not a bad deal offering singles/doubles, all with private bath, for up to L80,000/150,000.

Hotels & Pensioni – Castello This area to the east of San Marco, although close to the piazza, is less heavily touristed. From the train station catch vaporetto No 1 and get off at San Zaccaria.

A stone's throw east of San Marco is a delightful little establishment, *Hotel Doni* (☎ 522 42 67), Fondamenta del Vin, off Salizzada San Provolo. It has clean, quiet rooms for L65,000/95,000 with breakfast included. *Hotel Bridge* (☎ 520 52 87), just off Campo SS Filippo e Giacomo in Calle Rimpeto la Sacrestia, has doubles/triples for L90,000/120,000 with breakfast. *Albergo Corona* (☎ 522 91 74), north-east of Campo SS Filippo e Giacomo at Calle Corona 4464, has simple singles/doubles from L45,000/62,000 and triples from L85,000. An electric baggage carrier whisks luggage up the four flights. *Locanda Il Piave da Mario* (☎ 528 51 74) is just off Campo Santa Maria Formosa at Ruga Giuffa 4838/40. Singles/doubles are L75,000/110,000 with breakfast. *Locanda Silva* (☎ 522 76 43), Fondamenta del Rimedio 4423, south of Campo Santa Maria Formosa towards San Marco, has pleasant, simple singles/doubles without private bath for L55,000/85,000, and doubles with bath for L125,000.

Hotels & Pensioni – Dorsoduro, San Polo & Santa Croce *Hotel al Gallo* (☎ 523 67 61) on Calle Amai, just off Campo Tolentini in the Santa Croce area, is a couple of minutes walk from Piazzale Roma. Singles/doubles start at L60,000/95,000, and all have showers. *Locanda Salieri* (☎ 71 00 35), Fondamenta Minotto 160, just south of the Al Gallo, has singles/doubles from L65,000/95,000, breakfast included. Heading east, Fondamenta Minotto becomes Salizzada San Pantalon. At No 84 is the *Albergo Casa Peron* (☎ 528 60 38), which has rooms for L65,000/90,000, with own shower and breakfast but the loo's in the corridor.

Hotel dalla Mora (☎ 523 5703) is on a small canal just off Salizzada San Pantalon, near the Casa Peron. It has clean, airy rooms, some with canal views, and there is a terrace. Singles/doubles are L70,000/130,000 with private bathroom. Bookings are a must. The *Albergo Antico Capon* (☎ 528 52 92) on the lovely Campo Santa Margherita has a variety of rooms for anything up to L130,000. Ezra Pound favoured the *Antica Locanda Montin* (☎ 522 71 51), Fondamenta di Borgo, in Dorsoduro. It is small and comfortable, with rooms for L50,000/85,000, and has a popular if pricey restaurant.

Hotels & Pensioni – Lido *Pensione La Pergola* (☎ 526 07 84), Via Cipro 15 (just north off Gran Viale Santa Maria Elisabetta), has a range of rooms. Singles/doubles with bathroom cost L57,000/110,000 in peak season, and as little as half in the off season.

Hotels & Pensioni – Mestre Only 15 minutes away on the regular bus Nos 7 and 2 (the latter passes Mestre train station) or by train, Mestre is an economical, if drab, alternative to staying in Venezia. There are a number of good hotels, as well as plenty of cafés and places to eat around the main square. *Albergo Roberta* (☎ 92 93 55), near the train station at Via Sernaglia 21, has good-sized, clean rooms for L60,000/100,000. The *Giovannina* (☎ 92 63 96), Via Dante 113, has singles/doubles for L45,000/65,000.

Places to Stay – middle

Cannaregio The *Hotel Atlantide* (☎ 71 69 01), Calle della Misericordia 375a, has singles/doubles with bathroom for L100,000/140,000 (add L50,000 apiece in high season).

San Marco The *Serenissima* (☎ 520 00 11), Calle Goldoni 4486, is tucked away in the area between San Marco and the Ponte di Rialto. Singles/doubles are L107,000/138,000 or up to L145,000/198,000 with bathroom.

Castello *Hotel Riva* (☎ 522 70 34), Ponte dell'Angelo 5310, is on a lovely side canal. Singles/doubles with breakfast and private bathroom are L100,000/130,000. The location is nice, but there have been unflattering reports from readers about the reception. *Hotel da Bruno* (☎ 523 04 52), Salizzada San Lio 5726, just west of Campo Santa Maria Formosa, has singles/doubles from L150,000/190,000, including breakfast and showers.

An excellent deal, considering the prices of the other hotels along the waterfront, is the *Albergo Paganelli* (☎ 522 43 24), Riva degli Schiavoni 4182. Singles/doubles here are L130,000/190,000 at the most – with bathroom and breakfast. At that price you get canal views. *La Residenza* (☎ 528 53 15), Campo Bandiera e Moro, is in a 14th-century mansion and has delightful singles/doubles for L130,000/200,000. It's closed for much of the winter.

Dorsoduro, San Polo & Santa Croce Although this area is not the most picturesque in Venezia, the *Hotel Canal* (☎ 523 84 80), Fondamenta dei Tolentini, is a few minutes walk from Piazzale Roma and overlooks the Canal Grande. Singles/doubles with a bathroom, TV, phone and breakfast cost L90,000/120,000 in low season, ranging up to L150,000/180,000 in high season. In Dorsoduro, the *Albergo Accademia Villa Maravege* (☎ 521 01 88) on Fondamenta Bollani is set in lovely gardens, with views of the Canal Grande. This popular hotel has singles/doubles for up to L145,000/225,000.

The *Locanda Sturion* (☎ 523 62 43), Calle Sturion 679, is two minutes from the Ponte di Rialto. It has been a hotel on and off since the 13th century and has superb rooms starting at L100,000/150,000 in low season.

The *Pensione Seguso* (☎ 528 68 58), Fondamenta delle Zattere 779, is in a lovely quiet position facing the Giudecca Canal. Singles/doubles cost up to L140,000/190,000 with a bathroom and breakfast. Book ahead.

Mestre The three-star *Tritone* (☎ 93 09 55), Viale Stazione 16, has singles/doubles costing up to L140,000/200,000.

Places to Stay – top end

Cannaregio The *Hotel Abbazzia* (☎ 71 73 33) is in a restored abbey in Calle detta dei Cavalletti Priuli 68, a one-minute walk from the train station. Many of the lovely rooms face on to a central garden. Singles/doubles cost up to L200,000/260,000, with a bathroom and breakfast. Prices drop considerably out of season.

San Marco The luxury *Gritti Palace* (☎ 79 46 11; fax 520 09 42) is one of the most famous hotels in Venezia – its façade fronts onto the Canal Grande. If you can afford to pay up to L870,000 a double, you'll be mixing with royalty.

Castello Some of the city's finest hotels are on the Riva degli Schiavoni. The four-star *Londra Palace* (☎ 520 05 33; fax 522 50 32) has singles/doubles for up to L390,000/620,000 and most rooms have views over the water. The luxury-class *Danieli* (☎ 522 64 80; fax 520 02 08) nearby has rooms for up to L450,000/660,000, and most of them look out over the canal.

Giudecca The *Cipriani* (☎ 520 77 44; fax 520 39 30) is set in lavish grounds on Giudecca, with unbeatable views across to San Marco. In high season you will need to hand over up to L1,350,000 for a double oom. Prices drop by almost half in the low eason. Take the hotel's private boat from an Marco.

laces to Eat

f you've enjoyed the fine cooking of oscana and Emilia-Romagna and the basic down home' style of a Roman meal, you night find the fare in Venezia a bit disapointing. Search out the little trattorie tucked way in the side streets and squares, since nost of the restaurants around San Marco nd near the train station are tourist traps. Read the fine print if you want to eat seafood, s most fish is sold by weight. When considring a set price menu, make sure you know whether or not all service charges are ncluded – often they are not.

Many bars serve filling snacks with lunchime and pre-dinner drinks. Most also have a wide range of Venetian panini, with every maginable filling. *Tramezzi* (sandwich triangles) and huge bread rolls cost from L1500 o L5000 if you eat them standing up. A heaper alternative can be the many *bacari*, lso known as osterie. These are small bars erving local wines by the glass *(cichetti)* and nacks.

egional Cuisine The staples of Veneto uisine are rice and beans. Try *risi e bisi* risotto with peas) or *risotto nero*, coloured nd flavoured with the ink of cuttlefish seppia). Seafood is popular (but also expenive). Try *zuppa di pesce* (fish soup) or eppia with polenta. And don't miss a risotto r pasta dish with *radicchio trevisano* (red hicory). Tiramisù, the rich mascarpone lessert, is a favourite here.

estaurants, Trattorie & Pizzerie Better reas to look for places to eat include the ack streets of Cannaregio and San Polo, as vell as around Campo Santa Margherita in Dorsoduro.

Cannaregio It is best to head for the side treets to look for little trattorie and pizzerie, ut there are a couple of OK spots on the nain thoroughfare. *Trattoria alla Palazzina*, Cannaregio 1509, serves good pizza for L8000 to L10,000 and memorable homemade desserts. For a cheap set lunch at L16,000 (including service charge!), make for *Ristorante al Ponte*, Rio Terrà della Maddalena 2352.

On Fondamenta della Misericordia locals crowd into several trattorie and bars. Young people will enjoy *Paradiso Perduto*, at No 2539, a restaurant/bar with live music and tables outside in summer. For a Middle Eastern touch, try *Ristorante Arabo* at No 2520. *Trattoria Enoteca alla Bomba*, Calle de l'Oca, parallel to Strada Nova near Campo SS Apostoli, is a reasonably priced place – the set menu costs L24,000. A bit farther along is *Pizzeria Casa Mia*, which has pizzas and pasta for around L10,000 and main courses for around L18,000.

Around San Marco In Calle Bembo, the continuation of Calle dei Fabbri, *Antica Carbonera* is a small trattoria catering for the locals. Pasta starts at around L8000.

Noemi, beneath the hotel of the same name on Calle dei Fabbri, offers excellent food at reasonable prices. Pasta starts at L10,000 and main courses are from L15,000.

On Calle dei Fuseri, off Campo San Luca, is *Zorzi*, a vegetarian restaurant with main courses from L10,000. It also serves sandwiches and snacks. Farther along the same street beside a small canal at San Marco 1809, *Ristorante da Ivo* specialises in seafood and is recognised as one of Venezia's best restaurants. Consequently it's not cheap: a full seafood meal will cost around L80,000 to L100,000.

Vino Vino, San Marco 2007, is a popular bar/osteria at Ponte Veste near Teatro la Fenice. The menu changes daily and the pre-prepared food is good quality. A pasta or risotto costs L8000, a main dish L15,000, and there is a good selection of vegetables. Wine is sold by the glass for L2000.

Castello The *Trattoria alla Rivetta*, right next to the canal on Salizzada San Provolo, just before Campo San Provolo, serves Venetian dishes. Pasta costs around L9000, and a main dish is around L15,000. Wine is expensive at L11,000 a litre.

Pizzeria da Egidio in Campo Santa Maria Formosa has pizzas from L8000 and you can sit in the piazza. Just west of the campo is *Cip Ciap*, at the Ponte del Mondo Nuovo. It serves fantastic, filling pizza by the slice, as well as calzoni and vegetable pies.

Santa Croce & San Polo This is a great area for small, cheap places to eat. *Brodo di Giuggiole*, Fondamenta Minotto 159, is small and family-run and offers a good-value set-price menu. The *Trattoria alla Madonna*, Calle della Madonna, a few streets west of the Rialto off Fondamenta del Vin, is an excellent trattoria specialising in seafood. Prices are reasonable, but a full meal will cost L60,000 or more.

Crepizza, Calle San Pantalon 3757, serves pasta, pizza and fantastic crêpes for L8000 to L10,000. Across the street at No 3748 is *Da Silvio*, a good-value pizzeria and trattoria with outside tables in a garden setting. A full meal here will cost under L35,000.

Dorsoduro Typical regional fare is served at *L'Incontro*, Rio Terrà Canal 3062, between Campo San Barnaba and Campo Santa Margherita. The menu alters daily and a full meal will cost around L40,000. The restaurant at the *Antica Locanda Montin* hotel, Fondamenta di Borgo near Campo San Barnaba, has generally good food and a shady garden. A full meal is expensive for what you get at around L50,000.

Giudecca *Harry's Dolci*, Fondamenta San Biagio, is run by the Hotel Cipriani and has fantastic desserts. A meal in the restaurant will cost L60,000 or more. There is also a snack bar. *Trattoria al Redentore*, Campo A Giacomo 205b, is a cheaper alternative, where a meal will cost about L35,000.

Lido The *Ristorante All'Isola d'Oro*, Riviera Santa Maria Elisabetta 2, near the vaporetto landing, has average prices. Try the *osteria* next door for cichetti and roast chicken. *Trattoria da Scarso*, Piazzale Malamocca 4, is one of the better restaurants near the beach and offers a L18,000 set menu.

Murano The *Osteria dalla Mora*, Fondamenta Manin 75, looks out over one of the island's canals and is worth considering for lunch or dinner. A meal will cost around L25,000.

Burano The island's pretty, but the restaurant prices are less so. One of the better choices is *Ristorante Galuppi*, Via B Galuppi 470 – look for the dolls in the windows. A meal will cost about L40,000 a person.

Torcello The *Locanda Cipriani* is famous and expensive – expect to shell out L100,000. For something simpler, try *Al Trono di Attila*, Fondamenta Borgognoni 7a (between the ferry stop and the cathedral), where a full meal will cost around L40,000.

Chioggia *Ristorante Vecio Foghero*, Calle Scopici 91, has good pizzas and seafood. *Trattoria al Bersagliere*, Via Cesare Battisti 293, off Corso del Popolo, serves typical Chioggia cuisine. Pasta starts at L6000 and main courses at L10,000.

Mestre There is a *Brek* self-service restaurant at Via Carducci 54, where pasta starts at L5000 and main courses from L7000. *Da Bepi Venesian*, Via Sernaglia 27 (a couple of blocks from the train station), serves traditional dishes and a meal could cost L30,000.

Osterie Venezia's osterie are a cross between bars and trattorie, where you can sample cichetti (small glasses of wine or spirits) while eating finger-food such as stuffed olives and deep-fried vegetables in batter. These are generally washed down with a small glass of wine (*ombra*), and locals often choose to bar hop from osteria to osteria. They are a great way to experience a more down-to-earth side of Venezia.

Some osterie serve full meals. *Osteria al Mascaron*, on Calle Lunga, east of Campo Santa Maria Formosa, is a bar/osteria and trattoria. The cichetti are good, but a meal is overpriced. *Osteria alle Testiere*, on the other side of the campo on Calle del Mondo Nuovo, is another osteria/trattoria. Heading towards Cannaregio is *Osteria al Milion*, in Corta Prima del Milion, just behind the Chiesa di San Giovanni Crisostomo. The bar is popular but, again, the food a little expensive. The *Osteria dalla Vedova* (also called Trattoria Ca d'Or), Calle del Pistor, off Strada Nova in Cannaregio, is one of the oldest osterie in Venezia – the food is excellent and modestly priced – and L35,000 will cover you.

In the San Marco area, near Campo San Luca, *Enoteca Il Volto*, Calle Cavalli 4052, has an excellent wine selection and good snacks. On the San Polo side of the Ponte di Rialto, *Cantina do Mori*, on Sottoportego dei do Mori, offers good evening meals for about L25,000. A few steps away at Calle do Spade 860, the *Cantina do Spade* is Venezia's oldest eating house – L30,000 should see you through dinner. Another hidden Venetian jewel along similar lines is *Osteria da Alberto*, which changed address in early 1996 to Calle Gallina 5401 in Cannaregio. A stylish option well away from the madding crowd is *Da Codroma*, Fondamenta Brianti, Dorsoduro 2540.

Bars, Snacks & Cafés If you can cope with the idea of paying from L10,000 (some lucky people have reported being charged as much as L20,000!) for a cappuccino, spend an hour or so sitting at an outdoor table at Florian or Quadri, enjoying the atmosphere in Piazza San Marco, the world's most famous square. *Caffè Florian* is the most famous of the two – its plush interior has seen the likes of Lord Byron and Henry James taking breakfast (separately) before they crossed the piazza to *Caffè Quadri* for lunch. Both cafés have bars, where you can pay normal prices for a coffee or drink (taken on your feet) and still enjoy the elegant surroundings.

The world-famous *Harry's Bar*, Calle Vallaresso 1323, off Salizzada San Moisè, is on the western edge of Piazza San Marco. The Cipriani family, which started the bar, claims to have invented many Venetian specialities, including the Bellini cocktail. A meal at the restaurant upstairs will cost you at least L100,000, but it is one of the few restaurants in the city to have been awarded a Michelin star.

The *Black Jack Bar*, Campo San Luca, serves a decent Bellini, among other cocktails, for L3500. *Nave di Oro Vinaria*, Calle del Mondo Nuovo 5786b, off Salizzada San Lio, is open from 8 am to 1 pm and 5 to 8 pm and specialises in wines from the Veneto that are sold by the glass or mineral water by the bottle (to take home) served from huge *damigiane*. In the market area at Campo Beccarie is *Vini da Pinto*, a small bar frequented by stall holders. At Calle delle Rasse 4587, between Riva degli Schiavoni and Campo SS Filippo e Giacomo, is *Al Vecchio Penasa*, which offers an excellent selection of sandwiches and snacks at reasonable prices.

You'll find several alternatives for snacks and drinks on Campo Santa Margherita, including the *Green Pub* for a Guinness. *Il Caffè*, on the same square at No 2963, is a lively student bar. The *Bar ai Nomboli*, between Campo San Polo and the Frari, on the corner of Calle dei Nomboli and Rio Terrà dei Nomboli, has a great selection of gourmet sandwiches and tramezzini.

Along the main thoroughfare between the train station and San Marco, numerous bars serve sandwiches and snacks.

Gelaterie & Pasticcerie The best ice cream in Venezia is at *Gelati Nico*, Fondamenta delle Zattere 922. The locals take their evening stroll along the fondamenta while eating their gelati. *Gelateria il Doge*, Campo Santa Margherita, also has excellent gelati. One of Venezia's better cake shops is *Pasticceria Marchini*, just off Campo Santo Stefano, at Calle dello Spezier 2769.

Self-Catering The best *markets* take place on the San Polo side of the Ponte di Rialto. Grocery shops selling salami, cheese and bread are concentrated around nearby *Campo Beccarie*, which happens to lie next to the city's main fish market. There is a

Standa supermarket on Strada Nova and a *Mega 1 supermarket* off Campo Santa Margherita.

Entertainment

The Venezia Carnevale (see the Special Events section) is one of Italy's best known festivals, but exhibitions, theatre and musical events continue throughout the year in Venezia. Information is available in *Un Ospite di Venezia*, and the tourist office also has brochures listing events and performances for the entire year.

Cinemas The city doesn't have an English-language cinema. *Summer Arena*, a cinema -under-the-stars in Campo San Polo during July and August, features British and American films, but they are generally dubbed. The time to see foreign cinema in the original language is during the September film festival (see Special Events).

Bars *Caffè Poggi*, Rio Terrà della Maddalena 2104 in Cannaregio, is a great old-style bar for a sip of fragolino (a red or white wine with a tangy hint of strawberry), or you could try the nameless wine bar across the road by the bridge. *Paradiso Perduto* (See Cannaregio under Places to Eat) is a hip joint with live music. *Caffè Blue Music*, Dorsoduro 3778, is a cool student bar with live music on Fridays. It is as good a place as any to try the favourite Veneto drink, a *spritz*. This is one part sparkling white wine, one part soda water and one part bitter (Campari or one of several other variants), topped with a slice of lemon and, if you wish, an olive.

As far as nightclubs go, the city's spread is pretty dismal. A drive to Mestre is the best bet, or a boat to the Lido, but clubs tend to close there during winter.

Opera & Classical Music Until it was destroyed by fire in January 1996, Teatro la Fenice (☎ 521 01 61) was Venezia's premier opera and classical music stage. Performances are still organised but held in alternative venues. One is the Chiesa di Santa Maria della Pietà on the Riva degli Schiavoni; tickets can be purchased from Agenzia Kele & Teo (☎ 520 87 22), Ponte dei Baratteri, San Marco, or from the church two days before the event. A Contemporary Music Festival is held annually in October at the Teatro Goldoni.

Gambling The Casinò Municipale di Venezia has two locations. In winter it is at the Palazzo Vendramin Calergi, on the Canal Grande, and in summer it moves to the Palazzo del Casinò at the Lido. Vaporetto No 2, the so-called Casinò Express, takes you to both locations.

Things to Buy

When people shop in Venezia they tend to think of Murano glass and there is no shortage of workshops and showrooms full of the stuff, particularly between San Marco and Castello and on the island of Murano. Much of it is designed for tourist groups, so if you want to buy, shop around. Quality and prices vary dramatically. Always haggle, as the marked price is usually much higher than what the seller expects to get. If you do decide to buy Venetian glass, you can have the shop ship it home for you. Remember, this can take a long time and you are likely to have to pay duty when it arrives.

Carnevale masks make beautiful souvenirs. Again, quality and price are uneven. A workshop and showroom in a small street off Campo SS Filippo e Giacomo, towards San Marco, is worth a look, as is Ca' Macana, Calle delle Botteghe, Dorsoduro 5176. At the latter you can even see how masks are made.

Venezia is also noted for its *carta marmorizzata* (marbled paper). The oldest store is the Legatoria Piazzesi, Campiello della Feltrina 2551c, San Marco. There, they employ time-honoured methods to turn out high-quality (and high-priced) items. Il Pavone, Fondamenta Venier dai Leoni 721, Dorsoduro, is another good store.

Many shops (and artists in the city's many squares) sell simple watercolours of typical Venetian scenes. Veneziartigiana, Calle

Larga San Marco 412, is a collective selling works by Venetian artists.

If you want to buy yourself unusual pasta, for instance Curaçao blue fettucine, and other culinary delicacies try Grizzo, Salizzada S Giovanni Crisostomo, just north of the post office.

The main shopping area for clothing, shoes, accessories and jewellery is in the narrow streets between San Marco and the Rialto, particularly the Merceria and around Campo San Luca. The more upmarket shopping area is west of Piazza San Marco. Opening hours are roughly the same as in the rest of Italy, although many places open on Sundays during the tourist season.

Getting There & Away

Air Marco Polo airport (☎ 260 92 60 for flight info) is just east of Mestre and is served by flights from most major Italian and European cities, and from New York.

Alitalia (☎ 258 12 22) is at Via Sansovino 7 in Mestre; the Padova office of British Airways (☎ 049-66 04 44) is the closest to Venezia; Qantas, Canadian Airways and TWA are handled by Gastaldi Tours (☎ 290 51 11), Via Verdi 34 in Mestre.

Bus ACTV buses (☎ 528 78 86) leave from Piazzale Roma for surrounding areas including Mestre and Chioggia. There are also bus connections to Padova and Treviso. Tickets and information are available at the ticket office in the piazza.

Train The Stazione Santa Lucia (☎ 1478-8 80 88), known in Venezia as the *Ferrovia*, is directly linked by train to Padova, Verona, Trieste, Milano and Bologna, and thus is easily accessible from Firenze and Roma. You can also leave from Venezia for major points in Germany, Austria and the former Yugoslavia.

Orient Express The Venezia Simplon Orient Express runs between Venezia and London via Verona, Zürich and Paris twice weekly, although in winter there is only one service each week. Any travel agent in Venezia can assist, or call the headquarters in London on ☎ 0171-928 6000.

Car & Motorcycle The A4 passes through Mestre and is the quickest way to reach Venezia. Take the Venezia exit and follow the signs for the city. The A4 connects Trieste with Torino, passing through Milano. From the south, take the A13 from Bologna, which connects with the A4 at Padova. A more interesting route is to take the SS11 from Padova to Venezia. This is also the best road for hitchhikers.

Once you cross the bridge from Mestre, the Ponte della Libertà, cars must be left at one of the huge car parks in Piazzale Roma, or on the island of Tronchetto. Parking is not cheap and you will pay over L25,000 for every 24 hours. A cheaper alternative is to leave the car at Fusina near Mestre and catch vaporetto No 16 to the Zattere and then the No 5 either to San Marco or the train station. Ask for information at the tourist office just before the bridge to Venezia.

Avis is in Piazzale Roma (☎ 522 58 25) and also has a desk at the Marco Polo airport (☎ 541 50 30), and Eurodollar is at the same locations (☎ 528 95 51; 541 15 70).

Boat Minoan Lines (☎ 271 23 45), Porto Venezia, Zona Santa Marta, runs ferries to Greece (Corfu, Igoumenitsa and Patras) from Venezia three times a week in winter and daily in summer. Floor passengers pay L98,000 for a deck chair.

Kompas Italia (☎ 528 65 45), San Marco 1497, operates some ferry and hydrofoil services to Croatia in summer – much depends on the situation in the former Yugoslavia and destination programmes change each year.

Getting Around

The Airport The airport is accessible by regular *motoscafo* (motorboat) from San Marco and the Lido (L15,000), operated by the Cooperativa San Marco (☎ 522 23 03). There are also buses operated by the Società ATVO (☎ 520 55 30) from Piazzale Roma, which cost L5000, or you can take the regular ACTV city bus No 5, also from

Piazzale Roma. A water taxi from San Marco will cost more than L87,000.

Vaporetto Vaporetti are the city's mode of public transport. Ferry No 17 transports vehicles from Tronchetto, near Piazzale Roma, to the Lido.

From Piazzale Roma, vaporetto No 1 zigzags up the Canal Grande to San Marco and then the Lido. If you aren't in a hurry it is a great introduction to Venezia. There are faster and more expensive alternatives if you are in a hurry.

Single vaporetto tickets cost L4500 (plus L4500 for luggage!), even if you only ride to the next station. A 24-hour ticket is good value at L15,000 for unlimited travel. Better value still are the three-day (L30,000) and weekly (L55,000) tickets. Rolling Venezia passholders can get the three-day ticket for L20,000. Those tempted to ride without paying should note that ticket inspectors do occasionally make an appearance.

Tickets can be purchased at the ticket booths at most landing stations and should be validated in the machines at each landing station before you get on the boat. Otherwise you can buy them on the boat.

Routes and route numbers change regularly, so the following incomplete list should be taken as a guide only:

No 1
: Piazzale Roma, Ferrovia, Canal Grande, Lido

No 12
: Fondamente Nuove, Murano, Torcello, Burano

No 14
: San Zaccaria, Lido, Litorale del Cavallino (Punta Sabbioni & Treporti), Burano, Torcello (the one-way trip beyond Lido costs L5000)

No 17
: Car ferry from Tronchetto to Lido

No 52
: Circular route from San Zaccaria to Murano, the train station, Piazzale Roma, Zattere, Zitelle (HI hostel), San Zaccaria, Lido

No 52
: A variant on the above circular route that calls in at all Giudecca stops and San Giorgio

No 82
: San Zaccaria, San Marco, Canal Grande, Ferrovia, Piazzale Roma, Zattere, Giudecca, San Giorgio and (in summer only) Lido

N
: An all-stops night circuit taking in Piazzal Roma, Tronchetto, Giudecca, San Giorgio, Cana Grande, Lido

Traghetto The poor man's gondola, traghett are used by locals to cross the Canal Grand where there is no nearby bridge; they ar slowly being phased out, however. The operate between Calle Traghetto, near Sa Marco, and Fondamenta della Salute (until pm); between Campo San Samuele, north o the Ponte dell'Accademia, and Call Traghetto; between Calle Mocenigo, farthe north, and Calle Traghetto; betwee Fondamenta del Vin and Riva del Carbon near the Ponte di Rialto; and between Camp Santa Sofia and Campo della Pescaria, nea the produce market. The ride costs L600.

Water Taxis Water taxis are prohibitivel expensive, with a set L27,000 charge for maximum of seven minutes, an extra L800 if you order one by telephone, and variou surcharges which make a gondola ride seem cheap.

Gondola A gondola ride is the quintessenc of romantic Venezia, although at L80,000 fo 50 minutes (L100,000 after 8 pm) the *officia* price is a rather hefty return from the cloud to reality. The rates are for a maximum of six

VENETO

people – less romantic but more affordable. Prices are set for gondola rides but you can negotiate fees for additional services, such as a singer to serenade you during the ride.

Gondolas are available near main canals all over the city, or can be booked in the following areas: San Marco (☎ 520 06 85), Rialto (☎ 522 49 04), Piazzale Roma (☎ 522 05 81) and the train station (☎ 71 85 43).

Porters Getting from the vaporetto stop to your hotel can be difficult if you are heavily laden with luggage. There are several porter stands around the city with baggage carriers *(portabagagli)* who will escort you to your hotel. They are supposed to charge L9000 for one or two items and L3000 for each subsequent item, but haggling is the rule – a lot will depend on how far you want them to bear your goods and chattels. They can be found at points including the Ponte dell'Accademia (☎ 522 48 91), the train station (☎ 71 52 72), Piazzale Roma (☎ 520 30 70), the Ponte di Rialto (☎ 520 53 08) and San Marco (☎ 523 23 85).

Around the Veneto

THE BRENTA RIVIERA

Dotted along the Brenta river, which passes through Padova and spills into the Venetian lagoon, are more than 100 villas, built by wealthy Venetian families as summer homes; most are closed to the public. The most outstanding are the **Villa Foscari** (1571), built by Palladio at Malcontenta, and the **Villa Pisani**, also known as the Villa Nazionale, at Strà, which was built for Doge Alvise Pisani, used by Napoleon and was the site of the first meeting between Hitler and Mussolini. ACTV buses running between Padova and Venezia stop at or near the villas. See the Around Vicenza section for information on other Venetian villas.

The luxurious *Burchiello* barge plied the Brenta river between Venezia and Padova in the 17th and 18th centuries. Today, a reproduction barge ferries tourists for about L100,000, including lunch and short tours. Call ☎ 049-66 09 44 for information or try travel agents in Venezia, for example Intras, Piazza San Marco 145. At least two other ferries ply the Brenta – ask the Padova APT.

PADOVA

Although famous as the city of St Anthony and for its university, one of the oldest in Europe, Padova (Padua) is often seen as merely a convenient and cheap place to stay while visiting Venezia. The city offers a rich collection of art treasures, however, including Giotto's incredible frescoed chapel, and its many piazzas and arcaded streets are a pleasure to explore.

Padova's wealth grew during the 13th century when it was controlled by the counts of Carrara, who encouraged cultural and artistic prosperity and established the Stadium, the forerunner of the university.

Orientation

From the train station, it's a 10-minute walk across the square and up Corso del Popolo (later Corso Garibaldi) to the centre. Bus No 10 will also get you there. Piazza della Frutta and the adjoining Piazza delle Erbe form the lively heart of the old city, bustling with market activity – take some time to drool over all the fine foods. The Basilica del Santo (aka Basilica di Sant'Antonio) and the vast Prato della Valle are a good 20-minute walk south from the train station.

Information

Tourist Offices There is a tourist office at the train station (☎ 875 20 77), open Monday to Saturday from 9 am to 7.30 pm (9.20 am to 5.45 pm from November to March) and Sunday from 8.30 am to 12.30 pm (9 am to midday from November to March). There is another office on Piazza Eremitani (☎ 875 06 55), at the entrance to the Cappella degli Scrovegni (Scrovegni Chapel), open Tuesday to Sunday from 9.30 am to 12.30 pm and 1.30 to 4.30 pm.

Post & Communications The post office, Corso Garibaldi 33, is open from Monday to

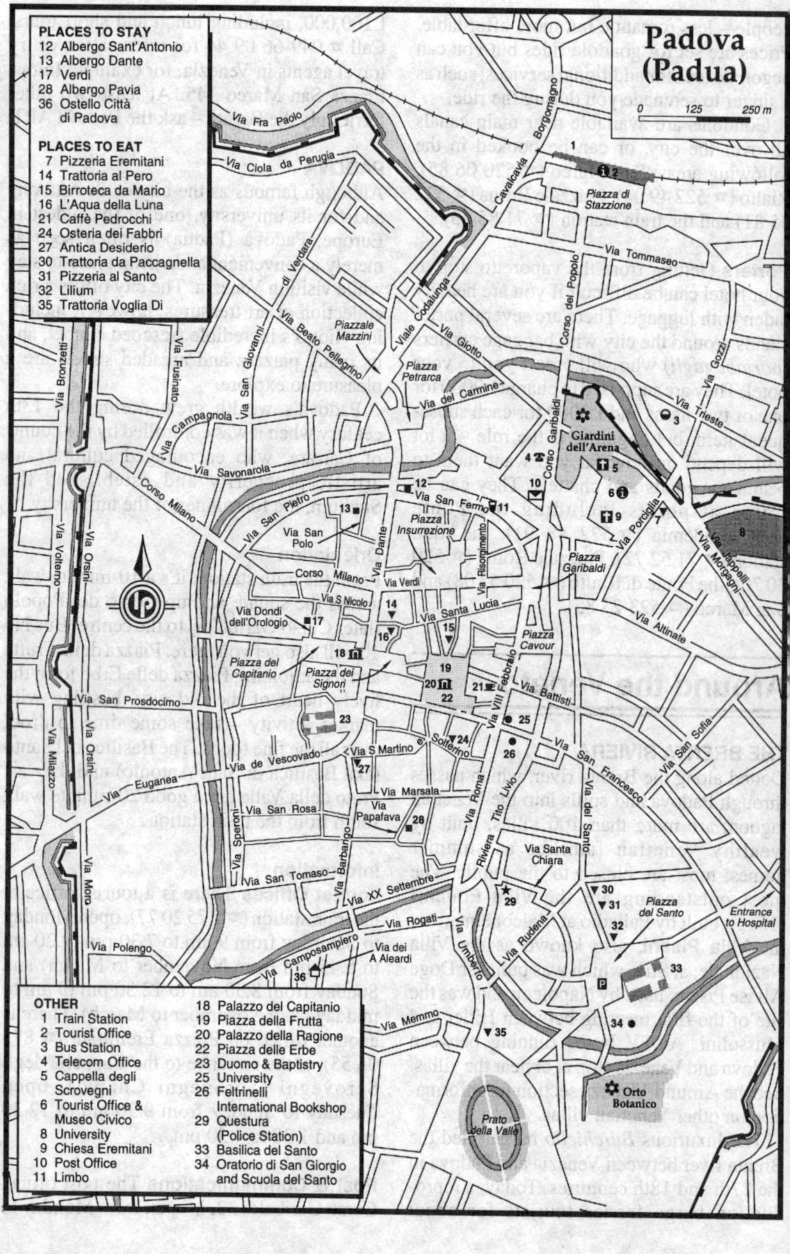

Padova (Padua)
0
125
250 m
PLACES TO STAY
12 Albergo Sant'Antonio
13 Albergo Dante
17 Verdi
28 Albergo Pavia
36 Ostello Città di Padova
PLACES TO EAT
7 Pizzeria Eremitani
14 Trattoria al Pero
15 Birroteca da Mario
16 L'Aqua della Luna
21 Caffè Pedrocchi
24 Osteria dei Fabbri
27 Antica Desiderio
30 Trattoria da Paccagnella
31 Pizzeria al Santo
32 Lilium
35 Trattoria Voglia Di
OTHER
1 Train Station
2 Tourist Office
3 Bus Station
4 Telecom Office
5 Cappella degli Scrovegni
6 Tourist Office & Museo Civico
8 University
9 Chiesa Eremitani
10 Post Office
11 Limbo
18 Palazzo del Capitanio
19 Piazza della Frutta
20 Palazzo della Ragione
22 Piazza delle Erbe
23 Duomo & Baptistry
25 University
26 Feltrinelli International Bookshop
29 Questura (Police Station)
33 Basilica del Santo
34 Oratorio di San Giorgio and Scuola del Santo
Via Fra Paolo
Via Ciola da Perugia
Borgomagno
Cavalcavia
Piazza di Stazzione
Via Tommaseo
Corso del Popolo
Viale Codalunga
Via Giotto
Via Gozzi
Via Trieste
Via del Carmine
Piazza Petrarca
Piazzale Mazzini
Via Beato Pellegrino
Via San Giovanni di Verdara
Via Fusinato
Via Bronzetti
Via Campagnola
Via Savonarola
Corso Milano
Via San Pietro
Giardini dell'Arena
Corso Garibaldi
Via Porciglia
Via Jappelli
Via Morgagni
Via San Fermo
Piazza Insurrezione
Via Risorgimento
Piazza Garibaldi
Via Altinate
Via Volterno
Via Orsini
Via San Polo
Via Dante
Via Verdi
Via S Nicolo
Via Dondi dell'Orologio
Via Santa Lucia
Piazza Cavour
Piazza del Capitanio
Piazza dei Signori
Via VIII Febbraio
Via Battisti
Via San Prosdocimo
Via Milazzo
Via S Martino e Solferino
Via de Vescovado
Via Euganea
Via San Sofia
Via San Francesco
Via Marsala
Via Papafava
Via San Rosa
Via Speroni
Via Barbarigo
Via Roma
Via Tito Livio
Via del Santo
Via Santa Chiara
Riviera
Via Moro
Via San Tomaso
Via XX Settembre
Via Rogati
Via Umberto
Via Rudena
Piazza del Santo
Entrance to Hospital
Via Polengo
Via Camposampiero
Via dei A Aleardi
Via Memmo
Orto Botanico
Prato della Valle

Saturday from 8.15 am to 7 pm (8.30 am to 6.30 pm on Sunday). Next door, the Telecom phone office opens Monday to Friday from 8.30 am to 12.30 pm and 4 to 7 pm. Address poste restante mail to 35100 Padova.

Padova's telephone code is ☎ 049.

Bookshop Padova is full of bookshops, and if you're looking for anything in languages other than Italian, try Feltrinelli International at Via San Francesco 14.

Emergency In an emergency, call ☎ 113. The questura (☎ 83 31 11) is at Via Santa Chiara, on the corner of Riviera Ruzante. Medical assistance is provided by the Complesso Clinico Ospedaliero (☎ 821 11 11), Via Giustiniani 1.

Things to See

A special ticket, available for L15,000 (L10,000 for students) at the main sites and tourist offices, allows you entry to the main monuments – worth considering if you intend to 'do' Padova thoroughly.

Cappella degli Scrovegni Many art lovers visit Padova just to see this chapel in the Giardini dell'Arena. It was commissioned by Enrico Scrovegni in 1303 as a burial place for his father, who had been denied a Christian burial because of his money-lending practices. Giotto's remarkable fresco cycle, probably completed between 1304 and 1306, illustrates the lives of Mary and Christ and is arranged in three bands. You can pick up an adequate guide to the frescoes as you enter. Among the most famous scenes in the cycle are the *Kiss of Judas* and the *Lamentation*. The series ends with the *Last Judgment* on the entrance wall and the Vices and Virtues are depicted around the lower parts of the walls. Keep in mind *when* the frescoes were done – Giotto was moving well away from the two-dimensional figures of his medieval contemporaries and presaging greater things to come.

The chapel is often full and in busier times attendants enforce strict time limits, usually of 20 to 30 minutes. The chapel is open daily except Monday from 9 am to 6 pm, and admission is L10,000. The ticket is also valid for the adjacent Museo Civico, whose collection of 14th to 18th-century Veneto art and forgettable archaeological artefacts includes a remarkable crucifix by Giotto.

Chiesa Eremitani This Augustinian church, completed in the early 14th century, was painstakingly rebuilt after being almost totally destroyed by bombing in WW II. The remains of frescoes done by Andrea Mantegna, in his 20s, are displayed in a chapel to the left of the apse. Most were lost in the bombing, the greatest single loss to Italian art during the war. The *Martyrdom of St James*, on the left, was pieced together from fragments found in the rubble of the church, while the *Martyrdom of St Christopher*, opposite, was saved because it had been removed before the war.

Historic Centre Via VIII Febbraio leads to the city's **university**, the main part of which is housed in the Palazzo Bò ('ox' in Venetian dialect, named after an inn that previously occupied the site). Established in 1222, the university is Italy's oldest after Bologna's. Europe's first anatomy theatre was opened here in 1594 and Galileo Galilei taught at the university from 1592 to 1610.

Continue along to Piazza delle Erbe and Piazza della Frutta, separated by the majestic **Palazzo della Ragione**, also known as the Salone, for the grand hall on the upper floor. Built in the 13th and 14th centuries, the building features frescoes by Giusto de' Menabuoi and Niccolò Mireto depicting the astrological theories of Pietro d'Abano. It is open daily, except Monday, from 9 am to 7 pm; in winter it opens from 9 am to 12.30 pm and from 3 to 6 pm. Price of entry depends largely on the nature of the temporary exhibits.

West from here is the Piazza dei Signori, dominated by the 14th-century **Palazzo del Capitanio**, the former residence of the city's Venetian ruler. South is the city's **duomo**, built from a much-altered design by Michelangelo. The 13th-century Romanesque **baptistry** (battistero) features a series of frescoes of Old and New Testament scenes by Giusto de' Menabuoi, influenced by Giotto.

The cathedral is open daily, except Monday, from 7.30 am to noon and 3.30 to 7.30 pm, while the baptistery opens on the same days from 9.30 am to 12.30 pm and 3 to 6 pm. Entry to the baptistry is L3000.

Piazza del Santo In the piazza, in front of the basilica, is the *Gattamelata*, created by Donatello in 1453. This magnificent equestrian statue of the 15th-century Venetian condottiere Erasmos da Narni (whose nickname, Gattamelata, translates as 'Honeyed Cat') is considered the first great bronze of the Italian Renaissance.

The city's most celebrated monument is the **Basilica del Santo** (or di Sant'Antonio), which houses the corpse of the town's patron saint and is an important place of pilgrimage. Construction of what is known to the people of Padova as Il Santo began in 1232. The saint's tomb, bedecked by requests for the saint's intercession to cure illness or thanks for having done so, is in the Cappella del Santo in the left transept. There was a time when the area around the tomb was awash with crutches and other prosthetic devices of the grateful cured – it appears these have been reduced to a symbolic few. Look out for the saint's relics in the apse too. The sculptures and reliefs of the high altar are by Donatello.

On the south side of the piazza lies the **Oratorio di San Giorgio**, the burial chapel of the Lupi di Soranga family of Parma, with 14th-century frescoes. Next door is the **Scoletta (or Scuola) del Santo**, containing works believed to be by Titian. The former is closed for restoration and the latter open from 9 am to 12.30 pm and 2.30 to 5.30 pm (to 4.30 pm in winter). Admission is L3000.

Just south of Piazza del Santo, the **Orto Botanico** is purportedly the oldest botanical garden in Europe. It opens daily except holidays from 9 am to 1 pm and 2 to 6 pm (mornings only in winter) and entry costs L5000.

Places to Stay

Padova has no shortage of budget hotels, but they fill quickly in summer. The closest camping ground, *Camping Sporting Center* (☎ 79 34 00), is at Via Roma 123, at Montegrotto Terme, about 15 km from Padova, and can be reached by city bus M. The *Ostello Città di Padova* (☎ 875 22 19), Via A Aleardi 30, offers B&B for L19,000. Take bus No 3, 8 or 12 from the train station to Prato della Valle and then ask for directions.

The *Verdi* (☎ 875 57 44), Via Dondi dell'Orologio 7, has basic, clean singles/doubles for L39,000/52,000. *Albergo Pavia* (☎ 66 15 58), Via dei Papafava 11, has rooms for the same price.

The *Albergo Sant'Antonio* (☎ 875 13 93), Via San Fermo 118, at the northern end of Via Dante, has excellent singles/doubles, most with TV and phone, for L50,000/68,000 or L78,000/102,000 with a bathroom. Just nearby is the much simpler and cheaper *Albergo Dante* (☎ 876 04 08), Via San Polo 5, with rooms for L39,000/52,000.

The three-star *Leon Bianco* (☎ 875 08 14; fax 875 61 84), Piazzetta Pedrocchi 12, near Piazza della Frutta, has rooms from L119,000/155,000 in high season (which is most of the time!).

Places to Eat

Daily *markets* are held in the piazzas around the Palazzo della Ragione, with fresh produce sold in the Piazza delle Erbe and Piazza della Frutta, and bread, cheese and salami sold in the shops under the porticoes.

Pizzeria Eremitani, at the end of Via Porciglia near the bus station, has excellent pizzas from L8000. *Trattoria al Pero*, Via Santa Lucia 72, serves regional dishes and a full meal will come to around L20,000. Across the road at No 91, *L'Aqua della Luna* is a funky sort of place where you can get great pizzas and/or cocktails.

For vegetarian food (set menu of L19,000), try *Birroteca da Mario*, Via Breda 3. *Osteria dei Fabbri*, Via dei Fabbri 13, is another good choice, although more expensive. In the area around Prato della Valle, the best choice is *Trattoria Voglia Di*, Via Umberto I, just before the Prato. It serves a good set meal for L19,000, or you can eat a snack in the bar. *Pizzeria al Santo*, Via del Santo 163, has good pizzas from L7000. Nearby, *Trattoria da Paccagnella*, Via del Santo 113, is a comfortably elegant setting for fine Veneto cuisine – expect to pay about L30,000 a head. *Lilium*, at No 175, offers wonderful gelati and fine pastries.

Caffè Pedrocchi, just off Via VIII Febbraio, was the meeting place for 19th-century liberals and one of Stendhal's favourite haunts – unfortunately, it was closed for restoration at the time of writing.

Entertainment

The city hosts the Notturni d'Arte festival from July to September each year, featuring concerts and outdoor events; many are free. The tourist office has details. Some opera and theatrical performances are held at the *Teatro Comunale Verdi* (☎ 876 03 39), Via Livello 32. If you want to go dancing try *Limbo*, Via San Fermo 44.

Getting There & Away

Bus & Train SITA buses (☎ 820 68 34) depart from Piazzale Boschetti, 200 metres south of the train station, and head for Montegrotto, the Euganean Hills, Trieste, Venezia (L4800), Este, Mantova, Piacenza and Genova. By train (☎ 875 18 00), the city is connected to Milano, Venezia (L3400 in 2nd class; L6900 on the fast InterCity trains) and Bologna.

Car & Motorcycle The A4 (Milano-Venezia) passes to the north, while the A13, which connects the city with Bologna, starts at the southern edge of town. The two autostrade are connected by a ring road.

AROUND PADOVA

South-west of Padova, along the A13 or the SS16, are the **Colli Euganei** (Euganean Hills), dotted with vineyards and good walking trails: ask at the Padova tourist office for information about the trails and accommodation. The Consorzio Vini DOC dei Colli Euganei (☎ 049-521 18 96), Via Vescovi 35 in Luvigliano, can provide details of the vineyards.

If you are driving (which you pretty much have to, as public transport is abysmal in the area), follow the signposted Strada dei Vini dei Colli Euganei (Euganean Hills Wine Road), which will take you on a tour of many vineyards. Pick up a map and itinerary from the APT in Padova. Most of the vineyards are open to the public and some offer accommodation.

The tourist office in the medieval town of **Montagnana** (☎ 0429-8 13 20) is at Piazza Trieste. The youth hostel, *Rocca degli Alberi* (☎ 0429-81 07 62), Castello degli Alberi, is housed in a former castle and open from April to October. B&B is L15,000 and it is close to the town's train station.

VICENZA

Vicenza is the centre for Italian textile manufacture and a leader in the development and production of computer components, making it one of the country's wealthiest cities. Most tourists come to Vicenza to see the work of Andrea di Pietro della Gondola, better known as Palladio, whose designs have influenced architects worldwide. Vicenza flourished as the Roman Vicentia and in 1404 became part of the Venetian Republic, sharing the city's fortunes, as the many Venetian Gothic mansions demonstrate.

Orientation

From the train station, in the gardens of the Campo Marzo, walk straight ahead along Via Roma into Piazzale de Gasperi. From here, the main street, Corso Andrea Palladio, leads to the duomo and the centre of town.

Information

Tourist Office The APT office (☎ 32 08 54) is at Piazza Matteotti 12 and opens Monday to Saturday from 9 am to 12.30 pm and 2.30 to 6 pm; Sundays from 9 am to 1 pm.

Post & Communications The main post office is at Contrà Garibaldi, near the duomo.

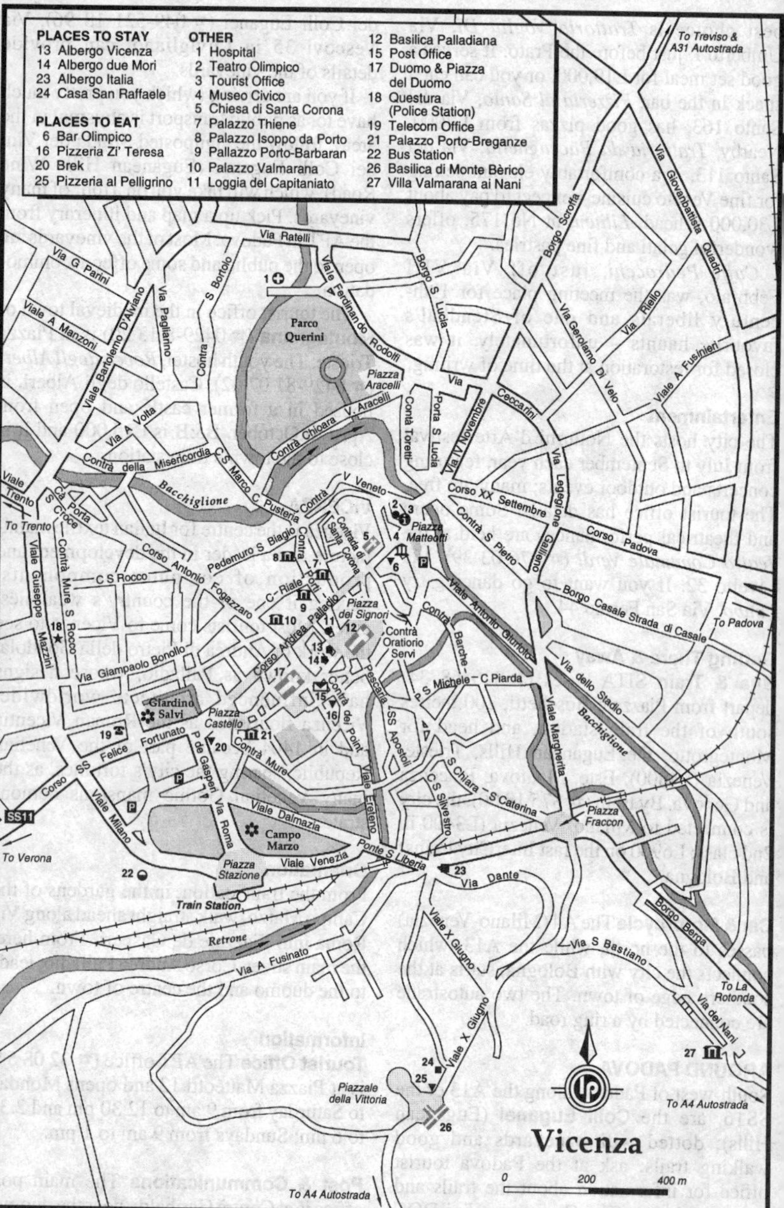
PLACES TO STAY
13 Albergo Vicenza
14 Albergo due Mori
23 Albergo Italia
24 Casa San Raffaele
PLACES TO EAT
6 Bar Olimpico
16 Pizzeria Zi' Teresa
20 Brek
25 Pizzeria al Pelligrino
OTHER
1 Hospital
2 Teatro Olimpico
3 Tourist Office
4 Museo Civico
5 Chiesa di Santa Corona
7 Palazzo Thiene
8 Palazzo Isoppo da Porto
9 Pallazzo Porto-Barbaran
10 Palazzo Valmarana
11 Loggia del Capitaniato
12 Basilica Palladiana
15 Post Office
17 Duomo & Piazza del Duomo
18 Questura (Police Station)
19 Telecom Office
21 Palazzo Porto-Breganze
22 Bus Station
26 Basilica di Monte Bèrico
27 Villa Valmarana ai Nani
To Treviso & A31 Autostrada
Via Ratelli
Via G Parini
Viale A Manzoni
Viale Bartolomeo D'Alviano
Via Pagliarino
Contrà S Bortolo
Viale Ferdinando Rodolfi
Parco Querini
Piazza Aracelli
Borgo S Lucia
Borgo Scroffa
Via Giovanbattista Quadri
Via Riello
Via Gerolamo Di Velo
Viale A Fusinieri
Via Ceccarini
Porta S Lucia
Contà Toretti
Via IV Novembre
Via Legegione Gallieno
Corso XX Settembre
Contrà S Pietro
Corso Padova
Borgo Casale Strada di Casale
To Padova
Via A Volta
Contrà Chioara
V. Aracelli
Contrà della Misericordia
C S Marco
C Pusteria
Bacchiglione
Viale Trento
To Trento
Ca Porta
S Croce
Contrà V Veneto
Piazza Matteotti
Corso Antonio Fogazzaro
Pedemuro S Biagio
Contrada di Santa Corona
C S Rocco
C- Riale
Contrà Porti
Piazza dei Signori
Viale Antonio Giuriolo
Contrà Barche
Contrà Oratiorio Servi
Viale Giuseppe Mazzini
Contrà Mure S Rocco
Corso Andrea Palladio
Via Giampaolo Bonollo
Giardino Salvi
Piazza Castello
Contrà Mure
Contrà dei Point
Pescaria
P S Michele
C Piarda
SS Apostoli
Via dello Stadio
Viale Margherita
Bacchiglione
Corso SS Felice Fortunato
P de Gaspari
Via Roma
Viale Milano
SS11
To Verona
Viale Dalmazia
Campo Marzo
Viale Eretenio
S Chiara
S Caterina
C.S Silvestro
Piazza Fraccon
Ponte S Liberia
Viale Venezia
Piazza Stazione
Train Station
Via Dante
Retrone
Via A Fusinato
Viale X Giugno
Borgo Berga
Via S Bastiano
To La Rotonda
Via dei Nani
To A4 Autostrada
Piazzale della Vittoria
Vicenza
0 200 400 m
To A4 Autostrada

Address poste restante mail to 36100 Vicenza. A Telecom office is at Piazzale Giusti and is staffed Monday to Friday from 9 am to 1 pm and 4 to 7 pm.

The telephone code for Vicenza is ☎ 0444.

Emergency In a police emergency, call ☎ 113. The questura (☎ 33 75 11) is at Viale Mazzini 24. For urgent medical assistance, go to the Ospedale Civile (☎ 99 37 23), Via Rodolfi, north of the city centre from Piazza Matteotti, or call ☎ 118 for an ambulance.

Things to See

In Piazza Castello there are several grand edifices, including the **Palazzo Porto-Breganze** on the southern side, designed by Palladio and built by Scamozzi, one of the city's leading 16th-century architects. The main street, Corso Andrea Palladio, runs north-east from the square and is lined with fine buildings. Piazza dei Signori, nearby, is dominated by the immense **Basilica Palladiana**, built by Palladio from 1549 over an earlier Gothic building – the slender 12th-century bell tower is all that remains of the original structure. The basilica is open Tuesday to Saturday from 9.30 am to midday and 2.30 to 5 pm, and Sunday from 10 am to midday. Palladio's **Loggia del Capitaniato**, on the north-western side of the piazza on the corner of Via del Monte, was left unfinished at his death and shows his flair for colour.

South-west from the basilica is the **duomo**, a dull church destroyed during WWII and later rebuilt (some of its artworks were saved). Contrà Porti, which runs north off Corso Andrea Palladio, is one of the city's most majestic streets. The **Palazzo Thiene** at No 12, by Lorenzo da Bologna, was originally intended to occupy the entire block. Palladio's **Palazzo Porto-Barbaran** at No 11 features a double row of columns. He also built the **Palazzo Isoppo da Porto** at No 21, which remains unfinished. His **Palazzo Valmarana**, at Corso Antonio Fogazzaro 18, is considered one of his more eccentric creations. Across the Bacchiglione river is the **Parco Querini**, the city's largest park.

North along Corso Andrea Palladio and left into Contrada di Santa Corona is **Chiesa di Santa Corona**, begun in 1261 by the Dominicans to house a relic from Christ's crown of thorns. Inside are the *Baptism of Christ* by Giovanni Bellini and *Adoration of the Magi* by Veronese.

Corso Andrea Palladio ends at the **Teatro Olimpico**, started by Palladio in 1580 and completed by Scamozzi after Palladio's death. Considered one of the purest creations of Renaissance architecture, the theatre design was based on Palladio's studies of Roman structures. Scamozzi's remarkable street scene, stretching back from the main façade of the stage, is modelled on the ancient Greek city of Thebes. He created an impressive illusion of depth and perspective by slanting the streets upward towards the rear of the set. The theatre was inaugurated in 1585 with a performance of *Oedipus Rex*, but soon fell into disuse – the ceiling caved in and it remained abandoned for centuries until 1934, when it was restored and reopened. Since then, the theatre has become a prized performance space for opera and other theatre – it is one of the few working theatres where the performers and audience are eyeball to eyeball. It is open Tuesday to Saturday in summer from 9 am to 12.30 pm and 2.15 to 5 pm; Sundays and holidays from 9.30 am to 12.30 pm and 2 to 7 pm; in winter, closing times are 15 minutes earlier. Entry costs L5000. The nearby **Museo Civico** in the Palazzo Chiericati, open the same hours, contains works by local artists as well as by the two Tiepolos and Veronese. Admission is L3000.

South of the city, the **Basilica di Monte Bèrico** on Piazzale della Vittoria, set on top of a hill, presents magnificent views over the city. The basilica was built in the 18th century to replace a 15th-century Gothic structure, itself raised on the supposed site of two appearances by the Virgin Mary in 1426. An impressive 18th-century colonnade runs most of the way along Viale X Giugno to the church on the top of the hill – very handy when it's pouring rain in autumn. Or catch city bus No 9.

A 20-minute walk part of the way back

down Viale X Giugno and then east along Via San Bastiano will take you to the **Villa Valmarana ai Nani**, featuring brilliant frescoes by Giambattista and Giandomenico Tiepolo. The 'ai nani' ('dwarfs' in Italian) refers to the statues perched on top of the gates surrounding the property. The villa is open every afternoon from mid-March to early November – check at the tourist office or call ☎ 54 39 76. Entry costs L8000.

Signs mark the path to Palladio's Villa Capra, better known as **La Rotonda**. It is one of Palladio's most admired – and copied – creations, having served as a model for similar buildings across Europe and the USA. From March to November the gardens (admission L5000) are open on Tuesday, Wednesday and Thursday from 10 am to midday and 3 to 6 pm and the villa (admission L10,000) opens on Wednesday for the same hours. Otherwise, groups of 25 or more (L20,000 a person) can book a visit to the villa and gardens on ☎ 32 17 93. Bus No 8 stops nearby.

Places to Stay

Many hotels close during the summer, particularly in August, so book ahead. At other times you should have no problems getting a room.

The closest camping ground, the *Campeggio Vicenza* (☎ 58 23 11), Strada Pelosa 239, is near the Vicenza Est exit from the A4. An HI youth hostel is planned soon for Vicenza.

The *Albergo Italia* (☎ 32 10 43), Viale Risorgimento 2, near the train station, has singles/doubles with a bathroom for L60,000/90,000. The *Albergo Vicenza* (☎ 32 15 12), Stradella dei Nodari 6-7, near Piazza dei Signori, has rooms with a bathroom for L65,000/90,000. The *Albergo due Mori* (☎ 32 18 86), nearby at Contrà do Rode 26, has rooms for L60,000/103,000 in the high season. One of the best choices is the *Casa San Raffaele* (☎ 32 36 63), Viale X Giugno 10, in a former convent behind the colonnade leading to Monte Bèrico, with singles/doubles with bathroom for L55,000/80,000.

Places to Eat

A large produce market is held each Tuesday and Thursday in Piazza delle Erbe. A bright little place for tasty tramezzini is *Bar Olimpico*, Corso Andrea Palladio 10. *Brek*, Corse Palladio 10, is good for a cheap lunch. *Pizzeria Zi' Teresa*, Contrà San Antonio 1, has good pizzas from L8000, as does *Pizzeria al Pellegrino* at Piazzale della Vittoria.

Entertainment

Concerts are held in summer at the Villa Valmarana ai Nani; check at the tourist office for details. For information about performances in the Teatro Olimpico, contact the APT or call ☎ 32 37 81.

Getting There & Away

FTV buses (☎ 22 31 15) leave from the bus station, just near the train station, for Padova, Thiene, Asiago, Bassano, Verona and towns throughout the nearby Berici mountains. Trains (☎ 32 50 46) connect the city with Venezia, Milano, Padova, Verona, Treviso and smaller towns in the north. By car, the city is on the A4 connecting Milano with Venezia. The SS11 connects Vicenza with Verona and Padova, and this is the best route for hitchhikers. There is a large car park near Piazza Castello and the train station.

Getting Around

The city is best seen on foot, but bus Nos 1, 2, 3 and 7 connect the train station with the city centre.

AROUND VICENZA

As Venezia's maritime power waned in the 16th century, the city's wealthy inhabitants turned their attention inland, acquiring land to build sumptuous villas (see also the Brenta Riviera section earlier in this chapter). Forbidden from building castles by the Venetian senate, which feared a landscape dotted with well-defended forts, the city's patricians set about building thousands of villas, of which about 3000 remain. Most are inaccessible to the public and many are run-down.

The APT in Vicenza can provide reams of information about the villas, including a booklet entitled *Vicenza – the Villas*. The De Agostini map, *Ville Venete*, sells for about L8000 from newspaper stands and is one of the few complete maps. Drivers should have little trouble planning an itinerary. If you don't have a car, take the FTV bus north from Vicenza to Thiene, passing through Caldogno and Villaverla, and then continue on to Lugo.

The Villa Godi-Valmarana, now known as the **Malinverni**, at Lonedo di Lugo, was Palladio's first villa. A good driving itinerary is to take the SS11 through Montecchio Maggiore and continue south for Lonigo, Pojana Maggiore and then head north for Longare and back to Vicenza. A round trip of 100km, the route takes in about a dozen villas.

A few km south of Pojana Maggiore you'll find an HI youth hostel at Montagnana (see the Around Padova section for details).

Check with the APT in Vicenza for details of the Concerti in Villa Estate, a series of classical concerts held in villas around Vicenza each summer. Also ask about accommodation, which is available in some villas.

VERONA

Wander the quiet streets of Verona on a winter's night, and you might almost be forgiven for believing the tragic love story of Romeo and Juliet to be true. Get past the Shakespearean hyperbole, however, and you'll find plenty to keep you occupied in what is doubtless one of Italy's most beautiful cities. Known as *piccola Roma* (little Rome) for its importance in the days of the empire, its truly golden era came during the 13th and 14th centuries under the della Scala family (also known as the Scaligeri). The period was noted for the savage family feuding about which Shakespeare wrote his play.

Orientation

Old Verona is small, and it's easy to find your way around. There is a lot to see and it is a popular base for exploring surrounding towns. Buses leave for the centre from outside the train station; otherwise walk to the right, past the bus station, cross the river and walk along Corso Porta Nuova to Piazza Brà, 15 minutes away. From the piazza, walk along Via Mazzini and turn left at Via Cappello to reach Piazza delle Erbe.

Information

Tourist Offices The main tourist office (☎ 59 28 28) is at Via Leoncino 61, on the corner of Piazza Brà, facing the Roman arena. It opens Monday to Saturday from 8 am to 8 pm (closing one hour earlier in winter) and on Sunday from 9 am to noon (in summer only). Another tourist office at the train station (☎ 800 08 61) opens daily from 8 am to 7 pm.

Money Banks dot the town centre, including the Banca Popolare di Bergamo on Piazza Brà, one of several with an automatic exchange machine. American Express is represented by Fabretto Viaggi (☎ 800 90 40), Corso Porta Nuova 11. Thomas Cook is represented by CIT (☎ 59 21 45) at Piazza Brà 2.

Post & Communications The main post office, Piazza Viviani 7, opens Monday to Friday from 8 am to 5 pm, Saturday to 1 pm. Address poste restante mail to 37100 Verona. You'll find telephones at the train station as well as Telecom phone offices on Piazza delle Erbe and Via Leoncino.

Verona's telephone code is ☎ 045.

Laundry There are Onda Blu laundrettes at Via XX Settembre 62a and Via Mantovana 16.

Emergency & Medical Services The city's Guardia Medica (☎ 91 32 22) provides medical services from 8 am to 8 pm and usually comes to you. Otherwise, the Ospedale Civile Maggiore (☎ 807 11 11) is at Piazza A Stefani, north-west from Ponte Vittoria.

In an emergency, call ☎ 113. The questura (☎ 809 06 11) is at Lungadige Porta Vittoria, near Via San Francesco.

Things to See

Roman Arena This pink marble Roman amphitheatre, in the bustling Piazza Brà, was

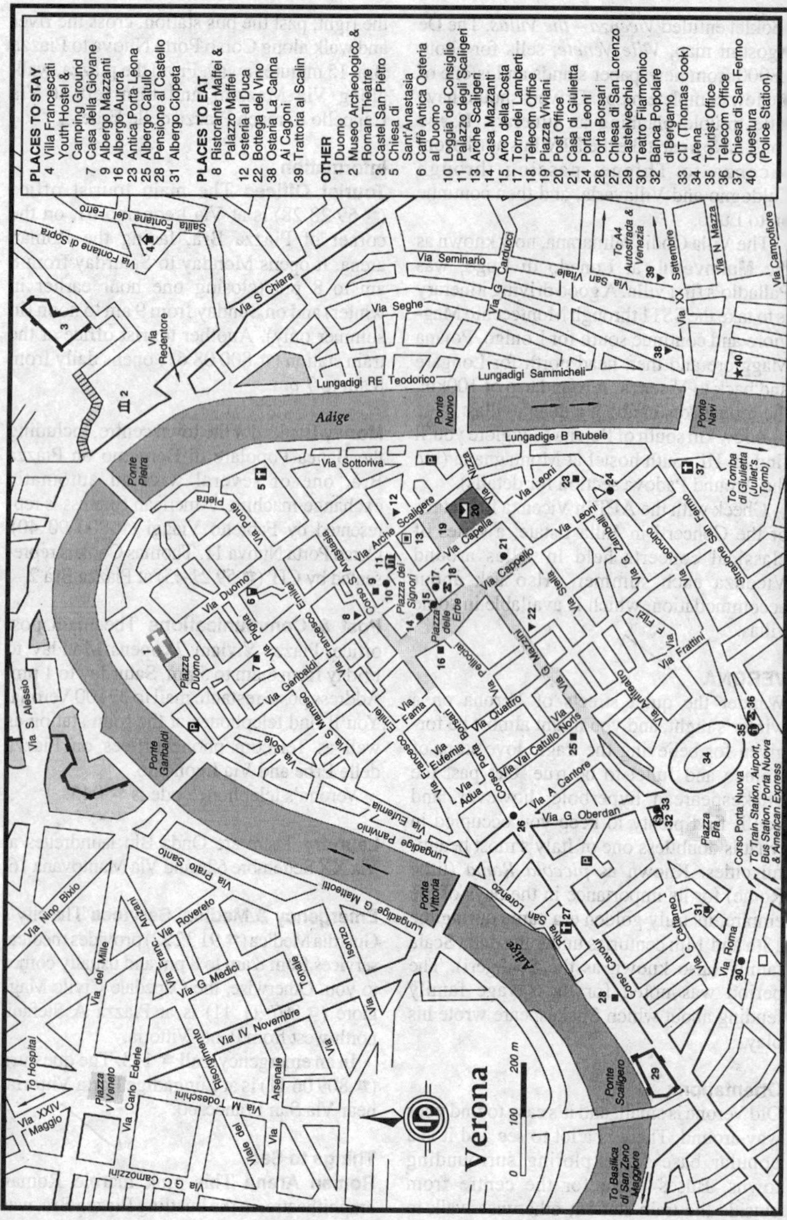
Verona
0 100 200 m
PLACES TO STAY
4 Villa Francescati Youth Hostel & Camping Ground
7 Casa della Giovane
9 Albergo Mazzanti
16 Albergo Aurora
23 Antica Porta Leona
25 Albergo Catullo
28 Pensione al Castello
31 Albergo Ciopeta
PLACES TO EAT
8 Ristorante Maffei & Palazzo Maffei
12 Osteria al Duca
22 Bottega del Vino
38 Osteria La Canna Ai Cagoni
39 Trattoria al Scalin
OTHER
1 Duomo
2 Museo Archeologico & Roman Theatre
3 Castel San Pietro
5 Chiesa di Sant'Anastasia
6 Caffè Antica Osteria al Duomo
10 Loggia del Consiglio
11 Palazzo degli Scaligeri
13 Arche Scaligeri
14 Casa Mazzanti
15 Arco della Costa
17 Torre dei Lamberti
18 Telecom Office
19 Piazza Viviani
20 Post Office
21 Casa di Giulietta
24 Porta Leoni
26 Porta Borsari
27 Chiesa di San Lorenzo
29 Castelvecchio
30 Teatro Filarmonico
32 Banca Popolare di Bergamo
33 CIT (Thomas Cook)
34 Arena
35 Tourist Office
36 Telecom Office
37 Chiesa di San Fermo
40 Questura (Police Station)
Adige
Ponte Pietra
Ponte Nuovo
Ponte Navi
Ponte Garibaldi
Ponte Vittoria
Ponte Scaligero
Piazza Duomo
Piazza dei Signori
Piazza delle Erbe
Piazza Brà
Piazza V Veneto
To A4 Autostrada & Venezia
To Tomba di Giulietta (Juliet's Tomb)
To Train Station, Airport, Bus Station, Porta Nuova & American Express
To Basilica di San Zeno Maggiore
To Hospital

VENETO

built in the 1st century AD and is now Verona's opera house. The third-largest Roman amphitheatre in existence, it could seat around 20,000 people. It is remarkably well preserved, despite a 12th-century earthquake that destroyed most of its outer wall. The arena is open from 8 am to 7.15 pm and entry is L6000. See the Verona Entertainment section for information about opera and plays at the Arena.

Casa di Giulietta Along Via Mazzini, Verona's main shopping street, is Via Cappello and 'Juliet's house' at No 23. Romeo and Juliet may have been fictional, but here you can swoon beneath what popular myth says was her balcony or, if in need of a new lover, approach a bronze statue of Juliet and rub her left breast for good luck. It is even doubtful there was ever a feud between the Cappello and Montecchi families, on whom Shakespeare based the play. The house was closed for restoration at the time of writing. If the theme excites you sufficiently, you could also search out Juliet's 'tomb' (Tomba di Giulietta) at Via del Pontiere 5. Also housed here is the Museo degli Affreschi. It opens Tuesday to Sunday from 8.15 am to 7.15 pm and admission is L5000.

Piazza delle Erbe Originally the site of a Roman forum, this piazza remains the lively centre of the city today, but the permanent market stalls in its centre detract from its beauty. The square is lined with some of Verona's most sumptuous buildings, including the Baroque **Palazzo Maffei**, at the northern end, with the adjoining 14th-century **Torre del Gardello**. On the east side is **Casa Mazzanti**, a former della Scala family residence whose fresco-decorated façade stands out.

Separating Piazza delle Erbe from **Piazza dei Signori** is the **Arco della Costa**, beneath which is suspended a whale's rib. Legend says it will fall on the first 'just' person to walk beneath it. In several centuries, it has never fallen, not even on the various popes who have paraded beneath it. Ascend the nearby 12th-century **Torre dei Lamberti** by elevator (L4000) or on foot (L3000) for a great view of the city. It is open daily, except Monday, from 9.30 am to 7.15 pm.

In Piazza dei Signori, the 15th-century **Loggia del Consiglio**, the former city council building, is regarded as Verona's finest Renaissance structure. It is attached to the **Palazzo degli Scaligeri**, once the main residence of the della Scala family.

Through the archway at the far end of the piazza are the **Arche Scaligere**, the elaborate tombs of the della Scala family, which unfortunately may only be viewed from outside.

North from here is the Gothic **Chiesa di Sant'Anastasia**, started in 1290, but not completed until the late 15th century. Inside are numerous artworks, including a lovely fresco in the sacristy, by Pisanello, of *St George Setting out to Free the Princess*. The 12th-century **duomo** combines Romanesque (lower section) and Gothic (upper section) styles and has some very interesting features. Look for the sculpture of Jonah and the Whale on the south porch and the statues of two of Charlemagne's paladins, Roland and Oliver, on the west porch. In the first chapel of the left aisle is an *Assumption* by Titian, in an altar frame by Jacopo Sansovino.

There is a combined entrance ticket (L6000) to these two churches that also includes the churches of San Zeno, San Fermo and San Lorenzo. The churches are open Monday to Saturday from 10 am to 4 pm, but hours vary a lot on Sunday and holidays.

Across the River Across Ponte Pietra is a **Roman theatre**, built in the 1st century AD and still used today for concerts and plays. Take the lift at the back of the theatre to the convent above, which houses an interesting collection of Greek and Roman pieces in the **Museo Archeologico**. On a hill high behind the theatre and museum is the **Castel San Pietro**, built by the Austrians on the site of an earlier castle. Both the museum and theatre open daily, except Monday, from 9 am to 3 pm. Entrance is L5000, which covers the theatre and museum.

Castelvecchio South-west from Piazza delle Erbe, on the banks of the Adige, is the 14th-century fortress of Cangrande II (of the della Scala family). The fortress was damaged by bombing during WWII and restored in the 1960s. It now houses a museum with a diverse collection of paintings, frescoes, jewellery and medieval artefacts. Among the paintings are works by Pisanello, Giovanni Bellini, Tiepolo, Carpaccio and Veronese. Also of note is a 14th-century equestrian statue of Cangrande I. The museum opens daily except Monday from 8 am to 7.15 pm and entry costs L5000. The **Ponte Scaligero** spanning the Adige river was rebuilt after being destroyed by WWII bombing. Just to the north of the fort, along Corso Cavour, you can visit the Romanesque **Chiesa di San Lorenzo**.

Basilica di San Zeno Maggiore A masterpiece of Romanesque architecture, this church in honour of the city's patron saint was built mainly in the 12th century, although its apse was rebuilt in the 14th century and its bell tower, a relic of an earlier structure on the site, was started in 1045. The basilica's magnificent rose window depicts the Wheel of Fortune. Before going inside, take a look at the sculptures on either side of the main doors. The doors themselves are decorated with bronze reliefs of biblical subjects. The highlight inside is Mantegna's triptych of the *Madonna and Saints*, above the high altar.

Other Attractions Near the Casa di Giulietta, in Via Leoni, is the **Porta Leoni**, one of the gates to Roman Verona. The other is **Porta Borsari** at the bottom end of Corso Porta Borsari. At the river end of Via Leoni is **Chiesa di San Fermo**, which is actually two churches: the Gothic church was built in the 13th century over the original 11th-century Romanesque structure.

Places to Stay

The beautifully restored HI youth hostel, the *Villa Francescati* (☎ 59 03 60), Salita Fontana del Ferro 15, should be your first choice. B&B is L18,000 a night. Next door is a *camping ground*. To reserve a space speak to the hostel management. Catch bus No 72 from the train station.

The *Casa della Giovane* (☎ 59 68 80), Via Pigna 7, off Via Garibaldi, is for women only and costs up to L22,000 for a bed in a small dormitory. Catch bus No 70 and ask the driver where to get off.

About the cheapest place in a central location is *Albergo Catullo* (☎ 800 27 86), Via Valerio Catullo 1. Basic singles/doubles without private bath cost L43,000/65,000, and they also have more expensive doubles with bath.

At Corso Cavour 43, *Pensione al Castello* (☎ 800 44 03 (☎ 800 44 03),), has rooms with private bathroom for as much as L70,000/100,000. *Albergo Ciopeta* (☎ 800 68 43), Vicolo Teatro Filarmonico 2, near Piazza Brà, is a great little place, but you'll need to book well in advance. Its singles/doubles cost L70,000/100,000.

One of the best located hotels in the city is the *Albergo Aurora* (☎ 59 47 17), Piazzetta XIV Novembre 2, but its overpriced rooms cost L60,000/110,000 for singles/doubles without bathroom in low season. The *Albergo Mazzanti* (☎ 800 68 13), Via Mazzanti 6, just off Piazza dei Signori is also in a good spot. If you can get low-season prices, the rooms are small but clean and not too pricey at L47,000/67,000, or L77,000/97,000 with a bathroom. Add up to 50% for high season. *Antica Porta Leona* (☎ 59 54 99), Corticella Leoni 3, is an excellent hotel, not far from the Casa di Giulietta. Its lovely rooms cost L140,000/200,000 in high season.

Places to Eat

Known for its fresh produce, its crisp Soave (a dry white wine) and its boiled meat, Verona offers good eating at reasonable prices.

The *Osteria al Duca*, Via Arche Scaligere

VENETO

2, in the so-called Casa di Romeo (actually the former home of the Montecchi, one of the families on which Shakespeare's play is based), has a solid set menu for L19,000, but its reputation is greater than its cooking. More expensive but locally recommended is the *Bottega del Vino*, Vicolo Scudo di Francia 3a. The frescoes alone are worth seeing. *Ristorante Maffei* in the Palazzo Maffei, Piazza delle Erbe 38, has pasta from L12,000 and main dishes from L22,000.

Head east across the river for a couple of other treats. *Ostaria La Canna Ai Cagoni*, Via Scrimiari 5, offers spadellato (pan-sauteed pasta with various meats, cheese and rucola). *Trattoria al Scalin*, Via San Vitale 6, is polenta heaven for vegetarians. First and second course cost only L7000.

Entertainment

Throughout the year the city hosts musical and cultural events, culminating in the season of opera and drama from July to September at the *Arena* (tickets from L30,000). There is a programme of ballet and opera in winter at the 18th-century *Teatro Filarmonico* (☎ 800 28 80), Via dei Mutilati 4, just south of Piazza Brà, and Shakespeare is performed at the Roman theatre in summer. Information and tickets for these events are available at the Ente Lirico Arena di Verona (☎ 800 51 51), Piazza Brà 28.

Caffè Antica Osteria al Duomo, Via Duomo 7, is a cosy tavern with mandolins, balalaikas and other string instruments hanging on the wall. On Wednesdays and Fridays you can join in for a singalong. Otherwise, just pop in for a drop of fragolino.

Getting There & Away

Verona-Villafranca airport (☎ 809 56 66) is just outside the town and accessible by bus and train. Flights from all over Italy and some European cities arrive here. City buses depart for the airport from the bus station near Porta Nuova.

The main intercity bus station (☎ 800 41 29) is in front of the train station, in an area known as Porta Nuova. Buses leave for Mantova, Ferrara and Brescia. Verona has rail links with Milano, Venezia, Padova, Mantova, Modena, Firenze, Roma, Austria and Germany and is at the intersection of the Serenissima A4 (Milano-Venezia) and Brennero A22 autostradas.

Getting Around

Bus Nos 11, 12, 13 and 72 (bus Nos 91 or 98 on Sundays and holidays) connect the train station with Piazza Brà, and bus No 70 with Piazza delle Erbe. Otherwise it's a 15 to 20-minute walk along Corso Porta Nuova. Cars are banned from the city centre in the mornings and early afternoon, but you will be given entry if you are staying at a hotel. Free car parks are at Via Città di Nimes (near the train station), Porta Vescovo and Porta Palio, from where there are buses into the city centre. For a taxi, call ☎ 53 26 66.

TREVISO

A small, pleasant city with historical importance as a Roman centre, Treviso is worth a stopover if you are heading north for the Dolomiti. There is, however, no decent cheap accommodation in the city. If you can pay higher rates, Treviso can make a good base from which to see the smaller towns leading up into the Alps. A prosperous town, Treviso claims Luciano Benetton as its favourite son. The company's factories can be found around the city.

Information

The APT's information office (☎ 54 76 32) is at Piazzetta Monte di Pietà 8, adjacent to Piazza dei Signori. It opens Monday to Friday from 8.30 am to 12.30 pm and 3 to 6 pm, and on Saturday to 1 pm.

Treviso's telephone code is ☎ 0422.

Things to See & Do

The APT promotes Treviso as the *città d'acqua* (city of water) and compares it with Venezia. While the Sile river, which weaves through the centre, is quite beautiful in parts, the city is not a patch on La Serenissima.

Boat cruises on the *Silis* and *Altino* (☎ 78 86 63/71) operate on the Sile between Treviso and the Venetian lagoon, but only in summer.

The city's other claim to fame is as the *città dipinta* (frescoed city). Get a copy of *Treviso Città Dipinta* from the APT and follow the fresco itinerary, taking in the **Cattedrale di San Pietro**, with frescoes by Pordenone, the **Chiesa di San Nicolò**, with frescoes by Tomaso da Modena, and the deconsecrated **Chiesa di Santa Caterina**, where there is a fresco cycle by Tomaso.

Places to Stay & Eat

The cheapest central accommodation option is *Al Cuor* (☎ 41 09 29), Piazzale Duca d'Aosta 1, but it's rather unsavoury, and well overpriced with singles/doubles starting at L35,000/58,000, or L50,000/78,000 with a bathroom. Otherwise you'll be looking at L75,000/100,000 at the handful of places in central Treviso – the best choice is *Albergo alle Beccherie* (☎ 54 08 71), Piazza Ancilotto 8 (near Piazza dei Signori). It's also known as the *Campeol* and has a good restaurant. Ristorante al Dante, Piazza Garibaldi 6, is a good budget options, with pasta from L8000.

Getting There & Away

The bus station is at Lungosile Mattei, near the train station. Lamarca Trevigiani buses link Treviso with other towns in the province, and ACTV buses go to Venezia. Trains (☎ 54 13 52) arrive at Piazzale Duca d'Aosta and go to/from Venezia, Belluno, Padova and major cities to the south and west. By car, take the SS53 for Venezia and Padova.

BELLUNO

Belluno is a beautiful little town at the foot of the Dolomiti and makes a good base for exploring the mountains. It is worth a day trip from Venezia either by train or bus and is also easily accessible from Treviso.

The tourist office, the Azienda di Promozione Turistica delle Prealpi e Dolomiti Bellunesi (☎ 0437-94 00 83), Via Rodolfo Psaro 21, produces a feast of information on walking, trekking, skiing and other sporting endeavours and should be visited if you are planning to head into the Dolomiti. The Comunità Montana Bellunese (☎ 0437-94 02 83), Via San Lucano 7, can assist with details on Alpine *rifugi* and mountain guides.

The *Camping Park Nevegal* (☎ 0437-90 81 43), Via Nevegal 263, is about 10 km from the town at Nevegal and is reached by Autolinee Dolomiti bus from Belluno. The *Casa per Ferie Giovanni XXIII* (☎ 0437-94 44 60), Piazza Piloni 11, near the centre of Belluno, has singles for L36,000 and only a few doubles for L62,000. The *Albergo Taverna* (☎ 0437-2 51 92), Via Cipro 7, has singles/doubles for L30,000/60,000. Most of the town's restaurants are around the central Piazza dei Martiri.

Autolinee Dolomiti buses (☎ 0437-94 12 37), Piazzale della Stazione, depart from the train station on the western edge of town for Agordo, Cortina d'Ampezzo, Feltre and smaller towns in the mountains and south of town. Trains (☎ 0437-94 44 38) are less regular to northern towns but there are services to Cortina as well as to Treviso and Venezia.

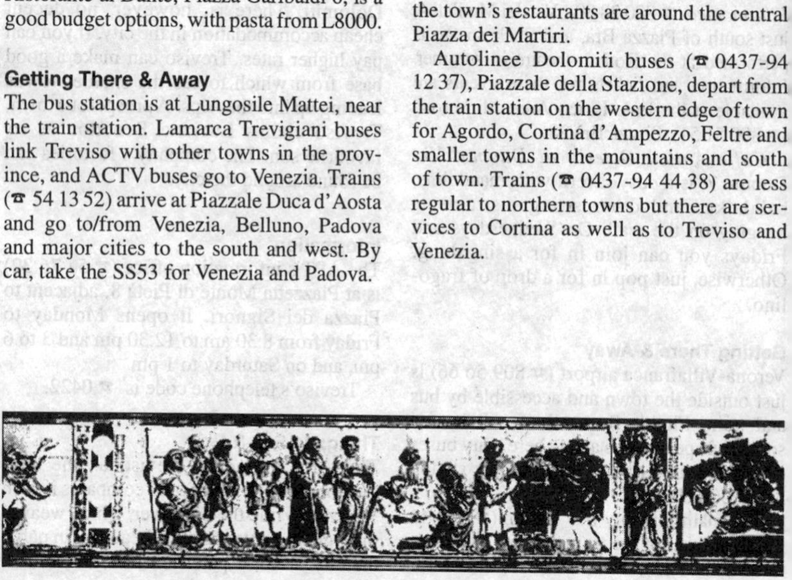

Friuli-Venezia Giulia

Made up of some of the last areas to join the Italian state after unification, Friuli-Venezia Giulia could be seen as a distant backwater – and not a few of Roma's politicians see it just that way. The region marks the front line between the three great European cultural groupings: it is here that the Latin, Slav and Germanic worlds have for centuries run up against each other, often violently.

There's little more than a series of lagoons and flat wetlands along the Adriatic coast, while the Friulian plains and Giulian plateaux lead up to pine-covered Alps in the north, bordered by the Veneto to the west, Austria to the north and Slovenia in the east.

Roman rule was followed by that of the Visigoths, Attila's Huns, the Lombards and Charlemagne's Franks, who all left their mark. The Patriarchate of Aquileia, formed in the second half of the 10th century, unified the local church and remained autonomous for several centuries. Parts of Friuli went to Venezia in 1420, but the easternmost area, including Gorizia, was only briefly touched by its influence. By 1797, the whole region was under the Habsburg Austrians. Most of Friuli joined Italy in 1866, but it was not until after WWI that Gorizia, Trieste (in a roughly defined area known as the Giulia), Istria and Dalmatia were included – and at what cost. The Latin-Germanic-Slav triangle found its bloodiest expression in the trenches of WWI – Italy's 700,000 dead came from as far afield as Sardegna and Sicilia, but they fell nearly to a man in what would subsequently become Friuli-Venezia Giulia.

After WWII Italy was obliged to cede Dalmatia and the Istrian peninsula to Tito's Yugoslavia in 1947, keeping Trieste. The Iron Curtain passed right through the frontier town of Gorizia. Today, road signs in the area around the town are in Italian and Slovene and you can still stumble across the occasional Slovene monument to Yugoslav partisans along the back lanes of the province. The Slovene community is strong but feels, not without reason, that Roma pays little heed to its needs – for years there has been talk of bilingual education for Italian Slovenes, with no result.

Relations between Italy and Slovenia are cordial at best. Each side is critical of the other's treatment of their respective Slovene and Italian minorities. Italy is also miffed that its eastern neighbour tends to turn north towards Austria and Germany in order to expand trade rather than looking towards Roma.

HIGHLIGHTS

- Buffet lunch in Trieste and a long afternoon coffee at Caffè San Marco
- The Romanesque basilica in Aquileia
- Lombard art in the pretty town of Cividale del Friuli
- Skiing and hiking in the northern Carnia Alps
- Crossing from Trieste into Slovenia to see the Lipizzaner horse farm

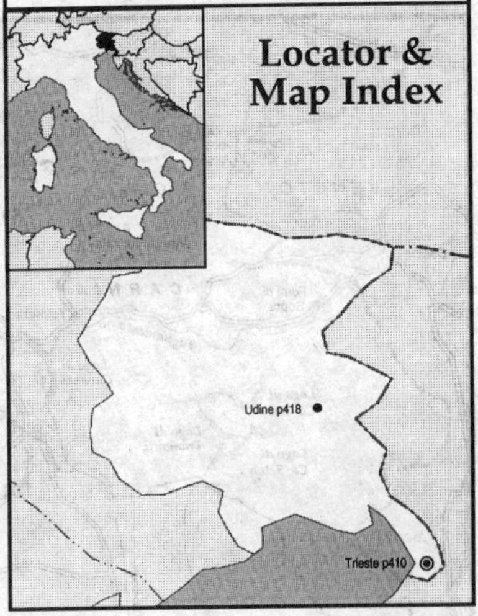

Heading west from the frontier, the road signs are in Italian and Friulian. Udine bears the marks of Venetian intervention, while Trieste is largely a neoclassical creation of Habsburg Austria.

The region is relatively unexplored, and its cities and towns are worth a few days of your time. You can mix urban culture with nature by heading for the Adriatic beaches, northern ski slopes or forest walking tracks.

TRIESTE

Sitting snugly between the Adriatic Sea and Slovenia, Trieste is an odd city. The faded grandeur of its largely homogeneous architecture is owed entirely to its days as the great southern port for the Austro-Hungarian Empire in the 18th and 19th centuries. The city is a kind of microcosm of one of Western Europe's major preoccupations – migrant pressure from east and south. What could be more incongruous, or more eloquent, than the sight of Croatian shoppers (bus and carloads flock to Trieste daily) bargaining fiercely with illegal black African immigrants hawking their wares in the streets?

Strangely attractive, although hardly strong on specific tourist sights, Trieste is not

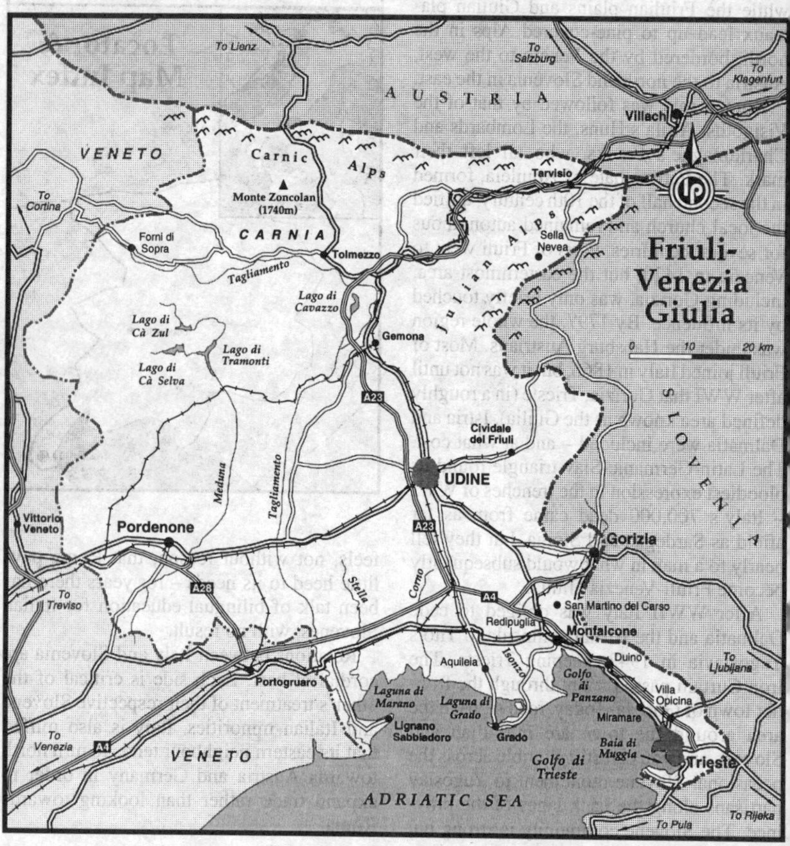

a bad place to end an Italian tour and embark on a foray into Eastern Europe – war in the former Yugoslavia permitting. The city closes down almost completely in August, including many restaurants and hotels.

History

Known in antiquity as Tergeste, the fortified settlement was occupied by a succession of Venetian tribes, Gauls and Celts. The city grew to prominence under the Romans in the 2nd century BC as a port and trading centre; however, when the Romans founded Aquileia to the west, Trieste fell into an obscurity that was to last until the 18th century, when the Austrian empress Maria Theresa saw its potential as a port. As the city developed, much of its medieval heart was levelled to make way for a new layer of neoclassical buildings. When Trieste became part of Italy in 1918, the government found the city no match for its ports to the south, and once again it fell into decline.

The city is known as Trst to the Slavs, and its nationality has often been a bone of contention. The poet and ultra-nationalist Gabriele d'Annunzio launched some of his madcap escapades into Yugoslavia from this city after WWI, and in 1945 the Allies occupied Trieste pending settlement of Italy's border disputes with Belgrade. They remained there until 1954. Today, traffic through the port is growing, although its main purpose is as an unloading point for the massive oil tankers supplying a pipeline to Austria.

Orientation

The train and bus stations are at the northern edge of Trieste's historic centre, in Piazza della Libertà. Head straight south along any main street and you'll be in the grid of the 18th-century Borgo Teresiano, where several budget hotels are located, as well as plenty of bars and restaurants. South of the grid (about a 20-minute walk from the train station) is the hilltop Castello di San Giusto. The town's main museums are a little farther south-west, while the principal shopping boulevards stretch east off Via Giosue Carducci.

Information

Tourist Offices The APT office (☎ 42 01 82) at the train station is open Monday to Friday from 9 am to 7 pm and Saturday to 2 pm. The main tourist office (☎ 679 61 11) is at Via San Nicolò 20, but its opening hours are shorter. There is also a small information booth at Stazione Marittima. Check out www.fvgpromo.it on the Internet to search for information.

Foreign Consulates The British Consulate (☎ 30 28 84) is at Vicolo delle Ville 16. The USA has a consular agency (☎ 66 01 77) at Via Roma 15. France (☎ 36 69 68) is represented at Piazza Unità d'Italia 7. The Federal Republic of Yugoslavia (☎ 41 01 25) has a consulate at Strada Friuli 54, and Slovenia (☎ 30 78 55) at Via San Giorgio 5. Croatia (☎ 77 51 42) has a consulate at Piazza Goldoni 9.

Money Branches of the Banca Nazionale del Lavoro have ATMs that accept Visa. There are exchange booths at the train and bus stations (open daily from 9 am to 7 pm) and Stazione Marittima.

Post & Communications The main post office is on Piazza Vittorio Veneto. It is open Monday to Saturday from 8 am to 7 pm. The postcode is 34100.

The staffed Telecom office at Via Pascoli 9 is open Monday to Friday from 8.30 am to 12.30 pm and 4 to 7 pm. There are unstaffed offices at the train station and Piazza Nicolò Tommaseo 4b. The telephone code for Trieste is ☎ 040.

Travel Agencies CTS (☎ 36 18 79), Piazza Dalmazia 3b, can advise on travel in the Balkans.

Emergency & Medical Services For a police emergency, call ☎ 113. The questura (☎ 37 901) is at Via Tor Bandena 6.

The Ospedale Maggiore (☎ 399 11 11) is in

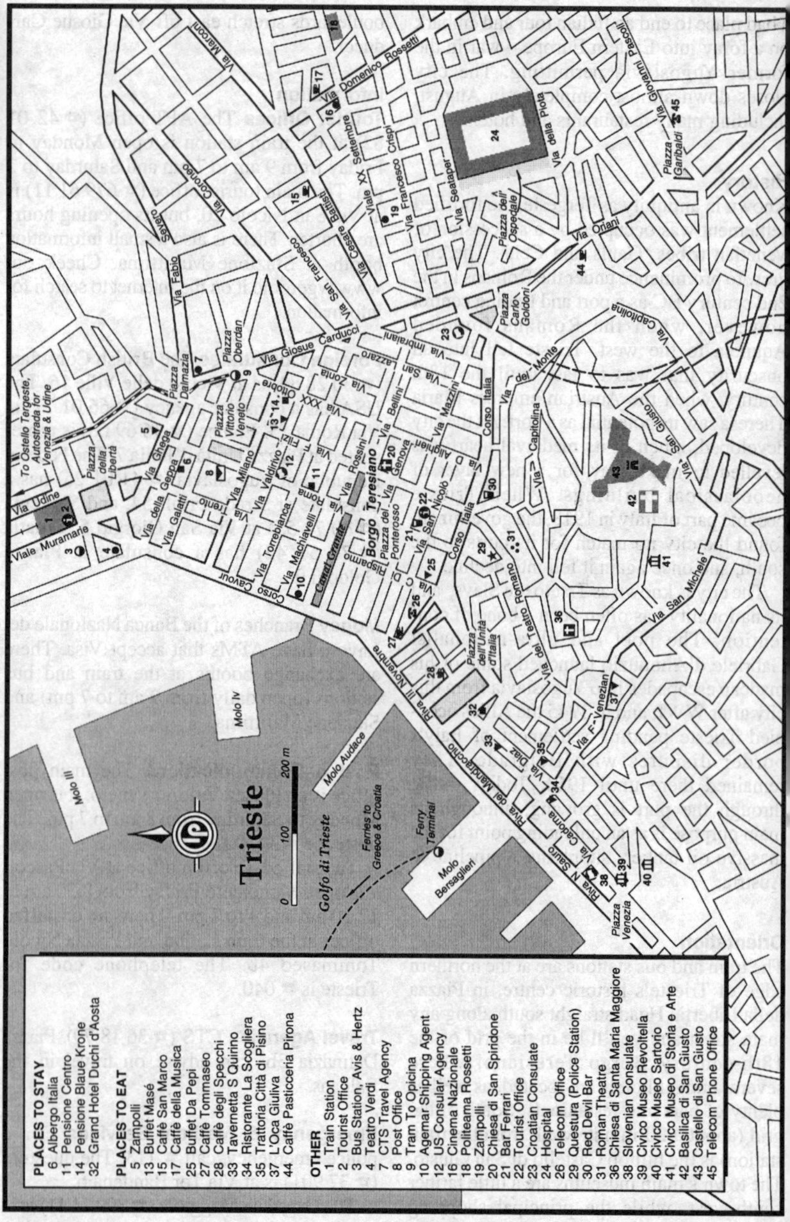
Trieste
0
100
200 m
Golfo di Trieste
Ferries to Greece & Croatia
Ferry Terminal
Molo Bersaglieri
Molo Audace
Molo IV
Molo III
Canal Grande
Borgo Teresiano
Piazza Oberdan
Piazza Dalmazia
Piazza Vittorio Veneto
Piazza della Libertà
Piazza dell'Unità d'Italia
Piazza Carlo Goldoni
Piazza dell'Ospedale
Piazza Garibaldi
Piazza Venezia
Piazza del Ponterosso
To Ostello Tergeste, Autostrada for Venezia & Udine
Via Udine
Viale Miramare
Corso Cavour
Riva III Novembre
Riva del Mandracchio
Riva N Sauro
Corso Italia
Via Giosue Carducci
Via Cesare Battisti
Viale XX Settembre
Via Domenico Rossetti
Via Francesco Crispi
Via della Piccola
Via Giovanni Pascoli
Via Oriani
Via Capitolina
Via del Monte
Via San Giusto
Via San Michele
Via del Teatro Romano
Via F Venezian
Via Cadorna
Via Diaz
Via Mazzini
Via San Nicolò
Via Roma
Via Ghega
Via della Geppa
Via Galatti
Via Milano
Via Valdirivo
Via Torrebianca
Via Machiavelli
Via Rossini
Via Genova
Via Bellini
Via San Lazzaro
Via Imbriani
Via Zonta
Via Fabio Severo
Via Coroneo
Via Marconi
Via San Francesco
Via XXX Ottobre

PLACES TO STAY
6 Albergo Italia
11 Pensione Centro
14 Pensione Blaue Krone
32 Grand Hotel Duchi d'Aosta

PLACES TO EAT
5 Zampolli
13 Buffet Masé
15 Caffè San Marco
17 Caffè della Musica
25 Buffet Da Pepi
27 Caffè Tommaseo
28 Caffè degli Specchi
33 Tavernetta S Quirino
34 Ristorante La Scogliera
35 Trattoria Città di Pisino
37 L'Oca Giuliva
44 Caffè Pasticceria Pirona

OTHER
1 Train Station
2 Tourist Office
3 Bus Station, Avis & Hertz
4 Teatro Verdi
7 CTS Travel Agency
8 Post Office
9 Tram To Opicina
10 Agemar Shipping Agent
12 US Consular Agency
16 Cinema Nazionale
18 Politeama Rossetti
19 Zampolli
20 Chiesa di San Spiridone
21 Bar Ferrari
22 Tourist Office
23 Croatian Consulate
24 Hospital
26 Telecom Office
29 Questura (Police Station)
30 Red Devil Bar
31 Roman Theatre
36 Chiesa di Santa Maria Maggiore
38 Slovenian Consulate
39 Civico Museo Revoltella
40 Civico Museo Sartorio
41 Civico Museo di Storia e Arte
42 Basilica di San Giusto
43 Castello di San Giusto
45 Telecom Phone Office

Piazza dell'Ospedale, south-east of Via Giosue Carducci. For an ambulance, call ☎ 118.

Colle di San Giusto

With commanding views across the city and out to sea, this hill is topped by a rambling 15th-century **castle**, largely rebuilt over earlier fortifications by the city's Venetian rulers from 1470 onwards. Apart from wandering around the walls, you can visit the **museum**, which houses a small collection of arms and period paraphernalia. Entry to the castle site costs L2000, and it is open from 9 am to sunset. Entry to the museum costs L3000, and it is open Tuesday to Sunday from 9 am to 1 pm.

The **Basilica di San Giusto**, completed in 1400, is the synthesis of two earlier Christian basilicas and blends northern Adriatic and Byzantine styles. The interior contains 14th-century frescoes depicting St Justus, the town's patron saint. Down the road a little, the **Civico Museo di Storia e Arte** has religious artefacts and Egyptian oddments, and opens daily except Monday from 9 am to 1 pm. Entrance is L2000. The **Orto Lapidario** (Stone Garden), behind the museum, has a collection of bits of classical statues and pottery.

Bus No 24 connects the hill with the Stazione Centrale train station. Otherwise, you could walk up from the waterfront area, taking Via F Venezian, Via San Michele and Via San Giusto. Car access is by Via Capitolina.

Borgo Teresiano Area

Going back down Via Capitolina you come to Corso Italia, the main business thoroughfare. The area of straight boulevards to the north, known as the Borgo Teresiano, was designed by Austrian urban planners in the 18th century for Empress Maria Theresa. The rather pathetic-looking **Canal Grande** that runs through this area marks the northern end of the harbour. The Serbian Orthodox **Chiesa di San Spiridione**, on the street of the same name, was completed in 1868 and has glittering mosaics.

At its southern end, Corso Italia spills into the grand **Piazza dell'Unità d'Italia**, which is bordered by the most elegant buildings, the results of Austrian town-planning efforts.

Farther in from the waterfront, and also accessible off Corso Italia, is Via del Teatro Romano. Built under Emperor Trajan and only rediscovered in 1938, the **Roman theatre** is today in poor condition. The nearby Baroque **Chiesa di Santa Maria Maggiore** is one of Trieste's finest churches.

Museums

The city's chief museum, the **Civico Museo Revoltella**, is at Via Diaz 27. The museum and art gallery are worth seeing, but visits are guided. Technically open from 10 am to 1 pm and 3 to 8 pm (closed Tuesday and Sunday afternoon), the hours in fact seem erratic. Entry is L2000.

Nearby, the **Civico Museo Sartorio**, Largo Papa Giovanni XXIII, contains an assortment of 19th-century furnishings and decorative art. It is open every day except Monday from 9 am to 1 pm, and admission costs L2000.

Activities

The APT runs a walking tour (in Italian) each Sunday morning from April to December. The tour starts at Stazione Marittima, Molo Bersaglieri 3 – check beforehand for the latest times and prices. The same office organises tours in summer of the Carso area on Saturday afternoons for L10,000 per

Risiera di San Sabba

This was once a rice-husking plant at the southern end of Trieste on Via Valmaura. In 1943 the Germans (with local Fascist help) built a crematorium here and turned it into Italy's only extermination camp. It is believed 20,000 people perished here. Yugoslav partisans closed it when they liberated the city in 1945, and 20 years later it became a national monument and museum. It is open Tuesday to Sunday from 9 am to 1 pm. You can get there by bus No 10. ■

person (these include a visit to the Grotta Gigante – see Around Trieste, later in this chapter). Local boat operators run harbour tours from just opposite Piazza dell'Unità d'Italia on Sunday from L5000 a person.

Places to Stay

Finding a room is generally easy, although in August many hotels close. Note that the cheaper places can fill with Croatians in town on shopping sprees. The closest camping ground to the city centre is *Obelisco* (☎ 21 16 55) on the SS58 in Villa Opicina. Take bus No 2 or No 4 from Piazza Oberdan. The *San Bartolomeo* (☎ 27 41 82), Lazzaretto di Punta Sottile, at Muggia, can be reached by bus No 7. The HI *Ostello Tergeste* (☎ 22 41 02), Viale Miramare 331, is 5km from the train and bus stations towards Venezia and can be reached by bus No 36. B&B is L18,000 and it opens all year.

The *Pensione Centro* (☎ 63 44 08), Via Roma 13, has rooms from L30,000/60,000. *Pensione Blaue Krone* (☎ 63 18 82), Via XXX Ottobre 12, offers simple rooms starting at L38,000/55,000.

The two-star *Albergo Italia* (☎ 36 99 00), Via della Geppa 15, has rooms from L110,000/140,000. To do it in style, try the *Grand Hotel Duchi d'Aosta* (☎ 760 00 11; fax 36 60 92) at Piazza dell'Unità d'Italia 2.

Ask at the APT about 'T For You', a weekend discount deal involving some of the city's better hotels.

Places to Eat

Local Cuisine Friulian cuisine has been influenced by many cultures but poverty has contributed the most. One typical dish, brovada, could see you eating turnips fermented with the dregs of pressed grapes. Otherwise gnocchi (potato, pumpkin or bread dumplings) is popular, as are polenta and bolliti (boiled meats), eaten in restaurants called *buffets*. Wines from the eastern hills of Friuli, stretching from near the city on the border up into the Alps, are considered the region's best. Finish dinner with a resentin, coffee in a cup rinsed with grappa.

Restaurants If you're in the castello area head for *L'Oca Giuliva*, Via Venezian 27 where L25,000 should ensure a good feed. The *Ristorante La Scogliera*, Via Cadorna 14a, has pasta from L7000.

Closer to Piazza dell'Unità d'Italia *Tavernetta S Quirino*, Via A Diaz 3b, has something of the atmosphere of a small English pub, and serves cheap, modest meals. The surrounding area is traditional fishers' territory, as some of the street names suggest. Try *Trattoria Città di Pisino*, Via Alberto Boccardi 7c, for fish.

One of Trieste's best restaurants is the *Antica Trattoria Suban* (☎ 5 43 68), Via Comic 2, in business since 1865. Take bus No 6 from the train station and expect to pay around L40,000 a head.

Cafés & Bars Triestini take their coffee seriously. The elegant *Caffè San Marco*, Via Cesare Battisti 18, rebuilt after WWI, is by far the most atmospheric – a favourite with students, chess players, newspaper readers and anyone in the mood for Austrian-style kaffeeklatsch.

Others of the ilk that have lost charm through refurbishing include *Caffè Tommaseo*, Riva III Novembre, and *Caffè degli Specchi*, Piazza dell'Unità d'Italia 7. Another pleasant stop is *Caffè della Musica* on Via Domenico Rossetti, while James Joyce used to seek inspiration in *Caffè/Pasticceria Pirona*, Largo Barriera Vecchia 12.

Bars are an odd mix, some reflecting a standard Italian model and others feeling more like the beer houses of Mitteleuropa. *Bar Ferrari*, Via San Nicolò, is decent.

For gelati, you can't go past *Zampolli*, Viale XX Settembre 25, which turns out ice-cream creations shaped like pasta and meat dishes. They look bad, but taste great. There's another outlet at Via Ghega 10.

Buffets About the most authentic buffet in town is *Buffet Da Pepi*, Via Cassa di Risparmio 3b. Another with a deliberately Germanic ambience is the *Buffet Masé*, Via Valdirivo 32, where you can wash down a plate of German sausage with a huge mug of ınich lager – perfect on a freezing winter ght.

ıtertainment

ıe *Teatro Verdi* (☎ 36 78 16), Piazza bertà 11, is the main venue for the city's era, while the *Politeama Rossetti* (☎ 56 72), Viale XX Settembre 45, is the principal ıge for drama. To taste the Slovene side of ieste's cultural life, see what's on at *Teatro oveno* (Kulturni Dom), Via Petronio 4.

For some live rock music, check out *Red evil* bar, Via Donota 4.

etting There & Away

r Some international flights and domestic ghts to Roma, Genova and southern Italy nd at Ronchi dei Legionari international rport (☎ 0481-77 32 25) on Via Aquileia.

us All national and international buses erate from the bus station in Piazza della bertà. Autolinee Triestine (☎ 42 50 20) and ita (☎ 42 50 01) operate services to Udine, orizia, Duino, Cividale del Friuli, Venezia, enova and places in Slovenia and Croatia.

ain The train station (☎ 41 82 07) in Piazza ella Libertà handles trains to Gorizia, dine, Pordenone, Mestre and main cities to e east and in the south. There are regular ains to Zagreb (Croatia) and less regular ains to Slovenia and Budapest (Hungary).

ar & Motorcycle Trieste is at the end of the 4 (to Venezia and Milano) and connects ith the A23 to Austria. The SS14 follows e coast and connects the city with Venezia; continues into Slovenia, as does the SS15. vis (☎ 42 15 21) and Hertz (☎ 42 21 22) ave offices at the bus station.

oat Agemar (☎ 36 40 64), Via Rossini 2, is good place to enquire about ferries to roatia and Albania. Anek Lines runs a ımmer service to Patras, Igoumenitsa and orfu, leaving once or twice a week. driatica normally has twice-weekly runs to urrés, Albania (deck class L140,000 one ay in low season). In summer, Adriatica runs motorboats to Lignano and Grado, as well as to a couple of spots on the Croatian coast.

Getting Around

A bus runs from the bus station in Piazza della Libertà to the airport at regular intervals.

ACT operates buses throughout the city. Bus No 30 connects the train station with Via Roma and the waterfront, while Bus No 24 goes to the Castello di San Giusto. There are services to Miramare (No 36) and Villa Opicina (tram No 2 or bus No 4).

Taxi Radio Trieste (☎ 30 77 30) operates round the clock.

AROUND TRIESTE

About 7km north-west of Trieste is the **Castello Miramare**, a grand, white castle overlooking the coastline. It was ordered to be built by Archduke Maximilian of Austria in the mid-19th century, but he never occupied it. After a brief stint as emperor of Mexico for Napoleon III, he was executed by the Mexicans in 1867. His widow, Carlotta, who remained at the castle, went mad, and it was subsequently rumoured that anyone spending a night at Miramare would come to a bad end. In summer you can see a sound and light show *(suoni e lumi)* re-creating all of these events. Take bus No 36 from Trieste, or the train. It's open daily from 9 am to 6 pm (4 pm in winter) and admission costs L8000.

Villa Opicina, 5km from Trieste, boasts the **Grotta Gigante**, the world's largest accessible cave. The interior is spotlit with coloured globes, and the 90m-high cavern is worth the effort it takes to get there. Take the Villa Opicina tram from Piazza Oberdan to Villa Opicina and then the No 45 bus. In summer buy a biglietto cumulativo for L12,000, which includes the bus and tram tickets and the entrance fee. Out of season you'll have to pay separately for the transport and admission to the cave. Opening hours in summer are daily from 9 am to noon and 2 to 7 pm; in winter, opening hours are reduced.

If you reached Opicina in your own transport, consider heading 5km over the Slovenian border to **Lipica**, since 1580 the home of Austria's legendary white Spanish thoroughbreds, or Lipizzaners. The stud farm opens to visitors from May to September. You can see performances by the four-legged stars on Tuesday and Friday afternoons in July and August.

Several monuments to soldiers who died in WWI were built in the Il Carso Heights area in the 1930s. The **Redipuglia memorial** contains the remains of 100,000 dead and is as sobering a reminder of the idiocy of war as any of the WWI monuments littered across Europe. There is a museum and, a couple of km north, an Austro-Hungarian war cemetery. The area is sprinkled with other monuments, including one on **Monte di San Michele**, the scene of particularly bloody encounters (you can wander through the battlefield today), and the **Sacrario di Olsavia**, north of Gorizia. Redipuglia can be reached by bus or train from Trieste. Your own transport is the best bet for the other sites, which are in any case of less interest.

GORIZIA

That strangely un-Italian feeling you may have picked up elsewhere in Friuli-Venezia Giulia is no more evident than in Gorizia – right on the frontier of the Latin and Slav worlds, and with a long history of Ge manic/Austrian tutelage. Most locals spe Italian and Slovenian, many road signs a in both languages, Austrian-style ca culture (lots of rustling newspapers) rul and not a few of the GO number plates a from Nova Gorica, that post-WWII creati over the border. Only a short train or bus ri from Trieste or Udine, Gorizia is an interes ing and quirky place and a stop wor making. The Colleo area surrounding th town produces some of Italy's finest wh wines.

History

Settled before the arrival of the Romans, th hilltop castle and surrounding town we always on the periphery of someone else empire – Roman, Holy Roman and, from th early 16th century, that of the Austria Habsburgs (to whom it became known as th Nice of the empire). Apart from a brief sp under Venezia, Gorizia first came und Italian control after WWI. In the wake of th following world war, Italy and Yugoslav finally agreed to draw a line through the ci in 1947, leaving most of the old city in Itali hands, and spurring Tito's followers to ere the soulless Nova Gorica on the other side

Information

The helpful APT (☎ 53 38 70) is at Via

The Fall of Caporetto

The wanton spilling of young blood in the fight for a few cm of ground during WWI was not restricted to the killing fields of France and Russia. From May 1915, Italy decided to join the massacre, hoping to end the campaign for independence begun the century before by booting Austria off 'Italian' soil. The price of this folly to a nation barely 50 years old was 700,000 dead and more than a million wounded.

The main Italian front stretched from the Alps to the Adriatic Sea through Friuli and the Giulia, and Italy made substantial gains in its first offensive – approaching Gorizia (which did not fall until the following year) and advancing as far as Caporetto in the north (in modern Slovenia). From then on, typical trench warfare set in, with neither side making much progress. Some of the toughest fighting took place on the Carso Heights between Trieste and Gorizia, and the Isonzo river soon had the impact on the Italians that the Somme had on the Allies in France. In October 1917 disaster struck when the Austro-Hungarians (with the decisive aid of crack German units) crushed the Italians at Caporetto (Italians don't meet their Waterloo, they 'have a Caporetto'), pretty much throwing them back to their 1915 starting lines, where they hung on grimly until the collapse of the Central Powers the following year. ■

iaz 16. The main post office is on the corner f Corso Verdi and Via Oberdan. The elecom office, at Via Crispi 7, is open daily om 9 am to 10 pm. The telephone code is ☎ 0481.

Borgo Castello

Gorizia's main sight is its castle, the original ucleus of the town. It has undergone several ransformations and was restored in the 920s after suffering serious damage in WWI. Occasional exhibitions are held there, nd it makes a pleasant excursion. It is open Tuesday to Sunday from 9.30 am to 1 pm and to 7.30 pm. Entry costs L6000.

There is a small **war museum** about 50m way downhill, but you need Italian to benefit from the explanations. It opens Tuesday to Sunday from 10 am to 6 pm. The ntrance price of L6000 includes access to djacent art and textile museums.

Churches

The most outstanding of Gorizia's churches s **Sant'Ignazio** on Piazza della Vittoria. You can't miss the onion-shaped domes – another sign that you're in Mitteleuropa. The little 14th-century **Chiesa di Santo Spirito**, by the castle, is also worth a quick look.

Nova Gorica

It's a hoot to hop across into Slovenia for a brief look at the post-Tito republic. There's nothing much to see, but the difference between the two places has its own fascination, and you may want to visit the **Kostanjevica monastery**, the burial place of the last of the French branch of the Bourbon royal family. You can walk or drive across at two points – formalities are minimal, but have your passport handy.

Places to Stay & Eat

The *Albergo Sandro* (☎ 53 32 23), Via Santa Chiara 18, has good singles/doubles with bathroom for L45,000/65,000. There are a couple of good little trattorie in the centre of the old town below the castle.

Getting There & Away

Trains and buses connect with Trieste and Udine. Buses also run to Nova Gorica, from where you can get buses all over Slovenia. The bus station is on Via IX Agosto, off Corso Italia, while the train station is about a km south-west of the centre on Piazzale Martiri Libertà d'Italia, at the end of Corso Italia.

A branch of the A4 starts just south of Gorizia, and the SS56 connects the town to Udine. To avoid toll roads you can take the SS14 from Trieste or the SS55 from Monfalcone.

AQUILEIA

Once the fourth city of the Roman Empire, Aquileia was founded in 181 BC. Dubbed the 'Second Roma' within 100 years, the city was a major trading link between the imperial capital and the East. By the beginning of the Christian era, Aquileia was the richest market town in Italy and subordinate only to Roma, Milano and Capua. A patriarchate was founded here as early as the 4th century AD; in spite of repeated assaults by Huns, Lombards and others, Aquileia's religious importance ensured it a privileged position until as late as the 14th century – the 4th-century mosaics in the town's Romanesque basilica are quite extraordinary.

What is now a small town lies at the eastern end of the Venetian plains, and the local dialect is a good measure of the influence the expanding Venetian republic was to have on Aquileia.

Information

The APT office (☎ 91 94 91), Piazza Capitolo 4, opens daily from 1 April to 1 November. Aquileia's telephone code is ☎ 0431.

Things to See & Do

Head straight for the **basilica**, largely rebuilt after the 1348 earthquake. The long-hidden floor of the basilica's 4th-century predecessor is a precious and rare pictorial document of Christianity's early days, made up of mosaics depicting episodes in Christ's life,

Roman notables and animal scenes. The basilica is open daily from 9 am to 12.30 pm and 2.30 to 5.30 pm. Don't miss out on the two crypts (entry L3000). The Cripta degli Affreschi (near the altar) boasts some marvellously preserved 12th-century frescoes, while the Cripta degli Scavi reveals the floor mosaics of the 4th-century church. The bell tower, erected in 1030, was closed for restoration at the time of writing.

Scattered remnants of the **Roman town** include ruins of the one-time river port *(porto fluviale)*, forum, houses and markets.

Visit the **Distilleria Aquileia**, Via Julia Augusta 87a, where you can sample local products (for free), and view the grappa-making process.

Places to Stay

Camping Aquileia (☎ 9 10 37), at Via Gemina 10, is the most affordable camping ground and is open from mid-May to mid-September. The *Albergo Aquila Nera* (☎ 9 10 45), Piazza Garibaldi 5, has rooms starting from L30,000/50,000 in low season.

Getting There & Away

Aquileia is a short trip from Trieste and Udine, and regular buses from both cities call in on the way to Grado. The SS352 road heads north towards Udine and south to Grado.

GRADO

About 14km south of Aquileia, Grado is a not unpleasant Adriatic beach resort, spread along a narrow island backed by lagoons. The small medieval centre, criss-crossed by narrow *calles* (lanes), is a bright spot dominated by a Romanesque **basilica** and surrounded by cheery, tumbledown houses. For centuries the townspeople have made a living from fishing, a vocation they have not yet abandoned in spite of beachside tourism.

The APT office (☎ 0431-89 91) is at Viale Dante Alighieri 72. Grado is a day trip by bus from Udine or Trieste, but if you want to stay in summer, book ahead. There are several camping grounds and about 90 hotels, many of which close in winter. *Albergo Zuberti* (☎ 0431-8 01 96), Piazza Carpaccio 25, is one of the cheapest hotels open all yea[r]. Rooms start at L40,000/70,000 in lo[w] season.

LIGNANO

The Lignano area is pure resort, dispensin[g] with the trappings of old town centres. Lyin[g] on the tip of a peninsula facing the lagoon t[o] the north and the Adriatic to the south **Lignano Sabbiadoro** is the main town o[f] the area. The water here and in th[e] neighbouring resorts is generally clean, an[d] is about all there is of interest. The AP[T] office (☎ 0431-7 18 21), Via Latisana 42, a[t] Lignano Sabbiadoro, can assist with hotel and camping grounds, most of which fi[ll] during summer.

UDINE

The region's second-largest city, Udine' topsy-turvy history has left it heir to an oddl[y] mixed Italian, Slavic and Germanic culture The city lies at the heart of Friuli, and a some inhabitants still speak the local dialect the town authorities have recently put u[p] street names in dialect next to the officia[l] Italian signs.

Imperial Roma founded Udine as a way station. By the early 15th century, when i[t] first came under Venetian control, Udine ha[d] grown into a substantial city to rival nearb[y] Cividale and Aquileia. It is the Venetia[n] influence that most strikes the eye in the town's bright medieval centre. Napoleon's lieutenants briefly took control at the beginning of the 19th century, followed by the Austrians until 1866, when the city joined the Italian kingdom. Udine survived WWI[I] intact, but an earthquake in 1976 caused heavy damage and cost hundreds of lives. The great Renaissance painter Giambattista Tiepolo lived here for many years, leaving a number of works behind, notably in the duomo.

Orientation

The train station is on Viale Europa Unità at the southern edge of the old city centre. Walk along Via Roma, through Piazza Repubblica and along Via Carducci for the duomo. An

SHOOT

DAMIEN SIMONIS

'enezia
'op: Basilica di Santa Maria della Salute
3ottom: Ponte di Rialto

DAMIEN SIMONIS

Fondamenta di Borgo, Dorsoduro, Venezia

lternative route from Piazza Repubblica is o veer to the left along Via Dante and coninue to Piazza della Libertà. The massive 'iazza I Maggio is to the north-east.

nformation

Tourist Office The APT office (☎ 29 59 72), 'iazza I Maggio 7, opens Monday to Friday rom 9 am to 1 pm and 3 to 5 pm, and aturday to noon. It produces a good city nap and a booklet, *Udine Il Giracittà*, feauring walking-tour itineraries. It has lots of nformation on the rest of the region too.

Money The Banca Commerciale Italiana is entrally located in Piazza del Duomo, and here are plenty of other banks scattered hrough the city centre.

Post & Communications The main post office is at Via Vittorio Veneto 42 and opens Monday to Saturday from 8.15 am to 7.30 om. Poste restante mail can be addressed to 33100 Udine.

The Telecom office is at Via Savorgnana 15. It is open daily from 9 am to 9.30 pm, and staffed Monday to Friday from 9 am to 12.30 pm and 4 to 7.30 pm. The telephone ode for Udine is ☎ 0432.

Gay & Lesbian Information Arci Gay ☎ 0337-54 06 54) has a branch at Viale Venezia 464.

Emergency For a police emergency, call ☎ 113. The questura (☎ 59 41) is at Via D Prefettura 16. For medical attention, go to he Ospedale Civile (☎ 55 21), north of the ity centre in Piazza Santa Maria della Misericordia, or call an ambulance on ☎ 118.

Piazza della Libertà

A gem of the Renaissance, Piazza della Libertà lies at the heart of the old town, and nost sights of historical interest are clustered on or near it.

The 15th-century Palazzo del Comune town hall), also known as the **Loggia del Lionello** after its architect, is a clear eminder of Venetian influence, as is the

Clock tower of Loggia di San Giovanni

Loggia di San Giovanni opposite, featuring a clock with Moorish figures that strike the hours – similar to the Mori of Venezia's Torre dell'Orologio.

Castle

The **Arco Bollani** next to the Loggia di San Giovanni was designed by Palladio in 1556 and leads up to the castle, which was used by the Venetian governors. It now houses the **Galleria d'Arte Antica**, whose extensive art collection includes works by Caravaggio, Carpaccio and Tiepolo. The complex includes the **Museo Archeologico**, and is open Tuesday to Sunday from 9.30 am to 12.30 pm and 3 to 6 pm (closed Sunday afternoon); entrance is L4000. Also on the hill is the 12th-century **Chiesa di Santa Maria del Castello**, which originally stood within the walls of the medieval castle.

Duomo Area

Down Via Vittorio Veneto from Piazza della Libertà you reach the Piazza del Duomo and the 13th-century Romanesque-Gothic **duomo**, with several frescoes by Tiepolo. The **Museo del Duomo**, in the bell tower, contains frescoes by Viale da Bologna. To the right of the duomo is the **Oratorio della Purità**, with a beautiful ceiling painting of

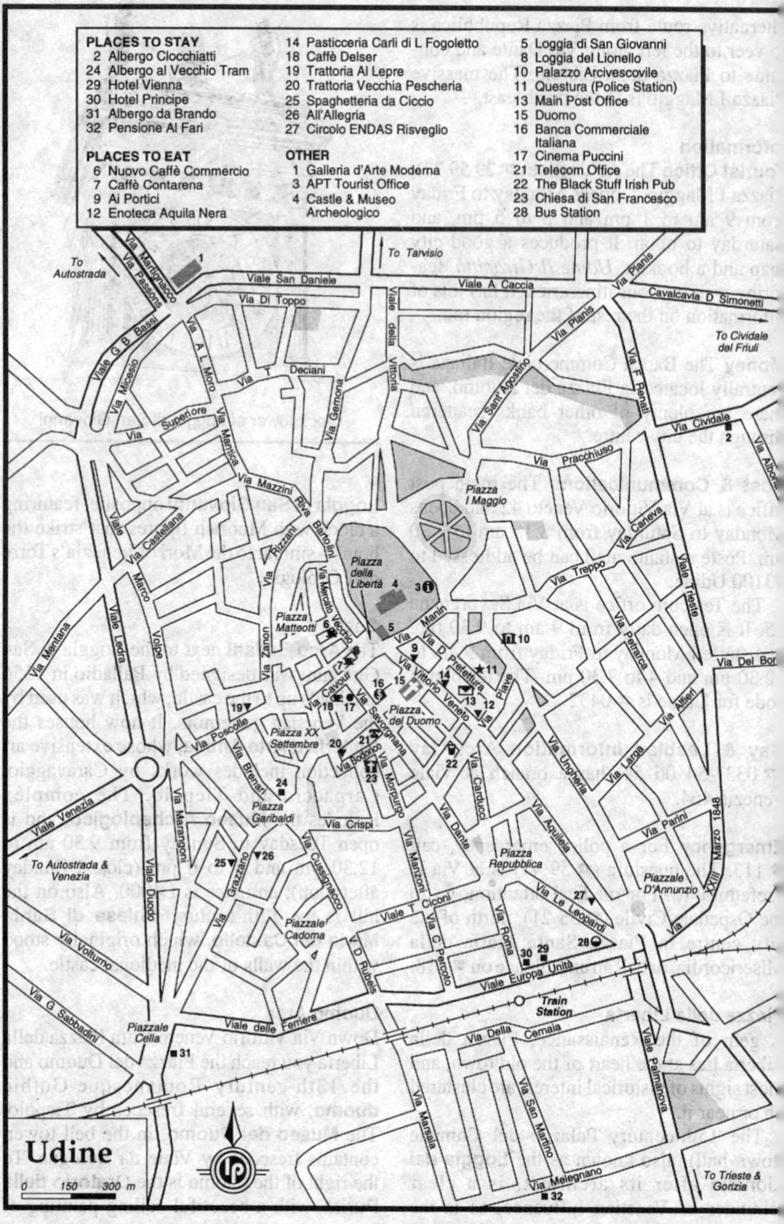
PLACES TO STAY
2 Albergo Clocchiatti
24 Albergo al Vecchio Tram
29 Hotel Vienna
30 Hotel Principe
31 Albergo da Brando
32 Pensione Al Fari
PLACES TO EAT
6 Nuovo Caffè Commercio
7 Caffè Contarena
9 Ai Portici
12 Enoteca Aquila Nera
14 Pasticceria Carli di L Fogoletto
18 Caffè Delser
19 Trattoria Al Lepre
20 Trattoria Vecchia Pescheria
25 Spaghetteria da Ciccio
26 All'Allegria
27 Circolo ENDAS Risveglio
OTHER
1 Galleria d'Arte Moderna
3 APT Tourist Office
4 Castle & Museo Archeologico
5 Loggia di San Giovanni
8 Loggia del Lionello
10 Palazzo Arcivescovile
11 Questura (Police Station)
13 Main Post Office
15 Duomo
16 Banca Commerciale Italiana
17 Cinema Puccini
21 Telecom Office
22 The Black Stuff Irish Pub
23 Chiesa di San Francesco
28 Bus Station
To Autostrada
To Tarvisio
To Cividale del Friuli
To Autostrada & Venezia
To Trieste & Gorizia
Viale San Daniele
Viale A Caccia
Cavalcavia D Simonetti
Via Martignacco
Via Passons
Viale G B Bassi
Via Di Toppo
Via A L Moro
Via T Deciani
Via Gemona
Viale della Vittoria
Via Planis
Via F Renati
Via Sant'Agostino
Via Cividale
Via Albona
Via Micesio
Via Superiore
Via Mantica
Via Pracchiuso
Via Mazzini
Riva Bartolini
Via Rizzani
Viale Castellana
Piazza I Maggio
Via Caneva
Viale Trieste
Via Treppo
Piazza della Libertà
Via Mercato Vecchio
Piazza Matteotti
Via Zanon
Via Manin
Via D Prefettura
Via Vittorio Veneto
Via Piave
Via Petrarca
Via Del Bon
Via Alfieri
Viale Ledra
Via Mentana
Via Volpe
Marco
Via Cavour
Via Savorgnana
Piazza del Duomo
Piazza XX Settembre
Via Poscolle
Via Bodoni
Via Brenari
Via Morpurgo
Via Carducci
Via Ungheria
Via Larga
Viale Venezia
Via Marangoni
Piazza Garibaldi
Via Crispi
Via Dante
Via Aquileia
Via Parini
Viale XXIII Marzo 1848
Via Grazzano
Via Cussignacco
Via Manzoni
Piazza Repubblica
Piazzale D'Annunzio
Viale Duodo
Via Le Leopardi
Viale T Ciconi
Via Roma
Via C Percoto
Via Volturno
Piazzale Cadorna
Via D Rubeis
Viale Europa Unità
Train Station
Via G Sabbadini
Piazzale Cella
Viale delle Ferriere
Via Della Cernaia
Viale Palmanova
Via Marsala
Via San Martino
Via Melegnano
Udine
0 150 300 m

the *Assumption* by Tiepolo. At the time of writing, the museum and much of the church were inaccessible, but you can request access to the Oratorio in the sacristy of the duomo.

North-east of Piazza del Duomo is the **Palazzo Arcivescovile** (Archbishop's Palace) on Piazza Patriarcato, where Tiepolo completed a remarkable series of frescoes depicting Old Testament scenes. The palace opens Wednesday to Sunday from 10 am to noon and 3.30 to 6.30 pm. Admission is L7000.

South of Piazza del Duomo on Via B Odorico is the 13th-century **Chiesa di San Francesco**. Although once one of Udine's most striking churches, it is now used as a gallery. A tiny ice-skating rink is erected in the square in front of the church in winter.

Galleria d'Arte Moderna

The Galleria d'Arte Moderna, Piazzale P Diacono 22, features a wide selection of well-known 20th-century art and also displays works by modern Friulian artists. It opens from 9.30 am to 12.30 pm and 3 to 6 pm, but is closed Sunday afternoon and all day Monday. Entry is L4000, but free on Sunday mornings.

Places to Stay

Udine has no youth hostel or camping ground, and rooms in many cheap hotels are taken by workers. A map outside the train station pinpoints all hotels. The *Albergo da Brando* (☎ 50 28 37), Piazzale Cella 16, west of the station, is the cheapest, charging L22,000 per person. The *Albergo Al Vecchio Tram* (☎ 50 25 16), Via Brenari 32, near Piazza Garibaldi, has decent, if slightly odorous, rooms from L32,000/52,000.

Pensione Al Fari (☎ 52 07 32), south of the train station at Via Melegnano 41, is more comfortable but in something of a residential backwater. Singles/doubles/triples range up to L40,000/60,000/68,000. *Albergo Cicchiatti* (☎ 50 50 47) is east of the city centre at Via Cividale 29, and charges about the same.

The *Hotel Vienna* (☎ 29 44 46), Viale Europa Unità 47, is almost opposite the train station and has singles/doubles from L80,000/100,000. The *Hotel Principe* (☎ 50 60 00) next door has singles/doubles starting from L95,000/145,000.

Places to Eat

Don't wait too late to eat out, as the city seems to shut down pretty early, especially during the week – no Latin excitement in the streets here. Things are generally pretty quiet by 9 pm.

Restaurants The city has a vegetarian restaurant, the *Circolo ENDAS Risveglio* (☎ 29 72 43), Via Aquileia 103, open for lunch and dinner (reservation required for the latter). *Ai Portici*, Via Veneto 10, behind the duomo, is a snack bar/restaurant where pasta starts at L8000. The *Trattoria Vecchia Pescheria*, Piazza XX Settembre, is a weird combination of traditional pizzeria and Chinese restaurant.

Via Grazzano is not a bad place to look. The *Spaghetteria da Ciccio* at No 18 does cheap, filling meals in a cosy atmosphere. Another place along here is the almost hidden *All'Allegria*, at No 11, which stays open comparatively late and serves local cuisine – count on spending about L35,000 a head.

Otherwise, the *Enoteca Aquila Nera*, on the corner of Via Vittoria Veneto and Via Piave, has first courses for L5000 and seconds for L6500 until midnight – you can wash the food down with a broad selection of wine. A good option is the *Trattoria al Lepre*, Via Poscolle 29b. Try the home-made tagliatelle ai funghi.

Cafés & Bars The 'in' crowd hangs out at *Caffè Contarena*, Via Cavour 1a. For an Austrian-style atmosphere and a good read of the newspaper day or night, head for *Caffè Delser*, Via Cavour 18a. The *Nuovo Caffè Commercio*, Via Mercato Vecchio 10, is also popular. The Germanic influence is clearly visible in the city's sweets; for great cakes and a coffee, try *Pasticceria Carli di L Fogoletto*, Via Vittorio Veneto 36, in a building dating from 1392.

All of Udine's youth, and a fair sprinkling of those more advanced in years, gathers nightly until 3 am for a pint or six at *The Black Stuff* Irish pub, Via Gorghi 3.

Getting There & Away

Bus The bus station (☎ 50 69 41) is opposite the train station, slightly to the east. Ferrari (☎ 50 40 12) operates services to smaller towns in the north of the region and to Trieste and Lignano. Saita (☎ 50 24 63) also serves Trieste and Grado. SAF (☎ 60 81 11) runs to most main centres in the region, and more distant destinations include Belluno, Padova, Venezia, Bolzano and even Taranto.

Train The train station (☎ 50 36 56) is on the main Trieste-Venezia train line and services are regular. Connections can be made to Milano and beyond, as well as to Vienna and Salzburg.

Car & Motorcycle The A23 passes the city to the west and connects the A4 with Austria. For hitchhikers, the SS56 leads to Trieste and the SS13 to Austria.

Getting Around

The train and bus stations are a few minutes from the city centre, but most ATM buses pass by. Take bus No 1 or No 3 for Piazza del Duomo. Radiotaxi (☎ 50 58 58) serves the city all hours.

CIVIDALE DEL FRIULI

A trip to Cividale del Friuli is a must if you make it to Udine. It is one of the most picturesque towns in the region, its small medieval centre managing to survive several devastating earthquakes. Julius Caesar founded the town in 50 BC and in the 6th century it became the seat of the first Lombard duchy. About 200 years later, its growing reputation drew the patriarch of Aquileia to Cividale.

The APT office (☎ 0432-73 13 98) at Largo Boiani 4 has information about Cividale, the Natisone valley and walking in several parks and the mountains to the north and east.

Cividale is at its most picturesque where the **Ponte del Diavolo** (Devil's Bridge crosses the emerald green Natisone rive Take a walk through the cobbled lanes to th **Tempietto Longobardo**, on Borgo Bros sano. This 'little temple', also known as th Oratorio di Santa Maria in Valle, was rebui after a 13th-century earthquake and is a exquisite example of Lombard artwork. It' open daily from 10 am to 1 pm and 3.30 t 5.30 pm (an hour longer in summer). Entr is L2000. The **duomo**, to the west, is not th most engaging cathedral, but you can con tinue exploring the Lombard theme in th tiny **museum** – the centrepiece is the Alta of Ratchis, a magnificent example of 8th century Lombard sculpture. Daily openin hours are 9.30 am to noon and 3 to 6 pm (t 7 pm in summer, afternoons only on Sunda and holidays).

The town has only three hotels. *Alberg Pomo d'Oro* (☎ 0432-73 14 89), Piazza Sa Giovanni 20, is the cheapest, with singles doubles for L60,000/90,000.

Trains and buses connect the town wit Udine and Trieste, or you can drive the 17kn from Udine on the SS54.

CARNIA

North of Udine, the Friulian lowlands grad ually give way to Alpine country on the wa to Austria. Known generically as the Carnia after the people who settled here in aroun the 4th century BC, the region's prime attrac tions are walking, hiking and skiing – and a agreeable, if only relative, absence of tour ists.

The eastern half is characterised by for bidding and rocky bluffs along the valley t **Tarvisio**. This Alpine resort, 7km short o the Austrian border (heading for Villach) an 11km from Slovenia, is not a bad base fo skiing and walking. The town itself is curiosity. The Saturday market attract hordes of Austrians; the bargains (everythin from alcohol to clothes) must be pretty good because Vienna's visitors are joined b bargain-hunters from as far afield as Buda pest, Zagreb and Ljubljana. A few km eas are a couple of fairly peaceful lakes, fron where you can take forest rambles.

For the more attractive, verdant western half of the Carnia, head off the main north-south road for Tolmezzo, a small town surrounded by industry. Don't bother stopping but make for the west (Forni di Sopra) or north (Monte Zoncolan, for instance). It's pretty, and comparatively undisturbed, area.

Information

The AAST office has branches in the towns of Tarvisio (☎ 0428-21 35), Via Roma 10; Forni di Sopra (☎ 0433-88 67 67), Via Cadore 1; and Piancavallo (☎ 0434-65 51 91). The Azienda Regionale delle Foreste (☎ 0432-29 47 11) at Via Manzini 41 in Udine can assist with maps and other information.

Activities

Skiing There are 18 skiing centres across northern Friuli-Venezia Giulia, the most important being (in a rough curve west to east) Piancavallo, Forni di Sopra, Ravascletto-Zoncolan, Sella Nevea and Tarvisio. Daily, weekly and season ski passes are available. A season ski pass (*Cartaneve*) is valid for the whole region and costs L540,000. The main centres have ski schools. There are some pretty decent downhill pistes, all starting at about 1700m or higher. Families tend to be attracted by these resorts and some effort is made to cater for children.

Walking & Hiking The Udine APT office produces *Rifugi Alpini*, a useful guide to *rifugi* in the region. It's in Italian, but you should be able to make out the salient details. Leaflets suggesting various walking routes are also available. There is plenty of scope: the Tarvisio APT alone has a brochure outlining some 70 walks in the area around the town, taking from one to seven hours. You can buy detailed walking maps in local newsagencies.

Cycling FS and some of the northern mountain communities have put together a useful guide to eight cycling itineraries in the Carnia. The rides are not too demanding and routes connect with train stations for those who want to ease up on the way. Older kids can cope with at least one of the more laid-back rides. Ask at the Udine APT office or hunt around the main train stations for the booklet *La Pedemontana col Treno*. Although it is written in Italian, you can follow the routes in conjunction with a decent map.

Places to Stay

Camping grounds are sparse. You can try *Da Cesco* (☎ 0428-29 18) at Camporosso, outside Tarvisio, or *Val del Lago* (☎ 0432-97 91 64) at Trasaghis.

Most towns have at least a few hotels, and a surprising number are in the one-star bracket. At the height of the season you are advised to book ahead – the Udine APT has a full list of the region's accommodation.

Getting There & Away

Tarvisio is connected by up to 10 trains a day to Udine (1¾ hours), and is the most easily accessible town in the region. Without your own transport, you'll need to rely on the Olivo bus line which operates often infrequent services throughout the Carnia. Drivers heading north from Udine can take the A23 or the SS13 – possibly one of the most boring roads in Italy, at least until you pass the chain of supermarkets between Udine and Gemona. The A23 is faster but is a tollway.

Emilia-Romagna & San Marino

Despite its convenient location between the big tourist draw cards of Toscana to the south and Lombardia and Veneto in the north, Emilia-Romagna is largely overlooked by the visiting masses. The regional capital, Bologna, was one of the most important medieval cities; its university is Europe's oldest, and turned out the likes of Dante and Petrarch. Bologna has also long been regarded as Italy's culinary capital, drawing on produce from the fertile plains along the Po valley and adding tortellini and lasagne to the Italian table. It is a sophisticated city, well worth a visit of several days, and makes a good base for short trips to Ferrara, Modena and Parma, all once important Renaissance towns.

The Adriatic towns of Ravenna, which boasts one of the world's best collection of Byzantine mosaics, and Rimini, with its beaches and nightlife, add to the region's diversity, as does the marshland of the Po delta, which Emilia-Romagna shares with Veneto.

A highlight for those interested in trekking is the Grande Escursione Appenninica (GEA), a 25-day hike that cuts a path through the Appennini, taking in *rifugi* and many of the dozens of medieval castles dotting the range.

Emilia, which stretches west of Bologna, and Romagna to the east were joined on Italian unification. Both former papal states, they each retain their own identity: the Emilians are an industrious people, and the Romagnoli are known for their entrepreneurial spirit, which finds a special expression in tourism.

Settled by the Etruscans, the area began to prosper after 187 AD, when the Romans built the Via Emilia. Apart from a period of Byzantine rule along the Adriatic coast and the medieval experience of the independent *comuni*, the real boom came with the Renaissance, when some of the country's most notable families ruled the various towns – the Farnese in Parma and Piacenza, the Este

HIGHLIGHTS

- Coffee and mime artists in car-free Piazza Maggiore, in the centre of old Bologna
- The mosaics at Ravenna, capital of the Byzantine Empire's western regions
- The cathedral at Modena, home town of Pavarotti, Ferrari and other big names
- Watching what inspired Fellini – people passing in the night – at his birthplace, Rimini

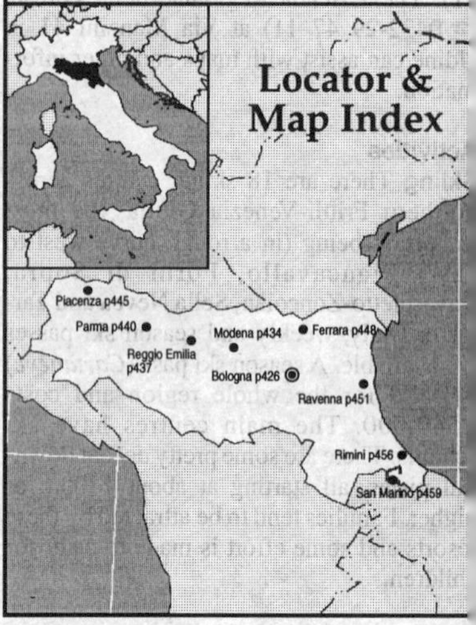

in Ferrara and Modena – and built opulen palaces and courts.

Transport along the Via Emilia is excellen and bus connections enable exploration into the mountains and north along the Po river The region's prosperity means prices are relatively high, but thanks to several youth hostels even a budget traveller can see the entire region without too much trouble Accommodation can be difficult to find, so it may be worth considering booking ahead

Squeezed in between Emilia-Romagna and Le Marche to the south is the tiny

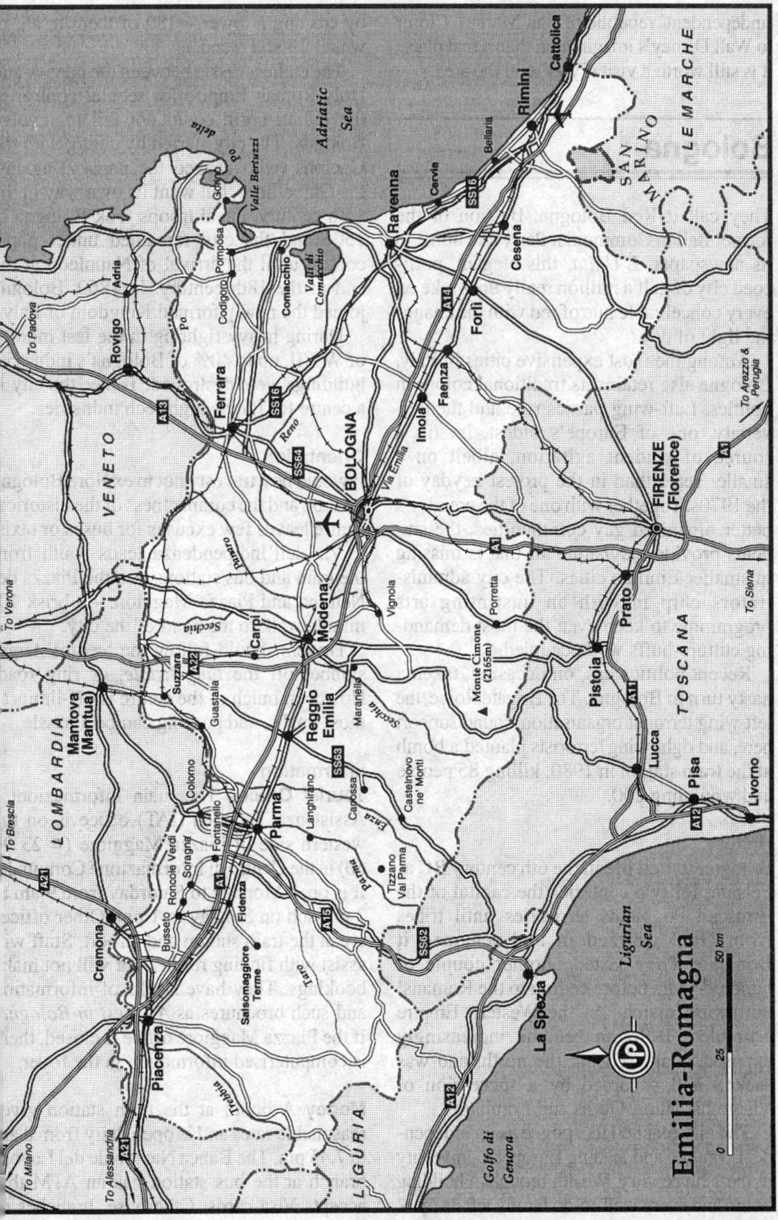

EMILIA-ROMAGNA

'independent' republic of San Marino. Closer to Walt Disney's imagination than a real place, it is still worth a visit if you're in the area.

Bologna

They call it Red Bologna. Bastion of the former Italian Communist Party and home to its newspaper, *L'Unità*, this elegant, porticoed city of half a million really does take on every conceivable hue of red with the changing light of day.

Among the most expensive cities in Italy, Bologna also retains its traditional colour in politics. Left-wing parties rule and the university, one of Europe's oldest, is still a source of student agitation, albeit on a smaller scale than in the protest heyday of the 1970s. Together with one of the country's better organised gay communities, the students provide a dynamic air that is missing in smaller Emilian cities. The city administrators chip in with an unstinting arts programme to keep even the most demanding culture-buffs well occupied.

Recent politics has, on occasion, taken a nasty turn in Bologna. The Brigate Rosse, the left-wing terrorist organisation, found support here, and right-wing terrorists planted a bomb at the train station in 1980, killing 85 people and wounding 200.

History

Bologna started life in the 6th century BC as Felsina, for two centuries the capital of the Etruscan Po plains territories until tribes from Gaul waltzed in and renamed it Bononia. They lasted another couple of hundred years before ceding to the Romans' northward march. As the Western Empire crumbled, Bologna became increasingly exposed to attack from the north, and was sacked and occupied by a succession of Visigoths, Huns, Goths and Lombards.

The city reached its apogee as an independent *comune* and leading European university in the 12th century. Wealth brought a building boom and every well-to-do family left its mark by erecting a tower – 180 of them in all, o which 15 still stand.

The endless tussle between the papacy an Holy Roman Empire for secular control o the Italian north could not fail to involv Bologna. The city started by siding with th Guelphs (who backed the papacy) agains the Ghibellines, but went its own way in th 14th century. Papal troops took Bologna i 1506 and the city remained under papa control until the arrival of Napoleon at th end of the 18th century. In 1860, Bologn joined the newly formed Kingdom of Italy.

During heavy fighting in the last month of WWII, up to 40% of Bologna's industria buildings were destroyed. Today, the city i a centre for Italy's high-tech industries.

Orientation

It would be a travesty not to explore Bologn on foot, and the compactness of the historica centre leaves few excuses for buses or taxis

Via dell'Indipendenza leads south fro the train and bus stations into the Piazza de Nettuno and Piazza Maggiore – a brisk 10 minute walk to the heart of the city.

Drivers should follow the 'centro' targe symbol off the *tangenziale*, or ring road However, much of the centre is off-limits t most traffic, and parking can be a hassle.

Information

Tourist Offices The main Informazioni e Assistenza Turistica (IAT) office is on th western side of Piazza Maggiore (☎ 23 9 60) in the Centro di Informazione Comunale It is open Monday to Saturday from 9 am t 7 pm and on Sunday to 1 pm. Other office are at the train station and airport. Staff wil assist with finding rooms, but will not mak bookings. They have stacks of informatio and such brochures as *A Guest in Bologna* If the Piazza Maggiore office is closed, ther is computerised information in the foyer.

Money A booth at the train station give reasonable rates and is open daily from 8 a to 7.45 pm. The Banca Nazionale del Lavor branch at the bus station has an ATM tha accepts Visa cards. Otherwise, branches o he major banks are on Via Rizzoli, the continuation of Via Ugo Bassi, and there is no shortage of ATMs.

Post & Communications The main post office is in Piazza Minghetti, south-east of Piazza Maggiore. It is open Monday to Friday from 8.15 am to about 7 pm and on Saturday to 12.30 pm. Poste restante mail can be addressed to 40100 Bologna.

Telecom offices, with attendants, are at Piazza VIII Agosto 24 and open daily from 8.30 am to 7.30 pm. Another (unstaffed) office at the train station is open 24 hours. Bologna's telephone code is ☎ 051.

Gay & Lesbian Information Arci Gay (☎ 657 01 00), Piazza di Porta Saragozza 2, arranges various events and provides information.

Medical Services In a medical emergency, call ☎ 118 or Ospedale Maggiore on ☎ 634 81 11. There is a 24-hour pharmacy in Piazza Maggiore, and the pharmacy at the train station is open until 11 pm on weeknights.

Emergency In a police emergency, call ☎ 113. The questura (☎ 640 11 11) is at Piazza Galileo 7.

Dangers & Annoyances The city is only just starting to have problems with street crime such as bag theft and pickpocketing. The area around the university, particularly Piazza Verdi, is a haunt for drug addicts and can be unsafe at night.

Other Information The CIT travel agency (☎ 26 61 24) is at Piazza del Nettuno 2 and CTS (☎ 22 76 46) has an office at Largo Respighi 2.

Feltrinelli has an Italian bookshop on Via dei Giudei, near the two leaning towers, and an international one at Via Zamboni 7b.

There is a coin laundrette, Lava & Lava, at Via Irnerio 35b, and Onda Blu laundries at Via San Donato 4 and Via Saragozza 34ab.

Piazzas Maggiore & Nettuno

The centre of Bologna's old city, Piazza Maggiore and the adjoining Piazza del Nettuno to the north are lined by some of Bologna's most graceful medieval and Renaissance monuments. Car-free but bustling nevertheless, the squares are a focal point of city life, with Bolognesi flocking to the cafés and often gathered around the mime artists and buskers who perform on the uneven stone pavement.

Fontana del Nettuno In the area between the two piazzas stands a mighty bronze Neptune, sculpted in 1566 by a Frenchman known to posterity as Giambologna. The four angels represent the winds and the four sirens the then known continents.

Palazzo Comunale Lining the western flank of the two piazzas is the town hall, sporting an immense staircase attributed to Bramante and built wide enough for horse-drawn carriages to chauffeur their occupants up to the 1st floor. In one courtyard you'll see a bronze statue of Pope Gregory XIII, a native of Bologna and responsible for the Gregorian calendar. You can visit two art

'I tell you, it was this big...'

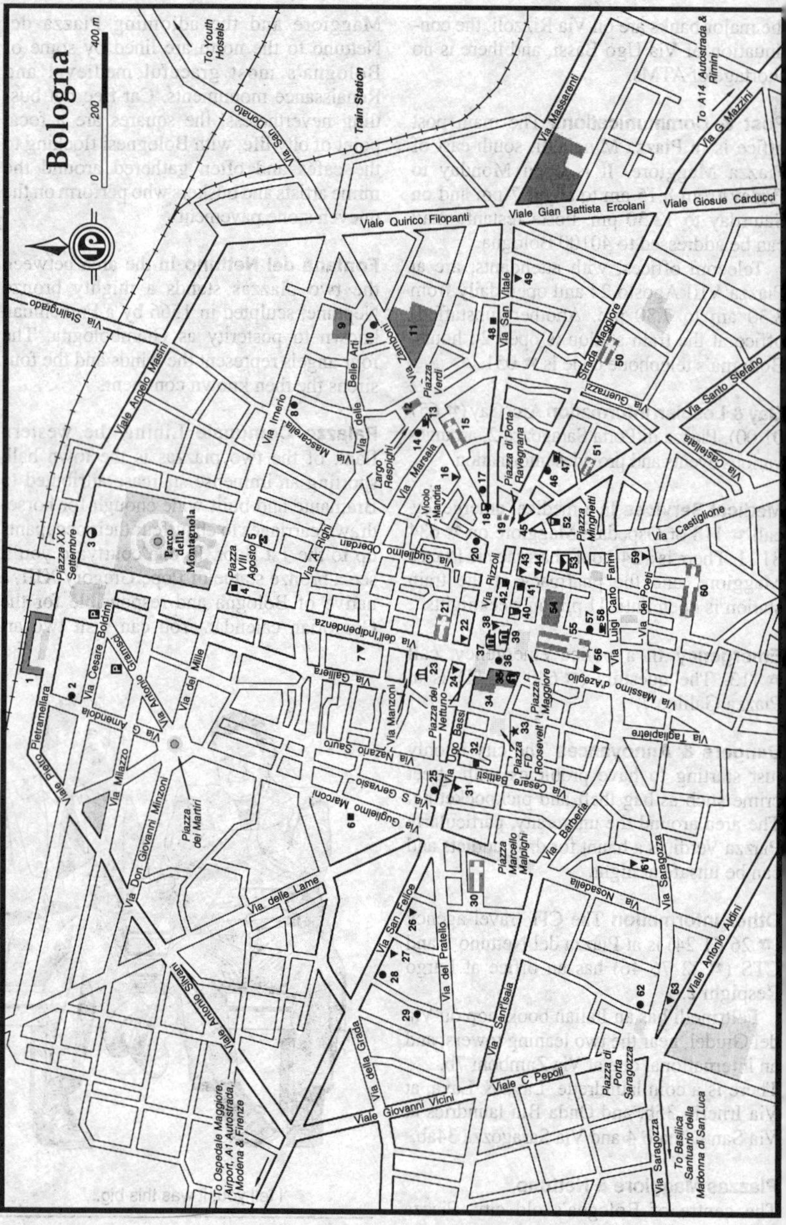
Bologna
0
200
400 m
To Youth Hostels
Train Station
Via San Donato
Via Stalingrado
Viale Angelo Masini
Viale Quirico Filopanti
Viale Gian Battista Ercolani
Viale Giosue Carducci
Via Massarenti
To A14 Autostrada & Rimini
Via G Mazzini
Via Santo Stefano
Via Castellata
Via Castiglione
Via Guerrazzi
Strada Maggiore
Via San Vitale
Via Zamboni
Piazza Verdi
Belle Arti
Via delle
Via Irnerio
Via Mascarella
Largo Respighi
Via Marsala
Vicolo Mandria
Piazza di Porta Ravegnana
Piazza Minghetti
Parco della Montagnola
Piazza VIII Agosto
Piazza XX Settembre
Via A Righi
Via Guglielmo Oberdan
Via Rizzoli
Via dell'Indipendenza
Via Galliera
Via Cesare Boldrini
Via Antonio Gramsci
Via dei Mille
Via G Amendola
Viale Pietro Pietramellara
Via Milazzo
Piazza dei Martiri
Via Don Giovanni Minzoni
Via Manzoni
Via Nazario Sauro
Via Guglielmo Marconi
Via S Gervasio
Piazza del Nettuno
Via Ugo Bassi
Via Cesare Battisti
Piazza FD Roosevelt
Piazza Maggiore
Via Luigi Carlo Farini
Via dei Poeti
Via Massimo d'Azeglio
Via Tagliapietre
Via Barberia
Piazza Marcello Malpighi
Via Nosadella
Via Saragozza
Via delle Lame
Via San Felice
Via del Pratello
Via Sant'Isaia
Viale Antonio Silvani
Via della Grada
Viale Giovanni Vicini
Viale C Pepoli
Piazza di Porta Saragozza
Viale Antonio Aldini
To Ospedale Maggiore, Airport, A1 Autostrada, Modena & Firenze
To Basilica Santuario della Madonna di San Luca
P

PLACES TO STAY

- 4 Albergo Donatello
- 6 Albergo Marconi
- 32 Albergo Panorama
- 41 Albergo Apollo
- 42 Albergo Garisenda
- 48 Albergo San Vitale

PLACES TO EAT

- 7 Diana
- 13 Caffè al Teatro
- 16 Self-Service la Mamma
- 22 Bar Canton de' Fiori
- 24 McDonald's
- 26 Gelateria Ugo
- 27 Pizzeria Bella Napoli
- 31 Pizzeria Altero
- 38 Gelateria la Torinese
- 43 Tamburini
- 44 Trattoria da Gianni
- 45 Vanes
- 47 Caffè Commercianti
- 49 Osteria du Madon
- 56 Ristorante Torre de' Galluzzi
- 58 Zanarini
- 59 Osteria dei Poeti
- 61 Osteria Senzanome
- 63 Trattoria da Boni

OTHER

- 1 Train Station & Tourist Office
- 2 Hertz
- 3 Main Bus Station
- 5 Telecom Office
- 8 Laundrette
- 9 Pinacoteca Nazionale
- 10 Farmacia dalla Maddalena
- 11 University & Palazzo Poggi
- 12 Teatro Comunale
- 14 CTS Travel Agency
- 15 Chiesa di San Giacomo Maggiore
- 17 Feltrinelli International Bookshop
- 18 Kinki Disco
- 19 Le Due Torri
- 20 Feltrinelli Bookshop
- 21 Cattedrale di San Pietro
- 23 Museo Civico Medioevale e del Rinascimento
- 25 Market
- 28 Cinema Adriano
- 29 Cinema Lumière
- 30 Chiesa di San Francesco
- 33 Questura (Police Station)
- 34 Palazzo Comunale
- 35 Tourist Office
- 36 Fontana del Nettuno
- 37 Palazzo del Re Enzo & CIT Travel Agency
- 39 Palazzo del Podestà
- 40 Osteria del Sole
- 46 British Council
- 50 Basilica di Santa Maria dei Servi
- 51 Basilica di Santo Stefano
- 52 Porto di Mano
- 53 Post Office
- 54 Museo Civico Archeologico
- 55 Basilica di San Petronio
- 57 Archiginnasio
- 60 Basilica di San Domenico
- 62 Cinema Tiffany

ollections, the **Collezioni Comunali** (good iews over Piazza Maggiore) and the new **Museo Morandi**, both open daily (except Monday) from 10 am to 6 pm. Admission to both is L8000, or L5000 to one. Note the huge panel outside the palazzo covered with photos of Italian partisans killed in the resistance to German occupation. Such displays are common in the cities and towns of Emilia-Romagna, which was a centre of fierce partisan activity.

Palazzo del Re Enzo Across from the Palazzo Comunale, this palace is named after King Enzo of Sicily, who was confined here for 20 years from 1249.

Palazzo del Podestà Beneath this fine example of Renaissance architecture and behind the cafés facing Piazza Maggiore are so-called whisper chambers. Stand diagonally opposite another person and whisper: the acoustics are amazing.

Basilica di San Petronio

Named after the city's patron saint, Petronius, Bologna's largest house of worship was started in 1392 to plans by Antonio di Vicenzo (who was in fact subordinated to Andrea da Faenza) but never finished.

Originally intended to be larger than the first St Peter's in Roma (the structure destroyed to make way for Roma's present basilica), San Petronio was effectively truncated by the papacy, which decreed it could not be larger than St Peter's and decided that much of the land should be used for a university. Walk along Via dell'Archiginnasio on the eastern side of the basilica and you will see the beginnings of apses poking out oddly from the building and the incomplete façade. Even so, the basilica is one of the largest in the world and a fine example of Gothic architecture.

The central doorway, by Jacopo della Quercia, dates from 1425 and features carvings from the Old and New Testaments and a beautiful *Madonna and Child*. The chapels inside contain frescoes by Giovanni da Modena and Jacopo di Paolo. A giant sundial, designed by Cassini in 1656, lines the floor of the north aisle.

Museo Civico Archeologico

Just east of the basilica along Via dell'Archiginnasio (entrance on Via de' Musei), this museum has impressive collections of Egyptian and Roman artefacts and one of Italy's best Etruscan displays, featuring two burial chambers unearthed near the city. It is open Tuesday to Friday from 9 am to 2 pm and Saturday and Sunday from 9 am to 1 pm and 3.30 to 7 pm. Admission is L5000.

Archiginnasio

Site of the city's first university and now its library, the Archiginnasio contains an anatomy theatre carved entirely from wood in 1647. It was destroyed during WWII and completely rebuilt. The theatre and the Sala della Stabat Mater, named after the hymn by Rossini first played here in 1842, can be visited for free. Just find the attendant.

Museo Civico Medioevale e del Rinascimento

Housed in the Palazzo Ghislardi-Fava at Via Manzoni 4, this museum has a collection of bronze statues and medieval coffin slabs, as well as some armour and a few frescoes by Jacopo della Quercia. It's open weekdays (closed on Tuesday) from 9 am to 2 pm and weekends from 9 am to 1 pm and 3.30 to 7 pm. Admission is L5000.

Le Due Torri

The two slender and highly precarious leaning towers that rise above Piazza di Porta Ravegnana are an unmistakable landmark. The taller of the towers is the **Torre degli Asinelli** at 97.6m. Raised by the family of the same name in 1109, it has 498 steps which can be climbed for marvellous views of the city, in spite of the 1.3m lean. Admission is L4000. The Garisenda family was even less cautious with foundations when erecting its tower, originally designed to compete with its neighbour and later sized down to 48m because of its 3.2m lean.

University Quarter

North-east of the towers along Via Zamboni is the **Chiesa di San Giacomo Maggiore** in Piazza Rossini. Built in the 13th century and remodelled in 1722, the church contains the Cappella Bentivoglio with frescoes by Lorenzo Costa. A little farther up the road is the **Teatro Comunale**, where Wagner's works were performed for the first time in Italy.

The university area is worth visiting for the cafés and bars alone. The university has several museums open to the public, mostly in the **Palazzo Poggi**, on the corner of Via Zamboni and Via San Giacomo, details of which can be obtained from the tourist office.

Pinacoteca Nazionale North of the university, at Via delle Belle Arti 56, this art museum concentrates on works by Bolognese artists from the 14th century on. The extensive exhibits include several works by Giotto and also Raphael's *Ecstasy of St Cecilia*. El Greco and Titian are also represented, but by comparatively little-known works. The gallery is open on Tuesday, Wednesday and Saturday from 9 am to 2 pm, Thursday and Friday from 9 am to 6 pm and Sunday to 1 pm. Admission is L8000.

Basilica di Santo Stefano

From the two towers, head south-east along Via Santo Stefano, long a residential area for Bologna's wealthy and lined with the elegant façades of their palazzi.

Where the street widens into what is more or less a piazza, you find yourself before the Basilica di Santo Stefano, actually a group of four churches (originally there were seven). On the right are the 11th-century Romanesque **Chiesa del Crocefisso** (Crucifix) and the octagonal **Chiesa del San Sepolcro** (Holy Sepulchre), whose shape suggests it started life as a baptistry. Crocefisso houses the bones of St Petronius, Bologna's patron saint. The basin in the small courtyard has long been popularly believed to be the one in which Pilate washed his hands after he condemned Christ to death. In fact it is an 8th-century Lombard artefact.

The city's oldest church is **San Vitale e Agricola**, which incorporates many recycled Roman ruins. The bulk of the building dates from the 5th century, and the tombs of the two saints, 100 years older still, once served as altars in the side aisles (today only one tomb remains). From the **Chiesa della Santa Trinità** you can pass to the modest medieval colonnaded cloister, off which a small **museum** contains a limited collection of paintings and frescoes. The complex is open from 9 am to midday and 3.30 to 6 pm.

Basilica di San Domenico

The basilica, south of the city centre, was erected in the early 16th century to house the remains of St Dominic, the founder of the Dominican order. St Dominic had only just opened a convent on the site when he died in 1221.

The **Cappella di San Domenico** contains the saint's elaborate sarcophagus, the reliefs of which illustrate scenes from his life. Designed by Nicolò Pisano in the late 13th century, the chapel was worked on by a host of artists over the following couple of centuries. The angel on the right of the altar was carved by Michelangelo when he was 19 and bears a resemblance to *David*, which he sculpted years later. The chapel is also decorated with several paintings of the saint, whose skull lies in a reliquary behind the sarcophagus. Ask an attendant to let you see the inlaid wood of the choir stalls behind the main altar of the church and the small **museum**.

When Mozart spent a month in the city's music academy, he played the odd sonata on the church's organ.

Chiesa di San Francesco

At the western end of Via Ugo Bassi, at Piazza Marcello Malpighi, the Chiesa di San Francesco is fronted by the elaborate tombs of the *glossatori* (law teachers). The church, one of the first in Italy to be built in the French Gothic style, was completed in the 13th century and contains the tomb of Pope Alexander V.

Santuario della Madonna di San Luca

The hilltop Basilica Santuario della Madonna di San Luca is visible from most parts of the city. Built in the mid-18th century, it houses a painting of the Virgin Mary supposedly painted by St Luke (hence the place's name) and transported from the Middle East to Bologna in the 12th century.

The sanctuary lies about 4km south-west of the city centre and is connected for part of the way by a long portico with 666 arches. Each April a statue of the Virgin is carried along the portico in an effort to stop the rains and bring on summer. Take bus No 20 from the city centre to Villa Spada, from where you can get a COSEPURI minibus (L2000 return) to the sanctuary.

Work

There is no shortage of foreign-language teachers in Bologna. If you want to try your luck, you could start with the British Council (☎ 22 51 42), Corte Isolani 8, or Inlingua (☎ 33 39 56), Viale XII Giugno 18.

Special Events

Each summer, the city sponsors Bologna Sogna (Bologna Dreams), a three-month festival of events involving museums and galleries, the university, and local and national performers. Torri da Estate is another summer programme and includes discos. Most events are free and a schedule is available at the tourist office.

Places to Stay

Budget hotels in Bologna are in short supply and it is almost impossible to find a single room. The city's busy trade-fair calendar means that hotels are often heavily booked, so always book in advance.

There are several camping grounds within driving distance of the city. Check with the tourist office. You could also ask for student accommodation, but only during university holidays.

Hostels The best options are the two HI youth hostels: *Ostello San Sisto* (☎ 51 92 02), Via Viadagola 14, charges L20,000 with breakfast and *Ostello Le Torri-San Sisto 2* (☎ 50 18 10), in the same street at No 5, charges L22,000. Take bus No 93 or 20b from Via Irnerio, off Via dell'Indipendenza near the station, and ask the driver where to alight. From there, follow the signs for the hostel.

There is one other hostel option for groups. The *Centro Europa Uno* (☎ 625 83 52; fax 45 03 59) at Via Emilia 297 in San Lazzaro di Savena, about 9km south-east of Bologna, offers sporting facilities and is targeted at families and groups. It is open from mid-March to mid-November and bookings are essential. Bus No 94 runs into central Bologna.

Hotels The pick of the city's cheaper hotels is *Albergo Garisenda* (☎ 22 43 69), Galleria del Leone 1, off Via Rizzoli, with rooms looking out over the leaning towers. Prices for singles/doubles start at L70,000/90,000. *Albergo Apollo* (☎ 22 39 55), Via Drapperie 5, also off Via Rizzoli, has singles/doubles from L51,000/85,000 and triples with bathroom for L145,000. *Albergo San Vitale* (☎ 22 59 66), Via San Vitale 94, has rooms with bathroom starting at L75,000/95,000.

On the opposite side of town, rooms at *Albergo Marconi* (☎ 26 28 32), Via Marconi 22, start at L45,000/70,000. *Albergo Panorama* (☎ 22 18 72), Via Livraghi 1, off Via Ugo Bassi, has roomy, clean singles/doubles for L49,000/81,000.

The city is jammed with expensive hotels catering to business people, but standards are sometimes poor. *Albergo Donatello* (☎ & fax 24 81 74), Via dell'Indipendenza 65, has singles/doubles for L120,000/160,000.

Places to Eat

Some know Bologna as La Grassa (the Fat), and the Bolognese are indeed serious about food and fussy about their pasta. The best pasta is tirata a mano, hand-stretched and rolled with a wooden pin, not a machine. It is cooked in many ways and eaten with a multitude of sauces. Everyone knows spaghetti bolognese, but the Bolognesi call the meat sauce ragù. Mortadella, known sometimes as Bologna sausage or baloney, hails from the area. The hills nearby produce the Riesling Italico and a full, dry Sauvignon.

Fortunately, it is cheap to eat in Bologna, particularly in the university district north of Via Rizzoli. The city has many good bars and osterie, where you can get cheap drinks and snacks. Some serve full meals and rarely levy a cover charge.

You can shop at the vast *Mercato Ugo Bassi*, Via Ugo Bassi 27, or the daily produce *market* just east of Piazza Maggiore, centred on speciality food shops along Via de' Fusari, Via Drapperie, Via Marchesana and Via Clavature.

Restaurants There are several self-service places about town. *La Mamma*, Via Zamboni 16, is open until 3 am and even has karaoke if you want to eat and sing. For a more classy version of the genre, head to *Tamburini*, Via Caprarie 1. Apart from selling some of Bologna's finest food products, it has a self-service restaurant where you can taste some of the goodies without having to cook them yourself. *Osteria du Madon*, Via San Vitale 75, serves mainly pasta and is quite cheap, with courses starting at L6000. *Osteria Senzanome*, Via Senzanome 42, is one of the best known osterie and serves a full meal for around L20,000. *Osteria dei Poeti*, Via dei Poeti 1a, is more expensive but the food's excellent. It's been in operation since 1600.

Local opinion is divided on the subject of Bologna's top pizza, but you won't go far wrong on price or quality at *Pizzeria Bella Napoli*, Via San Felice 40. Another good place for pizza is *Pizzeria Altero*, Via Ugo Bassi 10. *McDonald's* is on the corner of Via dell'Indipendenza and Via Ugo Bassi, if you feel that particular urge.

Vanes, Strada Maggiore 5c, near the two towers, specialises in pasta made at the restaurant. Pasta costs from L7000, pizzas from

L5000 and the cover charge is L2500. *Trattoria da Boni*, Via Saragozza 88, is very popular with Bolognesi on a budget, and *Trattoria da Gianni*, Via Clavature 18, is also recommended.

Ristorante Torre de' Galluzzi, Piazza Galluzzi behind the Basilica di San Petronio, has a set menu featuring local specialities. If you're aiming for the top, hit *Diana*, Via dell'Indipendenza, three blocks north of Piazza del Nettuno. It's considered the city's best restaurant, and a full meal will cost at least L70,000.

Cafés & Bars *Zanarini*, Via Luigi Carlo Farini 2, behind the Basilica di San Petronio, is one of the city's finest tearooms and specialises in unusual cakes. Some of its past glory is lost, but the grand décor makes a visit worthwhile, if a little expensive. In the past few years *Caffè Commercianti*, Strada Maggiore 23, has become something of a haunt for the city's intelligentsia, apparently inspired by Umberto Eco.

More modest and with plenty of student life is *Caffè al Teatro*, on the corner of Largo Respighi and Via Zamboni. Some places provide filling bar snacks – one is *Bar Canton de' Fiori*, Via dell'Indipendenza 1a.

Gelaterie *Gelateria Ugo*, Via San Felice 20, is one of the city's best ice-cream places. Also well established is *Gelateria la Torinese*, on Via Archiginnasio behind the Palazzo del Podestà.

Entertainment

Brochures are occasionally available from the tourist office, including *VIP a Bologna* and *Bologna Spettacolo News*. They have plenty of information on theatre, cinema and nightlife.

Cinema English-language films are screened at *Tiffany* (☎ 33 07 57), Piazza di Porta Saragozza 5, and *Lumière* (☎ 52 35 39), Via Pietralata 55a, which shows art-house movies in all languages. A similar place is the *Adriano*, Via San Felice 52.

Theatre & Music The *Teatro Comunale* (☎ 52 99 99), Piazza Verdi, is the main venue for opera, theatre and concerts, and has a year-round programme. Other drama theatres include the *Teatro Dehon* (☎ 30 74 88), Via Libia 59, and the *Teatro Duse* (☎ 23 18 36), Via Cartoleria 42.

Discos, Pubs & Nightclubs Bologna has one of the healthiest night scenes in Italy, bolstered by an active student population and gay community. For the latest info on what's on in club land, buy *Zero-in-Condotta* (L4000).

Osteria del Sole, Via Ranocchi 1d, first opened for business in about 1400 and it's the only place left in Bologna which maintains the centuries-old tradition of the osteria as watering hole only. It's also one of Bologna's few early openers, open from 8 am to 2 pm and 7 to 8.30 pm, although this is not set in stone. If you want to eat, arm yourself with goodies from the surrounding food shops.

Kinki, Via Zamboni 1, is a long-time favourite disco and goes lesbian and gay on Saturday nights. If techno, hip-hop and the very latest music trends are your thing, head for *Matis*, Via Rotta 10. Cover charges can be L30,000 at both places. At the handily located *Porto di Mano*, Vicolo Sampieri 3b, you can eat, drink and dance until the wee hours. Music ranges from hip-hop to acid jazz; there is no cover charge and it's one of the better inner-city spots.

More standard Italian-style discos include *Hobby One*, Via Mascarella 2a, and *Vertigo*, Via di San Luca 35. They all have a cover charge.

Things to Buy

If you're intending to do any shopping in Bologna, don't come on a Thursday, as all shops shut for the afternoon on that day. On weekends there's a flea market at the Parco della Montagnola. The main shopping streets are Via Ugo Bassi and Via Rizzoli, Via dell'Indipendenza and Via Massimo d'Azeglio. The most interesting shopping street is Via San Felice.

Getting There & Away

Air Bologna's Guglielmo Marconi airport (☎ 647 96 15), north-west of the city at Borgo Panigale, is serviced by mainly European airlines and there are flights to Roma, Venezia, southern Italy, Pisa, London, Paris and Frankfurt.

Bus Buses to regional centres such as Ravenna, Ferrara and Modena depart from the depot (☎ 24 21 50) in Piazza XX Settembre, around the corner from the train station. There are buses to Ancona and Milano, and international services to London, Paris, Amsterdam, Brussels, Prague and Warsaw.

Train Bologna is a major transport junction for northern Italy, and trains from most major cities stop here. The only hitch is that many are InterCity trains, which means you have to pay a supplement. The super-fast Pendolino (ETR 500) which runs between Roma and Milano stops here.

Car & Motorcycle The city is linked to Milano, Firenze and Roma by the A1 Autostrada del Sole. The A13 heads directly for Venezia and Padova, and the A14 for Rimini and Ravenna. The city is also on the SS9, which connects Milano with the Adriatic coast. The SS64 goes to Ferrara.

For car hire, all major companies are represented in the city. Most have offices at the airport. Try Avis (☎ 55 15 28) at Via Pietramellara, Europcar (☎ 24 71 01) at Via Boldrini 3B and Hertz (☎ 25 48 30) at Via G Amendola 17.

Getting Around

The Airport ATC bus No 91 connects the city with the airport. It leaves from in front of the train station.

Bus Bologna has an efficient bus system, run by ATC, which has information booths at the train station, bus depot and on Via Marconi, near Via Ugo Bassi. Bus Nos 11, 25 and 27 are among the many connecting the train station with the city centre.

Taxi To book a cab call ☎ 37 27 27.

PORRETTA

The tiny thermal spring town of Porretta Terme lies about 50km south of Bologna in the Appennini. Traditionally a sleepy resort for people wanting to take advantage of the therapeutic mineral waters, the town has in recent years become a focal point for soul music lovers from across Europe. Each year, during the third weekend in July, the town hosts the **Sweet Soul Music Festival**, a tribute to Otis Redding and a celebration of the Memphis sound. If you happen to be in the region at the time, it really is worth making the trip to Porretta for the festival, held over three nights in the town's Rufus Thomas Park. For information about the festival and about the town itself, contact the APT di Porretta (☎ 0534-22 02 1), Piazza della Libertà. Places to stay include the one-star *Trattoria Toscana* (☎ 0534-22 20 8), in Piazza della Libertà, or the three-star *Hotel Santoli* (☎ 0534-23 20 6), Via Roma. Trains leave hourly for Porretta from Bologna. The town is also accessible from Firenze, via Pistoia, by regular trains.

West of Bologna

MODENA

Some 40km north-west of Bologna, Modena was one of a series of Roman garrison towns established along the Via Emilia in the 2nd century BC, in this case on the site of an already extant Etruscan settlement.

Modena remained an obscure little place until it became a free city in the 12th century and passed to the Este family late in the following century. Prosperity finally came when it was chosen as the capital of a much-reduced Este duchy in 1598, after the family had lost Ferrara to the Papal States. Apart from a brief Napoleonic interlude, the Este remained in control until Italian unification.

Modena is home to Italy's favourite tenor, Luciano Pavarotti, and car manufacturers Ferrari, Maserati, Bugatti, Lamborghini and De Tomaso, who all do their bit to make this town of 200,000 one of the most affluent in the country.

Orientation

From the main train station in Piazza Dante, head down Viale Crispi and turn right into Corso Vittorio Emanuele II, which leads to the Palazzo Ducale. Walk around the palace to Piazza degli Estensi, and then straight ahead along Via L C Farini for Via Emilia, the main drag. The duomo and Piazza Grande are south of Via Emilia, and the bulk of offices, banks, hotels and restaurants are within easy walking distance of the centre.

Information

Tourist Office The Ufficio Informazioni Turistiche (☎ 20 66 60), Piazza Grande 17, provides a range of information for tourists and young people. It opens Monday to Saturday from 8.30 am to 1 pm and 3 to 7 pm (closed on Wednesday afternoon). Ask for the *Week-End in Modena* brochure, detailing 13 itineraries for the city and surrounding province.

Post & Communications The post office is at Via Emilia 86 and opens from 8.15 am to 7.30 pm. Poste restante mail can be addressed to 41100 Modena. The Telecom office is at Via L C Farini 26 and there's a smaller office on Via dell'Università 23. The telephone code for Modena is ☎ 059.

Medical Services You can call an ambulance on ☎ 118 or ☎ 22 22 08. The main hospital (☎ 43 72 71/2) is at Piazzale Sant'Agostino, opposite the Palazzo dei Musei. There is a night pharmacy (☎ 36 00 91) at via Emilia Est 416, far from the centre.

Emergency For the police, call ☎ 113. The questura (☎ 41 04 11) is at Viale delle Rimembranza 12.

Duomo

Dedicated to Modena's patron saint, St Geminiano, the duomo was started in 1099 and is one of the finest Romanesque cathedrals in Italy. The façade is adorned with precious bas-reliefs depicting scenes from Genesis by the 12th-century sculptor Wiligelmo. The carvings were a common way to inform the illiterate masses about the Old Testament. Although a rare practice in those times, Wiligelmo signed his work (to the left of the main door), as did the building's architect, Lanfranco, in the main apse. Note the beautiful carvings decorating the north door, which were inspired by the Breton cycle of King Arthur. They also feature typical medieval motifs depicting the months and agricultural scenes. The cathedral is open from 6.30 am to midday and 3.30 to 7 pm daily except Monday (it is not possible to visit during religious services). Much of Wiligelmo's work has been removed to the **Museo Lapidario del Duomo**, adjoining the duomo at Via Lanfranco 6. At the time of writing, the museum was closed for renovation.

The duomo's Romanesque **Torre Ghirandina** was started in 1169 and rises to 87m, culminating in a Gothic spire which has quite a lean. It's open during the summer on Sundays and holidays only from 10 am to 1 pm and 3 to 7 pm. Admission is L2000.

Palazzo dei Musei

Palazzo dei Musei, in Piazzale Sant' Agostino, houses several galleries, including the city's art collection and the Biblioteca Estense. The **Museo Lapidario Estense** contains Roman and medieval stonework, including sarcophagi; it was closed for renovation at the time of writing. The **Galleria Estense** (admission L8000) features most of the Este family collection and comprises works by Cosme' Tura, Bernini, Guercino, Guido Reni, Velasquez, Correggio and El Greco. The **Biblioteca Estense** has one of Italy's most valuable collections of books, letters and manuscripts, and includes the *Bible of Borso d'Este*, its 1200 pages illustrated by Ferrarese artists and considered the most decorated Bible in existence. It can be seen, but you must leave your passport at the desk. The **Museo Civico del Risorgimento** is a standard display chronicling Italian unification; it was closed for restoration at the time of writing. The **Museo**

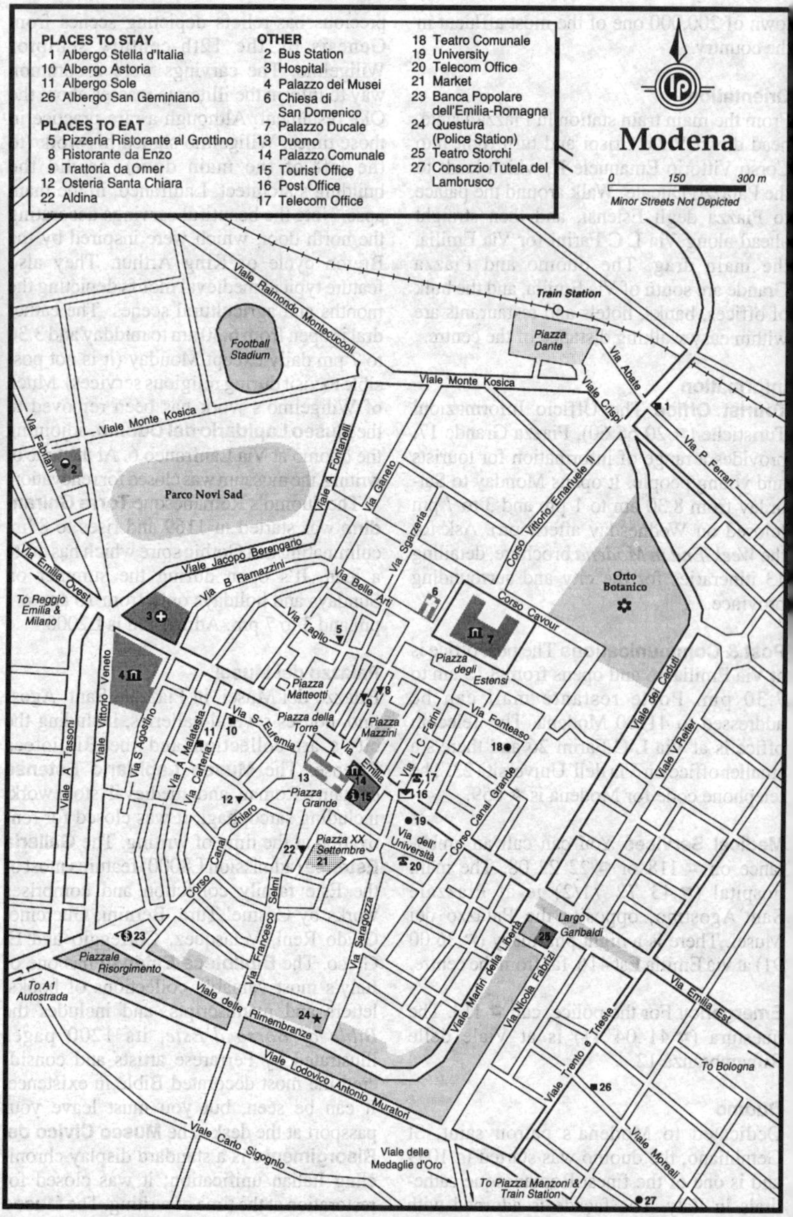
PLACES TO STAY
1 Albergo Stella d'Italia
10 Albergo Astoria
11 Albergo Sole
26 Albergo San Geminiano
PLACES TO EAT
5 Pizzeria Ristorante al Grottino
8 Ristorante da Enzo
9 Trattoria da Omer
12 Osteria Santa Chiara
22 Aldina
OTHER
2 Bus Station
3 Hospital
4 Palazzo dei Musei
6 Chiesa di San Domenico
7 Palazzo Ducale
13 Duomo
14 Palazzo Comunale
15 Tourist Office
16 Post Office
17 Telecom Office
18 Teatro Comunale
19 University
20 Telecom Office
21 Market
23 Banca Popolare dell'Emilia-Romagna
24 Questura (Police Station)
25 Teatro Storchi
27 Consorzio Tutela del Lambrusco
Modena
0
150
300 m
Minor Streets Not Depicted
Train Station
Piazza Dante
Viale Raimondo Montecuccoli
Football Stadium
Viale Monte Kosica
Via Abate
Viale Crispi
Via P Ferrari
Via Fabriani
Parco Novi Sad
Viale A Fontanelli
Via Ganeto
Via Sgarzeria
Corso Vittorio Emanuele II
Orto Botanico
Via Emilia Ovest
To Reggio Emilia & Milano
Viale Jacopo Berengario
Via B Ramazzini
Via Belle Arti
Corso Cavour
Via Taglio
Piazza degli Estensi
Viale Vittorio Veneto
Piazza Matteotti
Piazza della Torre
Piazza Mazzini
Via S Eufemia
Via Emilia
Via Fonteaso
Viale dei Caduti
Viale V Reiter
Via L C Farini
Viale A Tassoni
Viale Vittorio Veneto
Via S Agostino
Via A Malatesta
Via Carteria
Piazza Grande
Via Chiaro
Corso Canal Grande
Via dell' Università
Piazza XX Settembre
Corso Canal Chiaro
Via Francesco Selmi
Via Saragozza
Largo Garibaldi
Piazzale Risorgimento
To A1 Autostrada
Viale delle Rimembranze
Viale Martiri della Libertà
Via Nicola Fabrizi
Via Emilia Est
Viale Trento e Trieste
To Bologna
Viale Lodovico Antonio Muratori
Viale Carlo Sigognio
Viale delle Medaglie d'Oro
Viale Moreali
To Piazza Manzoni & Train Station

Civico Archeologico Etnologico (admission L4000) presents a range of Bronze Age exhibits, as well as items from Africa, Asia, Peru and New Guinea. The opening times vary for each museum, so check first at the tourist office.

Palazzo Ducale

Started in 1634 for the Este family, this grand baroque edifice is now home to Modena's military academy, whose cadets wear fuchsia-coloured uniforms (looking like they've stepped off a Quality Street chocolate tin) and are considered Italy's crack soldiers. The doors of the palace are thrown open to the public on Army Celebration Day (4 November) and every Sunday from 10.30 am to 12.30 pm – however, you need to book a week ahead; call ☎ 20 66 60.

Activities

If you're tiring of soaking up culture, the Apennini south of Modena offer lots of scope for outdoor activities, including walking, horse riding, canoeing and skiing. The tourist office has stacks of brochures, with details about walking trails and places to stay, including refuges and camping grounds.

Ask at the tourist office about booking tours of the Maserati and De Tomaso factories.

Special Event

The Settimana Estense in late June and early July is a week of banquets, jousts and other early Renaissance fun, with lots of locals flitting about in period costume.

Places to Stay

Modena is close enough to Bologna to make it a day trip, although the city does have reasonably cheap accommodation. *International Camping Modena* (☎ 33 22 52), Via Cave di Ramo 111, is a couple of km west of the city in Bruciata. Take bus No 19. It's open from April to the end of September.

Albergo Sole (☎ 21 42 45), Via Malatesta 45, west of Piazza Grande, has singles/doubles without bathroom for L35,000/60,000. *Albergo Astoria* (☎ 22 55 87) at Via Sant'Eufemia 43 has rooms for the same price. *Albergo Stella d'Italia* (☎ 22 25 84), Via Paolo Ferrari 3, has rooms from L50,000/80,000. *Albergo San Geminiano* (☎ 21 03 03), Viale Moreali 41, a 10-minute walk east of the city centre, has rooms from L60,000/95,000; it also has free parking.

Places to Eat

Like Bologna and Parma, Modena produces excellent prosciutto crudo (cured ham). The city's gastronomic speciality is zampone (stuffed pig's trotter). It also produces the bulk of Italy's balsamic vinegar, a rich aromatic vinegar using local wine that is sprinkled liberally over salads and meat dishes. Free guided visits to the acetaie (where they produce the vinegar) can be arranged through the tourist office. Tortellini are another speciality, as is Lambrusco, one of the more famous Italian sparkling reds, which should be drunk chilled and with everything. The city's Consorzio Tutela del Lambrusco, Via Schedoni 41, can tell you about vineyards and advise on tastings and opening times. The fresh produce *market* is just south of Piazza XX Settembre.

The trattoria *Aldina*, Via Albinelli 40, near the market, is open Monday to Saturday for lunch only and meals cost around L20,000. *Pizzeria Ristorante al Grottino*, Via Taglio 26, north of Piazza Matteotti, has pizzas from L6000 to L12,000. *Trattoria da Omer*, Via Torre 33, serves traditional Renaissance dishes that were prepared at the Este court, but a meal could cost L40,000 or more. *Ristorante da Enzo*, Via Coltellini 17, is one of the better restaurants, with main courses from L13,000 to L18,000. They make their own pasta on the premises. Try *Osteria Santa Chiara*, Via Ruggera 3, which serves local cuisine in a cosy old building for L40,000.

Entertainment

The city's better bars are along Via Emilia, near the duomo, but check prices, as a beer could cost L10,000.

Sipario in Piazza, held during July and August, features outdoor concerts and ballet in Piazza Grande, with tickets starting at around L10,000. Posters advertise upcoming events.

The opera season is performed in winter at the *Teatro Comunale* (☎ 22 51 83), Corso Canal Grande 85. Check out the *Teatro Storchi* (☎ 22 32 44), Largo Garibaldi 15, for drama.

Cinema Embassy, Vicolo dell'Albergo 8, sometimes screens English-language films.

Things to Buy

On the fourth weekend of every month, excluding July and December, a big antiques fair is held in Parco Novi Sad, 500m northwest of the city centre.

Getting There & Away

The bus station (☎ 30 88 00 01) is on Via Fabriani. ATCM and other companies connect Modena with most towns in the region and cities including Cremona and Milano.

The main train station is in Piazza Dante (national information number ☎ 1478-88088). There are services to Bologna, Mantova, Verona, Roma, Parma and Milano.

The city is at the junction of the A1 Autostrada del Sole, which connects Roma with Milano, and the A22, which heads north for Mantova, Verona and the Brenner pass.

Getting Around

ATCM's bus No 7 connects the train station with the bus station and the city centre. For a taxi, call ☎ 37 42 42. Bicycles can be rented next to the train station.

AROUND MODENA

Galleria Ferrari

Enzo Ferrari, who died in 1989, reckoned the Modenese possess a rare combination of the boldness and hard-headedness needed to build racing cars. His factory is in **Maranello**, 17km south of Modena (regular buses run from Modena), but visits are not allowed. The Galleria Ferrari (☎ 0536-94 32 04), the firm's museum, is at Via Dino Ferrari 43. It boasts one of the largest collections of Ferraris on show in the world and is open daily from 9.30 am to 12.30 pm and 3 to 6 pm (closed on Monday). Admission is L10,000.

Vignola

A lovely medieval village 22km south of Modena, Vignola offers visitors good food and a 14th-century castle, with frescoed rooms. During the spring, the countryside around the town is a mass of cherry blossoms.

Carpi

Once the centre of the Pio family territories, Carpi is an impressive Renaissance town, built using the characteristic local red bricks. It is 20km north of Modena and easily reached by train. Its elegant Pio palace incorporates a medieval castle and dominates one of the biggest squares in Italy, which is closed on one side by a system of ancient porticoes. Visit the 16th-century duomo and the Romanesque Chiesa di Santa Maria del Castello.

REGGIO EMILIA

Also known as Reggio nell'Emilia, this town started life in the 2nd century BC as a Roman colony along the Via Emilia, which splits it in two. Nothing remains of those days, and much of the present city was built by the Este family from 1406 during the 400 years it was in control.

Although most of us know the cheese from this area as Parmesan (as in Parma), it is in fact called *parmigiano-reggiano*, reflecting the fact that it's produced across both provinces.

Few tourists bother to stop here, but Reggio has a pleasant centre and makes a functional base for exploring the Apennines to the south – it certainly merits a look-in if you're passing through.

Information

Tourist Office The IAT (☎ 45 11 52) in Piazza Camillo Prampolini is 1km west of the train station, along Via Emilia San Pietro, and is open Monday to Saturday from 8.30

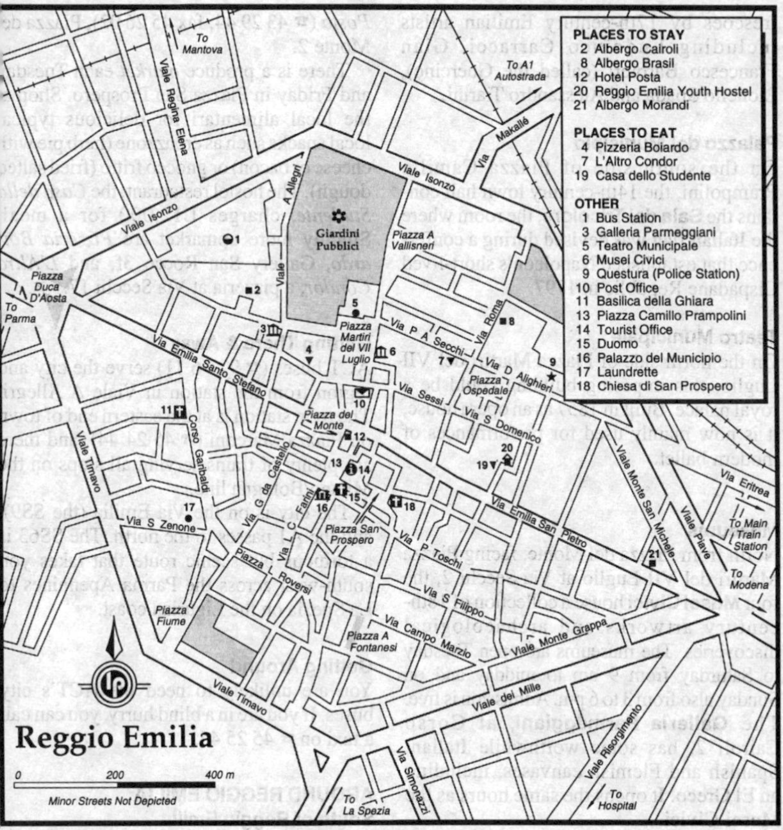

am to 1 pm and 2.30 to 6 pm, and on Sunday from 9 am to noon.

Post & Communications The post office is at Via Sessi 3, and poste restante mail can be addressed to 42100 Reggio Emilia. The telephone code for Reggio Emilia is ☎ 0522.

Medical Services Call ☎ 118 in an emergency. The Ospedale Santa Maria Nuova (☎ 29 61 11) is at Viale Risorgimento 80.

Emergency Call ☎ 113 in an emergency. The questura (☎ 45 87 11) is at Via Dante Alighieri 6.

Churches
The city's sights are concentrated around Piazza del Monte (former Piazza Cesare Battisti), Piazza Camillo Prampolini and Piazza San Prospero. The latter two are separated by the **duomo**, built in the 13th century in the Romanesque style and completely remodelled 300 years later. The 15th-century **Chiesa di San Prospero**, on the piazza of the same name, is fronted by lions of red marble and worth a quick look. Its striking octagonal bell tower was built in 1537. The Baroque **Basilica della Ghiara**, on Corso Garibaldi, houses recently restored

frescoes by 17th-century Emilian artists including Ludovico Carracci, Gian Francesco Barbieri (called the Guercino), Lionello Spada and Alessandro Tiarini.

Palazzo del Municipio
On the south side of Piazza Camillo Prampolini, the 14th-century town hall contains the **Sala del Tricolore**, the room where the Italian flag was devised during a conference that established Napoleon's short-lived Cispadane Republic in 1797.

Teatro Municipale
On the north side of Piazza Martiri del VII Luglio, this imposing building could be a royal palace. Built in 1857 as an opera house, it is now mainly used for performances of modern ballet.

Museums
North from Piazza del Monte, facing Piazza Martiri del VII Luglio at Via Secchi 2, the four **Musei Civici** house a collection of 18th-century artworks and archaeological discoveries. The museums are open Tuesday to Saturday from 9 am to midday and on Sunday also from 3 to 6 pm. Admission is free. The **Galleria Parmeggiani**, at Corso Cairoli 2, has some worthwhile Italian, Spanish and Flemish canvases, including an El Greco. It opens the same hours as the Musei Civici.

Places to Stay & Eat
The Reggio Emilia *youth hostel* (☎ 45 47 95), Via dell'Abbadessa 8, about 500m from the train station in the city centre, has B&B for L16,000. For a hotel, try *Albergo Morandi* (☎ 45 43 97), Via Emilia San Pietro 64, which has rooms with bathroom for L65,000/90,000. *Albergo Cairoli* (☎ 45 35 96), Piazza XXV Aprile 2, near the bus station, has rooms for L50,000/70,000, or L60,000/85,000 with bathroom. *Albergo Brasil* (☎ 45 53 76), Via Roma 37, has rooms for much the same price and will discount for longer stays. For sheer luxury in the centre, you can pay L190,000/250,000 at *Hotel Posta* (☎ 43 29 44; fax 45 26 02), Piazza del Monte 2.

There is a produce *market* each Tuesday and Friday in Piazza San Prospero. Shop at the local alimentari for delicious typical local snacks such as erbazzone (herb pie with cheese or bacon) or gnocco fritto (fried salted dough). The hostel restaurant, the *Casa dello Studente*, charges L12,000 for a meal. Slightly more upmarket are *Pizzeria Boiardo*, Gallery San Rocco 3f, and *L'Altro Condor*, a pizzeria at Via Secchi 17.

Getting There & Away
ACT buses (☎ 92 76 11) serve the city and region from the station in Viale A Allegri. The train station is at the eastern end of town on Piazza Marconi (☎ 45 24 44), and there are plenty of trains serving all stops on the Milano/Bologna line.

The city is on the Via Emilia (the SS9), and the A1 passes to the north. The SS63 is a tortuous but scenic route that takes you south-west across the Parma Apennines to La Spezia on the Ligurian coast.

Getting Around
You are unlikely to need the ACT's city buses. If you are in a blind hurry, you can call a taxi on ☎ 45 25 45.

AROUND REGGIO EMILIA

South of Reggio Emilia
South-west of the city along the SS63, the **Parco del Gigante** national park is spread along the province's share of the Apennines. There are numerous walking trails, well served by refuges. Climb or walk around the huge limestone rock called the **Pietra di Bismantova**. The tourist office at **Castelnovo ne' Monti** (☎ 0522-81 04 30), Piazza Martiri della Libertà 12b, can provide details of activities, hotels and camping.

The area's main attractions are three medieval castles, once owned by Matilda, the Countess of Canossa, famed for reconciling the excommunicated Emperor Henry IV with Pope Gregory VII in 1077. The castle of **Canossa**, built in 940, and rebuilt in the

13th century, is open to the public. It houses a small museum, open Thursday to Sunday from 9 am to 12.30 pm and in summer also from 3 to 7 pm. From Canossa you can see across to the castle of **Rossena**, which can be visited two days a week (check at Castelnovo's tourist office for details). The other castle, Bianello, is privately owned.

North of Reggio Emilia

A good base for exploring the Po valley area north of Reggio Emilia is **Guastalla**, as it has a *youth hostel* (☎ 0522-82 49 15), Via Lido Po 11. B&B costs L14,000. Trains and buses run from Reggio Emilia.

PARMA

Of the Emilian cities west of Bologna, Parma is the pick of the crop. Straddling the banks of a Po tributary – the 'Torrente Parma' – this well-off, orderly city should not be bypassed. The bicycle rules in the squares and cobbled lanes of the old town centre, and the surrounding countryside is home not only to Parmesan cheese and Parma ham (Italy's best prosciutto), but also to a smorgasbord of castles and walking tracks. The city itself is a little expensive, but the budget-conscious can stay at the hostel or camping ground.

Verdi and Toscanini composed many of their greatest works here, and Stendhal immortalised the city in *La Chartreuse de Parme*.

History

Originally Etruscan, Parma achieved importance as a Roman colony on what would become the Via Emilia. As the Romans' authority dwindled, Parma passed to the Goths and later the Lombards and Franks. In the 11th century, as the conflict between the Holy Roman Empire and the papacy gathered steam, Parma threw in its lot with the former, even furnishing two anti-popes. In the following centuries internal squabbling was largely responsible for the city's turbulent fate, as it fell to the Visconti family, the Sforzas, the French and finally the papacy.

The Farnese family ruled Parma in the pope's name from 1545 to 1731, when the Bourbons took control, making Parma one of the pawns in European power games. Don Phillip of Bourbon, son of Spain's Philip V, and his wife Louise Elisabeth, daughter of France's Louis XV, ushered in a period of peace and frenetic cultural activity. From the time of Napoleon's incursions into northern Italy at the beginning of the 19th century, Parma entered a period of instability that ended only with Italian unification. Some 60 years later, the barricades went up as Parma became the only Emilian city to oppose the infamous march on Roma by Mussolini's blackshirts in 1922.

Orientation

From the train station on Piazzale dalla Chiesa, head south along Via Verdi for the huge Palazzo della Pilotta. Cross Via Garibaldi for the duomo area, or walk south for Piazza Garibaldi, the main square.

Information

Tourist Office The IAT office (☎ 23 47 35) is in the Camera di San Paolo, in the convent of the same name off Via Melloni. It's open Monday to Saturday from 9 am to 12.30 pm and 3 to 5 pm and on Sunday to 12.30 pm. InformaGiovani (☎ 21 87 48) is now in the same building and has information for young people and disabled travellers.

Post & Communications The main post office is at Via Melloni 1b, off Via Garibaldi, and is open Monday to Friday from 8.15 am to 7 pm and Saturday to 12.30 pm. Poste restante mail can be addressed to 43100 Parma. The Telecom office is on Piazza Garibaldi; the telephones are down a flight of stairs in front of the office and are open daily from 7 am to midnight. The telephone code for Parma is ☎ 0521.

Medical Services For an ambulance, call ☎ 118, or the Guardia Medica on ☎ 29 25 55. The Ospedale Maggiore (☎ 9 67 20) is at Via Gramsci 14, west of the centre.

Emergency In an emergency, call ☎ 113.

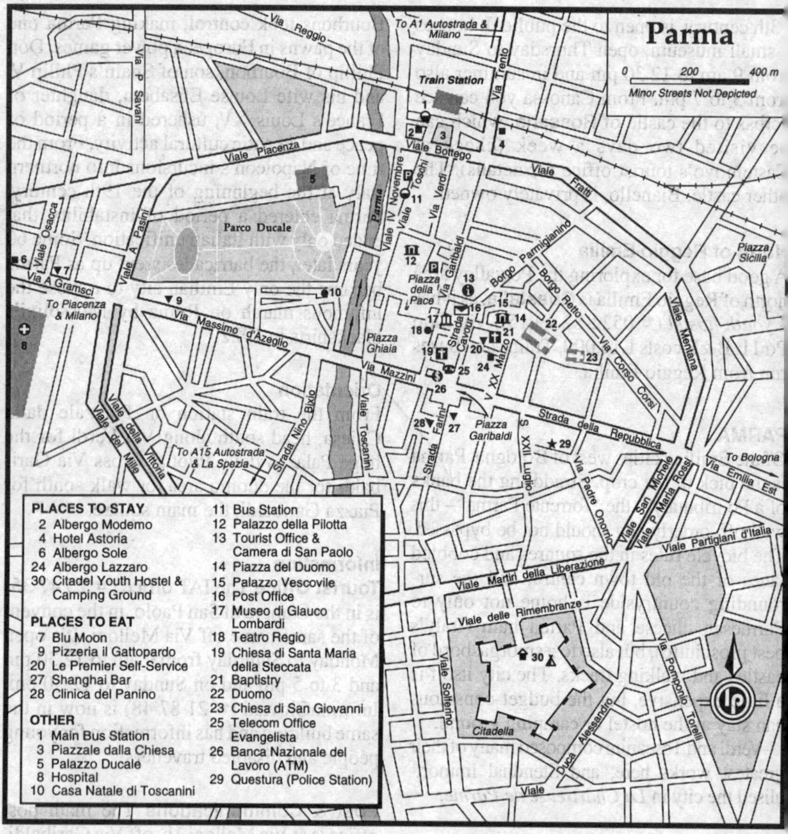

The questura (☎ 21 94) is at Borgo della Posta.

Piazza del Duomo

The **duomo** is a classic example of Po valley Romanesque design. It was begun in 1059 but largely rebuilt 60 years later after Parma was hit by an earthquake. Antonio Correggio's *Assunzione della Vergine* (Assumption of the Virgin) graces the inside of the cupola and took the painter six years to complete (from 1524). Take time to look at the restored wood inlay work in the Sagrestia dei Consorziali (sacristy) and, in the south transept, Benedetto Antelami's delicate sculpture, the *Deposizione* (Descent from the Cross), completed in 1178. The duomo is open daily from 9 am to 12.30 pm and 3 to 7 pm.

Antelami was also responsible for the striking pink marble **baptistry** on the south side of the square. Typically octagonal, it was completed in 1260, and represents the peak of Antelami's work. It is open daily from 9 am to 12.30 pm and 3 to 6 pm. Admission is L3000.

Palazzo della Pilotta

The hulk of this immense palace, shattered

by WWII air raids, looms over Piazza della Pace. Built for the Farnese family between 1583 and 1622, and supposedly named after the Spanish ball game of pelota played within its walls, it now houses several museums and picture galleries. The **Galleria Nazionale** is by far the most important. Its collection includes works by Antonio Correggio, Francesco Parmigianino, Fra Angelico and van Dyck, as well as a sculpture of Empress Marie-Louise, second wife of Napoleon, by Antonio Canova. The gallery is open daily from 9 am to 1.45 pm and tickets cost L12,000, which includes admission to the **Teatro Farnese**. The theatre, a copy of Andrea Palladio's Teatro Olimpico in Vicenza, is housed in the palace's fencing school. It was completely rebuilt after WWII bombing.

Upstairs, the **Museo Archeologico Nazionale** is devoted partly to Roman artefacts discovered around Parma and also hosts a display of Etruscan artefacts excavated in the Po plain. It is open daily, except Monday, from 9 am to 1.30 pm; admission is L4000.

The **Biblioteca Palatina**, first opened to the public in 1769, contains more than 700,000 volumes and 5000 manuscripts. The **Museo Bodoniano**, which can be visited only by appointment, is devoted to the life of Giambattista Bodoni, who designed the typeface that bears his name.

Piazza Garibaldi

More or less on the site of the ancient Roman forum, Piazza Garibaldi is the centre of Parma. The 17th-century Palazzo del Governatore at the northern end hides the **Chiesa di Santa Maria della Steccata**, which contains some of Francesco Parmigianino's most extraordinary work, including the frescoes on the arches above the altar. Many members of the ruling Farnese and Bourbons lie buried in this church, known to locals simply as La Steccata.

Chiesa di San Giovanni Evangelista

Just east of the duomo, this church and convent dedicated to St John the Baptist were constructed in the early 16th century on the site of a 10th-century church. The ornate Baroque façade was added a century later, and the magnificent decoration on the cupola is by Antonio Correggio. Parmigianino's contribution includes the adornment of the chapels. The church and cloisters are open from 6.30 am to midday and 3.30 to 8 pm.

Visit the convent's ancient pharmacy, the **Spezieria di San Giovanni**, accessible through a small door on the north side of the church. It opens daily from 9 am to 1.45 pm, and entry is L4000.

For more Correggio, head for the **Camera di San Paolo**, in the convent of the same name off Via Melloni. It's open daily from 9 am to 1.45 pm, and costs L4,000 to visit.

Museo di Glauco Lombardi

Waterloo meant different things to different people. While Napoleon headed into miserable exile, his second wife, Marie-Louise of Austria, got off pretty lightly. After her heady few years as Empress of the French, she was left with the dukedom of Parma, Piacenza and Guastalla. She ruled until 1847, with a moderation and good sense uncommon for the time.

Several of her belongings, including a portrait of her great husband, ended up in the hands of town notable and collector Glauco Lombardi. An eclectic assortment of Lombardi's artworks and other objects illustrative of life in Parma over the past few centuries now fill the Museo di Glauco Lombardi, on Via Garibaldi 15. It is open Tuesday to Sunday from 9 am to 2 pm and on Wednesday also from 3.30 to 5.30 pm. Admission is free.

West Bank

Spread along the west bank of the Parma (l'Oltretorrente) are the rambling gardens of the **Parco Ducale**, first laid out in 1560 around the Farnese family's **Palazzo Ducale**. The palace is now home to the local carabinieri, but groups can visit for free in the morning by calling ahead (☎ 23 00 23) – check at the tourist office. The lovely public gardens are open from dawn to dusk, except in summer, when you can stroll until midnight.

Just south of the park, at Via R Tanzi, is the **Casa Natale di Toscanini**, the birthplace of one of Italy's greatest modern conductors, Arturo Toscanini (1867-1957). His career began almost by accident during a tour in Brazil, when he was asked to take the podium in Rio de Janeiro after the Brazilian conductor had stormed off. In 1908 he joined the New York Metropolitan, and from then on split his time between Italy and the US, where he died. The house contains a small free museum dedicated to Toscanini's life and music. It opens Tuesday to Saturday from 10 am to 1 pm and 3 to 6 pm and on Sunday from 10 am to 1 pm.

While in a musical frame of mind, you could visit the tomb of Niccolò Paganini, a couple of km farther south in the Cimitero della Villetta.

EMILIA-ROMAGNA

Places to Stay

Cheap accommodation can be difficult to find most of the year, so bookings are advisable. Located within the walls of the giant former fortress, the city's youth hostel, the *Ostello Cittadella* (☎ 96 14 34), Parco Cittadella 5, charges L15,000 a night. It's open from the beginning of April to the end of October. Take bus No 9 or 12 from the train station or city centre and ask the driver for directions. There is a *camping ground* inside the fortress, run by the same management.

The *Albergo Sole* (☎ 99 51 07), Via Gramsci 15, has basic singles/doubles from L45,000/70,000. Take bus No 9 from the train station. *Albergo Lazzaro* (☎ 20 89 44), Via XX Marzo 14, the street leading away from the baptistry, has rooms from L53,000/75,000. The two-star *Albergo Moderno* (☎ 77 26 47), handy for the train station at Via A Cecchi 4, has rooms for L59,000/92,000 with bathroom, but the area is a little unpleasant. The *Hotel Astoria* (☎ 27 27 17), Via Trento 9, has all the mod cons and is near the train station – rooms cost L110,000/166,000.

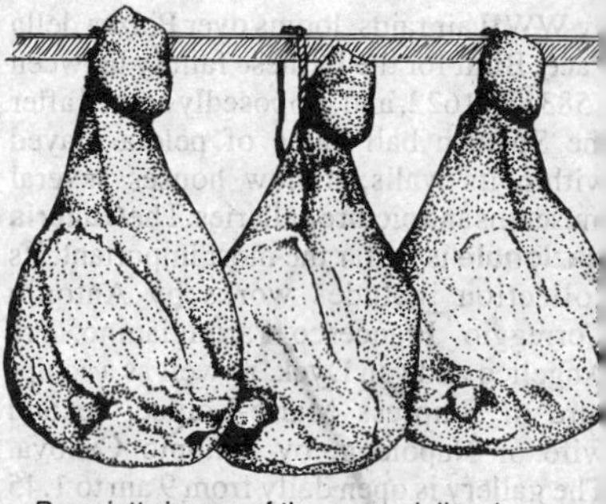

Prosciutto is one of the many delicacies you can sample in Parma

Places to Eat

The produce *market* in Piazza Ghiaia is open daily; it's near the river and south of the Palazzo della Pilotta. For a cheap lunch, the self-service restaurant *Le Premier*, Borgo San Biagio 6d, is open from midday to 2 pm only. Another decent snack place is *Clinica del Panino*, Borgo Palmia 2d.

Il Gattopardo, Via Massimo d'Azeglio 63a, is one of the city's more popular pizzerie, with big pizzas from L9000 to L14,000. If you're staying at Albergo Sole, *Blu Moon*, a couple of doors towards the city centre on Via Gramsci, has everything from seafood to pizzas. Main courses start at about L10,000. The *Albergo Lazzaro* has a restaurant that does a L16,000 vegetarian dish and L35,000 lunch. Parma has attracted plenty of Chinese chefs; the *Shanghai Bar* on Strada Farini 16 is just one of the city's ubiquitous Oriental restaurants.

Piazza Garibaldi is as good a spot as any for sipping your Campari and reading the paper.

Entertainment

Parma's opera, concert and theatre season runs from about October to April. A rich music and opera programme is offered by the *Teatro Regio* (☎ 21 86 78), Via Garibaldi 16a, while *Teatro Due* (☎ 23 02 42), Via Salnitrara 10, presents the city's top drama. In summer he city sponsors outdoor music programmes - enquire at the tourist office.

Getting There & Away

Bus TEP (☎ 21 41) operates buses throughout the region, including into the Appennini and to Soragna and Busseto (see the following section); they leave from just in front of the train station on Piazzale dalla Chiesa. Other services run to Mantova and Sabbioneta.

Train Parma is connected by frequent train services to Milano, Bologna, Brescia, La Spezia and Roma.

Car & Motorcycle Parma is just south of the A1 to Milano and east of the A15, which connects the A1 to La Spezia. It is on the Via Emilia (SS9), while the SS62 provides an alternative route parallel to the A15. There is a major car park in Piazza della Pace and plenty of meter parking near the station and along the main roads which encircle the historic centre. Traffic is restricted in the centre, which is a labyrinth of one-way streets.

AROUND PARMA

Verdi Country

Head north-west of Parma along the Via Emilia and branch north for Fontevivo and Fontanellato, where you will find one of the more interesting of Parma province's 25 castles. Sitting in its murky moat, the **Rocca di Sanvitale** was built in the 16th century by the family of the same name, more as a pleasure dome than a military bastion as the Sanvitale clan was inclined to more idle pursuits. Parmigianino had a part in the decoration. It is open from 9.30 to 11.30 am and 3 to 5 pm (longer in summer). Admission by guided tour costs L6000. Nine km farther on is Soragna, site of the **Rocca Meli Lupi**. It looks more like a stately home, but there are Parmigianino works and a display of period furniture. Opening times are similar to those at Sanvitale, but this castle is closed on Monday. Admission is L9000.

Roncole Verdi, site of the humble home where Giuseppe Verdi came into the world, is 10km on. The Casa Natale di Giuseppe Verdi is open daily except Monday from 9.30 am to midday and 2.30 to 5 pm (longer in summer). Admission costs L4000 if you don't have a L8000 cumulative ticket to all the Verdi sights.

Next stop is **Busseto**, a couple of km farther on. The Teatro Verdi is closed but you can visit a small museum dedicated to Verdi in the run-down Villa Pallavicino and, a few km outside Busseto, his villa at **Sant'Agata**.

TEP buses from Parma run along this route up to six times a day on weekdays.

> **The Small World of Don Camillo**
>
> If postwar Italy was dominated by the squaring off between the church-backed Christian Democrat party and the communists, no-one captured the essence of that conflict better than humorist Giovanni Guareschi. Emilia-Romagna, the stronghold of Italian communism, became the scene of Guareschi's village scraps between Don Camillo, the local curate with a direct line to God, and Peppone, the town mayor with a striking resemblance to Stalin. Their antics in what became known as Guareschi's Piccolo Mondo, published weekly in satirical magazines and later collected in several volumes (eg *Don Camillo* and *Don Camillo e il Suo Gregge)*, were a clever balance between comedy and political satire – so successful that several of the stories ended up on film.
>
> A free exhibition dedicated to Guareschi's Piccolo Mondo in the Sala delle Damigiane at Roncole Verdi is scheduled to remain open until the year 2000. ■

South into the Appennini

You could take several routes south of Parma to cross the Appennini into north-western Toscana, stopping at a castle on the way or hiking through the hills and around several glacial lakes.

One route roughly follows the Parma river towards Langhirano (a town of 6th-century Lombard origin, now the main production centre of the best quality ham). About 5km short of the town rises the majestic **Castello di Torrechiare**, one of many built or rebuilt by Pier Maria Rossi in the 15th century. He

EMILIA-ROMAGNA

romped with his lover Bianca Pellegrino in the Camera d'Oro (Golden Room), where he could look at a map of all his castles on the ceiling. The castle is open from 9 am to 1.45 pm daily except Monday and entry is L4000 (plus L2000 for a guide).

From Langhirano, follow the road down the west bank of the Parma, crossing the river at Capoponte and proceeding to **Tizzano Val Parma**, a charming Appennini town that offers pleasant walking in summer and skiing in winter (5km farther on at Schia). Farther south still, the heights around **Monchio delle Corti** offer views to La Spezia on a good day. It's a possible base for exploring some of the 20 glacial lakes that dot the southern corner of the province, bordering Toscana.

The mountains are in fact riddled with walking and cycling tracks and rifugi. If you'd prefer to be carried, there are several organisations in the province that arrange horse-riding excursions – the Parma IAT can point you to some of them. An interesting challenge is to follow the **Romea**, an ancient route for pilgrims heading south to Roma, from Collecchio to Fornovo, Bardone, Terenzo, Cassio and Berceto. All these villages have interesting Romanesque remains. The tourist office in Parma has an excellent trekking brochure for this route and can advise on appropriate maps.

Of the other 20 or so castles in the province, **Castello Bardi**, about 60km south-west of Parma (not on the above route), is also worth a mention. Soaring above the surrounding town, it dates to 898 AD, although most of the present structure was built in the 15th century.

Getting There & Away

TEP runs buses from Parma to most destinations throughout the province. On weekdays there are four a day to Bardi for instance, and at least as many to Monchio delle Corti via Langhirano. On weekends the La Spezia-Parma train service guarantees space for transporting bicycles.

PIACENZA

In the north-western corner of Emilia, just short of the Lombardia frontier, Piacenza is another prosperous town generally overlooked by tourists. Its few noteworthy monuments certainly make a stop worthwhile, but probably don't warrant an enormous effort to go out of your way.

Orientation

The train station is on the eastern edge of town. From here it's a 20-minute walk to the central square, Piazza dei Cavalli, or you can catch bus No 1, 6 or 8.

Information

The IAT office (☎ 32 93 24) in Piazzetta Mercanti 7 is open from 10 am to 1 pm and 4 to 7 pm (closed on Monday and Sunday afternoons). The telephone code for Piacenza is ☎ 0523.

Things to See

Piazza dei Cavalli is dominated by the impressive brick and marble 13th-century town hall, also known as **Il Gotico**. In front of the building, the two equestrian statues of the Farnese dukes Alessandro and his son Ranuccio, by Francesco Mochi, date from 1625 and are masterpieces of Baroque sculpture.

The **duomo**, on Via XX Settembre, was started in 1122 and is a sombre Romanesque building with frescoes by Guercino. The nearby **Basilica di Sant'Antonino** was built in the 11th century on the site of an earlier church. Its peculiar octagonal tower is claimed to be the oldest of its type in Italy.

The **Palazzo Farnese** in Piazza Cittadella was started in 1558 but never finished. It houses three little museums, of which the main one, the **Civico Museo**, is home to the Etruscan Fegato di Piacenza, a bronze liver which was used for divining the future. The other two are devoted to carriages and Italian unification memorabilia. All are open Tuesday to Sunday from 9 am to 12.30 pm, and on Thursday, Saturday and Sunday afternoons from 3.30 to 6 pm.

A few blocks south of Piazza dei Cavalli, the **Galleria d'Arte Moderna**, Via San Siro 13, contains a decent collection of 18th and

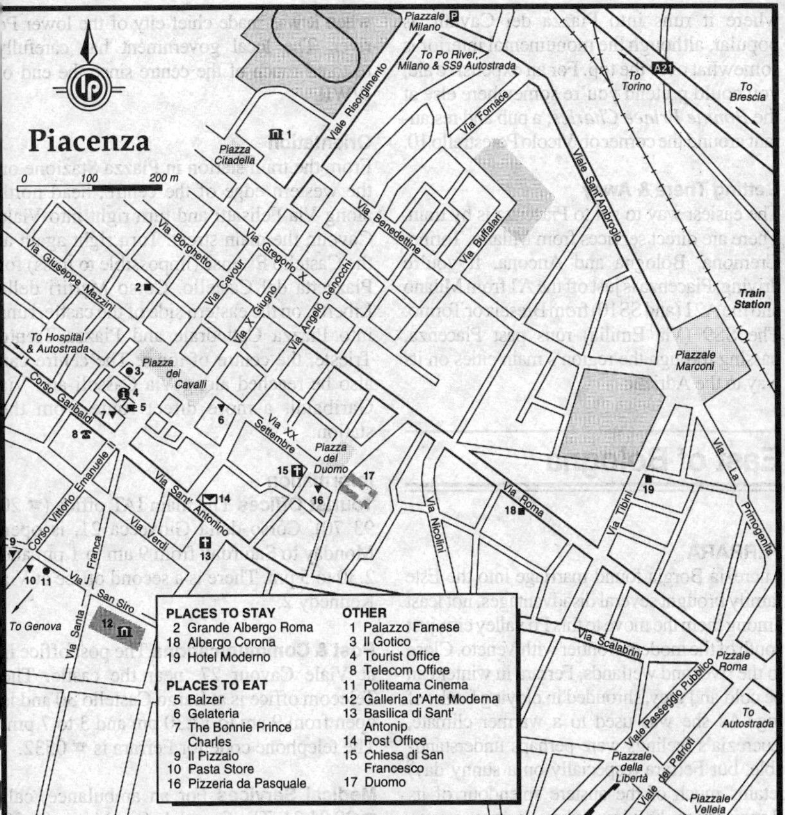

19th-century Italian art and sculpture. It opens from 10 am to midday and 3 to 5 pm (2 to 4 pm in winter).

Places to Stay & Eat

Budget accommodation is not one of Piacenza's strong points. *Albergo Corona* (☎ 32 09 48), Via Roma 141, has singles/doubles without bathroom from L40,000/50,000, but call ahead. *Hotel Moderno* (☎ 38 50 41), Via Tibini 31 (there's no sign), is nearest the train station and has rooms with bathroom for L55,000/70,000, but it's nothing special. If for some reason you want to spend big in Piacenza, you could try the overpriced *Grande Albergo Roma* (☎ 32 32 01), Via Cittadella 14, where singles/doubles are L180,000/220,000.

If you're just passing through, *Il Pizzaio*, Corso Vittorio Emanuele II, has pizza by the slice from about L5000, or else grab one at the *Ristorante Corona*, beneath the Albergo Corona, for about L10,000. The *Pizzeria da Pasquale* on Piazza del Duomo does a similar deal. More adventurous takeaway food can be bought from the nameless pasta store across the road from Il Pizzaio. The *Balzer* café, on Corso Vittorio Emanuele II where it runs into Piazza dei Cavalli, is popular, although the monumental interior is somewhat over the top. For an expensive ale, you could pretend you're somewhere else at the *Bonnie Prince Charles*, a pub and restaurant around the corner on Vicolo Perestrello 10.

Getting There & Away

The easiest way to get to Piacenza is by train. There are direct services from Milano, Torino, Cremona, Bologna and Ancona. If you're driving, Piacenza is just off the A1 from Milano and the A21 (and SS10) from Brescia or Torino. The SS9 (Via Emilia) runs past Piacenza, passing through the region's main cities on its way to the Adriatic.

East of Bologna

FERRARA

Lucrezia Borgia found marriage into the Este family brought several disadvantages, not least among them the move to this Po valley city, just south of the modern frontier with Veneto. Close to the river and wetlands, Ferrara in winter can be cold and grey, shrouded in cloying banks of fog. As she was used to a warmer climate, Lucrezia's feelings were perhaps understandable, but Ferrara (especially on a sunny day) retains much of the austere splendour of its Renaissance heyday, when it was strong enough to keep Roma and Venezia at arm's length.

History

The Este dynasty ruled Ferrara from 1260 to 1598, and their political and military prowess was matched by an uninterrupted stream of cultural activity. Petrarch, Titian, Antonio Pisanello and the poets Torquato Tasso and Ludovico Ariosto are just some of the luminaries who spent time here under the patronage of the Este dukes.

When the House of Este collapsed in 1598, Pope Clement VIII claimed the city and presided over its decline. Ferrara recovered some importance during the Napoleonic period when it was made chief city of the lower Po river. The local government has carefully restored much of the centre since the end of WWII.

Orientation

From the train station in Piazza Stazione on the western edge of the centre, head north along Via Felisatti and turn right into Viale Cavour, the main street. Turn right again at the Castello Estense (impossible to miss) for Piazzetta del Castello. Corso Martiri della Libertà, on the eastern side of the castle, runs into Piazza Cattedrale and Piazza Trento Trieste, the centre of town. The centre can also be reached along Via Cassoli and Via Garibaldi, a more direct route from the station.

Information

Tourist Offices The main IAT office (☎ 20 93 70), Corso della Giovecca 21, is open Monday to Saturday from 9 am to 1 pm and 2.30 to 5 pm. There is a second office at Via Kennedy 2.

Post & Communications The post office is at Viale Cavour 27, near the castle. The Telecom office is at Largo Castello 30 and is open from 9 am to 12.30 pm and 3 to 7 pm. The telephone code for Ferrara is ☎ 0532.

Medical Services For an ambulance, call ☎ 20 31 31. The Ospedale Sant'Anna (☎ 29 51 11) is at Corso della Giovecca 203.

Emergency In an emergency, call ☎ 113. The questura (☎ 29 43 11) is at Corso Ercole I d'Este 26, and the staff speak English.

Things to See & Do

The IAT publishes a useful mini-guide called *Ferrara* in various languages. It has information about the sights, as well as practical details. It is free when you purchase the L8000 cumulative ticket to some of the town's museums and monuments.

Castello Estense The imposing castle in the centre of town was started in 1385 for Nicolò

I d'Este, primarily to defend the family from riotous subjects who at one point rebelled over tax increases. By the middle of the following century, the Este family had begun to expand the fortress. Under Ercole I it became the dynasty's permanent residence.

Although sections are now used for government offices, many of the rooms, including the royal suites, are open for viewing. Highlights are the Sala dei Giganti (Giants' Room) and Salone dei Giochi (Games' Salon), with frescoes by Camillo and Sebastiano Filippi, the Cappella di Renée de France, and the dungeon. Here, in 1425, Duke Nicolò III d'Este had his young second wife, Parisina Malatesta, and his son, Ugo, beheaded after discovering they were lovers, providing the inspiration for Robert Browning's *My Last Duchess*. The castle is open daily, except Monday, from 9.30 am to 5.30 pm. Admission is L10,000.

Palazzo Municipale Linked to the castle, the town hall once also contained Este family apartments. The grand staircase by Pietro Benvenuti degli Ordani is worth seeing. Although closed to the public, you can see some of the rooms if you ask the attendant.

Cathedral Consecrated early in the 12th century, the cathedral features a mixture of Renaissance and Gothic styles. Note the array of columns along its south façade.

The **Museo della Cattedrale** contains a superb collection of Renaissance pieces, including 15th-century illustrated missals and works by Jacopo della Quercia and other Renaissance masters. It is open daily (except Sunday) from 10 am to midday and 3 to 5 pm, and admission is by donation. The bell tower was started in 1412 by the Florentine architect Leon Battista Alberti.

The city's former **ghetto** is centred on Via Vignatagliata, south of the cathedral.

Museums & Galleries North of the castle along Corso Ercole I d'Este there's the Palazzo dei Diamanti (Palace of the Diamonds), named after the shape of its rusticated façade and built for Sigismondo d'Este late in the 15th century by Biagio Rossetti. Regarded as the family's finest palace, the building now houses the **Pinacoteca Nazionale**, in which are hung works by artists of the Ferrarese and Bolognese schools, and a series of prints by Andrea Mantegna. The gallery is open on Sunday from 9 am to 1 pm and Tuesday to Saturday from 9 am to 2 pm. Entry is L8000.

Next door at No 19 is the **Museo del Risorgimento e della Resistenza**, a fairly standard display of decrees, letters and other memorabilia tracing Italian political history from the mid-19th century to WWII.

The **Museo Civico d'Arte Moderna e Contemporanea** is located in the Palazzo Massari at Corso Porta Mare 9, east of the Pinacoteca. It is open from 9 am to 1 pm and 3 to 6 pm. Admission is L4000.

The **Palazzina di Marfisa d'Este**, Corso della Giovecca 170, went up in 1559 and is worth a look for its decoration and furnishings. It is open daily from 9 am to 12.30 pm and 3 to 6 pm. Admission is L3000.

Lucrezia Borgia spent many of her Ferrara days in what is now the **Casa Romei**, on the corner of Via Praisolo and Via Savonarola, a typical Renaissance-style house. It is open daily, except Monday, from 8.30 am to 2 pm. Admission is L4000. She is buried in the nearby Monastero del Corpus Domini, along with several Este family members.

Via Borgo di Sotto leads to the 14th-century **Palazzo Schifanoia**, a sumptuous Este residence on Via Scandiana. The Salone dei Mesi (Room of the Months), featuring frescoes by Francesco del Cossa, ranks as the finest example of Ferrarese Renaissance mural painting. The palace is open daily from 9 am to 7 pm. Admission is L6000.

South of the palace, on the corner of Via Porta d'Amore and Via XX Settembre, is the **Palazzo di Ludovico il Moro**, housing the Museo Archeologico Nazionale. The palace was built by local architect Biagio Rossetti for the Duke of Milano. If it's not closed for renovations, take a look at the collection of Etruscan artefacts.

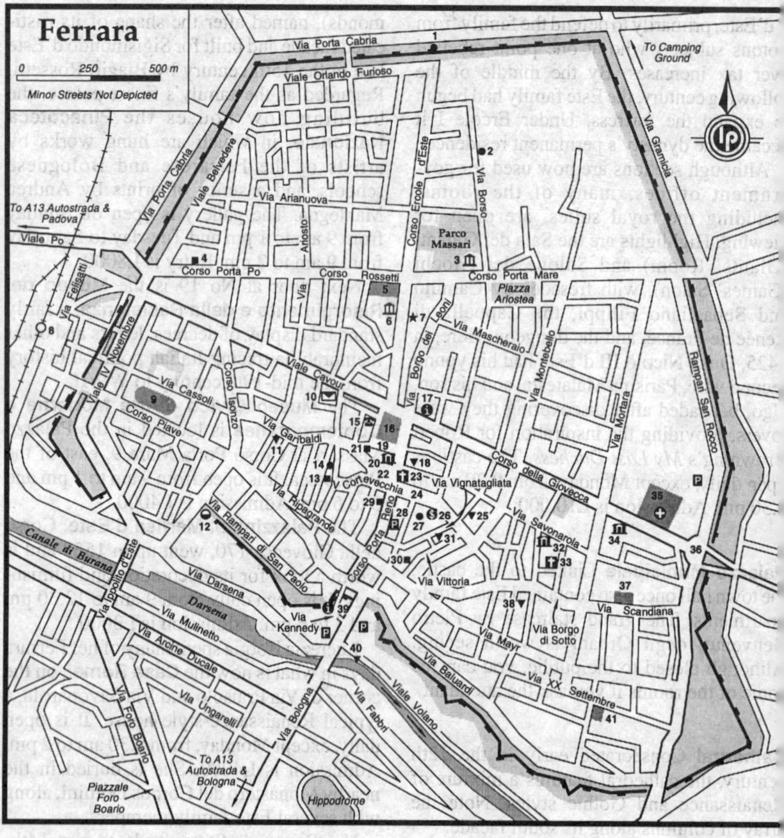

City Walls Although not terribly impressive, most of the 9km of ancient city walls are partly intact and a tour makes a pleasant walk. Start with the **Porta degli Angeli** in the north of the city – the surrounding area is leafy and tranquil.

Special Events

On the last Sunday of May each year, the eight *contrade* (districts) of Ferrara compete in the Palio, a horse race that momentarily turns Piazza Ariostea into medieval bedlam. Claimed to be the oldest such race in Italy, the first official competition was held in 1279.

The Ferrara Buskers' Festival, held late each August, attracts buskers from around the globe, primarily because the city pay travel and accommodation expenses for 20 of the lucky performers. Entry forms are available from the festival organisers (☎ 24 93 37; fax 75 41 91), or write c/o the Istituto di Cultura, Casa G Cini, Via Boccacanale di Santo Stefano 24.

Places to Stay

Accommodation is usually easy to find although many hotels close during August. The city's only camping ground is *Estense*

PLACES TO STAY
4 Albergo Bergamasco
13 Albergo Tre Stelle
21 Albergo Annunziata
29 Albergo Nazionale
30 Casa degli Artisti

PLACES TO EAT
11 Trattoria da Giacomino
18 Al Brindisi
25 Pizzeria Royal
31 Le Grazie
38 Il Cucco
40 Antica Trattoria del Volano

OTHER
1 Porta degli Angeli
2 Certosa (Cemetery)
3 Museo Civico d'Arte Moderna e Contemporanea
5 Pinacoteca Nazionale
6 Museo del Risorgimento e della Resistenza
7 Questura (Police Station)
8 Train Station
9 Stadium
10 Post Office
12 Bus Station
14 Market
15 Telecom Office
16 Castello Estense
17 Tourist Office
19 Palazzo Municipale
20 Piazzetta del Castello
22 Piazza Municipio
23 Piazza Cattedrale & Cathedral
24 Piazza Trento Trieste
26 Credito Romagnolo (ATM)
27 Ghetto
28 Parking (Foreign Cars)
32 Casa Romei
33 Monastero del Corpus Domini
34 Palazzina di Marfisa d'Este
35 Hospital
36 Piazzale Medaglie d'Oro
37 Palazzo Schifanoia
39 Tourist Office
41 Palazzo di Lodovico il Moro

☎ 75 23 96), Via Gramicia, north of the entre and outside the city walls. Take bus Jo 3 from the train station.

The best hotel deal is at *Casa degli Artisti* ☎ 76 10 38), Via Vittoria 66, a few minutes 'alk south of the cathedral, with ingles/doubles for L26,000/46,000. Book head. *Albergo Bergamasco* (☎ 20 49 56), Corso Porta Po 170 (next to a Chinese resaurant), is near the train station and has ooms from L30,000/60,000. *Albergo Tre telle* (☎ 20 97 48), Via Vegri 15, is central nd charges L30,000/40,000. *Albergo 'azionale* (☎ 20 96 04), Corso Porta Reno 2, has rooms from L55,000/90,000 with athroom. For well-located luxury, head to e four-star *Albergo Annunziata* (☎ 20 11 1), Piazza della Repubblica 5. Doubles start t L295,000.

'laces to Eat

'errara's cuisine is typical of the region, corporating meats and cheeses. One of the ocal specialities is cappelacci di zucca, a asta pouch filled with pumpkin that looks aguely like a small, floppy hat. Another raditional dish is tigella, a mixture of heeses and meats served with bread.

Pizzeria Royal, Via Vignatagliata 11, is a right place to eat pizza. *Trattoria da Giacomino*, Via Garibaldi 135, is good value nd popular with locals. A meal with wine will cost about L24,000. A little more expensive, and perhaps a little better as well, is the *Antica Trattoria del Volano*, Viale Volano 20. Try the cappelacci di zucca and rabbit. More upmarket still is *Il Cucco*, Via Voltacasotto, where you'll be looking at L40,000 for a meal. *Le Grazie*, Via Vignatagliata 61, in the ghetto, specialises in Jewish dishes. Main courses start at about L10,000. *Al Brindisi*, Via Adelardi 11, next to the cathedral, dates from 1435 and serves a salami-and-red-wine dish.

Getting There & Away

Bus The bus station is at Via Rampari di San Paolo. ACFT buses (☎ 24 06 79) operate services within the city and to surrounding towns such as Comacchio as well as the Adriatic beaches (some of these leave from the train station).

Train There are frequent services to Bologna, Venezia, Ravenna and other towns in the region.

Getting Around

Most traffic is banned from the city centre, but there is a small parking area for foreigners' cars on Corso Porta Reno (L3000 for the day). There are parking stations at the southern end of the centre on Via Bologna and the eastern edge near Piazzale Medaglie d'Oro. ACFT runs bus Nos 1, 2 and 9 from the train station to the city centre.

THE PO DELTA

Considering the incredibly polluted state of the Po river, the Po delta (Foci del Po), which straddles Emilia-Romagna and Veneto, should be an unpleasant place. However, the stretch of coast where the river spills into the Adriatic Sea is strangely alluring, particularly because the wetlands surrounding its two large lagoons – the Valli di Comacchio in the south and the Valle Bertuzzi in the north – have been designated nature reserves. The area provides some of Europe's best birdwatching, and after years of neglect by tourist authorities is now drawing quite a crowd. Despite this, swimming is banned, and many beaches have perennial problems with sludge-like algae caused by the dumping of phosphates upstream. Another problem is that the area is plagued by mosquitoes in summer, so be sure to have insect repellent, if not mosquito nets, on hand.

Information

Most towns in the area have tourist offices, although many are open in summer only, for example those at Comacchio (☎ 0533-31 01 47), Via Buonafede 12, and the Abbazia di Pomposa (☎ 0533-71 91 10) near Codigoro. The offices produce a wealth of information, including cycling itineraries, walking and horse-riding details, and tips on boat excursions, which are the best way to see the delta.

Things to See & Do

The **Abbazia di Pomposa**, 50km east of Ferrara, near Codigoro, is one of the oldest Benedictine abbeys in Italy, with a church dating from the 7th century. It is believed that the monk Guido d'Arezzo invented the musical scale here, and from the turn of the millennium the abbey was one of Italy's supreme cultural centres. Its decline began in the 14th century, and in 1652 the abbey was closed. The church is adorned with frescoes from the 14th-century Rimini school and works by Vitale di Bologna, and it contains a small museum with free admission. The complex is open daily from 9 am to pm. Musica Pomposa is a music festival staged at the abbey each July (☎ 0533-72 9 85 for information). Sporadic buses connect with Ravenna and Comacchio, but plan carefully or you could end up stranded.

Comacchio is a small fishing village that has but one attraction – the Trepponti (Triple Bridge), built in 1635 and crossing three canals. Don't stop unless you must, as the city's claim to be a mini-Venezia is a trifle exaggerated.

The delta's information office at **Ca Vecchia** (☎ 0544-44 68 66), a wildlife guardians' centre at Via Fossatone in the Stazione Pineta San Vitale park north of Ravenna, produces a map detailing the types of birds likely to be found in that part of the delta's Riserva Naturale and in the sanctuaries at Punte Alberete and Valle Mandriole. You can pick up the same map at the tourist office in Ravenna.

For boat trips, try the *Delfinus* (☎ 0533-38 12 65), which leaves from Lido degli Scacchi, east of Comacchio, or the *Principessa* (☎ 0533-99 98 15), which leaves from Gorino.

Places to Stay

If you want to stay in the area, a cheap option is the *Albergo Luciana* (☎ 0533-71 21 40), Via Roma 66, in Codigoro, which charges L35,000/48,000 for a single/double.

Getting There & Away

Moving around the area using public transport is difficult. From Ferrara to the Pomposa abbey, for instance, there is virtually nothing. You can get as far as Codigoro, but from there you're on your own. This makes a day trip from Ferrara without your own transport a frustrating prospect.

RAVENNA

Celebrated for the early Christian and Byzantine mosaics that adorn its churches and monuments, Ravenna was in fact the capital

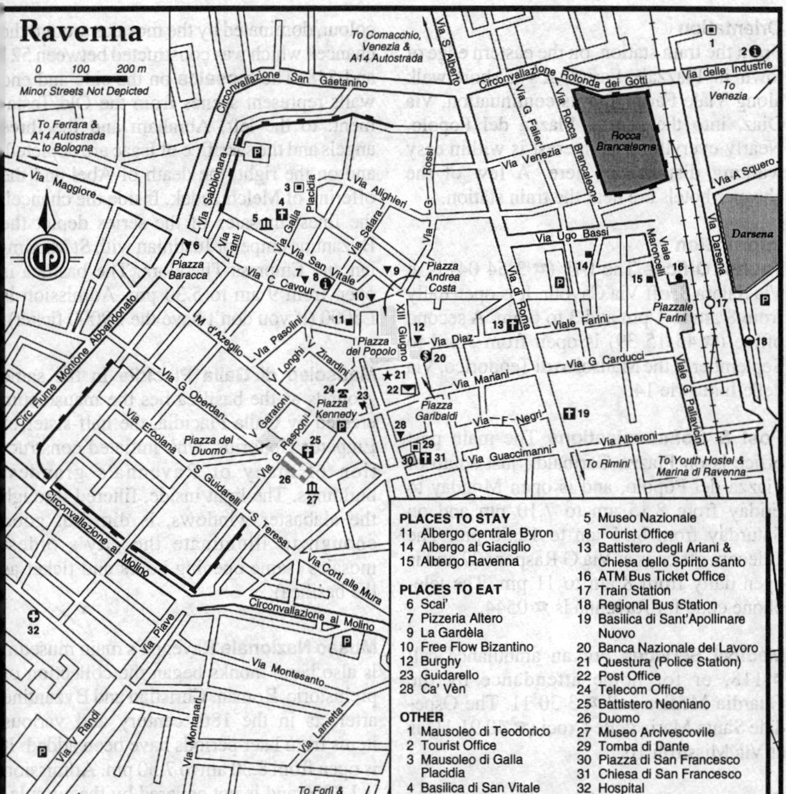

of the Byzantine Empire's western regions during the reign of Emperor Justinian and Empress Theodora.

The city had been the capital of the Western Roman Empire from 402 AD, when the ineffectual Emperor Honorius moved his court from Roma because Ravenna's surrounding malarial swamps made it easier to defend from northern invaders. The latter, however, simply walked around him and marched into Roma in 410. Honorius was unable, or unwilling, to react, preferring to vegetate in Ravenna until his death in 423 – the city finally succumbed 50 years later. The Byzantines arrived in 540 and ruled until the Lombards conquered the city in 752. Venetians controlled Ravenna from 1441 to 1509, when it was incorporated into the Papal States.

Under the Romans, Goths and Byzantines, Ravenna gradually rose to become one of the most splendid cities in the Mediterranean, and its mosaics are matched only by those of Istanbul; in his *Divine Comedy*, Dante described them as a symphony of colour. The city is close to Adriatic beaches, but they are hardly attractive, especially when effluent from the Po is a threat.

EMILIA-ROMAGNA

Orientation

From the train station, on the eastern edge of town in Piazzale Farini, it's a short walk along Viale Farini and its continuation, Via Diaz, into the central Piazza del Popolo. Nearly everything of interest is within easy walking distance of here. A few of the cheaper hotels are near the train station.

Information

Tourist Offices The IAT (☎ 3 54 04) is at Via Salara 8, off Via Cavour. It is open daily from 8 am to 1 pm and 3 to 6 pm. A second office (☎ 45 15 39) is open from April to September at the Mausoleo di Teodorico, Via delle Industrie 14.

Post & Communications The main post office is on Piazza Garibaldi, just south of Piazza del Popolo, and is open Monday to Friday from 8.15 am to 7.10 pm and on Saturday from 8.15 am to 12.50 pm. The Telecom office is at Via G Rasponi 22 and is open daily from 8 am to 11 pm. The telephone code for Ravenna is ☎ 0544.

Medical Services For an ambulance call ☎ 118, or for home attendance by the Guardia Medica call ☎ 3 30 11. The Ospedale Santa Maria delle Croci (☎ 40 91 11) is at Via Missiroli 10.

Emergency For police call ☎ 113. The questura (☎ 54 41 11) is on Piazza del Popolo.

Things to See

A *biglietto cumulativo* allows you into the six main monuments for L9000. If you intend to view the Museo Internazionale delle Ceramiche in Faenza as well, buy the ticket for L10,000. Opening times given below are summer times, which tend to be longer than those during the rest of the year.

Basilica di San Vitale Set back a little from the street of the same name and a few minutes walk north-west of the tourist office, the Basilica di San Vitale was consecrated in 547 by Archbishop Maximian. Its sombre exterior hides a dazzling internal feast of colour, dominated by the mosaics around the chancel, which was constructed between 521 and 548. The **mosaics** on the side and end walls represent scenes from the Old Testament: to the left, Abraham and the three angels and the sacrifice of Isaac are depicted and on the right, the death of Abel and the offering of Melchizedek. Inside the chancel the finest mosaics of the series depict the Byzantine emperor Justinian with St Maximian and Empress Theodora. The basilica is open from 9 am to 5.30 pm. Admission is L5000 (if you don't have the L9000 ticket).

Mausoleo di Galla Placidia In the same grounds as the basilica lies the mausoleum erected by Galla Placidia, the half-sister of Emperor Honorius, who initiated construction of many of Ravenna's grandest buildings. The light inside, filtered through the alabaster windows, is dim but good enough to illuminate the city's oldest mosaics (same opening hours and ticket as the basilica).

Museo Nazionale Ravenna's main museum is also here; monks began the collection of prehistoric, Roman, Christian and Byzantine artefacts in the 18th century and various items from later periods have been added. It is open from 8.30 am to 7.30 pm. Admission is L8000 and is not covered by the cumulative ticket.

Duomo The town's cathedral, in Via G Rasponi, was built in 1733 after its 5th-century predecessor was destroyed by earthquake. Although the cathedral itself is unremarkable, the small adjoining **Museo Arcivescovile** (Episcopal Museum) contains an exquisite 6th-century ivory throne of St Maximian and some beautiful mosaics. More mosaics, of Christ's Baptism and the apostles, can be seen in the neighbouring **Battistero Neoniano**. Thought to have started life as a Roman bathhouse, it was converted into a baptistry in the 5th century. The buildings are open from 9.30 am to 5.30 pm. Admission to both the museum and bap-

ıtry is L4000 (if you don't have the cumu-
tive ticket).

ımba di Dante As Dante showed in the *ivine Comedy* (much of it written in avenna), politics is a dodgy business. aving been exiled from Firenze in 1302, ante finally went to live in Ravenna, where : died in 1321. His tomb is next to the niesa di San Francesco, and there is a small **useum** (admission L3000). A mound aced over his sarcophagus during WWII to otect it from air raids is proudly marked ıd the area around the tomb has been :clared a *zona di silenzio*. Opening hours em flexible – ring the bell and see what the ıstodian has to say. To continue on a literary ɔte, Lord Byron lived in a house on Piazza San Francesco in 1819.

ther Churches Those appreciative of osaics will want to visit the **Basilica di ant'Apollinare Nuovo**, off Via di Roma, iginally built by the Goths in the 6th entury. The high walls in the nave are ɔvered with mosaics – on the right depict- g a procession of 26 martyrs and opposite procession of virgins. It is open from 9 am 7 pm, and admission is L4000 (without the ımulative ticket).

The Gothic **Battistero degli Ariani** is ehind the Chiesa dello Spirito Santo, in Via iaz.

Five km south-east of the city centre is the **asilica di Sant'Apollinare in Classe** (take ıs No 4 or the train to Classe). The basilica as built in the 6th century on the burial site : Ravenna's patron saint, St Apollinaris, ho converted the city to Christianity in the ıd century; it features a brilliant mosaic ver the altar.

osaic Courses

he Centro Internazionale di Studi per Insegnamento del Mosaico runs a series of vo-week mosaic courses during June, July ıd August, starting at L550,000. Contact ISIM (☎ 48 23 78), Via Corrado Ricci 29, r information.

Places to Stay

The city is an easy day trip from Bologna, but staying overnight is no problem (except in summer) as it has a hostel and a few cheap hotels. The closest camping areas are at Marina di Ravenna on the beach (take the ATM bus or follow the SS67). *Camping Piomboni* (☎ 53 02 30), Viale della Pace 421, and *Campeggio Rivaverde* (☎ 53 04 91), Viale della Nazione 301, have reasonably priced sites.

The HI youth hostel, the *Ostello Dante* (☎ 42 04 05), Via Aurelio Nicolodi 12, is 1km from the train station towards the beach, and is served by bus No 1. B&B is L24,000 and a meal L14,000. They have family rooms.

Albergo al Giaciglio (☎ 3 94 03), Via Rocca Brancaleone 42, is one of the cheaper alternatives, with rooms starting at L35,000/45,000. *Albergo Ravenna* (☎ 21 22 04), Viale Maroncelli 12, has rooms from L40,000/60,000 and is handy to the train station. They also have parking. Those with looser purse strings could do worse than the centrally located *Albergo Centrale Byron* (☎ 21 22 25), Via IV Novembre 14, which has singles/doubles from L95,000/120,000.

EMILIA-ROMAGNA

Places to Eat

The city's fresh-produce *market* (Mercato Coperto) in Piazza Andrea Costa, north of Piazza del Popolo, is the best bet for budget food. The self-service *Free Flow Bizantino*, in the same piazza, is also very cheap. *Pizzeria Arcobaleno*, Viale Farina, has good pizza by the slice. *Pizzeria Altero*, Via Cavour 31, has pizza by the slice from L1500, and the hamburger fast-food restaurant *Burghy*, in Piazza del Popolo, has a great view and cheap beers.

The *Ca' Vèn* enoteca, Via Corrado Ricci 24, has a good selection of local wines and serves traditional food at reasonable prices in a very nearly medieval atmosphere. At *La Gardèla*, Via Ponte Marino 1, and *Scai'*, Via Maggiore 2, you can eat a meal for about L30,000, while *Guidarello*, Via Gessi 9, specialises in local dishes and charges from L8000 for main courses.

Entertainment

The Ravennati let it all hang out for the annual blues festival in July, which attracts big US names. There is also a busy summer concert calendar, including jazz and opera, with many of the churches as venues. Enquire at the tourist office.

Things to Buy

To see local artisans constructing mosaics in the traditional way, visit **Akomena Studio Il Mosaico**, next to the Museo Nazionale at Via Benedetto Fiandrini 14, which specialises in copies of the city's finer works. Most are for sale.

Getting There & Away

Bus ATM buses (☎ 45 36 00) depart from Piazzale Farini at the train station for towns along the coast and north, in the Po delta area. Full information is available at the ticket office on the piazza.

Train Frequent trains connect the city with Bologna, Ferrara (where you can change for Venezia), Faenza, Rimini and the south coast.

Car & Motorcycle Ravenna is on a branch of the A14 Bologna-Rimini autostrada. Otherwise, the SS16 (Via Adriatica) heads south from Ravenna to Rimini and on down the coast. There are car parks at the train station and near the Basilica di San Vitale.

Getting Around

Ravenna is easy to cover on foot. To see the city by bicycle, hire one at Coop San Vitale in Piazzale Farini to the left of the station for L2000 an hour or L15,000 a day.

AROUND RAVENNA

Bicycle Tour

The Ravenna tourist office produces a slim brochure detailing a three-day tour beginning and ending in Cervia, on the coast south of the city, which takes you through pine forests and past lagoons in the coastal area up towards the Valli di Comacchio.

Faenza

This Romagnola town has been producin high-grade ceramics for hundreds of year and gave us the word faïence. A half-ho train ride from Ravenna, the **Museo Inte nazionale delle Ceramiche** is worth a visi It's open daily in summer from 9 am to 7 pr Admission is L6000.

Remembering Il Duce

It might seem a little odd that Italy's great dictator, Benito Mussolini, should have been born and raised in the red territory of the Romagna. Predappio, a village overloaded with monumental buildings erected by its most infamous son, is also the Fascist leader's final resting place; his remains were buried here in 1957. About 15km south of Forlì (a dull town 45 km north-west of Rimini along the Via Emilia), Predappio is the scene of pro-fascist celebrations each year, when the faithful few mark 31 October, the anniversary of the day Mussolini became prime minister in 1922. Many of the young skinheads and older faithful probably forget that their beloved icon, prior to donning the black shirt, started his political life as a card-carrying socialist and journalist who rarely missed a chance to wave the red rag. ■

You can get a L10,000 ticket in Ravenna that covers six monuments within that town as well as the Museo Faenza. There's a tourist office (☎ 0546-2 52 31) at Piazza del Popolo 1.

Mirabilandia

This huge amusement park, about 10km south of Ravenna, could be one for the kids. Free buses connect with local trains at the Savio station. For information, call freephone ☎ 1678-15 082.

RIMINI

Originally Umbrian, then Etruscan and Roman, Rimini sits at the centre of the Riviera del Sole and is now inhabited by beach-goers. The city continued to change hands through the Middle Ages, knowing Byzantine, Lombard and papal rule before ending up in the hands of the Malatesta family in the 13th century. Two centuries later Cesare Borgia added the city to his list of short-lived conquests, until it was ruled by Venezia and, finally, again by the Papal States. Rimini joined the Kingdom of Italy in 1860.

The charming old city centre was badly damaged during 400 bombing raids in WWII, but enough remains to warrant a quick look. The town's main attractions are the beach and its frenetic nightlife – young people flock there every weekend from as far as away as Roma. In summer, Rimini fills with Italian and, increasingly, foreign holiday-makers in search of a scrap of beach and nocturnal fun and games – they have more than 100 discos and clubs to choose from. In spite of all this, it remains a ritual family holiday destination for many Italians.

Orientation

The main train station is in Piazzale Cesare Battisti, on the northern edge of the old city centre. Via Dante becomes Via IV Novembre and leads to Piazza Tre Martiri. Corso d'Augusto heads north-west from here to the city's other main square, Piazza Cavour. To get to the beach, walk to the north-western edge of Piazzale Cesare Battisti and turn right into Viale Principe Amedeo di Savoia, which broadens into the Parco di Federico Fellini at the waterfront.

Information

Tourist Offices The IAT office (☎ 5 13 31) at Via Dante 86, is near the train station, open from 8 am to 8 pm. Another office (☎ 5 11 01) is at Piazzale di Federico Fellini 3 and has the same hours. The Comune di Rimini (☎ 70 41 10) operates the Centro di Informazione at Corso d'Augusto 156, which opens Monday to Friday from 8 am to 1 pm and 2 to 7 pm, and on Saturday to 1 pm. They all provide an array of brochures, including the *Book Istantaneo*, a useful guide to the city.

Money There are plenty of banks where you can change money. The Banca Nazionale del Lavoro and Cassa di Risparmio di Rimini, both on Corso d'Augusto, have ATMs that accept Visa and several other cards.

Post & Communications The main post office is on Largo Giulio Cesare and is open Monday to Friday from 8.10 am to 5.30 pm and on Saturday to 1 pm. There's a branch at Via Gambalunga.

The Telecom office is at Viale Trieste 1 and is open from 8 am to 9.30 pm. The telephone code for Rimini is ☎ 0541.

Medical Services In a medical emergency, call ☎ 38 70 01 for an ambulance. The Guardia Medica (☎ 38 70 01) operates at night and on weekends. In summer there is a tourist medical service at Piazzale Pascoli 2 from 8 am to 8 pm. The Ospedale Infermi (☎ 70 51 11) is at Viale Luigi Settembrini 2, south-east of the city centre along Viale Roma and Viale Ugo Bassi.

Emergency For police attendance, call ☎ 113. You'll find the questura (☎ 5 10 00) at Corso d'Augusto 152.

Castel Sigismondo

Brooding over the south-west corner of the old town, the castle takes its name from one of the Malatesta family, which ruled for a couple of centuries until Cesare Borgia took

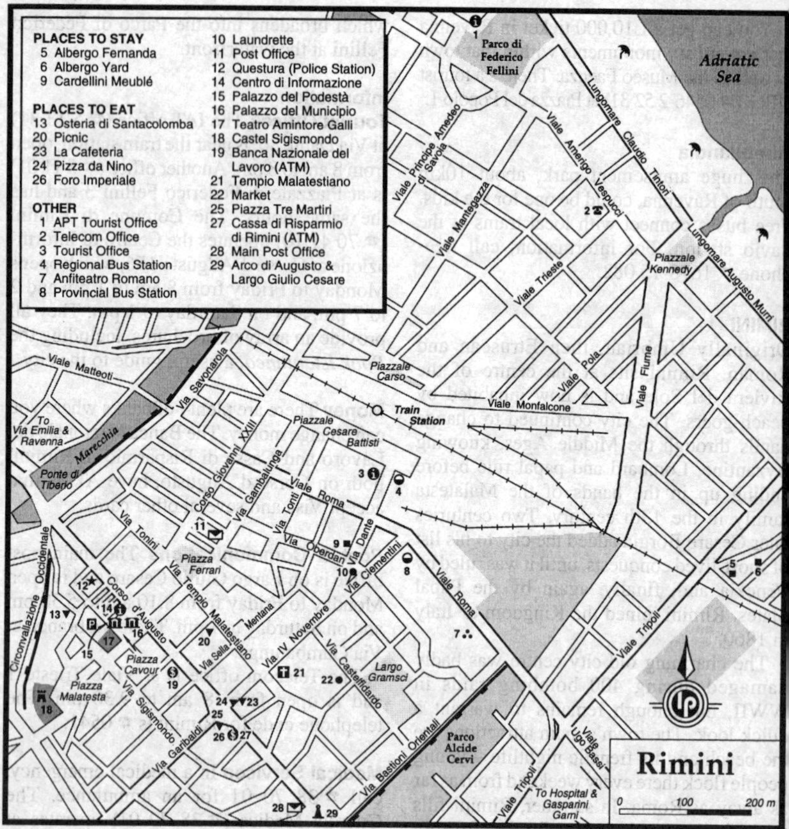

over in 1500. Sigismondo was the worst of a pretty bad lot, condemned to hell by Pope Pius II, who burned an effigy of him in Roma because of his shameful crimes, which included rape, murder, incest, adultery and severe oppression of his people – the usual stuff.

Otherwise known as the Rocca Malatestiana, the building houses the **Museo delle Culture Extraeuropee**, a collection of African, Asian and pre-Columbian art. It is open Monday to Friday from 8 am to 1.30 pm and on Tuesday and Thursday afternoons from 3.30 to 6 pm. Admission is L4000.

Roman Remains
About the only evidence left of the Roman presence in the city is the crumbly **Arco di Augusto** (Arch of Augustus) which was built in 27 BC, at the eastern end of Corso d'Augusto, and the modest **Ponte di Tiberio** (Tiberius' Bridge), at the western end of the same thoroughfare, built in the 1st century AD as testimony to the city's importance to the empire. Archaeologists have also dug up half of Piazza Ferrari to get at a possible Roman villa. The Roman forum lay where Piazza Tre Martiri is today.

Tempio Malatestiano

On Via IV Novembre, this so-called temple of the Malatesta clan is the city's grandest monument. Dedicated to St Francis, the 13th-century church was transformed into a personal chapel for the evil Sigismondo Malatesta and his beloved Isotta degli Atti, and is one of the more significant creations of the Renaissance. Most of the work on the unfinished façade was done by Leon Battista Alberti, one of the period's great architects. A crucifix inside is believed to be the work of Giotto, and the church contains a fresco by Piero della Francesca.

Piazza Cavour

This central square is lined with the city's finest palaces, including the **Palazzo del Municipio**, built in 1562 and rebuilt after being razed during WWII. The Gothic **Palazzo del Podestà** was built in the 14th century and is undergoing restoration. The **Teatro Amintore Galli** only went up in 1857, in the feverish years leading to unification.

Beaches

Most of the beaches along the coast are either rented to private companies, which in turn rent space to bathers, or are connected to the many nearby hotels. The average daily charge for a deck chair and umbrella is L16,000. Being the kind of resort it is, many people hire change facilities and chairs for a week or more. Two deck chairs and an umbrella in the front row with cabin facilities would cost L170,000 a week! These private areas are worth it if you have children. They all have bars and small playgrounds and often organise special activities. Otherwise, head for the public areas of the beach without the ubiquitous umbrellas – there is one near the pier.

The Po river pumps its heavily polluted waters into the Adriatic north of Rimini and this occasionally results in green algae washing onto the shores. Beaches have been closed over summer in the past, so check before you swim.

Sailboards can be hired from Bagno Nettuno on the beach near Piazzale Kennedy. Bicycles can also be hired at Piazzale Kennedy.

Theme Parks

Rimini is not just for sun-lovers and socialites; there are numerous theme parks for kids and their suffering parents. You could try **Italia in Miniatura** in Viserba, a fairly ambitious collection of reproductions of, well, bits of Italy – like the 6600sq metres given over to 1:5 scale models of some 120 buildings facing Venezia's Grand Canal and Piazza San Marco. Entry is L20,000 for adults, L18,000 for kids. Take bus No 8 from Rimini's train station.

Fiabilandia, in Rivazzura di Rimini, is a fantasy park full of weird and wonderful characters. It is expensive (around L20,000 a head) and not really suitable for very young children. Take bus No 9 from Rimini's train station.

There are also several **dolphinariums** in the area, including one right on the beach at Rimini (adults L14,000, kids over three years L10,000). There is another at Riccione, which charges the same entry fee. Take bus No 11 from Rimini. Waterparks in the area include **Acquafàn** at Riccione. Entry is L32,000 for adults and L20,000 for kids (over five years). There is a special 9 am bus from Marina Centro at Rimini.

Places to Stay

Unless you have booked well in advance, accommodation can be difficult to find and very expensive in summer, as proprietors often make full board compulsory. In winter, many of the 1500 hotels close and the city is dead. Your only hope in summer is the room-hawkers, sanctioned by the IAT, who frequent intersections on the outskirts of the city and offer rooms at so-called 'bargain' rates, which can be excessive. For booking ahead, ask the tourist office to send you a hotel list. Otherwise, try Adria Hotel Reservation (☎ 39 05 30).

The camping ground *Maximum Internazionale* (☎ 37 26 02), on Viale Principe Piemonte at Miramare, south-east of the city, is accessible by bus No 10 or 11 and is near

EMILIA-ROMAGNA

EMILIA-ROMAGNA

the water. *Camping Italia* (☎ 73 28 82), Via Toscanelli 112, is north-west of the centre at Viserba and can be reached by bus No 4.

The youth hostel, the *Ostello Urland* (☎ 37 32 16), Via Flaminia 300, is near the airport south-east of the city centre. Take bus No 124 from the train station, or the train to Stazione FS Miramare. B&B is L16,000 and a meal costs L14,000. The hostel is open from late April to the end of September.

The great majority of hotels close outside the main season. Those listed below are open all year.

The *Cardellini Meublé* (☎ 2 64 12), Via Dante 50, near the train station, charges from L90,000 per person for full board. *Gasparini Garni* (☎ 38 12 77), Via Boiardo 3, charges from L80,000 per person.

Albergo Fernanda (☎ 39 11 00), Via Griffa 2, on the eastern side of town across Viale Tripoli, has rooms starting at L30,000/50,000. Nearby, *Albergo Yard* (☎ 39 05 50), Via Carducci 47, offers rooms starting at L75,000 with a bathroom and breakfast included.

Places to Eat

The city is not noted for its culinary contribution to the Italian table and many restaurants offer cheap tourist menus. The produce *market*, Mercato Centrale Coperto, is at Via Castelfidardo. The self-service restaurant *Picnic*, Via Tempio Malatestiano 32, is one of the better budget deals. You can pick up cheap takeaway pizza at *Pizza da Nino*, Via IV Novembre 9. *La Cafeteria*, No 11 on the same street, has good snacks.

Osteria di Santacolomba, Via di Duccio 2, off Piazza Malatesta, is located in the former bell tower of an 8th-century church and serves traditional cuisine, with dishes starting at about L10,000.

A good place for people-watching and even a moderately priced meal is the *Foro Imperiale*, on Piazza Tre Martiri.

Entertainment

The area's discos and clubs are located north and south of Rimini proper. The most famous is *Cocorico*, at Riccione, a virtual mecca for Italian teenagers. Another is the *Paradise Club*, at Rimini. Ask at the tourist office for your type of club and also about the special buses which service the discos.

Getting There & Away

Air The city's Aeroporto Civile (☎ 37 31 32), Via Flaminia, is served by flights from Roma and Milano.

Bus There are regular buses to towns along the coast, including Riccione (Nos 11 and 124) and Cattolica (Nos 11 and 125). There are regular services to San Marino from Rimini's train station (L16,000 return). There's also a direct bus to Roma.

Train Trains run frequently down the coast to Ancona, Bari, Lecce and Taranto, and up the line through Bologna and on to Milano and Torino.

Car & Motorcycle You have a choice of the A14 (south into Le Marche or north-west towards Bologna and Milano) or the toll-free but often clogged SS16.

Getting Around

TRAM buses operate services throughout the city and to the airport. Bus Nos 10 and 11 pass the station and go through Piazza Tre Martiri, before heading for Piazzale di Federico Fellini. Bus No 124 runs between the train station and Riccione.

From the end of July to mid-September, TRAM operates special late-night bus services connecting the nightclubs with the city centre, train station and camping grounds. The buses run from about 10.30 pm to 4.30 am, after which you'll have to stay in the clubs or walk.

Taxis (☎ 5 00 20) charge a minimum of L7000, then L1700 a km. You are able to hire bicycles at Piazzale Kennedy, on the waterfront.

San Marino

Vhat did King Arthur say of Camelot in Monty Python's *The Holy Grail*? 'It's a silly place.' Lying 657m above sea level and only 0km from the Adriatic as the crow flies, the 1sq km Repubblica di San Marino seems a ittle silly as well (one can only speculate as o what Mexico's consul does here!). Everybody mocks this place, but it's perhaps a little infair. True, you are unlikely to see a greater lensity of kitsch souvenir stands in many other tourist centres, but San Marino is not lone in selling kitsch, and although there sn't an awful lot to see, the old town is pleasant and the views all around are quite pectacular.

If you're in Rimini, think of it as just another of the beach resort's theme parks. You can take pictures of the republic's soldiers, buy local coinage (a San Marino version of lira) and send mail with San Marino stamps. Be warned that at weekends, n summer especially, central San Marino can be choked with visitors.

History

There are innumerable legends describing he founding of this hilly city-state, including the one about a stone-cutter who was given the land on top of Monte Titano by a ich Roman woman whose son he had cured. At any rate, the 25,000 inhabitants of the mountain republic are the inheritors of 1700 years of revolution-free liberty: 'Welcome to the Country of Freedom', the signs proclaim. Everybody has left San Marino alone. Well almost. Cesare Borgia waltzed in early in the 16th century, but his own demise was just around the corner and his rule was shortlived. In 1739 one Cardinal Giulio Alberoni took over the republic, but the pope backed San Marino's independence and that was that. During WWII, the 'neutral' republic played host to 100,000 refugees until the Allies marched in, in 1944. San Marino joined the European Council in 1988 and the United Nations in 1992.

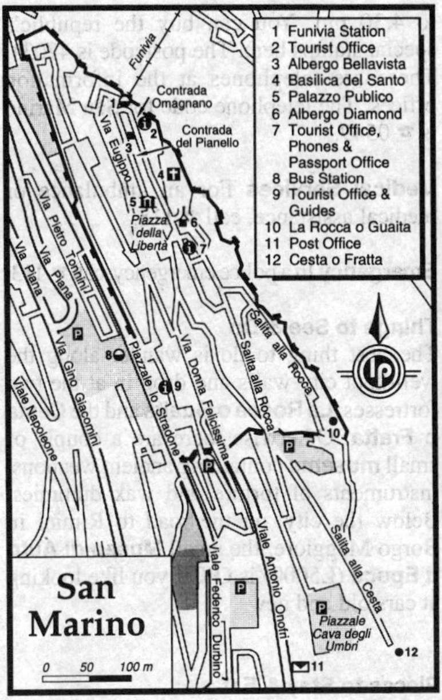

Orientation

If you arrive by car, you'll have to leave it at one of the numerous car parks and walk or take the series of stairs and elevators to the town. The car parks are expensive and the minimum fee is L7500 – even if you stay for only an hour.

Information

Tourist Offices In the capital, also called San Marino, the Ufficio di Stato per il Turismo (☎ 88 29 98), Palazzo del Turismo, Contrada Omagnano 20, is open daily from 8.15 am to 2.15 pm, as well as on Monday and Thursday afternoons. Two other offices, one at Contrada del Collegio 40 and the other just inside Porta di San Francesco, are open daily. The latter two will stamp your passport for a fee.

Post & Communications The main post office is at Viale Antonio Onofri 87 and is open from Monday to Friday from 8.15 am to 4.30 pm. You can buy the republic's special stamps here. The postcode is 47031. There are telephones at the information offices. The telephone code for San Marino is ☎ 0549.

Medical Services For an ambulance or medical assistance, call ☎ 118.

Emergency In a police emergency, call ☎ 113.

Things to See & Do

The best thing to do is wander along the well-kept city walls and drop in at the two fortresses, **La Rocca o Guaita** and the **Cesta o Fratta**. Otherwise there are a couple of small **musems** containing ancient weapons, instruments of torture and wax dummies. Below the city, on the road to Rimini in Borgo Maggiore, the small **Museo di Auto d'Epoca** (L5000) is OK if you like looking at cars old and new.

Places to Stay & Eat

There are *camping grounds* signposted off the main road (SS72) through the republic from Rimini. San Marino city has quite a few hotels should you decide to stay. The cheapest is the *Albergo Bellavista* (☎ 99 12 12), Contrada del Pianello 42-44, with rooms starting at L50,000/80,000. Only a sho walk away is the *Albergo Diamond* (☎ 99 1 03), Contrada del Collegio 50, with room starting at L60,000/90,000. Prices increas by about 20% in the high season.

The city centre is dotted with places offer ing set meals for L22,000 to L25,000. Th best thing about some of the cafés and snac bars is the views.

Things to Buy

Nothing is probably the best advice. Liquo stores claim to sell cut-price alcohol, but yo would want to be sure about what you poison is worth in Italy before buying her in the belief that you're getting duty-fre bargains.

Getting There & Away

Up to nine buses run daily to Rimini, an Busturs has a daily service to Urbino. Buse arrive at parking station No 1, in Piazzal Calcigni. There are no trains. If you ar driving, the SS72 leads into the city centr from Rimini. If all the car parks in the cit fill up, you are obliged to park near th *funivia* (cable car), and catch the latter to th centre (L6000 return). A trip along th winding roads leading south to Urbino in L Marche is recommended.

Toscana

The people of Toscana (Tuscany) can rightly claim to have just about the best of everything – architecture, the country's greatest collection of art, beautiful countryside bathed in soft pink hues, and some of Italy's finest fresh produce and best known wines. It was in Toscana, about 600 years ago, that the Renaissance began; this has had a long-lasting effect on European culture.

The works of Michelangelo, Donatello, da Vinci and other 15th and 16th-century Tuscan masters still influence artists worldwide. Tuscan architects – notably Brunel leschi, responsible for the magnificent dome of Firenze's cathedral, and Leon Battista Alberti, largely responsible for designing the façade of the Chiesa di Santa Maria Novella – have influenced architects through the centuries.

The literary works of Dante, Petrarch and Boccaccio planted the seeds for the Italian language, and today there still remains a sense of rivalry between the Sienese and the Florentines as to who speaks the purest Italian.

Most people are drawn to Toscana by the artistic splendour of Firenze and Siena or to view the Leaning Tower in Pisa. But Toscana also features some of Italy's most impressive hill towns, including San Gimignano, Volterra, Cortona and Montepulciano.

The Etruscan sites in the south – around Saturnia and Sovana – will take you away from the mainstream tourist itinerary. Southern Toscana also boasts some of the country's best beaches – on the Monte Argentario and on the island of Elba.

Walkers and nature lovers can enjoy the Alpi Apuane, the Garfagnana, the Mugello (north-east of Firenze) and the Parco Naturale della Maremma, near Grosseto.

Tuscan cuisine is dominated by bread and the extra virgin olive oil produced in the region's hills, which is close to Italy's finest. Bread features in every course, including dessert, where it can be topped with egg yolk and orange rind and sprinkled with a heavy layer of powdered sugar. *Crostini*, minced chicken liver canapés, and *fettunta*, a slab of toasted bread rubbed with garlic and dipped in oil, are popular antipasti, and hearty soups, such as *ribollita*, thickened with bread, are common starters. Meat and poultry are

HIGHLIGHTS

- The breath-taking Duomo in Firenze
- The gilded bronze doors of the Bapistry, the oldest building in the Tuscan capital
- A day in the Galleria degli Uffizi – the office building with the greatest collection of Italian art in the world
- Strolling or window-shopping for gold on the 14th-century Ponte Vecchio over the Arno
- A slice of *panforte* and a large draught of Sienese paintings in the glorious medieval city of Siena
- Eating, drinking and driving (not necessarily in that order) in the beautiful Chianti hills.

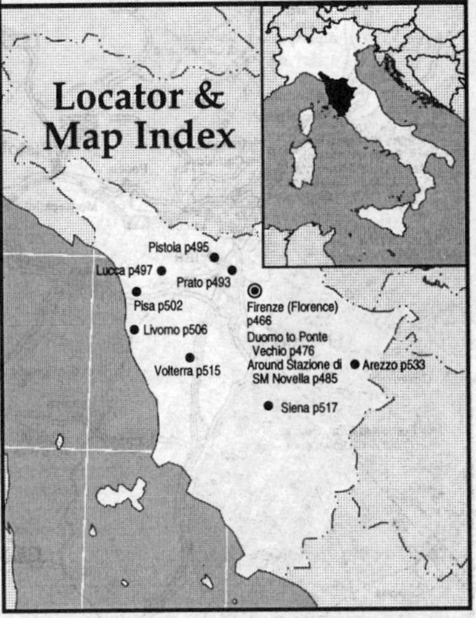

grilled, roasted or fried, and may come simply with a slice of lemon, which the Tuscans refer to as sauce. Traditional desserts are simple, such as biscuits flavoured with nuts or spices and served with a glass of the dessert wine *vin santo*.

The region's wines are among the country's best known: Chianti, the *vino nobile* of Montepulciano, and Brunello di Montalcino. Traditionally, most Tuscan wines are red, but in recent years the vineyards around San Gimignano have produced Vernaccia, a crisp white that is becoming more popular.

Travelling in Toscana is easy. The A1 and the main train line ensure good north-south connections and there are excellent train and bus services within the region. Most areas are easily accessible by public transport, but a car would provide flexibility and enable you to get to parts of Toscana few tourists see. Many of the cities have hotel associations which will book a room for you, although at certain times of the year – such as when the medieval-inspired Palio festival is being held in Siena – finding a room is almost impossible unless you have booked months in advance.

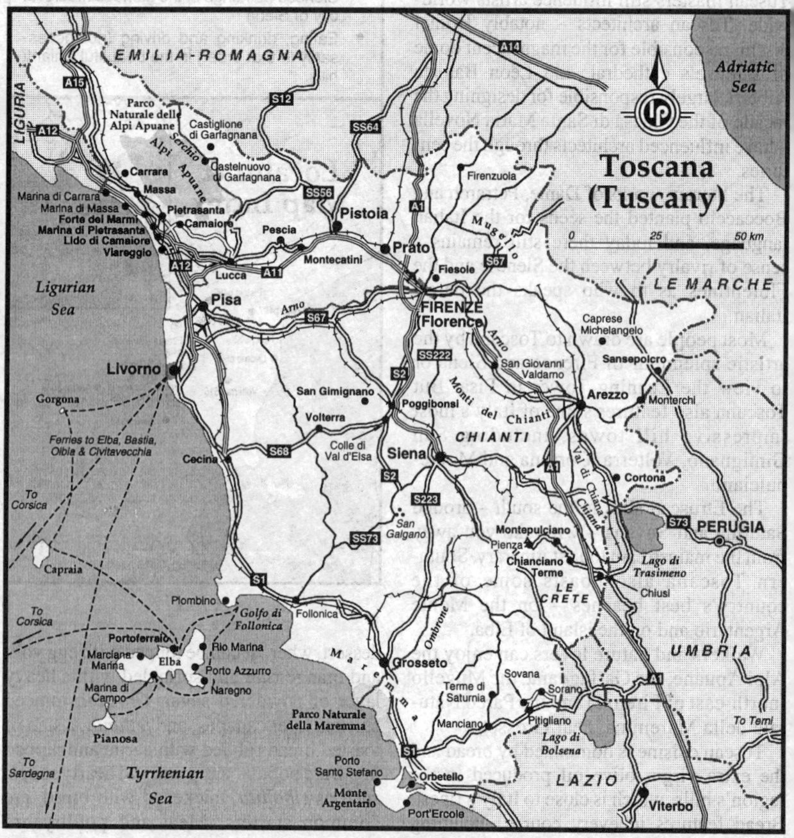

Firenze

Situated on the banks of the Arno river and set among low hills covered with olive groves and vineyards, Firenze (Florence) is immediately captivating. Cradle of the Renaissance and home of Dante, Machiavelli, Michelangelo and the Medici, the city is almost overwhelming in its wealth of art, culture and history. Despite the traffic, the intense and unrelenting summer heat, the pollution and the industrial sprawl on the city's outskirts, Firenze still attracts millions of tourists each year who come to view Michelangelo's *David* and the treasures of the Galleria degli Uffizi. The French writer Stendhal expressed a feeling of culture shock – a giddy faintness that left him unable to walk after he was dazzled by the magnificence of the Chiesa di Santa Croce. This condition is now known as Stendhalismo, or Stendhal's Disease, and Florentine doctors treat up to 12 cases a year.

You will need at least four or five days if you want more than a superficial impression of Firenze. You could spend at least one day in the Uffizi, and then there is the Galleria dell'Accademia, the sculpture collection in the Museo Nazionale del Bargello and the many richly embellished churches and palaces. Many people leave the city unsatisfied, perhaps expecting a pristine Renaissance museum. In fact, Firenze is a functioning city, complete with run-down palaces, chaotic traffic, pollution and litter.

If possible, avoid visiting Firenze during August when the weather is extremely hot, and when most Florentines depart for the coast. The best times to visit are May, June, September and October.

History

Firenze was founded as a colony of the Etruscan city of Fiesole in about 200 BC. The town later became the Roman Florentia, a strategic garrison settlement whose purpose was to control the Via Flaminia, which linked Roma to northern Italy and Gaul. Along with the rest of northern Italy, the city suffered during the barbarian invasions of the Dark Ages. In the early 12th century the city became a free *comune* and by 1138 it was ruled by 12 consuls who were assisted by the Council of One Hundred, drawn mainly from the prosperous merchant class. Agitation among differing factions in the city led to the appointment of a foreign head of state in 1207, known as the *podestà*, who replaced the council.

The first conflicts between the pro-papal Guelphs and the pro-imperial Ghibellines started towards the middle of the 13th century, with power passing from one faction to another for almost a century. The Guelphs eventually formed their own government, known as the Primo Popolo and overseen by a body of merchants called the Capitano del Popolo. In 1260, the Guelphs were ousted after Firenze was defeated by the Ghibelline Siena at the Battle of Montaperti, but the Guelphs regained control of the city in 1289.

By 1292, the increasingly turbulent nobility had been excluded from government, and by the turn of the century factions among upper-class Guelphs were grouped into two parties, the Neri (Blacks) and the Bianchi (Whites). When the latter were defeated, one

The *Medusa di Portonaccio* – an example of Etruscan art from the 7th century BC

TOSCANA

of the many members driven into exile in 1302 was the great Italian writer Dante.

In the period leading up to the mid-14th century, the system of government was further democratised until Firenze became a commercial republic controlled by the merchant class, which was strongly Guelph.

The great plague of 1348 cut the city's population by almost half. Subsequent financial problems caused great discontent among workers, who were eventually granted representation in the city's government. However, their representation was short-lived; from 1382 an alliance between the Guelphs and the city's wealthiest merchants seized power for the next 40-odd years.

During the latter part of the 14th century, Firenze was ruled by a caucus of Guelphs under the leadership of the Albizzi family. Opposed to them were the Ricci, Alberti and Medici families, who had the support of the lower classes. During this period, the Medici consolidated their influence and eventually became the papal bankers, with branches in 16 cities. After making claims to the leadership of the party in opposition to the Albizzi, Cosimo de' Medici was banished.

But Cosimo's political fortunes improved in his absence, mostly because of the sympathy the Medici enjoyed among the lower classes. He returned to Firenze a year later and became its ruler. Cosimo was described by contemporaries as serious but unassuming; he had a deep understanding of the arts and letters and was an extraordinarily generous patron. His eye for talent and his tact in dealing with artists saw the likes of Alberti, Brunelleschi, Lorenzo Ghiberti, Donatello, Fra Angelico and Filippo Lippi flourish under his patronage. Many of the city's finest buildings are testimony to his tastes.

Upon Cosimo's death in 1464, rule was assumed by his son, Piero il Gottoso (Peter the Gouty), and then by his grandson, Lorenzo Il Magnifico. Lorenzo's rule (1469-92) ushered in the most glorious period of Florentine civilisation and of the Italian Renaissance. His court fostered a great flowering of art, music and poetry, and Firenze became the cultural capital of Italy. Lorenzo favoured philosophers, but he maintained family tradition by sponsoring artists such as Botticelli and Domenico Ghirlandaio; he also encouraged da Vinci and the young Michelangelo, who was working under Giovanni di Bertoldo, Donatello's pupil.

Not long before Lorenzo's death in 1492, the Medici bank failed and, two years later, the Medici were driven out of Firenze. The city fell under the control of Girolamo Savonarola, a Dominican monk who led a puritanical republic until he fell from public favour and was burned as a heretic in 1498.

After Firenze's defeat by the Spanish in 1512, the Medici returned to the city but were once again expelled, this time by Emperor Charles V in 1527. The family made peace with Charles two years later; he not only permitted their return to Firenze, but married his daughter to Alessandro de' Medici, great-grandson of Lorenzo Il Magnifico, and made him Duke of Firenze in 1530. The Medici then ruled the city for another 200 years, gaining control of all Toscana during the period.

In 1737 the Grand Duchy of Toscana passed to the House of Lorraine, which retained control (apart from a brief interruption by the French under Napoleon from 1799 to 1814) until it was incorporated into the Kingdom of Italy in 1860. Firenze became the national capital a year later, but Roma assumed the mantle in 1875.

Firenze was badly damaged during WWII by the retreating Germans, who bombed all its bridges except the Ponte Vecchio. Devastating floods ravaged the city in 1966, causing inestimable damage to its buildings and artworks, some of which are still being restored. However, the salvage operation led to the widespread use of modern restoration techniques which have saved artworks throughout the country.

Orientation

Whether you arrive by train, bus or car, the central train station, Santa Maria Novella, is a good reference point. Budget hotels and pensioni are concentrated around Via Nazionale, to the east of the station, and

Savonarola

The Renaissance was a time of extraordinary contrasts. Artists, writers and philosophers of great talent flourished against a backdrop of violence, war, plague and extreme poverty. In Firenze, the court of Lorenzo de' Medici was among the most splendid and enlightened in Europe. Yet, in the streets and increasingly in Lorenzo's court itself, there were people who had begun to listen very intently to the fanatical preachings of a Dominican monk named Girolamo Savonarola. Born in Ferrara in 1452, Savonarola moved to Firenze in the last years of Lorenzo the Magnificent's rule. An inspired and eloquent orator, he preached against luxury, greed, the corruption of the clergy and against the Renaissance itself. To him both the church and the world were corrupt and he accused the ruling class of thinking only 'of new taxes, to suck the blood of the people'. When the Medici were expelled from Firenze after the French invasion of Italy in 1494 and a republic was proclaimed, Savonarola was appointed its legislator and under his severe, moralistic lead the city underwent a type of religious reform. His followers numbered some of the city's greatest humanist philosophers, as well as many of its most successful artists, but his enemies were numerous and powerful – not least the exiled Medici and the corrupt Pope Alexander VI, against whom the monk preached. The pope consequently excommunicated Savonarola in 1497. In the ensuing year, the Florentine public began to turn cold on the evangelistic preacher; he came under attack from the Franciscan monks and began to lose the support of political allies. After refusing to undergo the challenge of an ordeal by fire, Savonarola was arrested and on 22 May 1498, was hanged and burned at the stake for heresy in Piazza della Signoria. His ashes were thrown into the Arno river. ■

Piazza Santa Maria Novella, to the south. The main route to the city centre is Via de' Panzani and then Via de' Cerretani, about a 10-minute walk. You'll know you've arrived when you first glimpse the duomo.

Once at the Piazza del Duomo you will find Firenze easy to negotiate. Most of the major sights are within easy walking distance, and you can walk from one end of the city centre to the other in about 30 minutes. From Piazza San Giovanni around the baptistry, Via Roma leads to Piazza della Repubblica and continues as Via Calimala to the Ponte Vecchio. Take Via de' Calzaiuoli from Piazza del Duomo for Piazza della Signoria, the historic seat of government – don't be fooled by the lookalike of Michelangelo's *David* outside the Palazzo Vecchio; the real one is housed in the Galleria dell'Accademia. The Uffizi is on the piazza's southern edge, near the Arno river. Cross the Ponte Vecchio, or the Ponte alle Grazie farther east, to reach Piazzale Michelangelo in the south-east for a view over the city, one of the best vistas in Italy.

There is reasonably priced public parking around the imposing Fortezza da Basso, just north of the train station and a brisk 10-minute walk to the historic centre along Via XXVII Aprile and Via Cavour. The HI youth hostel is on the city's north-eastern fringe, accessible by bus No 17B from the station.

Firenze has two street-numbering systems: red or brown numbers indicate a commercial premises and black or blue numbers denote a private residence. When written, black or blue addresses are denoted by the number only, while red or brown addresses usually carry an 'r' after the number. Of course, there are exceptions, but check the colouring if you are trying to find an address.

Information

Tourist Offices The Comune di Firenze (city council) operates a tourist office (☎ 21 22 45) just outside the main train station in the covered area where buses stop. During high season it opens from Monday to Saturday from 8 am to 7.30 pm. It has another office (☎ 230 21 24) at Chiasso Baroncelli 17/19r, just off Piazza della Signoria. The main APT office (☎ 29 08 32; fax 276 03 83) is just north of the duomo at Via Cavour 1r, open from April to October from Monday to Saturday, 8.15 am to 7.15 pm, and on Sunday from 8.45 am to 1.45 pm. In other months it

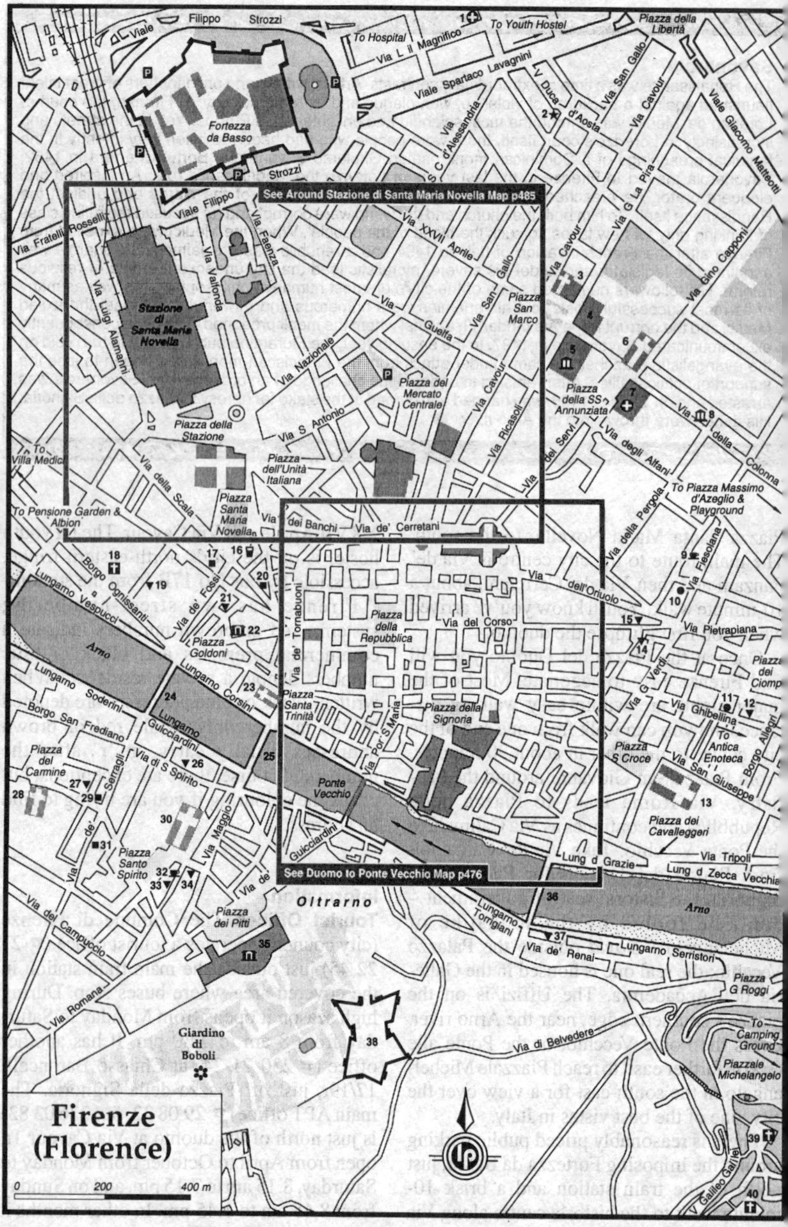
Firenze
(Florence)
0
200
400 m
Viale Filippo Strozzi
To Hospital
To Youth Hostel
Piazza della Libertà
Via L il Magnifico
Viale Spartaco Lavagnini
Fortezza da Basso
Strozzi
Via S C d'Alessandria
Duca d'Aosta
Via San Gallo
Via Cavour
Viale Giacomo Matteotti
Via G La Pira
Via Gino Capponi
See Around Stazione di Santa Maria Novella Map p465
Viale Filippo
Via Fratelli Rosselli
Via Faenza
Via XXVII Aprile
Via Valfonda
Via Luigi Alamanni
Stazione di Santa Maria Novella
Via Guelfa
Piazza San Marco
Via Nazionale
Piazza del Mercato Centrale
Piazza della SS Annunziata
Via della Colonna
Via S Antonio
Piazza della Stazione
Via Ricasoli
Via dei Servi
Via degli Alfani
To Villa Medici
Via della Scala
Piazza dell'Unità Italiana
Via della Pergola
To Piazza Massimo d'Azeglio & Playground
To Pensione Garden & Albion
Piazza Santa Maria Novella
Via dei Banchi
Via de' Cerretani
Via dell'Oriuolo
Via Fiesolana
Borgo Ognissanti
Lungarno Vespucci
Via de' Fossi
Via de' Tornabuoni
Piazza della Repubblica
Via del Corso
Via Pietrapiana
Arno
Piazza Goldoni
Lungarno Corsini
Piazza dei Ciompi
Lungarno Soderini
Via G Verdi
Via Ghibellina
Borgo San Frediano
Piazza Santa Trinità
Via Por S Maria
Piazza della Signoria
To Antica Enoteca
Borgo Allegri
Lungarno Guicciardini
Via di S Spirito
Piazza S Croce
Via San Giuseppe
Piazza del Carmine
Via de' Serragli
Ponte Vecchio
Via Maggio
Piazza dei Cavalleggeri
Guicciardini
Lung d Grazie
Via Tripoli
Lung d Zecca Vecchia
Piazza Santo Spirito
See Duomo to Ponte Vecchio Map p476
Oltrarno
Lungarno Torrigiani
Piazza dei Pitti
Via del Campuccio
Via de' Renai
Lungarno Serristori
Piazza G Roggi
Via Romana
Via di Belvedere
Giardino di Boboli
To Camping Ground
Piazzale Michelangelo
Viale Galileo Galilei
1
2
3
4
5
6
7
8
9
10
11
12
13
14
15
16
17
18
19
20
21
22
23
24
25
26
27
28
29
30
31
32
33
34
35
36
37
38
39
40
P

TOSCANA

PLACES TO STAY	34 Trattoria Casalinga	11 Casa Buonarroti
17 Pensione Ottaviani & Albergo Visconti	37 I Tarocchi	13 Chiesa di Santa Croce
20 Pensione Toscana & Pensione Sole		16 Fiddler's Elbow
29 Ostello Santa Monaca	**OTHER**	18 Chiesa di Ognissanti
31 Istituto Gould	1 Tourist Medical Service	22 Palazzo Rucellai
	2 Questura (Police Station)	23 Chiesa di Santa Trinità
PLACES TO EAT	3 Museo di San Marco	24 Ponte alla Carraia
9 Rex Caffè	4 University	25 Ponte Santa Trinità
12 Enoteca Pinchiorri	5 Galleria dell'Accademia	28 Chiesa di Santa Maria del Carmine
14 Natalino	6 Chiesa di SS Annunziata	30 Chiesa di Santo Spirito
15 Antico Noè	7 Spedale degli Innocenti	35 Palazzo Pitti
19 Sostanza	8 Museo Archeologico	36 Ponte alle Grazie
21 Da il Latini	10 Paperback Exchange Bookshop	38 Forte di Belvedere
26 Angelino		39 Chiesa di San Salvatore al Monte
27 Trattoria I Raddi		40 Chiesa di San Miniato al Monte
32 Cabiria		
33 Borgo Antico		

s open until 1.45 pm and is closed on Sunday.

At both offices you can pick up a map of the city, a list of hotels, and other useful information. Staff at the APT speak English, French, Spanish and German, and have extensive useful information about the city and its services, such as language and art courses, car and bike rental. The APT also offers a special service known as Firenze SOS Turista (☎ 276 03 82) from April to October. Tourists needing guidance on matters such as disputes over hotel fees etc can phone Monday to Saturday from 10 am to 1 pm and 3 to 6 pm.

The tourist offices will provide information about places to stay, but will not book rooms. See Places to Stay in this section for details about hotel booking services.

A good map of the city, on sale at newsstands, is the one with the white, red and black cover *(Firenze: Pianta della Città)*, which costs L8000.

Foreign Consulates The US Consulate (☎ 239 82 76) is by the Arno at Lungarno Vespucci 38, and the UK Consulate (☎ 28 41 33) is nearby at Lungarno Corsini 2.

Money A number of the main banks are concentrated around Piazza della Repubblica. Thomas Cook has an exchange office (☎ 28 97 81) at Lungarno Acciaioli 6r, near the Ponte Vecchio. From March to October it is open Monday to Saturday from 9 am to 7 pm and Sunday from 9 am to 1 pm. In other months it closes on weekdays at 6 pm and is closed on Sunday. There's a full American Express office and travel service (☎ 28 87 51) at Via de' Guicciardini 49r in the Oltrarno on the way to Palazzo Pitti. Another branch is at Via Dante Alighieri 22r.

Post & Communications The main post office is in Via Pellicceria, off Piazza della Repubblica, and is open daily from 7 am to 8 pm. Poste restante mail can be addressed to 50100 Firenze. Fax and telegram services are available, but only faxes sent from other post offices can be received. The APT has a list of private fax services in Firenze.

There is a Telecom office at Via Cavour 21, open daily from 8 am to 9.45 pm, and another at Stazione di Santa Maria Novella, open Monday to Saturday from 8 am to 9.45 pm.

You can connect to the Internet at Libreria Cima (☎ 247 72 45), Borgo degli Albizi 37r, for L10,000 an hour, or open an email address for L35,000 for six months or L50,000 for one year. It is open daily from 9.30 am to 7.30 pm, and on Tuesday, Thursday and Saturday it reopens at 9.30 pm and closes at 1 am. It has a caffè which has become a meeting place for foreigners.

The telephone code for Firenze is ☎ 055.

Travel Agencies Sestante CIT has offices at Via Cavour 56r (☎ 29 43 06) and at Piazza della Stazione 51r (☎ 28 41 45), where you can book train and air fares, organise guided tours etc.

Bookshops The Paperback Exchange, Via Fiesolana 31r, has a vast selection of new and second-hand books in English, including classics, contemporary literature, reference and bestsellers, as well as travel guides. It is closed Sunday. Feltrinelli International, Via Cavour 12r, opposite the APT, has a good selection of books in English, French, German, Spanish, Portuguese and Russian. Internazionale Seeber, Via de' Tornabuoni 70r, also has books in those languages.

Gay & Lesbian Information Arci Gay (☎ 28 81 26), Via Montebello 6, operates a phone information service from 5 to 7 pm.

Laundry Onda Blu, Via degli Affani 24bR, east of the duomo, is self-service and charges around L6000 for a 6.5kg load. There's another Onda Blu at Via Guelfa 22aR.

Medical Services The main public hospital is Ospedale Careggi (☎ 427 71 11), Viale Morgagni 85, north of the city centre. There is also the Ospedale Santa Maria Nuova (☎ 2 75 81), Piazza Santa Maria Nuova 1, just east of the duomo.

The Tourist Medical Service (☎ 47 54 11), Via Lorenzo il Magnifico 59, is open 24 hours a day and doctors speak English, French and German. An organisation of volunteer translators (English, French and German) called the Associazione Volontari Ospedalieri (☎ 234 45 67 or 40 31 26) will provide free translation once you've found a doctor. All public hospitals have a list of volunteers, but you may need to ask for it. The APT has lists of doctors, dentists etc of various nationalities.

All-night pharmacies include the Farmacia Comunale (☎ 28 94 35) inside the Stazione di Santa Maria Novella, and Molteni (☎ 28 94 90), in the city centre a Via de' Calzaiuoli 7r.

Emergency In an emergency (police medical and fire) call ☎ 113. The questur (☎ 4 97 71) is at Via Zara 2. There is an offic for foreigners, where you can report theft etc. There is an ambulance station (☎ 21 2 22) in Piazza del Duomo.

Lost property (☎ 36 79 43) and towed away cars can be collected from Vi Circondaria 19, north-west of the city centre

Dangers & Annoyances The most annoy ing aspect of Firenze is the crowds, closel followed by the summer heat. Pickpocket are very active in crowds and particularly o buses. Beware of the numerous bands o dishevelled women and children carryin newspapers or cardboard. A few will distrac you while the others rifle your bag an pockets. Carry a money pouch or wear money belt; never carry money in you pockets. The city has a small problem wit moped bandits who will try to grab handbags

Traffic in the city centre is heavy an chaotic, so watch out for aggressive, fas drivers in the narrow streets. Air pollutio can be a serious problem in Firenze, particu larly in summer, when locals are ofte

A Recipe for Stendhalismo

Any list of 'must sees' in Firenze is going to incite cries of protest. How can you recommend that a tour cover the Galleria degli Uffizi, the duomo and the baptistry, without including the Museo del Bargello, the Convento di San Marco and the churches of Santa Maria Novella, Santa Croce and SS Annunziata? And what about Masaccio's fresco cycle in Chiesa di Santa Maria del Carmine? Or Michelangelo's *David* in the Galleria dell'Accademia and his Medici tombs in the family chapel attached to the Basilica di San Lorenzo? Plan carefully, or you could end up with a severe case of Stendhalismo – see the introduction to Firenze. And make sure you carry plenty of L100, L200 and L500 coins for the machines to illuminate the frescoes in the churches. ■

warned to keep small children, people with respiratory problems and the elderly inside. If you fit one of these categories, stay informed about pollution levels through the tourist office or your hotel proprietor.

Walking Tour

Here is a suggested tour of churches that are important both architecturally and for the art treasures they contain. The walk is divided into two groups of four churches, one group for the morning and one for the afternoon, since most churches close for three to four hours in the middle of the day. The APT office at Via Cavour 1r has an updated list of opening hours.

First Group Start at the **Chiesa di Santa Maria Novella**, in the piazza of the same name, just south of the main train station. Begun in the late 13th century as the Florentine base for the Dominican order, the church was largely completed by around 1360, but work on its façade and the embellishment of its interior continued until well into the 15th century. The lower section of the lovely green and white marble façade is Gothic-Romanesque, while the upper section and the main doorway were designed by Alberti and completed in around 1470. The highlight of the Gothic interior is Masaccio's superb fresco of the **Trinity** (1428), one of the first artworks to use the then newly discovered techniques of perspective and proportion. It is about halfway along the north aisle.

The first chapel to the right of the choir, the Cappella di Filippo Strozzi, features lively frescoes by Filippino Lippi depicting the lives of St John the Evangelist and St Philip the Apostle. Another important work is Domenico Ghirlandaio's series of frescoes behind the main altar, painted with the help of artists who may have included the young student Michelangelo. Relating the lives of the Virgin Mary, St John the Baptist and others, the frescoes are particularly notable for their depiction of Florentine life during the Renaissance. Brunelleschi's famous crucifix hangs above the altar in the Cappella Gondi, the first chapel on the left of the choir.

The cloisters (entrance on the left of the façade) feature some of the city's best frescoes. The Chiostro Verde (Green Cloisters) is so named because green is the predominant colour of the fresco cycle by Paolo Uccello. The impressive Cappellone degli Spagnuoli (Spanish Chapel) contains frescoes by Andrea di Bonaiuto depicting significant religious events. The church is open daily from 7 am to 12.15 pm and 3 to 6 pm. The cloisters are open daily, except Friday, from 9 am to 2 pm. Admission is L5000.

From the Piazza Santa Maria Novella head east along Via dei Banchi and take the first street on the left, Via del Giglio. Cross Via de' Panzani and continue straight ahead until you reach the Piazza Madonna degli Aldobrandini and the Basilica di San Lorenzo. The streets in this area are lined with market stalls specialising in leather goods and knitwear.

The Medici commissioned Brunelleschi to rebuild the **Basilica di San Lorenzo** in 1425, on the site of a 4th-century basilica. It is considered one of the most harmonious examples of Renaissance architecture; Michelangelo prepared a design for the façade which was never executed. It was the Medici parish church and many family members are buried here. The two bronze pulpits are by Donatello, who died before they were completed. He is buried in the chapel featuring Filippo Lippi's *Annunciation*. The entrance to the basilica is in the busy Piazza San Lorenzo, off Borgo San Lorenzo. The basilica is open daily from 7 am to midday and 3.30 to 6.30 pm. The adjoining **Sagrestia Vecchia** (Old Sacristy) was also designed by Brunelleschi and its interior was largely decorated by Donatello.

Visit the **Biblioteca Laurenziana**, which can be reached through the cloister. It was commissioned by Cosimo de' Medici to house the Medici library and contains 10,000 volumes. The magnificent staircase was designed by Michelangelo. It is open daily from 9 am to 1 pm. Admission is free.

The **Cappelle Medicee** are entered via Piazza Madonna degli Aldobrandini. The

Cappella dei Principi (Princes' Chapel), sumptuously decorated with precious marble and semiprecious stones, was the principal burial place of the Medici rulers. The graceful and simple **Sagrestia Nuova** (New Sacristy) was designed by Michelangelo and was his first architectural work, although he left Firenze for Roma before its completion. It contains his beautiful sculptures *Night and Day*, *Dawn and Dusk* and the *Madonna with Child*, which adorn the Medici tombs. The chapels are open Tuesday to Saturday from 8.30 am to 1.50 pm (as well as alternating Mondays and Sundays). Admission is L10,000.

Next stop is the **Chiesa di SS Annunziata** in the piazza of the same name. From Piazza San Lorenzo walk east along Via dei Gori to reach Via Cavour, turn left and walk until you reach Piazza San Marco (two to three minutes), then turn right into Via Cesare Battisti to reach the Piazza della SS Annunziata. The church was established in 1250 by the founders of the Servite order and rebuilt by Michelozzo and others in the mid-15th century. It is dedicated to the Virgin Mary and in the ornate tabernacle, to your left as you enter the church from the atrium, is a so-called miraculous painting of the Virgin.

The painting, which is no longer on public view, is attributed to a 14th-century friar, and legend says it was completed by an angel. Also of note are frescoes by Andrea del Castagno in the first two chapels on the left of the church, a fresco by Perugino in the fifth chapel and the frescoes in Michelozzo's atrium, particularly the *Birth of the Virgin* by Andrea del Sarto and the *Visitation* by Jacopo Pontormo. The church is open daily from 7.30 am to 12.30 pm and 4 to 6.30 pm.

Head back to Piazza San Marco for the **Museo di San Marco** in the now deconsecrated Dominican convent and the Chiesa di San Marco. The piazza is the centre of the university area and is one of the most pleasant squares in the city. The church was founded in 1299, rebuilt by Michelozzo in 1437, and again remodelled by Giambologna some years later. It features several paintings, but they pale in comparison to the treasures contained in the adjoining convent.

Famous Florentines who called the convent home include the painters Fra Angelico and Fra Bartolomeo, as well as St Antoninus and Girolamo Savonarola. See the boxed aside on Savonarola earlier in this chapter. It is interesting to contemplate that Fra Angelico, who painted the radiant imaginative and joyous frescoes which adorn the walls of the convent, and Savonarola were of the same religious order – the latter arriving in Firenze almost 30 years after the painter's death in 1455. The convent is a museum of Fra Angelico's works, many of which were moved there from other locations in Firenze in the 1860s. The Ospizio dei Pellegrini (Pilgrim's Hospice) contains a number of his works, notably the *Tabernacolo dei Linaioli*, the *Last Judgment* (painted with his students) and *Descent from the Cross*. The chapter-house features more works by Fra Angelico including one of his greatest masterpieces, a fresco of the *Crucifixion*.

Upstairs are the monks' dormitory cells all decorated with frescoes by Fra Angelico and his assistants. At the top of the stairs is another of his masterpieces, a fresco of the *Annunciation*. Along the left corridor, in the cells on the left side, are several frescoes by the master (cells 1, 3, 4, 6, 7 and 9). The museum is open Tuesday to Saturday from 8.30 am to 1.50 pm (as well as alternating Mondays and Sundays). Admission is L8000.

The first part of the tour ends here. If you want to stop for a quick snack, head for Bondi, Via dell'Ariento 85, in the San Lorenzo market area, near Via Nazionale. It specialises in focaccia and pizza by the slice. For something more substantial you could try Caffè Za Za, Piazza del Mercato Centrale 20, or Mario's, a few doors down at Via Rosina 2r.

Second Group The second half of the tour starts at the remarkable **duomo**, with its pink, white and green marble façade, and Brunelleschi's famous dome, which domi-ates the Firenze skyline. No matter how nany times you have visited the city, the uomo will take your breath away. Named he Cattedrale di Santa Maria del Fiore, it vas begun in 1296 by the Sienese architect Arnolfo di Cambio, but took almost 150 ears to complete. It is the fourth-largest athedral in the world.

Brunelleschi won a public competition to lesign the enormous **dome**, the first of its ind since antiquity. Although now severely racked and under restoration, it remains a emarkable achievement of design. When Michelangelo went to Roma to work on the onstruction of the Basilica di San Pietro he s reported to have said, 'I go to build a greater dome, but not a fairer one'. The dome s decorated with frescoes by Vasari and Frederico Zuccari, and stained-glass windows by Donatello, Andrea del Castagno, Paolo Uccello and Lorenzo Ghiberti. The rescoes have recently been unveiled after a .11 billion restoration which took more than 5 years. You can climb up into the dome to get a closer look; enter to the left as you face he altar. The view from the summit over Firenze is unparalleled. The dome is open Monday to Saturday from 9.30 am to 6.20 om and the climb costs L8000.

The duomo's vast interior, about 155m ong and 90m wide, and its sparse decoration comes as a surprise after the visually tumultuous façade. The sacristies on each side of he altar feature enamelled terracotta lunettes over their doorways by Luca della Robbia. Lorenzo de' Medici hid in the north sacristy after his brother, Giuliano, was stabbed and killed by the Pazzi conspirators.

Also of note are the two frescoes in the north aisle commemorating the condottieri Sir John Hawkwood and Niccolò da Tolentino, who fought for Firenze. The former was painted by Paolo Uccello and the latter by Andrea del Castagno. Also in the north aisle is a painting of Dante with a depiction of the Divine Comedy, painted by Domenico di Michelino.

A stairway near the main entrance of the duomo leads to the crypt, where excavations have unearthed parts of the 5th-century Basilica di Santa Reparata, which originally stood on the site, and Brunelleschi's tomb. The duomo's marble façade in white, green and red marble was built in the 19th century in Gothic style to replace the original, uncompleted façade designed by Arnolfo di Cambio, which was pulled down in the 16th century. The duomo is open Monday to Friday from 10 am to 5 pm, Saturday to 4.45 pm and Sunday from 1 to 5 pm. Strict dress standards are enforced and guards will prevent visitors from entering during mass.

Giotto designed and began building the graceful and unusual **bell tower** next to the duomo in 1334, but died before it was completed. His work was continued by Andrea Pisano and Francesco Talenti. The first tier of bas-reliefs around the base of the tower

Lorenzo de' Medici & the Pazzi Conspiracy

Plots to ruin the Medici family were nothing new to Firenze, but in 1478 Lorenzo de' Medici lost his brother, Giuliano, and almost his own life in an incident known as the Pazzi conspiracy. The Pazzi were a wealthy Florentine family who had been denied the benefits of public office by the Medici. Jealous and bitter, Francesco de' Pazzi, who was actually a Catholic priest, formed a plan backed by Pope Sixtus IV to kill the Medici brothers and take power in Firenze. The audacious plan was put into effect in the Duomo during High Mass. When all heads were bowed as the host was raised, Francesco and an accomplice struck, stabbing Giuliano to death. Lorenzo escaped into the sacristy and survived the attack, but the city was in an uproar. A mob spent days hunting down the conspirators and anyone else believed to have been associated with the incident. Hundreds died, including most members of the Pazzi family. Surviving members were imprisoned or exiled, the Pazzi name was proscribed and female members of the family were forbidden to marry and have children (Lorenzo later revoked this order). ■

depicts the Creation of Man and the Arts and Industries, and was carved by Pisano, although it was believed to have been designed by Giotto. Those on the second tier depict the planets, cardinal virtues, the arts and the seven sacraments. The sculptures of the Prophets and Sybils in the niches of the upper storeys are actually copies of works by Donatello and others – the originals are in the duomo's museum. The bell tower is 82m high and you can climb its stairs daily between 9 am and 6.50 pm (until 4.20 pm in winter). Admission is L8000.

The Romanesque-style **baptistry** (battistero) is generally believed to have been built between the 5th and 12th centuries on the site of a Roman temple. It is one of the oldest buildings in Firenze and is dedicated to St John the Baptist. The octagonal building is decorated with stripes of white and green marble and is famous for its gilded bronze doors, particularly the celebrated east doors facing the duomo, the *Gates of Paradise* by Lorenzo Ghiberti. The bas-reliefs on its 10 panels depict scenes from the Old Testament. The south door, executed by Pisano and completed in 1336, is the oldest. The bas-reliefs on its 28 compartments deal predominantly with the life of St John the Baptist. The north door is also by Ghiberti, who won a public competition in 1401 to design it. The design was based on Pisano's earlier door and its main theme is also St John the Baptist. The *Gates of Paradise*, however, remain his consummate masterpiece. Dante was baptised in the baptistry. Most of the doors are copies – the original panels are being gradually removed for restoration and placed in the Museo dell'Opera del Duomo as work is completed. The baptistry is open Monday to Saturday from 1.30 to 6.30 pm and Sunday from 8.30 am to 1.30 pm. Admission is L3000.

The **Museo dell'Opera del Duomo**, behind the cathedral at Piazza del Duomo 9, features most of the art treasures from the duomo, baptistry and bell tower and is definitely worth a visit. Displays include the equipment used by Brunelleschi to build the dome, as well as his death mask. Perhaps its best piece is Michelangelo's *Pietà*, which h intended for his own tomb. Vasari recorde in his *Lives of the Artists* that, unsatisfie with the quality of the marble or his ow work, Michelangelo broke up the unfinishe sculpture, destroying the arm and left leg c the figure of Christ. A student of Michelan gelo later restored the arm and completed th figure of Mary Magdalene. The collection c sculpture is considered the city's second bes after that in the Museo del Bargello. Note i particular Donatello's carving of the prophe Habakkuk (taken from the bell tower) an his wooden impression of Mary Magdalen The museum is open daily, except Sunday from 9 am to 6.50 pm (it closes at 6.20 p in winter). Admission is L8000.

From the Piazza del Duomo, walk sout along Via del Proconsolo and turn left int Borgo degli Albizi and the area known a Santa Croce. When you reach Piazza S Pie Maggiore turn right and walk along Via M Palmieri. Across Via Ghibellina you wi pass Gelateria Vivoli in Via dell'Isola dell Stinche, one of the city's best gelateri where you can stop for an after-lunch pick me-up.

Continue straight ahead and turn left int Borgo de' Greci reaching the Francisca **Chiesa di Santa Croce** in the piazza of th same name. In Savonarola's day, the piazz was used for the execution of heretics, bu today it is lined with souvenir shops. Attrib uted to Arnolfo di Cambio, Santa Croce wa started in 1294 on the site of a Francisca chapel, and the façade and bell tower wer added in the 19th century. The three-nav interior of the church is grand, but austere The floor is paved with the tombstones o famous Florentines of the past 500 years an monuments to the particularly notable wer added along the walls from the mid-16t century.

Along the south wall (to your right as yo enter the church) is Michelangelo's tomb designed by Vasari, and a cenotaph dedicate to Dante, who is buried in Ravenna. Furthe along you will find a monument to the 18th century dramatist and poet Vittorio Alfieri b Antonio Canova, along with a monument t lachiavelli and a bas-relief, *Annunciation*, y Donatello.

The Cappella Castellani, in the right tran-ept, is completely covered with frescoes by gnolo Gaddi. In the Cappella Baroncelli at e end of the transept, frescoes by his father, addeo Gaddi, depict the life of the Virgin. gnolo Gaddi also painted the frescoes bove and behind the altar. Adjoining the acristy is a corridor by Michelozzo which ads to a Medici chapel, featuring a large tarpiece by Andrea della Robbia. The Bardi nd Peruzzi chapels, to the right of the hancel, are completely covered in frescoes y Giotto. In the central chapel of the north ansept (also a Bardi chapel) hangs a ooden crucifix by Donatello.

The **cloisters** were designed by Bru-elleschi just before his death in 1446 and re noted for their serenity. Brunelleschi's **appella dei Pazzi**, at the end of the first loister, is a masterpiece of Renaissance rchitecture. The **Museo dell'Opera di anta Croce**, off the first cloister, features a rucifix by Cimabue, which was badly amaged during the disastrous 1966 flood, hen more than 4m of water inundated the anta Croce area. The crucifix was almost ompletely destroyed and lost much of its aint. It has been partially restored.

In summer the church is open Monday to aturday from 8 am to 6.30 pm, and Sunday rom 8 am to 12.30 pm and 3 to 6.30 pm. In inter it is open Monday to Saturday from 8 m to 12.30 pm and 3 to 6.30 pm, and Sunday rom 3 to 6 pm. The museum is open daily, xcept Wednesday, from 10 am to 12.30 pm nd 2.30 to 6.30 pm. In winter opening hours re shorter in the afternoon, from 3 to 5 pm. Admission is L4000.

The walking tour now heads for two hurches in the **Oltrarno**, meaning literally the other side of the Arno'. From the top end f the piazza go left into Via dei Benci and ollow it to the river. Either cross here at the onte alle Grazie or follow the river to your ight to reach the Ponte Vecchio. Take Borgo Jacopo, on your right after you cross Ponte ecchio, and continue along it as it becomes ia di Santo Spirito. Cross Via de' Serragli and take the first left to reach Piazza del Carmine and the **Chiesa di Santa Maria del Carmine**. This 13th-century church was almost completely destroyed by a fire in the late 18th century. Fortunately the fire spared the magnificent frescoes by Masaccio which are in the Cappella Brancacci. Considered the painter's finest work, the frescoes had an enormous influence on Florentine art in the 15th century. Masaccio painted them in his early 20s and interrupted the task to go to Roma, where he died aged only 28. The cycle was completed some 60 years later by Filippino Lippi. Earlier frescoes in the cycle were painted by Masolino da Panicale. The frescoes were recently restored and their vibrant colours combined with Masaccio's vigorous style create a strong visual impact. Masaccio's work includes the famous *Expulsion of Adam and Eve from Paradise*, and *The Tribute Money* on the upper left wall. The chapel is open daily from 10 am to 5 pm. Admission is L5000.

Head back in the direction of the Ponte Vecchio, but take Via Santa Monica, which runs off the piazza. Cross Via de' Serragli and continue along Via Sant'Agostino until you come to Piazza Santo Spirito and the **Chiesa di Santo Spirito**. One of Brunelleschi's last commissions, the church is beautifully planned, with a colonnade of 35 columns and a series of semicircular chapels. The chapels' works of art include a *Madonna and Saints* by Filippino Lippi in the right transept. Santo Spirito is open daily, except Wednesday afternoon, from 8 am to midday and 4 to 6 pm. The piazza outside has developed somewhat of a bohemian feel and one of the most popular cafés for young people, Cabiria, is to your left as you leave the church.

Around Piazza della Signoria

The hub of the city's political life through the centuries and surrounded by some of its most celebrated buildings, the piazza has the appearance of an outdoor sculpture gallery. Ammannati's huge Fountain of Neptune sits beside the Palazzo Vecchio, and flanking the entrance to the palace are copies of Michelangelo's *David* (the original is in the

Galleria dell'Accademia) and Donatello's *Marzocco*, the heraldic Florentine lion (the original is in the Museo del Bargello). An equestrian statue of Cosimo de' Medici by Giambologna stands towards the centre of the piazza. A bronze plaque marks the spot where Savonarola was hanged and burnt at the stake in 1498.

The **Loggia della Signoria** was built in the late 14th century as a platform for public ceremonies and eventually became a showcase for sculptures. To the left of the steps is Benvenuto Cellini's magnificent statue of Perseus holding the head of Medusa (the statue was under restoration at the time of writing and will perhaps be placed inside the Uffizi). To the right is Giambologna's (Giovanni da Bologna) *Rape of the Sabine Women*, his final work and a famous example of Mannerist sculpture.

The **Palazzo Vecchio**, built by Arnolfo di Cambio between 1298 and 1314, is the traditional seat of Florentine government. Its **Torre d'Arnolfo** is 94m high and, with its striking crenellations, is as much a symbol of the city as the duomo. Built for the *signoria*, the highest level of Florentine republican government, it became the palace of Cosimo de' Medici in the mid-16th century, before he moved to the Palazzo Pitti. Vasari was commissioned by the Medici to reorganise the interior and created a series of sumptuous rooms. There is a beautiful courtyard by Michelozzo just inside the entrance and lavishly decorated apartments upstairs. The Salone dei Cinquecento was the meeting room of the Consiglio della Repubblica (Great Council) during Savonarola's time. It was later used for banquets and festivities and features frescoes by Vasari and Michelangelo's *Genius of Victory*, originally destined for Roma and Pope Julius II's tomb. The Studiolo, which was the study of Francesco I, was designed by Vasari and decorated by several Florentine Mannerist artists. Farther on is the Cappella di Signoria, decorated by Domenico Ghirlandaio in 1514. The palace is open Monday to Saturday from 9 am to 7 pm and Sunday from 8 am to 1 pm. Admission is L10,000.

Galleria degli Uffizi

Designed and built by Vasari in the second half of the 16th century at the request of Cosimo de' Medici, the Galleria degli Uffizi (Uffizi Gallery) is located in the **Palazzo degli Uffizi**, which originally housed the city's administrators, judiciary and guilds. It was, in effect, an office building (*uffizi* means offices). Vasari also designed the private corridor which links the Palazzo Vecchio and the Palazzo Pitti, through the Uffizi and across the Ponte Vecchio. Known as the **Corridoio Vasariano**, it is lined with paintings and can be seen only on a guided tour. Cosimo's successor, Francesco I, commissioned the architect Buontalenti to modify the upper floor of the Palazzo degli Uffizi to house the Medici's growing art collection. The gallery now houses the family's private collection, which was bequeathed to the city in 1737 by the last of the Medici, Anna Maria Ludovica, on condition that it never leave the city.

Although over the years sections of the collection have been moved to the Museo del Bargello and the city's Museo Archeologico, the Galleria degli Uffizi still houses the world's greatest collection of Italian and Florentine art. Paintings from Firenze's churches have also been moved to the gallery. Sadly, several of its artworks were destroyed and others badly damaged when a car bomb planted by the Mafia exploded outside the gallery's western wing in May 1993. Six people died in the explosion. Documents cataloguing the collection were also destroyed. A massive clean-up enabled the gallery to reopen quickly. At the time of writing, restoration work continued on damaged paintings and a number of rooms remained closed.

The gallery is arranged to illustrate the evolving story of Italian and, in particular, Florentine art. It is undergoing a major reorganisation and plans are afoot to expand the museum to other floors of the building. This will inevitably mean that works of art will be moved and rooms will be closed. More precise information was not available at the time of writing.

To avoid the crowds go when the gallery first opens, during lunchtime or late afternoon. The extraordinary wealth of the collection and the sheer number of famous works means one visit is not enough – if you are going to come down with Stendhalismo, it will be here! If you are in Firenze for three or four days and can afford the additional cost, try to spend at least two blocks of three or so hours in the gallery, spread over a few days. Several guidebooks to the gallery are on sale at vendors all over the city, and outside the entrance.

Before heading upstairs, visit the recently restored remains of the 11th-century Chiesa di San Piero Scheraggio, which was largely destroyed during the construction of the gallery, and its apse incorporated into the structure of the palace. Upstairs in the gallery proper, the first rooms feature works by Tuscan masters of the 13th and early 14th centuries. Room 2 is dominated by three paintings of the *Maestà* by Cimabue, Giotto and Duccio di Buoninsegna. All three were altarpieces in Florentine churches before being placed in the gallery. Also in the room is Giotto's polyptych *Virgin and Child with Angels and Saints*. Room 3 traces the Sienese school of the 14th century. Of particular note is Simone Martini's shimmering *Annunciation*, considered a masterpiece of the school, and Ambrogio Lorenzetti's triptych *Madonna and Child with Saints*. Rooms 5 and 6 house examples of the international Gothic style, among them *Adoration of the Magi* by Gentile da Fabiano. Room 7 features works by painters of the early 15th-century Florentine school, which pioneered the Renaissance. There is one panel from Paolo Uccello's *Battle of San Romano* (the other two are in the Louvre and London's National Gallery), as well as Piero della Francesca's *Portraits of Battista Sforza and Federico da Montefeltro*, and *Madonna and Child* painted jointly by Masaccio and Masolino. In the next room is Filippo Lippi's delightful *Madonna and Child with Two Angels*.

The Botticelli rooms, Nos 10 to 14, are considered the gallery's most spectacular. Highlights are the famous *Birth of Venus* and *Primavera*. Room 15 features Da Vinci's *Annunciation*, painted when he was a student of Verrocchio. Room 18, known as the Tribuna, houses the celebrated *Medici Venus*, a 1st-century BC copy of a 4th-century BC sculpture by the Greek sculptor, Praxiteles. The room also contains portraits of various members of the Medici. The great Umbrian painter, Perugino, who studied under Piero della Francesca and later became Raphael's master, is represented in Room 19, as well as Luca Signorelli. Room 20 features works from the German Renaissance, including Dürer's *Adoration of the Magi*. Room 21 has works by Giovanni Bellini and his pupil, Giorgione. Peek through the railings to see the 15th to 19th-century works in the Miniatures Room and then cross into the western wing, which houses works of Italian masters dating from the 16th century.

Room 25 features Michelangelo's *Holy Family* and in the next room are works by Raphael, including his *Leo X* and *Madonna del Cardellino*. Rooms 27 to 33 are still closed for repairs. In room 34 are works by Venetian artists, including Paolo Veronese's *Holy Family with St Barbara*. Room 35 is being used to display newly restored paintings, including Caravaggio's *Bacchus* and *Sacrifice of Isaac* and works by Velasquez and Titian. All the rooms after this were still closed at the time of writing. The gallery is open Tuesday to Saturday from 8.30 am to 7 pm and Sunday to 2 pm. Admission is L12,000 and the ticket office closes 55 minutes before closing time.

Around Ponte Santa Trinità

From the Uffizi head west along the Arno to the Ponte Santa Trinità, rebuilt after being destroyed by Nazi bombing. The original plan is believed to have been drawn by Michelangelo; the bridge itself was built by Ammannati. Head north along **Via de' Tornabuoni**, one of the city's most fashionable streets, lined with Renaissance palaces and high-class shops including Ferragamo, Gucci and Armani.

In the piazza of the same name, the 13th-century **Chiesa di Santa Trinità** features several significant works, including frescoes depicting the life of St Francis of Assisi by Domenico Ghirlandaio in the Cappella Sassetti (in the right transept). The altarpiece of the Annunciation in the fourth chapel of the south aisle is by Lorenzo Monaco, who was Fra Angelico's master. Monaco also painted the frescoes which adorn the walls of the chapel.

The Palazzo Davanzati, Via Porta Rossa 13, is a well preserved, 14th-century mansion that houses the **Museo dell'Antica Casa Fiorentina** (Florentine House Museum), featuring many of the original fittings. Th palace and museum were closed for restora tion at the time of writing and expected t open sometime in 1998. Just past the palac is the **Mercato Nuovo**, a loggia built in th mid-16th century to house the city's gold an silver trade and which today houses souveni stalls and leatherwork vendors.

Return to Via de' Tornabuoni and head nort for the **Palazzo Strozzi**, one of the mos impressive Renaissance palaces in Firenze The palace is used for art exhibitions. Th beautiful **Palazzo Rucellai**, designed b Alberti, is in Via della Vigna Nuova, whic

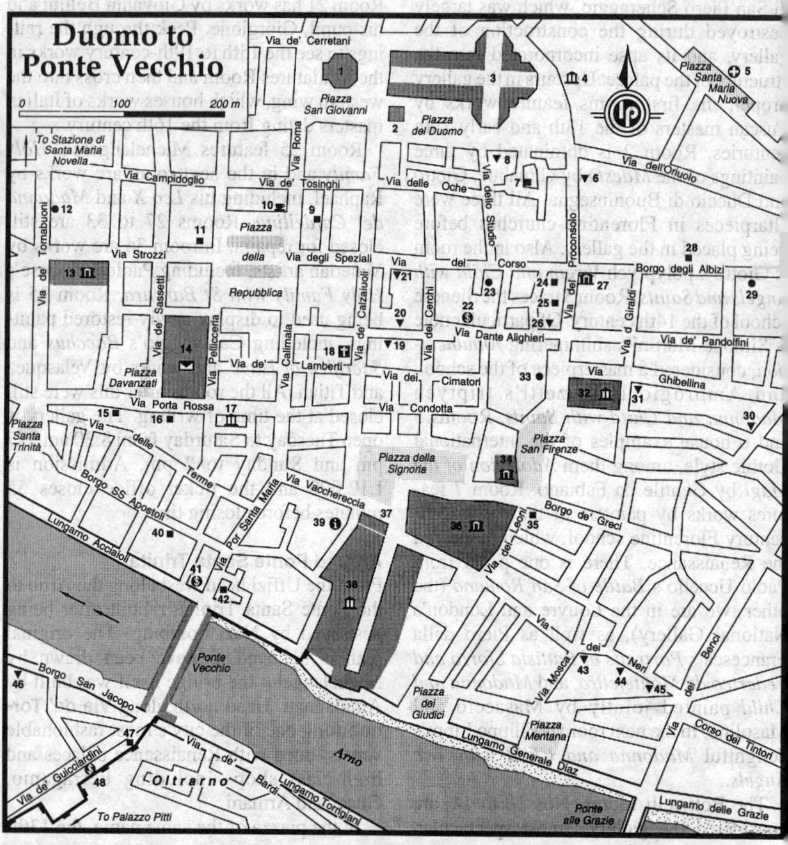

ranches off to the south-west. The palace ouses a photographic museum dedicated to he vast collection compiled by the Alinari rothers. It is open Tuesday to Sunday from 0 am to 7.30 pm. Admission is L8000.

Continue along Via della Vigna Nuova to each Piazza Goldoni and then turn right into Borgo Ognissanti to reach the 13th-century **hiesa di Ognissanti**. The church was nuch altered in the 17th century and has a Baroque façade, but inside are 15th-century vorks by Domenico Ghirlandaio and Botti-elli. Of interest is Ghirlandaio's fresco bove the second altar on the right of the Madonna della Misericordia, protector of the Vespucci family. Amerigo Vespucci, who gave his name to the American continent, is upposed to be the young boy whose head ppears between the Madonna and the old nan. Ghirlandaio's masterpiece, the *Last Supper*, covers most of a wall in the former nonastery's refectory. The church is open laily from 8 am to midday and 4 to 6 pm.

South of the Duomo

Take Via de' Calzaiuoli from Piazza del Duomo o reach the **Chiesa di Orsanmichele**. Orig-nally a grain market, the church was formed when the arcades of the market building were walled in the 14th century. The exterior is decorated with statues of the patron saints of the guilds of the city, commissioned over a period of 200 years and representing the work of many Renaissance artists. Some of the statues are now in the Museo Bargello. However, many splendid pieces remain, including *John the Baptist* by Lorenzo Ghiberti and a copy of Donatello's *St George*. The main feature of the interior is the splendid Gothic tabernacle, decorated with coloured marble, by Andrea Orcagna. The church is open from 9 am to midday and 4 to 6 pm.

Just west along Via degli Speziali is the Piazza della Repubblica. Originally the site of a Roman forum, it is now home to Firenze's most fashionable and expensive cafés.

Return to Piazza del Duomo, a little to the north-east of Piazza della Repubblica, and take Via del Proconsolo in the direction of the Arno. Near the intersection of Borgo degli Albizi is the **Palazzo Pazzi**, which is attributed to Brunelleschi and now houses offices. You can wander into the courtyard. From here, head west along Via del Corso to Via Santa Margherita and **Casa di Dante** at No 1, which has a small museum tracing

PLACES TO STAY

7 Albergo Firenze
9 Maxim
11 Pendini
15 Hotel Porta Rossa
16 Pensione TeTi & Prestige
24 Pensione Maria Luisa de Medici
25 Brunori
28 Albergo Bavaria
35 Bernini Palace
40 Pensione Alessandra
42 Aily Home
47 Pensione la Scaletta

PLACES TO EAT

6 Trattoria Le Mossacce
8 Osteria il Caminetto
10 Gilli
19 Gelateria Perchè No?
20 Ristorante Paoli
21 Festival del Gelato
26 Trattoria il Pennello
30 Gelateria Vivoli
31 Osteria del Gallo e Volpe
43 Trattoria da Benvenuto
44 Angie's Pub
45 Fiaschetteria
46 Osteria del Cinghiale Bianco

OTHER

1 Baptistry
2 Bell Tower
3 Duomo
4 Museo dell' Opera del Duomo
5 Hospital
12 Internazionale Seeber Bookshop
13 Palazzo Strozzi
14 Post Office & Telecom Office
17 Museo dell'Antica Casa Fiorentina & Mercato Nuovo
18 Chiesa di Orsanmichele
22 American Express
23 Casa di Dante
27 Palazzo Pazzi
29 Libreria Cima
32 Palazzo del Bargello & Museo del Bargello
33 Badia
34 Palazzo Gondi
36 Palazzo Vecchio
37 Loggia della Signoria
38 Galleria degli Uffizi
39 Comune di Firenze Tourist Office
41 Thomas Cook Exchange Office
48 American Express

Dante's life. It is open Monday to Friday, except Wednesday, from 9.30 am to 12.30 pm and 3.30 to 6.30 pm and on weekends to 12.30 pm. Admission is free.

Palazzo del Bargello Return to Via del Proconsolo and head towards the Arno for the Palazzo del Bargello, also known as the Palazzo del Podestà. Started in 1254, the palace was originally the residence of the chief magistrate and then a police station. During its days as a police complex, many people were tortured near the well in the centre of the medieval courtyard. It now houses the **Museo del Bargello** and the most comprehensive collection of Tuscan Renaissance sculpture in Italy. The museum is absolutely not to be missed. There are several works by Michelangelo on the ground floor, notably his drunken *Bacchus* (executed when the artist was 22), a marble bust of *Brutus*, a tondo of the *Madonna and Child* with the infant St John, and a *David* (or Apollo). Also on the ground floor are many works by Benvenuto Cellini. Don't miss Donatello's stunning bronze *David* on the 1st floor, the first free-standing sculpture since antiquity to depict a fully nude man. Among the many other works by Donatello are *St George*, removed from the façade of the Chiesa di Orsanmichele and replaced with a copy, and the *Marzocco*, which once stood in the Piazza della Signoria and was also replaced with a copy.

The museum is less popular than the Uffizi and Accademia galleries and attracts smaller crowds. It is open Tuesday to Saturday and on alternating Sundays and Mondays from 9 am to 1.50 pm. Admission is L8000.

The 10th-century **Badia**, opposite the Palazzo Bargello on Via del Proconsolo, was the church of a Benedictine monastery. It is worth a visit to see Filippino Lippi's *Appearance of the Virgin to St Bernard*, to the left of the entrance. Wander into the Renaissance cloister.

Around Piazza della SS Annunziata

Return to the duomo and head north-east along Via dei Servi for the Piazza della SS Annunziata, often described as the mos beautiful piazza in Firenze. Located in th university district, the piazza is usually fille with students rather than tourists. In it centre is Giambologna's equestrian statue o the Grand Duke Ferdinand I de' Medici.

The **Spedale degli Innocenti**, on th south-east side of the piazza, was founded i 1421 as Europe's first orphanage. Its portic was designed by Brunelleschi and decorate with terracotta medallions of a baby in swaddling cloths by Andrea della Robbia. Unde the portico to the left of the entrance is th small revolving door where unwanted children were left. A good number of people i Firenze with surnames such as degl Innocenti, Innocenti and Nocentini, can trac their family tree only as far back as th orphanage. A small gallery inside feature works by Florentine artists, including Luc della Robbia and Domenico Ghirlandaio. I is open Monday to Saturday from 8.30 am t 2 pm (closed Wednesday) and Sunday fron 8 am to 1 pm. Admission is L4000.

About 200m south-east of the piazza alon Via della Colonna is the **Museo Archeologico**, considered to be one of Italy's best Most of the Medici hoard of antiquities is o show, including the museum's highlight, collection of Etruscan artefacts. Th museum also features an impressive collection of Egyptian, Greek and Roma items, but many exhibits were badl damaged in the 1966 floods. It is ope Tuesday to Saturday from 9 am to 2 pm an on alternating Sundays and Mondays to pm. Admission is L8000.

Galleria dell'Accademia Take Via Cesar Battisti from Piazza della SS Annunziata t Piazza San Marco; the entrance to the galler is to the left on Via Ricasoli. No tour o Firenze could be complete without the inclusion of this gallery. It houses paintings b Florentine artists spanning the 13th to 16t centuries, but its main draw card i Michelangelo's *David*, carved from a singl block of marble when the artist was only 29 The colossal statue was originally placed i the Piazza della Signoria, and is now situate n an alcove at the end of the main hall on the ;allery's ground floor. Also in the hall are Aichelangelo's celebrated unfinished *Pris-ners* (or Slaves), intended for the tomb of Pope Julius II, and his *Pietà di Palestrina*, also unfinished.

The gallery is open Tuesday to Saturday rom 8.30 am to 6.50 pm and Sunday to 1.50 pm. Admission is L12,000.

Palazzo Medici-Riccardi Heading back towards the duomo, you will find this extraordinary palace on Via Cavour, just off Piazza San Lorenzo. It is typical of the Florentine Renaissance style and was started by Michelozzo for Cosimo de' Medici in 1444. The Medici residence from 1459 to 1540, it was the prototype for other buildings in the city, such as the Palazzo Pitti. It was remodelled in the 17th century by the Riccardi family. The chapel upstairs has beautiful frescoes by Benozzo Gozzoli, with regal scenes featuring members of the Medici clan. The Sala di Luca Giordano was built by the Riccardi family and is sumptuously decorated. The palace is open Monday to Friday (closed Wednesday) from 9 am to 1 pm and 3 to 5 pm and on weekends to midday. Admission is free.

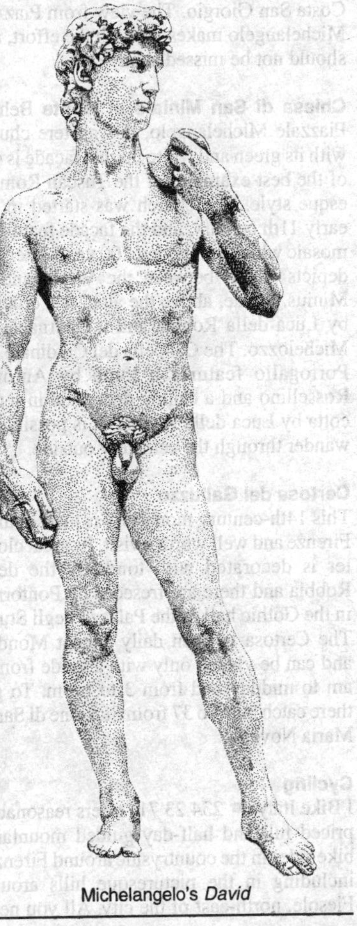

Michelangelo's *David*

Casa Buonarroti

North from Piazza Santa Croce along Via de' Pepi is the Casa Buonarroti, Via Ghibellina 70, which Michelangelo owned but never lived in. Upon his death, the house went to his nephew and eventually became a museum in the mid-1850s. The collection of memorabilia mostly comprises copies of Michelangelo's works and portraits of the master. On the 2nd floor is Michelangelo's earliest known work, *The Madonna of the Steps*. The museum is open daily from 9.30 am to 1.30 pm. Admission is L10,000.

The Oltrarno

Ponte Vecchio This famous 14th-century structure, lined with the shops of gold and silversmiths, was the only bridge to survive the bombs of the retreating Nazis. The shops originally housed butchers, but Cosimo de' Medici ordered them removed in favour of jewellers, whose trade was considered more appropriate and certainly more hygienic, since the butchers threw their leftovers directly into the river. Walk a few hundred metres along the Arno in either direction and then look back at the Ponte Vecchio for what has to be one of the most evocative views in Firenze. The view from the small piazza in the centre of the bridge is also impressive.

Palazzo Pitti This immense and imposing palace, south of the Arno on Via de' Guicciardini, was designed by Brunelleschi for the wealthy merchant Pitti family, which was a great rival of the Medici. Construction started in 1458, and almost a century later, in 1549, it was bought by Eleanora di Toledo, wife of Cosimo de' Medici, who expanded it by adding two wings. The Medici, followed by the grand dukes of Lorraine, lived in the palace. In the late 19th century it became a residence of the Savoy royal family, who presented it to the state in 1919.

The palace now houses four museums. The **Galleria Palatina** (Palatine Gallery) houses paintings from the 16th to 18th centuries, which are hung in lavishly decorated rooms. The works were collected by the Medici, and artists including Raphael, Filippo Lippi, Tintoretto, Paolo Veronese and Rubens are represented. It is a large collection and if visits to the Uffizi, Accademia and Bargello haven't yet worn you out, try to spend at least half a day in the Palatina. The apartments of the Medici, and later of the Savoy, show the splendour in which the rulers lived. The other three galleries are worth a look if you have plenty of time. The **Galleria d'Arte Moderna** (Modern Art Gallery) covers Tuscan works from the 18th until the mid-20th century, and the **Museo degli Argenti** (Silver Museum), entered from the garden courtyard, has a collection of glassware, silver and semiprecious stones from the Medici collections. The **Galleria del Costume** (Costume Gallery) has costumes from the 18th and 19th centuries. The Galleria Palatina is open Tuesday to Saturday from 8.30 am to 6.50 pm and Sunday to 1.50 pm. Admission is L12,000. The Museo degli Argenti opens Tuesday to Saturday and on alternating Sundays and Mondays from 8.30 am to 1.50 pm, and admission is L4000. The other two galleries open Tuesday to Sunday from 9 am to 2 pm and can be entered with the same L8000 ticket.

Take a break in the palace's Renaissance **Giardino di Boboli**, which were laid out in the mid-16th century and based on a design by the architect known as Il Tribolo. Buontalenti's noted artificial grotto, with a *Venus* by Giambologna, is interesting. The star-shaped **Forte di Belvedere**, built in 1590 at the southern end of the gardens, is worth a look.

Piazzale Michelangelo Via di Belvedere eventually leads to the piazzale from the Palazzo Pitti, but the road has been closed for some time. Rather than catch a bus, you can head back up Via de' Guicciardini to the river and then make the long, uphill walk along Costa San Giorgio. The view from Piazzale Michelangelo makes it worth the effort, and should not be missed at any cost.

Chiesa di San Miniato al Monte Behind Piazzale Michelangelo, this austere church with its green and white marble façade is one of the best examples of the Tuscan Romanesque style. The church was started in the early 11th century, and the façade features a mosaic which was added 200 years later and depicts Christ between the Virgin and St Minius. Inside, above the altar, is a crucifix by Luca della Robbia and a tabernacle by Michelozzo. The Cappella del Cardinale del Portogallo features a tomb by Antonio Rossellino and a ceiling decorated in terracotta by Luca della Robbia. It is possible to wander through the cemetery outside.

Certosa del Galluzzo

This 14th-century monastery is just south of Firenze and well worth a visit. Its great cloister is decorated with tondi by the della Robbia and there are frescoes by Pontormo in the Gothic hall of the Palazzo degli Studi. The Certosa is open daily except Monday and can be visited only with a guide from 9 am to midday and from 3 to 6 pm. To get there catch bus No 37 from Stazione di Santa Maria Novella.

Cycling

I Bike Italy (☎ 234 23 71) offers reasonably priced full and half-day guided mountain-bike rides in the countryside around Firenze, including in the picturesque hills around Fiesole, north-east of the city. All you need a reasonable amount of energy and a hardy ıckside.

If you are interested in cycling, ask for a ɔpy of *Viaggio in Toscana – Discovering* *oscana by Bike* at the APT office. For where rent a bike, see Car & Motorcycle in the ıllowing Getting Around section.

amily Activities

he tourist offices have information about ıild day-care services, courses and special :tivities for kids (organised for local young-ers, not tourists, so seek advice on those ıost suitable for your children). These ɔtions might come in handy if you are lanning a few days of hectic sightseeing and ɔur children have had enough of museums c.

There is a small playground in Piazza ɫassimo d'Azeglio, about five to 10 ıinutes walk east of the duomo. Beside the rno river, about 15 minutes walk to the west f Stazione di Santa Maria Novella, is a ıassive public park called Parco delle ascine.

Older children might find the Museo tibbert entertaining. It features a large col-ction of antique costumes and armaments om Europe, the Middle East and Asia. It is Via Federico Stibbert 26, north of the train ation, and is open daily from 9 am to 1 pm. dmission is L5000.

ourses

irenze has more than 30 schools offering ɔurses in Italian language and culture. umerous other schools offer courses in art, cluding painting, drawing, sculpture and t history, and there are also plenty of hools offering cooking courses.

While Firenze is one of the most attractive ties in which to study Italian language or t, it is one of the more expensive. For ıstance, Perugia, Siena and Urbino offer ɔod language courses at much lower prices.

The cost of language courses in Firenze ınges from about L450,000 to L900,000, epending on the school and the length of the ɔurse (one month is usually the minimum ıration).

Language courses available in Firenze include:

Dante Alighieri School for Foreigners
Via dei Bardi 12, 50125
(☎ 234 29 86)

Istituto Europeo
Piazzale delle Pallottole 1, 50122 (☎ 238 10 71)

Istituto di Lingua e Cultura Italiana per Stranieri Michelangelo
Via Ghibellina 88, 50122 (☎ 24 09 75)

Art courses range from one-month summer workshops (costing from L500,000 to more than L1,000,000) to longer term professional diploma courses. These can be expensive; some cost more than L6,500,000 a year. Schools will organise accommodation for students, upon request, either in private apartments or with Italian families.

Two art schools you might like to consider are:

Centro Lorenzo Medici
Via Faenza 43, 50122 (☎ 28 73 60)

Istituto per l'Arte e il Restauro
Palazzo Spinelli, Borgo Santa Croce 10, 50122
(☎ 234 58 98)

If you're interested in a cooking course, taught in English or French, try:

Cordon Bleu
Via di Mezzo 55r, 50123 (☎ 234 54 68)

Brochures detailing courses and prices are available at Italian cultural institutes throughout the world. The Firenze APT also has lists of schools and courses and will mail them on request. You can write in English to request information and enrolment forms – letters should be addressed to the segretaria.

Remember that many nationalities must to apply for a visa to study in Italy, so check with the Italian consulate in your country.

Organised Tours

Sestante CIT and American Express offer tours of the city. Call into one of their offices for information. Guides can be contacted through the APT office.

TOSCANA

Special Events

Major festivals include the Scoppio del Carro (Explosion of the Cart), when a cart full of fireworks is exploded in front of the duomo on Easter Sunday; the Festa del Patrono (the Feast of St John the Baptist) on 24 June; and the lively Calcio Storico (Football in Costume), featuring football matches played in 16th-century costume, held in June in Piazza della Signoria and ending with a fireworks display over Piazzale Michelangelo.

Every two years Firenze hosts the Internazionale Antiquariato, an antique fair attracting exhibitors from across Europe, at the Palazzo Strozzi, Via de' Tornabuoni. Call ☎ 28 26 35 for information. The next fair will be in September/October 1999.

Places to Stay

The city has hundreds of hotels in all categories and a good range of alternatives, including hostels and private rooms. There are more than 150 budget hotels in Firenze, so even in the peak season when the city is packed with tourists, it is generally possible to find a room. However, it is strongly advised that you book well in advance for the summer, and it is a good idea to do so throughout the year. Hotels and pensioni are concentrated in three main areas: near the main train station, near Piazza Santa Maria Novella and in the old city between the duomo and the river.

If you arrive at Stazione di Santa Maria Novella without a hotel booking, head for Consorzio ITA (Informazioni Turistiche e Alberghiere: ☎ 28 28 93), inside the station on the main concourse. Using a computer network, the office can check the availability of rooms and make a booking for a small fee; there are no phone bookings. The office is open daily from 8.30 am to 9 pm. Family Hotels (☎ 462 00 80), Via Faenza 77, will make bookings at associated hotels in Firenze and throughout Italy. It is open Monday to Friday from 8.30 am to 7 pm and Saturday 9 am to midday.

Contact the APT for a list of private rooms, which generally charge from L25,000 per person in a shared room an from L35,000 per person in a single roon Most fill with students during the school yea (from October to June), but are a good optio if you are staying for a week or longer.

When you arrive at a hotel, always ask fo the full price of a room before putting you bags down. Florentine hotels and pension are notorious for their bill-padding, particu larly in summer. Some may require an extr L10,000 for a compulsory breakfast and wi charge L3000 or more for a shower. Contac the APT's SOS Turista if you have any prob lems.

Prices listed here are for the high seaso and, unless otherwise indicated, are fo rooms without bathroom. A bathroom wi cost from L10,000 to L20,000 extra. Durin the low season (usually from mid-October t March, with exceptions for periods includ ing Christmas) prices drop dramatically.

Places to Stay – bottom end

Camping The closest camping ground to th city centre is *Parco Comunale di Campeggi Michelangelo* (☎ 681 19 77), Viale Miche angelo 80, just off Piazzale Michelangel south of the Arno. It opens 25 March to November. Take bus No 13 from the trai station. *Villa Camerata* (☎ 61 03 00), Via Augusto Righi 2-4, has a camping groun next to the HI hostel (see the next section Take bus No 17B, which leaves from th right of the main train station as you leav the platforms. The trip takes 30 minute. There is a camping ground at Fiesol *Campeggio Panoramico* (☎ 59 90 69) at Vi Peramonda 1, which also has bungalow. Take bus No 7 to Fiesole from the main trai station.

Hostels The HI *Ostello Villa Camera* (☎ 60 14 51), Viale Augusto Righi 2-4, considered one of the most beautiful hoste in Europe. B&B is L23,000, dinner L14,00 and there is a bar. Only members a accepted and reservations can be made b mail (essential in summer). Daytime closin is 9 am to 2 pm. Take bus No 17B, whic leaves from the right of the main train statio as you leave the platforms. The trip takes 30 minutes.

The private *Ostello Archi Rossi* (☎ 29 08 04), Via Faenza 94r, is another good option for a bed in a dorm room, and it is close to the train station. *Ostello Santa Monaca* (☎ 26 83 38), Via Santa Monaca 6, is another private hostel. It is a 15 to 20-minute walk south from the train station, through Piazza Santa Maria Novella, along Via de' Fossi, across the Ponte alla Carraia and directly ahead along Via de' Serragli. Via Santa Monaca is a few blocks from the river, on the right. A bed costs L24,000, and sheets and meals are available.

The *Ostello Spirito Santo* (☎ 239 82 02), Via Nazionale 8, is a religious institution near the main train station. The nuns accept only women and families, and charge L40,000 per person or L60,000 for a double. Call ahead to book. The hostel is open from July to October.

Istituto Gould (☎ 21 25 76), Via de' Serragli 49, has clean doubles for L38,000.

Hotels – east of Stazione di SM Novella Many of the hotels in this area are very well run, clean and safe, but there are also a fair number of seedy establishments. The area includes the streets around Piazza della Stazione and east to Via Cavour.

The *Pensione Bellavista* (☎ 28 45 28), Largo Alinari 15 (at the start of Via Nazionale), is small, but a knockout bargain if you can manage to book one of the two double rooms with balconies and a view of the duomo and Palazzo Vecchio. Singles/doubles cost up to L70,000/100,000, breakfast and use of the bathroom included.

Albergo Azzi (☎ 21 38 06), Via Faenza 56, has a very helpful management, which will arrange accommodation for you in other Italian cities. Simple, comfortable singles/doubles are L55,000/85,000, or L100,000 a double with bathroom. Dormitory beds cost L25,000 per person. Ask for a room away from the noisy Via Faenza and enjoy breakfast on the hotel's terrace. The same management runs *Albergo Anna* upstairs, where prices are slightly lower. There are several other budget pensioni in the same building and all are habitable. Across Via Nazionale at Via Faenza 20 is *Soggiorno Burchi* (☎ 41 44 54), which has doubles/triples with bathroom costing from L75,000/90,000.

The *Locanda Daniel* (☎ 21 12 93), Via Nazionale 22, has basic doubles for L79,000, breakfast included, and beds in a dorm room for L25,000 per person. One of the rooms has a panoramic view of the duomo. The owner will not take bookings, so arrive very early. In the same building is *Soggiorno Nazionale* (☎ 238 22 03), which has singles/doubles for up to L60,000/84,000, and triples for L114,000.

At No 24 is the *Pensione Ausonia & Rimini* (☎ 49 65 47), run by a young couple who go out of their way to help travellers. Singles/doubles are L70,000/95,000, a triple is L126,000. The price includes breakfast and use of the communal bathroom. Add about L20,000 to L25,000 for rooms with bathroom. A quad with bathroom is L180,000. The same couple runs the more expensive *Pensione Kursaal* downstairs.

Albergo Mary (☎ 49 63 10), Piazza della Indipendenza 5, has singles/doubles for L80,000/100,000.

Hotels – Around Piazza Santa Maria Novella This area is just south of the Stazione di Santa Maria Novella and includes Piazza Santa Maria Novella, the streets running south to the Arno and east to Via de' Tornabuoni.

La Mia Casa (☎ 21 30 61) at Piazza Santa Maria Novella 25 is a rambling place, filled with backpackers. Basic singles/doubles are L40,000/60,000 and triples/quads L75,000/90,000.

Via della Scala, which runs north-west off the piazza, is lined with pensioni. *La Romagnola* (☎ 21 15 97) at No 40 has large, clean rooms and a helpful management. Singles/doubles are L45,000/78,000. A triple room is a good deal at L100,000. The same family runs *La Gigliola* (☎ 28 79 81) upstairs, with rooms for about the same price. *La Scala* (☎ 21 26 29) at No 21 is small and has doubles/triples for L85,000/115,000.

The *Pensione Margareth* (☎ 21 01 38) at No 25 has pleasantly furnished singles/doubles for L65,000/85,000. A triple is L100,000 and use of the communal shower is L3000. *Pensione Montreal* (☎ 238 23 31) at No 43 has singles/doubles from L60,000/80,000 and triples for L120,000.

Pensione Sole (☎ 239 60 94), Via del Sole 8, is on the 3rd floor and there is no lift. Singles/doubles are L50,000/70,000 and triples/quads are L88,000/100,000, plus L3000 to use the communal shower. A double with bathroom costs L90,000. Ask for a quiet room. The *Pensione Toscana* (☎ 21 31 56), in the same building, has eccentrically decorated rooms for L75,000/120,000 with bathroom. The *Ottaviani* (☎ 239 62 23), Piazza degli Ottaviani 1, just off Piazza Santa Maria Novella, has singles/doubles for L50,000/70,000, breakfast included. In the same building is *Albergo Visconti* (☎ 21 38 77), with a pleasant terrace garden where you can have breakfast. Singles/doubles are L55,000/84,000 and a triple is L115,000. Add about L20,000 to the price if you want a private bathroom. At Piazza Vittorio Veneto 8, a five-minute walk west of the main train station and next to the Parco delle Cascine, is the *Garden* (☎ 21 26 69), which has doubles for L110,000. Most rooms overlook a pleasant garden.

TOSCANA

Hotels – Between the Duomo & the Arno

This area is a 15-minute walk south from Stazione di Santa Maria Novella in the heart of old Firenze. One of the best deals is the small *Aily Home* (☎ 239 65 05), Piazza Santo Stefano 81, just near the Ponte Vecchio. Doubles cost L60,000. It has five large rooms, three overlooking the bridge, and accepts bookings.

Albergo Firenze (☎ 21 42 03), Piazza dei Donati 4, just south of the duomo, has singles/doubles for L70,000/100,000 and breakfast is included. The *Brunori* (☎ 28 96 48), Via del Proconsolo 5, charges L37,000/72,000 for singles/doubles and an extra L5000 for showers. *Albergo Bavaria* (☎ 234 03 13), Borgo degli Albizi 26, has singles/doubles for up to L80,000/110,000. A double with bathroom is L130,000. The *Pensione TeTi & Prestige* (☎ 239 84 35), Via Porta Rossa 5, has singles/doubles for L60,000/L90,000 and charges an extra L10,000 per person for breakfast. The *Maxim* (☎ 21 74 74), Via dei Medici 4, has singles/doubles from L98,000/115,000 and offers substantial discounts in the low season. The *Pensione Maria Luisa de' Medici* (☎ 28 00 48), Via del Corso 1, is in a 17th-century palace. It has large rooms for up to five people (no singles) and the management caters for families. A double is L71,000, L94,000 with bathroom, and a triple is L100,000, or L115,000 with bathroom. Family rooms for four or five are reasonably priced.

Places to Stay – middle

East of Stazione di SM Novella The *Pensione Le Cascine* (☎ 21 10 66), Largo Alinari 15, near the train station, is a two-star hotel with nicely furnished rooms, some with balconies. Singles/doubles with bathroom cost L130,000/190,000.

The *Nuova Italia* (☎ 26 84 30), Via Faenza 26, is a very good choice. Its singles/doubles with bathroom cost up to L120,000/180,000. *Pensione Accademia* (☎ 29 34 51), Via Faenza 7, has very pleasant rooms and incorporates an 18th-century palace with magnificent stained-glass doors and carved wooden ceilings. Singles cost L100,000 and a double with bathroom is L130,000, breakfast and television included.

Hotel Bellettini (☎ 21 35 61), Via dei Conti 7, is a delightful small hotel with well furnished singles/doubles with bathroom for L105,000/170,000. Try for one of the rooms with a view.

Hotel Desirée (☎ 238 23 82), Via Fiume 20, close to the train station, has been recently renovated. Its very pleasant rooms all have bathroom and cost up to L130,000/170,000.

The *Giotto* (☎ 28 98 64), Via del Giglio 13, has doubles with bathroom for L140,000. The *Giada* (☎ 21 53 17) is in the middle of

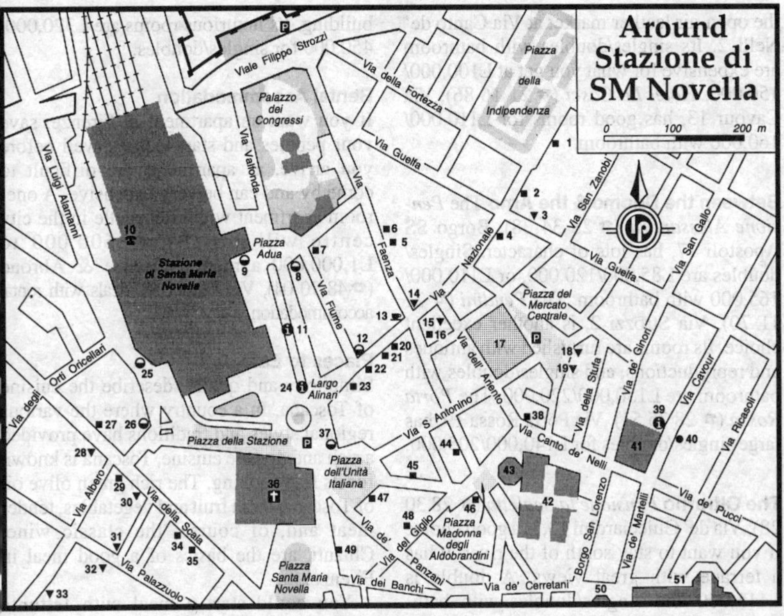

PLACES TO STAY

1 Albergo Mary
2 Pensione Ausonia & Rimini & Pensione Kursaal
4 Locanda Daniel & Soggiorno Nazionale
5 Ostello Archi Rossi
6 Albergo Azzi & Albergo Anna
7 Hotel Desirée
16 Nuova Italia
20 Atlantic Palace
21 Machiavelli Palace
22 Ostello Spirito Santo
23 Pensione Bellavista & Pensione Le Cascine
27 La Romagnola & La Gigliola
29 Pensione Montreal
34 Pensione Margareth
35 La Scala
38 Giada
44 Pensione Accademia
45 Albergo Majestic
46 Hotel Bellettini
47 Grand Hotel Baglioni
48 Giotto
49 La Mia Casa

PLACES TO EAT

3 Trattoria da Giovanni
13 Caffè degli Innocenti
14 Il Triangolo di Bermuda
15 Bondi
18 Mario's
19 Caffè Za Za
28 Trattoria il Giardino
30 La Grotta di Leo
31 Trattoria da Giorgio
32 Trattoria il Contadino
33 Ristorante Dino

OTHER

8 Lazzi Bus Station & Ticket Office
9 ATAF Local Bus Station
10 Telecom Office
11 Urban Bus Ticket & Information Office
12 CAT, CAP & COPIT Bus Station
17 Market
24 Comune di Firenze Tourist Office
25 ATAF Local Bus Station
26 SITA Bus Station
36 Chiesa di Santa Maria Novella
37 ATAF Local Bus Station
39 APT Tourist Office
40 Feltrinelli Bookshop
41 Palazzo Medici-Riccardi
42 Basilica di San Lorenzo
43 Cappelle Medicee
50 Baptistry
51 Duomo

the open-air leather market at Via Canto de' Nelli 2. Its singles/doubles with bathroom are expensive for what you get at L100,000/150,000. *Hotel Le Casci* (☎ 21 16 86), Via Cavour 13, has good rooms for L110,000/160,000 with bathroom.

Between the Duomo & the Arno The *Pensione Alessandra* (☎ 28 34 38), Borgo SS Apostoli 17, has lots of character. Singles/doubles are L85,000/120,000, or L110,000/165,000 with bathroom. The *Pendini* (☎ 21 11 70), Via Strozzi 2, is another excellent choice. Its rooms are furnished with antiques and reproductions, and singles/doubles with bathroom are L150,000/220,000. The *Porta Rossa* (☎ 28 75 51), Via Porta Rossa 19, has large singles/doubles for L140,000/205,000.

The Oltrarno *Pensione la Scaletta* (☎ 28 30 28), Via de' Guicciardini 13, is a good choice if you want to stay south of the river. It has a terrace with great views. A double is L115,000 and singles/doubles with bathroom are L90,000/150,000.

TOSCANA

Places to Stay – top end

Around Stazione di SM Novella The *Hotel Albion* (☎ 21 41 71), Via il Prato 22r, just west of the train station, has very comfortable singles/doubles for L150,000/200,000. The *Atlantic Palace* (☎ 21 30 31), Via Nazionale 12, has singles/doubles for up to L240,000/320,000 with breakfast included.

The *Machiavelli Palace* (☎ 236 00 08), Via Nazionale 10, is in a 17th-century palace. Many of its beautiful rooms have terraces. Singles/doubles are worth the price at L200,000/280,000. The four-star *Albergo Majestic* (☎ 26 40 21), Via del Melarancio 1, has very comfortable singles/doubles up to L300,000/400,000. *Grand Hotel Baglioni* (☎ 21 84 41), Piazza dell'Unità Italiana 6, has rooms from L280,000/370,000.

Between the Duomo & the Arno The *Bernini Palace* (☎ 28 86 21), Piazza San Firenze 29, is an excellent hotel in a historic building. Its luxurious rooms are L320,000/450,000 for singles/doubles.

Rental Accommodation

If you want an apartment in Firenze, save your pennies and start looking well before you arrive, as apartments are difficult to come by and can be very expensive. A one-room apartment with kitchenette in the city centre will cost from L600,000 to L1,000,000 a month. Firenze & Abroad (☎ 48 70 04), Via Zanobi 58, deals with rental accommodation.

Places to Eat

Simplicity and quality describe the cuisine of Toscana. In a country where the various regional styles and traditions have provided a rich and diverse cuisine, Toscana is known for its fine cooking. The rich green olive oil of Toscana, fresh fruit and vegetables, tender meat and, of course, the classic wine, Chianti, are the basics of a good meal in Firenze.

You could start a meal with fettunta (known elsewhere in Italy as bruschetta), a thick slice of toasted bread rubbed with garlic and soaked with olive oil. Try the ribollita, a very filling soup traditionally eaten by the poor of Firenze. It is basically a minestrone with lots of white beans which is reboiled with chunks of old bread and then garnished with olive oil. Another traditional dish is the deliciously simple fagiolini alla Fiorentina (green beans and olive oil). Firenze is noted for its excellent beefsteak, known as bistecca alla Fiorentina – thick, juicy and big enough for two people.

Many tourists fall into the trap of eating at the self-service restaurants which line the streets of the main shopping district between the duomo and the river. Be adventurous and seek out the little eating places in the Oltrarno and near Piazza del Mercato Centrale in the San Lorenzo area, where you'll eat more authentic Italian food. The market, open Monday to Saturday from 7 am to 2 pm (also Saturday from 4 to 8 pm), has fresh produce, cheeses and meat at reasonable prices.

Restaurants, Trattorie & Pizzerie Eating at a good trattoria can be surprisingly economical.

Near Stazione di SM Novella & Basilica di San Lorenzo *Mario's*, a small bar and trattoria at Via Rosina 2r, near Piazza del Mercato Centrale, is open only for lunch and serves pasta for around L6000 to L8000 and mains for L7000 to L9000. It is very popular. A few doors down, at Piazza del Mercato Centrale 20, is *Caffè Za Za*, another popular eating place. Prices are around the same as at Mario's.

Trattoria da Giovanni, Via Guelfa 94r, offers a L15,000 set menu, entrées from L2000 and pasta from L4000.

Around SM Novella & Ognissanti *La Grotta di Leo*, Via della Scala 41, is a pleasant trattoria with a L18,000 set menu or pizzas and pasta from L7000. *Trattoria il Giardino* at No 67 in the same street has a L20,000 set menu and serves good, hearty Tuscan dishes and cheap wine.

Nearby is the *Trattoria il Contadino*, Via Palazzuolo 55, with a L13,000 set menu, including wine. *Trattoria da Giorgio*, at No 54, also has a L13,000 set menu and the food is very good.

Ristorante Dino, Via Maso Finiguerra 6-8, is a good little trattoria, with pasta from L6000 and main courses from L10,000. The L2500 cover charge bumps up the price.

Da il Latini, Via dei Palchetti 4, just off Via del Moro, is an attractive trattoria serving pasta from L6000 and main courses from L12,000.

Sostanza, Via della Porcellana 25r, offers traditional Tuscan cooking and is one of the best spots in town for bistecca alla Fiorentina. A full meal will cost around L60,000 a head.

City Centre & Towards Santa Croce *Osteria il Caminetto*, Via dello Studio 34, south of the duomo, has a small, vine-covered terrace. Pasta costs around L7000 and a main from L9000 to L10,000. The L2000 cover charge plus a 10% service charge bumps up the price of a meal. *Trattoria Le Mossacce*, Via del Proconsolo 55r, serves pasta for around L9000 and a full meal with wine will cost up to L30,000.

Trattoria il Pennello, Via Dante Alighieri 4, is popular and quite cheap. Pasta starts at L5000 and a set meal costs L20,000. *Ristorante Paoli*, Via dei Tavolini 12, has magnificent vaulted ceilings and walls covered with frescoes, and food to match. It offers a L28,000 set menu and pasta from L8000, and the cover charge is L2500.

Trattoria da Benvenuto, Via Mosca 16r, on the corner of Via dei Neri, is excellent. Its menu changes regularly and a full meal will cost under L25,000. A quick meal of pasta, bread and wine will cost around L12,000. It is wise to reserve a table. Among the great undiscovered treasures of Firenze is *Angie's Pub*, Via dei Neri 35r, east of the Palazzo Vecchio, which offers a vast array of panini and focaccia, as well as hamburgers, Italian-style with mozzarella and spinach, and hot dogs with cheese and mushrooms. A menu lists the panini, but you can design your own from the extensive selection of fillings; try one with artichoke, mozzarella and mushroom cream. Prices start at around L4000. There is a good range of beers and no extra charge to sit down.

At *Fiaschetteria*, Via dei Neri 17r, you are even less likely to find a tourist. Try the excellent ribollita for L11,000. In Piazza San Pier Maggiore is a pleasant, reasonably priced little trattoria, *Natalino*.

Osteria del Gallo e Volpe, on the corner of Via Ghibellina and Via de' Giraldi, has pizzas from L5000 and pasta from L6000, and the cover charge is L2500. The *Sant' Ambrogio Caffè* at Piazza Sant'Ambrogio 7, along Via Pietrapiana, is a bar and restaurant where you can get a sandwich from L3000 or pasta from L7000.

One of the city's finest restaurants, *Enoteca Pinchiorri*, Via Ghibellina 87, is noted for its nouvelle cuisine Italian-style. A meal will cost around L150,000 a head.

Oltrarno *Osteria del Cinghiale Bianco*, Borgo San Jacopo 43, to the right as you

TOSCANA

cross Ponte Vecchio, specialises in Florentine food and offers a delicious onion soup and wild boar with polenta. Pasta starts at L7000 and main courses from L10,000, and the cover charge is L1500. *Angelino*, Via di Santo Spirito 36, is an excellent trattoria where you can eat a meal, including bistecca, for around L35,000. In Piazza Santo Spirito is the pizzeria *Borgo Antico*, a great location in summer, when you can sit at an outside table and enjoy the atmosphere in the piazza. *Cabiria* is a popular café which also has outdoor seating.

A five-minute walk farther west along Via del Campuccio will take you to Piazza Torquato Tasso and the small restaurant *Tranvai*. The great food and good value for money makes it worth the hike. A full meal will cost under L20,000.

Trattoria Casalinga, Via dei Michelozzi 9r, is a bustling, popular eating place. The food is great and a filling meal of pasta, meat or vegetables plus wine will cost under L25,000. Don't expect to linger over a meal, as there is usually a queue of people waiting for your table. *Trattoria I Raddi*, Via Ardiglione 47, just near Via de' Serragli, serves traditional Florentine meals and has pasta from L7000 and main courses from L12,000. *Il Cantinone di Gatto Nero*, Via di Santo Spirito 6r, specialises in crostini, starting at L3500. Pasta is from L4500 and the cover charge is L1500.

I Tarocchi, Via de' Renai 12-14r, is a popular pizzeria/trattoria serving excellent pizzas from L7000, regional dishes, including a good range of pasta, from L7000 to L10,000 and plenty of salads and vegetable dishes from L4000 to L7000.

Bars, Cafés & Snacks The streets between the duomo and the Arno harbour many pizzerie where you can buy takeaway pizza by the slice for around L2000 to L3000, depending on the weight. Another option for a light lunch is *Antico Noè*, a legendary sandwich bar through the Arco di San Piero, just off Piazza San Pier Maggiore. It is takeaway only.

Caffè degli Innocenti, Via Nazionale 57, near the leather market around Piazza del Mercato Centrale, has a great selection of prepared panini and cakes for around L3000 to L4000. *Bondi*, Via dell'Ariento 85, specialises in focaccia and offers a variety of toppings. They start at L2500 and pizza by the slice is also L2500.

The *Antica Enoteca*, Via Ghibellina 142, is one of the city's oldest bars and features hundreds of wines. The owners will gladly open any bottle and engage in a chat if you have the time. Wines start at L1500 a glass. The *Fiddler's Elbow*, Piazza Santa Maria Novella, is open from 4 pm to 1 am and is a popular spot for UK and US expatriates. *Rex Caffè*, Via Fiesolana 25r, in the Sant'Antonio area, is popular with the arts community.

Gilli, Piazza della Repubblica, is one of the city's finest cafés, and is reasonably cheap if you stand at the bar: a coffee at the bar is L1500, but at a table outside it is L5000.

Gelaterie People queue outside *Gelateria Vivoli*, Via dell'Isola delle Stinche, near Via Torta, to delight in the gelati that is widely considered the city's best. *Il Triangolo di Bermuda*, Via Nazionale 61, near the leather market, and *Perché No?*, Via dei Tavolini 19r, off Via de' Calzaiuoli, are both excellent. *Festival del Gelato*, Via del Corso 75, just off Via de' Calzaiuoli, offers 90 flavours, including a good selection of semi-frozen ice-cream desserts.

Entertainment

There are several publications which list the theatrical and musical events and festivals held in the city and surrounding areas. The free bimonthly *Florence Today*, the monthly *Firenze Information* and *Firenze Avvenimenti*, a monthly brochure distributed by the comune, are all available at the tourist offices. The APT publishes an annual booklet listing the year's events, as well as monthly information sheets. *Firenze Spettacolo*, the city's definitive entertainment publication, is available monthly for L2700 at newsstands. Posters at the tourist offices, the university and in Piazza della

Repubblica advertise current concerts and other events.

As for nightclubs, *La Dolce Vita*, Piazza del Carmine, south of the Arno, is frequented by foreigners and Italians alike. *Circus*, Via delle Oche 17, just south of the duomo, is one of the better nightclubs.

Cabiria, Piazza Santo Spirito, is a music bar which is very popular among young locals, particularly in summer when you can sit outside. Another popular bar, with live music and a DJ, is *Pongo*, Via Giuseppe Verdi 59r. Foreigners hang out at the *Fiddler's Elbow*, Piazza Santa Maria Novella.

Concerts, opera and dance are performed at various times of the year at the *Teatro Comunale*, Corso Italia 16, on the northern bank of the Arno. In May and June the theatre hosts Maggio Musicale Fiorentina, an international concert festival. Contact the theatre's box office (☎ 21 11 58).

There are also seasons of drama, opera, concerts and dance at the *Teatro Verdi* (☎ 21 23 20), Via Ghibellina 106, from January to April and October to December. There are concert series, organised by the Amici della Musica (☎ 60 84 20), from January to April and October to December at the *Teatro della Pergola*, Via della Pergola 18. Several other venues have theatre seasons, including the Teatro della Pergola during the winter.

Big rock and jazz concerts are held at *Tenax Rock Club* (☎ 30 81 60), Via Pistoiese 47. *Auditorium Flog* is another big concert venue, at Via Michele Mercati 24b.

A more sedate pastime is the evening stroll in Piazzale Michelangelo, overlooking the city (take bus No 13 from the station or the duomo). In May, visit the nearby iris garden when the flowers are in full bloom.

The city has many small art galleries and hosts travelling art shows. Check with the APT for details. The area around Piazza Sant'Ambrogio, along Via Pietrapiana, has many small galleries.

Things to Buy

It is said that Milano has the best clothes and Roma the best shoes, but Firenze without doubt has the greatest variety of goods. The main shopping area is between the duomo and the Arno, with boutiques concentrated along Via Roma, Via de' Calzaiuoli and Via Por Santa Maria, leading to the goldsmiths lining the Ponte Vecchio. Window-shop along Via de' Tornabuoni, where the top designers, including Gucci, Saint-Laurent and Pucci, sell their wares.

The open-air market (Monday to Saturday) near Piazza del Mercato Centrale offers leather goods, clothing and jewellery at low prices, but quality can vary greatly. You could pick up the bargain of a lifetime here, but check the item carefully before paying. It is possible to bargain, but not if you want to use a credit card. The flea market (Monday to Saturday) at Piazza dei Ciompi, off Borgo Allegri near Piazza Santa Croce, specialises in antiques and bric-a-brac.

Firenze is famous for its beautifully patterned paper, which is stocked in the many stationery and speciality shops throughout the city and at the markets.

Getting There & Away

Air Firenze is served by two airports, Amerigo Vespucci (☎ 37 34 98), a few km north-west of the city centre at Via del Termine 11, and Galileo Galilei (☎ 21 60 73, Firenze Air Terminal), near Pisa and about an hour by train or car from Firenze. Vespucci serves domestic and European flights. Galileo Galilei is one of northern Italy's main international and domestic airports and has regular connections to London, Paris, Munich and major Italian cities.

Most major European and some US airlines are represented in the city. Alitalia (☎ 2 78 88) is at Lungarno Acciaioli 10-12r; British Airways (☎ 21 86 55) is at Via Vigna Nuova 36r; and TWA (☎ 239 68 56) is at Via dei Vecchietti 4.

Bus The SITA bus station (☎ 478 22 31 for information in English, or ☎ 24 47 21 for information in French), Via Santa Caterina da Siena, is just to the west of Stazione di Santa Maria Novella. There is a direct, rapid service to Siena, and buses leave here for Poggibonsi, where there are connecting

TOSCANA

buses for San Gimignano and Volterra. There are direct buses to Arezzo, Castellina in the Chianti region, Faenza, Marina di Grosseto and other smaller cities throughout Toscana. Several bus companies, including CAP and COPIT, operate from Largo Alinari, at the southern end of Via Nazionale, with services to towns including Prato and Pistoia.

Lazzi (☎ 21 51 55), Piazza Adua 1, next to the station, runs services to Roma, Pistoia and Lucca. Lazzi forms part of the Eurolines network of international bus services. You can, for instance, catch a bus to Paris, Prague or Barcelona from Firenze. A detailed brochure of all Eurolines services is available from Lazzi. In collaboration with SITA, it operates a service called Alpi Bus, which runs extensive routes to the Alps. The buses depart from numerous cities and towns throughout Lazio, Umbria, Toscana and Emilia-Romagna for most main resorts in the Alps. A brochure detailing the services is available at the Lazzi office. See the Getting Around chapter at the beginning of this book for further details.

Train Firenze is on the Roma-Milano line, which means that most of the trains for Roma, Bologna and Milano are intercities or the pendolino, for which you have to pay a supplement. There are regular trains to and from Venezia (three hours) and Trieste. For Verona you will generally need to change at Bologna. To get to Genova and Torino, a change at Pisa is necessary. For train information, ring ☎ 1478-880 88 from 9 am to 5 pm (in Italian only), or pick up the handy train timetable booklet available at Stazione di Santa Maria Novella. There is a porter service operating from the train station; they charge L3000 per article to escort you to your hotel.

Car & Motorcycle Firenze is connected by the A1 to Bologna and Milano in the north, and Roma and Napoli in the south. The Autostrada del Mare (A11) connects Firenze with Prato, Lucca, Pisa and the coast, and a superstrada joins the city to Siena. Exits from the autostradas into Firenze are well signposted and there are tourist offices on the A1 both north and south of the city. From the north on the A1, exit at Firenze Nord and then simply follow the bulls-eye 'centro' signs. If approaching from Roma, exit at Firenze Sud.

The more picturesque S67 connects the city with Pisa to the west and Forlì and Ravenna to the east.

Hitchhikers should contact the International Lift Centre (☎ 28 06 26) in Firenze.

For car rental details, see the following Getting Around section.

Getting Around

The Airports The No 62 bus runs approximately every 20 minutes from the main train station to Amerigo Vespucci airport. The service from the airport runs from 6.30 am to 10.45 pm; from the train station it runs from 6 am to 10.20 pm. The trip takes 15 minutes. Buy a normal city bus ticket (L1500).

Regular trains leave from platform no 5 at the main train station for Galileo Galilei airport at Pisa. Check in your luggage 15 minutes before the train departs. Services are roughly hourly from 7.51 am to 5.05 pm from Firenze, and from 10.44 am to 5.44 pm from the airport (only until 4.44 pm on weekends).

Bus ATAF buses service the city centre and Fiesole, and the station for the most useful buses is in Piazza Adua as you exit from Stazione di Santa Maria Novella onto Via Valfonda. Useful buses leaving from the train station include:

No 7, for Fiesole
No 13, for Piazzale Michelangelo
No 62, for Amerigo Vespucci airport
No 71, night bus for the duomo and the Uffizi

Bus tickets can be bought at tobacconists or automatic vending machines at major bus stops before you get on the bus and must be validated in the machine as you enter. There is a small ticket booth near the train station exit on Via Valfonda where you can pick up a very useful brochure detailing bus routes.

Tickets cost L1500 for 60 minutes and L2000 for 120 minutes. A 24-hour ticket costs L6500.

Car & Motorcycle Traffic is restricted in the city centre. There are several major car parks and numerous smaller parking areas around the fringes of the city centre. If you are planning to spend the day in Firenze, your best option is to park at the Fortezza da Basso, which costs L1500 per hour. If you are arriving by car from the north you will eventually end up at the Fortezza – you just park your car on the street and pay the attendant in advance. From here it is a brisk 10-minute walk to the duomo. Closer to the centre are more expensive underground car parks at Piazza del Mercato Centrale (much too expensive for periods longer than a few hours) and Piazza della Stazione (L1500 first hour and from L2000 to L5000 for each consecutive hour). For shorter visits, there are several parking areas along the Arno river, which cost L2000 for the first hour and L3000 for each consecutive hour.

Rental Avis (☎ 21 36 29) is at Borgognissanti 128r, Europcar (☎ 236 00 72) at Borgognissanti 53r and Hertz (☎ 29 82 05), at Via Maso Finiguerra 33r. Alinari (☎ 28 05 00), Via Guelfa 85r, rents scooters, larger mopeds and bicycles. In summer it also sets up shop at several camping grounds – check at the APT for details. Mopeds/scooters cost from L18,000 to L35,000 for five hours, or from L25,000 to L40,000 per day.

You can rent a bike for L8000 for five hours, L15,000 per day or L25,000 per weekend. A mountain bike costs L20,000 for five hours, L30,000 per day or L60,000 for a weekend.

Taxi Taxis are outside Stazione di Santa Maria Novella, or call ☎ 47 98 or 43 90. The flagfall is L4000 and then L1300 per km.

AROUND FIRENZE

Fiesole

Perched in hills about 8km north-east of Firenze, between the valleys of the Arno and Mugnone rivers, Fiesole has attracted the likes of Boccaccio, Carducci, Giovanni Dupré, Marcel Proust, Gertrude Stein and Frank Lloyd Wright, all drawn by the lush olive groves and valleys – not to mention the spectacular view of Firenze. Fiesole was founded in the 7th century BC by the Etruscans and remained the most important city in northern Etruria. It is well worth visiting for the views and is a fabulous spot for a picnic and short walk.

The APT in Firenze, or in Fiesole (☎ 055-59 87 20), Piazza Mino da Fiesole 36, can assist with information about the town and can advise on accommodation, walks and other activities. Most other services are located around the tourist office.

Things to See & Do Opposite the tourist office in Piazza Mino da Fiesole is the **duomo**, started in the 11th century and altered in the 13th century, although a 19th-century renovation has eradicated many earlier features. Behind the duomo is the **Museo Bandini**, featuring an impressive collection of early Tuscan Renaissance works, including Taddeo Gaddi's *Annunciation* and Petrarch's beautifully illustrated *Triumphs*. The museum opens daily except Tuesday from 10 am to 7 pm in summer and to 6 pm in winter.

Opposite the entrance to the museum on Via Portigiana, the **Zona Archeologico** features a 1st-century BC Roman theatre which is used from June to August for the Estate Fiesolana, a series of concerts and performances. Also in the complex are a small Etruscan temple and Roman baths, which date from the same period as the theatre. The small archaeological museum is worth a look, as it includes exhibits from the Bronze Age to the Roman period. A cumulative ticket costing L6000 allows you admission to the archaeological zone and museum and the Museo Bandini. The archaeological zone and museum open from 9 am to 7 pm in summer and until 6 pm in winter, daily except Tuesday.

If you are planning a picnic, or just want a refreshing walk, head uphill along the main street from Piazza Mino da Fiesole to Via Corsica. Take Via Pelagaccio, which eventually becomes a dirt track as it weaves around the mountain overlooking Firenze and winds back into Fiesole. If you get lost, ask a local to redirect you.

Places to Stay & Eat The APT advises that you camp in designated areas. There is a camping ground at Fiesole, the *Campeggio Panoramico* (☎ 055-59 90 69), Via Peramonda 1, which also has bungalows. Take bus No 70 from Piazza Mino da Fiesole.

The city has several hotels but most are quite expensive. *Bencistà* (☎ 055-5 91 63), Via Benedetto da Maiano 4, about 1km from Fiesole just off the road to Firenze, is an old villa and from its terrace there is a magnificent view of Firenze. Half board is compulsory at L130,000 per person. It might bust the budget, but for one or two days it's well worth it. Ask for a room with a view.

The *Casa del Popolo di Fiesole*, Via Antonio Gramsci 25, up the hill from Piazza Mino da Fiesole, is a cheap pizzeria with great views from the terrace to the mountains to the north and east. Piazza Mino da Fiesole is full of expensive bars. The *Blu Bar* is one of the more popular.

TOSCANA

Getting There & Away Fiesole is easily reached from Firenze. ATAF bus No 7 from the Stazione di Santa Maria Novella in Firenze connects with Piazza Mino da Fiesole, the centre of this small town. If you are driving, find your way to Piazza della Libertà, north of the duomo, and then follow the signs to Fiesole.

The Medici Villas

The Medici built several opulent villas in the countryside around Firenze as their wealth and prosperity grew during the 15th and 16th centuries. Most of the villas are now enclosed by the city's suburbs and industrial sprawl, and are easily reached by taking ATAF buses from the train station. Ask for details at the APT in Firenze about bus numbers and opening times.

The **Villa Medicea La Petraia**, about 3.5km north of the city, is one of the finest. Commissioned by Cardinal Ferdinand de' Medici in 1576, this former castle was converted by Buontalenti and features a magnificent garden. The **Villa Medicea di Castello**, farther north of the city, was the summer home of Lorenzo the Magnificent, and it is possible to visit the park only. Other villas include the **Villa di Poggio a Caiano**, about 15km from Firenze on the road to Pistoia, and the Villa Medicea di Careggi, which is visitable by appointment only. The Firenze APT has full details of opening times for all the villas.

The Mugello

The area north-east of Firenze leading up to Firenzuola, near the border with Emilia-Romagna, is known as the Mugello and features some of the most traditional villages in Toscana. The Sieve river winds through the area and its valley is one of Toscana's premier wine areas.

Start with the APT in Firenze, or contact the Comunità Montana del Mugello (☎ 055-849 53 46), Via P Togliatti 45, Borgo San Lorenzo. The Consorzio Turistico Mugello (☎ 055-845 80 45), Divisione Partigiana Garibaldi, Borgo San Lorenzo, and Promomugello (☎ 055-845 87 42) can help with hotel information and bookings.

The Medici originated from the Mugello and held extensive property in the area. Several Medici family castles, villas and palaces dot the area, some of which are open to the public and others can be visited with a guide. The APT in Firenze has information, otherwise contact the Associazione Turismo Ambiente (☎ 055-845 87 93), Piazza Dante 29, Borgo San Lorenzo. If you're interested in a wineries tour, there is a so-called *strada del vino* (wine road) mapped out, which will take you through the areas producing Chianti Rufino and Colli Fiorentini. Again, the Firenze APT has details. Also ask about the various walking trails through the Mugello.

North & West Toscana

PRATO

Virtually enclosed in the urban and industrial sprawl of Firenze, 17km to the south-east, Prato is one of Italy's main centres for textile production. Founded by the Ligurians, the city fell to the Etruscans and later the Romans, and by the 11th century was an important centre for wool production. It is worth visiting on your way to the more picturesque cities of Pistoia, Lucca and Pisa to the west.

Orientation

The old city centre is small and surrounded by the city wall. The main train station, on Piazza della Stazione, is to the east of the city centre.

Information

The APT tourist office (☎ 2 41 12) is at Via B Cairoli 48-52, two blocks east of the central Piazza del Comune, and is open Monday to Saturday from 9 am to 1 pm and 4 to 7 pm (2.30 to 6 pm in winter). It's worth investing in the special L5000 ticket which allows admission to the Museo Civico, the Museo dell'Opera del Duomo and the less interesting Museo di Pittura Murale.

The main post office and Telecom office are at Via Arcivescovo Martini 8.

The questura (☎ 113 or 55 55) is well out of the centre at Via Cino 10. For medical emergencies, the Ospedale Misericordia e Dolce (☎ 43 41) is in Piazza dell'Ospedale, south-west of Piazza del Comune.

The postcode for Prato is 51100 and the telephone code is ☎ 0574.

Museo Civico

This museum, with its small but impressive collection of largely Tuscan paintings, is housed in the imposing medieval Palazzo Pretorio on Piazza del Comune. Among the

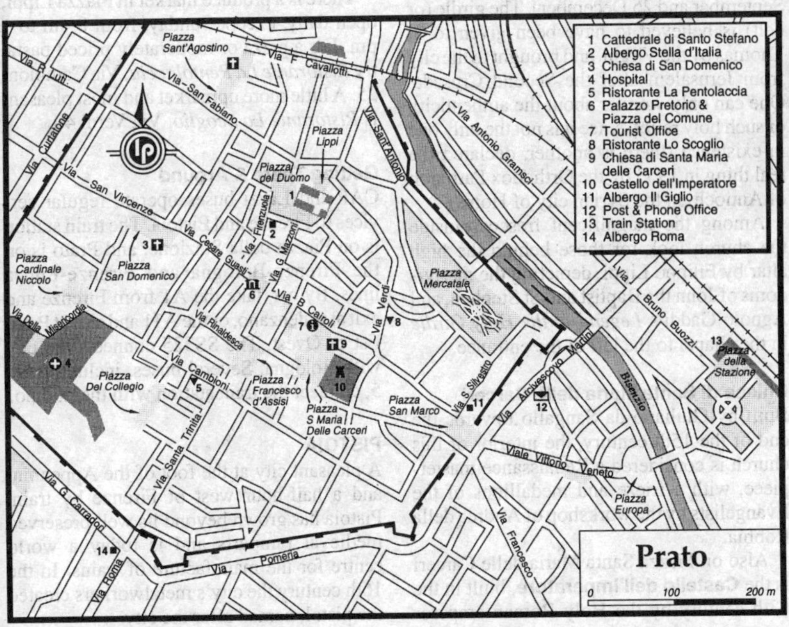

artists represented are Filippo Lippi and Vasari. The museum is open daily, except Tuesday, from 9.30 am to 12.30 pm and 3 to 6.30 pm (mornings only on Sunday).

Cattedrale di Santo Stefano

Along Via Mazzoni from Piazza del Comune is Piazza del Duomo and the 12th-century Cattedrale di Santo Stefano. The rather simple Pisan-Romanesque façade features a lunette by Andrea della Robbia and the white and green marble banding you have no doubt seen elsewhere in Toscana (Siena, Pistoia, Lucca). The most extraordinary element, however, is the oddly protruding **Pulpito della Sacra Cintola** jutting out over the piazza on the right-hand side of the main entrance. The eroded panels of the pulpit, designed by Donatello and Michelozzo in the 1430s, are in the **Museo dell'Opera del Duomo** next door. The pulpit was expressly added on so that the *sacra cintola* (sacred girdle) could be displayed to the people five times a year (Easter, 1 May, 15 August, 8 September and 25 December). The girdle (or belt) is believed to have been given to St Thomas by the Virgin, and brought to the city from Jerusalem after the Second Crusade. One can only wonder about the authenticity of such holy relics, since it is not the only one in existence (there is another, declared the real thing in 1953 by the Orthodox Patriarch of Antioch, in the Syrian city of Homs).

Among the magnificent frescoes inside the church look for those behind the high altar by Filippo Lippi, depicting the martyrdoms of John the Baptist and St Stephen, and Agnolo Gaddi's *Legend of the Holy Girdle* in the chapel to the left of the entrance.

Chiesa di Santa Maria delle Carceri

Built by Giuliano da Sangallo towards the end of the 15th century, the interior of this church is considered a Renaissance masterpiece, with a frieze and medallions of the Evangelists by the workshop of Andrea della Robbia.

Also on Piazza Santa Maria delle Carceri is the **Castello dell'Imperatore**, built in the 13th century by the Holy Roman emperor Frederick II. The castle is open daily, except Tuesday, from 9.30 to 11.30 am and 3.30 to 7 pm (3 to 5.30 pm in winter) and is closed on Sunday afternoons.

Chiesa di San Domenico

The main reason for dropping by this church is to have a look at the **Museo di Pittura Murale**, a collection of 14th to 17th-century frescoes and graffiti, reached through the church's cloister. It is open Monday to Saturday from 9 am to midday.

Places to Stay & Eat

The *Albergo Stella d'Italia* (☎ 2 79 10), overlooking the duomo at Piazza del Duomo 8, has singles/doubles from L48,000/75,000, while the *Albergo Roma* (☎ 3 17 77), Via Carradori 1, has rooms from L62,000/78,000. *Albergo Il Giglio* (☎ 3 70 49), Piazza San Marco 14, has rooms with bathroom from L70,000/92,000 (you may be able to bargain for a few cheaper rooms without bath).

There is a produce market in Piazza Lippi, open daily, except Sunday, from 8 am to 1 pm. For a pizza or moderately priced pasta, try *Ristorante La Pentolaccia*, Via Cambioni 25. A little more upmarket and most pleasant is *Ristorante Lo Scoglio*, Via Verdi 40.

Getting There & Around

CAP and Lazzi buses operate regular services to Firenze and Pistoia. The train station is on Piazza della Stazione, and Prato is on the Firenze-Bologna and Firenze-Lucca lines. By car, take the A1 from Firenze and exit at Calenzano, or the A11 and exit at Prato Est or Ovest. The SS325 connects the city with Bologna. Several buses, including No 5, connect the train station with the duomo.

PISTOIA

A pleasant city at the foot of the Appennini and a half-hour west of Firenze by train, Pistoia has grown beyond its well preserved medieval ramparts and is today a world centre for the manufacture of trains. In the 16th century the city's metalworkers created the pistol, named after the city.

Orientation & Information

Although spread out, the old city centre is easy to negotiate. From the train station in Piazza Dante Alighieri, head north along Via XX Settembre, through Piazza Treviso, and continue heading north to turn right into Via Cavour. Via Roma, branching off the north side of Via Cavour, takes you to Piazza del Duomo and the APT tourist office (☎ 2 16 22), which is open daily from 9 am to 1 pm and 3 to 6 pm.

The main post office is at Via Roma 5, and the Telecom phone office is on Corso Antonio Gramsci, near Via della Madonna. The latter is open Monday to Friday from 9 am to 1 pm and 4 to 7 pm.

For police, call ☎ 113. In medical emergencies, call ☎ 36 36. The public hospital (☎ 35 21) is in Viale Giacomo Matteotti, behind the old Ospedale del Ceppo.

The telephone code for Pistoia is ☎ 0573.

Piazza del Duomo

Much of Pistoia's visual wealth is concentrated on this central square. The Pisan-Romanesque façade of the **Cattedrale di San Zeno**, also known as the duomo, boasts a lunette of the Madonna and Child by

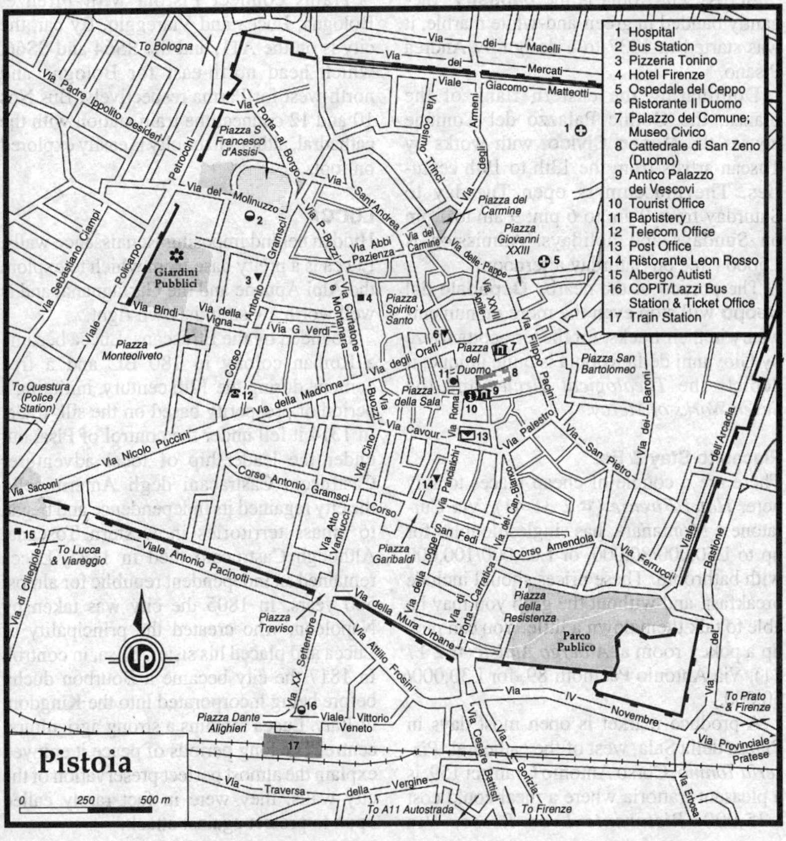

TOSCANA

Andrea della Robbia, who also made the terracotta tiles that line the barrel vault of the main porch. Inside, in the Cappella di San Jacopo, is the remarkable silver **Altarpiece of St James**. It was begun in the 13th century, with artisans adding to it over the ensuing two centuries until Brunelleschi contributed the final touch, the two half-figures on the left side.

The venerable building between the duomo and Via Roma is the **Antico Palazzo dei Vescovi**. There are guided tours four times a day through the wealth of artefacts dating as far back as Etruscan times which were discovered during restoration work.

Across Via Roma is the **baptistry**. Elegantly banded in green-and-white marble, it was started in 1337 to a design by Andrea Pisano.

Dominating the eastern flank of the piazza, the Gothic Palazzo del Comune houses the **Museo Civico**, with works by Tuscan artists from the 13th to 19th centuries. The museum is open Tuesday to Saturday from 9 am to 6 pm; 9 am to 1 pm on Sundays and holidays. Admission is L5000 (free on Saturday afternoon).

The portico of the nearby **Ospedale del Ceppo** will stop even the more monument-weary in their tracks, for the terracotta frieze by Giovanni della Robbia is quite unique; it depicts the *Theological Virtues* and the *Seven Works of Mercy*.

Places to Stay & Eat

There are a couple of cheap places to stay here. *Hotel Firenze* (☎ 2 31 41), Via Curtatone e Montanara, has singles/doubles for up to L50,000/80,000, or L65,000/100,000 with bathroom. These prices should include breakfast, and without the grub you may be able to talk them down a little. You can pick up a pokey room at *Albergo Autisti* (☎ 2 17 71), Via Antonio Pacinotti 89, for L30,000/50,000.

A produce market is open most days in Piazza della Sala, west of the cathedral. *Pizzeria Tonino*, Corso Antonio Gramsci 159, is a pleasant trattoria where a meal could cost L25,000. *Ristorante Leon Rosso*, Via Panciatichi 4, is very good but slightly more expensive, with pasta from L10,000. *Ristorante Il Duomo*, Via Bracciolini 5, has pasta from L8000 and a cheap selection of lunchtime self-serve dishes from L5000.

Getting There & Around

Buses connect Pistoia with most towns in Toscana. The main ticket office for COPIT and Lazzi buses is on the corner of Viale Vittorio Veneto and Via XX Settembre, and most buses leave from just outside (those for Firenze depart from Piazza Treviso). Other COPIT buses leave from Via del Molinuzzo, off Piazza San Francesco d'Assisi.

Trains connect Pistoia with Firenze, Bologna, Lucca and Viareggio. By car, the city is on the A11, and the SS64 and SS66, which head north-east for Bologna and north-west for Parma respectively. Bus Nos 10 and 12 connect the train station with the cathedral, although the city is easily explored on foot.

LUCCA

Hidden behind imposing Renaissance walls, Lucca is a pretty base from which to explore the Alpi Apuane and the Garfagnana, and is well worth a visit in its own right.

Founded by the Etruscans, Lucca became a Roman colony in 180 BC and a free comune during the 12th century, initiating a period of prosperity based on the silk trade. In 1314 it fell under the control of Pisa, but under the leadership of local adventurer Castruccio Castracani degli Anterminelli, the city regained its independence and began to amass territories in western Toscana. Although Castruccio died in 1325, Lucca remained an independent republic for almost 500 years. In 1805 the city was taken by Napoleon, who created the principality of Lucca and placed his sister, Elisa, in control. In 1817 the city became a Bourbon duchy before being incorporated into the Kingdom of Italy. Lucca remains a strong agricultural centre. The long periods of peace it enjoyed explain the almost perfect preservation of the city walls: they were in fact rarely called upon to protect against attack.

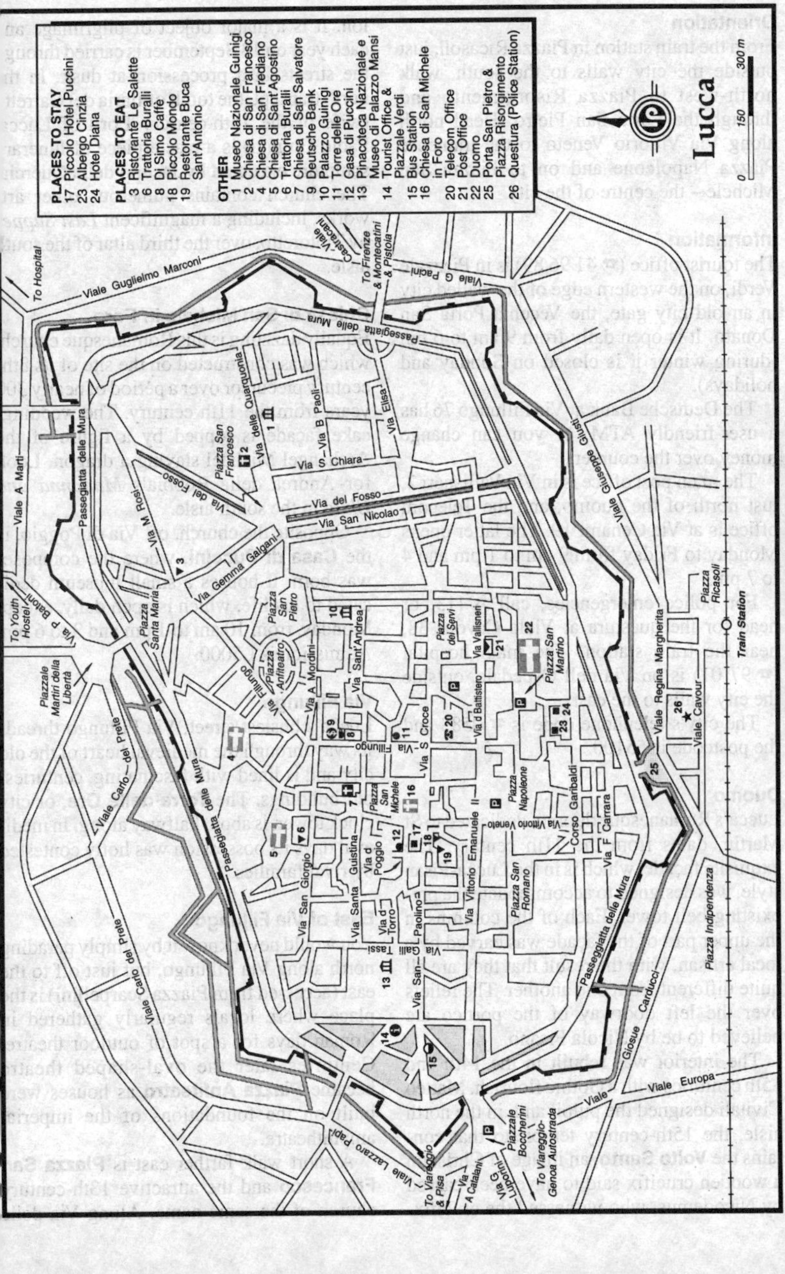
Lucca
0
150
300 m
PLACES TO STAY
17 Piccolo Hotel Puccini
23 Albergo Cinzia
24 Hotel Diana
PLACES TO EAT
3 Ristorante Le Salette
6 Trattoria Buralli
8 Di Simo Caffè
18 Piccolo Mondo
19 Restorante Buca Sant'Antonio
OTHER
1 Museo Nazionale Guinigi
2 Chiesa di San Francesco
4 Chiesa di San Frediano
5 Chiesa di Sant'Agostino
6 Trattoria Buralli
7 Chiesa di San Salvatore
9 Deutsche Bank
10 Palazzo Guinigi
11 Torre delle Ore
12 Casa di Puccini
13 Pinacoteca Nazionale e Museo di Palazzo Mansi
14 Tourist Office & Piazzale Verdi
15 Bus Station
16 Chiesa di San Michele in Foro
20 Telecom Office
21 Post Office
22 Duomo
25 Porta San Pietro & Piazza Risorgimento
26 Questura (Police Station)
To Hospital
Viale Guglielmo Marconi
Viale Castracani
To Firenze & Montecatini & Pistoia
Viale G Pacini
Passeggiata delle Mura
Viale A Marti
Via della Quarquonia
Via B Paoli
Via Elisa
Piazza San Francesco
Via S Chiara
Via del Fosso
Via San Nicolao
Via M Rosi
Via Gemma Galgani
Viale Giuseppe Giusti
Piazza Ricasoli
Train Station
To Youth Hostel
Via P Batoni
Piazzale Martiri della Libertà
Piazza Santa Maria
Piazza San Pietro
Via Sant'Andrea
Piazza Anfiteatro
Via Fillungo
Via A Mordini
Piazza dei Servi
Via Vallisneri
Piazza San Martino
Via d Battistero
Via S Croce
Viale Regina Margherita
Viale Cavour
Viale Carlo del Prete
Piazza San Michele
Piazza Napoleone
Corso Garibaldi
Via Vittorio Veneto
Via F Carrara
Via San Giorgio
Via Santa Giustina
Via d Poggio
Via Vittorio Emanuele II
Piazza San Romano
Via Paolino
Via d Torro
Via Galli Tassi
Via San Paolino
Piazza Indipendenza
Viale Giosue Carducci
Viale Europa
Piazzale Boccherini
To Viareggio-Genoa Autostrada
Via G Luporini
Via A Catalani
To Viareggio & Pisa
Viale Lazzaro Papi
TOSCANA

Orientation

From the train station in Piazza Ricasoli, just outside the city walls to the south, walk north-west to Piazza Risorgimento and through the Porta San Pietro. Head north along Via Vittorio Veneto to the immense Piazza Napoleone and on to Piazza San Michele – the centre of the city.

Information

The tourist office (☎ 41 96 89) is in Piazzale Verdi, on the western edge of the walled city in an old city gate, the Vecchia Porta San Donato. It is open daily from 9 am to 6 pm (during winter it is closed on Sunday and holidays).

The Deutsche Bank at Via Fillungo 76 has a user-friendly ATM, or you can change money over the counter.

The main post office is in Via Vallisneri 2, just north of the duomo, and the Telecom office is at Via Cenami 19. The latter opens Monday to Friday from 9 am to 1 pm and 4 to 7 pm.

For police emergencies, call ☎ 113, or head for the questura at Viale Cavour 38, near the train station. The main hospital (☎ 97 01) is on Via dell'Ospedale, outside the city walls to the east.

The city's telephone code is ☎ 0583 and the postcode is 55100.

Duomo

Lucca's Romanesque duomo, dedicated to St Martin, dates from the 11th century. The exquisite façade, which is in the Lucca-Pisan style, was designed to accommodate the pre-existing bell tower. Each of the columns in the upper part of the façade was carved by a local artisan, with the result that they are all quite different from one another. The reliefs over the left doorway of the portico are believed to be by Nicola Pisano.

The interior was rebuilt in the 14th and 15th centuries with a Gothic flourish. Matteo Civitali designed the pulpit and, in the north aisle, the 15th-century tempietto that contains the **Volto Santo**, an image of Christ on a wooden crucifix said to have been carved by Nicodemus, who witnessed the crucifixion. It is a major object of pilgrimage and each year on 13 September is carried through the streets in a procession at dusk. In the north transept, the tomb of Ilaria del Carretto (wife of the 15th-century Lord of Lucca Paolo Guinigi) is a masterpiece of funerary sculpture executed by Jacopo della Quercia. The church contains numerous other art works, including a magnificent *Last Supper* by Tintoretto, over the third altar of the south aisle.

Chiesa di San Michele in Foro

Equally dazzling is this Romanesque church which was constructed on the site of its 8th century precursor over a period of nearly 300 years from the 11th century. The wedding-cake façade is topped by a figure of the Archangel Michael slaying a dragon. Look for Andrea della Robbia's *Madonna and Child* in the south aisle.

Opposite the church, off Via di Poggio, is the **Casa di Puccini**, where the composer was born. It houses a small museum dedicated to his life, which is open daily, except Monday, from 10 am to 1 pm and 3 to 6 pm. Admission is L5000.

Via Fillungo

Lucca's busiest street, Via Fillungo threads its way through the medieval heart of the old city and is lined with fascinating, centuries-old buildings. The **Torre delle Ore**, or city clock tower, is about halfway along. In medieval days its possession was hotly contested by rival families.

East of Via Fillungo

You would never know it by simply parading north along Via Fillungo, but just off to the east (accessed from Piazza Scarpellini) is the place where locals regularly gathered in Roman days for a spot of outdoor theatre. Centuries later the oval-shaped theatre became **Piazza Anfiteatro** as houses were built on the foundations of the imperial amphitheatre.

A short walk farther east is **Piazza San Francesco** and the attractive 13th-century church of the same name. Along Via della

Quarquonia is the Villa Guinigi, which houses the **Museo Nazionale Guinigi** and the city's art collection. It is open daily, except Monday, from 9 am to 2 pm. Admission is L4000.

West of Via Fillungo

Another example of Lucca's adaptation of the Pisan-Romanesque style, the façade of the **Chiesa di San Frediano** features a unique (and much-restored) 13th-century mosaic. The main feature of the beautiful basilica's interior is the **Fonta Lustrale**, a 12th-century baptismal font decorated with sculpted reliefs. Behind it is an *Annunciation* by Andrea della Robbia.

Of some interest are the interior and artworks of the **Pinacoteca Nazionale e Museo di Palazzo Mansi**, Via Galli Tassi. It is open daily, except Monday, from 9 am to 2 pm. Admission is a bit expensive at L8000.

City Walls

If you have the time, do the 4km walk along the top of the city walls. These ramparts were raised in the 16th and 17th centuries and are similar to the defensive systems later developed by the French military engineer Vauban.

Courses

The Centro Koinè (☎ 49 30 40), Via A Mordini 60, offers Italian courses for foreigners. A two-week summer course is L610,000, while month-long courses, available all year, cost L830,000. The school can also arrange accommodation. Write for an information booklet, which contains an enrolment form.

Places to Stay

It is always advisable to book ahead, but if you're in a spot try the city's hotel association, the Sindacato Lucchese Albergatori (☎ 4 41 81), Via Fillungo 121, which may be able to help find a room. The city's HI youth hostel, the *Ostello Il Serchio* (☎ 34 18 11), Via del Brennero 673, is outside the walls to the north; take CLAP bus No 1 or 2 from Piazzale Verdi. B&B is L16,000. It is open from 10 March to 10 October.

Albergo Cinzia (☎ 49 13 23), Via della Dogana 9, has singles/doubles costing L30,000/45,000. *Hotel Diana* (☎ 49 22 02), Via del Molinetto 11, has singles for L45,000 and doubles with bathroom for up to L95,000. The three-star *Piccolo Hotel Puccini* (☎ 5 54 21), Via di Poggio 9, has singles/doubles with bathroom for up to L88,000/123,000.

Places to Eat

Lucca boasts a good selection of relatively cheap trattorie. For pizza by the slice, there is a small takeaway at Via Fillungo 5. *Piccolo Mondo*, Piazza dei Cocomeri 5, is a good spot for a cheap meal, with pasta from L6000. Just around the corner at Via della Cervia 3, *Ristorante Buca Sant'Antonio* is a rather classier affair where you'll need about L40,000 a head for a full meal. *Trattoria Buralli*, Piazza Sant'Agostino 9, offers a simple but filling tourist menu for L18,000. You'll also find several reasonably priced restaurants and pizza joints, including *Le Salette* on Piazza Santa Maria. *Di Simo Caffè*, Via Fillungo 58, is a grand bar and gelateria serving local specialities such as buccellato cakes.

Getting There & Away

CLAP buses (☎ 58 78 97) serve the region, including the Garfagnana. Lazzi (☎ 58 48 77) operates buses to Firenze, La Spezia, Carrara, Pisa, Torino and Roma. Both companies operate from Piazzale Verdi.

Lucca is on the Firenze-Viareggio-Pisa train line, and there are also services into the Garfagnana. By car, the A11 passes to the south of the city, connecting it with Pisa and Viareggio. The SS445 connects the city with the Garfagnana.

Getting Around

Most cars are banned from the city centre, although tourists are allowed to drive into the walled city and park in the residents' spaces (yellow lines) if they have a permit from one of the hotels. There are paid parking areas in piazzas Bernardini, San Martino, Napoleone and Boccherini.

CLAP buses connect the train station, Piazza del Giglio (near Piazza Napoleone) and Piazzale Verdi, but it is just as easy, and more pleasurable, to walk.

For a taxi, call ☎ 49 49 89.

THE GARFAGNANA

The heart of the Garfagnana is in the valley formed by the Serchio river and its tributaries. This is an excellent area for trekking, horse riding and a host of other outdoor pursuits, and the region is well geared for tourism. The tourist offices in Lucca or Pisa can advise, and the most useful organisation in the Garfagnana is the Consorzio Garfagnana Turistica, at the Comunità Montana (☎ 0583-64 49 11), Via Vittorio Emanuele 9, in Castelnuovo di Garfagnana. Pro Loco tourist offices in several smaller villages can help with details on hotels and mountain *rifugi*.

Walkers should pick up a copy of *Garfagnana Trekking*, which details a 10-day hike. Another booklet, *Garfagnana a Cavallo*, details guided horse treks that can cost L20,000 an hour or L90,000 a day. Details of these and other aspects of the mountains, including *agriturismo*, are available from the Azienda Agrituristica La Garfagnana (☎ 0583-6 87 05), Località Prade 25, in Castiglione di Garfagnana.

The Alpi Apuane

This mountain range is bordered on one side by the stretch of coastline known as the Versilia Riviera and on the other by the vast valley of the Garfagnana. Altitudes are relatively low, in comparison to the Alps farther north, but the Alpi Apuane are certainly not lacking in great walking possibilities: some trails afford spectacular views to the coastline and the Ligurian Sea. The landscape in some areas has been utterly destroyed by marble mining, an industry which has exploited these mountains since Roman times. No environmental laws have been in place to prevent mining companies from literally removing entire peaks in some places. But, in the end, the extent of interference in the natural landscape has created a new environment which has a certain aesthetic appeal. There is a good network of marked trails, as well as several rifugi in the Alpi Apuane. The 1:25,000 *Carta dei Sentieri e Rifugi*, published by Multigraphic of Firenze is a good map.

Information can be obtained from the Comunità Montana in Castiglione di Garfagnana.

MASSA & CARRARA

These two towns in the northern reaches of Toscana don't really warrant a visit unless you are interested in seeing Italy's famous marble quarries. Massa is the administrative centre of the province and is rather unattractive, although the beachfront extension, Marina di Massa, is very popular with holidaying Italians. You might wonder why, if you happen to stumble onto the overpopulated shores.

Carrara, however, is quite picturesque. At the foothills of the Alpi Apuane, the town appears to be dominated by snowcapped mountains – an illusion created by limestone formations and the vast quarries which virtually cover the hills. The texture and purity of Carrara's white marble is unrivalled and was chosen by Michelangelo for many of his masterpieces. He often travelled to the quarries to personally select blocks of the stone.

The APT has offices at Marina di Massa (☎ 0585-24 00 63), Via San Leonardo 500, and at Marina di Carrara (☎ 0585-63 22 18), Piazza Menconi 6B. There is a youth hostel on the coast at Marina di Massa, the *Ostello della Gioventù* (☎ 0585-78 00 34), Via delle Pinete 237, which charges L14,000 for a bed.

Both Massa and Carrara are accessible from the A12 and the S1 Via Aurelia; signs direct you to quarries you can visit and other attractions, such as museums.

PISA

Once a maritime power to rival Genova and Venezia, Pisa now draws its fame from an architectural project gone terribly wrong: its Leaning Tower. It is just about impossible to think of Pisa without the tilting bell tower and its graceful arcaded galleries leaping to mind, but the city offers lots more. Indeed, the tower is only one element of the fabulous trio of Romanesque buildings in the city's beautiful Campo dei Miracoli – along with Piazza San Marco in Venezia, one of Italy's most memorable squares.

Pisa has a centuries-old tradition as a university town and even today is full of young students. A perhaps unexpectedly beautiful city, it really deserves more than the usual one-day stopover planned by most tourists.

History

Possibly a settlement of Greek origin, Pisa became an important naval base during Roman times and remained a significant port for many centuries. The city's so-called Golden Days began late in the 9th century when it became an independent maritime republic and a rival of Genova and Venezia. This dominance peaked during the 12th and 13th centuries, when Pisa controlled Corsica, Sardegna and most of the Italian coast as far south as Civitavecchia. The majority of the city's finest buildings date from this period, as well as the distinctive Pisan-Romanesque architectural style.

Pisa's support for the Ghibellines during the tussles between the Holy Roman emperor and the pope brought the city into conflict with its mostly Guelph Tuscan neighbours, including Siena, Lucca and Firenze. The real blow, however, came when Genova's fleet inflicted a devastating defeat on Pisa in the Battle of Meloria in 1284. The city fell to Firenze in 1406, and the Medici encouraged great artistic, literary and scientific endeavour and re-established Pisa's university. The city's most famous son, Galileo Galilei, was later a teacher at the university.

Orientation

By train you'll arrive at Stazione Pisa Centrale, on the southern edge of the old city centre. The main intercity bus station is in Piazza Vittorio Emanuele II, a short walk north along Viale Gramsci. The medieval centre is about a 15-minute walk north, across the Arno river, and Campo dei Miracoli (also referred to as Piazza del Duomo) is about another 10-minute walk north-west. It is quicker to catch a city bus from outside the station. See Getting Around later in this section.

Information

Tourist Offices The main APT (☎ 56 04 64) is in the same building as the Museo dell'Opera del Duomo, on Campo dei Miracoli. It opens Monday to Saturday from 8 am to 8 pm (9.30 am to midday and 3 to 5.30 pm in the off season). The office at the train station (☎ 4 22 91) keeps longer hours in winter but has little more than a map and list of hotels – the most useful items for late night arrivals, however!

Money Avoid the exchange booths near the duomo. Change money at banks along Corso Italia, or at the train station.

Post & Communications The main post office is in Piazza Vittorio Emanuele II. Poste restante mail can be addressed to 56100 Pisa.

The Telecom telephone office at the train station opens daily from 8 am to 9.45 pm.

Pisa's telephone code is ☎ 050.

Laundry There's an Onda Blu at Via San Francesco 8a.

Emergency For police emergency, call ☎ 113. The questura (☎ 58 35 11) is at Via Mario Lalli. The Ospedali Riuniti di Santa Chiara (☎ 59 21 11) is a hospital complex at Via Roma 67. Call ☎ 118 for an ambulance.

Campo dei Miracoli

The Pisans can justly claim that the Campo dei Miracoli is one of the most beautiful squares in the world. Set among its sprawling lawns is surely one of the most extraordinary concentrations of Romanesque splendour – the duomo, the baptistry and the Leaning Tower. On any day the piazza is teeming with

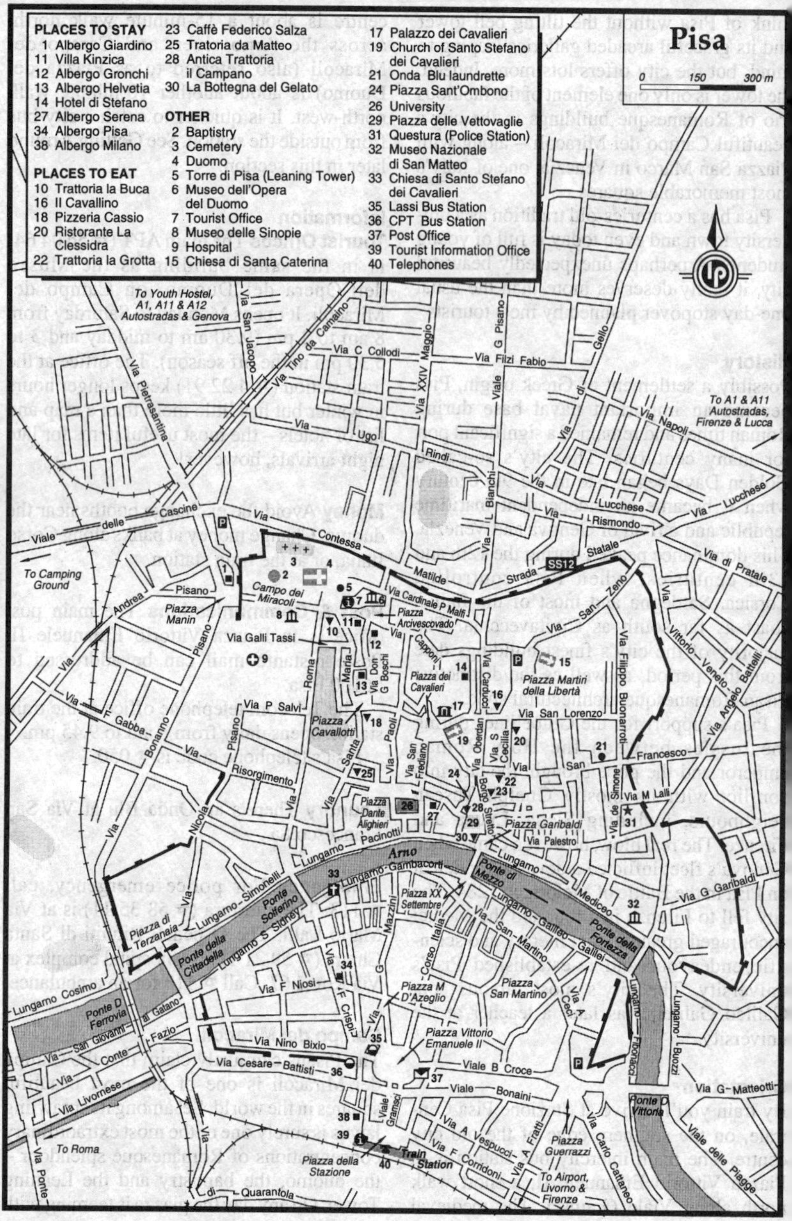
Pisa
0
150
300 m
PLACES TO STAY
1 Albergo Giardino
11 Villa Kinzica
12 Albergo Gronchi
13 Albergo Helvetia
14 Hotel di Stefano
27 Albergo Serena
34 Albergo Pisa
38 Albergo Milano
PLACES TO EAT
10 Trattoria la Buca
16 Il Cavallino
18 Pizzeria Cassio
20 Ristorante La Clessidra
22 Trattoria la Grotta
23 Caffè Federico Salza
25 Tratoria da Matteo
28 Antica Trattoria il Campano
30 La Bottegna del Gelato
OTHER
2 Baptistry
3 Cemetery
4 Duomo
5 Torre di Pisa (Leaning Tower)
6 Museo dell'Opera del Duomo
7 Tourist Office
8 Museo delle Sinopie
9 Hospital
15 Chiesa di Santa Caterina
17 Palazzo dei Cavalieri
19 Church of Santo Stefano dei Cavalieri
21 Onda Blu laundrette
24 Piazza Sant'Ombono
26 University
29 Piazza delle Vettovaglie
31 Questura (Police Station)
32 Museo Nazionale di San Matteo
33 Chiesa di Santo Stefano dei Cavalieri
35 Lassi Bus Station
36 CPT Bus Station
37 Post Office
39 Tourist Information Office
40 Telephones
To Youth Hostel, A1, A11 & A12 Autostradas & Genova
To A1 & A11 Autostradas, Firenze & Lucca
To Camping Ground
To Roma
To Airport, Livorno & Firenze
Via San Jacopo
Via Tino da Camaino
Via C Collodi
Via XXIV Maggio
Viale G Pisano
Via Filzi Fabio
Via di Gello
Via Pietrasantina
Via Ugo Rindi
Via Napoli
Via L Bianchi
Via Lucchese
Via Rismondo
Viale delle Cascine
Via Contessa Matilde
Strada Statale
SS12
Via di Pratale
Via San Zeno
Via Vittorio Veneto
Via Angelo Battelli
Via Andrea Pisano
Campo dei Miracoli
Piazza Manin
Via Cardinale P Maffi
Piazza Arcivescovado
Via Galli Tassi
Via Roma
Via Maria
Via Don G Boschi
Via Capponi
Via Carducci
Piazza Martiri della Libertà
Via Filippo Buonarroti
Piazza dei Cavalieri
Via F Gabba
Via Bonanno
Via Pisano
Via P Salvi
Piazza Cavallotti
Via Santa
Via Paoli
Via San Lorenzo
Via Oberdan
Via S Cecilia
Via San Francesco
Via San Frediano
Via Risorgimento
Via Nicola
Piazza Dante Alighieri
Borgo Stretto
Piazza Garibaldi
Via Palestro
Via M Lalli
Via de Simone
Lungarno Pacinotti
Arno
Lungarno Gambacorti
Lungarno Simonelli
Ponte Solferino
Lungarno S Sidney
Piazza di Terzanaia
Ponte della Cittadella
Ponte di Mezzo
Piazza XX Settembre
Lungarno Mediceo
Lungarno Galileo Galilei
Ponte della Fortezza
Via G Garibaldi
Via Mazzini
Corso Italia
Via San Martino
Piazza San Martino
Via Ceci
Lungarno Cosimo I
Ponte D Ferrovia
Via San Giovanni al Gatano
Via Fazio
Via Conte
Via Livornese
Via F Niosi
Via F Crispi
Via G
Piazza M D'Azeglio
Via Nino Bixio
Via Cesare Battisti
Piazza Vittorio Emanuele II
Viale B Croce
Lungarno Fibonacci
Lungarno Buozzi
Via G Matteotti
Ponte D Vittoria
Viale Bonaini
Via Gramsci
Via A Vespucci
Via F Corridoni
Via A Fratti
Piazza Guerrazzi
Via Carlo Cattaneo
Viale delle Piagge
Piazza della Stazione
Train Station
Via Quarantola
Via Ponte
P

people – students studying or at play, tourists wandering and local workers eating lunch.

There is a staggered pricing system for tickets to enter one or more of the monuments in and around the square. L10,000 gets you entry to two monuments, and L15,000 to four – the two museums, baptistry and cemetery. The duomo itself is not included and costs an extra L2000.

Duomo The majesty of Pisa's cathedral made it a model for Romanesque churches throughout Toscana and even in Sardegna. Begun in 1064, it is covered inside and out with the alternating bands of dark green and cream marble that were to become characteristic of the Pisan-Romanesque style. The main façade is adorned with four tiers of columns and its huge interior is lined with 68 columns in Classical style. The bronze doors of the transept, facing the Leaning Tower, are by Bonanno Pisano. The 16th-century bronze doors of the main entrance were designed by the school of Giambologna to replace the wooden originals, destroyed in a fire in 1596. The interior was also much redecorated after this devastating fire. Important works to survive the blaze include Giovanni Pisano's early 14th-century pulpit and an apse mosaic of *Christ in Majesty* completed by Cimabue in 1302. The duomo is open daily from 7.45 am to 1 pm and 3 to 7 pm (5 pm in winter).

Torre di Pisa The duomo's bell tower *(campanile)* was in trouble from the start: its architect, Bonanno Pisano, managed to complete only three tiers before the tower started to lean. The problem is generally believed to have been caused by shifting soil, and the 'leaning tower' *(torre pendente)* has continued to lean by an average of one mm a year ever since. Galileo climbed its 294 steps to experiment with gravity, but today it is no longer possible to follow in his footsteps. The tower has been closed since 1990 while the Italians try to work out how to stop its inexorable lean towards the ground – it now leans 5m off the perpendicular. In 1994 it was believed that a solution had been found – 600 tons of lead ingots to anchor the north foundation. The lean was stopped and the tower even began to straighten. However, in September 1995 the tower moved 2.5mm in one night, representing 10% of the total amount that had been corrected! No-one has any intention of straightening the Leaning Tower, and many believe it will fall down eventually whatever is done. The controversial Italian art historian, Vittorio Sgarbi, once said it would be 'better to see it fall and remember it leaning than see it straightened by mistake'.

Baptistry This unusual round structure was started in 1153 by Diotisalvi, remodelled and

The Torre di Pisa, now 5m off the perpendicular

TOSCANA

continued by Nicola and Giovanni Pisano more than a century later, and finally completed in the 14th century – which explains the mix of architectural styles. The lower level of arcades is in the Pisan-Romanesque style and the pinnacled upper section and dome are Gothic. Inside, the beautiful pulpit was carved by Nicola Pisano and signed in 1260, and the white marble font was carved by Guido da Como in 1246. The baptistery is open from 8 am to 7.30 pm (9 am to 4.30 pm in winter).

Cemetery Located behind the white wall to the north of the duomo, this exquisite cemetery is said to have soil that was shipped from Calvary during the Crusades. Many precious frescoes in the cloisters were badly damaged or destroyed during WWII Allied bombing raids. Among those saved were the *Triumph of Death* and *Last Judgment*, attributed to an anonymous 14th-century painter known as 'The Master of the Triumph of Death'. The cemetery is open daily from 8 am to 7.30 pm (9 am to 4.30 pm in winter).

Around Campo dei Miracoli

The **Museo delle Sinopie** houses reddish-brown sketches drawn onto walls as the base for frescoes, discovered in the cemetery after the WWII bombing raids. The *sinopie* have been restored and provide a fascinating insight into the process of creating a fresco, although they are really only worth visiting if you have a particular interest in the subject. The museum is open daily from 9 am to 1 pm and 3 to 7 pm (5 pm in winter).

The **Museo dell'Opera del Duomo** in Piazza Arcivescovado, near the Leaning Tower, features many artworks from the tower, duomo and baptistery, including a magnificent ivory carving of the *Madonna and Crucifix* by Giovanni Pisano. Another highlight is the bust known as the *Madonna del Colloquio*, by the same artist, taken from the exterior of the baptistery. It is open daily from 9 am to 1 pm and 3 to 7.30 pm (5.30 pm in winter).

The City

Head south along Via Santa Maria from the Campo dei Miracoli and turn left at Piazza Cavallotti for the splendid **Piazza dei Cavalieri**, which was remodelled by Vasari in the 16th century. The **Palazzo dell'Orologio**, on the north side of the piazza, occupies the site of a tower where, in 1288 Count Ugolino della Gherardesca, his sons and grandsons, were starved to death on suspicion of having helped the Genovese enemy at the Battle of Meloria. The incident was recorded in Dante's *Inferno*. The **Palazzo dei Cavalieri** on the north-eastern side of the piazza was redesigned by Vasari and features remarkable graffiti decoration. The piazza and palace are named for the Knights of St Stephen, a religious and military order founded by Cosimo de' Medici. Their church, **Santo Stefano dei Cavalieri**, was also designed by Vasari. The **Chiesa di Santa Caterina**, off Via San Lorenzo on Piazza Martiri della Libertà, is a fine example of Pisan Gothic architecture and contains works by Nino Pisano.

Wander south to the area around **Borgo Stretto**, the city's medieval heart. East along the waterfront boulevard, the Lungarno Mediceo, is the **Museo Nazionale di San Matteo**, one of Toscana's finest galleries. It features works by Giovanni and Nicola Pisano, Masaccio and Donatello. The gallery is open Tuesday to Saturday from 9 am to 7 pm and Sunday to 1 pm. Admission is L8000.

Cross the Ponte di Mezzo and head west to reach the **Chiesa di Santa Maria della Spina**, built in the early 14th century to house a thorn from Christ's crown.

Places to Stay

Pisa has a reasonable number of budget hotels for a small town, but many double as residences for students during the school year, so it can be difficult to find a cheap room. A camping ground, the *Camping Torre Pendente* (☎ 56 06 65), Via delle Cascine 86, is west of the duomo. The non-HI *Ostello della Gioventù* (☎ 89 06 22) is a long hike north-west of the duomo at Via Pietrasantina 15. A bed costs L14,000. Take bus No 3 from he train station (walking it from Campo dei Miracoli is a huge pain).

The *Albergo Serena* (☎ 58 08 09), Via D Cavalca 45, just off Piazza Dante Alighieri, has singles/doubles for up to L40,000/55,000. The *Albergo Helvetia* (☎ 55 30 84), Via Don Gaetano Boschi 31, near the duomo, has similarly priced rooms. *Hotel di Stefano* (☎ 55 35 59), Via Sant'Apollonia 35, near Via Carducci, has good rooms without private bath for up to L50,000/65,000.

The *Albergo Gronchi* (☎ 56 18 23), Piazza Arcivescovado 1, is a great bargain for its position alone, offers singles/doubles for L32,000/52,000. The *Albergo Giardino* (☎ 56 21 01), Piazza Manin 1, just west of Campo dei Miracoli, has rooms for L40,000/60,000 without private bath.

More upmarket is the *Villa Kinzica* (☎ 56 04 19; fax 55 12 04), Piazza Arcivescovado 2, with views of the Leaning Tower and singles/doubles with bathroom for L100,000/135,000.

Near the train station, the *Albergo Milano* (☎ 2 31 62), Via Mascagni 14, has comfortable rooms for L40,000/70,000 (doubles with bath can cost up to L92,000). The two-star *Albergo Pisa* (☎ 4 45 51), Via Manzoni 22, near Via Francesco Crispi, has a variety of rooms starting at L43,000/62,000.

Places to Eat

Being a university town, Pisa has a good range of cheap eating places. Head for the area north of the river around Borgo Stretto and the university. There is an open-air food market in Piazza delle Vettovaglie, off Borgo Stretto.

The *Antica Trattoria il Campano*, in an old tower at Vicolo Santa Margherita near Piazza Sant'Ombono, is full of atmosphere; a full meal is likely to set you back L35,000. *Trattoria la Grotta*, Via San Francesco 103, is another good choice and similarly priced.

Heading north, the *Ristorante La Clessidra*, Via Santa Cecilia 34, is a tad pricey (L35,000 or more for a full meal) but the food is excellent. *Trattoria la Buca* in Via Galli Tassi has pizzas from L8000. At *Pizzeria Cassio*, Piazza Cavallotti, you can also get decent pizza and pasta at moderate prices. *Trattoria da Matteo*, Via L'Arancio 48, has a cheap set menu for L17,000 as well as – you guessed it – pizza.

One of the city's finest bars is the *Caffè Federico Salza*, Borgo Stretto 46, with cakes, gelati and chocolates. Prices inside are one-third of those charged if you eat at the tables outside. Another is *Bar Duomo*, facing the Leaning Tower and very expensive. For great gelati, head for *La Bottega del Gelato* in Piazza Garibaldi, near the river.

Entertainment

The tourist office has a list of nightclubs and events in the city. Opera and ballet are staged at the Teatro Verdi (☎ 94 11 11), Via Palestro 40, from September to November. Cultural and historic events include the Gioco del Ponte, a festival of traditional costume held on the last Sunday in June. On 17 June, the Arno river comes to life with the Regata Storica di San Ranieri, a rowing competition commemorating the city's patron saint.

Getting There & Away

Air The city's Aeroporto Galileo Galilei (☎ 50 07 07), about 2km south of the city centre, is Toscana's main international airport and handles flights to major cities in Europe.

Alitalia (☎ 1478-6 56 43), British Airways (☎ 167-28 92 89) and other major airlines are based at the airport.

Bus Lazzi (☎ 4 62 88), Piazza Vittorio Emanuele II, operates services to Lucca, Firenze, Prato, Pistoia, Massa and Carrara. CPT (☎ 50 55 11), Piazza Sant'Antonio, also near the train station, serves Volterra, Livorno and Lucca.

Train The train station is on Piazza della Stazione (☎ 4 13 85) at the southern edge of town. The city is connected to Firenze and is also on the Roma-La Spezia line, with frequent services running in all directions.

Car & Motorcycle Pisa is close to the A12, which connects Parma to Livorno and is being extended south to Roma, although that may yet take some years to complete. The city is also close to the A11 (tollway) and S67 to Firenze, while the north-south S1, the Via Aurelia, connects the city with La Spezia and Roma.

Large car parks are all around Pisa, with one just north of the duomo perfect for day-trippers.

Getting Around

To get to the airport, take a train from the main station for the four-minute journey to the Stazione FS Pisa Aeroporto, or take city bus No 7, which passes through the city centre on its way to the airport. For a taxi call ☎ 54 16 00.

To get from the train station to the duomo take city bus No 1 or walk the 1.5km.

If you want to hire a bike while in Pisa, try Trattoria la Buca (see Places to Eat earlier in this section).

LIVORNO

Toscana's second-largest city, Livorno (Leghorn in English) is not worth a visit unless you are catching a ferry to Sardegna or Corsica. The city is a modern industrial

centre and was heavily bombed during WWII.

Orientation & Information

From the train station in Piazza Dante on the eastern edge of the city centre, walk west along Viale Carducci and then Via Grande into the central Piazza Grande. The main APT office (☎ 89 81 11) is at Piazza Cavour 6 (2nd floor) to the south. From Piazza Grande, continue west towards the waterfront, through Piazza Micheli, Piazza Arsenale and a smaller APT (☎ 89 53 20). A third office is near the main ferry terminal, known as Calata Carrara, near Stazione Marittima. The main office is open Monday to Friday from 9 am to 2 pm and Saturday to 1 pm. The smaller offices are open mornings and afternoons during summer only.

The main post office is at Via Cairoli 46, and the Telecom office at Largo Duomo 14 opens daily from 8 am to 9.45 pm.

For police emergency, call ☎ 113, or go to the questura (☎ 23 51 11) in the Palazzo del Governo, Piazza Unità d'Italia. The Ospedale Civile (☎ 40 11 29) is at Viale Alfieri 36, near the main train station.

The city's postcode is 57100 and the telephone code is ☎ 0586.

Things to See

The city does have a few worthy sights. The **Fortezza Nuova**, in the area known as Piccola Venezia because of its small canals, was built for the Medici in the late 16th century. Close to the waterfront is the city's other fort, the **Fortezza Vecchia**, built 60 years earlier on the site of an 11th-century building.

Livorno has two galleries of note in the east of the city: the **Museo Civico Giovanni Fattori**, Viale della Libertà 30, which features works by the 19th-century Livorno-based movement led by the artist Giovanni Fattori; and the **Museo Progressivo d'Arte Contemporanea**, also known as the Centro di Documentazione Visiva, Via Redi 22, which has a smattering of well known 20th-century works. Both galleries are open Tuesday to Sunday from 9 am to 1 pm. Admission at both is L6000. The city's unspectacular **cathedral** is just off Piazza Grande.

Places to Stay & Eat

Finding accommodation shouldn't be a problem. The *Albergo Stazione* (☎ 40 23 07), Viale Carducci 301, is near the main train station and has a range of singles/doubles costing up to L50,000/80,000 with private bath. *Albergo L'Amico Fritz* (☎ 40 11 49) is nearby at Viale Carducci 180 and is similarly priced. Near the waterfront at Scali d'Azeglio 28, *Pensione Dante* (☎ 89 34 61) has modest rooms without private bath for up to L44,000/58,000.

For produce, the market is on Via Buontalenti, and the area around Piazza XX Settembre is great for bars and cafés. *L'Angelo d'Oro*, Piazza Mazzini 15, is an inexpensive trattoria with pasta from L7000. The *Cantina Senese*, Borgo dei Cappuccini 95, is also a popular local eatery and just as inexpensive. For a quick pizza you could try *Pizzeria Umbria*, Via E Mayer 5, or there's Chinese food at the *Grande Cina*, No 9.

Getting There & Away

Bus ATL buses (☎ 88 42 62) depart from Largo Duomo for Cecina, Piombino and Pisa. Lazzi buses (☎ 89 95 62) depart from Piazza Manin for Firenze, Pisa, Lucca and Viareggio.

Train The main train station in Piazza Dante is on the Roma-La Spezia line and the city is also connected to Firenze and Pisa. Trains are less frequent to Stazione Marittima, a second station near the main port. It is usually easier to catch a train to the main train station and then a bus to the ports.

Car The A12 runs past the city and the S1 connects Livorno with Roma. There are several car parks near the waterfront.

Boat Livorno is a major west-coast port. Regular departures for Sardegna and Corsica leave from the Stazione Marittima (in an area called Calata Carrara, just north of Fortezza Vecchia). In addition, ferries also depart from a smaller terminal known as Porto Mediceo, near Piazza Arsenale, and occasionally from the Porto Nuovo. The first two can be easily reached by bus from the main train station. There third is several km north of the city along Via Sant'Orlando and not well served by public transport. Ask at the tourist office for directions.

Ferry companies operating from Livorno can be found in three locations:

Stazione Marittima
- Corsica Ferries (☎ 88 13 80), with regular services to Corsica (one-way deck-class fares to Bastia start at L38,000)
- Corsica Marittima (☎ 21 05 46), with services to Corsica (one-way deck-class fares to Bastia/Porto Vecchio start at L38,000/48,000)
- Sardinia Ferries (☎ 88 13 80), with regular services to Sardegna (one-way deck-class fares to Golfo Aranci, near Olbia, start at L42,000)
- Moby Lines (☎ 89 03 25), with services to Corsica (one-way deck-class fares to Bastia start at L36,000) and Sardegna (one-way deck-class fares to Olbia start at L42,000)

Porto Mediceo
- Toremar (☎ 89 61 13), with services to Isola di Capraia

Porto Nuovo
- Compagnia Sarda Navigazione Marittima (☎ 40 99 25), at Varco Galvani, Calata Tripoli, with ferries to Olbia (Sardegna)
- Sicil Ferry (☎ 40 98 04), at Varco Galvani, Calata Tripoli, with boats to Palermo (Sicilia)

Getting Around

To get from the train station to Piazza Arsenale and the Porto Mediceo, take ATL bus No 1. To reach the Stazione Marittima take bus No 18, and to get to the city centre take bus No 1, 2 or 8.

ISOLA D'ELBA

Made famous by Napoleon, who spent a year in exile on the island from May 1814, Elba now attracts more than one million tourists a year who come to swim in its glorious blue waters or lie on its beaches. One of the great attractions is the range of beaches: sandy, pebbly or rocky, crowded and serviced, or quiet and secluded. During August, however, the island is so crowded with tourists that even the most isolated beaches can get pretty crowded. Elba is also growing in popularity among walkers, and its mountainous terrain can provide some tough treks – although there are better places to walk in Toscana.

Just 28km long and 19km across at its widest point, Elba is well equipped for tourists, with plenty of hotels and camping grounds. The tourist hordes have only arrived in recent years, so the island is not (as yet) overdeveloped. Prior to the advent of tourism, its main industry was iron-ore mining. The main towns are Portoferraio on the north side and Marina di Campo on the south.

Orientation & Information

Most ferries arrive at Portoferraio, Elba's capital and its main transport hub. Ferries from Piombino travel less frequently to Rio Marina, Marina di Campo and Porto Azzurro. The main APT office (☎ 91 46 71) for the island is at Portoferraio, at Calata Italia 26, and can assist with accommodation information. If you plan to visit during the summer months, book well in advance. The local hotel association, the Associazione Albergatori Isola d'Elba (☎ 91 47 54), Calata Italia 20, will find you a room.

A tourist medical service operates during summer at: Portoferraio (☎ 91 42 12) at the public hospital, località San Rocco; Marina di Campo (☎ 97 60 61), Piazza Dante Alighieri 3; Rio Marina (☎ 96 24 07), Via Principe Amadeo; Marciana Marina (☎ 90 44 36), Viale Regina Margherita; and Capoliveri (☎ 96 89 95), Via Soprana.

If you're planning a walk, pick up a copy of *Trekking all'Elba*, a publication that lists walking trails and details each itinerary. For more information about walking, contact Il Genio del Bosco – Centro Trekking Isola d'Elba (☎ 93 03 35) at Portoferraio. The Comunità Montana at Viale Manzoni 4 has contour maps of the island, with paths clearly marked.

The postcode for the island is 57037, and the telephone code is ☎ 0565.

TOSCANA

Getting There & Away

Unless you have your own boat, the only way to get to Elba is by ferry from Piombino, or from Livorno via the island of Capraia. If you arrive in Piombino by train, there's a connecting train to the port. There are several companies – Toremar, Navarma and Elba Ferries – and all have offices at the ports of Piombino and Portoferraio. Unless it is the middle of August, you shouldn't have any trouble buying a ticket at the port. Prices are competitive, around L9000 per person and L40,000 for a small car. All lines offer a special deal on certain runs (indicated in timetables). The trip by ferry takes one hour. Elba Ferries has a faster catamaran, which carries cars and makes the trip in 25 minutes. Prices are from L13,000 per person and L53,000 for a small car.

Getting Around

Bus The island's bus company, ATL, runs regular services between the main towns. From Portoferraio, for instance, you can reach all of the main towns, including Marciana Marina, Marina di Campo, Capoliveri and Porto Azzurro, as well as smaller resorts and beaches such as Sant'Andrea, Cavo and Fetovaia. Ask at the tourist office for an updated timetable.

Car, Motorcycle & Bicycle The best way to get around Elba is to rent a mountain bike, scooter or motorcycle. In high season mountain bikes start at L20,000 a day and L98,000 for one week; mopeds are L35,000 a day and L147,000 per week; and Vespa scooters cost L65,000 per day and L300,000 per week. Cars are also available for rent, and there are two main companies: TWN Two Wheels Network has an office at Portoferraio (☎ 91 46 66), Viale Elba 32, and at Marciana Marina, Marina di Campo, Porto Azzurro and several other locations throughout the island. Happy Rent has an outlet at Portoferraio (☎ 91 46 65), Viale Elba 5, and at Marina di Campo and in the Capoliveri/Porto Azzurro area.

Portoferraio

Portoferraio is divided into two segments; the new section includes the port, but the old part, enclosed by a medieval wall, is much more interesting. It contains the **Villa dei Mulini**, which was one of the residences where Napoleon lived in exile. It features a splendid terraced garden and his library, and is open Monday to Saturday from 9 am to 7 pm and Sunday from 9 am to 1 pm. Admission is L8000.

The ticket also allows you admission to the **Villa Napoleonica di San Martino**, Napoleon's summer residence, set in hills about 5km south-west of the town. The villa houses a modest collection of Napoleonic paraphernalia and also hosts an annual exhibition based on a Napoleonic theme. The villa is open the same hours as the museum.

Places to Stay & Eat The closest camping grounds are about 4km west of town in Acquaviva. *Campeggio La Sorgente* (☎ 91 71 39) and *Acquaviva* (☎ 91 55 92) are easily found. The *Ape Elbana* (☎ 91 42 45), Salita de' Medici 2, in the old town, has singles/doubles with bathroom for up to L80,000/110,000. The *Villa Ombrosa* (☎ 91 43 63), Via De Gasperi 3, has singles/doubles with bathroom for L120,000/150,000.

The *Ristorante Villa Ombrosa* on Viale de' Gasperi serves Tuscan dishes and a full meal will cost around L40,000. Try the *Osteria Libertaria* at the port, on Calata Matteotti near the Torre della Lingua. It offers reasonably priced meals and you can sit outside with a view of the port, or in an internal courtyard garden.

Marciana Marina

About 15km west of Portoferraio, Marciana Marina is slightly less popular with tourists and is fronted by some pleasant pebble beaches. This town is also a perfect base for walking in the island's western region, where many of the best walking tracks are to be found. The inland villages of Marciana and Poggio are easily visited. From Marciana you can take the cable car to the summit of

Monte Capanne, from where you can see across Elba and as far as Corsica to the west.

In Marciana Marina, the *Albergo Villa Maria* (☎ 9 90 20), Piazza Sanzio, has rooms from L65,000/100,000. Farther west along the coast is the small resort town of **Sant'Andrea**, which remains unspoiled by the tourist hordes. It has a small sandy beach from where you can walk along the coast over rock formations, taking a swim if you get hot. Try the *Bellavista* (☎ 90 80 15), which has singles/doubles with bathroom from L75,000/100,000.

Marina di Campo

Elba's second-largest town, Marina di Campo, is on Campo Bay on the island's southern side. The beaches are among Elba's best and most crowded. Many camping grounds are located around the town and along the coastline, which means you shouldn't have too much trouble finding a site, except in the middle of summer. The *Albergo Thomas* (☎ 97 77 32), Viale degli Etruschi, is one of the cheapest hotels here and has doubles from L100,000. The *Elba* (☎ 97 62 24), Via Mascagni, has singles/doubles for L62,000/105,000. There are many cheap eateries close to the beach, including a couple of decent self-service restaurants.

Porto Azzurro & Capoliveri

Dominated by its fort, built in 1603 by Philip III of Spain and now a prison, Porto Azzurro is a pleasant resort town, close to some excellent beaches. *Albergo Villa Italia* (☎ 9 51 19), Viale Italia, has doubles from L85,000. For a good meal, try the *Ristorante Delfino Verde*, on the waterfront; a meal will cost around L40,000. From Porto Azzurro, take a short trip south to Capoliveri, certainly the island's most picturesque spot. Nearby are some great beaches: Barabarca, accessible only by a steep track which winds down a cliff, and Zuccale, more easily accessible and perfect for families. The beach of Naregno is a pleasant spot, if your scene is a hotel literally on the beachfront.

Central & Southern Toscana

CHIANTI

The beautiful hill country between Firenze and Siena forms the area known as Chianti. The Monti del Chianti, which rise into the Appennini, form Chianti's eastern boundary and comprise some of Toscana's loveliest countryside. Chianti is divided between the provinces of Firenze and Siena, into the areas known as Chianti Fiorentina and Chianti Senese. The area is famous for its internationally known wines, particularly the Chianti Classico, a blend of white and red grapes, recognisable by the Gallo Nero (Black Cockerel) symbol.

The Chianti landscape is stunning: a patchwork of forests, olive groves and vineyards, dotted with an extraordinary number of castles built by ancient Florentine and Sienese war lords, the Romanesque churches known as *pieve* and restored villas. The area has attracted many foreigners, who now call the Chianti home.

It is possible to catch buses around the Chianti countryside, but the best way to explore the area is by car. However, you might also like to do it by bicycle, or even on foot. You could take a few days to travel along the state road SS222, known as the Strada Chiantigiana, which runs between Firenze and Siena.

Budget accommodation is not the area's strong point, and you'll need to book well ahead, since it is a popular area for tourists year-round. However, if you have some extra funds and you're in search of a romantic spot, you shouldn't go past Chianti.

Getting information about the area is easy. Virtually every tourist office in Toscana has good information, but the best is at Radda in Chianti. The tourist office there also has a web site (see under Radda in Chianti in this section).

Chianti Fiorentino

About 20km south of Firenze on the

Chiantigiana is **Greve in Chianti**, the first good base for exploring the area. You can get there easily from Firenze on a SITA bus. The unusual triangular square, Piazza Matteotti, is the old centre of the town. An interesting provincial version of a Florentine piazza, it is surrounded by porticoes.

There is a tourist information office (☎ 055-854 52 43) at Via L Cini 1, 500m east of the piazza, open in summer from 10 am to 1 pm and 4 to 7 pm. They can provide maps and information in several languages, including English. If you're looking for a place to stay, try *Giovanni da Verrazzano* (☎ 055-85 31 89), Piazza Matteotti 28, with singles/doubles for L110,000/130,000. The *Del Chianti* (☎ 055-85 37 63), at No 86, is less interesting and charges L160,000/180,000.

Montefioralle is an ancient castle-village, only 2km west of Greve. It's worth the walk, particularly to see its church of Santo Stefano, which contains precious medieval paintings. From Montefioralle, follow the dirt road for a few hundred metres, then turn off to the right to reach the simple **Pieve di San Cresci**. From here you can descend directly to Greve.

Nearby, in a magnificent setting of olive groves and vineyards, is the evocative **Badia di Passignano**, founded in 1049 by Benedictine monks of the Vallombrosan order. The abbey is a massive towered castle encircled by cypresses.

The abbey church of San Michele has early 17th-century frescoes by the artist known as Passignano (so called because he was born here). In the refectory there's a *Last Supper* painted by Domenico and Davide Ghirlandaio in 1476. Take a look at the huge medieval chimney in the kitchen. It is possible to visit the abbey (☎ 055-807 16 22) on Saturday and Sunday from 3 to 5 pm, but you can try to persuade the monks to let you in at other times.

Food and drinks are available in the tiny village surrounding the abbey.

Travelling south along the Chiantigiana you will pass the medieval village of Panzano; after about 1km, you'll reach the Chiesa di San Leolino at the **Pieve di Panzano**. Built in the 10th century, it was rebuilt in Romanesque style in the 13th century and a portico was added in the 16th century. Inside, there is a painted table and a 14th-century triptych.

Chianti Senese

Castellina in Chianti is one of the best organised towns for tourists, with lots of hotels and restaurants. Its tourist information office (☎ 0577-74 02 01) is at the central Piazza del Comune 1.

You might prefer to head east to **Radda in Chianti**, which has retained much of its charm despite the tourist influx. It is also handy to many of Chianti's most beautiful spots. The excellent information office (☎ 0577-73 84 94) at Piazza Ferrucci 1 has an enthusiastic and very helpful staff; ask for Gioia Milani. They have loads of information about places to stay and eat in Chianti, as well as things to see and do, including suggestions for independent walking tours or organised tours to local wineries, where you can try the local wines before enjoying a traditional lunch. The tourist office has a site on the web at www.chianti.net.it and staff@chiantinet.it is their email address.

One of the cheapest forms of accommodation is a room in a private house. *Da Giovannino* (☎ 0577-73 80 56), Via Roma 6-8, is a real family house in the centre of Radda. You'll pay L50,000/80,000 for a single/double. The Radda tourist office can provide details about the apartments and the numerous farms and wineries offering accommodation. Prices start at around L100,000 a double.

Getting Around

Buses connect Firenze and Siena, passing

through Castellina and Radda, as well as other small towns.

SAN GIMIGNANO

From a distance, the towers of San Gimignano dominate the Val d'Elsa, a lush landscape of wheat fields, olive groves and vineyards. The towers, symbols of the power and wealth of the city's medieval families, once numbered as many as 72. Today, only 13 remain, but the city still carries the name San Gimignano delle Belle Torri (of the Fine Towers).

Originally an Etruscan village, the town later took its name from the Bishop of Modena, St Gimignano, who is said to have saved the city from the barbarians. It became a comune in 1199, but fought frequently with neighbouring Volterra and the internal battles between the Ardinghelli family (Guelph) and the Salvucci family (Ghibelline) over the next two centuries caused deep divisions. Most towers were built during this period as status symbols, the height depending on the family's wealth and power; although in the 13th century one particular podestà introduced a law which prohibited the building of towers higher than his (51 m).

In 1348, the plague decimated the town's population and weakened the power of its nobles, leading to the town's submission to Firenze in 1353. Today, San Gimignano is one of Europe's best-preserved medieval cities and has the feel of a museum. In summer and at weekends year-round it is crowded with tourists.

Orientation

The manicured gardens of Piazzale dei Martiri di Montemaggio, at the southern end of the town, are outside the medieval wall and next to the main gate, the Porta San Giovanni. From the gate, Via San Giovanni heads north until it meets Piazza della Cisterna and the connecting Piazza del Duomo, in the city centre. The other major thoroughfare, Via San Matteo, leaves Piazza del Duomo for the main northern gate, Porta San Matteo. The walled city is small and dominated by the cathedral, also known as th Collegiata, in Piazza del Duomo.

Information

Tourist Office The Associazione Pro Loc (☎ 94 00 08) is at Piazza del Duomo 1, o the left as you approach the cathedral. It i open daily from 9 am to 1 pm and 3 to 7 pr (closing at 6 pm in winter). The office has web site at: www.web.tin.it/sangimignano.

Post & Communications The post office i in Piazza delle Erbe 8, on the north side c the cathedral. Poste restante mail can b addressed to 53037 San Gimignano.

A Telecom office is at Via San Matteo 1 and is open 24 hours a day. There are als public phones at the tourist office.

The telephone code for San Gimignano i ☎ 0577.

Medical Services For medical assistance call the Confraternita della Misericordi (☎ 94 03 67), Via San Matteo. The Farmaci Comunale is in Piazza della Cisterna, or cal ☎ 95 50 80 for the night chemist.

Emergency For police attendance, cal ☎ 113. The carabinieri office (☎ 94 03 13) i behind the bus stop in Piazzale dei Martiri d Montemaggio.

Things to See & Do

Before you set out, buy the L16,000 ticke from the ticket offices of any of the city's sights which allows admission into most o San Gimignano's museums.

Start in the triangular Piazza della Cisterna, named after the 13th century cistern i its centre. The piazza is lined with houses anc towers dating from the 13th and 14th centuries. Adjoining it to the north is Piazza de Duomo, dominated by the duomo, anc facing it the late 13th-century **Palazzo de Podestà** and its tower, known as the **Torre della Rognosa**. To the left of the duomo is the Palazzo del Popolo, still operating as the town's town hall.

The Collegiata Up a flight of steps from the

piazza is the town's Romanesque cathedral, its simple façade belying the remarkable frescoes which cover the walls of its interior. There are five main cycles. On the left wall as you enter are scenes from the Old Testament by Bartolo di Fredi, dating from around 1367. On the right wall are scenes from the New Testament by Barna da Siena, completed in 1381. On the inside wall of the façade, as well as an adjoining wall, is a gruesome depiction of the Last Judgment by Taddeo di Bartolo (1393). It is fascinating to think of the impact the images of punishment for the seven deadly sins must have had on the pious of the 14th century. In the **Cappella di Santa Fina** are beautiful frescoes by Domenico Ghirlandaio depicting events in the life of the saint. Without the L16,000 general ticket, it costs L3000 to enter the chapel.

The cathedral and chapel are open daily from 9.30 am to 12.30 pm and 3 to 5.30 pm, but tourists cannot enter during mass times.

Palazzo del Popolo From the internal courtyard, climb the stairs to the **Museo Civico**, which features paintings from the Sienese and Florentine schools of the 12th to 15th century. Dante addressed the locals in 1299 in the Sala del Consiglio, urging them to support the Guelph cause. The room contains an early 14th-century fresco of the *Maestà*, by Lippo Memmi. Climb the palazzo's **Torre Grossa** for a spectacular view of the town and surrounding countryside.

The palace, tower and museum are open daily from 9.30 am to 7.30 pm in summer, with shorter hours during the rest of the year.

Other Sights The **Rocca**, a short walk to the west of Piazza del Duomo, is the atmospheric ruin of the town's fortress and there are great views across the valley.

At the northern end of the town is the **Chiesa di Sant'Agostino**, whose main attraction is the fresco cycle by Benozzo Gozzoli in the apse, depicting the life of St Augustine.

Places to Stay

San Gimignano has only a handful of hotels with eye-popping prices. However, the hostel and a camping ground come to the rescue. There are also numerous *affittacamere* (rooms for rent) at reasonable prices. The tourist office will provide details, but will not make bookings. The well organised Cooperativa Hotels Promotion (☎ 94 08 09), Via San Giovanni, just inside the gate of the same name, can place you in a hotel in the city. It will make arrangements months in advance and charges a L3000 fee.

The camping ground, *Il Boschetto di Piemma* (☎ 94 03 52), is at Santa Lucia, a couple of km south of the Porta San Giovanni, and is open from Easter to 15 October. Buses leave from Piazzale dei Martiri di Montemaggio. The non-HI *Ostello della Gioventù* (☎ 94 19 91), Via delle Fonti 1, is at the northern edge of town inside the wall. B&B is L22,000.

The hotel *Locanda Il Pino* (☎ 94 04 15), Via San Matteo 102, has doubles for L85,000 with bathroom. *Hotel La Cisterna* (☎ 94 03 28), in the magnificent Piazza della Cisterna, has singles/doubles from L80,000/125,000. Ask for a room in the medieval section, with a view across the valley.

Places to Eat

A produce market is held on Thursday mornings in Piazza della Cisterna and Piazza della Duomo. Try the wines at *Il Castello*, Via del Castello 20, a wine bar and restaurant which stays open until midnight; pasta starts at L5000. For sandwiches and snacks try *Antica Taverna*; just follow the signs from Via San Matteo.

Pizzeria Pizzoteca, Via dei Fossi, outside the walls to the left of Porta San Matteo, is one of the cheapest in town. The pizzas are fine, but the pasta can leave a lot to be desired. *La Stella*, Via San Matteo 77, has reasonable food, although they tend to exploit the tourists by providing small serves. A meal could cost L25,000. *Trattoria La Mangiatoia*, Via Mainardi 5, is one of the city's better restaurants, with pasta from about L9000.

At the other end of town is *Trattoria Chiribiri*, Piazzetta della Madonna 1, with pastas for around L8000. Nearby is *Pizza a Taglio*, with pizza by the slice.

Ice Festival, Via San Giovanni 113, and *Gelateria di Piazza*, Piazza della Cisterna 4, are great; the latter turns the local wine, Vernaccia, into a delicious ice cream.

Getting There & Around

San Gimignano is accessible from Firenze and Siena by regular buses, but you need to change at Poggibonsi. For Roma and areas such as Perugia and Assisi, you need to get to Siena and catch a bus from there. There's also a bus to Volterra. Bus timetables are posted on a pillar to the left as you face the Pro Loco office. Buses arrive in Piazzale dei Martiri di Montemaggio at the Porta San Giovanni. The closest train station is in Poggibonsi.

To reach San Gimignano by car, take the S68 from Colle di Val d'Elsa, which is on the S2 between Firenze and Siena, and follow the signs. The city is small and easily seen on foot. Signs direct you to large car parks outside the Porta San Giovanni.

TOSCANA

VOLTERRA

The Etruscan settlement of Velathri was an important trading centre, a status that continued under the Romans, who renamed the city Volaterrae. A long period of conflict with Firenze started in the 12th century and ended when the Medici took possession of the city in the 15th century.

Perched on top of a huge rocky plateau, Volterra looks almost forbidding because of its well preserved medieval ramparts. The city has long had a strong alabaster industry.

Orientation & Information

If you arrive by car, head for the main car park in Piazza Martiri della Libertà, on the south side of the city, where all buses arrive. From here it is only a short walk to the central Piazza dei Priori.

There is a small tourist office (☎ 8 61 50) at Via Turazza 2, which offers only an incomplete hotel list and little information about the town. The post office and Telecom office are on the northern side of Piazza dei Priori. For emergencies, call ☎ 113. The questura is in the Palazzo Pretorio in Piazza dei Priori.

The city's postcode is 56048, and the telephone code is 0588.

Piazza dei Priori

The Piazza dei Priori is recognised as one of Italy's finest medieval squares and is surrounded by austere palaces. The 13th-century **Palazzo dei Priori** is the oldest communal palace in Toscana and is believed to have been a model for Firenze's Palazzo Vecchio. The **Palazzo Pretorio**, also dating from the 13th century, is dominated by the Piglet's Tower, so named because of the wild boar sculpted on its upper section.

Behind the Palazzo dei Priori, along Via Turazza, is the **duomo**, built in the 12th and 13th centuries. Inside, highlights include a small fresco by Benozzo Gozzoli, the *Adoration of the Magi*, behind a nativity group in the oratory at the beginning of the left aisle. The 15th-century tabernacle on the high altar is by Mino da Fiesole. The 13th-century **baptistry** features a font by Andrea Sansovino. There is an interesting small collection of local art in the **Pinacoteca Comunale** in the Palazzo Minucci Solaini, Via dei Sarti 1. The Pinacoteca Comunale is open Tuesday to Sunday from 9.30 am to 6.30 pm, with slightly shorter hours during the winter months.

A special L10,000 ticket covers visits to this museum, as well as the Museo Etrusco Guarnacci, the Roman theatre and the Acropoli/Necropoli area in the Parco Archeologico.

The Museo dell'Opera del Duomo is located next to the duomo.

Museo Etrusco Guarnacci

All the exhibits in this fascinating Etruscan museum were unearthed locally, including a vast collection of some 600 funerary urns carved from alabaster, tufo and other materials. The urns are displayed according to the subjects depicted on their bas-reliefs and the period from which they date. It probably

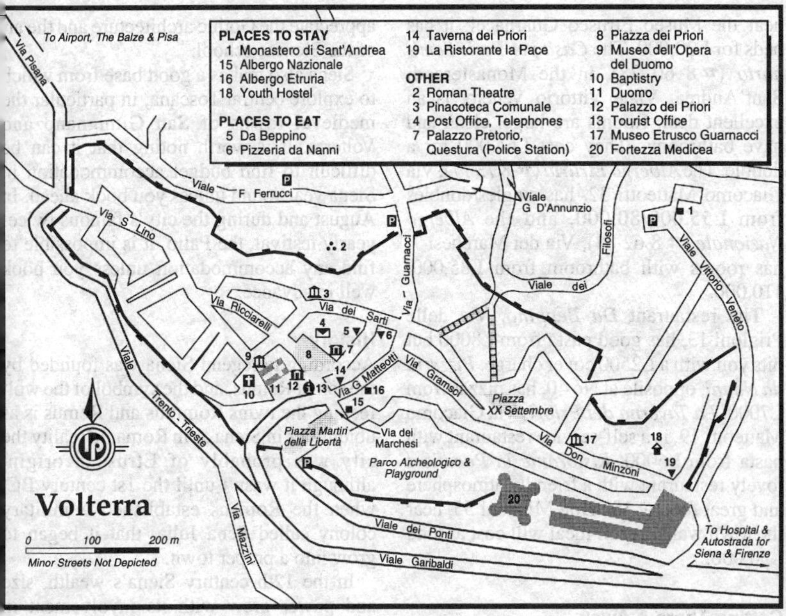

pays to be a bit choosy about which rooms to linger in, because one starts to merge into another after a while. Basically they get better as you go higher, with the best examples – those dating from later periods – on the 2nd and 3rd floors. The museum also houses two famous Etruscan relics: the **Ombra della Sera**, a strange, elongated nude figure, which would fit in well in any museum of modern art; and the urn of the **Sposi**, featuring an elderly couple, their faces depicted in portrait fashion rather than the stylised method usually employed.

The museum is open Tuesday to Sunday from 9.30 am to 1 pm and 3 to 6.30 pm in summer and from 10 am to 4 pm in winter. Admission is L8000.

Fortezza Medicea & Parco Archeologico

Farther along Via Minzoni is the entrance to the Fortezza Medicea, built in the 14th century and altered by Lorenzo the Magnificent, and now used as a prison.

Near the fort is the pleasant Parco Archeologico, whose archaeological remains have suffered with the passage of time. Little has survived, but it's a good place for a picnic. If you have small children, you can bring them here to play on the swings.

Other Sights

On the city's northern edge is a **Roman theatre**, a well preserved complex which includes a Roman bath.

The **Balze**, a deep ravine created by erosion, about a 20-minute walk north-west of the city centre, has claimed several churches since the Middle Ages, the buildings having fallen into its deep gullies. A 14th-century monastery is perched close to the precipice and is in danger of toppling into the ravine.

Places to Stay & Eat

The best deal is at the non-HI *Ostello della Gioventù* (☎ 8 55 77), Via Don Minzoni, near the Museo Etrusco Guarnacci; it has beds for L20,000. The *Casa per Ferie Seminario* (☎ 8 60 28), in the Monastero di Sant'Andrea, Viale Vittorio Veneto, is an excellent deal. Rooms are large, clean and have bathrooms. They cost L64,000 for a double. The *Albergo Etruria* (☎ 8 73 77), Via Giacomo Matteotti 32, has singles/doubles from L55,000/80,000, and the *Albergo Nazionale* (☎ 8 62 84), Via dei Marchesi 7, has rooms with bathroom from L85,000/110,000.

The restaurant *Da Beppino*, Via delle Prigioni 13, has good pasta from L8000 but hits you with a L2500 cover charge. *Pizzeria da Nanni*, opposite at No 40, has pizzas from L7000. *La Taverna dei Priori*, Via Giacomo Matteotti 19, is a self-service restaurant with pasta from L6000. *Ristorante la Pace* is a lovely restaurant with a friendly atmosphere and great food at Via Don Minzoni 55, near the town walls. A full meal will cost around L30,000.

Getting There & Away

Buses connect the city with Pisa, Siena, Firenze, Cecina and San Gimignano from Piazza Martiri della Libertà. For Siena and Firenze you need to change at Colle Val d'Elsa. There is a small train station in the nearby town of Saline, 9km to the south-west, which is connected to Volterra by bus. Trains run to Cecina, where you can catch trains on the main Roma-Pisa line. By car, take the S68 which runs between Cecina and Colle di Val d'Elsa.

SIENA

Siena is without doubt one of Italy's most enchanting cities. Its medieval centre is bristling with majestic Gothic buildings, such as the Palazzo Pubblico in the campo, Siena's main square, and a wealth of artworks is contained in its numerous churches and small museums. Like Firenze, Siena offers an incredible concentration of things to see, which simply can't be appreciated in a day trip. Try to plan at least an overnight stay, or better still allow yourself a few days to appreciate the Gothic architecture and the art of the Sienese school.

Siena also makes a good base from which to explore central Toscana, in particular the medieval towns of San Gimignano and Volterra. It is worth noting that it can be difficult to find budget accommodation in Siena year-round unless you book ahead. In August and during the city's famous twice-yearly festival, the Palio, it is impossible to find any accommodation unless you book well in advance.

History

According to legend Siena was founded by the son of Remus, and the symbol of the wolf feeding the twins Romulus and Remus is as ubiquitous in Siena as in Roma. In reality the city was probably of Etruscan origin, although it wasn't until the 1st century BC, when the Romans established a military colony called Sena Julia, that it began to grow into a proper town.

In the 12th century Siena's wealth, size and power grew with its involvement in commerce, banking and trade in European markets. Consequently, its rivalry with neighbouring Firenze also grew and led to numerous wars during the first half of the 13th century between Guelph Firenze and Ghibelline Siena. The conflict culminated in the victory of Siena over Firenze at the Battle of Montaperti in 1260. But it was a short-lived victory – only 10 years later the Tuscan Ghibellines were defeated by Charles of Anjou and for almost a century Siena was allied to Firenze, the chief town of the Tuscan Guelph League (supporters of the pope).

During this period Siena reached its peak under the rule of the Council of Nine, a group dominated by the middle class. Many of the fine buildings in the Sienese Gothic style, which give the city its striking appearance, were constructed under the direction of the Council of Nine, including the cathedral, the Palazzo Pubblico and the campo. The Sienese school of painting had its beginnings at this time with Guido da Siena and reached its peak in the early 14th century with the works of artists including Duccio di Buoninsegna, Simone Martini and Pietro and Ambrogio Lorenzetti.

A plague outbreak in 1348 killed 65,000 of the city's 100,000 people and led to a period of decline for Siena. The plague also put an end to an ambitious plan to dramatically enlarge the cathedral. At the end of the 14th century, Siena came under the control of Milano's Visconti family and in the 15th century was ruled by the autocratic patrician Pandolfo Petrucci, a period marked by a revival of the city's waning fortunes. Holy Roman Emperor Charles V conquered Siena in 1555 after a two-year siege that left thousands dead. Consequently, the city was handed over to Cosimo de' Medici, who barred the inhabitants from operating banks and thus curtailed Siena's power for good.

Siena was home to St Catherine, one of Italy's most famous saints. Today, the city relies heavily on tourism and on the success of its Monte dei Paschi di Siena bank, founded in 1472 and now one of the city's largest employers.

Orientation

Historic Siena, still largely surrounded by its

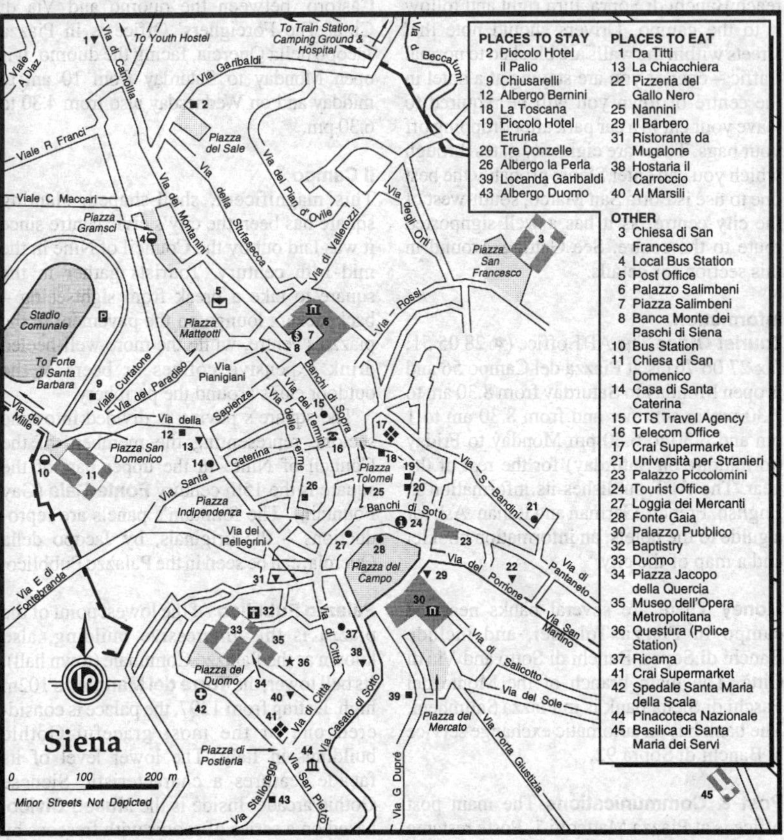

TOSCANA

medieval walls, is small and easily tackled by tourists on foot, even though the way in which streets swirl around the campo in semi-circles will confuse you for much of your stay. The fabulous Piazza del Campo is the city's heart and the main streets are the Banchi di Sopra, Via di Città and Banchi di Sotto. By bus you will arrive at Piazza San Domenico, which affords a panoramic view of the city. Walk east along Via della Sapienza and turn right into Banchi di Sopra to reach the campo.

From the train station you will need to catch a bus to Piazza Matteotti. Walk south-east out of the piazza on Via Pianigiani to reach Banchi di Sopra, turn right and follow it to the campo. Drivers should note that streets within the walls are blocked to normal traffic – even if you are staying at a hotel in the centre of town you will be required to leave your car in a car park after dropping off your bags. There are eight city gates through which you can enter Siena; probably the best one to use is Porta San Marco, south-west of the city centre, as it has a well signposted route to the centre. See Getting Around in this section for details.

Information

Tourist Office The APT office (☎ 28 05 51; fax 27 06 76) is at Piazza del Campo 56 and is open Monday to Saturday from 8.30 am to 7.30 pm in summer and from 8.30 am to 1 pm and 3.30 to 6.30 pm Monday to Friday (to midday on Saturday) for the rest of the year. The APT publishes its information in English, French, German and Italian. Ask for a guide to the hotels, an information booklet and a map of the city.

Money There are several banks near the campo in Piazza Tolomei, and include Banchi di Sopra, Banchi di Sotto and Via di Città. The main branch of the Monte dei Paschi di Siena bank is in Piazza Salimbeni. The bank has an automatic exchange service at Banchi di Sopra 92.

Post & Communications The main post office is at Piazza Matteotti 1. Poste restante mail can be addressed to 53100 Siena. The Telecom office is at Via dei Termini 40.

Siena's telephone code is ☎ 0577.

Laundry At the self-service laundry Onda Blu, Via del Casato di Sotto 17, you can wash and dry 6.5 kilos for L6000.

Medical Services For an ambulance call ☎ 28 00 28. The public hospital (☎ 29 08 07) is in Viale Bracci, just north of Siena at Le Scotte.

Emergency For the police, call ☎ 113. The questura (open 24 hours a day) is at Via del Castoro, between the duomo and Via di Città. The Foreigners' Office is in Piazza Jacopo della Quercia, facing the duomo. It is open Monday to Saturday from 10 am to midday and on Wednesday also from 4.30 to 6.30 pm.

Il Campo

This magnificent, shell-shaped, slanting square has been the city's civic centre since it was laid out by the Council of Nine in the mid-14th century. Tourists gather in the square to take a break from sightseeing – backpackers lounge on the pavement in the piazza's centre, while the more well-heeled drink expensive coffees or beers at the outdoor cafés around the periphery.

The square's paving is divided into nine sectors, representing the members of the Council of Nine. In the upper part of the square is the 15th century **Fonte Gaia** (Gay Fountain). The fountain's panels are reproductions – the originals, by Jacopo della Quercia, can be seen in the Palazzo Pubblico.

Palazzo Pubblico At the lowest point of the piazza is this impressive building, also known as the Palazzo Comunale (town hall). Its bell tower, the **Torre del Mangia**, is 102m high. Dating from 1297, the palace is considered one of the most graceful Gothic buildings in Italy. The lower level of its façade features a characteristic Sienese Gothic arcade. Inside is the **Museo Civico**, based on a series of rooms with frescoes by artists of the Sienese school. Of particular note is Simone Martini's famous *Maestà* in the Sala del Mappamondo. Completed and signed in 1315, it features the Madonna beneath a canopy, surrounded by saints and angels. It is one of the most important works of the Sienese school. In the Sala dei Nove is Ambrogio Lorenzetti's fresco series depicting *Allegories of Good and Bad Government*, which are among the most significant to survive from the Middle Ages. There is also a chapel with frescoes by Taddeo di Bartolo.

The opening hours for the Palazzo Pubblico and museum vary throughout the year: in July and August they open from 9 am to 7.30 pm Monday to Saturday and from 9 am to 1.30 pm on Sunday. At other times of the year they close as early as 6 pm. Admission is L6000, or L3000 for students. Climb to the top of the bell tower for a spectacular view (admission L5000). Opening hours for the tower also vary during the year but are roughly 10 am to 6 pm in summer and 10 am to 1 pm in winter.

Duomo

Although it has some Romanesque elements, the duomo is one of Italy's great Gothic churches. And it is certainly one of the most enchanting buildings in Italy. Begun in 1196, it was largely completed by 1215, although work continued on features such as the apse and dome well into the 13th century. Work then began on changing, enlarging and embellishing the structure. The magnificent façade of white, green and red polychrome marble was begun by Giovanni Pisano, who completed only the lower section, and was finished towards the end of the 14th century. The mosaics in the gables were added in the 19th century. The statues of philosophers and prophets by Giovanni Pisano above the lower section are copies, the originals being preserved in the adjacent Museo dell'Opera Metropolitana.

In 1339, the city's leaders launched a plan to enlarge the cathedral and create one of Italy's largest churches. Known as the New Cathedral, the remains of this unrealised project can be seen in Piazza Jacopo della Quercia, on the eastern side of the duomo. The plan was to build an immense new nave and the present church would have become the new transept. As it turned out, the plague of 1348 also put a stop to this ambitious plan, as the city's population was decimated.

The duomo's interior is incredibly rich with artworks and warrants an hour or more of your time. Its most precious feature is the inlaid-marble floor, decorated with 56 panels depicting historical and biblical subjects. The earliest panels are the graffiti designs in simple black and white marble, dating from the mid-14th century. The latest panels were completed in the 16th century. Many are roped off, while the most valuable are kept covered and revealed to the public only from 7 to 22 August annually.

The beautiful pulpit was carved in marble and porphyry by Nicola Pisano. Other artworks include a bronze statue of St John the Baptist by Donatello, in the north transept.

Through a door from the north aisle is another of the duomo's great treasures, the **Libreria Piccolomini**, which Pope Pius III (pope during 1503) built to house the books of his uncle, Enea Silvio Piccolomini, who was Pope Pius II. The walls of the small hall are covered by an impressive series of frescoes by Bernardino Pinturicchio, depicting events in the life of Piccolomini. In the centre of the hall is a group of statues known as the *Three Graces*, a 3rd century AD Roman copy of an earlier Hellenistic work. From mid-March to the end of October, the libreria is open from 9 am to 7.30 pm; at other times of the year it opens from 10 am to 1 pm and 2.30 to 5 pm. Admission is L2000.

Museo dell'Opera Metropolitana

This museum is next to the duomo, in what would have been the south aisle of the nave of the new cathedral. Its great artworks formerly adorned the duomo, including the 12 statues of prophets and philosophers by Giovanni Pisano which decorated the façade. However, the museum's main draw card is Duccio di Buoninsegna's striking early 14th-century *Maestà*, painted on both sides as a screen for the duomo's high altar. The front and back have now been separated and the panels depicting the Story of the Passion hang opposite the Maestà. It is interesting to compare Buoninsegna's work with Martini's slightly later *Maestà* in the Palazzo Pubblico. Other artists represented in the museum are Ambrogio Lorenzetti, Simone Martini and Taddeo di Bartolo. The collection also includes tapestries and manuscripts. The museum is open daily from 16 March to 30 September from 9 am to 7.30 pm, in October until 6 pm and for the rest of the year until 1.30 pm. Admission is L6000.

Battistero di San Giovanni

Behind the duomo and down a flight of stairs is the Battistero di San Giovanni. Its Gothic façade is unfinished, but its interior is heavily decorated with frescoes. The real attraction is a marble font by Jacopo della Quercia, decorated with bronze panels in relief depicting the life of St John the Baptist by artists including Lorenzo Ghiberti *(Baptism of Christ* and *St John in Prison)* and Donatello *(Herod's Feast)*. The baptistry has the same opening hours as the Museo dell'Opera Metropolitana, except that during the winter months it also opens from 2.30 to 5 pm. Admission is L3000.

Spedale Santa Maria della Scala

Located on the south-west side of Piazza del Duomo, this former pilgrims' hospital has frescoes by Domenico di Bartolo in the main ward. The building also houses the **Museo Archeologico**, which has an impressive collection of Roman and Etruscan remains. The Spedale is open from 10 am to 6.30 pm in summer, with reduced hours during the rest of the year. Admission is L5000. The museum opens Monday to Saturday from 9 am to 2 pm and Sunday from 9 am to 1 pm, and is closed the second and fourth Sunday of the month. Admission is L4000.

Pinacoteca Nazionale

Located in the 15th-century Palazzo Buonsignori, a short walk south of the duomo at Via San Pietro 29, this gallery houses numerous masterpieces by Sienese artists. Look for Duccio di Buoninsegna's *Madonna dei Francescani*, the *Madonna col Bambino* by Simone Martini and a series of Madonnas by Ambrogio Lorenzetti. The gallery is open Tuesday to Saturday from 9 am to 7 pm, Sunday from 8 am to 1 pm and Monday from 8.30 am to 1.30 pm. Admission is L8000.

Chiesa di San Domenico

This imposing Gothic church was started in the early 13th century, but has been much altered over the centuries. It is famous for its association with St Catherine of Siena, who took her vows in its Cappella delle Volte. In the chapel is a portrait of the saint painted during her lifetime. In the **Cappella di Santa Caterina**, on the south side of the church, are frescoes by Sodoma depicting events in the saint's life. St Catherine died in Roma and her body is preserved there in the Chiesa di Santa Maria Sopra Minerva. In line with the bizarre practice of collecting relics of dead saints, her head was given back to Siena. It is contained in a tabernacle on the altar of the Cappella di Santa Caterina.

The **Casa di Santa Caterina**, the house where St Catherine was born, is on Costa di Sant'Antonio, off Via della Sapienza. The rooms of the house were converted into small chapels in the 15th century and are decorated with frescoes and paintings by Sienese artists, including Sodoma. The house is open daily from 9 am to 12.30 pm and 3.30 to 6 pm. Admission is free.

Other Churches & Palaces

From the Loggia dei Mercanti north of the campo, take Banchi di Sotto to the east for the **Palazzo Piccolomini**, regarded as the city's finest Renaissance palace. The building houses the city's archives and a small museum which is open Monday to Saturday from 9 am to 1 pm. Admission is free. Farther east are the 13th-century **Basilica di Santa Maria dei Servi**, with a fresco by Pietro Lorenzetti, and the 14th-century **Porta Romana**.

Return to the Loggia dei Mercanti and

head north along Banchi di Sopra and past Piazza Tolomei, dominated by the 13th-century **Palazzo Tolomei**. Farther along there's the Piazza Salimbeni, featuring the **Palazzo Tantucci** to the north, the Gothic **Palazzo Salimbeni** to the east, the head office of the Monte dei Paschi di Siena bank and the Renaissance **Palazzo Spannocchi**. North-east of here, along Via Rossi, is the **Chiesa di San Francesco**.

West along Via del Paradiso is Piazza San Domenico, from where you can see the massive **Forte di Santa Barbara**, built for Cosimo de' Medici.

Courses

Language Siena's Università per Stranieri (University for Foreigners; ☎ 39-577-24 01 11, fax 39-577-28 31 63, email unistra4@unisi.it) is in Piazzetta Grassi 2, 53100 Siena. The school is open all year and the only requirement for enrolment is a high-school graduation/pass certificate. (The four-week summer courses have no prerequisites.) There are several areas of study and courses cost L725,000 for 10 weeks. Brochures can be obtained by making a request to the secretary of the university, or from the Italian Cultural Institute in your city.

Non-EU students are usually required to obtain a study visa in their own country; it is important to check with an Italian consulate in your country. See the Facts for the Visitor chapter for more details.

Music The Accademia Musicale Chigiana (☎ 4 61 52), Via di Città 89, offers classical music classes every summer, as well as seminars and concerts performed by visiting musicians, teachers and students as part of the Settimana Musicale Senese. Classes are offered for most classical instruments and range from L227,000 to L1,000,000. Enrolments must be completed by 4 April.

The Associazione Siena Jazz (☎ 27 14 01), Strada di Santa Regina 6, offers courses in jazz which start at L380,000; it's one of Europe's foremost institutions of its type.

Organised Tour

The *Treno Natura* is a great way to see the stunning scenery of the Crete Senese, south of Siena. The train line extends in a ring from Siena, through Asciano, across to the Orcia Valley and the Monte Antico station, before heading back towards Siena. The line, which opened in the early 1800s, was closed in 1994 and trains now run exclusively for tourists. Trains run on only Sunday during May, June, September and the first half of October. There are usually three per day, stopping at Asciano and Monte Antico, and there are coinciding trains from Firenze. Tickets cost L18,000. Check at the Siena APT or at Siena's train station for precise details.

Special Events

The Accademia Musicale Chigiana holds the Settimana Musicale Senese each July, as well as the Estate Musicale Chigiana in July, August and September. Concerts in these series are frequently held at the Abbazia di San Galgano (a former abbey about 20km south-west of the city and regarded as one of Italy's finest Gothic buildings) and at Sant'Antimo, near Montalcino. Concerts are also held throughout the year. For information, call ☎ 4 61 52. See also the Abbazia di San Galgano section in this chapter.

The city hosts Siena Jazz, an international festival each July and August, with concerts at the Fortezza Medici, as well as various sites throughout the city. For information, call ☎ 27 14 01.

Places to Stay

Siena offers a good range of accommodation, but budget hotels generally fill quickly, so it is advisable year-round to book in advance if you want to pay less than L100,000 a double. Forget about finding a room during the Palio unless you have a booking. For assistance in finding a room, contact the APT (☎ 28 05 51) or Siena Hotels Promotion (☎ 28 80 84; fax 28 02 90), Piazza San Domenico, which is open Monday to Saturday from 9 am to 8 pm in summer and 9 am to 7 pm in winter. Agriturismo is well organised around Siena, and the tourist

Il Palio

This spectacular event, held twice yearly on 2 July and 16 August in honour of the Virgin Mary, dates back to the Middle Ages and features a series of colourful pageants, a wild horse race around the Campo and much eating, drinking and celebrating in the streets. Ten of Siena's 17 town districts, or *contrade*, compete for the coveted *palio*, a silk banner. Each of the contrade has its own traditions, symbol and colours, and its own church and palio museum. The local rivalries which explode with each palio date back centuries and make the festival very much an event for the Sienese, even though the horse race and pageantry have, in recent years, attracted ever larger crowds of tourists. On festival days the Campo literally becomes a racetrack, with a ring of packed dirt around its perimeter serving as the course. From about 5 pm there are parades of contrade representatives in historical costume, each bearing their individual banners. The race is run at 7.45 pm in July and 7 pm in August. For not much more than one exhilarating minute, the 10 horses and their bareback riders tear three times around the Campo with a speed and violence that makes your hair stand on end. Even if a horse loses its rider it is still eligible to win and since many riders fall each year, it is the horses in the end who are the focus of the event. There is only one rule, that riders are not to interfere with the reins of other horses. Efforts by Benetton to sponsor the race have been unsuccessful, and the Sienese place incredible demands on the national TV network, RAI, for rights to televise the event. Book well in advance if you want to stay in Siena for the event, and join the crowds in the centre of the Campo at least four hours before the start, or even earlier if you want a place on the barrier lining the track. If you can't find a good vantage point, don't despair – the race is televised live and then repeated throughout the evening on TV. ■

TARTARUGA **DRAGO**

Two of the traditional banners of the contrade, districts of Siena which compete in il Palio

TOSCANA

office has a list of more than 60 establishments which rent rooms by the week or month.

The *Colleverde* camping ground (☎ 28 00 44) is north of the historical centre at Strada di Scacciapensieri 47 (take bus No 3 from Piazza Gramsci) and opens from late March to early November. The cost for one night is L13,000 for adults, L6500 for children and L18,000 for a site. The non-HI youth hostel *Guidoriccio* (☎ 5 22 12), Via Fiorentina, Località Stellino, is about 2km north-west of the city centre. B&B is L22,000 and a full meal is L15,000. Take bus No 10 or 15 from Piazza Gramsci. If driving, leave the city by Via Vittorio Emanuele II, which is an extension of Via di Camollia.

In town, try the *Tre Donzelle* (☎ 28 03 58), Via delle Donzelle 5, off Banchi di Sotto north of the campo. It has clean, simple singles/doubles for L40,000/66,000. A double with bathroom is L83,000. The *Piccolo Hotel Etruria* (☎ 28 80 88), close by at Via delle Donzelle 3, has pleasant rooms for up to L62,000/95,000 with bathroom. The *Locanda Garibaldi* (☎ 28 42 04), Via Giovanni Dupré 18, just south of the campo, has singles/doubles for L40,000/75,000. It also has a small trattoria with a cheap tourist menu.

Albergo Bernini (☎ 28 90 47), Via della Sapienza 15, has clean, simple singles/doubles with shower for up to L80,000/100,000. *Albergo la Perla* (☎ 4 71 44) is on the 2nd floor at Via delle Terme 25, a short walk north-west of the campo. Small but clean rooms with shower are L55,000/85,000.

The *Piccolo Hotel il Palio* (☎ 28 11 31), Piazza del Sale 19, a good 15-minute walk rom the campo, has rooms with bathroom or L120,000/150,000. *La Toscana* (☎ 4 60 7), at Via Cecco Angiolieri 12, has rooms or L53,000/80,000, or L80,000/120,000 vith bathroom. It could be cleaner for the rice, but is an option if other places are full. The *Cannon d'Oro* (☎ 4 43 21), Via dei Montanini 28, has rooms with bathroom for .90,000/110,000. The three-star *Albergo Duomo* (☎ 28 90 88), Via Stalloreggi 34, has ovely rooms, many with views, which cost rom L130,000/200,000. Just off Piazza San Domenico, at Viale Curtatone 15, is the *Chiusarelli* (☎ 28 05 62), which has very leasant singles/doubles with bathroom for .87,000/125,000. It is in a handy location if you have a car.

Places to Eat

The Sienese claim that most Tuscan cuisine has its origins in Siena, and that the locals are still using methods introduced to the area by he Etruscans, namely simple cooking methods and the use of herbs. Among the city's many traditional dishes are soups such as ribollita; *panzanella*, a summer salad of soaked bread, basil, onion and tomatoes; pappardelle con la lepre, pasta with hare; and the succulent steaks of the Chianina, cooked over a charcoal grill. Bread is made without salt, as throughout Toscana. Panforte, a rich cake of almonds, honey and candied melon or citrus fruit, has its origins in the city. Loosely translated, panforte is heavy bread, and it was created as sustenance for the crusaders to the Holy Land.

In the Piazza del Campo is the cheap self-service *Ciao & Spizzico*. *Hostaria il Carroccio*, Via Casato di Sotto 32, off the campo, has excellent pasta for around L10,000 and the bistecca is priced at L4000 an etto (100g). *Pizzeria del Gallo Nero*, Via del Porrione 67, also off the campo, has good pizzas from L7500 and there is no cover or service charge.

La Chiacchiera, Costa di Sant'Antonio 4, off Via Santa Caterina, is very small but has a good menu with local specialities. Pasta costs from L7000 and a litre of house wine is L5000. A full meal will cost about L25,000. *Al Marsili*, Via del Castoro 3, is one of the city's best restaurants and has dishes from L8000 for a first course and from L15,000 for a second. The 15% service charge and L4000 cover charge bump up the price of a meal. *Ristorante da Mugulone*, Via dei Pelligrini 8, is another excellent restaurant, with local specialities. It is a good place to try the bistecca (L4800 an etto). Pasta costs from L10,000 and second courses cost between L10,000 and L40,000. Service and cover charges are high.

About a 10-minute walk north of the campo, in a less frenetic neighbourhood, are several trattorie and alimentari. *Da Titti*, Via di Camollia 193, is a no-frills establishment with big wooden bench-tables where full meals with wine cost around L20,000. *Pizzeria Il Riccio*, nearby at Via Malta 44, has pasta for around L7000 and big pizzas from L6000. There's a L2000 cover charge, plus 10% for service.

There are *Crai* supermarkets scattered around the town centre, including at Via di Città 152-156 and in Via Cecco Angiolieri, opposite the La Toscana hotel. *Nannini*, Banchi di Sopra 22, is one of the city's finest cafés and pasticcerie.

Things to Buy

Ricama, a shop at Via di Città 61, promotes the crafts of Siena, in particular embroidery, and is worth a visit.

Getting There & Away

Bus Regular buses leave from Piazza San Domenico for Firenze, San Gimignano and Volterra (change at Colle Val d'Elsa), Pienza, Buonconvento, Montalcino and other destinations in the Crete Senese, as well as towns in the Chianti area. Daily buses also connect Siena with Perugia and Roma, leaving from Piazza San Domenico. The Siena APT has timetables.

Train Siena is not on a major train line, so from Roma it is necessary to change at Chiusi, and from Firenze at Empoli, making buses a better alternative. Trains arrive at Piazza F Rosselli, north of the city centre.

Car & Motorcycle Take the S2, a fast highway known as a *superstrada*, which connects Firenze and Siena. Alternatively, take the SS222, also known as the Chiantigiana, which meanders its way through the hills of Chianti. From the Firenze-Siena superstrada, the best exit to take is San Marco and then follow the signs marked 'centro'.

Getting Around
Tra-in operates city bus services from a base in Piazza Gramsci. From the train station, catch bus No 3 to Piazza Gramsci, about a 10-minute walk from the Piazza del Campo. No cars, apart from those of residents, are allowed in the city centre. There are large car parks at the Stadio Comunale and around the Fortezza Medici; both are just north of Piazza San Domenico. Technically, even to just drop off your luggage at your hotel it is necessary to get a special permit to enter the city by car. This can be obtained from the *vigili* in Piazza San Domenico, but only if you have a hotel booking. Otherwise, phone your hotel for advice. For a taxi, call ☎ 4 92 22, or after 9 pm, ☎ 28 93 50.

ABBAZIA DI SAN GALGANO

About 20km south-west of Siena on the SS73 is the ruined 13th-century San Galgano abbey, one of the country's finest Gothic buildings in its day and now a very atmospheric ruin. A former Cistercian abbey, its monks were among Toscana's most powerful, forming the judiciary and acting as accountants for the *comuni* of Volterra and Siena. They presided over disputes between the cities, played a significant role in the construction of the duomo in Siena and built for themselves an opulent church. By the 16th century the monks' wealth and importance had declined and the church had deteriorated to the point of ruin. The walls remain standing but the roof collapsed long ago. The abbey is definitely worth a diversion if you are driving, but visiting by public transport is quite difficult. The best option is the bus service between Siena and Massa Marittima, a little farther south-west. The Accademia Musicale Chigiana in Siena sponsors concerts at the abbey during summer. See Special Events in the Siena section.

On a hill overlooking the abbey is the tiny, round Romanesque **Cappella di Monte Siepi**. Inside are very badly preserved frescoes by Ambrogio Lorenzetti, which depict the life of St Galgano, a local soldier who had a vision of St Michael on this site. A real-life 'sword in the stone' is under glass in the floor of the chapel, put there, legend has it, by San Galgano.

If you have your own transport, drive via Monticiano towards the S223 road. Stop off at **Tocchi**, a tiny village with a restored castle nearby, where you can spend the night. You can enjoy an excellent meal of fresh local produce at *Posto di Ristoro a Tocchi* (☎ 0577-75 71 26). A meal will cost around L35,000, B&B from L40,000 a head. You can also get here on the Tra-in bus which travels between Siena and Monticiano. Continue across the valley towards **Murlo**, an interesting medieval fortified village. This was once an important Etruscan settlement and experts claim that DNA tests show that the locals are close relatives of these ancient people.

LE CRETE

Just south-east of Siena, this area of rolling clay hills is a feast of classic Tuscan images – bare ridges topped by a solitary cypress tree flanking a medieval farmhouse, four hills silhouetted one against the other as they fade off into the misty distance. The area of Le Crete changes colour according to the season – from the creamy violet of the ploughed clay to the green of the young wheat, which then turns to gold. If you have the funds to spare, hire a car in Firenze or Siena and spend a few days exploring Le Crete. Another option is the *Treno Natura*, a tourist train which runs from Siena through Asciano and along the Val d'Orcia (see Organised Tour in the Siena section for details).

Apart from the scenery, one of the main attractions in the area is the **Abbazia di Monte Oliveto Maggiore**, a 14th-century Olivetan monastery, famous for the frescoes by Signorelli and Sodoma which decorate its Great Cloister. The frescoes illustrate events in the life of the very severe St Benedict. The fresco cycle begins with Sodoma's work on the east wall (immediately to the right of the entrance into the church from the cloisters), and continues along the south wall of the cloisters. The nine frescoes by Signorelli line the west side of the cloisters and Sodoma picks up again on the north wall. Note the decorations on the pillars between some of Sodoma's frescoes – they are among the earliest examples of 'grotesque' art, copied from decorations found in the then newly excavated Domus Aurea of Nero, in Roma. Take the time to study the exquisite wood intarsia of the church choir; you'll need a L500 coin for the lights.

The monastery is open daily from 9 am to 12.30 pm and 1.30 to 6 pm. It is possible to stay at the monastery from Easter to the end of September. It costs L25,000 per person; phone ☎ 0577-700 70 61 to make a booking.

From the monastery, if you have your own transport, head for **San Giovanni d'Asso**, where there's an interesting 11th-century church with a Lombard-Tuscan façade, and a picturesque *borghetto* with the remains of a castle. Continue on to Montisi and Castelmuzio. Along a side road just outside Castelmuzio is the **Pieve di Santo Stefano in Cennano**, an abandoned 13th-century church. Ask for the key at the adjacent farm buildings. Two km past Castelmuzio on the road to Pienza is the 14th-century Olivetan monastery of **Sant'Anna in Camprena**. In the refectory there are frescoes by Sodoma which can be visited on Friday, Saturday and Sunday from 3 to 4.30 pm. Phone ☎ 0755-74 83 03 for further information.

The route from Monte Oliveto Maggiore to Pienza runs almost entirely along a high ridge, with great views of Le Crete.

PIENZA

A superb example of Renaissance architecture, this town was designed and built in the mid-15th century by the Florentine architect Bernardo Rossellino, on the orders of Pope Pius II, Aeneas Silvius Piccolomini, who was born there in 1405. The pope even had the town's name changed from Corsignano.

There is a tourist information office (☎ 74 90 71) in the Palazzo Pubblico, on the town's main square, Piazza Pio II.

Pienza's telephone code is ☎ 0578.

Things to See & Do

All of the town's important buildings are grouped around Piazza Pio II, a short walk from the town's entrance along Corso Rossellino. The **duomo** has a collection of five altarpieces painted by Sienese artists of the period, as well as a superb marble tabernacle by Rossellino. The **Palazzo Piccolomini**, to your right as you face the duomo, was the pope's residence and is considered Rossellino's masterpiece. Of particular note is the *loggia* which affords an extraordinary view. The palace is open Tuesday to Sunday from 10 am to 12.30 pm and 3 to 6 pm; entry is with a guide only and costs L5000. Opposite is the Palazzo Ammannati. To the left of the duomo is the **Palazzo Borgia**, built by Cardinal Borgia, later Pope Alexander VI, and the **Museo del Cattedrale**, which is open to the public daily except Tuesday from 10 am to 1 pm and 4 to 6 pm.

It is worth visiting the 10th-century Romanesque **Pieve di Corsignano**, less than 1km out of town along Via Fonti from Piazza Dante Alighieri. Ask for the key at the tourist office in Pienza.

Places to Stay & Eat

Pienza is very touristy, and both food and accommodation are on the expensive side. Try *Camere Capelli Gioiella* (☎ 74 85 51), Via Dante Alighieri 3, which has doubles with bathroom for L80,000.

Albergo Il Chiostro di Pienza (☎ 74 84 00) is in the former convent and cloister of the adjacent Chiesa di San Francesco. Singles/doubles are L110,000/170,000. Its atmospheric restaurant offers a L15,000 light lunch. At *Trattoria La Cucina di Fiorella*, Via Condotti, you'll eat well for around L40,000 a head. *Il Prato*, on the western side of Piazza Dante Alighieri, is also a bit on the

TOSCANA

expensive side. It has a terrace with panoramic views. Sample the local wines while eating a sandwich at *Enoteca Le Crete*, to your right as you enter the town from Piazza Dante Alighieri.

Getting There & Away

A bus runs three times a day between Siena, Pienza and Montepulciano.

SAN QUIRICO D'ORCIA

This fortified medieval town on the Via Cassia is well worth a stopover. Its Romanesque **Collegiata**, dating from the 12th century, is notable for its three doorways, decorated with stone carvings. Inside is a triptych by Sano di Pietro. Wander through the **Horti Leononi**, a lovely Italian Renaissance garden at the other end of town.

A few km from San Quirico towards Roma is **Bagno Vignoni**, a tiny spa town dating back to Roman times. The hot sulphurous water bubbles up into a picturesque pool, built by the Medici in the town's main piazza.

Places to Stay & Eat

If you're interested in staying in the area, try the *Agriturismo AIOLE* (☎ 0577-88 74 54), Strada Provinciale 22 della Grossola, near Castiglione d'Orcia. B&B is L50,000 per person and dinner is L25,000 (which must be booked ahead).

Getting There & Away

San Quirico is accessible by bus from Siena, Buonconvento, Pienza and Montepulciano.

MONTALCINO

A pretty town, perched high above the Orcia valley, Montalcino is best known for its wine, the Brunello. Produced only in the vineyards surrounding the town, Brunello is said to be one of Italy's best red wines and has gained considerable international fame. There are plenty of *entoteche* (wine cellars) around the town where you can taste and buy Brunello, as well as the other local wine, the Rosso di Montalcino, although you'll pay a minimum of L25,000 for a Brunello.

There is a tourist information office (☎ 0577-84 93 31) at Costa Municipio 8, just off Piazza del Popolo, the town's main square.

A 14th-century fortress dominates the town. It can be visited from 9 am to 1 pm and 2 to 8 pm Tuesday to Sunday and there is an enoteca inside the castle where you can sample and buy the local wines.

Places to Stay & Eat

There are plenty of places to stay in Montalcino and the surrounding countryside, including hotels, apartments and agriturismo. In town, try *Il Giardino* (☎ 0577-84 82 57), Piazza Cavour, which has doubles with bathroom for L85,000. The *Fattoria dei Barbi* (☎ 0577-84 94 21), Località Podernuovi, off the road from Montalcino to Castelnuovo dell'Abate, has two apartments which cost from L700,000 per week in the high season. This agriturismo establishment also has an excellent restaurant, *La Taverna dei Barbi*, where you'll eat a memorable meal for around L50,000. In town, try *Trattoria Sciame*, Via Ricasoli, or *Osteria Porta al Cassero*, Via della Libertà 9. At both, you'll eat well for L25,000 to L30,000.

If you're planning a visit to Sant'Antimo, stop for lunch at *Osteria Bassomondo* (☎ 0577-83 56 19), at Castelnuovo dell'Abate.

Getting There & Away

Montalcino is accessible from Siena by regular buses (Azienda Consorziale Trasporto – Siena, departing from Piazza San Domenico in Siena).

SANT'ANTIMO

It is best to visit this superb Romanesque church in the morning, when the sun shines through the east windows to create an almost surreal atmosphere. Set in a broad valley, just below the village of **Castelnuovo dell'Abate**, the 12th-century church and the ruined buildings of its Cistercian abbey are strikingly beautiful. Built in pale stone, the church's exterior is simple, but there are numerous fascinating architectural and decorative features, particularly the stone carvings of the bell tower and the apse windows, which include a *Madonna and Child* and the various fantastic animals typical of the Romanesque style. The interior of the church is in pale travertine stone. Take the time to study the capitals of the columns lining the nave, including one representing Daniel in the lion's den (second on the right as you enter). There is a 13th-century wooden statue of the Madonna in the right aisle and above the altar is a painted wooden crucifix, also dating from the 13th century. Behind the altar, in the ambulatory, there are traces of frescoes. The bases and capitals of some of the columns are of alabaster, which creates a stunning effect when the morning sun shines through the apse windows.

Ask the attendant to let you into the sacristy, where there are monochrome frescoes depicting the life of St Benedict. The sacristy is in what is known as the Carolingian Chapel, which probably dates back to the 8th century. The 9th-century crypt beneath the chapel is closed to the public, but you can get a murky glimpse of it through the small round window at the base of the exterior of the chapel's apse.

Concerts are sometimes held here as part of Siena's Estate Musicale Chigiana (see Special Events in the Siena section).

There are three buses a day from Montalcino (Azienda Consorziale Trasporto-Siena) to Castelnuovo dell'Abate, from where you can walk to the church.

MONTEPULCIANO

Set atop a narrow ridge of volcanic rock, Montepulciano combines Toscana's superb countryside with some of the region's finest wines. This medieval town is the perfect place to spend a few quiet days. Stop by the various enoteche to sample the local wines.

Orientation & Information

However you arrive, you will probably end up at the Porta al Prato on the town's northern edge. From here, buses take you through the town to Piazza Grande. The 15-minute walk is mostly uphill but well worth the exercise. The tourist office (☎ 75 86 87) is at Via Ricci 9, just off Piazza Grande, where you can pick up *Montepulciano Perla del Cinquecento*, a useful guide to the town. The office is open Tuesday to Sunday from 10.30 am to 1 pm and 3.30 to 6.30 pm.

Montepulciano's telephone code is ☎ 0578.

Things to See & Do

Most of the main sights are clustered around Piazza Grande, although the town's streets provide a wealth of palaces and other fine buildings. It is virtually impossible to get lost, so go for a wander.

To the left as you enter the Porta al Prato, designed by the Florentine Antonio da Sangallo the Elder, you'll see the 18th-century Chiesa di San Bernardo. Nearby is the Palazzo Avignonesi by Giacomo da Vignola. Several other **palaces** line the street, including the Palazzo Bucelli at No 73, whose façade features Etruscan and Latin inscriptions. Sangallo also designed the Palazzo Cocconi at No 70.

Piazza Michelozzo features Michelozzo's Chiesa di Sant'Agostino and a medieval tower house, topped by the town clock and the bizarre figure Pulcinella (Punch of Punch & Judy fame) which strikes the hours.

Continue up the hill and take the first left past the Loggia di Mercato for Via del Poggiolo, which eventually becomes Via Ricci. The tourist office is on the right, in the Renaissance Palazzo Ricci. The town's **Museo Civico** is opposite in the Gothic Palazzo Neri-Orselli. The small collection features terracotta reliefs by the della Robbia family and some Gothic and Renaissance paintings. It is open daily from 9 am to 1 pm and Sunday to 2 pm. Admission is L3000.

Piazza Grande marks the highest point of the town and features the austere **Palazzo Comunale**, a 13th-century Gothic building remodelled in the 15th century by Michelozzo. From the top of the 14th-century tower, on a clear day, you can see the Monti Sibillini to the east and the Gran Sasso to the south-east. The tower is open Monday to Saturday from 8 am to 1.30 pm and the climb is free.

The other palaces in the piazza are the Palazzo Contucci, now a wine cellar, and the Palazzo Tarugi, attributed to Giacomo da Vignola, near the fountain. The **duomo**, dating from the 16th century, has an unfinished façade. There is a lovely triptych above the high altar, depicting the Assumption, by Taddeo da Bartolo.

Outside the town wall, about 1km from the Porta al Prato, is the pilgrimage **Chiesa di San Biagio**, a fine Renaissance church built by Antonio da Sangallo the Elder and consecrated in 1529 by the Medici pope Clement VII.

Places to Stay & Eat

You might consider visiting Montepulciano on a day trip when you discover the hotel prices. The *Albergo Il Marzocco* (☎ 75 72 62), Piazza Savonarola 18, has singles/doubles with bathroom from L70,000/100,000. The *Albergo Il Borghetto* (☎ 75 75 35), Via Borgo Buio 5, is very appealing and has rooms for L90,000/130,000.

Lo Spuntino, Via Roma 25, sells pizza by the slice. You'll eat well at either *Trattoria Il Pulcino* (for around L35,000) or *Trattoria Diva e Marceo* (L20,000 to L25,000), both in Via Gracciano nel Corso. *Il Cantuccio*, in the same street at No 67, is another excellent restaurant, where a meal will cost around L35,000.

Try the local red, vino nobile, at one of the town's several cantine. *Cantina del Redi* is downhill from Piazza Grande along Via Ricci. *Le Cantine Contucci* is in the Palazzo Contucci on Piazza Grande.

Getting There & Around

Tra-in operates eight bus services daily between Montepulciano and Siena, via Pienza. LFE buses connect with Chiusi.

The most convenient train station is at Chiusi-Chianciano Terme, 10km south-east, on the main Roma-Firenze line. Buses for Montepulciano meet each train, so it is the best way to get there from Firenze or Roma. Stazione di Montepulciano, about 5km to the north-east, has less frequent services.

By car, exit the A1 at Chianciano Terme and follow the SS166 for the 18km trip to Montepulciano. Most cars are banned from the town centre and there are car parks near the Porta al Prato. Small town buses weave their way from here to Piazza Grande.

CHIUSI

One of the most important of the 12 cities of the Etruscan League, Chiusi was once powerful enough to attack Roma, under the leadership of the Etruscan king Porsenna. These days it is a fairly sleepy country town, but highly recommended as a stopover. There is a Pro Loco information office (☎ 0578-22 76 67) at Via Porsenna 73, just off Chiusi's main piazza. It is open daily from 8.30 am to 12.30 pm (and 3.30 to 6.30 pm in summer).

Things to See & Do

Chiusi's main attractions are the **Etruscan tombs** which dot the countryside around the town. Chiusi is noted as having the most painted tombs after Tarquinia – unfortunately, almost all are in a serious state of disrepair and are closed to the public. Visits to accessible tombs are with a guide only; ask at the **Museo Archeologico**. The museum has a reasonably interesting collection of artefacts found in the local tombs. The museum is open daily in summer from 9 am to 8 pm. In other months, it opens Monday to Saturday from 9 am to 2 pm and Sunday from 9 am to 1 pm.

Also take a look at the Romanesque **duomo** and the adjacent **Museo della Cattedrale**, which has an important collection of 22 illustrated antiphonals (psalm books). The **Labirinto di Porsenna** is a series of tunnels underneath the Piazza del Duomo, which date back to Etruscan times and formed part of the town's water supply system. Since ancient times, legend has associated the labyrinth with the Etruscan king Porsenna: it supposedly hid his grand tomb. A section of the labyrinth was excavated in the 1980s and can be visited with a guide. It's well worth a visit, and tickets can be bought at the Museo della Cattedrale.

Places to Stay & Eat
The *Albergo La Sfinge* (☎ 0578-2 01 57), Via Porsenna, is the only hotel in Chiusi's historical centre. It has singles/doubles for L65,000/90,000 with bathroom. There are several agriturismo establishments in the countryside near Chiusi; contact the Pro Loco for details. Two options for a good meal are *Il Bucchero*, Via Bonci, off Via Porsenna, and *La Solita Zuppa*, in Via Porsenna, just near the Albergo La Sfinge.

Getting There & Away
Chiusi is easily accessible by public transport. Its train station, in the valley below the town, is on the main Roma-Firenze line. The town is just off the Autostrada del Sole (A1).

Southern Toscana

THE MAREMMA & ETRUSCAN SITES

The area known as the Maremma extends along the Tuscan coast from just north of Grosseto and south to the border with Lazio, incorporating the Parco Naturale della Maremma, also known as Parco dell'Uccellina, and Monte Argentario. It also extends inland to the towns of Sovana, Terme di Saturnia and Pitigliano, important because of their Etruscan remains.

Information
Grosseto is the main town in the Maremma area. Its APT tourist information office (☎ 0564-45 45 10) is at Via Monterosa 206. Information about the Parco Naturale della Maremma can be obtained at the Grosseto APT, or at Alberese, on the northern edge of the park, where there is an information office (☎ 0564-40 70 98). Other useful organisations are the Associazione Albergatori (☎ 0564-2 63 15), Via Matteotti 55, the local hotel association, which can help you find a bed in the province.

You can pick up a copy of *Gli Etruschi in Maremma* from the APT in Grosseto. It is a series of brochures which are enclosed in a folder and provide comprehensive information and itineraries. They also describe the history of the Etruscans in the Maremma area.

The individual towns in the area each have small tourist information offices which open daily only during summer.

Parco Naturale della Maremma
Definitely the main attraction in the area, the park incorporates the Monti dell'Uccellina and a magnificent stretch of unspoiled coastline. Entry to the park is limited and cars must be left in designated parking areas. Certain areas can be visited only on certain days and excursions into the park are always limited to set itineraries. Depending on your chosen route, you may see plenty of native animals (including deer, wild boar, foxes and hawks). Certain routes also provide access to the sea. It is necessary to buy a ticket at the visitors' centre in Alberese; they cost L7500 (which includes bus transport from Alberese to the park entrance) or L6000. There are no shelters, bars etc within the park, so make sure you carry water and are properly dressed.

The tourist office at Alberese is open on Wednesday, Saturday and Sunday from 6.30 am to 6 pm and on Monday, Tuesday, Thursday and Friday from 7.30 am to 6 pm.

Etruscan Sites
If you're heading inland by car, stop off briefly at **Manciano**, a former Sienese fortress, and **Montemerano**, a picturesque walled medieval town, where you can buy outstanding Tuscan olive oil at *La Piaggia*, an agriturismo establishment. Visit the town's Chiesa di San Giorgio, which is decorated with 15th-century frescoes of the Sienese School. **Saturnia** is more famous for its sulphur spring and baths at **Terme di Saturnia**, but its Etruscan remains, including part of the town wall, are worth a diversion. A tomb at Sede di Carlo, just north-east of the town, is one of the area's best preserved. Bring along a bathing

TOSCANA

costume and take advantage of the curative waters at the picturesque thermal baths.

Sovana This very pretty little town has more than its fair share of important Etruscan sites and historical monuments. Its two information offices are in the main square, Piazza del Pretorio. From March to October they open daily from 10 am to 1 pm and 3 to 7 pm, and from November to March only at weekends.

Sovana was the birthplace of Pope Gregory VII and there are medieval palaces and the remains of a fortress belonging to his family at the eastern end of the town. The **Chiesa di Santa Maria** in Piazza del Pretorio is a starkly simple Romanesque church featuring a magnificent 9th-century ciborium in white marble, one of the last remaining pre-Romanesque works left in Toscana. In the church there are also some early Renaissance frescoes. Walk along the Via del Duomo to reach the imposing Gothic-Romanesque duomo, at the far eastern end of the town. The original construction dates back to the 9th century, although it was largely rebuilt in the 12th and 13th centuries, and its façade was destroyed to build the adjoining presbytery in the 14th century. Of particular note is the duomo's marble portal and the capitals of the columns which divide the interior into three naves. Several of the capitals feature biblical scenes and are thought to be the work of the Lombard school, dating from the 11th century.

About 1km to the south of the town are a number of Etruscan tombs, the most important being the **Tomba Ildebranda**, the only surviving temple-style tomb, and the **Tomba della Sirena**. The area is famous for the spectacular *vie cave*, narrow walkways which were carved like mini-gorges into the rock. The walkways continue for km and date from Etruscan times. There are other tombs and several necropoli worth a visit.

If you'd like to stay in Sovana, try the *Hotel Etrusca* (☎ 0564-61 61 83), on Piazza Pretorio, which has singles/doubles for L50,000/70,000, or L70,000/120,000 with bathroom. The *Scilla* (☎ 0564-61 65 31), just off the piazza at Via del Duomo 5, has cheaper rooms for L32,000/55,000, or L40,000/65,000 with bathroom. Both hotels also have restaurants.

Sorano Perched high on a rocky spur, this small medieval town has largely retained its original form and is worth including in your itinerary. There's a small tourist information office just outside the main entrance to the historical centre; open daily from 10 am to 1 pm and 3 to 7 pm, June to September. The town's main attraction is the newly renovated **Castello Orsini**. there are guided tours from 10 am to 1 pm and 4 to 7 pm daily for L3000. You could also climb up **Masso Leopoldino** for a spectacular view of the surrounding countryside (you'll need to ask for a key at the tourist office).

A few km out of Sorano, on the road to Sovana, are the **Necropoli di San Rocco**, an Etruscan burial area.

Pitigliano The visual impact of this town is quite spectacular – it almost seems to grow out of a high rocky outcrop which rises from a deep gorge. There is a small tourist information office on Via Roma, just off Piazza della Repubblica, which opens daily in summer from 10 am to 1 pm and 3 to 6 pm and in winter opens only at weekends. The town itself is a pleasant stopover – its offerings include the 13th-century **Palazzo Orsini** and an imposing 16th-century aqueduct. There's a small museum in the palace. The town's cathedral dates back to the Middle Ages, but its façade is Baroque and its interior has been modernised. It is interesting to wander the town's narrow, medieval streets, particularly in the area known as the **Ghetto**, once home to a large Jewish population.

For a place to stay, try the *Guastini* (☎ 0564-61 60 65), Piazza Petruccioli 4, with singles/doubles for L60,000/90,000. The kitchen at *Trattoria dell'Orso*, Piazza Gregorio VII, is open all day.

Getting Around

Infrequent buses (Rama) leave from the train

TOSCANA

station at Grosseto for Terme di Saturnia, Pitigliano and Sovana. Buses also leave from Orbetello for Pitigliano and Sorano. If you have the funds, hire a car in Grosseto, or even in Roma, and explore the area for a few days.

MONTE ARGENTARIO

Situated on an isthmus some 120km northwest of Roma, Orbetello is a pleasant place, popular with Romans on weekends.

Orbetello's main attraction is its **cathedral**, which has retained its 14th-century Gothic façade despite being remodelled in the Spanish style in the 16th century. Other reminders of the Spanish garrison which was stationed in the city include the fort and city wall, parts of which are the original Etruscan wall. But the main attraction is the increasingly popular Monte Argentario and its two harbour towns, Port'Ercole and Porto Santo Stefano, both crammed with incredibly expensive boats and yachts.

Around the Peninsula

Monte Argentario is popular with Romans, but not many tourists go there. **Porto Santo Stefano** and **Port'Ercole** are resort towns for the wealthy, but Port'Ercole, in a picturesque position between two forts, retains some of its fishing village character. The main tourist office (☎ 0564-81 42 08) is in Porto Santo Stefano, in the Monte dei Paschi di Siena building, at Corso Umberto 55.

For a pleasant drive, follow the signs to Il Telegrafo, one of the highest mountains in the region, and turn off at the **Convento dei Frati Passionisti**, a church and convent with sensational views across to the mainland.

There are plenty of good beaches, usually of the pebbly or rocky (rather than sandy) variety. One of the most popular is the long sandy strip of **Feniglia**, between Orbetello and Port'Ercole. Near Port'Ercole the beach is serviced, which means it's clean but cluttered with deck chairs and umbrellas for rent. As you move further away the beach becomes less crowded but, as with most public beaches in Italy, it also gets dirtier.

Places to Stay & Eat

Accommodation on the peninsula is generally expensive, although there is a *camping ground* (☎ 0564-83 10 90) near Port'Ercole, on the northern fringe at the Feniglia beach. In Orbetello, there's a very decent pensione, *Tony & Judy* (☎ 0564-8 61 09), on Corso Italia. In Porto Santo Stefano, *Pensione Weekend* (☎ 0564-81 25 80), Via Martiri d'Ungheria 3, is a cosy place with doubles with bathroom from L105,000, breakfast included. *Albergo Belvedere* (☎ 0564-81 26 34), Via del Fortino 51, is a luxurious complex overlooking the water, with double rooms with bathroom from L160,000 in the high season, breakfast included. It also has a private beach. Also at Porto Santo Stefano is *Il Veliero*, Strada Panoramica 149, where an excellent meal will cost around L50,000. At Port'Ercole try *Il Pirata*, a good pizzeria on Lungomare Andrea Doria.

Trattoria Da Sirio, Via del Molo 5, on the waterfront in Porto Santo Stefano, has pizzas and pasta from L7000. *Pizzeria Rossi* , Via del Molo 9 has pizza for from L1500 a slice.

Getting There & Away

Rama buses connect most towns on the Monte Argentario with Orbetello (coinciding with the arrival of trains) and Grosseto. Follow the signs to Monte Argentario from the S1, which connects Grosseto with Roma.

Eastern Toscana

AREZZO

This city is one of the real surprises of Toscana. Famous among art lovers for the fresco cycle by Piero della Francesca in the Chiesa di San Francesco, Arezzo has a well preserved medieval centre, featuring one of the most beautiful Romanesque churches in Italy, the Pieve di Santa Maria. An important Etruscan town, it was later absorbed into the Roman Empire. A free republic from the 10th century, Arezzo supported the Ghibelline cause in the awful battles between pope and emperor and was eventually subjugated by the Guelph Firenze in 1384. During WWII, the city was heavily bombed due to its tactical importance as a road junction and many important buildings were damaged. Famous natives include the poet Petrarch, the writer Pietro Aretino and Vasari, most famous for his book *Lives of the Artists*.

A widely known antiques fair is held in Piazza Grande and the surrounding streets on the first Sunday of every month, which means accommodation can be difficult to find unless you book well ahead.

Orientation & Information

From the train station on the southern edge of the walled city, walk north-east along Via Guido Monaco to the garden piazza of the same name. The old city is to the north-east and the modern part to the south-east along Via Roma.

The APT office (☎ 37 76 78), near the train station in Piazza della Repubblica, is open Monday to Friday from 9 am to 1 pm and 3 to 6.30 pm, and Saturday from 9 am to 1 pm. The post office is at Via Guido Monaco 34.

The Ospedale Civile (☎ 118) is outside the city walls on Via A de Gasperi. For police emergencies, call ☎ 113 or head for the questura on Via Fra Guittone.

Arezzo's postcode is 52100, and the telephone code is ☎ 0575.

Chiesa di San Francesco

The apse of this 14th-century church houses one of the greatest works of Italian art, Piero della Francesca's fresco cycle of the *Legend of the True Cross*. This is the artist's masterpiece, painted between 1452 and 1456, and relates in 10 episodes the story of Christ's death on the cross. Unfortunately, the frescoes were badly damaged by damp and have been under restoration for some years. One section of the restoration has been completed, but at the time of writing it was open to the public by appointment only (contact the tourist office for information). The restoration project is not expected to be completed before 2000.

Pieve di Santa Maria

This 12th-century church has a magnificent Romanesque arcaded façade, which has been recently restored and is reminiscent of the cathedral at Pisa. Each column is of a different design. Over the central doorway are carved reliefs representing the months. The bell tower, erected in the 14th century, has 40 windows and has become something of an emblem for the city. The stark, beautiful interior of the church shows a Gothic influence, the only colour coming from the polyptych by Pietro Lorenzetti on the raised sanctuary at the rear of the church.

Piazza Grande & Around

This sloping piazza is lined with interesting buildings. The **Palazzo della Fraternità dei Laici** dates from 1375. It was started in the Gothic style and finished after the onset of the Renaissance. On the north-eastern side of the piazza is Vasari's loggia, built in 1573.

Via dei Pileati leads to **Casa di Petrarca**, former home of the poet, which contains a small museum and the Accademia Petrarca.

Duomo

At the top of the hill on Via Ricasoli is the duomo, started in the 13th century and not completed until the 15th century. The Gothic interior houses several artworks of note, including a fresco of Mary Magdalene by Piero della Francesca.

Chiesa di San Domenico & Around

It is worth the walk to the Chiesa di San Domenico to see the crucifix painted by Cimabue, which hangs above the main altar. This church is on Via Sassoverde. South on Via XX Settembre is the **Casa di Vasari**, built and sumptuously decorated by the architect himself. The house is open Monday to Saturday from 9 am to 7 pm and Sunday to 1 pm. Entry is free. Down the hill on Via San Lorentino is the **Museo Statale d'Arte Medioevale e Moderna**, which has a collection of works by local artists spanning the 13th to 18th centuries, including Luca Signorelli and Vasari. The gallery is open daily from 9 am to 7 pm and entry is L8000.

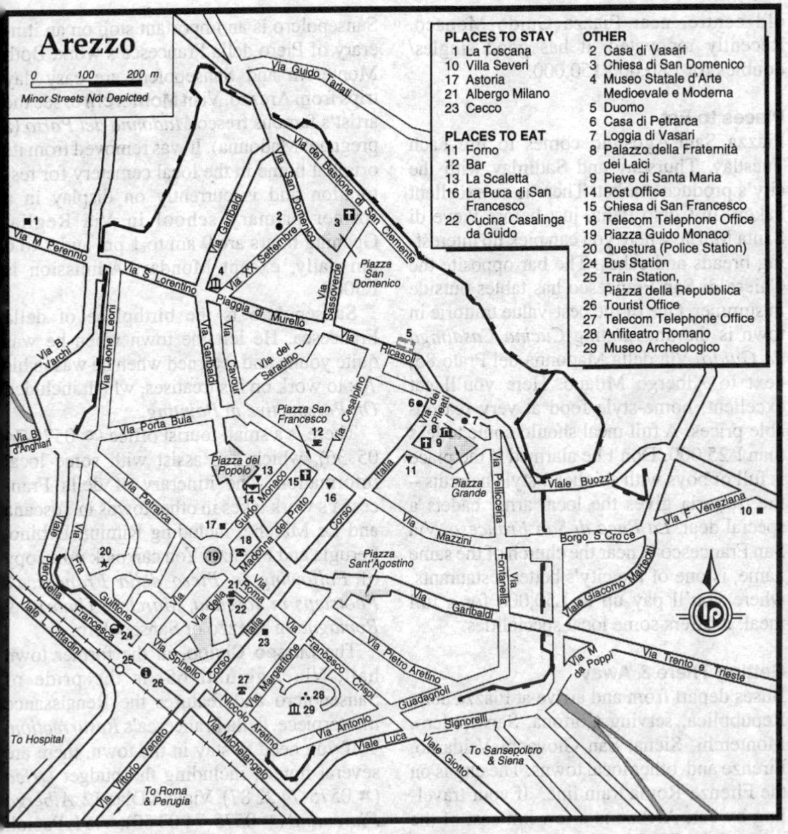

Museo Archeologico & Anfiteatro

Not far from the train station, the museum is in a convent overlooking the remains of the Roman amphitheatre. It houses an interesting collection of Etruscan and Roman artefacts, including locally produced craftwork. The museum is open Monday to Saturday from 9 am to 2 pm. Entry is L8000.

Places to Stay

The closest camping ground is *Camping Michelangelo* (☎ 0575-79 38 86) in Caprese Michelangelo, 35km north-east of Arezzo, It charges up to L7000 per person and L10,000 for a site. The non-HI youth hostel, the *Villa Severi* (☎ 2 90 47), Via F Redi 13, offers B&B for up to L20,000 in a wonderfully restored villa overlooking the countryside.

La Toscana (☎ 2 16 92), Via M Perennio 56, has simple rooms from L38,000/73,000. *Astoria* (☎ 2 43 61), Via Guido Monaco 54, has OK rooms for L38,000/98,000. The two-star *Cecco* (☎ 2 09 86), near the train station on the pedestrian-only Corso Italia, has singles/doubles for L40,000/65,000, or L65,000/90,000 with bathroom. *Albergo Milano* (☎ 2 68 36), Via della Madonna del Prato 83, is between the train station and the old centre, near Piazza Guido Monaco. Recently renovated, it has good singles/doubles for L80,000/150,000.

Places to Eat

Piazza Sant'Agostino comes to life each Tuesday, Thursday and Saturday with the city's produce market. There is an excellent bakery in Corso Italia, just before Pieve di Santa Maria, where you can pick up interesting breads and cakes. The bar opposite the Chiesa di San Francesco has tables outside in summer. One of the best-value trattorie in town is the unassuming *Cucina Casalinga da Guido*, Via della Madonna del Prato 85, next to Albergo Milano. Here you'll eat excellent, home-style food at very reasonable prices. A full meal should come to less than L25,000. Don't be alarmed if the place is full of boys with skinhead-style haircuts – the trattoria gives the local army cadets a special deal. *La Buca di San Franceso*, Via San Francesco 1, near the church of the same name, is one of the city's better restaurants, where you'll pay up to L50,000 for a full meal; it offers some local specialities.

Getting There & Away

Buses depart from and arrive at Piazza della Repubblica, serving Cortona, Sansepolcro, Monterchi, Siena, San Giovanni Valdarno, Firenze and other local towns. The city is on the Firenze-Roma train line. If your travelling by car, Arezzo is a few km east of the A1, and the SS73 heads east to Sansepolcro. Cars are banned from parts of the old city centre, and there are car parks near the train station and in Piazza del Popolo. The staff at the APT can advise on transport to neighbouring towns.

Getting Around

The easiest way is to walk, but some of the hills might get the better of you. There are several buses from the train station, which pass Piazza Guido Monaco, along Via Roma and into the old centre.

SANSEPOLCRO

Along with Arezzo and nearby Monterchi, Sansepolcro is an important stop on an itinerary of Piero della Francesca's work. Both Monterchi and Sansepolcro are easy day trips from Arezzo. Visit **Monterchi** to see the artist's famous fresco *Madonna del Parto* (a pregnant Madonna). It was removed from its original home in the local cemetery for restoration and is currently on display in a former primary school in Via Reglia. Opening hours are 9 am to 1 pm and 2 to 6 pm daily, except Monday. Admission is L5000.

Sansepolcro is the birthplace of della Francesca. He left the town when he was quite young and returned when he was in his 70s to work on his treatises, which included *On Perspective in Painting*.

There is a small tourist office (☎ 0575-74 05 36), which can assist with some local information. The itinerary of della Francesca's work takes in other towns in Toscana and Le Marche, including Rimini, Urbino, Perugia and Firenze. You can pick up a copy of *Following in Piero della Francesca's Footsteps in Toscana, Marches, Umbria & Romagna* in Arezzo or Sansepolcro.

The **Museo Civico**, in the former town hall, Via Aggiunti 65, is the pride of Sansepolcro and features the Renaissance masterpiece, della Francesca's *Resurrection*.

If you need to stay in the town, there are several hotels, including the budget *Orfeo* (☎ 0575-74 22 87), Viale A Diaz 12. *Albergo Fiorentino* (☎ 0575-74 03 50), Via L Pacioli 60, has singles/doubles with bathroom for L55,000/85,000.

SITA buses connect Arezzo with Sansepolcro hourly, and the town is on the Terni-Perugia train line.

CORTONA

Set into the side of a hill covered with olive groves, Cortona offers stunning views across the Tuscan countryside and has changed little since the Middle Ages. It was a small settlement when the Etruscans moved in during the 8th century BC and it later became a Roman town. In the late 14th century, it attracted the likes of Fra Angelico, who lived and worked in the city for about 10 years.

Luca Signorelli and the artist known as Pietro da Cortona were born here. The city is small, easily seen in a couple of hours, and well worth visiting for the sensational view.

Orientation & Information

Piazzale Garibaldi, on the southern edge of the walled city, is where buses arrive. It has a large car park, and also offers some of the best views in the city. From the piazza, walk straight up Via Nazionale to Piazza della Repubblica, the centre of town.

The APT (☎ 63 03 52), Via Nazionale 42, can assist with a hotel list and the useful *Cortona*, a complete guide to tourist essentials. It is open Monday to Saturday from 8 am to 1 pm and 3 to 6 pm, and on Sunday from 9 am to 1 pm from July to September. In an emergency, call ☎ 113.

Cortona's telephone code is ☎ 0575.

Things to See

Start in Piazza della Repubblica with the crenellated **Palazzo Comunale**, which was renovated in the 16th century. To the north is Piazza Signorelli, named after the artist and dominated by the 13th-century **Palazzo Pretorio**, also known as the Casanova Palace, whose façade was added in the 17th century. Inside is the **Museo dell'Accademia Etrusca**, which displays substantial local Etruscan finds, including an elaborate 5th-century BC oil lamp. The museum is open daily, except Monday, from 10 am to 1 pm and 4 to 7 pm. Admission is L5000.

Little is left of the Romanesque character of the **duomo** north-west of Piazza Signorelli. The duomo was completely rebuilt late in the Renaissance and again in the 18th century. Opposite is the **Museo Diocesano** in the former church of Gesù. Its fine collection includes works by Luca Signorelli and a beautiful *Annunciation* by Fra Angelico.

At the eastern edge of the city centre is the **Chiesa di Santa Margherita**, which features the magnificent Gothic tomb of St Margaret. Farther up the hill is the 16th-century **fortezza**, built for the Medici by Laparelli, the architect who built the fortress city of Valletta in Malta.

Places to Stay & Eat

The city has several cheap hotels and a hostel, and finding a room shouldn't be a problem at any time of the year. The HI *Ostello San Marco* (☎ 60 13 92), Via Maffei 57, just a short walk east of Piazzale Garibaldi, has B&B for L15,000. It is open from 1 March to 15 October. The *Betania* (☎ 6 28 29), Via Severini 50, is a monastery which offers rooms from L24,000 per person. The *Albergo Italia* (☎ 63 02 54), Via Ghibellina 5, just off Piazza della Repubblica, is in an old palace and has singles/doubles from L40,000/55,000, or L60,000/80,000 with bathroom.

There is a produce market in Piazza della Repubblica each Saturday and several grocery shops around the area. *Trattoria Dardano*, Via Dardano 24, is a good trattoria where you can eat for around L20,000. *Il Cacciatore*, Via Roma 11, is one of the city's better restaurants and offers local specialities. A meal could cost around L35,000.

Getting There & Away

LFI buses connect the city with Arezzo from Piazzale Garibaldi at regular intervals. The city is served by two train stations. Trains from Arezzo stop at the Camucia-Cortona station, in the valley below Cortona, and trains for Roma stop at Terontola, about 5km to the south of the Camucia-Cortona station. Shuttle buses connect both stations with Piazzale Garibaldi, and a board opposite the APT entrance details schedules. By car, the city is on the north-south SS71 which runs to Arezzo, and it is close to the superstrada that connects Perugia to the A1.

Umbria & Le Marche

Dotted with splendid medieval hill towns and offering a chance to flee the madding crowds in isolated valleys or mountains, the regions of Umbria and Le Marche need to be explored rather then simply visited. Umbria certainly offers some star attractions – the beautifully preserved medieval town of Perugia, St Francis' home town of Assisi and the extraordinary cathedral at Orvieto. The main attraction of Le Marche is Urbino, home of the painter Raphael and Duca Federico de Montefeltro. But in both regions there is a host of smaller, lesser known towns and villages and plenty of opportunities for nature lovers, walkers and mountain bikers to escape from the standard tourist attractions and get some exercise. This is also prime hang-gliding territory.

HIGHLIGHTS

- Hang-gliding over the Piano Grande
- Traditional Umbrian cuisine with *tartufi neri*
- Signorelli's fresco cycle *The Last Judgment* in Orvieto's magnificent duomo
- Visiting Assisi, one of the region's most beautiful towns, out of tourist season
- Spoleto's Festival dei Due Mondi in summer
- Corpus Domini celebrations in Orvieto and Spello

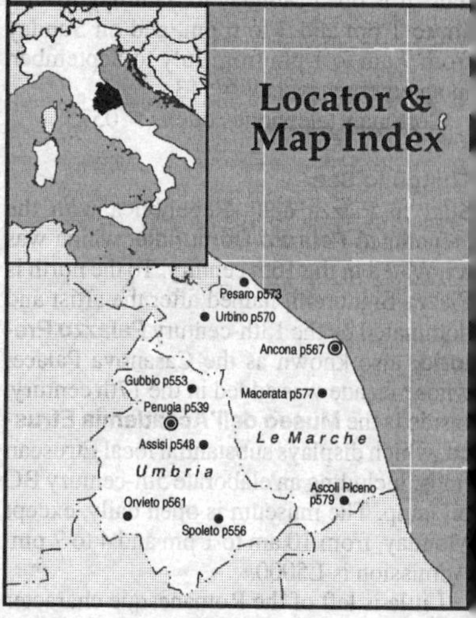

Umbria

One of the few landlocked Italian regions, Umbria likes to think of itself as Italy's green heart. In spring the countryside is splashed with the red, pink, yellow, purple and blue of wildflowers, and in summer it explodes with the vibrant yellow of the sunflowers harvested to make cooking oil. The rolling mountains of the Appennini in the north and east descend into hills, many capped by medieval towns, and eventually flatten out into lush valleys along the Tevere river. With the exception of the industrial blight around Terni in the south, most towns are unspoilt and have preserved their medieval centres.

The Romans named Umbria after the Umbrii, the Iron Age tribe who occupied the region. The Roman naturalist Pliny described the Umbrii as the oldest tribe in Italy but little more is known about them. The Etruscans later settled the west bank of the Tevere river, founding the towns of Perugia and Orvieto, and eventually creating 12 powerful city-states.

The barbarian invasions of the 5th and 6th centuries AD ended Roman rule and caused the Umbrians to retreat to the hill towns that gave rise to fortified medieval cities such as Gubbio and Todi. Domination by the Goths, the Lombards and various ruling families, as well as centuries of Guelph-Ghibelline rivalry, led to a long decline that left Umbria ripe for papal rule from the early 16th century.

St Francis was born in Assisi in the east of the region, and after his death the town

UMBRIA

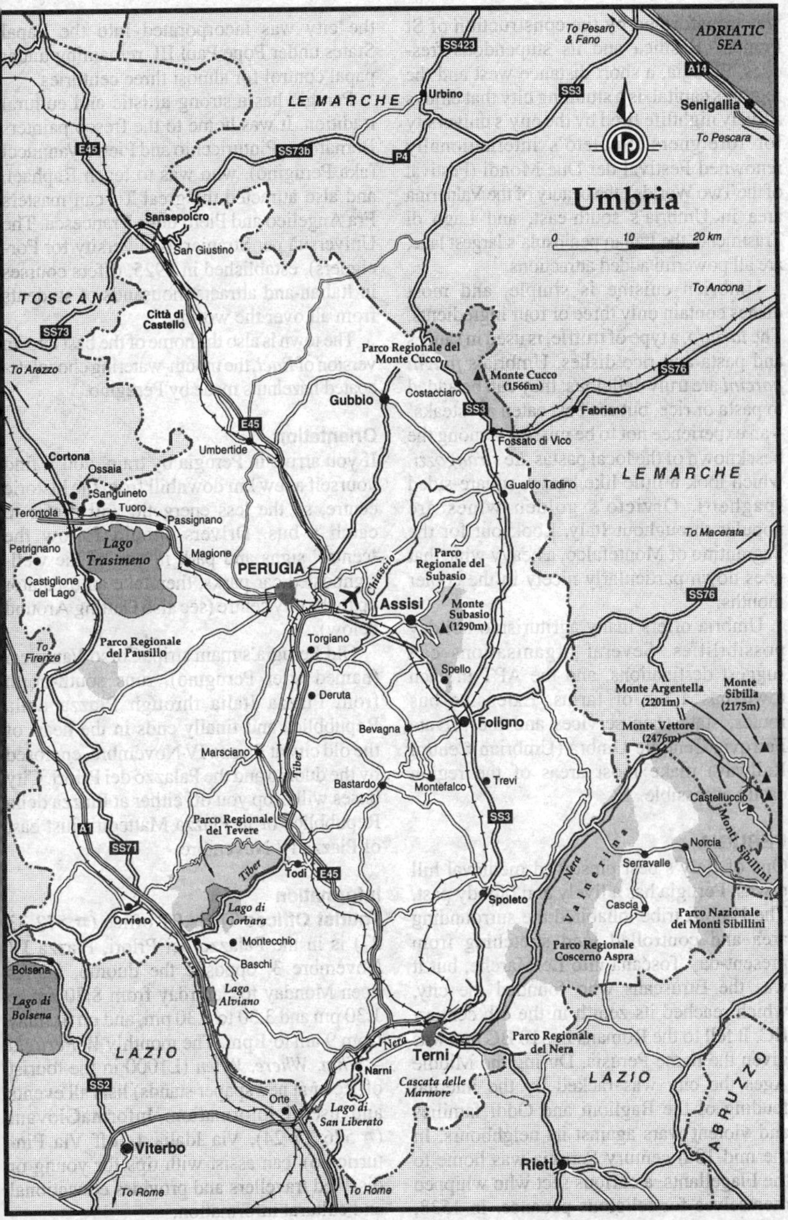
Umbria
0
10
20 km
ADRIATIC SEA
To Pesaro & Fano
SS423
A14
SS3
Urbino
LE MARCHE
Senigallia
To Pescara
E45
SS73b
P4
Sansepolcro
San Giustino
TOSCANA
Città di Castello
SS73
To Arezzo
To Ancona
Parco Regionale del Monte Cucco
Monte Cucco (1566m)
SS76
Costacciaro
Gubbio
SS3
Fabriano
Fossato di Vico
E45
Umbertide
Cortona
Ossaia
Sanguineto
Terontola
Tuoro
Passignano
Gualdo Tadino
LE MARCHE
Lago Trasimeno
Petrignano
Magione
Castiglione del Lago
PERUGIA
Chiascio
Parco Regionale del Subasio
To Macerata
Assisi
Monte Subasio (1290m)
SS76
Torgiano
Parco Regionale del Pausillo
To Firenze
Spello
Deruta
Monte Argentella (2201m)
Monte Sibilla (2175m)
Foligno
Bevagna
Monte Vettore (2476m)
Marsciano
Tiber
Bastardo
Montefalco
Trevi
Castelluccio
Monti Sibillini
SS3
Parco Regionale del Tevere
A1
SS71
Norcia
Tiber
Todi
E45
Serravalle
Nera
Valnerina
Spoleto
Cascia
Orvieto
Lago di Corbara
Parco Nazionale dei Monti Sibillini
Montecchio
Parco Regionale Coscerno Aspra
Bolsena
Baschi
Lago di Bolsena
Lago Alviano
Parco Regionale del Nera
LAZIO
Nera
Terni
Narni
ABRUZZO
SS2
Cascata delle Marmore
LAZIO
Orte
Lago di San Liberato
Viterbo
Rieti
To Rome
To Rome

UMBRIA

was transformed by the construction of St Francis' Basilica and its stupendous frescoes. Perugia, a short distance west and the region's capital, is a stunning city that enjoys a lively nightlife fired by the city's university for foreigners. Spoleto's internationally renowned Festival dei Due Mondi (Festival of the Two Worlds), the beauty of the Valnerina area in Umbria's south-east, and Lago di Trasimeno, the Italian peninsula's largest lake, are all powerful added attractions.

Umbrian cuisine is simple, and most dishes contain only three or four ingredients. The *tartufo*, a type of truffle, is used in sauces and pasta and rice dishes. Umbria's *funghi porcini* are truly delicious; they can be added to pasta or rice, but are best eaten as 'steaks' – an experience not to be missed. Among the best known of the local pastas are *strangozzi*, which look a little like heavy, square-sided spaghetti. Orvieto's golden wines are popular throughout Italy. Look out for the Sagrantino of Montefalco, a heavy wine that goes down particularly nicely in the cooler months.

Umbria offers many agriturismo holiday possibilities. Several organisations can suggest destinations, and the APT in each town has a list of farms. Extensive bus routes, state train services and the private Ferrovia Centrale Umbra (Umbrian Central Railway) make most areas of the region easily accessible.

PERUGIA

One of Italy's best preserved medieval hill towns, Perugia has a lively and bloody past. The Umbrii tribe inhabited the surrounding area and controlled land stretching from present-day Toscana into Le Marche, but it was the Etruscans who founded the city, which reached its zenith in the 6th century BC. It fell to the Romans in 310 BC and was given the name Perusia. During the Middle Ages the city was racked by the internal feuding of the Baglioni and Oddi families and violent wars against its neighbours. In the mid-13th century Perugia was home to the Flagellants, a curious sect who whipped themselves for religious penance. In 1538, the city was incorporated into the Papal States under Pope Paul III, remaining under papal control for almost three centuries.

Perugia has a strong artistic and cultural tradition. It was home to the fresco painters Bernardino Pinturicchio and Pietro Vannucci (aka Perugino), who was to teach Raphael, and also attracted the great Tuscan masters Fra Angelico and Piero della Francesca. The Università per Stranieri (University for Foreigners), established in 1925, offers courses in Italian and attracts thousands of students from all over the world.

The town is also the home of the best known version of *Baci*, the mouth-watering chocolate-coated hazelnuts made by Perugino.

Orientation

If you arrive in Perugia by train, you'll find yourself a few km downhill from the historic centre, so the less energetic will prefer to catch a bus. Drivers should follow the 'centro' signs and park in one of the well-signposted car parks, then take an escalator up to the city centre (see also Getting Around below).

Old Perugia's main strip, Corso Vannucci (named after Perugino), runs south-north from Piazza Italia through Piazza della Repubblica and finally ends in the heart of the old city at Piazza IV Novembre, enclosed by the duomo and the Palazzo dei Priori. City buses will drop you off either at Piazza della Repubblica or in Piazza Matteotti, just east of Piazza IV Novembre.

Information

Tourist Offices The APT office (☎ 572 33 27) is in the Palazzo dei Priori, Piazza IV Novembre 3, opposite the duomo, and is open Monday to Saturday from 8.30 am to 1.30 pm and 3.30 to 6.30 pm, and on Sunday from 9 am to 1 pm. The monthly *W Perugia – What, Where, When* (L1000 in the tourist office or at newspaper stands) lists all events and useful information. InformaGiovani (☎ 576 17 24), Via Idalia 1 (off Via Pinturrichio), can assist with tips for young or disabled travellers and provides educational and cultural information.

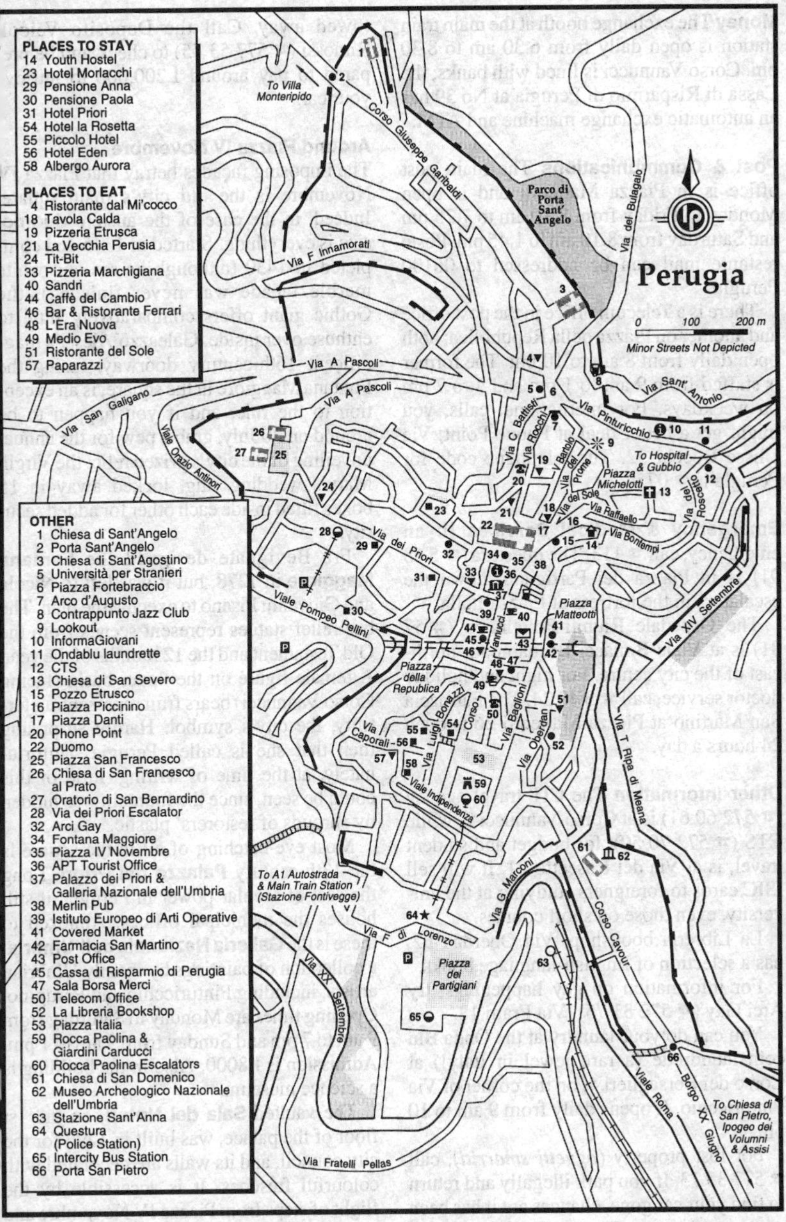

PLACES TO STAY
14 Youth Hostel
23 Hotel Morlacchi
29 Pensione Anna
30 Pensione Paola
31 Hotel Priori
54 Hotel la Rosetta
55 Piccolo Hotel
56 Hotel Eden
58 Albergo Aurora
PLACES TO EAT
4 Ristorante dal Mi'cocco
18 Tavola Calda
19 Pizzeria Etrusca
21 La Vecchia Perusia
24 Tit-Bit
33 Pizzeria Marchigiana
40 Sandri
44 Caffè del Cambio
46 Bar & Ristorante Ferrari
48 L'Era Nuova
49 Medio Evo
51 Ristorante del Sole
57 Paparazzi
OTHER
1 Chiesa di Sant'Angelo
2 Porta Sant'Angelo
3 Chiesa di Sant'Agostino
5 Università per Stranieri
6 Piazza Fortebraccio
7 Arco d'Augusto
8 Contrappunto Jazz Club
9 Lookout
10 InformaGiovani
11 Ondablu laundrette
12 CTS
13 Chiesa di San Severo
15 Pozzo Etrusco
16 Piazza Piccinino
17 Piazza Danti
20 Phone Point
22 Duomo
25 Piazza San Francesco
26 Chiesa di San Francesco al Prato
27 Oratorio di San Bernardino
28 Via dei Priori Escalator
32 Arci Gay
34 Fontana Maggiore
35 Piazza IV Novembre
36 APT Tourist Office
37 Palazzo dei Priori & Galleria Nazionale dell'Umbria
38 Merlin Pub
39 Istituto Europeo di Arti Operative
41 Covered Market
42 Farmacia San Martino
43 Post Office
45 Cassa di Risparmio di Perugia
47 Sala Borsa Merci
50 Telecom Office
52 La Libreria Bookshop
53 Piazza Italia
59 Rocca Paolina & Giardini Carducci
60 Rocca Paolina Escalators
61 Chiesa di San Domenico
62 Museo Archeologico Nazionale dell'Umbria
63 Stazione Sant'Anna
64 Questura (Police Station)
65 Intercity Bus Station
66 Porta San Pietro
Perugia
0 100 200 m
Minor Streets Not Depicted
To Villa Monteripido
Corso Giuseppe Garibaldi
Parco di Porta Sant' Angelo
Via del Bulagaio
Via F Innamorati
Via A Pascoli
Via San Galigano
Viale Orazio Antinori
Via Sant' Antonio
Via Pinturicchio
Via C. Battisti
Via Rocchi
Via Bartolo
Via del Prome
Piazza Michelotti
To Hospital & Gubbio
Via del Roscetto
Via del Sole
Via Raffaello
Via Bontempi
Via dei Priori
Viale Pompeo Pellini
Piazza Matteotti
Via XIV Settembre
Piazza della Repubblica
Vannucci
Corso
Via Baglioni
Via Luigi Bonazzi
Via Caporali
Via Oberdan
Viale Indipendenza
Via T Ripa di Meana
To A1 Autostrada & Main Train Station (Stazione Fontivegge)
Via G. Marconi
Corso Cavour
Via F di Lorenzo
Via XX Settembre
Piazza dei Partigiani
Viale Roma
Borgo XX Giugno
To Chiesa di San Pietro, Ipogeo dei Volumni & Assisi
Via Fratelli Pellas

UMBRIA

Money The exchange booth at the main train station is open daily from 6.30 am to 8.30 pm. Corso Vannucci is lined with banks; the Cassa di Risparmio di Perugia at No 39 has an automatic exchange machine and ATM.

Post & Communications The main post office is in Piazza Matteotti and is open Monday to Friday from 8.10 am to 7.25 pm and Saturday from 8.10 am to 1.45 pm. Poste restante mail can be addressed to 06100 Perugia.

There is a Telecom office in the post office and another on Piazza della Repubblica; both open daily from 8 am to 10 pm. The former is staffed from 9 am to 1 pm and 4 to 7 pm on weekdays. For international calls, you might get a better deal at Phone Point, Via Ulisse Rocchi 32. The telephone code for Perugia is ☎ 075.

Emergency & Medical Services In an emergency, call ☎ 113. The questura (☎ 5 68 91) is in Piazza dei Partigiani, down the escalators in the fortress at Piazza Italia.

The Ospedale Riuniti-Policlinico (☎ 57 81) is at Viale Bonacci Brunamonti, north-east of the city centre. For night and holiday doctor service, call ☎ 3 40 24. The Farmacia San Martino at Piazza Matteotti 26 is open 24 hours a day.

Other Information The CIT travel agency (☎ 572 60 61) is at Corso Vannucci 2, while CTS (☎ 572 70 50), for budget and student travel, is at Via del Roscetto 21. It will sell ISIC cards to foreigners studying at the university, even those on short courses.

La Libreria bookshop, Via Oberdan 52, has a selection of English-language books.

For information on gay happenings, try Arci Gay (☎ 572 31 75), Via Fratti 18.

You can do your laundry at the Onda Blu coin laundrette (a rare jewel in Italy!) at Corso dei Bersaglieri 4, on the corner of Via Pinturicchio. It opens daily from 9 am to 10 pm.

For lost property *(oggetti smarriti)*, call ☎ 577 35 73. If you park illegally and return to find your car gone, chances are it has been towed away. Call the Deposito Veicoli Rimossi (☎ 577 53 75) to check and be prepared to pay around L200,000 to retrieve your car.

Around Piazza IV Novembre

The imposing façades betray that Piazza IV Novembre is the old city's main square. Indeed, in the case of the austere **duomo** size is everything. Started in 1345 and completed in 1430 (although its red and white marble façade was never finished), the Gothic giant offers comparatively little to enthuse over inside. Galeazzo Alessi's magnificent 16th-century doorway, facing the Fontana Maggiore in the square, is an exception to the rule, and if you happen to be around on 30 July, grab a pew for the annual unveiling of the city's prized relic: the Virgin Mary's wedding ring, locked away in 15 boxes fitted inside each other for added security.

Fra Bevignate designed the **Fontana Maggiore** in 1278, but it was left to Nicola and Giovanni Pisano to execute the plan. The bas-relief statues represent scenes from the Old Testament and the 12 months of the year. A female figure on the upper basin (facing Corso Vannucci) bears fruit representing fertility, the city's symbol. Hardly surprising then that she is called Perugia. Unfortunately, at the time of writing, little of this could be seen, since the fountain was hidden by shrouds of restorers' plastic.

Most eye-catching of all in the square is the 13th-century **Palazzo dei Priori**. Long the seat of secular power in Perugia, it still houses the municipal offices. Annexed to these is the **Galleria Nazionale dell'Umbria**, a collection of paintings by mainly Umbrian artists, including Pinturicchio and Perugino. Opening times are Monday to Saturday from 9 am to 7 pm and Sunday from 9 am to 1 pm. Admission is L8000. Also in the building is a science museum.

The vaulted **Sala dei Notari**, on the 1st floor of the palace, was built in 1296 for the city council, and its walls are decorated with colourful frescoes. It is accessible by the flight of steps from Piazza IV Novembre and open daily (closed on Monday from October to May) from 9 am to 1 pm and 3 to 7 pm. Admission is free.

In the Corso Vannucci side of the palace is the **Collegio della Mercanzia**, the seat of the city's powerful Renaissance-era merchants. They formed one of several *arti*, or guilds, that still exist today (though their power is a shadow of what it was). Reflecting their one-time prestige is the impressive early 15th-century, carved-wood panelling inside. Look at the designs closely and it will be hard to escape the impression that they were influenced by Islamic artistry – possibly imported from the Orient via Venezia.

A few doors up in the same building is the **Collegio del Cambio**, constructed in 1450 for another guild, the city's moneychangers, and decorated with magnificent frescoes by Perugino. Admission to the Collegio della Mercanzia is Monday to Saturday from 9 am to 1 pm and 2.30 to 5.30 pm (mornings only on Sunday and holidays). The hours for the Collegio del Cambio are Monday to Saturday from 9 am to 12.30 pm and 2.30 to 5 pm and Sunday from 9 am to 12.30 pm. These hours change from November to the end of March, when both are open daily from 8 am to 2 pm (Sunday from 9 am to 1 pm). There are exceptions on certain days, so check first. A ticket for both *collegi* costs L6000, or you can pay L5000 for the Collegio del Cambio and L2000 for the Collegio della Mercanzia.

West of Corso Vannucci

Follow Via dei Priori west down to Piazza San Francesco. The 15th-century **Oratorio di San Bernardino** has a façade decorated with bas-reliefs by Agostino di Duccio. Next to it is the ruined **Chiesa di San Francesco al Prato**, destroyed over the centuries by various natural disasters. It is used as an atmospheric location for concerts.

Towards the Università per Stranieri

The **Pozzo Etrusco** (Etruscan Well), between Piazza Danti and Piazza Piccinino, dates from the 3rd century BC. From here take Via del Sole to the **Cappella di San Severo**, which features Raphael's *Trinity with Saints*, thought to be his first fresco, and frescoes by Perugino. The L3000 ticket admits you to the well and the chapel. Frankly, unless you are desperate to see what *might* be Raphael's first fresco or happen to be an aficionado of large, brown, wet, dank holes in the ground, your L3000 would probably be better spent on a gelato. As one smart-mouthed eight-year-old remarked on leaving the *pozzo*, 'that was *well* worth it!' Chapel and well open daily from 10.30 am to 1.30 pm and 2.30 to 6.30 pm (to 4.30 pm only in winter).

From the church, walk back into Piazza Michelotti and turn right into the small Piazza Rossi Scotti, from which you can enjoy a lovely view across the countryside. Take the steps down to Piazza Fortebraccio and the Università per Stranieri, housed in the Baroque Palazzo Gallenga. To the left is the **Arco d'Augusto**, one of the ancient city gates. Its lower section is Etruscan, dating from the 3rd century BC, and the upper part is Roman and bears the inscription 'Augusta Perusia'. The loggia on top dates from the Renaissance.

Around Corso Garibaldi

North along Corso Giuseppe Garibaldi is the **Chiesa di Sant'Agostino**, with a beautiful 16th-century choir by Baccio d'Agnolo. Small signs denote the many artworks carried off to France by Napoleon and his merry men. Farther north along the same thoroughfare, Via del Tempio branches off to the Romanesque **Chiesa di Sant'Angelo**, said to stand on the site of an ancient temple. The columns inside the round church were taken from earlier buildings. Corso Garibaldi continues through the 14th-century wall by way of the **Porta Sant'Angelo**. A 10-minute walk takes you to the **Villa Monteripido**, home of the Giuditta Brozzetti fabric company where you can buy hand-woven linens, produced using centuries-old techniques.

South of the Centre

At the southern end of Corso Vannucci are the tiny **Giardini Carducci**, with lovely views of the countryside. The gardens stand atop a once massive 16th-century fortress, now known as the **Rocca Paolina**, built by Pope Paul III over a medieval quarter formerly inhabited by some of the city's most powerful families. Destroyed by the Perugini after Italian unification, the ruins remain a symbol of defiance against oppression. A series of escalators runs through the Rocca and you can wander around inside the ruins, which are often used for exhibitions.

Along Corso Cavour, the early 14th-century **Chiesa di San Domenico** is the city's largest church. Perhaps unfortunately, its Romanesque interior, made light by the immense stained-glass windows, was replaced by austere Gothic fittings in the 16th century. Pope Benedict XI, who died after eating poisoned figs in 1325, lies buried here. The convent which adjoins it is the home of the **Museo Archeologico Nazionale dell'Umbria**, which has an excellent collection of Etruscan pieces and a section on prehistory. It is open Monday to Saturday from 9 am to 1.30 pm and 2.30 to 7 pm and Sunday to 1 pm. Admission is L4000.

Continuing along Corso Cavour you come to the Porta San Pietro. Keep going along Borgo XX Giugno for the 10th-century **Chiesa di San Pietro**, reached through a fresco-decorated doorway in the first courtyard. The interior is an incredible mix of gilt and marble, and contains a *Pietà* by Perugino.

About 5km south-east of the city, at Ponte San Giovanni, is the **Ipogeo dei Volumni**, a 2nd-century BC Etruscan burial site discovered in 1840. An underground chamber contains a series of recesses holding the funerary urns of the Volumnio family. Unless you're a big fan of the Etruscans, you'll probably find the tombs at Cerveteri or Tarquinia in Lazio more interesting. It is open Monday to Saturday from 9.30 am to 12.30 pm and 4.30 to 6.30 pm (3 to 5 pm in winter) and Sunday from 9.30 am to 12.30 pm only. Admission is L4000 and visits are limited to five people at a time, so there can be delays. Take the ASP bus from Piazza Italia to Ponte San Giovanni and walk from there.

Courses

The list of courses available to locals and foreigners in and around Perugia could constitute a book in itself. You can learn Italian, take up ceramics, study music or spend a month cooking. The APT has details of all courses available.

The Università per Stranieri (☎ 5 74 61) is Italy's foremost academic institution for foreigners and offers courses in language, literature, history, art and other subjects. It runs a series of degree courses as well as one, two, three-month and intensive courses. The basic language course costs L350,000 per month. For information, write to the Università per Stranieri, Palazzo Gallenga, Piazza Fortebraccio 4, Perugia 06122.

The Istituto Europea di Arti Operative (☎ 6 50 22), Via dei Priori 14, runs courses in graphic design, drawing, painting, fashion and industrial and interior design.

To study in Perugia you may need to apply for a student visa in your country before arriving in Italy. See the Visas & Embassies section in the Facts for the Visitor chapter.

Special Event

The Umbria Jazz Festival attracts international performers for 10 days each July, usually around the middle of the month. Check with the APT for details. Tickets range from L15,000 to L50,000 and can be bought in advance from Sala Borsa Merci (☎ 573 02 71), Via Mazzini 9. Check out www.krenet.it/uj on the Internet for info.

Places to Stay

Perugia has a good selection of reasonably priced hotels, but if you arrive unannounced during Umbria Jazz, or in August, expect problems. For agriturismo throughout Umbria try Agriturist Umbria (☎ 3 20 28), Via Savonarola 38; Terranostra Umbria (☎ 500 95 59), Via Campo di Marte 10; or Turismo Verde Umbria (☎ 500 29 53), Via Campo di Marte 14.

Camping The city has two camping grounds, both in Colle della Trinità, 5km north-west of the city and reached by bus No 36. They are 'aradis d'Été (☎ 517 04 88) and *Il Rocolo* ☎ 517 85 50). The latter opens from 15 June o 15 September only.

Iostel The non-HI youth hostel, the *Centro nternazionale per la Gioventù* (☎ 572 28 0), Via Bontempi 13, charges L15,000 a ight. Sheets (for the entire stay) are an extra .2000. Its TV room has a fresco-decorated eiling and the views from the terrace are antastic. It closes from mid-December to nid-January.

'ensioni & Hotels Visitors have more than 0 hotels to choose from in Perugia. *Penione Anna* (☎ 573 63 04), Via dei Priori 48, ıas simple singles/doubles for up to .36,000/58,000 (and up to L55,000/90,000 vith private bath). *Pensione Paola* (☎ 572 8 16), Via della Canapina 5, is five minutes rom the centre, down the escalator from Via lei Priori; it has rooms for L40,000/60,000. 'ust off Corso Vannucci, at Via Bonazzi 25, s the *Piccolo Hotel* (☎ 572 29 87), with loubles only, for L55,000, or L75,000 with athroom.

The two-star *Albergo Aurora* (☎ 572 48 9), Viale Indipendenza 21, has singles/ loubles with bathroom for L70,000/95,000 and a couple of cheaper singles without orivate bathroom). *Hotel Morlacchi* (☎ 572 3 19), Via Tiberi 2, has singles/doubles for .65,000/90,000, L120,000 for a triple with oathroom.

Hotel Priori (☎ 572 33 78), Via Vermiglioli 3, at the corner of Via dei Priori, is n a great location and has pleasant singles/ doubles for L90,000/120,000 with bathroom. *Hotel Eden* (☎ 572 81 02), Via Caporali 9, has bright, clean singles/doubles for L60,000/85,000. *Hotel la Rosetta* (☎ & fax 572 08 41), Piazza Italia 19, is one of Perugia's better hotels. Its singles/doubles cost up to L105,000/245,000.

Religious Institutions About 10 religious institutions and orders offer accommodation in Perugia. Generally rates are cheap and stays must be of at least two days. They have a curfew of 9 pm (10 pm in summer). The tourist office can provide a list.

Rental Accommodation If you are planning to study in Perugia, the Università per Stranieri will organise accommodation for L400,000 to L800,000 a month, depending on your needs. The weekly *Cerco e Trovo* (L2000 at newspaper stands) lists all available rental accommodation, and the APT can help with holiday houses and *affittacamere*, rooms rented on a weekly or monthly basis.

Places to Eat

Being a student city, Perugia offers many budget eating options. For great pizza by the slice, there's *Pizzeria Marchigiana*, Via dei Priori 3, just below Corso Vannucci. A student pizza haunt is *Pizzeria Etrusca*, Via Ulisse Rocchi 31.

Good places for a sit-down pizza are *L'Era Nuova*, Via Baldo 6, and *Tit-Bit*, Via dei Priori 105. A pizza will cost from L6000 to L10,000 at either restaurant. For a cheap, filling meal, try the *Tavola Calda* in Piazza Danti.

Ristorante dal Mi'Cocco, Corso G Garibaldi 12, has a L26,000 set menu featuring local specialities and is popular with students. *Ristorante Ferrari*, downstairs from the bar of the same name at Corso Vannucci 43, has excellent antipasto, good pizzas and a three-course menu. A meal will cost around L30,000.

For something light and a little funky, try a whimsical pasta or salad at *Paparazzi*, Via Bonazzi 45, while dancing away at the disco – you can pick up the monthly programme of theme nights any time.

Going a little further upmarket, *La Vecchia Perusia*, Via Ulisse Rocchi 9, has fine local cuisine. It can fill quickly, so be prepared to wait. A full meal will come close to L40,000. Further upmarket still is the popular *Ristorante del Sole*, Via Oberdan 28. It's actually down a side alley and, if you aren't dazzled by the views, you'll probably want to just roll around in the antipasto and dessert displays. The food tastes as good as it looks, but expect to pay up to L50,000 for a full meal with wine.

There is a covered *market* downstairs from Piazza Matteotti which is open daily, except Sunday, from 7 am to 1.30 pm. You can buy fresh produce, bread, cheese and meat.

Cafés & Bars *Sandri*, Corso Vannucci 32, retains a medieval air and is the city's finest café. Prices are very reasonable. *Caffè del Cambio* at No 29 is a trendy bar, as is *Medio Evo* on Corso Vannucci at Piazza della Repubblica.

Entertainment

The Estate Perugina programme features concerts during August. The box office is in Piazza della Repubblica and is open daily from 5 pm to 8 pm. Venues are near by.

For late-night drinks you could try a Guinness at the *Shamrock Pub*, by the entrance to the Pozzo Etrusco, or check out the *Merlin Pub*, Via del Forno 19, just off Via Fani. The *Contrappunto Jazz Club*, in Via Scortici 4, is one of the best clubs.

Keep an eye on the noticeboards at the Universitá per Stranieri, as the university often organises free concerts and excursions.

Getting There & Away

Bus Most buses terminate at Piazza dei Partigiani (take the escalators from Piazza Italia) for Roma (Stazione Tiburtina) and Fiumicino airport, Firenze (Via Stazione), Siena (train station), L'Aquila and cities throughout Umbria, including Assisi, Gubbio and nearby Lago di Trasimeno. Buses also head into Le Marche and as far south as Cosenza in Calabria. The bus to Roma is faster and cheaper than the train, and the bus station is more convenient to the historic centre than the train station. Full timetables are available at the tourist office.

Train The main train station, Stazione Fontivegge (☎ 500 74 67), is in Piazza Vittorio Veneto, a few km downhill from the city centre and easily accessible by frequent buses. The city is not on the main Roma-Firenze train line, so you generally need to change at Foligno for Roma or at Terontola for Firenze and the north. There are one or two direct trains each day to Roma and Firenze.

The private Ferrovia Centrale Umbra railway (☎ 572 39 47) operates from Stazione Sant'Anna in Piazzale G Bellucci and serves Umbertide, Sansepolcro, Terni and Todi.

Car & Motorcycle From Roma, leave the A1 at the Orte exit and follow the signs for Terni. Once there, take the SS3bis for Perugia. From the north, exit the A1 at Valdichiana and take the dual-carriageway SS75b for Perugia. The SS75 to the east connects the city with Assisi. Hertz (☎ 500 24 39) is at Stazione Fontivegge.

Getting Around

From Stazione Fontivegge catch any bus heading for Piazza Matteotti or Piazza Italia (including Nos 20, 26, 27, 28, 29 and 33) to get to the centre. Tickets cost L1500 and must be bought before you board, and validated in the machine as you enter.

If you arrive in Perugia by car, following the 'centro' signs along the winding roads up the hill should bring you to Piazza Italia, where you can leave your car in a metered parking spot (either on the piazza or on the hill immediately preceding it). You are only allowed to stay for an hour, but on Sunday you can park for as long as you please without paying.

The remainder of the city centre is largely closed to normal, non-resident traffic, although tourists may drive to their hotels. Escalators to large car parks downhill include the one in Via dei Priori (open from 6.45 am to 12.30 pm) that leads to the car parks in Piazza della Cupa and Via Pellini, and the series of escalators that descend through the Rocca Paolina to Piazza dei Partigiani (open from 6.15 am to 1 pm). The supervised car park here costs L1200 for the first hour and L1700 for every hour after. If you intend to use the car park long term, get an *abbonamento* for tourists – this costs

L14,000 for the first two days and then L9000 a day.

LAGO DI TRASIMENO

The fourth-largest lake in Italy, Lago di Trasimeno is not a bad location for swimming, fishing and other water sports, but hardly comparable with the country's northern lakes.

The only blemish is the autostrada on its northern fringe, an area that in 217 BC witnessed one of the bloodiest battles in Roman history as Hannibal's Carthaginians routed Roman troops under Consul Flaminius, killing 16,000. The battlefield extended from Cortona and Ossaia ('the place of bones'), in Toscana, to the small town of Sanguineto ('the bloody'), just north of the lake.

Passignano (or Passignano sul Trasimeno) is the most popular spot by the lake for holidaying Italians, so book accommodation ahead in summer. More enticing is **Castiglione del Lago**, up on a chalky promontory on the lake's western side, dotted with olive trees and dominated by a 14th-century castle.

Information

In Passignano, the tourist office (☎ 82 76 35), Via Roma 25, can assist with accommodation and water sports. It opens daily from 10 am to noon and 3 to 6 pm (morning only on Sunday). In Castiglione del Lago, the tourist office (☎ 965 24 84), Piazza Mazzini 10, is open Monday to Friday from 8.30 am to 1.30 pm and 3.30 to 7 pm, Saturday from 9 am to 6 pm (with a two-hour break from 1.30 pm) and Sunday from 9 am to 1 pm. It can advise on the many agriturismo options and good walking tracks.

The telephone code for the lake region is ☎ 075.

Things to See & Do

Water sports, walking and horse riding are the main reasons to visit the lake. The scenery is agreeable but hardly Umbria's best and the only other attraction is Castiglione del Lago and its **cathedral**, which contains several frescoes by Perugino.

The lake's main inhabited island, **Isola Maggiore**, near Passignano, was reputedly a favourite with St Francis and is noted for its lace and embroidery production. Boats run to the island from the main towns and, although there are no camping grounds, you may pitch a tent.

Ask at one of the tourist offices for *Tourist Itineraries in the Trasimeno District*, a booklet of walking and horse-riding tracks. For horse riding you could contact the Maneggio Oasi (☎ 0337-65 37 95) in Localitá Orto, Castiglione del Lago, or Poggio del Belveduto (☎ 82 90 76) at Passignano. You'll find other riding centres around the lake.

Places to Stay

Passignano Two camping grounds, the *Kursaal* (☎ 82 80 85), Viale Europa 41, and the *Europa* (☎ 82 74 05) in San Donato, are open from April to October. *Pensione del Pescatore* (☎ 82 71 65), Via San Bernardino 5, has singles/doubles for L50,000/80,000 in high season.

Castiglione del Lago The *Listro* camping ground (☎ 95 11 93), Via Lungolago, is open from April to September and costs L7000 per person and per tent. About the cheapest hotel you'll find is *Albergo Fazzuoli* (☎ 95 11 19), Piazza Marconi 11, where rooms cost L60,000/80,000.

Getting There & Away

Passignano is close to the autostrada and served by regular trains from Perugia and Terontola, making it the most accessible part of the lake. The ASP bus from Perugia to Tuoro, a few km west of Passignano, also stops here.

Castiglione del Lago is on the Firenze-Roma line, but board a local train as the Intercities don't stop there. You can also take the ASP bus from Perugia bound for Passignano.

Getting Around

SPNT (☎ 82 71 57) operates regular ferry services between the main towns. The

UMBRIA

company has information offices on the waterfront at each town, where you can pick up a timetable. The return trip to Isola Maggiore from Passignano is L8500.

DERUTA

About 15km south of Perugia, on the SS3bis to Terni, Deruta is famed for its richly coloured and intensely patterned pottery. The Etruscans and Romans worked the clay around Deruta, but it was not until the majolica glazing technique, with its bright blue and yellow metallic oxides, was imported from Majorca in the 15th century that the ceramics industry took off.

There is not much else to Deruta, but it is probably the place to buy ceramics, as prices are lower than in Perugia and other towns. Watch out for low-quality, mass-produced stuff as you browse through the large showrooms in town.

Regular ASP buses connect the town with Perugia, and it has a handful of hotels.

TODI

Originally an Etruscan frontier settlement, Todi ended up as a prosperous *comune* in the early Middle Ages – a prosperity reflected in the grandness of its central Piazza del Popolo.

Set atop a craggy hill, Todi seems to have ignored the 20th century, the growing stream of tourists notwithstanding, and getting there by public transport can be quite a slog.

UMBRIA

Information

The APT del Tuderte (☎ 894 38 67) in Piazza del Popolo is open morning and late afternoon. The town's telephone code is ☎ 075.

Things to See & Do

The 13th-century **Palazzo del Capitano** in Piazza del Popolo features an elegant triple window and houses the city's recently restored Pinacoteca (picture gallery) and Museo Archeologico. They are open daily from 9 am to 1 pm and 3 to 6 pm. Admission is L6000. Also facing the square are the 13th-century **Palazzo del Popolo** and gloomy **Palazzo dei Priori**.

The **duomo**, at the north-western end of the square, has a magnificent rose window and intricately decorated doorway. The 8th-century crypt is worth visiting for the inlaid wooden stalls in the chancel. Spend an hour or two wandering through the medieval labyrinth and popping into some of the other churches.

Special Event

The Todi Festival, held for 10 days each August, is a mixture of classical and jazz concerts, theatre, ballet and cinema.

Places to Stay & Eat

If you are planning to stay, expect to spend a lot of money on accommodation. For agriturismo, contact Agritop-Umbria (☎ 894 26 27), Via Paolo Rolli 3. The cheapest hotel in Todi is the *Tuder* (☎ 894 21 84), Via Maesta dei Lombardi 13, with singles/doubles at L90,000/130,000 in high season. The *Villa Luisa* (☎ 894 85 71), Via A Cortesi 147, has rooms for L100,000/150,000.

The *Ristorante Umbria*, Via Santa Bonaventura 13, behind the tourist office, is reasonably expensive but worth it for the view from the terrace over the countryside. If you'd prefer a pizza (and good views if you snaffle the right tables), try *Ristorante Cavour*, Corso Cavour 21.

Getting There & Away

ASP buses from Perugia terminate in Piazza Iacopone, just south of Piazza del Popolo. Todi is on the Ferrovia Centrale Umbra line; the train station is inconveniently located 3km from the town centre in the valley, although city bus No B makes connections. By road, the city is easily reached by taking the SS3bis between Perugia and Terni.

ASSISI

Despite the millions of tourists and pilgrims it attracts every year, St Francis' home town remains a beautiful and tranquil refuge. From Roman times, its inhabitants have been aware of the visual impact of their city, perched halfway up Monte Subasio. From the valley its pink and white marble buildings shimmer in the sunlight.

St Francis (San Francesco) was born here in 1182 and his spirit hovers over every aspect of the city's life. He renounced his father's wealth in his late teens to pursue a life of chastity and poverty, founding the order of mendicant friars known as the Order of Minors (the Franciscans after his death), which attracted a huge following in Europe. One of his disciples, St Clare (Santa Chiara), born in 1193, was the founder of the Franciscans' female Order of the Poor Clares.

St Francis' Basilica is the city's, and possibly Umbria's, main draw card. Don't be put off by the prospect of huge crowds, but do check before coming to Assisi that your trip doesn't coincide with a religious celebration, when hotels are likely to be booked out.

Orientation

Piazza del Comune is the centre of Assisi. At the north-western edge of this square, Via San Paolo and Via Portica both eventually lead to St Francis' Basilica. Via Portica also leads to the Porta San Pietro and the Piazzale dell'Unità d'Italia, where most intercity buses stop, although ASP buses from smaller towns in the area terminate at Piazza Matteotti. The train station is 4km south-west of the city (use the shuttle bus), in Santa Maria degli Angeli.

Information

Tourist Offices The APT office (☎ 81 25 34), Piazza del Comune 12, is open Monday to Friday from 8 am to 2 pm and 3.30 to 6.30 pm, Saturday from 9 am to 1 pm and 3.30 to 6.30 pm and Sunday from 9 am to 1 pm. It has all the information you need on hotels, sights and events. There is a small branch office (☎ 81 67 66) just outside Porta Nuova.

Money The Cassa di Risparmio di Perugia on Piazza del Comune has an ATM and automatic banknote exchange machine.

Post & Communications There are post offices just inside Porta San Pietro and by Porta Nuova. They are open Monday to Friday from 8.10 am to 6.25 pm and on weekends to 1 pm. Poste restante mail can be addressed to 06081 Assisi.

The Telecom office, open daily from 8 am to 10 pm, is next to the tourist office on Piazza del Comune. The telephone code for Assisi is ☎ 075.

Emergency In an emergency, call ☎ 113. The questura, or *commissariato della pubblica sicurezza* as it is known here, is in Piazza del Comune – call ☎ 81 22 15. The Ospedale di Assisi (☎ 813 92 27) is about 1km south-east of Porta Nuova, in Fuori Porta.

Basilica di San Francesco

This basilica, comprising two churches, one built on top of the other, suffered extensive damage when two earthquakes struck Umbria and Le Marche in September 1997. Four people died when sections of the vaulted ceiling collapsed. The full extent of the damage was still being assessed at the time of writing.

The lower church was started two years after the saint's death in 1228; two years later work began on the upper church on a patch of land known as the Hill of Hell because death sentences were carried out there. The two churches were erected as a compromise after dissent among the Franciscans, some of whom protested against plans for an enormous monument. Appropriately, the name of the hill was changed to Paradise Hill.

The **upper church** (enter from Piazza Superiore di San Francesco) contains Giotto's sequence of 28 frescoes depicting the life of St Francis. Fortunately these frescoes, though cracked, appear to have sustained minor damage. It has long been claimed that these frescoes are by Giotto, but the latest theories indicate at least three major artists were at work here: Pietro Cavallini, an as yet unidentified colleague and, it appears, a young Giotto – possibly the author of the final six scenes. Above the cycle is a series of 32 frescoes depicting

UMBRIA

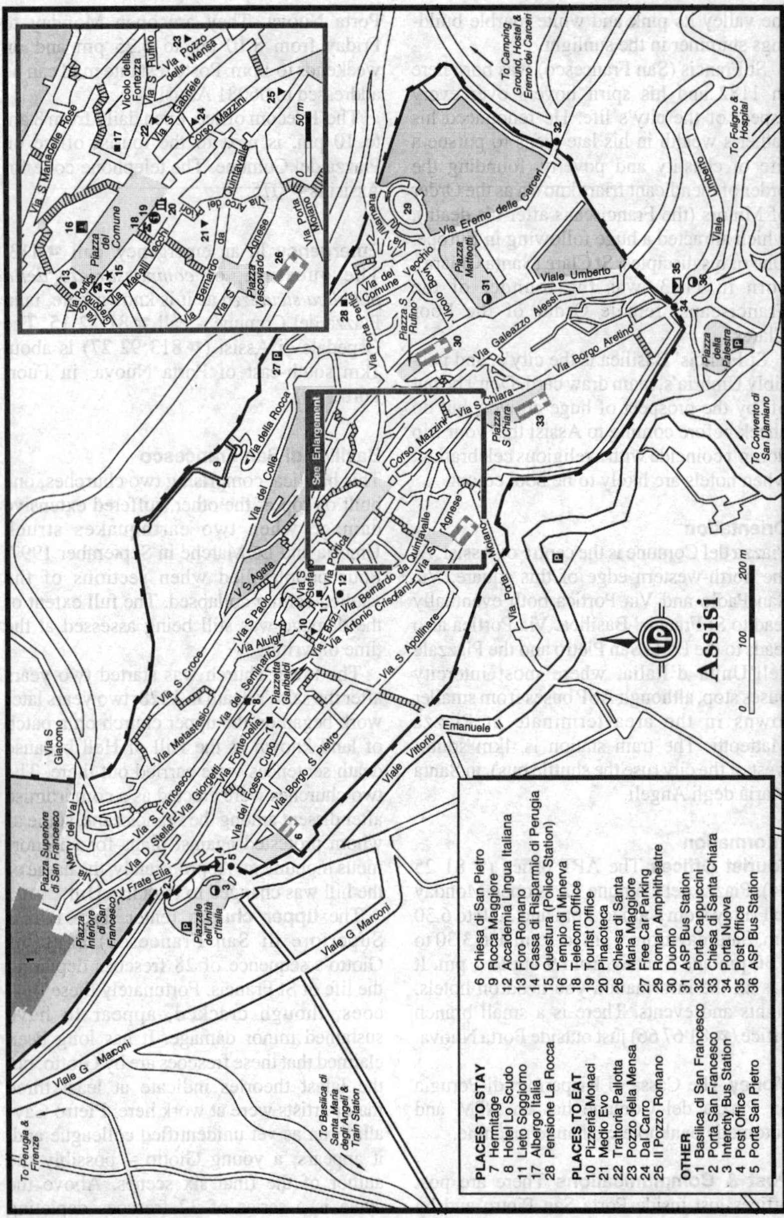
Assisi
See Enlargement
To Camping Ground, Hostel & Eremo dei Carceri
To Foligno & Hospital
To Convento di San Damiano
To Basilica di Santa Maria degli Angeli & Train Station
To Perugia & Firenze
Piazza del Comune
Piazza Superiore di San Francesco
Piazza Inferiore di San Francesco
Piazzale dell'Unità d'Italia
Piazza Matteotti
Piazza S Chiara
Piazza S Rufino
Piazzetta Garibaldi
Piazza Vescovado
Piazza della Palestra
Viale Umberto
Viale Vittorio Emanuele II
Viale G Marconi
Via S Francesco
Corso Mazzini
Via Eremo delle Carceri
Via Borgo Aretino
Via Galeazzo Alessi
Via Porta Moiano
Via S Apollinare
PLACES TO STAY
7 Hermitage
8 Hotel Lo Scudo
11 Lieto Soggiorno
17 Albergo Italia
28 Pensione La Rocca
PLACES TO EAT
10 Pizzeria Monaci
21 Medio Evo
22 Trattoria Pallotta
23 Pozzo della Mensa
24 Dal Carro
25 Il Pozzo Romano
OTHER
1 Basilica di San Francesco
2 Porta San Francesco
3 Intercity Bus Station
4 Post Office
5 Porta San Pietro
6 Chiesa di San Pietro
9 Rocca Maggiore
12 Accademia Lingua Italiana
13 Foro Romano
14 Cassa di Risparmio di Perugia
15 Questura (Police Station)
16 Tempio di Minerva
18 Telecom Office
19 Tourist Office
20 Pinacoteca
26 Chiesa di Santa Maria Maggiore
27 Free Car Parking
29 Roman Amphitheatre
30 Duomo
31 ASP Bus Station
32 Porta Cappuccini
33 Chiesa di Santa Chiara
34 Porta Nuova
35 Post Office
36 ASP Bus Station
0 100 200 m
0 50 m

scenes from the Old Testament, also attributed to Pietro Cavallini.

Unfortunately parts of the frescoes by Cimabue in the apse and transepts were destroyed in the earthquakes. They included the *Crucifixion*, *Visions of the Apocalypse*, *Life of the Virgin* and *Scenes from the Life of St Peter*.

The **lower church** did not appear to have been as badly damaged as the upper church. This church's walls are also covered with frescoes. Those by Simone Martini showing the *Life of St Martin*, in the first chapel on the left as you face the altar, are the highlight.

Along the left wall of the left transept are celebrated frescoes by Pietro Lorenzetti depicting scenes of the Crucifixion and the life of St Francis. Other frescoes above the main altar depict the virtues upon which the Franciscan order was founded – poverty, chastity and obedience. They are attributed to one of Giotto's pupils, dubbed the Maestro delle Vele. In the right transept are works by Cimabue and, below, more scenes by Simone Martini. A small chapel, reached by stairs on the right side of the church, contains various mementos of St Francis' life, including his shirt and sandals, and fragments of his celebrated *Canticle of the Creatures*. Descend the stairs in the middle of the church for the crypt with St Francis' tomb and those of four of his companions. The crypt was rediscovered in 1818, as the coffin had been hidden in the 15th century for fear of desecration.

Dress rules are applied rigidly in the churches – absolutely no shorts, miniskirts or low-cut dresses. The complex was closed for repairs at the time of going to press. Check with the tourist office for further information.

The basilica's **Tesoreria** (Treasury), accessible from the lower church, contains a rich collection of relics given to the Franciscans over the years. The Tesoreria was also closed following the earthquakes. Again, contact the tourist office for information.

Other Attractions

From the basilica, take Via San Francesco back to Piazza del Comune, once the site of a **Roman forum**, parts of which have been excavated. Access is from Via Portica, and admission to the forum and a small museum is L4000. It opens daily from 10 am to 1 pm and 3 to 7 pm (2 to 5 pm in winter). The **Tempio di Minerva** facing the same square is now a church but retains its impressive pillared façade. Wander into some of the shops on the piazza, which open their basements to reveal Roman ruins. The city's **Pinacoteca Comunale**, in the town hall on the southern side of the piazza, features Umbrian Renaissance art and frescoes from Giotto's school. It keeps the same hours as the Foro Romano and admission is L4000. For L10,000 you can get a joint ticket for the forum, Pinacoteca and the Rocca (see later in this section).

Off Via Bernardo da Quintavalle is Piazza Vescovado and the Romanesque **Chiesa di Santa Maria Maggiore**, formerly the city's cathedral and interesting for its rose window. South of Piazza del Comune along Corso Mazzini and Via Santa Chiara is the pink-and-white 13th-century Romanesque **Chiesa di Santa Chiara**, with a deteriorating but nonetheless striking façade. The body of St Clare is in the crypt. If you believe in talking crosses, cast a glance at the Byzantine crucifix that is said to have told St Francis to re-establish the moral foundations of the Church.

North-east of the church, in Piazza San Rufino, the 13th-century Romanesque **duomo**, remodelled by Galeazzo Alessi in the 16th century, contains the font at which St Francis was baptised. The façade is festooned with grotesque figures and fantastic animals typical of this architectural style.

Dominating the city is the massive 14th-century **Rocca Maggiore**, a hill fortress offering fabulous views over the valley and Perugia. It is open daily from 10 am to sunset and admission is L5000, although most of the fortress is closed for a long restoration that will eventually see it converted to an immense art gallery.

A 30-minute walk south from Porta Nuova, the **Convento di San Damiano** was built on the spot where the crucifix spoke to St Francis and where he wrote his *Canticle of the Creatures*. The convent on this pleasant, bucolic site was founded by St Clare.

About 4km east of the city and reached via the Porta Cappuccini is the **Eremo dei Carceri**, to which St Francis retreated after hearing the word of God. The *carceri* (prisons) are the caves that functioned as hermits' retreats for St Francis and his followers. Apart from a few fences and tourist paths, everything has remained as it was in St Francis' time, and a few Franciscans actually live here.

In the valley south-west of the city, near the train station, the imposing **Basilica di Santa Maria degli Angeli** was built around the first Franciscan monastery. St Francis died on 3 October 1226 in its **Cappella del Transito**.

Activities

The APT office has a map produced by the CAI of walks on nearby Monte Subasio (1290m). None is too demanding, and the smattering of religious shrines and camping grounds could make for an enjoyable couple of days.

Courses

If you favour Assisi over Perugia as a place to live and learn Italian, contact the Accademia Lingua Italiana (☎ & fax 81 52 81), Via Giotto 5. It runs a variety of language and culture courses and can arrange accommodation. Its web site at www.krenet.it/alia/ has information.

Special Events

The Festival of St Francis falls on 3 and 4 October and is the main religious event of the city's calendar. Easter week is celebrated with processions and performances. The Ars Nova Musica festival, held from late August to mid-September, features local and national performers. The colourful Festa di Calendimaggio celebrates the coming of spring in perky medieval fashion, and is normally held over several days at the end of the first week of May.

Places to Stay

Assisi is well geared for tourists but in peak periods, such as Easter, August/September and the Festival of St Francis on 3 and 4 October, you will need to book well in advance. Even outside these times many of the hotels will often be full. The tourist office has a full list of private rooms, religious institutions (of which there are 17), flats and agriturismo in and around Assisi. Otherwise keep an eye out for *camere* ('rooms') signs as you wander the streets. If you fail to find anything in Assisi itself, consider staying in Santa Maria degli Angeli, 4km away – this way you are near the train station and a half-hourly shuttle bus to central Assisi.

There is a non-HI *hostel* and *camping ground* just east of town at Fontemaggio (☎ 81 36 36 for both), reached by walking about 2km uphill along Via Eremo dei Carceri. Beds at the hostel are L17,000 and sites start at L6500 a person. The HI youth hostel, the *Ostello della Pace* (☎ 81 67 67), Via Valecchie 171, is open from 1 March to 1 September. B&B is L20,000, or L25,000 in family rooms. It is on the bus line between Santa Maria degli Angeli and Assisi.

Pensione La Rocca (☎ 81 22 84), Via Porta Perlici 27, has singles/doubles for L33,000/53,000 or L47,000/70,000 with private bath. *Albergo Italia* (☎ 81 26 25), Vicolo della Fortezza, just off Piazza del Comune, has singles/doubles for L30,000/50,000, or L45,000/69,000 with bathroom. The two-star *Lieto Soggiorno* (☎ 81 61 91), Via A Fortini 26, near Piazza del Comune, has rooms starting at L45,000/75,000 and doubles with bathroom for L95,000. Closer to the Basilica di San Francesco is *Hotel La Scudo* (☎ 81 31 96), Via San Francesco 3. Simple but decent rooms with bath and shower go for up to L60,000/85,000. The three-star *Hermitage* (☎ 81 27 64; fax 81 66 91), Via degli Aromatari 1, off Via Fontebella, has rooms for L100,000/150,000 and offers car parking.

Places to Eat

For a tasty pizza for L8000 try *Pizzeria Monaci*, by the steps on Piazzetta Garibaldi

If pennies are everything, *Il Pozzo Romano*, Via Sant'Agnese 8, has pizza for L7000 and under. In the same complex as the camping ground at Fontemaggio is *La Stalla*, where you can eat a filling meal under an arbour for about L30,000. *Dal Carro*, Vicolo dei Nepis 2, off Corso Mazzini, is a good bet – the strongozzi alla norcina are a marvel and so is the homemade dessert, tiramisú. Try also *Trattoria Pallotta*, Via San Rufino 4, where a meal will cost around L30,000. *Pozzo della Mensa*, Via Pozzo della Mensa 11, also specialises in Umbrian dishes and a full meal will come to about L40,000. One of the better restaurants is *Medio Evo*, Via Arco dei Priori 4, where an excellent meal will cost about L50,000.

Getting There & Away

ASP buses connect Assisi with Perugia, Foligno and other local towns, leaving from the terminus in Piazza Matteotti. Most ASP buses stop in Largo Properzio, just outside the Porta Nuova. Piazzale dell'Unità d'Italia is the terminus for buses for Roma, Firenze and other major cities.

Although Assisi's train station is 4km away at Santa Maria degli Angeli, train is the best way to get to many places as the frequency of departures is greater than for buses. It is on the Foligno-Terontola line and is about 35 minutes from Perugia. Change at Terontola for Firenze and at Foligno for Roma.

By car, take the SS75 from Perugia, exit at Ospedalicchio and follow the signs.

Getting Around

A shuttle bus operates every half-hour between Assisi and the train station. Normal traffic is subject to restrictions in the city centre and daytime parking is all but banned. If you object to paying for one of the several car parks dotted around the city walls (and connected to the centre by orange shuttle buses), head for the road that leads up to the Rocca (close to Pensione La Rocca) – there are no restrictions beyond the 'P' for parking sign. This leaves you a fairly short, if steep, walk from the duomo and Piazza del Comune.

SPELLO

Spello's proximity to Perugia and Assisi makes it well worth a quick morning or afternoon trip. Emperor Augustus developed much of the land in the valley, but the Roman ruins are some distance from the town and your time would be better spent wandering Spello's narrow cobbled streets.

There is a small tourist office at Piazza Matteotti 3, or you can pick up info at the APT in Assisi.

The Augustan **Porta Venere** leads to the gloomy **Chiesa di Sant'Andrea** on Piazza Matteotti, where you can admire a fresco by Bernardino Pinturicchio. A few doors down is the 12th-century **Chiesa di Santa Maria Maggiore** and the town's real treat, Pinturicchio's beautiful frescoes in the Cappella Baglioni. Also of note is the pavement (dating from 1566) made of tiles from Deruta.

The people of Spello celebrate the feast of Corpus Domini in June (the date changes each year) by skilfully decorating stretches of the main street with fresh flowers in colourful designs. If you want to enjoy it, come on the Saturday evening before the Sunday procession to see the floral fantasies being laid out (from about 8.30 pm on) and participate in the festive atmosphere. The Corpus procession begins at 11 am on Sunday – but the crowds can make it a stifling event.

Hotels are expensive and there are cheaper options in Assisi and Perugia. *Affittacamere Merulli* (☎ 0742-65 11 84), Via Belvedere, has simple singles/doubles for L40,000/60,000. Otherwise, you can try *Il Cacciatore* (☎ 0742-65 11 41), Via Giulia 42, which has rooms with bathroom for L70,000/100,000. It also has a restaurant with a large terrazza, perfect for a summer lunch. A classy alternative is the exquisite 18th-century *Hotel Palazzo Bocci* (☎ 0742-30 10 21), Via Cavour 17, where double rooms cost from L180,000.

ASP buses running between Perugia and Foligno serve the town, and there are also connections to Assisi. Trains are a better option, as Spello is on the line connecting Perugia, Assisi and Foligno. A shuttle bus connects the station with central Spello. By car, Spello is on the SS75 between Perugia and Foligno.

AROUND SPELLO

Those with time and (better still) their own wheels, could do worse than undertake a few excursions in the area south-west of Spello. **Bevagna**, about 8km west of Foligno (through which you'll need to pass on public transport), is a charming, medieval hamlet with a couple of Romanesque churches on the central Piazza Silvestri. It comes to life in the last week of June for the Mercato delle Gaite, a bit of a medieval lark where olde-worlde taverns open up and medieval-era handcrafts are brought back to life. The town also boasts a few remnants of its Roman days, including some impressive mosaics at the site of former Roman hot baths.

Seven km south, **Montefalco** is also known as the Ringhiera dell'Umbria for its expansive views. Again, the town is a pleasant medieval backwater graced with several churches. The deconsecrated Chiesa di San Francesco now serves as an overpriced art gallery. Do not leave here without trying the local Sagrantino wine.

GUBBIO

Hitched onto the steep slopes of Monte Ingino and overlooking a picturesque valley, the centuries-old *palazzi* of Gubbio exude a warm ochre glow in the late afternoon sunlight. It does not require a great effort of imagination to feel you have stepped back into the Middle Ages when meandering along the town's quiet, treeless lanes.

Gubbio is famous for its Eugubian Tables, which date from the 3rd century BC and constitute the best existing example of ancient Umbrian script. An important ally of imperial Roma and a key stop on the Via Flaminia, the town declined during the barbarian invasions. In the 14th century it fell into the hands of the Montefeltro family of Urbino and was later incorporated into the Papal States.

Like many hill towns from Toscana to Le Marche, Gubbio has taken on the feel of a museum, but a day spent here would be spent well.

Orientation

The city is small and easy to explore. The immense traffic circle known as Piazza Quaranta Martiri, at the base of the hill, is where buses to the city terminate, and it also has a large car park. The square was named in honour of 40 local people who were killed by the Nazis in 1944 in reprisal for partisan activities. From here it is a short, if somewhat steep, walk along Via della Repubblica to the main square, Piazza Grande, also known as the Piazza della Signoria. Corso Garibaldi and Piazza Oderisi are to your right as you head up the hill.

Information

The APT tourist office (☎ 922 06 93) in Piazza Oderisi is open Monday to Friday from 8.15 am to 1.45 pm and 3.30 to 6.30 pm (to 6 pm in winter), Saturday from 9 am to 1 pm and Sunday from 9.30 am to 12.30 pm. You can also get info at Easy Gubbio, Via della Repubblica 13, near Piazza Quaranta Martiri.

The main post office, Via Cairoli 11, is open Monday to Saturday from 8.10 am to 5 pm. The Telecom office is at Easy Gubbio and the telephone code for Gubbio is ☎ 075.

For police emergencies, call ☎ 113, or try the local police at the Pretura, Via XX Settembre 97. The Ospedale Civile (☎ 9 23 91) is in Piazza Quaranta Martiri.

Chiesa di San Francesco

Attributed to Perugia's Fra Bevignate, this church on Piazza Quaranta Martiri features impressive frescoes by a local artist, Ottaviano Nelli. Wander into the **Chiostro della Pace** (Cloister of Peace) in the adjoining convent to view some ancient mosaics.

Piazza Grande

Gubbio's grandest buildings look out over

Piazza Grande, dominated above all by the 14th-century **Palazzo dei Consoli**, attributed to Gattapone. The crenellated façade and tower can be seen from all over the town. The building houses the **Museo Civico**, with the Eugubian Tables, discovered in 1444 near the Roman theatre west of Piazza Quaranta Martiri. The seven bronze tablets date from 300 to 100 BC and are the main source for research into the ancient Umbrian language. Upstairs is the picture gallery, which features works from the Gubbian school. The museum and gallery are open daily from 10 am to 1.30 pm (to 1 pm in winter) and 3 to 6 pm (to 7 pm in August, 2 to 5 pm in winter). Admission is L4000. Across the square is the **Palazzo Pretorio**, built along similar lines to its grander counterpart and now the city's town hall.

Duomo & Palazzo Ducale

Via Ducale leads up to the 13th-century pink duomo, a plain beast with a fine 12th-century stained-glass window, a fresco attributed to Bernardino Pinturicchio and not much else. The Palazzo Ducale opposite was built by the Montefeltro family as a scaled-down version of their grand palace in Urbino, and its walls hide an impressive Renaissance courtyard. It opens Monday to Saturday from 9 am to 1.30 pm and 2.30 to 7 pm (Sunday mornings only), and entry is L4000.

Other Monuments

From Piazza Grande, Via dei Consoli leads north-west to the 13th-century **Palazzo del Bargello**, the city's medieval police station and prison. In front of it is the **Fontana dei Pazzi**, so named because of a belief that if you walk around it three times, you will go mad – on summer weekends the number of tourists carrying out this ritual is indeed cause for wondering about their collective sanity. At Via San Giuliano 1-3, just south of Palazzo Bargello, a rather crumbly 15th-century mansion houses the **Antica Fabbrica**

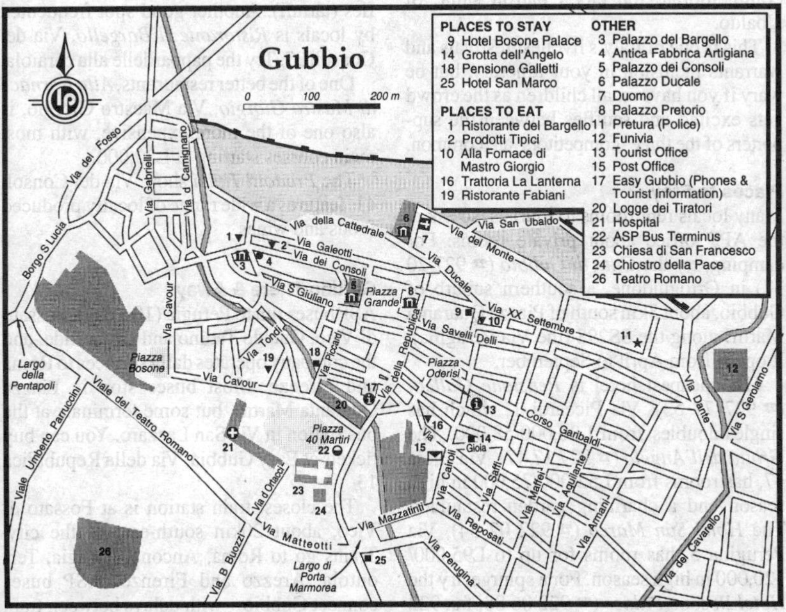

UMBRIA

Artigiana, an exuberant display of fine ceramics – in the Middle Ages one of the city's main sources of income.

South of Piazza Quaranta Martiri, off Viale del Teatro Romano, are the overgrown remains of a 1st-century AD **Roman theatre**. Most of what you see is the result of reconstruction.

From Via San Gerolamo you can ride the curious birdcage funicular *(funivia)* to the **Basilica di Sant'Ubaldo**, an uninspiring church that houses the three huge 'candles' used during the Corsa dei Ceri (see the following Special Event section).

Special Event

The Corsa dei Ceri (Candles Race) is held each year on 15 May. The event starts at 5.30 am and involves three teams, each carrying a *cero* (these 'candles' are massive wooden pillars weighing about 400kg, each bearing a statue of a 'rival' saint) and racing through the city's streets. It is all very complicated, but there is lots of festivity, all intended to commemorate the city's patron saint, St Ubaldo.

This is one of Italy's liveliest festivals and warrants inclusion in your itinerary, but be wary if you have small children as the crowd gets excited and scuffles between the supporters of the three 'competitors' are common.

Places to Stay

Many locals rent rooms to tourists, so ask at the APT office about private rooms. For camping, try the *Città di Gubbio* (☎ 927 20 37) in Ortoguidone, a southern suburb of Gubbio, about 3km south of Piazza Quaranta Martiri along the SS298 (the Via Perugina). It opens from April to September.

The cheapest hotel is *Pensione Galletti* (☎ 927 77 53), Via Piccardi 1, which has singles/doubles from L36,000/58,000. The *Grotta dell'Angelo* (☎ 927 17 47), Via Gioia 47, has rooms from L52,000/75,000 in high season and a charming garden restaurant. The *Hotel San Marco* (☎ 922 02 34), Via Perugina 5, has rooms for up to L95,000/120,000 in high season. For a splurge, try the *Hotel Bosone Palace* (☎ 922 06 88; fax 922 05 52), Via XX Settembre 22, a 14th-century palace rebuilt in the 18th century. Singles/doubles start at L95,000/120,000 in low season, but doubles can rocket as high as L200,000 or more in peak periods.

Out of town on the state road connecting Gubbio and Perugia is *Oasi Verde Mengara* (☎ 92 01 56). It's an agriturismo establishment, where half board costs up to L70,000 and full board L85,000. Its fine restaurant is open to the public and you can eat a memorable and very filling meal for around L30,000. Oasi Verdi Mengara is easily accessible from Gubbio on the regular ASP bus to Perugia. It stops right outside the hotel/restaurant.

Places to Eat

Ristorante Fabiani, Piazza Quaranta Martiri 26, is a good traditional trattoria where a meal will cost around L30,000. You'll pay about the same at the *Trattoria La Lanterna*, Via Gioia 23, where local specialities are on hand and many meals feature delicious truffles (tartufi). Another good spot frequented by locals is *Ristorante Il Bargello*, Via dei Consoli 37. Try the pappardelle alla ceraiola.

One of the better restaurants, *Alla Fornace di Mastro Giorgio*, Via Maestro Giorgio, is also one of the more expensive, with most main courses starting at L20,000.

The *Prodotti Tipici* shop, Via dei Consoli 41, features a wide range of locally produced foods and wines.

Getting There & Away

ASP buses run to Perugia (10 a day), Fossato di Vico, Gualdo Tadino and Umbertide, and the company operates daily services to Roma and Firenze. Most buses stop in Piazza Quaranta Martiri, but some terminate at the bus station in Via San Lazzaro. You can buy tickets at Easy Gubbia, Via della Repubblica 13.

The closest train station is at Fossato di Vico, about 20km south-east of the city. Trains go to Roma, Ancona, Perugia, Terontola, Arezzo and Firenze. ASP buses connect Gubbio – with delays between train and bus connections of anything between five minutes and an hour.

By car and motorcycle, take the SS298 from Perugia, or the SS76 from Ancona, and follow the signs. Parking in the large car park in Piazza Quaranta Martiri costs L1000 an hour.

Getting Around

Walking is best, but ASP buses connect Piazza Quaranta Martiri with the funicular station and most main sights.

AROUND GUBBIO

Parco Regionale del Monte Cucco

East of Gubbio, this park is a haven for outdoor activities and is dotted with caves, many of which can be explored. It is well set up for walkers, rock climbers and horse riders and has many hotels and mountain *rifugi*. **Costacciaro**, reached by bus from Gubbio, is a good base for exploring the area, and is the starting point for a walk to the summit of Monte Cucco (1566m).

Information is available from the APT office in Gubbio. The Centro Escursionistico Naturalistico Speleologico (☎ 075-917 04 00), Via Galeazzi 5 in Costacciaro, can also help with information about exploring local caves, walking and mountain-bike routes. The CAI produces a walking map entitled *Carta dei Sentieri Massiccio del Monte Cucco*. It is possible to rent mountain bikes at the Coop Arte e Natura (☎ 075-917 07 40), Via Stazione 2 in the village of Fossato di Vico, about 8km south of Costacciaro.

There are several horse-riding schools around Gubbio that arrange lessons or treks. Rio Verde (☎ 075-917 01 38) is north-east of the city in a hamlet called Fornace. They open in summer only. A farm where you can stay is the *Azienda Agraria Allevamento San Giovanni* (☎ 075-925 66 46), south-east at Torre Calzolari. Ask for directions when you arrive in these towns.

Alte Valle del Tevere

The northernmost reaches of Umbria, clamped in between Toscana and Le Marche and known as the Alta Valle del Tevere (Upper Tevere Valley), hardly constitute the region's showcase, but there are a few odds and ends to keep you occupied. Among the more interesting spots are **Città di Castello**, which was a powerful comune during the Renaissance, **Umbertide**, with a couple of castles and dominated by a 14th-century fortress (closed to the public), and **San Giustino**, whose centre is graced by the Castello Bufalini. The area is connected to Perugia by the private Ferrovia Centrale Umbra railway and the occasional bus. SITA buses also connect to nearby Arezzo and thence on to Firenze, in Toscana. It's best to explore the area on your own wheels.

SPOLETO

Each June and July, this otherwise quiet town takes centre stage for a parade of cultural and often snobbish sophistication, the Festival dei Due Mondi. The Italian-American composer Gian Carlo Menotti, with his American partner Thomas Schippers, set up the festival in Spoleto in 1958 after inspecting more than 30 other towns for their suitability. Did the fact that Menotti was born here at all influence his choice? The festival has given the city a worldwide reputation and brought great wealth to the small population who bask in the reflected glory of this international celebration of drama, music and dance.

If you plan to visit Spoleto during the festival, book accommodation and tickets months in advance. When the festival ends, Spoleto goes back to sleep, but it is nonetheless an enchanting town to spend a day exploring.

Orientation

The old part of the city is half a km south of the main train station – take the orange shuttle bus marked Circolare D for Piazza della Libertá in the centre, where you'll find the tourist office and the Roman-era theatre. Piazza del Mercato, a short walk north-east of Piazza della Libertá, marks the engaging heart of old Spoleto. Between here and Piazza del Duomo you'll find the bulk of the city's monuments and some fine shops.

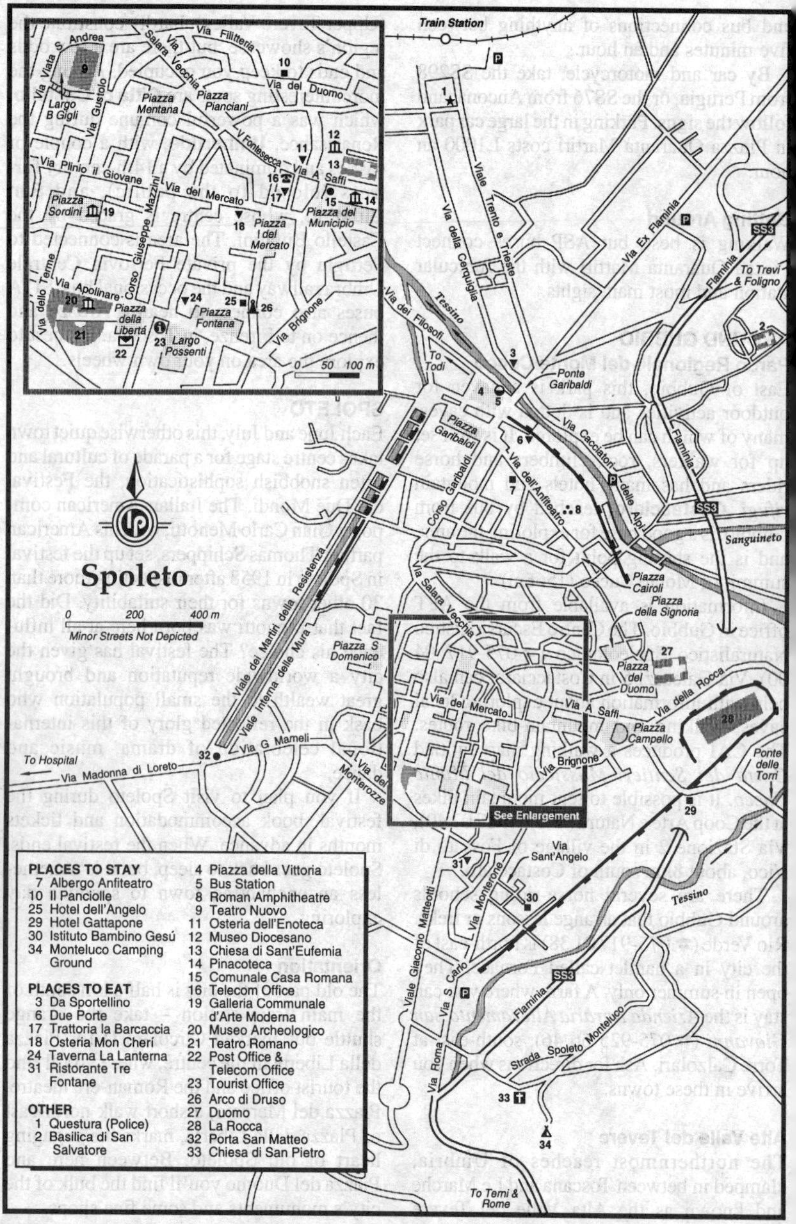
Spoleto
0 200 400 m
Minor Streets Not Depicted
PLACES TO STAY
7 Albergo Anfiteatro
10 Il Panciolle
25 Hotel dell'Angelo
29 Hotel Gattapone
30 Istituto Bambino Gesú
34 Monteluco Camping Ground
PLACES TO EAT
3 Da Sportellino
6 Due Porte
17 Trattoria la Barcaccia
18 Osteria Mon Cheri
24 Taverna La Lanterna
31 Ristorante Tre Fontane
OTHER
1 Questura (Police)
2 Basilica di San Salvatore
4 Piazza della Vittoria
5 Bus Station
8 Roman Amphitheatre
9 Teatro Nuovo
11 Osteria dell'Enoteca
12 Museo Diocesano
13 Chiesa di Sant'Eufemia
14 Pinacoteca
15 Comunale Casa Romana
16 Telecom Office
19 Galleria Communale d'Arte Moderna
20 Museo Archeologico
21 Teatro Romano
22 Post Office & Telecom Office
23 Tourist Office
26 Arco di Druso
27 Duomo
28 La Rocca
32 Porta San Matteo
33 Chiesa di San Pietro
Train Station
Viale Trento e Trieste
Via della Cerquiglia
Via Ex Flaminia
Flaminia
SS3
To Trevi & Foligno
Tessino
Via dei Filosofi
To Todi
Ponte Garibaldi
Piazza Garibaldi
Via Cacciatori delle Alpi
Corso Garibaldi
Via dell'Anfiteatro
Sangnineto
Viale dei Martiri della Resistenza
Viale Interna delle Mura
Via Salara Vecchia
Piazza Cairoli
Piazza della Signoria
Piazza S Domenico
Piazza del Duomo
Via della Rocca
Via del Mercato
Via A Saffi
Piazza Campello
Via Brignone
Ponte delle Torri
See Enlargement
Via G Mameli
To Hospital
Via Madonna di Loreto
Via del Monterozze
Via Sant'Angelo
Via Monterone
Viale Giacomo Matteotti
Via S Carlo
Via Roma
Strada Spoleto Monteluco
To Terni & Rome
Via Viata S Andrea
Via Filitteria
Via Salara Vecchia
Largo B Gigli
Via Gustolo
Piazza Mentana
Piazza Pianciani
Via del Duomo
V Fontesecca
Via Plinio il Giovane
Via del Mercato
Piazza Sordini
Corso Giuseppe Mazzini
Piazza I del Mercato
Piazza del Municipio
Via delle Terme
Via Apolinare
Piazza della Libertà
Piazza Fontana
Largo Possenti
Via Brignone
0 50 100 m

Information

Tourist Office The APT office (☎ 22 03 11), Piazza della Libertà 7, has loads of information about the town and good city maps. It is open daily from 9 am to 1 pm (on weekends and holidays 10 am to 1 pm) and from 4.30 to 7.30 pm. You can also email the office: turispo@mail.caribusiness.it.

Post & Communications The main post office faces Piazza della Libertà, although the entrance is off Viale Giacomo Matteotti. It is open Monday to Saturday from 8.15 am to 7 pm. The post code for the town centre is 06049.

The main Telecom office is at Via A Saffi 6, and opens daily from 8 am to 10 pm. The tourist office also has a range of national telephone books. The telephone code for Spoleto is ☎ 0743.

Emergency In an emergency, call ☎ 113, or head for the questura (☎ 4 03 24) on Viale di Trento e Trieste (a block from the train station). The casualty section of Ospedale di Madonna di Loreto (☎ 22 10 71) is on Via Madonna di Loreto, west of Porta San Matteo. For an ambulance, call ☎ 4 48 88.

Roman Spoleto

Pick up a map and walking itinerary from the APT office, and make the **Roman theatre** on the western edge of Piazza della Libertà your first stop. The 1st-century theatre has been rebuilt many times and is used for performances in summer. Have a quick look at the ceramics collection in the **Museo Archeologico** next to the theatre. The theatre and museum are open Monday to Saturday from 9 am to 1.30 pm and 2.30 to 7 pm, and Sunday from 9 am to 1 pm. Admission costs L4000.

East of Piazza della Libertà, around Piazza Fontana, are more Roman remnants, including the **Arco di Druso e Germanico**, which marked the entrance to the old forum. The excavated **Casa Romana** (Roman house) on Via di Visiale dates from the 1st century AD. It is open daily, except Monday, from 10 am to 1 pm and 3 to 6 pm. To get in you have to buy a L5000 ticket that also covers entry to the Pinacoteca (see the Other Attractions section) round the corner and the **Galleria Comunale d'Arte Moderna**, in Palazzo Spada off Corso Mazzini.

The city boasts a **Roman amphitheatre**, one of the country's largest, although it is enclosed within a military barracks and closed to the public. Wander along Via dell'Anfiteatro, off Piazza Garibaldi, in search of a glimpse.

Spoleto's Churches

A short walk through Piazza del Municipio takes you to the 12th-century **Chiesa di Sant'Eufemia** in the grounds of the Archbishop's palace. The church is notable for its *matronei*, galleries set high above the main body of the church to segregate the female congregation. Artists from the 15th-century Sienese school left behind some striking frescoes. Entry costs L5000, which includes access to the **Museo Diocesano** next door.

From here, it is a quick stroll to the **duomo**, consecrated in 1198 and remodelled in the 17th century. The Romanesque façade is fronted by a Renaissance porch. In the 11th century, huge blocks of stone salvaged from Roman buildings were put to good use in the construction of the rather sombre bell tower. Inside, the first chapel to the right of the nave was decorated by Bernardino Pinturicchio, and Annibale Carracci completed an impressive fresco in the right transept. The frescoes in the domed apse were executed by Filippo Lippi and his assistants. Lippi died before completing the work, and Lorenzo de Medici travelled to Spoleto from Firenze and ordered Lippi's son, Filippino, to build a mausoleum for the artist. This now stands in the right transept of the cathedral. At No 8 Piazza del Duomo stands the house where composer Gian Carlo Menotti was born.

Other Attractions

The **Pinacoteca Comunale** is in the town hall in Piazza del Municipio. Unfortunately, you must be guided around the gallery, although the sumptuous building and some impressive works by Umbrian artists compensate a little. Opening hours are the same as for the Casa Romana, which is covered by the same L5000 ticket.

Dominating the city is **La Rocca**, a former papal fortress that, until 1982, was a high-security prison housing such notables as Pope John Paul II's attempted assassin, Ali Agca. It is closed for restoration.

Along Via del Ponte is the **Ponte delle Torri**, erected in the 14th century on the foundations of a Roman aqueduct. The bridge is named after the towers on the far side.

If you feel like a walk, cross the bridge and follow the lower path, Strada di Monteluco, for the **Chiesa di San Pietro**. The 13th-century façade, the church's main attraction, is liberally bedecked with sculpted animals.

Special Events

Events at the Festival dei Due Mondi, held from late June to mid-July, range from cinema and theatre to ballet and art exhibitions. Tickets cost from L10,000 to L200,000, depending on the performance and whether you want luxury seats or standing room, and generally sell out by March.

For information and tickets, head for the Teatro Nuovo (☎ 4 40 97 or ☎ 4 02 56), Largo B Gigli. Bookings can be made from outside Italy by writing to: Associazione Festival dei Due Mondi, c/o Teatro Nuovo, 06049 Spoleto, Italy. You will first need to contact the office for a programme.

Places to Stay

The city is well served with cheap hotels, private rooms, hostels and camping grounds, although if you're going for the festival you will need to book a room months in advance.

The closest camping ground is *Monteluco* (☎ 22 03 58), just behind the Chiesa di San Pietro, open from April to September. It charges L9000 per person and L8000 for a tent in high season. *Camping Il Girasole* (☎ 5 13 35) is about 10km north-west of Spoleto in Petrognano. Buses connect with the town from Spoleto's train station.

There are also agriturismo options around Spoleto. The tourist office has a booklet with all the details.

The *Istituto Bambino Gesù* (☎ 4 02 32) is a religious hostel, just off Via Monterone at Via Sant'Angelo 4; it has singles/doubles for L40,000/80,000.

The *Albergo Anfiteatro* (☎ 4 98 53), Via dell'Anfiteatro 14, has rooms from L55,000/75,000. *Il Panciolle* (☎ 4 56 77), Via del Duomo 3, is in a good location and has rooms with bathroom from L60,000/90,000. *Hotel dell'Angelo* (☎ 22 23 85), Via Arco di Druso 25, is similarly priced.

One of the best located hotels is *Hotel Gattapone* (☎ 22 34 47; fax 22 34 48), Via del Ponte 6, with rooms overlooking Ponte delle Torri from L130,000/160,000.

Places to Eat

Spoleto is one of Umbria's main producers of the tartufo nero (black truffles), used in a variety of dishes. However, trying them can be a costly exercise – so check the price before digging in.

A great place in the town centre is *Taverna La Lanterna*, Via della Trattoria 6. It does a variety of Umbrian pasta dishes and a full meal should not cost much more than L25,000. *Osteria dell'Enoteca*, Via A Saffi 7, has a good-value tourist menu incorporating local dishes for just L18,000. Or you could buy some Umbrian wine and food products. Nearby, the *Trattoria la Barcaccia*, Piazza Fratelli Bandiera 2, offers a L25,000 tourist menu. For pizza, try *Ristorante Tre Fontane*, Via Egio 15, which offers pleasant garden dining.

Outside the old town, *Due Porte*, Piazza della Vittoria 14, is a good, cheap restaurant where pasta costs from L7000. *Da Sportellino*, Viale della Cerquiglia 4, has main courses from L15,000.

Getting There & Away

Most Società Spoletina Trasporti (SSIT) buses (☎ 21 22 11) depart from Piazza della Vittoria for Monteluco, Foligno, Terni, Roma, Bastardo, Assisi, Perugia and dozens of smaller towns. Trains from the main station (☎ 4 85 16), Piazza Polvani, connect with Roma, Ancona, Perugia and Assisi. The city is on the SS3, basically the old Roman Via Flaminia, which runs from Terni to Foligno. From Terni, it's a short trip to the A1. Car parks are located at all main approaches to the city.

Getting Around

The city is easily seen on foot, although local buses weave through the streets. Orange shuttle bus Circolare D runs between the train station, Piazza Garibaldi and Piazza della Libertá.

THE VALNERINA

Incorporating most of the lower eastern parts of Umbria, along the Nera river, the Valnerina is a beautiful area. Stretching north to the barren summit of Monte Sibilla (2175m) in neighbouring Le Marche, it makes for great walking territory. It also offers a couple of hang-gliding schools in one of the best areas in Europe to learn.

If you want to spend a few quiet days wandering around the valley, try the hotel *Agli Scacchi* (☎ 0743-9 92 21), a pleasant little establishment in the pretty medieval village of **Preci**. It has singles/doubles for L55,000/80,000 and half board for up to L75,000 per person.

The area is criss-crossed by walking trails and you might try to pick up a copy of the aptly titled *20 Sentieri Ragionati in Valnerina* (20 Well-Thought-Out Routes in Valnerina).

If you are driving, the APT Valnerina-Cascia (☎ 0743-7 11 47), Piazza Garibaldi 1, in Cascia, is a good place to start. Tourist bodies in Umbria and Le Marche have erected road signs on the roadside to identify driving itineraries.

Getting There & Away

Spoleto is the best point from which to head into the Valnerina. Spoleto's SSIT bus company (☎ 0743-21 22 11) operates several buses a day to the terminal at Via della Stazione in Norcia, from where connecting bus services along the Valnerina to Preci and Cascia depart. Getting to Castelluccio is not so easy, as there are two services from Norcia on Monday and Saturday only.

By car, the SS395 from Spoleto and SS209 from Terni connect with the SS320 and then the SS396, which passes through Norcia. The area can also be reached from Ascoli Piceno in Le Marche.

Norcia

This fortified medieval village is the main town in the valley and a transport hub of sorts; it also produces what is considered to be the country's best salami. Like the rest of the Valnerina, Norcia has suffered badly from earthquakes over the centuries. There is a small tourist office in the central Piazza San Benedetto.

Activities For information on walking and other activities in the surrounding area, head for the Casa del Parco (☎ 0743-61 70 90), Via Solferino 22. It is open daily from 9.30 am to 12.30 pm and 3 to 6 pm.

Hang-gliders should aim for Castelluccio (see the Around Norcia section).

Places to Stay *Da Benito* (☎ 0743-81 66 70), Via Marconi 5, has rooms which cost from L50,000/75,000. The *Hotel Garden* (☎ 0743-81 66 87), Via XX Settembre 2, has rooms for L80,000/150,000 (much less out of season).

Around Norcia

If you have a car, don't miss the opportunity to visit the vast **Piano Grande**, a high plateau north-east of Norcia, under Monte Vettore (2476m). It becomes a sea of colour as flowers bloom in early spring.

Perched above the plain is the tiny, hilltop village of **Castelluccio**. If you want to stay overnight, *Albergo Sibilla* (☎ 0743-87 01 13), Via Piano Grande 2, has singles/doubles for up to L55,000/90,000. About 10km north of Castelluccio at Monte Prata there's a free *camping ground* (☎ 0737-98 28), which opens from 15 June for the summer months. Free-camping in the plain itself doesn't seem to be a problem.

The area forms part of the **Parco Nazionale dei Monti Sibillini**, where you can indulge several outdoor whims. Before heading off into the Monti Sibillini, at least buy Kompass map No 666 (scale 1:50,000) of walking trails. If you want to learn hang-gliding, contact Pro Delta (☎ 0743-82 11 56), Via delle Fate 3 in Norcia (in summer only). Another school is Fly Castelluccio, but the office (☎ 0736-25 56 30) is based at Via Iannella 31, Ascoli Piceno, in the neighbouring region of Le Marche. A beginners course of five days will cost about L700,000. This is also mountain-bike territory. To hire bikes you could try the Associazione Pian Grande (☎ 0743-81 72 79), Pian Grande di Castelluccio di Norcia.

TERNI

Terni is a major industrial city, virtually obliterated in WWII bombing raids and subsequently rebuilt. St Valentine was born here, and was bishop of Terni until his martyrdom in 269 AD. Public transport users might need to pass through here on the way to the Valnerina, Norcia and the Monti Sibillini.

Terni's tourist office (☎ 0744-42 30 47) is south of the main train station and just west of Piazza C Tacito at Viale Cesare Battisti 7, near Largo Don Minzoni. It is closed during the middle of the day and on Sunday.

If you arrive in Terni by train and need to get to the bus station in Piazza Europa, or vice versa, catch local bus No 1 or 2.

UMBRIA

Cascate delle Marmore

About 6km east of Terni, this waterfall was created by the Romans in 290 BC when they diverted the Velino river into the Nera river. These days, the waterfall provides hydroelectric power and its flow is confined to certain times of the day. It is worth catching a bus to see it, particularly to witness the arrival of the water after it has been switched on. The falls operate on weekends all year round, usually for an hour or so before midday and again for a couple of hours in the late afternoon and early evening. They also operate for a couple of hours (mostly afternoons around 4 pm) on weekdays from mid-March to the end of August. The water is illuminated in the course of a sound-and-light show. Whenever the fall is switched on, the SS79 road connecting Terni with Roma resembles a car park as drivers stop to gawk at the spectacle. Ask at the Terni tourist office for the exact times that the water is turned on. Local bus No 24 runs to the falls. A number of short walking tracks around the falls allow you to get close up.

ORVIETO

The phalanxes of high-season tourists who crowd into Orvieto are drawn first and foremost by the magnificent duomo, one of Italy's finest Gothic buildings. The town rests on top of a craggy cliff, pretty much in the same spot as its precursor, the Etruscan League city of Velsina. Although medieval Orvieto is the magnet, Etruscan tombs testify to the area's antiquity.

Orientation

Trains pull in at Orvieto Scalo, the modern, downhill extension of the town. From here you can catch bus No 1 up to the old town, or the funicular railway to Piazza Cahen, from where you can walk straight ahead along Corso Cavour, turning left into Via del Duomo to reach the duomo. There's also plenty of parking in Piazza Cahen and in several parking stations outside the old city walls.

Information

The APT office (☎ 34 17 72) is at Piazza del Duomo 24 and is open Monday to Friday from 8 am to 2 pm and 4 to 7 pm, Saturday from 10 am to 1 pm and 4 to 7 pm, and Sunday from 10 am to midday and 4 to 6 pm. It can be hard to even get a decent map out of them.

The post office is at Via Cesare Nebbia, off Corso Cavour, and is open Monday to Saturday from 8.10 am to 6 pm. The post code for the town centre is 05018. There is an unstaffed Telecom phone office at Corso

Cavour 119, open daily from 8 am to 10 pm. The telephone code for Orvieto is ☎ 0763.

In a police emergency, call ☎ 113, or contact the questura (☎ 34 47 93) in Piazza Cahen. The hospital (☎ 30 91) is in Piazza del Duomo. In a medical emergency, call ☎ 34 02 44.

Duomo

Little can prepare you for the visual feast of this most remarkable edifice. Started in 1290, the cathedral was originally planned in the Romanesque style, but as work proceeded and architects changed, Gothic features were incorporated into the structure. The black-and-white marble banding of the main body of the church, reminiscent of other great churches you may already have seen in Tuscan cities like Siena and Pisa, is overshadowed by the rainbow riches of the façade. A harmonious blend of mosaic and sculpture, plain stone and dazzling colour, it has been likened to a giant outdoor altar screen.

Pope Urban IV ordered that the cathedral be built after the so-called 'Miracle of Bolsena' in 1263. A Bohemian priest who was passing through the town of Bolsena (near Orvieto) had doubts about transubstantiation but, while celebrating mass, his uncertainty was dispelled when blood began to drip from the Host onto the altar linen. The linen was presented to Pope Urban IV, in Orvieto at the time, who declared the event a miracle and set the wheels in motion for the construction of the cathedral. He also declared the new feast day of Corpus Domini.

The building took 30 years to plan and three centuries to complete. It was probably started by Perugia's Fra Bevignate and continued by Lorenzo Maitani (responsible for Firenze's duomo), Andrea Pisano, Nino Pisano, Andrea Orcagna and Michele Sammichelli.

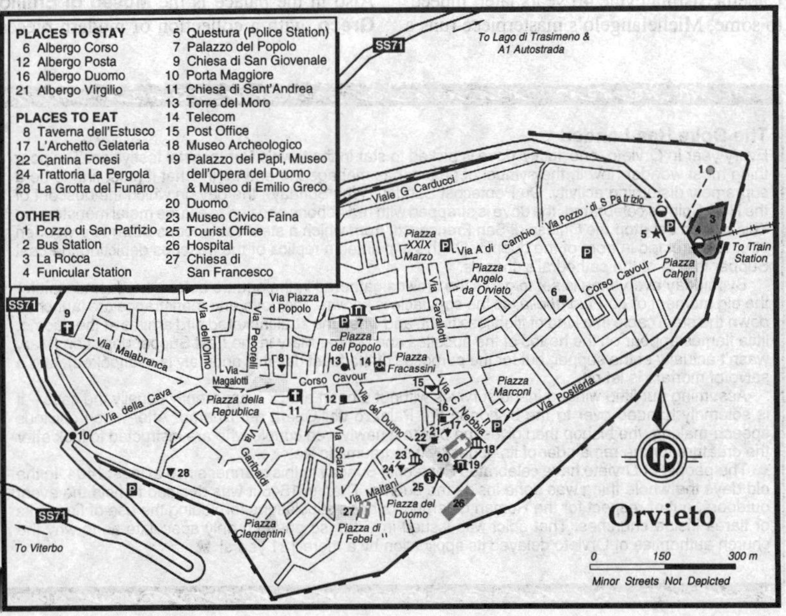

The **façade** appears almost unrelated to the main body of the church, and has greatly benefited from painstaking restoration, completed in 1995. The three huge doorways are separated by fluted columns and the gables are decorated with mosaics that, although mostly reproductions, seem to come to life in the light of the setting sun and in the evening under spotlights. The area between the doorways features 14th-century bas-reliefs of scriptural scenes by Maitani and his pupils, while the rose window is by Andrea Orcagna. The great bronze doors, the work of Emilio Greco, were added in the 1960s.

After the splendour of the exterior, the interior may at first come as something of a disappointment. Brace yourself, however. Reopened in late 1996 after years of painstaking restoration, Luca Signorelli's fresco cycle, *The Last Judgment*, in the Cappella di San Brizio (right of the altar), shimmers with life. Signorelli began work on the series in 1499, and Michelangelo is said to have taken inspiration from it when he began the Capella Sistina cycle 40 years later. Indeed, to some, Michelangelo's masterpiece runs a close *second* to Signorelli's work. Not to be ignored in the chapel are ceiling frescoes by Fra Angelico. You need a ticket (L3000) to get in; pick it up at the tourist office.

The **Cappella del Corporale** houses the blood-stained linen, preserved in a silver reliquary decorated by artists of the Sienese school. The walls feature frescoes by Ugolino di Prete Ilario depicting the miracle.

The duomo opens daily from 7.30 am to 12.45 pm and 2.30 to 7.15 pm in summer – the hours contract a little in winter. Be aware, however, that the chapels close when mass is being said.

Around the Duomo

Next to the cathedral, in the **Palazzo dei Papi**, is the **Museo dell'Opera del Duomo**, which houses a clutter of religious relics from the cathedral, as well as Etruscan antiquities and works by artists such as Simone Martini and the three Pisanos: Andrea, Nino and Giovanni. The museum seems to have been closed for an eternity of restoration. Also in the palace is the **Museo di Emilio Greco**, with a collection of modern pieces

The Dove Has Landed

Every year in Orvieto, one 'lucky' dove is picked to star in the town's Pentecostal festivities. The poor thing must wonder how it, the symbol of peace, has managed to end up in what it must find to be a supremely disturbing activity. On Pentecost Sunday (Whit Sunday), the day on which the descent of the Holy Spirit is celebrated, the dove is strapped with red ribbons and tied to a large metal monstrance. This is then set atop the Chiesa di San Francesco, from which a steel cable loops down to a wooden structure erected in front of the duomo. On this is painted a replica of the frescoes depicting the Last Supper in one of the cathedral's chapels.

By midday everything is set to go as the crowds gathered in the square before the duomo wait for the big moment of *La Palombella*, as the spectacle is known. The dove and monstrance are launched down the steel cable in a kind of flightless flight, and when the straitjacketed bird arrives at the duomo, little flames appear on the heads of the apostles and Mother Mary in the Last Supper depiction (Mary wasn't actually at the supper, but for the purposes of the feast day this anomaly is overlooked), and a salvo of mortars is let off.

Assuming our little winged friend survives without a heart attack – apparently usually the case – it is solemnly handed over to the bishop in the Palazzo dell'Opera del Duomo. After much officious speech-making, the bishop then gives the bird to a newly wed couple who are instructed to look after the creature for the remainder of its hopefully less traumatic life.

The people of Orvieto have celebrated Pentecost Sunday in this manner since at least 1404. In the old days the whole thing was done inside the duomo. Then in 1846 it was decided to hold the event outdoors, out of respect for the Roman Lateran Council's stipulations forbidding the use of fireworks or flares inside churches. That edict was issued in 1725, so one can only speculate as to why the church authorities of Orvieto delayed its application by a mere 121 years! ■

donated by the creator of the duomo's bronze doors. It opens Tuesday to Sunday from 10.30 am to 1 pm and 3 to 7 pm (2 to 6 pm in winter). Entry costs L5000 (or L8000 for a combined ticket including the Pozzo di San Patrizio – see below). Around the corner, you can see Etruscan antiquities in the **Museo Archeologico**. It opens daily and admission is L4000.

In the unlikely event that your thirst for Etruscan widgets isn't quenched, try the **Museo Civico Faina** opposite the duomo. Most of the stuff in here was found in 6th-century BC tombs near Piazza Cahen. It keeps similar hours to the Emilio Greco museum and entry is a rather steep L7000.

Other Attractions

Head along Via del Duomo to Corso Cavour and you'll see the stout **Torre del Moro**, which for L5000 you can climb for sweeping, pigeon-eye views of the city. Back on ground level you can continue west for Piazza della Repubblica, where you'll stumble upon the 12th-century **Chiesa di Sant'Andrea** and its curious octagonal bell tower. As with many Italian churches, it was built over a Roman structure, which in turn had incorporated an Etruscan building. You can see the ancient foundations in the crypt. The piazza, once Orvieto's Roman forum, is at the heart of what remains of the medieval city.

North of Corso Cavour, the 13th-century Romanesque-Gothic **Palazzo del Popolo** presides over the square of the same name. At the north-western end of town is the 11th-century **Chiesa di San Giovenale**, its interior brightened by 13th and 14th-century frescoes.

Standing watch at the town's easternmost tip is the 14th-century **Rocca**, part of which is now a public garden. Below the fortress, the **Pozzo di San Patrizio** is a well sunk in 1527 on the orders of Pope Clement VII. More than 60m deep, it is lined by two spiral staircases for water-bearing mules. It is open daily from 10 am to 7 pm (6 pm in winter) and admission is L6000.

Places to Stay

You should have no trouble getting a room here at any time of the year, but it is always a good idea to book ahead in summer and at weekends. The closest camping grounds are about 10km east of the town, on Lago di Corbara near Baschi. Try the *Orvieto* (☎ 0336-69 10 26), which charges L8000 per person and L7000 a tent.

In Orvieto, one of the best deals is *Albergo Duomo* (☎ 34 18 87), Via di Maurizio 7, where singles/doubles are L40,000/60,000, L60,000/85,000 with bathroom; some rooms overlook the duomo. *Albergo Posta* (☎ 34 19 09), Via L Signorelli 18, has rooms for about the same price. *Albergo Corso* (☎ & fax 34 20 20), at Corso Cavour 343, has singles/doubles at L95,000/135,000 in high season, and the three-star *Albergo Virgilio* (☎ 34 18 82; fax 34 37 97), Piazza del Duomo 5, overlooks the duomo and has rooms for L120,000/165,000 in high season.

Places to Eat

One of the most pleasant places for a snack is *Cantina Foresi*, Piazza del Duomo, a wine cellar with local wines and tables in the piazza, as well as good sandwiches. A popular pizza haunt is the *Taverna dell'Etrusco*, Via della Misericordia 7. You also have a choice of Umbrian dishes. Orvieto tends to be a little expensive on the food front, but you can't go wrong at the *Trattoria La Pergola*, Via dei Magoni 9a. A fine meal in the back garden will cost about L30,000 – try the ombrichelli or the melt-in-your-mouth gnocchi al modo nostro.

La Grotta del Funaro is an excellent but more pricey restaurant at Via Ripa Serancia 41, virtually dug into the city walls. Expect to pay around L40,000 a head.

L'Archetto, Piazza del Duomo 14, has mouth-watering gelati.

Getting There & Away

All buses depart from Piazza Cahen. COTRAL connects the city with Viterbo and Bagnoregio. ATC buses (☎ 34 22 65) connect with Baschi, Montecchio, Bolsena,

Perugia and Todi. SIRA runs a daily service to Roma.

Trains run to Roma and Firenze, and you can change at Terontola for Perugia. By car, the city is on the A1, and the SS71 heads north for Lago di Trasimeno.

Getting Around

A century-old funicular railway connects Piazza Cahen with the train station, with carriages leaving daily every 15 minutes from 7.15 am to 8.30 pm. Once in Orvieto, the easiest way to see the city is on foot, although ATC bus No A connects Piazza Cahen with Piazza del Duomo, and No B with Piazza della Repubblica.

AROUND ORVIETO

The Etruscans produced wine in the district, the Romans continued the tradition, and today the Orvieto Classico wines are among the country's most popular. You can visit 17 vineyards and sample the produce. Unfortunately, you need a car, as ATC bus services to most small towns near the vineyards are irregular at best.

Grab a copy of *Andar per Vigne* from the APT office, or pop into the Consorzio Tutela Vino Orvieto Classico e Orvieto (☎ 34 37 90), Corso Cavour 36, for details of its driving tour of the local vineyards.

Le Marche

Characterised by undulating countryside and peppered with barely 'discovered' medieval towns and villages, Le Marche forms a narrow and little travelled band between the Appennini and the Adriatic Sea. Now that Toscana has outpriced itself and Umbria is well on the road to doing the same, Le Marche is becoming increasingly popular with Italians and foreigners intent on buying old farm houses for renovation. Most visitors come for the Renaissance splendour of Urbino, or to catch a ferry from Ancona, but the rest of the region deserves at least a few days exploration.

In the south-west, the treeless Monti Sibillini form an impressive and, in parts, forbidding stretch of the Appennini, with plenty to keep even the most die-hard walker busy for days. Unfortunately, much of the coastline has been overdeveloped, with rows of characterless seaside hotels and the sand swamped with beach umbrellas in summer, but some of the nooks and crannies outside Ancona and around Senigallia and Pesaro are among the best the Adriatic has to offer.

The small hill towns, however, are the region's most enchanting feature. Urbino and Macerata are the better known, but the hilly countryside is littered with curious little towns and villages, often crowned by an ancient castle or medieval monastery, always ripe for poking around. In the south, Ascoli Piceno boasts a historic centre of elegant squares and several grand monuments in a web of narrow cobbled lanes.

One of Italy's earliest tribes, the Piceni, were the first inhabitants of the area, which later fell under Roman control. The region prospered in the Middle Ages and boomed during the 15th and 16th centuries, when the powerful Montefeltro family ruled Urbino. Le Marche attracted great Renaissance architects and painters, and Urbino gave the world the genius of Raphael and Donato Bramante.

Local cuisine draws inspiration from two sources. Inland mountain dishes comprise fish, beef, lamb, mushrooms and truffles, while on the coast, sole and prawns resembling lobsters are popular. *Brodetto* is a tempting fish stew common along the coast, while *vincisgrassi*, a rich lasagne with meat sauce, chicken livers and black truffles, is popular inland. The region is a small wine producer, with one of the best drops being the Vernaccia di Serrapetrona, a sparkling red.

The A14 and SS16 (Via Adriatica) hug the coastline, while the inland roads are good and provide easy access to all towns. Bus services inland are frequent and regular trains ply the coast on the Bologna-Lecce line.

ANCONA

Most visitors to Ancona go there only in order to head off elsewhere, namely by ferry to Greece, Turkey or the former Yugoslavia. A major point of trade with the East since the Middle Ages, Ancona remains the mid-Adriatic's largest port, doing a healthy business in tourists as well as road freight. The old centre was heavily bombed in WWII, but it still has a few faded gems to offer the listless voyager waiting for a boat.

Orientation

All trains arrive at the main station in Piazza Nello e Carlo Rosselli, and some continue the 1.5km north to the ferry terminal, Stazione Marittima (or Molo Santa Maria). From Largo Dogana, near the ferry terminal, walk uphill to the central Piazza Roma and on to the city's grand Piazza Cavour. There are several hotels near Piazza Roma, and a cluster around the main train station. What remains of the old town stretches in an arc around the waterfront.

Information

Tourist Offices The main APT office (☎ 3 49 38) is inconveniently placed at the eastern

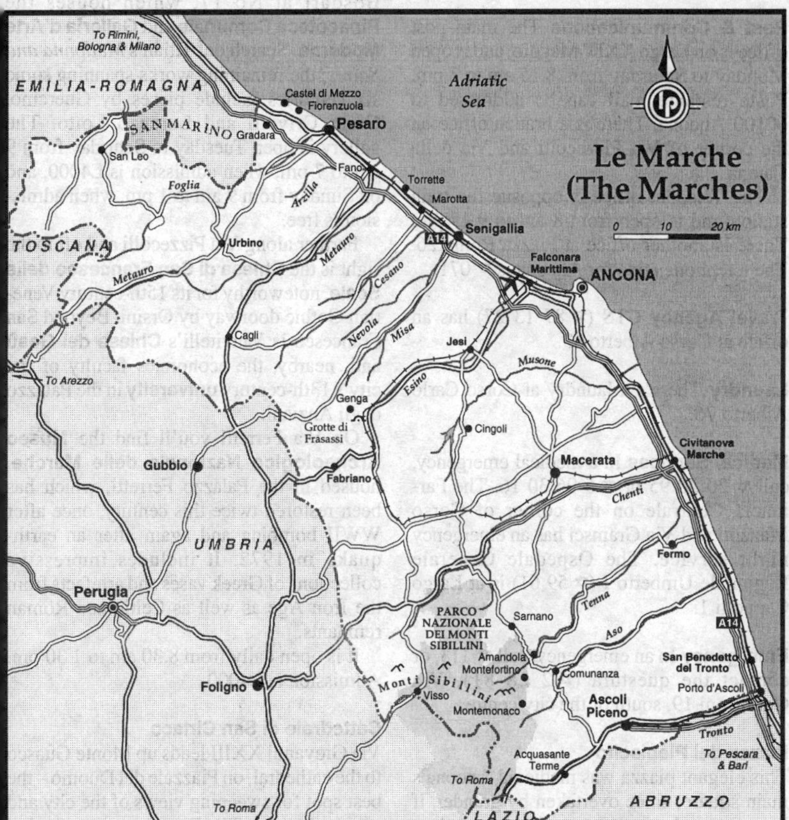

end of town at Via Thaon de Revel 4. It is open Monday to Friday from 8.30 am to 1.30 pm, as well as Tuesday and Thursday from 3.30 to 6.30 pm. Branch offices open daily at the train station and Stazione Marittima in summer.

Foreign Consulate France has a consulate (☎ 20 68 66) at Via Marsala 12.

Money There are exchange booths at the main train station and Stazione Marittima, but rates are not especially good. There is also an ATM good for Visa and MasterCard at the ferry terminal.

Post & Communications The main post office is on Largo XXIV Maggio, and is open Monday to Saturday from 8.15 am to 7 pm. Poste restante mail can be addressed to 60100 Ancona. There is a branch office on the corner of Via Pizzecolli and Via della Catena.

The Telecom office is opposite the train station and is open from 8 am to 9.45 pm. There is another office at Piazza Roma 26. The telephone code for Ancona is ☎ 071.

Travel Agency CTS (☎ 87 13 27) has an office at Corso Alberto 83.

Laundry There's a laundry at Corso Carlo Alberto 76.

Medical Services In a medical emergency, call ☎ 20 20 95 or ☎ 5 96 30 16. The Farmacia Centrale on the corner of Corso Mazzini and Via Gramsci has an emergency night service. The Ospedale Generale Regionale Umberto I (☎ 59 61) is at Largo Cappelli 1.

Emergency In an emergency, call ☎ 113, or contact the questura (☎ 2 28 81), Via Gervasoni 19, south of the city centre.

Piazza del Plebiscito

This elegant piazza was medieval Ancona's main square, since overtaken by grander, if less atmospheric, piazzas in the modern town. **La Prefettura**, the former police station, is housed in a 15th-century palace noted for its beautiful courtyard and dominating the piazza. At its eastern end stands the Baroque **Chiesa di San Domenico**, containing the superb *Crucifixion* by Titian and *Annunciation* by Guercino. Near the church is the 13th-century city gate, the **Arco Ferretti**. Most of the buildings overlooking the piazza went up in the 18th century, largely replacing their medieval precursors.

Museums & Churches

From the Prefettura take Via Pizzecolli north through the old city's ramparts to the Palazzo Bosdari at No 17, which houses the **Pinacoteca Comunale** and **Galleria d'Arte Moderna**. Search out Titian's *Madonna and Saints*; the remaining works spanning some six centuries include pieces by Guercino, Carlo Crivelli and Lorenzo Lotto. The gallery is open Tuesday to Saturday from 9 am to 7 pm, when admission is L4000, and on Sunday from 9 am to 1 pm, when admission is free.

Farther along Via Pizzecolli and off to the right is the **Chiesa di San Francesco delle Scale**, noteworthy for its 15th-century Venetian Gothic doorway by Orsini. Beyond San Francesco is Vanvitelli's **Chiesa del Gesù** and, nearby, the economics faculty of the city's 13th-century **university** in the Palazzo degli Anziani.

On Via Ferretti you'll find the **Museo Archeologico Nazionale delle Marche**, housed in the Palazzo Ferretti, which has been restored twice this century, once after WWII bombing and again after an earthquake in 1972. It includes impressive collections of Greek vases and artefacts from the Iron Age as well as Celtic and Roman remnants.

It is open daily from 8.30 am to 1.30 pm. Admission is L4000.

Cattedrale di San Ciriaco

Via Giovanni XXIII leads up Monte Guasco to the cathedral, on Piazzale del Duomo – the best spot for sweeping views of the city and across the port. The Romanesque cathedral was built on the site of a Roman temple and has Byzantine and Gothic features. The small **museum** (☎ 2 83 91) adjoining the church contains the 4th-century sarcophagus of Flavius Gorgonius, a masterpiece of early Christian art. The museum is open only by prior booking for guided visits. Tickets cost L2000.

Waterfront

North of Piazza Dante Alighieri along the esplanade of Lungomare Luigi Vanvitelli is the **Arco di Traiano** (Trajan's Arch), erected in 115 AD. Vanvitelli's **Arco Clementino** (Clementine Arch), dedicated to Pope Clement XII, is farther on. South of Piazza Dante Alighieri you'll hit the small Piazza Santa Maria and the disused, tumbledown **Chiesa di Santa Maria della Piazza**, which retains a few scraps of 5th and 6th-century pavement mosaics.

Places to Stay

Many people bunk down at the ferry terminal, although the city has many cheap hotels. *Albergo Dorico* (☎ 4 27 61), opposite the train station at Via Flaminia 8, has rooms with bathroom for L35,000/60,000. *Albergo*

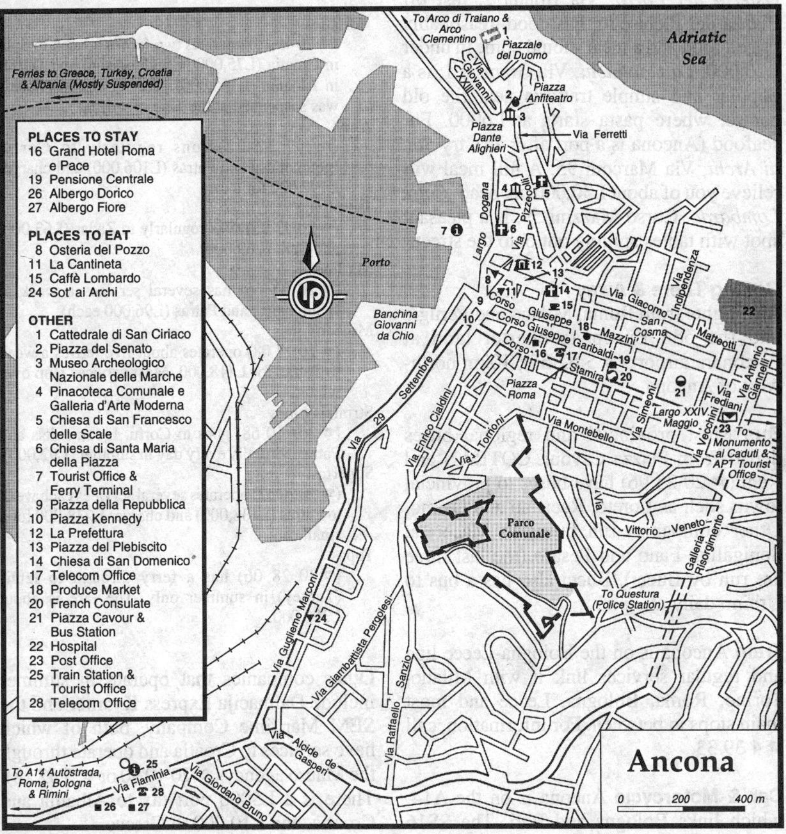

LE MARCHE

Fiore (☎ 4 33 90), a few doors down at Piazza Rosselli 24, is similar. In the centre of town, *Pensione Centrale* (☎ 5 43 88), Via Marsala 10, has rooms for L35,000/50,000 or doubles with bathroom for L80,000. *Albergo Cavour*, Viale della Vittoria 7, has singles/doubles for L38,000/65,000. The three-star *Grand Hotel Roma e Pace* (☎ 20 20 07; fax 207 47 36), Via Leopardi 1, has rooms with all mod cons and breakfast for L95,000/160,000.

Places to Eat

The produce *market* at Corso Mazzini 130 has fresh fruit, vegetables and other food. *Osteria del Pozzo*, Via Bonda 2, just off Piazza del Plebiscito, has good, reasonably priced food and a meal should come in under L20,000. *La Cantineta*, Via Gramsci 1, is a popular and simple trattoria near the old centre, where pasta starts at L6000. For seafood (Ancona is a port after all), try *Sot' ai Archi*, Via Marconi 95. A full meal will relieve you of about L30,000 per head. *Caffè Lombardo*, Corso Mazzini 59, is a pleasant spot with tables spilling out onto the street.

Getting There & Away

Air Flights from Roma, Milano and Perugia and the odd European charter land at Falconara airport (☎ 5 62 57), 10km northwest of Ancona.

Bus Most provincial and regional buses depart from Piazza Cavour. COTRAN and Reni (☎ 20 25 96) have buses to provincial towns such as Loreto, Recanati and Osimo. Other companies run buses to Macerata, Senigallia, Fano and Pesaro (the last three are run by Bucci). Bucci also has a bus to Urbino daily at 2 pm.

Train Ancona is on the Bologna-Lecce line and regular services link it with Milano, Torino, Roma, Bologna, Lecce and most main stops in between. For information, call ☎ 4 39 33.

Car & Motorcycle Ancona is on the A14, which links Bologna and Bari. The SS16 coastal road runs parallel to the autostrad and is a more pleasant (toll-free) alternative The SS76 connects Ancona with Perugia an Roma.

Boat Ferry operators have booths at th Stazione Marittima. Timetables are subjec to change, prices fluctuate with the season and some lines come and go – check at th APT office or at the terminal. Most line offer discounts on return fares, and the boat are generally roll-on roll-off car ferries Prices listed here are for one-way deck clas in the high season:

Adriatica
: (☎ 20 49 15) operates two ferries a week to Spli in Croatia (L75,000 in high season) and Durre in Albania (L155,000). The service to Albani was suspended at the time of writing.

Anek
: (☎ 207 32 22) runs regularly to Corfu Igoumenitsa and Patras (L106,000) and charge L192,000 for a car.

Jadrolinija
: (☎ 20 43 05) runs regularly to Zadar (L63,000 and Split (L69,000).

Marlines
: (☎ 20 25 66) has several services a week to Igoumenitsa and Patras (L96,000 each).

Minoan Lines
: (☎ 20 17 08) operates about five ferries a week to Patras for L118,000. Most services stop ove winter.

Strintzis Lines
: (☎ 207 10 68) goes to Corfu, Igoumenitsa and Patras, virtually every day in summer (L92,000)

Superfast
: (☎ 20 20 33) operates several services each week to Patras (L138,000) and charges L238,000 for a small car.

Topas
: (☎ 20 28 06) has a ferry through to Izmi (Turkey) in summer only. The fare is abou L300,000.

Other companies that operate in summer include Dalmacija Express Kvarner and the SEM Maritime Company, both of which have services to Croatia and operate through the Mauro agency (☎ 20 40 90 or ☎ 5 52 18). There is a L5000 port tax to Albania and Croatia, and L10,000 to Greece.

Getting Around

About six ATMA buses, including No 1, connect the train station with Stazione Marittima and the city centre (look for the bus stop with the big sign displaying Centro and Porto). For a taxi, call ☎ 4 33 21.

AROUND ANCONA

Loreto

The story goes that angels transferred the house of the Virgin Mary from Palestine to this spot towards the end of the 13th century. Why the angels should have done such a thing is unclear, but a church was soon built over the site and later expanded to become today's **Santuario della Santa Casa**, an important site for pilgrims. Restoration began in 1468, and additions have been made ever since. The house itself, whatever its origin, is beneath the dome inside the sanctuary and is open all day. Loreto lies about 28km south of Ancona and can be reached easily by bus from there. The train station (Bologna-Lecce line) is a few km away, but shuttle buses connect it with the town centre.

Beaches

If you are hanging about Ancona for any length of time, head about 20km south along the coast road (buses from Piazza Cavour) for **Sirolo** and **Numana**, below Monte Conero. These beaches are among the Adriatic's more appealing, although they fill up in summer.

URBINO

Urbino is the jewel of Le Marche and one of the best preserved and most beautiful hill towns in Italy. It enjoyed a period of great splendour under the Montefeltro family from the 12th century, and reached its zenith under Duca Federico da Montefeltro, who hired some of the greatest Renaissance artists and architects to construct and decorate his palace and other parts of the town. The architects Donato Bramante, born in Urbino, and Francesco di Giorgio were among his favourites. Painters in particularly good grace with the duke included Piero della Francesca, who developed his theories on mathematical perspective in Urbino, Paolo Uccello, Justus of Ghent and Giovanni Santi (the father of Raffaello d'Urbino, the great Raphael, who was born in the city).

After Duca Federico lost his right eye and broke his nose in a tournament, he insisted on being portrayed only in profile. The most famous result of this caprice was executed in 1466 by della Francesca and hangs in the Galleria degli Uffizi in Firenze.

The city can be a pain to reach by public transport, but should not be missed. The area to the north, particularly the winding road to San Marino and on into Emilia-Romagna, is a treat, and there are plenty of hotels in the small towns along the way.

Orientation

Buses arrive at Borgo Mercatale on the walled city's western edge. From there it is a short walk up Via G Mazzini to Piazza della Repubblica and then back south to Via Veneto for Piazza Duca Federico and the sprawling Piazza del Rinascimento. Drivers will most likely arrive at Piazzale Roma on the city's northern edge, where cars can be parked free of charge. Via Raffaello connects the piazza with Piazza della Repubblica.

Information

Tourist Office The APT (☎ 24 41), Piazza Duca Federico 35, is open Monday to Saturday from 9 am to 1 pm. From April to September it's also open in the afternoons from 3 to 6 pm and on Sunday mornings from 9 am to 1 pm.

Money There are several banks. The Banca Nazionale di Lavoro in Via Vittorio Veneto has an ATM which is good for several cards including Visa and MasterCard.

Post & Communications The main post office is at Via Bramante 18, open Monday to Saturday from 8.30 am to 6.30 pm. The post code for the town centre is 61029.

The Telecom office, at Via Puccinotti 4, opposite the Palazzo Ducale, is open from 8 am to 10 pm. There's another office at Piazza

LE MARCHE

di San Francesco 1. The telephone code for Urbino is ☎ 0722.

Medical Services For medical assistance, call ☎ 118 or ☎ 32 80 89. The Ospedale Civile (☎ 30 11) is at Via B da Montefeltro. There is a pharmacy at Piazza della Repubblica 9.

Emergency Call the police on ☎ 113.

Palazzo Ducale

The grand residence of Urbino's ruling dynasty was completed in 1482, and still dominates the heights of Urbino. Elegant and balanced, it is the most complete and refined early Renaissance palace in Italy. Dalmatian architect Luciano Laurana drew up the original design, but several masters had a hand in its construction, including the ruling Duca Federico who commissioned it. From Corso Garibaldi you get the best view of the complex with its unusual **Facciata dei Torricini**, a three-storey loggia in the form of a triumphal arch, flanked by circular towers. The palace now houses the Galleria Nazionale delle Marche, a formidable art collection, and the less inspiring Museo Archeologico.

A monumental staircase, one of Italy's first, leads to the piano nobile and the Ducal Apartments. The best preserved room is Duca Federico's **Studiolo**. Intricately worked intarsia (inlaid wood) decorates the entire room, creating illusory perspectives and depicting books which look real, cupboard doors that seem to be hanging open and even a letter that appears to be lying in a desk drawer.

Amongst the paintings in the **Galleria Nazionale delle Marche**, look out for Piero della Francesca's masterpiece, *Flagellation*, and *The Ideal City*, long held to be by Piero but now attributed to Laurana. Another highlight is the remarkable portrait of Federico and his son Guidobaldo, attributed to the

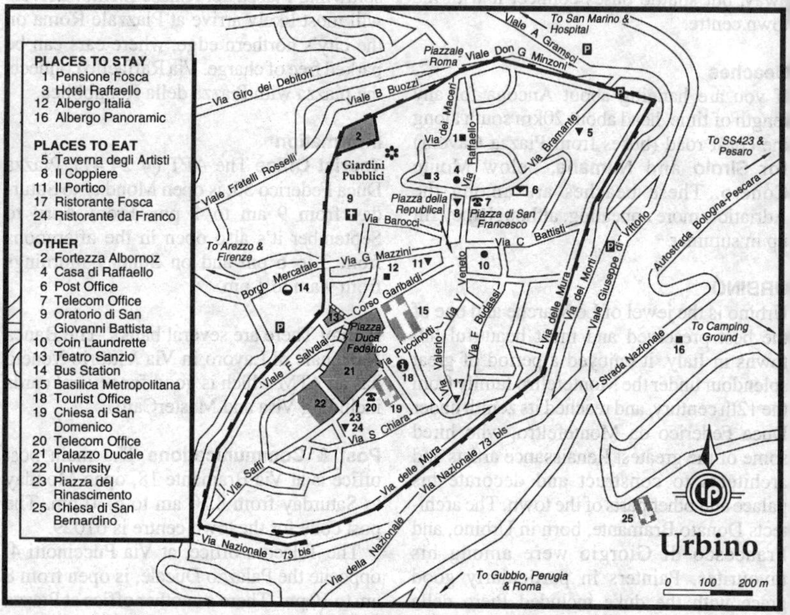

Spanish artist Pedro Berruguete. The art collection, which continues on the second floor, also features several works by the Urbino artist Federico Barocci, including a large number of drawings.

The mildly interesting **Museo Archeologico**, on the far side of the Cortile d'Onore, the palace courtyard, is worth a look-in – you may as well, as admission is included in the L8000 ticket. The palace is open Tuesday to Saturday from 9 am to 7 pm and Sunday and Monday from 9 am to 2 pm. However, a booking system introduced in 1997 for peak tourism periods means that at certain times of the year you need to make a reservation for entry at 20-minute intervals. This can only be done in person at the booking office which is open Tuesday to Saturday from 8.30 am to 5.40 pm and Sunday and Monday from 8.30 am to 12.40 pm. If in doubt, ask at the ticket office or APT for details.

Basilica Metropolitana

Rebuilt in the early 1800s in the neoclassical style after an earthquake destroyed Francesco di Giorgio Martini's original Renaissance building, the interior of Urbino's cathedral commands greater interest than its austere façade. Particularly memorable is Frederico Barocci's *Last Supper*. The cathedral's **Museo Albani** contains further paintings, including Andrea da Bologna's *Madonna del Latte*, along with an engaging assortment of articles collected from Urbino's churches over the centuries. The basilica is next to the Palazzo Ducale, and is open daily from 9.30 am to midday and 3 to 6 pm. Admission is L3000.

Churches & Oratories

Opposite the Palazzo Ducale, the medieval **Chiesa di San Domenico** is notable for its lunette, the panel above the 15th-century doorway, by Luca della Robbia.

The 14th-century **Oratorio di San Giovanni Battista** on Via Barocci features brightly coloured frescoes by Lorenzo and Giacomo Salimbeni. It's open Monday to Saturday from 10 am to 12.30 pm and 3 to 5.30 pm and Sunday from 10 am to 12.30 pm. Admission is L3000. A few steps away, the **Oratorio di San Giuseppe** (same hours, admission L2000) boasts a stucco *Nativity* by Federico Brandani.

The **Chiesa di San Bernardino**, outside the city walls to the east along Viale Giuseppe di Vittorio, houses the mausoleum of the Dukes of Urbino, designed by Donato Bramante and Francesco di Giorgio Martini. It's open daily from 8.30 am to 12.30 pm and 2.30 to 6.30 pm.

Casa di Raffaello

If you want to have a look at where Raphael first saw the light of day, the house of his birth is north of Piazza della Repubblica at Via Raffaello 57. It is open Monday to Saturday from 9 am to 1 pm and 3 to 7 pm, and Sunday from 10 am to 1 pm. Admission is L5000.

Courses

The university offers an intensive course in language and culture for foreigners during August at a cost of L600,000, and can arrange accommodation for L250,000 for the month. For information call ☎ 30 52 50 (mornings only) or write to the Segreteria dell'Università, Via Saffi 2, Urbino 61029. You can get details and make a booking from about March to May.

Places to Stay

The tourist office has a full list of private rooms. *Campeggio Pineta* (☎ 47 10), the only camping ground, is 2km east of the city in San Donato. *Pensione Fosca* (☎ 25 42), Via Raffaello 61, has singles/doubles for L39,000/55,000. *Albergo Italia* (☎ 27 01), Corso Garibaldi 32, is behind the Palazzo Ducale and has singles/doubles from L40,000/58,000, or L53,000/80,000 with bathroom. *Albergo Panoramic* (☎ 26 00), outside the city just off the Strada Nazionale, has rooms from L50,000/70,000 but is awkward to reach without your own transport. Heading up the scale in price, *Hotel Raffaello* (☎ 47 84), Via Santa Margherita 40, charges L100,000/150,000 for singles and L150,000/200,000 for doubles.

Places to Eat
There are numerous bars around Piazza della Repubblica and near the Palazzo Ducale that sell good panini. Try *Pizzeria Galli*, Via Vittorio Veneto 19, for takeaway pizza by the slice. *Bar Europa*, at No 34, also sells pizza slices. For bruschetta, salads and light meals try *Il Portico*, Via Mazzini 7, which is both a bookshop and osteria. *Ristorante da Franco*, just off Piazza Rinascimento and next to the university, has a self-service section for lunch for less than L20,000. You can eat well at *Ristorante Fosca*, Via F Budassi 64, for around L25,000 a head. Try the strozzapreti al pesto, worm-like shreds of pasta designed to choke priests – sounds horrid but they're delicious. *Taverna degli Artisti*, Via Bramante 52, has good pasta and meat dishes; a meal will set you back around L30,000 but it will cost you less if you choose one of their giant pizzas, served on huge wooden slabs and big enough to feed an army. For more elegant dining, head for *Il Coppiere* at Via Santa Margherita 1 – a meal in the cosy 1st-floor restaurant will cost about L40,000.

Entertainment
The *Teatro Sanzio* hosts a variety of drama and concerts, particularly from July to September. Pick up a brochure at the tourist office.

Getting There & Away
Bus The bus station is in Borgo Mercatale. SAPUM (☎ 2 23 33) and Bucci (☎ 3 24 01) operate up to 10 services a day between Urbino and Pesaro. Bucci also has two buses a day to Roma and services to Ancona and Arezzo. Busturs has services to San Marino and Rimini. Check with the APT office or consult the board under the portico near Caffè Belpassi, Piazza della Repubblica, for schedules.

Train Take the bus for Pesaro to pick up trains there.

Car & Motorcycle A superstrada and the SS423 connect the city with Pesaro, and the SS73 connects the city with the SS3 for Roma.

Getting Around
Most vehicles are banned from the walled city. Small shuttle buses operate between Piazzale Roma, Borgo Mercatale and Piazza Rinascimento. Taxis (☎ 25 50) operate from Piazza della Repubblica. There are car parks outside the city gates. Your car will be towed away on Saturday mornings from Piazzale Roma, as that is market day.

AROUND URBINO
San Leo
Machiavelli, who knew a thing or two about such matters, thought the fortress of San Leo, about 60km north-west of Urbino, quite 'impregnable'. He was probably right – it is difficult to see how the walls perched defiantly on a high outcrop of stone could be assailed.

Part of the Montefeltro duchy, San Leo was first fortified by the Romans, who erected a temple to Jupiter here. The temple was later replaced by the 12th-century **duomo**, and nearby you can also admire the pre-Romanesque **Pieve**, an 11th-century basilica. The Papal States converted the fort into a prison and the Fascists used it as an aircraft-spotting post during WWII.

Without a car, San Leo is a little difficult to reach. Although in Le Marche, the most reliable bus route is actually from Rimini, in Emilia-Romagna.

PESARO
Like other resort towns on the Adriatic, Pesaro offers an expanse of beach, the remains of a medieval centre and not much else. In mid-summer you can't move for the crowds, and out of season the waterfront has a sad air about it – maybe it's all the tacky concrete hotel blocks boarded up for the winter. It is, however, a handy transport junction, and the best place to get a bus for Urbino, an hour's drive inland.

Orientation
The train station is at the southern edge of

he centre, away from the beach. Walk along /iale del Risorgimento, through Piazza .azzarini and continue to Piazza del Popolo, he town's main square. Via Rossini takes 'ou to Piazza della Libertà and the water-ront.

nformation

The APT office (☎ 6 93 41), at Piazzale della Libertà, is open daily from 9 am to 1 pm and .30 to 6.30 pm in summer (July to Septem-)er) and Monday to Friday from 9.30 am to pm (also Tuesday and Thursday from 3.30 .o 6.30 pm) for the rest of the year.

Money There are plenty of banks. The Banca Nazionale del Lavoro on Piazza del Popolo has an ATM good for several cards including Visa.

Post & Communications The main post office is in Piazza del Popolo and is open Monday to Saturday from 8.15 am to 7.40 pm. The post code for the town centre is 61100.

The Telecom office is in Piazza Matteotti, south-east of Piazza del Popolo, and is open daily from 7 am to 11 pm in summer (the

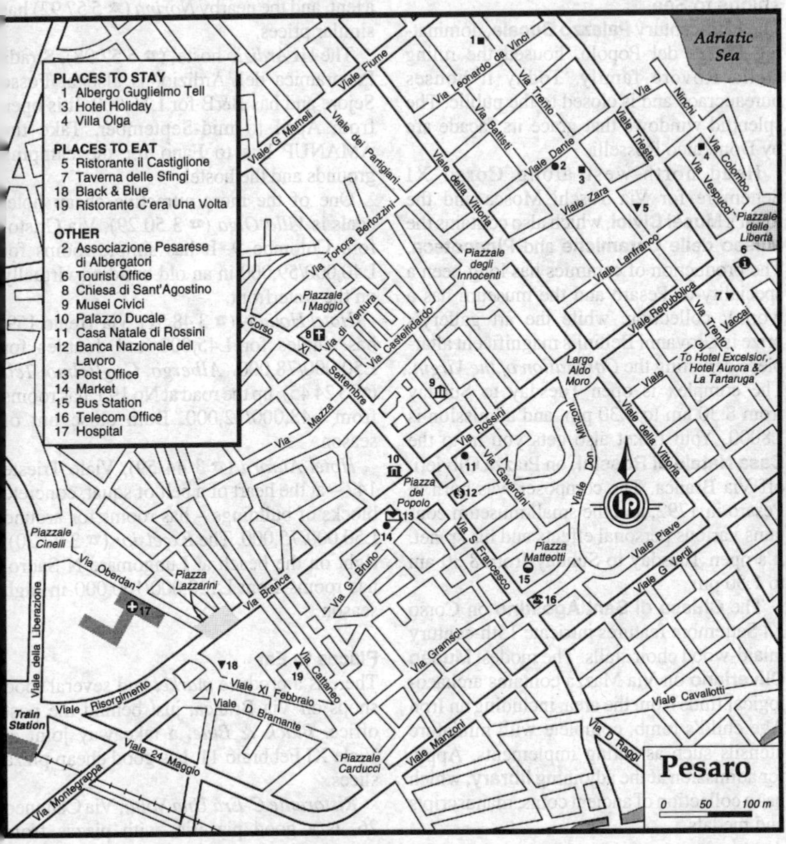

hours are reduced off season). The telephone code for Pesaro is ☎ 0721.

Laundry There's an Onda Blu laundry at Piazza 1, Maggio 12.

Medical Services For an ambulance, call ☎ 41 12 22 or ☎ 6 41 18; or try *pronto soccorso* on ☎ 3 29 57. Ospedale San Salvatore (☎ 36 11) is at Piazzale Albani.

Emergency For the police, call ☎ 113, or contact the questura (☎ 38 61 11) at Via Bruno 5.

Things to See

The 15th-century **Palazzo Ducale**, dominating Piazza del Popolo, housed the ruling Della Rovere family. Today it houses bureaucracy and is closed to the public. The splendid windows that grace its façade are by Domenico Rosselli.

Head north-west along Corso XI Settembre for Via Toschi Mosca and the town's **Musei Civici**, which also contains the **Museo delle Ceramiche** and **Pinacoteca**. The production of ceramics has long been a speciality of Pesaro and the museum has a worthy collection, while the art gallery's prize is Giovanni Bellini's magnificent altarpiece depicting the *Coronation of the Virgin*. The complex is open Tuesday to Sunday from 8.30 am to 1.30 pm, and admission is L8000. Your ticket also gets you in to the **Casa Natale di Rossini**, on Piazza Olivieri, off Via Branca. The composer was born in Pesaro in 1792, and the small museum contains various personal effects and his spinet. It's open Tuesday to Sunday from 8.30 am to 1.30 pm.

The **Chiesa di Sant'Agostino** on Corso XI Settembre features intricate 15th-century inlaid-wood choir stalls. The modest **Museo Oliveriano** on Via Mazza contains archaeological finds from the area, including an Iron Age child's tomb, complete with miniature utensils such as eating implements. Apply for admission at the adjoining **library**, which has a collection of ancient coins, manuscripts and medals.

Places to Stay

The town's hotel association, the Associazione Pesarese di Albergatori (☎ 6 79 59), has an office at Viale Dante Alighieri 40 and will help you find a room. The APT office has a lengthy list of apartments, although most are more expensive than hotels. Many hotels close from October to April, and the camping grounds may well do the same. If you can, go first to the APT office to find out what's still open.

The closest camping grounds are about 5km south of the town centre at Fosso Sejore. The *Marinella* (☎ 5 08 76) on the SS16 has sites for up to L14,000 a person and L26,000 a tent, and the nearby *Norina* (☎ 5 57 92) has similar prices.

The HI *Ardizio* hostel (☎ 5 57 98), Strada Panoramica dell'Ardizio, is also at Fosso Sejore and has B&B for L16,000. It is open from April to mid-September. Take the AMANUP bus to Fano for the camping grounds and the hostel.

One of the more attractive cheap hotel deals is *Villa Olga* (☎ 3 50 29), Via Cristoforo Colombo 9. It has simple rooms for L40,000/59,000 in an old building virtually on the waterfront.

Hotel Holiday (☎ 3 48 51), Via Trento 159, has singles for L45,000 and doubles for L50,000/78,000. *Albergo Guglielmo Tell* (☎ 3 24 45), up the road at No 195, has rooms from L48,000/72,000. Both close out of season.

Hotel Aurora (☎ 3 44 59), Viale Trieste 147 – at the heart of a belt of squat, concrete blocks of buildings – has rooms for around L50,000/75,000. The *Excelsior* (☎ 3 27 20), right on the beach at Lungomare N Sauro, has rooms from L120,000/160,000 in high season.

Places to Eat

There is a produce *market* and several food shops on Via Branca, just behind the post office. *Black & Blue*, a takeaway joint at Viale XI Febbraio 11, has good cheap pizza slices.

Ristorante C'Era Una Volta, Via Cattaneo 26, is a good pizzeria, with pizzas from

L7000. *Taverna delle Sfingi*, Viale Trieste 219, is one of the better restaurants near the beach, and a meal will set you back about L30,000. At about the same price, *La Tartaruga*, Viale Trieste 31, serves typical local dishes. If you're prepared to part with about L50,000, you could eat at *Ristorante il Castiglione*, Via Trento 148, a posh place with the air of a small castle set in rambling gardens.

Entertainment

In honour of Rossini, the town hosts a series of concerts each August at the theatre bearing his name in Piazza Lazzarini. The APT office has programmes.

Getting There & Away

Bus The main bus station is in Piazza Matteotti. AMANUP buses (☎ 69 92 60) connect Pesaro with Gradara, Cattolica, Carpegna, Fosso Sejore, Fano, Ancona, Senigallia and most small towns in the region. There are up to 10 buses a day to Urbino. Bucci operates a service to Roma daily at 6 am.

Train Pesaro is on the Bologna-Lecce line and you can connect for Roma by changing trains at Falconara Marittima, just before Ancona; for information, call ☎ 3 30 09.

Car & Motorcycle Pesaro is on the A14 and the SS16.

Getting Around

Most AMANUP buses connect the train station with Piazza Matteotti, including bus Nos 1, 3, 4, 5, CD and CS.

For a taxi in the centre, call ☎ 3 14 30, and at the train station, ☎ 3 11 11.

AROUND PESARO

If you want slightly more secluded beaches than the Pesaro waterfront, take the Strada Panoramica Adriatica coast road heading north from Pesaro to Cattolica in Emilia-Romagna. The walled, hilltop town of **Gradara** boasts an impressive 14th-century castle, but its beaches can be as crowded as Pesaro. The smaller fishing towns of **Castel di Mezzo** and **Fiorenzuola** are appealing and quieter, even during summer. Fighting in WWII was heavy around here, as the Allies struggled to break the Germans' Gothic Line, which ran from Pesaro to La Spezia, on Italy's western coast. There is a **British war cemetery** 2km east of Gradara.

FANO

Only 12km south of Pesaro, Fano is a fairly sedate beach resort that nevertheless fills up in the summer rush. The ancient village took its name from the Fanum, the Temple of Fortune, and its pleasant historic centre retains several reminders of its Roman and medieval past, warranting a brief stop if you're passing through.

Information

The APT office (☎ 80 35 34) is at Viale Cesare Battisti 10 in Fano. There are other offices (summer only) in the smaller towns of Torrette (☎ 88 47 79), Via Boscomarina 10, and Marotta (☎ 9 65 91), Viale Colombo 31. The telephone code is ☎ 0721.

Things to See

A **triumphal arch** built in 2 AD for Augustus still stands despite losing part of its masonry to surrounding buildings over the centuries. Sections of the Roman and medieval **walls** also remain. The 16th-century **Corte Malatestiano** contains a museum with works by local artists over the centuries.

Places to Stay

Cheap accommodation is in short supply along this stretch of coastline, making Pesaro a more economical base. Five campsites on the southern end of Fano's seashore all charge L5000 to L7000 per person and up to L15,000 per tent. Try the *Fano* (☎ 80 26 52), or pick up the accommodation list from the APT office.

AROUND FANO

If you're staying a while, a couple of excursions inland are worth considering. **Mondavio** is a charming Renaissance town about 35km south of Fano. Several buses run from Fano; if driving, take the SS16 south to Marotta, from where you head inland to San Michele; Mondavio is a few km to the north.

Some 38km south-west of Fano is **Mombaroccio**, a pleasant 15th-century hill town. The main attraction is the view from the old castle walls. Take the SS3 west from Fano and turn north at Calcinelli.

SENIGALLIA

Senigallia's aptly named Spiaggia di Velluto (Velvet Beach) is reputedly one of the Adriatic's best lidos.

The APT office (☎ 792 27 25), Piazzale Morandi 2, is between the beach and the train station. The telephone code is ☎ 071.

Apart from sea and sand, the main draw is the **Rocca Roveresca**, whose four stout, crenellated towers make it hard to miss. Built for Duca Federico da Montefeltro's son-in-law, its plush Renaissance interior makes a visit well worthwhile if you have a spare hour or two.

Places to Stay

If you're having trouble finding a room, which in summer would come as no surprise, try the hotel and camping association (☎ 6 53 43) at Via Brofferio 4 for assistance.

The *Helios* camping ground (☎ 6 91 79), Lungomare Italia 3, has sites from L5000 per person and L16,000 per tent in the high season. The *Liana* (☎ 6 52 06), Lungomare Leonardo da Vinci 54, is about the same price. The *Albergo Villa Serena* (☎ 792 22 04), Via Sardegna 4, is one of the better cheap deals, with rooms from L40,000. *Albergo del Sole* (☎ 6 34 67), on the waterfront at Lungomare Alighieri 118, has singles/doubles from L50,000/60,000.

Getting There & Away

Autolinee Bucci buses operate along the SS16 road to Ancona, Fano and Pesaro, but there are also plenty of trains on the same stretch.

GROTTE DI FRASASSI

In September 1971 a team of climbers stumbled across an aperture in hill country around Genga, about 40km south-west of Ancona, and decided to drop in. What they found were the biggest known caves in Europe – a spectacle of stalactites and stalagmites – some of them 1.4 million years old.

Three years later they were opened to the public, with a 1.5km-long trail carefully laid through five chambers. The first chamber, the **Ancona Abyss**, is almost 200m high, 180m wide and 120m long, and could easily accommodate Milano's duomo.

Groups are taken through the caves every couple of hours for about an hour, and tickets cost L16,000. The ticket area and car park are just outside San Vittore Terme, and the entrance to the caves is 600m farther west. For L50,000, you can get rigged up in caving gear to explore the remaining chambers. This has to be booked well in advance, however; call the Consorzio Grotte di Frasassi (☎ 0732-97 30 39). Should you need to stay, there are a couple of hotels in San Vittore Terme and Genga.

Take the SS76 from Ancona, or the train for Genga (Roma-Ancona line), about 2km from the ticket area (a shuttle bus runs from the train station in summer).

MACERATA

This bustling provincial capital is one of Italy's better kept secrets. Situated atop a rise between the Potenza river valley to the north and the Chienti river in the south, Macerata was established in the 10th century. It is as impressive as many Umbrian and Tuscan hill towns but lacks the tourists, and makes a good base for exploring the surrounding countryside – some of the region's most picturesque.

Orientation

Piazza della Libertà is the focal point of the medieval city, contained within 14th-century walls above the sprawl of the more modern development. Buses arrive at the huge Giardini Diaz, a stone's throw from the Porta Romana (the main gate) and the tourist office. A shuttle bus links the train station, which is west of the city centre, to Piazza

DAMIEN SIMONIS

DAMIEN SIMONIS

DAMIEN SIMONIS

DAMIEN SIMONIS

The Veneto
Top: Sign at the ferry landing, Isola di Torcello, Venezia
Middle: Taking a break from the tourists, Venezia
Bottom: Via Roma, Verona
Right: Gondolier, Venezia

DAMIEN SIMONIS

DAMIEN SIMONIS

Friuli-Venezia Giulia
Top: Natisone river, Cividale del Friuli
Bottom: Old pharmacy, Piazza Garibaldi, Udine

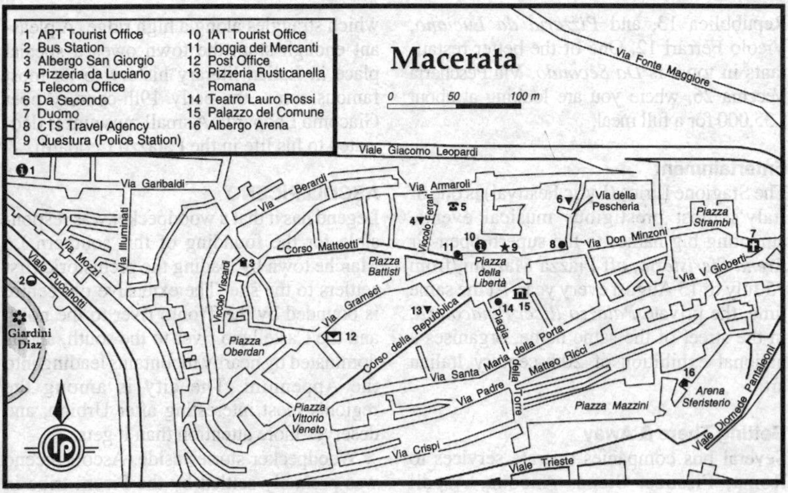

della Libertà. There is parking virtually right around the walls and you may even find a space on one of the main squares inside the old city.

Information

Tourist Offices The main APT office (☎ 23 15 47) is at Via Garibaldi 87, above the Standa supermarket, and is open Monday to Friday from 9 am to 1 pm, and from 3 to 6 pm on Tuesday and Thursday as well. A second office is in Piazza della Libertà (☎ 23 48 07), open all day in summer and otherwise mornings only.

Post & Communications The Telecom office is at Galleria del Commercio 33. The city's post code is 62100 and the telephone code is ☎ 0733.

Medical Services For an ambulance, call ☎ 23 14 44.

Emergency For the police, call ☎ 113.

Things to See

Piazza della Libertà is adorned by one of the city's finest buildings, the 16th-century Renaissance **Loggia dei Mercanti**, built by the Farnese pope, Paul III. In the courtyard of the **Palazzo del Comune** are archaeological remains from Helvia Ricina, a Roman town 5km from Macerata, which was destroyed by the Goths.

Corso della Repubblica, the main boulevard where locals take their late-afternoon strolls, spills into Piazza Vittorio Veneto. Here you will find the **Pinacoteca**, with a good collection of early Renaissance works, including a 15th-century *Madonna* by Carlo Crivelli. The gallery is open Tuesday to Saturday from 9 am to 1 pm and 5 to 7.30 pm, and on Sunday from 9 am to 1 pm.

The rather ordinary Baroque **duomo** is unfinished and worth visiting only if you have some spare time.

Places to Stay & Eat

Albergo Lauri (☎ 23 23 76), Via T Lauri 6, has singles from L35,000/55,000 and doubles from L60,000/90,000. *Albergo Arena* (☎ 23 09 31), Vicolo Sferisterio 16, has singles from L40,000/65,000 and doubles from L60,000/95,000.

Several pizzerie serve quick takeaway food, including *Rusticanella Romana*, Corso della

Repubblica 13, and *Pizzeria da Luciano*, Vicolo Ferrari 12. One of the better restaurants in town is *Da Secondo*, Via Pescheria Vecchia 26, where you are looking at about L35,000 for a full meal.

Entertainment

The Stagione Lirica (Lyric Festival) is one of Italy's most prestigious musical events, attracting big names to the superb open-air *Arena Sferisterio*, off Piazza Mazzini, from 15 July to 15 August every year. At the same time, the private *Palazzo Ricci Pinacoteca*, in the street of the same name, organises a national exhibition of 20th-century Italian art.

Getting There & Away

Several bus companies operate services to Roma, Firenze, Siena, Ancona, Ascoli Piceno, Civitanova Marche and Foligno. The train station (☎ 24 03 54) is in Via Corridoni. The SS77 connects the city with the A14 to the east and roads for Roma in the west.

AROUND MACERATA

About 20km north-east on the road to Ancona, **Recanati** is a pretty little town which straggles along a high ridge. A pleasant enough stop, the town owes a special place in Italian literary history to its most famous son – the early 19th-century poet Giacomo Leopardi. A small museum is dedicated to his life in the Palazzo Leopardi.

Giacomo Leopardi

Born in Recanati on 29 June 1798, of well-to-do parents, Giacomo Leopardi became the greatest romantic poet to emerge from Italy. From 1822, when he left home for the first time, Leopardi travelled extensively through Italy until his death in Napoli in 1837, although he returned to Recanati regularly during his life. The most penetrating of his poetry, often erudite and always demanding, reflects the pain, anxiety and fragile, bitter-sweet moments of joy or simple remembrance that seem to have been the substance of the man's life. Leopardi was steeped in a classical education from a precocious age and his verse, however much it belongs to the stormy age of the romantics, remains firmly planted in the disciplined framework of classicism. The pick of his work is the *Canti*, first published between 1824 and 1835, and now a standard element of Italian literary education. ■

ASCOLI PICENO

Legend has it that a woodpecker was responsible for the founding of this southern Le Marche town by leading the prehistoric first settlers to the site. The extensive old centre is bounded by the Tronto river to the north and the Castellano river to the south, and is dominated by nearby mountains leading into the Appennini. The city is among the region's most interesting after Urbino, and deserves more attention than it gets.

Woodpecker stories aside, Ascoli Piceno was probably settled by the Piceni tribe in the 6th century BC. The salt trade eventually brought the city into contact with the Romans, to whom it fell after clamorous defeats in the battlefield in 268 BC. By the sixth century AD, the Goths and then the Lombards had come to supplant the Romans. The city flourished in the Middle Ages, despite being ransacked by troops of Holy Roman Emperor Frederick II after a long siege in 1242.

Orientation

The old town and its modern extension are separated by the Castellano river. The train station is in the new town, east of the river. From here, head west across the Ponte Maggiore and along Corso Vittorio Emanuele and past the duomo. Any of the narrow cobbled lanes north will eventually take you to Piazza del Popolo, the heart of the medieval city.

Information

Tourist Office The AAST (☎ 25 72 88), at Piazza del Popolo 1, is open Monday to Friday from 8 am to 1.45 pm and 3 to 6.30 pm, and Saturday from 9 am to 12.30 pm and 3 to 6.30 pm.

Post & Communications The main post

office is on Via Crispi, east along Corso Mazzini from Piazza del Popolo. It is open Monday to Saturday from 8.15 am to 7.40 pm. The post code is 63100.

The Telecom office is on Corso Vittorio Emanuele and is open Monday to Friday from 9 am to 1 pm. The telephone code for Ascoli Piceno is ☎ 0736.

Medical Services For an ambulance, call ☎ 35 81.

Emergency In a police emergency, call ☎ 113.

Piazza del Popolo

The heart of medieval Ascoli and the town's forum in Roman times, Piazza del Popolo is dominated on the western side by the 13th-century **Palazzo dei Capitani del Popolo**. The seat of Ascoli's rulers, it was burned to the ground in 1535 during a bitter local feud and rebuilt 10 years later. The statue of Pope Paul III above the main entrance was erected in recognition of his efforts to bring peace to the town, but the building's colourful history did not end there, as it was the headquarters for the local branch of the Fascists from 1938 and became the seat of the partisan Comitato di Liberazione in 1945.

Closing off the piazza to the north, the **Chiesa di San Francesco** was started in 1262 and features a 15th-century wooden crucifix and 16th-century works by Cola dell'Amatrice. Virtually annexed to the church is the **Loggia dei Mercanti**. It looks suspiciously Tuscan, but was in fact built by Lombard masons in the 16th century. Merchants hawk their wares there to this day.

Pinacoteca

The largest art gallery in Le Marche is inside the 17th-century Palazzo Comunale on Piazza Arringo, south of Piazza del Popolo.

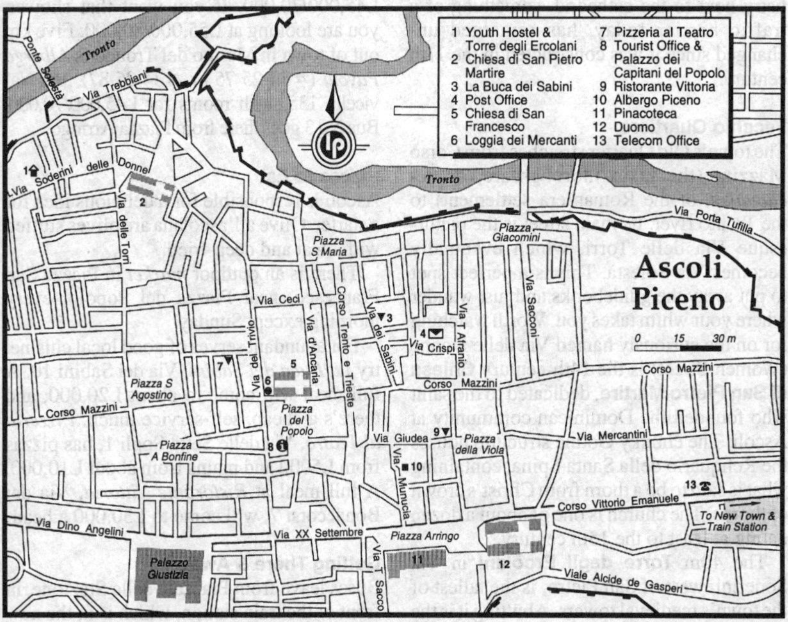

The Pinacoteca boasts 400 works, including paintings by Van Dyck, Titian, Carlo Crivelli and even Turner. Among the prints and drawings is an etching by Rembrandt. The gallery was founded in 1861 with works taken from churches and religious orders that were suppressed in the wake of Italian unification. It is open from Tuesday to Sunday from 9 am to 1 pm. Admission is L2500. In summer it is also open in the afternoon. Across Piazza Arringo, the **Museo Archeologico** has a collection of implements used by the ancient Piceni tribe. It is open the same hours as the gallery and admission is free.

Duomo

Standing on the eastern flank of Piazza Arringo, Ascoli's cathedral is a lavish example of Baroque excess, embellished in what some connoisseurs consider to be a less than tasteful manner. In compensation for the overkill, you will encounter what is possibly Carlo Crivelli's best work, *Virgin and Saints*, in the **Cappella del Sacramento**. The baptistry next to the cathedral, something of a traffic barrier today, has remained unchanged since it was constructed in the 11th century.

Vecchio Quartiere

The town's Old Quarter stretches from Corso Mazzini (the main thoroughfare, or *decumanus*, of the Roman-era settlement) to the Tronto river. Its main street is the picturesque Via delle Torri, which eventually becomes Via Solestà. This is a perfect spot to put away the guidebooks and just wander where your whim takes you. Worth watching for on the curiously named Via delle Donne (Women Street) is the 14th-century **Chiesa di San Pietro Martire**, dedicated to the saint who founded the Dominican community at Ascoli. The chunky Gothic structure houses the Reliquario della Santa Spina, containing what is said to be a thorn from Christ's crown of thorns. The church is one of about a dozen dating at least to the 15th century.

The 40m **Torre degli Ercolani** in Via Soderini, west of San Pietro, is the tallest of the town's medieval towers. Abutting it is the **Palazzetto Longobardo**, a 12th-century Lombard-Romanesque defensive position and now a youth hostel. Just north is the well-preserved **Ponte di Solestà**, a single-arched Roman bridge.

Special Events

The town's big festival is the Quintana, a medieval pageant held on the first Sunday of every August. Hundreds of locals dressed in traditional costume fill the town centre for jousting, parades and other medieval doings. The summer months also come alive with shows and concerts during the city's Stagione Lirica.

Places to Stay

The town's HI *Ostello de' Longobardi* (☎ 25 90 07), Via Soderini 26, charges L13,000 for B&B. Otherwise, your options for budget accommodation are not extensive. The central *Albergo Piceno* (☎ 25 25 53), Via Minucia 10, offers singles/doubles without even the possibility of taking a shower for L45,000/70,000. If you want that shower, you are looking at L55,000/80,000. Five km out of town in Marino del Tronco is *Albergo Pavoni* (☎ 34 25 75 or ☎ 34 25 87), Via Navicella 135, with rooms for L45,000/70,000. Bus No 3 goes there from Piazza Arringo.

Places to Eat

Ascoli is responsible for a delicious idea for a starter. Olive all'ascolana are olives stuffed with meat and deep-fried.

There is an outdoor *market* in Piazza San Francesco, near Piazza del Popolo, every morning except Sunday.

For abundant serves of good local cuisine, try *La Buca dei Sabini*, Via dei Sabini 10. A full meal will come to about L20,000, and there's a cheap, self-service lunch. *Pizzeria al Teatro*, Via delle Sette Sogli 1, has pizzas from L5000 and mains from about L10,000. A full meal at *Ristorante Vittoria*, Via dei Bonaccorsi 7, will come to L30,000 a head.

Getting There & Away

Buses leave from Piazzale della Stazione, in front of the train station, which is in the new part of town on the eastern side of Fiume Castellano. Cotravat (☎ 34 22 43) has three buses a day to Roma, and serves Ancona as well as small towns in the Tronto river area. Cameli (☎ 25 90 91) also has buses to Roma. Mazzuca (☎ 40 22 67) serves Montemonaco, Amandola and other towns near the Monti Sibillini range. Amadio (☎ 34 18 38) has a service to Firenze via Perugia and Siena, and the Abruzzo bus company ARPA (☎ 34 10 49) serves Pescara and Teramo (change here for L'Aquila).

A spur train line connects Ascoli Piceno with Porto d'Ascoli and San Benedetto del Tronto on the Adriatic, which is on the Bologna-Lecce line.

By car, the SS4 connects Ascoli Piceno with Roma and the Adriatic coast.

MONTI SIBILLINI

Rising bare and forbidding in the lower south-west of Le Marche, and reaching into neighbouring Umbria, the stark Monti Sibillini range is one of the most beautiful stretches of the Appennini. Dotted with caves and lined with walking trails, the mountains are also the scene of more energetic sporting activities such as hang-gliding and horse riding. The range is littered with rifugi and offers reasonable skiing in winter.

Amandola makes a good base to explore the area, but lacks cheap accommodation. It is one of the prettiest villages in Le Marche and is just north of **Montefortino**, which is a good base for walking as it's reasonably close to the serious walking areas around Montemonaco, at the base of Monte Sibilla.

Montemonaco is an out-of-the-way town and not easily reached by public transport, although you'll be surprised by the number of tourists in summer. Many are there for the Gola dell'Infernaccio (Gorge of Hell), one of the easiest and most spectacular walks in Le Marche.

To reach the range, take the SS4 from Ascoli Piceno and follow the signs. Buses connect the area with Ascoli Piceno and various cities throughout Le Marche. See also the Valnerina section in the Umbria chapter for details about hang-gliding and how to get to the mountains from Umbria.

Information

If approaching from the north, along the SS78 from Ancona, stop at the AAST in Sarnano (☎ 0733-65 71 95) in Piazza Perfetti 17. It might have limited walking and climbing information, but there is nothing at the AAST in Ascoli Piceno. The CAI publishes a detailed guide in Italian to the mountains, complete with maps, *Parco Nazionale dei Sibillini – Le Più Belle Escursioni*, by Alberico Alesi and Maurizio Calibani.

Places to Stay

There is a camping ground just south of Montefortino at Cerrentana. The *Montespino* (☎ 0736-85 92 38) has sites for L8000 a person and L10,000 a tent, and opens from 1 June to 30 September. Montemonaco has quite a few rooms at good rates. The *Albergo Sibilla* (☎ 0736-85 61 44), Via Roma 52, charges L65,000/75,000 per person. The *Rifugio della Montagna* (☎ 0736-85 63 27), in Foce, just near Montemonaco, has singles/doubles from L30,000/60,000.

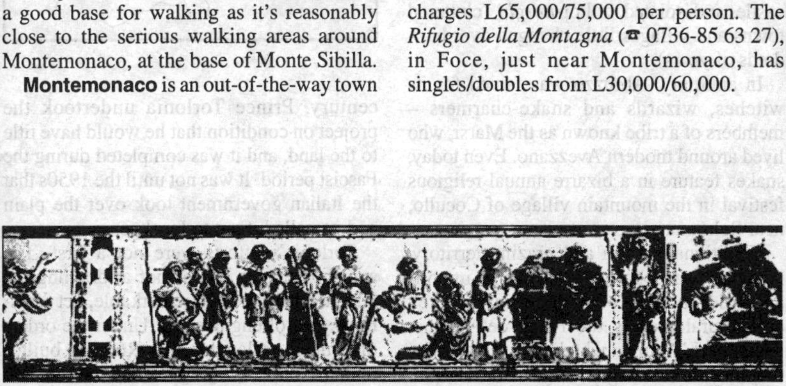

Abruzzo & Molise

Abruzzo, along with neighbouring Molise, is one of the few parts of Italy to be spared the influx of mass tourism. Although neither region is as rich in artistic and cultural heritage as their more illustrious neighbours, there is still plenty to explore, particularly in Abruzzo.

Until administratively divided in 1963, Abruzzo and Molise were known as the Abruzzi, a term still commonly used to describe the two. The earthquake-prone region was particularly hard-hit in 1915, when a massive jolt left 30,000 people dead.

Abruzzo

The wild beauty of Abruzzo's mountain terrain is captivating – the bald, craggy peaks of the Gran Sasso d'Italia are capped by the Corno Grande (at 2914m the highest mountain in the Appennini) and have perilous drops of up to 1000m. Farther south, wolves and bears still roam protected in the forests of the Parco Nazionale d'Abruzzo.

The region is not just for nature-lovers. The medieval towns of L'Aquila and Sulmona are well worth visiting, and the countryside is speckled with an array of castles and isolated, hilltop *borghi* (cluttered towns and villages little changed over hundreds of years).

In antiquity, Abruzzo was famed for its witches, wizards and snake-charmers – members of a tribe known as the Marsi, who lived around modern Avezzano. Even today, snakes feature in a bizarre annual religious festival in the mountain village of Cocullo, near Sulmona.

Traditionally farm and grazing territory, Abruzzo's sheep farmers still play an important role in the local economy. A key agricultural area is the Piana del Fucino, south of L'Aquila, which was created by draining the vast Lago Fucino in the late 19th century. Prince Torlonia undertook the project on condition that he would have title to the land, and it was completed during the Fascist period. It was not until the 1950s that the Italian government took over the plain and parcelled it out to local peasants.

HIGHLIGHTS

- Trekking and skiing in the Gran Sasso d'Italia
- Chocolate *torrone* (nougat) in L'Aquila
- Wildlife and villages of the Parco Naturale d'Abruzzo
- Little-visited Roman ruins at Saepinum
- Year-round boats to the Isole Tremiti from Termoli
- Snake-Charmers' Procession in Cocullo

Torlonia's efforts were not a first. The ancient Romans had a shot at draining the lake in what proved a remarkable, yet disastrous, feat of engineering. Under the orders of Emperor Claudius, the Romans built a tunnel about 10km long to drain the lake into

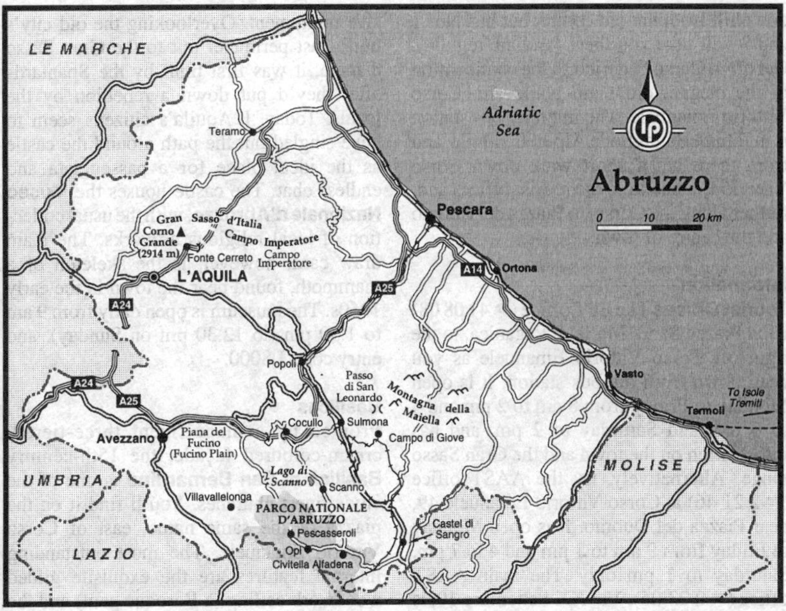

a neighbouring valley. Unfortunately, when the outlet tunnel was opened, it proved too small for the massive volume of water in the lake and thousands of spectators, including the emperor himself, almost drowned.

L'AQUILA

The evening sun casts an opaque rose light across the Gran Sasso d'Italia just to the north of L'Aquila – an encouraging counterpoint to the somewhat gloomy regional capital. In spite of repeated earthquakes, the medieval core of the city remains an interesting place to explore, but L'Aquila's curious beginnings are perhaps more intriguing still. Emperor Frederick II founded the town in 1240, it is said, by drawing together the citizens of 99 villages. Whether true or not, the number 99 became a symbol. The citizens of L'Aquila ('the Eagle', a reference to the eagle in the imperial coat of arms) established 99 churches and 99 piazzas, as well as a fountain with (almost) 99 spouts. Earthquakes, especially one in 1703, have destroyed most of the churches and piazzas, but the medieval fountain survives and, every evening, the town hall bell chimes 99 times.

L'Aquila's people have a rebellious spirit but have frequently backed the wrong horse. King Manfred destroyed the city in 1266 because the people supported the Pope, and it came close to a repeat under siege by the Aragonese, in the fight over the Kingdom of Napoli against the House of Anjou. Twice L'Aquila rose against Spanish rule in the 16th and 17th centuries (the first time allied with Francis I of France), and both times the city was crushed. The 1703 earthquake all but finished L'Aquila off, but revolt finally proved fruitful when, in 1860, the city was made regional capital for its efforts towards national unity.

Orientation

L'Aquila's train station is some distance

downhill from the old centre, but bus Nos 1 and 3 will take you there (and are regular). Get off in Corso Federico II, the continuation of the elegant old main boulevard, Corso Vittorio Emanuele. The intercity bus station is in Piazza Battaglione Alpini L'Aquila, and from there it's a short walk down Corso Vittorio Emanuele to the tourist offices and, farther along the Corso, to Piazza del Duomo and the centre of town.

Information

Tourist Offices The EPT office (☎ 41 08 08) is on Piazza Santa Maria di Paganica, to the right off Corso Vittorio Emanuele as you head down from the bus station. It is open Monday to Friday from 8 am to 2 pm and 4 to 6 pm, and Saturday to 2 pm, and has information on the town and the Gran Sasso range. Alternatively, try the AAST office (☎ 2 21 46) at Corso Vittorio Emanuele 49, near Piazza del Duomo. It is open Monday to Friday from 9 am to 1 pm and 4 to 7 pm, Saturday to 1 pm only. The main AAST office (☎ 2 23 06), Via XX Settembre 10, is open Monday to Saturday from 9 am to 1 pm and 3.30 to 6.45 pm (in summer also on Sunday mornings).

Post & Communications The main post office is in Piazza del Duomo, and opens Monday to Saturday from 8.15 am to 7.40 pm. The postcode for central L'Aquila is 67100.

The Telecom office is at Via Salustio 7 and is open daily from 8 am to 10 pm. The town's telephone code is ☎ 0862.

Emergency For immediate police attendance call ☎ 113, or track down the Questura (☎ 43 01) at Via Strinella 2, well out of the centre. The public hospital, the Ospedale San Salvatore (☎ 77 81), is north of the old town centre on Corso Vittorio Emanuele. For an ambulance call ☎ 118.

Castle

This massive edifice of steep, blanched battlements sunk deep into a now empty moat is without a doubt L'Aquila's most impressive monument. Overlooking the old city's north-east perimeter out to the Gran Sasso d'Italia, it was first built by the Spaniards after they'd put down a rebellion by the locals. Today, L'Aquila's citizens seem to have singled out the path around the castle as the ideal place for a passeggiata and endless chat. The castle houses the **Museo Nazionale d'Abruzzo**, with the usual collection of local religious artworks. The main draw card, however, is the skeleton of a mammoth, found near the town in the early 1950s. The museum is open daily from 9 am to 1.30 pm (to 12.30 pm on Sunday), and entry costs L8000.

Basilicas

Fronted by a magnificent three-tiered, cream-coloured façade, the 15th-century **Basilica di San Bernardino** is one of the city's finest churches. You'll find it on the piazza of the same name, east of Corso Vittorio Emanuele. The most outstanding internal features are the exquisite gilded woodwork ceiling (a Baroque gem) and the intricate detail of the relief decoration of St Bernardino's mausoleum, the work of local craftsman Silvestro dell'Aquila. St Bernardino, originally of Siena, spent his last years in L'Aquila, where he died.

The Romanesque **Basilica di Santa Maria di Collemaggio**, south-east of the town centre along Viale di Collemaggio, has an equally imposing façade, its rose windows encased by a quilt pattern of pink and white marble. The basilica was built at the instigation of a hermit, Pietro da Morrone, who was elected pope at the age of 80 in 1294. Pietro took the name Celestine V, but this unworldly and trusting man was no match for the machinations of courtiers and politicians and he was eventually forced to abdicate. His successor, Pope Boniface VIII, saw Celestine as a threat and threw him into prison, where he died. As founder of the Celestine order, he was canonised seven years later and his tomb is inside the basilica.

Fontana delle 99 Cannelle

A symbol of the city, the 'Fountain of the 99

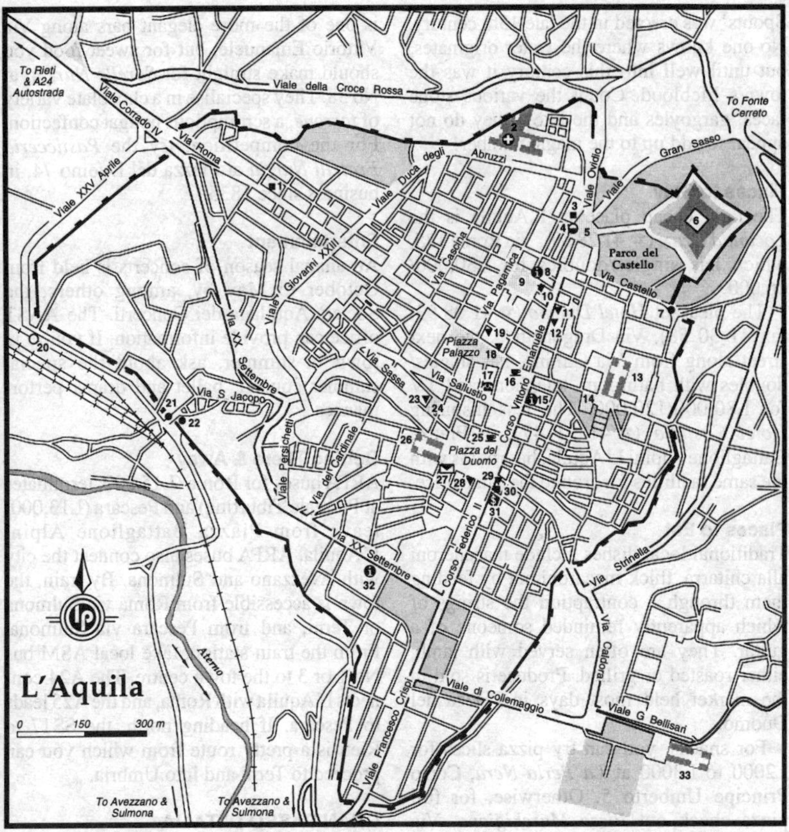

PLACES TO STAY
1 Locanda Orazi
3 Hotel Castello
30 Hotel Duomo

PLACES TO EAT
10 Trattoria del Giaguaro
11 Pizza Marchigiana
12 Pizzeria Due Mari
16 Gran Caffè Eden
18 La Perla Nera
19 Ristorante la Mimosa
23 Trattoria San Biagio
25 Sorelle Nurzia
28 Ristorante Renato
29 Pasticceria Fratelli Nurzia

OTHER
2 Hospital
4 Intercity Bus Station
5 Piazza Battaglione Alpini L'Aquila
6 Castello & Museo Nazionale d'Abruzzo
7 Porta Castello
8 EPT Tourist Office
9 Piazza Santa Maria Paganica
13 Basilica di San Bernadino
14 Piazza San Bernardino
15 AAST Tourist Office
17 Telecom Office
20 Train Station
21 Porta Rivera
22 Fontana della 99 Cannelle
24 Piazza San Biagio
26 Duomo
27 Post Office
31 BNL Bank (ATM)
32 AAST Head Tourist Office
33 Basilica di Santa Maria di Collemaggio

Spouts' was erected in the late 13th century. No-one knows where the water originates, but until well into this century it was the town's lifeblood. Count the various stone faces, gargoyles and the like – they do not appear to add up to the magic number!

Places to Stay

The only cheap place in L'Aquila is the *Locanda Orazi* (☎ 41 28 89), Via Roma 175, which has singles/doubles for L30,000/46,000.

The pleasant *Hotel Duomo* (☎ 41 08 93; fax 41 30 58), Via Dragonetti 6, the next street along from Via Cimino, has singles/doubles with bathroom, telephone and TV for L80,000/120,000. The less inspiring *Hotel Castello* (☎ 41 91 47), in Piazza Battaglione Alpini L'Aquila, has rooms with the same facilities for around the same price.

Places to Eat

Traditional local dishes include maccheroni alla chitarra, thick macaroni cut by feeding them through a contraption the strings of which apparently reminded someone of a guitar. They are often served with lamb, either roasted or grilled. Produce is sold in the market held most days in Piazza del Duomo.

For snacks, you can try pizza slices for L2000 to L3000 at *La Perla Nera*, Corso Principe Umberto 5. Otherwise, for full pizza check out *Pizza Marchigiana*, Via Vittorio Emanuele 117, or *Pizzeria Due Mari* at No 109.

At *Trattoria San Biagio*, Piazza San Biagio, along Via Sassa from Piazza del Duomo, you can dine well on local specialities for around L25,000. Another good choice for a low-priced meal is *Trattoria del Giaguaro*, Piazza Santa Maria Paganica 4. *Ristorante la Mimosa* (☎ 41 34 41), tucked away at Via Navelli 22, is more expensive at around L35,000 for a full meal, but offers excellent food. Another, more expensive option is *Ristorante Renato* (☎ 2 55 96), Via dell'Indipendenza 9.

Cafés, Bars & Pasiccerie *Gran Caffè Eden* is one of the more elegant bars along Via Vittorio Emanuele, but for sweet food you should make straight for *Sorelle Nurzia*, at No 38. They specialise in a chocolate variety of *torrone*, a scrumptious nougat confection. For the competition, try the *Pasticceria Fratelli Nurzia* at Piazza del Duomo 74, in business since 1835.

Entertainment

An annual season of concerts is held from October to May by, among others, the Società Aquilana dei Concerti. The AAST office can provide information. If you're in town in summer, ask about the special summer concert, ballet and drama performances.

Getting There & Away

ARPA buses for Roma (L15,500; terminates at Piazzale Tiburtina) and Pescara (L13,000) leave from Piazza Battaglione Alpini L'Aquila. ARPA buses also connect the city with Avezzano and Sulmona. By train, the town is accessible from Roma via Sulmona or Terni, and from Pescara via Sulmona. From the train station, take local ASM bus No 1 or 3 to the town centre. The A24 connects L'Aquila with Roma, and the A25 leads to Pescara. If heading north, the SS17 to Rieti is a pretty route from which you can proceed to Terni and into Umbria.

GRAN SASSO D'ITALIA

The rocky peaks of the Gran Sasso d'Italia are close to L'Aquila. Try the city's tourist offices for details on walking trails and *rifugi*. A cable car leaves **Fonte Cerreto** every 30 minutes for Campo Imperatore (2117m), providing access to decent walking trails and a small, but popular, ski resort of the same name. Chair and ski lifts operate on the runs at **Campo Imperatore** and there is more skiing at nearby Monte Cristo, as well as Campo Felice.

There is a camping ground, the *Funivia del Gran Sasso* (☎ 0862-60 61 63), at Fonte Cerreto, and a network of mountain rifugi in the area. Hotel accommodation is limited and expensive, and includes the *Nido delle*

Aquile (☎ & fax 0862-60 63 36), at Fonte Cerreto, which has singles/doubles starting at L80,000/120,000, and the *Campo Imperatore* (☎ 0862-40 00 00; fax 41 32 01), at Campo Imperatore, which has doubles from L120,000 to L150,000.

From L'Aquila, take bus No 6 (six daily) from Via Castello to the cable car at Fonte Cerreto.

SULMONA

Sulmona, the birthplace of Ovid, is an understated but charming little town, hemmed in by mountains. The medieval centre invites one to wander, and the town is well placed to serve as a base for exploring southern Abruzzo.

Its modern claim to fame is the *confetti* industry – the making of elaborate flower-shaped arrangements of sugar almonds, a must at traditional Italian weddings.

Orientation & Information

The town's main street, Corso Ovidio, runs from the small park at Piazzale Tresca to the vast Piazza Garibaldi, a five-minute walk.

Sulmona's AAST office (☎ 5 32 76), Corso Ovidio 108, is open Monday to Saturday from 8 am to 2 pm. The town's telephone code is ☎ 0864.

Things to See

Sulmona's main attraction is the **Palazzo dell'Annunziata** on Corso Ovidio, which combines Gothic and Renaissance styles. Note the beautifully carved frieze halfway up the façade. The building houses a small museum dedicated to the work of Sulmona's Renaissance goldsmiths. Next to the palace is a Baroque church of the same name, rebuilt after the 1703 earthquake. Also along Corso Ovidio, in Piazza XX Settembre, is a statue of Ovid.

Piazza Garibaldi is the scene of a colourful market every Wednesday and Saturday morning. When the bustle of the market clears, you can take a closer look at the austere Renaissance **Fontana del Vecchio** and the medieval **aqueduct**, which borders the piazza on two sides. The most interesting feature of the **Chiesa di San Martino**, also on the square, is its Gothic entrance. In the adjacent Piazza del Carmine, the Romanesque portal is all that remains of the **Chiesa di San Francesco della Scarpa**, destroyed in the 1703 earthquake.

Ovid

The Augustan poet, considered by some as being second only to Virgil, has a mixed and not altogether flattering reputation. Born in Sulmona in 43 BC and sent at an early age to Roma to study rhetoric and make himself a comfortable career in the cesspit of Roman politics, Ovid preferred to write poetry instead. His early erotic verse, such as *Amores* and *Ars Amatoria*, gained him quick popularity in Roman high society. Possibly his most ambitious work was the *Metamorphosis*, a kind of extended cover version of a whole gamut of Greek myths which culminated in descriptions of Caesar's transformation into a star and the apotheosis of Augustus, ruler at the time. This last piece of sycophancy did not stop the emperor from banishing him to the Black Sea in 8 AD for reasons which are not entirely clear. He died in Tomi, in modern Romania, 10 years later. ■

Places to Stay & Eat

The *Locanda di Giovanni* (☎ 5 13 97) at Via Peligna 8, along Via Mazara from Corso Ovidio, has singles/doubles for L30,000/60,000. The pleasant *Hotel Italia* (☎ 5 23 08) in Piazza San Tommaso, through Piazza XX Settembre from Corso Ovidio, has rooms with bathroom for L50,000/80,000.

For a square meal with no frills (about L25,000 a head), try the *Ristorante Stella* at Via Mazara 18. For more ambience (and with more money!) head for the *Ristorante Italia*, Piazza XX Settembre 23.

Getting There & Away

ARPA buses link Sulmona to L'Aquila (nine daily), Pescara (five daily), Napoli (two daily), Scanno (10 daily) and other nearby towns. From Piazza Tresca, walk along Via di Circonvallazione Orientale to reach the bus station, off Via Japasseri. ARPA buses also head for Castel di Sangro and Pescasseroli, which are in the Parco Nazionale d'Abruzzo.

Regular trains connect the town with Roma and Pescara. The train station is about 2km downhill from the historic centre, and the half-hourly bus No A runs between the two.

AROUND SULMONA

Cocullo

The tiny mountain village of Cocullo only warrants a visit on one day of the year – the first Thursday in May, when its inhabitants celebrate the feast day of St Dominic in a truly original and weird fashion. A statue of the saint is draped with live snakes and carried in procession through the town, accompanied by townspeople also carrying live snakes. Known as the Processione dei Serpari (Snake-Charmers' Procession), the festival has pagan origins and is an unforgettable experience.

The village has no accommodation, but is close to Sulmona and Scanno and linked to both by ARPA bus. Plan to arrive in the village early on the day of the festival, as it has attracted increasingly large crowds in recent years. Festivities usually start at around 10 am, culminating in the procession at midday and then continuing throughout the afternoon.

Ask at the tourist offices in Sulmona or Scanno for details on buses to Cocullo, since services are increased for the event.

Scanno

This village was assaulted by various photographers after WWII, and made into an example of traditionalism in the modern world. As a result, Scanno has become something of a minor tourist mecca for Italians. The handful of elderly women who still skittle about in traditional costume must, you can't help thinking, take some affront at having become individual mobile tourist 'sights'.

Scanno was long a centre of wool production, and for centuries an exclusive supplier to the Franciscan order. Today the cheerfully jumbled medieval village is surrounded by an outcrop of uninspired modern 'suburbia', not a little of which is given over to hotel space.

The place is worth the effort, especially if you have made it this far into Abruzzo. The drive south from Sulmona through the Gole di Saggitario (the Saggitarius Gorges) and past the peaceful Lago di Scanno is delightful, and beyond Scanno the road takes you right into the Parco Nazionale d'Abruzzo.

Information The AAST office (☎ 7 43 17), Via Santa Maria della Valle 12, is on the edge of the medieval town centre. The telephone code for Scanno is ☎ 0864.

Places to Stay & Eat If you plan to stay overnight, there is a camping ground at the Lago di Scanno, the *Camping I Lupi* (☎ 74 01 00), which opens from June to September. The town is crammed with hotels. Try the *Pensione Nilde* (☎ 7 43 59), Via del Lago, which has singles/doubles for L45,000/70,000, or the *Pensione Margherita* (☎ 7 43 53), Via Tanturri, which has rooms with own bath for L45,000/80,000. The *Hotel Vittoria* (☎ 74 71 79), Via Domenico di Rienzo 46, is a more upmarket option at L70,000/110,000 with private bathroom. Most will want to charge for full board, but there is no obligation.

For a meal, *Ristorante Gli Archetti*, at Via Silla 8, and the *Trattoria Lo Sgabello*, Via dei Pescatori 45, both in the medieval village, are decent spots.

Getting There & Away ARPA buses connect Scanno with Sulmona. An ARPA bus leaves Piazza della Repubblica in Roma for Scanno. Contact the EPT office in Via Parigi, Roma, for information.

Ski Fields

Some modest ski fields lie east of Sulmona. About 18km of tortuous driving brings you to **Campo di Giove**, around which you'll find 15km of downhill runs and some cross-country trails. It is the first in a series of small ski areas (the next is at Passo San Leonardo, about 10km north of Campo di Giove) leading up into the Montagna della Maiella and the surrounding nature reserves.

PARCO NAZIONALE D'ABRUZZO

Established in 1923 with a former royal hunting reserve as its nucleus, the Parco Nazionale d'Abruzzo now incorporates about 40,000 hectares of the Appennini (plus an external protected area of 60,000 hectares). It is the last refuge in Italy of the Marsican brown bear and the Apennine wolf, although it is difficult to spot one of these now rare native animals. At last count there were an estimated 80 bears roaming wild here. The park is also home to golden eagles, a herd of chamois and the odd wildcat. There are plans to reintroduce the lynx, which became extinct in this area around the turn of the century. The park's forests and meadows are perfect for family excursions and long-distance walks, but leaving the marked trails is prohibited.

The most convenient base is the town of **Pescasseroli** (telephone code ☎ 0863), in the centre of the park. The tourist office (☎ 91 04 61), at Via Piave 9, is open daily except Sunday from 9 am to 1 pm and 4.30 to 6.30 pm. Before setting off for the park, buy a detailed map of the park at the Ufficio di Zona (☎ 9 19 55), Via Consultore 1; the map includes the walking trails and locations of rifugi. The Ufficio di Zona (visitors' centre) is open daily from 10 am to noon and 3 to 6 pm; for L10,000 you can visit its museum and zoo (more a veterinary station for sick and wounded animals), where you can see at least one of most of the park's species up close, including a wolf, a Marsican brown bear and a lynx. The majority of these animals are later released back into the wild.

Another possible base is the mountain village of **Civitella Alfadena**, on the park's eastern edge. Less touristy than Pescasseroli, it has a visitors' centre and a large enclosure *(area faunistica)* housing six wolves in semi-captivity. In a smaller enclosure lurks a pair of lynx.

Places to Stay & Eat

Free-camping is forbidden in the park, but there are several camping grounds, including the *Campeggio dell'Orso* (☎ 91 29 55), near the village of Opi. There are also rifugi in the park, but few are open and you must obtain permission and a key from the Ufficio di Zona (aka Centro di Visita; ☎ 94 92 61), Via Colle di Marcandrea, Villavallelonga.

In Pescasseroli the *Hotel Pinguino* (☎ 91 25 80), Via Collachi 2, has singles/doubles with bathroom and half board for L60,000/100,000. The *Hotel Cristiana* (☎ 91 07 95), just outside the town in Collachi, has singles/doubles for L50,000/70,000. For the hungry, *Ristorante La Capannina*, Via Cabinovia 1, offers tasty grub for about L30,000 a head. If it's just a pizza you want, try *Pizzeria San Francesco* on Via Isonzo.

If you want to stay overnight in Civitella Alfadena, the best choice is the *Albergo La Torre* (☎ 0864-89 01 21), in the centre of the old town at Via Castello 3, which has rooms for L30,000 per person.

Getting There & Away

Pescasseroli, Civitella Alfadena and other villages in the park are linked by ARPA bus to Avezzano (and from there to L'Aquila) and Castel di Sangro (reached from Sulmona by bus or train). In summer an ARPA bus leaves from Piazza della Repubblica in Roma for Pescasseroli (go to the EPT office in Via Parigi, Roma, for information).

PESCARA

A heavily developed beach resort and commercial centre, Pescara's only attraction is the beach and even that is nothing to write home about. However, travellers to Abruzzo are likely to pass through Pescara since it is also the main transport hub of the region, with trains connecting it to Bologna, Ancona, Roma and Bari, and buses running from it to towns throughout Abruzzo.

The tourist office can provide information about the jazz festival held in the second half of July at the Teatro D'Annunzio, in the public park by the beach east of the city centre. If you're desperate for something to do, you could visit the Museo Ittico, a fishery museum on the waterfront at Via Raffaele Paolucci.

Orientation & Information

From the train station and intercity bus station in Piazzale della Repubblica, the beach is a short walk north-east down Corso Umberto I.

Tourist Offices The EPT (☎ 421 17 07) is at Via Nicola Fabrizi 171. It is open Monday to Saturday from 9 am to noon. In summer another information booth normally opens at the train station.

Post & Communications The post office is at Corso Vittorio Emanuele II 106, to the right off Piazzale della Repubblica, and opens Monday to Saturday from 8.15 am to 7.40 pm. The postcode for central Pescara is 65100.

The Telecom office is at Piazza del Sacro Cuore 20 and is open daily from 8 am to 10 pm. The telephone code for Pescara is ☎ 085.

Medical & Emergency Services In a police emergency, call ☎ 113. The public hospital, the Ospedale Civile (☎ 42 51), is at Via Renato Paolini, south-west of the train station, off Via del Circuito.

Places to Stay & Eat

The *Internazionale* camping ground (☎ 6 56 53) is by the beach on Lungomare Cristoforo Colombo (take bus No 10 from the train station). A fairly simple place is *Pensione Roma* (☎ 421 16 57), Via Piave 142. Don't expect any frills, but singles/doubles cost up to L25,000/50,000. Near the station, at Via Michelangelo Forti 14, is *Hotel Alba* (☎ 38 91 45), which has decent rooms with bathroom for L65,000/100,000 (less for a stay of a few days). The *Hotel Natale* (☎ 422 28 85), Via del Circuito 175, has pleasant singles/doubles for L50,000/80,000, and bargaining is possible.

For a reasonably priced meal, try the *Pinguino*, Corso Manthonè 36, across the Pescara river. A meal at *Cantina di Jooz*, in the parallel Via delle Caserme, will cost around L40,000.

Getting There & Away

Bus ARPA buses leave from Piazzale della Repubblica for L'Aquila, Sulmona and anywhere else you like in Abruzzo. SATAM has a daily service to Napoli (about five hours), while Eagle Lines buses pass through twice a week on the long haul from Taranto in Puglia to Udine in Friuli. Timetables are posted at the ticket office in the piazza.

Train Pescara is on the main train line along the Adriatic coast and is easily accessible for towns such as Bologna, Ancona, Foggia and points farther south, as well as L'Aquila, Sulmona and Roma.

Car & Motorcycle You can choose between the A14 and often busy SS16 heading north or south along the coast. Those heading for Roma, L'Aquila or Sulmona should take the A25 or SS5.

Boat A ferry to Split in Croatia may be operating again by the time you read this. Check with Agenzia Sanmar (☎ 6 52 47) at the ferry terminal, just south of the Pescara river.

Molise

Hived off in 1963 from its bigger northern sibling, Abruzzo, Molise is a small, hilly and rather undistinguished region. A kind of cultural bridge from north to south, it has a low ranking on the tourist trail.

Largely rural and repeatedly shaken by devastating earthquakes, its towns are prosaic and of little interest. In fact, the traveller moving north to south will notice, perhaps for the first time, those great clumps of hideous concrete blocks that seem to pass for a kind of standard in modern Mediterranean 'architecture', whether in southern Italy, Spain, Morocco or Egypt.

It's not all bad news. You can wander through the Roman provincial town of Saepinum, south-west of Campobasso, and there are good walking opportunities in the Monti del Matese. Excavations in Isernia have unearthed what is believed to be the oldest village in Europe, and the small beach resort of Termoli is a jumping-off point for the Isole Tremiti, bunched together off the coast of northern Puglisa (see the Puglia section of the Puglia, Basilicata & Calabria chapter).

CAMPOBASSO

Molise's regional capital, Campobasso is predominantly modern and basically unappealing, but makes a good base for exploring nearby Saepinum. The national carabinieri training school is here, as is a high-security prison.

The EPT office (☎ 41 56 62) is at Piazza della Vittoria 14, open Monday to Saturday from 8.30 am to about 1.30 pm. From the train station, turn left into Via Cavour, right into Via Gazzani and left again into Corso Vittorio Emanuele to reach it. Campobasso's telephone code is ☎ 0874.

You can kill a couple of hours wandering up into the older part of town to take a look at the Romanesque churches of **San Bartolomeo** (13th century) and **San Giorgio** (12th century). The castle you can see from a distance looks impressive until you get close.

If you need a bed for the night, try the *Albergo Belvedere* (☎ 6 27 24), Via Colle delle Api 32, which has singles/doubles for up to L37,000/55,000 and triples for L68,000. From the train station, take bus No 1N and ask the driver to let you off at the hotel.

Campobasso is connected by bus to Termoli, Isernia and Pescara. By train it can be reached from Roma via Sulmona, or from Napoli via Benevento.

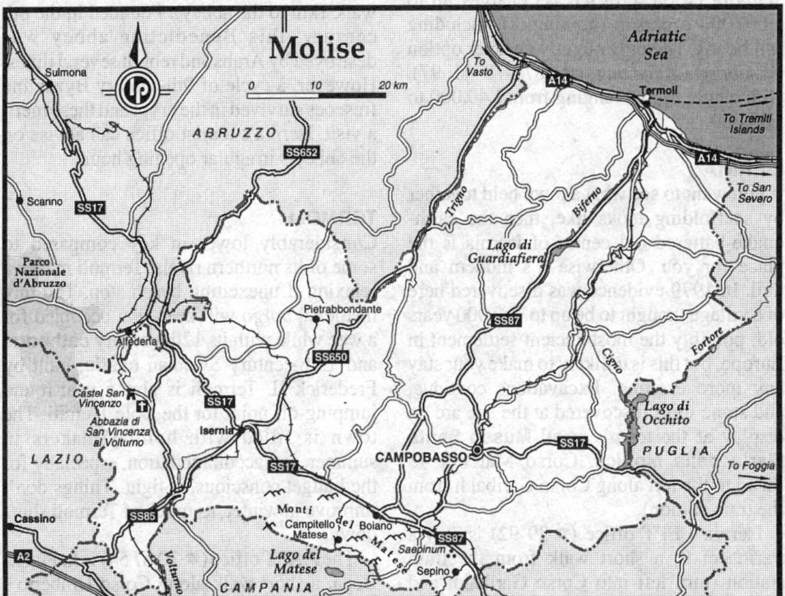

AROUND CAMPOBASSO

One of the least visited Roman ruins in Italy, **Saepinum** is handy to Campobasso and worth a visit. An unimportant provincial town, it survived into the 9th century before being sacked by Arab invaders. Surrounded by small farms, the ruins are quite well preserved and include the town walls, a temple, a triumphal arch and the foundations of numerous houses.

To reach Saepinum by public transport, you will need to take one of the infrequent provincial buses to Altilia, next to the archaeological zone, or Sepino, a 3km walk away.

The **Monti del Matese**, south-west of Campobasso, offer good hiking in summer and adequate skiing in winter. Take a bus from Campobasso to Campitello Matese, or a train from Campobasso or Isernia to Boiano. From either point there are trails into the mountains.

Campitello Matese is the centre for winter sports and has several hotels, but there's nothing cheap about them. *Lo Sciatore* (☎ 0874-78 41 37) charges up to L110,000 a person (no singles), including full board. The only slightly cheaper option is *Albergo Kristiana* (☎ 0874-78 41 97), with single rooms ranging from L40,000 to L80,000.

ISERNIA

If you want to see what a town held together by scaffolding looks like, then the earthquake-battered old centre of Isernia is the place for you. Otherwise it's modern and dull. In 1979 evidence was discovered here of a village thought to be up to 700,000 years old, possibly the most ancient settlement in Europe, but this is unlikely to make your stay any more exciting. Excavations continue, and stone tools discovered at the site are on display at the town's small **Museo Santa Maria della Monica**, Corso Marcelli 48 (head to the left along Corso Garibaldi from the train station).

Isernia's EPT office (☎ 39 92) is at Via Farinacci 9, a short walk from the train station (turn left into Corso Garibaldi and right into Via Farinacci). It is open Monday to Saturday from 8 am to 2 pm. The town's telephone code is ☎ 0865.

For a place to stay, try the *Hotel Sayonara* (☎ 5 09 92), Via G Berta 131, which has singles/doubles with bathroom for L50,000/70,000. Try bargaining if you plan to stay for several nights.

Isernia is easily reached by bus from Campobasso and Termoli and by train from Sulmona, Pescara and Campobasso.

AROUND ISERNIA

Provincial buses will take you to local hilltop villages. Of interest are the remains of a pre-Roman village, including a Greek-style theatre, just outside **Pietrabbondante**, about 30km north-east of Isernia. It was settled by the Samnites, who controlled the area before Roman domination. Three buses a day connect Isernia and Pietrabbondante.

Near Castel San Vincenzo, about 20km north-west of Isernia, is the **Abbazia di San Vincenzo al Volturno** (take the bus for Castel San Vincenzo from Isernia and then walk 1km to the abbey). Founded in the 8th century, this Benedictine abbey was destroyed by Arabs and rebuilt several times. However, a cycle of 9th-century Byzantine frescoes survived in the crypt and these merit a visit. Isernia's tourist office can advise on the abbey's irregular opening hours.

TERMOLI

Considerably lower in key compared to some of its northern rivals, Termoli makes a relaxing if unexciting beach stop. The tiny medieval *borgo* will keep you occupied for a wee while with its 12th-century **cathedral** and 13th-century Swabian **castle**, built by Frederick II. Termoli is also a year-round jumping-off point for the Isole Tremiti. The town is filled with holiday-makers in summer, and accommodation, especially for the budget conscious, is tight. Things don't improve in winter, as much of Termoli shuts down.

The AAST office (☎ 70 67 54) is in Piazza Bega, a short walk along Corso Umberto I from the train station. It opens Monday to

Saturday from 8.15 am to 1 pm. The town's telephone code is ☎ 0875.

Places to Stay & Eat

There are camping facilities at *Cala Saracena* (☎ 5 21 93), Via SS Europa 2, No 174 (also known as SS16 to Pescara). It can be reached by local bus from the train station.

At Via Mascilongo 34 is the *Affittacamere Porreca* (☎ 70 42 48). It has singles/doubles/triples for L30,000/50,000/75,000 – don't let the abrupt manner of the staff put you off.

Hotel Meridiano (☎ 70 59 46) overlooks the beach on Lungomare Cristoforo Colombo and has singles/doubles with bathroom for L65,000/85,000. Like many hotels in Termoli, it closes in winter.

For a reasonable fish meal and some rough wine, try *Da Antonio* at Corso Umberto I 59. A very full meal will cost about L30,000.

Getting There & Away

Bus SATI buses connect Termoli to Campobasso and Pescara, and Isernia can be reached with the Cerella company. The main intercity bus station is in Piazza Bega. Buses also connect the town with Roma, Milano and Napoli (the tourist office has full details of bus timetables).

Train Termoli is on the main Bologna-Lecce train line along the Adriatic coast.

Car & Motorcycle Termoli is on the A14 and SS16 that follow the coast north to Pescara and beyond and south to Bari.

Boat Termoli is the only place from where you can get a daily ferry all year round to the Isole Tremiti (see the Puglia section of the Puglia, Basilicata & Calabria chapter). Enquire at Adriatica Navigazione (☎ 70 53 41), Corso Umberto I, 93; Navigazione Liberal del Golfo, care of Agenzia Di Brino (☎ 70 39 37), Piazza Bega; or at ticket booths at the ferry terminal. There is at least one departure a day (Tuesday and Saturday at 7 am and 2 pm, the other days at 9 am), and tickets are L26,000 return. Hydrofoils run from June to September.

ALBANIAN TOWNS

Several villages to the south of Termoli form an Albanian enclave dating back to the 15th century. These include Campomarino, Portocannone, Ururi and Montecilfone. Although the inhabitants shrugged off their Orthodox religion in the 18th century, locals still use a version of Albanian incomprehensible to outsiders as their first language. The towns can be reached by bus from Termoli.

Campania

Presided over by the magnificent, chaotic capital of the south, Napoli, Campania has everything the traveller could want. With the only true metropolis in the Mezzogiorno (literally midday, the evocative name for the country's south), Campania is also blessed with some of the country's most dramatic coastline, a sprinkling of magical islands and a rich heritage in ancient ruins.

In the shadow of Vesuvio (Mt Vesuvius) lie the ruins of Pompeii and Herculaneum, Roman cities buried by the volcano and so preserved for posterity – both a short excursion south of Napoli. There is plenty more for the classicist to explore, including the Campi Flegrei (Phlegraean Fields) to the north, with its reminders of the world celebrated in the writings of Homer and Virgil and, in the south, the Greek temples of Paestum, among the best preserved in the world.

Many writers have sought to do justice to the natural beauty of the Amalfi coast, farther south of Pompeii, and the islands in the Golfo di Napoli (Bay of Naples), particularly Capri. Inland is the grand palace of the Spanish Bourbons in Caserta, set in magnificent gardens and modelled on Versailles.

Campania is alive with myth and legend. Sirens lured sailors to their deaths off Sorrento, the islands in the Golfo di Napoli were the domain of mermaids, and Lago Averno (Lake Avernus], in the Campi Flegrei, was believed in ancient times to be the entrance to the underworld. Odysseus (Ulysses), Aeneas and other characters of classical story-telling and history have left their mark (real or imagined) here.

Napoli is the most densely populated area of Campania, although the city itself started life humbly, first as a Greek settlement and later as a pleasure resort for Roma's high society. Little touched by the eruption of 79 AD that wiped out Pompeii and neighbouring towns, Napoli also survived the fall of Roma and several Barbarian assaults. It was an independent city state ruled by dukes until southern Italy came under the sway of the Normans in the mid-12th century. The short-lived kingdom of the Normans, with its capital in Palermo, changed hands and dimensions regularly, but always comprised the bulk of southern Italy, including all Campania. Under Spanish Bourbon rule in

HIGHLIGHTS

- Losing yourself among the Graeco-Roman artefacts in Napoli's important Museo Archeologico Nazionale
- Walking in the landscaped garden of the Reggia di Caserta, built by the Bourbons and modelled on Versailles
- Spying on the ancient Roman lifestyle at perfectly preserved Pompeii
- Wandering the lanes and exploring the Grotta Azzurra on the isle of Capri
- Gazing down at the sparkling Amalfi coast from hill-top Ravello's Villa Rufolo, after lazing on the beach or exploring the shops in pretty Positano
- Exploring another world amid the Greek temples and red poppy fields of Paestum

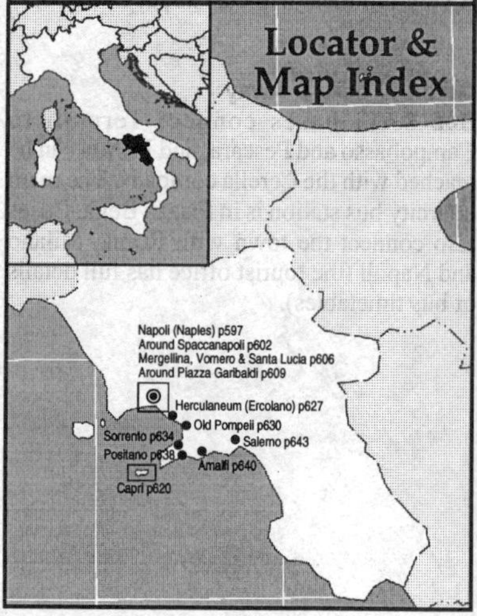

he 18th century, Napoli was one of the great :apitals of Europe.

Campanian cooking is simple, its greatest :ontribution to world cuisine is the pizza. In Napoli especially, you can pick up a quick ›izza anywhere, and savour its unmistak- ıble, rich, tomato sauce.

Campania produces a number of decent wines, including various tipples under the ıame of Greco di Tufo. You will probably be more interested in the bright-yellow lemon iqueur *(limoncello)* which is produced along the Sorrento and Amalfi coasts and on Capri and the other islands in the Golfo di Napoli. It is best taken in small, icy doses in summer, and it's definitely an acquired taste.

Napoli is on the main train line from Roma and is a regional transport hub, which makes travel quite easy and cheap. Most places that are of interest to the traveller in Campania are accessible by train. This is an advantage as tracking down buses can become tiresome.

For the more adventurous and energetic there are some interesting walks in the mountains of the Costeria Amalfitana, on the Sorrento peninsula and in the Picentini mountains.

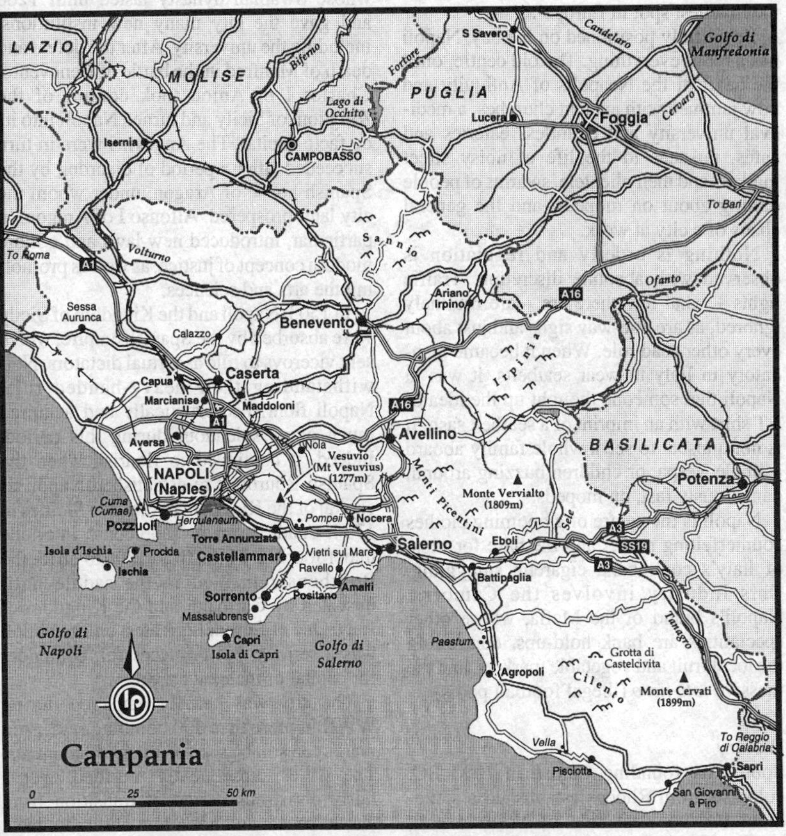

CAMPANIA

Napoli

A man who has seen Napoli (Naples), said Goethe, can never be sad. The third-largest city in Italy, Napoli defies description. *Cook's Tourist's Handbook* of 1884 declared: 'Naples is an ill-built, ill-paved, ill-lighted, ill-drained, ill-watched, ill-governed and ill-ventilated city'. Napoli has made big strides forward, but to many people's way of thinking, the observations of a century ago retain a grain of truth. There is another side to the coin, however, and for all the carping, Cook's concludes that the city 'is, perhaps, the loveliest spot in Europe'.

Beautifully positioned on the bay, Napoli has a bit of everything. The old centre, once the heart of the Neapolis of Antiquity and now jammed with ancient churches, a medieval university and countless eateries and cafés, pulsates to the life of noisy street markets and their clientele, swarms of people darting about on mopeds, and the general chaos of a city at work.

Nothing is orderly and regulation is observed with absolute discretion. Traffic lights – what few there are – are routinely ignored, as are one-way signs and just about every other road rule. When it became mandatory in Italy to wear seatbelts, it was in Napoli that someone thought up the idea of a T-shirt with an imprint of a seatbelt sash. It is not unusual to see a whole family aboard a single Vespa, or children buzzing around, dangerously fast, on mopeds.

Napoli is the centre of a booming clothes counterfeiting racket and the base for most of Italy's contraband cigarette smuggling. This industry involves the Camorra, Napoli's brand of the Mafia, whose other specialities are bank hold-ups, controlling the local fruit and vegetable markets, and the massive *toto nero* (illegal football pools).

History

Soon after founding Cumae in 1000 BC, colonists from Rhodes established a settlement on the west side of Vesuvio and, according to legend, named it after the siren Parthenope. Several centuries later, Phoenician traders and Greeks from Athens attracted by the splendour of the coast expanded the settlement and christened it Neapolis (new city). It prospered as a centre of Greek culture and later, under Roman rule, became a favourite for such notables as Pompey, Caesar and Tiberius.

After successive waves of invasion by the Goths and a couple of spells associated with Byzantium, Napoli was an independent dukedom for about 400 years until taken by the Normans in 1139. They, in turn, were replaced by the German Hohenstaufens, whose Swabian dynasty lasted until 1266 and gave the city many new institutions, including the university. After the defeat and death of Manfred in the battle of Benevento, Charles I of Anjou took control of the Kingdom of Sicily and turned Napoli into its de facto capital. The Angevins were in turn succeeded, after a period of disorder, by the Spanish house of Aragon, under whom the city later prospered. Alfonso I of Aragon, in particular, introduced new laws and a more modern concept of justice, as well as promoting the arts and sciences.

In 1503, Napoli and the Kingdom of Sicily were absorbed by the Spanish empire, which sent viceroys to rule as virtual dictators. Notwithstanding their heavy-handed rule, Napoli flourished artistically and acquired much of its splendour during this period. Indeed, it continued to flourish when the Spanish Bourbons re-established Napoli as capital of the Kingdom of the Two Sicilies in 1734. Aside from a Napoleonic interlude under Joachim Murat from 1806 to 1815, the Bourbons remained in the saddle until unseated by Garibaldi and the Kingdom of Italy. One of Europe's greatest cities, Napoli was a serious, but unsuccessful, contender for capital of the new nation.

The city was heavily damaged during WWII in more than 100 bombing raids, and marks can still be seen on many monuments. The Allies subsequently presided over a fairly disastrous period of transition from war to peace, and not a few observers have attributed the initial boom in the city's organised crime, at least in part, to members of the occupying forces. A severe earthquake in 1980 and a dormant, but not extinct, Vesuvio looming to the east, remind Neapolitans of their city's vulnerability.

Orientation

Napoli stretches along the waterfront and is divided into *quartieri* (districts) – most street signs bear the name of the district as well. The main train station, Stazione Centrale, and the bus station are off Piazza Garibaldi, just east of Spaccanapoli, the old city. The piazza and its side streets form an enormous and unwelcoming transport terminus and street market. The area is distinctly seedy. Quite a few of the cheaper hotels, some of which double as brothels, are here.

A wide shopping street, Corso Umberto I, skirts the southern edge of Spaccanapoli, the ancient heart of Napoli, on its way southwest from Piazza Garibaldi to Piazza Bovio and on to the huge Piazza Municipio, dominated by the unmistakable Castel Nuovo. From the waterfront behind the castle you can find boats to the bay islands, Palermo and other long-distance destinations.

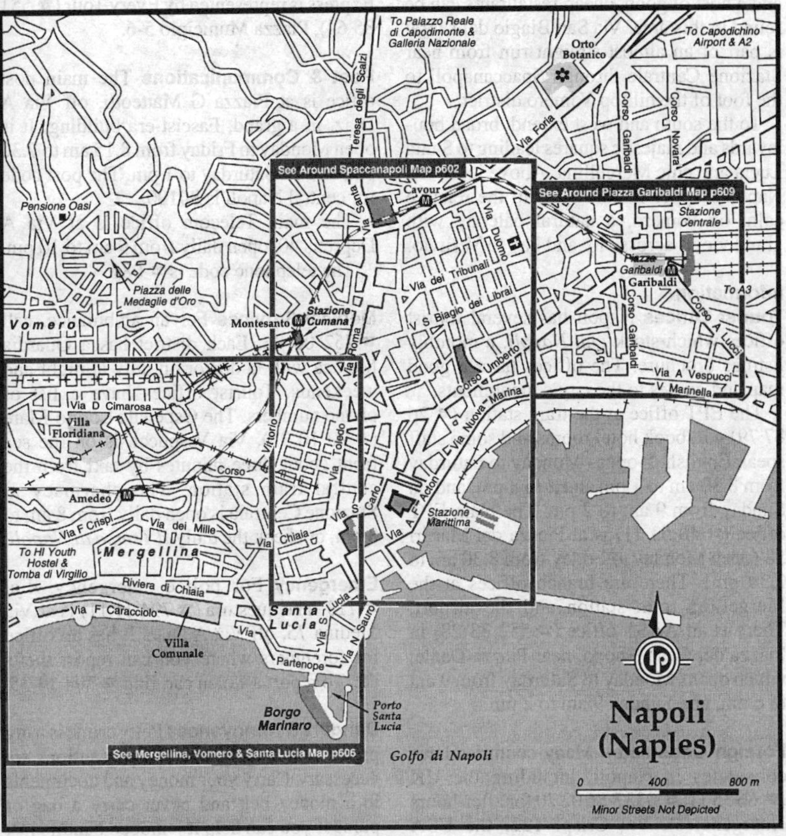

The Palazzo Reale, the former royal palace, is next to the castle. From the palace, head north for Napoli's main street, Via Toledo, which becomes Via Roma for a short stretch after it crosses Piazza Carità, to reach Piazza Dante, on the western boundary of Spaccanapoli. The road continues as Via Santa Teresa degli Scalzi and then Corso Amedeo di Savoia, before reaching the Parco di Capodimonte north of the centre.

The extensions of two of Napoli's more original streets, Via Benedetto Croce (which becomes Via San Biagio dei Librai) and Via dei Tribunali, eventually meet Via Roma. Most street life, many of the city's artisans and a host of good, cheap restaurants can be found in this area. Via San Biagio dei Librai is part of an almost straight run from near Stazione Centrale through Spaccanapoli to the foot of the hilltop Vomero district.

To the south and west extend broad boulevards and majestic squares leading to Santa Lucia and chic Mergellina. Above it all, sits Napoli's upper middle class in the relative calm of Vomero, a natural balcony with grand views across city and bay to Vesuvio.

Information

Tourist Offices Napoli has several tourist offices which stock *Qui Napoli*, a monthly listings brochure. The offices have a good map and guides to the city's monuments.

The EPT office at the train station (☎ 26 87 79) will book hotel rooms and some staff speak English. It opens Monday to Saturday from 8.30 am to 1 pm and 2 to 8 pm, and on Sunday from 9 am to 2 pm. The main EPT office (☎ 40 53 11) is at Piazza dei Martiri 58 (open Monday to Friday from 8.30 am to 2.30 pm). There are branch offices at the Mergellina train station and the airport. There is an AAST office (☎ 552 33 28) in Piazza del Gesù Nuovo, near Piazza Dante, which opens Monday to Saturday from 9 am to 6 pm, and Sunday 9 am to 2 pm.

Foreign Consulates Many countries have consulates in Napoli, including the UK (☎ 66 35 11; ☎ 0337-86 02 70 for after-hours emergencies), Via Crispi 122; the USA (☎ 583 81 11), Piazza della Repubblica; and France (☎ 761 22 75), also at Piazza della Repubblica 2.

Money The city is full of exchange booths, although the rates offered are usually lower than at banks. Some banks charge commission to change travellers' cheques, so ask first. Visa, MasterCard or Eurocheques can be used at many banks with ATMs, including the Banca Nazionale del Lavoro at Via Firenze 39 and Monte dei Paschi di Siena, around the corner on Corso Novara. Banks open Monday to Friday from about 8 am to 1 pm and then 3 to 4.30 pm. American Express is represented by Every Tour (☎ 551 85 64), Piazza Municipio 5-6.

Post & Communications The main post office is at Piazza G Matteotti, off Via A Diaz, in a grand, Fascist-era building. It is open Monday to Friday from 8.15 am to 7.30 pm, and on Saturday to 1 pm. The post code for central Napoli is 80100.

The main Telecom office is at Via A Depretis 40, open daily from 9 am to 10 pm.

The telephone code is ☎ 081.

Medical Services For an ambulance, call ☎ 752 06 96. Each district has a Guardia Medica with a doctor on duty at night and weekends. Tourist offices have a list of phone numbers. The Ospedale Loreto-Mare (☎ 20 10 33), Via Vespucci, is on the sea front about three minutes by taxi from the central train station. The pharmacy at Stazione Centrale is open daily from 8 am to 8 pm, or check the daily *Il Tempo di Napoli*.

Emergency For police emergency, dial ☎ 113. The questura (☎ 794 11 11) is at Via Medina 75, off Via A Diaz. It has an office for foreigners where you can report thefts etc. To report a stolen car, ring ☎ 794 14 35.

Dangers & Annoyances Petty crime is a big problem in Napoli, so a few precautions are necessary. Carry your money and documents in a money belt and never carry a bag or purse if you can help it – moped bandits just love them. Be very careful of pickpockets on crowded buses.

Women should be careful about walking alone in the streets at night, particularly near Stazione Centrale and Piazza Dante. Never venture into the dark side streets at night unless you are in a group. The area west of Via Toledo and as far north as Piazza Carità can be particularly threatening.

Take care when crossing roads. There are few functioning traffic lights and pedestrian crossings and Neapolitans rarely stop anyway. When facing a green light they drive with caution, believing that those facing the red light will not stop. Vehicles and pedestrians simply slip around each other in a kind of unwritten code of road 'courtesy' that can be a little unnerving at first.

Car and motorcycle theft are also problems in Napoli, so think twice before bringing a vehicle to the city.

Other Information The student travel centre, CTS (☎ 552 79 60), is at Via Mezzocannone 25.

There's a decent newspaper stand selling foreign language newspapers and magazines downstairs from the main train station, before the turnstyles to the Metropolitana.

Walking Tour

You'll never walk all of Napoli in a day, but the following itinerary will take you through the heart of it and help you get your bearings. Use public transport during your stay. The buses, the Metropolitana and funiculars are simple to use.

Starting from Piazza Garibaldi, head a short way down Corso Umberto I before veering right into Via Egiziaca a Forcella. Cross Via P Colletta and follow the main street as it veers to the left. Where this runs into the busy cross street, Via Duomo, you have the **Chiesa di San Giorgio Maggiore** on your left and, two blocks north up Via Duomo, the **duomo** itself. Virtually opposite is the **Chiesa dei Girolamini**. Walk back south to where you emerged on Via Duomo. The continuation west of Via Duomo is Via San Biagio dei Librai, one of the liveliest roads in Spaccanapoli. You'll pass the **Ospedale delle Bambole** (Dolls' Hospital) and the churches of **SS Filippo e Giacomo** and **Sant'Angelo a Nilo**.

On Piazza San Domenico Maggiore stands the important church of the same name. Note that the not-to-be-missed **Cappella di San Severo** is just off this square in a lane east of the church. Here you are faced with at least two choices:

You could head south along Via Mezzocannone past the **university** and rejoin Corso Umberto I, turning right and following it into Piazza Bovio. From here, Via A Depretis leads south-west to Piazza Municipio and the round-towered **Castel Nuovo**. West from here you will come to an elegant series of squares and the surrounding **Palazzo Reale**, the **Teatro San Carlo**, the **Galleria Umberto I** and the **Chiesa di San Francesco di Paola**. From here you could follow the waterside around to Santa Lucia and beyond to Mergellina, or turn north up **Via Toledo** (named after the Spanish Viceroy who had it laid out as part of his urban expansion programme in the mid-16th century) from Piazza Trento e Trieste, leading back to Spaccanapoli.

Alternatively, from Piazza San Domenico Maggiore continue west along Via B Croce past the **Palazzo Filomarino** and the **Basilica de Santa Chiara** as far as Piazza del Gesù Nuovo, and the **Chiesa del Gesù Nuovo** (as well as the AAST office). Then backtrack to the first intersection, and turn left (north) along Via S Sebastiano. At the next intersection on your left a short street leads down to the **Port'Alba**, a city gate built in 1625, and Piazza Dante. Ahead of you is Piazza Bellini and to your right Piazza Luigi Miraglia. The latter becomes Via dei Tribunali and heads east to Via Duomo. It was the **decumanus**, or main street, of the original Greek, and later Roman, town. Two-thirds of the way along stood the Greek **agora**, or central market and meeting place, in what is now Piazza San Gaetano.

Piazza Bellini, by the way, is a good place to rest your weary feet in one of several cafés, and while you're at it you could inspect the remains of the ancient Greek city walls under the square. After that you could then proceed farther north along Via Santa Maria di Costantinopoli right up to the grand **Museo Archeologico Nazionale**.

Spaccanapoli

Duomo Built on the site of earlier churches, which were themselves preceded by a temple of Neptune, this grand cathedral was begun by Charles I of Anjou in 1272. Largely destroyed in 1456 by an earthquake, it has undergone numerous alterations. The neo-Gothic façade is the result of late 19th-century cosmetic surgery. Above the wide central nave inside is an ornately decorated panel ceiling.

Of central importance to Napoli's religious (some would say superstitious) life is the 17th-century Baroque **Cappella di San Gennaro** (St Januarius; also known as the Cappella del Tesoro, or Chapel of the Treasury), to the right after you enter the church. Now under restoration, the chapel houses the head of the saint, as well as two phials of his congealed blood, kept behind the opulent high altar. St Januarius, the city's patron saint, was martyred at Pozzuoli, near Napoli, in 305 AD and tradition holds that two phials of his congealed blood liquefied when his body was transferred back to Napoli. Three times a year, thousands gather in the duomo to pray for a miracle, namely, that the blood will again liquefy and save Napoli from any potential disaster. The saint is said to have saved the city from disaster on numerous occasions, although the miracle failed to occur in 1941 when Vesuvio erupted. See the Special Events section later in the chapter for more information.

The next chapel contains an urn with the saint's bones and various other relics. Below the cathedral's high altar lies the **Cappella Carafa**, also known as the Crypt of St Januarius, a Renaissance chapel built to house the saint's relics.

To the left and rear of the cathedral, a passageway leads to what is effectively a separate church, the 10th-century **Basilica di Santa Restituta**. Also much altered over time, it is now part of the duomo's so-called archaeological zone, to which entrance costs L5000. It's open Monday to Saturday from 9 am to noon and 4.30 to 7 pm and Sunday from 9 am to midday.

Around the Duomo Virtually opposite the cathedral is the entrance to the **Chiesa dei Girolamini**, or San Filippo Neri, a rich Baroque church. Its 18th-century façade (now closed) actually faces Via dei Tribunali. A small picture gallery in the adjoining convent features works from the 16th to 18th centuries, open from 9.30 am to 12.30 pm and 2 to 5.30 pm (entrance is free).

Duck around the corner into Via dei Tribunali and soon you'll find the **Chiesa di San Lorenzo Maggiore** before you, to the left in Piazza San Gaetano. The piazza is laid over what was originally the Greek **agora** and then the Roman **forum**, the centre of the ancient city. The interior of the church, begun by Provençal architects under the Franciscans in the 13th century, is French Gothic. Catherine of Austria, who died in 1323, is buried here, and her mosaic-covered tomb is among the most eye-catching of the church's adornments. You can pass through to the cloisters of the neighbouring convent, where Petrarch sojourned in 1345. There is also a museum housing relics, dating back as far as Greek Neapolis, which were discovered during excavations. Entrance is free.

Across Via dei Tribunali is the **Chiesa di San Paolo Maggiore**, built in the late 16th century on the site of a temple of the Dioscuri. The opulent interior houses the tomb of San Gaetano (St Cajetan).

While you're in the area, the **Chiesa di San Giorgio Maggiore**, where Via San Biagio dei Librai meets Via Duomo, is worth a quick look for its austere interior.

Across the road is the 15th-century **Palazzo Cuomo**, built by Tuscan artists. The building was moved several metres in 1881 when the street was being widened. It now contains the Museo Gaetano Filangieri, with an extensive collection of arms, furniture and china, as well as paintings of the Neapolitan school. It opens Tuesday to Saturday from 9 am to 2 pm and until 1 pm on Sunday, and entrance is L5000.

Via San Biagio dei Librai Take a look at the **Ospedale delle Bambole**, at No 81. This 'dolls' hospital' looks a little macabre, with little heads piled up in the windows, but you'd be hard pressed to find too many places like it anywhere in the world for buying or repairing dolls. In fact, this whole street, and its continuation, Via B Croce, the parallel Via dei Tribunali to the north and the labyrinth of side alleys, is thronged with craftspeople of all sorts. Here you'll find not only goldsmiths and other jewellers, but the makers of the famous Neapolitan *presepi* (Christmas nativity scenes) – some of them extraordinarily elaborate.

Farther along from the dolls' hospital is the **Palazzo Marigliano**, which features a magnificent Renaissance entrance hall and façade. You then pass the **Palazzo di Carafa di Maddaloni** and **Chiesa di SS Filippo e Giacomo** with their contrasting Renaissance and Rococo styles.

The entrance to the **Chiesa di Sant'Angelo a Nilo** is on Vico Donnaromita 15, off Via San Biagio dei Librai. Built in 1385 and remodelled in the 18th century, the church contains the monumental Renaissance tomb of one Cardinal Brancaccio, to which Donatello contributed.

The Gothic **Chiesa di San Domenico Maggiore**, along Via B Croce in the piazza bearing its name, was completed in 1324 by the Dominican order and was favoured by the Aragonese nobility. The church's interior, a cross between Baroque and 19th-century neo-Gothic, features some fine examples of Renaissance sculpture. In the sacristy are 45 coffins of the princes of Aragon and other nobles.

The deceptive simplicity of the **Cappella di San Severo**, in Via de Sanctis, a narrow lane east of the church, is a dazzling contrast to the treasure chest of sculpture inside. Giuseppe Sanmartino's *Veiled Christ*, for instance, still confounds experts, who cannot agree on how he created the apparently translucent veil. Also baffling is Corradini's *Pudicizia* (Modesty), which makes no attempt to hide the erotic. Known as the Cappella di Santa Maria della Pietà dei Sangro, the chapel is the tomb of the princes of Sangro di San Severo, open from 10 am to 5 pm, except Tuesday, Sunday & holidays, when it closes at 1.30 pm. Entrance is L6000.

To Piazza del Gesù Nuovo From Piazza San Domenico Maggiore the road continues west, following the course of the old Roman main street under the name of Via Benedetto Croce. Croce, Italy's foremost philosopher and historian in the first half of this century, lived and died in the **Palazzo Filomarino**, a grand Renaissance building on the right just before you reach Via San Sebastiano.

Across Via San Sebastiano you come to the **Basilica di Santa Chiara**, a church and convent partly incorporating a Roman wall that was extended around the convent to protect the nuns. Built between 1310 and 1328 under the Angevin dynasty, it suffered from earthquakes and Baroque alterations in the 18th century ('overloaded with excessive ornamentation' according to one British observer late last century). Incendiary bombs burned out the church and destroyed many works of art in 1943. Since the end of the war it has been returned more or less to its original spare Gothic appearance and is one of Napoli's principal medieval monuments. The **nuns' cloisters** behind the church consist of four paths that form a cross, bordered by a long parapet entirely covered in decorative ceramic tiles, depicting 64 landscapes and scenes from the nuns' lives.

A few steps west, Piazza del Gesù Nuovo opens before you, with its *guglia*, a kind of ground-level Baroque steeple, dripping with opulent sculptural decoration. You'll see several of these around the city. The 16th-century **Chiesa del Gesù Nuovo**, on the north side of the piazza, is one of the city's greatest examples of Renaissance architecture, particularly the lozenge-shaped rustication of its façade. The interior was redecorated in Neapolitan Baroque style by Cosimo Fanzango after a fire in 1639.

The **Chiesa di Sant'Anna dei Lombardi**,

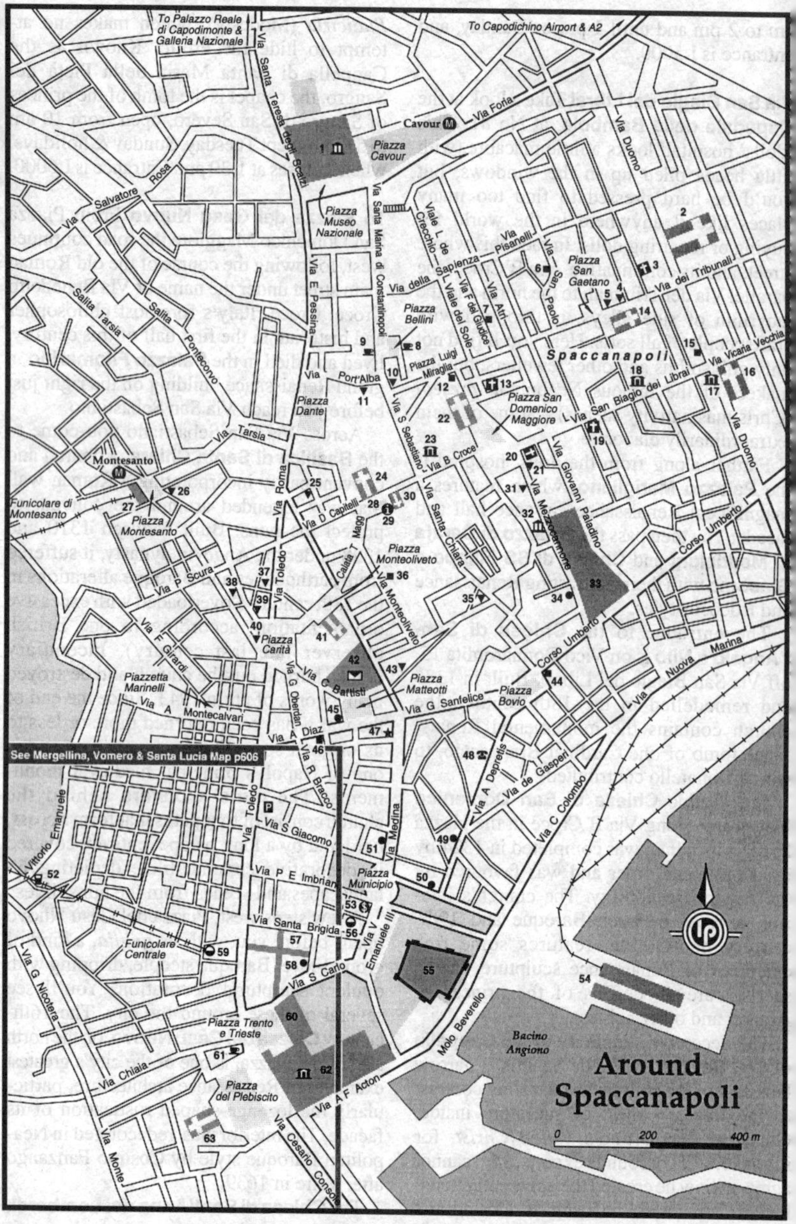

Around Spaccanapoli
To Palazzo Reale di Capodimonte & Galleria Nazionale
To Capodichino Airport & A2
Via Santa Teresa degli Scalzi
Via Foria
Cavour
Piazza Cavour
Via Duomo
Via Salvatore Rosa
Via Santa Maria di Constantinopoli
Piazza Museo Nazionale
Via E Pessina
Viale L de Crecchio
Via Pisanelli
Via San Paolo
Piazza San Gaetano
Via dei Tribunali
Via della Sapienza
Via F del Giudice
Via Atri
L Viale del Sole
Salita Tarsia
Salita Pontecorvo
Piazza Bellini
Piazza Luigi Miraglia
Spaccanapoli
Via Vicaria Vecchia
Via San Biagio dei Librai
Via Port'Alba
Piazza Dante
Piazza San Domenico Maggiore
Via S Sebastiano
Via Tarsia
Montesanto
Via B Croce
Via Giovanni Paladino
Via Mezzocannone
Funicolare di Montesanto
Piazza Montesanto
Via Roma
Via D Capitelli
Calata T Magg
Via Santa Chiara
Corso Umberto
Piazza Monteoliveto
Via P Scura
Via Toledo
Via Monteoliveto
Via F Girardi
Piazza Carità
Piazzetta Marinelli
Via A Montecalvari
Via G Oberdan
Via C Battisti
Piazza Matteotti
Via G Sanfelice
Piazza Bovio
Via Nuova Marina
Via A Diaz
Via R Bracco
See Mergellina, Vomero & Santa Lucia Map p606
Via A Depretis
Via de Gasperi
Via C Colombo
Via S Giacomo
Via Medina
Vittorio Emanuele
Via P E Imbriani
Piazza Municipio
Via Santa Brigida
Via V Emanuele III
Funicolare Centrale
Via S Carlo
Via G Nicotera
Piazza Trento e Trieste
Molo Beverello
Bacino Angiono
Via Chiaia
Piazza del Plebiscito
Via A F Acton
Via Cesario Console
Via Monte
0
200
400 m

PLACES TO STAY

6 Bellini
7 Alloggio Fiamma
12 Soggiorno Imperia
15 Duomo
36 Candy
44 Hotel Orchidea
46 Oriente Grand Hotel

PLACES TO EAT

4 Pizzeria di Matteo
5 Trattoria da Carmine
8 Intra Moenia
9 Caffè dell'Epoca
10 Ristorante Bellini
11 Pizzeria Port'Alba
21 La Campagnola
25 Ristorante Hong Kong
26 Friggitoria Fiorenzano
31 Il Pizzicotto
35 Minipizza
37 La Taverna del Buongustaio
38 Pizzeria al 22
39 Lo Sfizietto
40 Gelateria della Scimmia
43 La Nova Club
61 Gambrinus

OTHER

1 Museo Archeologico Nazionale
2 Duomo
3 Chiesa dei Girolamini
13 Cappella di San Severo
14 Chiesa di San Lorenzo Maggiore
16 Chiesa di San Giorgio Maggiore
17 Palazzo Cuomo
18 Palazzo Marigliano
19 Chiesa di SS Filippo e Giacomo
20 Chiesa di Sant'Angelo a Nilo
22 Chiesa di San Domenico Maggiore
23 Palazzo Filomarino
24 Chiesa del Gesù Nuovo
27 Stazione Cumana
28 Piazza del Gesù Nuovo
29 AAST Tourist Office
30 Basilica di Santa Chiara
32 Museo della Mineralogia & Museo Zoologico
33 University
34 CTS Travel Agency
41 Chiesa di Sant'Anna dei Lombardi
42 Main Post Office
45 Tourcar Travel Agency
47 Questura (Police Station)
48 Telecom Office
49 Gastaldi Travel Agency
50 CIT Travel Agency
51 Alitalia
52 Otto Jazz Club
53 Every Tour (American Express)
54 Stazione Marittima
55 Castel Nuovo & Museo Cirico
56 SITA Bus Station
57 Galleria Umberto I
58 Box Office (Ticket Sales)
59 Funicular to Vomero (Closed)
60 Teatro San Carlo
62 Palazzo Reale
63 Chiesa di San Francesco di Paola

south-west of Piazza del Gesù Nuovo, was founded in 1414 by Origlia and features fine Renaissance sculpture, including a superb terracotta *Pietà* (1492) by Guido Mazzoni.

Near the train station, the **Basilica del Carmine Maggiore**, on the waterfront in Piazza del Carmine, was the scene of the 1647 Neapolitan Revolution led by Masaniello. Inside is the much-worshipped *Madonna Bruna* (Brown Madonna). Each year on 16 July a fireworks display celebrates the festival of the Madonna by simulating the burning of the church – the *incendio simolato del campanile*.

Museo Archeologico Nazionale

Housed in a vast red building that dominates the northern fringe of Spaccanapoli, the archaeological treasures of Napoli's principal museum form one of the most comprehensive collections of Graeco-Roman artefacts in the world. You could easily lose yourself in here for several hours. Originally a cavalry barracks and later seat of the city's university, the museum was established by Charles of Bourbon in the late 18th century to house the rich collection of antiquities he had inherited from his mother, Elizabeth Farnese, as well as the treasures which had been discovered at Pompeii and Herculaneum. It also contains the Borgia collection of Etruscan and Egyptian relics.

Many items from the Farnese collection of classical sculpture are featured on the ground floor, including the impressive *Farnese Bull* in the room of the same name. It is most likely a Roman copy of a Greek original dating from 150 BC, and is an enormous group of figures depicting the death of Dirce, Queen of Thebes, who in Greek mythology was tied to a bull and torn apart over rocks. The group was carved from a single block of marble and later restored by Michelangelo.

On the mezzanine floor is a gallery of mosaics, mostly from Pompeii, including the *Battle of Alexander*, the best known depiction of the great Macedonian emperor. It once paved the floor in the Casa del Fauno at Pompeii and is just one of a series of remarkably detailed and lifelike pieces depicting animals, scenes from daily life, musicians and even Plato with his students. In all, the mosaics are an eloquent expression of ancient artistic genius.

The 1st floor is largely devoted to discoveries from Pompeii, Herculaneum, Stabiae and Cumae. The displays range from numerous murals and frescoes rescued from the sites, through to gladiators' helmets, household items, ceramics and glassware. One room is dedicated to an extraordinary collection of vases of mixed origins, many of them carefully reassembled. The Egyptian collection is in the basement.

The museum is on Piazza Museo Nazionale and is open Tuesday to Saturday from 9 am to 2 pm and Sunday until 1 pm, and entrance is L12,000. In summer it often stays open to 7 pm.

City Centre & Santa Lucia

Castel Nuovo When Charles I of Anjou took over Napoli and the Swabians' Sicilian kingdom, he found himself in control not only of his new southern Italian acquisitions, but possessions in Toscana, northern Italy and Provence. It made sense to base the new dynasty in Napoli rather than Palermo, and Charles launched an ambitious construction programme to expand the port and city walls. His plans included converting a Franciscan convent into the castle that still stands in Piazza Municipio. Also dubbed the Maschio Angioino, its crenellated round towers make it one of the most striking buildings in Napoli. The 'New Castle' was erected in three years from 1279, but what you see today was the result of renovations by the Aragonese two centuries later, as well as a meticulous restoration effort prior to WWII. The heavy grey stone that dominates was imported from Majorca. The two-storey Renaissance triumphal arch at the entrance, the Torre della Guardia, completed in 1467, commemorates the triumphal entry of Alfonso I of Aragon into Napoli.

Spread across several halls on the ground, 1st and 2nd floors is the **Museo Civico**. Frescoes and sculpture from the 14th and 15th centuries, on the ground floor, are of most interest. The other two floors offer a range of paintings, either by Neapolitan artists or overwhelmingly with Napoli or Campania as subjects, covering the 17th through to the early 20th centuries. The castle and museum are open Monday to Saturday from 9 am to 7 pm. Entrance to the museum is L7000.

North-east of the Castel Nuovo on Piazza Bovio is the **Fontana di Nettuno**, dating from 1601. Bernini sculpted its sea creatures and Naccherini the figure of Neptune.

Piazza Trieste e Trento This is one of Napoli's more elegant squares, fronted on the north-eastern side by Italy's largest and oldest opera house, the **Teatro San Carlo**, famed for its perfect acoustics. Built in 1737 by Charles of Bourbon (40 years before La Scala, locals proudly boast), San Carlo was destroyed by fire in 1618 and later restored. It is home to one of the oldest ballet schools in Italy. Stendhal wrote, 'There is nothing in Europe to compare with it, or even give the faintest idea of what it is like.' It is open in the early morning and mid-afternoon, although an attendant might show you through at other times.

Across Via San Carlo is one of the four entrances to the imposing but somewhat-worse-for-wear glass atrium of the **Galleria Umberto I**. Built in 1890 and opened in 1900, it seems a rather humble cousin of Milano's truly impressive Galleria Vittorio Emanuele II.

Palazzo Reale Facing onto the grand **Piazza del Plebiscito**, this magnificent palace was built around 1600. It was completely renovated in 1841, but suffered extensive damage during WWII. The statues of the eight most important kings of Napoli were inserted into niches in the façade in 1888.

After entering the courtyard, a huge double staircase under a dome leads to the royal apartments, which house the Museo del Palazzo Reale, a rich collection of furnishings, porcelain, tapestries, statues and paintings. The museum is open Tuesday to Sunday from 9 am to 1.30 pm and also from to 7.30 pm on weekends. Entrance is L8000.

The palace has also, since 1925, been home to the **Biblioteca Nazionale**, which includes the vast Farnese collection brought to Napoli by Charles of Bourbon, with more than 2000 papyri discovered at Herculaneum and fragments of a 5th-century Coptic Bible. Entry is free.

The **Chiesa di San Francesco di Paola**, at the eastern end of the piazza, was begun by Ferdinand I in 1817 to celebrate the restoration of his kingdom after the Napoleonic interlude. Flanked by semicircular colonnades, the church is based on Roma's Pantheon and is a popular wedding spot.

Castel dell'Ovo The so-called Castle of the Egg is on the small rocky island off Santa Lucia known as Borgo Marinaro and connected by bridge from Via Partenope. Folklore has it that the name came about after part of the island collapsed, likened by locals to Virgil's story of the breaking of an egg. The castle occupies the site of a Roman villa. Built in the 12th century by the Norman king, William I, the castle became a key fortress in the defence of Campania. You can wander through the small lanes on the island (mostly occupied by restaurants), but the castle, restored in the 1970s, is opened only for meetings and exhibitions.

The **Fontana dell'Immacolatella**, at the end of Via Partenope, dates from the 17th century and features statues by Bernini and Naccherini.

Mergellina

West of Santa Lucia, Via Partenope spills into Piazza della Vittoria, marking the beginning of the so-called Riviera di Chiaia, which runs along the northern edge of the **Villa Comunale**, a large park marked off on the seaward side by Via Caracciolo. The **Acquario** (aquarium) in the park was founded in the late 19th century by German naturalist Anton Dohrn. Its 30 tanks contain specimens of sea life exclusively from the Golfo di Napoli area. Ask to see the frescoes on the first floor. In summer, the acquarium opens Monday to Saturday from 9 am to 6 pm and Sunday from 10 am to 6 pm, and in winter Monday to Saturday 9 am to 5 pm and to 2 pm on Sunday. Entrance is L3000.

Close by at Riviera di Chiaia 200 is the **Museo Pignatelli**, an old patrician residence containing mostly 19th-century furnishings, china and other nick-nacks. A pavilion set in gardens houses a coach museum and contains English and French carriages. Both museums are open Tuesday to Sunday from 9 am to 2 pm. Entrance is L4000.

Farther west, a short stroll from Piazza Sannazzaro and the Mergellina train station, is the **Tomba di Giacomo Leopardi**, the 19th-century poet who died in Napoli in 1837, and an Augustan-age Roman monument that has come to be known as the **Tomba di Virgilio**, although it has nothing to do with the ancient bard, who died in Brindisi in 19 BC. The tombs lie behind the Chiesa di Santa Maria di Piedigrotta, and can be visited daily from 9 am to 1 pm.

Vomero

Visible from all over the city, the Vomero hill (pronounced Vómero) is a bit of a world apart, a serene and well-to-do residential quarter that rises above the chaos of the great metropolis below. Several funicular lines connect Vomero with the city.

Castel Sant'Elmo Commanding spectacular views across the city and bay, this austere, star-shaped castle was built over a stronghold first established in 1329. The present structure was built under Spanish vice-regal rule in 1538. Impressive though it is, the castle has seen little real action, serving more often than not as a prison. It opens Tuesday to Sunday from 9 am to 2 pm; entrance is L4000. These details can vary when temporary exhibitions are being held.

Certosa di San Martino Barely 100m down the road from the castle lies this Carthusian monastery, established in the 14th century and rebuilt in the 17th century by Fanzango in Neapolitan Baroque style. It houses the **Museo Nazionale di San Martino**, which

CAMPANIA

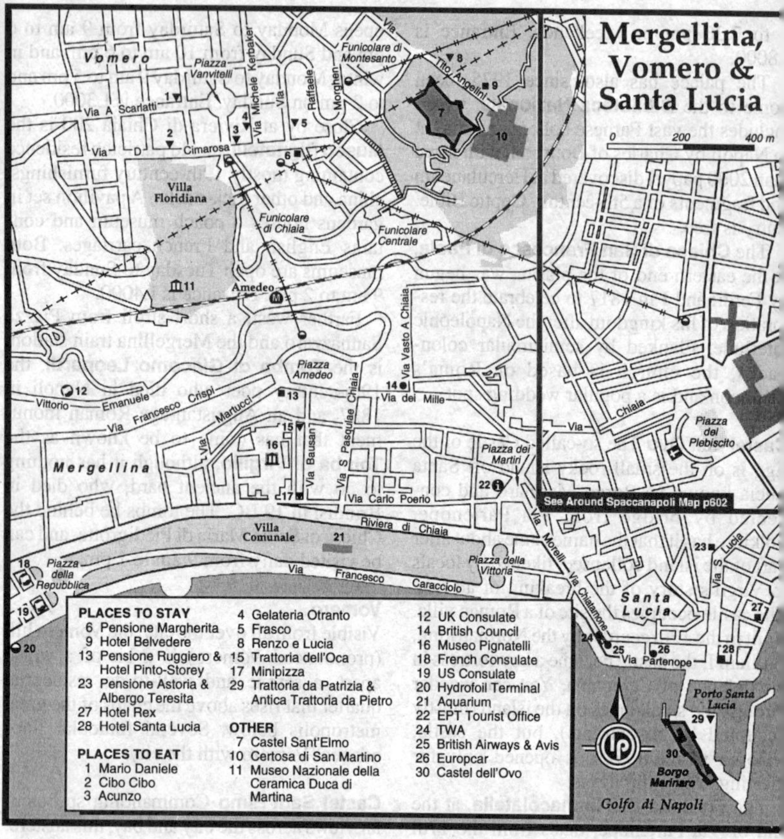

features a section on naval history, an area dedicated to the history of the Kingdom of Naples, as well as an extensive art collection. Of particular interest is the Sezione Presepiale, several rooms devoted to a collection of Neapolitan *presepi*, elaborate nativity scenes sculpted in the 18th and 19th centuries. Not all of the monastery is open to the public, but you can enjoy the tranquil Baroque Chiostro Grande, or main cloisters, whose manicured gardens are ringed by elegant porticoes.

Adjacent is the monastery's church, virtually an art gallery in itself, whose original Gothic character is still evident. It contains exquisite marblework, and a good number of frescoes and paintings, particularly by 17th century Neapolitan artists. There is a magnificent view from the terraced gardens and from Largo San Martino (the car park) outside. The museum is open Tuesday to Sunday from 9 am to 2 pm, and entrance is L8000.

Villa Floridiana The verdant grounds of this public park spread down the slopes from Via Domenico Cimarosa in Vomero to Mergellina. The stately home at the bottom end of the gardens was built in 1817 by Ferdinand I for his wife, the Duchess of Floridia. Today it contains the **Museo Nazionale della Ceramica Duca di Martina**, which holds an extensive collection of European, Chinese and Japanese china, ivory, enamels and Italian majolica. The museum opens Tuesday to Saturday from 9 am to 2 pm and Sunday to 1 pm. Entrance is L4000. The park is open daily except Monday from 9 am to one hour before sunset, and entrance is free.

Capodimonte

Palazzo Reale di Capodimonte A royal estate built by Charles of Bourbon on the northern edge of the city, the palace is set in extensive parklands that were once the nobles' hunting grounds. Since 1957 it has housed the National Gallery of Napoli, one of Europe's foremost museums. Visit the royal apartments on the first floor of the palace.

Museo e Gallerie di Capodimonte Occupying the entire 2nd floor of the palace, the **Galleria Nazionale** has a fine collection of works, mainly by Italian artists, including many of the big names. Featured are Simone Martini, Masaccio, Botticelli, Pinturicchio, Filippino Lippi, Signorelli, Mantegna, Sodoma, Bellini, as well as several Titians and works by Caravaggio. There are some cartoons (for frescoes) by Michelangelo and Raphael, as well as an impressive range from the 18th-century Neapolitan school.

On the first floor is the **Galleria dell'Ottocento**, which focuses mainly on 19th-century artists from southern Italy. The Royal Apartments, also on the 1st floor, house an extensive collection of armour, ivories, bronzes, porcelain and majolica, tapestries and other works of art.

The palace is open Tuesday to Saturday from 10 am to 6 pm and until 2 pm on Sunday. Entrance is L8000. Entrance to the park surrounding the palace is free.

Catacombe di San Gennaro The catacombs are just below the palace – enter from Via di Capodimonte. Dating from the 2nd century, they are quite a different experience from the dark, claustrophobic catacombs characteristic of Roma: a mix of tombs, corridors and broad vestibules held up by columns and arches and decorated with frescos and mosaics. St Januarius was buried here. Guided tours begin daily at 9.30, 10.15, 11 and 11.45 am, and cost L3000.

Orto Botanico

Head north along Via Duomo to Via Foria and turn right to reach the Orto Botanico (☎ 44 97 59) at No 223, near Piazza Carlo III. The botanical gardens were founded in 1807 by Joseph Bonaparte and are part of the Napoli university. Visits are by appointment.

Family Activities

Kids of all ages will enjoy visiting Napoli's various castles. They will also enjoy a visit to the acquario (see under Mergellina) and older kids should appreciate the archaeological museum (see Museo Archeologico Nazionale). The **Museo Nazionale Ferroviario**, in a restored railway building on the waterfront at Corso San Giovanni a Teduccio, is another option. It was founded by Ferdinand II of Bourbon last century to house his collection of railway memorabilia, including engines and carriages. It opens Monday to Saturday from 9 am to 2 pm and entrance is free.

The **Museo della Mineralogia**, on Via Mezzocannone 8 between Via B Croce and Corso Umberto I, features minerals, meteorites and quartz crystals collected from the Vesuvio region. The building also contains the **Museo Zoologico**. Both open Monday to Friday from 9 am to 1 pm and weekends from 10 am to 1 pm. Entrance to each museum is L1000, or L2000 for families.

Work

The Centro di Lingua e Cultura Italiana (☎ 551 33 61), Vico Santa Maria dell'Aiuto 17, is one of several language schools in the city. If you want to teach English, start your enquiries at the British Council (☎ 66 74 10), Via Crispi 92.

Organised Tours

Excursions to the bay islands and inland to Pompeii and Vesuvio are organised by CIT (☎ 552 54 26), Piazza Municipio 70; Cima Tours (☎ 554 06 46), Piazza Garibaldi 114; and Tourcar (☎ 552 33 10), Piazza Matteotti 1. A half-day tour to Pompeii is about L50,000. The AAST sometimes organises free tours of city sights on Sunday at 10.30 am. Check at the AAST office.

For something completely different, you could head underground. A warren of cisterns, wells and stone quarries lies below the city's surface splendour, and can be visited with the Libera Associazione Escursionisti Sottosuolo (☎ 40 02 56), Via Santa Teresinella degli Spagnoli 24. At the time of writing they met at Bar Gambrinus (Piazza Trieste e Trento) on Saturday and Sunday at 10 am and Thursday at 9 pm.

Special Events

Napoli's main festivals honour St Januarius. On the first Sunday in May, on 19 September and on 16 December each year, thousands gather in the duomo to pray that the saint's blood, held in two vials, will liquefy: a miracle said to save the city from potential disasters. Get there early, as police turn back the crowds when the duomo is full. See the Things to See section for more information.

Other important festivals are the Madonna del Carmine on 16 July, held in Piazza del Carmine, which culminates in a fireworks display, and the Madonna di Piedigrotta (5-12 September). At Christmas, thousands of elaborate nativity scenes are erected around the city.

Places to Stay

Napoli is surprisingly cheap compared with the north of the country, although most of the budget hotels are clustered around Stazione Centrale in a rather unsavoury area. The EPT office at Stazione Centrale will recommend and book hotels, and you should avoid the hawkers who may harass you around the station – they are on commission and generally pushing less reputable establishments. Many cheaper hotels double as brothels.

Room prices should always be read in Italy as a guide rather than gospel truth, but this is even more the case in Napoli. The following prices are a fair indication. Some hotels unfortunately only have doubles, and are not always willing to knock down prices for single travellers. The closest camping ground is in Pozzuoli – see the Pozzuoli section.

Hostel The HI *Ostello Mergellina Napoli* (☎ 761 23 46), Salita della Grotta 23, in Mergellina, is modern and safe. B&B is L22,000 and a meal L12,000. It is open all year and imposes a minimum three-night stay in summer. Take bus No 152 from Stazione Centrale or the Metropolitana to Mergellina and follow the signs.

Pensioni & Hotels – Around Stazione Centrale The *Hotel Zara* (☎ 28 71 25), Via Firenze 81, is clean and safe with singles/doubles from L35,000/ 50,000. Via Firenze is off Corso Novara, to the right as you exit the station. The *Albergo Ginevra* (☎ 28 32 10), Via Genova 116, the second street to the right off Corso Novara, is another reliable hotel with doubles only, starting at L50,000. The *Casanova Hotel* (☎ 26 82 87), Corso Garibaldi 333, through Piazza Garibaldi and past Piazza Principe Umberto, has singles/doubles for about L30,000/55,000 and triples with shower for L75,000. *Holiday Hotel* (☎ 28 39 00), Via Silvio Spaventa 18, just off Piazza Garibaldi, has singles/doubles from L45,000/75,000.

Moving up the price scale, the three-star *Prati* (☎ 554 18 02), Via C Rosaroll 4, has singles/doubles from L90,000/140,000 up. It is one of the area's best hotels.

Pensioni & Hotels – Around Spaccanapoli Many hotels in this area are near Piazza Dante, which you can reach by bus No R2 from Stazione Centrale, or by the Metro (take the train from track No 4 and get off at Piazza Cavour – from there the area is a five-minute walk – see the Getting Around section for more information).

You could easily miss *Soggiorno Imperia*

ROB FLYNN

RICHARD STEWART

LAUREN SUNSTEIN

Toscana
Top: View from San Gimignano
Middle: Firenze as seen from the Forte di Belevedere
Bottom: Palazzo Vecchio with a copy of Michelangelo's *David*, Firenze

DAMIEN SIMONIS

DAMIEN SIMONIS

DAMIEN SIMONIS

DAMIEN SIMONIS

Umbria

Top: Village of Vallo di Nera, east of Spoleto on the Spoleto-Norcia road
Middle, Bottom & Right: Ceramics, Gubbio

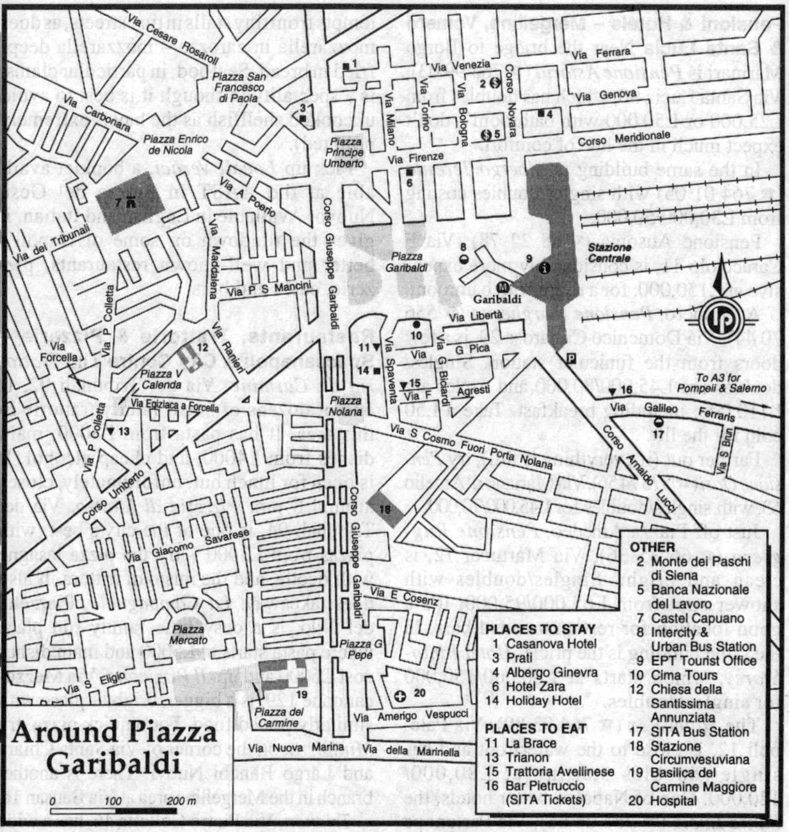

Around Piazza Garibaldi

(☎ 45 93 47), Piazza Luigi Miraglia 386, as it isn't signposted. It is through the Port'Alba from Piazza Dante. Spacious if spartan singles/doubles are L40,000/60,000. *Alloggio Fiamma* (☎ 45 91 87), Via Francesco del Giudice 13, is nearby. It has basic rooms at L25,000 a head and is really only recommendable in terms of price. An acceptable deal is *Candy* (☎ 552 13 59), Via Carrozzieri a Monteoliveto 13, south of Piazza del Gesù Nuovo. It has basic singles/doubles for L30,000/40,000.

A popular spot tucked away in the heart of Spaccanapoli is the *Bellini* (☎ 45 69 96), Via San Paolo 44, with singles/doubles for L30,000/50,000. Just down from the cathedral is the *Duomo* (☎ 26 59 88), Via Duomo 228, with doubles/triples for L60,000/90,000. Don't be put off by the entrance.

Hotel Orchidea (☎ 551 07 21), Corso Umberto 7, is just outside the rabbit warren of Spaccanapoli and has good doubles with bathroom, some overlooking the bay, for L100,000.

For the looser wallet, the *Oriente Grand Hotel* (☎ 551 21 33), Via A Diaz 44, is one of the city's finest hotels, with singles/doubles starting at L140,000/170,000 and spiralling upwards.

Pensioni & Hotels – Mergellina, Vomero & Santa Lucia Near the bridge to Borgo Marinari is *Pensione Astoria* (☎ 764 99 03), Via Santa Lucia 90, which has doubles from L25,000 or L50,000 with bathroom – don't expect much in the line of comfort.

In the same building is *Albergo Teresita* (☎ 764 01 05) with singles/doubles costing from L30,000/50,000.

Pensione Ausonia (☎ 68 22 78), Via F Caracciolo 11, is considerably more expensive at L150,000, for a room with bathroom.

At Vomero, *Pensione Margherita* (☎ 556 70 44), Via Domenico Cimarosa 29, is a few doors from the funicular station. Singles/doubles are L45,000/80,000 and triples are L110,000, including breakfast. Take a L50 coin for the lift.

Farther out (if everything is full), try *Pensione Oasi* (☎ 578 7456), Via Mariano d'Amelio 63, with singles/doubles for L45,000/70,000.

Just off Piazza Amedeo, *Pensione Ruggiero* (☎ 66 35 36), Via Martucci 72, is clean and bright. Singles/doubles with shower start from L65,000/95,000. It's a good location for restaurants and bars. In the same building is the pricier *Hotel Pinto-Storey*, which starts at L80,000/150,000 for singles/doubles.

The *Hotel Rex* (☎ 764 93 89), Via Palepoli 12, is close to the waterfront and has singles/doubles starting at L80,000/120,000. One of Napoli's better hotels, the *Santa Lucia* (☎ 764 06 66), Via Partenope 46, overlooks the bay and Vesuvio in sumptuous style. Singles/doubles cost from L135,000/200,000 depending on the view. For even better views, the *Hotel Belvedere* (☎ 578 81 69), Via Tito Angelini 51, stands below the walls of the Castel Sant'Elmo and has sweeping vistas of the city and bay.

Places to Eat

Neapolitan street food is among Italy's best. The pizza with mozzarella cheese and fresh tomato sauce is standard fare, as is the related calzone, a puffed up version with the topping becoming a filling instead. Misto di frittura – deep-fried potato, eggplant and zucchini flowers – tempts from tiny stalls in tiny streets, as does mozzarella in carozza – mozzarella deep-fried in bread. Seafood, in particular clams, is a speciality (although it is best to avoid uncooked shellfish as the bay is extremely polluted).

Pick up *Locali Veraci*, a booklet available at the AAST in Piazza del Gesù Nuovo. Available in English and Italian, it gives the rundown on some of Napoli's better and well-known restaurants, pizzerie, cafés and bars.

Restaurants, Trattorie & Pizzerie – Spaccanapoli & City Centre The *Trattoria da Carmine*, Via dei Tribunali 92, is one of dozens of small family trattorie in this area. It has pasta from L3000, main dishes from L4000, and cheap alcohol. It is open for lunch but, unfortunately, closes around 8 pm. *Pizzeria di Matteo*, Via dei Tribunali 94, is one of the city's best, with pizzas from L3000 – try the pizza lasagne with ricotta, and the misto di frittura. It also does takeaway. *La Campagnola*, Piazzetta del Nilo, is a cosy little family run place where pasta starts at L5000 and main dishes cost L6000 and up. *Il Pizzicotto*, Via Mezzocannone 129, is a bigger, brighter place with similarly priced food. For a quick pizza, try *Minipizza*, on the corner of Via Santa Chiara and Largo Banchi Nuovi. There is another branch in the Mergellina area at Via Bausan 1a.

Trianon, Via Pietro Colletta 46, has a wide selection of pizzas from L5000 and is close to Stazione Centrale. It's been going since 1925 and was for a long time a favourite with Italian celebrities such as film director Vittorio de Sica and comic actor Totò. *Trattoria Avellinese*, Via Silvio Spaventa 31-35 is just off Piazza Garibaldi and specialises in cheap seafood. Just up the road, *La Brace* at No 14 is a recommended no-nonsense eatery where you can fill up for not more than L25,000.

Ristorante Bellini, Via Santa Maria di Costantinopoli 79-80, is one of Napoli's better restaurants and a full meal will cost upwards of L35,000. Seafood is a house speciality. Virtually around the corner, at Via

Port'Alba 18 is *Pizzeria Port'Alba*. Founded in 1830, it is one of the oldest pizzerie in Napoli.

Near the central post office is *La Nova Club*, at Piazza Santa Maria La Nova 9. It offers excellent food at reasonable prices – you can even tell the waiter your upper limit and he will help you order accordingly. You might need to ring the doorbell. *La Taverna del Buongustaio*, tucked in west of Via Toledo at Vico Basilico Puoti 8, is about as basic a place as you'll find. It specialises in seafood and is cheap. It's closed Sunday. *Pizzeria al 22*, off Piazza Carità at Via Pignasecca 22, has takeaway pizzas from L4000.

If you want something other than Italian, *Ristorante Hong Kong*, Vico Quercia 5A, off Via Roma near Piazza Dante, does good Chinese for about L15,000 a head.

Restaurants, Trattorie & Pizzerie – Santa Lucia The restaurants on Borgo Marinari are generally overpriced, but try *Trattoria da Patrizia*, Via Luculliana, with the red Coke chairs, which offers pasta from L6000. *Antica Trattoria da Pietro* is a couple of doors down and much the same.

Restaurants, Trattorie & Pizzerie – Mergellina & Vomero Head for the area around Piazza Amedeo. The surrounding streets down to the waterfront are filled with bars, cafés and restaurants of varying descriptions, as well as some Neapolitan nightlife. A full meal at *Trattoria dell'Oca*, Via Santa Teresa 11, will be about L15,000. For Spanish and Latin American fare, try *El Bocadillo*, Via Martucci 50.

In front of the Certosa di San Martino, *Renzo e Lucia*, Via Tito Angelini 33a, offers spectacular views over the city and lofty prices to match. Pasta costs from L10,000 and pizza from L7000, with a L3000 cover charge. To reach the restaurant, you could go for a 30-minute uphill walk (not recommended at night) from Via Roma or take bus No VS, VD or V3 from Piazza Vanvitelli.

The *Acunzo*, Via Domenico Cimarosa 60, has pizzas and pasta and a full meal can cost L16,000. *Frasco*, nearby at Via Morghen 12, is one of Vomero's more popular spots, with pizzas and pasta from about L8000. It has a pleasant garden for al fresco dining in summer and pasta from L6000. *Mario Daniele*, Via A Scarlatti 104, is a bar with a restaurant upstairs. For a light meal in a bright new place, or just a drink at the bar, *Cibo Cibo*, Via Cimarosa 150, is a good spot.

Food Stalls *Friggitoria Fiorenzano* in Piazza Montesanto is one of several food stalls scattered throughout the Spaccanapoli area that sells deep-fried vegetables for L200 apiece – the eggplant slices are especially good. For more substantial snacks and deep fried food, *Lo Sfizietto*, on the corner of Vico Basilico Puoti and Via Pignasecca, has goodies for under L1000.

Cafés If sitting around in a bar is your idea of fun, one of the more interesting is *Intra Moenia*, Piazza Bellini 69-70, an arty/gay/leftist café/bookshop in one of the city's more beautiful piazzas. Virtually across the road at Via Constantinopoli 81, the *Caffè dell' Epoca* has been going since 1886. For something more elegant, head for *Gambrinus*, where Via Chiaia runs into Piazza Trento e Trieste.

Gelaterie & Pasticcerie For good gelati, head for *Gelateria della Scimmia*, Piazza Carità 4, or *Gelati Otranto*, in Vomero at Via M Kerbaker 43. A local tip for the best gelati in Napoli is *Remy Gelo* in Mergellina.

Sfogliatelle is the great Neapolitan pastry, a vaguely sweet ricotta-filled number that tastes best straight out of the oven. *Attanasio*, Vico Ferroviario 1-4, near Stazione Centrale, is famous throughout Italy for them. Just ask around for shops selling pastries.

Entertainment

The monthly *Qui Napoli* and the local newspapers are the only real guides to what's on. The Box Office (☎ 551 91 88), Galleria Umberto I 16, sells tickets for most sporting and cultural events. Enquire there or at the tourist office about what is happening during your stay.

Cinema Finding films in English is not easy, but you might have luck at *Cinema Amedeo*, Via Martucci 69, something of an art-house place with lots of classics.

Theatre & Music The *Teatro San Carlo* has year-round performances of opera, ballet and concerts. Tickets start at L15,000 and spiral upwards, and always sell quickly. The booking office is at the theatre (☎ 797 21 11). Adjacent to the theatre in the Palazzo Reale (to the left of the main entrance and up the grand staircase) is the *Teatro di Corte*, which is slightly avant-garde but still expensive. Watch out for posters; you can book at the theatre.

In July, there is a series of free concerts called Luglio Musicale a Capodimonte outside the Capodimonte Palace.

Bars & Nightclubs Young, hip Neapolitans stand around their cars and mopeds eating gelati at Piazza Amedeo, which can be fun to watch, and the city jumps with jazz joints and trendy (some might say tacky) clubs. Some clubs charge hefty entrance or membership fees (say L80,000), which usually include a drink.

The area around Piazza Amedeo is worth investigating, as there are several watering holes, clubs and live music venues sprinkled in among the trattorie and cafés. Try Via Martucci, where you'll find the *Jam Club* (No 87), *Il Picaro* (No 81), *Wonky Club* (No 43), *New Callegher* (No 39), *Baboon Club* (No 32) and *Kafafà* (No 49).

The *Otto Jazz Club*, Piazzetta Cariati 23, features Neapolitan jazz.

Exclusive, also known as Kiss Kiss, Via Sgambati 59, in Vomero, is well-established and expensive, while *La Belle Epoque*, Via Andrea d'Isernia 33, near the Riviera di Chiaia, has rock, blues, jazz and soul on different nights.

There are several venues for live music. The *Palapartenope* (☎ 570 68 06), Via Barbagallo, gets Italian and international acts. Heading out of town, *Havana* (exit No 12 from the Tangenziale to Pozzuoli) hosts live acts and also the plastic stuff, mostly garage and underground material. Similar is *Dynamik Area*, on the Strada Provinciale Grumo/Sant'Arpino in Frattamaggiore.

Spectator Sport

For football, Napoli's home matches are played at the Stadio San Paolo in the western suburb of Mostra d'Oltremare. Call ☎ 61 56 23 for details.

Things to Buy

They say you can buy anything in Napoli, and you can see why after a little time spent wandering around the city centre. From designer stores to improvised stalls with goods fresh off the back of a truck, Napoli certainly seems to have it all.

In particular, Napoli is renowned for its gold, and Christmas items such as nativity scenes and *pastori* (shepherds). The former can take on enormous proportions, becoming fantastic models of all Bethlehem. Most artisans are in Spaccanapoli, in particular along Via dei Tribunali, Via B Croce and the side streets and lanes. Many goldsmiths and *gioiellerie* (jewellery shops) are clustered around Via San Biagio dei Librai, and their wares are well advertised. Be warned, some inflate prices for tourists. If you like old dolls, head for the Ospedale delle Bambole, Via San Biagio dei Librai 81.

The city's more exclusive shops are in Santa Lucia, behind Piazza del Plebiscito, along Via Chiaia to Piazza dei Martiri and down towards the waterfront. Young people shop along Via Roma and Via Toledo.

Street markets selling just about everything are scattered across the city centre, including Piazza Garibaldi and along Via Pignasecca, off Piazza Carità.

Getting There & Away

Air Capodichino airport (☎ 789 62 28), Viale Maddalena, about 5km north-east of the city centre, is southern Italy's main airport and links Napoli with most Italian and several major European cities.

Airlines represented in Napoli include:

Alitalia
(☎ 542 53 33; ☎ 1478 6 56 42 for international flights), Via Medina 41-42

British Airways
(☎ 780 29 52), at the airport

TWA
(☎ 764 58 28), Via Cervantes 55

Qantas, handled by Gastaldi Travel
(☎ 552 30 01), Via Depretis 108

Bus Buses leave for Italian and some European cities from Piazza Garibaldi in front of Stazione Centrale. Look carefully or ask, because there are no signs.

SITA (☎ 552 21 76) has a daily service to Bari, departing from outside the SITA ticket office in Via Pisanelli. It also operates a service to Germany. Marino (☎ 871 23 72) has two buses to Bari. Miccolis (☎ 521 23 04) has three buses to Taranto, Lecce and Brindisi, while CLP (☎ 531 17 06) has four buses to Foggia.

Within Campania, SITA runs buses from Via Pisanelli, or Via G Ferraris to Pompeii, Herculaneum, the Amalfi coast and Salerno. You can pick up tickets and buses either from the main office at Via Pisanelli (near Piazza Municipio), or from Via G Ferraris, near Stazione Centrale (tickets at Bar Pietruccio, Via G Ferraris 5). Regular buses leave for Caserta, Benevento and Avellino from Piazza Garibaldi.

Curreri (☎ 801 54 20) has a Capodichino airport-Sorrento bus.

Train Napoli is the hub for the south and many trains originating in the north pass through Roma and terminate here. The city is served by regionale, diretto, espresso, Intercity, EuroCity and the superfast Pendolino (ETR 500) trains. They arrive and depart from Stazione Centrale (☎ 554 31 88) at Piazza Garibaldi. There are up to 30 trains a day to Roma.

Car & Motorcycle Napoli is on the major north-south Autostrada del Sole, known as the A1, to Roma and Milan and the A3 to Salerno and Reggio di Calabria. The A30 acts as a ring road through Campania, while the A16 heads east to Bari.

When approaching the city, the autostradas meet the Tangenziale di Napoli, a major ring road around the city. The multi-lane ring road, Tangenziale Ovest di Napoli, hugs the city's northern fringe, meeting the A1 for Roma and the A2 to Capodichino airport in the east, and continues for Pozzuoli and the Phlegraean Fields to the west. The A3 for Salerno and Calabria can be reached from Corso Arnaldo Lucci, south-east of Piazza Garibaldi.

For rental information, see the following Getting Around section.

Boat Ferries and hydrofoils leave for Capri, Sorrento, Ischia, Procida, Forio and Casamicciola from the Molo Beverello in front of the Castel Nuovo. Ferries to Palermo, Cagliari, Milazzo and the Aeolian Islands leave from the Stazione Marittima, next to the Molo Beverello. Some hydrofoils leave for the bay islands from Mergellina, and Alilauro and SNAV also operate to most destinations from Mergellina.

Ferry companies and the routes they service are as follows:

SNAV
(☎ 761 23 48), Via Caracciolo 10 (Mergellina), runs hydrofoils to Capri (L15,500 one way), Procida (L13,500) and Casamicciola, in Ischia (L16,500). In summer there are daily services to the Aeolian Islands.

Alilauro
(☎ 761 10 04), Via Caracciolo 11 (Mergellina), operates boats and hydrofoils to Ischia (L8500 and L15,000 one way respectively) and hydrofoils to Sorrento (L13,000 one way).

Caremar
(☎ 551 38 82), Molo Beverello, serves Capri (L8300 one way by ferry; L15,000 one way by hydrofoil), Ischia (same fares) and Procida (L7000 return by ferry).

Navigazione Libera del Golfo
(☎ 552 72 09), Molo Beverello, services Capri (L28,000 return) and Sorrento (once daily).

Tirrenia
(☎ 720 11 11) has a daily service to Palermo at 8 pm (high season fare is L68,000 one way in an airline-style seat; L95,000 for a bed in a second-class cabin; L130,000 for a small car), and to

Cagliari (L72,000 one way in an airline-style seat; L100,000 in a second-class cabin; L140,000 for a small car) on Thursday. From Palermo and Cagliari there are connections to Trapani and on to Tunisia.

Siremar
(☎ 761 36 88, or contact Tirrenia), part of the Tirrenia group, operates a service to the Aeolian Islands and Milazzo. The service is infrequent in the off-season, and up to five days a week in the high season.

Linee Lauro
(☎ 551 33 52), linked with Alilauro, has summer boat services direct from Napoli to Trapani (Sicilia) and Tunis. One-way high season fares to Tunis are L120,000 (deck class), L140,000 (airline-style seat) and L220,000 (bed in 2nd-class cabin). They also have direct runs to Sardinia and Corsica in summer.

Getting Around

The Airport Take bus No 14 from Stazione Centrale, or CLP's airport bus (☎ 531 17 06) every 30 minutes from Piazza Municipio, Via Depretis, Piazza Borsa or Piazza Garibaldi (L3000).

Bus & Tram Most city ANM buses operating in the central area depart from and terminate in front of Stazione Centrale, although the bus stops there are not well signposted. The city does not prepare a bus map, and it is impossible to find decent information. There is an ANM bus information office at Stazione Centrale and another at Piazza Dante. Tickets (L1200) can be bought from ANM booths and tobacconists. They are valid for 90 minutes for one trip on the Metro, one trip on the funicular and unlimited bus trips within that time. A daily tourist ticket is good value at L4000.

A useful bus is the No R2, which starts and terminates at Stazione Centrale and passes Via Diaz, Via Toledo and Corso Umberto I and Piazza Dante in the city centre. Other buses and their routes include:

No C1
from Piazza Gesù to Corso Umberto and back

No C4
around Mergellina, along the waterfront to the city centre, Piazza Diaz, Piazza Amedeo and back to Mergellina

No 14 & 14R
from Piazza Garibaldi to the airport and the city's north

No 24
from the Parco Castello and Piazza Trieste e Trento along Via Toledo, Via Roma to Capodimonte

No R3
from Parco Castello, along the Riviera di Chiaia and westwards, past Mergellina

No 109
from Parco Castello through Piazza Dante past the museum, Capodimonte and farther north

No 110
from Stazione Centrale to the museum and Capodimonte

No 137R
from Piazza Dante north to Capodimonte, farther north and then back to Piazza Dante

Night buses include:

No 401
connects Stazione Centrale with the Riviera di Chiaia, through the city centre, and returns to the station

No 403S
from Stazione Centrale to Mergellina through the city centre, and returns along the same route

No 401
round trips from Stazione Centrale through the city centre

Trams No 1 and 1B operate from east of Stazione Centrale, through Piazza Garibaldi, the city centre and along the waterfront to Riviera di Chiaia. Tram No 2B travels from Piazza Garibaldi to the city centre along Corso Garibaldi.

Train The city has four train systems. For a long time the only Metropolitana (underground railway) line has been little more than an ordinary train running from Gianturco, east of Stazione Centrale, with stops at Stazione Centrale, Piazza Cavour, Piazza Amedeo, Mergellina, Fuorigrotta, Campi Flegrei (the Phlegraean Fields), Pozzuoli and Solfatara. Tickets (L1500) on this line are good for one trip only. A new underground line has been partly completed with EU funds. It runs north from Piazza Vanvitelli to Piazza Medaglie d'Oro and seven stops beyond, but will only become truly useful to travellers when the extension connecting Piazza Garibaldi, the duomo, Piazzas Bovio, Carità and Dante, the Museo Archeologico Nazionale and Piazza Vanvitelli is completed. Tickets on the new stretch cost L1200.

The Circumvesuviana (☎ 779 21 11), about 400m south-west of Stazione Centrale in Corso Garibaldi (take the underpass from Stazione Centrale), operates trains to Sorrento via Pompeii (L3000), Herculaneum and other towns along the coast. There are about 40 trains a day running between 5 am and 11 pm.

The Ferrovia Cumana and the Circumflegrea (☎ 551 33 28), based at Stazione Cumana in Piazza Montesanto, 500m south-west of Piazza Dante, operate services to Pozzuoli and Cuma (Cumae) every 20 minutes.

Funicular Railway The Funicolare Centrale from Via Toledo connects the city centre with Vomero (Piazza Fuga). The Funicolare di Chiaia travels from Via del Parco Margherita to Via Domenico Cimarosa, also in Vomero. The Funicolare di Montesanto travels from Piazza Montesanto to Via Morghen. All three can be used to reach the Certosa di San Martino and the Vomero area. The Funicolare di Mergellina connects the waterfront at Via Mergellina with Via Manzoni. Tickets cost L1000.

Car & Motorcycle Forget it unless you have a death wish. Park your car at one of the car parks, most of which are staffed, and walk around the city centre. Try Supergarage, Via Shelley 11, in the city centre.

Apart from the headaches you will suffer trying to negotiate the city's chaotic traffic, car theft is a major problem in Napoli. Although it is said that Neapolitans observe some caution when driving behind or near cars with foreign numberplates, the risk of being in an accident is quite high if you fail to deal with the local system of not (necessarily) stopping at traffic lights.

Rental Avis has offices at Via Partenope 33 (☎ 764 56 00) and Stazione Centrale (☎ 554 30 20); and Europcar (☎ 764 58 59) is at Via Partenope 38. Both have offices at the airport.

It is impossible to rent a moped in Napoli because of theft. You can hire them at Sorrento.

Taxi Taxis generally ignore kerb-side arm wavers. You can arrange one through Radiotaxi (☎ 556 44 44) or else at taxi stands on most piazzas in the city. The minimum fare is L6000, and a short trip can cost up to L20,000 because of traffic delays.

Around Napoli

CAMPI FLEGREI

The area west of Napoli is known as the Campi Flegrei (Phlegraean – 'Fiery' – Fields), a classical term for the volcanic activity that has made it one of the globe's most geologically unstable areas. It includes the towns of Pozzuoli, Baia and Cumae, and it was partly through this region that Greek civilisation arrived in Italy. Homer believed the area to be the entrance to Hades, and Virgil too wrote of it in *The Aeneid*. Now part of suburban Napoli, it bears some reminders of the Greeks and Romans and is easily accessible and worth a half-day trip.

Getting There & Away

Although there is an ANM bus from Piazza Garibaldi in Napoli, and also CTP and SEPSA buses from near Stazione Centrale, train is a more straightforward bet. See the Napoli Getting Around section for details of the Metropolitana, Ferrovia Cumana and Circumflegrea rail services.

The Tangenziale di Napoli runs through the area. Exit at Pozzuoli. Alternatively, take Via Caracciolo along the Napoli waterfront for Posillipo.

Caremar (☎ 526 13 35) runs frequent ferries to Ischia and Procida, as well as one hydrofoil per day to Procida. Another company is Traghetti Pozzuoli (526 77 36). You can take your car across on the ferries. Signs will direct you to the port.

Pozzuoli

Now a grubby-looking suburb of Napoli, Pozzuoli still has some impressive Roman ruins. The tourist office (☎ 081-526 50 68), Via Campi Flegrei 3, is about 1km uphill from the train station.

Things to See Close to the remains of the Roman port of Puteoli is the **Tempio di Serapide** (Temple of Serapis), which was simply a market of shops and, according to some sources, skilfully designed toilets. It has been badly damaged over the centuries by the seismic activity known as bradyseism ('slow earthquake') which raises and lowers the ground level over long periods. The nearby church of Santa Maria delle Grazie, along Via Roma, is sinking at a rate of about 2cm a year because of this.

The **duomo** was built over a temple of Augustus and earthquake activity and excavation have revealed six columns from the temple.

North-east along Via Rosini are the substantial ruins of the **Anfiteatro Flavio**, which had seating for 40,000 people and could be flooded for mock naval battles. It's open daily from 9 am to one hour before sunset and entrance is L4000.

Farther along, Via Rosini becomes Via Solfatara and continues to the **Solfatara Crater**, about a 2km walk (or jump on any city bus heading uphill). Known to the Romans as the Forum Vulcani and bearing some remnants of ancient spa buildings, the crater occasionally ejects steam jets and bubbling mud. The entire crater is a layer of rock supported by the steam pressure beneath. Pick up a boulder, cast it into the air and listen to the rumblings as it hits the ground. The site is open daily from 9 am to one hour before sunset and entrance is L6000.

To the south of the crater is the **Chiesa di San Gennaro**, where Napoli's patron saint was beheaded in 305 AD.

There is a crowded camping ground (☎ 526 74 13) at Via Solfatara 47.

Baia & Cuma

Twenty minutes north-west of Pozzuoli, on the Ferrovia Cumana or by SEPSA bus, is Baia, once a fashionable Roman bathing resort, the remains of which are now submerged about 100m from the shore. You can take a glass-bottomed boat out to the extensive ruins. From April to September, there are frequent boats on weekends.

Beyond Baia is Bacoli with more Roman remains, and Cuma (Cumae), the earliest Greek colony in Italy. A visit to the **Antro della Sibilla Cumana** [Cave of the Cumaean Sybil], home of one of the ancient world's greatest oracles, is a must. Inland is the **Lago di Averno** (Lake Avernus), the mythical entrance to the underworld where Aeneas descended to meet his father. Cumae is easily accessible from Baia by a regular bus service. The site is open from 9 am to 5 pm in summer (closing earlier during winter months) and entrance is L8000.

CASERTA

Probably founded by the Lombards in the 8th century on the site of a Roman emplacement atop Monte Tifata, the town spread into the plains below from the 12th century on. The construction of the Bourbons' grand palace assured the town a certain grandeur it otherwise would never have known.

The tourist office (☎ 32 11 37) in the Palazzo Reale produces a guide to the palace. The telephone code is 0823.

Palazzo Reale

Also known as the Reggia di Caserta, this splendid palace was built by the Bourbons of Napoli and modelled on Versailles. Work started in 1752 after Charles III of Bourbon decided he would build himself a palace similar to Versailles. Neapolitan Luigi Vanvitelli, commissioned for the job, established his reputation as one of the leading architects of the time after working on the palace.

Covering 51,000 square metres, with a façade stretching 250m, the building is of massive proportions, with 1200 rooms, 1790 windows and 34 staircases. After entering by Vanvitelli's immense staircase, you follow a path through the royal apartments, most of them richly decorated with tapestries, furniture, mirrors and crystal. After the library is a room containing a vast collection of Nativity scenes played out in several huge cabinets, featuring hundreds of hand-carved characters.

A walk in the elegant landscaped **gardens** is a must. Some 3km long, the best bet is probably to take the special bus to the far end (L1500 return), marked by a waterfall and the so-called fountain of Diana, and amble your way back. Guides take groups through one garden, the **Giardino Inglese**, which is sprinkled with rare plants, little lakes and fake Roman ruins – all very much the taste of the day.

Entrance to the apartments costs L8000 and they are open daily from 9 am to 1 pm. The gardens are open daily until 4 pm and entrance costs L4500.

Getting There & Away

CPTC buses connect Caserta with Napoli (Piazza Garibaldi) about every half-hour from 8 am to 8 pm. Some Benevento services also stop in Caserta. Caserta is on the main train line between Roma and Napoli and the Reggia is close to the station.

AROUND CASERTA

About 2km north-west of the palace (buses run from the train station), is the **San Leucio silk factory**, built by Ferdinand IV and still operating today. A few km to the west in Capua (take a CPTC bus) are the still impressive ruins of the **Arco d'Adriano** (Hadrian's Arch), under which passed the Via Appia, and the nearby **amphitheatre**, restored in 119 AD by Emperor Hadrian. About 10km to the north-east lies **Caserta Vecchia** (CPTC bus), the decayed nucleus of the original town, where you can see the remains of the 9th-century castle and the 13th-century cathedral.

BENEVENTO

A provincial capital about 60km from Napoli, Benevento is on the Via Appia. After a period as a Lombard duchy, when it controlled much of southern Italy, the town was transferred to the control of the papacy in the 11th century and remained mostly under papal rule until 1860.

The Battle of Benevento

At the close of 1250, Emperor Frederick II died in Puglia, leaving his kingdom in southern Italy to his son Conrad, who was, at the time, in Germany. For the next eight years, Conrad and his son fought the papacy for control of the kingdom until Manfred, a bastard son of Frederick, finally took the reins and eventually asserted his mastery over the entire kingdom. Roma, however, was not idle and, in 1265, reached an agreement with Charles I of Anjou, brother of King Louis IX of France, which gave the Frenchman the kingdom in the name of the Church in exchange for the extirpation of Manfred and his Swabians.

Manfred assembled an army to meet the threat and, on 25 February, he was waiting for the French on the Grandella plain north of Benevento. Charles had hoped to take the city by surprise and so have control of the road to Napoli. His 30,000 troops exhausted by the long march, he now decided to stay put. Manfred, with only half that number of men, calculated that his only real chance was to attack immediately, abandoning his favourable, defensive position. At dawn the following day, his Saracen archers and German cavalry stormed Charles' camp, but when the latter's French horsemen entered the fight, things began to go awry. Manfred, seeing his chances of victory fade, charged into the mêlée, but at this vital instant he was abandoned by many of his barons. Manfred and a handful of diehards pressed on. Every one of them fell. Manfred was 34, and with him passed the short, but illustrious, Swabian line. ■

Information

The tourist office (☎ 31 06 61) is at Via Nicola Sala 31. The telephone code is 0824.

Things to See

The town was heavily bombed in WWII and the Romanesque **Duomo** had to be largely rebuilt. Its elaborate façade was severely damaged. South-west of the cathedral is a Roman theatre, dating from Hadrian's time but oft restored since. The **Arco di Traiano** (Trajan's Arch), built in 114 AD, commemorated the opening of the Via Traiana. The **obelisk** in Piazza Matteotti is a reminder of the Napoleonic period. The **Chiesa di Santa Sofia**, near the piazza, adjoins what was once a Benedictine abbey. Founded in 762, its main entrance dates from the 12th century. The abbey contains the **Museo del Sannio**, which houses remnants of a temple dedicated to Isis, dating from 88 AD, along with a gallery devoted to medieval paintings.

Places to Stay

Should you need to stick around overnight, the *Albergo Genova* (☎ 42 926), Via Principe di Napoli 103, is the cheapest hotel at L25,000/40,000 for a single/double and is close to the train station.

Getting There & Away

Infrequent FBN trains and buses operate from Napoli along the Valle Caudina, and FS trains operate via Caserta. Buses also link Benevento with Roma and Campobasso. Benevento is on the SS7 (the Via Appia) and close to the A16.

AVELLINO

About 60km east of Napoli and connected by buses every 20 minutes, Avellino is a largely modern town of 60,000 inhabitants. The EPT office (☎ 74 732) is at Piazza Libertà 50. The telephone code is ☎ 0825.

The attraction in the area is the vertiginous summit of **Monte Vergine** and the sanctuary devoted to the Virgin Mary, north of the city. A young pilgrim, Guglielmo di Vercelli, erected a church here in the 12th century, and so began a tradition of pilgrimage that continues to the present day. His remains were finally laid to rest in the crypt of a modern basilica here in 1807. From the summit (1493m) you can see Napoli on a clear day, and the twisting drive up from Avellino is pleasant. If you are in the province in winter, skiing is possible, but not great, at Lago Laceno, south-east of Avellino.

Although best reached with your own transport, buses do run from Avellino to the sanctuary daily in summer. There is a funicular that links the sanctuary from the town of Mercogliano. A day excursion from Napoli is the best idea, as accommodation options in Avellino are poor.

The Golfo di Napoli

CAPRI

Despite the boatloads of tourists who pour onto the Marina Grande each day and restaurants that boast *würstl* (German sausages), real English butter and Maxwell House coffee, Capri remains an enchanting island haven in the Golfo di Napoli (Bay of Naples). Its breathtaking caves, luxuriant vegetation and the charming narrow laneways of its small towns have attracted visitors for centuries. The best time to visit is spring (April to early June), or mid-autumn (October) after the summer crowds have ebbed away.

History

Already inhabited in the Old Stone Age, Capri was eventually occupied by the Greeks. Roma's Emperor Augustus made it his private playground and his successor Tiberius retired there in 27 AD. Augustus is believed to have founded the world's first palaeontological museum, in the Villa Augustus, to house fossils and Stone Age artefacts unearthed by his workers.

Tiberius, a victim of Tacitus' pen, has gone down in history as something of a porn king on the island, although there is little evidence to back the lurid claims concerning the emperor's orgies. The mud stuck, however, and until modern times his name has been equated by the islanders with evil. When the eccentric Swedish doctor Axel Munthe first began picking about the ruins of Roman palaces and villas on the island late last century, locals would observe it was all *'roba di Timberio'* (Tiberius' stuff).

Despite their sleepy, bucolic appearances, the people of Capri and Anacapri have always been at loggerheads and are always ready to trot out their respective patron saints to ward off the *malocchio* (Evil Eye) of their rivals.

Orientation

About 5km from the mainland, Capri is a mere 6km long and 2.7km wide. As you approach, there is a lovely view of the town of Capri with the dramatic slopes of Monte Solaro (589m) to the west, hiding the village, Anacapri.

All hydrofoils and ferries arrive at Marina Grande, a small settlement that is virtually part of Capri. Buses connect the port with Capri and Anacapri, departing from Via Marina Grande (L1500), just to the right as you leave the pier. A funicular (L1500) also connects the marina with Capri. Otherwise, follow Via Marina Grande for a 3km uphill hike.

Via Marina Grande reaches a junction at Capri with Via Roma, which, to the left, is the town's main strip and leads to Piazza Umberto I and the centre. To the right of the junction is Via Provinciale di Anacapri, which eventually becomes Via G Orlandi as it reaches Piazza Vittoria.

Information

There are three AAST tourist offices: at Marina Grande, Banchina del Porto (☎ 837 06 34), open Monday to Saturday 9 am to 1 pm and 3.30 pm to 7 pm; at Piazza Umberto I, in the centre of Capri (☎ 837 06 86), open Monday to Saturday 9 am to 7 pm; and at Piazza Vittoria in Anacapri (☎ 837 15 24), open Monday to Saturday, 9 am to 3 pm. The offices at Marina Grande and Capri open on Sunday from 8.30 am to 2.30 pm in summer. They provide a vague map and walking guide as well as a publication, *Capri È*, listing restaurants and other useful information. *A Capri*, with historical and cultural information, is available periodically.

Post & Communications The main post office is on Via Roma, to the left as you enter Capri. Another post office is at Viale de Tommaso in Anacapri. Capri's post code is 80073, and Anacapri's 80071.

There are Telecom telephone offices at Piazza Umberto I in Capri and at Piazza Vittoria 4, in Anacapri. The telephone code for the island is 081.

Medical Services In summer there is a tourist medical service (☎ 837 50 19) at Via Capri 30, Anacapri. Throughout the year, a Guardia Medica (☎ 837 50 19) operates at Via Cimino, Capri at nights and on weekends and public holidays. There is also a public hospital (☎ 838 11 11) and *pronto soccorso* (emergency first aid – ☎ 837 81 49). There is a helicopter ambulance (☎ 584 14 81).

Emergency For the police, call ☎ 113. The questura (☎ 837 72 45) is at Via Roma 70.

Grotta Azzurra

Capri's craggy coast is studded with more than a dozen grottoes, most accessible and spectacular, but none as stunning as this, the Blue Grotto. Two Germans, writer Augustus Kopisch and painter Ernst Fries, are credited with discovering the grotto in 1826, but they merely rediscovered and renamed what the locals had long called Grotta Gradola. Remains of Roman work inside, including a carved ledge towards the rear of the cave, were found later.

It is believed the cave sank to its present height, about 15 to 20m below sea level, blocking every opening except the 1.3m-high entrance. This causes the refraction of sunlight off the sides of the cavity, creating the magical blue colour and a reflection of light off the white sandy bottom, giving anything below the surface a silvery glow.

Boats leave from the Marina Grande and a round trip will cost about L25,000 (which includes the cost of a motorboat to the grotto,

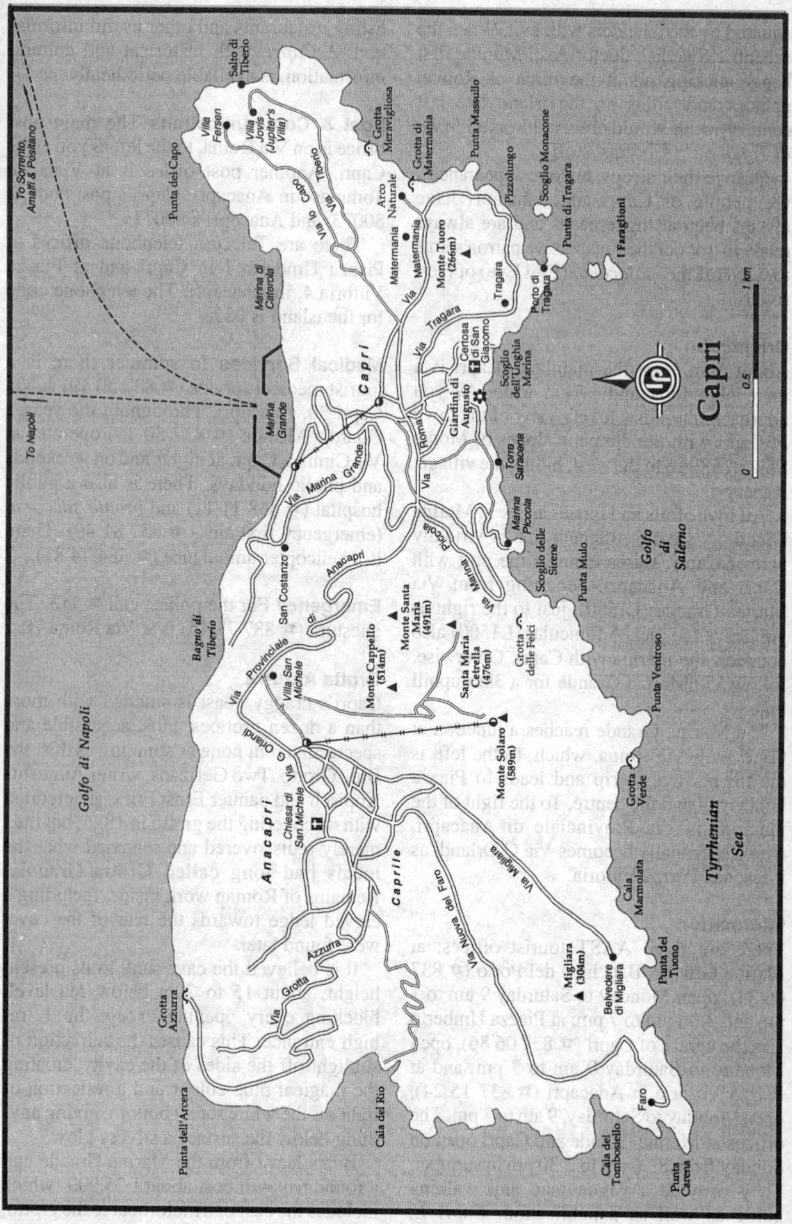
Capri
0
0.5
1 km
To Sorrento, Amalfi & Positano
To Napoli
Golfo di Napoli
Golfo di Salerno
Tyrrhenian Sea
Capri
Anacapri
Caprile
Punta del Capo
Salto di Tiberio
Villa Fersen
Villa Jovis (Jupiter's Villa)
Via Tiberio
Via lo Capo
Grotta Meravigliosa
Grotta di Matermania
Arco Naturale
Matermania
Via Matermania
Punta Massullo
Pizzolungo
Scoglio Monacone
Punta di Tragara
I Faraglioni
Porto di Tragara
Tragara
Via Tragara
Monte Tuoro (266m)
Marina di Caterola
Marina Grande
Via Marina Grande
Via Roma
Certosa di San Giacomo
Giardini di Augusto
Scoglio dell'Unghia Marina
Torre Saracena
Marina Piccola
Via Marina Piccola
Scoglio delle Sirene
Punta Mulo
San Costanzo
Via Provinciale di Anacapri
Bagno di Tiberio
Monte Santa Maria (491m)
Monte Cappello (514m)
Santa Maria Cetrella (476m)
Grotta delle Felci
Villa San Michele
Via G Orlandi
Monte Solaro (589m)
Punta Ventroso
Chiesa di San Michele
Grotta Verde
Via Migliara
Via Nuova del Faro
Cala Marmolata
Migliara (304m)
Belvedere di Migliara
Punta del Tuono
Via Grotta Azzurra
Grotta Azzurra
Punta dell'Arcera
Cala del Rio
Faro
Cala del Tombosiello
Punta Carena

rowing boat into the grotto and the entrance fee). It is only slightly cheaper to catch a bus from Anacapri (L1500 each way, and double that if you're coming from Capri), since you'll still have to pay for the rowing boat and entrance fee. The visit itself is worth the money. The 'captains' expect a tip, but you've already paid enough. Tours start at 9 am. The grotto is closed if the sea is too choppy, so before making your way there, check with the tourist office that it's open.

It is possible to swim into the grotto before 9 am and after 5 pm, but do so only in company and if the sea is completely calm. Because of tidal flows through the small entrance, it can be quite dangerous, but locals, despite their fear of the dragons and witches, believed to inhabit the cave, have swum in it for centuries.

Around Capri Town

From Piazza Umberto I, in the centre of Capri, an afternoon can be whiled away wandering through the narrow laneways with their tiny houses and villas. In the square itself, the 17th-century **Chiesa di Santo Stefano** contains remnants from the Roman villas. Head down Via D Birago, or Via V Emanuele, for the **Certosa di San Giacomo**, a Carthusian monastery with cloisters dating from the 14th century. It is open Tuesday to Sunday from 9 am to 2 pm. The nearby **Giardini di Augusto** (Gardens of Augustus) command one of the better views of the **Faraglioni**, the rock stacks along the south coast.

The **Museo del Centro Caprese I Cerio**, at Piazzetta Cerio 8a, houses a collection of Neolithic and Palaeolithic fossils discovered on the island. It was closed for restoration at the time of writing.

Villa Jovis

East of the town centre, an hour's walk along Via Tiberio leads to Villa Jovis (Jupiter's Villa), the residence of Emperor Tiberius. The largest and best preserved of the Roman villas on the island, it was in its heyday a vast complex including imperial quarters, entertainment areas, baths, grand halls, gardens and woodland. It is open from 9 am to one hour before sunset and entry costs L4000.

The stairway behind the villa leads to **Salto di Tiberio** (Tiberius' Leap), a cliff from where he is believed to have had out-of-favour subjects pitched into the sea. A pleasant walk down Via Matermania passes the **Arco Naturale**, a rock arch formed by the pounding sea. From there you can head farther down a long series of steps and follow the path south and back east into town, passing Punta di Tragara and the Faraglioni on the way.

Anacapri

Villa San Michele Many of the island's visitors are lured here, above all by the words of one of its most troubled inhabitants, Doctor Axel Munthe (see the boxed aside for more details). The house he built here on the ruined site of a Roman villa remains immortalised in his book *The Story of San Michele*. The villa houses Roman sculptures from the period of Tiberius' rule and is a short walk north of Piazza Vittoria in Anacapri. Opening hours are daily from 9 am to 6 pm in summer, 10.30 am to 3.30 pm in winter, and entrance is L6000. The pathway behind the villa offers superb views over Capri and the (usually closed) stairway of 800 steps was the only link between Anacapri and the rest of the island until the mountain road was built in the 1950s.

Monte Solaro

From Piazza Vittoria in Anacapri, take the chair lift to the top of Monte Solaro (L5500 one way, L7000 return, from 9 am to two hours before sunset) where, on a (rare) clear day, you can see for miles. From Anacapri, take a bus to Faro (L1500), a less crowded spot, with one of Italy's tallest lighthouses.

Activities

For scuba diving, try Servizi al Mare (Sea Service Centre; ☎ 837 02 21), Marina Piccola, Via Mulo 63, which represents a host of companies, including the Capri Diving Club (☎ 837 34 87). The club runs NAUI certificate courses.

The centre hires out canoes and motorised dinghies, and can take you water-skiing. Alberino Gennaro (☎ 837 71 18), Via Colombo, also rents scuba equipment. For sailboards and Hobie Cats, contact Banana Sport (☎ 837 51 88) at Marina Grande. For a real treat, ask about submarine voyages around the island aboard the *Tritone*. You can book in at the SNAV ticket booth at the Marina Grande, or call ☎ 837 56 46 for information. You're looking at L70,000 for an hour, and it operates from May to September only.

The main places to swim are at a small inlet west of Marina Grande; Bagno di Tiberio, where the emperor dipped; a rocky area at Marina Piccola; off concrete ledges at the Blue Grotto (only after 5 pm); and, farther west of the grotto, below the restaurants. There are no private beaches on the island and the best areas can only be reached by hired boat or by traversing tracks, particularly around Pizzolungo.

Places to Stay

Hotel rooms are at a premium in summer, and many close during winter. There are few really cheap rooms at any time of year. Beware of the compulsory breakfast in summer and haggle for a better price in the low season.

During the summer months, and occasionally in winter, hundreds of young people flock to Capri to party on Friday and Saturday nights, usually around Piazza Umberto I. So if you want peace and quiet at night, avoid this area!

Camping is forbidden and offenders are either prosecuted or 'asked' to relocate to a hotel. You might want to enquire at the tourist office about renting a room in a private home.

Marina Grande The *Italia* (☎ 837 06 02), Via Marina Grande, has singles/doubles from L64,000/84,000 and ranging up to L154,000 for doubles with shower. Nearby, the *Belvedere e Tre Re* (☎ 837 03 45), Via Marina Grande, has good views, with singles/doubles from L40,000/75,000.

Capri All rooms have views over the bay at *ABC* (☎ 837 06 83), Via M Serafina, at L50,000/75,000. The *Stella Maris* (☎ 837 04 52), Via Roma 27, just off Piazza Umberto I, is right in the noisy heart of town. Singles/doubles are L65,000/95,000 and triples/quads are an additional 30%. *Villa Luisa* (☎ 837 01 28), Via D Birago 1, has rooms with great views from L85,000 a double. The Liberty-style *Esperia* (☎ 837 02 62), Via Sopramonte, is a crumbling villa with spectacular views. Doubles with bathroom start at about L120,000.

La Reginella (☎ 837 56 19) is pleasantly located on Via Matermania and has singles/doubles with bathroom starting at L65,000/120,000. *La Vega* (☎ 837 04 81), Via Occhio Marino, has doubles with bathroom from L200,000. There is a spectacular view from the hotel pool.

Anacapri The *Loreley* (☎ 837 14 40), Via G Orlandi, is one of the better deals, starting at L50,000/90,000 for singles/doubles with bathroom, breakfast included, and L30,000 per person in a triple room. Some rooms afford views across to Napoli. *Caesar Augustus* (☎ 837 33 95), Via G Orlandi, has the best view in town, with a terrace overlooking the bay. The hotel is generally not cheap, with singles/doubles with bathroom starting at L100,000/180,000 but, in the off season, may significantly discount smaller vacant rooms. Anacapri virtually closes during winter.

Places to Eat

Food is good and reasonably priced and even the expensive-looking bread and cheese shops aren't exorbitant. Insalata caprese, a delicious salad of fresh tomato, basil and mozzarella, has its origins here. Some of the local wines are a bit rough but generally good. The *Sfizi di Pane*, Via le Botteghe 4, has local breads and cakes and the *cheese shop* opposite sells caprese cheese, a cross between mozzarella and ricotta.

Capri *Ristorante Settanni*, Via Longano 5, has a bay view and pasta from about L8000.

La Cisterna, Via M Serafina 5, is one of several cosy restaurants in the alleys off Piazza Umberto I and has pizza from L5000. Another nearby is *Il Tinello*, Via l'Abate 1-3. *Da Giorgio* and *Moscardino*, virtually beside each other at Via Roma 34 and 28, have the best views in town and a cover charge to match (L3000, plus 12% service charge). A full meal at either is likely to set you back about L40,000. One of the island's best traditional restaurants is *La Capannina*, Via le Botteghe 12, but a meal could cost up to L70,000 a person.

On the way to Arco Naturale, *Ristorante le Grottelle*, Via Arco Naturale, has pasta from L7000 and mains from L9000. Locals do their fruit and vegetable shopping at the small market, the *mercatino*, below the Capri bus stop (take the stairs).

Anacapri *Il Solitario*, Via G Orlandi 54, set in a garden, has pasta from L7000. *La Giara*, Via G Orlandi 69, has good pizzas from L7000, as well as a full menu. *Trattoria Il Saraceno*, Via Trieste e Trento 18, serves ravioli caprese at L8000, and the owners serve their own wine. *Pizzeria Materita*, Via G Orlandi 140, has pizzas from L7000 and faces onto Piazza Diaz, as does *Mamma Giovanna*, Via Boffe 3-5, with pasta from L6000.

Entertainment

For a drink you could head for Guarracino, Via Castello 7. In Anacapri, sit on *Piazza Diaz* or shoot pool at *Bar Materita*, Via G Orlandi 140. Nightlife is a bit thin on the ground. In Capri, try *Atmosphere* or *Number Two*, Via Camerelle 61b and 1, and the slightly more modern (if that is possible) *Pentothal*, Via Vittorio Emanuele 45. In Anacapri, the *Zeus* and *New Planet* discos, at Via G Orlandi 103 and 101, might get your blood rushing. The only other option is *Underground*, at No 259.

The main non-religious festival is from 1 to 6 January when local folk groups perform in Piazza Diaz and Piazza Umberto I.

Things to Buy

The island is covered with ceramic tiles displaying street names and numbers and romantic scenes. Massimo Goderecci, Via P Serafino Cimino 8, just off Piazza Umberto I, takes credit for most of these and will bake you a tile for about L100,000.

The island is famous for its perfume and limoncello. The former smells like lemons and the latter tastes like vodka. Visit Limoncello Capri, Via Capodimonte 27, in Anacapri, and taste the liqueur. The perfumeries are ubiquitous.

Getting There & Away

See the Napoli & Sorrento Getting There & Away sections for details of ferries and hydrofoils. Call Eli Ambassador (☎ 789 62 73) for helicopter flights between the island and Napoli, which can cost several hundred thousand lira.

Getting Around

You can take your car or moped to Capri, but there is no hire service on the island. The best way to get around is by bus, with tickets costing L1500 on the main runs between Marina Grande, Capri, Anacapri, Grotta Azzurra and Faro. Buses run between Capri and Anacapri until past midnight. A funicular links Marina Grande with Capri (L1500).

A taxi ride between any of the villages can cost up to L20,000 and, from the Marina to Capri, about L12,000 – the open-topped 1950s Fiats are very inviting. For a taxi in Capri, call ☎ 837 05 43; and in Anacapri, call ☎ 837 11 75.

ISCHIA

Ischia manages to retain some sense of its past, despite being the largest and most developed of the islands in the Grotto di Napoli and a major tourist destination. Away from the uglier towns, people still work the land as if they'd never seen a tourist, itself an improbable proposition. Although Ischia is especially loved by Germans today, it was the Greeks who first colonised the island in the 8th century BC, calling it Pithecusa. The largely volcanic island is noted for its thermal springs and in summer is frequented as much for the curative powers of its waters and muds as for its beaches.

The main centres are the touristy town of Ischia and Ischia Porto, Casamicciola Terme, Forio and Lacco Ameno, all fairly unattractive and overcrowded compared to the picturesque towns of Ischia Ponte, Serrara Fontana, Barano d'Ischia and Sant'Angelo. Sant'Angelo is very picturesque, as well as quiet – no cars are allowed in the town. Hotel prices and camping make the island affordable, and its size means you might just be able to get away from the August crowds.

Orientation & Information

Ferries dock at Ischia Porto, the main tourist centre. It is about a half-hour walk from the pier to Ischia Ponte, an attractive older centre that culminates in the islet bearing the castle.

The tourist office (☎ 99 11 46), Via Iasolino (Banchina Porto Salvo) at the main port, is open Monday to Saturday from 8.30 am to 9 pm and until 1 pm on Sunday in summer. The times are flexible and in winter they tend to open in the mornings only. Expect to find it closed from 1.30pm to about 3.30 pm for the lunch break. Get a hotel list, which has the tourist office's best attempt at a map.

There are several banks and exchange booths around the island. The Monte dei Paschi di Siena, Via Sogliuzzo 50, has an ATM.

For police, call ☎ 99 13 36, and for medical assistance go to the hospital (☎ 99 40 44) at Lacco Ameno. The telephone code for the island is ☎ 081.

Things to See & Do

The ruins of the **Castello d'Ischia**, an Aragonese castle complex on a small islet that includes a 14th-century cathedral and several smaller churches, make for an interesting visit while you are in Ischia Ponte (L6000, plus L1500 for the lift).

Monte Epomeo (788m) is the island's highest mountain and can be reached on foot from Panza and Serrara Fontana (about 1½ hours). It offers superb views of the Golfo di Napoli.

Among the better beaches is the Lido dei Maronti, south of Barano. If you're interested in diving, Dimensione Blu (☎ 98 56 08), Via Iasolina 106, in Ischia Porto, hires out equipment and runs courses.

Places to Stay

Call the tourist office in advance for room availability during summer. From October to May, prices can drop considerably. Few hotels open in winter. During the peak period, watch for the compulsory breakfast and extra charge for showers.

Camping There are three camping grounds on the island, open in high season only. Perhaps the best placed is *Mirage* (☎ 99 05 51), at Lido dei Maronti 37 on the beach south of Barano. The others are *La Valle dell'Eden* (☎ 98 01 58) in Casamicciola Terme and *Eurocamping dei Pini* (☎ 98 20 69), Via delle Ginestre 28, Ischia.

Hotels The simple *Locanda Sul Mare* (☎ 99 15 08), Via Iasolino 68, is handy to the port and has singles/doubles from L35,000/L45,000. *Villa Antonio* (☎ 98 26 60), Via San Giuseppe della Croce, a 20-minute walk from the port, has singles/doubles with bathroom and breakfast included, for L65,000/L130,000. Prices drop by 30% out of season.

In Sant'Angelo, try the *Conchiglia* (☎ 99 92 70), Via Chiaia delle Rose. It is perched over the water and prices start at L45,000 per person for bed and breakfast in a room with bathroom. In July and August, half board is compulsory, from L85,000 per person. On the promontory of Sant'Angelo, the *Pensione Francesco* (☎ 99 93 76), Via Nazario Sauro 42, offers bed and breakfast for L50,000 per person.

In Barano, *Da Franceschina* (☎ 99 01 09), Via Corrado Buono 51, has singles/doubles for L40,000/65,000 and obligatory half board for L40,000 per person in August.

Places to Eat

Cicco e Domingo, Via Luigi Mazzella 80, in

Ischia, is a pleasant trattoria with solid seafood dishes and pasta. A full meal with wine will cost you about L25,000 a person. *Pirozzi*, Via Seminario 53, Ischia Ponte, has pizzas from L7000.

Getting There & Away

See the Napoli Getting There & Away section for details. You can catch ferries direct to Capri and Procida from Ischia.

Getting Around

The main bus station is at Ischia Porto, and the most useful lines are the CS (Circo Sinistra, Left Circle) and CD (Circo Destra, Right Circle), which circle the island in opposite directions, passing through each town and leaving every 30 minutes. All hotels and camping grounds can be reached by these buses, but ask the driver for the closest stop. Taxis and microtaxis (Ape three-wheelers) are also available.

The best way to see the island is by car or moped. You can either bring your own on to the island, or rent them. Autonoleggio Ischia (☎ 99 24 44), Via A De Luca 61, has Fiats from L90,000 and scooters from L35,000 a day, with free helmets. Fratelli del Franco (☎ 99 13 34), Via A De Luca 121, rents out mopeds. Both also have mountain bikes. The vehicles cannot be taken off the island.

PROCIDA

The pinks, whites and yellows of Procida's tiny cubic houses cluttered along the water-front make for a colourful introduction to the island. The beauty of the Golfo di Napoli's smallest island is immediately apparent. There are only a few hotels and six camping grounds, making it attractive for backpackers, particularly during the peak tourist season in July/August when the other islands are crowded.

Orientation & Information

Marina Grande is the hop-off point for ferries and hydrofoils and forms most of the tourist showcase. There is an information office (☎ 810 19 68) right by the boat ticket office on Via Roma. The telephone code for the island is 081.

Things to See & Do

The 16th-century Palazzo Reale d'Avalos, more recently a prison, dominates the island and is worth exploring. It is possible to explore the island on foot, but the island's narrow roads are usually full of cars – one of Procida's only drawbacks. Walk or catch a bus to Chiaolella for lunch, then explore Vivara, a smaller island reached by bridge. It is a nature reserve and a good place for birdwatching or simply strolling. The Procida Diving Centre (☎ 896 83 85) rents boats and diving equipment and will organise tours around the island by boat.

Special Events

Visit Procida at Easter to see the fascinating procession of the Misteri on Good Friday. This remains one of Italy's most authentic and colourful Easter festivals. Locals dress in special costumes – the men wear blue tunics and white hoods covering their heads and faces, and many carry young children dressed as the Madonna Addolorata. Preparations for the procession begin months in advance, as plans and designs are prepared for the misteri, basically life-size scenes using plaster and papier mâché figures, which illustrate the events leading up to the crucifixion of Christ – many with considerable artistic licence. The evening before the procession, wander through the narrow streets of Procida town and, without too much trouble, you'll come across locals putting the finishing touches on the misteri. On Thursday night there is a re-enactment of the Last Supper at the church of Congreca dei Turchini. Good Friday's activities begin before dawn at the Chiesa di San Michele a Terra Murata and the procession departs from the castello at around 8 am. Men carry the misteri on huge wooden platforms, very slowly, as they need to put the platforms down every few minutes.

Places to Stay & Eat

Camping grounds are dotted around the

island. The *Vivara* (☎ 896 92 42), Via IV Novembre, and *La Caravella* (☎ 896 92 30) are on the eastern side of the island, while *Privato Lubrano* (☎ 896 94 01) and *Graziella* (☎ 896 77 47), both in Via Salette, are near the better beaches of Ciraccio on the western side.

For a hotel, try the *Riviera* (☎ 896 71 97), which has singles/doubles for L55,000/100,000, or the *Crescenzio* (☎ 896 72 55) with singles/doubles with breakfast and bathroom for L45,000/90,000, both at Marina di Chiaolella. The Crescenzio has a very pleasant restaurant overlooking the small harbour.

The *Savoia* (☎ 896 76 16) near Centane, has doubles from L65,000. A great place to stay if you're travelling with family or friends is *La Rosa dei Venti* (☎ 896 83 85), Via Vincenzo Rinaldi 32. It's a group of self-contained cottages sleeping up to six people, set in a large garden on a clifftop overlooking the sea. The cost can be as little as L35,000 per person if you fill a cottage. Ask at the port, or ask the bus driver, for directions.

Good restaurants can be found along the waterfront near the port, including *L'Approdo*, where you'll eat good, fresh seafood at reasonable prices. They also have pizzas. *Il Cantinone* is another good choice, with meals for around L25,000. For a coffee and cake head for the Bar *Il Cavaliere*. There are grocery shops in the area around Via Vittorio Emanuele.

Getting There & Away

Procida is linked by boat and hydrofoil to Napoli, Pozzuoli and Ischia. See the Napoli and Pozzuoli Getting There & Away sections for details.

Getting Around

SEPSA runs a limited bus service, with the L2 and C1 buses making return trips to most parts of the island from the port, where the ferries and hydrofoils arrive. L1 buses connect the port and Chiaiolella. The small Ape open micro-taxis can be hired for two to three hours for about L20,000 or L30,000, depending on how hard you bargain. You can hire boats from Barcheggiando (☎ 810 19 34), although the local fishers will take you out for L10,000 to L20,000 per person, depending on the size of your group.

South of Napoli

HERCULANEUM

According to the legend, this Greek settlement was founded by Hercules (hence the name). Whatever the truth of this, it later passed to the Samnites before becoming a Roman town in 89 BC. Twelve km south of Napoli, Herculaneum (modern Ercolano) is a congested, tangled suburb of the city. Herculaneum was a peaceful fishing and port town of about 4000, and something of a resort for wealthy Romans and Campanians.

History

The fate of the city paralleled that of nearby Pompeii. Destroyed by earthquake in 63 AD, it was completely submerged in the 79 AD eruption of Vesuvio. The difference was that Herculaneum was buried by a river of volcanic mud, not the tufa stone and ash that rained on Pompeii. The mud helped preserve it for posterity. When the town was rediscovered in 1709, amateur excavations were carried out intermittently until 1874 and much of the material found was carted off to Napoli to decorate the houses of the well-to-do or to end up in museums. Serious archaeological work was begun in 1927 and excavation continues today.

Orientation

Ercolano's main street, Via IV Novembre, leads from the Stazione Circumvesuviana at the modern town's eastern edge to Piazza Scavi and the main ticket office for the excavations – an easy walk.

Information

There is a tourist office (☎ 081-788 12 43) at Via IV Novembre 84, but it has little more to offer than a brochure with a map of the ruined city. The *Amedeo Maiuri* guide to Herculaneum sells at some tourist stands for L10,000, and is considered one of the better ones.

The Ruins

The site is divided into 11 islands or *insulae*, carved up in a classic Roman grid pattern. From the main entrance and ticket office you follow a path above and around the site until you arrive at the entrance to the ruins proper in the south-west corner. To leave the site, you must go all the way back to the ticket office. After your tickets have been checked, you will probably be gently assailed by would-be guides – if you really want one, make sure you understand what kind of fee or 'gift' is expected at the end. Some of the houses are closed, but an attendant may be able to open them on request. The two main streets, the *decumani*, are crossed by several *cardos*. On entering, you first encounter the **Casa di Aristide** on your left on Cardo III. Immediately next door is the **Casa d'Argo**, a well preserved example of a Roman noble family's house, equipped with a porticoed garden, *triclinium* (dining area) and a partly excavated peristyle hall.

The most extraordinary mosaic to have survived intact is in the *nyphaeum* (fountain and bath) in the **Casa del Nettuno ed Anfitrite**, on Cardo IV. Neptune and Amphitrite are depicted in colours so rich they make you realise what the interior of other well-to-do households must have been like. If mosaics are your thing, make your way to the city's public baths, **Terme del Foro**, with separate sections for men and women. The floor mosaics are in pristine condition. While women passed from the *apodyterium* (changing rooms; note the naked figure of Triton adorning the mosaic floor) through the *tepidarium* to the *calidarium* (steam bath), men had the added bracing option of the *frigidarium* – a cold bath. You can still see the benches where bathers sat, and the wall shelves for clothing.

The **Casa del Atrio Mosaico**, an impressive mansion on Cardo IV, also has extensive floor mosaics – time and nature have left the floor uneven to say the least.

Behind it, and accessible from Cardo V, the **Casa dei Cervi** (House of the Deer) is probably the most imposing of the nobles' dwellings. The two-storey villa, built around a central courtyard, contains various murals and still-life paintings, as well as the marble groups of deer assailed by dogs. In one of the rooms stands a statue of a drunken Hercules.

On the corner of the Decumanus Inferiore and Cardo V is **Casa del Gran Portale**, named after the elegant brick Corinthian columns that flank its main entrance. Inside are some well-preserved wall-paintings.

Off the main street, the Decumanus Maximus, is the **Casa del Bicentenario**, so named because it was excavated 200 years after digging at Herculaneum first began. A room upstairs contains a crucifix, indicating that there might have been Christians in the town before 79 AD. As you exit the ruins, to the left along Corso Ercolano, you will see the remains of a **theatre**, dating from the Augustan period.

The archaeological area is open daily from 9 am to one hour before sunset in summer, but closes as early as 2.45 pm in winter. Entrance is L12,000.

Places to Stay & Eat

Like Pompeii, Herculaneum is a convenient day trip from Napoli. Otherwise, the *Albergo Belvedere* (☎ 081-739 07 44) is close to the train station and has decent singles/doubles for L45,000/60,000. There are several bars around the entrance where you can buy panini and other snacks – the one across the road from the ancient site, on the right-hand corner of Via IV Novembre, is fine.

Getting There & Away

SITA buses stop at Herculaneum on the Napoli-Pompeii route. However, the easiest way to get from central Napoli or Sorrento to Herculaneum is by train on the Circumvesuviana (see the Napoli Getting Around section). By car, take the A3 from Napoli, exit at Ercolano Portico, and follow the signs to car parks near the main entrance to the site.

VESUVIO

The still active volcano dominates the landscape, looming ominously over Napoli. The last eruption in 1944 blasted open the cone and the plume of smoke that had long been a constant reminder of the peril also disappeared. This may have eased the minds of some, but living in the shadow of Vesuvius is akin to staying on the fault line in Los Angeles – scientists consider more eruptions a sure thing.

Its name is probably derived from the Greek *besubios* or *besbios*, which means fire. The volcano erupted with such ferocity on 24 August 79 AD that it all but destroyed the towns of Pompeii and Herculaneum, and pushed the coastline out several km. The subsequent 2000 years have witnessed regular displays of the mountain's wrath, the more destructive being those of 1631, 1794 (when the town of Torre del Greco was destroyed), 1906 and, most recently, 1944, when poverty-stricken Napoli was struggling back onto its feet under Allied occupation.

To reach the summit of Vesuvio you can catch a Trasporto Vesuviano bus from Piazza Esedra in Pompeii (which also stops at

Danger Brewing
Vesuvio is not Europe's most active volcano, but it is potentially its most dangerous. More than 1.5 million people live around and on its slopes. A major eruption, particularly if accompanied by a cloud of burning ash and poisonous gases (as occurred during the 79 AD eruption which destroyed Pompeii and Herculaneum), could cause the loss of many lives.

An emergency plan, covering a worst case scenario, recommends the evacuation of 600,000 people in the event of an eruption. But there are many theories about what would happen in the event of a disaster in an area noted for disorganisation which verges on lawlessness. Even the authors of the plan warn of the possibility of shoot-outs and people being crushed by crowds if they panic.

The volcano last erupted in 1944, during the allied occupation of Napoli and, since then, it has remained ominously silent – a cause for concern, since the longer it remains dormant, the greater the risk of a violent eruption. Seismologists monitor Vesuvio around the clock and scientists are using computer simulations of past eruptions in an effort to predict the potential force of new ones. This close monitoring, combined with Vesuvio's tendency to give plenty of warning of impending eruptions, gives emergency planners, and local residents, at least some comfort. ■

Herculaneum). There are four a day leaving at 9 am, 10 am, 12.20 pm and 1.20 pm from Pompeii. If you are travelling by car, take the A3 and exit at Ercolano Portico. You can follow the signs through the town, but a road map would also be handy.

The bus will take you to the summit car park, from where you walk a distance of about 1.5km (it takes 30 minutes if you're quick). Work on a funicular railway to replace the long out-of-service chairlift is yet to get underway. You must pay L5500 to enter the summit area and to be accmpanied by a guide, although it is possible to sneak through unaccompanied. Once there, you can walk around the top of the crater. There are several bars at the summit car park. Those with cars can drive on past the turn-off for the summit car park and head closer up to the crater.

L'osservatorio Vesuviano (Vesuvius Observatory), on the road to the summit, was commissioned by Ferdinand II of Bourbon in 1841 and is open to the public.

POMPEII

Ever since Pliny the Younger wrote his moving letters to Tacitus describing the eruption of Vesuvio that buried Pompeii (Pompei) in 79 AD, the city has been the stuff of books, scholarly and frivolous, and a perfect subject for the big screen. Much of the site, the richest insight into the daily life of the Romans, is open to the public and requires at least three or four hours to visit.

History

Founded in the 7th century BC by the Campanian Oscans on a prehistoric lava flow of Vesuvio, Pompeii eventually fell to the Greeks, and later, in the 5th century BC, came under the influence of the Samnites, a southern Italian people related to the Oscans. It became a Roman colony in 80 BC and prospered as a major port and trading town, adorned with grand temples, villas and palaces, until it was devastated by an earthquake in 63 AD. Pompeii had been largely rebuilt when Vesuvio, overshadowing the town to the north, erupted in 79 AD and buried it under a layer of lapilli (burning fragments of pumice stone). Although the town was completely covered by the shower, only about 2000 of its 20,000 inhabitants are believed to have perished. Later, Emperor Titus considered rebuilding the city and Severus plundered a little, but Pompeii gradually receded from the public eye.

The Pompeii area was completely abandoned during the period of Saracen raids and its remains were further shaken by subsequent earthquakes. In 1594, the architect Domenico Fontana stumbled across the ruins during the construction of a canal. Though

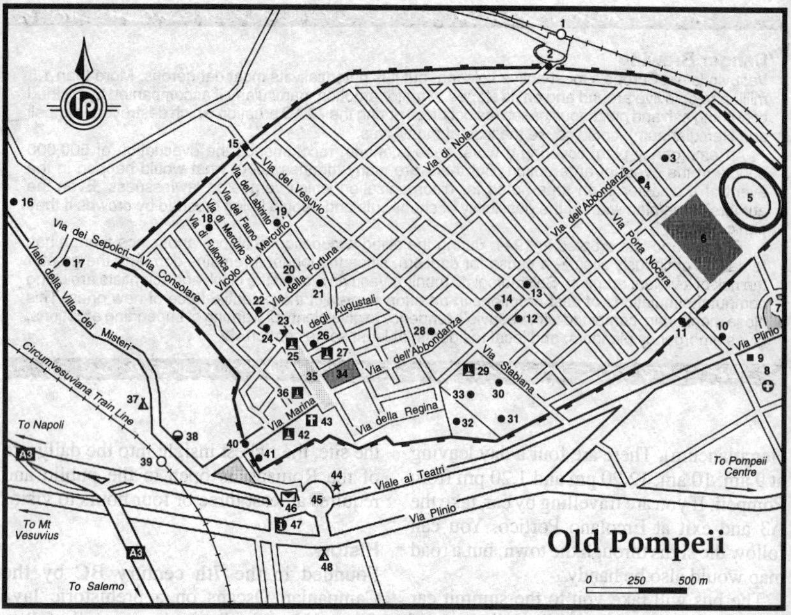

the discovery was recorded, substantial excavation was not conducted until 1748, in the time of Charles of Bourbon, who was interested above all in retrieving items of value. Credit for most of the major discoveries belongs to Giuseppe Fiorelli, who worked under the auspices of the Italian government from 1860.

Work continues, but most of the ancient city has been uncovered. Many of the mosaics and murals have been removed to the Museo Archeologico Nazionale in Napoli and other museums around the world. The exception is the Villa dei Misteri (Villa of the Mysteries), whose frescoes remain *in situ*. They are the single most important series on the site.

Orientation

Arriving by train, you are deposited at either of the main entrances to the site; by car, signs direct you to the excavations and car parks. There are several camp sites, hotels and none-too-cheap restaurants in the vicinity, although the choice is better in and near the modern town of Pompeii itself.

Information

Tourist Offices & Guides There are two AAST offices, one in modern Pompeii at Via Sacra 1 (☎ 850 72 55), open Monday to Saturday from 8 am to 7.30 pm. The other office is just outside the excavations at Piazza Porta Marina Inferiore 12 (☎ 861 09 13), near the Porta Marina entrance. Pick up a map and a copy of the handy *NTR (Notiziario Turistico Regionale)*.

A good guidebook is essential as it is easy to miss important sites. *How to Visit Pompeii* (L7000) is small but comprehensive. The Guide d'Agostini – Pompeii (L12,000) is probably the best.

The tourist offices warn against the dozens of unauthorised guides who swoop at tourists, charging exorbitant prices for brief and generally inaccurate tours. Authorised

PLACES TO STAY
9 Pensione Minerva
37 Camping Zeus
48 Camping Pompeii

PLACES TO EAT
23 Snack Bar

OTHER
1 Stazione Pompei-Santuario
2 Porta Nola Entrance
3 Villa di Giulia Felice
4 Casa di Venere
5 Amphitheatre
6 Palestra Grande
7 Piazza Anfiteatro & Entrance
8 First Aid Post
10 Necropoli
11 Porta Nocera
12 Casa di Menandro
13 Casa di Sacerdote Amandus
14 Casa di Cryptoportico
15 Porta di Vesuvio
16 Villa dei Misteri
17 Villa di Diomede
18 Casa di Apollo
19 Casa dei Vettii
20 Casa del Fauno
21 Lupanaro
22 Casa del Poeta Tragico
24 Terme del Foro
25 Tempio di Giove
26 Market
27 Tempio di Vespasiano
28 Terme Stabiane
29 Tempio di Iside
30 Teatro Piccolo
31 Caserma dei Gladiatori
32 Foro Triangolare
33 Teatro Grande
34 Edificio di Eumachia
35 Forum
36 Tempio di Apollo
38 Bus Station
39 Stazione Pompeii - Villa dei Misteri
40 Porta Marina Entrance
41 Antiquario
42 Tempio di Venere
43 Basilica
44 Police Booth
45 Piazza Esedra & Main Entrance
46 Post Office
47 Tourist Office

guides wear identification tags and belong to one of two cooperatives, Coop Touring (☎ 536 91 01) and Gata (☎ 861 56 61). A group of up to 20 people can take a guide from the latter company for two hours at a cost of L115,000 (L3000 more for each person extra). Also be warned that some of the official attendants on the site, who should open many of the closed sites upon request, are more than keen to escort women on their own to out-of-the-way ruins, a situation that could turn nasty.

The Ruins

The town was surrounded by a wall with towers and eight gates, through several of which you can now gain access to the town. The western sea gate, the **Porta Marina**, was considerably closer to the water before the eruption. Immediately as you enter you see on the right the remains of an imperial villa with long porticoes. The **antiquarium** above it contains remnants gathered from the city and, in one room, body casts formed by hollows left in the hardened tufa by decayed corpses, depicting their final moments of horror.

Farther along Via Marina you pass the striking **Tempio di Apollo**, built originally by the Samnites in the Doric style, and enter the **foro**, the centre of the city's life. To the right as you enter is the **basilica**, the city's law courts and exchange. Dating back to the 2nd century BC, it was one of Pompeii's greatest buildings. Among the fenced-off ruins to the left as you enter are more gruesome body casts. The various buildings around the forum include the **Tempio di Giove** (Temple of Jupiter), one of whose two flanking triumphal arches remains, the **market**, where you can see the remains of a series of shops, and the **Edificio di Eumachia**, which features an imposing marble doorway.

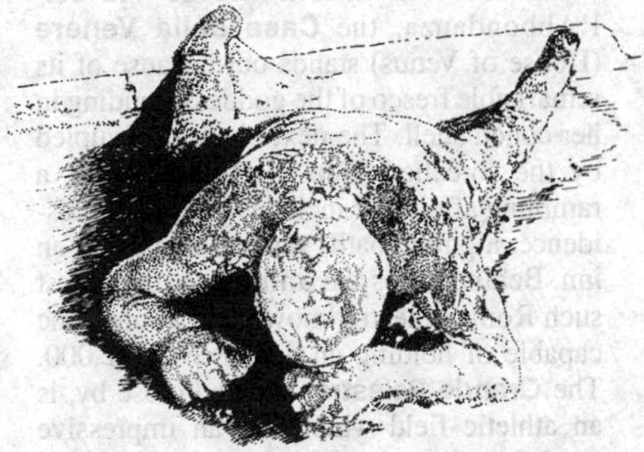

Casts of the fleeing residents were left in the hardened tufa after their corpses decayed

Taking the street to the right of the edificio di Eumachia, Via dell'Abbondanza, wander along and turn right into Via dei Teatri and enter the **Foro Triangolare**, which is surrounded by the remains of a Doric colonnade. To your left is the entrance to the **Teatro Grande**, originally built in the 2nd century AD and capable of seating 5000. Adjoining it is the more recent **Teatro Piccolo**, also known as the Odeon, which is used for music and mime. The **Caserma dei Gladiatori** (Gladiators' Barracks) behind the theatres is surrounded by a portico of about 70 columns. You may wander around the theatres, but the attendants become testy if they see you climbing on the ruins.

From the pre-Roman **Tempio di Iside** (Temple of Isis), rebuilt after the 63 AD earthquake and dedicated to the Egyptian goddess, return to Via dell'Abbondanza, which intersects Via Stabiana. The **Terme Stabiane** is a large complex with many rooms, some featuring original tiling and murals. Several body casts are located here. Farther along Via dell'Abbondanza are the newer excavations. An attempt has been made in this area to keep frescoes (now behind glass) and artefacts exactly where they were found in some of these buildings. Look for the **Casa del Criptoportico**, the **Casa di Sacerdote Amandus** (House of the Priest Amandus) and the **Casa di Menandro**, all well preserved.

Towards the eastern end of Via dell'Abbondanza, the **Casa della Venere** (House of Venus) stands out because of its remarkable fresco of the goddess standing in her conch shell. The next block is occupied by the so-called **Villa di Giulia Felice**, a rambling affair that includes her private residence, a public bath, various shops and an inn. Behind it lies the **anfiteatro**, the oldest such Roman theatre known and at one time capable of holding an audience of 12,000. The **Grande Palestra**, situated close by, is an athletic field which has an impressive portico and the remains of a swimming pool in its centre.

Return along Via dell'Abbondanza and turn right into Via Stabiana (which becomes Via Vesuvio) to see some of Pompeii's grandest houses. The **Casa del Fauno**, one of the best, featured a magnificent mosaic now in Napoli's Museo Archeologico. A couple of blocks south-west along Via della Fortuna, the **Casa del Poeta Tragico** still contains some decent mosaics. The nearby **Casa dei Vettii**, on Vicolo di Mercurio, sports some well-preserved paintings and statues. Across the road from the Casa del Fauno along Vicolo Storto was the **Lupanaro**, a brothel with eye-opening murals. A good place for Pompeii's rakes to make for after the Lupanaro was probably the **terme di foro** (forum baths) a short walk away in Via Terme.

From the baths you could continue to the end of Via della Fortuna and turn right into Via Consolare, which takes you out of the town through Porta Ercolano at Pompeii's north-western edge. Once past the gate, you pass the Villa di Diomede and come to the **Villa dei Misteri**, one of the most complete structures left standing in Pompeii. The Dionysiac Frieze around the walls of the large dining room, one of the largest paintings from the ancient world, depicts the initiation of a bride-to-be into the cult of Dionysus (the Greek god of wine).

The **Museo Vesuviano**, Via San Bartolomeo, south-east of the excavations, contains an interesting array of artefacts.

The archaeological zone is open from 9 am to one hour before sunset. Entrance is L12,000.

Places to Stay

Pompeii is best visited on a day trip from Napoli, Sorrento or Salerno as, apart from the excavations, there is little else to see.

Camping Zeus (☎ 861 53 20) is near the Stazione Pompeii-Villa dei Misteri and has sites from L6000 per person and L10,000 for tent space. *Camping Pompei* (☎ 862 28 82), Via Plinio, has bungalows from L50,000 a double. There are some 25 hotels around the site and in the nearby modern town. *Pensione Minerva* (☎ 863 25 86), Via Plinio 23, has simple rooms with bathroom for L45,000. The *Motel Villa dei Misteri* (861 35

93), near the villa itself, has doubles for L80,000. Heading up the scale, the *Hotel Vittoria* (☎ 536 81 66) is a pleasant, old building a short walk from the entrance and has singles/doubles with bathroom for L70,000/110,000, breakfast included.

Places to Eat

For meals, you are best off making the effort to get into town. Via Roma, the continuation of Via Plinio, is a busy street with several options. *Á Dó Giardiniello*, at No 89, is a no-nonsense pizzeria with prices starting at L4000. *Ristorante Tiberius*, Villa dei Misteri 1B, near the villa, has pasta from L6000.

Getting There & Away

Bus SITA (see the Napoli Getting There & Away section) operates regular services between Napoli and Pompeii, while ATACS (see the Salerno Getting There & Away section) runs from Salerno. Marozzi (see the Roma Getting There & Away section) runs services between Pompeii and Roma. Buses arrive at Stazione Pompeii-Villa dei Misteri.

Train The quickest route from Napoli is on the Circumvesuviana (see the Napoli Getting Around section) to Sorrento. Get off at Pompeii-Villa dei Misteri, near the Porta Marina entrance. Alternatively, take the Circumvesuviana for Poggiomarino, exiting at Pompeii-Santuario.

Car & Motorcycle Take the A3 from Napoli, a trip of about 23km, otherwise you could spend hours weaving through narrow streets and traffic snarls all the way. Use the Pompeii exit, and follow the signs to Pompei Scavi. Car parks are clearly marked.

SORRENTO

Back in 1884, *Cook's Tourist's Handbook* to southern Italy noted soberly that Sorrento, birthplace of the great 16th-century poet Torquato Tasso, 'is a good stopping place', adding that the surrounding ravines make for charming walks 'especially in the evening, when they have such a weirdness and gloominess that the people light the lamps in the oratories perched on the rocks, to keep away hobgoblins and foul fiends'.

The foul fiends have long since been replaced by reliable hordes of British and German tourists, who, it appears, concur with Cook's century-old assessment. A pleasant enough town, Sorrento is handy for Capri (15 minutes away) and the Amalfi coast. The road to Pompeii is pretty in parts but has unfortunately been spoiled by expanding residential and industrial sprawl.

To the ancient Greeks, the area around Sorrento was the Temple of the Sirens. Sailors of Antiquity were powerless to resist the beautiful song of these maidens-cum-monsters who, without fail, would lure them and their vessels to their doom on reefs. Homer's Odysseus (Ulysses) was determined to hear the other-worldly melodies, and so strapped himself to the mast of his ship as he sailed past the fatal place.

Orientation

Piazza Tasso, bisected by Sorrento's main street, Corso Italia, is the centre of town. The train station is about 250m east of the piazza, along Corso Italia, while the Marina Piccola, where ferries and hydrofoils arrive, is a similar distance northwards along Via Luigi de Maio. A walk from the port involves climbing about 200 steps to reach the piazza. Corso Italia becomes the SS145 on the way east to Napoli, and changes its name to Via del Capo when it heads west.

Information

Tourist Office The AAST office (☎ 807 40 33), Via Luigi de Maio 35, inside the Circolo dei Forestieri (Foreigners' Club) office/restaurant complex, is open from Monday to Saturday from 8.30 am to 2 pm and 4 to 7 pm (slightly shorter hours out of season).

Money The Deutsche Bank, Piazza Angelina Lauro, has an ATM that accepts credit cards. American Express is at Acampora Travel (☎ 807 23 63), Piazza A Lauro 12.

Post & Communications The post office is at Corso Italia 210 and the local

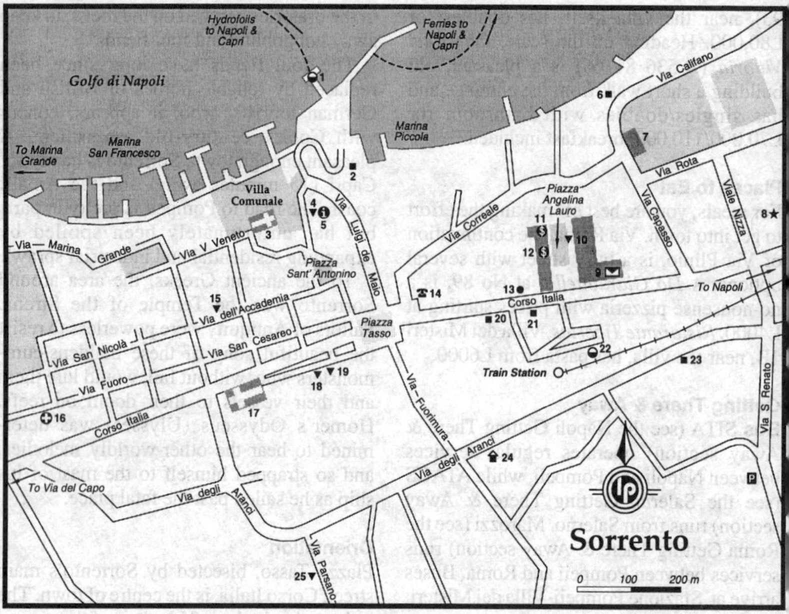

PLACES TO STAY
- 2 Excelsior Grand Hotel Vittoria
- 6 Loreley et Londres
- 20 Albergo City
- 21 Albergo Nice
- 23 Pensione Linda
- 24 La Caffetteria Youth Hostel

PLACES TO EAT
- 4 Foreigners' Club
- 10 Self Service Angelina Lauro
- 15 Giardinello
- 18 Gatto Nero
- 19 Osteria La Stalla
- 25 Caruso

OTHER
- 1 Hydrofoil Terminal
- 3 Chiesa di San Francesco
- 5 Tourist Office
- 7 Palazzo Correale
- 8 Questura (Police Station)
- 9 Post Office
- 11 Deutsche Bank (ATM)
- 12 American Express
- 13 Sorrento Rentacar
- 14 Telecom Office
- 16 Hospital
- 17 Cathedral
- 22 Bus Station

postcode is 80067. The Telecom office is in Piazza Tasso 37, near Via Correale and the local telephone code is 081.

Medical Services Contact the Ospedale Civile (☎ 533 11 11), which is on Via Fuoro, west of Piazza Tasso.

Emergency In an emergency call ☎ 113.

Things to See & Do

The **cathedral** on Corso Italia has a Romanesque façade and its rather odd bell tower rests on an archway supported by four ancient columns. The 18th-century **Palazzo Correale** has some interesting murals and houses the **Museo Correale**, which contains a small collection of 17th and 18th-century Neapolitan art, as well as an odd assortment of Greek and Roman artefacts. The gardens offer views of the bay and steps lead down to the water.

The **Chiesa di San Francesco**, near the Villa Comunale park and the tourist office, boasts a beautiful, if modest, cloister and is set in lovely gardens – the views up and down the coast are breathtaking.

If you want a **beach**, head for Marina Grande, a 15-minute walk west from Piazza Tasso, which has small strips of sand and is very popular. The jetties nearby, with ubiquitous umbrellas and deck chairs, will cost up to L25,000 a day. Bagni Regina Giovanna, a 20-minute walk west along Via del Capo (or take the bus for Massalubrense), is more picturesque, set among the ruins of the Roman Villa Pollio Felix. To the east is a small beach at Marinella. It is possible to hire pedal cars at Marina Grande.

From May to October, Forza 7 (☎ 878 90 08) at Marina Piccola hires out a variety of boats, starting at L25,000 an hour (or L20,000 for three hours or more) and organises boat cruises. Goldentours International (☎ 878 10 42), Corso Italia 38E, offers package tours to the Amalfi coast, Pompeii, Capri and other destinations.

Special Events

The Sorrento Film Festival, regarded as the most important in the country for Italian-produced cinema, is held annually, usually in September/October. The city's patron saint, Sant'Antonio, is remembered on 5 February each year with processions and huge markets. The saint is credited with having saved Sorrento during WWII when Salerno and Napoli were heavily bombed.

To encourage people to visit the city during the winter months, the town organises dozens of free events between December and March, a period known as Sorrento Inverno. Details are available from the tourist office.

Places to Stay

Most accommodation is in the town centre or clustered along Via del Capo about 3km west of the centre (many with views over the bay). To reach this area, catch the SITA buses for Sant'Agata or Massalubrense from the train station. Book early for summer.

Camping The *Campogaio – Santa Fortunata* (☎ 807 35 79), Via del Capo 39A, has camp sites from L8000 to L15,000 and charges L8500 per person. Nearby is the *Nube d'Argento* (☎ 878 13 44), Via del Capo 21, which is slightly dearer. Catch the SITA bus for both camping grounds.

Hostel The hostel *La Caffetteria* (☎ 807 29 25), is run by the comune. It is at Via degli Aranci 160 and is near the train station. It opens year round and beds with breakfast cost L23,000 per person. Otherwise, private singles/doubles are L40,000/70,000.

Hotels The *Albergo City* (☎ 877 22 10), Corso Italia 221, has singles/doubles with bathroom from L60,000/85,000. *Albergo Nice* (☎ 878 16 50), Corso Italia 257, has singles/doubles for L72,000/95,000 with bathroom, and charges an extra L10,000 for breakfast. *Pensione Linda* (☎ 878 29 16), Via degli Aranci 125, is a very pleasant establishment, with singles/doubles with bathroom for L40,000/70,000. *Loreley et Londres* (☎ 807 31 87), Via Califano 12, overlooks the sea and has singles/doubles with bathroom from L80,000/110,000.

Near Marina Grande is *Elios* (☎ 878 18 12), Via del Capo 33, which has singles/doubles with views from L45,000/ 70,000. *Desirée* (☎ 878 15 63), next door at Via del Capo 31, has singles/doubles from L70,000/120,000 and triples/quads from L150,000/180,000, all with bathrooms and including breakfast. The hotel has an elevator to a private beach. *Pensione La Tonnarella* (☎ 878 11 53), at the same address, has doubles with bathroom from L160,000.

For a touch of Sorrento's former glory, try the venerable old *Excelsior Grand Hotel Vittoria* (☎ 807 10 44), which takes up a huge block overlooking the ferry terminal. Rooms here start at about L250,000.

Places to Eat

One of the cheapest options is *Self Service*

Angelina Lauro, Piazza Angelina Lauro, with pasta from L5000. It offers a full English breakfast and is one of several snack places on the square. *Giardinello*, Via dell'Accademia 7, has pizzas from about L6000. *Osteria la Stalla*, Via Pietà 30, has main courses from L10,000. *Gatto Nero*, a cosy little place a couple of doors down, will do you a full meal with wine for about L25,000. *Caruso*, Via Sant'Antonio 12, one of the town's best restaurants, is also one of the more expensive, and you could easily go through L45,000 per person.

The *Foreigners' Club* is at Via Luigi de Maio 35, in the same building as the AAST. It offers bay views and cheap food.

Entertainment

Outdoor concerts are held during the summer months in the cloisters of *San Francesco*. Nightclubs include the *Kan Kan*, Piazza Sant'Antonino 1, which is about the best of a bad bunch and is not overrun by the tourist hordes.

Getting There & Away

SITA buses leave from outside the Circumvesuviana train station, and their office is located near the bar in the station. They service the Amalfi coast, Napoli and Sant'Agata. It is possible to catch the buses throughout the town, although you must buy tickets from shops bearing the blue SITA sign.

For more details on bus and train, see the Napoli Getting There & Away and Getting Around sections.

The city can be reached by the SS145, which meets a spur from the A3 at Castellammare. See the following section for information on rental cars in Sorrento.

Navigazione Libera del Golfo (☎ 807 18 12) and Alilauro (☎ 807 30 24) run hydrofoils to Capri, while Caremar (☎ 807 30 77) operates ferries. The 15-minute run in the fast boats costs L9000 one way and L18,000 return. The ferry costs L10,000 return. Alilauro has up to six boats a day to Napoli (L14,000 one way), and Navigazione Libera del Golfo has one.

Getting Around

Sorrento Rentacar (☎ 878 13 86), Corso Italia 210, rents scooters from L50,000 for 24 hours or L280,000 for a week. Its cheapest car, a Fiat Uno, will set you back L98,000 a day plus petrol, or L460,000 for five days. This is one of several rental companies, and it is worth shopping around. For a taxi, call ☎ 878 22 04.

COSTIERA AMALFITANA

The 50km stretch of coastline from Sorrento to Salerno (the Amalfi Coast) is one of the most beautiful in Europe. A narrow asphalt ribbon bends and winds along cliffs that drop into crystal-clear blue waters, connecting the beautiful towns of Positano, Amalfi and the hillside village of Ravello. The coast is jam-packed with wealthy tourists in summer, prices are inflated and finding a room is impossible. The moral is that you are much better off coming during spring and autumn. The coast all but shuts down over winter, but you can still find places to stay. The area is famous for its ceramics.

Getting There & Away

Bus SITA operates a service along the Amalfi coast from the Sorrento train station to Salerno and vice versa, with buses leaving every 50 minutes. Tickets must be bought in advance from the bar at the Sorrento train station or the SITA bus station in Salerno, or else in bars near the bus stations in the towns along the coast (Piazza Flavio Gioia in Amalfi and Via G Marconi in Positano). Buses also leave from Roma for the Amalfi coast, terminating at Salerno (see the Roma Getting There & Away section for details).

Train Take the Circumvesuviana from Napoli to Sorrento or the train to Salerno, and then the SITA bus along the coast.

Car & Motorcycle The road is breathtakingly beautiful, if a little hairy at times as buses from each direction crawl past each other on narrow sections. In summer, it becomes a 50km traffic jam and can take hours to navigate as the hordes flock to the coast. From Napoli, take the A3 and exit near Castellammare, or follow the signs to Sorrento. The coast road, the SS145, passes through Sorrento and becomes the SS163 Amalfitana. A short cut over the hills beyond Meta can save about 30 minutes. Follow the signs to Vietri sul Mare or Amalfi if you approach from Salerno. Hitching is generally quite easy.

Boat Navigazione Libera Del Golfo (☎ 081-552 72 09), based in Napoli, operates hydrofoils between Amalfi, Positano and Capri, and Alilauro (☎ 081-761 10 04) serves the coast from both Salerno and Napoli. Amalfi Navigazione (☎ 089-87 31 90), Via Nazionale 17, Amalfi, operates services between Amalfi and Positano, Capri and Salerno, as does Avenire (☎ 089-87 76 19), also in Amalfi. Most companies operate in summer only.

Positano

Exuding a rather Moorish flavour, Positano is the most picturesque of the coast towns, and some might think the most precious, with its cute houses and expensive shops.

Positano is virtually divided in two by the cliff which bears the Torre Trasita tower. West is the smaller and more pleasant Spiaggia del Fornillo beach area and the less expensive side of town, and east is the Spiaggia Grande, which gives way to the village centre.

Navigating is easy, if steep. Via G Marconi, part of the Costeria Amalfitana road, runs north around and above the town, which itself cascades inside this fold in the mountain down to the water. The one-way Viale Pasitea winds down off Via G Marconi from the west to the centre, and changes name to Via Cristoforo Colombo as it climbs back up to the main road on the east side.

Information The small APT office (☎ 089-87 50 67), Via del Saraceno 4, near Spiaggia Grande, caters mainly to Italians and Germans, but its map is printed in English too. It is open Monday to Saturday from 8 am to 2 pm in summer; the same hours from Monday to Friday for the rest of the year.

For changing money, the Ufficio Cambio is in Piazza dei Mulini, although the Deutsche Bank, Via C Colombo 75, may offer better rates and has an ATM.

The post office is on Via G Marconi where it meets Viale Pasitea. It's open Monday to Saturday from 8.20 am to 2 pm.

The post code is 84017 and the telephone code is ☎ 089.

In a police emergency, call ☎ 113. The carabinieri (☎ 87 50 11) are on Via G Marconi where it intersects with Viale Pasitea.

For medical emergencies at night, on Sunday or holidays, ring the Guardia Medica on ☎ 81 14 44. Their headquarters is on Via G Marconi, near Via Cristoforo Colombo.

Things to See & Do Positano's main sight is the **Chiesa di Santa Maria Assunta**, just back from the Spiagga Grande. Inside you'll find a 13th-century Byzantine *Black Madonna*. The church is closed in the afternoons.

Boating isn't cheap. Head for the 'To Rent' signs on the Spiaggia Grande, and expect to pay from L18,000 an hour for a rowing boat or L40,000 an hour for a small motor boat, both cheaper by the half or full day.

Hiring a chair and umbrella on the fenced-off **beaches** can cost around 25,000 lire per day, but the crowded public areas are free.

Places to Stay Positano has several one-star hotels, although in summer they are usually booked well in advance. Out of peak season, haggle with the guest-starved proprietors. Ask at the tourist office about rooms in private houses, which are generally expensive, or apartments for rent.

All of the following hotels have rooms with private bathrooms. The pick of the cheaper hotels is the *Villa Maria Luisa* (☎ 87 50 23), Via Fornillo 40, which has large doubles with terraces and magnificent views for L80,000. Half board at L80,000 per person is obligatory in late July and August. Single travellers may be able to talk their

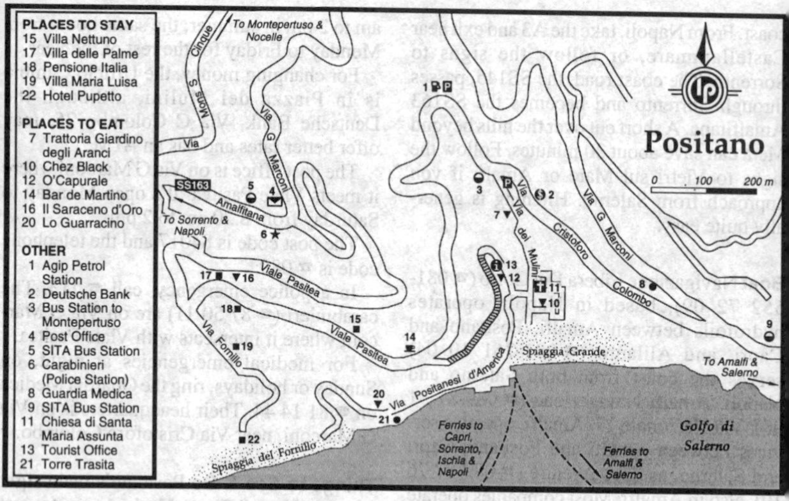

hosts down out of season. The *Pensione Italia* (87 50 24), off Viale Pasitea, is one of about 20 affittacamere in Positano. It has doubles only for L80,000. The *Villa delle Palme* (☎ 87 51 62), around the corner, charges L100,000 a double in low season and L110,000 in the peak period, breakfast included.

The *Villa Nettuno* (☎ 87 54 01), Viale Pasitea 208, has doubles from L90,000 and L110,000 in the high season and most rooms have balconies, or open onto a terrace. *Hotel Pupetto* (☎ 87 50 87), overlooking the beach at Fornillo, has doubles for L140,000 in the low season and L180,000 in the high season; all rooms have views.

Places to Eat Most restaurants are overpriced for the food they serve and you should always check the cover and service charges before you sit down. Many restaurants close over winter, making a brief reappearance for Christmas and New Year. *Il Saraceno d'Oro*, Viale Pasitea 254, has pizzas from L5000 and is close to most of the cheaper hotels. *Lo Guarracino*, Via Positanesi d'America, on the waterfront path connecting the two beaches, has pasta from about L7000.

Near the main beach, *O'Capurale*, Via Regina Giovanna, serves local dishes, with pasta from L8000. Overlooking the beach is *Chez Black*, Spiaggia Grande, a popular spot specialising in seafood. A full meal could cost up to L45,000. *Trattoria Giardino degli Aranci*, Via dei Mulini 22, although still not cheap, is a little more modest and serves solid meals. A great place for a coffee is the *Bar de Martino*, which has commanding views of the town and sea.

Getting Around Dozens of small stairways throughout the town make walking relatively easy, if you don't mind a climb. A small orange bus does a complete circuit of the town, passing along Viale Pasitea, Via C Colombo and Via G Marconi. Stops are clearly marked, and tickets can be bought on board. The bus also stops near the Amalfitana road at the town's western edge, where you can meet the SITA bus.

Around Positano

The hills overlooking Positano offer some great walks if you tire of lazing on the beach. The tourist office at Positano has a brochure listing four routes, including the **Sentiero**

degli Dei (Trail of the Gods), which heads into the hills from the hamlet of Nocelle and on to the Agerola, towards Amalfi. From the small village of Montepertuso, you can reach Santa Maria al Castello and Monte Sant'Angelo e Tre Pizzi (1444m). The latter is quite a hike.

Visit **Nocelle**, a tiny and still relatively isolated village above Positano, accessible by a short walking track from the end of the road from Positano. Have lunch at *Trattoria Santa Croce* (☎ 089-81 12 60), which has a terrace with panoramic views. It is open for lunch and dinner in summer, but at other times of the year it is best to phone and check in advance. Nocelle is accessible by local bus from Positano, via Montepertuso; buses run roughly every half-hour in summer from 7.50 am to midnight.

Praiano is not as scenic as Amalfi, but has more budget options, including the only camping ground on the Amalfi coast. The camping ground, *La Tranquillità* (☎ 87 40 84), is along the coastal road on the Amalfi side of Praiano and has a pensione and bungalows, as well as a small camping ground, a restaurant and a swimming pool. A camp site for two people costs L40,000, and a double room or bungalow costs from L60,000 to around L100,000. In August, half board is compulsory at L90,000 per person. The SITA bus stops outside the pensione.

Amalfi

At its peak in the 11th century, Amalfi was a supreme naval power, a bitter enemy of the northern maritime republics, Pisa and Genova, and had a population of 70,000. Its navigation tables, the *Tavole Amalfitane*, formed the world's first maritime code and governed all shipping in the Mediterranean for centuries.

Amalfi was founded in the 9th century and soon came under the rule of a doge. Thanks to its connections with the Orient, the city claims to have introduced to Italy such modern wonders as paper, coffee and carpets. The small resort still bears many reminders of its seafaring and trading heyday and is now one of Italy's most popular seaside spots.

Orientation & Information Most hotels and restaurants are around Piazza Duomo, or along Via Genova and its continuation, Via Capuano, which snakes north from the duomo.

The AST office (☎ 87 11 07), at Corso Roma 19 on the waterfront, opens year round Monday to Saturday from 8 am to 2 pm.

The post office is at Corso Roma 29. It's open Monday to Friday from 8.15 am to 6.30 pm, and Saturday to 12.15 pm. Amalfi's post code is 84011 and the telephone code is ☎ 089. The Deutsche Bank on the Marina Grande has an ATM.

Medical Services For medical treatment, go to the Municipio Pronto Soccorso (☎ 87 27 85), Piazza Municipio, near the tourist office.

Emergency If you need the police ring ☎ 113, or go to the questura (☎ 87 10 22) at Via Casamare 19.

Things to See The **Duomo Sant'Andrea**, an imposing sight at the top of a sweeping flight of stairs, dates from early in the 10th century, but the façade has been rebuilt twice. Although the building is a hybrid, it is the Arab-Norman style of Sicilia that predominates, particularly in the two-tone masonry and the bell tower. The interior is mainly Baroque and the altar features statues believed to be by Gianlorenzo Bernini and Naccherini, along with 12th and 13th-century mosaics.

The **Chiostro del Paradiso** next door was built in the 13th century, in Arabic style, to house the tombs of noted citizens. It opens from 9 am to 8 pm, with a break of about two hours from 1 pm. Entrance is L1000.

The **Museo Civico**, behind Corso Roma in the town hall building, contains the *Tavole Amalfitane* and other historical documents. It opens Monday to Saturday from 8 am to 2 pm. The restored **Arsenale** of the former republic, the only ship building depot of its kind in Italy, is to the left of Porta della Marina.

Two paper mills still operate in Amalfi. One is at Via Cartoleria 2. The other is also on Via Cartoleria, but is further away from Piazza Duomo. It's called the Cartier d'Amatruda, it still makes paper in the traditional way, and can be visited. The town also has a **paper museum** in Valle dei Mulini set up in a 13th-century paper mill (the oldest in Amalfi), and is open daily, except Monday and Friday, from 9 am to 1 pm.

The many ceramics shops, mostly clustered around Piazza Duomo, testify to Amalfi's traditional promotion of this art. Visit the Bottega d'Arte in Piazza Duomo and see items being made and glazed.

About 6km along the coast towards Positano is the **Grotta dello Smeraldo**, so-called for the emerald colour of its sandy bottom. Just a shadow of the Blue Grotto at Capri, it can be reached by SITA bus from either direction along the Amalfi coast. It opens

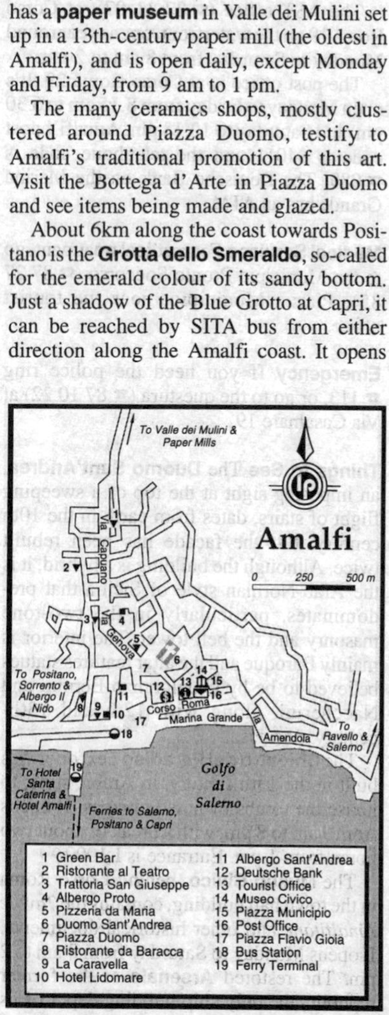

daily from 9 am to 4 pm and entrance is L5000. On 24 December and 6 January, skin divers make their traditional pilgrimage to the ceramic crib in the grotto.

The Regatta of the Four Ancient Maritime Republics, which rotates between Amalfi, Venezia, Pisa and Genova, is held on the first Sunday in June. Amalfi last hosted it in 1997 and should next host it in 2001.

Activities In the hills above Amalfi, on the way to Ravello, are dozens of small paths and stairways connecting the towns with mountainside villages. The CAI in Salerno publishes a map with eight long walks in the area stretching from Salerno to Sorrento. A book titled *Walks from Amalfi – The Guide to a Web of Ancient Italian Pathways* (L10,000) is available from most bookshops in the town.

Boats can be hired in summer at the Marina Grande area, the Spiaggia Santa Croce and the Grotta dello Smeraldo.

Places to Stay The HI *Ostello Beata Solitudo* (☎ 081-802 50 48), Piazza G Avitabile, in Agerola (off the road to Positano) is open all year. A bed costs L13,000. *A'Scalinatella* (☎ 87 14 92), in Atrani on Piazza Umberto I, a 15-minute walk south of Amalfi, also has hostel-style accommodation for L15,000 per person (L20,000 in August).

In Amalfi itself, the *Albergo Proto* (☎ 87 10 03), Salita dei Curiali 4, has doubles/triples in high season for L100,000/140,000 (with bathroom and breakfast), less L10,000 with bathroom. Out of season, prices drop by more than 30%. *Hotel Lidomare* (☎ 87 13 32), in Piazza Piccolomini off Piazza Duomo, has spacious and homey singles/doubles from L55,000/110,000, including breakfast. *Hotel Amalfi* (☎ 87 24 40), Via dei Pastai 3, has singles/doubles for about L50,000/80,000, cheaper in the low season. Full board is obligatory in summer. The *Albergo Sant'Andrea* (☎ 87 10 23), off Piazza Duomo, has singles/doubles from L63,000/105,000 in summer.

Il Nido (☎ 87 11 45), about 2km west of

the centre, has attractive doubles from L90,000, but no singles. Compulsory half board in high season costs a steep L80,000 per person. The *Santa Caterina* (☎ 87 10 12), Strada Amalfitana 9, is one of the best hotels on the coast and is the place to stay if you want to splurge. It is set in extensive grounds and commands a magnificent view of the coast. An added attraction is its salt-water swimming pool by the sea. Lovely rooms cost upwards of L300,000.

Places to Eat The *Green Bar*, Via Capuana 46, is a cheap takeaway place where you can pick up a decent slice of pizza for L2000. *Pizzeria da Maria*, Via Lorenzo d'Amalfi, has pizzas from L5000. *Trattoria San Giuseppe*, Salita Ruggiero II 4, off Via Amalfi, has excellent pasta and decent second courses for around L25,000 all up. *Trattoria da Baracca*, overlooking Piazza dei Dogi, is almost as good, and prices are similar. For a sit-down pizza, you could do worse than *Ristorante al Teatro*, Via Marini 19, where you're looking at about L8000. *La Caravella*, Via Matteo Camera 12, is one of Amalfi's finest restaurants, but L50,000 per person is about the minimum you'll pay.

Ravello

Ravello sits like a natural balcony overlooking the Golfo di Salerno from where you can peer down on Amalfi and the nearby towns of Minori and Maiori. The 7km drive from Amalfi along the Valle del Dragone passes through the soaring mountains and deep ravines that characterise the area – watch the hairpin turns. You can continue inland across the mountains and down to Nocera to link up with the A3 to Napoli and Salerno.

Ravello's tourist office (☎ 85 79 77), in Piazza Vescovado, is open Monday to Saturday from 8 am to 8 pm in summer (to 7 pm for the rest of the year), and has limited information. The town's telephone code is ☎ 089.

Things to See & Do The **duomo** in Piazza Vescovado dates from the 11th century and features an impressive marble pulpit with six lions carved at its base. There is a free museum in the crypt containing religious artefacts. Overlooking the piazza is the **Villa Rufolo**. Its last resident was the German composer Wagner, who wrote the third act of *Parsifal* there. The villa was built in the 13th century for the wealthy Rufolos and housed several popes, as well as Charles I of Anjou. From the terraces there is a magnificent view over the gulf. The villa's gardens are the setting for the Festivale Musicale di Ravello each July, when international orchestras and guests play a selection that always features Wagner. Tickets start at L40,000 and can go as high as L250,000 for some performances. The festival includes major international performers and is the centrepiece of a summer series of musical events. The city hosts a smaller Wagner festival in early July, and the patron saint, San Pantaleon, is celebrated with fireworks in late July.

Away from the Piazza Vescovado is the **Villa Cimbrone**, built this century and set in beautiful gardens.

You can visit the city's vineyards: the Casa Vinicola Caruso, Via della Marra; Vini Episopio, at the Hotel Palumbo, Via Toro; and Vini Sammarco, Via Nazionale. Or you can arrange to visit places where limoncello, the local lemon liqueur, is produced – ask at the tourist office.

Places to Stay & Eat Accommodation and food are too expensive to make Ravello an overnight option for most budget travellers. Book well ahead if you're planning to visit Ravello during the concert series in July. The small *Toro* (☎ 85 72 11), Viale Wagner 3, has doubles with bathroom from L95,000. The delightful *Parsifal* (☎ 85 71 44), Via d'Anna 5, in a former convent, has obligatory half board in high season at L125,000 per person. Otherwise doubles cost L136,000 with breakfast out of high season.

The *Pizzeria la Colonna*, Via Roma 20, serves regional cuisine, with pasta from L8000. *Cumpà Cosimo*, Via Roma 42-44, is a little more expensive, but the food is excellent. A meal will cost from L30,000.

Getting There & Away To reach the town by car, take the Amalfitana for Salerno and turn off about 2km after Amalfi. SITA operates about 15 buses in each direction daily from Piazza Flavio Gioia in Amalfi, departing from 6 am to about 9 pm. Cars are not permitted in the town centre, but there is adequate parking in supervised car parks.

From Amalfi to Salerno

If you're coming from the north, life on the Amalfi coast doesn't end at the town of Amalfi. The 20km drive on to Salerno, although marginally less exciting than the 16km stretch to Positano and beyond, is dotted with a series of little towns that could make useful alternative bases.

Atrani, a bare km away round a point, is a pretty extension of Amalfi with a little beach. Farther on are the towns of **Minori** and **Maiori**. Although lacking much of the charm of its better-known partners up the road, both have plenty of hotels and Maiori has a fairly decent-sized beach. Perhaps most attractive on this run is the fishing village of **Cetara**. Shortly before you hit Salerno (see the following section), you pass through **Vietri sul Mare**, set on a rise commanding views over Salerno. If all else fails, you could even use this as a local base without really feeling cheated. It is also a good place to buy the local ceramics. The town has plenty of workshops and showrooms and, if you shop around, you'll find some good buys.

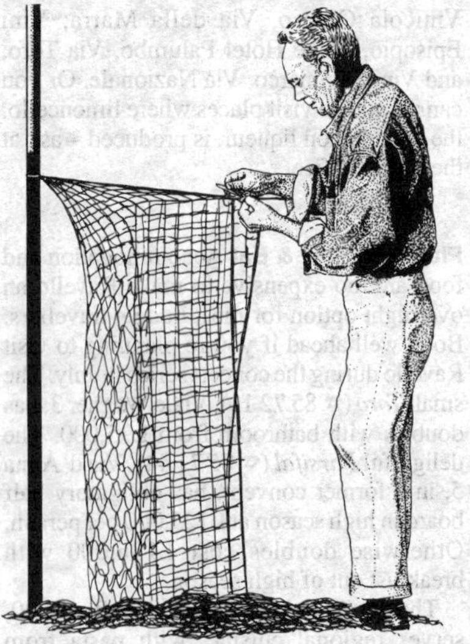

Fishing remains a premier source of income in the coastal towns near Napoli.

SALERNO

After the picturesque little towns of the Amalfi, the urban sweep of Salerno and its port along the Baia di Salerno (Bay of Salerno) might come as a shock. One of southern Italy's many victims of earth tremors and even landslides, Salerno was left in tatters by heavy fighting that followed landings by the American 5th Army just to the south of the city in 1943. With the exception of a mildly charming, tumbledown medieval quarter, the city today is largely unexciting. It is, however, an important transport junction and a possible base for exploring the Amalfi coast to the north and Paestum and the Cilento coast to the south.

Originally an Etruscan and later a Roman colony, Salerno flourished with the arrival of the Normans in the 11th century. Robert Guiscard made it the capital of his dukedom in 1076 and under his patronage the Scuola Medica Salernitana gained fame as one of medieval Europe's greatest medical institutes.

Orientation

The train station is in Piazza Vittorio Veneto, at the eastern end of town. You'll find most intercity buses and a number of hotels in this area too. Salerno's main shopping strip, the car-free Corso Vittorio Emanuele, leads off to the north-west to the medieval part of town. Running parallel and closer to the sea is Corso Garibaldi, which becomes Via Roma as it heads north-west out of the city for the Costiera Amalfitana. The tree-lined Lungomare Trieste on the unattractive waterfront changes its name to Lungomare Marconi at the massive Piazza della Concordia on its way out of town south-east towards Paestum.

Information

Tourist Office The EPT office (☎ 089-23 14 32) is near the train station in Piazza Vittorio Veneto and opens Monday to Saturday from 8 am to 8 pm (generally closing around 1.30 pm for an hour). There is another tourist office (☎ 089-22 47 44) at the other end of town, at Via Roma 258, open daily except Sunday from 9 am to 1 pm and 4.30 to 7 pm.

Money The Banca Nazionale del Lavoro, at Corso Garibaldi 208, has an ATM, as do two branches of Monte dei Paschi di Siena, one at Via Roma 118 and the other in Corso Vittorio Emanuele.

Post & Communications The main post office is at Corso Garibaldi 203 and is open Monday to Saturday from 8.15 am to 7.15 pm. The post code for central Salerno is 84100.

The Telecom office is at Corso Garibaldi 31. The telephone code for Salerno is 089.

Medical Services The Ospedale Ruggi d'Aragona (☎ 67 11 11) is at Via San Leonardo.

Emergency In an emergency, call the police on ☎ 113. The questura (☎ 61 31 11) is at Piazza Amendola.

Duomo

The city's cathedral, in Piazza Alfano north of Via dei Mercanti, is dedicated to St Matthew the Evangelist, whose remains were brought to the city in 954 and later buried in the crypt. Flanked by a Romanesque bell tower and an atrium featuring 28 Roman columns, the church was erected by the Normans under Robert Guiscard in the

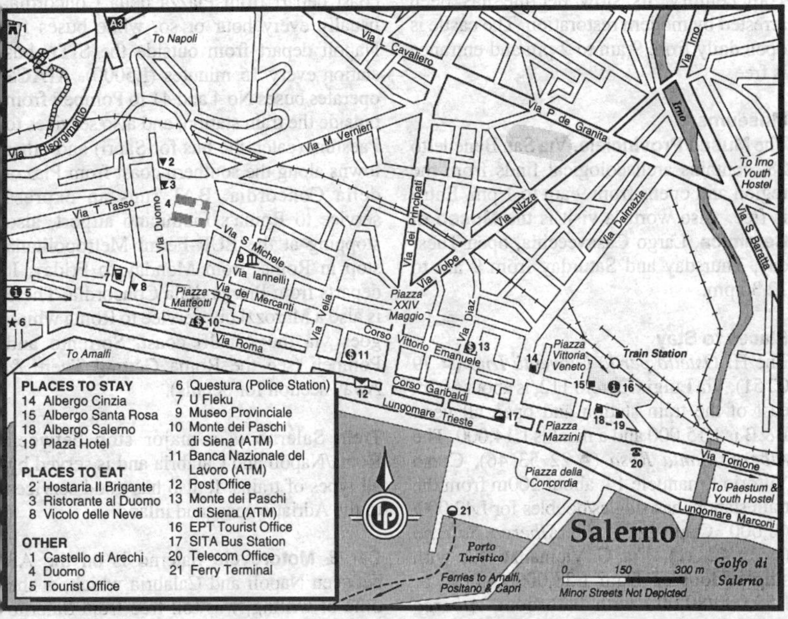

11th century and remodelled in the 18th century. It sustained severe damage in the 1980 earthquake. The Cappella delle Crociate (Chapel of the Crusades), so called because crusaders' weapons were blessed here, is also named after Pope Gregory VII. He lived in exile in Salerno until his death in 1085, and is buried under the altar. The 12th-century mosaic and sculptural decoration on the left side of the central nave is among the most eye-catching. The **Museo Diocesano** next door, with a modest collection of artworks encompassing items dating back as far as the Norman period, and even a few fragments of Lombard sculpture, is open from 9 am to 1 pm and 4 to 7 pm.

Castello di Arechi

A walk to the Castello di Arechi along Via Risorgimento is rewarded with good views, if you can ignore the industrial sprawl beneath you. Arechi II, the Lombard duke of Benevento, built the castle over a Byzantine fort. Last renovated by the Spanish in the 16th century, its slow decline has been arrested by modern restoration. The castle is open daily from 9 am to 2 pm and entrance is free.

Museums

The **Museo Provinciale,** Via San Benedetto 28, contains archaeological finds from the region and opens from 9 am to 1 pm. Entry is free. Also worth a visit is the **Museo di Ceramica**, Largo Casavecchia, open Tuesday, Thursday and Saturday from 9 am to 12.30 pm.

Places to Stay

The HI *Ostello per la Gioventù Irno* (☎ 79 02 51), Via Luigi Guercio 112, is about 500m east of the train station and open all year. B&B is L15,000 and a meal is L14,000. The *Albergo Santa Rosa* (☎ 22 53 46), Corso Vittorio Emanuele 14, about 200m from the train station, has singles/doubles for L42,000/60,000. Opposite is the *Albergo Salerno* (☎ 22 42 11), Via G Vicinanza 42, with singles/doubles from L38,000/66,000, or L58,000/80,000 with bathroom. *Albergo Cinzia* (☎ 23 27 73), Corso V Emanuele 74, has very basic singles/doubles for L35,000/55,000. Pricier is the *Plaza Hotel* (☎ 22 44 77), Piazza Ferrovia 42, at L80,000/120,000 for singles/doubles with bathroom, telephone and TV.

Places to Eat

The 500-year-old *Pizzeria del Vicolo delle Neve*, Vicolo delle Neve 24, off Via dei Mercanti, serves traditional fare, and a meal could cost about L20,000. For a soothing ale afterwards, you could try the *U Fleku* beerhouse at No 5.

The *Ristorante al Duomo* has a terrace overlooking Piazza al Duomo, but you're looking at about L30,000 for two courses and wine. A little more modest is the nearby *Hostaria il Brigante*, about 20 paces away at Via Fratelli Minguiti 2.

Getting There & Away

Bus The SITA bus station (☎ 22 66 04) is at Corso Garibaldi 117. Buses for the Amalfi coast depart from Piazza della Concordia, usually every hour or so, while buses for Napoli depart from outside the SITA bus station every 15 minutes (L5000). ATACS operates buses No 4 and 41 to Pompeii from outside the train station, and also services to Paestum (catch the bus for Sapri) and other towns along the southern coast from Piazza della Concordia. BAT runs an express service to Roma's Fiumicino airport, also stopping at the EUR-Fermi Metropolitana stop in Roma, from Monday to Friday. It departs from Piazza della Concordia. There is also a Marozzi bus service to Roma which goes via the Amalfi coast, Sorrento and Pompeii (see the Roma Getting There & Away section for details).

Train Salerno is a major stop between Roma/Napoli and Calabria and is served by all types of trains. It also has good services to the Adriatic coast and inland.

Car & Motorcycle Salerno is on the A3 between Napoli and Calabria which, at the time of writing, was toll free from Salerno south. From Roma, you can bypass Napoli by taking the A30.

Boat Ferries run from Salerno to Capri, Positano and Amalfi from April through to October, and to Ischia in summer only. They are operated by Cooperativa Sant'Andrea (☎ 87 31 90). Hydrofoils to these destinations, operated by Alilauro, run in summer only. Contact the tourist office for latest details.

Getting Around

Most hotels are around the train station and Corso Vittorio Emanuele, the main drag, is a mall, so walking is the most sensible option. ATACS buses run from the train station through the town centre.

PAESTUM

The evocative image of three Greek temples standing in fields of poppies is not easily forgotten and makes the trek to this archaeological site well worth the effort. The temples are among the world's best preserved monuments of the ancient Greek world, remnants of Magna Graecia, as the Greeks called their colonies in southern Italy and Sicilia. The small town is close to some of Italy's better beaches and just south of where US forces landed in 1943. The modern town of Capaccio, about 3km from the site, is supposed to be renamed Paestum some time this decade.

Paestum, or Poseidonia as the city was originally known, was founded in the 6th century BC by Greek settlers from Sybaris, on the Golfo di Taranto farther south. Conquered by the Lucanians from Basilicata in the 4th century BC, it came under Roman control in 273 BC and became an important trading port. The town was gradually abandoned after the fall of the Roman Empire, periodic outbreaks of malaria and savage raids by the Saracens in 871. The temples were rediscovered in the late 18th century by road builders who subsequently ploughed right through the ruins. The road did little to alter the state of the surrounding area, which remained full of malarial swamps and teeming with snakes and scorpions until well into the 20th century.

This state of affairs belongs to the past and the site is now easily traversed by foot. All public transport is within walking distance. The tourist office (☎ 0828-81 10 16), Via Aquilia, opposite the main site, has maps.

The Ruins

The first temple you come across when you enter the site from the northern end, near the tourist office, is the **Tempio di Cerere** (Temple of Ceres), which dates from the 6th century BC. It is the smallest of the three and was used as a Christian church for a time. The basic outline of the **forum** is evident as you head south. Among the buildings, parts of which remain, are the Italic temple, the Greek theatre, the Bouleuterion, where the senate met and, farther south, the amphitheatre, through which the road was built.

The **Tempio di Nettuno** (Temple of Neptune), dating from about 450 BC, is the most impressive of the remains, the largest and best preserved, with only parts of the inside walls and roof missing. From a distance, its structure gives the impression that the columns are leaning outward. Virtually next door, the so-called **basilica** is the oldest surviving monument in Paestum, dating from the middle of the 6th century BC. With nine columns across and 18 along the sides, it is a majestic building. In the front of the building you can make out remains of a sacrificial altar.

The city was ringed by 4.7km of walls, built and rebuilt by Lucanians and Romans. The most intact section is west of the ruins, but the area to the east makes for a pleasant walk through the local farmland.

The **Museo di Paestum**, opposite the site, houses a collection of metopes, including 33 of the original 36 from the **Tempio di Argive Hera** (Temple of Argive Hera), 9km north of Paestum, making up one of the best collections of ancient architecture in the world. It also features wall paintings from tombs on the site. Entrance to both the museum (closed first and third Monday on the month) and the ruins is L10,000. The ruins open daily from

Metope, relief from the Tempio di Argive Hera

9 am to 6 pm in summer, closing earlier during the rest of the year.

Places to Stay & Eat

Paestum is a short trip from Salerno, which offers a better range of accommodation. There are more than 20 camping grounds in the area, including *Intercamping Apollo* (☎ 0828-81 11 78), Via Principe di Piemonte 2, close to the ruins and near the beach. There is a HI hostel nearby at Agropoli (see Agropoli). *Albergo Villa Rita* (☎ 0828-81 10 81), Via Principe di Piemonte 39, is pleasantly located back from the main road but close to the ruins. Smart singles/doubles cost L80,000/97,000 including breakfast in summer and L60,000/87,000 out of season. There are a few cafés and snack bars near the temples, or you could eat at the *Ristorante Museo* or *Ristorante delle Rose* on Via Magna Grecian, which runs between the temples and the museum.

Getting There & Away

Bus ATACS runs buses from Salerno to Paestum (and on to Agropoli), departing hourly from Piazza della Concordia.

Train Paestum is on the train line from Napoli through Salerno to Reggio di Calabria. Many trains stop at the Stazione di Capaccio, nearer the new town (about 3km from the site), and less frequently at the Stazione di Paestum, a short walk from the temples. Trains are less frequent than the ATACS buses.

Car & Motorcycle Take the A3 from Salerno and exit for the SS18 at Battipaglia, or follow the coast road out of Salerno. Paestum is 36km from Salerno.

AROUND PAESTUM

The World Wide Fund for Nature has a wildlife sanctuary about 12km inland from Paestum on the Sele river, one of the few protected natural environments in southern Italy. Consisting mainly of wetlands and home to a wide variety of birds, the area is known as the **Woods of Diana**, after the Roman goddess of the hunt. Virgil wrote about the area, the roses of Paestum and the woodlands. The sanctuary (☎ 0828-97 46 84) is open from September to April, and signs direct you there from the SS18.

The **Grotte di Castelcivita**, 40km east of Paestum, were discovered late last century, and are heavily promoted as a tourist destination. You can wander for about 1700m through the labyrinth of chambers, shafts, stalagmites and stalactites. The **Grande Cascata** (Great Waterfall) is magnificent. Entry is with a guide only and tours leave hourly from 10 am to 6.30 pm daily, year round. For information, call ☎ 0828-77 23 97. Catch the Pecori bus from Piazza della Concordia in Salerno. There's one in the morning and another will take you back in the afternoon. By car, the caves can be reached via the SS166, which leaves the SS18 north of Paestum.

COSTIERA CILENTANA

South of the Golfo di Salerno, the coastal plains begin to give way to more rugged territory, a foretaste of what lies farther on in the stark hills and mountains of Basilicata and the more heavily wooded peaks of Calabria. This southernmost tract of the Campania littoral is known as the Costiera Cilentana (Cilento Coast) and, with some exceptions, lends itself little to summer seaside frolics, although skin-divers will perhaps appreciate some of the rocky points. Despite a desultory spattering of camp sites and the like, the beaches are not as popular as those farther north or south, into Basilicata and Calabria. ATACS buses leave Salerno for Sapri, on the regional boundary marking off Campania from Basilicata, and trains south from Salerno also stop at most towns. By car, take the SS18 which connects Agropoli with Velia via the inland route, or the SS267, which hugs the coast.

Agropoli

At first sight, the sprawl of this modern coastal town south of Paestum does not augur well, but the small medieval core of Agropoli, perched on a high promontory overlooking the sea and topped by a crumbling old castle, is a rewarding stop. If you can find a place to stay, it could even be a base for travel to the temples at Paestum and also to the clean, sandy beaches to the north.

To join cycling excursions around Agropoli, contact Amici della Bicicletta, Via Salerno 14 (☎ 0974-82 34 90).

The *Camping Villaggio Arco delle Rose* (☎ 0974-83 82 27), Via Isca Solofrone, is a tacky tourist resort village but has camping sites. There is an HI youth hostel, *La Lanterna* (☎ 0974-83 80 03), just out of Agropoli, at Via Lanterna 8, località San Marco. It opens from March to October and has B&B for L15,000. Family rooms cost L16,000 per person and meals are L14,000. The *Hotel Carola* (☎ 0974-82 30 05), Via Pisacane 1, near the harbour, has singles/doubles for L65,000/85,000, but closes from November to March. The *Ristorante U Sghizu*, Piazza Umberto I, the main square in the old town, bakes a pizza for L4500 or more. A full meal will cost around L20,000.

Velia

The ruins of the Greek settlement of Elea, founded in the mid-6th century BC and later a popular spot for wealthy Romans, are worth a visit if you have the time. Its decline matches that of Paestum, but as the town was never an important trading centre, it was considerably smaller than its northern rival and its ruins are in a far worse state.

The closest town with accommodation is Ascea, with several camping grounds and hotels. *Camping Alba* (0974-97 23 31) near Marina di Ascea, is close to the sea and a few km downhill from the main town. *Albergo Elea* (☎ 0974-97 15 77) has singles/doubles for L44,000/65,000 and is near the water.

The train station for Ascea is at Ascea Marina. To get to the ruins, wait for a local bus to Castellamare di Velia or hitchhike.

South to Sapri

If you've made it as far as Ascea, consider pursuing the coast road south into Basilicata (see the Maratea section in the Puglia, Basilicata & Calabria chapter). From Ascea to Sapri, a dowdy seaside town a few km short of Basilicata, the road climbs, dips and curves its way through country that, while not Italy's prettiest, is rarely dull. **Pisciotta**, 12km south of Ascea, is an attractive medieval village and another 25km or so further on are some striking white sandy **beaches** south of Palinuro (in and around which are campsites and the odd hotel). A little further on is Marina di Camerota, where the road turns steeply inland to pass through San Giovanni a Piro, with a small medieval centre. From there, it's another 25km to Sapri. If you get this far you should really make the effort to continue the short distance into Basilicata.

Puglia, Basilicata & Calabria

A good number of visitors to Italy, drawn by the beauty of the Amalfi coast and Capri, summon up the gumption to proceed south of Roma to Napoli, but few venture much beyond the boundaries of Campania.

While you won't find the sumptuous artistic treasures of Roma or Firenze in these southern regions, the Mezzogiorno beyond Campania nevertheless retains many reminders of the march past of several civilisations since the Greeks first established the colonies of Magna Graecia along the coast of Calabria, Basilicata and Puglia.

Of the three, Puglia came out best from the eras of Norman, Swabian, Angevin and Spanish rule, all of which left behind a surprisingly diverse heritage in churches, fortresses and other monuments. The same rulers pretty much left Basilicata and Calabria to their own devices. That sense of abandonment created a vacuum that has all too often allowed petty overlords to maintain an often violent grip on their local territories. The 'Ndrangheta of Calabria, a vicious organised-crime syndicate, keeps much of the region's population obedient with fear and even today is an eloquent expression of that abandonment.

Although great strides towards improving living standards have been made since the end of WWII, especially in Puglia, much remains to be done. These regions have dramatic natural beauty and foreign travellers are a definite minority – a welcome change.

HIGHLIGHTS

- The Romanesque cathedrals, particularly the one at Trani
- Climbing to the hilltop Castel del Monte, 13th-century hunting lodge of King Frederick
- Trulli – circular stone houses with conical roofs, in the pretty town of Alberobello
- The baroque architecture of Lecce
- The sassi of Matera – cave dwellings where thousands of peasants languished in Basilicata
- Driving along Basilicata's Tyrrhenian coast Walking and skiing in Calabria's Sila Massif mountain range
- Visiting the Museo Nazionale at Reggio di Calabria – make sure you see the Bronzi di Riace

Puglia

Encompassing the 'spur' and 'heel' of Italy's boot, Puglia (Apulia) is bordered by two seas, the Adriatic to the east and the Ionian (known as the Golfo di Taranto), to the south.

Puglia's strategic position as the peninsula's gateway to the east made it a major thoroughfare and a target for colonisers and invaders.

The ancient Greeks founded Magna Graecia in a string of settlements on the Ionian coast, including Taranto, which was

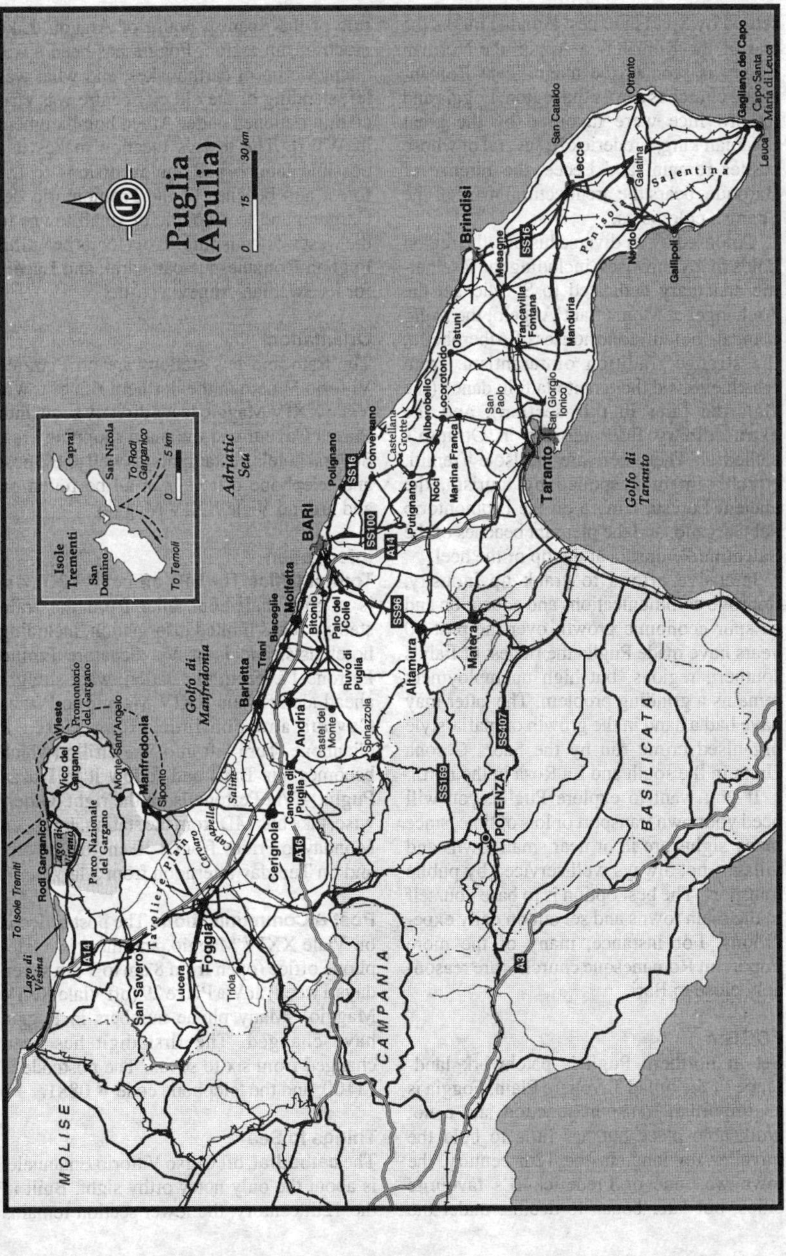
Puglia
(Apulia)
0 15 30 km
Isole
Tremeti
San
Domino
Caprai
San Nicola
To Rodi
Garganico
To Termoli
0 5 km
Adriatic
Sea
Golfo di
Manfredonia
Golfo di
Taranto
MOLISE
CAMPANIA
BASILICATA
To Isole Tremiti
Lago di
Vesina
Rodi Garganico
Lago di
Varano
Parco Nazionale
del Gargano
Vico del
Gargano
Wieste
Promontorio
del Gargano
Monte Sant'Angelo
Manfredonia
Siponto
Tavoliere Plain
San Savero
Foggia
Lucera
Triola
Cervaro
Carapelle
Saline
Cerignola
Canosa di
Puglia
Barletta
Andria
Castel del
Monte
Spinazzola
Trani
Bisceglie
Molfetta
Ruvo di
Puglia
Bitonio
Palo del
Colle
BARI
Altamura
Matera
POTENZA
Polignano
Conversano
Castellana
Grotte
Putignano
Alberobello
Locorotondo
Noci
Martina Franca
Ostuni
San
Paolo
Taranto
San Giorgio
Ionico
Francavilla
Fontana
Manduria
Mesagne
Brindisi
Lecce
San Cataldo
Otranto
Galatina
Nardò
Gallipoli
Penisola Salentina
Gagliano del Capo
Capo Santa
Maria di Leuca
Leuca
A14
A16
SS16
SS100
SS96
SS169
SS407
A3

PUGLIA

settled by Spartan exiles. Brindisi marks the end of the Roman Via Appia; the Norman legacy is seen in the magnificent Romanesque churches across the region; Foggia and its province were favoured by the great Swabian king, Frederick II, several of whose castles remain; and Lecce, the Firenze of Baroque, bears the architectural mark of the Spanish colonisers.

Coloured by its diverse history, the region holds many surprises, including the fascinating sanctuary dedicated to St Michael the Archangel at Monte Sant'Angelo; the *trulli*, conical-roofed, stone houses of Alberobello; the strange tradition of tarantism, from which evolved the tarantella folk dance (see Galatina later in this section); and the extraordinary floor mosaic in Otranto's cathedral. Then there are the Isole Tremiti, which remain unspoiled by tourism, the ancient Foresta Umbra on the Promontorio del Gargano, and the pleasant beaches of the Salentine Peninsula at the tip of the heel.

Intensive efforts to crank up industry, improve communications and education and so spur economic growth over the past 30 years have made Puglia the richest of Italy's southern regions, but high unemployment remains a grinding problem. The latter may have had a hand in the growth of mafia-style organised crime run by the Sacra Corona Unita in the south and La Rosa in the north.

If you want to explore Puglia, you will need your own transport or lots of time, since many sights are in or near small towns and villages not always well serviced by public transport. The best option is to base yourself in the main towns and set out on daily expeditions. For instance, many of the more important Romanesque churches are reasonably close to Bari.

FOGGIA

Set in northern Puglia's patchwork landscape of the broad Tavoliere Plain, Foggia is an important transport junction and a not unlikeable place but has little to hold the traveller for long. In the 12th century, the town was one of Frederick II's favourite cities, but later began to decline under the rule of the Spanish house of Aragon. Like much of the region, Foggia has been a frequent victim of earthquakes, and what was left standing of the old city centre was efficiently flattened under Allied bombardment in WWII. The town's location makes it a possible launch pad for excursions to the forest and beaches of the Promontorio del Gargano and to a couple of small towns to the west worth visiting: Troia for its beautiful Puglian-Romanesque cathedral, and Lucera for its Swabian-Angevin castle.

Orientation

The train and bus stations are on Piazzale Vittorio Veneto in the northern rim of town. Viale XXIV Maggio leads directly south into Piazza Cavour and the main shopping area. Several hotels, restaurants, as well as the post and telephone offices, can all be found on and around Viale XXIV Maggio.

Information

Tourist Office The EPT office (☎ 72 31 41) is a good half-hour hike from the train station. It has limited information, including hotel lists, and is at Via Senatore Emilio Perrone 17. From the station, walk straight ahead along Viale XXIV Maggio to Piazza Cavour and continue along Corso P Giannone. Turn left into Via Cirillo (which becomes Via Bari) and follow it to Piazza Puglia – Via Perrone is on the right. Otherwise, take bus MD from the station. It is open Monday to Friday from 8.30 am to 1.30 pm, and on Tuesday afternoon from 5 to 7 pm.

Post & Communications The post office is on Viale XXIV Maggio, and there is a telephone office (open from 8 am to 9 pm seven days a week) at Via Piave 29 (off Viale XXIV Maggio). Many phone numbers in Foggia have changed. The first digit has been changed from six to seven. The postcode is 71100, and the telephone code ☎ 0881.

Things to See

The **cathedral**, off Corso Vittorio Emanuele, is about the only noteworthy sight. Built in the 12th century, the lower section remains true to the original Romanesque style. The top half, the noticeably different Baroque of six centuries later, was grafted on after an earthquake. Most of the cathedral's treasures were lost in the quake, but you can see a Byzantine icon preserved in a chapel inside the church. The icon was supposedly discovered in the 11th century by shepherds, in a pond over which burned three flames. The flames are now the symbol of the city.

The **Musei Civici** in Piazza Nigri (take Via Arpi to the right off Corso Vittorio Emanuele) houses archaeological finds from the province, including relics from the Roman and medieval town of Siponto. Three portals in the side of the building, one featuring two suspended eagles, are all that remain of Frederick II's local palace.

Places to Stay & Eat

Near the station, *Albergo Venezia* (☎ 77 09 03), Via Piave 40, is basic, with singles starting at L25,000 without bath and top-of-the-range doubles going for L65,000. A little farther away and a little more expensive is the *Albergo Centrale* (☎ 77 18 62), Corso Cairoli 5. The *Hotel Europa* (☎ 72 67 83), Via Monfalcone 52, has more upmarket singles/doubles starting at L100,000 150,000.

There are several trattorie in side streets to the right off Viale XXIV Maggio (walking away from the station). *Ristorante Margutta*, Via Piave 33, has pizzas from L6500. You'll eat well at *Ristorante L'Angolo Preferito*, Via Trieste 21, for about L20,000.

Getting There & Away

Bus Buses leave from Piazzale Vittorio Veneto, in front of the train station, for towns throughout the province of Foggia. SITA has buses to Vieste on the Promontorio del Gargano (up to six daily), Monte Sant' Angelo (eight a day), Lucera (five a day), Manfredonia and Campobasso (in Molise; twice daily). Four direct services (CLP) also connect Foggia with Napoli. Tickets are available at window 10 in the train station, except for Napoli (buy tickets on the bus). ATAF runs buses to Manfredonia, Vieste, Troia and Barletta (buy tickets from the tobacconist's at the station).

Train Foggia is connected by train to other major towns in Puglia, including Bari, Brindisi and Lecce. The town is easily accessible from points along the Adriatic coast, including Ancona and Pescara.

Car & Motorcycle Take the SS16 south for Bari or north for the Adriatic coast to Termoli, Pescara and beyond. The Bologna-to-Bari A14 also passes Foggia. The SS90 south-west will put you on the road to Napoli.

Central Foggia is a confusing tangle of one-way streets. Follow the 'stazione' signs for the train station and get oriented from there, especially if you are planning to stay.

LUCERA

Less than 20km west of Foggia (and a much more pleasant place to spend the night), Lucera has the distinction of having been re-created as an Arab city by Frederick II.

Surrounded, like Foggia, by the flat plains of the Tavoliere, the site was first settled by the Romans in the 4th century BC and named Luceria Augusta. The fall of empire meant decay for the town, but Frederick II resuscitated it in the 13th century. Arab bandits had become a growing problem in Sicilia and Frederick decided to remove the thorn from his side by relocating all of them to Puglia. Some 20,000 ended up in Lucera, where the emperor allowed them to build mosques and practise Islam freely. He recruited his famous Saracen bodyguard from the Arabs of Lucera, who accompanied him on his journeys between castles and even to the crusades.

Charles I of Anjou conquered Lucera in 1269, and the new French arrivals replaced many of the town's mosques with Gothic churches. Both sides got along tolerably well until Charles II decided to have the Arabs slaughtered in 1300.

Things to See

The imposing **castle** was built by Frederick

PUGLIA

II in 1233. Its external walls were later added by Charles of Anjou, forming a pentagon topped with 24 towers. The remains stand in the north-east corner of the enclosure. Excavations have also revealed the remains of Roman buildings. The castle is open daily until dusk. Admission is free, but the guard will expect a small tip.

The **duomo**, in the centre of the old town, was begun by Charles II of Anjou in 1300 and is considered the best example of Angevin architecture in southern Italy. The Gothic **Chiesa di San Francesco** was also erected by Charles II. On the eastern outskirts of town is a poorly maintained 1st-century BC **Roman amphitheatre**, open from 7 am to 1 pm and 2 pm until dusk. Admission is free, but tip the guard.

PUGLIA

Places to Stay

The pick here is the *Albergo Al Passetto* (☎ 0881-52 08 21), next to the old city gate at Piazza del Popolo. Singles/doubles with bath cost L33,000/60,000, and there is a restaurant downstairs.

Getting There & Away

Lucera is easily accessible from Foggia (a 30-minute trip) by SITA and FS buses, which terminate in Piazza del Popolo.

TROIA

The village of Troia, 18km south of Lucera, has nothing to do with the Troy of legend. However, its beautiful Puglian-Romanesque **cathedral** merits the (hardly strenuous) effort of getting here. The façade is splendidly decorated with a rose window and in among the gargoyles and other creatures that adorn the exterior of the church are hints of Oriental influence – look particularly for the geometric designs across the top of the eastern façade. The bronze doors are also of particular note.

If you want to stay, try the *Albergo Alba d'Oro* (☎ 0881-97 09 40) at Viale Kennedy 30, on the way out of town towards Lucera. It has singles/doubles with bathroom for L35,000/60,000.

MANFREDONIA

Founded by the Swabian king Manfred, Frederick II's illegitimate son, this port town has little to attract tourists other than its usefulness as a transport junction on the way to the Promontorio del Gargano. Intercity buses terminate in Piazza Marconi, a short walk along Corso Manfredi from the AAST office (☎ 58 19 98) at No 26. It is open Monday to Saturday from 8.30 am to 1.30 pm and also from 3 to 6 pm on Tuesday and Thursday. You can get limited information on the promontory. The telephone code is ☎ 0884.

Things to See

If you have time to kill, head to the other end of Corso Manfredi for a look at the majestic **castle** started by Manfred and completed by Charles of Anjou (open daily except Monday from 9 am to 1 pm and 5 to 7 pm). The **Museo Nazionale del Gargano** inside has a display of ancient artefacts discovered in the area around Manfredonia.

About 2km south of town is **Siponto**, an important port from Roman to medieval times, which was abandoned in favour of Manfredonia because of earthquakes and malaria. Apart from the **beaches**, the only thing of interest is the distinctly Byzantine looking 11th-century Romanesque **Chiesa di Santa Maria di Siponto.**

Places to Stay & Eat

There are four campsites south of town. Of the hotels in town, *Albergo Sipontum* (☎ 54 29 16), Viale di Vittorio 229, is cheapest at L35,000/65,000. Rooms at *Hotel Azzurro* (☎ 58 14 98), at No 56, start at L55,000/80,000. For a good meal, try *Al Fuego*, Via dei Celestini, just off Corso Manfredi.

Getting There & Away

SITA buses connect Manfredonia with Foggia, Vieste and Monte Sant'Angelo, leaving from Piazza Marconi. Tickets and timetable information are available at Bar Impero in Piazza Marconi, near the corner of Corso Manfredi.

PROMONTORIO DEL GARGANO

The 'spur' of the Italian boot is made up of limestone mountains, ancient forest and beautiful beaches. For centuries an important destination for religious pilgrims, the Promontorio del Gargano (Gargano Promontory) has more recently become a popular tourist playground. Its beach resorts, including Vieste and Peschici, are developing rapidly to accommodate the annual influx of sun-and-fun seekers.

The ancient beeches and oaks of the **Foresta Umbra** in the promontory's mountainous interior make up one of Italy's last remaining original forests. Walkers will find plenty of well-marked trails and there are several picnic areas. The visitors' centre comes complete with stuffed examples of the forest's wildlife. Public transport to and from the forest can be tricky, but not impossible.

The promontory also has two important religious sanctuaries: that of the Archangel Michael at Monte Sant'Angelo, and the burial place of Padre Pio at San Giovanni Rotondo.

Monte Sant'Angelo

For centuries this isolated mountain ridge town overlooking the south coast of the Gargano has been the last stop on a gruelling pilgrimage . The object of devotion is the Santuario di San Michele. Here, in 490 AD, the Archangel Michael is said to have appeared in a grotto before the Bishop of Siponto. The legend goes that a local man who had lost his prize bull eventually found it at the entrance to a cave. He could not make the animal move, so shot an arrow at it. But the arrow turned and hit the man, who then went to the bishop for advice. St Michael later appeared to the bishop at the grotto, ordering him to consecrate a Christian altar there in place of a pagan shrine.

During the Middle Ages, the sanctuary marked the end of the pilgrim Route of the Angel, which began in Normandy and passed through Roma. In 999 AD, Holy Roman Emperor Otto III made a pilgrimage to the sanctuary to pray that prophecies of the end of world in the year 1000 would not be fulfilled. The sanctuary's fame grew after the much-predicted apocalypse did not eventuate.

Information There is a Pro Loco tourist office in the town's main street, Via Reale Basilica, which can provide limited information about the town. It's open in summer only, from 9 am to 1 pm and 2.30 to 5 pm Monday to Saturday.

Things to See & Do Like so many great destinations of pilgrimage, the **Santuario di San Michele** has lately become big tourist business. Those who forget the religious nature of the place are quickly reminded: dress rules are strictly enforced (absolutely no shorts, miniskirts or revealing tops – even bare arms are frowned upon), and don't be surprised if you are asked to put on a special coat to cover offending exposed skin. You enter through a double archway, above which is carved in Latin: 'This is an awesome place; it is the House of God and the Gate of Heaven'.

Once inside, a flight of stone steps leads down to the grotto. As you descend, note the graffiti that fills the walls, some of it the work of 17th-century pilgrims. Archangel Michael is said to have left a footprint in stone inside the grotto, so it became customary for pilgrims to carve outlines of their feet and hands and leave accompanying messages. Magnificent Byzantine bronze and silver doors open onto the grotto itself.

Inside, a 16th-century statue of the archangel covers the spot where he is said to have left his footprint. The main altar stands at the site of the first altar consecrated by the bishop of Siponto to St Michael, and behind it is a small fountain of legendary 'healing' waters which you can no longer drink. Also in the grotto is a beautiful marble bishop's chair, resting on two lions.

Once outside, head down the short flight of steps opposite the sanctuary to the **Tomba di Rotari**, once thought to be the tomb of a 7th-century Lombard king, but more likely a 12th-century baptistry. Little more than the façade and rose window remain of the

PUGLIA

Chiesa di San Pietro next door, destroyed by an earthquake in the 19th century. The adjacent 11th-century **Chiesa di Santa Maria Maggiore** is closed to the public.

Commanding the highest point of the town is a Norman **castle**, long closed for restoration.

The serpentine alleyways and jumbled houses of this town are perfect for a little aimless ambling. Take the time to head for the **belvedere** for sweeping views of the coast to the south.

Places to Stay & Eat Finding rooms can be decidedly difficult in Monte Sant'Angelo. Ask at the tobacconist's near the sanctuary if there are any cheap beds to be had. The only hotel is the comfortable if charmless three-star *Rotary Hotel* (☎ 0884-56 21 46), Via Pulsano, 1km downhill from town, which has rooms for L55,000/75,000.

Via Reale Basilica is lined with takeaways and trattorie, including the *Trattoria San Michele* at No 59, and *Ristorante Garden Paradise* at No 51. While in town, try the local sweets, ostie ripiene (literally, 'stuffed Hosts') – two wafers (like Hosts used in the Catholic Communion) with a filling of almonds and honey.

Getting There & Away Monte Sant'Angelo is accessible from Foggia, Manfredonia, Vieste and San Giovanni Rotondo by SITA bus. If you have your own transport, you can take the road to/from Vico del Gargano, which cuts through the Foresta Umbra.

San Giovanni Rotondo

When Padre Pio, an ailing Capuchin priest in need of a cooler climate, arrived in 1916, San Giovanni Rotondo was a tiny, isolated medieval village in the heart of the Gargano. In the following years, Pio gained a reputation as a mystic and miracle-worker and San Giovanni Rotondo underwent something of a miraculous transformation itself, expanding well beyond its original limits. Up to 200,000 pilgrims crowd into the town every year to pay homage to the priest and spend up in the souvenir shops. Aside from the 14th-century **Chiesa di Sant'Onofrio**, a **baptistry** and the 16th-century **Chiesa di Santa Maria delle Grazie**, you can visit the **tomb of Padre Pio** in the modern church (Santuario) nearby.

If you want to stay, there are more than 20 hotels, although pilgrims can fill a good number of them early.

SITA buses run five times daily to and from Monte Sant'Angelo, and hourly from Manfredonia.

Vieste

The most popular seaside resort on the promontory and the best equipped with tourist facilities, Vieste is a bright little place. The better beaches are away from town, between Vieste and Peschici, particularly in the area known as La Salata, where there are three camping grounds.

Orientation & Information Intercity buses terminate in Piazza Manzoni, a few minutes walk along Via XXIV Maggio from the entrance to the old town and the AAST office (☎ 70 74 95), Corso Fazzini 8, near Piazza Kennedy by the sea. The office is open in summer from 8 am to 9 pm Monday to Saturday. Out of season it is open from Monday to Saturday from 8.30 am to 1.30 pm.

The post office is in Piazza Vittorio Veneto, and there are rows of public telephones there too. The town's telephone code is ☎ 0884.

Things to See & Do The old town, with its whitewashed houses and winding medieval streets, offers a couple of sights of interest, although tourists come here for the beaches rather than the history. The **duomo** is Puglian-Romanesque, but underwent alterations in the 18th century.

Head down Via Cimaglia to the **Chianca Amara** (Bitter Stone), on which thousands of citizens were beheaded when the Turks sacked Vieste in the 16th century. Nearby, at the town's highest point, is a **castle**, built by Frederick II, now occupied by the military and closed to the public.

If you want to head for a beach and don't

have your own transport, the **Spiaggia del Castello** is just south of the town.

Places to Stay Most of Vieste's many hotels and pensioni are scattered along the beachfront roads to the north and south of town. Camping grounds (more than 70) abound, particularly along Lungomare E Mattei to the south. A good one is *Campeggio Capo Vieste* (☎ 70 63 26), at La Salata on the road between Vieste and Peschici. It is accessible by Ferrovie del Gargano bus. Another good option is the *Villaggio Baia di Campi* (☎ 70 61 59), near Pugnochiuso on the coast road between Vieste and Mattinata.

The *Pensione al Centro Storico* (☎ 70 70 30) is at Via Mafrolla 32 in the medieval centre (from Via XXIV Maggio, walk through Piazza Vittorio Emanuele and then follow Via Pola). It has singles/doubles for up to L60,000/90,000. The *Vela Velo Club* (☎ 79 63 03) is at Lungomare Europa 19, north of the old town. It charges by the person, up to L80,000 in the high season, which covers B&B, use of the private beach and a bicycle; out of season you should be able to pay for the room only. The *Hotel del Seggio* (☎ 70 81 23) is at Via Vieste 7, in the old town. A pleasant hotel, it has a private pool and sunbathing terraces. It charges up to L140,000 a double in the high season.

Places to Eat For a snack, try *Il Fornaio*, Piazza della Libertà, at the end of Via Fazzini near the entrance to the old town, which serves pizza by the slice. A panoramic spot for a cool drink is *Sapori di Mare*, overlooking the sea in Piazzetta Petrone, downhill along Via Cimaglia. *La Ripa*, Via Cimaglia 16, is a pleasant little rustic trattoria, where a full meal will cost about L25,000. Otherwise, try *Taverna al Cantinone*, on the corner of Vico Caruso and Via Mafrolla, where a good meal will cost around L30,000. A cosy place is the *Locanda La Macina*, Via Alessandro III 49, near the duomo. Also close by is the *Enoteca Vesta*, Via Duomo 14, for those wanting to sip local vintages.

Getting There & Away SITA buses connect Vieste with Foggia and Manfredonia, while the Ferrovie del Gargano bus and train network connects the town with Peschici and Rodi Garganico, as well as other towns on the promontory. Buses terminate in Piazza Manzoni and timetables are posted outside the town hall nearby. Bus services connecting the towns along the coast are frequent in summer and almost non-existent at other times of the year.

Vieste's port is just north of the old town, about a five-minute walk from the tourist office. Boats to the Isole Tremiti are run by two companies, Adriatica and Motonave, both of which have ticket offices at the port. The cost is L47,000 return on the fast *monostab* boat. It is also possible to make a boat tour of the coast near Vieste, which includes visits to some of the area's grottoes. Enquire at the port for timetables and tickets.

Peschici

A short, pretty drive just in from the coast separates Vieste from the next popular stop. On a rocky outcrop above a sparkling bay, Peschici is a fast-developing resort, but to date remains relatively unspoiled.

Strongly recalling villages of the Greek islands, with whitewashed houses and a sunny aspect, Peschici has cobbled alleyways with suggestive names – Vico Purgatorio (Purgatory Lane), Via Malconsiglio and Via Buonconsiglio (Bad Advice and Good Advice Streets). Their origins are anyone's guess; Vico Stretto (Narrow Lane) is more straightforward.

Peschici's sandy beaches and hotels fill up in summer, so book well in advance.

Orientation & Information While the medieval part of town clings to the clifftop at the point of the bay, the newer parts of town extend inland and around the bay. Buses arrive at the sports ground uphill from the town's main street, Corso Garibaldi. Turn right into the Corso and walk straight ahead to reach the old town.

The Pro Loco tourist office (☎ 96 44 25), Corso Garibaldi 57, near the entrance to the old town, can provide information about accommodation, but little else. The town's telephone code is ☎ 0884.

Places to Stay Peschici has several hotels and pensioni, but prices are usually on the expensive side, particularly in summer. Numerous campsites dot the coast on either side of Peschici. Try the *Baia San Nicola* (☎ 96 42 31), close to town, or *Camping Parco degli Ulivi* (☎ 96 34 04), a few km west on the road to Rodi Garganico.

The pick in old Peschici is the *Locanda al Castello* (☎ 96 40 38), Via Castello 29, right by the seaward cliffs. It has singles/doubles with bath starting at L50,000/80,000. It also has *Albergo La Pineta* (☎ 96 41 26), Viale Libetta 77, which has rooms for L40,000/65,000, while the *Hotel Timiana* (☎ 96 43 21) next door has rooms for L45,000/85,000. These two are in the new town.

Places to Eat To stock up on supplies, shop at the *Supermercato Crai* at the far end of Corso Garibaldi from the medieval section. The *Locanda al Castello* has a good, reasonably priced pizzeria and trattoria. Other restaurants in the old part of town include *Ristorante La Taverna*, at Via Malconsiglio 6 off Via Castello, where a full meal will cost up to L40,000, and *Ristorante Vecchia Peschici*, Via Roma 31, where an excellent meal on the terrace overlooking the sea costs around L35,000.

Getting There & Away Peschici is accessible by Ferrovie del Gargano buses from Vieste and Rodi Garganico. From April to September, daily boats leave Peschici's port for the Isole Tremiti. For information and tickets, go to Ondazzurra (☎ 96 42 34) at Corso Umberto I.

Rodi Garganico

Closing off the stretch of beach resorts in the north-west of the promontory is what was once a simple fishing village. Rodi Garganico and the beach stretching east to the hamlet of San Menaio are rapidly filling up with hotels, campsites and apartments, and the area is the least agreeable of the resorts. Should you really want to go, Ferrovie del Gargano buses link it with Peschici and other towns in the promontory.

ISOLE TREMITI

This small archipelago about 40km north of the Promontorio del Gargano consists of three main islands: San Domino, San Nicola and Capraia. Until the 1930s a convict station, the islands are becoming increasingly popular, but for now remain relatively low-key. Out of season most of the islands' tourist facilities close down and the 370 or so permanent residents resume their isolated, quiet lives.

The islands have an ancient history. Legend says that Diomedes, a Greek hero of the Trojan War, was buried here and that a rare local species of bird, the Diomedee, continues to mourn his death. Early in the 11th century, the Abbey of Santa Maria (Abbazia e Chiesa di Santa Maria) was founded on San Nicola by Benedictine monks, who wielded power in the region until the arrival of the Spanish Bourbons in the 18th century. King Ferdinand IV used the abbey as a jail, a tradition continued by the Fascists, who sent political exiles to the islands in the 1920s and 1930s.

Easily defensible, San Nicola was always the administrative and residential centre of the islands, while the lusher San Domino was used to grow crops. With the risk of pirate attack no longer a preoccupation, you will find most of the islands' accommodation and other facilities on San Domino.

Depending on the boat you catch, you will arrive on either San Domino or San Nicola. Don't panic if you think you have been dropped off on the wrong island, since small boats regularly make the brief crossing (L1800 one way – no exact timetable, you just have to wait). Confirm the departure point of your boat. Phone numbers on the island have the telephone code ☎ 0882.

Things to See

San Nicola It is interesting to wander around the abbey on San Nicola, noting in particular the **Chiesa di Santa Maria**, which features an 11th-century floor mosaic, a painted wooden Byzantine crucifix brought to the island in 747 AD, and a black Madonna, which was almost certainly transported here from Constantinople in the Middle Ages.

San Domino San Domino has the only sandy beach on the islands and it becomes extremely crowded in summer. However, numerous small coves where you can swim off the rocks dot the coastline. Some are accessible on foot, while others can be reached only by boat.

If you are feeling energetic, a walking track around the island starts at the far end of San Domino village, past Pensione Nassa. Alternatively, you could hire a bicycle from IBIS Cicli at Piazzetta San Domino. Motorised rubber dinghies are available for hire at the port for about L130,000 a day (go to the Il Piràta bar). Boats leave from San Domino's small port on tours of the island's grottoes; tickets cost L20,000.

Places to Stay & Eat

You will need to book well in advance for summer. If you intend to arrive out of season, phone to check that hotels are open. In the high season, most hotels require that you pay for full board – a good idea, since the options for eating out are not extensive.

On San Domino, *Al Faro* (☎ 46 34 24), Via della Cantina Sperimentale, has singles/doubles for around L50,000/70,000, while *Locanda La Nassa* (☎ 46 33 45) has doubles for up to L100,000. *Hotel Gabbiano* (☎ 46 34 10) has a terrace restaurant overlooking San Nicola from San Domino, and very pleasant rooms for around L130,000 a double, or L105,000 per head for full board, or L90,000 for half board.

On San Nicola, you could eat at *Diomedea*, where a simple meal will cost around L20,000.

Getting There & Away

Adriatica Navigazione runs a year-round daily ferry between the islands and Termoli (in Molise). From October to April the same ferry calls in at Vieste once a week. The return fare is L26,600. From late May to late September, *aliscafi* (hydrofoils) also run between Termoli and the islands, with occasional runs to Ortona (in Abruzzo). The return fare Termoli to Tremiti is L46,800.

There are regular services from the towns on the Gargano coast to the islands during the peak summer period, generally by the so-called *monostab*, a sleek high-speed cruise boat. It links Manfredonia to Vieste, Rodi Garganico and the Isole Tremiti. Services are reduced out of season.

Tickets can be purchased at the ports (preferably 24 hours in advance) or at the following agents:

Manfredonia
: Antonio Galli e Figlio (☎ 0884-54 28 88), Corso Manfredi 4

Vieste
: Gargano Viaggi (☎ 0884-70 85 01), Piazza Roma 7

Peschici
: Ondazzurra (☎ 0884-96 42 34), Corso Umberto I

Rodi Garganico
: Agenzia Marittima VI.Pl.Sas (☎ 0884-96 63 57), Corso Madonna della Libera 22

Tremiti
: Ditta P Domenichelli (☎ 0882-46 30 08), Via degli Abbati 10

Termoli (Molise)
: Intercontinental Viaggi (☎ 0875-70 53 41), Corso Umberto I 93

Ortona (Abruzzo)
: Agenzia Marittima Fratino e Figli (☎ 085-906 38 55), Via Porto 34

Vasto (Abruzzo)
: Massacesi – Agenzia Viaggi e Marittima (☎ 0873-36 26 80), Piazza Diomede 3

TRANI

A vigorous facelift and a magnificent portside cathedral have made Trani one of those little jewels that turn up where you least expect to find them. Some 40km north-west along the coast from Bari, this compact and easily manageable town makes a good base for exploring this part of Puglia. Barletta, Molfetta and the Castel del Monte.

Trani was important in the Middle Ages – the modern world's earliest written maritime code, the Ordinamenta Maris, was drawn up here in 1063– and it flourished during the rule of Frederick II.

Orientation

The train and bus stations are in Piazza XX Settembre. From here, Via Cavour leads past the tourist office to the main central square, the tree-lined Piazza della Repubblica. Continue along Via Cavour to Piazza Plebiscito and the public gardens and, to the left, the port area. Across the small harbour is the cathedral, spectacularly located on a small promontory.

Information

A few metres down Via Cavour from the train station is the AAST office (☎ 58 88 25) at No 140, open Monday to Friday from 8.30 am to 12.30 pm and 3.30 to 5.30 pm (until noon only on Saturday). A booth on Piazza della Repubblica, when staffed, has similar hours. The town's telephone code is ☎ 0883.

Cathedral

Started in 1097 on the site of a Byzantine church, the cathedral was not completed until the 13th century. Dedicated to St Nicholas the Pilgrim (San Nicola Pellegrino), it is one of the most beautiful churches in Italy. Its simple but imposing façade is decorated with blind arches. The bronze doors of the main portal were cast around 1180 by Barisano da Trani, an accomplished artisan of whom little is known, other than that he also cast the bronze doors of the cathedral at Ravello and the side doors of the cathedral at Monreale.

The grand interior of the cathedral was recently restored to its original Norman austerity. Light shines through alabaster windows, giving the interior an eerie glow. Near the main altar, take a look at the remains of a 12th-century floor mosaic, similar in style to the one at Otranto. Below the church is the crypt, a forest of ancient columns, where the bones of St Nicholas are kept beneath the altar.

Around the Cathedral

The cathedral crypt opens onto the Byzantine **Chiesa di Santa Maria della Scala**. Of note here is the *Madonna Dolorata,* a life-size statue of the Madonna, dressed in black velvet, a dagger protruding from her heart. Down another flight of stairs is the **Ipogèo San Leucio**, a chamber believed to date back to the 6th century.

Near the cathedral is the 13th-century **castle**, built by Frederick II. It was altered by the Angevins and until recently was used as a prison.

Around the Port

Several interesting palaces and churches are sprinkled over the port area. Note the 15th-century Gothic **Palazzo Caccetta** and the nearby 12th-century **Chiesa di Ognissanti** (All Saints' Church), both in Via Ognissanti close to the cathedral. The Templars built the church as part of a hospital complex used for knights injured in the crusades. Also worth searching out is the **Palazzo della Quercia**, in Piazza Quercia at the other end of the port zone.

Places to Stay

By far the most evocative place to spend a night is the *Hotel Regia* (☎ 58 45 27), Piazza Duomo 2, in the 18th-century Palazzo Filisio just across the road from the cathedral. Singles/doubles with bathroom cost from L40,000/75,000. The hotel was closed for renovations at the time of writing, but was expected to reopen in 1998. About 3km out of town (accessible by blue bus for Corato from the station) is the *Hotel Capirro* (☎ 58 07 12), a characterless place with secure singles/doubles for L40,000/70,000 (with TV and telephone). Further upmarket, the *Hotel Royal* (☎ 58 87 77), Via De Robertis 24, has rooms starting at L80,000/120,000.

Places to Eat

To pick up supplies, shop at the *market*, held every morning Monday to Saturday in Piazza della Libertà, to the left along Via Pagano from Piazza della Repubblica.

Attached to the Hotel Regia is a restaurant/pizzeria, where you can eat a reasonably priced meal.

Pizzeria Al Faro, Via Statuti Marittimi 50, at the port, is a good choice – try their seafood pizza. *La Darsena*, at the port in the 18th-century Palazzo Palumbo, is more expensive.

The *Caffè Nautico Club*, Via Statuti Marittimi 18, is actually a private club but also an excellent little restaurant. If you are lucky, you might find that the owner/chef is willing to whip up a delightful seafood meal for around L35,000.

Closer to the centre of town, *Ristorante La Nicchia*, Corso Imbriani 22, serves up some very decent nosh for around L25,000.

Getting There & Away

Bus AMET buses connect Trani with points along the coast and inland, including Barletta, Canosa di Puglia, Ruvo di Puglia and Andria. Timetables and tickets are available at Agenzia Sprint, opposite the train station in Piazza XX Settembre, and at the tourist office.

Three buses from Trani leave in time to connect with the 8.30 am service from Andria to Castel del Monte (see the next section). The return run to Andria leaves the castle at 3 pm. Check with the tourist office for updated times.

Train Trani is on the main train line between Bari and Foggia and is easily reached from towns along the coast.

Car & Motorcycle The SS16 runs through Trani, linking it to Bari and Foggia, or you can hook up with the A14 Bologna-Bari autostrada.

AROUND TRANI

Barletta

About 13km north-west along the coast from Trani, Barletta is more faithful to the stereotype of a grubby neglected port town. It is worth a quick visit for its cathedral, castle and the so-called *Colossus*, a rather stout Roman-era bronze statue in the town centre.

Orientation & Information From the train station, walk down Via Giannone across the gardens to Corso Garibaldi then turn right to reach Barletta's centre. From the bus station in Via Manfredi, walk to Piazza Plebiscito and turn into Corso Vittorio Emanuele. The AAST office (☎ 53 13 73) is on Piazza Roma.

The telephone code for Barletta is ☎ 0883.

Things to See The 12th-century Puglian-Romanesque **duomo**, along Corso Garibaldi from the town centre, is among the region's better preserved examples of this architectural style. Restoration work that was due to end in 1993 is still under way and the cathedral is closed.

The imposing waterside **castle** was built initially by the Normans, rebuilt by Frederick II and fortified by Charles of Anjou. It is supposedly open from 9 am to 1 pm and 4 to 7 pm (summer) or 3 to 4 pm (winter). Entry costs L3000.

Back in the town centre, just off Corso Garibaldi in Corso Vittorio Emanuele, is the **Colossus**, a 5.11m bronze Roman statue believed to be of Emperor Valentinian I. The statue was plundered during the sacking of Constantinople in 1203 and snapped up by Barletta after the ship carrying it sank off the Puglian coast. The statue stands next to the 12th-century **Basilica del Santo Sepolcro** (Basilica of the Holy Sepulchre). Originally Romanesque, this church subsequently underwent Gothic and Baroque facelifts. The manner in which it appears to have sunk below the level of the square is uncannily reminiscent of the duomo in Modena (Emilia-Romagna).

Special Event The main event on the town's calendar is the Disfida (Challenge) of Barletta, held annually on the last Sunday in July. One of Italy's best known medieval pageants, it re-enacts a duel between 13 Italian and 13 French knights on 13 February 1503, when the town was besieged by the French. The Italians won, and in return the chivalrous French decamped.

Getting There & Away From the bus station in Via Manfredi, ATAF buses link Barletta with Foggia; there are regular AMET buses to Trani and Molfetta; and SITA buses head for Manfredonia and Bari. Barletta is on both the Bari-Foggia coastal train line and the Bari-Nord line and is easily accessible from Trani and other points along the coast, as well as inland towns.

Castel del Monte

The Castel del Monte, standing like a royal crown on a hilltop, is one of Puglia's most prominent landmarks and visible for miles around. It is situated in the Murge, a long limestone plateau stretching west and south of Bari. You have to be fairly enthusiastic to make the journey to the castle without your own transport, but it is worth the effort.

The stronghold was built by Frederick II, probably for his own pleasure and to his own design, in the mid 13th century, during the last 10 years of his life. It appears that the castle's most bellicose use was as a hunting lodge – in Frederick's day the surrounding country was heavily forested and teeming with game.

The castle is built on an octagonal base, each corner equipped with an octagonal tower. There is no moat or other system of defence, apart from its high walls and slit windows. Completely restored some years ago, its interconnecting rooms have decora-

A Little Romanesque Tour of Puglia

Of 18 important Romanesque churches in Puglia, only nine have been preserved in the original style. These include the cathedrals at Bari, Altamura, Barletta, Bitonto, Molfetta, Ruvo di Puglia and Trani. Another church that should be added to the list is the Basilica di San Nicola in Bari, used as a model for many of the churches built in the Puglian-Romanesque style and of exceptional architectural value.

With some careful planning, you can visit all these churches on day trips from Bari, although the town of Trani is worth a visit in its own right. If you want to make a full tour of the towns and cities where the churches are located, consider hiring a car for two or three days. This would also enable you to take in a couple of the less important Romanesque churches in the province, and include a trip to the Castel del Monte, the stunning octagonal castle of Frederick II of Swabia, about 40km west of Bari.

The itinerary starts in **Bari** with the Basilica di San Nicola, built in the 11th century on the ruins of a Byzantine palace to house the miracle-working bones of St Nicholas, stolen by Bari mariners from their resting place in Myra (in what is now Turkey). The basilica has a stark, imposing façade, simply decorated with blind arches and mullioned windows, and flanked by two bell towers. Look for the Lion's Doorway on the basilica's north side, decorated with beautiful sculptures and bas-reliefs depicting chivalric scenes. Inside the three-naved interior is a splendid 12th-century tabernacle, as well as a bishop's throne, known as Elia's Pulpit, sculpted in the second half of the 12th century. The remains of St Nicholas are housed in the crypt, under the transept.

Bari's 12th-century cathedral was built on the remains of a Byzantine cathedral. It retains its elegant Romanesque shape and bell tower, but has been much altered and added to over the centuries.

The cathedrals of Bitonto, Ruvo di Puglia and Molfetta lie west of Bari and can be reached easily by public transport. **Trani** and **Barletta** are farther along the coast; Trani makes the better base – see the Trani and Around Trani sections for more details. If you have the time, take a look also at the cathedrals in **Conversano** and **Palo del Colle.**

The cathedral of **Bitonto** is a particularly stunning example of Puglian-Romanesque architecture and one of the most beautiful in the region. Built in the late 12th century on the model of San Nicola in Bari, it is dedicated to St Valentine. Note the carved animals and plants that decorate the capitals on the side walls. The cathedral has been closed for some time and is not expected to reopen in the foreseeable future because of work being carried out under its main pavement. While in Bitonto, spare a moment to inspect the 17th-century Chiesa di Purgatorio, near the cathedral. Above the main door people are depicted burning in purgatory, and to the sides are two large figures of Death, dancing in what seems to be delight at these poor souls' fate. You can get to Bitonto from Bari on the private Bari-Nord train line. From the station, walk directly ahead along Via Matteotti (about 1km) until you reach the medieval part of town. You'll see an Angevin tower and there are signs directing you to the cathedral, with tourist maps posted at various points.

The graceful cathedral in **Ruvo di Puglia** has a particularly striking façade and boasts a fine rose

tive marble columns and fireplaces, and the doorways and window frames are adorned with corallite stone. The castle is open in summer from 8.30 am to 7 pm Monday to Saturday, and from 9 am to 1 pm on Sunday. From October to March it opens from 8.30 am to 2 pm Monday to Saturday, and from 9 am to 1 pm on Sunday, although opening times can vary slightly at the whim of the guardians. Admission costs L4000.

Getting There & Away The easiest way to get to the castle is via Andria. A bus leaves Piazza Municipio in Andria at 8.30 am Monday to Saturday for the castle, returning at 3 pm, and the town is an easy trip by bus from Trani, or via the Bari-Nord train line from Bari. The Andria-Spinazzola bus (several a day) passes close to the castle – ask the driver to let you off at the right spot. See also the Getting There & Away section under Trani.

BARI

Unless you are planning to catch a ferry to Greece, Bari won't be high on your destination list. But it does offer a handful of interesting sights and can make a good base for exploring neighbouring towns such as Ruvo di Puglia, Molfetta, Bitonto, Altamura and even Alberobello and the trulli area. The city's Stop Over in Bari programme makes

window and three portals. The delicately carved central portal features columns supported by griffins, resting on (now very worn) lions, themselves supported by telamons. Ruvo is on the Bari-Nord train line. Otherwise you can take a Ferrotramviaria bus from Bari's Piazza Eroi del Mare (approximately every half-hour daily, except Sunday), which arrives at Cortugno, just off Ruvo's main piazza. The same bus also goes to Bitonto, Andria and Barletta. From the bus stop, walk to the left through the piazza and turn right into Corso Giovanni Jatta. Once you reach the park, turn right and then right again when you reach the tower, which is at the rear of the cathedral.

Rose window from the Cattedrale di Ruvo di Puglia

Molfetta is worth a stop not only for its impressively simple cathedral, but also for its largely abandoned, tumbledown medieval centre. Known as the Duomo Vecchio, the cathedral was started in 1150 and completed at the end of the 13th century. It has a stark, undecorated white façade flanked by two bell towers. The interior is a mix of Romanesque, Byzantine and Muslim architecture. The medieval quarter, or Borgo Vecchio, stretches out behind the cathedral and is in a state of great disrepair, although sections are being restored. Molfetta is on the main Bari-Foggia train line, about 20 minutes from Bari. From the station, ask for directions to Via Dante and the port (*il porto*), near which you'll find the cathedral at Via Chiesa Vecchia.

Altamura is about 45 minutes south-west of Bari and easily accessible on the Appulo-Lucane train line (see the Getting There & Away section under Bari). Its 13th-century cathedral was erected during the reign of Frederick II but was badly damaged by an earthquake in 1316, and later suffered some Baroque renovations when the beautiful medieval main portal and elegant rose window were moved from their original position to what had been the apse. The cathedral is in the old town's main street, Via Federico II di Svevia. From the train station, walk straight ahead along Viale Regina Margherita to Piazza Unità d'Italia and enter the old town through Porta Bari. Ferrovie Appulo-Lucane buses also connect Bari and Altamura, arriving in Piazza Santa Teresa. From the piazza, turn right and walk to Piazza Unità d'Italia. ■

it still more attractive for under-30s (see the Information section).

Capital of Puglia and the second most important city in the south after Napoli, it can be a frenetic sort of place – the peak-hour traffic is choking. It was an important Byzantine town and flourished under the Normans and later under Frederick II. Bari is a long way from the North Pole, but it is here that St Nicholas of Myra, otherwise known as Father Christmas, was finally laid to rest. His remains, contained in a liquid known as the manna (said to have miraculous powers), were stolen from Turkey in 1087 and interred in the Basilica di San Nicola, built especially for the purpose. It is still an important place of pilgrimage.

Occupied by the Allies during WWII, the port city was heavily bombed by the Germans.

Orientation

Bari is surprisingly easy to negotiate. The FS and Bari-Nord train stations are at the vast Piazza Aldo Moro, in the newer (19th-century) section of the city, about a 10-minute walk south of the old town (called Bari Vecchia). The main tourist office is off the same square. Via Crisanzio, a block north of Piazza Aldo Moro and running east to west, has a fair choice of hotels.

This newer part of Bari is on a grid plan. Any of the streets heading north from Piazza Aldo Moro, including Via Sparano, will take you to Corso Vittorio Emanuele II, which separates the old and new cities. Corso Cavour is the main shopping strip.

Information

Tourist Offices The APT office (☎ 524 22 44) is to the right as you leave the train station, just off Piazza Aldo Moro, and opens from 9 am to 1 pm and 4 to 8 pm Monday to Saturday (from October to April it's open mornings and Tuesday evenings only).

If you are under 30 you can take advantage of Stop Over in Bari, an initiative that aims to attract youth tourism to the city. The programme operates from June to September, offering a package that includes low-priced accommodation in small hotels or private homes, or free accommodation in the Pineta San Francesco camping ground; free use of the city's buses; free admission to museums; cut-rate meals; a free bike service; and information centres for young travellers.

Stop Over's main office, OTE (☎ 521 45 38), is at Via Nicolai 47, and there is an information booth on Piazza Aldo Moro and at the ferry terminal. The staff are helpful, speak English and have loads of information about the town. While only under-30s can take advantage of the package, anyone is welcome to seek information. Ring the above number to make a booking, or go to one of Stop Over's outlets when you arrive. OTE has a home page on the Internet, where you can get updated information. The address is www.inmedia.it/StopOver.

Foreign Consulates Some 26 countries have diplomatic representatives in Bari, including:

France
  Via Amendola 138 (☎ 521 00 17)
Germany
  Corso Cavour 40 (☎ 524 40 59)
Netherlands
  Viale Ennio 2 (☎ 536 92 22)
United Kingdom
  Via Dalmazia 127 (☎ 554 36 68)

Money There is no shortage of banks, many with ATMs that will accept Visa, MasterCard and Eurocheque cards. Alternatively, there are exchange booths at the main train station and the ferry terminal – watch the exchange rates. American Express's representative is Morfimare (☎ 521 00 22), Corso di Tullio 36-40.

Post & Communications The main post office is in Piazza Cesare Battisti, on Via Cairoli. Its counters are open from 8.20 am to 6.30 pm, Monday to Saturday. The postcode for central Bari is 70100. There is a Telecom office at Via Marchese di Montrone 123, open seven days a week from 8 am to 9.45 pm. Bari's telephone code is ☎ 080.

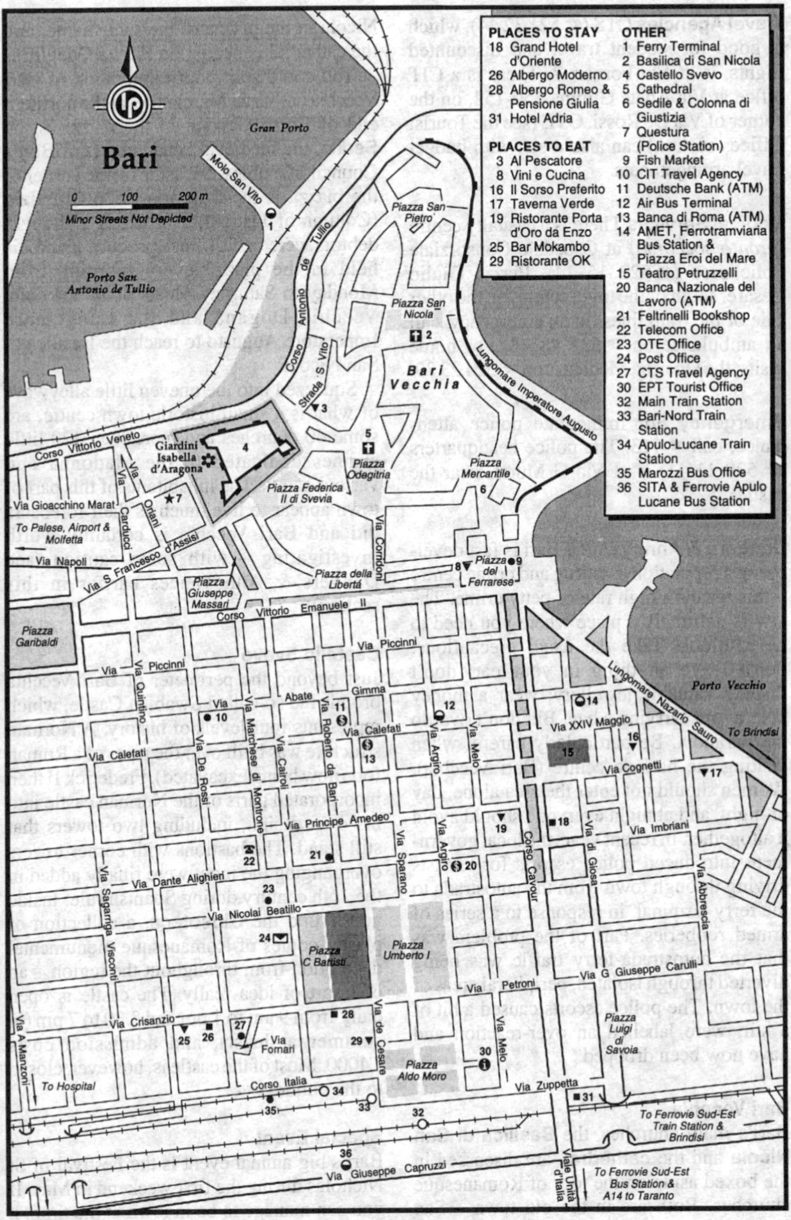
Bari
0 100 200 m
Minor Streets Not Depicted
PLACES TO STAY
18 Grand Hotel d'Oriente
26 Albergo Moderno
28 Albergo Romeo & Pensione Giulia
31 Hotel Adria
PLACES TO EAT
3 Al Pescatore
8 Vini e Cucina
16 Il Sorso Preferito
17 Taverna Verde
19 Ristorante Porta d'Oro da Enzo
25 Bar Mokambo
29 Ristorante OK
OTHER
1 Ferry Terminal
2 Basilica di San Nicola
4 Castello Svevo
5 Cathedral
6 Sedile & Colonna di Giustizia
7 Questura (Police Station)
9 Fish Market
10 CIT Travel Agency
11 Deutsche Bank (ATM)
12 Air Bus Terminal
13 Banca di Roma (ATM)
14 AMET, Ferrotramviaria Bus Station & Piazza Eroi del Mare
15 Teatro Petruzzelli
20 Banca Nazionale del Lavoro (ATM)
21 Feltrinelli Bookshop
22 Telecom Office
23 OTE Office
24 Post Office
27 CTS Travel Agency
30 EPT Tourist Office
32 Main Train Station
33 Bari-Nord Train Station
34 Apulo-Lucane Train Station
35 Marozzi Bus Office
36 SITA & Ferrovie Apulo Lucane Bus Station
Gran Porto
Molo San Vito
Porto San Antonio de Tullio
Corso Antonio de Tullio
Piazza San Pietro
Piazza San Nicola
Bari Vecchia
Strada S. Vito
Lungomare Imperatore Augusto
Giardini Isabella d'Aragona
Corso Vittorio Veneto
Piazza Odegitria
Piazza Federica II di Svevia
Piazza Mercantile
Via Gioacchino Marat
To Palese, Airport & Molfetta
Via Napoli
Via S Francesco d'Assisi
Via Carducci
Via Oriani
Piazza Giuseppe Massari
Piazza della Libertà
Via Corridoni
Piazza del Ferrarese
Corso Vittorio Emanuele II
Piazza Garibaldi
Via Piccinni
Via Quintino
Via Abate Gimma
Via Calefati
Via De Rossi
Via Marchese di Montrone
Via Cairoli
Via Roberto da Bari
Via Argiro
Via Melo
Via XXIV Maggio
Lungomare Nazario Sauro
Porto Vecchio
To Brindisi
Via Cognetti
Via Principe Amedeo
Via Sparano
Corso Cavour
Via di Giosa
Via Imbriani
Via Abbrescia
Via Dante Alighieri
Via Nicolai
Beatillo
Via Sagarriga Visconti
Piazza C Battisti
Piazza Umberto I
Via G Giuseppe Carulli
Via Petroni
Piazza Luigi di Savoia
Via Crisanzio
Via Fornari
Via de Cesare
Via A Manzoni
Piazza Aldo Moro
To Hospital
Corso Italia
Via Zuppetta
To Ferrovie Sud-Est Train Station & Brindisi
To Ferrovie Sud-Est Bus Station & A14 to Taranto
Viale Unità d'Italia
Via Giuseppe Capruzzi

PUGLIA

Travel Agencies CTS (☎ 521 32 44), which is good for student travel and discounted flights, is at Via Fornari 7. There is a CIT office at Via Abate Gimma 150-152, on the corner of Via De Rossi. OTE (see the Tourist Offices section) can also assist with budget travel arrangements.

Medical Services There is a casualty centre *(pronto soccorso)* at Ospedale Consorziale Policlinico (☎ 522 15 14), Piazza Giulio Cesare, south of the town centre, on the other side of the train lines. In an emergency, call an ambulance on ☎ 534 48 48. For home visits, the Guardia Medica is on ☎ 524 23 89.

Emergency For immediate police attendance, call ☎ 113. The police headquarters (☎ 529 11 11) is at Via G Murat, near the castle.

Dangers & Annoyances Bari is fast developing a reputation as a drug and crime centre – this means a high rate of petty crime. The city is definitely a place where you need to be cautious. Take the usual precautions: don't leave anything in your car; don't display valuable jewellery; wear a money belt; avoid carrying a bag. But don't overdo the paranoia. Be particularly careful when visiting the historic centre (Bari Vecchia). Women should not enter the area alone, day or night, and at night everyone should avoid it altogether. In recent years the local government introduced police escorts for tourists driving through town from the autostrada to the ferry terminal, in response to a series of armed robberies. Part of the problem was that the autostrada-ferry traffic was being diverted through isolated, peripheral areas of the town. The police escorts caused a bit of a stir, were labelled an over-reaction and have now been dropped.

Bari Vecchia

Bari's main churches, the **Basilica di San Nicola** and the **cathedral**, are discussed in the boxed aside on the tour of Romanesque churches. Both are in the old town – San Nicola in the piazza of the same name, and the cathedral is nearby on Piazza Odegitria.

You could start your exploration of Bari Vecchia at Piazza Mercantile, at the northern end of Corso Cavour. In the piazza is the **Sedile**, the medieval headquarters of Bari's Council of Nobles. Set aside in one corner of the piazza is the **Colonna della Giustizia** (Column of Justice), to which it is thought debtors were tied. A fresh produce market is held in the piazza every morning from Monday to Saturday. Head along Via della Vecchia Dogana and the Lungomare Imperatore Augusto to reach the Basilica di San Nicola.

Squeezed into the uneven little alleyways of what is a small historic town centre, are some 40 churches and more than 120 little shrines dedicated to the Madonna and various saints. The inhabitants of this part of town appear to live much as their forebears did and Bari Vecchia is certainly worth investigating – with some caution (see Dangers & Annoyances earlier in this section).

Castello Svevo

Just beyond the perimeter of Bari Vecchia broods the so-called Swabian Castle, which represents four levels of history. A Norman structure was built over the ruins of a Roman fort (now being excavated). Frederick II then incorporated parts of the Norman castle into his own design, including two towers that still stand. The bastions with corner towers overhanging the moat were finally added in the 16th century during Spanish rule. Inside you'll find the **Gipsoteca**, a collection of plaster copies of Romanesque monumental decoration from throughout the region – an odd sort of idea really. The castle is open daily from 9 am to 1 pm and 3.30 to 7 pm (in summer at least), and admission costs L4000. Most of the castle is, however, closed to the public.

Special Event

Bari's big annual event is the Festival of St Nicholas during the first weekend in May. If you can manage to be in town at the time, it is quite a spectacle. On the Saturday evening a procession of people in Norman costume leaves the castle for the Basilica di San Nicola, where they re-enact the delivery of the saint's bones to the Dominican friars. The next day, with a statue of the saint in pride of place, a procession of boats sets off along the coast.

Places to Stay

If you are aged under 30, take advantage of the Stop Over programme (see the Information section earlier). If not, there are several reasonably priced options. The HI youth hostel, the *Ostello del Levante* (☎ 530 02 82), is just west of Bari by the sea at Palese. B&B is L16,000 a night and a meal costs L14,000. The hostel closes from 20 December to 15 January. The No 1 bus goes there from outside Teatro Petruzzelli on Corso Cavour.

If you choose to stay in a hotel, it is best to pay a bit more for security. The following are all reliable. *Albergo Romeo* (☎ 523 72 53), Via Crisanzio 12, has singles/doubles for L50,000/80,000 and triples for L110,000, all with bathroom. In the same building is *Pensione Giulia* (☎ 521 82 71), where rooms cost L50,000/70,000 or L65,000/90,000 with bathroom and breakfast.

Hotel Adria (☎ 526 6 99), Via L Zuppetta 10, to the right of the station, has rooms which cost L40,000/70,000 without bathroom, or L65,000/95,000 with. Back on Via Crisanzio is the *Albergo Moderno* (☎ 521 33 13), No 60, which has rooms for L80,0000/137,000. The *Grand Hotel d'Oriente* (☎ 524 40 11), Corso Cavour 32, is a lovely, old-style hotel, with grand prices: L150,000/270,000, breakfast included.

Places to Eat

You will find it difficult to eat a meal more cheaply in Bari than at *Vini e Cucina*, Strada Vallisa, just off Piazza del Ferrarese in the old city (it's best to avoid the area at night; see the Dangers & Annoyances section). It's hard to get much more basic than its cave-like atmosphere and paper tablecloths, though you come close at *Ristorante OK*, Via de Cesare 19, off Piazza Aldo Moro. A two-course lunch with wine here costs around L15,000.

Taverna Verde, Via Cognetti 18, has excellent pizzas and very reasonably priced pasta and main dishes. A full meal will come to under L35,000. Nearby, *Il Sorso Preferito*, Via Vito Nicola de Nicolò 40, is a roomy old restaurant with loads of character. Again, you're looking at about L35,000.

Ristorante Porta d'Oro da Enzo, Via Principe Amedeo 12, off Corso Cavour, has excellent food for less than L30,000 for a full meal. *Al Pescatore*, Piazza Federico II di Svevia 8, is next to the castle and specialises in seafood and Puglian dishes. A full meal will cost around L50,000.

For excellent ice cream, head for *Bar Mokambo*, Via Crisanzio 72.

Getting There & Away

Air Bari's airport (☎ 538 23 70) is several km west of the city centre and services domestic flights. You can get there on the Bari-Nord train line. There is also an Alitalia airport bus, which leaves from a terminal at Via Calefati 37 and from the train station. Buses depart 80 minutes before flight times and you must show your plane ticket.

Bus Intercity buses leave from several locations around the town, depending on where you are going and with which company. SITA buses (☎ 574 18 00) depart from Via Capruzzi, on the south side of the main train station. Buy tickets at window No 1 at the train station.

Buses serve towns including Andria, Bitonto, Castellana and Ruvo di Puglia. Ferrovie Apulo-Lucane buses (☎ 572 52 01) serve Altamura, also from Via Capruzzi.

Ferrovie del Sud-Est (FSE) buses (☎ 553 02 74) leave from Largo Ciaia, south of Piazza Aldo Moro, for places including Polignano, Ostuni and Taranto.

AMET buses leave Piazza Eroi del Mare for Andria, Barletta, Molfetta and Trani, and Ferrotramviaria buses leave from the same piazza for Barletta, Ruvo di Puglia, Trani and Bitonto.

Marozzi buses (☎ 521 03 65) for Roma leave from Piazza Aldo Moro. The company's office is at Corso Italia 32.

Note: It is not unheard of for enterprising locals to organise private buses in summer to ferry tourists direct to Castel del Monte (see the Around Trani section) from Bari – check with the tourist office.

PUGLIA

Train As with buses, an array of train lines connects Bari with the outside world.

From the main station (☎ 521 68 01) national FS trains go to Milano, Bologna, Pescara, Roma and cities throughout Puglia, including Foggia, Brindisi, Lecce and Taranto.

There are also private train lines. The Bari-Nord line connects the city with the airport, Bitonto, Andria and Barletta, and the station is next to the main station in Piazza Aldo Moro. The Apulo-Lucane line links Bari with Altamura, Matera and Potenza in Basilicata. The station is in Corso Italia, just off Piazza Aldo Moro.

FSE trains head for Alberobello, Castellana, Locorotondo, Martina Franca and Taranto, leaving from the station in Via Oberdan – cross under the train tracks south of Piazza Luigi di Savoia and head east along Via Giuseppe Capruzzi for about half a km. You can also pick up an FSE train for Martina Franca from the main station on platform 10.

Car & Motorcycle Bari is on the A14 autostrada, which heads north-west to Foggia and south to Taranto and connects with the A16 to Napoli at Canosa di Puglia. Exit at Bari-Nord to reach the centre of town. The easiest way to orient yourself is to follow the 'centro' signs to the centre and then the 'stazione' signs for the main train station and Piazza Aldo Moro.

Boat Ferry traffic to and from Bari is busy year-round, especially to Greece, but also to Albania, Croatia and Egypt. All ferry companies have offices at the ferry terminal, accessible from the train station on bus No 20. Fares to Greece from Bari tend to be only marginally cheaper than from Brindisi, and the trip is two hours longer.

Once you have bought your ticket and paid the embarkation tax, you will be given a boarding card, which must be stamped by the police at the ferry terminal.

The main companies and routes they served at the time of writing were:

Adriatica
: (☎ 553 03 60), c/o Agestea at the ferry terminal or Via Liside 4. It has boats to Durrës on Monday, Wednesday, and Saturday (L110,000 deck class; L120,000 *poltrona* (airline-type chair); L155,000 for a bed in a shared cabin; L180,000 car).

European Seaways
: (☎ 523 04 20), Corso De Tullio 26 and at the ferry terminal, has two boats a week to Çesme (Turkey) via Greece from June to September (L180,000 deck class; L200,000 poltrona; from L240,000 to L530,000 for a bed in a shared cabin; L310,000 car). The trip takes 38 hours.

Jadrolinija
: (☎ 521 28 40), c/o P Lorusso & Co at the ferry terminal and at Via Piccinni 133. It runs a weekly ferry to Dubrovnik (L69,000 deck class; L77,000 poltrona; L116,000 for a bed in a shared cabin; L96,000 car).

Poseidon Lines
: (☎ 521 00 22), c/o Morfimare at the ferry terminal and 36-40 Corso de Tullio. Also has frequent ferries to Patras and Igoumenitsa (deck class L59,000; car L105,000). Poseidon has onward links to Israel and Cyprus. You can sleep in your campervan on the deck and pay deck class.

Ventouris Ferries
: (☎ 524 43 88), c/o Pan Travel at the ferry terminal, or at Via San Francesco d'Assisi 95. It has regular services to Corfu and Igoumenitsa (deck class L65,000; poltrona L100,000; bed in shared cabin L155,000; car L125,000) and to Patras (deck class L85,000; poltrona L115,000; bed in shared cabin L175,000; car L135,000). These are high season (roughly July-September) fares; they come down by up to L20,000 for the rest of the year.

Note: There is a L10,000 embarkation fee to Greece and L5000 to Albania and Croatia. It may be possible to get boats to Bar in Montenegro.

Getting Around

Central Bari is compact – a 15-minute walk

will take you from Piazza Aldo Moro to the old town. Useful city buses are No 20 from the train station to the ferry terminal, and No 1 from Teatro Petruzzelli to the youth hostel.

THE TRULLI AREA

Trulli are unusual, circular houses made of whitewashed stone without mortar, with conical roofs. The roofs, topped with pinnacles, are tiled with concentric rows of grey slate, known locally as *chiancarella*. Many trulli have astrological or religious symbols painted on the roof.

The trulli area, in the Itria Valley, extends from Conversano and Goia del Colle in the west to Ostuni and Martina Franca in the east, but the greatest concentration of these houses is in and around Alberobello.

Alberobello

This pretty town virtually exists for tourism these days but, with whole quarters covered with nothing but trulli, it is quite unique. It was declared a zone of historical importance in 1924 and many of the trulli are no longer private dwellings, given over rather to souvenir and wine shops, boutiques and restaurants.

The Pro Loco tourist office is just off Piazza del Popolo at Corso Vittorio Emanuele 15 in the town centre. The telephone code is ☎ 080.

A few km west of the town is the **Chiesa di Santa Maria di Barsento**, accessible only if you have a vehicle (or by hitching). Founded in 591 AD as an abbey, the small complex features one of the oldest churches in Puglia. It is now part of a farm, but the owner is proud to show tourists around the property – which he makes available for wedding receptions. Take the road from Alberobello to Putignano, and after 6km turn left into the road for Noci. After 3km you will see Barsento (signposted) to your right.

Places to Stay *Camping dei Trulli* (☎ 932 36 99) is just out of town on Via Castellana Grotte. Charges are L6000 per person and up to L18,000 for a site. In the town centre, at Piazza Ferdinando IV 31, is *Hotel Lanzillotta* (☎ 72 15 11), which has singles/doubles for L55,000/85,000. The town's top hotel is the *Hotel dei Trulli* (☎ 932 35 55; fax 932 35 60), Via Cadore 32, which is a complex of trulli. They are self-contained, with bathroom and living area, and the cost is L170,000 per person per day for half board.

Trulli are also available for rent through various agencies, with charges ranging from around L100,000 a day and L600,000 a week. For further information contact Agenzia Immobiliare Fittatrulli (☎ 72 27 17), Via Duca d'Aosta 14, Alberobello.

Getting There & Away The easiest way to get to Alberobello is on the FSE private train line (Bari-Taranto). From the station, walk straight ahead along Via Mazzini, which becomes Via Garibaldi, to reach Piazza del Popolo.

Grotte di Castellana

These spectacular limestone caves are among Puglia's prime attractions, and justifiably so. The series of subterranean caves, with their at times breathtaking formations of stalactites and stalagmites, were known as far back as the 17th century and were probably partially investigated in the 18th century. In the 1930s Italian speleologist Franco Anelli explored about 3km of the caves, and today tourists can follow his path with a guide. After descending by elevator to a huge cavern known as La Grave, you are taken on a tour through several caves, culminating in the magnificent **Caverna Bianca**.

The caves are open daily all year, from 8.30 am to 12.30 pm and 2.30 to 6.30 pm (only in the morning from October to March) and tours leave roughly every hour. You can enter only with a guide, but in the low season they are usually prepared to make the tour even for one person only. There are two tours: a 1km, one-hour trip (L15,000) that does not include the Caverna Bianca, and the full 3km, two-hour trip (L27,000). At the time of writing it was possible to make only the one-hour tour. Call the Grotte di Castellana information office (☎ 080-496 55 11) for further information.

You can reach the Grotte on the FSE train line (Bari-Taranto). The station is about 150m from the entrance.

Martina Franca

Founded in the 10th century by refugees fleeing the Arab invasion of Taranto, Martina Franca flourished in the 14th century after it was granted tax exemptions (*franchigie*, hence the name Franca) by Philip of Anjou.

The town is at the edge of the trulli area and you'll see few of the conical constructions here, but it has an interesting historical centre, with a medieval quarter and several specimens of Baroque architecture.

Orientation & Information The FSE train station is downhill from the historic centre. City buses go to Piazza XX Settembre and the entrance to the old town, or you can walk to the right along Viale della Stazione, continuing along Via Alessandro Fighera to Corso Italia; continue to the left along Corso Italia to Piazza XX Settembre. The tourist office (☎ 70 57 02) is at Piazza Roma 37, where you can get a map of the town and advice on accommodation. The telephone code is ☎ 080.

Things to See Next to the tourist office on Piazza Roma is the 17th-century **Palazzo Ducale**, a vast edifice now used as the municipal offices. Several frescoed rooms on the 3rd floor are open to the public (free entry).

From the piazza, follow the narrow Corso Vittorio Emanuele into Piazza Plebiscito and the heart of the historic centre. Of note here is the Baroque façade of the 18th-century **Chiesa di San Martino**.

Special Event The town stages the annual Festival of the Itria Valley in July and August, with concerts and opera. Information and tickets are available through the tourist office.

Places to Stay & Eat The cheapest accommodation options are both out of the town. *La Cremaillere* (☎ 70 00 52) is about 6km away at San Paolo on the road to Taranto. It charges from L70,000 for doubles with bathroom. *Da Luigi* (☎ 90 13 24) is about 3km out on the road to Taranto and charges L40,000/60,000 for rooms with bathroom. Both are accessible by FSE bus from Piazza Crispi.

In town all hotels are expensive, including the *Park Hotel San Michele* (☎ 880 70 53), Viale Carella 9, which charges L130,000/200,000.

For a meal, try *Trattoria La Tavernetta*, Corso Vittorio Emanuele 30.

Getting There & Away The easiest way to reach the town is on the FSE train line (Bari-Taranto). FSE buses also connect the town with Taranto, Alberobello, Castellana Grotte and Bari, arriving in Piazza Crispi, off Corso Italia.

Ostuni

This stunning town of stark, whitewashed buildings is set on three hills east of Martina Franca and about 40km north-west of Brindisi. The seemingly disordered tangle of narrow cobblestone streets, many little more than arched stairways between the houses, is strongly reminiscent of a North African Arab *medina*. Rising above it all in sombre brown stone is the 15th-century Gothic **cathedral**. Its distinctive cupolas, covered in green, yellow and white slate tiles, act like a beacon among the surrounding buildings.

Ostuni's AAST office (☎ 97 12 68) is in Piazza della Libertà, downhill from the cathedral in the newer part of town. It is open Monday to Friday from 9.30 am to 12.30 pm and 6.30 to 9 pm. The town's telephone code is ☎ 0831.

From Piazza della Libertà, take the narrow Via Cattedrale uphill to the cathedral. From the tiny piazza in front of the cathedral, turn right for a view across to the Adriatic, or turn left to get lost in Ostuni's whitewashed lanes.

Places to Stay & Eat Ostuni is an easy day trip from Brindisi, but if you want to stay, try the *Albergo Tre Torri* (☎ 33 11 14), Corso Vittorio Emanuele 298. It has rooms for L41,000/62,000. *Hotel Orchidea Nera* (☎ 30 13 66), Via Mazzini, near the train station, has singles/doubles for L65,000/90,000.

There are some excellent eating places in the old town. The *Osteria del Tempo Perso* is tucked away behind the cathedral. To find it, head up Via Cattedrale and, when you reach the wall of the cathedral, turn right through the archway into Largo Giuseppe Spennati and follow the signs to the restaurant.

Getting There & Away Società Trasporti Pubblici (STP) buses run between Ostuni and Brindisi about every two hours, arriving in Piazza Italia in the newer part of Ostuni. STP buses also connect the town with Martina Franca. However, the easiest way to reach Ostuni is on the main train line from Brindisi or Bari. The No 1 city bus will take you from the station into the centre.

BRINDISI

Travellers associate Brindisi with waiting. The major embarkation point for ferries from Italy to Greece, the city swarms with people in transit. What's more, there really is very little to do here other than wait. Most backpackers gather at the train station, at the port in the ferry terminal, or in Piazza Cairoli in between the two. If your budget extends beyond minimum rations, you could while away a few hours in a trattoria.

Settled in ancient times and taken over by Roma in 3 BC, Brindisi is a natural safe harbour that prospered under the Romans and retained its importance until after the period of the crusades. Invasion, plague and earthquake brought about decline, but today it is again a busy merchant and passenger port.

Orientation

The port is about a 10-minute walk from the train station along Corso Umberto I, which becomes Corso Garibaldi. There are numerous takeaway food outlets along the route, as well as a bewildering array of ferry companies and travel agents.

Information

Tourist Office There is a tourist information office at Lungomare Viale Regina Margherita 12, a short walk from the end of Corso Garibaldi and the ferry terminal (turn left once you reach the waterfront). It is open Monday to Saturday from 8.30 am to 12.30 pm and 4.30 to 7.30 pm. Another, the EPT (☎ 56 21 26) is at Via Cristoforo Colombo 88, close to the train station.

Money There are numerous exchange offices between the station and the port. Check the rates and choose the best. Otherwise, good old-fashioned banks abound. The Banco Ambrosiano Veneto next to the post office has an ATM that accepts Visa, MasterCard and some other cards, as does Monte dei Paschi di Siena at Corso Garibaldi 112.

Post & Communications The main post office is on Piazza Mercato, and opens Monday to Saturday from 8.15 am to 7.40 pm. The postcode for central Brindisi is 72100.

PUGLIA

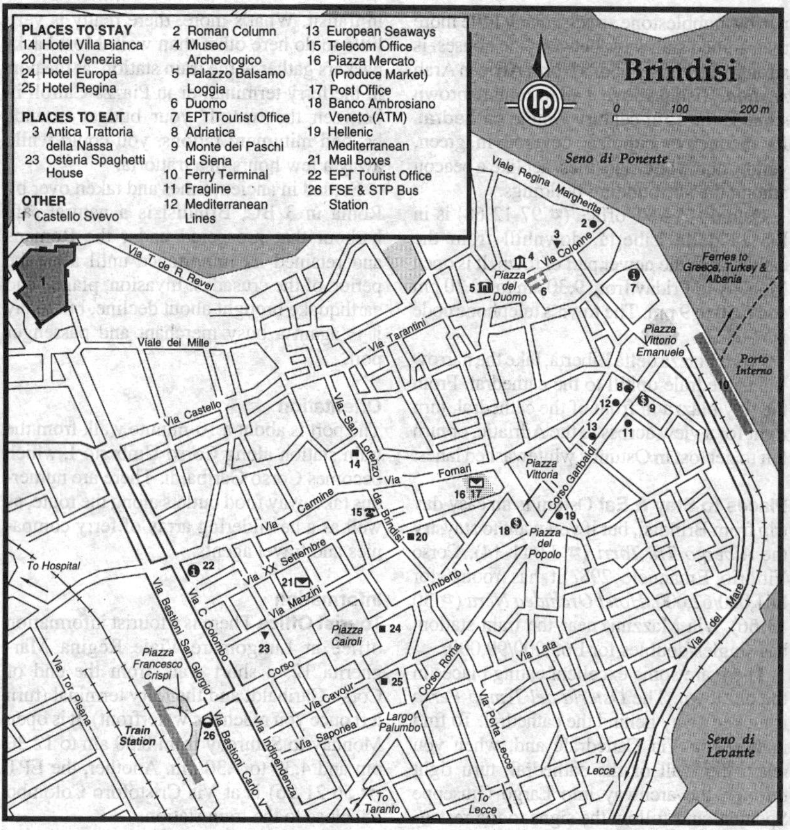

The Telecom office is at Via XX Settembre 6. It opens from 9.15 am to 12.50 pm and 3.30 to 6.30 pm. The telephone code is ☎ 0831.

Medical Services The public hospital, Ospedale Generale Antonio di Summa (☎ 51 05 10), is at Piazza Antonio di Summa, west of the train station, between Via Appia and Via Arione. The same number is good for ambulances.

Emergency For police attendance, call ☎ 113.

Dangers & Annoyances Brindisi is a thieves' paradise – try not to be an angel to them. Valuables should be carried in a money belt, and nothing of remote interest should be left unattended in your car. Women are advised not to walk through the town alone at night.

Brindisi is extremely busy in summer, so if you arrive by car, allow extra time for the eternal traffic jam around the port.

One word on taxis – you do not need one. Travellers arriving late in the evening are perfect victims for the line that, 'If you get a taxi, you might just make the last ferry'.

Keep your cool, and walk right down to the port (if your bags will allow it), as the roundabout ride in the taxi will probably take longer. When you arrive and the ferry has inevitably left, you will of course be offered further rides to hotels.

Things to See & Do

For the Romans, Brindisi was the end of the line or, more specifically, of the Via Appia. For centuries, two great columns marked the end of the imperial highway. One remains, near the waterfront (the other was removed to Lecce and only its pedestal remains). Tradition has it that the Roman poet Virgil died in a house near here after returning from a voyage to Greece.

A little farther in from the waterfront, the modest **duomo** was originally built in the 11th century but substantially remodelled about 700 years later. Next door is a small **Museo Archeologico**. Across the quiet little square is Palazzo Balsamo, an otherwise undistinguished building that sports a noteworthy **loggia**.

If you are hanging around Brindisi for any length of time, you might cast your eye over the **Castello Svevo**, another of Frederick II's monuments to militarism. Turn left from the train station and walk straight on to get there.

The town's main sight is the **Chiesa di Santa Maria del Casale**, 4km north of the centre. Built by Prince Philip of Taranto around 1300, it is a Romanesque church with Gothic and Byzantine touches. To get there, follow Via Provinciale San Vito round the Seno di Ponente bay. The road becomes first Via E Ciciriello and then Via R de Simone.

Places to Stay

The *Ostello per la Gioventù* (☎ 41 31 23) is about 2km out of town at Via N Brandi 2. B&B costs L18,000 a night. Take bus No 3 or 4 from Via Cristoforo Colombo near the train station.

Hotel Venezia (☎ 52 75 11), Via Pisanelli 4, has singles/doubles for L25,000/40,000. Turn left off Corso Umberto I onto Via San Lorenzo da Brindisi. The *Hotel Villa Bianca* (☎ 52 12 48), Via Armengol 21 (farther on along Via San Lorenzo da Brindisi), has rooms for L35,000/55,000, and doubles with bathroom for L60,000. The *Hotel Europa* (☎ 52 85 46), Piazza Cairoli, has clean, basic singles/doubles for L40,000/60,000, and L65,000/80,000 with bathroom. More upmarket is the *Hotel Regina* (☎ 56 20 01), Via Cavour 5 (take Via Cappellini off Piazza Cairoli and turn left), which charges L90,000/120,000.

Places to Eat

To pick up supplies for the boat trip, shop at the *Sidis supermarket* in Piazza Cairoli. A colourful fresh food *market* is held every morning from Monday to Saturday in Piazza Mercato, just around the corner from the post office. There are plenty of takeaway outlets between the train station and port.

For a proper feed, head for the side streets off this route. The *Osteria Spaghetti House*, Via Mazzini 57, near the station, has down-to-earth meals for around L20,000. The *Antica Trattoria della Nassa*, Via Colonne 49, has good meals for around L30,000.

Entertainment

Musical and cultural events are held in Brindisi throughout the year, including Estate Insieme in July and August. Get a brochure from the tourist office if you are in town for a while.

Getting There & Away

Bus STP (☎ 52 37 31) and FSE buses connect Brindisi with Ostuni and towns throughout the Salentine Peninsula. Most leave from Via Bastioni Carlo V in front of the train station.

Marozzi has three daily express buses to Roma (Stazione Tiburtina). The trip takes up to nine hours. Appia Travel (☎ 52 16 84), on the waterfront at Viale Regina Margherita 8-9, sells tickets.

Train Brindisi is on the main FS train line, with regular services to Bari, Lecce and Taranto, as well as to Ancona, Bologna, Milano, Napoli and Roma.

Car & Motorcycle Brindisi is easy to reach by road. Watch out for the superstrada exit for the 'porto' or 'Grecia' (Greece). In summer the port area becomes one big traffic jam, so allow plenty of time to board your ferry.

Boat Ferries leave Brindisi for Greek destinations including Corfu (nine hours), Igoumenitsa (10½ hours), Patras (approximately 17 hours) and Cefalonia approximately 16 hours). From Patras there is a bus to Athens. Ferries also service Turkey and Albania. The main companies are given below:

Adriatica (☎ 52 38 25), Corso Garibaldi 85-87 and at the ferry terminal, is one of the few companies to run ferries to Greece (Corfu, Igoumenitsa and Patras) year-round (deck class L100,000; airline-type chair L120,000; bed in shared cabin L165,000; car L115,000). The price is the same for all three destinations, while it can vary with other companies.

European Seaways (☎ 59 03 21), care of Discovery, Corso Garibaldi 96-98, has departures from Brindisi for Çeşme (Turkey) year round. Prices are the same as from Bari (see under Bari), starting from L180,000 for deck class.

Fragline (☎ 59 03 34), Corso Garibaldi 88, runs ferries to Corfu, Igoumenitsa and Patras from March to October. Its fares are among the most competitive, with deck class from L38,000 to L75,000.

Hellenic Mediterranean Lines (☎ 52 85 31), Corso Garibaldi 8, has boats from March to September, and offers a wide range of destinations in Greece. Its prices are similar to those offered by Adriatica.

Illyria Lines (☎ 59 02 05), care of Agenzia Ionian, Via de Flagilla 12, has three services a week to Durrës and four a week to Vlora.

Vergina Ferries (☎ 56 81 90), care of Angela Gioia Agenzia Marittima, Corso Garibaldi 83, operates boats to Patras from April to October.

Companies sometimes change hands or names, and many only operate in summer. When you get to Brindisi, shop around. Most agents can sell tickets for most lines – ask to see the company brochures if you are in any doubt about what you are paying.

Adriatica and Hellenic are among the most reliable. They are the only lines that can officially accept Eurail passes and Inter-Rail passes, which means you pay nothing to go deck class with Inter-Rail and L19,000 with Eurail. With both passes you pay a L29,000 supplement for an airline-style seat or L45,000 for a cabin bed (plus the L19,000 if you are travelling with a Eurail pass). If you want to use your Eurail or Inter-Rail pass, you may need to reserve some weeks in advance, particularly in summer. You can usually get a discount (of up to 20%) on the return leg if you buy it with the outgoing trip.

You must check in at least two hours prior to departure, or risk losing your reservation (a strong possibility in the high season). You have to pay a L12,000 port tax.

Several companies offer travellers with campervans the option of paying deck class and sleeping in their vehicles on the open deck.

Fares increase by up to 40% in July and August (prices listed in this section are for the high season – ferry services also increase during this period).

Bring warm clothing and a sleeping bag if you are planning to travel deck class. The airline-type chairs are packed into rooms that are generally noisy and smoky. Cabins range from four-bed shared arrangements without bathroom to first-class cabins with private services. All boats have snack bars and restaurants but, to save money, buy supplies in Brindisi.

Bicycles can usually be taken free of charge. At the time of writing, Adriatica's fares for other vehicles to Corfu/Igoumenitsa were L50,000 for motorcycles, L115,000 for cars, and L210,000 for minibuses and caravans.

LECCE

Baroque architecture can be grotesque, but never in Lecce. The style here is so refined and particular to the city that the Italians call it *barocco leccese*, Lecce Baroque. There is a more prosaic explanation for why the Leccesi went to such ornate lengths. The local stone is particularly malleable, but after it's been quarried it hardens – the perfect building and sculpting material.

A graceful and intellectual city, close to both the Adriatic and Ionian seas, Lecce makes an agreeable base from which to explore the Penisola Salentina.

It is worth whiling away a few days in Lecce. Certainly there are enough Baroque churches and palazzi to keep you busy, and the numerous bars and restaurants are a pleasant surprise in such a small city.

History

A settlement of ancient origins, Lecce was overrun in the 3rd century BC by the Romans, who named it Lupiae. While relatively little is known of this period, Lecce boasts the remains of an imposing Roman amphitheatre, which stand in the main square, Piazza Sant'Oronzo. The city passed to the Byzantines, Normans and Swabians, but it was in the 16th to 18th centuries that it really came into its own, when it was embellished with splendid Renaissance and, most notably, Baroque buildings.

Orientation

The train station is about 1km south-west of Lecce's historic centre. To get to the centre, walk straight ahead from the station and turn right into Viale Gallipoli, then left at Piazza Argento into Viale Francesco Lo Re. At the end of this street, turn left again to reach Piazza Sant'Oronzo and the city centre. Regular local buses run from the station to Viale Marconi (get off when you see the castle). From the STP bus station in Via Adua, turn left and walk to the Porta Napoli. Turn right and follow Via G Palmieri, turn left into Via Vittorio Emanuele and continue until you reach Piazza Sant'Oronzo.

If you have a car, the easiest point to enter the city centre is through the Porta Napoli, a 16th-century gate into the old city, just off the ring road. From the gate, follow Via Principe di Savoia and turn right into Corso Umberto I to reach Piazza Sant'Oronzo.

Information

Tourist Office The AAST information office (☎ 24 80 92) is in the Castello Carlo V, Via XXV Luglio. It is open Monday to Friday from 9 am to 1 pm and 5.30 to 7.30 pm, Saturday to 1 pm only.

Money Branches of the main banks are in Piazza Sant'Oronzo, including the Banca Nazionale del Lavoro at No 39, which has an ATM friendly to Visa and MasterCard.

Post & Communications The main post office is in Piazza Libertini, along Via Salvatore Trinchese from Piazza Sant'Oronzo. The postcode for central Lecce is 73100.

There is a Telecom office, with telephones outside, at Via Oberdan 13. The telephone code for Lecce is ☎ 0832.

Medical Services The public hospital, Ospedale Vito Fazzi (☎ 66 11 11), is in Via San Cesario, 2km south of the centre on the road to Gallipoli. For an ambulance, call ☎ 66 54 11.

Emergency For immediate police attendance, call ☎ 113.

Basilica della Santa Croce

Little can prepare you for the opulence of the most celebrated example of Lecce Baroque. Artists including Cesare Penna, Francesco Antonio Zimbalo and Giuseppe Zimbalo worked for 150 years through the 16th and 17th centuries to decorate the building, creating an extraordinarily ornate façade, divided in two by a large balcony supported by 13 caryatids and fantastic figures. The interior is more faithful to the Renaissance style but merits a look if you can recover from the impact of the exterior. Giuseppe Zimbalo also left his mark in the former **Convento dei Celestini**, north of the basilica and now known as the Palazzo del Governo.

Piazza del Duomo

Although it falls short of the Basilica della Santa Croce, the Baroque feast continues in Piazza del Duomo. The almost unassuming 12th-century **duomo** was completely restored in the Baroque style by Giuseppe Zimbalo, who was also responsible for the

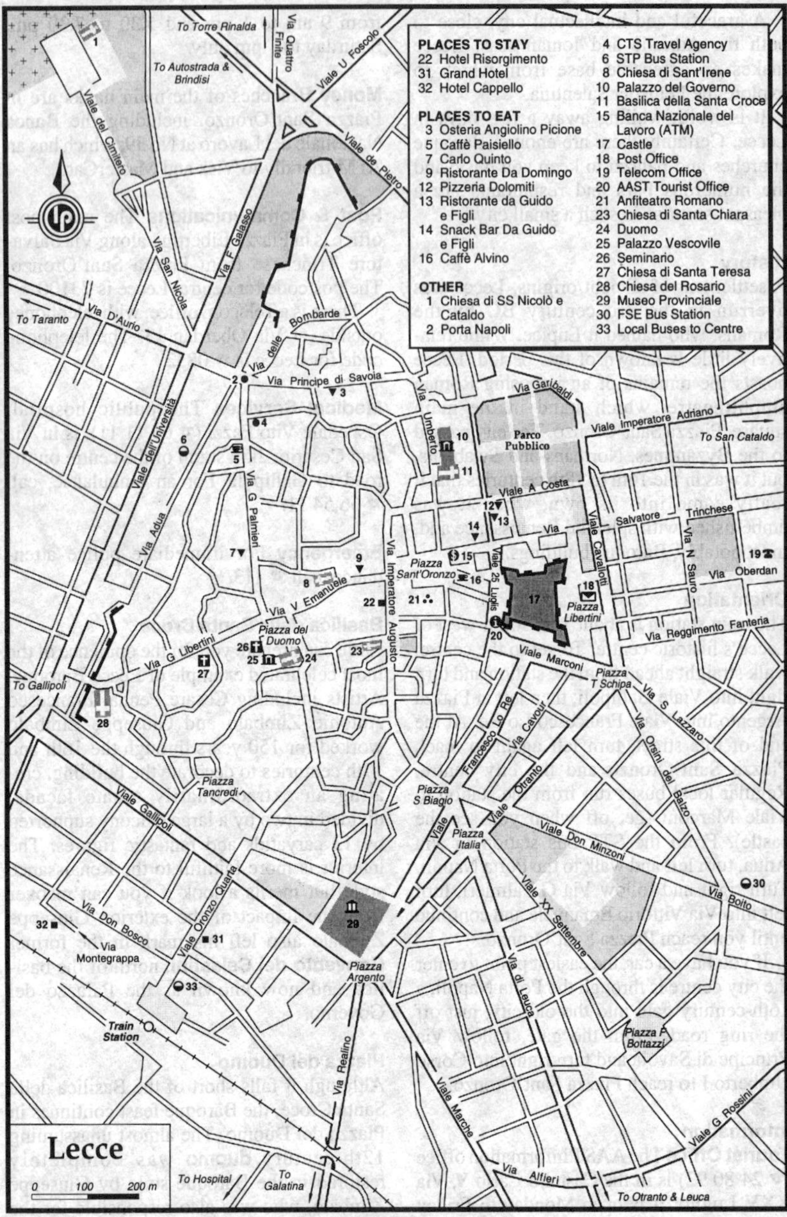
PLACES TO STAY
22 Hotel Risorgimento
31 Grand Hotel
32 Hotel Cappello
PLACES TO EAT
3 Osteria Angiolino Picione
5 Caffè Paisiello
7 Carlo Quinto
9 Ristorante Da Domingo
12 Pizzeria Dolomiti
13 Ristorante da Guido e Figli
14 Snack Bar Da Guido e Figli
16 Caffè Alvino
OTHER
1 Chiesa di SS Nicolò e Cataldo
2 Porta Napoli
4 CTS Travel Agency
6 STP Bus Station
8 Chiesa di Sant'Irene
10 Palazzo del Governo
11 Basilica della Santa Croce
15 Banca Nazionale del Lavoro (ATM)
17 Castle
18 Post Office
19 Telecom Office
20 AAST Tourist Office
21 Anfiteatro Romano
23 Chiesa di Santa Chiara
24 Duomo
25 Palazzo Vescovile
26 Seminario
27 Chiesa di Santa Teresa
28 Chiesa del Rosario
29 Museo Provinciale
30 FSE Bus Station
33 Local Buses to Centre
To Torre Rinalda
To Autostrada & Brindisi
Via Quattro Finite
Viale U Foscolo
Viale del Cimitero
Viale de Pietro
Via F Galasso
Via San Nicola
To Taranto
Via D'Aurio
Via delle Bombarde
Via Principe di Savoia
Via Umberto
Via Garibaldi
Viale Imperatore Adriano
To San Cataldo
Parco Pubblico
Viale dell'Università
Via G Palmieri
Viale A Costa
Viale Cavallotti
Salvatore
Trinchese
Via N Sauro
Via
Via Oberdan
Via Adua
Viale Imperatore Augusto
Piazza Sant'Oronzo
Viale 25 Luglio
Piazza Libertini
Via V Emanuele
Via Reggimento Fanteria
Via G Libertini
Piazza del Duomo
Viale Marconi
Piazza T Schipa
Via S Lazzaro
To Gallipoli
Francesco Lo Re
Via Cavour
Via Orsini del Balzo
Viale Otranto
Piazza Tancredi
Piazza S Biagio
Viale
Piazza Italia
Viale Don Minzoni
Viale Gallipoli
Viale XX Settembre
Via Boito
Via Don Bosco
Viale Oronzo Quarta
Via Montegrappa
Via di Leuca
Piazza Argento
Train Station
Via Realino
Piazza F Bottazzi
Viale Marche
Viale G Rossini
Lecce
0 100 200 m
To Hospital
To Galatina
Via Alfieri
To Otranto & Leuca

70m-high **bell tower**. Also in the piazza is the 15th-century **Palazzo Vescovile** (Episcopal Palace), which was reconstructed in 1632. Of note is its beautiful 1st-floor loggia. Opposite the cathedral is the **Seminario** (seminary), designed by Giuseppe Cino and completed in 1709. Its elegant façade features two levels of windows balanced by a fine portal. Cino also designed the well in the seminary courtyard.

Other Churches

On the way from the duomo to Piazza Sant'Oronzo, in Corso Vittorio Emanuele, you'll see another example of Lecce Baroque, the **Chiesa di Sant'Irene**, completed in 1639. Other Baroque churches of interest include the **Santa Teresa** and the **Rosario** (the last work of Giuseppe Zimbalo) in Via Libertini, and the **Santa Chiara** in Piazza Vittorio Emanuele. The **Chiesa di SS Nicolò e Cataldo** was built by the Normans in 1180 and rebuilt in 1716 by Cino, who retained the Romanesque rose window and portal. The church is along Via San Nicola from the Porta Napoli.

Roman Remains

Excavated below the level of Piazza Sant'Oronzo is the 2nd-century AD **Roman amphitheatre**, discovered in the 1930s. It's in reasonable condition, and open from 8.30 am to 4 pm (to 2 pm on Sunday). Admission is free. Virtually next door stands the **Colonna di Sant'Oronzo**, one of the two columns that marked the end of the Via Appia at Brindisi. After it was moved to Lecce a statue of the city's patron saint was placed on top of it.

Museo Provinciale

In Viale Gallipoli near the train station, this museum houses a collection of Roman artefacts and religious treasures from later periods. It's open Monday to Friday from 8.30 am to 1.30 pm and 2 to 7 pm. Admission is free.

Places to Stay

Cheap accommodation is non-existent in Lecce, but you could try campsites elsewhere in the Salentine Peninsula. Near Lecce is *Torre Rinalda* (☎ 38 21 62), near the sea at Torre Rinalda. It costs L10,800 per person and L14,000 for a site. You can get there by STP bus from the terminal in Via Adua. Another option is Lecce's only *affitacamere* (rooms for rent), *Goffredo Andreina* (☎ 30 46 54), Via Taranto 31, with singles for L32,000, doubles L60,000 and triples L80,000.

In town, try the *Hotel Cappello* (☎ 30 88 81), Via Montegrappa 4, near the station. Singles/doubles are L50,000/80,000 with bathroom. The *Grand Hotel* (☎ 30 94 05), near the station at Viale Oronzo Quarta 28, has rooms for L72,000/125,000 with bathroom and breakfast. *Hotel Risorgimento* (☎ 24 21 25), Via Imperatore Augusto 19, is just off Piazza Sant'Oronzo. Its very pleasant rooms cost L80,000/150,000 with bathroom.

Places to Eat

Eating in Lecce is a pleasure and needn't be expensive. There is a fresh produce *market* every morning from Monday to Saturday in Piazza Libertini. *Caffè Alvino* at Piazza Sant'Oronzo 30 is a good café for breakfast, and *Caffè Paisiello*, on Piazzetta Bonifacio IX, is another of the many fine cafés around town.

Da Guido e Figlio, Via Trinchese 10, is popular for a quick bite from 11.30 am to 3.30 pm Monday to Saturday. The restaurant of the same name around the corner at Via XXV Luglio 14 serves good local food at around L8000 for pasta and L10,000 for a main. For a decent pizza, eat in or out, try *Pizzeria Dolomiti*, Viale A Costa 5. A cheerful, moderately priced place with a garden dining area is the *Ristorante Da Dominga*, Viale Vittorio Emanuele 48. *Osteria Angiolino Picione*, Via Principi di Savoia 24, serves typical local food at around L15,000 for a full meal.

Entertainment

In summer there are numerous musical and cultural events, notably the Estate Musicale Leccese in July and August, and a series of classical concerts in August and September. Seasons of theatre and music continue throughout the year and information is available at the AAST office.

Getting There & Away

Bus STP buses connect Lecce with towns throughout the Salentine Peninsula, including Galatina and Leuca; they leave from the terminal in Via Adua. FSE buses for towns including Gallipoli, Otranto and Taranto leave from Via Boito, the continuation of Viale Don Minzoni, off Viale Otranto.

Train Lecce is directly linked by train to Bari, Brindisi, Roma, Napoli and Bologna. FSE trains also depart from the main station for Taranto, Bari, Otranto, Gallipoli and Martina Franca.

Car & Motorcycle Brindisi is 30 minutes away from Lecce by superstrada, and the SS7 goes to Taranto.

Getting Around

The historic centre of Lecce is easily seen on foot. However, useful buses include Nos 1, 3 and 4, which run from the train station to Viale G Marconi. Ask the bus driver to let you off near Piazza Sant'Oronzo.

GALATINA

The small town of Galatina, 18km south of Lecce, is almost the only place where the ritual of tarantism is still practised. Each year, on the feast day of Saints Peter and Paul (29 June), the ritual is performed at the (now deconsecrated) church dedicated to the saints.

Galatina is accessible by STP bus from Lecce.

OTRANTO

Founded in antiquity and long a base of Byzantine power in Italy, Otranto is the easternmost settlement in Italy. In 1480, the Byzantines' successors in Constantinople, the Turks, landed in Otranto and massacred the inhabitants in an event known to history as the Sack of Otranto.

Otranto makes a good place to start a coastal tour of the Penisola Salentina (Salentine Peninsula). It's obviously easier for those with their own transport, but travellers without wheels will find that local bus companies manage to link all the towns in the peninsula. Otranto itself is overrun in summer with Italian holiday-makers.

Information

The tourist office (☎ 80 14 36) has two branches: in the Castello Aragonese and at Via Rondachi 8 next to the basilica. The telephone code in Otranto is ☎ 0836.

Things to See

First built by the Normans in the 11th century and subsequently subjected to several facelifts, the Romanesque **cathedral**, has several attractions, including a restored 12th-century floor mosaic. Depicting the tree of life and other scenes of myth and legend, it is a masterpiece unrivalled in southern Italy. 'Rex Arturis', or King Arthur as he is more commonly known to Anglo-Saxons, is depicted on horseback near the top of the mosaic. An earlier mosaic from the 4th century, discovered 40cm below the surface, is to be put on display.

In the chapel to the right of the altar is one of the south's more bizarre sights. The walls are lined with glass cases filled with hundreds of skulls and other bones, the remains of the victims (they say there were 800) of the terrible Sack of Otranto. It is said that the town never really recovered from the slaughter. The cathedral is open from 8 am to noon and 3 pm to sunset. Next door is a small **museum**, open from 10 am to 1 pm and 3 to 5 pm.

The tiny Byzantine **Chiesa di San Pietro** contains some well-preserved Byzantine paintings.

The Aragonese **castle**, at the eastern edge of town beside the port, is typical of the squat, thick-walled forts you'll find in coastal towns throughout Puglia. Built in the late 15th century, it is characterised by cylindrical towers that widen towards the base. The castle is in the process of restoration.

Places to Stay & Eat

There are several campsites in or near Otranto. The *Hydrusa* (☎ 80 12 55) near the port is basic and cheap. Of the dozen or so hotels in the area, *Il Gabbiano* (☎ 80 12 51), Via Porto Craulo 5, is one of the cheapest at L46,000/L84,000 for singles/doubles. The *Bellavista* (☎ 80 10 58), Via Vittorio Emanuele 19, has rooms for around the same price.

There are fruit and grocery shops along Corso Garibaldi, on the way from the port to the town centre. A bright place for a meal or just a drink is *La Duchesca* on the cheery square in front of the castle.

Getting There & Away

A Marozzi bus runs daily from Roma to Brindisi, Lecce and Otranto, arriving at the port. Otranto can be reached from Lecce by FSE train or bus.

Ferries leave from here for Corfu and Igoumenitsa in Greece. For information and reservations for both ferries and the Marozzi bus, go to Ellade Viaggi (☎ 80 15 78) at the port.

AROUND OTRANTO

The road south from Otranto takes you along a wild coastline. The land here is rocky, and when the wind is up you can see why it is largely treeless. This is no Costa Azzura or Amalfi coast, but it gives you a feeling which is rare in Italy – that of being well off the beaten tourist track. Many of the towns here started life as Greek settlements and the older folk still speak Greek in some parts. There are few monuments to be seen but the occasional solitary tower appears, facing out to sea. When you reach **Santa Maria di Leuca**, you've hit the bottom of the heel of Italy, and the dividing line between the Adriatic and Ionian seas. Here, as in other small Salentine towns, summer sees an influx of Italians in search of seaside relaxation, and the Ionian side of the Penisola Salentina in particular is spattered with reasonable beaches. There are few cheap hotels in the area, but you'll stumble across a lot of campsites around the coast.

GALLIPOLI

Jutting into the Ionian Sea 50km north-west of Santa Maria di Leuca, the picturesque old town of Gallipoli is actually an island connected to the mainland and modern city by a bridge. An important fishing centre, it has a history of strong-willed independence, being the last Salentine settlement to succumb to the Normans in the 11th century. The Cooperativa Kale' Polis (☎ 0833-26 40 86), Piazza Imbriani, near the port, will help with information about the town.

The entrance to the medieval island-town is guarded by an Angevin **castle**. On the other side of the bridge, in the modern part of the town, is the so-called **Fontana Ellenistica**. Reconstructed in the 16th century, it is doubtful that any of what you see is truly Hellenistic. Through the maze of narrow lanes in the old town you will find the 17th-century Baroque **cathedral**, crammed with paintings by local artists. A little farther west, the **Museo Civico** contains a mixed bag of ancient artefacts, paintings and other odds and ends. A walk around the town perimeter is a pleasant diversion.

Should you want to stay, the pick is the *Pensione Al Pescatore* (☎ 0833-26 43 31), Riviera Colombo, in the old town. Spacious, modern rooms cost L55,000/90,000. You can also get dinner there for around L40,000. Otherwise, try *Trattoria La Tonnara*, Via Garibaldi 7, near the cathedral (around L35,000 a head). It is one of several restaurants in the old town.

FSE buses and trains link Gallipoli to Lecce. There are train stations at the port and in the modern town at Via XX Settembre.

TARANTO

In an ideally protected location, the port of Taranto has always looked to the sea. Founded around the beginning of the 7th century BC by exiles from Sparta, Taras, as it was then known, became one of the wealthiest and most important colonies of Magna Graecia. At the height of its power, the city was home to some 300,000 people. In the 3rd century BC it was conquered by Roma and its name changed to Tarentum, although Greek customs and laws were maintained.

Taranto is Italy's second naval port after La Spezia, and during WWII the bulk of Italy's fleet was bottled up here by the British. One of the city's more interesting claims to fame is that it is alleged to be the point where the first cat landed on European shores.

Orientation

Taranto can be divided in two. The old city is on an island between the port and train station to the west and the new city to the east. You'll find the more expensive hotels, tourist office and banks in the modern grid of the new city.

From the train station, take bus Nos 1,2 or 8 to the centre of the new town. It is not advisable to walk through the old city with a backpack or luggage.

If you arrive in Taranto by car, particularly from the east, you will find the drive from the state road into the centre of town a long one. Simply follow the familiar 'centro' signs and aim to reach Lungomare Vittorio Emanuele III, a good point of reference.

Information

Tourist Office Taranto's EPT office (☎ 453 23 92) is at Corso Umberto I 113, on the corner of Via Acclavio. It is open Monday to Friday from 9.30 am to 1 pm and 5 to 7 pm (4.30 to 6.30 pm in winter), and Saturday from 9.30 am to 1 pm.

Post & Communications The main post office is on Lungomare Vittorio Emanuele III, a short distance from the Canale Navigabile that separates the new and old cities. The postcode is 74100.

There is a public Telecom office slightly farther along the Lungomare. The telephone code is ☎ 099.

Medical Services The public hospital, the Ospedale SS Annunziata (☎ 98 51), is on Via Bruno. Follow the Lungomare Vittorio Emanuele III and turn left at Via de Noto.

Emergency For immediate police attendance, call ☎ 113.

Dangers & Annoyances Travellers need to be alert in Taranto, particularly in the old city. Carry all valuables in a money belt and be especially cautious at night in the old city. Women should try to be indoors before the evening crowds disperse.

Città Vecchia

Taranto's old city is in an extremely dilapidated state, although recent years have seen some efforts to renovate its palaces and churches. The **Castello Aragonese**, at the island's southern extreme on the Canale Navigabile, was completed in 1492. It is occupied by the Italian navy.

The 11th-century **duomo**, in the centre of the old city on Via del Duomo, is one of the oldest Romanesque churches in Puglia. Remodelled in the 18th century, its three-nave interior is divided by 16 ancient marble columns with Romanesque and Byzantine capitals. Its Cappella di San Cataldo is a fine example of Baroque architecture and is decorated with frescoes and inlaid marble. The whole cathedral is dedicated to San Cataldo, Taranto's patron saint.

Visit the **fish markets** on Via Cariati, where the morning's remarkably varied catch is on display. Taranto has been famous since antiquity for its seafood, in particular its shellfish.

Museo Nazionale

In the new city, the archaeological museum at Corso Umberto I 41 is one of the most important in Italy. It houses a fascinating collection that traces the development of Greek Taras and includes sculpture and pottery, as well as a display of magnificent gold jewellery found in local tombs. The museum also houses Roman sculpture and mosaics. It is open daily from 9 am to 2 pm. Admission is L8000.

Places to Stay

The city's only really cheap hotels are in the old city, on Piazza Fontana near the bridge leading to the train station. Women on their own should not stay in this area. The *Hotel Sorrentino* (☎ 470 74 56), at No 7, is reasonable and has singles/doubles for L45,000/60,000 with bathroom.

In the new city is *Albergo Pisani* (☎ 453 40 87), Via Cavour 43, which is safe and clean and has singles/doubles for L40,000/75,000. A little more upmarket, the *Hotel Plaza* (☎ 459 07 75), Via D'Aquino 46, has better rooms starting at L110,000/140,000.

Places to Eat

A fresh produce *market* is held every morning from Monday to Saturday in Piazza Castello, just across the Canale Navigabile. For a meal, try the *Trattoria da Mimmo*, Via Giovinazzi, or the *Trattoria Gatto Rosso* at Via Cavour 2. Both offer good food for around L25,000 a full meal.

At the *Birreria*, Via d'Aquino 27, you can choose between self-service, pizza or the full menu, and all prices are very reasonable. For fresh seafood at moderate prices, head straight for *Ristorante Gambrinus*, Via Cariati 24. A dish costs around L10,000, and with the fish markets just opposite, how can you go wrong?

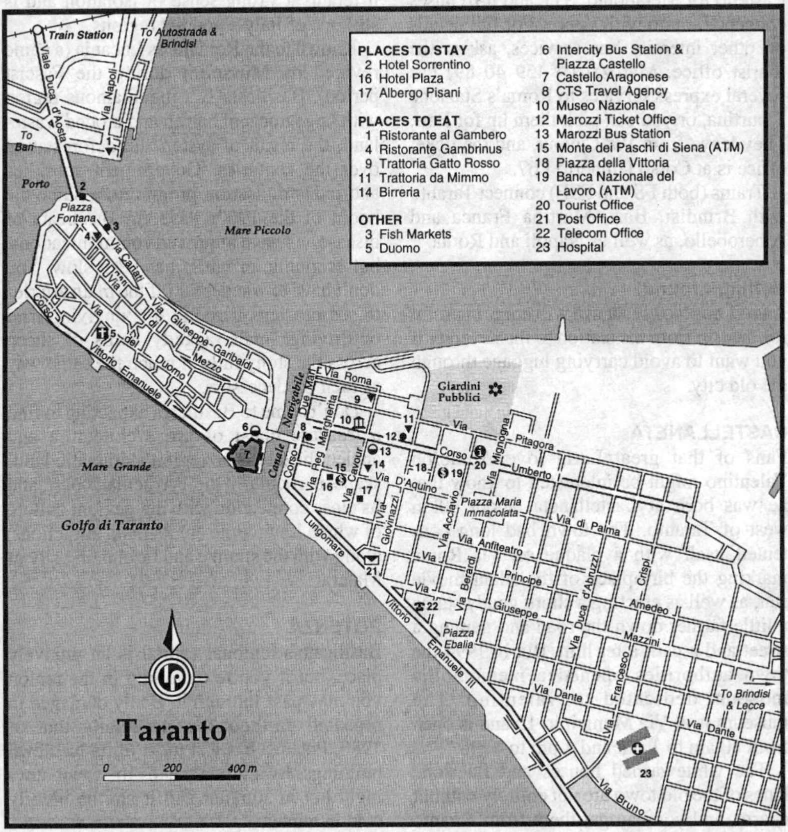

Ristorante al Gambero in Piazzale Democrate, across the Ponte Porta Napoli overlooking the old city, is the pricey version. You won't get away for under L50,000 for a full meal.

Getting There & Away

FSE buses connect Taranto with Martina Franca, Alberobello, Castellana Grotte and Bari (leaving from Piazza Castello), as well as Ostuni (leaving from Via Magnaghi, in the east of the new city) and smaller towns in the area. SITA buses leave from Piazza Castello for Matera (stopping at Castellaneta) and Metaponto. Chiruzzi buses also leave Piazza Castello for Metaponto. STP and FSE buses connect Taranto with Lecce. For full details on other intercity bus services, ask at the tourist office. Marozzi (☎ 459 40 89) has several express services to Roma's Stazione Tiburtina, or you can pick them up for Bari. They leave from Via Cavour, and the ticket office is at Corso Umberto I 67.

Trains (both FS and FSE) connect Taranto with Brindisi, Bari, Martina Franca and Alberobello, as well as Napoli and Roma.

Getting Around

AMAT bus Nos 1, 2 and 8 will come in useful for the trip from the station to the new city if you want to avoid carrying luggage through the old city.

CASTELLANETA

Fans of that great Latin lover Rudolph Valentino might be interested to know that he was born at Castellaneta, about 40km west of Taranto. The town had long contented itself with a plaque on Via Roma marking the birthplace of the silent movie star, as well as erecting a short, gaudy statue a little farther down the road and naming a street and a park after him. But in 1994 the town authorities opened a memorabilia **museum** dedicated to Valentino. The museum is at Via Municipio 19 and is open from 10 am to 1 pm and 4 pm to 6 pm.

The whitewashed houses and flagstone lanes of the old town are not entirely without charm, and you can get there from Taranto by the SITA bus for Matera (from Piazza Castello). It is also on the FSE train line.

Basilicata

This small and much neglected region stretches across Italy's 'instep', incorporating the provinces of Potenza and Matera and brief strips of coastline on the Tyrrhenian and Ionian seas. Basilicata is no longer the desolate, malaria-ridden land of poverty-stricken peasants so powerfully described by Carlo Levi in his novel *Christ Stopped at Eboli*, but it retains a strong sense of isolation and is still one of Italy's poorest regions.

Known to the Romans as Lucania (a name revived by Mussolini during the Fascist period), Basilicata is a mountainous region with large tracts of barren and eroded wasteland, the result of systematic deforestation over the centuries. Government subsidies and industrialisation programmes since the boom of the 1960s have rid Basilicata of disease and have improved communications, but economic progress has been slow. You don't have to wander far off the main arteries to see peasants working this ungiving land or driving small raggedy herds of sheep across the stony hills in much the same way as their predecessors.

Don't come to Basilicata expecting to find a treasure chest of art, architecture and ancient history. The region's dramatic landscape, particularly the Tyrrhenian coast, and its close connection with the peasant culture of which Levi wrote are its main attractions, along with the strange and fascinating city of Matera.

POTENZA

Basilicata's regional capital is an unlovely place, but if you're travelling in the region you may pass through it. Badly damaged in repeated earthquakes, especially that of 1980, Potenza has lost most of its medieval buildings. Its altitude makes the town cloyingly hot in summer and it can be bitterly cold in winter.

The centre of town straggles east to west across a high ridge. To the south lie the main FS and FCL train stations, and local buses make the run up to the centre.

Information
The APT office (☎ 2 18 12) is at Via Alianelli 4, just off the main square, Piazza Pagano.

The post office is at Via IV Novembre. You can find telephones outside the neighbouring INPS building. The telephone code is ☎ 0971.

The Banca Popolare del Materano, Via Vescovado 30, is open from 8.30 am to 1.30 pm and 3.15 to 4 pm.

Things to See
In the old centre of town a couple of modest churches remain, including the **duomo**, originally erected in the 12th century but rebuilt in the 18th century. North of the town centre is the **Museo Archeologico Provinciale**, housing a collection of ancient artefacts found in the region, but it has been closed for years and no-one knows if it will ever reopen.

Places to Stay & Eat
About the cheapest place to stay is *La Casa dello Studente* (☎ 44 27 08), Piazza Don Bosco, with basic rooms at L25,000/35,000. At the town's other small hotels you'll have to pay at least L50,000/70,000 for a single/double. The *Monticchio*, Via Caserma Lucana 32, is a reasonable restaurant, where a meal will cost about L20,000.

Getting There & Away
The transport system in the region is provided by so many different companies that it is best to check with the tourist office to find the best means to reach your destination. The following is a brief guide.

Bus Various companies operate out of several places; getting sensible information

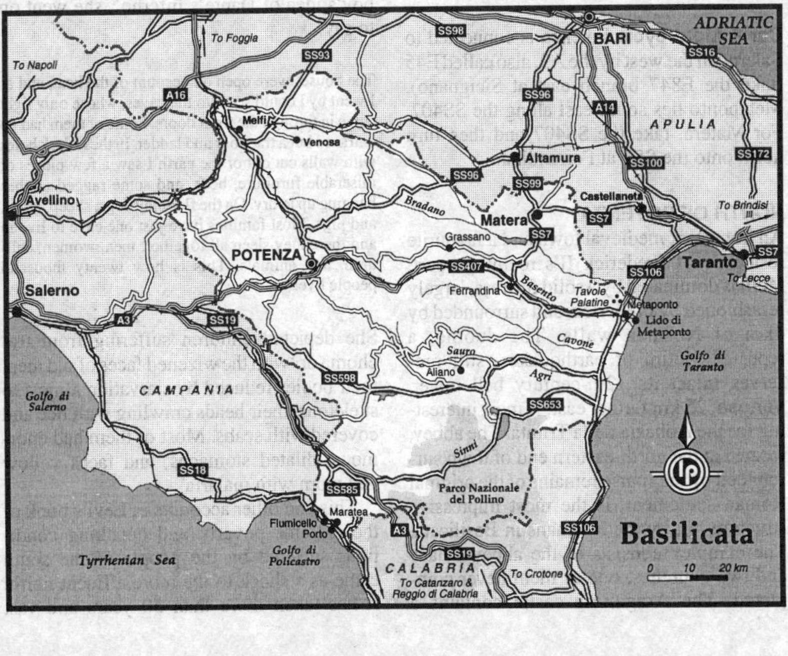

can be a trial. SITA (☎ 5 79 01) has an office at Corso Umberto I 69, and its buses also leave from Via Crispi. It has one service a day to Matera, and several buses a day to Venosa, Melfi and Metaponto. Grassani has two buses to Matera, leaving at about 6.30 am and 2 pm. Otherwise, Ferrovie Apulo-Lucane has a bus to Matera at about 5.45 am which goes from the Ferrovie Calabro-Lucane train and bus station, near the FS Potenza Inferiore station. The bus on this trip is not always able to catch the connection in Ferrandina.

Train To pick up a train on the main FS line from Taranto to Napoli and Foggia, go to Potenza Inferiore (☎ 5 46 30). If you want to go to Bari or Matera use the Ferrovie Apulo-Lucane at the Potenza Superiore station (☎ 2 35 16). There are regular services to Taranto, Metaponto, Salerno and Foggia (a different line), and occasionally direct to Napoli. To get to Matera, change at Ferrandina on the Metaponto line.

Car & Motorcycle Potenza is connected to Salerno in the west by the A3, also called E45 (take the E847 branch east at Sicignano). Metaponto lies south-east along the SS407. For Matera, take the SS407 and then turn north onto the SS7 at Ferrandina.

NORTH OF POTENZA

An important medieval town and a favourite residence of Frederick II's roaming court, **Melfi** is dominated by a solid fortress, largely refashioned by Frederick, and surrounded by 4km of Norman walls. The duomo, a repeated victim of earthquakes, still preserves intact its 12th-century bell tower. **Venosa**, 25 km farther east, is most interesting for the Abbazia della Trinità. The abbey, located at the north-eastern end of town surrounded by the sparse remains of the original Roman settlement, is the most impressive structure left by the Normans in Basilicata. The complex consists of the abbey palace and two churches, one of them never completed. The Aragonese castle contains a small archaeological museum. Melfi and Venosa can be reached by bus from Potenza.

MATERA

This ancient city evokes powerful images of a peasant culture that lasted until well after WWII. Its famous *sassi* – the stone houses built in the two ravines that slice through Matera – were home to more than half of the populace (about 20,000 people) until local government built new residential areas in the late 1950s and relocated the entire population. Probably the most striking account of how these people lived is given in Carlo Levi's *Christ Stopped at Eboli*.

Levi, a doctor who loved to paint and write, quotes the reactions of his sister to the conditions she observed while passing through Matera on her way to visit him in nearby Aliano, where he was forced to live in the years 1935/36 as punishment for his critical comments on the fascist regimen. Describing the stone dwellings of Sasso Caveoso and Sasso Barisano as 'a schoolboy's idea of Dante's Inferno', she went on to say:

> The houses were open on account of the heat, and as I went by I could see into the caves, whose only light came in through the front doors. Some of them had no entrance but a trapdoor and ladder. In these dark holes with walls cut out of the earth I saw a few pieces of miserable furniture, beds, and some ragged clothes hanging up to dry. On the floor lay dogs, sheep, goats, and pigs. Most families have just one cave to live in and there they sleep all together; men, women, children, and animals. This is how twenty thousand people live.

She depicted children suffering from trachoma or 'with the wizened faces of old men, their bodies reduced by starvation almost to skeletons, their heads crawling with lice and covered with scabs. Most of them had enormous, dilated stomachs, and faces yellow and worn with malaria'.

This and other accounts in Levi's book of the extreme poverty and appalling conditions suffered by the people of the south came as a shock to the more affluent north. It has taken more than 50 years and vast amounts of development money to eradicate malaria and starvation in Basilicata. Today, people are returning to live in the sassi – but now it is a trend, rather than a necessity. Many of the primitive stone dwellings are being renovated, with a new population of artists, writers and other 'interesting' types moving in.

Orientation

The centre of the new city is Piazza Vittorio Veneto, a short walk down Via Roma from the train station and intercity bus station off Piazza Matteotti. The ravine housing the sassi zone opens up to the east of Piazza V Veneto.

Information

Tourist Office The APT office (☎ 33 19 83) is in Via Viti de Marco 9, off Via Roma. It is open Monday to Saturday from 8 am to 2 pm and Monday and Thursday also from 3.30 to 6.30 pm, and can put you in contact with one of several groups that provide guides to the sassi. One such group, the Coop Amici del Turista (☎ 31 01 13), has an office in Piazza San Pietro in Sasso Caveoso (this office was temporarily closed at the time of writing, and the coop was operating out of Via Bruno Buozzi 99). The coop organises guided tours, in English too, for groups of one to four people for L45,000 an hour, L80,000 for two hours and L110,000 for three hours. For groups of five to 10 people the cost is L55,000 an hour.

If you would like to read about the sassi, an excellent book is *Sassi e Secoli (Stones and Centuries)* by R Guira Longa. It is available in English from Libreria dell'Arco, Via Ridola 36, near Sasso Caveoso.

Post & Communications The main post office is in Via del Corso, off Piazza Vittorio Veneto. The postcode is 75100.

The Telecom office, just before the post office, is open Monday to Friday from 9 am to 12.30 pm and 2.30 to 6 pm. The telephone code is ☎ 0835.

Money The Banca di Roma, Via Roma 57, has a fairly reliable ATM that accepts Visa and MasterCard.

Medical Services The public hospital (☎ 24 32 12) is in Via La Nera, south of the city centre. If you need a doctor to come to you, call the Guardia Medica on ☎ 24 35 38.

Emergency For police attendance, call ☎ 113.

The Sassi

The two Sassi wards, known as **Barisano** and **Caveoso**, had no electricity, running water or sewerage system until well into this century. The oldest sassi are at the top of the ravine, and the dwellings in the lower sections of the ravine, which appear to be the oldest, were in fact established this century. As space ran out in the 1920s, the population started moving into hand-hewn or natural caves, an extraordinary example of civilisation in reverse.

The sassi zones are accessible from several points around the centre of Matera. There is an entrance just off Piazza Vittorio Veneto, or follow Via delle Beccherie to Piazza del Duomo and follow the tourist itinerary signs to enter either Barisano or Caveoso. Sasso Caveoso is also accessible from Via Ridola, by the stairs next to the Hotel Italia.

Caveoso is the most picturesque area to wander around, and the most important rock churches are here, including **Santa Maria d'Idris** and **Santa Lucia alla Malva**, both with amazingly well preserved Byzantine frescoes. As you enter Caveoso, you might be approached by young boys wanting to act as tour guides. They generally don't speak any English, but for a few thousand lire will lead you to some of the more interesting sassi. You can take a formal tour too if you wish (see the Tourist Office section).

Town Centre

Recent excavations in Piazza Vittorio Veneto have yielded some remarkable discoveries. Beneath the piazza lie the ruins of parts of

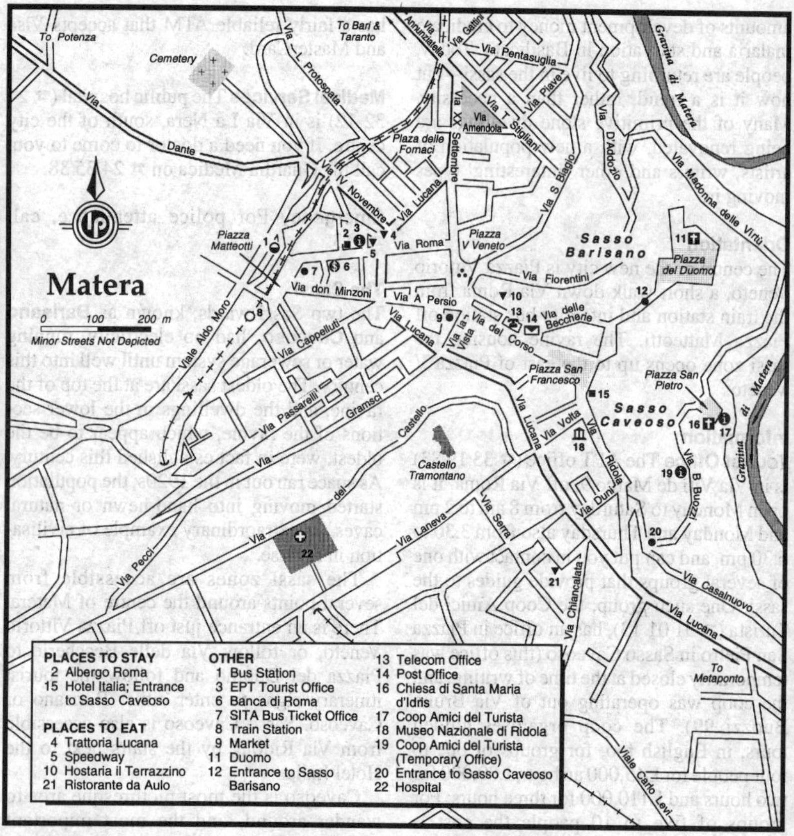

Byzantine Matera, including a rock church with frescoes, a castle, a large cistern and numerous houses. Access to the excavations is restricted.

The 13th-century Puglian-Romanesque **cathedral**, in Piazza del Duomo, overlooking Sasso Barisano, is also worth a visit.

The **Museo Nazionale Ridola** at Via Ridola 24 (☎ 31 12 39) is in the ex-convent of Santa Chiara, dating from the 17th century, and houses an interesting collection of prehistoric and classical artefacts. It is open daily from 9 am to 7 pm. Entry costs L4000.

Special Event

Matera celebrates the feast day of Santa Maria della Bruna (the city's patron saint) on 2 July. The festival culminates in a colourful procession from the cathedral, and a statue of the Madonna is carried along in an ornately decorated cart. When the procession ends (and the statue has been removed), the crowd descends on the cart in a ceremony known as the *assalto al carro*, tearing it to pieces in order to take away relics.

Places to Stay & Eat

There are few budget options here. Try the

Albergo Roma (☎ 33 39 12), Via Roma 62, which has simple but clean singles/doubles for L40,000/60,000. The pleasant *Hotel Italia* (☎ 33 35 61), Via Ridola 5, has rooms with bathroom for L120,000/150,000.

There is a *Divella supermarket* virtually opposite the APT office, or you can pick up supplies in Piazza Vittorio Veneto at the *Casa del Pane*. A fresh produce *market* is held daily just south off Piazza Vittorio Veneto. For a quick snack and a beer, try *Speedway*, Via Roma 50.

Ristorante da Aulo, off Via Anza di Lucana, is economical and serves cuisine typical of Basilicata. *Trattoria Lucana*, Via Lucana 48, has a good selection of vegetables and a full meal will cost around L35,000. Try the house specialities, such as orecchiette alla materana, a fresh pasta with a tomato, eggplant and courgette sauce. *Hostaria il Terrazzino* is in Vico San Giuseppe 7, behind the Telecom office. It has a good reputation and the typical local food is excellent. A full meal will cost L35,000 plus.

Getting There & Away

The bus station is in Piazzale Aldo Moro, near the railway station of Ferrovie Apulo-Lucane.

Bus SITA (☎ 33 28 62) buses connect Matera with Taranto (six a day), Potenza (leaves at about 2 pm) and Metaponto (up to five daily services to the beach in summer; only one in winter), as well as the many small towns in the province. Grassani (☎ 72 14 43) has two buses a day to Potenza at 6.25 am and 2.30 pm (1½ hours).

A Marozzi bus connects Roma and Matera at 8 am, 4 pm and midnight (6½ hours). Ask for tickets and information at the Kronos Travel Agency (☎ 33 46 53), Piazza Matteotti 8. SITA and Marozzi run a joint special service leaving directly for the northern cities of Siena, Firenze, Prato, Pistoia and Pisa via Scalo Grassano and Potenza. It leaves at 10.35 pm and booking is essential.

Train The city is on the private Ferrovie Apulo-Lucane line, which connects with Bari and Altamura. FAL runs regular trains and buses to Bari (L4400) from its station off Piazza Matteotti (☎ 32 28 61). To get to Potenza, you can take an FAL bus to Ferrandina and connect with an FS train, or go to Altamura to link up with FAL's Bari-Potenza run.

Car & Motorcycle If arriving from Bari or Taranto, follow Via Nazionale, which becomes Via Annunziatella, until you reach Via XX Settembre, which connects with Piazza Vittorio Veneto and the city centre. From Metaponto, follow Via Lucana into the city centre.

ALIANO

Not one of Italy's – or even Basilicata's – great tourist stopovers, this tiny hilltop village south of Matera might attract those who have read Carlo Levi's novel *Christ Stopped at Eboli* and have their own transport. When he was exiled to Basilicata during 1935-36 for his opposition to Fascism, Levi lived first in Grassano and then in Aliano. In the novel, he called the town Gagliano, and little has changed since he was interned here. The landscape is still as he described it, an 'endless sweep of clay, with the white dots of villages, stretching out as far as the invisible sea'.

Wander to the edge of the old village to see the house where he stayed, or you can try getting information at the Pro Loco office (☎ 0835-56 80 74), Via Stella 65. Two museums have been established in the town, one devoted to Levi and another to the peasant tradition of the area.

Although the town's inhabitants are no longer stricken with poverty and malaria, the wheels of progress have turned slowly and you are just as likely to see the locals riding a donkey as driving a car. For the extra keen, Aliano is accessible by a SITA bus that leaves from Matera, but you will have to change in Pisticci Scalo.

METAPONTO

Founded by Greek colonisers between the 8th and 7th centuries BC, the city of

Metaponto prospered as a commercial and grain-producing centre. One of the city's most famous residents was Pythagoras, who established a school here after being banished from Crotone (in what is now Calabria) towards the end of the 6th century BC.

After Pythagoras died, his house and school were incorporated into a Temple of Hera. The remains of the temple – 15 columns and sections of pavement – are known as the Tavole Palatine (Palatine Tables), since knights, or paladins, are said to have gathered there before heading off to the crusades. The columns were thought to have been the legs of their giant tables.

Overtaken politically and economically by Roma, Metaponto met its end as a result of the Second Punic War. Hannibal had made it his headquarters after Roma retook Tarentum (Taranto) in 207 BC and he is said to have relocated the town's population to spare it the fate of the people of Tarentum, who were sold into slavery by the Romans for having backed the Carthaginians.

Modern Metaponto's only real attraction is a sandy beach, Lido di Metaponto, that attracts loads of summer holiday-makers. It's about 3km east of the train station.

Information

In summer an EPT tourist booth (☎ 74 19 33) opens at Piazzale Lido, behind the beach. Metaponto's telephone code is ☎ 0835.

Things to See

You either have to be keen on ancient ruins or have your own transport to make traipsing around the sparse ruins worth your while. From the train station walk straight ahead for about 2km. Signposted to your right is the **Parco Archeologico**, and to the left is the **Museo Archeologico Nazionale** (☎ 74 53 27); it's a 1km walk to either. The park is actually the site of ancient Metapontum, where you can see what little remains of a **Greek theatre** and the Doric **Tempio di Apollo Licio**. The museum is a modern and well-presented collection of artefacts from the site. It is open daily from 9 am to 7 pm (officially at least) and admission costs L4000.

Once back on the main road between Metapontum and the museum, you have a 3km trek to the most memorable reminder of this ancient city-state, the **Tavole Palatine**. Follow the slip road for Taranto onto the SS107 highway. The temple ruins are located north, just off the highway, behind the old Antiquarium that used to house the museum.

Places to Stay

There are several camping grounds and the tourist office can point you to private rooms. Be aware that virtually nothing opens during winter. *Camping Magna Grecia* (☎ 74 18 55), Via Lido, is close to the sea. *Hotel Kennedy* (☎ 74 19 60), Viale Ionio 1, has singles/doubles for L60,000/80,000. The *Sacco* (☎ 74 19 30), Via Olimpia 12, charges about L75,000 a double.

Getting There & Away

Metaponto is accessible from Taranto's Piazza Castello by SITA or Chiruzzi buses, and from Matera by SITA bus. Metaponto is on the Taranto-Reggio di Calabria line, and trains also connect with Potenza, Salerno and occasionally Napoli. The station is 3km west of the Lido di Metaponto. If you don't want to walk, you could wait for one of the SITA or Chiruzzi buses to pass by on the way to the beach.

TYRRHENIAN COAST

Basilicata's Tyrrhenian coast is short (about 20km) but sweet. The SS18 threads its way between craggy mountains on the inland side and cliffs that drop away into the sea to the west, making for one of the prettiest drives on the Tyrrhenian coast – but one that curiously peters out virtually as soon as you leave Basilicata in either direction.

About halfway between the Campanian and Calabrian frontiers and a short, steep ride up from the coast lies the small town of **Maratea**. Watched over by a 22m-tall statue of Christ (at the Santuario di San Biagio), Maratea has been done no harm by tourism. The high part of town, as so often along the south Tyrrhenian coast, forms the historic core, below which has spread an as yet unobtrusive extension.

Maratea is the administrative centre of a series of coastal villages, the prettiest of which are probably **Fiumicello** and **Porto**. Most of the accommodation is down in these coastal settlements, and each has at least one small protected beach.

The AAST office (☎ 87 69 08) is at Piazza Gesù 32 in Maratea. A booth (☎ 87 60 50) also opens in Porto during summer. The telephone code in Maratea is ☎ 0973.

One of the cheapest places is the fairly simple *Albergo Fiorella* (☎ 87 69 21) in Fiumicello. The *Villa degli Aranci* (☎ 87 63 44) is prettier, but rooms start at about L85,000/100,000. Half board is compulsory in summer, at L80,000 per person.

SITA buses link Maratea to Potenza. They also run up the coast to Sapri, in Campania, and south to Praia a Mare, in Calabria. Non-express trains on the Salerno-Reggio di Calabria line call in at Maratea train station, below the town, and several of the coastal settlements. Local buses connect the coastal towns and Maratea train station with the old centre of Maratea.

Calabria

With some of the country's better beaches and a brooding, mountainous interior, the 'toe' of the Italian boot represents for many travellers little more than a train ride down the Tyrrhenian coast on the way to or from Sicilia. Although it may not loom large on the average visitor's list of Italian destinations, Calabria is worth a little exploration. The beaches are among the cleanest in Italy and lovers of ancient history can explore the sparse reminders of the civilisation of Magna Graecia. The downside is the spread of ugly holiday villages along parts of the Ionian and Tyrrhenian coasts, and sometimes you have to settle for pebbles rather than sand. Along the roads heading inland you'll encounter some magnificent natural beauty and, every now and then, picturesque and long ignored medieval villages huddled on hilltops.

Sparsely inhabited in Paleolithic times, the area was first settled by Greeks from Sicilia who founded a colony at what is now modern Reggio di Calabria. The process of colonisation spread along the Ionian coast, with Sibari and Crotone the most important settlements. Siding with Hannibal against Roma turned out to be a mistake, and with the general's departure for Carthage in 202 BC, the cities of Magna Graecia came under Roma's permanent control. Later, as Roma faded away, the Byzantines took superficial control. Their ineffectual rule, and the appearance of Arab raiders (the so-called Saracens) off the coast, favoured a decline in the area which was never really arrested; Calabria continued to be a backwater for a succession of Norman, Swabian, Aragonese, Spanish and Bourbon rulers based in Napoli. Although the brief Napoleonic incursion at the end of the 18th century and the arrival of Garibaldi and Italian unification inspired hope for change, Calabria remained chained to a virtually feudal treadmill.

The province's history of misery has sparked numerous revolts. It also caused, from the 1870s onwards, the rise of highway robbery, which has slowly grown into pervasive organised crime. For many, the only answer has been to get out, and for at least a century, Calabria has seen its young people emigrate to the north or abroad in search of work.

While mostly tacky, the many tourist villages along the coast can offer excellent package deals and should not be rejected out of hand. There are plenty of camping grounds along the coast, but with the exception of some of the more popular coastal towns, budget accommodation is thin on the ground, and much of it closes from October to April. Where possible, arm yourself with provincial hotel lists from tourist offices before venturing off into the backblocks. If you plan to visit in summer, book in advance or at least try to turn up early.

The food is simple, peasant fare and relies heavily on what is produced in the region. It

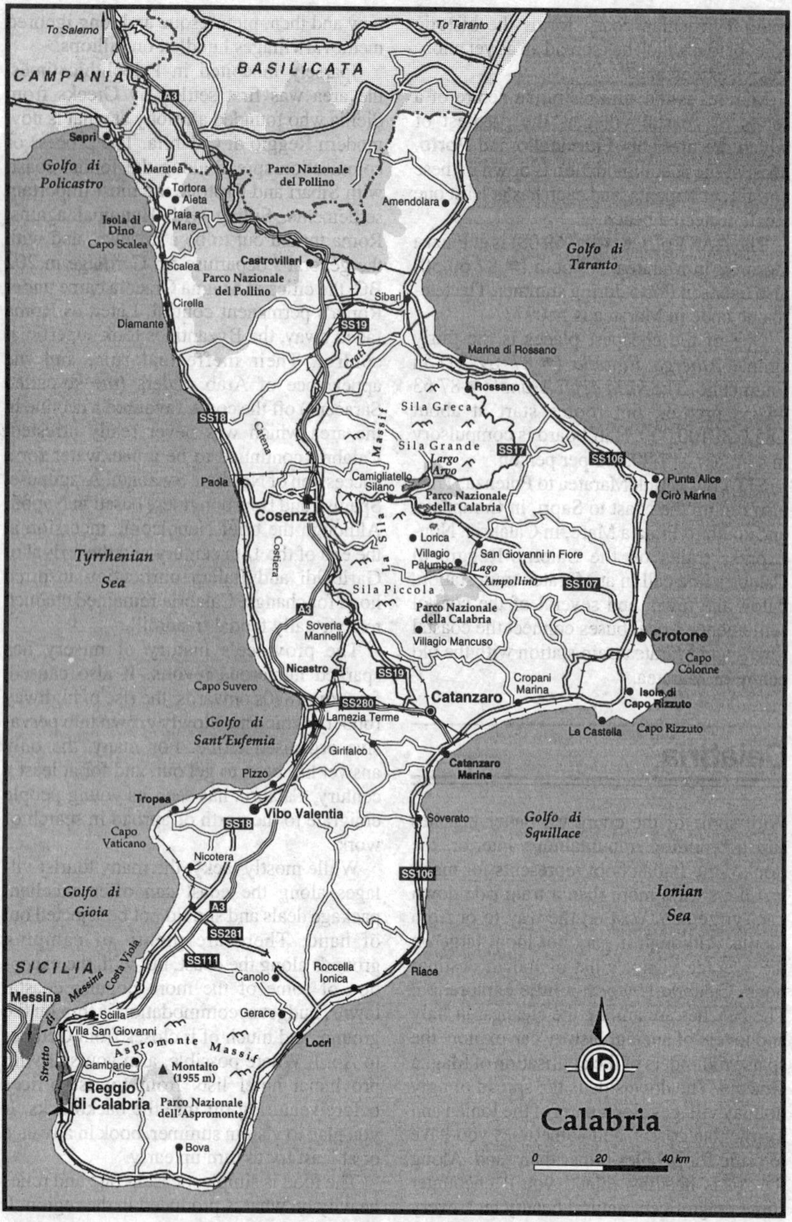
To Salerno
To Taranto
CAMPANIA
BASILICATA
A3
Sapri
Golfo di Policastro
Maratea
Tortora
Aieta
Parco Nazionale del Pollino
Amendolara
Isola di Dino
Praia a Mare
Capo Scalea
Scalea
Castrovillari
Parco Nazionale del Pollino
Golfo di Taranto
Cirella
Sibari
Diamante
SS19
Crati
Marina di Rossano
Rossano
Sila Greca
SS18
Catena
Massif
Sila Grande
SS17
SS106
Largo Arvo
Punta Alice
Cirò Marina
Paola
Camigliatello Silano
Parco Nazionale della Calabria
Cosenza
La Sila
Lorica
Costiera
Tyrrhenian Sea
Villagio Palumbo
San Giovanni in Fiore
Lago Ampollino
SS107
Sila Piccola
A3
Parco Nazionale della Calabria
Soveria Mannelli
Villagio Mancuso
Crotone
Capo Colonne
Nicastro
SS19
Cropani Marina
Capo Suvero
Catanzaro
Isola di Capo Rizzuto
SS280
Lamezia Terme
Golfo di Sant'Eufemia
La Castella
Capo Rizzuto
Girifalco
Catanzaro Marina
Pizzo
Tropea
Vibo Valentia
SS18
Soverato
Golfo di Squillace
Capo Vaticano
Nicotera
SS106
Golfo di Gioia
Ionian Sea
A3
SS281
SS111
SICILIA
Costa Viola
Roccella Ionica
Canolo
Riace
Messina
Stretto di Messina
Scilla
Gerace
Villa San Giovanni
Aspromonte Massif
Locri
Gambarie
Montalto (1955 m)
Reggio di Calabria
Parco Nazionale dell'Aspromonte
Bova
Calabria
0
20
40 km

would not be unusual to eat in a restaurant where the owners themselves have produced the salami, cheese and vegetables and the grapes for the wine.

You can get pretty much anywhere by public transport, but it is not always fast or easy. The national FS railway operates between the main cities and around the coast. The private Ferrovie della Calabria links Catanzaro and Cosenza and serves smaller towns between the two by train and bus. Blue provincial buses, belonging to a plethora of small private companies, connect most towns – sooner or later.

CATANZARO

Long the hub of Calabria, Catanzaro replaced Reggio di Calabria as the regional capital in the early 1970s. Despite this, it is overlooked by tourists – and it is not difficult to see why. Catanzaro is set atop a rocky peak 13km in from the Ionian coast on the way north to La Sila. It can be pleasant enough wandering the heart of the old city, but there is precious little to draw you there apart from the town's transport connections.

Evidence of the city's Byzantine origins is virtually non-existent. Positioned to deter raiders and prevent the spread of malaria, Catanzaro has suffered repeatedly from a different curse – earthquake. As a result of the severe jolts of 1688, 1783 and 1832 there's nothing much of historical interest left standing.

Orientation

The train station for the private Calabrian railway, Ferrovie della Calabria, is just north of the city centre. Walk south along Via Indipendenza for Piazza Matteotti, the main square. Corso Mazzini takes you farther south through the middle of old Catanzaro. The FS station is about 2km south and downhill from the centre – you'll need to take a local bus.

Information

The APT administration office (☎ 85 11) in the Galleria Mancuso, just north of Piazza Prefettura, can help with information, but you're better off going to the APT office on Piazza Prefettura (☎ 74 17 64). Both open from 8 am to 1.30 pm Monday to Friday and 3 to 5.30 pm on Monday and Wednesday afternoons.

The main post office, in Piazza Prefettura, opens from 8.30 am to 5 pm Monday to Saturday. The city's postcode is 88100. The public telephone office is on Via Buccarelli, and the telephone code is ☎ 0961.

There is a CTS travel agency (☎ 72 45 30) at Via E Scalfaro 5.

The main hospital (☎ 72 67 19) is on Viale Pio X, north of the Ferrovie della Calabria train station. In a police emergency, call ☎ 113, or contact the police headquarters (☎ 72 73 46) in Piazza Cavour.

CALABRIA

Things to See

Wander south along Corso Mazzini for the older and more interesting parts of the city. Of its churches, the Baroque **Basilica dell'Immacolata** is the most impressive. The **duomo**, farther south, was almost completely rebuilt after the last war and is quite ordinary. The **Chiesa di San Domenico** (also known as the Chiesa del Rosario) nearby contains several attractive Renaissance paintings by comparative unknowns.

The city's **Museo Provinciale** is inside the Villa Trieste, a large garden on the eastern edge of town near Via Jannoni. The museum has a large collection of coins and some local archaeological finds, but has been closed for some time and seems set to stay that way. **Catanzaro Marina**, also known as Catanzaro Lido, is the city's access to the sea and one of the Ionian coast's major resorts. Although heavily developed, it is less tacky than others and the beaches stretching off in both directions are among the best on the coast.

Places to Stay & Eat

If you are coming from Cosenza, the HI youth hostel *La Pineta* (☎ 0968-66 21 15) is at Soveria Mannelli on the SS19 inland Catanzaro-Cosenza road, 43km north of Catanzaro. It is set in woodlands within striking distance of La Sila, and B&B costs

L19,500. It's 4km from the nearest train station but buses between Cosenza and Catanzaro can drop you nearby.

Catanzaro has few hotels and they are generally expensive. The *Albergo Belvedere* (☎ 72 05 91), Via Italia 33, has rooms from L50,000/90,000. It's in a decent location if you can get a room with a view. The *Grand Hotel* (☎ 70 12 56), Piazza Matteotti, has bland but comfortable rooms for L160,000/190,000 with breakfast.

The best bets for cheap food are the city's bars, where you can grab a cheap sandwich. The self-service *Lo Stuzzichino*, Piazza Matteotti, has pasta from about L6000. More substantial meals can be found at *Ristorante La Griglia*, at Via Poerio 26, off Piazza Garibaldi. *Ristorante la Corteccia*, on Via Indipendenza 30, is in much the same league, while *Il Ghiottone*, across the road, is not a bad bar and pizzeria.

Getting There & Away

Air The airport, Sant'Eufemia Lamezia, is at Lamezia Terme (☎ 0968-41 41 11), about 35km west of Catanzaro. It links the region with major Italian cities and a small number

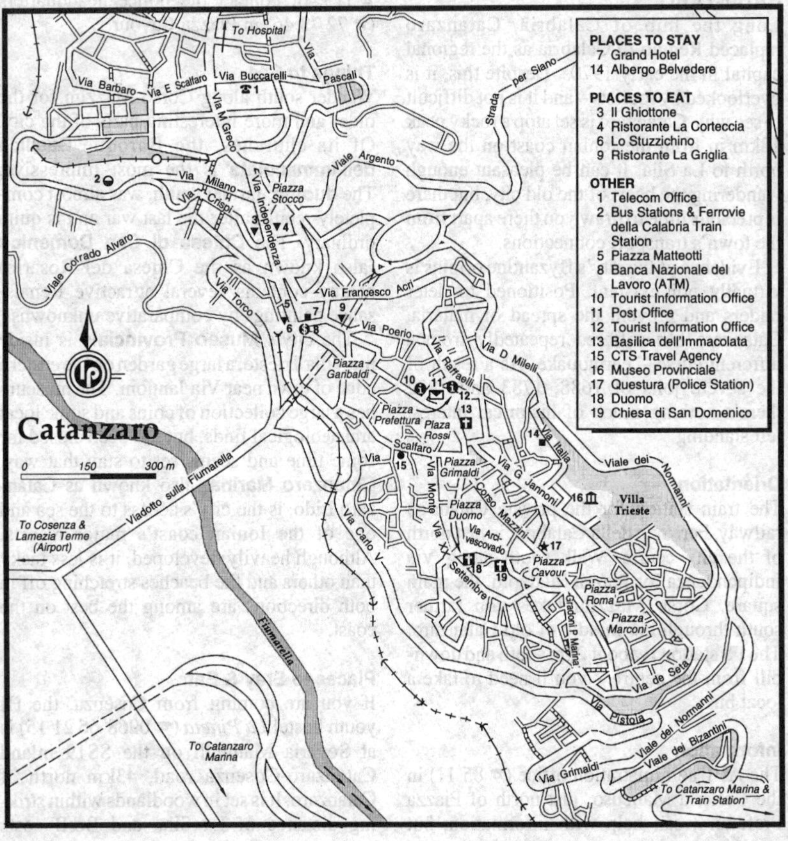

of flights serve international destinations like Munich, London and Frankfurt.

Bus FC buses depart from the Ferrovie della Calabria train station to towns throughout the province, Catanzaro Marina, other cities on the Ionian coast and into La Sila. Various other small companies have terminals throughout the town.

Train The FC railway runs trains between the city and Catanzaro Marina (also known as Catanzaro Lido), where you can pick up an FS train to Reggio di Calabria or north-east along the Ionian coast. From the Catanzaro city FS station, trains connect with Lamezia Terme, Reggio di Calabria, Cosenza and even Napoli, Roma, Milano and Torino.

Car & Motorcycle By car, leave the A3 autostrada at Lamezia Terme and head east on the SS280 for the city. If approaching from along the Ionian coast, follow the 'centro' signs off the SS106.

Getting Around

City buses connect the FS train station with the city centre, including Nos 10, 11, 12 and 13. The Circolare Lido line connects the city centre, the FS train station and Catanzaro Marina.

IONIAN COAST

Wilder and less crowded than the Tyrrhenian seaboard, the Ionian coast nevertheless has its fair share of tourist villages – unappealing resorts that fill up in the summer months. There is something brooding and resistant to outsiders about this territory, especially if you venture into the hills and valleys away from the coast. Much of the land near the sea is under cultivation, interspersed with ramshackle villages or, more often, the growing blight of half-built housing and holiday villas.

Most of the tourist villages, hotels and campsites close for up to eight months of the year, so finding accommodation can be tricky. Add to that the woes of travelling on the slow trains or infrequent buses along the coast and the area might start to seem unappealing. Don't despair. There are dozens of small hill towns to explore and some of the beaches are quite good. You can get a list of camping grounds and hotels from tourist offices in the provincial capitals. Your own vehicle is a decided advantage, but you *can* get to most places by public transport.

Locri

Locri is a small, modern and unimpressive town about 100km south of Catanzaro, but it's a potential base for exploration into the hills. The IAT office (☎ 0964-2 96 00), Via Fiume 1, is open from 8 am to 8 pm Monday to Saturday. The *Albergo Orientale* (☎ 0964-20 261), Via Tripodi 31 in the centre, has singles/doubles at L40,000/60,000 in the low season. It is the cheapest of three hotels in town.

Gerace

About 10km inland from Locri on the SS111, Gerace is an immaculately preserved medieval hill town which, perhaps sadly, is becoming a routine stop on the tourist circuit. It boasts Calabria's largest Romanesque **cathedral**, high up in the town. It was first laid out in 1045, and subsequent alterations have robbed it of none of its majesty. There is a Pro Loco tourist office (☎ 0964-35 68 88) at Piazza Tribuna 10. *Ristorante a Squella*, Viale della Resistenza 8, is an excellent traditional restaurant, and a meal will cost about L25,000.

Farther inland still is the town of **Canolo**, a small hamlet seemingly untouched by the 20th century. Buses connect Gerace with Locri.

Isola di Capo Rizzuto

Forty km north-east of Catanzaro Marina is Isola di Capo Rizzuto, one of the best locations along the Ionian coast for camping. *La Fattoria* (☎ 0962-79 11 65), Via del Faro, is one of about 15 grounds near the small town. The *Pensione Aragonese* (☎ 0962-79 50 13), Via Discesa Marina, is about 10km south-west of town on the waterfront and opposite a rather lonely looking Aragonese castle at

Le Castella. It has doubles only, for L60,000, and for L100,000 you can have full board.

At the northern tip of this zone, whose shore was declared a marine reserve in 1991, is **Capo Colonne**, marking the site of the Greek fortress complex of Hera Lacinia. Only a solitary column belonging to a Doric temple remains to testify to the spot's former splendour.

Crotone

About 10km north of Isola di Capo Rizzuto, Crotone was founded by the Greeks in 710 BC and reached its zenith in the following century, when it virtually controlled all Magna Graecia. In more recent times it has regained influence as one of the region's heavyweight industrial centres and ports – something you can hardly fail to notice as you enter the town.

The APT office (☎ 0962-2 31 85) is at Via Torino 148.

The town's **Museo Archeologico Statale**, Via Risorgimento, is one of Calabria's better museums. It's open daily except Monday from 9 am to 7 pm. Nearby is a 15th-century **castle**, typical of the cylindrically towered fortresses erected by the Aragonese in southern Italy's main coastal cities.

Albergo Italia (☎ 0962-2 39 10), Piazza Vittoria 12, has comfortable enough rooms ranging from L35,000 to L70,000, and is open all year round.

North of Crotone

The coastline from Crotone to Basilicata is the region's least developed, partly because the beaches are not terribly good (mostly grey pebble and stone affairs) and public transport is generally irregular, although the coast road is decent (and being upgraded).

Cirò Marina About 30km north of Crotone, Cirò Marina is a decent-sized town with plenty of hotel rooms and good beaches despite the huge cement breakwaters nearby. The *Albergo Atena* (☎ 0962-3 18 21), Via Bergamo, has singles/doubles from L45,000/70,000. The *Punta Alice* (☎ 0962-3 11 60) camping ground is at **Punta Alice**, a couple of km north of the town.

Rossano Rossano, 56km north of Cirò, is really two towns – Lido Sant'Angelo, the standard beach resort and coastal extension of the modern plains town of Rossano Scalo, and the original hill town itself, 6km inland.

The transformation over such a short drive is remarkable. The snaking road takes you through verdant countryside, an invitation in itself to head farther inland to a tranquil and picturesque old town, once an important Italian link in the Byzantine empire's chain.

Various reminders of Rossano's ties to the city of Constantinople remain. The **cathedral**, remodelled several times, conserves a 9th-century Byzantine fresco of the Madonna. For more proof, try the **Museo Diocesano** next door, which houses a precious 6th-century codex containing the gospels of Saints Matthew and Mark in Greek. The museum is open daily from 10 am to noon and 5 to 7 pm, except Sunday when it is closed in the afternoon (entry is L2000). Ask around for the custodian if you're having trouble getting in.

The *Albergo Scigliano* (☎ 0983-51 18 46), Viale Margherita 257, near the station, has singles/doubles from L90,000/150,000 with breakfast, and there is a camping ground, the *Camping Torino* (☎ 0983-51 00 80), at Marina di Rossano.

Rossano is on the Taranto-Reggio di Calabria train line. If you want to head inland, the SS177 makes a pretty drive across La Sila to Cosenza, although it could be a bit dangerous, especially for women on their own.

Sibari About 25km farther north, among reclaimed farmland, is the town of Sibari, near what was once the seat of the ancient Sybarites, about whose wealth and genius much has been written. This once great Greek city state was destroyed by Crotone under Pythagoras in the 6th century BC, and excavations since the 1960s have brought only a glimmer of its glory to light (there is a small museum).

COSENZA

Seated at the confluence of two rivers, the Crati and Busento, the medieval core of Cosenza is an unexpected pleasure, with its narrow *vicoletti* (alleys), some no more than steep stairways, winding past elegant, if much decayed, multi-storeyed apartment houses.

A university town since 1968, Cosenza is without doubt the most attractive of Calabria's three provincial capitals, and possibly the only one that seriously merits a stop. What's more, if you're coming from the north, it has the appeal of being a gateway into La Sila and on across to the Ionian coast. As a transportation hub, the city makes a good base for the mountains.

Orientation

The main drag, Corso Mazzini, runs south off Piazza Fera (near the bus station) and intersects Viale Trieste before meeting Piazza dei Bruzi. What little there is in terms of accommodation, food, banks and tourist assistance is all within about a 10-minute walking radius of the intersection. Head farther south still and cross the Busento river to reach the medieval part of town.

Information

Tourist Offices There are two APT offices, one on Piazza Rossi (☎ 39 05 95) at the roundabout north of Viale della Repubblica (useful for drivers coming in off the A3), the other (☎ 2 7485) at Corso Mazzini 92, near Viale Trieste. Among the odds and ends on offer is a guide (with map) to the 'agriturismo' accommodation throughout the province. These places in the country are worth considering as an alternative to the usual hotel grind, and often have horse-riding facilities and similar activities. The office in Piazza Rossi is open Monday to Friday from 7.30 am to 8 pm.

Post & Communications The main post office is at Via Vittorio Veneto on the city centre's western edge. The Telecom office is at the bus station off Piazza Fera. The postcode for Cosenza is 87100, and the telephone code is ☎ 0984.

Medical Services The hospital, the Ospedale Civile (☎ 68 11), is on Via Felice Migliori, behind the post office.

Emergency In a police emergency, call ☎ 113, or contact the police headquarters (☎ 7 26 13) at Via Frugiuele 10.

Things to See

A short walk south of the Busento river along Corso Telesio is the 12th-century **duomo**, rebuilt in the Baroque style (although hardly in the most florid fashion) in the 18th century. The cathedral is unexceptional, but on the left is a Baroque chapel in the process of restoration. It contains a copy of a 13th-century Byzantine Madonna. From the cathedral you can follow Via del Seggio through an enchanting little medieval quarter to the 13th-century **Chiesa di San Francesco d'Assisi**, in which you'll find a chapel of the original structure behind the right transept. The cloister also bears some remnants of the first building.

Farther south along Corso Vittorio Emanuele is the **castle**, built by the Normans, rearranged by Frederick II and the Angevins in 1222 and left in disarray by several earthquakes. The views are its best feature.

At the southern edge of the old city centre is Piazza XV Marzo, an appealing square fronted by the Accademia Cosentina which houses the city's **Museo Civico**, containing local finds. Entry is free and it is open Monday to Saturday from 9 am to 1 pm. South of the piazza stretches a huge public garden, the **Villa Vecchia**.

Places to Stay & Eat

Accommodation can be a prickly business in Cosenza – there are only four hotels. The cheapest option is the *Albergo Bruno* (☎ 7 38 89), Corso Mazzini 27, which has singles/doubles from L50,000/70,000, or L30,000/55,000 without bathroom. Rooms are functional and spacious. The *Excelsior* (☎ 7 43 83), on Piazza Matteotti 14, by the old train station, has rooms from L60,000/90,000. *Hotel Centrale* (☎ 7 36 81), Via del Tigrai 3,

CALABRIA

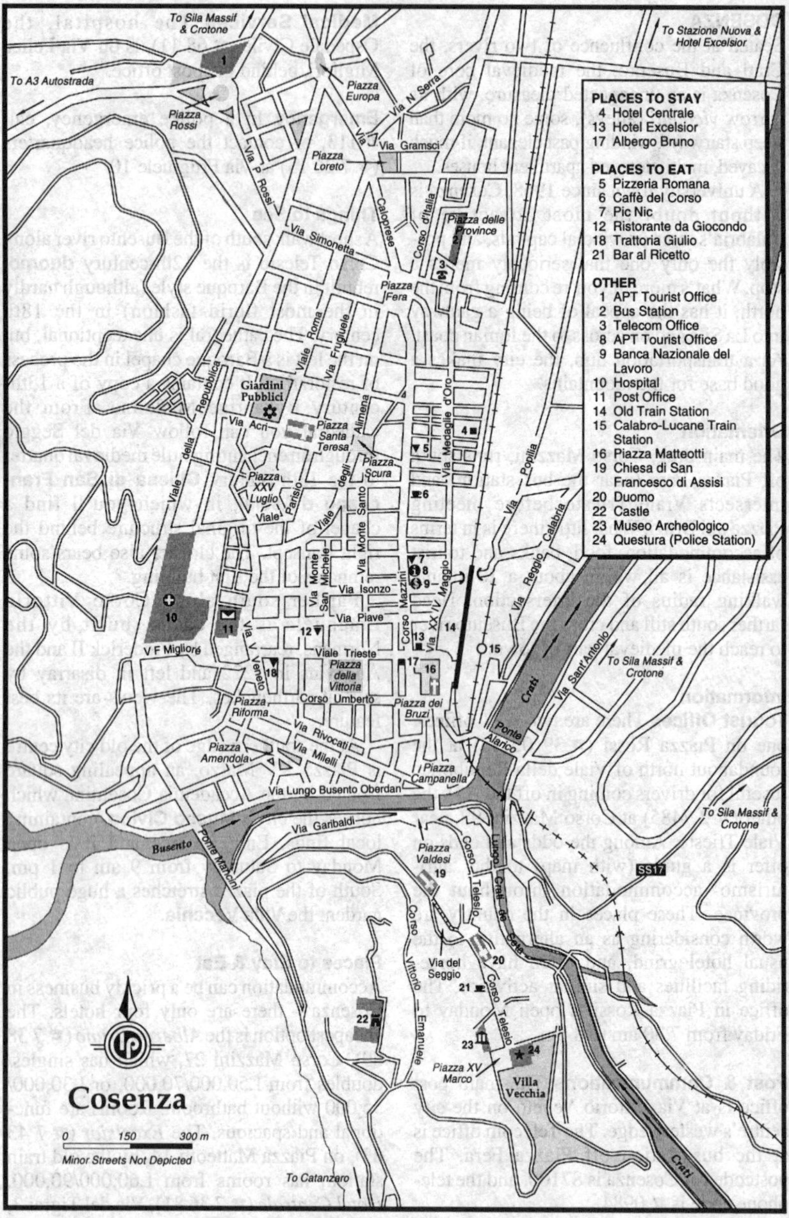
Cosenza
PLACES TO STAY
4 Hotel Centrale
13 Hotel Excelsior
17 Albergo Bruno
PLACES TO EAT
5 Pizzeria Romana
6 Caffè del Corso
7 Pic Nic
12 Ristorante da Giocondo
18 Trattoria Giulio
21 Bar al Ricetto
OTHER
1 APT Tourist Office
2 Bus Station
3 Telecom Office
8 APT Tourist Office
9 Banca Nazionale del Lavoro
10 Hospital
11 Post Office
14 Old Train Station
15 Calabro-Lucane Train Station
16 Piazza Matteotti
19 Chiesa di San Francesco di Assisi
20 Duomo
22 Castle
23 Museo Archeologico
24 Questura (Police Station)
To Sila Massif & Crotone
To A3 Autostrada
To Stazione Nuova & Hotel Excelsior
Piazza Europa
Piazza Rossi
Via N Serra
Via Gramsci
Piazza Loreto
Via P Rossi
Calopresse
Corso d'Italia
Piazza delle Province
Via Simonetta
Piazza Fera
Viale Roma
Via Frugiuele
Viale della Repubblica
Giardini Pubblici
Via Acri
Piazza Santa Teresa
Alimena
Piazza Scura
Piazza XXV Luglio
Via Parisio
Viale degli
Via Monte Santo
Via Medaglie d'Oro
Via Popilia
Via Reggio Calabria
Via Monte San Michele
Via Isonzo
Via Piave
Corso Mazzini
Via XXIV Maggio
V F Migliori
Via V Veneto
Viale Trieste
Piazza della Vittoria
Corso Umberto
Piazza Riforma
Piazza dei Bruzi
Via Sant'Antonio
To Sila Massif & Crotone
Crati
Ponte Alarico
Via Rivocati
Via Milelli
Piazza Amendola
Piazza Campanella
Via Lungo Busento Oberdan
Via Garibaldi
Busento
Ponte Mancini
To Sila Massif & Crotone
SS17
Piazza Valdesi
Corso Telesio
Lungo Crati de Seta
Corso Vittorio Emanuele
Via del Seggio
Piazza XV Marco
Villa Vecchia
0 150 300 m
Minor Streets Not Depicted
To Catanzaro

has singles/doubles starting at L88,000/118,000. See the preceding Information section for agriturismo options.

You can grab a snack at *Pic Nic*, Corso Mazzini 108, or *Pizzeria Romana* at No 190. *Trattoria Giulio*, Viale Trieste 93, is an informal place for simple meals. For something a little more substantial, head for *Ristorante da Giocondo*, Via Piave 53, where a reasonable meal will cost about L30,000. In the old town, try *Bar al Ricetto*, on Corso Telesio 29, for a quick bite. *Caffè del Corso*, on Corso Mazzini, is a bright spot for a coffee and pastry.

Getting There & Away

Bus The city's main bus station is just east of Piazza Fera. Services leave for Catanzaro, towns throughout La Sila and Paola. Autolinie Preite has half a dozen buses daily along the north Tyrrhenian coast as far as Praia a Mare, and SITA goes to Maratea in Basilicata.

Train The national FS Stazione Nuova is about 2km north-east of the city centre. Trains go to Reggio di Calabria, Salerno, Napoli and Roma, as well as most destinations around the Calabrian coast. The Ferrovie Calabro Lucane line serves La Sila and other small towns around Cosenza.

Car & Motorcycle Cosenza is off the A3 autostrada. The SS107 connects the city with Crotone and the Ionian coast, across La Sila.

Getting Around

You're unlikely to need a bus in town, but it is best to get ATAC bus No 27 and 28 to or from the Stazione Nuova train station. For a taxi, call ☎ 2 88 77.

LA SILA

Though less spectacular than many of the mountain ranges farther up the peninsula, La Sila (the Sila Massif) is still magnificent and offers good walking. The highest peaks are around 2000m; much of them are covered in what amounts to a vast forest, but there is some winter skiing in the central Sila Grande. Other main areas are the Sila Greca, north of the Grande, and the Sila Piccola to the south. Sadly, there are few mountain *rifugi* and camping in the national parks is forbidden.

The main towns are Camigliatello Silano and San Giovanni in Fiore, both accessible by bus along the SS107 that connects Cosenza with Crotone, or by the train which runs between Cosenza and San Giovanni in Fiore. You will find accommodation in various towns throughout La Sila and at several tourist resorts, including the Villaggio Palumbo and Villaggio Mancuso. Skiers can use lifts around Camigliatello Silano and near Lorica, on Lago Arvo.

Information

Unfortunately, the tourist offices can help you with little more than vague maps and accommodation lists. Any brochures they have will almost certainly be in Italian only.

Camigliatello Silano

Ordinary enough in summer, Camigliatello looks quite cute under snow. It is a popular local skiing resort, but won't host any international competitions. A few lifts operate on Monte Curcio about 3km to the south. One summertime activity that might interest the kids is a **steam train** excursion that runs from Camigliatello to San Giovanni in Fiore. It leaves every Saturday and Sunday and costs L20,000 return. Occasionally it runs in winter too. For information, enquire at the Calabro-Lucane train station.

The town has about 15 hotels, including the *Miramonti* (☎ 0984-57 90 67), near the tourist office on Via Forgitelle, which has singles/doubles from L40,000/55,000. *Mancuso* (☎ 0984-57 80 02), Via del Turismo, has rooms for about the same price, while the three-star *Aquila & Edelweiss* (☎ 0984-57 80 44), Viale Stazione 11, has rooms from L60,000/90,000.

San Giovanni in Fiore

Although this is the biggest town in La Sila, it really has little to recommend it. The provincial accommodation guide lists a lot of hotels here, but most of them are scattered

CALABRIA

about small villages around – some as far away as Lorica, 20km to the south-west.

Lorica

A peaceful little spot on Lago Arvo amid thick woods, Lorica is a minor ski resort, with a lift operating nearby. There are several camp sites in the area including *Camping Lorica* (☎ 0984-53 70 18), on the lake. Otherwise try *Albergo La Trota* (☎ 0984-53 71 66), which has rooms for L50,000/80,000. You may have to pay full board in ski season.

Villaggio Palumbo

About 15km south of San Giovanni in Fiore, this is a tourist village resort on Lago Ampollino. There is a similar venture about 25km farther south on the road to Catanzaro, **Villaggio Mancuso**. They both offer weekend package deals including food and accommodation, and are set up for skiing, horse-riding and the like.

REGGIO DI CALABRIA

As you gaze across the strait from the elegant tree-lined Lungomare Matteotti to the twinkling night lights of Messina in Sicilia, you could almost be forgiven for thinking you are in a rather romantic spot. However as you drive through miles of half-built and semi-inhabited concrete slum tenements, you can hardly feel anything but pity for the bulk of this city's people. Rocked repeatedly by earthquakes, the last time devastatingly in 1908, this once proud ancient Greek city has plenty of other woes as well, among them, organised crime. You may notice an awful lot of Carabinieri and Alpine soldiers (Italy's elite troops) in the streets. Wander up to Piazza Castello where heavily armed guards surround the law courts and you begin to gauge the depth of the problem.

Orientation

The main train station is at the southern edge of town in Piazza Garibaldi, where most buses also terminate. Walk north along Corso G Garibaldi, the city's main street, for the tourist office and other services. Corso Garibaldi is a kind of de facto pedestrian zone in the evening, as streams of Reggians parade in the ritual *passeggiata*.

Information

Tourist Offices The APT office has branches at the train station (☎ 2 71 20), the airport (☎ 64 32 91) and on the autostrada near the Rosano Ovest exit. In town the head office is on Via Roma (☎ 2 11 71) and there's a branch at Corso Garibaldi 329 (☎ 89 20 12), in the Teatro Comunale building. Most offices purport to open from 8 am to 8 pm, Monday to Saturday, but it's perhaps wiser to use the 2 pm closing time of the head office as a guide.

Post & Communications The main post office is at Via Miraglia 14 near Piazza Italia, and is open from 8.15 am to 6 pm Monday to Saturday. The city's postcode is 89100. The Telecom office is on Via Marina and the telephone code is ☎ 0965.

Money There is no shortage of banks in Reggio. The Banca Nazionale del Lavoro, Corso Garibaldi 431, is one of several with a user-friendly ATM.

Medical Services The city's hospital, Ospedali Riuniti (☎ 39 71 11), is at Via Melacrino. For an ambulance, call ☎ 2 00 10 or ☎ 2 44 44. For the Guardia Medica (visiting doctors, at night and on holidays), call ☎ 34 71 05.

Emergency For the police, call ☎ 113, or head to their headquarters (☎ 41 11) on Via Santa Caterina.

Things to See & Do

Reggio was completely rebuilt after the 1908 earthquake that devastated southern Calabria and few historic buildings remain. Apart from wandering along Lungomare Matteotti and gazing at Sicilia or participating in one of the most serious passeggiatas you're likely to see, there's little to see or do.

The big exception is housed in a predictably pompous Fascist-era building on Piazza de Nava, at Corso Garibaldi's northern end. The

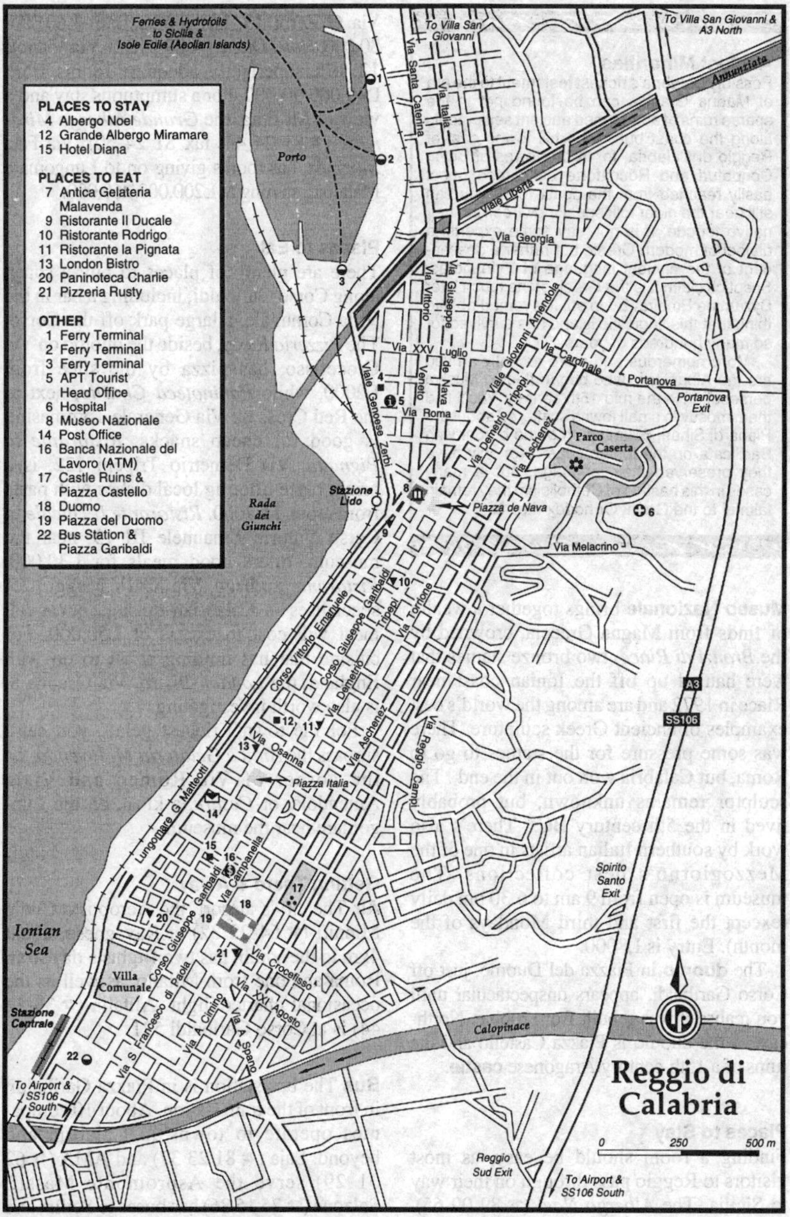
Ferries & Hydrofoils to Sicilia & Isole Eolie (Aeolian Islands)
PLACES TO STAY
4 Albergo Noel
12 Grande Albergo Miramare
15 Hotel Diana
PLACES TO EAT
7 Antica Gelateria Malavenda
9 Ristorante Il Ducale
10 Ristorante Rodrigo
11 Ristorante la Pignata
13 London Bistro
20 Paninoteca Charlie
21 Pizzeria Rusty
OTHER
1 Ferry Terminal
2 Ferry Terminal
3 Ferry Terminal
5 APT Tourist Head Office
6 Hospital
8 Museo Nazionale
14 Post Office
16 Banca Nazionale del Lavoro (ATM)
17 Castle Ruins & Piazza Castello
18 Duomo
19 Piazza del Duomo
22 Bus Station & Piazza Garibaldi
Porto
To Villa San Giovanni
To Villa San Giovanni & A3 North
Annunziata
Via Santa Caterina
Via Italia
Viale Libertà
Via Georgia
Via Vittorio Veneto
Via Giuseppe de Nava
Via XXV Luglio
Viale Genoese Zerbi
Via Roma
Viale Giovanni Amendola
Via Cardinale
Portanova
Portanova Exit
Via Demetrio Tripepi
Via Aschenez
Parco Caserta
Stazione Lido
Piazza de Nava
Rada dei Giunchi
Via Melacrino
Corso Vittorio Emanuele
Corso Giuseppe Garibaldi
Via Demetrio Tripepi
Via Torrione
A3
SS106
Via Reggio Campi
Via Osanna
Via Aschenez
Piazza Italia
Lungomare G Matteotti
Via Campanella
Spirito Santo Exit
Ionian Sea
Villa Comunale
Corso Giuseppe Garibaldi
Via Crocefisso
Via XXI Agosto
Stazione Centrale
Via S Francesco di Paola
Via A Cimino
Via A Spano
Calopinace
Reggio di Calabria
To Airport & SS106 South
0 250 500 m
Reggio Sud Exit
To Airport & SS106 South

Ancient Minorities

Possibly Calabria's richest testament to the era of Magna Graecia can be found not in the sparse ruins of abandoned ancient settlements along the coast but in the hill towns east of Reggio di Calabria, for in the towns of Bova, Condofuri and Roccaforte del Greco (most easily reached from the coast road) you can still hear the older folk speaking Greek as their native tongue. It is not, say some experts, a dialect of modern Greek, but rather a descendant of the ancient language of Pythagoras. Sceptics claim it is the Greek of the much later Byzantine Empire. Even so, it is remarkable to think that this linguistic island has survived for so many hundreds of years.

More numerous and more recently arrived are the Albanians, who began fleeing Muslim persecution in the mid-15th century. You'll find them mostly in small towns scattered about the Piana di Sibari, 50km south of the border with Basilicata on the Ionian coast. Not only have they preserved their language, but in many cases in this bastion of Catholicism they remain faithful to the Greek Orthodox rite. ■

Museo Nazionale brings together a wealth of finds from Magna Graecia, crowned by the *Bronzi di Riace*, two bronze statues that were hauled up off the Ionian coast near Riace in 1972 and are among the world's best examples of ancient Greek sculpture. There was some pressure for the statues to go to Roma, but Calabria won out in the end . The sculptor remains unknown, but probably lived in the 5th century BC. There's also work by southern Italian artists in one of the Mezzogiorno's best collections. The museum is open from 9 am to 6.30 pm daily (except the first and third Mondays of the month). Entry is L8000.

The **duomo** in Piazza del Duomo, just off Corso Garibaldi, appears unspectacular until you realise it was rebuilt from rubble. North-east of the duomo is Piazza Castello and the ruins of a 15th-century Aragonese **castle**.

Places to Stay

Finding a room should be easy, as most visitors to Reggio pass through on their way to Sicilia. The *Albergo Noel* (☎ 89 09 65), Via G Zerbi 13, has rooms from L60,000/80,000. *Hotel Diana* (☎ 89 15 22), Via Vitrioli 12, offers perfectly adequate rooms from L45,000/90,000. For a sumptuous stay and a view of Mt Etna, the *Grande Albergo Miramare* (☎ 81 24 44; fax 81 24 50), Via Fata Morgana, has rooms giving on to Lungomare Matteotti, starting at L200,000/260,000.

Places to Eat

There are plenty of places to buy a snack along Corso Garibaldi, including a bar in the Villa Comunale, a large park off the Corso. The *Pizzeria Rusty*, beside the duomo on Via Crocefisso, has pizza by the slice from L2000, while *Paninoteca Charlie*, next to the Red Cross on Via Generale Tommasini, is good for cheap snacks. *Ristorante la Pignatta*, Via Demetrio Tripepi 122, is a bright place offering local dishes with pasta from around L7000. *Ristorante Il Ducale* in Corso Vittorio Emanuele III 13, near the museum, offers good meals for L30,000. *Ristorante Rodrigo*, Via XXIV Maggio 25, specialises in Calabrian cuisine, but a full meal will cost in excess of L50,000. For cuisine that has nothing at all to do with England, the *London Bistro*, Via Osanna 8, is also worth investigating.

For the town's richest gelati, you can't surpass the *Antica Gelateria Malavenda*, on the corner of Via Romeo and Viale Amendola, or *Cesare*, a kiosk on the Lungomare near the museum.

Getting There & Away

Air The city's airport, the Aeroporto Civile Minniti (☎ 64 22 32) at Ravagnese, about 4km to the south, has two flights a day from Roma and one from Milano, as well as the occasional charter flight. Alitalia (☎ 33 14 44) is at Corso Garibaldi 521.

Bus The bus station is in Piazza Garibaldi, in front of the train station. About 10 companies operate to towns in Calabria and beyond. Saja (☎ 81 23 37) and AMA (☎ 62 01 29) serve the Aspromonte Massif; Salzone (☎ 75 15 86) has buses to Scilla; and

Lirosi (☎ 5 75 52) has two daily runs to Roma and one to Catanzaro.

Train Trains stop at Stazione Centrale (green number 1478/ 8 80 88), and less frequently at Stazione Lido, near the museum. Reggio is the terminus for trains from Milano, Firenze, Roma and Napoli.

Car & Motorcycle The A3 ends at Reggio di Calabria. If you are heading south, the SS106 hugs the coast round the 'toe' and up along the Ionian Sea.

Boat Up to 20 hydrofoils run by SNAV (☎ 2 95 68) leave the port just north of Stazione Lido for Messina every day (L4200 one way; three only on Sunday). Some boats proceed on to the Isole Eolie. The FS national railways run up to 19 big hydrofoils a day from the port to Messina (L4200 one way).

Car ferries cross to Messina around the clock from Villa San Giovanni, 20 minutes farther north along the rail line. FS railways run boats that carry cars and trains across (L1500 for foot passengers), while the private company Caronte operates car and truck ferries from a little farther north. During the day, there is usually a crossing every 20 minutes. Caronte charges L32,000 one way for a standard car, L57,000 return (valid 60 days). Passengers don't pay; motorcycles cost L10,000 each way. The crossing takes about 20 minutes.

Island Seaways runs a direct service from Reggio to Malta leaving every Sunday at 1 pm. A return fare for deck class is L230,000. For information, contact the Fratelli Labate Travel Agency (☎ 89 20 32), Via Bruno Buozzi 31, or the Forum Travel Agency in Roma (☎ 06-482 04 24).

Getting Around

Orange local buses cover most of the city. To get to the airport, take bus No 15, 19, 111, 113, 114 or 115.

ASPROMONTE MASSIF

Inland from Reggio di Calabria rises the Aspromonte massif. Its highest peak, **Montalto** (1955m), is dominated by a huge bronze statue of Christ, and offers sweeping views across to Sicilia.

The tourist office in Reggio may have information and a map of the Montalto area, now a national park, which has some walking trails, albeit not quite as spectacular, or difficult, as those in La Sila.

To reach the Aspromonte's main town of Gambarie, take city bus No 127 from Reggio di Calabria. Most of the roads inland from Reggio eventually hit the main SS183 road that runs north to the town.

TYRRHENIAN COAST

Tamer and more developed than Calabria's Ionian coast, the region's western seaboard is a mixture of the good, the bad and the ugly. Certain stretches, particularly in the popular north, are crammed with tacky package resorts that attract holidaying Italians by the thousand each summer. But there are several small towns that are pleasant to stay in, along with the odd cove with a protected sandy beach.

The drive along the Costa Viola, from Rosarno to Scilla and on towards Reggio di Calabria, is one of Italy's great coastal drives, with breathtaking views of Sicilia.

The best sources of information about the coast are the tourist offices in Reggio di Calabria and Cosenza. They will probably recommend that you stay at one of the tourist villages – don't be immediately put off. Although most are reminiscent of *Carry On...* films, many offer excellent value and all have private beaches, generally some of the best on the coast.

As elsewhere in Calabria, cheap accommodation can be a little difficult to find. Out of season, most hotels, campsites and tourist villages close. In summer many of the hotels are full, although you should have an easier time with the campsites.

Most coastal towns are on the main train line between Reggio and Napoli, and the SS18 road hugs the coast for much of the way. The A3 from Reggio di Calabria to Salerno is farther inland.

CALABRIA

Scilla

After the urban confusion of Reggio and Villa San Giovanni, the SS18 brings you to one of the most striking stretches of Calabria's coastline. The highlands of the Aspromonte extend right to the coast, and the views from the cliffs across to Sicilia can fuel the imagination.

If you're coming from the north, the drive is still better (especially if you take it slowly on the SS18). Wedged in here and arching around a small beach is the picturesque town of Scilla, its northern end dominated by the rock associated with Scylla, the mythical sea monster who drowned sailors as they were trying to navigate the Stretto di Messina (and if she didn't get them, Charybdis, across in Sicilia, would).

The HI hostel has closed. You could try the *Pensione le Sirene* (☎ 0965-75 40 19), Via Nazionale 55, with rooms for L44,000/78,000. Just north of the castle, there is a row of houses built into the water which are worth seeing.

Nicotera

About 50km north, Nicotera is dominated by a medieval castle. At least one camping ground functions all year round here, *Camping Sayonara* (☎ 0963-8 19 44) at Nicotera Marina, with good ocean views. It charges about L10,000 per person, plus the cost of a site.

About 20km north-west of the town at **Capo Vaticano** are several tourist villages, including the *Costa Azzurra* (☎ 0963-66 31 09). It closes in winter and generally imposes a full-board arrangement.

Tropea

Just north of Capo Vaticano, Tropea is a pretty little town perched high above a small beach. The almost (but not quite) twee town centre is becoming a minor tourist attraction in itself. There is a Pro Loco tourist office (☎ 6 14 75) in the centre. The telephone code is ☎ 0963.

Most of the 10 or so hotels are in the higher price bracket, although *La Perla* (☎ 6 13 68), Viale Crigna 27, has singles/doubles from L80,000/130,000 and is open all year. The *Stromboli* tourist village (☎ 66 90 93) charges from L80,000 to L140,000 a person for full board on a sliding scale from winter to super-high season (August).

The SAV bus line operates in this area, connecting the resorts with Tropea and Pizzo, which both have train stations.

Pizzo

In the bars of Pizzo, you will find possibly Italy's best *tartufo*, a type of chocolate ice-cream ball.

Inside the town's **duomo** lies the tomb of Joachim Murat, king of Napoli from 1808 until 1815, when he was defeated by the Austrians and the Bourbons were restored to the Neapolitan throne. Although he was the architect of various enlightened reforms, the locals seemed to prefer the Bourbon devil they had known and showed no great concern when Murat was imprisoned and executed here after one last attempt to regain power in September 1815.

Just north of the town, the **Chiesa di Piedigrotta** was literally carved into the sandstone near the beach by Neapolitan shipwreck survivors in the 17th century. The church was later added to (the statue of Fidel Castro kneeling before a medallion of Pope John XXIII is an obvious recent addition), but the place is crumbling away, and there is no move afoot to stop the rot.

Wander through Piazzetta Garibaldi, the picturesque old centre of Pizzo overlooking the water, before settling in at *Bar Ercole* for an ice-cream fix. For a typical seafood meal, *La Nave*, in a rusting boat on the waterfront, has good main courses from L20,000.

Paola

The 80km coast between Pizzo and Paola is mostly overdeveloped and ugly. Paola is the main train hub for Cosenza, about 25km inland, and is a large, comparatively nondescript place. Watched over by a crumbling castle, its main attraction is the **Santuario di San Francesco di Paola**. The saint, who lived and died in Paola in the 15th century, was known as a miracle-worker in his lifetime, and the sanctuary he and his followers carved out of the bare rock has for centuries been the object of pilgrimage. You can wander through these spartan chambers but there is precious little to see, and a church and monastery has been erected over them. A chapel in the church contains a reliquary of the saint. The sanctuary is open from 6 am to 12.30 pm and 2 to 5.30 pm.

The *Albergo Elena* (☎ 0982-61 24 74), Via San Leonardo, has rooms from L50,000/80,000, although towns farther north along the coast might be preferable.

Diamante to Praia a Mare

Diamante and Cirella mark the southern end of a largely uninterrupted stretch of wide, grey pebbly beach that continues for about 30km to Praia a Mare, just short of Calabria's regional boundary with Basilicata. Although popular with the locals, it is for the most part uninspiring. Backed by rows of campsites and growing development projects, the coast here lacks much of the scenic splendour to the north in Basilicata or indeed south towards Reggio di Calabria.

Il Fortino (☎ 0985-8 60 85), at Via Vittorio Veneto in Cirella, is one of several campsites and so-called tourist villages along the coast here.

If you do find the coast a little flat, head for Scalea and the hills. The old centre of **Scalea**, about 15km south of Praia, is one of the more eye-catching towns along the northern coast. Climb the stairway lanes past the muddle of tumbledown houses, or stop in Piazza de Palma for a beer at the Tarì Bar.

Back in the anonymous modern urbanscape below, you could stay at the *Camping la Pantera Rosa* (☎ 0985-2 15 46) on Corso Mediterraneo. In August it costs L21,800 per person plus tent space, but the price drops on either side of this high season.

Praia a Mare

A couple of km short of the border with Basilicata, Praia a Mare is a modern and not terribly appealing town built to serve Italian holiday-makers. At least the surrounding landscape takes a more dramatic tone here, with the SS18 coastal highway climbing away behind the town up into Basilicata. The **Isola di Dino**, just off the coast south of the town, is blessed with an easily accessible **grotto** every bit as impressive as Capri's better known Grotta Azzurra, and the grey beach is expansive.

If you plan to stay in Praia, *La Mantiniera* (☎ 0985-77 90 23) is at the southern end of town in the Fiuzzi area. The *Hotel Rex* (☎ 0985-7 21 91), Via C Colombo, a couple of blocks back from Praia's beach, charges L53,000 per person for full board. However, you might be better off up the road in Maratea, across the regional frontier in Basilicata (see the section on Maratea).

Autolinee Preite operates five or six buses a day in each direction between Cosenza and Praia a Mare. SITA goes north to Maratea.

Aieta & Tortora

The hill villages of **Aieta** and **Tortora**, about 12 and 6km inland from Praia, belong to another world. Infrequent local buses serve both villages, but this is really only a practical excursion for people with their own transport or a lot of time and patience. The towns are precariously perched upon ridges that must have been hard going before asphalt days. Aieta is higher up than Tortora, and the journey constitutes much of the reward for going there. When you arrive, walk up to the 16th-century Palazzo Spinello at the end of the road and take a look into the ravine behind it.

Sicilia

Think of Sicilia (Sicily) and two things come to mind: beaches and the Mafia. There is no doubt its beaches are beautiful and that organised crime has a powerful impact on Sicilian society. But the island is too diverse to be so easily summed up. It is a place of contrasts, from the crumbling grandeur of the capital, Palermo, to the upmarket glitz of the tourist resort, Taormina. There are Greek ruins at Siracusa, Agrigento, Selinunte and Segesta; and the volcanic Isole Eolie off Sicilia's north coast have a wild beauty matched only by the spectacular Mt Etna on the island's east coast.

Sicilia is the largest island in the Mediterranean and its strategic location made it a prize for successive waves of invaders. As well as Greek temples, there are Roman ruins, Norman churches and castles, Arab and Byzantine domes and splendid Baroque churches and palaces.

HIGHLIGHTS

- Glowering at Mt Etna from below its steaming craters
- Marvelling at the mosaics and tile designs of an Arab-Norman masterpiece – the Cappella Palatino in Palermo
- Visiting the stunning Norman cathedral at Monreale
- The Parco Archeologico and the Museo Archeologico Paolo Orsi in Siracusa, the ancient Greek city that once rivalled Athens
- Taking a bus ride through pretty countryside from the 'mosaic town' of Piazza Armerina to the Villa Romana del Casale
- The Valle dei Templi, an ancient Greek site overlooking the Mediterranean at Agrigento

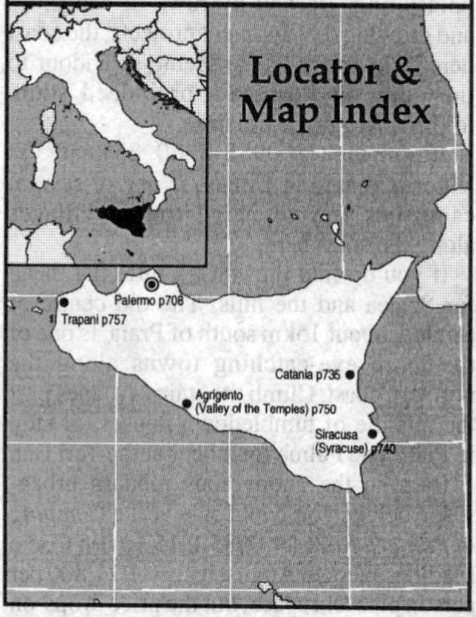

History

It is believed the earliest settlers were the Sicanians, Elymians and Siculians, who came from various points around the southern Mediterranean; they were followed by the Phoenicians. Greek colonisation began in the 8th century BC with the foundation of Naxos. The cities of Siracusa, Catania, Messina and Agrigento grew and still dominate the island. By 210 BC, Sicilia was under Roman control, with power eventually passing to the Byzantines and then to the Arabs, who had settled in by 903 AD.

Norman conquest of the island began in 1060, when Roger I of Hauteville captured Messina. Mastery of Sicilia subsequently passed to the Swabians and the Holy Roman emperor Frederick II, known as Stupor Mundi (Wonder of the World). In the 13th century, the French Angevins provided a period of misrule that ended with the revolt known as the Sicilian Vespers in 1282. The island was handed over to the Spanish Aragon family and, in 1503, to the Spanish crown. After short periods of Savoy and Austrian rule in the 18th century, Sicilia again came under the control of the Spanish Bourbons of Napoli in 1734, who united the island with southern Italy in the Kingdom of the Two Sicilies.

On 11 May 1860, Giuseppe Garibaldi

Garibaldi, in taking Sicilia and Napoli for Italy, won the imagination of the Italian people and made them realise independence was attainable

landed at Marsala with his One Thousand and began the conquest that eventually set the seal on the unification of Italy. Life did not greatly improve for the people and between 1871 and 1914 more than one million Sicilians emigrated, mainly to the USA.

In 1943, some 140,000 Allied troops under General Dwight Eisenhower landed in south-eastern Sicilia. Initially blocked by dogged Italian and German resistance, Eisenhower's field commanders entered Messina within six weeks, after heavy fighting had devastated many parts of the country. The Allied occupation lasted until early 1944. In 1948 Sicilia became a semi-autonomous region, and unlike other such regions in Italy, it has its own parliament and legislative powers.

The Mafia

The overt presence of the Italian army in Sicilia (you'll see armed soldiers at 'strategic' spots here and there) has done little to dent the Mafia's activities. However, since the arrest of the Sicilian 'godfather' Salvatore ('Totò') Riina in 1993, and his successor, Giovanni 'The Pig' Brusca, in 1996, Mafia pentiti (grasses, or turncoats) have continued to blow the whistle on fellow felons, politicians, businessmen and others, right up to former prime minister Giulio Andreotti. Andreotti stood accused at two separate trials in 1997 of supporting the Sicilian Mafia, helping fix court cases and ordering, or consenting to, the murder of an investigative journalist. He says the case is a conspiracy against him. Some fear the pentiti are inventing confessions to settle private scores, but there must be something in it, otherwise the Cosa Nostra, as the Sicilian Mafia is known, would not have opened a campaign to 'discourage' pentiti by bumping off their relatives. The most famous pentito of them all, Tommaso Buscetta, has lost something like 33 relatives, his wife and three sons included. There were more than 1000 pentiti in 1997, waiting to give evidence in return for immunity or leniency and protection. However, evidence has surfaced that some pentiti have been carrying on with their criminal activities while under state protection – which has thrown the witness protection programme into confusion. The Italian author Luigi Barzini once wrote: 'The phenomenon has deep roots in history, in the character of the Sicilians, in local habits. Its origins disappear down the dim vistas of the centuries.'

Sicilians feel offended that the image abroad of their proud island is one portrayed in blood. There is no need to fear that you will be caught in the crossfire of a gang war while in Sicilia. The 'men of honour' are little interested in the affairs of foreign tourists. (See Mafia in the Facts About the Country chapter.)

Orientation & Information

Although some industry has developed and tourism is a fast-growing sector, the island's economy is still largely agricultural and the people remain strongly connected to the land. Along the east coast especially, there is mile upon mile of citrus groves.

The coastal landscape ranges from rugged and windswept shores to long stretches of sandy beach, while rolling hills, mountains and dry plateaus dominate the interior. The temperate climate brings mild weather in winter, but summer is relentlessly hot and the beaches swarm with holiday-makers. The best times to visit are spring and autumn, when it is warm enough for the beach but not too hot for sightseeing.

Sicilian food is spicy and sweet – no doubt part of the island's Oriental heritage. The focus along the coast is on seafood, notably swordfish, and fresh produce. Some say fruit and vegetables taste better in Sicilia. The cakes and pastries can be works of art, but are very sweet. Try the *cassata*, a rich cake filled with ricotta and candied fruits (there is also cassata ice cream); *cannoli*, tubes of pastry filled with cream, ricotta or chocolate; and *dolci di mandorle*, the many varieties of almond cakes and pastries. Like the Spaniards, Sicilians have a penchant for marzipan, which they make just as well as their Iberian cousins. Then there is granita, a drink of crushed ice flavoured with lemon, strawberry or coffee, to name a few flavours – perfect on a hot Sicilian day.

Dangers & Annoyances Sicilians are generally welcoming and sociable but women might find the local men a little too friendly. Female tourists should take a hint from local women and avoid walking around at night alone in the bigger cities such as Palermo, Catania and Messina. Exercise caution elsewhere too.

You won't have to worry about confronting the Godfather but petty criminals abound, especially in the bigger centres. Pickpockets and motorcycle-mounted snatch thieves are the worst, and the latter love handbags and small day packs. If you have to carry one of these items, keep a firm hold on it. Don't wear jewellery and keep all your valuables in a money belt or in your hotel.

Car theft is a problem in Palermo, so using private, guarded car parks is advisable.

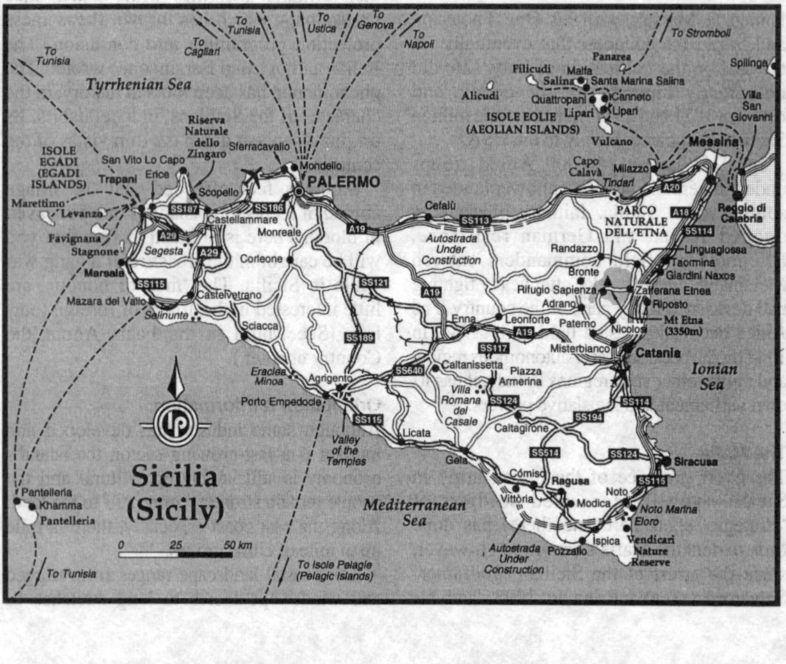

Things to Buy

As in Spain and Portugal, the Arabs brought to Sicilia a rich tradition of ceramic production. Although the modern products are doubtless directed at tourists, as souvenirs go, they are evocative of the island. Simple designs with blues and yellows as base colours best reflect the artisanal roots of the ceramics; more luridly decorated plates, vases, pots and bowls can be found all over the island. Or you could go for a ceramic *trinacria*, a face surrounded by three legs representing the three-pointed island. Major ceramics centres include Caltagirone and Santo Stefano di Camastra.

Since the 18th century, Sicilia's *carretti* (carts) have been a byword for the island. Used for transport until the arrival of the motorcar, the wooden carts were lovingly sculpted and bedecked with brightly coloured illustrations of mythic events, local characters or even family histories. You'd be lucky to see one in action now, but they are occasionally hauled out as tourist attractions. For the ultimate in memento kitsch, however, you could always buy one of the models on sale in virtually all souvenir shops.

Getting There & Away

Air Flights from all over Italy land at Palermo and Catania. The airports are also serviced by flights from major European cities. Palermo's airport is at Punta Raisi, about 32km out of the city, while Catania's airport is 7km out. Buses run from both airports into the respective city centres. See the Palermo and Catania Getting There & Away sections for further details. The easiest way to obtain information on flights to/from Sicilia is from any Sestante CIT or Alitalia office throughout Italy.

Bus Direct bus services from Roma to Sicilia are operated by two companies – SAIS and Segesta. In Roma, the buses leave from Stazione Tiburtina. The Segesta bus runs direct to Palermo and on to Trapani, leaving Roma at 8 am on Tuesday, Thursday and Saturday. One-way tickets to Palermo cost L50,000. The SAIS bus runs between Roma (leaves 8 pm daily) and Messina (4.30 am), Catania (6 am) and Agrigento (9.30 am). The bus connects in Catania with others to Palermo, Siracusa, Ragusa and Enna. Going the other way, the bus leaves Agrigento daily at 4.15 pm and Messina daily at 9.30 pm, arriving in Roma at 6.30 am. One-way tickets to Catania cost L75,000. In Roma, enquire at Saistours (☎ 06-482 50 66), Piazza della Repubblica 42, or go to Bar La Favorita, Via Guido Mazzoni 42, near the bus station at Piazzale Tiburtina. See Palermo and Roma Getting There & Away sections for more details.

Train Direct trains run from Milano, Firenze, Roma, Napoli and Reggio di Calabria to Messina and on to Palermo, Catania and other provincial capitals – the trains are transported from the mainland by ferry from Villa San Giovanni. Be prepared for long delays on Intercity trains on this route.

Boat Regular car/passenger ferries cross the strait between Villa San Giovanni (Calabria) and Messina. Hydrofoils run by the railways, and snappier jobs run by SNAV, connect Messina directly with Reggio di Calabria. See the Messina and Reggio di Calabria sections for details.

Sicilia is also accessible by ferry from Genova, Livorno, Napoli and Cagliari, and from Malta and Tunisia. The main company servicing the Mediterranean is Tirrenia and its services to/from Sicilia include Palermo-Cagliari, Palermo-Genova, Palermo-Napoli, Catania-Livorno, Trapani-Cagliari and Trapani-Tunisia.

Grandi Traghetti runs ferries from Livorno and Genova to Palermo, and from there on to Malta and Tunisia. Grimaldi runs luxury cruise boats from Palermo to Genova, Malta and Tunisia.

Ustica Lines runs summer ferries from Trapani to Kelibia in Tunisia (via Pantelleria) and to Napoli via Ustica.

Ferry prices are determined by the season and jump considerably in summer (Tirrenia's high season varies according to destination, but is generally from July to September).

Timetables can change dramatically each year. Tirrenia publishes an annual booklet listing all routes and prices, which is available at Tirrenia offices and agents throughout Italy.

In summer, all routes are busy and, unless you book in advance, you may literally miss the boat. Tickets can be booked through the company concerned or travel agencies throughout Italy. Offices and telephone numbers for the ferry companies are listed in the Getting There & Away sections for the relevant cities.

The following is a guide to fares, based on high-season travel on Tirrenia at the time of writing. For an airline-type chair, fares were: Genova-Palermo L109,700 (22 hours), Napoli-Palermo L69,100 (10½ hours), Palermo-Cagliari L60,000 (14 hours) and Trapani-Tunisia L92,000 (eight hours). For a 2nd-class cabin (shared with up to three other people and often segregated by gender) fares were: Genova-Palermo L123,900, Napoli-Palermo L79,000, Palermo-Cagliari L84,000 and Trapani-Tunisia L116,000.

Fares for cars vary according to the size of the vehicle. High-season charges for the Palermo-Cagliari route ranged from L103,000 to L159,700; a small caravan cost L43,500, while motorcycles under 200cc were L30,500 (L47,000 for 200cc and above) and bicycles L18,000.

There are also ferry and hydrofoil services from Sicilia to the small groups of islands off the coast (the Isole Eolie, the Isole Egadi, the Pelagie, Pantelleria and Ustica). See the relevant Getting There & Away sections in this chapter for details.

SICILIA

Getting Around

Bus The best mode of public transport in Sicilia is the bus. Numerous companies run services connecting the main towns around the coast including Messina, Catania, Siracusa, Agrigento, Trapani and Palermo. Services also connect these cities with the smaller towns along the coast and in the interior. The companies with the most extensive networks are SAIS and AST. See the Getting There & Away and Getting Around sections for each town.

Train The coastal train service between Messina and Palermo and between Messina and Siracusa is efficient and the run between Palermo and Agrigento is also generally OK. However, train services elsewhere to the interior can be infrequent and slow, and it is best to do some research before deciding between train and bus. The service from Noto to Ragusa, for instance, is picturesque but very slow.

Car & Motorcycle There is no substitute for the freedom your own vehicle can give you, especially for getting to places not well served by public transport. Roads are generally good and autostradas connect most major cities. It is possible to hitchhike in Sicilia, but don't expect a ride in a hurry. Single women should not hitchhike under any circumstances.

Palermo

At one time an Arab emirate and seat of a Norman kingdom, and in its heyday regarded as the grandest city in Europe, Palermo today is in a remarkable state of decay. It was heavily bombed in WWII and has been much neglected since. It is noted more for the Mafia trials of the 1980s, the assassinations in 1992 of the top anti-Mafia judges, Giovanni Falcone and Paolo Borsellino, and the upsurge in gangland killings in the mid-1990s. It was in Palermo that former prime minister Giulio Andreotti went on trial in 1995 for alleged involvement with Cosa Nostra.

Beneath the grime, enough evidence of its golden days remains for Palermo to be a compelling city to visit, if only as a crossroads between east and west. Cultural cross-fertilisation finds expression in the city's architectural mix, obvious in such monuments as the adjacent churches of La Martorana and San Cataldo.

Palermo's superb position by the sea at the foot of Monte Pellegrino, with the fertile

Conca d'Oro valley behind it, has long made it a rich prize for Sicilia's colonisers. Around the 8th century BC the Phoenicians established the town of Ziz here, on the site of a prehistoric village. It remained a relatively minor town under Roman, and later Byzantine, domination and it was not until 831 AD, when it was conquered by the Arabs, that the city truly flourished and became a jewel of the Islamic world.

When the Normans took control in 1072, things only improved. The seat of the kingdom of Roger I of Hauteville, Palermo was hailed as one of the most magnificent and cultured cities of 12th-century Europe. For more than half a century after Roger's death the monarchy foundered, eventually passing to the German Hohenstaufens and the Holy Roman emperor Frederick II, still remembered as one of Sicilia's most enlightened rulers. After his death, Palermo and all of Sicilia passed to the French Anjou family, themselves later deposed following the Sicilian Vespers revolt, which started in Palermo. By then eclipsed by Napoli, Palermo sank into a long, slow decline.

Raised from Rubble

Moves are afoot to do something about the decrepit state of Palermo's historical centre and many monuments are have been or are being restored. The area around Via Alloro, for instance, is literally being raised from the rubble – it was subject to intensive bombing during WWII, due to its proximity to the port – and is worth exploring. This area, known as the Kalsa, was founded in the late 10th century and is one of the oldest quarters of Palermo. You'll need to be very wary of thieves. ■

Orientation

Palermo is a large but manageable city. The main streets of the historical centre are Via Roma and Via Maqueda, which extend from Stazione Centrale in the south to Piazza Castelnuovo, a vast square in the northern, modern part of town and a 20-minute walk from the train station. Around Stazione Centrale are most of the cheaper pensioni and hotels. It's a grimy and chaotic area, but behind the decaying palaces lining the main streets is a fascinating maze of narrow lanes and tiny piazzas where you will find markets and trattorie and, unfortunately, get an even better idea of just how decrepit Palermo is. Tourists need to be on their guard in these side streets, which are favourite haunts of bag snatchers, pickpockets and worse.

The area around Piazza Castelnuovo seems a world away, with its malls, outdoor cafés and designer shops. Intersecting Via Maqueda and Via Roma are Via Vittorio Emanuele and Via Cavour, the main thoroughfares to the port and Stazione Marittima (about a 10-minute walk east of Via Roma).

Information

Tourist Offices The main APT office (☎ 58 61 22) is at Piazza Castelnuovo 35. The staff speak English and you can pick up a map of the city and a monthly calendar of cultural, theatrical and musical events. Ask for the *Palermo Flash Guide* booklet. The office is open Monday to Friday from 8 am to 8 pm and Saturday to 2 pm. The branch office at Stazione Centrale was due to reopen at the time of writing. There is a branch office at Punta Raisi airport.

Foreign Consulates The UK consular agent (☎ 58 25 33) is at Via Cavour 117. France (☎ 58 50 73) is represented at Via Segesta 9 and Germany (☎ 58 33 77) at Via Emerico Amari 124. Although the US maintains an office (☎ 611 00 20) at Via Re Federico 18B, it mainly handles Italians' US pension problems.

Tunisia has a consulate (☎ 32 12 31) at Piazza Ignazio Florio 2. Most foreigners can travel as tourists to Tunisia visa-free, but it is worth dropping in (9 am to midday) to make sure. Australians may need a visa.

Most consulates are open Monday to Friday from about 9 am to midday (some to 1 pm).

Money The exchange office at Stazione Centrale is open daily from 8 am to 8 pm, and there's another at the airport (Banco di

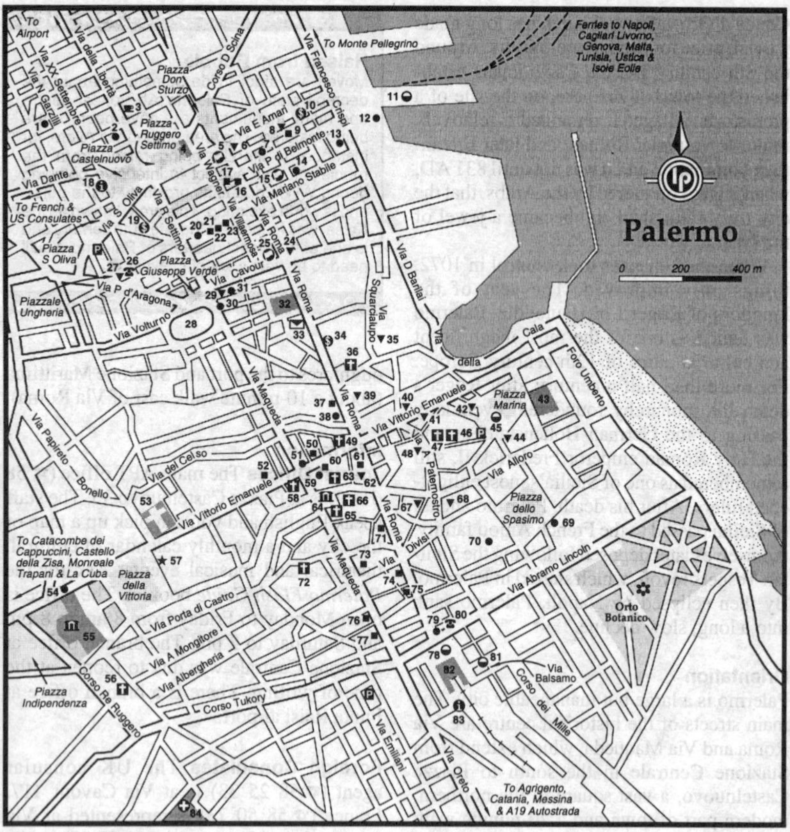

Sicilia). Banks are generally open from 8.30 am to 1.15 pm. Several have ATMs, including the Banca Nazionale del Lavoro, Via Roma 297, and the Monte dei Paschi di Siena off Via Sant'Oliva. American Express is represented by Ruggieri & Figli (☎ 58 71 44), Via Emerico Amari 40.

Post & Communications The main post office is at Via Roma 322. It is open from 8.10 am to 7.30 pm (on Saturday to 1.30 pm) and has fax and telex services. The post code for central Palermo is 90100.

There is a Telecom office virtually opposite Stazione Centrale in Piazza G Cesare. It is open daily from 8 am to 9.30 pm. The Telecom office on Piazzale Ungheria is open Monday to Saturday from 8 am to 8 pm.

The telephone code for Palermo is ☎ 091.

Travel Agencies Sestante CIT (☎ 58 63 33), where you can book train, ferry and air tickets, is at Via della Libertà 12. There is a CTS travel agent (☎ 611 07 13) at Via N Garzilli 28/G. A bit more convenient is Record Viaggi (☎ 611 09 10), Via Mariano Stabile 168 (between Via Ruggero Settimo and Via Roma).

PLACES TO STAY

- 9 Hotel Principe di Belmonte
- 16 Grand Hotel Le Palme
- 17 Hotel Petit
- 21 Hotel Libertà, Hotel Elite & Hotel Boston-Madonia
- 22 Hotel Tonic
- 23 Hotel Liguria
- 37 Hotel Moderna
- 50 Grande Albergo Sole
- 52 Centrale Palace Hotel
- 60 Albergo da Luigi
- 61 Hotel Le Terrazze
- 71 Albergo Corona
- 73 Hotel Sicilia
- 74 Albergos Piccadilly & Concordia
- 75 Albergo Rosalia Conca d'Oro
- 76 Albergo Orientale
- 77 Pensione Vittoria

PLACES TO EAT

- 3 Roney
- 6 Osteria lo Bianco
- 8 Hostaria Al-Duar
- 24 Hostaria da Sella
- 27 Charleston
- 29 Dal Pompiere
- 35 I Grilli
- 39 Trattoria Shanghai & Vucciria Market
- 40 Casa del Brodo
- 41 Ristorante Vittorio Emanuele
- 42 La Cambusa
- 44 Trattoria Il Crudo e Il Cotto
- 48 Antica Focacceria di San Francesco
- 62 Hostaria da Ciccio
- 67 Trattoria dai Vespri
- 68 Trattoria Stella

OTHER

- 1 CTS Travel Agency
- 2 CIT Travel Agency
- 4 Teatro Politeama
- 5 German Consulate
- 7 Pietro Barbaro (SNAV Agents)
- 10 American Express
- 11 Stazione Marittima
- 12 Tirrenia
- 13 Siremar
- 14 Grandi Traghetti & Grimaldi
- 15 Tunisian Consulate
- 18 APT Tourist Office
- 19 Monte dei Paschi di Siena
- 20 Record Viaggi Travel Agency
- 25 UK Consulate
- 26 Telecom Office
- 28 Teatro Massimo
- 30 Feltrinelli Bookshop
- 31 Opera dei Pupi
- 32 Museo Archeologico Regionale
- 33 Post Office
- 34 Banca Nazionale del Lavoro
- 36 Chiesa di San Domenico
- 38 Teatro Biondi
- 43 Palazzo Chiaramonte
- 45 AST Bus Station
- 46 Chiesa di San Francesco d'Assisi
- 47 Oratorio di San Lorenzo
- 49 Chiesa di San Matteo
- 51 Quattro Canti
- 53 Duomo
- 54 Porta Nuova
- 55 Palazzo dei Normanni & Cappella Palatina
- 56 Chiesa di San Giovanni degli Eremiti
- 57 Questura (Police Station)
- 58 Chiesa di San Giuseppe dei Teatini
- 59 Fontana Pretoria
- 63 Chiesa di Santa Caterina
- 64 Palazzo del Municipio
- 65 Chiesa di San Cataldo
- 66 La Martorana
- 69 Lo Spasimo
- 70 La Magione
- 72 Chiesa del Gesù
- 78 Urban Bus Station
- 79 Night Pharmacyion
- 80 Telecom Office
- 81 Intercity Bus Station
- 82 Stazione Centrale
- 83 APT Tourist Office
- 84 Hospital

Bookshops & Newsstands Feltrinelli, Via Maqueda 459, has a foreign language section which includes English. Several stands around Piazza Giuseppe Verdi sell foreign newspapers.

Medical Services In an emergency, phone the Public Hospital (Ospedale Civico), Via Carmelo Lazzaro, on ☎ 666 22 07, or ring for an ambulance on ☎ 30 66 44. There is an all-night pharmacy, Lo Cascio, near Stazione Centrale at Via Roma 1.

Emergency Ring the police on ☎ 113. The questura (☎ 21 01 11), where you should go to report thefts and other crimes, is in Piazza della Vittoria.

Dangers & Annoyances Despite a strong police presence in Palermo's historical centre, petty crime continues to be a major problem. Avoid wearing jewellery or carrying a bag, and keep your valuables in a money belt. The risk of being robbed is particularly high in the area from the Vucciria market towards the port. Women should not walk alone in the historical centre at night and all travellers would be best advised not to walk around in the area between Via Roma and the port at night.

Quattro Canti

The busy intersection of Via Vittorio Emanuele and Via Maqueda marks the Quattro Canti (the 'Four Corners' of Palermo), the centre of the oldest part of town. Each

Opening Times
Opening times of the principal sights are constantly changing. As a vague rule of thumb, most churches open from about 8 or 9 am to midday and again for a couple of hours from 3 pm. Museums generally open from 9 am to 1 pm and some open in the afternoon from 3 to 5 pm.

corner is marked by a 17th-century Spanish Baroque façade decorated with a fountain and a statue. On the south-west corner is the Baroque **Chiesa di San Giuseppe dei Teatini**, its interior dripping with marble.

Piazza Pretoria
This piazza hosts the eye-catching **Fontana Pretoria**, which was created by Florentine sculptors in the 16th century. At the time of its unveiling, the shocked populace named it the Fountain of Shame because of its nude figures. Take time to study the numerous figures which decorate its every corner. Closing off the east side of the piazza is the Baroque **Chiesa di Santa Caterina**, while the **Palazzo del Municipio**, also known as the Palazzo delle Aquile because of the eagle sculptures that guard each corner of the roof, fronts the southern edge of the square.

SICILIA

Chiesa di San Matteo
On the north side of Via Vittorio Emanuele, just before it crosses Via Roma, this Baroque church has a richly decorated interior. The four statues in the pilasters of the dome represent the Virtues and were carved by Giacomo Serpotta in 1728.

La Martorana
This is one of Palermo's most famous churches and is located in Piazza Bellini, a few steps south of Piazza Pretoria. It is also known as Chiesa di Santa Maria dell' Ammiraglio. Although the original 12th-century structure has been much altered, it retains its Arab-Norman bell tower and the interior is richly decorated with Byzantine mosaics. Totally in keeping with the decoration, the Greek eastern rite Mass is still celebrated here. Try to time your visit to avoid the many weddings celebrated in the church.

Chiesa di San Cataldo
Next to La Martorana is this tiny, simple church dating from the period of the Norman domination of Sicilia. Its battlements and red domes are another fusion of Arab and Norman styles. You'll need to get the key from the custodian who sits at a small table to the right as you enter La Martorana.

Duomo
Despite its hotchpotch of styles, Palermo's duomo, west of the Quattro Canti along Via Vittorio Emanuele, is certainly grand.

Built in the second half of the 12th century, the duomo has been modified many times since, most disastrously in the 18th century when the dome was added, spoiling the architectural harmony of the building. In the same period the interior was restored. The only part conserved in purely original Norman style is the apse, although the church remains an impressive example of Norman architecture. Arab influences in some of the geometric decoration are unmistakable and the graceful Gothic towers distract the eye from that dome. Inside are royal tombs, and among those interred in porphyry sarcophagi are Roger II, Henry VI of Hohenstaufen, Constance de Hauteville and Frederick II of Hohenstaufen. The ashes of St Rosalia, patron saint of Palermo, are contained in a silver urn in one of the church's numerous chapels.

Palazzo dei Normanni
Across the Piazza della Vittoria and the gardens is the Palazzo dei Normanni, also known as the Palazzo Reale (Royal Palace). Built by the Arabs in the 9th century, it was extended by the Normans and restructured by the Hohenstaufens. It is now the seat of Sicilia's regional government.

Enter from Piazza Indipendenza to see the **Cappella Palatino**, a magnificent example of Arab-Norman artistic genius, built during the reign of Roger II and decorated with

Byzantine mosaics. The chapel was once described as 'the finest religious jewel dreamt of by human thought', its mosaics rivalled only by those of Ravenna and Istanbul. While the mosaics demonstrate the Byzantine influence on Palermitan art, the geometric tile designs are a clear reminder of Arab input. The carved wooden ceiling is a classic example of intricate, Arab-style stalactite design. The chapel is open Monday to Friday from 9 am to midday and 3 to 5 pm and Saturday from 9 am to midday. It is open for one hour on Sunday from midday to 1 pm, but overrun by tour groups, so it's better to visit on another day, if possible. Admission is free.

The **Sala di Ruggero** (King Roger's Room), the king's former bedroom, is also worth visiting as it is decorated with 12th-century mosaics. It is only possible to visit the room with a guide (free of charge). Go upstairs from the Cappella Palatino. There are guided tours of the palace itself, but you'll need to book a few days in advance by sending a fax to 091-656 17 37.

Next to the palace is the **Porta Nuova**, built to celebrate the arrival of Charles V in Palermo in 1535.

Chiesa di San Giovanni degli Eremiti

Just south of the palace, this church is a simple and tranquil refuge from the chaos outside. Located in Via dei Benedettini, St John of the Hermits is yet another example of the Sicilian Arab-Norman architectural mix. Built under Roger II, it is topped by five red domes and set in a pretty, atmospheric garden with cloisters. The bare interior of the now deconsecrated church features some badly deteriorated frescoes.

Museo Archeologico & Around

A block north of the main post office on Via Roma is the Museo Archeologico Regionale. To enter, turn left into Via Bara all'Olivella and into Piazza Olivella. The museum houses a collection of Greek metopes from Selinunte, the Hellenistic *Bronze Ram of Siracusa* and finds from archaeological sites throughout the island. Although there is not a lot to see, apart from the metopes, the museum is definitely worth a visit. It is open Monday to Saturday from 9 am to 1.30 pm (also on Tuesday and Friday from 3 to 6.30 pm) and on Sunday and holidays to 12.30 pm. Admission is L2000.

About 200m south on Via Roma is the **Chiesa di San Domenico**. The grand 17th-century structure houses the tombs of many important Sicilians and a wealth of paintings.

Towards Piazza Marina

Plunge into the streets heading towards the waterfront from the intersection of Via Vittorio Emanuele and Via Roma and you'll find a few more architectural gems. The **Oratorio di San Lorenzo**, Via dell' Immacolatella, is decorated with stuccoes by Giacomo Serpotta (his greatest work). Caravaggio's last known piece, a Nativity, once hung over the altar. It was stolen in 1969 and has never been recovered. Virtually next door, the 13th-century **Chiesa di San Francesco d'Assisi** features a fine rose window and Gothic portal that have survived numerous restorations and restructuring.

Palazzo Chiaramonte

This imposing 14th-century palace in Piazza Marina boasts an imposing façade that served as a model for many other buildings in Sicilia. The island's Grand Parliament sat here in the 16th century and, for many years, so did the Holy Office of the Inquisition.

Lo Spasimo

South of Piazza Marina, across Via Alloro, this complex of buildings includes the Chiesa di Santa Maria dello Spasimo, a typical example of the late-Gothic style, although it was actually built during the Renaissance. Building work on the church extended as far as the walls and the soaring apse, but it has stood for centuries without a roof and its interior is host to a couple of tall Ailanthus altissima trees. Restored and opened to the public in 1995, the complex is an atmospheric venue for concerts, performances and exhibitions. Across a vast piazza from Lo Spasimo is the **Chiesa della SS**

Trinità, also known as La Magione, a fine Norman church, dating from 1193.

Catacombe dei Cappuccini

For centuries, Sicilians of a certain social standing who didn't want to be forgotten on their death were embalmed by Capuchin monks. The catacombs in the Capuchin convent on Piazza Cappuccino, west of the city centre, contain the mummified bodies and skeletons of some 8000 Palermitans who died between the 17th and 19th centuries. Although time has been unkind to most (some are just skeletons with suits on), a few are remarkably intact. Rosalia Lombardi, who died at the age of two in 1920, has auburn hair tied in a yellow bow, and looks as though she could be sleeping – even if she is rather pallid. The catacombs are open daily from 9 am to midday and from 3 to 5 pm. You'll be required to make a donation on entry – L2000 or L3000 is acceptable.

La Zisa

In the same area is this 12th-century Arab-Norman castle. The name, which means 'the Splendid', testifies to its magnificence. It was built for William I and completed by William II, and is open Monday to Saturday from 9 am to 1.30 pm (also on Tuesday and Friday from 3 to 5 pm) and on Sunday and holidays to 12.30 pm. Admission is free.

La Cuba

Built in 1180, this castle was once part of an enormous park planned by William II, which also incorporated La Zisa. La Cuba has long been engulfed by an army barracks on Via Calatafimi, but you can visit it Monday to Saturday, 9 am to 1 pm (Monday and Thursday also from 3 to 5 pm) and the first and third Sunday of the month from 9 am to 1 pm.

Teatro Massimo

Overlooking Piazza Giuseppe Verdi, the proud and haughty 19th-century Teatro Massimo has finally been partially reopened following a restoration programme that has been in progress for 20 years. At the time of writing, the theatre was about to host its first season in decades.

Markets

Palermo's historical ties with the Arab world and its proximity to North Africa are reflected in the noisy street life of the city's ancient centre. Nowhere is this more evident than in its markets, which make a truly Oriental assault on all the senses.

Several markets are spread through the tangle of lanes and alleys of central Palermo, but the most famous is the **Vucciria**, winding south from the Chiesa di San Domenico. Here you can purchase anything your stomach desires (and several items it may recoil at – slippery tripe and all sorts of fishy things) as well as a host of off-the-back-of-a-truck-style bargains. This is another place where it is a bad idea to carry bags or purses: keep your money in a money belt.

Places to Stay

You should have little trouble finding a room in Palermo at whatever price you choose. The tourist office will make recommendations, but not bookings.

Head for Via Maqueda or Via Roma, between the station and Quattro Canti, for the bulk of the cheap rooms, some of which are in old apartment buildings. Rooms facing onto either street will be noisy. Women on their own should be wary about staying in the area near the train station. Prostitutes from time to time bring clients to the cheaper hotels, though as a rule this is not really a problem. The area around Piazza Castelnuovo offers a higher standard of accommodation with fewer budget options (catch bus No 101 or 107 from the train station to Piazza Sturzo).

Places to Stay – bottom end

Camping The best camping ground is *Trinacria* (☎ 53 05 90), Via Barcarello 25, by the sea at Sferracavallo. It costs L6500 per person, plus L13,000 for a tent place. Catch bus No 628 from Piazzale A De Gasperi (which can be reached by bus No 101 from Stazione Centrale).

Hotels Near the train station, try the *Albergo Orientale* (☎ 616 57 27), Via Maqueda 26, in an old and somewhat decayed building with a once grand courtyard. Basic singles/doubles are L25,000/40,000 and triples are L60,000. Just around the corner is *Albergo Rosalia Conca d'Oro* (☎ 616 45 43), Via Santa Rosalia 7, with ancient, but clean singles/doubles for L35,000/50,000 and triples for L75,000. The *Pensione Vittoria* (☎ 616 24 37), Via Maqueda 8, is close to the station and has still more spartan singles/doubles for L25,000/38,000, or L35,000/50,000 with bathroom.

There are a few hotels in one building at Via Roma 72. The *Albergo Piccadilly* (☎ 617 64 70) has clean rooms (even if there are holes in the bedspreads) for L30,000/50,000, while the *Albergo Concordia* (☎ 617 15 14) is also reasonable value at L30,000/50,000. The *Albergo Corona* (☎ 616 23 40), Via Roma 118, has clean, pleasant rooms for L32,000/50,000; a double with a bathroom is L60,000. *Albergo da Luigi* (☎ 58 50 85), Via Vittorio Emanuele 284, is next to the Quattro Canti. It has rooms for L25,000/50,000, and with a bathroom for L40,000/60,000 or more, depending on the room – ask for one with a view onto the Piazza Pretoria and its fountain.

Hotel Sicilia (☎ 616 84 60), Via Divisi 99, on the corner of Via Maqueda, has large rooms of a reasonable standard, although they can be quite noisy. Singles/doubles L45,000/65,000, and triples are L75,000, all with a bathroom.

Around Piazza Castelnuovo, *Hotel Petit* (☎ 32 36 16), Via Principe di Belmonte 84, has comfortable rooms for L35,000/55,000 or for L50,000/65,000 with a bathroom. A triple with bathroom is L90,000. The *Hotel Liguria* (☎ 58 15 88), Via Mariano Stabile 128, offers a good standard of accommodation. Rooms are L35,000/50,000 and doubles with a bathroom are L65,000.

Places to Stay – middle

Near Via Vittorio Emanuele, at Via Roma 188, *Hotel Le Terrazze* (☎ 58 63 65) is an agreeable and clean establishment with great views of the city. Rooms are L50,000/65,000 or L60,000/80,000 with a bathroom. Farther north on Via Roma at No 276, the *Hotel Moderno* (☎ 58 86 83) offers good rooms for L65,000/95,000 and triples for L120,000 with a bathroom.

Near Piazza Castelnuovo, the *Albergo Libertà* (☎ 32 19 11), Via Mariano Stabile 136, is a good choice. It has singles/doubles for L45,000/70,000 or for L70,000/90,000 with a bathroom; triples with bathroom are L120,000. There are several other hotels in the same building. The *Hotel Elite* (☎ 32 93 18) has singles/doubles for L75,000/95,000 and triples for L125,000, all with a bathroom. The *Hotel Boston-Madonia* (☎ 58 02 34) has doubles with bathroom for L85,000, which you can have as singles for about L60,000. Hotel Tonic (☎ 58 17 54), Via Mariano Stabile 126, has decent singles/doubles with bathroom for L60,000/85,000.

Hotel Principe di Belmonte (☎ 33 10 65), Via Principe di Belmonte 25, has rooms for L45,000/85,000, or for L70,000/90,000 with a bathroom.

Places to Stay – top end

The *Centrale Palace Hotel* (☎ 33 66 66; fax 33 48 81), Via Vittorio Emanuele 327, is an excellent choice. It has elegantly furnished rooms and full services; breakfast is included. Singles are L130,000, doubles L200,000 and triples L260,000. Renovations are under way to turn it into a 4-star hotel, so prices will go up. The *Grande Albergo Sole* (☎ 58 18 11; fax 611 01 82), Via Vittorio Emanuele 291, has attractive rooms for L150,000/ 200,000.

The four-star *Grand Hotel Le Palme* (☎ 58 39 33; fax 33 15 45), Via Roma 398, at the Piazza Castelnuovo end of town, is one of the ritziest hotels in Palermo. Its beautiful rooms cost L180,000/240,000, including breakfast.

Places to Eat

With more than 300 officially listed restaurants and eateries to choose from in the city and surrounding area, you should have little trouble finding something to suit your taste and budget.

Palermo's cuisine takes advantage of the fresh produce of the sea and the fertile Conca d'Oro valley. One of its most famous dishes is the tasty pasta con le sarde, with sardines, fennel, peppers, capers and pine nuts. Swordfish is served here sliced into huge steaks. A reflection of Sicilia's proximity to North Africa is the infiltration of couscous, basically a bowl of steamed semolina with a sauce.

Palermitans are late eaters and restaurants rarely open for dinner before 8 pm.

Inexpensive Restaurants *Dal Pompiere*, Via Bara all'Olivella 107, just up the road from the Opera dei Pupi puppet theatre, has a simple, but filling, set-menu lunch for L10,000. The *Hostaria la Sella*, Via Cavour 97, also has a good lunch for L14,000.

If you want to try an age-old Palermo snack – a panino with milza (veal innards) and ricotta cheese – head for the *Antica Focacceria di San Francesco*, Via Paternostro 58. It's one of the city's oldest eating houses and worth seeking out; it serves pizza slices and similar snacks.

Another Palermitan institution is the *Casa del Brodo*, Via Vittorio Emanuele 173. For more than 100 years it has been serving up various broths and boiled meat dishes, all much appreciated by locals. It has a L22,000 tourist menu.

Osteria lo Bianco, Via E Amari 104, off Via Roma at the Castelnuovo end of town, has a menu that changes daily. A full meal will cost under L20,000. *Trattoria Stella*, Via Alloro 104, is in the courtyard of the old Hotel Patria. In summer, the entire courtyard is filled with tables. A full meal will come to around L35,000.

Trattoria dai Vespri, Piazza Santa Croce dei Vespri 8, off Via Roma, past Chiesa di Santa Anna, has outside tables and excellent food for around L30,000 for a full meal. Meat and seafood are cooked on an outdoor barbecue in summer.

Hostaria da Ciccio, Via Firenze 6, just off Via Roma, is one of Palermo's best-loved cheaper eating places – and the food really is great. A meal will cost from around L30,000.

Trattoria Shanghai, right in the middle of the Vucciria market, is an atmospheric little place with tables on a terrace overlooking the market. Despite its Chinese name, the trattoria serves typical Sicilian food, which is reasonably priced but not the best you can eat in Palermo.

La Cambusa and *Trattoria Il Crudo e Il Cotto*, both in Piazza Marina, near the port,

SICILIA

Unravelling the History of Noodles

The legend goes that Marco Polo discovered noodles in China and was so impressed that he introduced them to Italy. Nice story, but that particular historical recipe for the rise and rise of pasta as a national staple should probably not be swallowed.

Rather, it seems more likely Italian pasta was born in Sicilia. First come the ingredients. The durum wheat used to make a decent pasta noodle was apparently unknown in Italy until the Arabs introduced it to Sicilia when they conquered the island in the 9th century. It seems the spaghetti variant was an early version of the noodle – an illustrated Arabic handbook on healthy living depicts great swathes of the thin noodles draped over ladder-like stands to dry. Al-Idrissi, an Arab visitor to the island in the 12th century (long after the Arab occupation had come to an end), described the place in glowing terms and remarked that so much of this 'string-like food made of flour' was produced that he thought you could feed half the world on it!

The word 'pasta' itself appears to come from ancient Greek. Given the long-standing Greek presence in Sicilia, that is hardly surprising. Apparently, the tubes of pasta that have come to be known as *maccheroni* also emerged in Sicilia – some claim the word is from the Greek *makaria*. The Sicilian love of pasta grew to such proportions that the island's inhabitants were known to haughty Neapolitans in the Middle Ages as *sicilianu manciamaccaruna* – Sicilian maccheroni-munchers! ■

Gelato

It is difficult to get a bad gelato in Italy. Instead, the challenge is to find the best! It is not surprising that many travellers to Italy become obsessed with the country's ice-cream, it really is so good and comes in so many flavours that it seems a shame not to eat at least two or three a day. Serious gelato eaters should search out the *gelaterie* which make their ice-cream on the premises, particularly the few establishments which actually make their gelato from scratch, using fresh ingredients (many places use industrial powdered flavours these days).

You only need to try one of the fruit flavours in order to be able to tell the difference. Most Italians would agree that the best gelato in the country is found in Sicilia and if you locate a good gelateria, which makes its own ice-cream with fresh ingredients, you will realise that you have probably never before eaten a gelato *that* good! ■

are popular and serve good meals for around L30,000. The former sometimes has a set all-inclusive seafood menu for L35,000. Not far away, the *Ristorante Vittorio Emanuele*, at No 150 on the street of the same name, has a limited but tasty menu.

If you feel like a Tunisian night out, with couscous and other typical North African dishes, try the *Hostaria Al-Duar*, Via Ammiraglio Gravina 31A, the first street south of Via E Amari. It has a L15,000 set menu.

Expensive Restaurants Most of the posher restaurants are on the outskirts of Palermo or in nearby towns. *I Mandarini* (☎ 671 21 99) is at Pallavicino, near Mondello beach, at Via Rosario da Patanna 18. The food is good and a meal will cost at least L40,000. The locals head for Mondello to eat seafood. Try *La Barcaccia* (☎ 45 40 79), Via Piano di Gallo 4. Again, you will be lucky to eat for under L40,000. A popular but pricey fish restaurant at Sferracavallo is the *Al Delfino* (☎ 53 02 82). Don't expect much change from L100,000.

The *Charleston* is one of Palermo's classiest restaurants. Its main establishment is in Palermo at Piazzale Ungheria 30. In summer it generally closes and its Mondello branch takes over, with outdoor eating on Viale Regina Elena. Expect to pay around L100,000 per head for a memorable meal.

Cafés In Via Principe di Belmonte (which is closed to traffic between Via Ruggero Settimo and Via Roma) there are numerous cafés with outdoor tables where you can linger over breakfast or lunch. If you want to spend less, buy a panino in one of the many bars along Via Roma. For an expensive afternoon tea, head for *Roney*, Via della Libertà 13, Palermo's most fashionable and best-known pasticceria. *I Grilli* is a popular cocktail bar (and restaurant) in Piazza Cavallieri di Malta, north-east of the Vucciria market.

Markets The *Vucciria market* is held daily, except Sunday, in the narrow streets between Via Roma, Piazza San Domenico and Via Vittorio Emanuele. Here you can buy fresh fruit and vegetables, meat, cheese and seafood. Or you can just watch as huge, freshly caught swordfish and tuna are sliced up and sold in minutes. Numerous stalls sell steaming-hot boiled octopus. Although the best known, the Vucciria is far from the only such market around town. For other grocery supplies, try the *Standa supermarket* at Via della Libertà 30.

Entertainment

Theatre For opera and ballet, the main venue is the Teatro Politeama (☎ 605 33 15) on Piazza Ruggero Settimo. There is a summer programme of the Teatro Massimo. If your Italian is up to it, you can see plays at the Teatro Biondi (☎ 58 87 55) on Via Roma. *Il Giornale di Sicilia* has a daily listing of what's on.

Opera dei Pupi Something of a Sicilian speciality, the Opera dei Pupi, Via Bara all'Olivella 95, just south of Via Cavour, makes for an enchanting performance experience. It's a good break for young kids, and the elaborate old puppets will endear them-

SICILIA

selves to adults too. You can generally expect shows to be staged on weekends. At No 40, in the same street, is one of several artisans who makes and repairs the puppets.

Getting There & Away

Air The airport is at Punta Raisi, 32km west of Palermo, and is a terminal for domestic and European flights. For information about domestic flights, ring Alitalia on ☎ 1478 6 56 41 and for international flights, ring ☎ 1478 6 56 42. Alitalia has an office (☎ 601 93 33) at Via della Libertà 39. It is usually possible at any time of the year to hunt down charter flights to major European cities such as London – shop around.

Bus The main Intercity bus station is around Via Paolo Balsamo, to the east of the train station.

Segesta (☎ 616 79 19), Via Balsamo 26, has a daily direct service to Roma (L50,000 one way). It also runs frequent buses to Trapani (two hours). SAIS (☎ 616 60 28), Via Balsamo 16, runs services to Roma, with a change at Catania, costing L92,000 one way. SAIS also services Catania (more than 20 a day), Enna (six a day), Piazza Armerina (four a day), Siracusa (six a day), Messina (via Catania; 10 a day) and Cefalù (two a day). For Marsala, go to Salemi (☎ 617 54 11), Via Rosario Gregorio 44. Cuffaro and Fratelli Camilleri between them have about 10 buses a day to Agrigento.

Away from the main terminal, AST (☎ 688 27 83), Piazza Marina 31, runs three daily buses to Ragusa.

Numerous other companies service points throughout Sicilia and most have offices in the Via Paolo Balsamo area. Their addresses and telephone numbers, as well as destinations, are listed in *Palermo Flash Guide*, available at the tourist office.

Train Regular trains leave from Stazione Centrale for Milazzo, Messina, Catania, Siracusa and Agrigento, as well as nearby towns such as Cefalù. There are also Intercity trains for Reggio di Calabria, Napoli and Roma. Train timetable information is available in English at the station. There is a Transalpino office inside the station, as well as baggage-storage and bathing facilities.

Car & Motorcycle Palermo is accessible by autostrada from Messina (only partially completed) and from Catania (which passes Enna). Trapani and Marsala are also easily accessible by autostrada, while Agrigento and Palermo are linked by a good state road through the interior of the island.

Rental Europcar (☎ 32 19 49) has an office at Via Cavour 77A, as well as others at the train station (☎ 616 50 50) and the airport (☎ 59 12 27). All major rental companies are represented in Palermo.

Boat Ferries leave from Molo Vittorio Veneto, off Via Francesco Crispi, for Cagliari (Sardegna), Napoli, Livorno and Genova (see the Getting There & Away section at the beginning of this chapter for further details). The Tirrenia office (☎ 33 33 00) is at the port in Palazzina Stella Maris, Calata Marinai d'Italia. Siremar (☎ 58 26 88) runs ferries and hydrofoils to Ustica and the Isole Eolie; its office is at Via F Crispi 118. SNAV, represented by the Pietro Barbaro agency (☎ 33 33 33) at Via Principe Belmonte 55, also runs a summer service to the Isole Eolie.

Grandi Traghetti, part of the Grimaldi Group, (☎ 58 93 31), Calata Marinai d'Italia, at the port, runs ferries from Palermo to Genova and Livorno. Its more upmarket line, Grandi Navi Veloci, runs ferries to Malta and Tunisia. The one-way fare for a bed in a shared cabin from Palermo to either Malta or Tunisia is L194,000 in the high season. The direct trip to Malta is 12 hours and to Tunis 9 hours. There is also a service to Malta, via Tunisia, which takes 33 hours, including a 12-hour stop in Tunis.

The *deposito bagagli* at the ferry terminal is open daily from 7 am to 8 pm.

Getting Around

The Airport Taxis to the airport cost upwards of L60,000. The cheaper option is to catch one of the regular blue buses run by Prestìa e Comandè, which leave from outside Stazione Centrale, in front of the Hotel Elena, from 5.25 am to 9.15 pm roughly every hour (a timetable is posted at the bus stop, to your right as you leave the station). Buses also stop in Piazza Ruggero Settimo, in front of the Teatro Politeama. The trip takes one hour and costs L4500.

Bus Palermo's city buses (AMAT) are efficient, and most stop in front of the train station. Tickets must be purchased before you get on the bus and are available from tobacconists or the booths at the terminal. They cost L1500 and are valid for one hour. A day pass costs L5000. Useful routes are:

No 107
: from the train station along Via Roma to the Teatro Politeama, near Piazza Castelnuovo, and on to the Giardino Inglese up Via della Libertà

No 101
: from the train station along Via Roma to the Politeama and on past the Giardino Inglese to Piazza A De Gasperi, from where there are connecting buses to Mondello and Sferracavallo

No 812
: from near the Politeama to Monte Pellegrino

No 833
: (summer only), from Piazza Don Sturzo to Mondello, along the coast

No 603
: (year-round), Piazza de Gaspari to Mondello

No 614
: from Piazza A De Gasperi to Mondello

No 628
: from Piazza A De Gasperi to Sferracavallo

No 12
: from Piazza Giuseppe Verdi to Monte Pellegrino

No GT
: from Piazza Giuseppe Verdi to Mondello

No 139
: from the train station to the port

No 105
: from under the trees diagonally left across the piazza from the train station to Piazza dell'Indipendenza, from where there are connecting buses to Monreale and the Convento dei Cappuccini

No 389
: from Piazza dell'Indipendenza to Monreale

No 327
: from Piazza dell'Indipendenza to the Convento dei Cappuccini

No 124
: from the Politeama to reach the Castello della Zisa

Metropolitana Palermo's metro system won't be of much use to most people, as its 10 stations radiating out from Stazione Centrale are a good hike from any destinations of tourist interest. There is talk of expanding the system to Punta Raisi airport, which would be useful. A single trip ticket costs L1500.

Car & Motorcycle If you have dealt with Roma or Napoli in your own vehicle, Palermo will present no difficulties. Theft of and from vehicles is a problem, however, and you are advised to use one of the attended car parks around town if your hotel has no parking space. You'll be looking at L15,000 to L20,000 for 24 hours. Some hotels have small car parks, but they are often full; check with your hotel proprietor.

AROUND PALERMO

There are beaches north-west of the city at Mondello and Sferracavallo, but if you're really into spending some time by the sea, you'd be better off heading farther afield, to Scopello, for example. **Mondello** is popular with Palermitans, who crowd the beachfront Viale Regina Elena for the evening stroll. There are numerous seafood restaurants and snack stalls along the avenue. For bus information, see the Palermo Getting Around section.

Between Palermo and Mondello is Monte Pellegrino and the **Santuario di Santa Rosalia**. Palermo's patron saint, St Rosalia lived as a hermit in a cave on the mountain, now the site of a 17th-century shrine. The water, which is channelled from the roof of the cave into a large font, is said to have miraculous powers. Whatever your beliefs, this is a fascinating place to visit, but remember that it is a shrine, not a tourist haunt. The sanctuary is open daily from 7 am to 7 pm. See the Getting Around section in Palermo for bus details.

On the northern side of Monte Pellegrino, at Addaura, is the **Grotta dell'Addaura**, where several cave drawings from the Paleolithic period have managed to survive into the 20th century. It is possible to visit the cave, but you'll need to make arrangements through the Palermo APT.

Monreale

An absolute must is a visit to the **cathedral** at Monreale, about 8km south-west of Palermo and accessible by frequent city buses. See Getting Around in the Palermo section earlier in this chapter.

The magnificent 12th-century Norman cathedral was built for William II. It is said he did not want to be inferior to his grandfather, Roger, who was responsible for the cathedral at Cefalù and the Cappella Palatino at Palermo. Considered the finest example of Norman architecture in Sicilia, the cathedral in fact incorporates Norman, Arab, Byzantine and classical elements and, despite renovations over the centuries, remains substantially intact. The central doorway has bronze doors by Bonanno Pisano and its north door is by Barisano di Trani. The interior of the cathedral is almost entirely covered by dazzling gilded mosaics, the work of Byzantine artisans, representing the complete cycle of the Old and New Testaments. Over the altar is a towering mosaic of Jesus Christ.

Outside the cathedral is the entrance to the cloisters, which were part of a Benedictine abbey once attached to the church. There are 228 twin columns with polychrome ornamentation. Each of the Romanesque capitals is different, depicting plants, animals and fantastic motifs. The capital of the 19th column on the west aisle depicts William II offering the cathedral to the Madonna.

The cathedral is open daily from 8 am to midday and 3.30 to 6 pm. The cloisters are open Monday to Saturday from 9 am to 1 pm (Monday, Wednesday and Friday also 3 to 6 pm) and Sunday from 9 am to 12.30 pm. Admission is L2000.

Solunto

About 17km east of Palermo are the remains of the Hellenistic-Roman town of Solunto. Although the ancient city is only partially excavated, what has been brought to light is well worth the trip. Founded in the 4th century BC on the site of an earlier Phoenician settlement, Solunto was built in a particularly panoramic position, on Monte Catalfano, overlooking the sea. Wander along the main street, the Decumanus, and take detours up the steep, paved sidestreets to explore the ruined houses, some of which still sport their original mosaic floors. Take particular note of the theatre and the House of Leda (if you can find it), which has an interesting floor mosaic. A new museum was due to be opened at the site in 1998.

The site is open Monday to Saturday, 9 am to 7 pm and Sunday from 9 am to 12.30 pm. To get there, take the train from Palermo to the Santa Flavia-Solunto-Porticello stop and ask for directions. It's about a half-hour uphill walk.

Ustica

Almost 60km north of Palermo lies the lonely island of Ustica. In 1980, a passenger jet crashed near the island in mysterious circumstances, leaving 81 people dead. Investigators suspect the military was involved, and a dozen officers of the Italian airforce officers stand accused of a cover-up.

Ustica is otherwise a tranquil place with barely more than 1000 inhabitants, most living in the mural-bedecked village of the same name. The best months to come are June and September. To visit during August is sheer lunacy. Parts of the rocky coast have been declared a Riserva Marina (marine reserve), and the limpid waters, kept sparkling clean by an Atlantic current through the Straits of Gibraltar, are ideal for diving.

There is an information office (☎ 844 94 56) for the Riserva Marina on Piazza della Vittoria, part of an interlocking series of squares in the centre of the village. It is open from 8 am to 8 pm and staff can advise on activities – they have a list of the island's dive centres. For police, call the carabinieri on ☎ 844 90 49. The Pronto Soccorso, for medical emergencies, is on ☎ 844 92 48.

The island's telephone code is ☎ 091.

Activities Among the most rewarding dive sites are the Secca Colombara, to the north of the island, and the Scoglio del Medico, to the west. Note that Zone A of the marine reserve, taking in a good stretch of the western coast north of Punta dello Spalmatore, is protected. Fishing, diving and even swimming are forbidden in the area without permission. The reserve's information office can organise sea-watch diving excursions into the zone. The only dive hire outlet, Ailara Rosalia (☎ 844 91 62), Banchina Barresi, operates in summer. Otherwise, bring your own gear.

You can also hire a boat and cruise around the island, visiting its many grottoes and tiny beaches. Osteodes (☎ 844 92 10), Via Magazzino 5, is one of several agents which can organise boat trips, or you could try Ariston da Bartolo (☎ 844 95 42) to hire a boat or dinghy.

Places to Stay & Eat There are eight hotels and several affittacamere on Ustica. The *Pensione Clelia* (☎ 844 94 34), Via Magazzino 7, is a decent place with rooms for L35,000/65,000. In the high season, prices rocket to L88,000 per head for full board. It has a good little restaurant and the town centre has many others.

Getting There & Away From April to December there is at least one Siremar hydrofoil a day from Palermo. A car ferry runs daily throughout the year (in winter there is nothing on Sunday). One-way passenger fares are L28,500 (hydrofoil) and L16,700 (ferry) in the high season. The Siremar office (☎ 844 90 02) is on Piazza Capitano V di Bartolo, in the centre of Ustica.

Getting Around Orange minibuses run around the island from the village, or you could hire a moped at the Hotel Ariston in town.

NORTH COAST

Parco delle Madonie

This 40,000 hectare park, between Palermo and Cefalù, incorporates the Madonie mountain range and some of the highest mountains in Sicilia after Etna (the highest peak in the range is Pizzo Carbonara at 1979m). Instituted in 1989 by the Regione Sicilia, the park also takes in several small towns and villages and plenty of farms and vineyards. It is an area where people live, rather than simply a nature reserve – so you can combine hiking with visits to some of the more interesting towns in the park, such as Geraci Siculo and Petralia Soprana and Sottana. There are information offices of the Ente Parco delle Madonie (the body responsible for the park) at Petralia Sottana (☎ 0921-8 02 01) and Isnello (☎ 0921-6 27 95). There is also an Internet site at www.comunec.it/parks.html with details about the park and several one-day walks, as well as information about transport and accommodation.

There are several *rifugi* in the park, including the *Rifugio Ostello della Gioventù* (☎ 0921-4 99 95), Piano della Battaglia, località Mandria Marcate. The *Madonie* (☎ 0921-4 11 06), Corso Paolo Agliata 81, at Petralia Sottana, is another option. If you're looking for something more characteristic, there are some excellent agriturismo-style establishments in the area. *Tenuta Gangivecchio* (☎ 0921-8 91 91) is in a former Benedictine convent, dating from the 14th century, just out of the town of Gangi, towards the interior of Sicilia. Children under 10 aren't accepted at Easter and New Year. Half board is from L100,000. *Flugy Barone d'Aspermont* (☎ 0921-7 41 28), near San Mauro Castelverde and close to Cefalù, offers accommodation in small apartments with kitchens. Half board costs from L85,000 per person.

Transport could be a problem in the Madonie unless you have a car. The towns within the park are serviced by SAIS and AST buses from Palermo, but if you want to reach some of the more secluded parts of the park, you might find that hitching a ride is the only option.

Cefalù

Just over an hour by train or bus from Palermo, Cefalù is an attractive beachside village backing onto the rocky frontage to the Madonie mountains. Something of a tourist magnet, it is unspoiled and makes for a relaxing day trip from the capital.

The AAST tourist office (☎ 2 10 50) is at Corso Ruggero 77 and is open Monday to Friday from 8 am to 2 pm and 4 to 7 pm and Saturday to 2 pm. From the train station, turn right into Via Moro to reach Via Matteotti and the old town. If you are heading for the beach, turn left and walk along Via Gramsci, which becomes Via V Martoglio. Cefalù's telephone code is ☎ 0921.

Things to See & Do Roger II built the **cathedral** in the 12th century to fulfil a vow to God after his fleet was saved during a violent storm off Cefalù. The twin pyramid towers of the cathedral stand out over the town centre, but the real beauty is inside. A towering figure of Christ Pancrator in the apse is the focal point of the elaborate Byzantine mosaics. The columns of the twin aisles support Arab-style pointed arches and have beautiful capitals.

SICILIA

Off Piazza del Duomo, in Via Mandralisca, is the private **Museo Mandralisca**. Its collection includes Greek ceramics and Arab pottery, as well as paintings, notably the *Portrait of an Unknown Man* by Antonello da Messina. Opening hours vary according to the time of year, but are roughly 9 am to 12.30 pm and 4 to 6 pm daily. It opens to midnight in July and August. Admission is L5000.

From the old town's main street, Via Matteotti, look for the sign pointing uphill to the **Tempio di Diana** and make the one-hour climb to the castle. Both are ruins that can be visited, but the main attraction is the panoramic view.

Places to Stay & Eat There are several camping grounds in the area, including *Costa Ponente Internazionale* (☎ 2 00 85), about 4km west of the town at Contrada Ogliastrillo. It costs L8500 per person and up to L17,000 for a site. Catch the bus from the train station heading for Lasari.

In town, the only really cheap option is *Locanda Cangelosi* (☎ 2 15 91), Via Umberto I, 26 with singles/doubles for L28,000/40,000. *La Giara* (☎ 2 15 62), Via Veterani 40, uphill from the beach and off Corso Ruggero, has rooms for L60,000/90,000. *Baia del Capitano* (☎ 2 00 05) is in an olive grove near the beach at Mazzaforno, a few km out of town towards Palermo. Its pleasant rooms are L120,000/150,000.

Trattoria La Botte, Via Veterani 6, just off Corso Ruggero, serves full meals for around L25,000. Otherwise, there are plenty of restaurants and several bars along Via Vittorio Emanuele.

Getting There & Away SAIS buses leave Palermo for Cefalù twice daily (see the Palermo Getting There & Away section). Trains are more frequent, if a little slow.

Tindari

Farther along the coast towards Milazzo, at Capo Tindari, are the ruins of ancient Tyndaris, founded in 396 BC as a Greek settlement on a rocky promontory. It was later occupied by the Romans and destroyed by Arab invaders. Today, fragments remain of the city's ramparts, as well as a Greek theatre and Roman buildings, including a house and public baths. A museum houses a collection of Hellenistic statues as well as Greek and Roman pottery. The site is open from 9 am to one hour before sunset. Entry is free.

Nearby is the **Santuario della Madonna Nera**. Built in this century to house a statue of a black Madonna revered since Byzantine times, the sanctuary is a place of pilgrimage.

To get to Tindari, catch a train to Patti (on the Palermo-Messina line) and then a bus to the site from outside the station (three a day, with increased services in summer).

Milazzo

This is not the prettiest sight in Sicilia, but most people aiming for the Isole Eolie pass through here. You could head to the northern end of town for a peek at the 16th-century Spanish **castle**, open in summer daily, except

Monday, from 10 am to 7 pm, with shorter hours in winter.

There are several hotels near the port if you get stuck for the night. The *Central* (☎ 090-928 10 43), Via del Sole 8, has basic rooms for L35,000/60,000.

Milazzo is easy to reach by bus or train from Palermo and Messina. See Getting There & Away in the Messina section. Intercity buses terminate in Piazza della Repubblica, a five-minute walk back along Via Crispi to the port. The train station is a little farther away, connected to the port by bus No 01.

If you have your own transport, the drive north along the coast from Messina to Capo Peloro and then round to the east is pretty, and there are some reasonable **beaches** between the cape and Acquarone. Where the coast road meets the A20 heading for Milazzo, take the tollway, as the SS113 can be incredibly congested from this point.

Isole Eolie

The seven islands of this volcanic archipelago stretching north of Milazzo range from the developed tourist resort of Lipari and the understated jet-set haunt of Panarea, to the rugged Vulcano, the spectacular scenery of Stromboli and its fiercely active volcano, the fertile vineyards of Salina, and the solitude of outlying Alicudi and Filicudi. Also known as the Lipari Islands, the Isole Eolie (Aeolian Islands) have been inhabited since the Neolithic era, when people travelled there for the valuable volcanic glass, obsidian.

The ancient Greeks believed the islands were the home of Aeolus, the god of the wind, and Homer wrote of them in his *Odyssey*. Characterised by their rich colours and volcanic activity, the rugged coastlines are at times lashed by violent seas. As attractive as all this may appear to the modern traveller, the Isole Eolie have traditionally made for a difficult living environment. From the 1930s to 50s many inhabitants migrated to Australia (often referred to here as the eighth Isole Eolie), virtually abandoning the outer islands and leaving behind only a small contingent on the others.

Cinema fans might like to see Nani Moretti's *Caro Diario* (Dear Diary). Part of this quirky film is set in the islands, and Moretti captures their essence well.

You will need to book accommodation well in advance in the July-August high season. The best time to come is in May and early June or late September and into October. Ferries and hydrofoils operate all year, but winter services are much reduced and sometimes cancelled – to the outer islands at any rate – due to heavy seas.

The post code for the Isole Eolie is 98055 and the telephone code is ☎ 090.

Getting There & Away

Ferries and hydrofoils leave regularly from Milazzo and all the ticket offices are along Via L Rizzo, at the port. Note that there is a L1500 port fee for vehicles. All prices quoted below were one-way fares in the high season at the time of writing.

Both SNAV and Siremar run hydrofoils (L18,500) to Lipari and on to the other islands. SNAV hydrofoils also connect the islands with Messina (L32,500) and Reggio di Calabria (L33,700) all year round, as well as Napoli and Palermo, in summer only.

Siremar runs ferries from Milazzo for about half the price of the hydrofoil (L11,100; cars from L28,700 to L67,700, depending on size), but they are slower and less regular. Siremar also runs ferries to Napoli. NGI Traghetti also runs a limited car ferry service for around the same rates.

Getting Around

Regular hydrofoil and ferry services operate between the islands, but they can be disrupted to the outer islands by heavy seas. Lipari's two ports are separated by the castle – hydrofoils arrive at and depart from Marina Corta, while Marina Lunga services ferries. Siremar and SNAV have ticket offices in the same building at Marina Corta. Siremar also has a ticket office at Marina Lunga. Full timetable information is available at all offices. On the other islands, ticket offices are at or close to the docks.

Examples of one-way fares and sailing times from Lipari are:

Alicudi
: L25,200, 1½ hours (hydrofoil); L16,200, 3¼ hours (ferry)

Panarea
: L11,900, 30 minutes (hydrofoil); L7000, one hour (ferry)

Stromboli
: L23,700, 50 minutes (hydrofoil); L13,900, 2¾ hours (ferry)

LIPARI

The largest and most developed of the islands, Lipari is also the most popular with tourists. The main town, of the same name, is typically Mediterranean, with pastel-coloured houses huddled around its two harbours. A thriving exporter of obsidian in ancient times, it is now a centre for mining pumice-stone (another volcanic product), and it's the best equipped base for exploring the archipelago.

Orientation

Lipari town's two harbours, Marina Lunga and Marina Corta, are on either side of the cliff-top castle, which is surrounded by 16th-century walls, and the town centre extends between them. The main street, Corso Vittorio Emanuele, runs roughly north-south to the west of the castle. Hydrofoils dock at Marina Corta, from where you should walk to the right across the piazza to Via Garibaldi and follow the 'centro' signs for Corso Vittorio Emanuele.

Information

Tourist Office The AAST office (☎ 988 00 95) is at Corso Vittorio Emanuele 202. It is the main tourist office for the archipelago, although offices open on Stromboli, Vulcano and Salina in summer. It will assist with accommodation, which is useful in the busy summer months. Pick up a copy of *Ospitalità in blu*, which contains details of accommodation and services on all the islands. The office is open Monday to Saturday from 8 am to 2 pm and 4.40 to 10 pm and Sunday and holidays from 8 am to 2 pm in summer. Out of season it closes at 7.30 pm on weekdays.

Money There are several banks in Lipari, including the Banca del Sud in Corso V Emanuele. You should have no trouble using Visa, MasterCard or Eurocheque cards for cash advances. Outside banking hours, exchange facilities can be found at the post office and several travel agencies.

Note that banking facilities on the other islands are limited.

Post & Communications The post office is at Corso V Emanuele 207, near the tourist office, and is open Monday to Friday from 8 am to 6.30 pm and on Saturday to 1 pm. Public telephones can be found throughout the township.

Medical Services Contact the hospital (☎ 9 88 51) or Pronto Soccorso (First Aid) on ☎ 988 52 67.

Emergency For police attendance call ☎ 113.

Things to See & Do

The **castle**, surrounded by massive walls built in the 16th century after Turkish pirates raided Lipari, stands on the site of an ancient acropolis that is now part of the **Parco Archeologico**. Buildings dating to before 1700 BC have been unearthed. Also within the castle complex is the **cathedral**, built by the Normans and sent up in flames during the 1544 pirate raid. Rebuilt a century later, the interior is Baroque. Excavations have uncovered part of the original 12th-century Norman cloisters.

The **Museo Archeologico Eoliano** boasts well-organised exhibits that trace the volcanic and human history of the islands and include a collection of Neolithic pottery. It is open Monday to Friday from 9 am to 2 pm and Sunday to 1 pm. Admission is free.

It is worth exploring the island, in particular for views of Salina, Alicudi and Filicudi from the rugged, windy cliffs of Lipari's north-west corner. Sunbathers and swimmers head for **Canneto**, a few km north of Lipari town. The beach is accessible by a track just north of Canneto. Farther north are the pumice mines of **Pomiciazzo** and **Porticello**, where there is another beach. The village of Quattropani and the lookout known as Quattrocchi, south of Pianoconte, are good spots to drink in the views.

Scuba diving and sailing are popular. For information on courses, contact the Centro Nautico Eoliano (☎ 981 21 10), Salita San Giuseppe 8, or the tourist office.

Places to Stay

Lipari provides plenty of options for a comfortable stay, from budget level to luxurious. However, prices soar in summer, particularly in August. If all else fails in peak season, tourist office staff will billet new arrivals in private homes on the island. Don't reject offers by touts when you arrive, as they often have decent rooms in private houses.

To rent an apartment, contact the tourist office for a list of establishments.

Places to Stay – bottom end

The island's camping ground, the *Baia Unci* (☎ 981 19 09), is at Canneto, about 2km out of Lipari township and accessible by bus from the Esso service station at Marina Lunga. It isn't cheap at L15,000 per person and L25,000 for a tent/caravan site. The HI *youth hostel* (☎ 981 15 40), Via Castello 17, is inside the walls of the castle. B&B costs L15,500 per person, plus L2000 for a hot shower, and L15,000 for a meal – or you can cook your own. It is open from March to October.

Cassarà Vittorio (☎ 981 15 23), Vico Sparviero 15, off Via Garibaldi near Marina Corta, costs L40,000 per person, or L45,000 with private bathroom. There are two terraces with views, and use of the kitchen is L5000. The owner can be found (unless he finds you first) at Via Garibaldi 78, on the way from the port to the city centre. *Locanda Salina* (☎ 981 23 32), Via Garibaldi 18, is also very close to Marina Corta. It has reasonable singles/doubles for L40,000/60,000 or doubles with a bathroom for L75,000. Ask for a room with a view of the sea. *Enzo il Negro* (☎ 981 24 73), at Via Garibaldi 29, has spotless, comfortable digs for up to L45,000 per person in the high season. All rooms have a bathroom and balcony and there is a large terrace.

Places to Stay – middle

Pensione Neri (☎ 981 14 13), Via G Marconi 43, off Corso V Emanuele, is in a lovely old, renovated villa. In the low season, a double costs L80,000 and triples/quads L100,000/120,000; in summer, prices jump to L110,000 a double, L140,000 a triple and L170,000 a quad. All rooms have a bathroom.

The *Hotel Oriente* (☎ 981 14 93) is next door at Via Marconi 35. It has a bar and garden and very comfortable rooms. Prices vary according to the season and range from L50,000 to L90,000 for a single, L70,000 to L150,000 for a double, L95,000 to L200,000 for a triple, and L120,000 to L250,000 for a quad. All rooms include a bathroom and breakfast.

A new tourist residence, *Costa Residence Vacanze* (☎ 981 17 84), at San Leonardo, has one and two-room apartments for L226,000/320,000 per day.

Places to Stay – top end

Lipari's top hotel is the *Villa Meligunis* (☎ 981 24 26) in Via Marte, on a hill overlooking Marina Corta. Room rates range from L150,000 to L300,000, depending on season. The price includes breakfast.

Places to Eat

Try pasta prepared with the island's excellent capers and be prepared to spend big to eat the day's sea catch, particularly swordfish. The waters of the archipelago abound in fish, including tuna, mullet, cuttlefish and sole, all of which end up on restaurant tables at the end of the day. The local wine is the sweet, white Malvasia.

People with access to a kitchen can shop for supplies at the grocery shops along Corso V Emanuele.

'OK, who had an entrée *and* a main?'

Although prices go up in the high season, you can still eat cheaply by sticking to the pizzerie along Corso V Emanuele. *Il Galeone*, Corso V Emanuele 222, has good pizzas for around L8000 or a set lunch for L17,000. *Zum Willi*, on the corner of Corso V Emanuele and Via Umberto I, is basically a bar that serves pizzas for L6000 to L10,000. For a more complete meal, eat at *Trattoria d'Oro*, Corso Umberto I 28-32. For an à la carte meal you'll pay around L30,000, and there is a good set menu for L20,000.

Da Bartolo, Via Garibaldi 53, is certainly one of the island's better trattorie and a good choice for seafood. A full meal is worth around L35,000. Cheaper and just as good is *Dal Napoletano*, at No 12, where L25,000 should see you through a good meal with a glass of Malvasia (on the house) to finish.

Near Marina Corta, in Via Roma, there are a couple of no-nonsense trattorie, including *Nenzyna*, where you can eat for around L20,000.

Getting There & Away

See the Getting There & Away section for the Isole Eolie.

Getting Around

Urso Guglielmo buses leave from the Esso service station at Marina Lunga for Canneto (10 a day, more frequently in summer), Porticello (seven a day) and Quattrocchi (eight a day). The company also offers special round trips of the island. Contact the tourist office for timetables.

Boats and scooters are available for hire at Foti Roberto (☎ 981 23 52), Via F Crispi 31, to the right as you leave Marina Lunga. A Vespa costs L38,000 a day and a moped is L28,000 a day. A motorised rubber dinghy costs L120,000 a day.

Viking (☎ 981 25 84), Vico Himera 3 (with a ticket booth at Marina Corta), conducts boat tours of all the islands, including one to Stromboli by night for L45,000 to see the Sciara del Fuoco.

VULCANO

Just south of Lipari, and the first port of call for ferries and hydrofoils from Milazzo, Vulcano is known for its therapeutic mud baths and hot springs. To the ancients, the island of Thermessa, Terasia or Hiera – as Vulcano was variously known – must have inspired a good deal of respect, if not downright fear. Not only did the god of fire, Vulcan, have his workshop here, but Aeolus, the god of the wind, also swirled about.

Of Vulcano's three volcanoes, the oldest lies on the southern tip of the island and was already extinct in ancient times. The youngest, Vulcanello, next to the mud baths at the north-east end of the island, rose from the sea in the 2nd century BC, according to Pliny. The only active volcano is the Gran Cratere, which has a number of fumaroles and whose broad, smoking crater broods over the port. A tranquil place, the Gran Cratere hasn't blown for more than four centuries but you'll notice on arrival the all-pervading stench of sulphurous gases.

Orientation & Information

Boats dock at the Porto di Levante. To the right, as you face the island, is the small Vulcanello peninsula. All facilities are concentrated between the Porto di Levante and the Porto di Ponente, where you will find the Spiaggia Sabbia Nera (Black Sand Beach), the only smooth, sandy beach on the islands.

A tourist office (☎ 985 20 28) is open in summer only.

Things to See & Do

Climbing the **Gran Cratere** is the main attraction. Follow the signs south along Via Provinciale out of town. A track is then signposted off the road. Take the left fork and head up – about an hour's scramble. The views from the top are reward enough for the sweat.

Even if you don't need a skin cure, a wallow in the hot, sulphurous mud pool of the **Laghetto di Fanghi** can be a relaxing way to pass the time, if slightly offensive to the nose (don't wear your best bathing costume, as you'll never get the smell out). It's next to Vulcanello, and when you've had enough you can hop into the water at the adjacent beach where underwater hot springs create a natural jacuzzi effect.

Paddle boats are usually available for hire on the beach.

Viking offers a boat trip around the island for around L20,000 per person. Information is available on Lipari.

Places to Stay & Eat

The *Pensione Agostino* (☎ 985 23 42), Via Favaloro 1, is close to the mud baths (and their smell) and has doubles for up to L85,000 with a bathroom, depending on the season. *Pensione la Giara* (☎ 985 22 29), Via Provinciale 18, is towards the Gran Cratere. A pleasant spot, its rooms cost around L90,000 a double, although the management prefers to charge by the week. *Sea House Residence* (☎ 985 22 19), which is very close to the mud baths, is a complex of self-contained two, three, four and five-bed apartments in a garden setting. Prices start at L114,000 per day for a double in the off-season and rise to L228,000 in August. It is open from April to October.

For a decent meal, try *Da Maurizio* or *Da Vincenzino*, both in Via Porto di Levante. Another good option is *Il Caimano*.

Getting There & Away

Vulcano is an intermediate stop between Milazzo and Lipari and a good number of vessels go both ways throughout the day.

Getting Around

Scooters and bicycles are available for rent from Pino Marturano (☎ 985 24 19), Via Comunale Levante, near the Porto di Levante. The proprietor of Gioelli del Mare (☎ 985 21 70) at Porto di Levante organises bus tours around the island for groups of at least 12 people. Make a booking and hope a large enough group will form.

SALINA

Just north-west of Lipari, Salina is the most fertile of the islands and consists of two extinct volcanoes, Monte dei Porri and Monte Fosse delle Felci. Its high coastal cliffs are topped with vineyards, where most of the islands' Malvasia wine is produced.

Orientation & Information

Boats dock at Santa Marina Salina, where you will find most accommodation, or at Rinella, a fishing hamlet on the south coast. The other main villages on the island are Malfa, on the north coast, and Leni, slightly inland from Rinella.

In summer there are AAST booths at Rinella, Malfa and Santa Marina Salina. For medical assistance, call ☎ 984 40 05. For the police, phone ☎ 984 30 19.

Things to See & Do

If you are feeling energetic, you could climb the Fosse delle Felci volcano. From Santa Marina Salina, head for Lingua, a small village 3km south, from where paths lead up the mountain.

The **Santuario della Madonna del Terzito** at Valdichiesa, just south of Malfa, is a place of pilgrimage, particularly around the Feast of the Assumption on 15 August.

Rinella is a popular underwater fishing spot. For information, contact the tourist office or the Centro Nautico Salina (☎ 980 90 33), Via Rotabile 2, at the port at Leni, which also operates as a dive centre (week-long courses for about L600,000) and rents out motorised rubber dinghies for up to

L180,000 a day. Boats are also available for rent from Nautica Levante (☎ 984 30 83), Via Risorgimento, Santa Marina Salina.

Places to Stay & Eat

The *Camping Tre Pini* (☎ 980 9155) is on the beach at Rinella. It costs L12,000 per person, plus L22,000 for a site. *Pensione Mamma Santina* (☎ 984 30 54) is at Via Sanità 40 in Santa Marina Salina. Head for Via Risorgimento (the narrow main street of town) and walk north for a few hundred metres. The pensione is uphill along a winding lane to your left. Singles/doubles are L35,000/60,000 and a double with a bathroom is L110,000. In summer, half board is obligatory at L105,000 per person. Two blocks farther north along Via Risorgimento and again uphill to the right is *Catena de Pasquale* (☎ 984 30 94), Via F Crispi 17. Its six rooms all have a bathroom, terrace and cooking facilities. You'll pay from L40,000 to L60,000 per person, less if you're in a group of three or more.

Hotel L'Ariana (☎ 980 90 75) is in a turn-of-the-century villa at Via Rotabile 11, overlooking the sea at Rinella. It has terraces and a bar. Half board ranges from L70,000 in the low season to L112,000 in the high season (L140,000 with bathroom); full board is from L95,000 to L160,000.

There are several restaurants clustered around the docks at Santa Marina, or you could try the one at the Albergo Punta Barone, with views out to sea, at the northern exit of town.

SICILIA

Getting There & Away

Hydrofoils and ferries service Santa Marina and Rinella. You'll find ticket offices at both.

Getting Around

Regular buses run from Santa Marina Salina to Malfa and Lingua, and from Malfa to Leni and Rinella. Timetables are posted at the ports. Motorcycles are available for rent from Antonio Bongiorno (☎ 984 34 09), Via Risorgimento 240, Santa Marina Salina. A Vespa costs L38,000 a day and a moped L33,000 a day – less if you hire for longer periods.

PANAREA

Easily the most picturesque of the Isole Eolie, tiny Panarea is 3km long and 2km wide. Boats dock at San Pietro, where you'll find most of the accommodation.

After wandering around San Pietro, head south to Punta Milazzese, about a half-hour walk (there is a small beach along the way), to see the Bronze Age village discovered in 1948. Pottery found at the site is now in the museum at Lipari. Rent a boat at the port to explore the coves and beaches of the island, which are otherwise inaccessible.

The *Locanda Rodà* (☎ 98 30 06) in Via San Pietro, uphill from the port and to the left, is about as close as you'll come to a cheap hotel. It charges L70,000/100,000 in the peak months, or more likely half board at L110,000. It has a pizzeria/trattoria that charges average prices. *La Sirena* (☎ 98 30 12), at Via Drautt 4, on the way to the Bronze Age village, has doubles with bathroom for L90,000, and a pleasant trattoria. In the same area is *Trattoria da Nunzio*, with a terrace overlooking the sea. A meal at any of these places should cost no more than L35,000.

Hydrofoils and the occasional ferry link the island with Stromboli to the north and Salina (and on to Lipari and Milazzo) to the south.

STROMBOLI

Stromboli's almost constant eruptions of fiery molten rock make an unforgettable spectacle at night. Lava flow is confined to the Sciara del Fuoco (Trail of Fire) on the volcano's north-western flank, leaving the villages of San Bartolo, San Vincenzo and Scari (which merge into one town) to the east and Ginostra to the south quite safe. Until the massive eruption of 1930, some 5000 people lived on the island, but most took fright and left. Permanent residents now number about 500. The volcano's most recent eruption was in March 1996 and, although minor, left several people injured.

The most captivating of the islands,

Stromboli is inconveniently placed and boat services are prone to disruption. There's a fair choice of accommodation and a stay is more than recommended.

Orientation & Information

Boats arrive at Scari/San Vincenzo, downhill from the township. Accommodation is a short walk up the Scalo Scari to Via Roma, or, if you plan to head straight for the crater, follow the road along the waterfront (see the following section for details).

A tourist office is open in summer. The post office is in Via Roma, and the only bank, in Via Nunziante at Ficogrande, is open only from June to September. Otherwise, exchange facilities are available at the travel agency, Le Isole e Terme d'Italia, in Via Roma near the port.

Climbing the Volcano

From the port, follow the road along the waterfront, continuing straight past the beach at Ficogrande. Once past the village the path heads uphill, deviating after about 20 minutes to a bar/pizzeria and observatory. Alternatively, follow it through a slightly confusing section of reeds until it starts to ascend to the crater. About halfway up is a good view of the Sciara del Fuoco, although in daylight the glow of the molten lava is imperceptible. The path eventually becomes quite steep and rocky. Note the warning signs at the summit and do not go too close to the edge of the crater. The round trip from the village should take about four hours.

The climb is a totally different experience at night, when darkness throws the molten lava of the Sciara del Fuoco and volcanic explosions into dramatic relief. It is possible to make the climb during the day without a guide, although the tourist office says it is forbidden. Night climbers are strongly advised to go with a guide.

Experienced guides can be contacted through the Alpine Guides office (☎ 98 62 63), just off Piazzale San Vincenzo. They take groups of 10 people or more to the crater daily at 4 pm (depending on weather conditions and whether a group can be formed), returning at 11.30 pm (about L20,000 per person). Contact the office around midday to make a booking. For the night climb, you will need heavy shoes and clothing for cold, wet weather, a torch (flashlight), food and a good supply of water. Even during the day, you will need heavy, wet-weather clothing, as conditions are unpredictable.

The Società Navigazione Stromboli (☎ 98 61 35) organises nightly boat trips to view the Sciara del Fuoco from the sea. The boat, named Pippo, leaves at 10 pm from Ficogrande. Viking offers a similar boat trip, starting in Lipari and departing from the Stromboli ferry port for the Sciara del Fuoco at 8 pm. The same boat also heads out to **Strombolicchio**, a towering rock rising out of the sea north of San Vincenzo. The rock is a popular spot for underwater fishing.

Water Sports

The Centro Mare Stromboli (☎ 98 61 56), Via V Nunziante 26 (on the way to the volcano), has canoes, sailboards, catamarans and sailing boats for rent. It also offers windsurfing and sailing courses. La Sirenetta Diving Center (☎ 98 60 25), Via Marina 33, at La Sirenetta park Hotel, offers diving courses.

Alternatively, make your way to the beach of rocks and black volcanic sand at Ficogrande to swim and sunbathe.

Places to Stay & Eat

There's nothing much in the dirt cheap bracket on Stromboli. *Locanda Stella* (☎ 98 60 20), Via Fabio Filzi 14, has doubles for L60,000 and charges L135,000 for obligatory full board in July/August. This is about as low as prices come. You will also find a few affittacamere, charging from L40,000 per person for a room in the high season. A good one is *Barbablù* (☎ 98 61 18), Via Vittorio Emanuele 17, a pleasant pensione charging L90,000 to L150,000 a double, depending on the season. Cheaper is the *Casa del Sole* (☎ 98 60 17), Via Soldato Cincotta, off the road to the volcano, before you reach Ficogrande. It has singles/doubles for L30,000/60,000.

Hotel Villaggio Stromboli (☎ 98 60 18), Via Regina Elena, has rooms for L110,000/180,000 in the high season. It is on the beach front and has a terrace bar/restaurant.

For a reasonably priced meal, try *La Trottola* in Via Roma. The *Punta Lena* on the Lungomare, walking away from the port towards the volcano, is more expensive and has a terrace overlooking the sea. The pizzeria at the observatory, about 20 minutes walk up the lower slope of the volcano, is also reasonable.

Getting There & Away

Ticket offices for SNAV and Siremar are at the port. Bear in mind the cost of the trip and distance if you're considering a day visit – which in any case will rob you of the opportunity of a night climb up the volcano. Heavy seas can cause cancellation of ferry and hydrofoil services.

FILICUDI & ALICUDI

You will need a strong desire to get away from it all to stay on either of these islands west of Lipari. Facilities are limited (severely on Alicudi) and boats can be cancelled due to heavy seas, even in summer.

Filicudi is the larger of the two and its attractions include the Grotta del Bue Marino (Grotto of the Monk Seal) and La Canna rock pinnacle, about 1km off the island towards Alicudi. On Capo Graziano, south of the port, are the remains of a prehistoric village dating to 1800 BC. Boats are available for rent if you want to explore the grotto, and scuba diving courses are available in summer.

The island has two hotels. *La Canna* (☎ 988 99 56), Via Rosa 43, just uphill from the port, has doubles for L80,000 and half board for L85,000 per person in the high season. *Phenicusa* (☎ 988 99 46) in Via Porto has rooms for L55,000/80,000 and full board for up to L130,000.

Alicudi is the farthest from Lipari and the least developed of the Aeolian group. There is only one hotel and restaurant, the *Ericusa* (☎ 988 99 02) in Via Regina Elena. Doubles cost L100,000 and half board is L95,000 per person. It is open only during the summer months and bookings are strongly advised.

While on the island, trek up Monte Filo dell'Arpa to see the crater of the extinct Montagnola volcano and the Timpone delle Femmine, huge fissures where women are said to have taken refuge during pirate raids.

The East Coast

MESSINA

For most, Messina is the point of arrival in Sicilia, and you could hardly imagine a less auspicious introduction. Devastated many times over the centuries, the modern city is pretty much bereft of any hint of its past. Known to the ancient Greeks as Zankle (Sickle) for its beautiful, curved harbour, Messina grew into a splendid city as a Greek colony and later thrived under Roman, Byzantine and Norman patronage. Since the 18th century, Messina has been something of a disaster area, hit first by plague, then cholera, and finally by earthquakes, including the massive 1908 jolt that all but destroyed the city and killed more than 80,000 people in the region. The city had barely been rebuilt when it was flattened by bombing during WWII.

If for any reason you're stuck in Messina, don't despair. The city centre, with its wide avenues, is a pleasant place to wander around, and there remain a couple of vestiges of happier days.

Orientation

The train station is on Piazza della Repubblica, at the southern end of the long waterfront. FS car and truck ferries also arrive here. The main Intercity bus station is outside the train station, to the left in the piazza. To get to the city centre from Piazza della Repubblica, walk either straight across the piazza and directly ahead along Via I Settembre to the Piazza del Duomo, or turn left into Via G La Farina and take the first right into Via Cannazzaro to reach Piazza Cairoli.

SICILIA

Those coming by hydrofoil from Reggio di Calabria arrive about 1km north of the city on Corso Vittorio Emanuele II, while drivers on the private car ferry from Villa San Giovanni land a few km farther along, just north of the trade fair area (Fiera).

Information

Tourist Office There is an information office (☎ 67 29 44) in Piazza della Repubblica, to the right as you leave the train station, open Monday to Thursday from 8 am to 2 pm and 2.30 to 6 pm and Friday and Saturday to 2 pm only. The AAPIT office (☎ 64 02 21) is a bit farther along at Via Calabria 301. Both have extensive information on Messina, its province and Sicilia in general.

Money There are numerous banks in the city centre – several with ATMs – and an exchange booth at the timetable information office at the train station.

Post & Communications The main post office is in Piazza Antonello, on Corso Cavour near the cathedral. It is open Monday to Saturday from 8.30 am to 6.30 pm. The post code for central Messina is 98100.

There is a Telecom office in Corso Cavour, near Via Cannazzaro. The telephone code for Messina is ☎ 090.

Travel Agency The CTS student travel group has an agency (☎ 292 67 61) located at Via U Bassi 93.

Medical Services The public hospital, the Ospedale Piemonte (☎ 22 21), is in Viale Europa; at night, ring ☎ 67 50 48. A booklet available at the tourist office lists pharmacies open at night on a rotation basis.

Emergency For police attendance, call ☎ 113.

Things to See & Do

The Norman **duomo**, built in the 12th century, was almost completely destroyed by the combined effects of the 1908 earthquake and WWII bombing. Rebuilt virtually from scratch, its fine 15th-century doorway is one of the few original elements. The clock tower houses what is believed to be the world's largest astronomical clock, which strikes at midday.

In the Piazza del Duomo is the **Fontana di Orione**, an elegant 16th-century work by Angelo Montorsoli. Nearby, in Piazza Catalani, off Via Garibaldi, is the 12th-century **Chiesa della Santissima Annunziata dei Catalani**, a jewel of Arab-Norman construction. The statue in front of it is a monument to Don John of Austria, who beat the Turks at the Battle of Lepanto in 1571. Farther north, where Via Garibaldi spills into Piazza dell'Unità d'Italia, is Messina's other great fountain, the 16th-century **Fontana del Nettuno**.

The **Museo Regionale** is a long walk along Viale della Libertà (or take bus No 8 from the train station), and houses works of art including the *Virgin & Child with Saints* by Antonello da Messina, born here in 1430. It is open daily from 9 am to 1 pm and occasionally from 4 to 7 pm. Admission is L3000.

Places to Stay & Eat

The *Roma* (☎ 67 55 66), Piazza del Duomo 3 (just off Corso Cavour), has basic singles/doubles for L18,000/35,000. A warning: there is no hot water.

Two OK hotels which have hot water and are convenient for the train station are *Touring* (☎ 293 88 51) and *Mirage* (☎ 293 88 44), at Via N Scotto 17 and 1, respectively. They both charge around L35,000/65,000 for singles/doubles, though the Mirage is slightly better. Both have more expensive rooms with bathroom.

Hotel Monza (☎ 67 37 55), Viale San Martino 63, is of a higher standard and charges L66,000/110,000 for singles/doubles with bathroom.

La Trappola, Via dei Verdi 39, is near the university area. Its good meals are reasonably priced, but not rock-bottom. *Trattoria al Padrino*, Via Santa Cecilia 54, is a simple place, where a meal will cost about L30,000.

SICILIA

Getting There & Away

Bus SAIS (☎ 77 19 14) runs a regular service (approximately every hour; last bus leaves at 8 pm) to Taormina (L5100 one way), Catania (L9500 one way) and Catania's airport. The company's office and bus station are at Piazza della Repubblica 6, to the left as you leave the train station. There is a direct connection to Roma (see Getting There & Away at the beginning of this chapter). Giuntabus (☎ 67 37 82) runs a service to Milazzo (for ferries and hydrofoils to the Isole Eolie) roughly every hour from Via Terranova 8, on the corner of Viale San Martino.

Train Regular trains connect Messina with Catania, Taormina, Siracusa, Palermo and Milazzo, but buses are generally faster. The train stations for Milazzo and Taormina are inconveniently located some distance from the city centre.

Car & Motorcycle If you arrive in Messina by FS ferry with a vehicle (see below), it is simple to make your way out of town. For Palermo (or Milazzo and the Isole Eolie), turn right as you exit the docks and follow Viale Garibaldi along the seafront. After about 1km, turn left into Viale Boccetta and follow the green autostrada (tollway) signs for Palermo. To reach Taormina, Siracusa etc, turn left from the docks into Via La Farina and follow the autostrada signs for Catania.

If you arrive by private ferry, turn right along Viale della Libertà for Palermo and Milazzo, and left for Taormina and Catania – follow the green autostrada signs. You can also take the SS114 (busy in summer).

Boat The FS railway runs car ferries to Villa San Giovanni, about 10km north of Reggio di Calabria, from next to the train station. The private Caronte company does the same run from docks a few km up the waterfront, just north of the Fiera (trade fair centre). It costs L35,000 one way to take a small car on Caronte and FS prices are similar. The trip takes about 20 minutes, with departures around the clock.

There are also big FS hydrofoils to Reggio di Calabria (L5000 one way), and SNAV (☎ 36 40 44) runs up to 20 hydrofoils on weekdays to Reggio di Calabria (L7000 one way; 15 minutes). SNAV hydrofoils also connect Messina with the Isole Eolie.

SOUTH TO TAORMINA

Those driving the Messina-Taormina route should consider a brief excursion into the foothills of the Monti Peloritani. Head for **Savoca**, 4km of winding road inland from the grey pebble beaches of Santa Teresa di Riva, which take you through lemon groves and almond stands to a quiet village with a couple of medieval churches and a Capuchin monastery, which contains **catacombs**. Some eerie-looking skeletons in raggedy 18th-century rig are all that remain of local nobles who paid good money for this kind of 'immortality'. The catacombs are open from 9 am to 1 pm and 4 to 7 pm from April to September; 9 am to midday and 3 to 5 pm the rest of the year. Admission costs L3000. STAT buses run between Savoca and Santa Teresa di Riva.

TAORMINA

Spectacularly located on a terrace of Monte Tauro, dominating the sea and with views westwards to Mt Etna, Taormina is easily Sicilia's most picturesque town. From its foundation by the Siculians, Taormina remained a favourite destination for the long line of conquerors who followed. Under the Greeks, who moved in after Naxos was destroyed during colonial wars in the 5th century BC, Taormina flourished. It later came under Roman dominion and eventually became the capital of Byzantine Sicilia, a period of grandeur that ended abruptly in 902 AD when the town was destroyed by Arab invaders. Taormina remained an important centre of art and trade throughout the subsequent periods of Norman, Spanish and French rule.

Long ago discovered by the European jet set, Taormina is an expensive and heavily touristed town. It is well served by hotels, pensioni and eating places, but some travellers might find the glitz and kitsch a little overwhelming. It would be a shame to miss this place though, as its magnificent setting, Greek theatre and nearby beaches remain as seductive as they were for the likes of Goethe and DH Lawrence.

Orientation

The train station (Taormina-Giardini) is at the bottom of Monte Tauro, and you'll need to get an SAIS bus up to the bus station (for local and Intercity buses – where you'll arrive anyway if you catch the bus from Messina) in Via Pirandello. A short walk uphill from there brings you to the old city entrance and Corso Umberto I, which traverses the town.

Information

Tourist Office The AAST office (☎ 2 32 43) is in the Palazzo Corvaja, just off Corso Umberto I, near Largo Santa Caterina. It is open daily from 8 am to 2 pm and 4 to 7 pm.

Money There are several banks in Taormina, mostly along Corso Umberto I. You'll also find exchange places along the same street. Check on commissions. Several banks, such as the Monte dei Paschi di Siena on Piazza del Duomo, have user-friendly ATMs. American Express is represented by La Duca Viaggi (☎ 62 52 55), Via Don Bosco 39.

Post & Communications The main post office is in Piazza Sant'Antonio, just outside the Porta Catania, at the far end of Corso Umberto I from the tourist office. There are public telephones in the Avis Rent-a-Car office, Via San Pancrazio 6, to your right off Via Pirandello at the entrance to the old town. Taormina's post code is 98039 and the telephone code is ☎ 0942.

Newspapers If you're anxious for news from home, try the tobacconist at Via Bagnoli Croci 62, or the newsagent at Corso Umberto I 245, just inside Porta Catania.

Medical Services There is a free night-time medical service in summer for tourists (☎ 62 54 19) in Piazza San Francesco di Paola. The hospital, the Ospedale San Vincenzo (☎ 5 37 45), is in Piazza San Vincenzo, just outside the Porta Catania. Call the same number for an ambulance.

Emergency For the police, call ☎ 113.

Things to See & Do

The **Greek theatre** at the end of Via Teatro Greco, off Corso Umberto I, was built in the 3rd century BC. Later expanded and remodelled by the Romans, what you see is pretty much a Roman structure, despite its name. In the final years of the empire the amphitheatre was given over solely to gladiator fighting – the sword was mightier at the box office than the pen. The structure has been much tampered with over the centuries – the family of the Spanish Costanza d'Aragona built its home in the 12th century over part of the theatre (to the right as you face the stage). However, it remains a most atmospheric place. Film buffs might note that Woody Allen filmed the Greek chorus scenes here for his film *Mighty Aphrodite*. The view of Mt Etna and the sea through what was once the stage area is breathtaking. There are concerts here in summer. The theatre is open from 9 am to 8 pm in summer and closes at 4.30 pm in winter. Admission is L2000.

From the theatre, wander down to the beautiful **villa comunale** (public gardens) on Via Bagnoli Croci. Opening hours are similar to the theatre. Take a picnic and enjoy the panorama.

Back in the town centre is the **Odeon**, a small Roman theatre, badly preserved and partly covered by the adjoining Chiesa di Santa Caterina. It was discovered and excavated in the late 19th century and is believed to have been erected on the site of a Greek temple of Apollo. Taormina's **duomo**, in the Piazza del Duomo along Corso Umberto I, was built in the early 15th century.

There are several mansions in Taormina, including the **Palazzo Corvaja**. Begun by the Arabs as a defence tower in the 11th century, it was extended several times and includes halls dating from the 14th and 15th centuries. The **Palazzo Duca di Santo Stefano**, at the other end of town, is an important example of Sicilian Gothic architecture, with a fanciful mix of Arab and Norman styles. The nearby **Badia Vecchia** (Old Abbey) is a 14th-century Gothic building, again with Norman-Arab elements.

Just wandering along the main drag, Corso Umberto I, you can see a smattering of stately old buildings, some dating to the 15th century.

The peak of Monte Tauro is adorned by the lonely, windswept ruins of the town's medieval castle, 3km from the town centre along the road to Castelmola (see the Around Taormina section) or accessible by climbing the linking stairs. The views are great.

You can reach the beaches at **Isola Bella** and **Mazzarò** directly under Taormina by cable car from Via Pirandello. It costs L2000 and runs from 8.30 am to 9 pm in winter and until 1.30 am in summer. Both beaches are largely taken up by private operators (a space with deckchairs and umbrella costs up to L20,000 a day), but there is some space for free bathing. SAIS buses also connect the beaches with the upper town.

SICILIA

Organised Tours

CST (☎ 2 33 01), Corso Umberto I 101, runs excursions to various locations. Destinations include Mt Etna (L33,000), Agrigento (L70,000), Siracusa (L68,000) and Lipari (L80,000). These are winter prices; expect rises in summer. SAT (☎ 2 46 53), Corso Umberto I 73, also runs tours to Mt Etna.

Special Events

Festivals, theatre and music concerts are organised throughout the summer. The Raduno del Costume e del Carretto Siciliano, featuring parades of traditional Sicilian carts and folkloric groups, is usually held in autumn – ask at the tourist office.

Places to Stay

Taormina has plenty of accommodation, but in summer you should book in advance as rooms fill rapidly, particularly during August (a good time to stay away). In winter you can sometimes get prices brought down a tad. You can camp near the beach at *Campeggio San Leo* (☎ 2 46 58), Via Nazionale, at Capo Taormina. The cost is L7000 per person per night.

There are numerous private rooms in Taormina and the tourist office has a full list. At *Pensione Ingegneri* (☎ 62 54 80), Via Timeo 8 (next to the Odeon), you will pay L35,000 per person. *Il Leone* (☎ 2 38 78), Via Bagnoli Croci 127, near the gardens, charges L29,000/46,000 for singles/doubles (a L5000 breakfast is compulsory if you stay for one night only). Some rooms have terraces and great views of the sea.

Pensione Svizzera (☎ 2 37 90), Via Pirandello 26, on the way from the bus station to the town centre, has simple, pleasant singles/doubles with a bathroom for L60,000/100,000, breakfast included. Farther up the same road, the *Pensione Inn Piero* (☎ 2 31 39), at No 20, has comfortable rooms with a bathroom for L48,000/72,000.

Pensione Villa Gaia (☎ 2 31 85), Via Fazzello 34, is near the duomo and has rooms for L45,000/80,000. It is closed in winter.

Hotel Villa Carlotta (☎ 2 37 32), Via Pirandello 81, is about 10 minutes walk downhill from the town. A beautifully furnished establishment, it has rooms with terrace and bathroom for around L85,000/130,000, including breakfast.

Villa Fiorita (☎ 2 41 22), Via Pirandello 39, is one of Taormina's nicer middle-range hotels. It is well-furnished and comfortable, with a garden, swimming pool, terraces and rooms with sea views. Doubles cost from L150,000.

Hotel Villa Belvedere (☎ 2 37 91), Via Bagnoli Croci 79, has a swimming pool and garden and all rooms and terraces face Mt Etna. Singles/doubles with full services cost up to L140,000/228,000

If you want to stay near the beach at Mazzarò, try the *Villa Caterina* (☎ 2 47 09), Via Nazionale 155, which has pleasant rooms for L48,000/80,000 or L110,000 per person for full board.

Places to Eat
Those on a tight budget will be limited in their choice of eating places. There are several gourmet grocery shops along Corso Umberto I, where prices are high. Alternatively, head for the side streets between Via Teatro Greco and the public gardens, where you can buy picnic supplies at several grocery and pastry shops. There is a *Standa supermarket* in Via Apollo Arcageta, just up from the post office. Quite a few restaurants close in winter.

For a quick takeaway, you could do worse than *Myosotis*, Corso Umberto I 113. It has pizzas, arancini (deep fried orange rice balls stuffed with meat and peas), and panini for around L3000. For a light meal try *Shelter Pub*, Via Fratelli Bandiera 10, off Corso Umberto I. *Time Out*, Via San Pancrazio 19, is a decent little bar and eatery.

For pizza, *Mamma Rosa* at Via Naumachia 10 is a safe bet at L8000 to L10,000.

Trattoria Rosticepi, Via San Pancrazio 10, at the top of Via Pirandello, has good meals for under L25,000 per person. *Ritrovo Trocadero*, at Via Pirandello 1, makes pizzas which will appeal to tourists – with names like Hawaiian, Mexicano etc – for around L6000 to L11,000. For an excellent meal in lovely surroundings, head for *Ristorante La Piazzetta*, Via Paladini 5, in a tiny piazza downhill from Corso Umberto I. A full meal will cost L30,000 or more. Next door is *Shatulle*, a bar/crêperie. *Il Baccanale*, on Piazzetta Filea, off Via Giovanni di Giovanni, is a popular restaurant moderately priced by Taormina standards.

For a quiet drink, head for *Arco Rosso*, Via Naumachia 7, off Corso Umberto I, or walk farther down to the busier *Da Peppe*, Via Calapitrulli 3. Many of the cafés on Corso Umberto I charge extortionately in the high season.

Getting There & Away
Bus The bus is the easiest means of reaching Taormina. SAIS (☎ 62 53 01) services leave for Messina (1½ hours; L5100) and Catania (about the same) at least hourly from about 5 am to 7 pm.

Train There are also regular trains, but the awkward location of Taormina's station is a strong disincentive. If you arrive this way, catch an SAIS bus up to the town. They run roughly every half an hour to 90 minutes (much less frequently on Sunday).

Car & Motorcycle Taormina is on the A18 tollway and SS114 between Messina and Catania. Parking can be a problem in Taormina, particularly in summer.

There are several car rental agencies in Taormina, including Avis, Hertz and Maggiore. California (☎ 2 37 69), Via Bagnoli Croci 86, rents cars and motorcycles at reasonable prices. A small car will cost upwards of L300,000 a week. A Vespa costs L28,000 a day or L180,000 a week, while a moped costs L23,000 a day or L150,000 a week.

AROUND TAORMINA
Panorama fanatics should head 5km up the hill to **Castelmola**, literally the high point of the area, with a ruined castle and sweeping views of, well, everything. Several buses run from Taormina.

There is an **archaeological park** south of Taormina at Giardini-Naxos (follow the 'scavi' signs), the site of the first Greek settlement in Sicilia. Founded in 735 BC, it was destroyed by Dionysius, the tyrant of Siracusa, in 403 BC. There is not a lot to see, but the park is a pleasant green refuge. It is open Monday to Saturday from 9 am to one hour before sunset and Sunday to 1 pm. Admission is free. Regular buses leave from the Taormina bus station in Via Pirandello for Giardini-Naxos. Giardini's AAST tourist office (☎ 0942-5 10 10) is at Via Tysandros 76E.

Fans of Francis Ford Coppola's *The Godfather* might be interested to know that the wedding scene was shot at **Forza d'Agrò**, near Taormina (three buses a day from Taormina).

A relatively short drive (SAIS buses from Taormina at 9.15 am and 1.45 pm weekdays only) will get you to the **Gole Alcantara**, a series of modest lava gorges on the river of the same name, a few km short of Francavilla. You could stop in here on your way to Mt Etna. Admission to the gorges costs L3500, and you can hire wading boots (cost L10,000), which you'll need if you want to do anything more than peer into the gorges.

CATANIA

Catania's crumbling appearance, chaotic traffic and reputation as a major crime centre may make it seem an intimidating and uninviting place on arrival (the ugly location of the train and bus stations doesn't help), but the city merits the benefit of the doubt. You may end up using it as a base for visiting Mt Etna, so take the time to look around its grand, if poorly maintained, Baroque palaces and churches. It is well served by hotels and pensioni, and the food is good and cheap.

A busy industrial and commercial port town, Catania has an unfortunate history. Situated at the foot of Mt Etna, it was partially destroyed in a massive eruption in 1669 and, as reconstruction proceeded, was shaken to the ground in 1693 by an earthquake that devastated much of south-eastern Sicilia. The 18th-century project to rebuild the city in grand Baroque style was largely overseen by the architect Giovanni Vaccarini.

SICILIA

Orientation

The main train station and Intercity bus terminal are near the port at Piazza Giovanni XXIII. From here, Corso Martiri della Libertà heads west towards the city centre, about a 15-minute walk. Follow the road to Piazza della Repubblica and continue along Corso Sicilia to Via Etnea, the main thoroughfare running north off Piazza del Duomo. Most sights are concentrated around and west of Piazza del Duomo, while the commercial centre of Catania is farther north around Via Pacini and Via Umberto I.

Information

Tourist Office The AAPIT office (☎ 730 62 11) is at Via Cimarosa 10. It is open Monday to Friday from 9 am to 1 pm and 3 to 7 pm and Saturday from 9 am to 1 pm. There are branches at the train station (☎ 730 62 55) on platform No 1, open roughly the same hours, and at the airport (☎ 730 62 66), open daily from 8 am to 10 pm.

Money Banks are concentrated along Corso Sicilia, including the Deutsche Bank and Banca Nazionale del Lavoro, both with reliable ATMs. There is an exchange office at the train station. American Express is represented by La Duca Viaggi (☎ 31 61 55), Via Etnea 65. They have another office at Piazza Europa 1.

Post & Communications The main post office is at Via Etnea 215, between Via Pacini and Via Umberto I. The Telecom office, Corso Sicilia 67, is open Monday to Saturday from 9 am to 1 pm and 4 to 7.30 pm and Sunday from 9 am to 12.30 pm. The post code for central Catania is 95100, and the telephone code is ☎ 095.

Travel Agency There is a CTS travel agent (☎ 715 04 34) at Via P Garofalo 3.

Medical Services Go to the Ospedale Vittorio Emanuele, Via Plebiscito 268, off Via Vittorio Emanuele II, or try the Ospedale Garibaldi on Viale Mario Rapisardi. There's a late night pharmacy on Via Vittorio Emanuele II, opposite Piazza Cutelli.

Emergency For the police, call ☎ 113.

Piazza del Duomo & Around

Catania's most atmospheric square is easy to identify, as its centrepiece is the **Fontana dell'Elefante**, which was assembled by Vaccarini. The lava statue, carved possibly in the days of Byzantine rule, carries an Egyptian obelisk on its back. The architect worked on the square after the 1693 earthquake. He remodelled the 11th-century **duomo**, incorporating the original Norman apses and transept, and designed the **Palazzo del Municipio** (town hall) on the north side of the piazza. It features an elegant Baroque façade and, in keeping with a theme, is also known as the Palazzo degli Elefanti. Across Via Vittorio Emanuele II from the duomo is

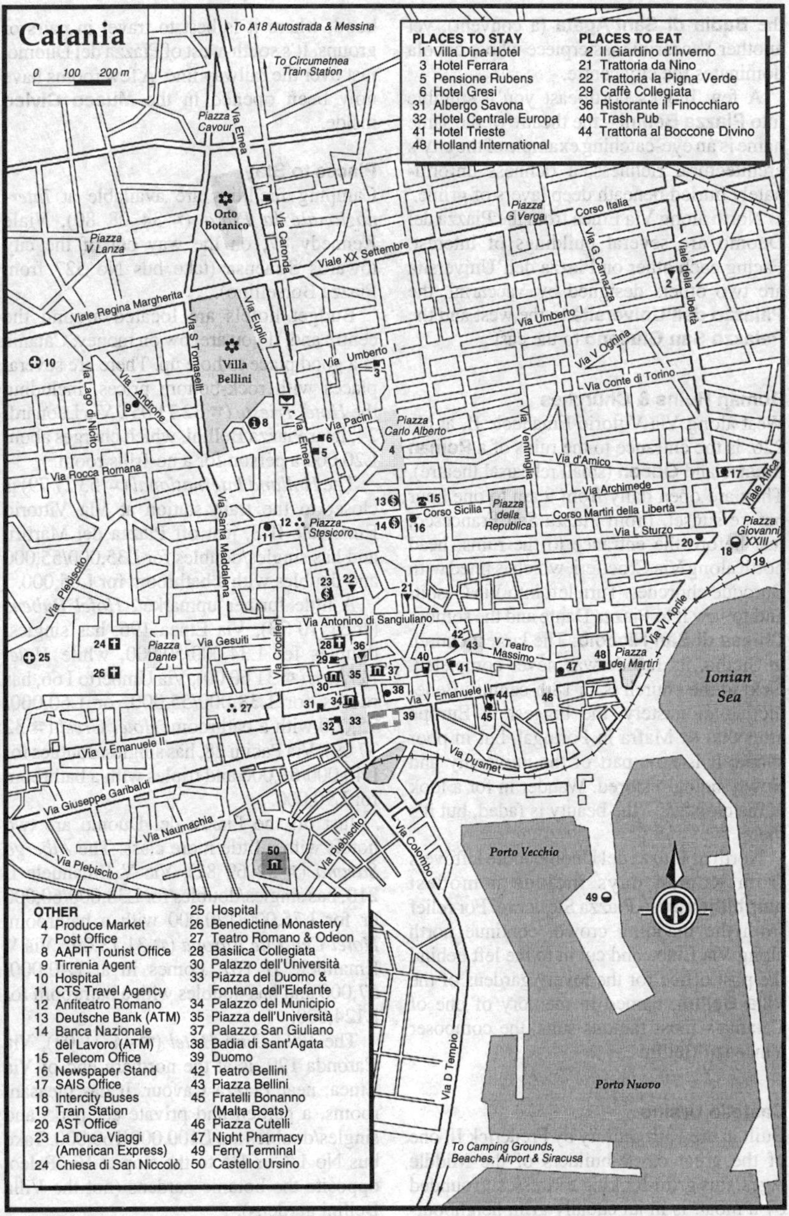
Catania
0 100 200 m
To A18 Autostrada & Messina
To Circumetnea Train Station
PLACES TO STAY
1 Villa Dina Hotel
3 Hotel Ferrara
5 Pensione Rubens
6 Hotel Gresi
31 Albergo Savona
32 Hotel Centrale Europa
41 Hotel Trieste
48 Holland International
PLACES TO EAT
2 Il Giardino d'Inverno
21 Trattoria da Nino
22 Trattoria la Pigna Verde
29 Caffè Collegiata
36 Ristorante il Finocchiaro
40 Trash Pub
44 Trattoria al Boccone Divino
Piazza Cavour
Via Etnea
Orto Botanico
Piazza V Lanza
Via Caronda
Viale XX Settembre
Piazza G Verga
Corso Italia
Via G Carnazza
Viale della Libertà
Viale Regina Margherita
Via S Tomaselli
Via Euplio
Villa Bellini
Via Umberto
Via V Ognina
Via Conte di Torino
Via Lago di Nicito
Via Androne
Via Pacini
Piazza Carlo Alberto
Via Ventimiglia
Via d'Amico
Viale Africa
Via Rocca Romana
Via Archimede
Corso Sicilia
Piazza della Repubblica
Corso Martiri della Libertà
Piazza Stesicoro
Via L Sturzo
Piazza Giovanni XXIII
Via Santa Maddalena
Via Plebiscito
Via Antonino di Sangiuliano
Via VI Aprile
Via Crociferi
Via Gesuiti
Piazza Dante
V Teatro Massimo
Piazza dei Martiri
Ionian Sea
Via V Emanuele II
Via Dusmet
Via Giuseppe Garibaldi
Via Naumachia
Via Plebiscito
Via Colombo
Porto Vecchio
Via D Tempio
Porto Nuovo
To Camping Grounds, Beaches, Airport & Siracusa
OTHER
4 Produce Market
7 Post Office
8 AAPIT Tourist Office
9 Tirrenia Agent
10 Hospital
11 CTS Travel Agency
12 Anfiteatro Romano
13 Deutsche Bank (ATM)
14 Banca Nazionale del Lavoro (ATM)
15 Telecom Office
16 Newspaper Stand
17 SAIS Office
18 Intercity Buses
19 Train Station
20 AST Office
23 La Duca Viaggi (American Express)
24 Chiesa di San Niccolò
25 Hospital
26 Benedictine Monastery
27 Teatro Romano & Odeon
28 Basilica Collegiata
30 Palazzo dell'Università
33 Piazza del Duomo & Fontana dell'Elefante
34 Palazzo del Municipio
35 Piazza dell'Università
37 Palazzo San Giuliano
38 Badia di Sant'Agata
39 Duomo
42 Teatro Bellini
43 Piazza Bellini
45 Fratelli Bonanno (Malta Boats)
46 Piazza Cutelli
47 Night Pharmacy
49 Ferry Terminal
50 Castello Ursino

the **Badia di Sant'Agata** (a convent), yet another Vaccarini masterpiece whose cupola dominates the city centre.

A few blocks north-east you'll stumble into **Piazza Bellini** – the theatre of the same name is an eye-catching example of the city's architectural richness, a richness unfortunately buried beneath deep layers of grime.

North along Via Etnea from the Piazza del Duomo are several buildings of interest. Facing each other on Piazza dell'Università are two others designed by Vaccarini, the **Palazzo dell'Università** to the west and the **Palazzo San Giuliano** to the east.

Roman Ruins & Churches

West along Via Vittorio Emanuele II, at No 226, is the entrance to the ruins of a **Roman theatre** and **Odeon** (small rehearsal theatre). They are open daily from 9 am to one hour before sunset. From Piazza San Francesco, just before the entrance to the ruins, head north along Via Crociferi, which is lined with Baroque churches. Turn left into Via Gesuiti and follow it to Piazza Dante and the sombre **Chiesa di San Niccolò**. The largest church in Sicilia, its façade was never completed. Next to the church is an 18th-century Benedictine monastery, the biggest in Europe after that of Mafra in Portugal, but in poor shape. It is now part of the university and slowly being restored. Wander in for a look at the cloisters – the beauty is faded, but it's there.

North of Piazza del Duomo more leftovers from Roman days include a modest **amphitheatre** in Piazza Stesicoro. For relief from the madding crowd, continue north along Via Etnea and cut in to the left behind the post office for the lovely gardens of the **Villa Bellini**, named in memory of one of Catania's most famous sons, the composer Vincenzo Bellini.

Castello Ursino

Built in the 13th century by Frederick II, one of the great castle-builders of the Middle Ages, this grim-looking fortress, surrounded by a moat, is in an equally grim neighbourhood, where it is best to travel in pairs or groups. It's south-west of Piazza del Duomo, just over the railway line. A few rooms have now been opened in the **Museo Civico** inside.

Places to Stay

Camping facilities are available at *Internazionale la Plaja* (☎ 34 08 80), Viale Kennedy 47, on the way out of the city towards Siracusa (take bus No 527 from Piazza Borsellino).

Budget hotels are located around the centre and, if you are low on money, Catania is a good place to hole up. There are several places with rock-bottom prices, including the *Hotel Trieste* (☎ 32 71 05), Via Leonardi 24, near Piazza Bellini, which charges about L20,000 a person for a no-frills room.

The *Holland International* (☎ 53 27 79) is closer to the train station at Via Vittorio Emanuele II 8, just off Piazza dei Martiri, and has singles/doubles for L35,000/55,000 and doubles with a bathroom for L65,000.

A little further upmarket, *Hotel Rubens* (☎ 31 70 73), Via Etnea 196, has singles/doubles for L34,000/50,000, while *Hotel Ferrara* (☎ 31 60 00), Via Umberto I 66, has rooms for L38,000/55,000, or L60,000/75,000 with a bathroom. *Hotel Gresi* (☎ 32 37 09), Via Pacini 28, has singles/doubles for L40,000/61,000 and triples with a bathroom for L90,000.

Just off the Piazza del Duomo are two hotels with a little more class. The *Albergo Savona* (☎ 32 69 82), Via V Emanuele II 210, has singles/doubles for L38,000/60,000 or for L75,000/120,000 with a bathroom. *Hotel Centrale Europa* (☎ 31 13 09), Via V Emanuele II 167, comes in at L40,000/57,000 and has doubles with a bathroom for L124,000.

The *Villa Dina Hotel* (☎ 44 71 03), Via Caronda 129, is at the northern end of Via Etnea, near Piazza Cavour. It has pleasant rooms, a garden and private car park, and singles/doubles are L100,000/160,000. Take bus No 1-4 or 1-5 to the stop at Via Paleo, opposite the botanic gardens (not the Villa Bellini gardens).

DAMIEN SIMONIS

DAMIEN SIMONIS

DAMIEN SIMONIS

JOHN GILLMAN

Top Left: Hanging out in Piazza del Duomo, Orvieto, Umbria
Top Right: Priest in Piazza del Duomo, Spoleto, Umbria
Bottom Left: Views of Gubbio from the top of Palazzo dei Consoli, Umbria
Bottom Right: Wildflowers in the Monti Sibillini, Le Marche

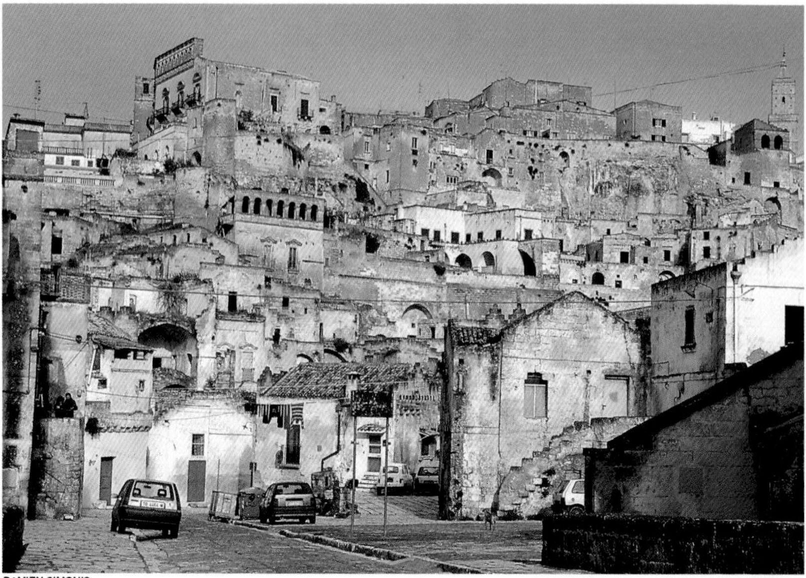
DAMIEN SIMONIS

LAUREN SUNSTEIN

LAUREN SUNSTEIN

STEFANO CAVEDONI

Top: Sassi, Matera, Basilicata
Middle & Bottom: Trulli, Puglia
Right: The whitewashed town of Ostuni, Puglia

Places to Eat
Every morning except Sunday, Piazza Carlo Alberto is flooded by the chaos of a produce *market*, one of several in Catania. You can pick up supplies of bread, cheese, salami, fresh fruit and all manner of odd and ends.

Eating out can be pleasant and inexpensive in Catania. Students head for the area around Via Teatro Massimo, where there are several sandwich bars and 'pubs'. The area between here and the duomo is littered with small restaurants and trattorie, but some open only for lunch.

One eatery with a solid L15,000 lunch menu is the *Trattoria al Boccone Divino*, Via Vittorio Emanuele II 101. In the evening, you could track down the no-fuss *Trattoria la Pigna Verde*, Via Carcaci 17, where you can get local dishes and eat well for about L20,000.

Trattoria Da Nino, Via Biondi 19, has reasonably priced, good meals. Pricier but very pleasant is the *Ristorante Il Finocchiaro*, Via Cestai 8. In a similar price bracket is *Il Giardino d'Inverno*, Via Asilo Sant'Agata 34, about 500m north of the train station and west off Viale della Libertà. A full meal costs about L40,000.

One of the city's better restaurants is the *Costa Azzurra*, Via de Cristoforo 4, by the sea at Ognina, north-east of the city. It specialises in seafood and is expensive. Bus Nos 332 and 334 leave from Piazza Europa for Ognina. Catch bus No 3-6 from the train station to Piazza Europa.

There are several decent cafés along Via Etnea, especially down the Piazza del Duomo end. For a touch of elegance, look in at the *Caffè Collegiata*, at No 3 on the street of the same name. For a Guinness, try *Trash Pub*, Piazza Scammacca 3.

Getting There & Away
Air Catania's airport, Fontanarossa, is 7km south-west of the city centre and services domestic and European flights (the latter all via Roma or Milano). In summer you may be able to dig up the odd direct charter flight to London or Paris. Take the special Alibus from outside the train station.

Bus Intercity buses terminate in the area around Piazza Giovanni XXIII, in front of the train station. SAIS (☎ 53 61 68), Via d'Amico 181, services Messina, Taormina, Noto, Siracusa, Palermo (two hours 40 minutes via autostrada; L16,000), Agrigento and Enna, and has a service to Roma. AST (☎ 53 17 56), Via Luigi Sturzo 220, also services these destinations and many smaller provincial towns around Catania, including Nicolosi and the cable car on Mt Etna. Etna Trasporti, at the same address as SAIS, runs buses to Piazza Armerina, Ragusa and Gela.

Train Frequent trains connect Catania with Messina and Siracusa (both 1½ hours) and there are less frequent services to Palermo (3¼ hours), Enna (1¾ hours) and Agrigento (an agonisingly slow four hours). The private Circumetnea train line circles Mt Etna, stopping at the towns and villages on the volcano's slopes. See the Mt Etna Getting There & Away section.

Car & Motorcycle Catania is easily reached from Messina on the A18 and from Palermo on the A19. From the A18, signs for the centre of Catania will bring you to Via Etnea.

Boat Tirrenia (☎ 31 63 94), Via Androne 61, runs car ferries to Livorno, in Tuscany, four days a week. Gozo Channel, represented by Fratelli Bonanno (☎ 31 06 29) at Via Anzalone 7, runs boats to Malta. The ferry terminal is south of the train station along Via VI Aprile.

Getting Around
Many of the more useful AMT city buses terminate in front of the train station. These include: Alibus, station-airport; Nos 1-4 and 1-6, station-Via Etnea; and Nos 4-7 and 4-6, station-Piazza del Duomo. In summer, a special service ('D') runs to the beaches from Piazza G Verga.

MT ETNA
Dominating the landscape in eastern Sicilia between Taormina and Catania, Mt Etna (approximately 3350m) is Europe's largest

live volcano and one of the world's most active. Eruptions occur frequently, both from the four live craters at the summit (one, the Bocca Nuova, was formed in 1968) and on the slopes of the volcano, which is littered with crevices and old craters.

The volcano's most devastating eruption occurred in 1669 and lasted 122 days. A massive river of lava poured down its southern slope, engulfing a good part of Catania and dramatically altering the landscape. In 1971 an eruption destroyed the observatory at the summit, and another in 1983 finished off the old cable car and tourist centre (you can see where the lava flow stopped on that occasion). Nine people died in an explosion at the south-east crater in 1979, and two died and 10 were injured in an explosion at the crater in 1987. Its most recent eruption was in 1992, when a stream of lava pouring from a fissure in its south-eastern slope threatened to engulf the town of Zafferana Etnea. The town was saved, but not before one family lost their home and others much of their farm land.

The unpredictability of the volcano's activity means people are no longer allowed to climb to the craters. Only a rope marks the point where it becomes unsafe, but it would be foolish to ignore the warning signs and go any farther.

On the north side of the volcano is a Pro Loco tourist centre at Linguaglossa (☎ 64 30 94), Piazza Annunziata. It has information about skiing and excursions to the craters, as well as an exhibition of the flora, fauna and rocks of the Parco Naturale dell'Etna. It is possible to hire a 4WD and guide to tour the volcano. On the south side, try the tourist office in Catania for information. The telephone code for the area is ☎ 095.

To the Craters

South With a daily bus link from Catania via Nicolosi, the south side of the volcano presents the easier option for an ascent towards the craters. From the Rifugio Sapienza (the closest the surfaced road comes to the summit) a cable car functions year-round from 9 am to 3.30 pm (L25,000 return). In summer, 4WD vehicles then take you through the eerie lava-scape close to the 3000m level. The all-in price for cable car, 4WD and guide was L58,000 return at the time of writing. In winter you are expected to ski back down (snow permitting) – there is no transport beyond the cable car. A day ski pass costs L42,000.

Some tourists make the long climb from the rifugio to the top (3½ to four hours on a track winding up under the cable car and then following the same road used by the minibuses).

North Several ski lifts operate at Piano Provenzana, snow permitting (a day ski pass costs up to L25,000). From the lifts you're looking at about an hour's walk to come close to the top – a difficult proposition on snow. Enquire about hiring a guide and the feasibility of the walk in winter at the Linguaglossa Pro Loco.

In summer, the lifts don't operate but 4WDs make the same journey. Again, consider a guide for the hour's scramble from where the vehicles stop. The return trip with a guide costs L55,000.

Places to Stay

There's a camping ground at Nicolosi (☎ 91 43 09), Via Goethe. The *Rifugio Sapienza* (☎ 91 10 62) near the cable car has beds for L35,000 a night and full board for L75,000 a day.

At Piano Provenzana, a small ski resort, the *Rifugio Nord-Est* (☎ 64 79 22) has beds for L35,000 a night.

There are small hotels at Piano Provenzana and in some of the towns along the Circumetnea train line, including Linguaglossa. For details, contact the Catania tourist office.

Getting There & Away

Having your own transport will make life much easier around Mt Etna, but there are some public transport options. The easier approach is from the south.

South An AST bus (095-53 17 56) for

Rifugio Sapienza leaves from Via L Sturzo in front of the main train station in Catania at 8.15 am, travelling via Nicolosi. It returns from the rifugio at 4 pm. The AST office in Nicolosi (☎ 91 15 05) is at Via Etnea 32. You can also drive this route (take the Via Etnea north out of town and follow the signs for Nicolosi and Etna).

North SAIS and FCE buses connect Linguaglossa with Fiumefreddo on the coast (from where other SAIS buses run north to Taormina and Messina and south to Catania). Unless the FCE puts on a winter ski-season or summer bus to Piano Provenzana, your only chance from Linguaglossa is your thumb. If driving, follow the signs for Piano Provenzana out of Linguaglossa.

Around the Mountain Another option is to circle Mt Etna on the private Circumetnea train line. It starts in Catania at the train station in Corso delle Province, opposite Corso Italia. Catch bus No 628, 448 or 401 back from the main train station to Corso delle Province. The line runs around the mountain from Catania to the coastal town of Riposto, passing through numerous towns and villages on its slopes, including Linguaglossa. You can reach Riposto (or neighbouring Giarre) from Taormina by train or bus if you want to make the trip from that end.

Catania-Riposto is about a 3½-hour trip, but you needn't go that far. If leaving from Catania, consider finishing the trip at Randazzo (two hours), a small medieval town noted for the fact that it has consistently escaped destruction despite its proximity to the summit. Randazzo is itself mildly interesting, with a couple of churches to punctuate a brief stroll along a few quiet streets, some lined with Aragonese apartments. A good example of lava architecture are the walls of the Norman Cattedrale di Santa Maria, while the Chiesa di Santa Maria della Volta preserves a squat 14th-century bell tower.

An FS railway branch line connects Randazzo with Taormina/Giardini Naxos, but services are subject to cancellation. The infrequent SAIS buses are more reliable.

South-East Sicilia

SIRACUSA

Once a powerful Greek city to rival Athens, Siracusa (Syracuse) is one of the highlights of a visit to Sicilia. The city was founded in 734 BC by colonists from Corinth, who established their settlement on the island of Ortygia. Ruled by a succession of tyrants from the 5th century BC, Siracusa became a dominant sea power in the Mediterranean, prompting Athens to attack it in 413 BC. In one of history's great maritime battles, the Athenian fleet was sent to the bottom of the sea.

Siracusa reached its zenith under the rule of Dionysius and attracted luminaries from all around, Plato among them. He apparently so bored Dionysus with his diatribes that the tyrant ended up trying to sell the philosopher as a slave.

The Romans marched into Siracusa in 212 BC, but the city remained important and enlightened under the new administration. Less sensitive handling came from the barbarians in the 5th century AD, later succeeded by an empire more in the old style, that of the Byzantines. Siracusa's fate followed that of much of the island, witnessing the arrival of the Arabs, Normans, Swabians, French and Spaniards over the centuries.

The Greek mathematician Archimedes was born here and the apostle Paul converted the city to the Christian faith.

Orientation

The main sights of Siracusa are in two areas: on the island of Ortygia and 2km across town in the Neapolis Parco Archeologico (archaeological zone). From the train station, walk east along Via Francesco Crispi to Piazzale Marconi. Heading straight through the piazza to Corso Umberto will bring you to Ortygia, just a five-minute walk. Alternatively, turn left from Piazzale Marconi into

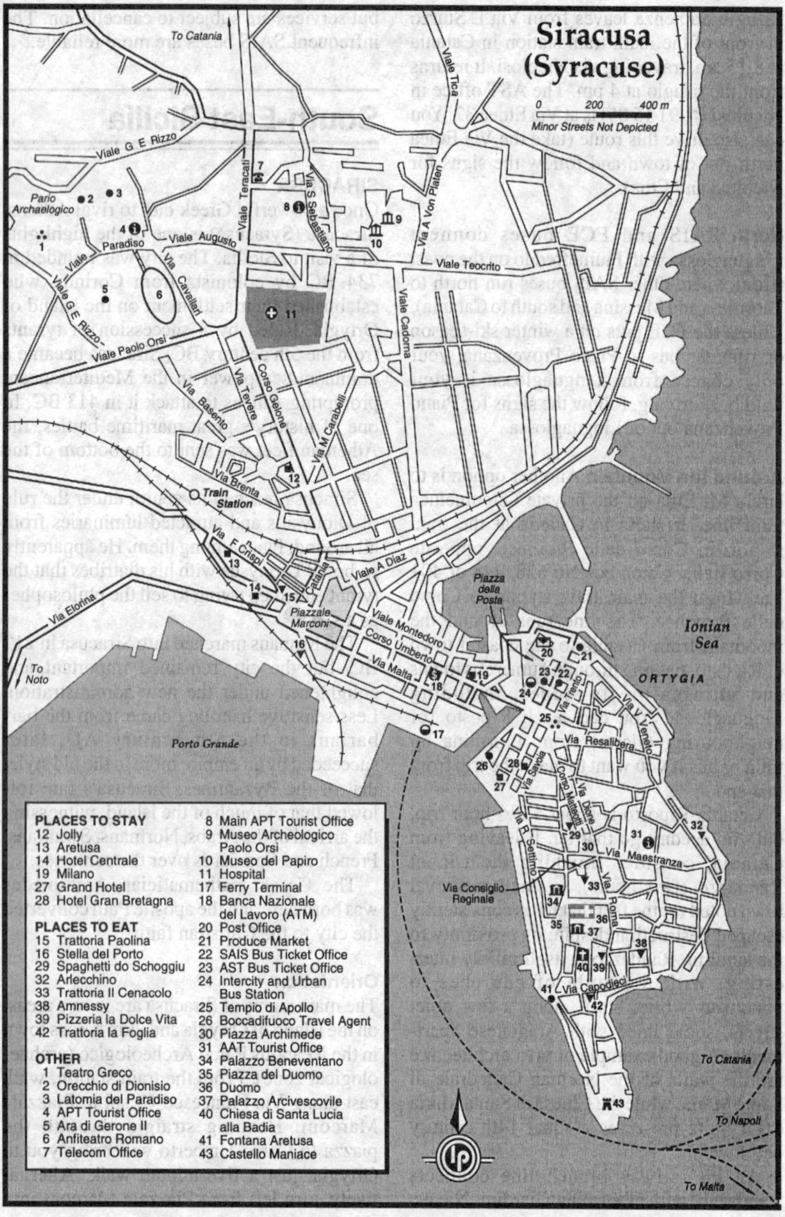
Siracusa
(Syracuse)
0 200 400 m
Minor Streets Not Depicted
To Catania
Viale Tica
Viale G E Rizzo
Viale Teracati
Via S Sebastiano
Viale A Von Platen
Parco Archaelogico
Viale Paradiso
Viale Augusto
Via Cavallari
Viale Teocrito
Viale Cadorna
Viale Paolo Orsi
Via Teracati
Via Tevere
Corso Gelone
Via Basento
Via M Carabelli
Via Brenta
Train Station
Via F Crispi
Catania
Viale A Diaz
Via Elorina
To Noto
Piazzale Marconi
Viale Montedoro
Corso Umberto
Via Malta
Piazza della Posta
Ionian Sea
ORTYGIA
Porto Grande
Via Trento
Via V Veneto
Via Resalibera
Via Savoia
Corso Matteotti
Via Dione
Via R Settimo
Via Maestranza
Via Consiglio Reginale
Via Roma
Via Capodieci
To Catania
To Napoli
To Malta
PLACES TO STAY
12 Jolly
13 Aretusa
14 Hotel Centrale
19 Milano
27 Grand Hotel
28 Hotel Gran Bretagna
PLACES TO EAT
15 Trattoria Paolina
16 Stella del Porto
29 Spaghetti do Schoggiu
32 Arlecchino
33 Trattoria Il Cenacolo
38 Amnessy
39 Pizzeria la Dolce Vita
42 Trattoria la Foglia
OTHER
1 Teatro Greco
2 Orecchio di Dionisio
3 Latomia del Paradiso
4 APT Tourist Office
5 Ara di Gerone II
6 Anfiteatro Romano
7 Telecom Office
8 Main APT Tourist Office
9 Museo Archeologico Paolo Orsi
10 Museo del Papiro
11 Hospital
17 Ferry Terminal
18 Banca Nazionale del Lavoro (ATM)
20 Post Office
21 Produce Market
22 SAIS Bus Ticket Office
23 AST Bus Ticket Office
24 Intercity and Urban Bus Station
25 Tempio di Apollo
26 Boccadifuoco Travel Agent
30 Piazza Archimede
31 AAT Tourist Office
34 Palazzo Beneventano
35 Piazza del Duomo
36 Duomo
37 Palazzo Arcivescovile
40 Chiesa di Santa Lucia alla Badia
41 Fontana Aretusa
43 Castello Maniace

Via Catania, cross the railway and follow the busy shopping street, Corso Gelone, to Viale Paolo Orsi and the Parco Archeologico. If you arrive by bus, you'll be dropped in or near Piazza della Posta in Ortygia. Most accommodation is in the newer part of town, to the west, while the better eating places are in Ortygia.

Information

Tourist Offices The main APT office (☎ 677 10), Via San Sebastiano 43, opens Monday to Saturday from 8 am to 7 pm and Sunday from 8 am to 1 pm. There's also a branch office at the Parco Archeologico.

The AAT (☎ 46 42 55), on Ortygia at Via Maestranza 33, deals specifically with Siracusa and is probably the most convenient office at which to pick up a map and hotel list. It is open Monday to Saturday from 8.30 am to 1.45 pm and 4.30 to 7.30 pm.

Money Numerous banks line Corso Umberto, including the Banca Nazionale del Lavoro at No 29, which has ATMs. There are others on Corso Gelone. The rates at the train station exchange booth are generally poor.

Post & Communications The post office is in Piazza della Posta, to your left as you cross the bridge to Ortygia. It is open Monday to Friday from 8 am to 7 pm and Saturday to 1 pm.

The Telecom office, Viale Teracati 46, is open Monday to Saturday from 8 am to 7.15 pm. The post code for Siracusa is 96100 and the telephone code is ☎ 0931.

Medical Services The public hospital is in Via Testaferrata. For medical emergencies, ring ☎ 6 85 55.

Emergency For immediate police assistance, ring ☎ 113.

Ortygia

The island of Ortygia is the spiritual and physical heart of the city. Its buildings are predominantly medieval, with some Baroque palaces and churches. The 7th-century **duomo** was built on top of a Greek temple of Athena, incorporating most of the original columns of the temple in its three-aisled structure. The duomo is a melting pot of architectural styles. Rebuilt after various earthquakes, it has a Gothic/Catalan ceiling, a Baroque façade and Baroque chapels and altars. The towers on the left side of the church's exterior were built by the Arabs, who used the building as a mosque. Some of the columns on the left side have shifted on their bases, the result of an earthquake in 1542.

Piazza del Duomo, once the site of the Greek acropolis, is lined with Baroque palaces, including the **Palazzo Beneventano** and the **Palazzo Arcivescovile** (Archbishop's Palace), and is among the finest Baroque squares in Italy. At the southern end is the **Chiesa di Santa Lucia alla Badia**, dedicated to St Lucy, the city's patron saint, who was martyred at Siracusa during the reign of the Roman emperor Diocletian. The church's Baroque façade is decorated with a wrought-iron balustrade.

Walk down Via Picherali to the waterfront and you'll find the **Fontana Aretusa**, a natural freshwater spring only metres from the sea. Greek legend says the nymph Arethusa, pursued by the river god Alpheus, was turned into a fountain by the goddess Diana so she could escape. Undeterred, Alpheus then turned himself into the river that feeds the spring. Next to the spring is the Foro Vittorio Emanuele II, where locals take their evening constitutional. At the entrance to Ortygia, in Piazza Pancali, lies the **Tempio di Apollo** (Temple of Apollo). Little remains of the 6th-century BC Doric structure, apart from the bases of a few columns.

Parco Archeologico

For the classicist, Siracusa is summed up in one image – that of the sparkling white, 5th-century BC **Teatro Greco**, hewn out of the rock in what for the Greek settlers was Neapolis, or the New City. A masterwork, the ancient theatre could seat 16,000 people.

Near the theatre is the **Latomia del Paradiso** (Garden of Paradise), which was a former limestone quarry run by the Greeks along the lines of a concentration camp, where prisoners cut blocks of limestone in subterranean tunnels for building projects. Most of the area remained covered by a 'roof' of earth, which collapsed during the 1693 earthquake. After this, the garden of citrus and magnolia trees was created.

In the garden is the **Orecchio di Dionisio** (Ear of Dionysius), a grotto 23m high and 65m deep, in the shape of an ear. It was named by Caravaggio, who, during a visit in the 17th century, was much impressed by its extraordinary acoustics. Caravaggio mused that the tyrant must have taken advantage of them to overhear the whispered conversations of his prisoners. Next to it, the **Grotta dei Cordari** (Cordmakers' Cave) is so named because it was used by cordmakers to practise their craft. The cave has been closed for some years.

Back outside this area and opposite the APT tourist office you'll find the entrance to the 2nd-century AD **Roman amphitheatre**. The structure was used for gladiator fighting and horse races. Roman punters used to park their chariots in the area between the amphitheatre and Viale Paolo Orsi. The Spaniards, little interested in archaeology, largely destroyed the site in the 16th century, using it as a quarry to build the city walls on Ortygia. West of the amphitheatre is the 3rd-century BC **Ara di Gerone II** (Altar of Hieron II). The monolithic sacrificial altar was a kind of giant abattoir where 450 oxen could be killed at one time.

The Parco Archeologico is open daily from 9 am to one hour before sunset (in the depths of winter until 3 pm). Admission is L2000 and you can stay for up to an hour after the ticket window shuts. To get here, catch a bus (No 1 and several others) from Riva della Posta on Ortygia.

Museo Archeologico Paolo Orsi

This museum is located in the grounds of the Villa Landolina, about 500m east of the Parco Archeologico, off Viale Teocrito. It contains the best organised and most interesting archaeological collection in Sicilia and certainly merits a visit. It is divided into three sections: Section A deals with proto and prehistoric Sicilia; Section B has an excellent collection from the ancient Greek colonies of Megara Hyblea and Siracusa itself; and Section C looks at Syracusan subcolonies such as Eloro, as well as several Hellenised indigenous towns, and Agrigento and Gela. The museum's collection also provides a fascinating and informative window on the important settlements of Pantalica, Megara Hyblea and Eloro. The museum is open daily from 9 am to 1 pm (also from 3.30 to 6.30 pm Wednesday and Friday). Admission is L2000.

Museo del Papiro

This small museum, at Viale Teocrito 66, has exhibits including papyrus documents and products. The plant grows in abundance around the Ciane river, near Siracusa, and was used to make paper in the 18th century. The museum is open Tuesday to Sunday from 9 am to 2 pm.

Special Events

Since 1914, in every even-numbered year, Siracusa has hosted a festival of Greek classical drama in May and June. Performances are given in the Greek theatre and prices range from around L20,000 for unreserved seats in the rear to L80,000 for reserved seats close to the stage. Tickets are available from the APT office or at a booth at the entrance to the theatre. You can call for information on ☎ 6 53 73.

Places to Stay – bottom end

Camping There are camping facilities at *Agriturist Rinaura* (☎ 72 12 24), about 4km west of the city; catch bus No 21, 22 or 24 from Corso Umberto. It costs L6000 per person and around L17,000 for a site (including electricity and car space). *Fontane Bianche* (☎ 79 03 33) is about 18km south-west of Siracusa, at the beach of the same name. It is slightly more expensive than Agriturist Rinaura and is open from April to October. Catch bus No 21 or 22.

Hostel The non-HI *Ostello della Gioventù* (☎ 71 11 18), Viale Epipoli 45, is 8km west of Siracusa; catch bus No 11 or 25 from Piazza Marconi. Beds are L20,000.

Hotels Close to the train station is the *Hotel Centrale* (☎ 6 05 28), Corso Umberto 141. It has small, basic singles/doubles for L25,000/40,000. The *Milano* (☎ 6 69 81), Corso Umberto 10, near Ortygia, has no-frills rooms for L30,000/50,000 or L40,000/65,000 with a bathroom.

The two-star *Aretusa* (☎ 2 42 11), Via Francesco Crispi 73-81, is close to the train station and has comfortable singles/doubles for L40,000/60,000. With a bathroom, you're looking at L47,000/70,000.

The *Hotel Gran Bretagna* (☎ 6 87 65), Via Savoia 21, is pleasant and has rooms for L46,000/76,000 or L52,000/89,000 with a bathroom.

Places to Stay – middle to top end

The *Scala Greca* (☎ 75 39 22; fax 75 37 78) is north of the Parco Archeologico at Via Avola 7 and has singles/doubles with a bathroom for L75,000/103,000. It is, like several other better hotels, quite a distance from the centre. The *Jolly* (☎ 46 11 11; fax 46 11 26), is a very good choice. It is near both the station and the Parco Archeologico, at Corso Gelone 45. Fully-serviced, sound-proofed rooms cost up to L200,000/230,000.

The newly-restored *Grand Hotel* (☎ 46 46 00; fax 46 46 11), on Ortygia at Viale Mazzini 12, has top-class rooms for L200,000/250,000.

Places to Eat

In the streets near the post office, there's a produce *market* daily, except Sunday, until 1 pm. There are several grocery shops and supermarkets along Corso Gelone.

For snacks, try the excellent takeaway pizza and focaccia at *Casa del Pane*, Corso Gelone 115.

In the new part of town, the *Stella del Porto*, Via Tripoli 40, off Via Malta, is a simple trattoria with a small menu concentrating on seafood. Try the spaghetti with swordfish (pesce spada). A full meal will cost about L20,000. *Trattoria Paolina*, in Corso Umberto near the Hotel Centrale, serves up big plates of pasta for around L7000.

Spaghetti do Schoggiu is at Via Scinà 11, just off Piazza Archimede. It has pasta from L6000 and mains for around L10,000. *Pizzeria la Dolce Vita*, Via Roma 112, has outside tables in a small courtyard, and occasionally puts on live entertainment. *Amnessy* is a pleasant pizzeria/restaurant and bar in a corner of Piazza San Giuseppe; it charges average prices. *Trattoria Il Cenacolo* is tucked away in a tiny piazza off Via Consiglio Reginale, south of Piazza del Duomo. It serves good food at around L25,000 for a full meal. There's an atmospheric 'pub' across the square.

At *Trattoria la Foglia*, Via Capodieci 29, off Largo Aretusa, the eccentric owner/chef and her vegetarian husband serve whatever seafood and vegetables are fresh on the day, and cook their own bread. A full meal will cost around L40,000. *Arlecchino* is near the waterfront at Via dei Tolomei 5. It is one of the city's better restaurants and you'd be lucky to get away with paying less than L45,000 a head.

Getting There & Away

Bus Unless you're coming from Catania or Messina, you'll find buses faster and more convenient than trains. SAIS buses (☎ 6 67 10) leave from Riva della Posta or near their office at Via Trieste 28, a block in. They connect with Catania and its airport, Palermo (three-four hours; L20,000), Enna and surrounding small towns, including Noto. SAIS also has a daily service to Roma, leaving Siracusa at 6.30 am and connecting with the Roma bus at Catania.

AST buses leave for Catania, Piazza Armerina, Noto, Modica and Ragusa from their office (☎ 46 27 11) at Riva della Posta 11.

Train More than a dozen trains depart daily for Messina (three hours) via Catania (1½ hours). Some go on to Roma, Torino, Milano and other long-distance destinations. There is only one direct connection to Palermo, leaving at 6.40 am and taking five hours. If you insist on using trains and miss this one, you'll have to go to Catania and wait for a connection. There are several slow trains to Modica and Ragusa.

Car & Motorcycle By car, if arriving from the north, you will enter Siracusa on Via Scala Greca. To reach the centre of the city, turn left at Viale Teracati and follow it around to the south; it eventually becomes Corso Gelone. There is ongoing confusion over the superstrada connection between Catania, Siracusa and towns such as Noto farther along the coast. An autostrada is supposed to connect the towns but starts and ends virtually in the middle of nowhere some km out of Siracusa. You'll need to follow the signs to find it.

Boat Maltese companies run summer ferry and catamaran services to Siracusa. For information try the Boccadifuoco travel agency (☎ 46 38 66), Viale Mazzini 8.

Getting Around
Only a few km separate the Parco Archeologico and Ortygia, about a 20-minute walk. Otherwise, buses Nos 1 and 2 make the trip from the Piazza della Posta.

NOTO
Flattened by the 1693 earthquake, Noto was rebuilt in grand Baroque style by its noble families. The warm gold and rose hues of the local stone tone down the heavily embellished palaces and churches, and the town is very picturesque. However, many of Noto's most important buildings are in a state of extreme disrepair – the result of decades of neglect and plenty of minor earth tremors. The town was shocked in early 1996 when the dome and roof of its splendid baroque cathedral collapsed – apparently local authorities knew that the dome was cracked, but nothing was done. Fortunately, no-one was in the church at the time, but the absence of the dome has dramatically altered the town's skyscape, since the original designers of Baroque Noto had taken particular account of the visual impact of the town as a whole.

Noto is also good for your tastebuds and particularly known for its cakes and pastries. Be aware that accommodation is a problem.

Orientation & Information
Intercity buses drop you in the Porta Reale, at the beginning of Corso Vittorio Emanuele, the town's main street. You can get a map at the APT tourist office (☎ 83 67 44), along the corso in Piazza XVI Maggio (8 am to 2 pm and 3.30 to 7 pm). For police call ☎ 113. In a medical emergency call ☎ 57 12 22. The public hospital is in Via dei Mille, on the way out of town towards Noto Antica.

Noto's telephone code is ☎ 0931.

Things to See & Do
The collapse of the cathedral dome revealed that most previous restoration work done on the city's monuments had been very superficial – a significant problem, since the local white *tufo* stone is very soft and, as a building material, requires constant maintenance. The situation is so bad that several buildings remain standing only because they're held up by wooden supports. Lots of money has been allocated in the past, only to remain unspent, or to evaporate into the ether. However, it seems that this time the authorities are serious and numerous projects are under way to restore the cathedral and other important buildings in the city centre. There has also been a move to have Noto added to UNESCO's World Heritage List.

Most of the important monuments line Corso Vittorio Emanuele. Overlooking Piazza XVI Maggio are the **Chiesa di San Domenico** and the adjacent **Dominican convent**, both designed by Rosario Gagliardi, a Sicilian architect who made a big contribution to the town's reconstruction. Back towards the Porta Reale is the **Palazzo Villadorata** (also known as Palazzo Nicolaci), on Via Corrado Nicolaci. On the third Sunday in May the street is transformed into a sea of flowers for the **Infiorata**, a festival to welcome the spring. Each of the palace's richly sculpted balconies is different, sporting a veritable menagerie of centaurs, horses, lions, sirens and tragic masks. Once the home of the princes of Villadorata, it is now partly used as municipal offices and some rooms are open to the public.

The **cathedral** stands at the top of a sweeping staircase overlooking Piazza Municipio. The façade is imposing, but less extravagant than most of Noto's other Baroque monuments. Next to the cathedral is the **Palazzo Landolina**, now abandoned, but belonging to the Sant'Alfano, Noto's oldest noble family. Across the piazza is the **Palazzo Ducezio**, Noto's town hall, which has been buried in scaffolding for years.

Farther along the corso are the **Chiesa del Santissimo Salvatore** and an adjoining monastery. The interior of the church is the most impressive in Noto. The monastery was reserved for the daughters of local nobility. The fountain suspended on a wall next to the monastery was left there after Noto's streets were lowered in 1840 to facilitate the movement of carriages.

If you are interested in taking home a few pieces of Sicilian ceramics, All'Angolo, on the corner of Piazza dell'Immacolata and Corso Vittorio Emanuele has an excellent selection of pieces from Caltagirone and Santo Stefano di Camastra.

Places to Stay

There are only two hotels in Noto. The *Albergo Stella* (☎ 83 56 95), on the corner of Via F Maiore and Via Napoli, near the public gardens, has singles/doubles for L35,000/70,000. *Al Canisello* (☎ 83 57 93), Via Principe Umberto 94, has rooms for around the same price.

The remaining tourist accommodation is by the sea at Noto Marina, a 15-minute drive or bus trip (although buses run only in summer). Hotels include the *Residence Korsal* (☎ 81 21 19), which has rooms for L45,000/65,000, and the *President* (☎ 81 23 30), with a higher standard of rooms for L120,000/200,000.

Places to Eat

The people of Noto are serious about their food, so take time to enjoy a meal and follow it up with a visit to one of the town's excellent bars/pasticcerie. *Caffè Sicilia*, Corso V Emanuele 125, and *Corrado Costanzo*, round the corner at Via Silvio Spaventa 9, are neck and neck when it comes to the best gelato and dolce in Noto. Both make superb dolci di mandorle (almond cakes and sweets), real cassata cake and torrone (nougat), as well as heavenly gelati and granita – try the one made with fragolini (tiny wild strawberries).

Trattoria del Carmine, Via Ducezio 9, serves excellent home-style meals for about L25,000 a head, as does *Trattoria Il Giglio*, Piazza Municipio 8-10. *Ristorante Il Barocco*, off Via Cavour in Ronco Sgadari, near Via Nicolaci, is one of Noto's finest restaurants and has a lovely internal courtyard. There is a set menu for L25,000; otherwise you'll pay around L50,000 for à la carte.

Getting There & Away

Noto is easily accessible by AST and SAIS buses from Catania and Siracusa (see the Getting There & Away sections for those cities). From June to August only, buses run frequently between Noto and Noto Marina (in winter there is a school bus service).

AROUND NOTO

The beach at **Noto Marina** is pleasant and, as yet, has not been subject to the overdevelopment characteristic of most Italian resorts. Nearby, and accessible only by car or by making the 45-minute walk, is **Eloro**, the site of a Greek settlement later occupied by the Romans. Uncompleted excavations have revealed a city square and sacred area. On either side of the hill where the sparse ruins lie are long, sandy beaches comparatively free of the usual crowds. Unfortunately, a storm-water drain spills into the sea at the beach to the south of Eloro.

Farther along the coast is the **Vendicari** nature reserve, a haven for water birds. Birdwatchers are well catered for by special observatories and there is a superb, long, sandy beach that is popular in summer but never overcrowded. It is possible to reach the park by the SAIS bus connecting Noto and Pachino.

If you have a car, there are several interesting places to visit within an hour or two of Noto. At **Palazzolo Acreide**, the site of the ancient Akrai, one of the early colonies of Greek Siracusa, there is a moderately interesting Parco Archeologico with the ruins of a Greek theatre, temples and a series of interesting rock carvings called **santoni**, figures connected to ancient goddess worship. About 30km from Palazzolo are the necropoli of **Pantalica**, which are definitely worth a visit. This has been identified as the site of ancient Hybla, one of the oldest settlements in eastern Sicilia, dating back to the Bronze Age. The necropoli are located in a deep gorge. It is possible to walk down into the gorge – even to swim in its icy waters. Of interest are the sparse ruins of the *anaktoron*, a monumental royal palace, similar to a Mycenaean *megaron*.

SICILIA

Closer to Noto is the **Cava d'Ispica**, just outside the town of Ispica, a Parco Archeologico above a deep gorge. There are traces of prehistoric, Byzantine, and medieval settlements. The area was abandoned after the 1693 earthquake.

AST buses leave from Piazza della Posta in Siracusa for Palazzolo Acreide and Ispica. There are also regular trains from Siracusa for Ispica. AST buses leave from Siracusa for Ferla and Sortino, 11 and 6km from Pantalica respectively. There are no buses connecting these towns to Pantalica itself. The Siracusa APT has timetables and more information.

RAGUSA & RAGUSA IBLA

This prosperous provincial capital is virtually two towns in one: Ragusa Ibla, a curious cocktail of medieval and Baroque, and the 18th-century 'new' town, simply known as Ragusa.

Orientation & Information

The lower town, Ibla, has most of the sights, but transport and accommodation are in the newer upper town. The train station is in Piazza del Popolo and the Intercity bus station is in the adjacent Piazza Gramsci. From the train station, turn left and head along Viale Tenente Lena, across the bridge (Ponte Nuovo) and straight ahead along Via Roma to reach Corso Italia, the upper town's main street. Turn right on Corso Italia and follow it to the stairs to Ibla, or follow the winding road to the lower town.

The tourist office (☎ 62 14 21) is at Via Capitano Bocchieri 33 on the 1st floor of the Palazzo Rocca, open Monday to Saturday from 7.30 am to 2.30 pm. The public hospital, the Ospedale Civile (☎ 62 39 46 for the Guardia Medica), is across Piazza del Popolo from the train station. For an ambulance, call ☎ 62 14 10. For police attendance, ring ☎ 113.

The telephone code for Ragusa is ☎ 0932.

Things to See & Do

The stairs linking the upper and lower towns are next to the **Chiesa di Santa Maria delle Scale**. The church was rebuilt after the 1693 earthquake and retains parts of the original 15th-century structure including the bell tower and doorway. Take in the panoramic view of Ibla before heading down the stairs.

The **Basilica di San Giorgio**, at the top of a flight of stairs in the Piazza del Duomo, dominates Ibla. Designed by Rosario Gagliardi and built in the late 18th century, it has the boisterous, 'wedding-cake' appearance of high Baroque.

Follow Corso XXV Aprile downhill, past the **Chiesa di San Giuseppe**, which bears similarities to San Giorgio, until you reach the **Giardino Ibleo**, the town's pleasant public gardens, where you can have a picnic.

In the upper town, visit the early 18th-century **duomo** in Piazza San Giovanni on Corso Italia, and the **Museo Archeologico Ibleo** in Via Natalelli, off Via Roma. The museum is open Monday to Saturday from 9 am to 1 pm and 3 to 6 pm. Admission costs L2000.

Places to Stay

All of Ragusa's accommodation is in the

upper town and there are no budget hotels. *Hotel San Giovanni* (☎ 62 10 13), Via Traspontino 3, has singles/doubles for L40,000/60,000, or L60,000/96,000 with a bathroom. To get there from Piazza del Popolo, head down Viale Leonardo da Vinci, turn left at Via Ingegnere Migliorisi and follow it to the footbridge.

At Corso Italia 40 is *Hotel Rafael* (☎ 65 40 80), a pleasant establishment with rooms with bathroom for L80,000/120,000. Nearby, at Corso Italia 70, is *Hotel Montreal* (☎ 62 11 33), with good singles/doubles with bathroom for L75,000/100,000.

Places to Eat

There is a *Standa supermarket* at Via Roma 187, near the bridge. *Trattoria la Bettola*, Largo Camerina, downhill to the left off Piazza del Duomo, is pleasant, and meals are priced at around L25,000. *La Rusticana*, at Via XXV Aprile 68, is another reasonable little place. *U Saracinù*, Via del Convento 9, off Piazza del Duomo, has a L25,000 tourist menu; otherwise a full meal will come to around L35,000.

Getting There & Away

Ragusa is accessible by not-so-regular trains from Siracusa, Noto and Agrigento. Buses are better. Etna Trasporti, a subsidiary of SAIS (information and tickets at Gran Bar Puglisi, Via Dante 94, opposite the train station) runs eight buses per day to Catania.

AST (☎ 62 12 49) services Catania by way of Siracusa (three buses a day). It also serves Palermo (three buses a day) and runs more regularly to Noto and Siracusa (seven a day). An AST timetable is posted at the spot in Piazza Gramsci where AST buses stop.

Getting Around

City buses Nos 1 and 3 run from Piazza del Popolo in the upper town to Piazza Pola and the gardens in the lower town.

MODICA

About 20km east of Ragusa, Modica seems to be a close cousin. It has the same sun-bleached colour and is also divided into two sections: Modica Alta (High Modica) and, you guessed it, Modica Bassa (Low Modica).

The highlight is the **Chiesa di San Giorgio** in the upper part of town (local buses run by from the lower end), easily one of the most extraordinary Baroque churches in the province. A majestic stairway sweeps up to a daringly tall façade, erected by Rosario Gagliardi in the early 18th century – it looks as if it was meant to be a tower. There are regular AST buses from Ragusa.

Central Sicilia & the South Coast

ENNA

Situated high on a commanding ridge in the sun-scorched centre of Sicilia, Enna is somewhat isolated from the main tourist route around the coast. Known since Greek times as the 'umbilicus' of Sicilia, the journey itself is rewarding, from whichever direction you approach. The exercise becomes more tempting still if combined with an excursion to nearby Piazza Armerina for the extraordinary mosaics of the Villa Romana (see the Piazza Armerina section later in this chapter).

Enna, 931m above sea level, has been an ideal defensive position and lookout post since prehistoric times. First settled by the Sicani, Enna later became Greek, submitting to the tyranny of Siracusa in 307 BC and thereafter falling into Carthaginian and Roman hands. In Byzantine times it became a fortress and one of the main bulwarks against the Arabs, who nonetheless managed to capture the town in 859 AD. Today it is an important agricultural and mining centre.

Orientation

The principal road into the town is Via Pergusa, which eventually links with Via Roma, the main street of historic Enna. The Intercity bus station is on Viale Diaz. To get to the town centre, turn right from the terminal and follow Viale Diaz to Corso Sicilia,

SICILIA

turn right again and follow it to Via Sant'Agata to the left, which heads down to Via Roma.

Information

The AAPIT office (☎ 52 82 28) is at Via Roma 413. The staff are helpful and you can pick up a map and information on the city and province. The office is open Monday to Saturday from 9 am to 1 pm. The AAST office (☎ 50 08 75), next to the Albergo Sicilia in nearby Piazza Colajanni, has information mainly on the city itself and is open daily from 8 am to 2 pm and every evening, except Monday and Saturday, from 4 to 7 pm.

The post office is at Via Volta 1, just off Piazza Garibaldi, and the post code for Enna is 94100. Public telephones are scattered about the town, or you can try the Albergo Sicilia. The telephone code for Enna is ☎ 0935.

There are several banks on Piazza VI Dicembre, a short walk downhill from the AAPIT.

In an emergency, call the police on ☎ 113. For medical assistance, go to the Ospedale Civile Umberto I in Via Trieste, or ring ☎ 4 51 11. Out of hours, the Guardia Medica is on ☎ 50 08 96.

Castello di Lombardia

Enna's most visible monument, the medieval castle, crowns the town's highest point at the eastern end. Built by the Swabians and altered by Frederick III of Aragon, it was one of the most important defensive structures in medieval Sicilia. It retains six of its original 20 towers and the views of the surrounding countryside are spectacular – you can make out Etna in the distant north-east. Closer and across the valley rises the town of Calascibetta, erected by the Arabs in the 9th century. It forms the northern sentinel over a valley which now contains the Palermo-Catania A19 autostrada and railway. The castle, now part theatre, is open daily from 8 am to 6 pm.

Duomo

Back along Via Roma, the 14th-century duomo retains, despite remodelling in the 15th and 16th centuries, its Gothic apse and transept. Behind the duomo on Via Roma is the **Museo Alessi**, which houses the contents of the cathedral's treasury. It was closed at the time of writing. Across Via Roma in Piazza Mazzini, the **Museo Archeologico** (also known as Museo Varisano) has a small collection of ancient artefacts found in the area. It is open daily from 9 am to 6.30 pm and admission is free.

Towers

In Piazza Vittorio Emanuele, the most impressive element of the **Chiesa di San Francesco** is its 15th-century bell tower, adorned with fine Gothic windows. The tower once formed part of the city's defence system. You could head over to the chunky **Torre di Federico** in the public gardens (villa comunale) in the new part of town, also part of the old system. The octagonal tower, standing 24m high, was once linked by a secret passage to the castle.

For a pleasant evening stroll, head for Piazza Francesco Crispi and wander along Viale Marconi to enjoy the view.

Special Event

During Holy Week at Easter, Enna is the setting for colourful, traditional celebrations. On Good Friday, thousands of people wearing hoods and capes of different colours participate in a solemn procession to the duomo.

Places to Stay & Eat

There is no cheap accommodation, so be prepared. Enna itself has only one hotel, the *Albergo Sicilia* (☎ 2 46 22), Piazza Colajanni. Singles/doubles with breakfast are L79,000/119,000. For other options, catch city bus No 4 from Piazza V Emanuele to Lago di Pergusa (a small, touristy lake with beaches about 10km south). Cheapest is the *Miralago* (☎ 54 12 72), with rooms at L40,000/60,000. It is the first place you pass on the right before entering the town proper along Via Nazionale.

There is a *market* every morning from Monday to Saturday in Via Mercato

Sant' Antonio, where you can find fresh fruit, bread and cheeses etc. *Knulp*, Via Restivo 14, is a bar where snacks, including some creative sandwiches, are served. *Da Gino* is a pleasant trattoria/pizzeria on Viale Marconi. It has outdoor tables and a view, and prices are reasonable. *Ristorante Centrale*, Piazza VI Dicembre 9, is more expensive. *Al Rupe* is set into the hillside, just below the castle, and serves reasonable food. It has tables on an open terrace with great views of Enna and the surrounding area.

Getting There & Away

SAIS buses (☎ 50 09 02) connect Enna with Catania (and on to Roma), Palermo and Siracusa. It is possible to reach Agrigento via Caltanisetta. Buses terminate in Viale Diaz. Regular SAIS buses also run to Piazza Armerina. Don't take a train – the station is miles away at the foot of the mountain-top town.

PIAZZA ARMERINA

A pleasant town less than an hour by bus or car from Enna, Piazza Armerina boasts an interesting Baroque **cathedral**. This self-proclaimed *città dei mosaici* (city of mosaics) is the nearest town to the wonderful treasure that lies in the Villa Romana del Casale, an imperial Roman villa some 5km away.

The AAST tourist office (☎ 68 02 01) is at Via Cavour 15, in the town centre, uphill along Via Umberto I or Via Garibaldi from the Intercity bus stops. It is open from 8 am to 2 pm and 4.30 to 7.30 pm. Get the brochure on the villa here; it explains the layout of the ruins and the mosaics and is often unavailable at the site. SAIS buses connect Enna and Piazza Armerina (about 10 a day). There is also a daily AST bus from Siracusa.

Villa Romana del Casale

Built between the end of the 3rd and mid-4th century AD, the villa was probably the home or hunting lodge of a Roman dignitary. Buried under mud in a 12th-century flood, it remained hidden for 700 years before its magnificent floor mosaics were revealed.

Covering about 3500sq metres, the villa was designed in line with the lie of the hill on which it stands, creating three main areas. The mosaics cover almost its entire floor and are considered unique for their narrative style of composition, range of subjects and variety of colours – much of them clearly influenced by African themes.

The villa is well organised to cope with hordes of tourists and, by following the raised walkways, you will see all the main areas. The most captivating of the mosaics include the erotic depictions in what was probably a private apartment on the north side of the great peristyle. One of the richest mosaics in terms of colour and action, the *Little Hunt*, is in the largest room. Next door is the villa's most famous piece, illustrating 10 girls clad in what must have been the world's earliest bikinis.

The east side of the peristyle opens onto a long corridor, its floor carpeted with the splendid mosaic of the *Great Hunt*, depicting the chase for exotic wild animals. On the other side of the corridor is a series of apartments, whose floor illustrations reproduce scenes from Homer, as well as mythical subjects such as Arion playing the lyre on a dolphin's back, and Eros and Pan wrestling. There is also a lively circus scene.

The villa is open daily from 9 am to one hour before sunset. Admission is L2000. Three ATAN buses leave hourly for the villa from Piazza Generale Cascino in Piazza Armerina from 9 am, and another three from 4 pm. If you have a car, you will be charged L2000 to park outside the entrance.

Places to Stay & Eat

If you want to stay in Piazza Armerina, about the cheapest accommodation is the *Villa Romana* (☎ 68 29 11), Via A De Gasperi 18, which has singles/doubles starting at L40,000/60,000. *Hotel Mosaici* (☎ 68 54 53) is 3km out of town on the way to the villa. It has rooms for L40,000/55,000. For a decent meal, try *Dal Goloso*, Via Garao 4, just off Piazza Garibaldi near the tourist office.

MORGANTINA

About 16km north-east of Piazza Armerina, just beyond the town of Aidone, the remains of what started life as a rich Siculian town have been unearthed. What you see of its agora, theatre and other buildings owes more to subsequent Greek occupation than to the Siculians, however. That the remains are not more spectacular is largely the fault of the Romans, who destroyed the town in 211 BC. Set in pleasant country with wide views to Etna, the Morgantina site is an easy detour if you have your own transport, but a difficult proposition without.

AGRIGENTO

This pleasant medieval town, set high on a hill, overlooks both the Mediterranean and the spectacular Valley of the Temples, a significant ancient Greek site. Founded in 582 BC by settlers from Gela, themselves originally from Rhodes, the town became powerful in the 5th century BC when it was ruled by tyrants, and most of the temples date from then. The Greek poet Pindar described the town as 'the most beautiful of those inhabited by mortals'.

Sacked and destroyed by the Carthaginians in 406 BC, it was rebuilt and conquered by the Romans in the 3rd century BC. The newcomers renamed the town Agrigentum and it continued to prosper under Byzantine and Arab rule. On the road between Agrigento and Porto Empedocle is Caos, where the playwright Luigi Pirandello (1867-1936) was born.

The Greek temples are the obvious reason to come to Agrigento, but it would be a shame to overlook the town itself.

Orientation

Intercity buses arrive in Piazza Rosselli, just off the north side of Piazza Vittorio Emanuele. The train station is slightly south in Piazza Marconi. Lying between the two is the green oasis of Piazzale Aldo Moro, at the

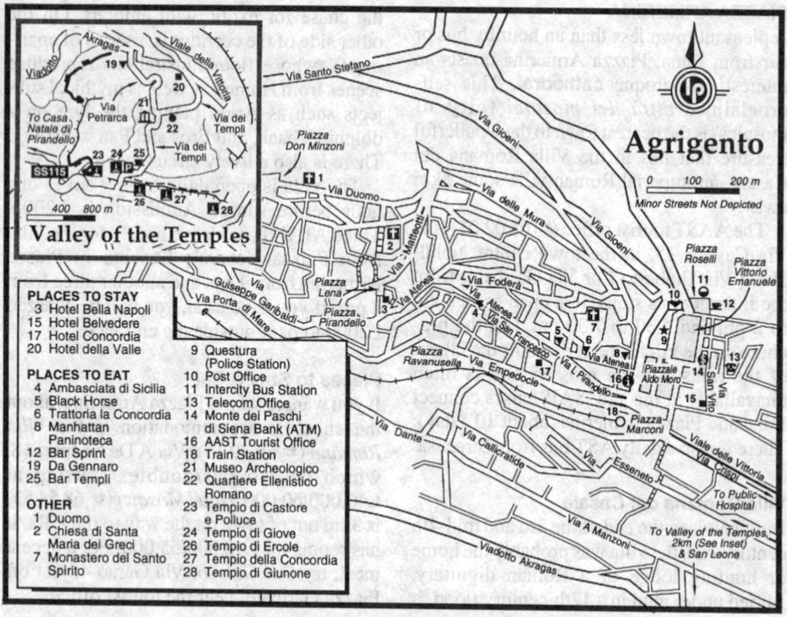

eastern end of Via Atenea, the main street of the medieval town. Frequent city buses run to the Valley of the Temples below the town. See the Getting Around section.

Information

Tourist Office The AAST office (☎ 2 04 54), Via Cesare Battisti 15, is open Monday to Saturday from 8.30 am to 1.45 pm and (excluding Saturday) 4 to 7 pm.

Money Banks are generally open from 8.30 am to 1.30 pm (larger banks also open from 3 to 4 pm) and the Monte dei Paschi di Siena on Piazza Vittorio Emanuele has an ATM. Out of hours there's an exchange office at the post office and another at the train station – watch the rates.

Post & Communications The post office, in Piazza Vittorio Emanuele, is open Monday to Friday from 8 am to 7 pm and Saturday to 11 am. The post code for central Agrigento is 92100.

There is a Telecom office at Via A de Gasperi 25, open Monday to Friday from 9 am to 12.30 pm and 4.30 to 7.45 pm. The telephone code for Agrigento is ☎ 0922.

Newspapers & Magazines You can get foreign newspapers and magazines near the bar in the Valley of the Temples.

Medical Services The public hospital, Ospedale San Giovanni di Dio (☎ 49 21 11), is on Via Atenea. For an ambulance, call ☎ 40 13 44.

Emergency For police attendance, call ☎ 113.

Valley of the Temples

The five main Doric temples along the 'valley' (actually a ridge) were constructed around the 5th century BC and are in various states of ruin, due to earthquakes and vandalism.

The area is divided into two sections. East of the Via dei Templi are the most spectacular temples. The first you will come to is the **Tempio di Ercole** (Temple of Hercules), built towards the end of the 6th century BC and believed to be the oldest of the temples. Eight of its 38 columns have been raised and you can wander around the remains of the rest. The **Tempio della Concordia** (Temple of Concord) is the only one to survive relatively intact. Built around 440 BC, it was transformed into a Christian church in the 6th century AD. Its name is taken from a Roman inscription found nearby. The **Tempio di Giunone** (Temple of Juno) stands high on the edge of the ridge, a five-minute walk to the east. Part of its colonnade remains and there is an impressive sacrificial altar.

This section of the valley is not enclosed and can be visited at any time.

Across the Via dei Templi is what remains of the massive **Tempio di Giove** (Temple of Jupiter), actually never completed. Now totally in ruin, it covered an area measuring 112m by 56m, with columns 20m high. Between the columns stood *telamoni* (colossal statues), one of which was reconstructed and is now housed in the Museo Archeologico. A copy lies on the ground among the ruins, giving an idea of the immense size of the structure. Work began on the temple around 480 BC and it was probably destroyed during the Carthaginian invasion in 406 BC. The nearby **Tempio di Castore e Polluce** (Temple of Castor & Pollux) was partly reconstructed in the 19th century, although probably using pieces from other constructions.

This area is open daily from 9 am to one hour before sunset and entry is free. The temples are lit up at night.

The **Museo Archeologico**, on Via dei Templi just north of the temples, has a collection of artefacts from the area worth inspecting. It is open Monday, Wednesday, Thursday and Saturday from 8 am to 1 pm and Tuesday and Friday from 8 am to 5 pm. Admission is free.

Opposite the museum, the **Quartiere Ellenistico-Romano** (Hellenistic-Roman quarter) constituted part of urban Agrigento. Some of its structures date to the 4th century

BC, while others were built as late as the 5th century AD.

West of the temples is the country house in Caos where Luigi Pirandello was born. Now a small museum, the **Casa Natale di Pirandello** is open daily from 9 am to 1.30 pm and 3 to 6 pm. Take bus No 1 from the station. The house is just short of Porto Empedocle, and overlooks the sea.

Medieval Agrigento

Wandering around the town's narrow, winding streets is relaxing after a day among the temples. The **Chiesa di Santa Maria dei Greci**, uphill from Piazza Lena, at the end of Via Atenea, is an 11th-century Norman church built on the site of a 5th-century BC Greek temple. Note the remains of the wooden Norman ceiling and some Byzantine frescoes.

A not so relaxing walk farther uphill is to the fragile-looking **duomo** in Via Duomo. Built in the year 1000, it has been restructured many times. The bell tower was erected in the 15th century and the panelled ceiling inside dates to the 17th century.

Back towards Piazza Vittorio Emanuele, the **Monastero del Santo Spirito** was founded by Cistercian nuns at the end of the 13th century. Giacomo Serpotta is responsible for the stuccoes in the chapel. There is a small ethnographic museum above the old church which is open from 9 am to 1 pm. You can buy cakes and pastries from the nuns. See the Places to Eat section.

Special Event

The town's big annual shindig is the Festival of the Almond Blossom, a folk festival held on the first Sunday in February in the Valley of the Temples.

Places to Stay

You can camp by the sea at San Leone, a few km south of Agrigento, at *Camping Nettuno* (☎ 41 62 68), which is open all year. Take bus No 2 or 2/ from Agrigento, or drive down Via dei Templi, continue along Viale Emporium towards the sea and turn left at Lungomare Akragas.

The *Hotel Bella Napoli* (☎ 2 04 35), Piazza Lena 6, is uphill off Via Bac Bac. It has clean, basic singles/doubles for L35,000/55,000 or L44,000/77,000 with a bathroom. The *Hotel Belvedere* (☎ 2 00 51), Via San Vito 20, is in the newer part of town, uphill from Piazza Vittorio Emanuele. It has rooms for L30,000/55,000 and doubles with a bathroom for L80,000. The *Hotel Concordia* (☎ 59 62 66) is just off Via Atenea at Piazza San Francesco 11, where the daily produce market is held. It has rooms for L30,000/50,000 or L44,000/77,000 with a bathroom.

Most of Agrigento's better hotels are out of town around the Valley of the Temples or near the sea. *Hotel Akrabello* (☎ 60 62 77) is in the Parco Angeli area, east of the temples. It is modern and comfortable and has rooms for up to L130,000/180,000.

Hotel della Valle (☎ 2 69 66) is in Via dei Templi. It has lovely rooms with full services, a pool and gardens; rooms cost up to L110,000/220,000. *Hotel Kaos* (☎ 59 86 22) is by the sea, about 2km from the temples. It is a large resort complex in a restored villa. Rooms cost up to L150,000/200,000.

Places to Eat

A good choice for a light lunch is the *Manhattan Paninoteca*, up Salita M Angeli from Via Atenea. For the best pastries, and just for the experience, go to *Santo Spirito* at the end of Via Foderà. The nuns have been making heavenly cakes and pastries to a secret recipe for centuries, and their dolce di mandorle (almond cake) is particularly special (and expensive). Press the door bell and say 'Vorrei comprare qualche dolce', and see how you go.

The *Black Horse*, Via Celauro 8, serves good, reasonably priced meals. *Ambasciata di Sicilia*, Via Giambertoni 2, offers typical Sicilian fare, and an enjoyable meal will cost under L30,000. Another reasonable place specialising in fish is the *Trattoria la Concordia*, Via Porcello 6.

If you have a car, head for *Trattoria Kokalos*, Via C Magazzeni, east of the temples, where they dish up the area's best pizza.

One of Agrigento's better restaurants is *Le Caprice*, between the town and temples. A full meal will cost between L40,000 and L50,000. Take any bus heading for the temples and get off at the Hotel Colleverde, from where it's a short walk (signposted). *Da Gennaro*, Via Petrarca, again downhill from the town, also maintains high standards. A full meal, including seafood, will cost around L70,000.

Getting There & Away

Bus For most destinations, bus is the easiest way to get to and from Agrigento. The Intercity station is in Piazza Roselli, just off Piazza Vittorio Emanuele, and timetables for most services are posted in Bar Sprint in the piazza. Autoservizi Cuffaro and Camilleri & Argento both run buses to Palermo. SAIS buses serve Roma, Catania, and Caltanissetta. Information about SAIS buses can be obtained at Via Ragazzi 99.

Train Trains run to Palermo (two hours), Catania (3½ hours) and Enna. For Palermo, the train is fine, if a little slow. For anywhere else you should consider the bus.

Car & Motorcycle Agrigento is easily accessible by road from all of Sicilia's main towns. The SS189 links the town with Palermo, while the SS115 runs along the coast, west towards Sciacca and east for Gela and eventually Siracusa. For Enna, take the SS640 via Caltanissetta. There is plenty of parking at Piazza Vittorio Emanuele in the centre.

Getting Around

City buses run down to the Valley of the Temples from in front of the train station. Take bus No 1, 1/, 2, 2/ or 3 and get off at either the museum or farther downhill at Piazzale dei Templi. The Green Line (Linea Verde) bus runs every hour from the train station to the duomo, for those who prefer not to make the uphill walk. Tickets cost L1200 and are valid for 1½ hours.

ERACLEA MINOA

A colony within a colony, Eraclea Minoa lies about halfway between Agrigento and Selinunte to the west, atop a wild bluff overlooking a splendid, sandy beach. Founded by Selinunte in the 6th century BC, the ruins are comparatively scanty and the 4th-century theatre's seating has been covered in moulded plastic to protect the crumbling remains. Buses running between Sciacca and Agrigento will drop you at the turn-off, from where it's a 4km walk. In summer, buses go from Cattolica Eraclea (which can be reached from Agrigento and Sciacca) to the site.

ISOLE PELAGIE

Some 240km south of Agrigento, this tiny archipelago (Pelagic Islands) lies farther from mainland Sicilia than Malta, and in many respects has more in common with nearby Tunisia or Libya than Italy. Indeed Libya's Colonel Gaddafi is so convinced of this that he launched a couple of wobbly missiles its way in 1987. Of the three islands, which rise on the African continental shelf, only Lampedusa is of any interest. Linosa has nothing to offer and Lampione is little more than an uninhabited pimple on the sometimes rather tempestuous surface of the Canale di Sicilia, the stretch of the Mediterranean separating Africa from Sicilia.

Lampedusa, a rocky, sparsely covered and, in winter, wind-whipped place, is becoming increasingly popular with Italians looking for an early tan, and the water is enticingly warm. Of the several beaches on the south side of the 11km-long island, the best known is the so-called Isola dei Conigli (Rabbit Island), where Caretta-Caretta turtles lay their eggs between June and August. These timid creatures generally only come in when no-one's about. There are several dive rental outlets; for more information go first to the Pro Loco tourist office (☎ 97 14 77) at Piazza Comm-Brignone 12. The telephone code for the islands is ☎ 0922. Hourly orange minibuses run from near the Pro Loco to the beach, or you could hire a Vespa from one of several outlets around town (look for the *autonoleggio* signs).

Cheap accommodation can be hard to

find. The little pensioni are often full in summer and closed in winter. You could try the *Albergo Alba d'Amore* (☎ 97 02 72), west along the waterfront from the port near the expensive Hotel Medusa – a good half-hour walk that takes you past Via Roma (the main drag) and over the rise to the fishing port along Via Marconi. It has singles/doubles for L25,000/40,000, but like most places makes at least half board compulsory in summer.

A Siremar ferry leaves Porto Empedocle (7km south-west of Agrigento) daily, except Friday, at midnight. It takes six hours to reach Linosa and another two to reach Lampedusa; the one-way fare to the latter is L47,800. A car up to 3.5m long costs L78,100. You can buy tickets at the Siremar booth (☎ 63 66 83) in the port. Orange buses from Agrigento arrive at Piazza Italia, from where it's a quick walk down Via Quattro Novembre to the port entrance (the last ferry from Porto Empedocle leaves for Agrigento at about 9 pm). Boats from Lampedusa (and Linosa) leave daily, except Saturday (10 am from Lampedusa). Trips can be cancelled due to bad weather, especially in winter. There are also flights between Lampedusa and Palermo.

SCIACCA

Sciacca started life as a Roman settlement but only really took off with the arrival of the Arabs. The Normans fortified this prosperous farming town, which later came to be ruled alternately by local feuding families. Today a bustling fishing port, the centre of town has a few monuments worthy of a quick look, including the **duomo**, which was erected by the Normans in the 12th century, the peculiar 15th-century **Steripinto** building, the neo-Gothic **Palazzo San Giacomo** and the ruins of a **castle** dominating the town. The time to come is February, when the townsfolk let their hair down for Carnevale. The AAST tourist office (☎ 0925-2 27 44) is at Corso Vittorio Emanuele 84. The *Paloma Blanca* (☎ 0925-2 51 39), Via Figuli 5 on the east side of town, has rooms for L40,000/ 70,000. Buses for Palermo leave from Viale della Vittoria (tickets at No 22). Others, run by the Lumia company, serve Trapani,Agrigentoanddestinationsbetween from Via Agatocle.

SELINUNTE

The ancient Greek city of Selinus, founded in the 7th century BC, was long a prosperous and powerful city, but its standing rivalry with Segesta to the north was to be its undoing. In 409 BC, the latter called in a powerful ally, Carthage, whose troops utterly destroyed Selinunte. The city later recovered under the tutelage of Siracusa and then Carthage, but in 250 BC its citizens delivered the *coup de grâce* to prevent it passing to the Romans. What they left standing, mainly temples, was finished off by an earthquake in the Middle Ages.

One of the more captivating ancient sites in Italy, Selinunte once fairly bristled with temples. They are known today simply by the letters A to G, O and M. Five are huddled together in the acropolis at the western end of the site, accessible by road from the ticket office, across the depression known as the Gorgo di Cottone – once Selinunte's harbour. Of particular note is **Temple C** – several of the metopes in Palermo's archaeological museum came from this temple, and there is also a reconstruction of the temple's clay roof at the museum.

Temple E, reconstructed in 1958 amid much criticism, stands out for its recently acquired completeness. Built in the 5th century BC, it is the first of three temples you'll come to at the eastern end of the site, close to the ticket office. The more outstanding metopes in Palermo's archaeological museum came from this temple. **Temple G**, the northernmost, was built in the 6th century BC and, although never completed, was one of the largest in the Greek world. Today it is a massive pile of rubble, but evocative nonetheless.

Selinunte is close to the village of Marinella di Selinunte, where you can find accommodation. *Il Maggiolino* (☎ 0924-4 60 44) is one of a couple of camping grounds;

charges are L6000 per person, L4000 per tent and L5000 per car. The *Pensione Costa d'Avorio* (☎ 0924-4 62 07), Via Stazione 10, has singles/doubles for L25,000/40,000 or L30,000/50,000 with a bathroom. It also has a trattoria. *Hotel Alceste* (☎ 0924-4 61 84), Via Alceste 23, has more upmarket rooms for L60,000/ 90,000 with a bathroom.

There are some pleasant little restaurants along the beachfront. Try the *Lido Azzurro*, also known as Baffo's, where you can eat good pizzas, pasta and fresh seafood virtually beside the water's edge.

Buses link Marinella to Castelvetrano, which can be reached by Lumia buses from Agrigento, Mazara del Vallo, Marsala and Trapani.

North-West Sicilia

MARSALA

Best known for its sweet dessert wines, Marsala is a surprisingly pleasant town, with an interesting historical centre. If you have a car, it's a good alternative to Trapani as a base for exploring Sicilia's north-west. Founded as Lilybaeon on Cape Lilibeo by Carthaginians who had fled nearby Mozia (or Motya) after its destruction by Siracusa, the city was eventually conquered by the Arabs, who renamed it Marsa Allah (Port of God). It was at Marsala that Garibaldi landed with his One Thousand in 1860.

Information

Marsala's APT tourist office (☎ 71 40 97) is at Via XI Maggio 100, just off Piazza della Repubblica, in the centre of town. It is open Monday to Saturday from 8 am to 2 pm and 3 to 7 pm. For a medical emergency, call ☎ 95 14 10. The public hospital is in Piazza San Francesco, just west of the city centre. You can call the police on ☎ 113. The telephone code for Marsala is ☎ 0923.

Things to See & Do

Visit the **duomo** in Piazza della Repubblica, built in the 17th and 18th centuries, and its **Museo degli Arazzi**, at Via Garraffa 57. In the museum are eight 16th-century tapestries, woven for the Spanish king Philip II and depicting scenes from the war of Titus against the Jews. The **Museo Lilibeo**, in Via Boeo by the sea (follow Via XI Maggio to Piazza Vittoria and turn left along Via N Sauro), houses a partly reconstructed Carthaginian warship, which may have seen action in the First Punic War. It was found off the coast north of Marsala in 1971. The museum is open daily from 9 am to 1.30 pm, as well as from 4 to 7 pm on Wednesday and Saturday. North of the museum, along Viale Vittorio Veneto, is the partly excavated **Insula Romana**, which was a 3rd-century AD Roman house.

Pay a visit to Marsala's open-air fresh produce **market**, open every morning except Sunday in a piazza off Piazza dell' Addolorata, next to the municipal offices (the *comune)*. In this small, lively marketplace, you're likely to be serenaded by a fruit vendor.

Tipplers should head to **Florio** on Lungomare V Florio (bus No 16 from Piazza del Popolo) – this is the place to buy the cream of Marsala's wines. At 4 pm Florio opens its doors to visitors to explain the

How Sweet it Is

The Marsala wine was 'discovered' by Englishman John Woodhouse, who after landing in the city in 1773 and tasting the local product, decided it should be marketed throughout Europe. His first competitor was Benjamin Ingham, who established his own factory in the town and began exporting the wine to the USA and Australia.

One particularly interesting figure in the Marsala-producing business was Ingham's nephew, Joseph Whitaker, who bought the island of San Pantaleo, where the ancient site Mozia was based, and built a villa there (it is still in his family today). Whitaker was responsible for renewing interest in the archaeological site of Mozia and for the few excavations carried out. His former villa is now the museum of Mozia, which houses finds from the ancient city, including the statue *Il Giovinetto di Mozia*. ■

process of making Marsala and give you a taste of the goods. There are several other producers in the same area and all have an *enoteca* (wine bar), where you can select a bottle or two (usually open from about 9 am to 12.30 pm).

If you're travelling with small children, they might enjoy a break at the small playground in Piazza della Vittoria, at the end of Via XI Maggio.

Special Events

Marsala's most important annual religious event is the *Processione del Gioved i Santo* (Holy Thursday procession). A tradition dating back centuries, the procession features actors depicting the events leading up to Christ's crucifixion. Many children participate in the procession, dressed in colourful costume as saints. If you're visiting the area at Easter, be sure to attend both this procession and Trapani's own version on Good Friday.

Places to Stay & Eat

The *Garden* (☎ 98 23 20), near the train station at Via Gambini 36, has basic singles/doubles for L50,000/75,000. *Hotel CAP 2000* (☎ 98 90 55), Via Trapani 161, is outside the historical centre, on the road to Trapani..It has rooms with bathroom, phone and TV for L90,000/150,000. Another option is the *Azienda Agrituristica Samperi* (☎ 72 13 13), Contrada Fornara 13, an agritourism establishment just south of Marsala. The *Trattoria Garibaldi*, Piazza dell'Addolorata 5, specialises in fish and a full meal will come to about L35,000. You can also eat well, for a bit less, at *Trattoria da Pino*, Via San Lorenzo 27.

Getting There & Away

Buses head for Marsala from Trapani (AST or Lumia; eight a day), Agrigento (Lumia; four a day) and Palermo (Salemi). Palermo buses arrive at Piazza del Popolo, off Via Mazzini, in the centre of town. All other buses stop in Piazza Pizzo. The Agrigento buses generally stop at Castelvetrano, from where you can get another to Selinunte.

Trains serve Marsala from Trapani and Palermo, although from the latter you have to change at Alcamo Diramazione.

From June to September, Sandokan (☎ 71 20 60) runs a boat service to the Isole Egadi.

BETWEEN MARSALA & TRAPANI

The site of ancient **Mozia**, situated on the island of San Pantaleo in the lagoon known as the Stagnone, is about 11km north along the coast from Marsala, a scenic drive or bus trip. The island is accessible by boat (L4000 return until around 6 pm; mornings only in winter – there's a L500 charge to access the island). Mozia was the site of one of the most important Phoenician settlements in the Mediterranean, coveted for its strategic position and eventually destroyed by Dionysus the Elder, tyrant of Siracusa in 379 BC. Today, it is the island's picturesque position in the area known as the *saline* (salt flats) that attracts visitors. The salt flats extend along the coast between Marsala and Trapani, and are dotted with windmills and piles of salt covered with terracotta tiles. Very little remains of the city which once covered Mozia, but it is interesting to follow the path around the island to visit the various excavations, including the ancient port and dry dock, as well as numerous buildings. Note the submerged road at the port, which connects the island to the mainland. There is a museum (admission L4000) on the island – its main treasure is the *Giovinetto di Mozia*, a 5th-century BC Phoenician statue of a young boy. Bus No 11 from Piazza del Popolo runs in summer only; bus No 4 drops you close to the boat and runs all year.

The island and lagoon form part of the Stagnone nature reserve, a noted humid zone which has a large population of water birds. The *saline* form part of an adjacent nature reserve known as the *Saline di Trapani e Paceo*, which includes a small museum at Nùbia, a few km south of Trapani. There are plans to develop better facilities for tourists in the area of the *saline* – such as cycling and walking tracks.

TRAPANI

Although not one of Sicilia's top attractions, Trapani is a comfortable base from which to explore the north-west. From the ancient Greek city of Segesta and the medieval town of Erice to the beaches of the Golfo di Castellammare, the Riserva Naturale dello Zingaro and the Isole Egadi, this small corner is a smorgasbord of Sicilia's main delights.

A Carthaginian and later a Roman city, Trapani thrived as a trading centre under Arab and Norman rule and, after the arrival of the Spanish, enjoyed a period as western Sicilia's most important town. Since then, slow decline has reduced it to a coastal backwater, kept afloat by moderate sea traffic and some fishing. A handful of Baroque churches and piazzas warrant some exploration and the town's Easter celebrations are a high point of the year.

Orientation

The main bus station is in Piazza Montalto, with the train station around the corner in Piazza Umberto I. The cheaper hotels are in the heart of the old centre, about 500m west. Make for Piazza Scarlatti down Corso Italia.

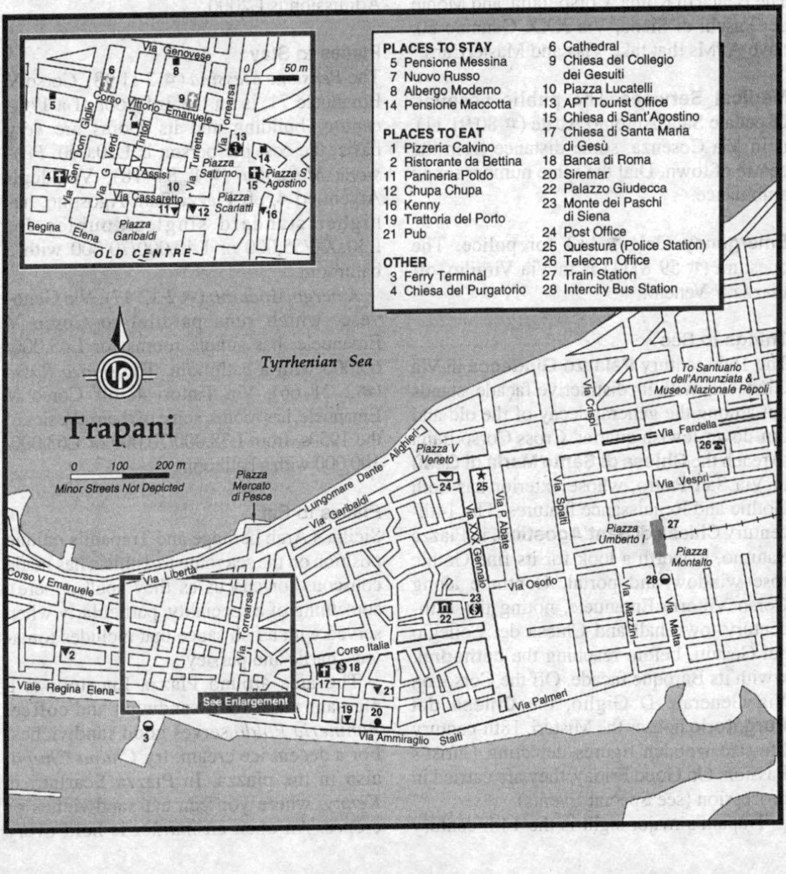

SICILIA

Information

Tourist Office The APT office (☎ 2 90 00) is in Piazzetta Saturno, off Piazza Scarlatti. It is open Monday to Saturday from 8 am to 8 pm and Sunday mornings from 9 am to midday. It is usually shut for a couple of hours from 2 pm and closes earlier in winter.

Post & Communications The main post office is in Piazza Vittorio Veneto and is open Monday to Saturday from 8.20 am to 7 pm. The post code for central Trapani is 91100 and the telephone code is ☎ 0923.

Money There are several banks in the town. The Banca di Roma, Corso Italia, and Monte dei Paschi di Siena, Via XXX Gennaio 80, have ATMs that take Visa and MasterCard.

Medical Services The public hospital, Ospedale Sant'Antonio Abate (☎ 80 91 11), is in Via Cosenza, some distance from the centre of town. Dial the same number for an ambulance.

SICILIA

Emergency Call ☎ 113 for police. The questura (☎ 59 8111) is in Via Virgilio, off Piazza V Veneto.

Things to See

The 16th-century **Palazzo Giudecca** in Via Giudecca, with its distinctive façade, stands out among the general decay of the old and run-down Jewish quarter. Cross Corso Italia to reach the **Chiesa di Santa Maria di Gesù** in Via San Pietro, whose exterior has both Gothic and Renaissance features. The 14th-century **Chiesa di Sant'Agostino**, in Piazza Saturno, is worth a look for its fine Gothic rose window and portal. Continue along Corso Vittorio Emanuele, noting the 17th-century town hall and Chiesa del Collegio dei Gesuiti, before reaching the **cathedral**, wwith its Baroque façade. Off the Corso, on Via Generale D Giglio, the **Chiesa del Purgatorio** houses the Misteri, 18th-century life-size wooden figures depicting Christ's Passion. On Good Friday, they are carried in procession (see Special Events).

Trapani's major sight is the 14th-century **Santuario dell'Annunziata**, some distance from the centre in Via A Pepoli. Remodelled in Baroque style in the 17th century, it retains its original Gothic rose window and doorway. The Cappella della Madonna, behind the high altar, contains the venerated *Madonna di Trapani*, carved, it is thought, by Nino Pisano.

The adjacent **Museo Nazionale Pepoli**, housed in a former Carmelite monastery, has an archaeological collection, statues and coral carvings. It is open Tuesday to Saturday from 9 am to 1.30 pm and also on Tuesday and Thursday from 3 to 6 pm. On Sunday it is open from 9 am to 12.30 pm. Admission is L2000.

Places to Stay

The *Pensione Messina* (☎ 2 11 98), Corso V Emanuele 71, is on the 3rd floor of a 17th-century building and its rooms are very basic; the cost per person is L20,000. *Pensione Maccotta* (☎ 2 84 18), Via degli Argentieri 4, off Piazza Sant'Agostino, has higher standard singles/doubles for L30,000/55,000 or L40,000/70,000 with a bathroom.

Albergo Moderno (☎ 2 12 47), Via Genovese, which runs parallel to Corso V Emanuele, has simple rooms for L45,000/60,000 with a bathroom. The *Nuovo Russo* (☎ 2 21 66), Via Tintori 4, off Corso V Emanuele, has rooms, some of them classics of the 1950s, from L38,000/70,000 or L63,000/100,000 with a bathroom.

Places to Eat

Sicilia's Arab heritage and Trapani's unique position on the sea route to Tunisia has made couscous (or cuscus as they spell it here), something of a speciality, particularly when served with a fish sauce that includes tomatoes, garlic and parsley.

The area around Piazza Lucatelli is a pleasant place for a sandwich and coffee. *Panineria Poldo* serves good sandwiches. For a decent ice cream, try *Chupa Chupa*, also in the piazza. In Piazza Scarlatti is *Kenny*, where you can eat sandwiches or crêpes. An open air *market* is held every morning from Monday to Saturday in Piazza Mercato di Pesce, on the north waterfront.

Pizzeria Calvino, Via N Nasi 77, towards the port off Corso V Emanuele, is the town's favourite takeaway pizza and pasta place. You can eat a set lunch at the self-service *pub*, Via della Luce 8, for L12,000. *Trattoria del Porto*, Via Ammiraglio Staiti 45, on the south waterfront, is more upmarket, with good meals for around L35,000. Similarly priced is the *Ristorante Da Bettina*, Via San Francesco d'Assisi 69.

Getting There & Away

Air Trapani has a small airport, 16km out of town at Birgi. AST buses leave from Piazza Montalto to coincide with flights. Segesta has a daily bus for the island's main airport at Punta Raisi. Its timetable changes regularly, so check with the tourist office.

Bus Express buses connect Trapani with Palermo (Segesta) and Agrigento (Lumia). They terminate in Piazza Garibaldi on the south waterfront. All other Intercity buses use Piazza Montalto, from where AST buses serve Erice (approximately every hour), Castellammare del Golfo (four a day), Castelvetrano (seven a day), Marsala and Mazara del Vallo (four a day) and San Vito Lo Capo (six a day). Autoservizi Tarantola runs a bus service to Segesta and Calatafimi.

Train Trains connect Trapani to Palermo, Castelvetrano and Marsala. For Segesta, you can either get off at Segesta Tempio (one train a day) or Calatafimi (plenty) on the way to Palermo. The stations are roughly equidistant from the ancient Greek site.

Boat Siremar runs ferries and hydrofoils to the Isole Egadi. The high-season one-way fare to the main island, Favignana, is L9200 on the hydrofoil (journey time is 20 minutes). Tickets are cheaper on the slower car ferries. Siremar's ticket office (☎ 2 77 80) is at Via Ammiraglio Staiti 61. The same company runs a daily ferry to Pantelleria at midnight. There is no service on weekends except in summer. The high-season fare for the six-hour trip is L59,000. The boat returns (usually) at 11 am.

Volaviamare (☎ 2 40 73) also runs hydrofoils to the Isole Egadi – tickets can be purchased at the docks.

Ustica Lines runs regular hydrofoils to the Isole Egadi (L9200), as well as a service from Napoli to Ustica, via Trapani and the Isole Egadi (L149,000 one way). It also has a ferry to Pantelleria (L59,000) and to Kelibia in Tunisia (L89,000). Get tickets at Egatours, Via Ammiraglio Staiti 13, opposite the Ustica Lines embarkation point.

Tirrenia runs weekly ferries to Tunisia from Trapani, leaving on Monday at 9 am. Tickets for the 7½-hour trip cost L92,000 for an airline-type seat and L116,000 for a bed in a second-class cabin in the high season. There is also a weekly Tirrenia service to Cagliari, leaving on Tuesday at 9 pm. Tickets cost L60,000 for an airline-style seat and L84,000 for a bed in a second-class cabin. Tickets can be purchased at Salvo Viaggi (☎ 2 18 96), Corso Italia 48.

ERICE

This dramatic medieval town, 750m above the sea, is about 40 minutes from Trapani by bus and should not be missed on any account. Settled by the Elymians, an ancient mountain people who also founded Segesta, it was an important religious site associated with the goddess of fertility – first the Carthaginian Astarte, then the Greek Aphrodite and finally the Roman Venus. It has unfortunately become a bit of a tourist trap (watch out for exorbitant charges for food and drinks), but manages to maintain a relatively authentic medieval atmosphere.

The tourist office (☎ 86 93 88) is at Viale Conte Pepoli 56. The telephone code is ☎ 0923.

The triangular-shaped town is best explored by pottering around its narrow streets and peeking through the doorways into courtyards. At the top of the hill stands the Norman **Castello di Venere** (Castle of Venus). It was built in the 12th to 13th centuries over an ancient temple of Venus. The castle is open Monday to Saturday from 8 am to 6.45 pm, and on Sunday from 8 am to 1 pm; entry is free. Not much more than a ruin, the castle is upstaged by the panoramic vistas north-east to San Vito Lo Capo and Monte Cofano and west to Trapani.

Of the several churches and other monuments in the small, quiet town, the 14th-century **Chiesa Matrice**, in Via V Carvini just inside Porta Trapani, is probably the most interesting by virtue of its separate bell tower with mullioned windows. The interior of the church was remodelled in neo-Gothic style in the 19th century, but the 15th-century side chapels were conserved.

If you want to stay overnight, there is an HI youth hostel, *G Amodeo* (☎ 55 29 64), just out of town and open all year. B&B is L19,000 and a meal costs L14,000. Otherwise the options are expensive. The *Edelweiss* (☎ 86 91 58), Cortile Vincenzo 5, has singles/doubles for L100,000/130,000. For a meal, the atmospheric *Ristorante La Pentolaccia*, Via G Guarnotti 17, is set inside a former 16th-century monastery.

There are regular AST buses (hourly in summer) to Trapani (Piazza Montalto).

SICILIA

SEGESTA

The ancient Elymians must have been great aesthetes if their choice of sites for cities is any indication. Along with Erice and Entella, they founded Segesta on and around Monte Barbaro. The Greeks later took over, and it is to them that we owe the two outstanding survivors: the theatre high up on the mountain with commanding views out to sea (how did spectators concentrate on the show with such a backdrop?) and the temple.

The city was in constant conflict with Selinunte in the south and this rivalry led it to seek assistance from a succession of allies, including Carthage, Athens, Siracusa and the Romans, and eventually Selinunte was destroyed. Time has done to Segesta what violence inflicted on Selinunte, and little remains save the theatre and the never completed Doric **temple**, the latter dating from around 430 BC and remarkably well preserved. The Hellenistic **theatre** is also in a fair state of repair and the only structure inside the old city walls to have survived intact. Nearby are ruins of a castle and church built in the Middle Ages. The site is open daily from 9 am to an hour before sunset. A shuttle bus runs every half-hour from the entrance 1.5km uphill to the theatre.

During July and August of every odd-numbered year (alternating with Siracusa), performances of Greek plays are staged in the theatre. For information, contact the tourist office in Trapani.

Segesta is accessible by Autoservizi Tarantola bus from Piazza Montalto in Trapani (approximately every two hours from 8 am to 7.30 pm in summer), or from Palermo (Piazza Marina) by Trepanum buses (☎ 0923-51 12 32). Otherwise catch an infrequent train from Trapani or Palermo to Segesta Tempio; the site is then a 20-minute walk away.

GOLFO DI CASTELLAMMARE

Saved from development and road projects by local protests, the tranquil and wildly beautiful **Riserva Naturale dello Zingaro** is the star attraction on the gulf. A stroll up the coast between San Vito Lo Capo and the little fishing village of Scopello will take about four hours along a clearly marked track. There are also several trails inland, which are detailed on maps available for a small fee at the information offices at the park's two entrances (near Scopello and near San Vito Lo Capo). **Punta della Capreria** is a pebble beach in a tiny cove about 15 minutes walk from the Scopello entrance to the park.

Once home to tuna fishers, **Scopello** now hosts mainly tourists – although its sleepy village atmosphere remains unspoilt. Its port is interesting to visit, with an abandoned *tonnara* (tuna processing plant) and *faraglione* (rock towers rising out of the sea).

Camping grounds include *Camping Soleado* (☎ 0923-97 21 66) and *Camping La Fata* (☎ 0923-97 21 33) at San Vito Lo Capo; and *Camping Baia di Guidaloca*

(☎ 0924-54 12 62) and *Camping Ciauli* (☎ 0924-3 90 49) on the coast road south of Scopello. There are numerous pensioni and hotels at touristy **San Vito Lo Capo** and at **Castellammare del Golfo**, a busy coastal town with an interesting medieval core 10km south of Scopello. The tourist office at Trapani has a full list. In Scopello itself, the *Pensione Tranchina* (☎ 0924-54 10 99), Via Diaz 7, is an excellent choice. It has comfortable rooms with bathroom for L35,000/60,000 and full board from L90,000 per person. The hotel also has a restaurant which serves whatever fish is fresh that day – unless you're a hotel guest you'll need to make a booking to eat there.

AST buses run to San Vito Lo Capo and Castellammare del Golfo from Trapani's Piazza Montalto. From Castellammare it is possible to catch a bus to Scopello. There is no road through the Zingaro park.

ISOLE EGADI

For centuries the Egadi islanders have lived from tuna fishing. Nowadays tourism looks set to be the main earner – even the *mattanza*, the almost ritual slaughtering of tuna, is becoming a spectator sport (see the aside). Made up of three islands (Egadi Islands), the archipelago is only a short hop from Trapani.

Windswept Monte Santa Caterina dominates the otherwise flat main island of **Favignana**. It is pleasant to explore, with plenty of rocky coves and crystal-clear water. Wander around the abandoned tuna processing plant at the port – called a *tonnara*. It was closed at the end of the 1970s due to the general crisis in the local tuna fishing industry. A lack of funding has blocked plans to turn the building into a complex which would include a school and art and craft shops.

Levanzo, 4km north of Favignana, is known for the **Grotta del Genovese**, whose walls bear Paleolithic etchings of bison and deer, and a series of fascinating figures dating from the Neolithic period. The figures of women and men were 'painted' using animal fat and carbon. Interestingly, there is also a representation of a tuna fish – indicating that tuna fishing in the Isole Egadi is indeed an ancient tradition. If you have the time, this is an experience not to be missed. Contact the custodian, Signore Castiglione, on ☎ 92 40 32. Alternatively, ask at the Pro Loco on Favignana. The custodian will take you to the cave by small boat – on the way back, ask him to drop you off at the small beach known as *i faraglione*.

Marettimo, the most distant of the islands, is also the least modern. A few

La Mattanza

A centuries-old tradition, the Isole Egadi's *mattanza* (the ritual slaughter of tuna) survives despite the ever-decreasing number of tuna fish which swim into the local waters each year. Schools of tuna have for centuries used the waters of western Sicilia as a mating ground, and locals can recall the golden days of the islands' fishing industry, when it was not uncommon to catch giant breeding tuna of 200 and 300kg. Fish that size are rare these days and the annual catch is increasingly smaller, due to general overfishing of tuna worldwide. But, even though the Egadi's fishing industry is in severe crisis as a result, the tradition of the mattanza goes on.

Now that the slaughter of tuna can no longer support the islands' economy, it is reinventing itself as a tourist attraction. From around 20 May to 10 June, tourists flock to the Isole Egadi to witness the event. For a fee you can join the fishers in their boats and watch them catching the tuna at close hand – note that you'll need a strong stomach. This is no ordinary fishing expedition: the fishers organise their boats and nets in a complex formation designed to channel the tuna into a series of enclosures which culminate in the *camera della morte* (room of death). Once enough tuna are imprisoned there, the fishers close in and the *mattanza* begins (the word is derived from the Spanish word for killing). It is a bloody affair – up to eight or more fishers at a time will sink huge hooks into a tuna and drag it aboard. Anyone who has seen Rossellini's classic *Stromboli* will no doubt recall the famous mattanza scene. ■

hundred people live mostly in the tiny village on the east coast, and there are no roads. You can go with fishing boats along the coast or follow mule tracks into the hills. There is a Pro Loco tourist office (☎ 92 16 47) at Piazza Matrice 8 in Favignana town. or contact Signora Guccione at the Albergo Egadi in Favignana. You'll find dive hire outlets and bicycles for rent around town and the small harbour. The telephone code is ☎ 0923.

There are plenty of accommodation options on Favignana, although during the period of the *mattanza* and in August, you'll have trouble finding a bed without a booking. Many local people rent out rooms. Try the *Bouganville* (☎ 92 20 33), Via Cimabue 10, which has singles/doubles for L38,000/65,000. The *Villaggio Quattro Rose* (☎ 92 12 23), Località Mulino a Vento, has camping facilities and bungalows. *Albergo Egadi* (☎ 92 12 32), Via Colombo 17, just off Favignana town's main piazza, has comfortable singles/doubles for L50,000/90,000 and also offers half and full board. It has an acclaimed restaurant, where you'll eat one of your best meals in Italy, at very reasonable prices.

Levanzo has only two pensioni. The *Paradiso* (☎ 92 40 80), on the seafront, charges L43,000/75,000 for rooms with a bathroom. It has a restaurant where you'll eat very well for around L25,000 a head. There are no hotels on Marettimo, but you should be able to dig up a room with the locals. In summer, you'll probably be asked to pay full board wherever you stay.

Ferries and hydrofoils run between the islands and to Trapani. See the Trapani section for more details.

PANTELLERIA

Known to the Carthaginians as Cossyra, the island fell to the Romans in 217 BC and five centuries later to the Arabs. The Arab presence lives on in the names of various localities. Pantelleria is a curious place that lies closer to Tunisia than it does to Sicilia. It has sea and sunshine and a mountainous, volcanic interior, with thermal springs and remnants of several ancient settlements, such as Mursia, a few km south of the main town.

There is nothing cheap here, especially in summer, when it is best to book ahead. The *Albergo Agadir* (☎ 91 11 00), Via Catania 1, offers simple rooms for L35,000/60,000. You can also rent *dammusi*, the characteristic domed houses of the island. Siremar boats go to Trapani (see the Trapani section for more transport details) and Alilauro's summer season Trapani-Tunisia boat generally calls in at Pantelleria on the way.

SICILIA

Sardegna

The second largest island in the Mediterranean, Sardegna (Sardinia) has always been considered an isolated, far-away land. Even today, its people and culture maintain a separate identity from the mainland, which they call *il continente* (the continent).

The island is dotted with some 7000 *nuraghi*, the conical-shaped megalithic stone fortresses that are the only remnants of the island's first inhabitants – the Nuraghic people. These people lived in separate communities led by warrior-king shepherds, and their culture flourished from around 1800 BC. Sardegna's coast was visited by Greeks and Phoenicians, first as traders then as invaders, and the island was colonised by the Romans. They, in turn, were followed by the Pisans, Genoese, Spanish, Austrians and, finally, the Royal House of Savoia, the future kings of a united Italy. In 1948 Sardegna became a semiautonomous region. The Italian government's Sardegnan Rebirth Plan of 1962 influenced the development of tourism, industry and agriculture.

Despite the succession of invaders and colonisers, it is often said that the Sardinians (known as the Sardi) were never really conquered, they simply retreated into the hills. The Romans were prompted to call the island's central-eastern mountains the Barbagia (from the Latin word for barbarian) because of the uncompromising lifestyle of the warrior-shepherds, who never abandoned their Nuraghic customs. Even today, the Sardinians of the interior speak an ancient Latin-based dialect and proudly maintain traditional customs and costume. Many of the island's shepherds exist in almost complete isolation, until about 10 years ago still living in the traditional conical-shaped shelters of stone and wood called *pinnettas*. These days the shelters are used as refuges by trekkers.

Sardegna's cuisine is as varied as its history. Along the coast most dishes feature seafood and there are many variations of *zuppa di pesce* (fish soup) and pasta. Inland you will find *porcheddu* (roast sucking pig), kid goat with olives, and even lamb's trotters in garlic sauce. The Sardi eat *pecorino* (sheep's-milk cheese) and you will rarely find Parmesan here. The preferred bread throughout the island is the paper-thin *carta musica*, also called *pane carasau*, often sprinkled with oil and salt.

Sardegna's 'savage, dark-bushed, sky-exposed land' described by DH Lawrence has incredibly beautiful gorges and highlands, and km of unspoiled coastline with salt lakes and herons. Hunters have always

HIGHLIGHTS

- Visiting the Su Nuraxi fortress at Barumini
- Lazing on the Costa Verde's unspoilt beaches
- Climbing into the magnificent Gola di Gorropu
- The various isolated coves and beaches accessible only by boat from Cala Gonone or on foot

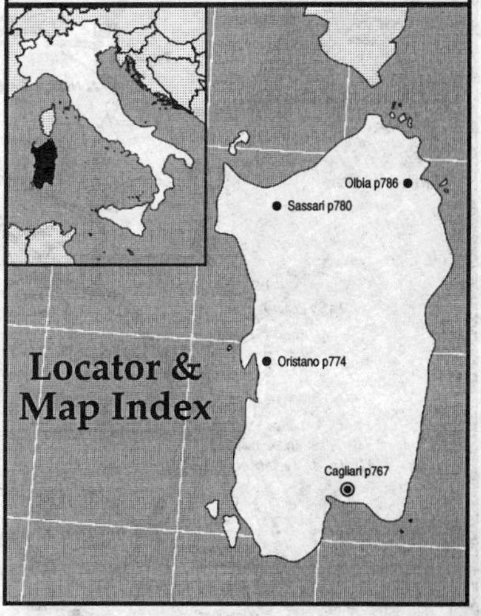

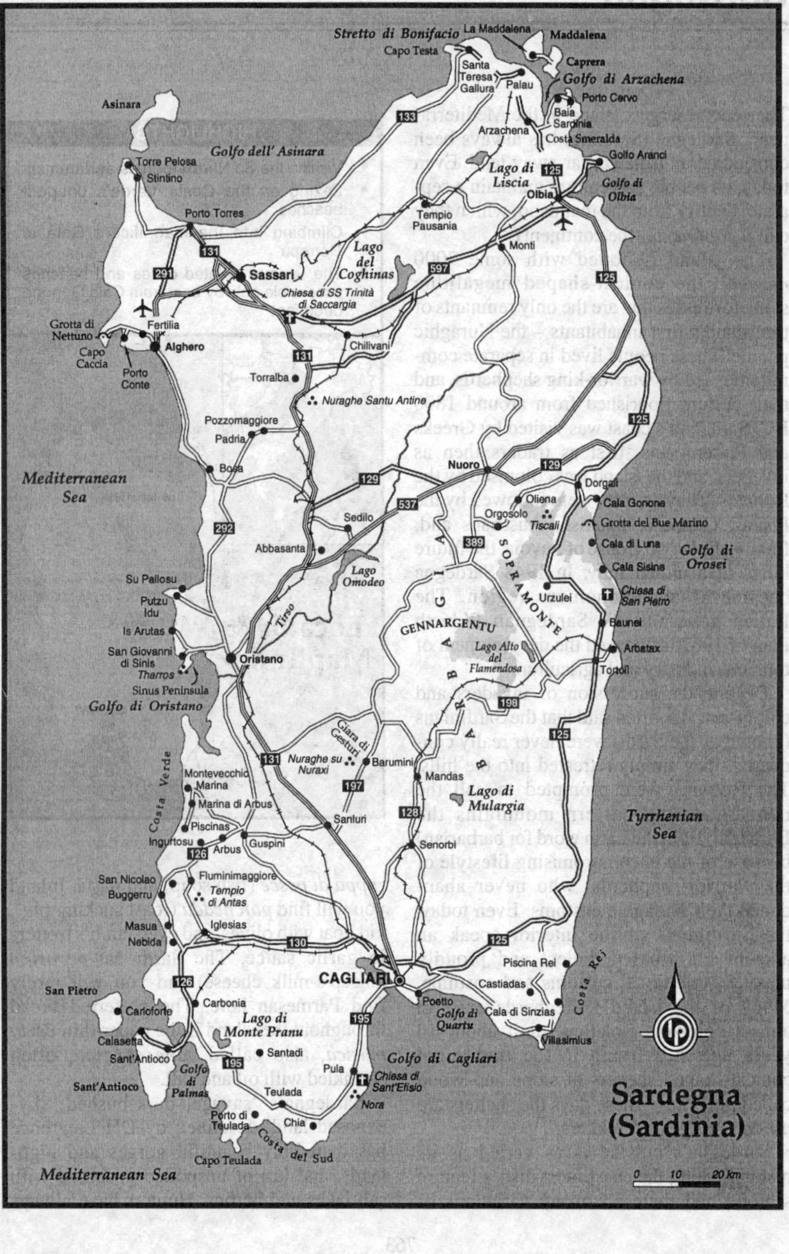
Sardegna
(Sardinia)
Stretto di Bonifacio
La Maddalena
Maddalena
Capo Testa
Caprera
Santa
Teresa
Gallura
Palau
Golfo di Arzachena
Porto Cervo
Baia
Sardinia
Arzachena
Costa Smeralda
Golfo Aranci
Asinara
Golfo dell' Asinara
Lago di
Liscia
Golfo di
Olbia
Olbia
Torre Pelosa
Stintino
Porto Torres
Tempio
Pausania
Monti
Lago
del
Coghinas
Sassari
Chiesa di SS Trinità
di Saccargia
Grotta di
Nettuno
Fertilia
Alghero
Capo
Caccia
Porto
Conte
Chilivani
Torralba
Nuraghe Santu Antine
Pozzomaggiore
Padria
Bosa
Mediterranean
Sea
Nuoro
Dorgali
Cala Gonone
Oliena
Orgosolo
Tiscali
Grotta del Bue Marino
Sedilo
Cala di Luna
Golfo di
Orosei
Cala Sisine
Abbasanta
Lago
Omodeo
SOPRAMONTE
BARBAGIA
Su Pallosu
Putzu
Idu
Urzulei
Chiesa di
San Pietro
Baunei
Tirso
Is Arutas
GENNARGENTU
San Giovanni
di Sinis
Tharros
Oristano
Lago Alto
del
Flamendosa
Arbatax
Tortolì
Sinus Peninsula
Golfo di Oristano
Giara di
Gesturi
Nuraghe su
Nuraxi
Barumini
Costa Verde
Montevecchio
Marina
Mandas
Lago di
Mulargia
Marina di Arbus
Sanluri
Tyrrhenian
Sea
Piscinas
Ingurtosu
Guspini
Arbus
Senorbì
San Nicolao
Fluminimaggiore
Buggerru
Tempio
di Antas
Masua
Iglesias
Nebida
Piscina Rei
Costa Rei
CAGLIARI
Castiadas
San Pietro
Carloforte
Carbonia
Poetto
Golfo di
Quartu
Cala di Sinzias
Lago di
Monte Pranu
Calasetta
Villasimius
Sant'Antioco
Santadi
Golfo di Cagliari
Golfo
di
Palmas
Pula
Chiesa di
Sant'Efisio
Sant'Antioco
Teulada
Nora
Porto di
Teulada
Chia
Costa del Sud
Capo Teulada
Mediterranean Sea
133
125
131
291
597
131
129
537
292
389
198
131
197
128
126
130
125
126
195
195
0
10
20 km

SARDEGNA

been active in Sardegna, but some wildlife remains, notably the wild pig, the Golden and Bonelli's eagles, the Peregrine falcon, pink flamingos, the Sardegnan deer and a colony of griffon vultures on the west coast. Miniature horses are raised on the Giara di Gesturi plain, in the south-west. Unfortunately, the famous colony of Mediterranean monk seals at the Grotta del Bue Marino, near Cala Gonone, has not been sighted for some years.

The island offers visitors a wide range of attractions, from spectacular beaches and archaeological treasures to the isolated interior, perfect for the more adventurous traveller. If you do venture into the interior, you will find the people incredibly gracious and hospitable, although you might find it difficult to make initial contact. Try to avoid coming to the island in August, when the weather is very hot and the beaches are overcrowded. Warm weather generally continues from April to October.

Getting There & Away

Air The airports at Cagliari, Olbia, Alghero and Arbatax-Tortolì link Sardegna with major Italian and European cities.

Boat The island is accessible by ferry from Genova, Civitavecchia, Napoli, Palermo, Trapani, Bonifacio (Corsica) and Tunisia, as well as Toulon and Marseille in France. The departure points in Sardegna are Olbia, Golfo Aranci, Palau and Porto Torres in the north, Arbatax on the east coast and Cagliari in the south.

The main ferry company is Tirrenia, although Ferrovie dello Stato (FS) runs a slightly cheaper ferry service between Civitavecchia and Golfo Aranci. Other companies include Moby Lines, also known as Sardegna Lines, which runs ferries between Sardegna and Corsica, as well as from Livorno to Olbia. Brochures detailing Moby Lines and Tirrenia services are available at most travel agencies. Note that timetables change dramatically every year and that prices fluctuate according to the season.

Addresses and telephone numbers for Tirrenia's offices in Sardegna are listed throughout this chapter. It also has offices throughout Italy, including Roma (☎ 06-474 20 41), Via Bissolati 41; Civitavecchia (☎ 0766-2 88 01); and Genova (☎ 010-25 80 41). Moby Lines has offices and agents throughout the island. In Livorno it operates through the agency LV Ghianda (☎ 0586-89 03 25), Via Vittorio Veneto 24.

Refer to the chart for details on Tirrenia ferry services. Fare prices are listed in the following order: *poltrona* (seat) in a 2nd-class cabin; bed in a 2nd-class cabin; and bed in a 1st-class cabin. The cost of taking a small car can be up to L138,000.

Moby Lines offers special fares for daytime passages in the low season. At the time of writing, the fare was L260,000 return (Livorno-Olbia) for a car and two people.

Getting Around

Bus The main bus companies are ARST, which operates extensive services throughout the island, and PANI, which links the main towns. Other companies include Ferrovie di Sardegna (FDS) and Ferrovie Meridionale Sardegna (FMS). Buses are generally faster than trains.

Train The main Ferrovie dello Stato (FS) train lines link Cagliari with Oristano, Sassari and Olbia, and are generally reliable. The private railways which link smaller towns throughout the island can be very slow. However, the Trenino Verde (Green Train) which runs from Cagliari to Arbatax through the Barbagia is a relaxing way to see part of the interior (for more details, see Getting There & Away in the Cagliari section).

Car & Motorcycle The only way to really explore Sardegna is by road. Rental agencies are listed under Cagliari and some other towns around the island.

Hitching You might find hitchhiking laborious because of the light traffic once you get away from the main towns. Hitchhiking is not recommended and women should not hitchhike alone, or even in groups, under any circumstances.

Cagliari

The capital of the island, Cagliari is a surprisingly attractive city, notable for its interesting Roman and medieval sections, its beautiful beach – Poetto – and its wide marshes populated by numerous species of birds, including pink flamingos. The city warrants a day of sightseeing and is a good base for exploring the southern coast. Believed to have been founded by Phoenicians, Cagliari became an important Carthaginian port town before coming under Roman control. As with the rest of the island, the city passed through the hands of various conquerors, including the Pisans, Spanish and the Piemontese House of Savoia, before joining the unified Italy. Cagliari was savagely bombed during WWII, suffering significant destruction and loss of life.

Orientation

If you arrive by bus, train or boat you will find yourself at the port area of Cagliari. The main street along the harbour is Via Roma, and the old city stretches up the hill behind it to the fortified area. At the north-western end of Via Roma, to the left as you leave the port, is Piazza Matteotti and the AAST tourist office, the ARST intercity bus station and the train station. Most of the budget hotels and restaurants are close to the port area.

SARDEGNA

Information

Tourist Offices The AAST information booth (☎ 66 92 55) in Piazza Matteotti is open from 8 am to 8 pm daily during summer, and from 8 am to 2 pm in other months. It has a reasonable amount of information about the town and will advise on accommodation. There is also a provincial tourist information booth at the airport (☎ 24 02 00), open from 8.30 am to 1 pm and 3.30 to 9 pm daily in the high season. There is an office of the Ente Sardo Industrie Turistiche (ESIT, ☎ 167-013153, which covers all of Sardegna, at Via Goffredo Mameli 97. It opens from 8 am to 8 pm daily during summer.

Money There are several major banks on Largo Carlo Felice, which runs uphill from Piazza Matteotti; they open from 8.30 am to 1.30 pm and 2.30 to 3.30 pm, Monday to Friday. Otherwise, there is an exchange office at the train station, open daily from 7 am to 8 pm, and at the airport, open 8 am to 1 pm Monday to Saturday.

Post & Communications The main post office is in Piazza del Carmine, up Via la Maddalena from Via Roma, and open from 8 am to 4.30 pm Monday to Saturday. You can also change money there. The 24 hour Telecom office is at Via G Angioj, off Piazza Matteotti. The postcode for central Cagliari is 09100.

The telephone code for Cagliari is ☎ 070.

Travel Agency There is a CTS office (☎ 48 82 60) at Via Cesare Balbo 4.

Medical Services For an ambulance, call ☎ 27 23 45. The closest public hospital to the centre of town is the Ospedale Civile (☎ 601 82 67), Via Ospedale, between the church of San Michele and the Anfiteatro Romano.

Emergency For immediate police attendance, call ☎ 113. To report thefts, you should go to the police headquarters (☎ 4 44 44) at Via Amat 9.

Things to See & Do

The **Museo Archeologico Nazionale** at Piazza Arsenale, in the new Cittadella dei Musei, has a fascinating collection of Nuraghic bronzes. It is open daily except Monday from 9 am to 7 pm from April to October and from 9 am to 2 pm and 3.30 to 8 pm for the rest of the year. Entry is L4000. On the 2nd floor is the **Pinacoteca Nazionale**, whose collection includes local

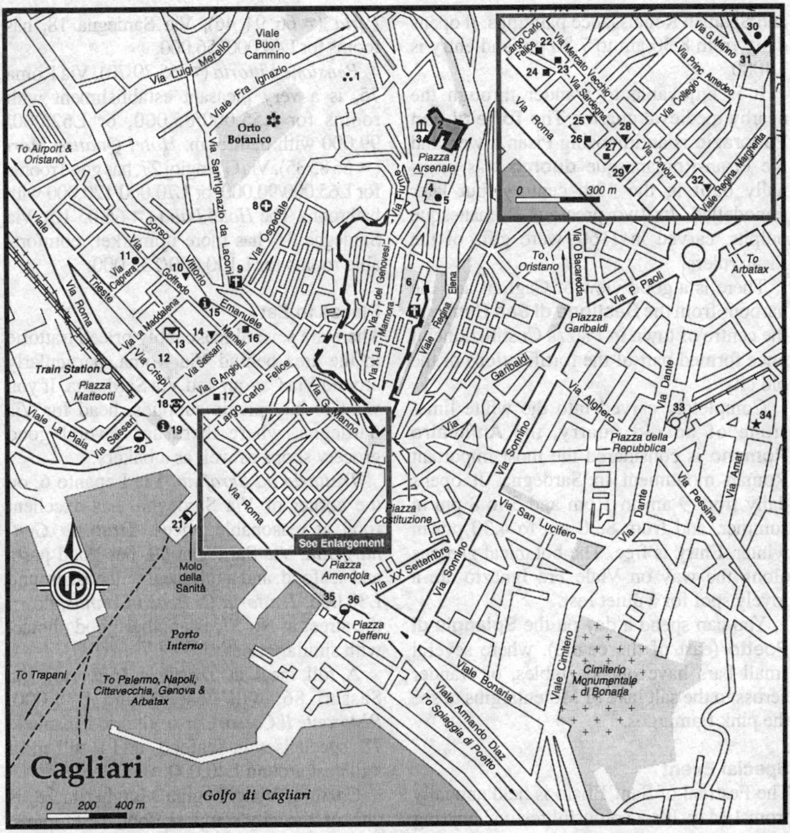

PLACES TO STAY
- 16 Locanda Firenze
- 17 Hotel Quattro Mori
- 22 Albergo Centrale
- 23 Albergo La Perla
- 24 Hotel Italia
- 26 Pensione Vittoria
- 27 Locanda Miramare

PLACES TO EAT
- 10 Ristorante Il Corso
- 14 Trattoria Umberto
- 25 Trattoria Ci Pensa Cannas
- 28 Trattoria Gennargentu
- 29 Trattoria da Serafino
- 32 Corsaro

OTHER
- 1 Anfiteatro Romano
- 2 Cittadella dei Musei
- 3 Museo Archeologico Nazionale, Pinacoteca Nazionale
- 4 Piazza Indipendenza
- 5 Torre di San Pancrazio
- 6 Piazza Palazzo
- 7 Duomo
- 8 Hospital
- 9 Chiesa di San Michele
- 11 Alitalia Office
- 12 Piazza del Carmine
- 13 Post Office
- 15 ESIT Tourist Office
- 18 Telecom Office
- 19 AAST Tourist Office
- 20 ARST Bus Station
- 21 Ferry Terminal
- 30 Bastione di San Remy
- 31 Piazza dei Martiri
- 33 Ferrovie Complementari della Sardegna Train Station
- 34 Questura (Police Station)
- 35 Piazza Darsena
- 36 PANI Bus Station

and Spanish Renaissance paintings. It opens daily from 8.30 am to 7.30 pm and entry is L4000.

It is enjoyable to wander through the nearby medieval quarter. The **Torre di San Pancrazio** is an imposing Pisan tower, and the Pisan-Romanesque **duomo** was originally built in the 13th century, but later remodelled. Its two precious Romanesque pulpits, carved in 1160, were gifts of the Pisan rulers.

There is a good view of Cagliari and the harbour from the **Bastione di San Remy**, in the centre of town in Piazza Costituzione; it once formed part of the fortifications of the old city.

Completely carved into the white limestone of an old quarry, the **Anfiteatro Romano** is considered the most important Roman monument in Sardegna. It opens daily from 9 am to 1 pm and 5 to 8 pm in summer, and from 8.30 am to 4.30 pm in winter. Entry is free. The botanical gardens along the way on Viale Fra Ignazio are a lovely spot for a quiet rest.

You can spend a day on the **Spiaggia di Poetto** (east of the centre), where several small bars have outside tables, or wander across to the salt lake of Molentargius to see the pink flamingos.

Special Event

The Festival of Sant'Efisio is held annually from 1 May. It's a colourful festival, mixing the secular and the religious, and the highlight is when an effigy of the saint is carried in procession to the small church of Sant'Efisio in the nearby town of Nora (see the Around Cagliari section).

Places to Stay

There are numerous budget hotels in the old city near the station. Try the pleasant *Locanda Firenze* (☎ 65 36 78), Corso Vittorio Emanuele 50, which has singles/doubles for L40,000/54,000. *Locanda Miramare* (☎ 66 40 21), Via Roma 59, has singles/doubles for L50,000/65,000. *Albergo Centrale* (☎ 65 47 83), Via Sardegna 4, charges L40,000/60,000, and the nearby *Albergo La Perla* (☎ 66 94 46), Via Sardegna 18, has rooms for L44,000/ 56,000.

Pensione Vittoria (☎ 65 79 70), Via Roma 75, is a very pleasant establishment with rooms for L55,000/85,000, or L62,000/ 99,000 with bathroom. *Hotel Quattro Mori* (☎ 66 85 35), Via G Angioj 27, has good rooms for L65,000/90,000, or L70,000/120,000 with bathroom. The *Hotel Italia* (☎ 66 05 10), Via Sardegna 31, has more upmarket, comfortable rooms for L100,000/135,000.

Places to Eat

There are several reasonably priced trattorie in the area behind Via Roma, particularly around Via Cavour and Via Sardegna. If you want to buy picnic supplies, head for Via Sardegna, where there are several good grocery shops as well as a bakery.

Trattoria da Serafino, Via Lepanto 6, on the corner of Via Sardegna, has excellent food at reasonable prices. *Trattoria Gennargentu*, Via Sardegna 60, has good pasta and seafood, and a full meal will cost around L30,000. *Trattoria Ci Pensa Cannas*, down the street at No 37, is another good choice, with similar prices.

A full meal at *Trattoria Umberto*, Via Sassari 86, will cost around L30,000. *Ristorante Il Corso*, Corso Vittorio Emanuele 78, specialises in seafood, and a full meal will cost around L40,000.

Corsaro, Viale Regina Margherita 28, is one of the city's top seafood restaurants. During summer it transfers to the Marina Piccola at Poetto beach. A full meal will cost at least L80,000.

Getting There & Away

Air Cagliari's airport (☎ 24 00 47) is 8km north-west of the city at Elmas. ARST buses leave regularly from Piazza Matteotti to coincide with flights. Alitalia is at Via Caprera 14 (☎ 60 10 7) and the airport (☎ 24 00 79).

Bus ARST buses leave from the bus station (☎ 1678-65042, toll-free) in Piazza Matteotti for nearby towns, including Pula, the Costa del Sud and Teulada south-west of Cagliari, as well as Villasimius and the Costa

JOHN GILLMAN

JOHN GILLMAN

JOHN GILLMAN

DAMIEN SIMONIS

Top Left: Cliff-top housing, Calabria
Top Right: Farmer in Gerace, Reggio di Calabria
Bottom Left: Windowsill in Gerace, Reggio di Calabria
Bottom Right: Hunting for dinner at a market in Sicllia

DAMIEN SIMONIS

DAMIEN SIMONIS

STEFANO CAVEDONI

STEFANO CAVEDONI

STEFANO CAVEDONI

Top Left & Right: Traditional Sicilian art and donkey decorations in Monreale, Sicilia
Bottom Left: Woman in traditional costume, Orgosolo, Sardegna
Middle Right: Townsfolk in traditional costume join in a folk dance, Oliena, Sardenga
Bottom Right: Gold jewellery worn as part of traditional costume at Quartu Sant'Elena, near Cagliari, Sardegna

Rei to the east. Granturismo PANI buses leave from farther along Via Roma at Piazza Darsena for towns such as Sassari, Nuoro, Oristano and Porto Torres. The PANI ticket office (☎ 65 23 26) is at Piazza Darsena 4.

Train Regular trains leave for Oristano, Sassari, Porto Torres and Olbia. The private Ferrovie Complementari della Sardegna train station is in Piazza della Repubblica.

For information about the Trenino Verde, which runs along a scenic route between Cagliari and Arbatax, contact the ESIT tourist office (see Tourist Offices) or Ferrovie Complementari directly (☎ 58 00 75). The most interesting and scenic section of the route is between Mandas and Arbatax.

Boat Ferries arrive at the port just off Via Roma. Bookings for Tirrenia can be made at the Stazione Marittima in the port area (☎ 66 87 88). The office opens from 9 to 11.30 am and from 3 to 6 pm (7 pm for the line to Sicilia). Ferries connect Cagliari with Palermo, Trapani, Napoli, Civitavecchia and Genova, as well as Tunisia (via Trapani). See the Getting There & Away section at the beginning of this chapter for further information.

Car & Motorcycle If you want to rent a car or motorcycle, try Hertz (☎ 66 81 05), Piazza Matteotti 1, or Ruvioli at Elmas airport (☎ 24 03 23).

Getting Around

The only reason you will need to use public transport in Cagliari is if you want to head for the beach at Poetto. Take bus PF or PQ from Piazza Matteotti.

AROUND CAGLIARI

The Costa Rei

There are good beaches within day-trip distance of Cagliari on the largely undeveloped Costa Rei. The area is dotted with camping grounds and (generally expensive) hotels.

Villasimius is a good place to base yourself, and is near reasonable beaches. Try the *Albergo Stella d'Oro* (☎ 070-79 12 55), Via Vittorio Emanuele 25, which has singles/doubles for L45,000/75,000, but half board is obligatory in August (L125,000 per person). Nearby, on the beach, is *Camping Spiaggia del Riso* (☎ 070-79 10 52); costs are L11,000 per person and L13,000 for a site. Other camping grounds include *Cala di Sinzias* (☎ 070-99 50 37), on the coast near Castiadas, and, farther north, *Piscina Rei* (☎ 070-99 10 89).

Slightly farther along the coast from Villasimius is the *Hotel Cormoran* (☎ 070-79 81 01), in the locality of Campus, a lovely resort hotel with a private sandy beach. Prices for full board range up to L250,000 in the high season. Bungalows for two people are available for around L1,600,000 per week, and bungalows for five people for up to L2,400,000 per week in the high season. For full details on camping and other accommodation along the coast, contact the tourist office at Cagliari. Regular daily ARST buses connect Cagliari with Villasimius and places along the Costa Rei, including camping grounds.

Nora

Founded in the 9th century BC by the Phoenicians, Nora was considered important for its strategic position and eventually came

SARDEGNA

Tirrenia Ferry Services

Destination	*Fares*	*Duration*
Genova-Porto Torres or Olbia	L76,700/97,600/124,700	12½ hours
Genova-Cagliari	L102,900/129,900/170,900	19 hours
Civitavecchia-Olbia	L40,700/56,000/77,800	7 hours
Civitavecchia-Cagliari	L71,500/89,500/119,500	13½ hours
Napoli-Cagliari	L52,000/72,000/93,000	15 hours
Palermo-Cagliari	L47,000/66,000/85,000	12½ hours

under Roman control. The ruins of the city extend into the sea and offer evidence of both civilisations, including temples, houses, a Roman theatre and baths. The ruins are open daily for free from 9 am to 8 pm in summer, and from 9 am to 6 pm out of season. To get to the ruins, take an ARST bus from Cagliari to Pula, then a local bus (Autolinee Murgia) to Nora (only three a day).

The Costa del Sud

The small town of **Chia** marks the start of the beautiful Costa del Sud, which is protected from further development by special ordinances – private homes can be built only in certain zones. There is one large hotel complex which blights the coastline about halfway between Chia and Teulada, the four star *Grand Hotel Baia delle Ginestre* (☎ 070-927 30 05). Half board per person per week costs from L900,000, depending on the season. Apartments are also available for rent.

Those happy to settle for something simpler can camp at *Camping Comunale Portu Tramatzu* (☎ 070-927 10 22), just past Porto di Teulada. The camping ground is by the sea and has a supermarket, bar, pizzeria and restaurant. Costs are L11,000 per person and L10,000 for a site, and it is open from April to October. To get to the camping ground, take the ARST Cagliari-Teulada bus, get off at Porto di Teulada and then walk the short distance from the port to the camping ground (signs will point you in the right direction).

Your only other option is the *Hotel Sebera* (☎ 070-927 08 76), a pleasant establishment in the town of **Teulada**, in the central piazza where buses stop. Full board costs L75,000/ 90,000.

At **Porto di Teulada** there is a very pleasant bar/trattoria which specialises in fresh seafood. You can enjoy lunch in a small courtyard for around L40,000 a head.

Regular ARST buses connect Cagliari with Chia, and about eight a day continue on to Teulada.

If you have a car, make a detour to the **Is Zuddas caves** (☎ 0781-95 59 83), near Santadi. The series of caves has interesting stalagmite and stalactite formations, and is open from June to September daily from 9 am to midday and 2.30 to 6 pm (closing earlier in winter). Entry is L10,000.

Another deviation would include the remains of the Phoenician/Carthaginian city on **Monte Sirai**, just out of Carbonia (☎ 0781-6 40 44). This 7th-century BC fort town commanded a view for miles around. The site is still being excavated, and is open from 9 am to 1 pm and 4 to 8 pm (9 am to 5 pm in winter); entry is free.

Southern Sardegna

SANT'ANTIOCO & SAN PIETRO

These islands, off the south-west coast of Sardegna, feature sandy beaches and quiet coves, as well as the pleasant towns of Calasetta on Sant'Antioco and Carloforte on San Pietro, both with whitewashed or pastel-coloured houses lining narrow streets. The town of Sant'Antioco is more developed.

Information

The Pro Loco tourist office (☎ 8 20 31) in the town of Sant'Antioco is in Piazza della Repubblica. It can provide information and advice on accommodation, including apartments for rent. You can request information by writing (in English) to the Associazione Turistica Pro Loco, 09017 Sant'Antioco. The nearby island of San Pietro has a separate tourist office (☎ 84 00 59) at Carloforte.

The telephone code for the Sant'Antioco and San Pietro islands is ☎ 0781.

Places to Stay

Both islands have good camping facilities. Try the *Campeggio Tonnara* (☎ 80 90 58) at Calasapone on Sant'Antioco, or *La Caletta* (☎ 85 21 12) on San Pietro. Both grounds are by the sea, away from the towns, and are accessible by the orange FMS buses which service both islands.

In Sant'Antioco, try the *Hotel Moderno* (☎ 8 31 05), Via Nazionale 82, which has singles/doubles for L60,000/90,000 with bathroom. You will need to book well in advance. In Calasetta, the best choice is the *Fiby Hotel* (☎ 8 84 44), Via Solferino 83, a very pleasant establishment with rooms with bathroom for L70,000/85,000. It also offers half board for L95,000 per person and full board for L105,000.

In Carloforte on San Pietro there are few choices and only the camping grounds are cheap. The *Hieracon Hotel* (☎ 85 40 28), Corso Cavour 62, fronting the port, charges L105,000 per person for half board in the high season and L90,000 a double in other months.

Places to Eat

There is a Coop supermarket in the town of Sant'Antioco on the corner of the Lungomare and Via d'Arborea. In Carloforte you can pick up supplies at the Mercato Super Crai in Via Diaz.

In Sant'Antioco there are several good trattorie and restaurants, including the pizzeria/restaurant *Il Cantuccio*, Viale Trento, near Piazza Repubblica. In Calasetta, try *L'Anfora*, Via Roma 121, or *Da Pasqualino*, Via Roma 99. A full meal at either will cost around L30,000. In Carloforte, the *Barone Rosso*, Via XX Settembre 26, is the place to go for a sandwich; otherwise, try *Ristorante Da Vanino*, on the waterfront, a short walk from the yacht harbour.

Getting There & Away

Sant'Antioco is connected to the mainland by a land bridge, and is accessible by FMS bus from Cagliari and Iglesias. Regular ferries connect Calasetta and Carloforte.

Getting Around

Orange FMS buses link the small towns on Sant'Antioco and the camping grounds and localities on San Pietro. On Sant'Antioco you can rent a scooter (L65,000 a day), moped or bicycle (L48,000 a day) from in front of the Coop supermarket in the town of Sant'Antioco and make your own tour of the island. At Carloforte, go to SARINAV, Lungomare 6, where scooters cost L100,000 a day. From both outlets you can also rent motorised rubber dinghies for around L250,000 a day.

IGLESIAS

This mining centre, slightly inland from Sardegna's south-western coast, is left off most tourist itineraries, but it's well worth a stopover. Iglesias is in a zone rich in minerals, including lead, zinc and some silver and gold, and its mining history extends back to Roman and Carthaginian times. From the 13th century it was occupied by the Pisans, who called it Argentaria (the Place of Silver) after the rich silver deposits discovered there in that period. However, it was the Spanish Aragons who left a greater mark on the town.

You will have to do without tourism advice while in Iglesias because the town is unprepared for the tourists who do pass through. If you require any information, ask at the municipal offices (from 8 am to 2 pm Monday to Saturday) in Piazza del Duomo in the centre of town.

Iglesias' telephone code is ☎ 0781.

Things to See

The **duomo**, in Piazza del Duomo, opposite the municipal offices, dates from the period of Pisan domination and was built in the Romanesque-Gothic style. Nearby, in Piazza San Francesco, is the Gothic **Chiesa di San Francesco**. Above the old town, along Via Campidano, there are the remains of Pisan towers and fortified walls.

Places to Stay & Eat

The *Artu* (☎ 2 24 92), Piazza Quintino Sella 15, east of the old part of town, has singles/doubles with bathroom for L65,000/105,000. There are numerous pastry shops, takeaways and grocery shops in the shopping area around Via Martini and Via Azuni, a short walk from Piazza del Duomo. For a meal, try *Stalla* in Via Musio, off Via Azuni.

Getting There & Away

The bus station is in Via Oristano, off Via XX Settembre, south-east of the old town, and tickets can be purchased at Sulcis Agenzia

Viaggi, Via Roma 52 (which is parallel to Via Oristano). Regular FMS buses link Iglesias with Cagliari, Carbonia, Sant'Antioco and Calasetta. Two FMS buses a day head for Arbus, from where you can pick up connections to the Costa Verde. Iglesias is also accessible by train from Cagliari, Carbonia and Oristano, and the train station is in Via Garibaldi, a 15-minute walk along Via Matteotti from the town centre.

AROUND IGLESIAS

About 15km north of Iglesias towards Fluminimaggiore is the Phoenician-Roman **Tempio di Antas**. Set in a wide, picturesque valley, the small temple was dedicated to a god of fertility and hunting by the Phoenicians, while the Romans dedicated it to a local Nuraghic divinity. Six columns remain standing. If you don't have a car, take the FMS bus from Iglesias for Fluminimaggiore and get off just after the village of Sant'Angelo. The temple is then a 3km walk away along a dirt road.

Western Sardegna

THE COSTA VERDE

This magnificent stretch of coastline remains almost entirely unspoiled, despite the fact that much of the area has been extensively mined. Former mining towns such as Buggerru, Masua and Nebida are now seeking to make their fortunes as small coastal resorts.

The Costa Verde starts just north of Buggerru and continues to Montevecchio Marina. Laws have been passed to protect much of the coastline from development, and the area remains a paradise for lovers of secluded beaches. Discreet campers will find that they can free-camp in the area without any hassle. The isolation of much of the coast makes it difficult, but not impossible, for people to reach without their own transport.

Buggerru is a good place to make your base. It doesn't have any hotels as yet, but there is space set aside for camping by the waterfront, and you can free-camp along the coast to the south of the town. Many residents rent out rooms and apartments, and by asking at one of Buggerru's bars or supermarkets you will easily find a bed for the night (although most will be booked out in August).

North of Buggerru there's the long, sandy beach of **San Nicolao**. This is a clean public beach, something of a rarity in Italy, and the rows of deck chairs and umbrellas characteristic of the 'privatised' beaches in other parts of the country are missing. Buggerru and San Nicolao are accessible by FMS bus from Iglesias.

In the heart of the Costa Verde is **Piscinas**, at the mouth of the Piscinas river. This magnificent unspoiled beach is backed by a vast protected area of 200m-high sand dunes, which support a rich variety of wildlife. An organised parking area for campervans has been established behind the dune area, just off the road from Ingurtosu, although at the time of writing it was not open. Camping is strictly prohibited on the beach and in the sand dunes.

The only hotel in the area is set right on the beach. *Le Dune* (☎ 070-97 71 30) is an atmospheric hotel featuring the mineral deposits of the mines which once lined the Piscinas valley. It offers excellent food and can organise guided tours to the island's most important archaeological sites. Out of season, full board costs from L120,000 per person and half board is from L110,000. Prices are as high as L190,000 per person in peak periods.

To reach Piscinas from Guspini, take the road for Ingurtosu, then take the dirt road to the right where you see the sign for Le Dune. It is possible to catch an ARST bus between Guspini and Ingurtosu – ask the driver where to get off. ARST buses also run from Cagliari and Oristano for Guspini. The distance from the turn-off to the sea is 7km, but if you're on foot the walk is interesting, since you'll pass the ruins of the numerous mines which once operated in the valley. The hotel will pick you up from the airport in Cagliari if you can spare the L150,000 fare.

Marina di Arbus, also known as Gutturu Flumini, is several km north and is more developed. Accommodation possibilities here include *Camping Costa Verde* (☎ 070-97 70 09), which charges L12,000 per person and L19,000 for a site. Apartments are available for rent at *Residence Piscinas* (☎ 070-97 71 37) for a minimum of one week. A two person apartment will cost from L600,000, and an apartment for four people over L900,000.

Getting to Marina di Arbus is not simple by public transport. You will need to catch an ARST bus from Oristano, or an FMS bus from Iglesias to Arbus, then a bus from Via della Repubblica to Marina di Arbus – which operates only in summer and only twice a day at 7.30 am and 2.30 pm, returning to Arbus in the evening.

ORISTANO

Like much of interest in Sardegna, the city of Oristano and its province should be approached with the attitude that they are to be 'discovered'. Originally inhabited by the Nuraghic people, the area around what is now Oristano was colonised by the Phoenicians, who established the port town of Tharros, later controlled by Carthaginians and then Romans.

Oristano is believed to have been founded sometime in the 7th century AD by the people of Tharros, who abandoned their ancient town, probably to escape raids by Moorish pirates. Oristano grew to prominence in the 14th century, particularly during the rule of Eleonora d'Arborea, who opposed the Spanish occupation of the island and drew up a body of laws known as the *Carta de Logu*, a progressive legal code which was eventually enforced throughout the island. The code is also considered important because it recorded the ancient Sardegnan language, in which it was written.

Orientation

A good point from which to orient yourself is Piazza Roma, not far from the PANI bus stop, off Via Tirso in Via Lombardia, and a five-minute walk from the ARST bus station in Via Cagliari, just off Piazza Mannu. The train station is a 20-minute walk away in Piazza Ungheria. To reach Piazza Roma from here, follow Via Vittorio Veneto to Piazza Mariano and then take Via Mazzini.

Information

Tourist Offices A mobile tourist office opens daily in Piazza Roma during summer and has loads of information on the town and the province and will advise on accommodation and transport. Pick up a copy of the booklet *Oristano & Its Province*, rarely updated but available in English, which includes a map of the town. There is a Pro Loco office (☎ 7 06 21) in Via Vittorio Emanuele 8, open from 9 am to midday and 5 to 8 pm Monday to Friday. The EPT office (☎ 7 31 91) at Via Cagliari 278 is open Monday to Friday from 8 am to 2 pm and also on Tuesday and Wednesday from 4 to 7 pm.

Post & Communications The main post office is on Via Liguria, north-west of Piazza Roma along Via Tirso, and opens Monday to Saturday from 8.15 am to 7.30 pm. The postcode for central Oristano is 09170. There are Telecom public telephones in Piazza Eleonora d'Arborea.

Oristano's telephone code is ☎ 0783.

Medical Services For an ambulance, call ☎ 7 82 22. There is a public hospital (☎ 31 71) at Via Fondazione Rockefeller, along Viale San Martino from Piazza Mannu.

Emergency For immediate police assistance, call ☎ 113. The police headquarters are in Via Carducci.

Things to See

In Piazza Roma is the 13th-century **Torre di Mariano II**, which is also known as the Tower of San Cristoforo. From here, walk along Corso Umberto until you get to **Piazza Eleonora d'Arborea**, where you will find a 19th-century statue of Oristano's heroine. The neoclassical **Chiesa di San Francesco** is adjacent. Of note inside the church are a

15th-century polychrome wooden crucifix, a 14th-century marble statue of San Basilio by Nino Pisano and a 16th-century polyptych by Pietro Cavaro.

Follow Via Eleonora d'Arborea or Via Duomo to reach the **duomo**, built in the 13th century but completely remodelled in the 18th century. It has a Baroque bell tower, topped by a multicoloured dome.

Also of interest is the 14th-century **Convento & Chiesa di Santa Chiara**, between Via Parpaglia and Via Garibaldi. About 3km south of Oristano at Santa Giusta, and easily accessible by local ARST buses, is the **Basilica di Santa Giusta**. Built around 1100, the church is Romanesque, with Pisan and Lombard influences.

Special Event

The most important festival in Oristano is the colourful Sa Sartiglia, held on the last Sunday of carnival (late February or early March) and repeated on Shrove Tuesday. Probably one of the island's most beautiful festive events, the Sartiglia had its origins in a military contest performed by the knights of the Second Crusade. It developed into a festival during the period of Spanish domi-

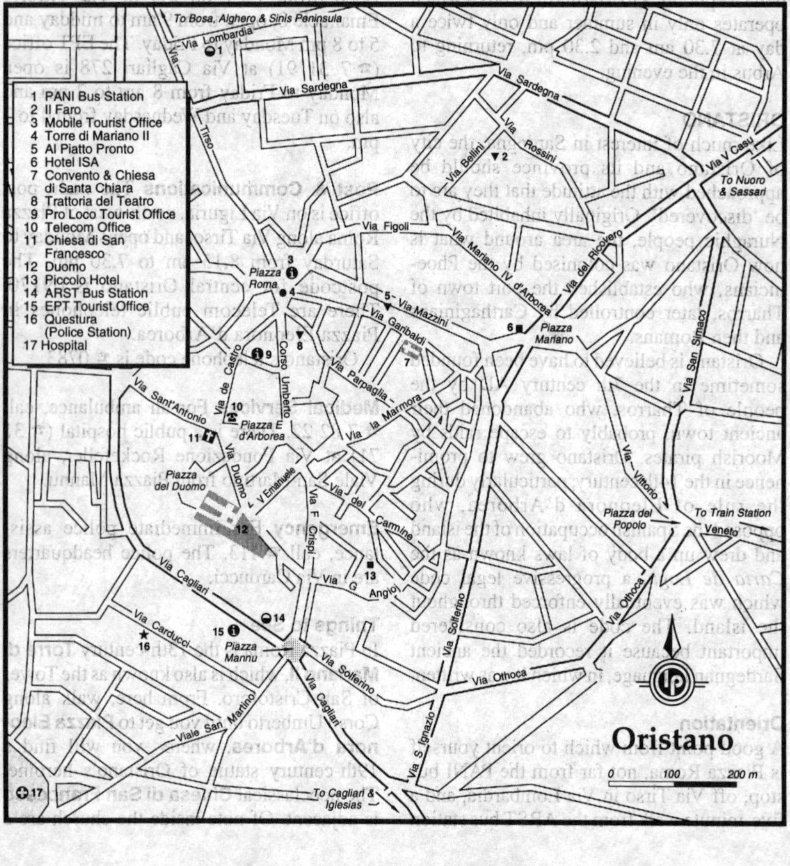

nation and now involves masked, costumed riders who parade through the town before participating in a tournament, where they must pierce the centre of a silver star with their swords while riding at full speed.

Places to Stay & Eat

Oristano is not exactly bursting with hotels and there are no budget options. There is a camping ground, the *Camping Torregrande* (☎ 22 22 8) at Marina di Torre Grande, about 7km west of Oristano (regular ARST buses connect the two towns – see the following Getting There & Away section). It is open from May to October, but may be full during August.

In town is the *Piccolo Hotel* (☎ 7 15 00), Via Martignano 19, with singles/doubles for L60,000/100,000. *Hotel ISA* (☎ 36 01 01) is half a km from the station at Piazza Mariano 50 and has rooms for L75,000/120,000 with private bathroom.

Agriturismo is very well organised in the province, with B&B costing around L30,000 a head and half board around L50,000. It is organised by the Consorzio Agriturismo di Sardegna (☎ 7 39 54).

For a quick snack or meal, try *Al Piatto Pronto* at Via Mazzini 21, near Piazza Roma, which has a wide range of pre-prepared dishes. *Trattoria del Teatro*, Via Parpaglia 11, has full meals for around L40,000, while *Il Faro*, Via Bellini 25, is considered one of Oristano's better and more expensive restaurants, with a meal costing L90,000.

Getting There & Away

The terminal for ARST buses, which service the province, is on Via Cagliari, opposite the EPT tourist office. Regular buses head for Marina di Torre Grande, Putzu Idu and Su Pallosu; during summer only they also service San Giovanni di Sinis and the ruins of Tharros. Four buses a day leave for Bosa.

The PANI bus stop is in Via Lombardia, outside the Blu Bar at No 30 (where you can check on timetables). There are connections to Cagliari, Sassari and Nuoro.

Oristano is accessible by train from Cagliari, Sassari and Olbia.

Getting Around

Oristano is easy to negotiate on foot, although urban bus No 2 Circolare Destra (clockwise) or Sinistra (anticlockwise) is handy for getting around.

AROUND ORISTANO

Just west of Oristano is the **Sinis Peninsula**, with some lovely sandy beaches (which have been awarded a coveted Blue Flag for cleanliness by the EU), the opportunity to see lots of flamingos, and the ruins of the ancient Phoenician port of Tharros. If you have the time, spend a few days relaxing here. There are only a couple of hotels, but rooms are available for rent and there are several places participating in the local agriturismo programme. Check at the tourist office in Oristano for details.

At the village of **San Giovanni di Sinis** is the 5th century Byzantine church of the same name, where mass is still celebrated. Nearby is the tiny church of **San Salvatore**, built over a pagan temple and in a tiny village of whitewashed houses with pastel-coloured doors.

Tharros, just out of San Giovanni at the southernmost end of the peninsula, was originally a Phoenician and later a Roman port town. These important ruins, discovered in 1851 by an English archaeologist, yielded significant treasures and are well worth a visit. They are open from 9 am to 1 pm and 4 to 7 pm, and entrance is free. For information, call ☎ 0783-37 00 19.

San Giovanni and Tharros can be reached from Oristano by regular ARST buses during summer.

At the northern end of the peninsula are the villages of **Putzu Idu** and **Su Pallosu**, both offering peaceful surroundings and lovely beaches. Between the two villages are marshes which are home to hundreds of pink flamingos, as well as other water birds. The loveliest beach on the peninsula is nearby at **Is Arutas**.

If you want to stay at Putzu Idu, try *Da Cesare* (☎ 0783-5 20 15), which has singles/doubles available for around L105,000/120,000. Half board is obligatory in the high season, costing L130,000 per person. A short walk away is the quieter Su Pallosu and the *Hotel Su Pallosu* (☎ 0783-5 80 21), which has rooms for L80,000/110,000. The friendly owner, Michele Carta, offers special deals on half board at certain times of the year.

Both villages and the beach of Is Arutas are accessible by ARST bus from Oristano.

An event of particular interest, especially for those who want to experience Sardegna's wilder side, is the Sa Ardia in **Sedilo**. This spectacular festival is held on 6 and 7 July in honour of St Constantine, and features a dangerous horse race through the town. Thousands of spectators crowd into Sedilo to witness the event, and some of them fire guns into the ground and air to excite the horses further. Needless to say, there are serious injuries every year. The race starts at 6 pm on 6 July and is repeated the following morning at about 7 am. Information about the event is available at the provincial tourist office in Oristano. Sedilo is about 50km north-east of Oristano, near Abbasanta and Lago Omodeo.

On the road connecting Oristano and Sedilo, a few km before Paulilatino, you will find the important Nuraghic **Pozzo Sacro di Santa Cristina**. Near Abbasanta there's the **Nuraghe Losa**, one of the best conserved nuraghe in Sardegna.

SARDEGNA

BOSA

The only town of the Nuoro province on the west coast, Bosa is fast becoming a popular tourist destination, but it is yet to show signs of becoming 'touristy'. The town's historical centre has a pleasant architectural balance which is uncommon in Sardegna. The Pro Loco tourist office (☎ 37 61 07) has information on accommodation and other services. A medical service for tourists is available – call ☎ 37 46 15.

Bosa's telephone code is ☎ 0785.

Things to See & Do

Bosa has a fascinating town centre with lovely little squares and elegant Baroque churches. The imposing medieval castle was built in 1112 by the Malaspina, a noble Tuscan family, to control the valley of the Temo river. The Temo, with its 8km of navigable waters, made a local tanning industry possible. Also of interest is the Romanesque church of San Pietro Extramuros.

The coastline between Bosa and Alghero is stunning, with rugged cliffs dropping down to unspoiled beaches. The coastline is accessible between **Sa Badrucche** and the Spanish guarding tower called **Torre Argentina**. These beaches are often crowded on summer weekends, but the area remains a paradise for walkers in all seasons. However, the only way to really explore the coast is by car or motorcycle. Don't leave anything in your car: thieves patrol the coast looking for easy targets like unattended cars loaded with luggage.

Also near Bosa is one of the last habitats of the griffon vulture. It is quite an experience if you are lucky enough to spot one of these huge birds. Their wingspan can reach 2m.

Places to Stay and Eat

There are hotels in Bosa and at nearby Bosa Marina, an anonymous, modern resort town at the mouth of the Temo river. Nearest to the centre is *Hotel Perry Clan* (☎ 37 37 98), Via Alghero 3, with singles/doubles charges L50,000/80,000 with bathroom. *Hotel Mannu* (☎ 37 53 06), also in Via Alghero, has clean, modern rooms and a good restaurant. It charges L70,000/100,000 for a single/double and L40,000 for a seafood meal. All the hotels in Bosa can organise guided tours and boat and bicycle rental, as well as a shuttle service to the best beaches on the rocky coastline.

For a good meal try *Tatore*, Piazza IV Novembre 13b, where you'll spend around L50,000. A more economical option is *Taverna Sant'Ignazio*, Via Sant'Ignazio 33, in the medieval quarter of Sas Costas.

Getting There & Away

Regular ARST buses connect Bosa with Sassari and Oristano, arriving and departing from Piazza IV Novembre (locals call it Piazza Monumento). There is a daily bus connection to Olbia, which coincides with the Civitavecchia ferry.

Central Sardegna

AROUND BARUMINI

There are innumerable Nuraghic sites on the island, but some of the most interesting are in the interior and are often very difficult to reach without your own transport. The most important is the **Su Nuraxi** fortress, 1km west of Barumini and about 60km north of Cagliari. This vast complex consists of a castle and village, and is open from 9 am to about 8 pm (closing earlier in winter); entry is free. On a day trip you will probably spend most of your time travelling if you need to use public transport.

A better option than spending hours trying to juggle bus timetables is to head for the nearby town of **Gergei** (10km east of Barumini) and the delightful *Hotel Dedoni* (☎ 0782-80 80 60), Via Marconi 50. The hotel offers a very high standard of accommodation at reasonable prices: L50,000 per person for B&B, and L65,000 for full board. The hotel organises excursions in the area, also in connection with the Trenino Verde, and can send a car to pick you up in Cagliari or Olbia for about L80,000.

Although Gergei itself is a pretty anonymous place, it is a perfect base from which to explore the Su Nuraxi site, as well as the nearby plain of **Giara di Gesturi**, inhabited by wild ponies. North of Gergei is the **Giara di Serri**, a high-plain area which, like the Giara di Gesturi, is a great place for hiking. Also in this area is the Nuraghic sanctuary of **Santa Vittoria di Serri**, less well known than Su Nuraxi but certainly worth visiting. Of particular interest in this ancient complex is the *recinto delle feste*, a large enclosure lined with small 'rooms' where, it is believed, cult objects and other goods were displayed and sold. A few km south of Barumini, off the road for Cagliari, are the spiky ruins of a 12th-century castle, protruding from a hill at **Las Plássas**.

There is an ARST bus from Cagliari to Barumini, but to return you will need to catch an FDS bus to Sanluri and then an ARST bus to Cagliari. FDS buses also serve Gergei. To avoid being stranded, check the latest bus timetables at the Cagliari tourist office. The Trenino Verde which runs between Cagliari and Arbatax passes nearby at Mandas. The section between Mandas and Arbatax is the most scenic part of the railway, so it might be worthwhile catching the train there if you have the time.

Northern Sardegna

ALGHERO

Situated on the island's north-west coast, in the area known as the Coral Riviera, Alghero is one of the most popular tourist resorts in Sardegna. The Catalan Aragonese won the town from Genova in 1354, and even today the locals speak a dialect strongly linked to the Catalan language. Alghero is a good base from which to explore the magnificent coastline that links it to Bosa in the south, and the famous Grotta di Nettuno in the north (see the Around Alghero section).

Orientation

Alghero's historical centre is on a small promontory jutting into the sea, with the new town stretching out behind it and along the coast to the north. Intercity buses arrive in Via Catalogna, next to a small park just outside the historical centre. The train station is about 1km north, on Via Don Minzoni, and connected to the centre by a regular bus service.

Information

Tourist Office The AAST office (☎ 97 90 54) is at Piazza Porta Terra 9, near the port and just across the gardens from the bus station. You can pick up a map of the town and ask for assistance to find a hotel. The old town and most hotels and restaurants are in the area west of the tourist office.

Post & Communications The main post office is at Via XX Settembre 108. There is a row of public telephones on Via Vittorio Emanuele at the opposite end of the gardens from the tourist office.

The telephone code for Alghero is ☎ 079.

Medical Services From 1 July to 10 September there is a tourist medical service (☎ 93 05 33) on Piazza Venezia Giulia in Fertilia, just north of Alghero. It is open from 9 am to 12.30 pm and 4.30 to 7.30 pm, although for emergencies you can telephone 24 hours a day. Otherwise go to the Ospedale Civile (☎ 99 62 33) in Via Don Minzoni.

Emergency For immediate police attention, call ☎ 113.

Things to See & Do

Wander through the narrow streets of the old town and around the port. The most interesting church is the **Chiesa di San Francesco**, Via Carlo Alberto. The **cathedral** has been ruined by constant remodelling, but its bell tower remains a fine example of Gothic Catalan architecture.

There are three defensive towers in the town. The **Torre del Portal**, in Piazza Porta Terra, was furnished with a drawbridge and moat, and was one of the two entrances to the walled town. The **Torre de l'Esperó Reial** was one of the bastions of Alghero's fortified wall. The octagonal **Torre de Sant Jaume** is also known as the Dog's Tower, since it was used as a pound for stray dogs.

Special Events

In summer Alghero generally stages the Estate Musicale Algherese in the cloisters of the church of San Francesco. A festival, complete with fireworks display, is held annually on 15 August for the Feast of the Assumption.

Places to Stay

It is virtually impossible to find a room in August, unless you book months in advance. At other times of the year you should have little trouble. Camping facilities include *Camping Calik* (☎ 93 01 11) in Fertilia, about 6km north of town, where charges in the high season are L18,000 per person plus site and L4000 for electricity. The HI *Ostello dei Giuliani* (☎ 93 03 53) is at Via Zara 1, in Fertilia. Take bus AF from Via Catalogna to Fertilia. B&B is L14,000 a night and a meal is L14,000. It is open all year.

In the old town, *Hotel San Francesco* (☎ 98 03 30) at Via Ambrogio Machin 2 has singles/doubles for L60,000/110,000, with bathroom. *Pensione Normandie* (☎ 97 53 02), Via Enrico Mattei 6, is out of the centre. Follow Via Cagliari (which becomes Viale Giovanni XXIII). It has slightly shabby, but large, rooms for L37,000/65,000.

The *Miramare* (☎ 97 93 50), Via G Leopardi 15, south along the Lungomare Dante from the old town, has good rooms with bathroom for up to L80,000/110,000. *La Margherita* (☎ 97 90 06), Via Sassari 70, has rooms with bathroom for up to L90,000/125,000.

Places to Eat

There are numerous supermarkets, including *Mura* in Via Lamarmora. For good sandwiches, head for *Paninoteca al Duomo*, next to the cathedral in Piazza Civica. The best ice cream is at *Paradiso 2*, through the Porta a Mare from Piazza Civica.

Ristorante La Piconia, Via Principe Umberto 29, is also a pizzeria. A full meal will cost around L30,000. *Trattoria Il Vecchio Mulino*, Via Don Deroma 3, is a pleasant establishment, where a full meal will cost about L30,000. A cheaper option is the *pizzeria* just off Via Roma at Vicolo Adami 17; takeaway pizza by the slice costs about L3000. At Vicolo Adami 25 is *La Posada del Mar*, which serves good pasta for around L10,000 and pizzas for around L9000. *La Lepanto*, Via Carlo Alberto 135, overlooks the sea. A good full meal will cost around L50,000.

La Palafitta is literally on the beach known as Spiaggia di Maria Pia, a few km north of Alghero, on the way to Fertilia. Look for the sign and then walk through the small area of pine trees to the restaurant. A full meal will cost around L35,000 and you can follow it up with a moonlit walk along the beach.

Getting There & Away

The airport, inland from Fertilia, services domestic flights from major cities throughout Italy. Regular buses leave from Piazza della Mercedes to coincide with flights.

Intercity buses terminate in Via Catalogna, next to the public park. ARST buses leave for Sassari and Porto Torres; FDS buses service Sassari as well and there is a special service to Olbia to coincide with ferry departures. FDS also runs a service between Alghero and Bosa. Regular buses leave for Capo Caccia and Porto Conte. Timetables are posted in the bar beside the bus-stop area. Trains connect Alghero with Sassari.

Getting Around

Urban bus No AF runs hourly between Alghero and Fertilia from 8 am to 10 pm. The more regular A0 goes only as far as the Maria Pia beach. Regular FDS buses run between the port and the train station, a distance of about 1km.

If you want to rent a bicycle or motorcycle to explore the coast, try Velosport (☎ 97 71 82), Via Vittorio Veneto 90. A bike will cost about L20,000 a day, a moped L45,000 and a scooter L75,000. Cicloexpress (☎ 98 69 50), Via Garibaldi Porto, has mountain bikes for L18,000 per day, bicycles for L12,000, mopeds for L25,000 and Piaggio 125 cc scooters for L50,000.

AROUND ALGHERO

There are good beaches north of Alghero, including the **Spiaggia di San Giovanni** and the **Spiaggia di Maria Pia**, easily accessible on the Alghero-Fertilia bus.

The **Grotta di Nettuno** (Neptune's Cave) on Capo Caccia, west of Alghero, is accessible by regular boats operated by various companies from Alghero's port (L15,000), or by the SFS bus from Via Catalogna (L6300 return). For some services you will need to change at Porto Conte.

If you have your own means of transport, explore the Capo Caccia area and visit the **Nuraghe di Palmavera**, about 10km out of Alghero on the road to Porto Conte, and the **Necropoli di Anghelu Ruju**, on the road to Porto Torres.

SASSARI

The capital of Sardegna's largest province, Sassari is also the island's second-largest city after Cagliari. It is a pleasant town, but is best regarded as a convenient stopover on the way to the northern coast. However, it is certainly worth visiting in May for the Sardegnan Cavalcade, one of Sardegna's most important festivals.

Orientation

Sassari has a compact centre concentrated around its cathedral, but most services are in the busy newer part of town in the area around the vast 18th-century Piazza Italia. Most intercity buses arrive in Emiciclo Garibaldi; to reach Piazza Italia, head up Via Brigata Sassari to Piazza Castello and turn right.

The train station is about 10 minutes walk from the centre. From the station, turn left to reach Piazza Sant'Antonio and then right along Corso Vittorio Emanuele to reach Piazza Castello.

Information

Tourist Offices The AAST office (☎ 23 35 34) is at Viale Umberto 72, near the Museo Sanna. It opens Monday to Friday from 8 am to 2 pm, and on Thursday and Wednesday also from 4 to 7 pm. The EPT information office (☎ 29 95 44), Via Caprera 36, has the same hours.

Money There is a branch of the Banca Commerciale Italiana in Piazza Italia, where you can exchange travellers cheques and obtain cash advances on Visa and MasterCard.

Post & Communications The main post office is at Via Brigata Sassari 13, just off Piazza Castello. There is a Telecom office in front of this post office, open Monday to Friday from 9 am to 12.30 pm and 4 to 7.30 pm.

Sassari's telephone code is ☎ 079.

SARDEGNA

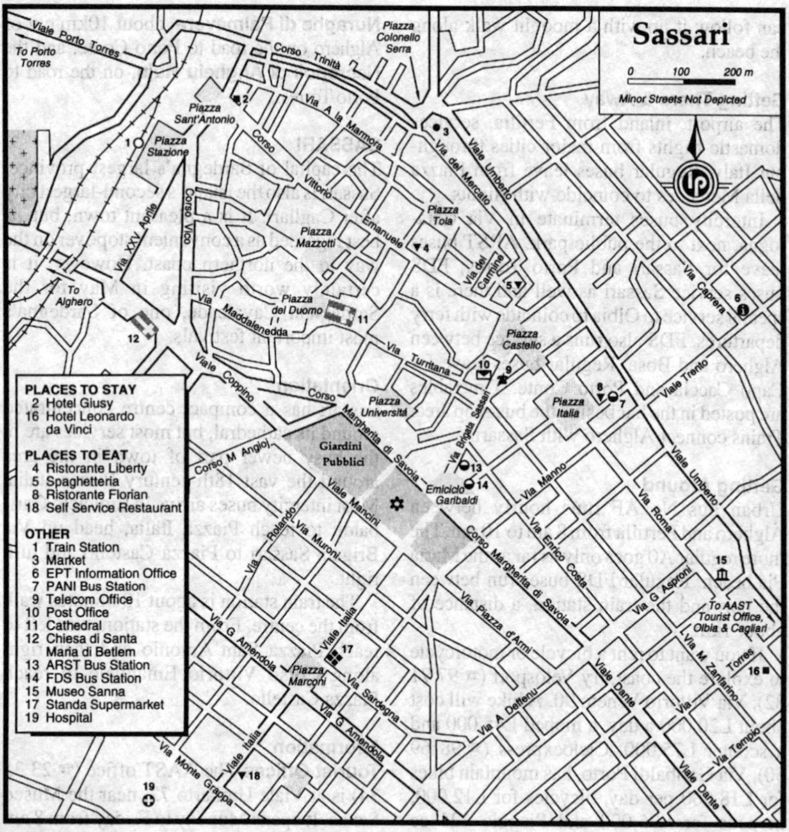

Medical Services The public hospital, Ospedale Civile (☎ 22 05 00), is in Via E de Nicola, off Viale Italia.

Emergency For immediate police attendance, call ☎ 113.

Things to See

Sassari's **cathedral** is in the old town on Piazza del Duomo. Built in Romanesque style in the 13th century, it was remodelled and given a Baroque façade in the 17th century. Also worth a look is the **Chiesa di Santa Maria di Betlem**, on Viale Coppino near the station, which has a 13th-century façade and lovely 14th-century cloisters.

Museo Sanna, Via Roma 64, is of considerable interest for its Nuraghic collection, as well as its display of traditional costumes.

Special Event

The Cavalcata Sarda (Sardegnan Cavalcade) is generally held on the second-last Sunday in May (although the day can change from year to year). It attracts participants from all over the island, who dress in traditional costume and participate in a large and quite colourful parade, followed by equestrian competitions. It's well worth visiting Sassari during the festival.

Places to Stay

Hotels and pensioni are not abundant in Sassari and if you plan to arrive in high summer, or for the Cavalcade, it is advisable to book a room. The *Hotel Giusy* (☎ 23 33 27), Piazza Sant'Antonio 21, is close to the station and has singles/doubles with bathroom for L50,000/70,000. At Via Roma 79 there's the more upmarket *Hotel Leonardo da Vinci* (☎ 28 07 44), which has quality singles/doubles for L110,000/160,000 and triples for L210,000, including breakfast and private bathroom.

Places to Eat

An outdoor fresh-produce market is held every morning from Monday to Saturday in Via del Mercato, near Piazza Colonnello Serra. Alternatively, shop at the Standa supermarket on the corner of Viale Italia and Via Sardegna. You can get good sandwiches at either of the sandwich shops in Via Turritana, off Via Brigata Sassari.

There is a *Spaghetteria* at Via Usai 10a, off Largo Felice Cavallotti, where a dish of pasta costs between L5000 and L12,000. A new *self-service restaurant* is in Viale Italia, near the hospital, where you can eat for L20,000. *Ristorante Liberty* is in a restored palace in Piazza Sauro, off Corso Vittorio Emanuele. A full meal will cost around L35,000. *Ristorante Florian*, off Piazza Italia at Via Bellieni 27, has a good reputation. A full meal will cost around L60,000.

Getting There & Away

ARST buses leave from Emiciclo Garibaldi piazza, connecting with flights at Fertilia airport. Tickets can be purchased at the Sarda Viaggi travel agency, Via Brigata Sassari 30. ARST buses also connect with towns such as Alghero, Bosa and Pozzomaggiore. There are also regular buses to Porto Torres (28 a day), Santa Teresa Gallura (31 a day) and Nuoro. Timetable information and tickets are available at the ARST office in the piazza at the southern end of Via Brigata Sassari.

FDS buses run to Alghero, Fertilia, Bosa, Olbia, Palau and Porto Torres. You can check timetables at the company's ticket office at Emiciclo Garibaldi 26.

PANI buses connect Sassari with Oristano, Nuoro and Cagliari, leaving from Piazza Italia. The PANI ticket office is at Via Bellieni 25, next to Ristorante Florian.

Trains connect Sassari to Porto Torres, Olbia, Oristano and Cagliari.

Getting Around

It is easy to make your way around the centre of town on foot, but the No 8 is a useful bus as it heads from the station to Piazza Italia, travelling along Corso Vittorio Emanuele and Via Roma. If arriving by car, you will find the familiar 'centro' signs to direct you to the centre, where there are numerous supervised daytime car parks.

AROUND SASSARI

The **Chiesa di SS Trinità di Saccargia**, a splendid Romanesque-Pisan church built in 1116, is set in a bare landscape near the town of Codrongianus, about 18km south-east of Sassari along the SS131. You should have little trouble reaching Codrongianus by ARST bus from Sassari, but then you have to walk the 2km to the church.

The **Nuraghe Santu Antine** is just off the SS131 near Torralba, about 40km south of Sassari. Said to be the most beautiful nuraghe in Sardegna, it is well worth a visit. By public transport, it can be reached from Sassari by the ARST bus heading for Padria, which stops at Torralba.

PORTO TORRES

Unless you are arriving or leaving by ferry, there is no reason to visit this port town and major petrochemical centre. To the north-west is the fast-developing beach resort of Stintino, a former fishing village which has managed to retain some of its past atmosphere.

The town's main street is Corso Vittorio Emanuele, which is directly in front of you as you face away from the port. The tourist office (☎ 51 50 00), Piazza XX Settembre 2, opens daily from May to mid-September only from 8.30 am to 1.30 pm and 4.30 to 7.30 pm (until midday on Sunday); in April and the second half of September it's open only in the morning.

Porto Torres' telephone code is ☎ 079.

Places to Stay & Eat

If you find it necessary to spend the night in Porto Torres, try the *Albergo Royal* (☎ 50 22 78), Via Sebastiano Satta 8, which has singles/doubles for L60,000/110,000 with bathroom and triples for L120,000 in summer (prices drop by half out of season). There are numerous places where you can buy sandwiches or snacks, including take-away pizza by the slice at Via Ponte Romano 54. For a simple meal, try *Poldiavolo* in Piazza XX Settembre 7, in front of the tourist office.

Getting There & Away

Regular ARST buses connect Porto Torres with Sassari and Stintino. The bus station is in Piazzale Colombo at the port and the ticket office is at the Acciaro Bar, Corso Vittorio Emanuele 38. Regular trains connect Porto Torres with Sassari. A new train station has been built about 2km to the west of the port.

Tirrenia runs daily ferries to Genova (three a day in summer). Its office (☎ 51 41 07) is in the ferry terminal at the port. The French line SNCM runs four or five ferries per month to Toulon and Marseille, some via Bastia in Corsica from the end of March to September. The agent for SNCM in Porto Torres is Agenzia Paglietti Petertours (☎ 51 44 77), Corso Vittorio Emanuele. In France the company has offices in Marseille, at 61 Blvd des Dames (☎ 08-36 67 95 00), and in Toulon, 21 & 49 Ave de l'Infanterie de Marine (☎ 04-94 16 66 66). In Corsica, it can be contacted through SNCM Corsica (☎ 04-95 54 66 99), Noveau Port BP 57, Bastia.

STINTINO

A picturesque fishing village turned tourist resort, Stintino is very crowded in summer. A few km west of the town, facing Asinara Island, is a magnificent sandy beach, the **Spiaggia di Pelosa**, at Torre Pelosa.

If you want to spend a few days in Stintino, try the *Albergo Silvestrino* (☎ 079-52 30 07), Via Sassari 14, in the centre of the village. It has singles/doubles with bathroom for L65,000/100,000, and half board for L105,000 (L130,000 in August) per person (closed in January). The *Hotel Lina* (☎ 079-52 30 71), Via Lepanto 38, which faces the village's small port, has doubles only. They cost L80,000.

Stintino is accessible from Porto Torres by ARST bus (five a day in summer).

SANTA TERESA GALLURA

Together with Palau, about 26km to the east, this seaside resort is an affordable alternative to the jet-set hangouts on the Costa Smeralda. It is a very pleasant spot to pass a few relaxing days, especially if the magnificent coves, rock pools and small beaches of nearby Capo Testa appeal. From the town you can see across the Stretto di Bonifacio to Corsica, and you can catch one of the regular ferries which make the crossing to Bonifacio on Corsica's southern tip.

Information

Santa Teresa's AAST office (☎ 75 41 27) is in the town centre at Piazza Vittorio Emanuele 24, open daily in summer from 8.30 am to 1 pm and 3.30 to 8 pm. The helpful staff can provide loads of information and will assist in finding accommodation. You can ring ahead for information on hotels, as well as rooms and apartments for rent, or you can write (in English) to: AAST, Piazza V Emanuele 24, 07028 Santa Teresa Gallura, Sassari.

You can exchange money daily from 8 am to 10 pm at the port; otherwise there's a bank in Piazza V Emanuele.

For medical attention, go to the Guardia Medica in Via Carlo Felice, on the corner of Via Eleonora d'Arborea, a short walk from the town centre.

Santa Teresa's telephone code is ☎ 0789.

Things to See & Do

The main reason for a visit to this area is to

spend time on the beach. There is the small **Spiaggia Rena Bianca** next to the town, but it is recommended that you head for **Capo Testa**, a small cape connected to the mainland by an isthmus, about 5km west of Santa Teresa. There are lovely little beaches on either side of the cape, as well as a large sheltered rock pool. The road ends just below the lighthouse; the path to the right leads to the rock pool, and the path to the left leads to a small cove and sandy beach. The cape is actually a military zone, but you'll only have problems if you try to get to the lighthouse.

Motorised rubber boats for up to six people are available for rent at Santa Teresa's port for L150,000 to L180,000 a day, or L90,000 for half a day. GULP Immobiliare, Via Nazionale 58 (☎ 75 56 89), rents apartments and villas, cars, boats, bicycles and motorcycles, which are handy for exploring the area. A mountain bike costs around L25,000 a day, a moped L40,000 and a scooter L60,000.

Places to Stay

Santa Teresa offers extensive accommodation possibilities, including rooms and apartments for rent (contact the tourist office). It is advisable to book if you plan to arrive during late July or August.

Camping facilities are all out of town. Try *La Liccia* (☎ 75 51 90), about 6km from Santa Teresa towards Palau, 400m from the beach; charges are L16,000 per adult and L11,500 for a child, and they include the site.

In town, *Albergo Da Cecco* (☎ 75 42 20), Via Po 3 (take Via XX Settembre from the tourist office and turn right at Via Po), has pleasant singles/doubles for L80,000/110,000 with bathroom. *Hotel Bacchus* (☎ 75 45 56), Via Firenze 5, is a quiet place in the new town which is known for its restaurant. It has singles/doubles for L80,000/100,000 and half board for L135,000. The *Hotel del Porto* (☎ 75 41 54), Via del Porto 20, on the port, has singles/doubles for L55,000/80,000.

At Capo Testa there's the *Bocche di Bonifacio* (☎ 75 42 02), which has singles/doubles for L60,000/85,000 and half board for L100,000 per person.

Places to Eat

There are plenty of good bars and sandwich shops where you can buy sandwiches, including *Poldo's Pub*, Via Garibaldi 4. For good pizza, try *Pizzeria La Cambusa* in Via Firenze. *Marinaro*, at the Hotel Marinaro, Via Angioj, has good meals for around L30,000. Restaurant *La Torre* in Via del Mare charges about L35,000 for a seafood meal. If visiting Capo Testa, try the trattoria at the *Bocche di Bonifacio* hotel.

Getting There & Away

Regular ARST buses connect Santa Teresa with Olbia, Golfo Aranci and Palau, arriving in Via Eleonora d'Arborea, off Via Nazionale and only a short walk to the centre. There are also two buses a day to Sassari. Tickets can be purchased at the Bar Black & White on Via Nazionale.

Ferry services to Corsica are run by two companies, Moby Lines (☎ 75 52 60) and Saremar (☎ 75 47 88), both of which have small offices at the port. Both companies run several services a day.

PALAU & AROUND

Close to the Costa Smeralda, Palau is little more than a conglomeration of expensive hotels and private apartment blocks and is much less pleasant than Santa Teresa.

Just off the coast are the islands of **La Maddalena**, site of a US navy base, and **Caprera**, which was given to the hero of Italian unification, Giuseppe Garibaldi, by King Victor Emmanuel II. Garibaldi spent his last years there and it is possible to visit his house. Most of the island is a nature reserve, which means that camping is forbidden, although it is the site of a Club Méditerranée (see the following Places to Stay section).

La Maddalena has an attractive main town, La Maddalena, and several good beaches, and is popular with campers. The two islands are connected by a road bridge.

Information

Palau's tourist office (☎ 70 95 70) is at Via Nazionale 96. It has little tourist information, but can assist with accommodation, including apartments and rooms for rent. La Maddalena's tourist office (☎ 73 63 21) is at Piazza Barone de Geneys.

The telephone code for the Palau area is ☎ 0789.

Places to Stay

Just east of Palau is the seaside *Camping Capo d'Orso* (☎ 70 81 82), on the cape of the same name. It charges L6500 per person and L13,500 for a site, and also has caravans and bungalows for rent at L110,000 and L160,000 per day, respectively.

In the town there are numerous hotels and rooms for rent, but you should book ahead for July and August. The *Hotel Serra* (☎ 70 95 19), Via Nazionale 17, has singles/doubles for L50,000/75,000 with bathroom. *La Roccia* (☎ 70 95 28), Via dei Mille 15, has singles/doubles for L60,000/90,000. If you're looking for luxury accommodation, try the *Hotel Palau* (☎ 70 84 68), Via Baragge, which has doubles for up to L280,000.

On La Maddalena there is *Villaggio Camping La Maddalena* (☎ 72 80 51) at Moneta, and *Campeggio Abbatoggia* (☎ 73 91 73) on the other side of the island at Lo Strangolato, close to a lovely beach. Both are reasonably cheap and accessible by local bus from the town of La Maddalena. In town, *Hotel Il Gabbiano* (☎ 72 25 07), Via Giulio Cesare, has singles/doubles for L90,000/ 115,000 with bathroom. The *Club Méditerranée* (☎ 72 70 78) on Caprera charges around L700,000 per person per week for full board.

Places to Eat

In Palau, you can buy supplies at the Minimarket da Gemma, Via Nazionale 66. There are several decent places to eat, including *L'Uva Fragola*, Piazza Vittorio Emanuele, just off Via Nazionale near the port, which serves good pizzas, as well as salads for around L15,000. *Da Robertino*, Via Nazionale 22, is a good trattoria where a full meal will cost around L40,000. At *La Taverna*, Via Rossini, off Via Nazionale, you can eat an excellent seafood meal for around L70,000.

Getting There & Away

Palau is easily accessible by ARST bus from Sassari, Santa Teresa Gallura and Olbia. SFS and Autoservizi Caramelli buses connect Palau with places along the Costa Smeralda, including Baia Sardegna and Porto Cervo. Buses stop at Palau's small port. Timetables are posted inside the small ferry terminal at the port. Linee Lauro operates a new service with a company called Traghetti Isole Sarde (TRIS) that connects Palau with Genova and Napoli three days a week from April to January. Call the office in Palau (☎ 70 95 05), Via Fonte Vecchia 11, for more details.

Getting Around

Ferries make the short crossing between Palau and La Maddalena every 20 minutes during summer, less frequently in the off season. It is not possible to take your car to La Maddalena; there is a car park just outside Palau, where you can leave the car if you want to catch a ferry to La Maddalena, and a bus shuttle service will take you to the port. While it is not obligatory to use the car park, it may be difficult to find a parking spot in town during summer.

Once on the island, catch one of the blue local buses which leave from the port every half-hour and make the round trip of the island. Buses for Caprera leave from the piazza at the end of Via Giovanni Amendola, to the right of the port.

COSTA SMERALDA

For the average tourist, the Costa Smeralda (Emerald Coast) is basically out of reach. There are no hotels of less than three stars, which means that prices for a double room start at around L160,000 a day. The coast was purchased in 1962 by a group of international investors led by Prince Karim Aga Khan, and was basically developed from scratch. Its resorts include Baia Sardegna, Liscia di Vacca and Porto Cervo, all bearing a stronger resemblance to Disneyland than seaside towns. The coastline is certainly beautiful, but it is not the real Sardegna, and unless you have money to burn, or very rich friends with an apartment, it is better to spend the day on one of its beaches and continue your journey.

Those who would like to stay on the Costa Smeralda can obtain information about accommodation from the tourist office at Arzachena (☎ 0789-8 26 24), Via Paolo Dettori 43 (inside the ERSAT building).

The coast is accessible by ARST, SFS and Autoservizi Caramelli buses from Palau and Olbia.

OLBIA

This busy port and industrial centre will very likely be the first glimpse of Sardegna for many tourists. It is a major port for ferries arriving from Civitavecchia, Genova and Livorno, and while it is not particularly unpleasant, it is not particularly interesting either and is best passed through quickly.

Orientation

If arriving by ferry, you will find yourself at a well-organised port complete with a new ferry terminal and a local bus (No 3) to take you into the centre of town (only about 1km). Trains run from the main station to the port to coincide with ferry departures. Intercity buses terminate at the end of Corso Umberto at Via XX Settembre. Head west along Corso Umberto to reach the town centre. The train station is close by in Via Pala, off Piazza Risorgimento.

Information

Tourist Office The AAST office (☎ 2 49 79) is at Via Catello Piro 1, off Corso Umberto, and opens from 8 am to 2 pm and 4 to 8 pm in summer. The staff are very keen to help and will advise in English on places to stay and eat, and can provide information about accommodation and places to visit throughout Sardegna.

Money There are three major banks on Corso Umberto, including the Banca Commerciale Italiana at No 191, where you can obtain cash advances on both Visa and MasterCard.

Post & Communications The main post office is in Via Acquedotto, off Piazza Matteotti, and there is a Telecom office at Via de Filippi 14. Poste restante mail can be addressed to 07026 Olbia.

Olbia's telephone code is ☎ 0789.

Medical Services The public hospital, the Ospedale Civile (☎ 5 22 00), is in Viale Aldo Moro, about a 15-minute walk from the centre along Via Porto Romano and Via Gabriele d'Annunzio.

Emergency For immediate police attendance, call ☎ 113.

Places to Stay

The *Albergo Terranova* (☎ 2 23 95), Via Giuseppe Garibaldi 3, has singles/doubles for L38,000/60,000. The *Hotel Minerva* (☎ 2 11 90), Via Mazzini 7, has doubles for L60,000, and singles/doubles with bathroom for L45,000/70,000.

The *Hotel Gallura* (☎ 2 46 48), Corso Umberto 145, is a pleasant establishment, with singles/doubles with bathroom costing L80,000/110,000. The *Hotel Centrale* (☎ 2 30 17), Corso Umberto 85, has rooms for L100,000/140,000.

Places to Eat

If you want to stock up on food supplies, head for the Mercato Civico in Via Acquedotto. At *Il Golosone*, Corso Umberto 41, you can buy good sandwiches, crêpes and gelati. For an excellent meal, try *Trattoria il Gambero*, Via Lamarmora 6, off Piazza Matteotti; a full meal will cost over L40,000. One of Olbia's better restaurants is the *Ristorante Gallura* at the Hotel Gallura, Corso Umberto 145; a full meal here will cost around L90,000.

Getting There & Away

Air Olbia's airport, a few km south-east of the town, services flights to and from Italy's main cities. City bus No 8 heads to the airport.

Bus ARST buses depart from both the port (coinciding with ferry arrivals) and the bus station in the centre for Arzachena and the resorts of the Costa Smeralda, Palau, Santa Teresa Gallura, and the towns of Sassari and Nuoro.

Train There are train connections to major towns, including Sassari, Cagliari and Oristano.

Boat Tirrenia ferries make the 7½ hour night crossing to Civitavecchia five times a day in the high season. The company has an office at the ferry terminal (☎ 2 46 91) and at Corso Umberto 17 (☎ 2 85 33). This is an extremely busy route and it is very important to book at least three weeks in advance during the summer months, particularly if you want to take a car.

Ferries run by Navarma Lines (also known as Moby Lines) connect Olbia with Livorno twice a day in the high season (the daytime trip is sometimes offered at a special price for two people and a car). The company

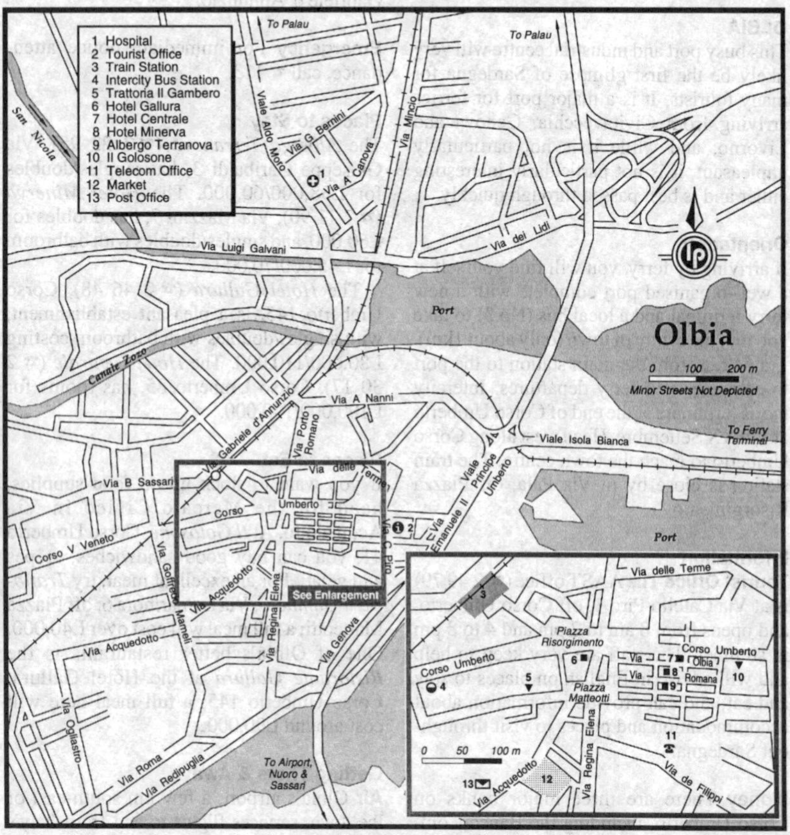

has an office at the ferry terminal (☎ 2 79 27) and another at Corso Umberto 1 (☎ 2 35 72).

If you are taking a car on a ferry, you will find clear signs directing you to the port and to your point of embarkation. From the town centre, head for Viale Principe Umberto and then Viale Isola Bianca to reach the port.

GOLFO ARANCI

Golfo Aranci is a ferry terminal on the promontory north-east of Olbia, where FS ferries from Civitavecchia dock. You can catch a train directly to Olbia, or take an ARST bus to Olbia, Palau or Santa Teresa Gallura. It is possible to buy a ticket in Roma (at Stazione Termini or any Sestante CIT office) which covers the cost of the train trip to Civitavecchia, the ferry crossing and the train to Olbia. Ferries run by Sardegna Ferries connect Golfo Aranci with Livorno (day and night services) and Civitavecchia (daytime service) from April to September. For booking and information call the Livorno office on ☎ 0586-88 13 80, Golfo Aranci on ☎ 0789-46 78 0 or Civitavecchia on ☎ 0766-50 07 14. There are special prices for daytime trips on some days for two people and a car.

Eastern Sardegna

NUORO PROVINCE

This province, about halfway up the east coast of Sardegna, encompasses the area known as the Barbagia. It has unspoiled, isolated beaches, spectacular gorges and great trekking routes, as well as important Nuraghic sites. More than in any other part of Sardegna, this is where you'll be able to get a real sense of the island's traditional culture. Although tourism in the area is increasing, the people remain strongly connected to the traditions which have been swept aside by tourism in other parts of the island. Shepherds still tend their flocks in remote areas of the province, often living alone in stone or wooden shacks and having little contact with the outside world. It is common to see older women in the traditional black, ankle-length dresses of the area, their heads covered by Spanish-style black, fringed shawls. It's recommended to visit the area in spring when the patron saint feast days are frequent. On these occasions the young people dress in beautifully embroidered traditional costumes and perform ancient folk dances.

The locals remain fairly aloof, and it is important when visiting the smaller, more remote towns to behave respectfully. If you manage to befriend a local, you will find them incredibly hospitable and helpful.

Larger towns in the area are accessible by bus, but a car is a necessity to explore the smaller villages and the mountains. A surprisingly cheap way to explore parts of the area is by trekking with an organised guide.

Nuoro is the capital of the province and the gateway to the beautiful coastline around Cala Gonone, Baunei and Urzulei's dramatically beautiful highlands and gorges, and the Gennargentu and Sopramonte mountain ranges.

Now endangered, the mouflon is a small wild sheep found in the mountains of Sardegna

SARDEGNA

Nuoro

Orientation There is not a lot to see and do in Nuoro, but it is a good starting point for an exploration of the Barbagia. The old centre of town is around Piazza delle Grazie, Corso Garibaldi and Via Italia, near the tourist office. From Piazza delle Grazie, walk along Via IV Novembre and Via Dante. ARST buses terminate in Via Lucania, near the train station. The station is about a 15-minute walk from Piazza delle Grazie along Via La Marmora (turn left as you leave the station).

Information The EPT office (☎ 3 00 83) is at Piazza Italia 19 and is open Monday to Friday from 10.30 am to 1 pm, and on Thursday and Wednesday also from 4 to 7 pm. The main post office is in Piazza Crispi, between Corso Garibaldi and Piazza Dante, and there is a Telecom office at Via Brigata Sassari 6.

Nuoro's telephone code is ☎ 0784.

Things to See While in town, take a look at the neoclassical **cathedral** in Piazza Santa Maria della Neve, and the monument and square dedicated to the local poet Sebastiano Satta. The **Museo della Vita e delle Tradizioni Popolari Sardi** (Museum of the Life & Traditions of the Sardegnan People), at Via Antonio Mereu 56, south of the cathedral, is well worth a visit. It opens from 9 am to 1 pm and 3 to 7 pm in winter and from 9 am to 7 pm in summer, and houses a collection of traditional costumes and masks.

SARDEGNA

Places to Stay There are no rock-bottom budget options, but you could try *Mini Hotel* (☎ 3 31 59), Via Brofferio 13, a pleasant little place which has singles/doubles with bathroom for L60,000/75,000. It is off Via Roma, near Piazza Sebastiano Satta. *Hotel Grillo* (☎ 3 86 78), Via Monsignor Melas 14, is in an ugly building, but its rooms are pleasant. Singles/doubles with bathroom are L76,000/99,000, and triples are L129,000.

Places to Eat To pick up supplies, shop at the Conad supermarket in Via Trieste, just near Piazza Italia, or at the great little grocery shop at Corso Garibaldi 168 and the cheese shop next door. Otherwise try *Pizzeria del Diavolo*, Corso Garibaldi 134.

Getting There & Away ARST buses connect Nuoro with Cagliari (two a day), Olbia (six a day) and Sassari (three a day), as well as towns throughout the province, including Oliena (hourly), Orgosolo (10 a day), Dorgali and Cala Gonone (seven a day), and Baunei (two a day). PANI buses head for Cagliari, Sassari and Oristano. The train reaches Macomer and Bosa on the west coast, where there are connections with the main north-south line.

Oliena

The value of visiting Oliena, or Orgosolo farther south (see the following section), is to get a better idea of how people live in Sardegna's interior. Neither town offers much in the way of tourist facilities or sights, although both, in their own way, provide an 'alternative' travel experience.

Oliena is about 12km south-east of Nuoro, and is easily accessible by regular ARST bus. For the more adventurous, it is a place from which to set out on a trekking exploration of the Sopramonte area to the south or to the isolated Nuraghic site at **Tiscali**, either alone or, better, with a guide. Remember that there are very few clearly marked trails and that the area is full of goat tracks – so orientation is a serious problem.

On Easter Sunday morning a traditional festival takes place; it is called S'Incontru, and dates back to the period of Spanish domination. In separate processions, the women of the town carry a statue of the Madonna and the men carry a statue of Christ on the cross. They meet in Oliena's main piazza and the place goes crazy, as every man and boy in town greets the *incontru* by shooting a gun into the air.

For information on guided treks, contact Levamus Viaggi (☎ 0784-28 51 90), Corso Vittorio Emanuele 27. They speak English and offer a wide range of possibilities, from a one day 4WD guided tour to a guided trek in the Sopramonte. Ask for Murena, a local guide who also operates a *rifugio* near Tiscali and can take you on a three day trek from there, through the Gola di Gorropu to the beach at Cala di Luna. Murena doesn't speak English, but this shouldn't be a problem.

Barbagia Insolita (☎ 0784-28 81 67), Via Carducci 25 in Oliena, organises guided tours to out-of-the-way areas in the Barbagia by Land Rover, as well as on foot. You can choose between demanding treks or more manageable walks to places including Tiscali, the Gola di Gorropu, Monte Corrasi and the Codula di Luna valley.

Places to Stay Accommodation options are limited. Try *Ci Kappa* (☎ 0784-28 87 33), Via Martin Luther King 2, which has singles/doubles for L60,000/85,000. It also has a good pizzeria/restaurant. A few km east of town, near the beautiful Lanaittu valley, is *Su Gologone* (☎ 0784-28 75 12). The hotel is in a lovely setting and is a paricularly good option for people wanting to explore the area as it organises guided tours, treks and even horse-riding expeditions. Singles/doubles cost L105,000/150,000 with bathroom out of season. Half board costs up to L115,000 per person and full board up to L145,000. Its restaurant serves excellent traditional local dishes and is justifiably renowned throughout the island.

Orgosolo

About 18km farther south, Orgosolo is famous for its tradition of *banditismo* (banditry), although this is not a subject you will find the locals willing to discuss openly. This tradition was immortalised by the 1963 Italian film *The Bandits of Orgosolo*. One of the town's more notorious *banditi* was released from prison in 1992 and acted as an unofficial negotiator in the much-publicised kidnapping of the son of a Costa Smeralda hotelier (and a relative of the Aga Khan). The child was eventually released in the countryside close to the town.

Orgosolo is also interesting for the series of leftist and nationalistic murals which decorate the façades of many of its buildings. The idea of a local art teacher, Francesco del Casino, a native of Siena who has lived in Orgosolo for many years, the murals started appearing in 1973. Generally designed by him, they have been painted by local students as well as other artists. The murals originally reflected fairly extreme political views on a range of international issues, such as Vietnam, South Africa and the Palestinian question; they now deal mainly with social issues.

Places to Stay & Eat Try the *Petit Hotel* (☎ 0784-40 20 09), Via Mannu, which has singles/doubles for L40,000/55,000 with bathroom. Just out of town is *Ai Monti del Gennargentu* (☎ 0784-40 23 74), which has doubles for L45,000 with bathroom.

A local group organises lunches in the countryside just outside town, where you can enjoy one of Sardegna's most traditional dishes, porcheddu (roast sucking pig). The travel agency Avitur (☎ 0789-5 32 30), Corso Vittorio Emanuele 142 in Olbia, organises guided trips by bus from Olbia to Orgosolo, including the lunch, for L80,000 a head. Otherwise you can arrange to attend a lunch by contacting the organisers in Orgosolo directly on ☎ 0784-40 20 71. The cost for lunch only is L30,000 a head.

Orgosolo is accessible by ARST bus from Nuoro.

Cala Gonone & Around

This fast-developing seaside resort is an excellent base from which to explore the coves along the coastline, as well as the Nuraghic sites and rugged terrain inland. There is a Pro Loco tourist office (☎ 9 33 87) in Viale del Bue Marino, where you can pick up maps, a list of hotels, and information to help you explore the area. There is also a tourist office in the nearby town of **Dorgali**, which you will probably need to pass through on your way to Cala Gonone. It is in Via La Marmora (☎ 9 62 43).

If you are travelling by car, you will need a detailed road map of the area. One of the best is published by the Istituto Geografico de Agostini. The tourist office has maps which detail the locations of the main sights.

The telephone code for Cala Gonone and Dorgali is ☎ 0784.

Things to See & Do From Cala Gonone's small port, catch a boat to the **Grotta del Bue Marino** (Cave of the Monk Seal), where a guide will take you on a 1km walk to see vast caves with stalagmites, stalactites and lakes. They were one of the last habitats of the rare monk seal which has not been sighted for some years. The return boat trip plus entrance to the caves costs from L17,000.

There are also boats for the beautiful **Cala di Luna** (L18,000). This isolated beach is accessible only by boat or on foot (a combined return fare for the grotta and Cala di Luna is L30,000). In August the beach is crowded with day-tripping sunbathers and camping is forbidden. At other times it is deserted and you can ask for permission to camp near the restaurant, Su Neulagi (☎ 9 33 92). If the weather is unsuitable for swimming, walk along the **Codula di Luna**, a long valley stretching from Cala di Luna almost to Urzulei. Other boats head farther along the coast to the beach at **Cala Sisine** (L22,000).

There is a walking track along the coast linking Cala Gonone and Cala di Luna (about two hours). The Dorgali tourist office has information about other trails in the area, including how to reach the Nuraghic village of Tiscali (see Oliena section).

If you want to explore the spectacular **Gola di Gorropu** (Gorropu Gorge), about 15km south of Dorgali, you could ask at the Dorgali tourist office about hiring a guide, since you'll need to use ropes and harnesses to descend some sections of the gorge. However, it is possible to walk into the gorge from its northern entrance for about 1km before it becomes impossible to proceed.

To get to the entrance, head south from Dorgali along the road for Urzulei for a couple of km. After the turn-off to the left for Cala Gonone, there is a dirt road to the right, which heads for the Hotel Sant'Elene (see Places to Stay). Follow this into the valley for about 8km (don't head uphill for the hotel) and you'll get to a small bridge. Here you'll have to park the car and continue on foot. Walk for about an hour and a half, to reach two small lakes and the entrance to the gorge – one of the most spectacular and romantic landscapes in Sardegna. The huge boulders scattered around the entrance to the gorge are a reminder that nature can be harsh as well as beautiful in Sardegna. Even if you have your own car, allow a full day for the expedition, which will give you enough time for the walk, a picnic and a swim in the lakes. If you're on foot, but want to explore the gorge, you could stay at the Hotel Sant'Elene and walk to its entrance from there.

Gruppo Ricerche Ambientali (☎ 9 43 85 at Dorgali) organises guided treks in the Gola di Gorropu, the Codula di Luna and sections of the Grotta del Bue Marino not normally open to the public. There are several Nuraghic sites in the area and, the Dorgali tourist office can provide maps and advice on how to reach them. See also the Oliena section for information about a guided trek that approaches this area from the west.

Boat Marine Charter (☎ 9 69 52), Via Cavour 3 in Dorgali or at the port (☎ 9 35 46), runs charter-boat cruises for one day or longer periods for groups only. For diving courses, contact Dimensione Mare (☎ 9 67 66), Via La Marmora, Dorgali.

Places to Stay & Eat Try *Camping Cala Gonone* (☎ 9 31 65), Via Collodi 1, which charges up to L24,900 per person. Free-camping is strictly forbidden in the area.

Hotels include the *Piccolo Hotel* (☎ 9 32 32), Via Cristoforo Colombo, near the port, which has very pleasant rooms for L60,000/99,000 with bathroom. *Hotel La Playa* (☎ 9 31 06), Via Collodi, has rooms for up to L95,000/135,000. At *Pop Hotel* (☎ 9 33 00), near the port, half board is L105,000 and full board L125,000. They also manage an inexpensive restaurant.

Just out of Dorgali, at Monte Sant'Elene, is the *Hotel Sant'Elene* (☎ 9 45 72), Località Sant'Elene. Singles/doubles go for L60,000/110,000, and triples are L150,000. It also has an excellent restaurant with a reasonably priced tourist menu.

Due Chiacchiere is a trattoria/pizzeria

overlooking the sea at Via Acquadolce 13, near the port in Cala Gonone; a full meal will cost around L30,000. More expensive is the nearby *Ristorante Il Pescatore*, where you will pay around L40,000 or more.

Getting There & Away An ARST bus will get you from Nuoro to Cala Gonone, via Dorgali. ARST buses also connect Cala Gonone with Oliena. It should be noted that services are drastically reduced to Cala Gonone out of season.

Baunei

The reason for coming to this small village between Urzulei and Arbatax is to explore the high plain and valley around the ancient **Chiesa di San Pietro**. This beautiful area has an almost magical atmosphere, and is where you can see evidence of the ancient Nuraghic civilisation. The rustic church, for centuries a place of pilgrimage, stands isolated in the countryside and is surrounded by a wall lined with pilgrims' shelters. Nearby are the Nuraghic *betili*, conical sacred stones which were carved to indicate feminine forms.

To get to the church from Baunei, you need to take a small road north from the centre of town. A sign indicates San Pietro, but you'll probably need to ask directions. It is about 8km to the church. On the way is *Golgo* (☎ 0337-81 18 28), a restaurant designed to blend into its natural surroundings. You can camp here for L7000 a day if you want to explore the area. A filling, traditional-style Sardegnan meal will cost up to L35,000. The complex opens from Easter to the end of September.

From the church, a trail continues on for more than 10km to Cala Sisine; otherwise head back to Golgo and take the walking trail down to the sea at Cala Goloritze (one hour). The beauty of the scenery will take your breath away.

For guided tours and trekking in the area call Societa' Gorropu (☎ 0782-64 92 82), a group of young expert guides based in Urzulei at Via Cagliari 4. They can take you on an exciting descent of the Gorropu Gorge with ropes for expert climbers.

Baunei is accessible by ARST bus from Nuoro, Dorgali and Cagliari.

Arbatax

If you're planning to explore the Barbagi this small port town, not far from Baunei, towards Cagliari, is probably the most convenient place to arrive by ferry. Tirrenia ferries dock here from Civitavecchia twice a week. If you're heading north to Baunei, Cala Gonone, Dorgali or Nuoro, you will need to catch an ARST bus or walk 4km to Tortolì, where you can catch the direct once-daily ARST bus for Nuoro (via Lanusei). At the time of writing, the bus left from Tortolì at 3.30 pm, but it's best to check at the tourist offices in Dorgali or Nuoro for up-to-date information. Buses leave from Arbatax for Cagliari two or three times a day, not necessarily coinciding with ferry arrivals.

Another, more extravagant, option would be to catch the Trenino Verde to Cagliari (see Getting There & Away in Cagliari section). You could also try *Il Gabbiano* (☎ 0782-62 35 12), in the Porto Frailis area, a few km away, which has singles/doubles with bathroom for L60,000/L85,000.

Glossary

AAST – Azienda Autonoma di Soggiorno e Turismo, the local tourist office
acque alte – high water (flooding that occurs in Venezia during winter, when the sea level rises)
ACI – Automobile Club Italiano, the Italian automobile club
aereo – aeroplane
affittacamere – rooms for rent (cheaper than a *pensione*, and not part of the classification system)
affresco – fresco; the painting method in which watercolour paint is applied to wet plaster
agriturismo – tourist accommodation on farms
AIG – Associazione Italiana Alberghi per la Gioventù, Italy's youth hostel association
albergo – hotel (up to five stars)
albergo diurno – day hotel, with public bathing facilities
alimentari – grocery shop
aliscafo – hydrofoil
alloggio – lodging (cheaper than a *pensione*, and not part of the classification system)
alto – high
ambulanza – ambulance
anfiteatro – amphitheatre
appartamento – apartment, flat
apse – domed or arched area at the altar end of a church
APT – Azienda di Promozione Turistica, the provincial tourist office
arco – arch
assicurato/a – insured
atrium – forecourt of a Roman house or a Christian basilica
autobus – bus
autostazione – bus station/terminal
autostop – hitchhiking
autostrada – freeway, motorway

bagno – bathroom; also toilet
baldacchino – canopy supported by columns over the altar in a church
basilica – in ancient Rome, a building used for public administration, with a rectangular hall flanked by aisles and an *apse* at the end; later, a Christian church built in the same style
battistero – baptistry
benzina – petrol
bicicletta – bicycle
biglietteria – ticket office
biglietto – ticket
binario – platform
bivacco – unattended hut
borgo – ancient town or village
broletto – town hall
busta – envelope

cabinovia – two-seater cable car
CAI – Club Alpino Italiano, for information on hiking and mountain refuges
calle – street (Venezia)
camera – room
camera doppia – double room with twin beds
camera matrimoniale – double room with a double bed
camera singola – single room
campanile – bell tower
cappella – chapel
carabinieri – military police (see *polizia*)
carta marmorizzata – marbled paper
carta telefonica – phonecard
cartoleria – paper-goods shop
cartolina – postcard
casa dello studente – accommodation for students available on campus during holidays
casa religione di ospitalità – accommodation in religous institutions in cities and in monasteries in the country
castello – castle
cattedrale – cathedral
cena – evening meal
centro – centre
centro storico – (literally, historical centre) old town
chiesa – church

chiostro – cloister; covered walkway, usually enclosed by columns, around a quadrangle
cicchetti – small glass of wine or spirits
cin cin – cheers (a drinking toast)
cinquecento – 16th century
circo – oval or circular arena
CIT – Compagnia Italiana di Turismo, the Italian national tourist/travel agency
codice fiscale – tax number
colazione – breakfast
colonna – column
comune – equivalent to a municipality or county; town or city council; historically, a commune (self-governing town or city)
contrada – district
coperto – cover charge
corso – main street, avenue
cortile – courtyard
CTS – Centro Turistico Studentesco e Giovanile, the student/youth travel agency
cupola – dome

deposito bagagli – left luggage
digestivo – after-dinner liqueur
distributore di benzina – petrol pump (see *stazione di servizio*)
duomo – cathedral

ENIT – Ente Nazionale Italiano per il Turismo, the Italian state tourist office
EPT – Ente Provinciale per il Turismo, the provincial tourist office
espresso – express mail; express train; short black coffee

farmacia – pharmacy
farmacia di turno – late-night pharmacy
ferramenta – hardware shop
ferrovia – train station
festa – festival
fiume – river
fondamenta – street beside a canal
fontana – fountain
foro – forum
francobollo – postage stamp
fresco – see *affresco*
FS – Ferrovie dello Stato, the Italian state railway
funicolare – funicular railway
funivia – cable car

gabinetto – toilet, WC
gettoni – telephone tokens
golfo – gulf
grotta – cave

intarsia – inlaid wood, marble or metal

lago – lake
largo – (small) square
lavanderia – laundrette
lavasecco – dry-cleaning
lettera – letter
lettera raccomandata – registered letter
lido – beach
locanda – inn, small hotel (cheaper than a *pensione*)
loggia – covered area on the side of a building; porch
lungomare – seafront road; promenade

malghe – Alpine huts where graziers make butter and cheese in summer
mare – sea
merceria – haberdashery shop
mercato – market
monte – mountain, mount
motorino – moped
motoscafo – motorboat
municipio – town hall

navata centrale – nave; central part of a church
navata laterale – aisle of a church
nave – ship
necropolis – (ancient) cemetery, burial site

oggetti smarriti – lost property
ospedale – hospital
ostello – hostel
osteria – snack bar/cheap restaurant

pacco – package, parcel
palazzo – palace; a large building of any type, including an apartment block
panino – bread roll with filling
parco – park
passaggio ponte – deck class
passeggiata – traditional evening stroll

pasta – cake; pasta; pastry or dough
pasticceria – shop selling cakes, pastries and biscuits
pensione – small hotel, often with board
permesso di soggiorno – residence permit
piazza – square
piazzale – (large) open square
pietà – (literally, pity or compassion) sculpture, drawing or painting of the dead Christ supported by the Madonna
polizia – police
poltrona – (literally, armchair) airline-type chair on a ferry
polyptych – altarpiece consisting of more than three panels (see *triptych*)
ponte – bridge
portico – portico; covered walkway, usually attached to the outside of buildings
porto – port
posta aerea – air mail
presepio – nativity scene
pronto soccorso – first aid, casualty ward

quattrocento – 15th century
questura – police station

raccomandata – registered mail
resentin – coffee in a grappa-rinsed cup
rifugio – mountain/Alpine refuge
rio terrà – a street following the course of a filled-in canal
riva – river bank
riva alta – high river bank
rivo – a stream
rocca – fortress

sagra – festival
salumeria – delicatessen
santuario – sanctuary
sassi – stone houses
scalinata – stairway
scavi – excavations
lo sci – downhill skiing
sci di fondo – cross-country skiing
sci alpinismo – ski mountaineering
seicento – 17th century
Settimana Bianca – White Week: a skiing package deal combining accommodation, food and lift ticket
servizio – service fee
sestiere – city section (Venezia)
sottoportego – street continuing under a building (like an extended archway)
spiaggia – beach
spiaggia libera – public beach
stazione – station
stazione di servizio – service/petrol station
stazione marittima – ferry terminal
strada – street, road
suoni e lumi – sound and light show
superstrada – expressway; highway with divided lanes

teatro – theatre
telamoni – large statues of men, used as columns in temples
telegramma – telegram
tempio – temple
terme – thermal baths
tesoro – treasury
tombaroli – tomb robbers
torre – tower
torrente – stream
torrone – nougat
traghetto – ferry
tramezzini – sandwiches
trattoria – cheap restaurant
travertino – travertine; light-coloured limestone, used extensively as a building material in both ancient and modern Rome because of large deposits in the area
treno – train
triptych – painting or carving on three panels, hinged so that the outer panels fold over the middle one, often used as an altarpiece (see *polyptych*)
trompe l'œil – painting or other illustration designed to 'deceive the eye', creating the impression that the image is real

ufficio postale – post office
ufficio stranieri – (police) foreigners' bureau

via – street, road
via aerea – air mail
via ferrata – climbing trail with permanent steel cables to aid walkers
villa – town house or country house; also the park surrounding the house

Index

MAPS

TEXT

Map references are in **bold** type
References to works of art are in *italic* type

LONELY PLANET JOURNEYS

JOURNEYS is a unique collection of travel writing – published by the company that understands travel better than anyone else. It is a series for anyone who has ever experienced – or dreamed of – the magical moment when they encountered a strange culture or saw a place for the first time. They are tales to read while you're planning a trip, while you're on the road or while you're in an armchair, in front of a fire.

JOURNEYS books catch the spirit of a place, illuminate a culture, recount a crazy adventure, or introduce a fascinating way of life. They always entertain, and always enrich the experience of travel.

THE GATES OF DAMASCUS

Lieve Joris

Translated by Sam Garrett

This best-selling book is a beautifully drawn portrait of day-to-day life in modern Syria. Through her intimate contact with local people, Lieve Joris draws us into the fascinating world that lies behind the gates of Damascus. Hala's husband is a political prisoner, jailed for his opposition to the Assad regime; through the author's friendship with Hala we see how Syrian politics impacts on the lives of ordinary people.

Lieve Joris, who was born in Belgium, is one of Europe's leading travel writers. In addition to an award-winning book on Hungary, she has published widely acclaimed accounts of her journeys to the Middle East and Africa. *The Gates of Damascus* is her fifth book.

'Expands the boundaries of travel writing' **– Times Literary Supplement**

KINGDOM OF THE FILM STARS

Journey into Jordan

Annie Caulfield

Kingdom of the Film Stars is a travel book and a love story. With honesty and humour, Annie Caulfield writes of travelling in Jordan and falling in love with a Bedouin. Her book offers fascinating insights into the country – from the traditional tent life of nomadic tribes to the first woman MP's battle with fundamentalist colleagues. *Kingdom of the Film Stars* unpicks some of the tight-woven Western myths about the Arab world, presenting cultural and political issues within the intimate framework of a compelling love story.

Annie Caulfield, who was born in Ireland and currently lives in London, is an award-winning playwright and journalist. She has travelled widely in the Middle East.

'Annie Caulfield is a remarkable traveller. Her story is fresh, courageous, moving, witty and sexy!' **– Dawn French**

LONELY PLANET PHRASEBOOKS

Building bridges,
Breaking barriers,
Beyond babble-on

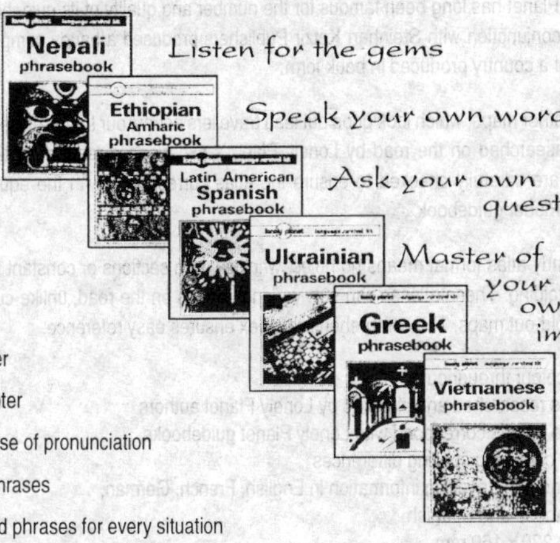

Listen for the gems

Speak your own words

Ask your own questions

Master of your own image

- handy pocket-sized books
- easy to understand Pronunciation chapter
- clear and comprehensive Grammar chapter
- romanisation alongside script to allow ease of pronunciation
- script throughout so users can point to phrases
- extensive vocabulary sections, words and phrases for every situation
- full of cultural information and tips for the traveller

'...vital for a real DIY spirit and attitude in language learning' **– Backpacker**

'the phrasebooks have good cultural backgrounders and offer solid advice for challenging situations in remote locations' **– San Francisco Examiner**

'...they are unbeatable for their coverage of the world's more obscure languages'* – *The Geographical Magazine

---

Arabic (Egyptian)
Arabic (Moroccan)
Australia
Australian English, Aboriginal and Torres Strait languages
Baltic States
Estonian, Latvian, Lithuanian
Bengali
Brazilian
Burmese
Cantonese
Central Asia
Central Europe
Czech, French, German, Hungarian, Italian and Slovak
Eastern Europe
Bulgarian, Czech, Hungarian, Polish, Romanian and Slovak
Ethiopian (Amharic)
Fijian
French
German
Greek
Hindi/Urdu
Indonesian
Italian
Japanese
Korean
Lao
Latin American Spanish
Malay
Mandarin
Mediterranean Europe
Albanian, Croatian, Greek, Italian, Macedonian, Maltese, Serbian and Slovene
Mongolian
Nepali
Papua New Guinea
Pilipino (Tagalog)
Quechua
Russian
Scandinavian Europe
Danish, Finnish, Icelandic, Norwegian and Swedish
South-East Asia
Burmese, Indonesian, Khmer, Lao, Malay, Tagalog (Pilipino), Thai and Vietnamese
Spanish (Castilian)
Basque, Catalan and Galician
Sri Lanka
Swahili
Thai
Thai Hill Tribes
Tibetan
Turkish
Ukrainian
USA
US English, Vernacular, Native American languages and Hawaiian
Vietnamese
Western Europe
Basque, Catalan, Dutch, French, German, Irish, Italian, Portuguese, Scottish Gaelic, Spanish (Castilian) and Welsh

LONELY PLANET TRAVEL ATLASES

Lonely Planet has long been famous for the number and quality of its guidebook maps. Now we've gone one step further and in conjunction with Steinhart Katzir Publishers produced a handy companion series: Lonely Planet travel atlases – maps of a country produced in book form.

Unlike other maps, which look good but lead travellers astray, our travel atlases have been researched on the road by Lonely Planet's experienced team of writers. All details are carefully checked to ensure the atlas corresponds with the equivalent Lonely Planet guidebook.

The handy atlas format means no holes, wrinkles, torn sections or constant folding and unfolding. These atlases can survive long periods on the road, unlike cumbersome fold-out maps. The comprehensive index ensures easy reference.

- full-colour throughout
- maps researched and checked by Lonely Planet authors
- place names correspond with Lonely Planet guidebooks – no confusing spelling differences
- legend and travelling information in English, French, German, Japanese and Spanish
- size: 230 x 160 mm

Available now:
Chile & Easter Island • Egypt • India & Bangladesh • Israel & the Palestinian Territories • Jordan, Syria & Lebanon • Kenya • Laos • Portugal • South Africa, Lesotho & Swaziland • Thailand • Turkey • Vietnam • Zimbabwe, Botswana & Namibia

LONELY PLANET TV SERIES & VIDEOS

Lonely Planet travel guides have been brought to life on television screens around the world. Like our guides, the programmes are based on the joy of independent travel, and look honestly at some of the most exciting, picturesque and frustrating places in the world. Each show is presented by one of three travellers from Australia, England or the USA and combines an innovative mixture of video, Super-8 film, atmospheric soundscapes and original music.

Videos of each episode – containing additional footage not shown on television – are available from good book and video shops, but the availability of individual videos varies with regional screening schedules.

Video destinations include: Alaska • American Rockies • Australia – The South-East • Baja California & the Copper Canyon • Brazil • Central Asia • Chile & Easter Island • Corsica, Sicily & Sardinia – The Mediterranean Islands • East Africa (Tanzania & Zanzibar) • Ecuador & the Galapagos Islands • Greenland & Iceland • Indonesia • Israel & the Sinai Desert • Jamaica • Japan • La Ruta Maya • Morocco • New York • North India • Pacific Islands (Fiji, Solomon Islands & Vanuatu) • South India • South West China • Turkey • Vietnam • West Africa • Zimbabwe, Botswana & Namibia

The Lonely Planet TV series is produced by:
Pilot Productions
The Old Studio
18 Middle Row
London W10 5AT UK

For video availability and ordering information contact your nearest Lonely Planet office.

Music from the TV series is available on CD & cassette.

PLANET TALK

Lonely Planet's FREE quarterly newsletter

We love hearing from you and think you'd like to hear from us.

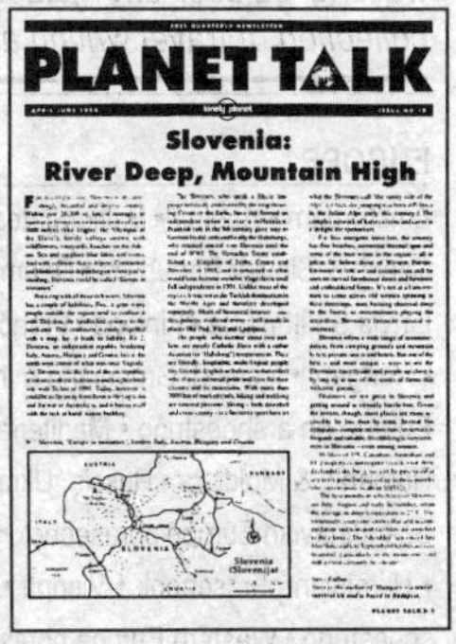

When...is the right time to see reindeer in Finland?
Where...can you hear the best palm-wine music in Ghana?
How...do you get from Asunción to Areguá by steam train?
What...is the best way to see India?

For the answer to these and many other questions read PLANET TALK.

Every issue is packed with up-to-date travel news and advice including:

- a letter from Lonely Planet co-founders Tony and Maureen Wheeler
- go behind the scenes on the road with a Lonely Planet author
- feature article on an important and topical travel issue
- a selection of recent letters from travellers
- details on forthcoming Lonely Planet promotions
- complete list of Lonely Planet products

To join our mailing list contact any Lonely Planet office.

Also available: Lonely Planet T-shirts. 100% heavyweight cotton.

LONELY PLANET ONLINE

Get the latest travel information before you leave or while you're on the road

Whether you've just begun planning your next trip, or you're chasing down specific info on currency regulations or visa requirements, check out Lonely Planet Online for up-to-the minute travel information.

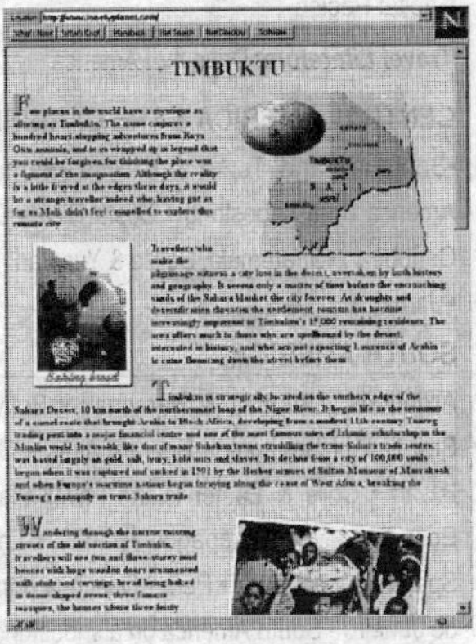

As well as travel profiles of your favourite destinations (including maps and photos), you'll find current reports from our researchers and other travellers, updates on health and visas, travel advisories, and discussion of the ecological and political issues you need to be aware of as you travel.

There's also an online travellers' forum where you can share your experience of life on the road, meet travel companions and ask other travellers for their recommendations and advice. We also have plenty of links to other online sites useful to independent travellers.

And of course we have a complete and up-to-date list of all Lonely Planet travel products including guides, phrasebooks, atlases, Journeys and videos and a simple online ordering facility if you can't find the book you want elsewhere.

www.lonelyplanet.com
or
AOL keyword: lp

LONELY PLANET PRODUCTS

Lonely Planet is known worldwide for publishing practical, reliable and no-nonsense travel information in our guides and on our web site. The Lonely Planet list covers just about every accessible part of the world. Currently there are nine series: *travel guides, shoestring guides, walking guides, city guides, phrasebooks, audio packs, travel atlases, Journeys – a unique collection of travel writing and Pisces Books - diving and snorkeling guides.*

EUROPE

Amsterdam • Austria • Baltic States phrasebook • Britain • Central Europe on a shoestring • Central Europe phrasebook • Czech & Slovak Republics • Denmark • Dublin • Eastern Europe on a shoestring • Eastern Europe phrasebook • Estonia, Latvia & Lithuania • Finland • France • French phrasebook • Germany • German phrasebook • Greece • Greek phrasebook • Hungary • Iceland, Greenland & the Faroe Islands • Ireland • Italian phrasebook • Italy • Lisbon • London • Mediterranean Europe on a shoestring • Mediterranean Europe phrasebook • Paris • Poland • Portugal • Portugal travel atlas • Prague • Romania & Moldova • Russia, Ukraine & Belarus • Russian phrasebook • Scandinavian & Baltic Europe on a shoestring • Scandinavian Europe phrasebook • Slovenia • Spain • Spanish phrasebook • St Petersburg • Switzerland • Trekking in Spain • Ukrainian phrasebook • Vienna • Walking in Britain • Walking in Italy • Walking in Switzerland • Western Europe on a shoestring • Western Europe phrasebook

Travel Literature: The Olive Grove: Travels in Greece

NORTH AMERICA

Alaska • Backpacking in Alaska • Baja California • California & Nevada • Canada • Chicago • Deep South • Florida • Hawaii • Honolulu • Los Angeles • Mexico • Mexico City • Miami • New England • New Orleans • New York City • New York, New Jersey & Pennsylvania • Pacific Northwest USA • Rocky Mountain States • San Francisco • Southwest USA • USA phrasebook • Washington, DC & the Capital Region

Travel Literature: Drive thru America

CENTRAL AMERICA & THE CARIBBEAN

• Bahamas and Turks & Caiços • Bermuda • Central America on a shoestring • Costa Rica • Cuba • Eastern Caribbean • Guatemala, Belize & Yucatán: La Ruta Maya • Jamaica

SOUTH AMERICA

Argentina, Uruguay & Paraguay • Bolivia • Brazil • Brazilian phrasebook • Buenos Aires • Chile & Easter Island • Chile & Easter Island travel atlas • Colombia Ecuador & the Galápagos Islands • Latin American Spanish phrasebook • Peru • Quechua phrasebook • Rio de Janeiro • South America on a shoestring • Trekking in the Patagonian Andes • Venezuela

Travel Literature: Full Circle: A South American Journey

ISLANDS OF THE INDIAN OCEAN

Madagascar & Comoros • Maldives • Mauritius, Réunion & Seychelles

AFRICA

Africa - the South • Africa on a shoestring • Arabic (Moroccan) phrasebook • Cairo • Cape Town • Central Africa • East Africa • Egypt • Egypt travel atlas • Ethiopian (Amharic) phrasebook • Kenya • Kenya travel atlas • Malawi, Mozambique & Zambia • Morocco • North Africa • South Africa, Lesotho & Swaziland • South Africa, Lesotho & Swaziland travel atlas • Swahili phrasebook • Tunisia Trekking in East Africa • West Africa • Zimbabwe, Botswana & Namibia • Zimbabwe, Botswana & Namibia travel atlas

Travel Literature: The Rainbird: A Central African Journey • Songs to an African Sunset: A Zimbabwean Story

MAIL ORDER

Lonely Planet products are distributed worldwide. They are also available by mail order from Lonely Planet, so if you have difficulty finding a title please write to us. North American and South American residents should write to 150 Linden St, Oakland CA 94607, USA; European and African residents should write to 10a Spring Place, London NW5 3BH; and residents of other countries to PO Box 617, Hawthorn, Victoria 3122, Australia.

NORTH-EAST ASIA

Beijing • Cantonese phrasebook • China • Hong Kong • Hong Kong, Macau & Guangzhou • Japan • Japanese phrasebook • Japanese audio pack • Korea • Korean phrasebook • Mandarin phrasebook • Mongolia • Mongolian phrasebook • North-East Asia on a shoestring • Seoul • Taiwan • Tibet • Tibet phrasebook • Tokyo

Travel Literature: Lost Japan

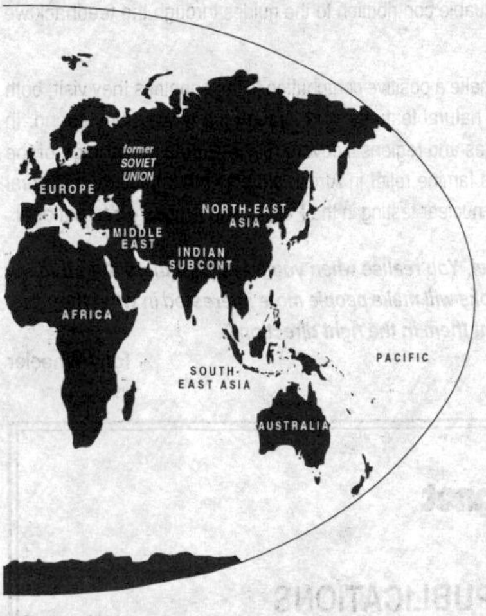

MIDDLE EAST & CENTRAL ASIA

Arab Gulf States • Arabic (Egyptian) phrasebook • Central Asia • Central Asia phrasebook • Iran • Israel & the Palestinian Territories • Israel & the Palestinian Territories travel atlas • Istanbul • Jerusalem • Jordan & Syria • Jordan, Syria & Lebanon travel atlas • Lebanon • Middle East • Turkey • Turkish phrasebook • Turkey travel atlas • Yemen

Travel Literature: The Gates of Damascus • Kingdom of the Film Stars: Journey into Jordan

ALSO AVAILABLE:

Brief Encounters • Travel with Children • Traveller's Tales

INDIAN SUBCONTINENT

Bangladesh • Bengali phrasebook • Delhi • Goa • Hindi/Urdu phrasebook • India • India & Bangladesh travel atlas • Indian Himalaya • Karakoram Highway • Nepal • Nepali phrasebook • Pakistan • Rajasthan • Sri Lanka • Sri Lanka phrasebook • Trekking in the Indian Himalaya • Trekking in the Karakoram & Hindukush • Trekking in the Nepal Himalaya

Travel Literature: In Rajasthan • Shopping for Buddhas

SOUTH-EAST ASIA

Bali & Lombok • Bangkok • Burmese phrasebook • Cambodia • Ho Chi Minh City • Indonesia • Indonesian phrasebook • Indonesian audio pack • Jakarta • Java • Laos • Lao phrasebook • Laos travel atlas • Malay phrasebook • Malaysia, Singapore & Brunei • Myanmar (Burma) • Philippines • Pilipino phrasebook • Singapore • South-East Asia on a shoestring • South-East Asia phrasebook • Thailand • Thailand's Islands & Beaches • Thailand travel atlas • Thai phrasebook • Thai audio pack • Thai Hill Tribes phrasebook • Vietnam • Vietnamese phrasebook • Vietnam travel atlas

AUSTRALIA & THE PACIFIC

Australia • Australian phrasebook • Bushwalking in Australia • Bushwalking in Papua New Guinea • Fiji • Fijian phrasebook • Islands of Australia's Great Barrier Reef • Melbourne • Micronesia • New Caledonia • New South Wales • New Zealand • Northern Territory • Outback Australia • Papua New Guinea • Papua New Guinea phrasebook • Queensland • Rarotonga & the Cook Islands • Samoa • Solomon Islands • South Australia • Sydney • Tahiti & French Polynesia • Tasmania • Tonga • Tramping in New Zealand • Vanuatu • Victoria • Western Australia

Travel Literature: Islands in the Clouds • Sean & David's Long Drive

ANTARCTICA

Antarctica

THE LONELY PLANET STORY

Lonely Planet published its first book in 1973 in response to the numerous 'How did you do it?' questions Maureen and Tony Wheeler were asked after driving, bussing, hitching, sailing and railing their way from England to Australia.

Written at a kitchen table and hand collated, trimmed and stapled, *Across Asia on the Cheap* became an instant local bestseller, inspiring thoughts of another book.

Eighteen months in South-East Asia resulted in their second guide, *South-East Asia on a shoestring*, which they put together in a backstreet Chinese hotel in Singapore in 1975. The 'yellow bible', as it quickly became known to backpackers around the world, soon became *the* guide to the region. It has sold well over half a million copies and is now in its 9th edition, still retaining its familiar yellow cover.

Today there are over 240 titles, including travel guides, walking guides, language kits & phrasebooks, travel atlases and travel literature. The company is the largest independent travel publisher in the world. Although Lonely Planet initially specialised in guides to Asia, today there are few corners of the globe that have not been covered.

The emphasis continues to be on travel for independent travellers. Tony and Maureen still travel for several months of each year and play an active part in the writing, updating and quality control of Lonely Planet's guides.

They have been joined by over 70 authors and 170 staff at our offices in Melbourne (Australia), Oakland (USA), London (UK) and Paris (France). Travellers themselves also make a valuable contribution to the guides through the feedback we receive in thousands of letters each year and on our web site.

The people at Lonely Planet strongly believe that travellers can make a positive contribution to the countries they visit, both through their appreciation of the countries' culture, wildlife and natural features, and through the money they spend. In addition, the company makes a direct contribution to the countries and regions it covers. Since 1986 a percentage of the income from each book has been donated to ventures such as famine relief in Africa; aid projects in India; agricultural projects in Central America; Greenpeace's efforts to halt French nuclear testing in the Pacific; and Amnesty International.

'I hope we send people out with the right attitude about travel. You realise when you travel that there are so many different perspectives about the world, so we hope these books will make people more interested in what they see. Guidebooks can't really guide people. All you can do is point them in the right direction.'

– Tony Wheeler

LONELY PLANET PUBLICATIONS

Australia
PO Box 617, Hawthorn 3122, Victoria
tel: (03) 9819 1877 fax: (03) 9819 6459
e-mail: talk2us@lonelyplanet.com.au

USA
150 Linden St
Oakland, CA 94607
tel: (510) 893 8555 TOLL FREE: 800 275-8555
fax: (510) 893 8563
e-mail: info@lonelyplanet.com

UK
10a Spring Place,
London NW5 3BH
tel: (0171) 428 4800 fax: (0171) 428 4828
e-mail: go@lonelyplanet.co.uk

France:
71 bis rue du Cardinal Lemoine, 75005 Paris
tel: 01 44 32 06 20 fax: 01 46 34 72 55
e-mail: bip@lonelyplanet.fr

World Wide Web: http://www.lonelyplanet.com
or ***AOL keyword: lp***